BLACKSTONE'S

CRIMINAL LAW
INDEX

CASE PRECEDENTS 1900-1997

BLACKSTONE'S

CRIMINAL LAW INDEX

CASE PRECEDENTS 1900–1997

Dr Maxwell Barrett

BLACKSTONE PRESS LIMITED

First published in Great Britain 1998 by Blackstone Press Limited,
Aldine Place, London W12 8AA. Telephone: 0181-740 2277

© Max Barrett, 1998

ISBN: 1 85431 737 7

British Library Cataloguing in Publication Data
A CIP catalogue record for this book is available from the British Library

Typeset by Style Photosetting Limited, Mayfield, East Sussex
Printed by Bell and Bain Limited, Glasgow

CONTENTS

INTRODUCTION

> The decisions . . . of courts are held in the highest regard, and are
> not only preserved as authentic records in the treasuries of the
> several courts, but are handed out to public view in the numerous
> volumes of *reports* which furnish the lawyer's library.[1]

So wrote Blackstone in 1765. Since then those 'numerous volumes of reports' to which he makes reference have multiplied in number to a level that is surely beyond anything he ever imagined. And it is not just that the total number of reports being published has increased in the past two and a half centuries. Mirroring the present tendency among lawyers towards ever greater specialisation into ever more specific fields of legal expertise has been a growing tendency among publishers in recent years to bring out law reports that concentrate on particular subject areas.

All of this has placed lawyers in something of a predicament. Even if it were economically feasible to subscribe to each of the many series of law reports and legal periodicals that have been or become available during this century alone (and even the most generously funded library would surely balk at such an enormous expense) the amount of overlap in coverage between the different sources could well mean that those cases to which particular lawyers need access are already handsomely covered in the publications to which they or their chambers or firm presently subscribe and that outside reference is so occasional it could be met by a reasonably priced publication which would not only index the reports to which those lawyers or their chambers or firms now subscribe but contain additional comprehensive references to alternative reports and journals that feature relevant case-law and to which occasional recourse might be necessary.

Economic feasibility aside, there is the matter of convenience. However well prepared they are on entering court every barrister and many solicitors have on occasion found themselves on their feet addressing or pressing a perhaps unanticipated argument which they wished they could support by reference to a convincing precedent. That precedent may well exist somewhere among the many sources of case-law now available. Indeed oftentimes a barrister or solicitor may have a very good notion of when a relevant case was decided or with what subject-matter the relevant case was concerned but simply cannot remember its name. Standing before the court, away from law reports and legal periodicals, practitioners would at such times undoubtedly find a one-stop, single-volume index relevant to the subject area being litigated, detailing the location and content of many thousands of cases and drawn from a very wide array of sources to be of real usefulness.

Of course such an index would also be of enormous benefit back in the office. It would in a single self-contained book provide lawyers with a cost-effective, hassle-free, easy-to-use means of accessing in their particular subject area many thousands of cases in many thousands of law report and law journal volumes and so open up a whole new world of precedents for them to call in aid when seeking to buttress whatever case they are called upon to make. And with lawyers working ever longer hours, many of them at home, such a reference work that gave immediate access to thousands of cases would be of considerable help there too.

---

[1] Blackstone, *Commentaries on the Laws of England* (Dawsons of Pall Mall, 1966), Volume I, p.71.

Such a reference work now exists. The publication of the first eight volumes of *Blackstone's Index of Case Precedents*, each volume being an entirely self-contained index to cases in one of eight subject areas means that there is now a reasonably priced, convenient and readily usable one-stop reference source for legal practitioners, academic lawyers and legal students who are seeking to locate a specific twentieth century precedent or trying to discover whether there is a relevant and helpful precedent in a particular area of the law.

Embracing Child Law, Criminal Law, Evidence, Family Law, Marriage Breakdown, Road Traffic Law, Sentencing, and Tort these first eight volumes of *Blackstone's Index* contain over 120,000 references to more than 40,000 cases decided by the English and Welsh courts (and by the Privy Council) throughout the twentieth century. Within the various volumes cases are listed alphabetically as well as by subject. The court which decided each case is also identified. In addition case-entries are followed by brief one or two sentence 'pointers' which seek to indicate in a little greater detail the content of the many decisions that have been indexed. These pointers do not, it should be noted, attempt to summarise the *ratio decidendi* of each case or indeed to encapsulate the entire array of issues that have been considered in a case. They are intended merely to provide a modicum of assistance to the reader in deciding whether it is worth moving on from having unearthed a case in *Blackstone's Index* to actually reading it in its entirety in a case report.

Blackstone's Index is uniquely comprehensive in indexing not only law reports but legal journals and periodicals as well. Cases have been extracted from the *All England Law Reports, Cox's Criminal Cases*, the *Criminal Appeal Reports, Criminal Appeal Reports (Sentencing), Criminal Law Review (Case and Comment), Family Court Reporter, Family Law Reports, Justice of the Peace Reports, Law Journal, Law Journal County Court Reporter, Law Journal Newspaper County Court Appeals, Law Journal Newspaper County Court Reports, Law Journal Reports, Law Reports (Appeal Cases, Chancery Division, Family Division, King's/Queen's Bench Division, Probate, Divorce and Admiralty Division), Law Times Reports, New Law Journal, New Law Journal Reports, Road Traffic Reports, Solicitors Journal, Times Law Reports* (old and new series), *Weekly Notes, Weekly Reporter* and *Weekly Law Reports*.

In short *Blackstone's Index of Case Precedents* represents a uniquely powerful low-cost reference tool through which the legal wisdom of the twentieth century is made readily available to lawyers heading into the twenty-first. In addition to publishing each volume of the work as a separate self-contained and easy-to-use book all eight volumes have been published on a CD-ROM.

HOW TO USE BLACKSTONE'S CRIMINAL LAW INDEX

This volume contains references to those Criminal Law cases decided by the English and Welsh courts (and the Privy Council) during the twentieth century which have been reported in the wide array of reports and periodicals that form the basis of *Blackstone's Index of Case Precedents*.

Like each other volume of a *Blackstone's Index* this volume is a self-contained reference source. In other words users of *Blackstone's Criminal Law Index* will not be referred to any other volume in their quest for a particular Criminal Law case.

On the whole *Blackstone's Criminal Law Index* embraces those areas of law that would feature in a typical Criminal Law syllabus at university. However, some additional categories which may be of interest to the practitioner such as 'Extradition' have also been included. As with all volumes of the *Index* cases primarily concerned with points of practice have not been included. Some civil cases which touch upon criminal law-related issues have been indexed.

Blackstone's Criminal Law Index is divided into two Parts. In Part I cases are grouped into subject categories. In Part II cases are listed alphabetically. Readers looking for cases by topic are recommended to consult Part I. Readers with a rough (or indeed exact) idea of a case name and who wish merely to discover where a specific case is located ought to consult Part II.

Each case is succeeded by a brief 'pointer'. The 'pointer' gives a better idea of what exactly each case is concerned with. It cannot be overemphasised that the 'pointer' does not represent an attempt to summarise the entirety of a case nor does it seek to give a one or two line *ratio decidendi* for each case. It is meant merely to provide a flavour of what has been decided in each case and to thereby enable the reader to make a somewhat more informed choice as to whether it is worth consulting a comprehensive account of the case in the relevant source or sources to which the reader is referred.

The Subject Index Cases in the subject index are grouped into generic categories such as DISHONESTY, HOMICIDE and SEXUAL OFFENCES. Cases are then listed under a variety of highly specific sub-headings. This has the double advantage that readers can either look up all the cases in a loosely defined area of interest or alternatively can very quickly zone in on the few cases decided in a much more tightly defined area of interest.

Either way the subject index is perfectly easy to use. It is preceded by two Tables of Contents. The first (entitled 'Generic Headings') lists the broad categories into which cases have been divided (DISHONESTY, HOMICIDE, SEXUAL OFFENCES). The second (entitled 'Generic Headings with Sub-Headings') lists the much more specific headings under which cases are listed within each generic category ('DISHONESTY (larceny)', 'HOMICIDE (murder)', 'SEXUAL OFFENCES (rape)'). The reader can turn to the 'Generic Headings' page, see in what generic category the case or type of case being looked for is most likely to be found and turn to the appropriate part of the subject index. Alternatively the reader can move on to (if the reader has not in fact gone straight to) the 'Generic Headings with Sub-Headings' page, find out the sub-headings under which cases are listed, decide which sub-heading most closely matches the reader's subject of inquiry and turn to the page indicated. As with any dictionary or index a degree of creative thinking may very occasionally be required of the reader in judging which category or sub-heading best matches the case or genre of case the reader is seeking to locate.

The Alphabetical Index The alphabetical index generally follows the traditional format adopted in the contents of case reports. Hence case names are on the whole listed both in forward and in reverse order. However, there is one important exception. Cases beginning '*R* v . . .' are listed only in reverse order. Thus users consulting the alphabetical index for, say, '*R* v *Abbott*' should look under '*Abbott, R* v'. Users seeking '*R* v *Robinson*' should look under '*Robinson, R* v' and so on.

Users should note that while every reasonable care has been taken to ensure that the case names and citations in the text of this work are accurate and that the text of the work is correct insofar as it indicates what was decided in each case mentioned the author accepts no responsibility for loss occasioned to any person acting or refraining from acting as a result of material contained in this publication.

ABBREVIATIONS USED

The following abbreviations are used in the text:

AC	*Law Reports (Appeal Cases)*
All ER	*All England Reports*
CA	Court of Appeal
CCA	Court of Criminal Appeal
CCR	Crown Cases Reserved
CC Rep	*Law Journal County Court Reports*
Ch	*Law Reports (Chancery Division)*
Cox CC	*Cox's Criminal Cases*
Cr App R	*Criminal Appeal Reports*
Cr App R (S)	*Criminal Appeal Reports (Sentencing)*
CrCt	Crown Court
Crim LR	*Criminal Law Review*
CyCt	County Court
FamD	*Law Reports (Family Division)*
FCR	*Family Court Reporter*
FLR	*Family Law Reports*
HC ChD	High Court (Chancery Division)
HC FamD	High Court (Family Division)
HC KBD	High Court (King's Bench Division)
HC PDAD	High Court (Probate, Divorce and Admiralty Division)
HC QBD	High Court (Queen's Bench Division)
HL	House of Lords
JP	*Justice of the Peace Reports*
KB	*Law Reports (King's Bench Division)*
LJ	*Law Journal/Law Journal Reports*
LJNCCR	*Law Journal Newspaper County Court Reports*
LJNCCA	*Law Journal Newspaper County Court Appeals*
LTR	*Law Times Reports*
Mag	Magistrates' Court
NLJ	*New Law Journal/New Law Journal Reports*
PC	Privy Council
Police Ct	Police Court
PDAD	*Law Reports (Probate, Divorce and Admiralty Division)*
QB	*Law Reports (Queen's Bench Division)*
RTR	*Road Traffic Reports*
SJ	*Solicitors Journal*
TrTb	Transport Tribunal
TLR	*Times Law Reports*
WN	*Weekly Notes*
WR	*Weekly Reporter*
WLR	*Weekly Law Reports*

ABBREVIATIONS USED

In addition the following letters are sometimes indicated alongside:

1. dt, g, i, t

These letters when they appear immediately after a page number indicate that the source to which the reader is being referred contains an additional reference to a British newspaper report of the case concerned.

dt	=	*Daily Telegraph*
g	=	*The Guardian*
i	=	*The Independent*
t	=	*The Times*

2. ccr

Not all County Court cases noted by the *Law Journal* were published separately from the main body of the *Journal*. Those notes of County Court reports contained within the *Journal* itself are indicated in the text of this *Index* by prefacing the page number from the relevant volume of the *Law Journal* with the abbreviation 'ccr' to show that the case is contained in the County Court Reporter section of the *Journal*.

3. LB

These letters may appear before the page number in a reference to the *Solicitors Journal* and indicate that the reference is to a page number in the *Lawyer's Brief* section of the relevant *Solicitors Journal*.

ACKNOWLEDGMENTS

Writing the first eight volumes of the *Blackstone's Index of Case Precedents* has been a challenging task rendered all the easier by the consistent kindness of family and friends and the very real generosity of many other people who have freely given their advice and assistance throughout the period in which the volumes were prepared.

My parents, Michael and Della Barrett, yet again provided me with that unqualified encouragement and support which they have afforded me in the past. My two brothers, Conor and Dr Gavin Barrett were similarly helpful.

In addition to my parents and brothers I was privileged throughout the period of writing the various volumes of the *Index* to have a close coterie of generous people around me who were eager to provide me with whatever assistance I needed. My very good friend Jennifer Powell proved herself to be a remarkable bastion of support to whom I owe a particular debt of gratitude. I am also deeply grateful to Sue Bate, the Law Librarian at Manchester University whose unfailing and undeserved kindness towards me has immeasurably facilitated and speeded the completion of this work. Professor Frank B. Wright, my onetime doctoral and later post-doctoral research supervisor at the European Occupational Health and Safety Legal Research Centre willingly provided useful and much-appreciated advice whenever it was solicited. My old friend Dr Jonathan Rush, not only undertook the onerous technical task of formatting the *Index* for publication both in book and CD-form but was a constant bedrock of support in many other ways. Bryan and Josie Hallows provided me with a warm and welcome retreat in the Cheshire countryside and so much more besides. So far as places to retreat to with my work were concerned I was in fact rather spoiled for choice with — regrettably as yet unavailed of — offers coming in from Duncan Lennox in San Francisco and from Anna Retoula, Christos Retoulas and Constantina Scholidi in Greece. Others among this 'support team' of friends included Fr Des Doyle, Fr Ian Kelly, Fr John McMahon, Stephano Pistillo and Martin Wai-Chung Leung. I must also acknowledge the very great assistance given to me by the library staff at Cambridge University, Manchester University, Salford University and Trinity College Dublin.

Last but far from least I would like to record my special thanks to Agapi Kapeloni, who when I began this work was my girlfriend, who somewhere along the way found herself changed in status to that of honorary research assistant and whose latest and most agreeable change in status was to become my wife.

Finally, I have taken reasonable care to ensure that the case names and citations in the text of this work are accurate and that the text of the work is correct insofar as it indicates what was decided in each case mentioned. However, I accept no responsibility for loss occasioned to any person acting or refraining from acting as a result of material contained in this publication.

Blackstone's Index of Case Precedents embraces cases from the turn of the twentieth century through to the early Autumn of 1997.

Dr Maxwell Barrett,
Dublin,
Feast of the Immaculate Conception, 1997.

GENERIC HEADINGS

ABDUCTION
ABORTION
ABSOLUTE OFFENCE
ACCOMPLICE
ACTING AS SOLICITOR
ADMINISTERING NOXIOUS THING
AFFRAY
ANIMAL
ARMY OFFENCE
ARREST
ARSON
ASSASSINATION
ASSAULT ON CONSTABLE
ASSAULT
ATTEMPT
AUCTION
AVIATION
AVOIDING FARE
BAIL
BANKRUPTCY
BANK
BIGAMY
BIRTH
BLACKMAIL
BLASPHEMY
BREACH OF PEACE
BREACH OF SANCTIONS
BROADCAST
CAUSING BODILY HARM WHEN IN
  CHARGE OF VEHICLE
CHILD-STEALING
CHILD
COMMON NUISANCE
COMMUNICATING FALSE
  INFORMATION
COMPUTER
CONDONATION
CONSPIRACY
CORPORATION
CORPSE
CORRUPTION
COUNTERFEIT
CRIMINAL CONVERSATION
CRIMINAL INJURIES COMPENSATION

CRIMINAL RECORD
CURRENCY
CUSTODY
DAMAGING/DESTROYING PROPERTY
DEATH
DECEPTION
DEFENCES
DEPORTATION
DESERTION
DISHONESTY
DOCK OFFENCE
DRUGS
DURESS
EDUCATION
ELECTION OFFENCE
EMBRACERY
ENDANGERING SAFETY OF RAIL
  PASSENGERS
ENGINE SETTING
ENTRAPMENT
ENVIRONMENT
ESCAPE
EVICTION/HARASSMENT
EXPLOSIVES
EXTRADITION
FALSE ACCOUNTING
FALSE IMPRISONMENT
FIREARMS
FORGERY
GRIEVOUS BODILY HARM
GROSS INDECENCY
HABEAS CORPUS
HANDLING
HARASSMENT
HIGHWAY
HIJACK
HOMICIDE
HOUSING
ILL-TREATMENT OF PATIENT
INCEST
INCITEMENT
INDUCEMENT
INTIMIDATION
INTOXICATION

GENERIC HEADINGS

JOINT ENTERPRISE
KEEPING UNCUSTOMED GOODS
KIDNAP
LANDLORD AND TENANT
LOTTERY
MENS REA
MILITARY
MISPRISION OF FELONY
NEWSPAPER PUBLISHER'S ADDRESS
OBSCENITY
OBSTRUCTING/PERVERTING THE
   COURSE OF JUSTICE
OBSTRUCTION OF HIGHWAY
OBSTRUCTION
OFFENCE UNDER STATUTORY ORDER
OFFENCE UNDER TEMPORARY
   STATUTE
OFFENCES AGAINST THE STATE
OFFENSIVE WEAPON
OPPORTUNITY
PAWNBROKER
PERJURY
PIRACY
PUBLIC ORDER
RAPE
RECKLESSNESS

RECOGNISANCE
RENT
REVENUE
REWARD
RIOT
SALE OF POISON
SEARCH AND SEIZURE
SEXUAL OFFENCES
SOLICITING
STREET COLLECTIONS
STREET TRADING
SUICIDE
UNAUTHORISED THEATRE
UNLAWFUL DEPOSIT ON HIGHWAY
UNLAWFULLY SOLICITING FOR
   REWARD
UNSOLICITED PUBLICATIONS
VACCINATION
VAGRANCY
VIOLENT DISORDER
WILFUL OBSTRUCTION OF
   CONSTABLE
WILFUL OBSTRUCTION OF OMNIBUS
   SERVANT
WINDOW-CLEANING
WITCHCRAFT
WOUNDING

GENERIC HEADINGS WITH SUB-HEADINGS

ABDUCTION (general)
ABORTION (attempt)
ABORTION (general)
ABSOLUTE OFFENCE (general)
ACCOMPLICE (accessory)
ACCOMPLICE (aiding and abetting)
ACCOMPLICE (assisting escape)
ACCOMPLICE (general)
ACCOMPLICE (inciting person to become
  accessory)
ACCOMPLICE (murder)
ACCOMPLICE (suicide)
ACTING AS SOLICITOR (general)
ADMINISTERING NOXIOUS THING
  (general)
AFFRAY (general)
ANIMAL (badger-fighting)
ANIMAL (bird)
ANIMAL (cruelty)
ANIMAL (custody)
ANIMAL (deer)
ANIMAL (dog)
ANIMAL (fish)
ANIMAL (general)
ANIMAL (hunt)
ANIMAL (killing cat)
ANIMAL (pigeon)
ANIMAL (poaching)
ANIMAL (rabbit)
ANIMAL (sheep)
ANIMAL (wild animals)
ARMY OFFENCE (general)
ARREST (citizen's arrest)
ARREST (escape from arrest)
ARREST (general)
ARREST (stop and search)
ARSON (attempt)
ARSON (general)
ASSASSINATION (encouraging
  assassination)
ASSAULT ON CONSTABLE (general)
ASSAULT (aggravated assault)
ASSAULT (assault on child)
ASSAULT (assault with intent to rape)

ASSAULT (assault with intent to resist arrest)
ASSAULT (assault with intent to rob)
ASSAULT (causing bodily harm)
ASSAULT (child)
ASSAULT (general)
ASSAULT (ill-treatment of patient)
ATTEMPT (abortion)
ATTEMPT (arson)
ATTEMPT (attempt to discharge firearm)
ATTEMPT (attempt to incite perjury)
ATTEMPT (attempt to obstruct/pervert the
  course of justice)
ATTEMPT (attempt to obtain by
  deception/false pretences)
ATTEMPT (attempt to procure)
ATTEMPT (attempt to procure act of gross
  indecency)
ATTEMPT (attempt to procure drugs)
ATTEMPT (attempt to procure woman to
  become prostitute)
ATTEMPT (attempt to steal)
ATTEMPT (attempt to supply drugs)
ATTEMPT (attempted false imprisonment)
ATTEMPT (attempted unlawful carnal
  knowledge of under-sixteen year old)
ATTEMPT (burglary)
ATTEMPT (false imprisonment)
ATTEMPT (general)
ATTEMPT (grievous bodily harm)
ATTEMPT (gross indecency)
ATTEMPT (handling)
ATTEMPT (incitement of child to gross
  indecency)
ATTEMPT (infanticide)
ATTEMPT (larceny)
ATTEMPT (murder)
ATTEMPT (rape)
ATTEMPT (rape per anum)
ATTEMPT (suicide)
ATTEMPT (theft)
ATTEMPT (to obtain by deception/false
  pretences)
AUCTION (conspiracy to effect auction)
AUCTION (general)

AVIATION (general)
AVOIDING FARE (general)
BAIL (conspiracy to effect public mischief)
BAIL (general)
BAIL (habeas corpus)
BAIL (indemnity)
BAIL (surety)
BANK (general)
BANKRUPTCY (general)
BANKRUPTCY (obtaining credit)
BIGAMY (general)
BIRTH (concealment)
BLACKMAIL (demanding with menaces)
BLACKMAIL (general)
BLACKMAIL (uttering threatening letter)
BLASPHEMY (blasphemous libel)
BLASPHEMY (general)
BREACH OF PEACE (general)
BREACH OF PEACE (wilful obstruction)
BREACH OF SANCTIONS (general)
BROADCAST (general)
BROADCAST (incitement to use unlicensed radio)
BROADCAST (unlicensed)
CAUSING BODILY HARM WHEN IN CHARGE OF VEHICLE (general)
CHILD (abandonment)
CHILD (assault)
CHILD (corporal punishment)
CHILD (cruelty)
CHILD (general)
CHILD (neglect)
CHILD (running away/leaving)
CHILD (tobacco sale)
CHILD (wilful neglect)
CHILD-STEALING (conspiracy to steal child)
CHILD-STEALING (general)
COMMON NUISANCE (general)
COMMUNICATING FALSE INFORMATION (general)
COMPUTER (data protection)
COMPUTER (failure to register as user)
COMPUTER (general)
CONDONATION (general)
CONSPIRACY (auction)
CONSPIRACY (conspiracy to abduct)
CONSPIRACY (conspiracy to breach toiletries regulations)
CONSPIRACY (conspiracy to cause explosion)
CONSPIRACY (conspiracy to cheat/defraud)
CONSPIRACY (conspiracy to commit public nuisance)
CONSPIRACY (conspiracy to contravene statute)

CONSPIRACY (conspiracy to corrupt public morals)
CONSPIRACY (conspiracy to effect public mischief)
CONSPIRACY (conspiracy to import drugs)
CONSPIRACY (conspiracy to import prohibited goods)
CONSPIRACY (conspiracy to intimidate)
CONSPIRACY (conspiracy to obstruct/ pervert the course of justice)
CONSPIRACY (conspiracy to obtain by deception/false pretences)
CONSPIRACY (conspiracy to outrage public decency)
CONSPIRACY (conspiracy to possess firearm)
CONSPIRACY (conspiracy to prevent burial)
CONSPIRACY (conspiracy to procure)
CONSPIRACY (conspiracy to procure execution of valuable security)
CONSPIRACY (conspiracy to produce drug)
CONSPIRACY (conspiracy to receive)
CONSPIRACY (conspiracy to rob)
CONSPIRACY (conspiracy to steal)
CONSPIRACY (conspiracy to steal child)
CONSPIRACY (conspiracy to supply drug)
CONSPIRACY (general)
CONSPIRACY (husband and wife)
CORPORATION (criminal insolvency)
CORPORATION (director)
CORPORATION (failure to keep books)
CORPORATION (false accounting)
CORPORATION (false business name)
CORPORATION (false prospectus)
CORPORATION (false statement)
CORPORATION (fraudulent trading)
CORPORATION (general)
CORPORATION (illegal insurance business)
CORPORATION (insider dealing)
CORPORATION (manslaughter)
CORPORATION (mens rea)
CORPORATION (shares)
CORPSE (conspiracy to prevent burial)
CORPSE (prevention of burial)
CORRUPTION (bribery)
CORRUPTION (general)
CORRUPTION (misbehaviour in public office)
COUNTERFEIT (general)
CRIMINAL CONVERSATION (general)
CRIMINAL INJURIES COMPENSATION (general)
CRIMINAL RECORD (general)
CURRENCY (general)
CUSTODY (general)

DAMAGING/DESTROYING PROPERTY
(arson)
DAMAGING/DESTROYING PROPERTY
(computer)
DAMAGING/DESTROYING PROPERTY
(criminal damage)
DAMAGING/DESTROYING PROPERTY
(damaging ancient monuments)
DEATH (certificate)
DECEPTION (accepting Bill of Exchange
with intent to defraud)
DECEPTION (acting as auditor when
disqualified)
DECEPTION (acting as solicitor)
DECEPTION (attempt to obtain by
deception/false pretences)
DECEPTION (breach of trust)
DECEPTION (conspiracy to cheat/defraud)
DECEPTION (conspiracy to obtain by
deception/false pretences)
DECEPTION (false instrument)
DECEPTION (false statement)
DECEPTION (forgery)
DECEPTION (fortune-telling)
DECEPTION (fraud)
DECEPTION (fraudulent appropriation)
DECEPTION (fraudulent conversion)
DECEPTION (fraudulent debtor)
DECEPTION (fraudulent declaration on
licence application)
DECEPTION (fraudulent inducement to
invest)
DECEPTION (fraudulent misrepresentation)
DECEPTION (general)
DECEPTION (going equipped to cheat)
DECEPTION (holy orders)
DECEPTION (house-to-house collection)
DECEPTION (immigration)
DECEPTION (impersonation of police)
DECEPTION (incitement to obtain property
by deception/false pretences)
DECEPTION (inducement to invest money)
DECEPTION (insurance fraud)
DECEPTION (making false statement)
DECEPTION (obtaining by deception/false
pretences)
DECEPTION (possession of changed
passport)
DECEPTION (pretending to be solicitor)
DECEPTION (theft)
DECEPTION (theft in breach of trust)
DECEPTION (train/tram fare)
DECEPTION (unlawful obtaining of benefit)
DECEPTION (unlicensed credit broker)
DECEPTION (unlicensed deposit-taking)

DEFENCES (alibi)
DEFENCES (automatism)
DEFENCES (battered woman syndrome)
DEFENCES (claim of right)
DEFENCES (diminished responsibility)
DEFENCES (drug addiction)
DEFENCES (drunkenness)
DEFENCES (duress)
DEFENCES (forgetfulness)
DEFENCES (hypoglycaemia)
DEFENCES (insanity)
DEFENCES (intoxication)
DEFENCES (lawful excuse)
DEFENCES (necessity)
DEFENCES (pre-menstrual syndrome)
DEFENCES (provocation)
DEFENCES (reasonable force)
DEFENCES (self-defence)
DEFENCES (sleep)
DEFENCES (uncontrollable impulse)
DEPORTATION (general)
DESERTION (general)
DISHONESTY (abstracting electricity)
DISHONESTY (advertisement)
DISHONESTY (aggravated burglary)
DISHONESTY (animus furandi)
DISHONESTY (appropriation)
DISHONESTY (asportation)
DISHONESTY (attempt)
DISHONESTY (attempted burglary)
DISHONESTY (attempted larceny)
DISHONESTY (attempted theft)
DISHONESTY (breaking and entering)
DISHONESTY (burglary)
DISHONESTY (cheque)
DISHONESTY (claim of right)
DISHONESTY (conspiracy to rob)
DISHONESTY (conspiracy to steal)
DISHONESTY (fish)
DISHONESTY (forcible detainer)
DISHONESTY (fraudulent conversion)
DISHONESTY (fraudulent misapplication)
DISHONESTY (going equipped)
DISHONESTY (intoxication)
DISHONESTY (invito domino)
DISHONESTY (larceny)
DISHONESTY (larceny by agent)
DISHONESTY (larceny by bailee)
DISHONESTY (larceny by finding)
DISHONESTY (larceny by trick)
DISHONESTY (larceny from the person)
DISHONESTY (larceny in presence of
husband)
DISHONESTY (larceny of deer)
DISHONESTY (larceny of fish)

DISHONESTY (larceny of fixture)
DISHONESTY (larceny of pigeon)
DISHONESTY (misapplication of service property)
DISHONESTY (misappropriation)
DISHONESTY (pawnbroker)
DISHONESTY (possession of housebreaking implements)
DISHONESTY (possession of stolen property)
DISHONESTY (receiving)
DISHONESTY (recent possession)
DISHONESTY (restitution)
DISHONESTY (robbery)
DISHONESTY (shoplifting)
DISHONESTY (stealing)
DISHONESTY (taking)
DISHONESTY (theft)
DISHONESTY (theft in breach of trust)
DISHONESTY (theft of valuable security)
DISHONESTY (treasure trove)
DISHONESTY (union official wilfully withholding moneys)
DISHONESTY (unlawful possession)
DOCK OFFENCE (general)
DRUGS (assisting in offfence)
DRUGS (attempt to procure)
DRUGS (attempt to supply)
DRUGS (causing/permitting premises to be used)
DRUGS (conspiracy to import)
DRUGS (conspiracy to produce)
DRUGS (conspiracy to supply)
DRUGS (cultivation/production)
DRUGS (general)
DRUGS (importation)
DRUGS (incitement to supply)
DRUGS (offer to supply)
DRUGS (possession)
DRUGS (possession with intent to supply)
DRUGS (procuring)
DRUGS (supply)
DRUGS (trafficking)
DRUGS (use)
DURESS (general)
EDUCATION (general)
ELECTION OFFENCE (general)
EMBRACERY (general)
ENDANGERING SAFETY OF RAIL PASSENGERS (general)
ENGINE SETTING (general)
ENTRAPMENT (general)
ENVIRONMENT (causing effluent to be discharged)
ENVIRONMENT (control of pollution)

ENVIRONMENT (depositing controlled waste)
ENVIRONMENT (depositing/leaving litter)
ENVIRONMENT (destroying controlled waste)
ENVIRONMENT (discharge of oil)
ENVIRONMENT (disposal of waste)
ENVIRONMENT (litter)
ENVIRONMENT (oil in navigable waters)
ENVIRONMENT (pollution)
ESCAPE (aiding and abetting)
ESCAPE (assisting escape)
ESCAPE (general)
ESCAPE (harbouring escapee)
ESCAPE (lawful custody)
ESCAPE (military service)
ESCAPE (prison)
EVICTION/HARASSMENT (general)
EXPLOSIVES (conspiracy to cause explosion)
EXPLOSIVES (general)
EXPLOSIVES (possession)
EXTRADITION (general)
FALSE ACCOUNTING (general)
FALSE IMPRISONMENT (attempt)
FALSE IMPRISONMENT (general)
FIREARMS (attempt to discharge)
FIREARMS (carrying in public place)
FIREARMS (certificate)
FIREARMS (conspiracy to possess)
FIREARMS (general)
FIREARMS (going about armed)
FIREARMS (imitation)
FIREARMS (possession)
FIREARMS (use with intent to resist arrest)
FORGERY (false instrument)
FORGERY (general)
FORGERY (possession of changed passport)
FORGERY (uttering)
GRIEVOUS BODILY HARM (assault occasioning)
GRIEVOUS BODILY HARM (attempt)
GRIEVOUS BODILY HARM (causing - with intent)
GRIEVOUS BODILY HARM (general)
GRIEVOUS BODILY HARM (incitement to cause)
GRIEVOUS BODILY HARM (mens rea)
GRIEVOUS BODILY HARM (sado-masochism)
GRIEVOUS BODILY HARM (unlawfully and maliciously causing)
GROSS INDECENCY (attempt to procure)
HABEAS CORPUS (bail)
HABEAS CORPUS (general)

HANDLING (attempt)
HANDLING (conspiracy to receive)
HANDLING (general)
HANDLING (incitement to receive)
HANDLING (possession)
HANDLING (receiving)
HANDLING (recent possession)
HARASSMENT (general)
HARASSMENT (tenant)
HIGHWAY (fire)
HIJACK (general)
HOMICIDE (attempted infanticide)
HOMICIDE (attempted murder)
HOMICIDE (capital murder)
HOMICIDE (constructive malice)
HOMICIDE (general)
HOMICIDE (incitement to murder)
HOMICIDE (incitement to solicit to murder)
HOMICIDE (infanticide)
HOMICIDE (intoxication)
HOMICIDE (manslaughter)
HOMICIDE (manslaughter, corporation)
HOMICIDE (motor manslaughter)
HOMICIDE (murder)
HOMICIDE (provocation)
HOMICIDE (sending letter threatening to
  murder)
HOMICIDE (shooting with intent to murder)
HOMICIDE (soliciting murder)
HOMICIDE (threat to kill)
HOMICIDE (uncontrollable impulse)
HOMICIDE (unlawful killing)
HOUSING (general)
ILL-TREATMENT OF PATIENT (general)
INCEST (general)
INCITEMENT (attempt to incite perjury)
INCITEMENT (attempted incitement of
  child to gross indecency)
INCITEMENT (encouraging assassination)
INCITEMENT (encouraging unlawful carnal
  knowledge of under-sixteen year old)
INCITEMENT (general)
INCITEMENT (incitement of gross
  indecency)
INCITEMENT (incitement to cause grievous
  bodily harm)
INCITEMENT (incitement to commit
  summary offence)
INCITEMENT (incitement to murder)
INCITEMENT (incitement to obtain by
  deception/false pretences)
INCITEMENT (incitement to receive)
INCITEMENT (incitement to solicit to
  murder)
INCITEMENT (incitement to supply drugs)

INCITEMENT (incitement to use unlicensed
  radio)
INDUCEMENT (inducement of unlawful
  act)
INTIMIDATION (general)
INTOXICATION (drunk and disorderly)
JOINT ENTERPRISE (attempted murder)
JOINT ENTERPRISE (general)
JOINT ENTERPRISE (homicide)
JOINT ENTERPRISE (husband and wife)
JOINT ENTERPRISE (manslaughter)
JOINT ENTERPRISE (murder)
JOINT ENTERPRISE (possession of drugs)
KEEPING UNCUSTOMED GOODS
  (general)
KIDNAP (general)
LANDLORD AND TENANT (unlawful
  eviction)
LOTTERY (general)
MENS REA (arson)
MENS REA (assault)
MENS REA (attempt)
MENS REA (attempted murder)
MENS REA (breaking and entering)
MENS REA (coercion)
MENS REA (contempt)
MENS REA (corporation)
MENS REA (doli incapax)
MENS REA (drunkenness)
MENS REA (epilepsy)
MENS REA (firearms)
MENS REA (forgery)
MENS REA (general)
MENS REA (grievous bodily harm)
MENS REA (handling)
MENS REA (homicide)
MENS REA (implied malice)
MENS REA (importation of drugs)
MENS REA (incitement to obtain by
  deception/false pretences)
MENS REA (intent to defraud)
MENS REA (intoxication)
MENS REA (larceny)
MENS REA (manslaughter)
MENS REA (mistake)
MENS REA (murder)
MENS REA (offences against the person)
MENS REA (rape)
MENS REA (suicide)
MENS REA (theft)
MENS REA (trespass)
MENS REA (wounding with intent)
MILITARY (condonation)
MILITARY (desertion)
MILITARY (general)

MILITARY (military service)
MILITARY (mutiny)
MISPRISION OF FELONY (general)
NEWSPAPER PUBLISHER'S ADDRESS
(general)
OBSCENITY (general)
OBSCENITY (importation of obscene goods)
OBSCENITY (indecent photographs)
OBSCENITY (obscene libel)
OBSCENITY (obscene publication)
OBSCENITY (obscene telephone call)
OBSCENITY (seizure/destruction of obscene
publication)
OBSCENITY (unlawful importation of
obscene material)
OBSTRUCTING/PERVERTING THE
COURSE OF JUSTICE (attempt to defeat)
OBSTRUCTING/PERVERTING THE
COURSE OF JUSTICE (attempt to
pervert)
OBSTRUCTING/PERVERTING THE
COURSE OF JUSTICE (conspiracy)
OBSTRUCTING/PERVERTING THE
COURSE OF JUSTICE (conspiracy to
intimidate)
OBSTRUCTING/PERVERTING THE
COURSE OF JUSTICE (general)
OBSTRUCTING/PERVERTING THE
COURSE OF JUSTICE (perverting)
OBSTRUCTION OF HIGHWAY (general)
OBSTRUCTION (of fire brigade officer)
OFFENCE UNDER STATUTORY ORDER
(general)
OFFENCE UNDER TEMPORARY
STATUTE (general)
OFFENCES AGAINST THE STATE
(assisting the enemy)
OFFENCES AGAINST THE STATE
(communicating with the enemy)
OFFENCES AGAINST THE STATE (coup
d'état)
OFFENCES AGAINST THE STATE
(diplomat)
OFFENCES AGAINST THE STATE
(internal security)
OFFENCES AGAINST THE STATE
(official secrets)
OFFENCES AGAINST THE STATE
(sedition)
OFFENCES AGAINST THE STATE
(treason)
OFFENSIVE WEAPON (general)
OFFENSIVE WEAPON (possession)
OPPORTUNITY (general)
PAWNBROKER (general)

PERJURY (attempt to incite perjury)
PERJURY (general)
PIRACY (general)
PUBLIC ORDER (breach of peace)
PUBLIC ORDER (busking)
PUBLIC ORDER (conspiracy to effect public
mischief)
PUBLIC ORDER (disorderly behaviour)
PUBLIC ORDER (disturbing religious
meeting)
PUBLIC ORDER (general)
PUBLIC ORDER (indecent behaviour in
church)
PUBLIC ORDER (indecent language)
PUBLIC ORDER (insulting behaviour)
PUBLIC ORDER (obscene language)
PUBLIC ORDER (procession)
PUBLIC ORDER (public mischief)
PUBLIC ORDER (public nuisance)
PUBLIC ORDER (threatening
behaviour/words)
PUBLIC ORDER (trespassory assembly)
PUBLIC ORDER (unlawful assembly)
PUBLIC ORDER (using indecent language)
PUBLIC ORDER (violent disorder)
PUBLIC ORDER (watching/besetting
premises)
RAPE (assault with intent to rape)
RECKLESSNESS (general)
RECOGNISANCE (arraignment)
RECOGNISANCE (breach)
RECOGNISANCE (estreatment)
RECOGNISANCE (forfeiture)
RECOGNISANCE (general)
RECOGNISANCE (insanity)
RECOGNISANCE (surety)
RENT (general)
REVENUE (general)
REWARD (general)
RIOT (general)
SALE OF POISON (general)
SEARCH AND SEIZURE (general)
SEXUAL OFFENCES (assault with intent to
rape)
SEXUAL OFFENCES (association/
conversation with prostitute)
SEXUAL OFFENCES (attempt to procure
gross indecency)
SEXUAL OFFENCES (attempt to procure
woman to become prostitute)
SEXUAL OFFENCES (attempted gross
indecency)
SEXUAL OFFENCES (attempted rape)
SEXUAL OFFENCES (attempted rape per
anum)

SUBJECT INDEX

ABDUCTION (general)

R v Alexander (1913-14) XXIII Cox CC 138; (1912) 76 JP 215; (1912-13) 107 LTR 240; (1911-12) XXVIII TLR 200 CCA Conviction quashed where trial judge actively encouraged accused to plead guilty to abduction charge.

R v Burns (James); R v Ralph (Michael Peter); R v Jackson (Stephen Ronald); R v Burns (Sidney) (1984) 79 Cr App R 173 CA Person could be prosecuted for conspiracy to commit offence though immune from prosecution for substantive offence.

R v Colville-Hyde [1956] Crim LR 117 Assizes On necessary elements of offence of abduction.

R v Duguid (1907-09) XXI Cox CC 200; (1906) 70 JP 294; (1906) 41 LJ 335; [1906] 75 LJKB 470; (1906) XCIV LTR 887; (1905-06) 50 SJ 465; (1905-06) XXII TLR 506; (1906) WN (I) 100 CCR Was criminal conspiracy on part of person agreeing with mother to remove her child from lawful custody.

R v Griffin [1993] Crim LR 515 CA On respective roles of judge/jury in child abduction case; was possible to find attempted abduction where had arranged boat trip and went to school to request control of children in local authority care.

R v Jarvis (James) (1901-07) XX Cox CC 249 Assizes Not abduction to passively acquiesce to proposal of under-sixteen year old unmarried girl to join her in her leaving home.

R v Jones (James William) [1973] Crim LR 621 CrCt Was not taking child out of possession of parents (contrary to Sexual Offences Act 1956, s 20) to seek to bring girls for walk, aim being to indecently assault them.

R v Kauffman (1904) 68 JP 189 CCC On elements of offence of abducting under-eighteen year old girl (Criminal Law Amendment Act 1885, s 7).

R v Powell (1914-15) XXIV Cox CC 229; (1915) 79 JP 272 CCC Need not intend to forever deprive parent of child to be convicted of child abduction.

R v Tegerdine [1983] Crim LR 163 CA Putative father was guilty of abduction of child albeit that did so from concern for child.

ABORTION (attempt)

R v Spicer (1955) 39 Cr App R 189; [1955] Crim LR 772 Assizes Could be convicted for procuring miscarriage where sought to do so though means used could not be successful.

ABORTION (general)

R v Bourne [1938] 3 All ER 615; [1939] 1 KB 687; (1938) 86 LJ 115; [1939] 108 LJCL 471 CCC On danger to life versus danger to health; on acts of abortionist versus those of surgeon.

R v Buck and Buck (1960) 44 Cr App R 213; [1960] Crim LR 760 Assizes Must be found guilty of (at least) manslaughter where death results from criminal abortion; person procuring criminal abortion that results in death is accessory before fact to manslaughter.

R v Lumley (1911-13) XXII Cox CC 635; (1912) 76 JP 208 CCC Abortionist guilty of murder/manslaughter if did/did not (nor could not reasonably) consider that death or grievous bodily harm would result from actions.

R v Marlow (1965) 49 Cr App R 49; [1965] Crim LR 35 CCC 'Noxious thing'/'poison' in Offences against the Person Act 1861, ss 58 and 59 not confined to abortifacients.

ABSOLUTE OFFENCE (general)

R v Mills [1963] 1 All ER 202; (1963) 47 Cr App R 49; [1963] Crim LR 181; (1963) 127 JP 176; (1963) 113 LJ 90; [1963] 1 QB 522; (1963) 107 SJ 38; [1963] 2 WLR 137 CCA Meaning of 'procuring' instruments to effect abortion (Offences Against the Person Act 1861, s 59).

R v Newton and Stungo [1958] Crim LR 469 CCC On offence of using instruments to procure miscarriage.

R v Smith [1973] Crim LR 700t CA On general need for medical evidence to support conviction of doctor for unlawful procuring of miscarriage.

R v Smith (John) [1974] 1 All ER 376; (1974) 58 Cr App R 106; (1974) 138 JP 175; (1973) 123 NLJ 723t; (1973) 117 SJ 774; [1973] 1 WLR 1510 CA Absence of good faith by doctor in decision-making may be found by jury absent expert evidence.

R v Sockett (Mary) (1908) 1 Cr App R; (1908) 72 JP 428; (1907-08) 52 SJ 729; (1907-08) XXIV TLR 893 CCA Woman whom seek to aid by procuring miscarriage need not actually be pregnant to support conviction under Offences Against the Person Act 1861, s 58 (second part).

R v Spicer (1955) 39 Cr App R 189; [1955] Crim LR 772 Assizes Could be convicted for procuring miscarriage where sought so to do though means used could not be successful.

R v Starkie (1921-22) 16 Cr App R 61; (1922) 86 JP 74; [1922] 2 KB 275; [1922] 91 LJCL 663; (1921-22) 66 SJ 300; (1921-22) XXXVIII TLR 181; (1922) WN (I) 10 CCA Admissibility of evidence pertaining to alternative counts in criminal abortion charge.

R v Turner (William) (1910) 4 Cr App R 203 CCA Person guilty of causing person to take noxious drug to procure miscarriage contrary to Offences Against the Person Act 1861, s 58, could be guilty of supplying same under s 59 of 1861 Act.

ABSOLUTE OFFENCE (general)

Chilvers v Rayner (1984) 78 Cr App R 59; [1984] 1 WLR 328 HC QBD False hallmarking contrary to Hallmarking Act 1973, s 1 an absolute offence (no mens rea required).

Davidson v Strong [1997] TLR 145 HC QBD Is strict liability offence to expose unfit animal for sale.

French v Hoggett (1967) 111 SJ 906; [1968] 1 WLR 94 HC QBD Sale of alcohol absent licence an absolute offence.

Gammon (Hong Kong) Ltd v Attorney General of Hong Kong [1984] 2 All ER 503; [1985] AC 1; (1985) 80 Cr App R 194; [1984] Crim LR 496; (1984) 128 SJ 549; [1984] TLR 308; [1984] 3 WLR 437 PC Strict liability in statutory offence permissible if statute concerned with public safety and strict liability furthers that goal.

Patel v Comptroller of Customs [1965] 3 All ER 593; [1966] AC 356; [1965] Crim LR 728; (1965-66) 116 NLJ 102; (1965) 109 SJ 832; [1965] 3 WLR 1221 PC Making false customs entry an absolute offence; burden of proving false rests on prosecution; dispute over country of origin not one of 'whence...goods brought'.

R v Blake [1997] 1 All ER 963; [1997] 1 Cr App R 209; [1997] Crim LR 207; (1996) TLR 13/8/96; [1997] 1 WLR 1167 CA Unlicensed broadcasting an absolute offence.

R v Cummerson (1968) 52 Cr App R 519; [1968] Crim LR 395t; [1968] 2 QB 534; (1968) 112 SJ 424; [1968] 2 WLR 1486 CA Making false statement under Road Traffic Act 1960, s 235(2) (a) an absolute offence.

R v Howells [1977] 3 All ER 417; (1977) 65 Cr App R 86; [1977] Crim LR 354t; (1977) 141 JP 641; (1977) 127 NLJ 370t; [1977] QB 614; (1977) 121 SJ 154; [1977] 2 WLR 716 CA Absolute liability if no certificate yet possess firearm; mistaken belief an antique no defence.

R v St Margaret's Trust, Ltd and others [1958] 2 All ER 289; (1958) 102 SJ 349 CCA Hire-purchaser breach of Hire-Purchase and Credit Sale Agreements (Control) Order 1956 an absolute offence.

R v Wells Street Magistrates' Court and Martin; ex parte Westminster City Council [1986] Crim LR 695 HC QBD Carrying out of unauthorised works affecting listed building an absolute offence under Town and Country Planning Act 1971.

ACCOMPLICE (accessory)

Davies v Director of Public Prosecutions [1954] 1 All ER 507; [1954] AC 378; [1954] Crim LR 305; (1954) 118 JP 222; (1954) 104 LJ 152; [1954] 2 WLR 343 HL Must be corroboration warning regarding accomplice's evidence; accomplice to be same must be party to crime charged.

Dick (Surujpaul called) v R [1958] 3 All ER 300; (1958) 42 Cr App R 266; [1958] Crim LR 806; (1958) 108 LJ 681; (1958) 102 SJ 757 PC Cannot be convicted accessory before fact when principals acquitted of substantive offence.

Director of Public Prosecutions for Northern Ireland v Maxwell [1978] 3 All ER 1140; (1979) 68 Cr App R 128 (also CCA/NI); [1979] Crim LR 40; (1979) 143 JP 63 (also CCA/NI); (1978) 122 SJ 758; [1978] 1 WLR 1350 HL May be accomplice if anticipate limited number of crimes but unaware of precise crime in which assisting.

Homolka v Osmond [1939] 1 All ER 154 HC KBD Accessory before the fact to misdemeanour is considered akin to principal offender.

Majara (Nkau) v R [1954] Crim LR 464; [1954] 2 WLR 771 PC On what constitutes being accessory after the fact in South Africa; headman's shortcomings in apprehension of ritual murderers which gave them chance to escape made him accessory after the fact to murder.

Pope v Minton [1954] Crim LR 711 HC QBD That person not at scene of offence when was perpetrated did not mean could not be accessory before the fact.

R v Andrews; R v Craig [1962] 3 All ER 961; (1963) 47 Cr App R 32; [1963] Crim LR 51; (1963) 127 JP 64; (1962) 106 SJ 1013; [1962] 1 WLR 1474 CCA On accessories after the fact.

R v Anthony [1965] 1 All ER 440; (1965) 49 Cr App R 104; [1965] Crim LR 160t; (1965) 129 JP 168; [1965] 2 QB 189; [1965] 2 WLR 748 CCA Can be accessory to felony of which principal not convicted/party to conspiracy though other conspirators unknown.

R v Aston (Roy Edward); R v Mason (Christine Janet) (1992) 94 Cr App R 180; [1991] Crim LR 701 CA Could not infer guilt of both parties charged of child's manslaughter where was no evidence to pointing to one over another.

R v Bainbridge [1959] 3 All ER 200; (1959) 43 Cr App R 194; [1959] Crim LR 653; (1959) 123 JP 499; (1959) 109 LJ 539; [1960] 1 QB 129; [1959] 3 WLR 656 CCA Precise knowledge of crime not necessary to be accessory before the fact.

R v Barnes; R v Richards [1940] 2 All ER 229; (1938-40) 27 Cr App R 154; (1940) 84 SJ 258; (1939-40) LVI TLR 379 CCA Separate trials a discretionary matter for judge; evidence of accomplice incriminating another admissible as not called by prosecution.

R v Bettles [1966] Crim LR 503t CCA Person was accessory before the fact if loaned car to another so that latter might commit a crime.

R v Brown [1965] Crim LR 108; (1964) 108 SJ 921 CCA Must intend through disposal of property to aid thief to avoid arrest to be guilty as accessory after the fact.

R v Bubb (1906) 70 JP 143 CCR Person charged with another (found guilty) as principal ought not to have been convicted as accessory after the fact.

R v Buck and Buck (1960) 44 Cr App R 213; [1960] Crim LR 760 Assizes Must be found guilty of (at least) manslaughter where death results from criminal abortion; person procuring criminal abortion that results in death is accessory before fact to manslaughter.

R v Bullock [1955] 1 All ER 15; (1954) 38 Cr App R 151; [1955] Crim LR 179; (1955) 119 JP 65; (1955) 99 SJ 29; [1955] 1 WLR 1 CCA Jury question indicating believed general unlawful purpose existed justified non-explanation by judge when answering of general versus particular unlawful purpose distinction.

R v Court [1954] Crim LR 622 CCA Adequate direction regarding possibility that certain witness might be accomplice.

R v Creamer [1965] 3 All ER 257; (1965) 49 Cr App R 368; [1965] Crim LR 552; (1965) 129 JP 586; (1965) 115 LJ 676; [1966] 1 QB 72; (1965) 109 SJ 648; [1965] 3 WLR 583 CCA Involuntary manslaughter if un/intended/foreseen death flows from unlawful act likely to do injury; person seeking/arranging such act an accessory before fact to manslaughter.

R v Davies (Michael John) (1954) 38 Cr App R 11 HL On what constitutes an accomplice; on need for corroboration warning in respect of accomplice.

R v Davis [1977] Crim LR 542 CA Successful appeal by person convicted of aiding and abetting burglary where person charged as burglar was acquitted.

R v Draper (Arthur Albert) (1928-29) 21 Cr App R 147 CCA If girl is sixteen or over she may be accomplice to incest - corroboration of her evidence therefore required.

R v Fallon [1993] Crim LR 591 CA On requirement that evidence of accomplice be corroborated.

R v Farid (Mohamed) (1943-45) 30 Cr App R 168; (1945) 173 LTR 68 CCA Corroboration warning necessary where evidence given against accused of involvement in other offences to which witness is accomplice (though not accomplice to offence charged).

R v Fisher (Charles) [1969] Crim LR 20t; (1968) 118 NLJ 1102t; (1968) 112 SJ 905; [1969] 1 WLR 8 CA Could be charged as accessory after the fact to felony where offence existed when was allegedly committed but had been abolished by time charged.

R v Fitzpatrick (Norman) (1925-26) 19 Cr App R 91 CCA That accused was accessory after fact does not prove was principal/accessory before fact; accused may give account of own state of mind at pertinent time: mens rea a question of fact.

R v Forman and Ford [1988] Crim LR 677 CrCt Police officer who does not act when other assaults prisoner is guilty of assault; where not proved which of two officers assaulted prisoner with whom were alone both must be acquitted (if one must have encouraged the other both are guilty).

R v Giannetto [1996] Crim LR 722; (1996) 140 SJ LB 167; (1996) TLR 19/7/96 CA Jury to be satisfied that accused guilty as principal or as accessory where Crown allege was one or the other.

R v Godspeed (1911) 75 JP 232 CCA Person charged with burglary and receiving can be found guilty as accessory before the fact to both.

R v Goodwin (Thomas Henry) (1909) 3 Cr App R 276 CCA Could be charged as receiver (under Larceny Act 1861, s 91) but convicted as accessory under Accessories and Abettors Act 1861, ss 1 and 2.

R v Grundy [1977] Crim LR 543 CA Jury ought to have been allowed consider defence by person who originally urged offence that he had expressly communicated withdrawal from same prior to it being committed.

R v Holley [1963] 1 All ER 106; (1963) 47 Cr App R 13; [1962] Crim LR 829g; (1963) 127 JP 71; (1963) 113 LJ 57/139; (1963) 107 SJ 116; [1963] 1 WLR 199 CCA Absent coercion by husband wife helping him in felony guilty as accessory after the fact.

R v Howe and another appeal [1987] 1 All ER 771; [1987] AC 417; (1987) 85 Cr App R 32; (1987) 151 JP 265; (1987) 137 NLJ 197; [1987] 2 WLR 568 HL Duress an objective defence not open to those charged with murder in first/second degree; accessory before fact using duress to get another to commit offence can be guilty of greater offence than other.

R v Howe and other appeals [1986] 1 All ER 833; (1986) 83 Cr App R 28; (1986) 150 JP 161; [1986] QB 626; [1986] 2 WLR 294 CA Duress open as defence to alleged aider and abettor not alleged principal; accessory before fact cannot be convicted of more serious crime than principal.

R v Hyde [1954] Crim LR 540 CMAC Conviction affirmed though related conviction of another not confirmed.

R v Jackson (1953) 103 LJ 232; (1953) 97 SJ 265; [1953] 1 WLR 591 CCA Non-rebuttal by prisoner of charge levelled at him not corroborative of accomplice's evidence against prisoner.

R v Jones [1948] 2 All ER 964; (1949) 113 JP 18; [1949] 1 KB 194; (1948) LXIV TLR 616; (1948) WN (I) 442 CCA On proper direction where charge of being accessory after the facts.

R v Kearon and Williamson [1955] Crim LR 183 Sessions Person could not be guilty of aiding and abetting offence where was too drunk to possess necessary intent.

R v Kemp [1968] Crim LR 32t CA Must be guilty of endeavouring to aid another to evade justice to be guilty as accessory after the fact.

R v Knowlden (Derek James); R v Knowlden (Harold) (1983) 77 Cr App R 94 CA Appropriate direction where defendant gives evidence detrimental to co-accused.

R v Levy (Beatrice) [1911-13] All ER 222; (1911-13) XXII Cox CC 702; (1911-12) 7 Cr App R 61; (1912) 76 JP 123; [1912] 1 KB 158; (1911) 46 LJ 753; [1912] 81 LJKB 264; (1912) 106 LTR 192; (1911-12) 56 SJ 143; (1911-12) XXVIII TLR 93; (1911) WN (I) 239 CCA On what constitutes being an accessory after the fact.

R v Lomas (1913-14) XXIII Cox CC 765; (1914) 78 JP 152; (1914) 110 LTR 239; (1913-14) 58 SJ 220; (1913-14) XXX TLR 125 CCA Not accessory to fact where simply provide tool knowing it is for criminal use.

R v MacDonald (Michael) (1928-29) 21 Cr App R 33 CCA Grave doubt whether accused's admission could corroborate accomplice's evidence.

R v Martin (Francis Augustus) (1910) 5 Cr App R 4 CCA Co-prisoner's evidence against party did not render former accomplice.

R v Maxwell (James Charles) (1979) 68 Cr App R 128; (1979) 143 JP 77; [1978] 1 WLR 1363 HL May be accomplice if anticipate limited number of crimes but unaware of precise crime in which assisting.

R v Pardoe [1963] Crim LR 263g CCA Successful appeal against conviction (despite guilty plea) as accessory after the fact to factory-breaking where facts did not merit conviction for same.

R v Pickford (Tom James) (1914) 10 Cr App R 269 CCA Prostitute need not be accomplice of man living on earnings of prostitution.

R v Poole and Blake [1959] Crim LR 45 Sessions On what constitutes being an accessory to receiving.

R v Powell [1956] Crim LR 255 CCA On necessary attributes of accessory after the fact.

R v Price [1968] Crim LR 329t; (1968) 112 SJ 330 CA On warning to be given as to evidence of accomplice (here to offence of using instrument with intent to procure miscarriage).

R v Revuelta [1959] Crim LR 777t CCA Successful appeal against conviction for being accessory after the fact to stealing.

R v Richards (Isabelle) [1973] 3 All ER 1088; [1974] Crim LR 96; (1974) 138 JP 68; [1974] QB 776; (1973) 117 SJ 852; [1973] 3 WLR 888 CA Person some distance from action not an abettor.

R v Rook [1993] 2 All ER 955; (1993) 97 Cr App R 327; [1993] Crim LR 698; (1993) 143 NLJ 238; [1993] TLR 87; [1993] 1 WLR 1005 CA Consequences of criminal enterprise need only be foreseeable, not intended, for accessory before fact to be liable; withdrawal from joint enterprise must be unequivocal before liability may be overcome.

R v Rose (Malcolm Joel) (1962) 46 Cr App R 103; [1962] Crim LR 252 CCA Not accessory after the fact to larceny where went to place stolen goods kept with view to purchasing same.

R v Rowley [1948] 1 All ER 570; (1946-48) 32 Cr App R 147; (1948) 112 JP 207 CCA Cannot plead guilty to being accessory after the fact until principal convicted.

R v Rudd (1948) LXIV TLR 240 CCA On effect of evidence of co-defendant; on extent of need for corroboration warning in respect of accomplice's evidence.

R v Russell (Marion) and Russell (Andrew Louis) (1987) 85 Cr App R 388; [1987] Crim LR 494 CA Could infer that parents jointly responsible for administering drug where no proof one rather than another guilty/one did not interrupt ill-treatment of child by other.

R v Smith (No 3) [1968] Crim LR 375t CA On effect of verdict of being not guilty of office breaking but guilty as accessory before the fact.

R v Thorley [1962] Crim LR 696 CCA On what it takes to be (unlike here) an accessory after the fact.

R v Vernon [1962] Crim LR 35; (1962) 112 LJ 76 CCA Thief might not be accomplice of handler.

R v Watson (1915-16) XXXII TLR 580 CCA Cannot be convicted as accessory after the fact where are only charged as being principal.

R v West [1962] 2 All ER 624; (1962) 126 JP 352; (1962) 112 LJ 488; (1962) 106 SJ 514 CCA Cannot summarily try alleged accessory before fact; rôle of examining justices/justices trying summarily; certificate of acquittal not certificate of jurisdiction.

Saqui v Lawrence and Stearns (1911) 80 LJCL 451 (also HC KBD) CA Porter who admitted burglars to house and was later given share of spoils a principal in second degree/guilty of theft.

Saqui v Lawrence and Stearns (1911) 80 LJCL 451 (also CA) HC KBD Porter who admitted burglars to house and was later given share of spoils an accessory before the fact.

Sneddon v Stevenson [1967] 2 All ER 1277; [1967] Crim LR 476t; (1967) 131 JP 441; (1967) 111 SJ 515; [1967] 1 WLR 1051 HC QBD Not accomplice where police officer places self in position to facilitate offence if offence to be committed.

Surujpaul called Dick v R [1958] 3 All ER 300 PC Cannot be convicted accessory before fact when principals acquitted of substantive offence.

ACCOMPLICE (aiding and abetting)

Ackroyds Air Travel, Ltd v Director of Public Prosecutions [1950] 1 All ER 933; (1950) 114 JP 251 HC KBD Conviction for aiding and abetting unlawful carrying of passengers for hire/reward (Civil Aviation Act 1946, s 23(1)).

Attorney-General's Reference (No 1 of 1975) [1975] 2 All ER 685; (1975) 61 Cr App R 118; [1975] Crim LR 449t; (1975) 139 JP 569; (1975) 125 NLJ 485t; [1975] QB 773; [1975] RTR 473; (1975) 119 SJ 373; [1975] 3 WLR 11 CA Covert act resulting in other unwittingly doing criminal act 'procured' criminal act.

Bentley v Mullen [1986] RTR 7 HC QBD Supervisor of learner driver convicted of aiding and abetting latter in not stopping after accident occurred.

Carmichael and Sons Ltd v Cottle [1971] Crim LR 45t; (1970) 120 NLJ 1040t; [1971] RTR 11; (1970) 114 SJ 867 HC QBD Persons hiring car to another could not be said to be using it/were not accessories before the fact to the car being used with threadbare tyres.

Carter Patersons and Pickfords Carriers Limited v Wessel [1947] 2 All ER 280; (1947) 111 JP 474; [1947] KB 849; (1947) 97 LJ 373; [1947] 116 LJR 1370; (1947) 177 LTR 448; (1947) 91 SJ 446; (1947) LXIII TLR 517; (1947) WN (I) 216 HC KBD Aider and abettor, a principal in second degree, can be treated as principal in first degree; robber passing his stolen goods to receiver can himself be convicted as receiver.

Carter v Richardson [1974] Crim LR 190; [1974] RTR 314 HC QBD Supervising driver validly convicted of aiding and abetting learner driver in offence of driving with excess alcohol.

Davies, Turner and Co Ld v Brodie [1954] 1 WLR 1364 HC QBD Accused not guilty of aiding and abetting (road traffic) offence where principal had given misleading good faith explanation of facts and accused had taken reasonable precautions.

John Henshall (Quarries), Ltd v Harvey [1965] 1 All ER 725; [1965] Crim LR 235t; (1965) 129 JP 224; (1965) 115 LJ 230; [1965] 2 QB 233; [1965] 2 WLR 758 HC QBD Knowledge of responsible company officer of facts of offence necessary to prove company aided/abetted offence.

Johnson v Youden and others [1950] 1 KB 544 HC KBD Cannot be guilty of aiding and abetting where unaware of facts making up offence; once aware of same it is no defence to one's actions that did not know were acting unlawfully.

Mohan (Ramnath) and Another v R [1967] 2 All ER 58; [1967] 2 AC 187; [1967] Crim LR 356; (1967) 111 SJ 95; [1967] 2 WLR 676 PC Person present aiding and abetting in offence - though had not arranged to do so - guilty as principal in second degree (here of murder).

Morris v Tolman [1922] All ER 182; (1921-25) XXVII Cox CC 345; (1922) 86 JP 221; [1923] 1 KB 166; [1923] 92 LJCL 215; (1923) 128 LTR 118; (1922-23) 67 SJ 169; (1922-23) XXXIX TLR 39 HC KBD Can be convicted as aider and abettor though principal acquitted (but not with respect to using vehicle for unlicensed purpose).

National Coal Board v Gamble [1958] 3 All ER 203; (1958) 42 Cr App R 240; [1958] Crim LR 682; (1958) 122 JP 453; (1958) 108 LJ 617; [1959] 1 QB 11; (1958) 102 SJ 621; [1958] 3 WLR 434 HC QBD Aiding and abetting where seller of unascertained goods completed sale despite knowing at weighing (passing) of property that conveyance of that weight an offence.

Poultry World, Ltd v Conder [1957] Crim LR 803t HC QBD Cannot be guilty of aiding/abetting offence unless know facts making up offence or are wilfully blind as to same.

R v Bland [1988] Crim LR 41; (1987) 151 JP 857 CA Aiding and abetting requires some form of constructive action so mere knowledge that boyfriend a drug-dealer not enough to support aiding and abetting conviction.

R v Brindley; R v Long [1971] 2 All ER 698; (1971) 55 Cr App R 258; [1971] Crim LR 276t; (1971) 135 JP 357; (1971) 121 NLJ 178t; [1971] 2 QB 300; (1971) 115 SJ 285; [1971] 2 WLR 895 CA Need not show accused knew identity of offender to sustain charge of assisting them.

R v Calhaem [1985] 2 All ER 266; (1985) 81 Cr App R 131; [1985] Crim LR 303; [1985] QB 808; (1985) 129 SJ 331; [1985] 2 WLR 826 CA 'Counsel' crime if advise or solicit other to act and does; need not be major reason for offence.

R v Clarkson and others [1971] 3 All ER 344; (1971) 55 Cr App R 445; [1972] Crim LR 586; (1971) 135 JP 533; (1971) 115 SJ 654; [1971] 1 WLR 1402 CMAC Intent to encourage and actual encouragement necessary where aiding and abetting rape.

R v Cogan; R v Leak [1975] 2 All ER 1059; (1975) 61 Cr App R 217; [1975] Crim LR 584t; (1975) 139 JP 608; (1975) 125 NLJ 623t; [1976] QB 217; (1975) 119 SJ 473; [1975] 3 WLR 316 CA Can be guilty of aiding/abetting rape even if principal acquitted of rape as believed consent.

R v Cross and Channon [1971] 3 All ER 641; (1971) 55 Cr App R 540; [1972] Crim LR 95; (1972) 136 JP 5 CA If unforeseen, prosecution may before evidence complete seek conviction under Criminal Justice Act 1967, s 4; adjournment for defendant if needs to prepare defence; jury to state whether find guilty of substantive/s 4 offence.

R v Daily Mirror Newspapers, Limited; R v Glover (Charles William) (1921-22) 16 Cr App R 131; (1922) 86 JP 151; [1922] 2 KB 530; (1922) 57 LJ 196; [1922] 91 LJCL 712; (1922) 127 LTR 218; (1921-22) 66 SJ 559; (1921-22) XXXVIII TLR 531 CCA Could not try limited company by indictment but might charge person for aiding and abetting limited company in criminal act.

R v Donald (John Thomas); R v Donald (Lesley) (1986) 83 Cr App R 49; [1986] Crim LR 535; (1986) 130 SJ 284 CA Could be convicted of assisting an offender who had not at time of assistance been convicted/admitted arrestable offence where was evidence had participated in same.

R v Dunnington [1984] 1 All ER 676; (1984) 78 Cr App R 171; [1984] Crim LR 98; (1984) 148 JP 316; [1984] QB 472; (1983) 127 SJ 822; [1983] TLR 569; [1984] 2 WLR 125 CA Is attempt where acts if completed would be aiding and abetting even if principal act only attempt.

R v Gommo [1964] Crim LR 469 CCA That passenger had been sitting next to driver who was disqualified was not per se evidence that knew of disqualification (and so was guilty of aiding and abetting offence of driving while disqualified).

R v Goodspeed (Charles) (1910-11) 6 Cr App R 133; (1910-11) 55 SJ 273; (1910-11) XXVII TLR 255 CCA Accessory before burglary can be receiver thereafter; that did not carry out promise to aid and abet burglars was not countermanding of promise.

R v Humphreys and Turner [1965] 3 All ER 689; [1966] Crim LR 98; (1966) 130 JP 45; (1965-66) 116 NLJ 159 CrCt Person can be convicted of aiding and abetting in crime of which principal offender acquitted.

R v JF Alford Transport Ltd; R v Alford; R v Paynes [1997] 2 Cr App R 326; (1997) 141 SJ LB 73; [1997] TLR 176 CA Failure to prove intention on part of company/its management to do what knew to be aiding and abetting tachograph offence merited quashing of conviction for same.

R v Jones (Kevin Edward); R v Mirrless (Neil Robert) (1977) 65 Cr App R 250 CA Must intend to and actually encourage assault to be guilty of assault occasioning actual bodily harm where did not physically partake in same.

R v Kearon and Williamson [1955] Crim LR 183 Sessions Person could not be guilty of aiding and abetting offence where was too drunk to possess necessary intent.

R v Leahy (Mark Anthony) [1985] Crim LR 99 CrCt On liability for aiding and abetting in offence where had been inciting person to strike X but person instead struck Y.

R v McCarthy [1964] 1 All ER 95; (1964) 48 Cr App R 111; [1964] Crim LR 225; (1964) 114 LJ 74; (1964) 108 SJ 17 [1964] 1 WLR 196; CCA On elements necessary to establish guilt of aiding and abetting offence (here of possession of explosive substance).

R v Morgan [1972] 1 All ER 348; (1972) 56 Cr App R 181; [1972] Crim LR 96t; (1972) 136 JP 160; (1971) 121 NLJ 1098; (1972) 116 SJ 76; [1972] 2 WLR 123 CA Need to set out offence of principal offender when charging assistant.

R v Moss (Robert Francis); R v Harte (Stephen Patrick) (1986) 82 Cr App R 116; [1985] Crim LR 659; (1986) 150 JP 26 CA On what constitute a 'prison' under Prison Act 1952, s 39.

R v Patel [1970] Crim LR 274 CA Person must know that other in possession of a dangerous drug before can be guilty of aiding and abetting in possession of same.

R v Payne [1965] Crim LR 543t CCA Were guilty of aiding and abetting corruption where were party to placing of false statement on local government forms (did not have to know content of statement).

R v Raven (Alfred John) and Dellow (Mabel Nelly) (1920) 84 JP 139 CCC Failed bigamy prosecution where first (foreign) marriage not proved to court's satisfaction.

R v Reed (Nicholas) [1982] Crim LR 819 CA On what it means to 'procure' something (here suicide).

R v Rourke [1956] Crim LR 326 Magistrates Doctor not guilty of aiding and abetting unlawful possession of drugs where prescribed heroin to patient who - unknown to him - was also obtaining same from another doctor.

R v Spinks [1982] 1 ALL ER 587; (1982) 74 Cr App R 263; [1982] Crim LR 231 CA That accused's out-of-court statements not be used against co-accused applies where alleged offender and person charged with assisting him tried together.

R v Whitefield (Arthur Armour Mallie) (1984) 79 Cr App R 36; [1984] Crim LR 97 CA To extricate oneself from unlawful common enterprise must unequivocally explain to others that are not party to enterprise and will not help at all.

R v Whitehouse [1977] 3 All ER 737; (1977) 65 Cr App R 33; [1977] Crim LR 689; (1978) 142 JP 45; (1977) 127 NLJ 369t; (1977) 121 SJ 171; [1977] QB 868; [1977] 2 WLR 925 CA Girl under 16 cannot aid and abet in incest; Court of Appeal may hear appeal that offence charged not an offence.

Saqui v Lawrence and Stearns (1911) 80 LJCL 451 (also HC KBD) CA Porter who admitted burglars to house and was later given share of spoils a principal in second degree/guilty of theft.

Saqui v Lawrence and Stearns (1911) 80 LJCL 451 (also CA) HC KBD Porter who admitted burglars to house and was later given share of spoils an accessory before the fact.

Smith v Baker [1972] Crim LR 25; [1971] RTR 350 HC QBD Not aiding and abetting in driving uninsured vehicle to sit in stolen car until no longer being driven and then run away when see police approaching.

Smith v Jenner [1968] Crim LR 99t; (1967) 117 NLJ 1296t; (1968) 112 SJ 52 HC QBD Successful appeal by driving instructor against conviction for aiding and abetting learner driver in unlicensed driving of car.

Smith v Reynolds and others; Smith v Hancock; Smith v Lowe [1986] Crim LR 559 HC QBD On elements of offence of aiding and abetting in obstruction of police officer.

Stanton (D) and Sons Ltd v Webber [1972] Crim LR 544; [1973] RTR 86; (1972) 116 SJ 666 HC QBD On what knowledge was necessary to prove employer guilty aiding/abetting worker-driver in unlicensed driving.

Thambiah v R [1965] 3 All ER 661; [1966] AC 37; [1965] Crim LR 721; (1965-66) 116 NLJ 131; (1965) 109 SJ 832; [1966] 2 WLR 81 PC Person helping other to prepare for commission of crimes can be guilty of abetting them when done; admission anytime between beginning and ending of investigation is inadmissible.

Thomas v Lindop (1950) 94 SJ 371; (1950) WN (I) 227 HC KBD On what it means to aid and abet an offence.

Thornton v Mitchell [1940] 1 All ER 339; (1940) 104 JP 108; (1940) 162 LTR 296; (1940) 84 SJ 257; (1939-40) LVI TLR 296; (1940) WN (I) 52 HC KBD Only driver can be guilty of driving without due care and attention; no conviction for aiding and abetting where principal acquitted of offence.

Tuck v Robson [1970] Crim LR 273t HC QBD On what constitutes 'aiding and abetting' offence.

ACCOMPLICE (assisting escape)

R v Abbott [1956] Crim LR 337t CCA Valid conviction for assisting prisoner (doing work outside prison) to escape.

ACCOMPLICE (general)

Nkambule (Gideon) and Others v R [1950] AC 379 PC Once satisfied crime was committed can under Swaziland law convict accused thereof on accomplice's evidence.

R v Heuser (Henry) (1910-11) 6 Cr App R 76 CCA Police officers party to entrapment are not accomplices.

ACCOMPLICE (inciting person to become accessory)

R v Bodin (Leif Viktor) and Bodin (Dolores Patricia) [1979] Crim LR 176 CA No offence of inciting someone to become accessory before the fact to an offence (assault).

ACCOMPLICE (murder)

Nkambule (Gideon) and Others v R [1950] AC 379 PC Once satisfied crime was committed can under Swaziland law convict accused thereof on accomplice's evidence.

ACCOMPLICE (suicide)

Attorney-General v Able and others [1984] 1 All ER 277; (1984) 78 Cr App R 197; [1984] Crim LR 35; [1984] QB 795; (1983) 127 SJ 731; [1983] TLR 294; [1983] 3 WLR 845 HC QBD Civil court will issue declaration on criminal law if declaration would not criminalise non-criminal behaviour; must know that giving euthanasia booklet to person considering suicide - which occurs imminently - to be assisting in suicide.

ACTING AS SOLICITOR (general)

Reynolds v Hoyle [1975] Crim LR 527; (1975) 125 NLJ 800t HC QBD Successful prosecution for unlawful conveyancing by unqualified person.

ADMINISTERING NOXIOUS THING (general)

R v Cunningham [1957] 2 All ER 412; (1957) 41 Cr App R 155; [1957] Crim LR 473t; (1957) 121 JP 451; (1957) 107 LJ 392; [1957] 2 QB 396; (1957) 101 SJ 503 CCA 'Maliciously' administering noxious thing means to do so intending/being reckless as to foreseen effect.

R v Cunningham [1957] Crim LR 326 Assizes On malice as an element of unlawfully and maliciously causing another to take a noxious thing.

R v Dones [1987] Crim LR 682 CCC Squirting ammonia at another was not 'administering a noxious thing' contrary to Offences against the Person Act 1861, s 24.

R v Gillard (Simon Paul) (1988) 87 Cr App R 189; [1988] Crim LR 531 CA On what it means to 'administer' noxious thing under Offences against the Person Act 1861, s 24 (includes spraying CS gas from spray can into face).

R v Hill (1986) 83 Cr App R 386; [1986] Crim LR 815 HL Test of criminality where charged with administering noxious thing is whether intended to harm victim's health.

R v Hill (Frederick Philip) (1985) 81 Cr App R 206; [1985] Crim LR 384 CA Must look to overall intent of accused in deciding if accused acted with intent to injure - keeping person awake need not mean intent to injure.

R v Marcus [1981] 2 All ER 833; (1981) 73 Cr App R 49; [1981] Crim LR 490; (1981) 145 JP 380; (1981) 131 NLJ 504; (1981) 125 SJ 396; [1981] 1 WLR 774 CA Quantity and quality relevant in deciding if substance noxious; 'noxious' does not only apply to bodily health injury.

R v Marlow (1965) 49 Cr App R 49; [1965] Crim LR 35 CCC 'Noxious thing' /'poison' in Offences against the Person Act 1861, ss 58 and 59 not confined to abortifacients.

R v Shillingford [1968] Crim LR 282t; (1968) 112 SJ 170 CA Is single offence of administering drug to stupefy woman even though single administration enabled several men to have sex with woman.

R v Shillingford (Holly); R v Vanderwall (Rayonne Niel) (1968) 52 Cr App R 188; (1968) 132 JP 264; (1968) 118 NLJ 421; [1968] 1 WLR 566 CA Is single offence of administering drug to stupefy woman even though single administration enabled several men to have sex with woman.

R v Weatherall [1968] Crim LR 115 CCC Failed prosecution for administration of noxious thing (portion of sleeping tablet in tea) with intent to injure, aggrieve, annoy as insufficient proof of intent and thing administered not shown to be noxious.

R v Wood [1975] Crim LR 236 CrCt Wife who surreptitiously placed sleeping tablets in husband's coffee to stop him from keeping her up at night not guilty of causing noxious thing to be taken.

AFFRAY (general)

Button v Director of Public Prosecutions; Swain v Director of Public Prosecutions [1965] 3 All ER 587; [1966] AC 591; (1966) 50 Cr App R 36; [1966] Crim LR 39; (1966) 130 JP 48; (1965-66) 116 NLJ 131; (1965) 109 SJ 872; [1965] 3 WLR 1131 HL Affray need not occur in public place to be affray.

Cobb v Director of Public Prosecutions (1992) 156 JP 746 HC QBD On what constitutes (must be proved to establish) offence of affray.

R v Allan and others [1963] 2 All ER 897; (1963) 47 Cr App R 243; (1963) 127 JP 511; (1963) 113 LJ 561; [1965] 1 QB 130; (1963) 107 SJ 596; [1963] 3 WLR 677 CCA Principal in second degree to affray must have physically encouraged affray.

R v Allen and others [1963] Crim LR 561t CCA On what constitutes offence of affray.

R v Button; R v Swain [1965] Crim LR 294t; (1965) 109 SJ 193; [1965] 2 WLR 992 CCA Affray occurs where fight between two or more persons in any place which puts fear into uninvolved third party.

R v Clark and others (1963) 47 Cr App R 203; [1963] Crim LR 839 Assizes Bar was a public place.

R v Davison [1992] Crim LR 31 CA On elements of offence of affray.

R v Dixon [1993] Crim LR 579 CA On elements of offence of affray.

R v Farmill (C); R v Gladman; R v Firth; R v Wood [1982] Crim LR 38 CrCt On elements of offence of affray (need for third party to be put in terror).

R v Fleming and Robinson [1989] Crim LR 658; (1989) 153 JP 517 CA Where only persons involved in alleged violent disorder are those charged at least three of them must be found guilty or all must be found not guilty.

R v Hosken [1974] Crim LR 48 CrCt Whether possess requisite mens rea for constructive manslaughter a subjective matter.

R v Jones (John McKinsie); R v Tomlinson (Eric); R v Warren (Dennis Michael); R v O'Shea (Kenneth Desmond Francis); R v Carpenter (John); R v Llywarch (John Elfyn) (1974) 59 Cr App R 120 CA On what constitutes 'intimidation' under Conspiracy and Protection of Property Act 1875, s 7; on constituent elements of unlawful assembly and of affray.

R v Jones and others [1974] Crim LR 663t; (1974) 124 NLJ 270t; (1974) 118 SJ 277 CA On elements of affray.

R v Kane and others [1965] 1 All ER 705; [1965] Crim LR 363; (1965) 129 JP 170 Assizes Public place is any place to which no real restrictions on public access.

R v Khan and Rakhman [1963] Crim LR 562t CCA Self-defence a defence to affray.

R v Mapstone and others [1963] 3 All ER 930; [1964] Crim LR 291; (1964) 128 JP 94; [1964] 1 WLR 439 Assizes On affray.

R v Morris and others (1963) 47 Cr App R 202; [1963] Crim LR 838 Assizes Dance hall was a public place.

R v Notman [1994] Crim LR 518 CA Actions must have been substantial cause of injury suffered to constitute assault; direction to convict of using threatening words/behaviour ought not to have been made where guilty plea to same rather than affray (offence charged) withdrawn.

R v Plastow (Bruce John) (1989) 88 Cr App R 48; [1988] Crim LR 604 CA Bystander's terror must be terror for own safety in offence of affray.

R v Robinson [1993] Crim LR 581 CA Mere words, albeit threateningly delivered, did not amount to affray.

R v Sanchez (1996) TLR 6/3/96 CA On elements of offence of affray.

R v Scarrow (Terence Roland); R v Brown (Douglas Stephen); R v Attlesey (William) (1968) 52 Cr App R 591 CA On what constitutes affray; can be convicted of affray though those charged fought with others not each other.

R v Sharp and another [1957] 1 All ER 577; (1957) 41 Cr App R 86; (1957) 121 JP 227; (1957) 107 LJ 169; [1957] 1 QB 552; (1957) 101 SJ 230; [1957] 2 WLR 472 CCA Fight where one acting in self-defence not affray; that would terrify reasonable person adequate proof of terror.

R v Sidhu and others [1976] Crim LR 379t; (1976) 126 NLJ 314t CA Affray conviction quashed in light of unsatisfactory evidence; 'accomplice'/'corroboration' alien concepts to offence of affray.

R v Summers (Stanley George) (1972) 56 Cr App R 604; [1972] Crim LR 635 CA On what constitutes an affray.

R v Taylor (Vincent) [1973] 1 All ER 78; (1973) 57 Cr App R 122; [1972] Crim LR 772t; (1973) 137 JP 91; (1972) 122 NLJ 918t; (1972) 116 SJ 800; [1972] 3 WLR 961 CA One person fighting unlawfully may be guilty of affray; if two charged with affray and one acquitted other may be convicted.

R v Worton [1990] Crim LR 124 CA Substitution of conviction of affray for one of violent disorder.

Reference by the Attorney-General under Section 36 of the Criminal Justice Act 1972 (No 3 of 1983) [1985] 1 All ER 501; (1985) 80 Cr App R 150; [1985] Crim LR 207; [1985] QB 242; (1985) 129 SJ 115; [1985] 2 WLR 253 CA On what constitutes affray in a public place.

Taylor v Director of Public Prosecutions [1973] 2 All ER 1108; [1974] Crim LR 98; [1973] AC 964; (1973) 57 Cr App R 915; (1973) 137 JP 608; (1973) 123 NLJ 746t; (1973) 117 SJ 544; [1973] 3 WLR 140 HL May be guilty of affray even if only person fighting unlawfully to terror of others.

ANIMAL (badger-fighting)

Crown Prosecution Service v Barry (1989) 153 JP 557 HC QBD Procuring fight between dog and badger not an offence under Protection of Animals Act 1911 as badger not a domestic/captive animal as the 1911 Act requires.

ANIMAL (bird)

Flower v Watts (1910) 45 LJ 391; (1909-10) XXVI TLR 495; (1910) WN (I) 146 HC KBD Possession in London of live larks lawfully caught in another place guilty of offence.

Harris v Lucas (1919) 83 JP 208; [1919] 88 LJCL 1082; (1918-19) XXXV TLR 486; (1919) WN (I) 147 HC KBD On deciding whether birds 'recently taken' for purposes of Wild Birds Protection Act 1880, s 1.

Hollis v Young (1908) 72 JP 199; (1908) XCVIII LTR 751; (1907-08) XXIV TLR 500 HC KBD State and colour of birds plus supporting evidence of witness could have grounded conviction for possession of recently taken wild birds contrary to Wild Birds Protection Act 1880, s 3.

Jipps v Lord and another [1982] TLR 277 CA On determining whether mechanically propelled boat used in pursuit of wild bird for purpose of killing same.

Kirkland v Robinson [1987] Crim LR 643 CA Possession of live birds contrary to Wildlife and Countryside Act 1981, s 1(2)(a), a strict liability offence.

Partridge v Crittenden [1968] Crim LR 325t; (1968) 118 NLJ 374t; (1968) 112 SJ 582; [1968] 1 WLR 1204 HC QBD Classified sales advertisement an invitation to treat not an offer for sale (so not guilty of offering to sell protected live wild bird).

R v Hopkins and another; ex parte Lovejoy (1911) 75 JP 341 HC KBD Issue of fact for magistrate whether bird recently taken.

Robinson v Everett and W and FC Bonham and Son Ltd [1988] Crim LR 699 HC QBD Rehearing ordered of prosecution for possession of dead wild bird.

Robinson v Hughes [1987] Crim LR 644 HC QBD On elements of offence of laying poison for wild birds in breach of Wildlife and Countryside Act 1981, s 5(1)(a).

Robinson v Kenworthy [1982] TLR 257 HC QBD On determining whether bird a 'wild bird' for purposes of the Protection of Birds Act 1954, s 1.

Starling v Brooks [1956] Crim LR 480t HC QBD Successful prosecution for confinement of budgerigars in small cages.

ANIMAL (cruelty)

Armstrong v Mitchell (1901-07) XX Cox CC 497; (1903) 67 JP 329; (1903) LXXXVIII LTR 870; (1902-03) XIX TLR 525 HC KBD Need not be cruelty to shoot at trespassing dog with intent to injure.

Bowyer v Morgan (1907-09) XXI Cox CC 203; (1906) 70 JP 252; (1906-07) XCV LTR 27; (1905-06) 50 SJ 377; (1905-06) XXII TLR 426 HC KBD Branding of sheep on nose with hot iron not cruelty.

Dee v Yorke (1914) 78 JP 359; (1913-14) XXX TLR 552 HC KBD Whether treatment of animal was cruelty a question of fact for justices.

Green v Cross (1910) 74 JP 357; (1910-11) 103 LTR 279; (1909-10) XXVI TLR 507 HC KBD Person unnecessarily leaving two-hour delay in releasing injured dog from vermin-trap could be guilty of cruelty.

Greenwood v Backhouse (1901-07) XX Cox CC 196; (1902) LXXXVI LTR 566 HC KBD Prosecution for cruelty to animals failed as no proof of guilty knowledge.

Hooker v Gray (1907-09) XXI Cox CC 437; (1907) 71 JP 337; (1907) XCVI LTR 706; (1906-07) XXIII TLR 472 HC KBD Party severely wounding cat, allowing to crawl away, then later killing it not guilty of cruelty.

Johnson v Needham (1911-13) XXII Cox CC 63; (1909) 73 JP 117; [1909] 1 KB 626; (1909) C LTR 493; (1908-09) XXV TLR 245; (1909) WN (I) 26 HC KBD Ill-treatment/abuse/torture of animals are separate offences.

North Staffordshire Railway Company v Waters (1914-15) XXIV Cox CC 27; (1914) 78 JP 116; (1914) 110 LTR 237 HC KBD Failed prosecution against railway company for cruel transport of animals.

Peterssen v RSPCA [1993] Crim LR 852 HC QBD On elements of offence of causing unreasonable suffering to animal (here conviction upheld for causing unreasonable suffering to sheep).

Potter v Challans (1911-13) XXII Cox CC 302; (1910) 74 JP 114; (1910) 102 LTR 325 HC KBD Prosecution failed to discharge burden of proof.

R v Cable and another; ex parte O'Shea (1906) 70 JP 246; (1906) 41 LJ 246; [1906] 75 LJKB 381; (1906) XCIV LTR 772; (1905-06) 50 SJ 391; (1905-06) XXII TLR 438; (1906) WN (I) 82; (1905-06) 54 WR 626 HC KBD General conviction for over-stocking animals with milk is good (no need for separate conviction in respect of individual animals).

R v Rawson and another (Justices); ex parte Morley (1909-10) 101 LTR 463 HC KBD One of four convictions for cruelty (to horses) allowed to stand where procedural irregularity required quashing of other three.

Rodgers v Pickersgill (1910) 74 JP 324; (1909-10) 54 SJ 564; (1909-10) XXVI TLR 493 HC KBD On what constitutes hunting of animals (so that Wild Animals in Captivity Act 1900, s 4 does not apply and are not guilty of cruelty).

Steele v Rogers (1912) 76 JP 150; (1911-12) XXVIII TLR 198 HC KBD Cruelty to stranded whale that would have been washed away with tide not offence under Wild Animals in Captivity Protection Act 1900.

Thielbar v Craigen (1907-09) XXI Cox CC 44; (1905) 69 JP 421; (1905-06) XCIII LTR 600; (1904-05) XXI TLR 745 HC KBD Creating situation in which lion could savage pony was unlawful cruelty to pony.

Waters v Braithwaite (1914-15) XXIV Cox CC 34; (1914) 78 JP 124; (1914) 110 LTR 266; (1913-14) XXX TLR 107 HC KBD Custom not defence to cruelty to animals charge.

Waters v Meakin (1915-17) XXV Cox CC 432; (1916) 80 JP 276; [1916] 2 KB 111; [1916] 85 LJKB 1378; (1916-17) 115 LTR 110; (1915-16) XXXII TLR 480; (1916) WN (I) 197 HC KBD Cruelty to rabbit conviction avoided by way of statutory protection afforded coursing meetings (Protection of Animals Act 1911, s 1(3) (b)).

White v Fox (1931-32) XLVIII TLR 641 HC KBD Deer hind not a domestic animal so hunting of same not breach of Protection of Animals Act 1911.

Whiting v Ivens (1915-17) XXV Cox CC 128; (1915) 79 JP 457; [1915] 84 LJKB 1878; (1915-16) 113 LTR 869; (1914-15) XXXI TLR 492 HC KBD Case against owner ought not to have been dismissed where was prima facie case of cruelty to animal.

ANIMAL (custody)

RSPCA v Miller [1994] Crim LR 516; [1994] TLR 131 HC QBD Whether have 'custody' of animal depends on particular facts of each case (holding leash of another's dog did not place it in leash-holder's custody).

ANIMAL (deer)

Threlkeld v Smith (1901-07) XX Cox CC 38; [1901] 2 KB 531; [1901] 70 LJK/QB 921; (1901-02) LXXXV LTR 275; (1900-01) XVII TLR 612; (1901-02) 50 WR 158 HC KBD Killing of deer outside place kept is killing deer lawfully come by (Larceny Act 1861, s 14) even though killer wrongly on third party's land.

White v Fox (1931-32) XLVIII TLR 641 HC KBD Deer hind not a domestic animal so hunting of same not breach of Protection of Animals Act 1911.

ANIMAL (dog)

Bates v Director of Public Prosecutions (1993) 157 JP 1004; [1993] TLR 118 HC QBD Having unmuzzled dangerous dog inside car in public place constituted offence of having unmuzzled dangerous dog in public place.

Bond v Belville [1963] Crim LR 103t HC QBD Valid dismissal of information in which had been alleged that hunt foxhounds had worried cattle.

Burton v Atkinson (1907-09) XXI Cox CC 575; (1908) 72 JP 198; (1908) XCVIII LTR 748; (1907-08) XXIV TLR 498 HC KBD Foxhound puppy not required to wear collar when on highway.

Cichon v Director of Public Prosecutions [1994] Crim LR 918 HC QBD Could not plead defence of necessity to having unmuzzled pit bull terrier in public place (allegedly unmuzzled to prevent discomfort in coughing).

Crawford v Coggan [1964] Crim LR 292t HC QBD Person charged with custody/control of dog has onus of proving are not in his custody/control; on elements of being a 'keeper' of a dog.

Cresswell v Sirl (1948) 112 JP 69; [1948] 1 KB 241; (1947) 97 LJ 648; [1948] 117 LJR 654; (1947) 91 SJ 653; (1947) LXIII TLR 620 CA On test of criminal liability for shooting of trespassing dog.

Director of Public Prosecutions v Kellet [1994] Crim LR 916; (1994) 158 JP 1138; [1994] TLR 399 HC QBD That had been drunk was no excuse for letting unmuzzled/untethered dangerous dog wander into public place.

Egan v Floyde (1910) 74 JP 223 HC KBD Failed prosecution for not having licence in respect of farm-dog seen in pursuit of rabbits but not encouraged by owner to do same.

Fellowes v Director of Public Prosecutions [1993] Crim LR 523; (1993) 157 JP 936; [1993] TLR 38 HC QBD Garden path not a 'public place' for purposes of Dangerous Dogs Act 1991.

Flack v Church (1918) 82 JP 59; (1917-18) XXXIV TLR 32 HC KBD Can be convicted twice under Dog Licences Act 1867, s 8, for non-possession of licence on different days of same year.

Greener v Director of Public Prosecutions (1996) TLR 15/2/96 HC QBD Could commit offence under Dangerous Dogs Act 1991 by omission.

Hobson v Gledhill [1978] Crim LR 45; (1978) 142 JP 250; (1977) 127 NLJ 1105; (1977) 121 SJ 757; [1978] 1 WLR 215 HC QBD Construction of Guard Dogs Act 1975, s 1(1).

Keddle v Payn [1964] 1 All ER 189; [1964] Crim LR 39; (1964) 128 JP 144; (1964) 114 LJ 25; (1963) 107 SJ 911; [1964] 1 WLR 262 HC QBD Dog could simultaneously be dangerous and not ferocious.

Kite v Napp [1982] TLR 294 HC QBD That dog bit people with bags a characteristic of that dog for purposes of the Animals Act 1971, s 2(2)(b).

Lamb v Gorham (1971) 115 SJ 831 HC QBD Valid finding by justices on basis of single incident that dog was dangerous dog.

Lancaster v Whalley [1957] Crim LR 245 Magistrates Successful prosecution for non-possession of dog licence.

Lee v Dalton and Stevens [1954] Crim LR 206 HC QBD Persons who allowed poultry to wander freely by day over unfenced/uncultivated land entitled to protection of Dogs (Protection of Livestock) Act 1953.

R v Bezzina; R v Codling; R v Elvin [1994] 3 All ER 964; (1994) 99 Cr App R 356; (1994) 158 JP 671; (1994) 138 SJ LB 11; [1993] TLR 629; [1994] 1 WLR 1057 CA Dangerous Dogs Act 1991, s 3(1) imposed strict liability on owners of dogs when latter are in public places and out of control.

R v Crown Court at Knightsbridge, ex parte Dunne; Brock v Director of Public Prosecutions [1993] 4 All ER 491; [1994] 1 WLR 296 HC QBD 'Type' not synonomous with 'breed'.

R v Dymock and another; R v Moger and another (1900-01) 45 SJ 597; (1900-01) XVII TLR 593; (1900-01) 49 WR 618 HC KBD Dog-owner need not be given choice of properly controlling dog before justices order its destruction; on format of dog destruction order.

R v Haringey Magistrates' Court; ex parte Cragg (1997) 161 JP 61; (1996) TLR 4/11/96 HC QBD Immediate re-seizure of dog and bringing of new dangerous dogs charge following acquittal of same owner on same charge was improper.

R v Jones; ex parte Daunton [1963] Crim LR 188; (1963) 127 JP 349; (1963) 113 LJ 138; (1962) 160 SJ 76 HC QBD Destruction order quashed where by time made owner named in order had made good faith transfer of dog to another.

R v Jones; ex parte Davidson [1963] 1 WLR 270 HC QBD Order for destruction of dog (under Dogs Act 1871, s 2) to be made against latest owner of animal.

R v Knightsbridge Crown Court, ex parte Dunne; Brock v Director of Public Prosecutions [1993] Crim LR 853; (1994) 158 JP 213; (1993) 143 NLJ 1479; [1993] TLR 418 HC QBD On determining what constitutes 'type' of dog 'known as the pit bull terrier' (Dangerous Dogs Act 1991, s 1).

R v Leicester Justices; ex parte Workman [1964] Crim LR 455t; (1964) 108 SJ 358; [1964] 1 WLR 707 HC QBD Person against whom dangerous dog order to be made is owner at date of proceedings.

R v Metropolitan Police and the Index of Exempted Dogs, ex parte Wheeler [1993] Crim LR 942 HC QBD Not tattooing pit bull terrier did not render certificate of exemption void.

R v Rawlings [1994] Crim LR 433 CA Whether person in charge of dog ought to have been left to jury where was looking after dog for another and was out shopping when dog got out.

R v Walton Street Justices, ex parte Crothers [1992] Crim LR 875; (1993) 157 JP 171; (1992) 136 SJ LB 221; [1992] TLR 323 HC QBD Person has been prosecuted for an offence for purposes of Dogs Act 1991 if prosecution started but discontinued; person ought to be afforded chance to be heard before destruction of property ordered.

Rafiq v Director of Public Prosecutions (1997) 161 JP 412 HC QBD That dog bit person absent previous indication of inclination to bite could of itself be basis for reasonable apprehension of injury.

Rhodes v Heritage (1951) 115 JP 303; (1951) 101 LJ 219; (1951) 95 SJ 255; [1951] 1 TLR 802; (1951) WN (I) 221 HC KBD Court of summary jurisdiction could not, pursuant to Dogs Act 1871, s 2, order dog to be destroyed.

Ross v Evans [1959] Crim LR 582; (1959) 123 JP 320; (1959) 109 LJ 418; [1959] 2 QB 79; (1959) 103 SJ 393; [1959] 2 WLR 699 HC QBD Dog not 'at large' when was attached to lead.

Sansom v Chief Constable of Kent [1981] Crim LR 617; (1981) 125 SJ 529 HC QBD Successful appeal against finding that dog which killed neighbour's two white pet rabbits was a dangerous dog.

Watson v Jones [1939] LJNCCR 9 CyCt On who is 'owner' of dog for purposes of Dogs Act 1906, s 1(1).

Williams v Richards [1971] Crim LR 41t; (1907) 71 JP 222; [1907] 2 KB 88; (1907) 42 LJ 249; [1907] 76 LJKB 589; (1907) XCVI LTR 644; (1970) 114 SJ 864; (1906-07) XXIII TLR 423; (1907) WN (I) 90 HC KBD That dog has killed sheep shows is dangerous for purposes of Dogs Act 1871, s 2.

Workman v Cowper [1961] Crim LR 394; (1961) 125 JP 254; (1961) 111 LJ 190; [1961] 2 QB 143; (1961) 105 SJ 130; [1961] 2 WLR 386 HC QBD Test for criminality in killing of dog running wild on land.

Workman v Leicester Justices [1964] Crim LR 39 39 HC QBD Justices had no jurisdiction to hear dangerous dog-owner complaint against person who came into possession of dog post-summons/pre-hearing.

ANIMAL (fish)

Alexander v Tonkin [1979] Crim LR 248; (1979) 123 SJ 111 HC QBD On when fishing complete for purposes of Sea Fisheries Regulation Act 1966, s 11(2).

Birkett v McGlassons Ltd [1957] Crim LR 197t; (1957) 101 SJ 149 HC QBD Failed prosecution for sale of salmon during close season.

Cain v Campbell [1978] Crim LR 292 CA Must intend to catch salmon to be guilty of offence under Salmon and Freshwater Fisheries Act 1975, s 19.

Champion v Maughan and another [1984] Crim LR 291; (1984) 128 SJ 220; [1983] TLR 755 HC QBD Placing fixed engine in tidal waters an absolute offence under Salmon and Freshwater Fisheries Act 1975, s 6(1)(a).

Clayton v Pearse (1903-04) 52 WR 495 HC KBD That had power to regulate nets meant had power to prohibit nets entirely.

Davies v Jones and others (1901-02) 46 SJ 319 HC KBD No evidence that tenant did not enjoy right of fishing under lease so conviction for taking of fish quashed.

Edwards v Morgan [1967] Crim LR 40t HC QBD Unless bailiff on duty exercising special responsibility under the Salmon and Freshwater Fisheries Act 1923 (for which must produce warrant) he is a constable and attack on same (as here) is attack on bailee in execution of his duty.

Friend v Brehout (1913-14) 58 SJ 741; (1914) WN (I) 283 HC KBD Bye-law prohibiting trawling in particular bay to safeguard crab-fishing in bay was valid.

Iremonger v Wynne [1957] Crim LR 624 HC QBD Parties acting jointly (one with light/one with gaff) were each guilty of aiding and abetting other in contravention of the Salmon and Fresh Water Fisheries Act 1923, s 1.

Large v Mainprize [1989] Crim LR 213 HC QBD Interpretation of 'recklessness' in context of prosecution for breach of the Sea Fishing (Enforcement of Community Control Measures) Order 1985, reg 3.

Leavett v Clark (1915) 79 JP 396; [1915] 3 KB 9; (1915) 50 LJ 253; [1915] 84 LJKB 2157; (1915-16) 113 LTR 424; (1914-15) XXXI TLR 424; (1915) WN (I) 211 HC KBD Taking of winkles was larceny of fish under Larceny Act 1861, s 24.

Moses v Raywood (1911) 80 LJCL 823 HC KBD Salmon net need not have been placed in water to be guilty of offence of using net to catch salmon contrary to Salmon Fishery Act 1865, s 36.

ANIMAL (general)

Percival v Stanton [1954] Crim LR 308; (1954) 98 SJ 114 HC QBD Net not a 'fixed engine' as was not fixed/secured by anchors.

R v Mallison (William) (1901-07) XX Cox CC 204; (1902) LXXXVI LTR 600 CCR Was larceny from smack-owner for skipper of smack to sell fish caught at sea and take proceeds for self.

R v Vasey and Lally (1905) 69 JP 455; [1905] 2 KB 748; (1905) 40 LJ 750; [1906] 75 LJKB 19; (1905-06) 50 SJ 14; (1905-06) XXII TLR 1; (1905) WN (I) 150; (1905-06) 54 WR 218 CCR On poisoning of fish in salmon river.

Ryan v Ross and another (1963) 113 LJ 383 HC QBD On elements of offence of possessing instrument used for taking salmon/trout with intent of committing fisheries offence.

Stead v Tillotson and another (1899-1900) 44 SJ 212; (1899-1900) XVI TLR 170; (1899-1900) 48 WR 431 HC QBD Taking dying trout with improperly licensed instrument is crime under Salmon Fishery Act 1873, s 22.

Wedderburn and others v The Duke of Atholl and others; The Duke of Atholl and others v The Glover Incorporation of Perth and others (1899-1900) XVI TLR 413 HL Was offence to use 'toot-and-haul' nets for salmon fishing on River Tay.

Wells v Hardy [1964] 1 All ER 953; [1964] Crim LR 405t; (1964) 128 JP 328; (1964) 114 LJ 440; (1964) 108 SJ 238; [1964] 2 WLR 958 HC QBD Construction of Larceny Act 1861, s 24 (unlawful and wilful taking of fish).

Wharton v Taylor [1965] Crim LR 432t HC QBD Person who did not have licence when fishing was guilty of unlicensed fishing even though subsequently obtained licence.

ANIMAL (general)

Barnard v Evans (1926-30) XXVIII Cox CC 69; (1925) 89 JP 165; [1925] 2 KB 794; [1925] 94 LJCL 932; (1925) 133 LTR 829; (1924-25) XLI TLR 682; (1925) WN (I) 234 HC KBD Conviction merited for unwarranted shooting and injuring of trespassing dog.

Cheshire County Council v Alan Helliwell and Sons (Bolton) Ltd [1991] Crim LR 210; (1991) 155 JP 425; [1990] TLR 766 HC QBD Transporting of animals while are unfit to travel a strict liability offence (Transport of Animals (Road and Rail) Order 1951).

Edgar v Spain (1899-1901) XIX Cox CC 719; (1901) LXXXIV LTR 631 HC KBD Interpretation of animal 'brought...for' slaughter clause of Cruelty to Animals Act 1849, s 8.

Nethaway v Brewer (1931) WN (I) 109 HC KBD On extent of duty under the Transit of Animals (Amendment) Order 1930 to clean conveyance after use same for transporting animals.

R v Isaacs [1994] Crim LR 517 HC QBD Test as to what constitutes 'unnecessary suffering' to animal is objective.

Smith v Baker (1961) 125 JP 53; (1960) 110 LJ 845; (1961) 105 SJ 17; [1961] 1 WLR 38 HC QBD Police officer can bring complaint under Dogs Act 1871, s 2.

Southern Water Authority v The Nature Conservancy Council [1991] Crim LR 769 HC QBD On who is an 'occupier' of land for purposes of Wildlife and Countryside Act 1981, s 28(1)(b).

ANIMAL (hunt)

Winder and others v Director of Public Prosecutions (1996) TLR 13/8/96 CA Running after hunt with intent of interfering with same an offence under the Criminal Justice and Public Order Act 1994, s 68.

ANIMAL (killing cat)

Nye v Niblett and others (1918-21) XXVI Cox CC 113; (1918) 82 JP 57; [1918] 1 KB 23; [1918] 87 LJCL 590; (1917-18) 117 LTR 722; (1917) WN (I) 314 HC KBD Need not show particular animal kept for domestic purpose if such animals normally so kept to sustain conviction under Malicious Damage Act 1861, s 41.

ANIMAL (pigeon)

Cotterill v Penn [1935] All ER 204; (1934-39) XXX Cox CC 258; (1935) 99 JP 276; [1936] 1 KB 53; (1935) 79 LJ 432; [1936] 105 LJCL 1; (1935) 153 LTR 377; (1935) 79 SJ 383; (1934-35) LI TLR 459; (1935) WN (I) 107 HC KBD That mistook breed of bird did not relieve liability for intended killing of particular bird under Larceny Act 1861, s 23.

Horton v Gwynne [1921] All ER 497; (1918-21) XXVI Cox CC 744; (1921) 85 JP 210; [1921] 2 KB 661; [1921] LJCL 1151; (1921) 125 LTR 309; (1921) WN (I) 144 HC KBD No defence to killing house pigeon that thought it was wild pigeon.

Smith v Dear (1901-07) XX Cox CC 458; (1903) 67 JP 244; (1903) LXXXVIII LTR 664 HC KBD Any person (not just owner) may prosecute for unlawful and wilful killing of house pigeon.

ANIMAL (poaching)

Jones v Evans [1978] Crim LR 230 CA Conviction for poaching rabbits.

R v Lines (1901-07) XX Cox CC 142; [1902] 1 KB 199; [1902] 71 LJCL 125; (1901-02) LXXXV LTR 790; (1901-02) 46 SJ 138; (1901-02) XVIII TLR 176; (1901) WN (I) 251; (1901-02) 50 WR 303 CCR Could not be indicted for misdemeanour of night-poaching unless were twice previously charged with night-poaching by self.

ANIMAL (rabbit)

Jenkins v Ash and another (1926-30) XXVIII Cox CC 665; (1929) 93 JP 229; (1929) 141 LTR 591; (1928-29) XLV TLR 479 HC KBD Cruelty to rabbit (coursing/hunting exemptions inapplicable).

ANIMAL (sheep)

Bingley v Quest (1907-09) XXI Cox CC 505; (1907) 71 JP 443; (1907-08) XCVII LTR 394 HC KBD Sheep dipping offence.

Peterssen v RSPCA [1993] Crim LR 852 HC QBD On elements of offence of causing unreasonable suffering to animal (here conviction upheld for causing unreasonable suffering to sheep).

ANIMAL (wild animals)

Director of Public Prosecutions v Barry [1989] Crim LR 645; (1989) 133 SJ 784 HC QBD Offence of procuring fighting of animal under Protection of Animals Act 1911, s 1(1)(c) included wild animals.

ARMY OFFENCE (general)

Cox v Army Council [1962] Crim LR 459; (1962) 112 LJ 256; (1962) 106 SJ 305; [1962] 2 WLR 950 HL Proper that army sergeant be convicted under Army Act 1955 of driving without due care and attention in Germany.

R v Cox (1962) 112 LJ 41; (1962) 106 SJ 17; [1962] 2 WLR 126 CMAC Proper that army sergeant be convicted under Army Act 1955 of driving without due care and attention in Germany.

ARREST (citizen's arrest)

R v Kelbie [1996] Crim LR 802 CA On making of citizen's arrest as defence to charge of assault occasioning actual bodily harm.

ARREST (escape from arrest)

R v Timmis (David) [1976] Crim LR 129 CrCt Person who ran away after breath test could be guilty of escape from arrest.

ARREST (general)

Abbassy and another v Commissioner of Police of the Metropolis and others [1990] 1 All ER 193; (1990) 90 Cr App R 250; (1989) 139 NLJ 1266; [1990] RTR 164; [1990] 1 WLR 385 CA Police officer exercising power of arrest without warrant need not specify offence for which being arrested but can indicate general nature of offence.

Alderson v Booth [1969] 2 All ER 271; (1969) 53 Cr App R 301; [1969] Crim LR 270t; (1969) 133 JP 346; (1969) 119 NLJ 225t; [1969] 2 QB 216; (1969) 113 SJ 268; [1969] 2 WLR 1252 HC QBD Any words clearly informing person that are under compulsion is valid arrest.

Anderton v Royle [1985] RTR 91 HC QBD Police station breath test results admissible though had not sought to administer preliminary breath test upon stopping defendant on road.

Barnard and another v Gorman [1941] 3 All ER 45; [1941] AC 378; (1941) 105 JP 379; (1941) 91 LJ 326; (1942) 92 LJ 52/59; [1941] 110 LJ 557; (1941) 165 LTR 308; (1940-41) LVII TLR 681; (1941) WN (I) 194 HL Under Customs Consolidation Act 1876, s 186 can arrest actual/suspected 'offender'.

Bentley v Brudzinski (1982) 75 Cr App R 217; [1982] Crim LR 825; [1982] TLR 122 HC QBD Unlawful arrest of person remaining with constable as volunteer meant assault on constable was not assault on constable in execution of duty.

Brooks v Director of Public Prosecutions of Jamaica and another [1994] 2 All ER 231; [1994] 1 AC 568; [1994] 2 WLR 381 PC DPP may ask judge to direct/agree to preferral of indictment; if after magistrate's refusal and no new evidence indictment only very exceptionally.

Bunyard v Hayes [1985] RTR 348; [1984] TLR 603 HC QBD Issue of lawfulness of arrest did not not affect culpability for failure to provide breath specimen.

Castorina v Chief Constable of Surrey (1988) 138 NLJ 180 CA On determining reasonableness of police arrest.

Chapman v Director of Public Prosecutions (1989) 89 Cr App R 190; [1988] Crim LR 843; (1989) 153 JP 27 HC QBD Conviction quashed where absence of evidence that entry onto premises to effect arrest was reasonable.

Coffin and another v Smith and another; R v Coates (1980) 71 Cr App R 221; [1971] Crim LR 370; [1971] RTR 74 CA Conviction quashed where validity of arrest/proper functioning of breathalyser not left to jury.

Da Costa Small v Kirkpatrick (1979) 68 Cr App R 186; [1979] Crim LR 41 HC QBD Unlawful arrest on warrant as warrant not physically in police officer's possession when effected arrest.

Da Costa Small v Kirkpatrick (1978) 128 NLJ 1125t CA Unlawful arrest on warrant as warrant not physically in police officer's possession when effected arrest.

Dawes v Director of Public Prosecutions [1995] 1 Cr App R 65; [1994] Crim LR 604; [1994] RTR 209; [1994] TLR 112 HC QBD Valid arrest for aggravated driving.

Director of Public Prosecutions v Godwin (1992) 156 JP 643; [1991] RTR 303 HC QBD Evidence as to excess alcohol in defendant's breath validly excluded on basis that obtained on foot of unlawful arrest.

Director of Public Prosecutions v Hancock and Tuttle [1995] Crim LR 139 HC QBD Officer making arrest under the Public Order Act 1986, s 5(4) must be the same officer who administered warning required under that section to offender.

Director of Public Prosecutions v Kitching [1990] Crim LR 394; (1990) 154 JP 293 HC QBD Police officer could arrest person for being drunk and disorderly in public place.

Edwards v Director of Public Prosecutions (1993) 97 Cr App R 301; [1993] Crim LR 854; [1993] TLR 184 HC QBD Was not valid arrest for obstruction of police officer in execution of duty where arrestee aided person in turn arrested by officer under false pretext.

Elias and others v Pasmore and others [1934] All ER 380; (1934) 98 JP 92; [1934] 2 KB 164; (1934) 77 LJ 94; (1934) 103 LJCL 223; (1934) 150 LTR 438; (1934) 78 SJ 104; (1933-34) L TLR 196; (1934) WN (I) 30 HC KBD Can search arrestee/take property relevant to crime; property seized may be retained until charges concluded; unlawful seizure of documents overlooked where are evidence of crime.

Erskine v Hollin [1971] Crim LR 243t; (1971) 121 NLJ 154t; [1971] RTR 199; (1971) 115 SJ 207 HC QBD Improper to arrest person and then wait for breathalyser to be brought to scene.

Evans v Macklen [1976] Crim LR 120 HC QBD Person in respect of whom warrant for arrest for sentencing purposes had been issued could be arrested by police officer without warrant.

Farrow v Tunnicliffe [1976] Crim LR 126 HC QBD Could under Misuse of Drugs Act 1971 remove suspect offender thereunder to another place to conduct search there.

Faulkner v Willetts [1982] Crim LR 453; [1982] RTR 159 HC QBD Valid arrest where constable's entry into house appeared from evidence not to be trespass.

Felix v Thomas [1966] 3 All ER 21; [1967] AC 292; (1965-66) 116 NLJ 1173; (1966) 110 SJ 528; [1966] 3 WLR 902 PC Person could be arrested on suspicion of having stolen goods 'in any [public/private] place'.

Fox v Chief Constable of Gwent [1985] 1 All ER 230; [1984] Crim LR 567; [1984] RTR 402; (1985) 129 SJ 49; [1984] TLR 406; [1985] 1 WLR 33 HC QBD Breath specimen admissible though obtained on foot of unlawful arrest.

Fox v Chief Constable of Gwent [1986] Crim LR 59; (1985) 129 SJ 757 HL Breath specimen admissible though obtained on foot of unlawful arrest.

G v Director of Public Prosecutions [1989] Crim LR 150 HC QBD On pre-requisites necessary for arrest to be valid under Town Police Clauses Act 1847, s 29/Police and Criminal Evidence Act 1984, s 25(3)).

Gelberg v Miller [1961] 1 All ER 291; [1961] Crim LR 251; (1961) 125 JP 123; (1961) 111 LJ 172; (1961) 105 SJ 89; [1961] 1 WLR 153 HC QBD Valid arrest without warrant where wilful obstruction of highway/know of factual basis for arrest.

Gorman v Barnard [1940] 3 All ER 453; (1940) 104 JP 368; [1940] 2 KB 570; (1940) 90 LJ 57; [1940] 109 LJCL 841; (1940) 163 LTR 207; (1939-40) LVI TLR 929; (1940) WN (I) 275 CA Can/cannot arrest actual/suspected offender under Customs Consolidation Act 1876, s 186.

Government of the Federal Republic of Germany v Sotiriadis and another [1974] 1 All ER 692; [1975] AC 1; [1974] Crim LR 250; (1974) 138 JP 305; (1974) 124 NLJ 176t; (1974) 118 SJ 148; [1974] 2 WLR 253 HL Date of apprehension is date of arrest after requesting state requisition; sufficiency of evidence.

Grant v Gorman [1979] Crim LR 669 (amended at [1980] Crim LR 184); [1980] RTR 119 HC QBD Valid arrest where warned that failure to provide specimen would result in arrest and refused specimen (though arrested for assault on constable who sought to effect arrest upon failure).

Groom v Director of Public Prosecutions [1991] Crim LR 713 HC QBD On what suffices as a 'warning' before arrest under Public Order Act 1986, s 5(4).

Gwyn-Jones v Sutherland [1982] RTR 102 HC QBD Conviction quashed as arrest for second failure to provide breath specimen invalid in that it took place not near where driving but outside hospital to which admitted and promptly released.

Hart v Chief Constable of Kent [1983] Crim LR 117; [1983] RTR 484; [1982] TLR 549 HC QBD Person whom police began but failed to physically restrain outside house was arrested outside house; police could without permission lawfully enter house in pursuit of escaped arrestee.

Holden v Chief Constable of Lancashire [1986] 3 All ER 836; [1987] QB 380; (1970) 130 SJ 985; [1986] 3 WLR 1107 CA Exemplary damages available for unconstitutional act per se.

Holgate-Mohammed v Duke [1984] 1 All ER 1054; [1984] AC 437; (1984) 79 Cr App R 120; [1984] Crim LR 418; (1984) 134 NLJ 523; (1984) 128 SJ 244; [1984] TLR 196; [1984] 2 WLR 660 HL Valid arrest by police officer where effected in honest belief that arrestee more likely to answer questions truthfully at police station.

In the matter of an application for a warrant of further detention [1988] Crim LR 296 Magistrates Interpretation of Police and Criminal Evidence Act 1984, s 42.

Isaacs v Keech (1926-30) XXVIII Cox CC 22; (1925) 89 JP 189; [1925] 2 KB 354; (1925) 94 LJCL 676; (1925) 133 LTR 347; (1924-25) XLI TLR 432; (1925) WN (I) 109 HC KBD Police officer can under Town Police Clauses Act 1847, s 28 arrest anyone whom genuinely believes guilty of inter alia importuning for prostitution.

Jones v Kelsey (1987) 85 Cr App R 226; [1987] Crim LR 392; (1987) 151 JP 429 HC QBD Constable could arrest person wanted for breach of community service order though not in possession of warrant at time - assault on constable doing same was therefore assault on constable in execution of duty.

Kelly v Dolbey [1984] RTR 67 HC QBD Arrest of driver after failed to inflate bag but crystals afforded negative reading was valid (though crystals later found at station to give positive reading): appellant properly convicted inter alia of failure to give specimen.

Knight v Taylor [1979] Crim LR 318; [1979] RTR 304 HC QBD Where two constables acting together one could request breath specimen and other could arrest upon failure to provide same.

Kynaston v Director of Public Prosecutions; Heron (Joseph) v Director of Public Prosecutions; Heron (Tracey) v Director of Public Prosecutions (1988) 87 Cr App R 200 HC QBD Was lawful entry of premises by police where knew offence committed, knew whom wanted to arrest, reasonably suspected were on premises and owner knew what police wanted.

Ledwith and another v Roberts and another [1936] 3 All ER 570; (1934-39) XXX Cox CC 500; (1937) 101 JP 23; [1937] 1 KB 232; [1937] 106 LJCL 20; (1936) 155 LTR 602; (1936) 80 SJ 912; (1936-37) LIII TLR 21; (1936) WN (I) 281 CA On arrest without warrant of 'suspected person or reputed thief'/'loose, idle or disorderly person' under Vagrancy Act 1824, ss 4, 6/Liverpool Corporation Act 1921, s 513.

Lewis and another v Chief Constable of the South Wales Constabulary [1991] 1 All ER 206 CA Arrest unlawful for non-advice of basis is lawful once arrestee advised of basis of arrest.

Lewis and anr v Chief Constable of Greater Manchester (1991) 141 NLJ 1486i CA May arrest for breach of peace on anticipatory basis.

McArdle v Egan and others [1933] All ER 611; (1934-39) XXX Cox CC 67; (1934) 98 JP 103; (1934) 150 LTR 412 CA Reasonable and probable cause to suspect person of felony justifies arrest without warrant: question whether had such cause a matter for judge.

McCarrick v Oxford and another [1982] Crim LR 750; [1983] RTR 117 CA Constable's refusing to visit home of person (whom arrested on suspicion of driving while disqualified) and there see letter stating disqualification suspended pending appeal did not render arrest invalid.

McConnell v Chief Constable of the Greater Manchester Police [1990] 1 All ER 423; (1990) 91 Cr App R 88; (1990) 154 JP 325; (1990) 134 SJ 457; [1990] 1 WLR 364 CA Police may exercise power of arrest in private premises if likely breach of peace by persons inside.

McKee v Chief Constable for Northern Ireland [1985] 1 All ER 1; (1984) 128 SJ 836; [1984] TLR 662; [1984] 1 WLR 1358 HL Necessary state of mind to justify constable's arresting suspected terrorist under emergency legislation could be grounded solely on superior's orders.

Michaels v Block (1917-18) XXXIV TLR 438 HC KBD On extent of power to arrest without warrant under Consolidated Defence of the Realm Regulations 1914, regulation 55.

Mohammed-Holgate v Duke [1983] 3 All ER 526; (1984) 78 Cr App R 65; [1983] Crim LR 734; [1984] QB 209; (1983) 127 SJ 616; [1983] TLR 502; [1983] 3 WLR 598 CA Reasonable belief person committed offence justifies police arrest in hope will get more information during detention period.

Murray v Ministry of Defence [1988] 2 All ER 521; (1988) 138 NLJ 164; (1988) 132 SJ 852; [1988] 1 WLR 692 HL Arrest can begin before formal words of arrest spoken; formal words usually to be said at moment of arrest.

Nawrot and Shaler v Director of Public Prosecutions [1988] Crim LR 107 HC QBD No offence of abusing constable and Justices of the Peace Act 1361 does not provide basis for arrest for such an offence.

Nicholas v Director of Public Prosecutions [1987] Crim LR 474 HC QBD On elements necessary to render arrest valid under Police and Criminal Evidence Act 1984 (ss 25 and 28(3) considered).

Nicholas v Parsonage [1987] RTR 199 HC QBD Police were acting in course of duty (and arrest was valid) where in course of conversation indicated offence for which would be arrested if failed to give name and address.

Nichols v Bulman [1985] RTR 236 HC QBD Invalid arrest meant obtaining blood/urine specimens impermissible.

North v Pullen [1962] Crim LR 97t; (1962) 106 SJ 77 HC QBD Brief delay in effecting arrest did not mean police constable not acting in execution of his duty when was head-butted by offender.

O'Hara v Chief Constable of the Royal Ulster Constabulary [1997] 1 All ER 129; [1997] AC 286; [1997] 1 Cr App R 447; [1997] Crim LR 432; (1997) 141 SJ LB 20; (1996) TLR 13/12/96; [1997] 2 WLR 1 HL On justifiability/justifying arrest without warrant under the Prevention of Terrorism (Temporary Provisions) Act 1984.

Ormiston v Great Western Railway Company [1917] 86 LJCL 759; (1917) 116 LTR 479; (1916-17) XXXIII TLR 171 HC KBD Railway company servant cannot arrest passenger for travelling without proper fare unless passenger refuses to show ticket and disclose name and address but what servant says in course of arrest can only be slanderous if is special damage.

Plange v Chief Constable of South Humberside Police [1992] TLR 137 CA Arrest invalid where arresting officer believes upon arrest that charge will not be made against arrestee.

R v Allen [1981] Crim LR 324; [1981] RTR 410 CA Police were trespassing once ordered by person (whom believed to have been in accident) to leave his property: arrest thereafter invalid.

R v Beckford (Junior) (1992) 94 Cr App R 43; [1991] Crim LR 918 CA Matter for determination in each case whether police search and entry powers post-arrest of person for drugs possession was justified.

R v Birdwhistle [1980] Crim LR 381; [1980] RTR 342 CA Breath specimen evidence admitted though may have been obtained on foot of unlawful arrest.

R v Bow Street Magistrates' Court; ex parte Van der Holst (1986) 83 Cr App R 114 HC QBD Admissibility of various pieces of evidence in extradition proceedings.

R v Bridger [1970] Crim LR 290 CA Fact of arrest not to be tried as preliminary issue.

R v Broomhead [1975] Crim LR 721; [1975] RTR 558 CA Police officer could validly arrest person on basis of results of second breath test.

R v Brosch [1988] Crim LR 743 CA On what constiutes an arrest.

R v Brown (Michael) (1977) 64 Cr App R 231; [1977] Crim LR 291t; (1977) 127 NLJ 114t; [1977] RTR 160 CA Was valid for policeman having formed opinion that defendant had excess alcohol taken to require breath test of him after detaining him but before arresting him.

R v Churchill [1989] Crim LR 226 CA Were entitled to resist unlawful force of police who upon appellant's arrest for burglary sought to forcibly/wrongfully take appellant's car keys.

R v Dixon [1980] RTR 17 CA Valid arrest where arrested as unfit through drink to drive but police indicated would not be charged with same and was later charged with driving with excess alcohol.

R v Drameh [1983] Crim LR 322 CrCt Cannot be arrested without warrant for offence of making off without payment (Theft Act 1978, s 3).

R v Estop (Peter John) (1976) 63 Cr App R 226; [1976] RTR 493 CA Not valid arrest where officers who had not seen accused arrested him an hour after alleged offence/in place different to that where alleged offence committed.

R v Forbes [1984] Crim LR 482; [1984] TLR 335 CA On power of arrest under Prevention of Crime Act 1953, s 1(3).

R v Francis [1972] Crim LR 549t; (1972) 122 NLJ 655t; (1972) 116 SJ 632 CA Malicious damage committed between 9pm and 6am an arrestable offence; police officer not required to know offence arrestable before could enter premises to arrest for same.

R v Garrett, ex parte Sharf and others (1917) 81 JP 145 (also HC KBD) CA No appeal to CA from KBD decision that persons on vessel detained for search for contraband could in time of war be arrested for alleged obtaining of passport by false statement.

R v Garrett; ex parte Sharf and others (1917) 81 JP 145 (also CA); (1917) 116 LTR 82; (1916-17) XXXIII TLR 188 HC KBD Persons on vessel detained for search for contraband could in time of war be arrested for alleged obtaining of passport by false statement.

R v Gordon (Elliston James) (1969) 53 Cr App R 614; [1970] Crim LR 408; [1970] RTR 125 CA Where delay in informing accused of reason for arrest sprang from accused's violent behaviour at time the arrest was valid.

R v Grant [1980] Crim LR 245; [1980] RTR 280 CA Arrest valid where clear from circumstances though not specifically told why arrested.

R v Hamilton [1970] Crim LR 400 Sessions Certificate of indictment granted that person committed for sentence who failed to appear might be arrested.

R v Hampson (Thomas) (1914-15) 11 Cr App R 75 CCA That tried to avoid being arrested did not prove guilty of offence charged.

R v Hatton (Francis) (1978) 67 Cr App R 216; [1978] Crim LR 95 CA Was valid arrest where arrest for second offence had taken place while already under arrest for intial offence.

R v Holmes, ex parte Sherman and another [1981] 2 All ER 612; (1981) 145 JP 337 HC QBD Requirement of charge as soon as possible after arrest is mandatory and cannot be qualified; 48 hours normal time for bringing before magistrate.

R v Horseferry Road Magistrates' Court, ex parte Bennett (No 2) [1995] 1 Cr App R 147 HC QBD Arrests to be effected in strict accordance with procedure.

R v Howell (Errol) (1981) 73 Cr App R 31; [1981] Crim LR 697; (1982) 146 JP 13; (1981) 131 NLJ 605; [1982] QB 416; (1981) 125 SJ 462; [1981] 3 WLR 501 CA On what constitutes a breach of the peace; on when can arrest for breach of the peace.

R v Inwood [1973] 2 All ER 645; (1973) 57 Cr App R 529; [1973] Crim LR 290; (1973) 137 JP 559; (1973) 123 NLJ 249t; (1973) 117 SJ 303; [1973] 1 WLR 647 CA Unless made clear to person that under arrest police cannot use force in restraining them.

R v Jackson (Kenneth) [1984] Crim LR 674; [1985] RTR 257 CA Could not use reasonable force to restrain person who already committed offence (not stopping/giving name and address) from committing another offence (fleeing scene); person allegedly acting in self defence as sought to flee scene had no reasonable belief for so acting (and in any event used excessive force in flight).

R v Jones; ex parte Moore [1965] Crim LR 222t; (1965) 109 SJ 175 HC QBD On procedure as regards requiring arrestee to enter into recognisance.

R v Kulynycz [1970] 3 All ER 881; (1971) 55 Cr App R 34; [1970] Crim LR 693; (1971) 135 JP 82; (1970) 120 NLJ 945t; (1970) 114 SJ 785 CA Unlawfulness of arrest does not colour everything thereafter; arrest unlawful if not informed of basis for arrest.

R v Lowe; R v Lowe (JD) [1973] 1 All ER 805; (1973) 57 Cr App R 365; [1973] Crim LR 238; (1973) 137 JP 334; (1973) 123 NLJ 107t; [1973] QB 702; (1973) 117 SJ 144; [1973] 2 WLR 481; [1986] Crim LR 49 CrCt Arrest unlawful where person not told why arrested and arresting officers considered accused to have been arrested for different offences.

R v Mayer [1975] RTR 411 CA Person arrested after provided breath test specimen did not have to be told why as was apparent from circumstances.

R v McKenzie (Weston George) and Davis (Jennifer Dorcas) [1979] Crim LR 164 CrCt Invalidity of arrest meant assault on constable was not assault on same in execution of his duty.

R v Morgan [1961] Crim LR 538t CCA Overnight detention of all persons arrested late at night was not good police practice.

R v Naylor (Angela) [1979] Crim LR 532 CrCt On extent of power of police to relieve person in custody of her property.

R v Nottingham Justices; ex parte Fraser [1995] TLR 279 HC QBD On relevant factors when justices deciding whether to issue warrant for arrest of defence witness.

R v Podger [1979] Crim LR 524 CrCt On extent of power of arrest in anticipation of breach of the peace.

R v Purdy [1974] 3 All ER 465; (1975) 60 Cr App R 30; [1974] Crim LR 597t; (1974) 138 JP 771; [1975] QB 288; (1974) 118 SJ 698; [1974] 3 WLR 357 CA Arrest under warrant lawful if warrant in immediate control (not possession) of arresting officer.

R v Redman [1994] Crim LR 914 CA Legal issues to be resolved before speeches delivered so that all lawyers address jury on same basis.

R v Rey (Frederick Brian) (1978) 67 Cr App R 244; [1978] RTR 413 CA Valid arrest for failure to provide specimen where had provided same but in inadequate amount.

R v Self [1992] 3 All ER 476; (1992) 95 Cr App R 42; [1992] Crim LR 572; (1992) 156 JP 397; (1992) 136 SJ LB 88; [1992] TLR 107; [1992] 1 WLR 657 CA Arrestable offence must be committed before resistance to arrest unlawful.

R v Spicer [1970] Crim LR 695; (1970) 114 SJ 824 CA Conspiracy to defraud not an arrestable offence.

R v Sullivan [1977] Crim LR 751 CA Conviction for failure to provide specimen quashed where arresting police officer had not told offender at time of arrest of reason for arrest.

R v Telfer [1976] Crim LR 562 CA On necessary level of detail about arrest to be communicated to arrestee upon arrest.

R v Veevers [1971] Crim LR 174; [1971] RTR 47; (1971) 115 SJ 62 CA Drunk driving conviction quashed where issue whether arrest valid (on which validity of breath test in part depends) not left to jury.

R v Way [1970] Crim LR 469; (1970) 120 NLJ 481; [1970] RTR 348; (1970) 114 SJ 418 CMAC That person's breath smelt of alcohol was not per se evidence that driving ability was impaired.

Re Sherman and Apps (1981) 72 Cr App R 266; [1981] Crim LR 335 HC QBD Accused must be charged/told will be prosecuted as soon as possible once evidence available; arrested person must be granted bail/brought before court as soon as possible.

Reynolds v Commissioner of Police for the Metropolis [1982] Crim LR 600; [1982] TLR 274 CA £12,000 damages merited in serious case of wrongful arrest/false imprisonment.

Riley v Director of Public Prosecutions (1990) 91 Cr App R 14; [1990] Crim LR 422; (1990) 154 JP 453 HC QBD Could not be guilty of assault on police officer in execution of duty where validity of arrest unproven.

Roberts v Jones [1969] Crim LR 90; (1968) 112 SJ 884 HC QBD Arrest of person in charge of motor car justified subsequent request that arrestee take breath test.

Sargent v West [1964] Crim LR 412t HC QBD On what amounts to reasonable exercise of power of search/arrest under the Metropolitan Police Act 1839, s 66.

Seneviratne v Bishop [1978] RTR 92 HC QBD Invalid arrest where constable failed to examine crystals after some air blown into breathalyser (though bag not filled).

Sharpe v Perry [1979] RTR 235 HC QBD Need not be roadside breath test when rresting person for being in charge of motor vehicle on road while unfit to drink (Road Traffic ct 1972, s 5(5)).

Siddiqui v Swain [1979] Crim LR 318; [1979] RTR 454 HC QBD Invalid arrest as no proof that policeman suspected driver had alcohol in body: arrest per se not evidence of suspicion.

Snook v Mannion [1982] Crim LR 601; [1982] RTR 321; [1982] TLR 158 HC QBD Defendant saying 'fuck off' to police on his property found not to be thereby revoking implied licence of police to enter thereon so his arrest was valid.

Stevenson v Aubrook and others [1941] 2 All ER 476; (1941) 91 LJ 254 HC KBD Arrest under Vagrancy Act 1824, s 6 for offence not actually committed an unlawful arrest.

Swales v Cox [1981] 1 All ER 1115; (1981) 72 Cr App R 171; [1981] Crim LR 235; (1981) 131 NLJ 372; [1981] QB 849; (1981) 125 SJ 133; [1981] 2 WLR 814 HC QBD Police may enter place using any necessary force to effect arrest.

Tims v John Lewis and Co, Ltd [1951] 1 All ER 814; (1951) 115 JP 265; [1951] 2 KB 459; (1951) 101 LJ 203; (1951) 95 SJ 268; [1951] 1 TLR 719; (1951) WN (I) 188 CA Upon arrest must be taken to police officer/justice of the peace forthwith.

Walker v Hodgkins (1983) 147 JP 474; [1983] TLR 149 HC QBD Justices could take into account normal laboratory procedure when deciding whether to accept evidence regarding blood specimens.

Ware and another v Matthews (1981) 131 NLJ 830 HC QBD Successful action for damages for arrest without reasonable cause for alleged unlawful taking of car.

Wershof v Commissioner of Police for the Metropolis [1978] 3 All ER 540; (1979) 143 JP 1; (1979) 68 Cr App R 82; [1978] Crim LR 424; (1978) 128 NLJ 486t; (1978) 122 SJ 279 HC QBD Arrest for wilful obstruction if obstruction likely to cause breach of peace/frustrate other arrest; officer acting in course of duty.

Wheatley v Lodge [1971] 1 All ER 173; [1971] Crim LR 40; (1970) 120 NLJ 1016t; (1970) 114 SJ 907 CA Arrest of non lip-reading deaf person valid if all that is reasonable is done by police officer.

Wheatley v Lodge (1971) 135 JP 176; [1971] RTR 22; [1971] 1 WLR 29 HC QBD Police officer arresting deaf person only obliged to do what reasonable person would have done in circumstances.

Willey v Peace [1950] 2 All ER 724; (1950) 114 JP 502; [1951] 1 KB 94; (1950) 100 LJ 483; (1950) 94 SJ 597; [1950] 66 (2) TLR 450 HC KBD Police officer may under Metropolitan Police Act 1839, s 66 arrest anyone reasonably suspects of conveying stolen property.

Wills v Bowley [1982] 2 All ER 654; [1983] 1 AC 57; (1982) 75 Cr App R 164; [1982] 3 WLR 10 HC QBD Police have power of arrest where reasonably suspect crime committed in their sight.

Wills v Bowley [1982] 2 All ER 654; [1983] 1 AC 57; (1982) 75 Cr App R 164; [1982] Crim LR 580; (1982) 146 JP 309; (1982) 126 SJ 411; [1982] TLR 286; [1982] 3 WLR 10 HL Police have power of arrest where reasonably suspect crime committed in their sight.

Wilson v Clark [1984] TLR 716 HC QBD On validity of arrest effected pursuant to the Immigration Act 1971.

Wiltshire v Barrett [1965] 2 All ER 271; [1965] Crim LR 295t; (1965) 129 JP 348; [1966] 1 QB 312; (1965) 109 SJ 274; [1965] 2 WLR 1195 CA Valid arrest if police officer has reasonable suspicion are committing road traffic offence/are released once discover innocent or no case.

Wimperis v Griffin [1973] Crim LR 533 HC QBD Arrest under Road Trfafic Act 1960 not rendered improper by virtue of immediately prior requst for breath specimen under the Road Safety Act 1967.

ARREST (stop and search)

R v McCarthy [1996] Crim LR 818 CA Police evidence validly admitted even though obtained after police stopped and searched car without informing persons therein that police suspected drugs being carried in car.

ARSON (attempt)

R v O'Toole (Michael) [1987] Crim LR 759 CA On requisite intent to be guilty of attempt (here attempted arson).

ARSON (general)

Attorney General's Reference (No 3 of 1992) [1994] 2 All ER 121; (1994) 98 Cr App R 383; [1994] Crim LR 348; (1993) 143 NLJ 1675; [1994] RTR 122; (1993) 137 SJ LB 278; [1993] TLR 576; [1994] 1 WLR 409 CA Intent to cause damage by fire and recklessness to endangerment of life establishes intent for attempted aggravated arson.

Hawkins v Wilson [1957] Crim LR 320 Magistrates Caravan not a building for purposes of Malicious Damage Act 1861, s 6.

R v Allwright [1991] TLR 107 CA On desirability of psychiatric report before sentencing for arson.

R v Arthur [1968] Crim LR 114; [1968] 1 QB 810; (1967) 111 SJ 925 Assizes Maliciously setting fire to dwelling house where person inside meant person other than accused (Malicious Damage Act 1861, s 2).

R v Caldwell (James) (1980) 71 Cr App R 237; [1980] Crim LR 572 CA Self-induced drunkenness relevant to deciding whether were criminally reckless.

R v Clark; R v Sharp [1991] Crim LR 625 CA Evidence of other criminal damage committed on same occasion as arson and not genuinely separable from latter was properly admitted.

R v Coles [1994] Crim LR 820 CA On recklessness in the context of arson; psychological evidence rightly excluded where went to matters that could be properly assessed by jury absent expert evidence.

R v Cooper (G); R v Cooper (Y) [1991] Crim LR 524 CA On difference between criminal damage to property with fire (arson) and without fire (criminal damage).

R v Cullen [1993] Crim LR 936 CA On recklessness in the context of arson.

R v Davis (1968) 52 Cr App R 227 Assizes Must be person apart from accused in house to be guilty of arson under the Malicious Damage Act 1861, s 2.

R v Denton [1982] 1 All ER 65; (1982) 74 Cr App R 81; [1982] Crim LR 107; (1982) 146 JP 138; (1981) 125 SJ 746; [1981] 1 WLR 1446 CA Damage to own property not arson even if tainted with intent to commit fraud.

R v Fitzaucher [1956] Crim LR 118 Assizes Was case to answer where fire caused either by accused or intruder and prosecution possessed of evidence proving fire not caused by intruder.

R v Fletcher, Fletcher and Zimnowodski [1962] Crim LR 551t CCA On whether/when death arising from arson will be murder.

R v Goodfellow (Kevin) (1986) 83 Cr App R 23; [1986] Crim LR 468 CA Manslaughter where do unlawful act that reasonable person would foresee exposed some other to chance of harm.

R v Hardie (Paul Deverall) (1985) 80 Cr App R 156; (1984) 128 SJ 851; [1984] TLR 511; [1985] 1 WLR 64 CA Self-induced drunkenness cannot be defence where recklessness alleged - taking of sedative drug need not raise same presumption.

R v Hunt (Anthony Gerald) (1978) 66 Cr App R 105; [1977] Crim LR 740 CA Using objective test could not defend arson with plea of lawful excuse (that set fire to premises to highlight that fire alarm system defective).

R v Lee (Robert Paul) [1996] 2 Cr App R 266; (1996) 140 SJ LB 38; [1995] TLR 715 CA Child's video-link evidence to court was valid as defendant charged with arson (being reckless as to threat to life) had threatened to the child.

R v Miller [1983] 1 All ER 978; [1983] 2 AC 161; (1983) 77 Cr App R 17; [1983] Crim LR 466; (1983) 133 NLJ 450; (1983) 127 SJ 223; [1983] TLR 192; [1983] 2 WLR 539 HL Actus reus of arson includes accidental starting of fire with intended/recklessness as to destruction/damage of property coupled with failure to put out fire/stop it damaging property.

R v Miller [1982] 2 All ER 386; (1982) 75 Cr App R 109; [1982] Crim LR 526; (1982) 146 JP 243; [1982] QB 532; (1982) 126 SJ 327; [1982] TLR 123; [1982] 2 WLR 937 CA Usually actus reus/mens rea to coincide; absent statute omission does not generally raise criminal liability; reckless/intended omission after unintended act is criminal.

R v Parker [1993] Crim LR 856 CA Unnecessary to prove that life actually endangered (merely had to prove recklessness to same) to be guilty of arson.

R v R (Stephen Malcolm) (1984) 79 Cr App R 334; [1984] TLR 502 CA Where charged with arson with intent to endanger life and issue of recklessness raised, in determining same by reference to ordinary man that ordinary man need not have peculiar charcteristics of accused.

R v Sangha [1988] 2 All ER 385; (1988) 87 Cr App R 88; (1988) 152 JP 293; (1988) 132 SJ 191; [1988] 1 WLR 519 CA Mens rea for arson is that reasonable person would see risk of fire damaging property or endangering life.

R v Spencer [1979] Crim LR 538 CA Five years' (not life) imprisonment for offender with personality disorder guilty of arson and theft but not an unceasing public menace.

R v Webb [1954] Crim LR 49 Sessions Person found guilty of arson on basis inter alia of police dog identification evidence.

ASSASSINATION (encouraging assassination)

R v Antonelli and Barberi (1906) 70 JP 4 CCC Valid conviction for inciting murder of sovereigns and rulers of Europe.

ASSAULT (aggravated assault)

Blackburn v Bowering [1995] Crim LR 38; [1993] TLR 551; [1994] 1 WLR 1324 CA Person pleading self-defence to be judged on facts however perceived them (whether reasonably or unreasonably) to be; must be guilty of assault to be guilty of aggravated assault.

ASSAULT (assault on child)

R v Hilton (John James) (1925-26) 19 Cr App R 29 CCA Interpretation of Children Act 1908, s 12(1).

ASSAULT ON CONSTABLE (general)

Bailey v Wilson [1968] Crim LR 617 Sessions Police officer making general enquiry was trespasser once remained on private property after told to leave; disorderly conduct to be offence must occur on public passageway: struggling from house/garden to police van not disorderly conduct.

Bentley v Brudzinski (1982) 75 Cr App R 217; [1982] Crim LR 825; [1982] TLR 122 HC QBD Unlawful arrest of person remaining with constable as volunteer meant assault on constable was not assault on constable in execution of duty.

Brazil v Chief Constable of Surrey (1983) 77 Cr App R 237; [1983] Crim LR 483; (1984) 148 JP 22; (1983) 127 SJ 712; [1983] TLR 253; [1983] 1 WLR 1155 HC QBD Was not assault on constable in execution of duty where police officer conducting search had not directed mind to whether search necessary/had not given reasons for search.

Daniel v Morrison (1980) 70 Cr App R 142; [1980] Crim LR 181 HC QBD No constraints imposed on power of detention under Metropolitan Police Act 1839, s 66 once reasonable suspicion of offences outlined therein.

Davis v Lisle (1934-39) XXX Cox CC 412; (1936) 100 JP 280; [1936] 2 KB 434; [1936] 105 LJCL 593; (1936) 155 LTR 23; (1936) 80 SJ 409; (1935-36) LII TLR 475 HC KBD Not guilty of assault/obstruction of police in course of duty as had at material time requested police to leave property so police were trespassers.

Director of Public Prosecutions v Hawkins [1988] 3 All ER 673; (1989) 88 Cr App R 166; [1988] Crim LR 741; (1988) 152 JP 518; (1988) 132 SJ 1460; [1988] 1 WLR 1166 HC QBD Is assault on officer in course of duty where person attacks officer who fails to say why arresting either immediately or when reasonably practicable.

Donnelly v Jackman [1970] 1 All ER 987; (1970) 54 Cr App R 229; [1970] Crim LR 219; (1970) 134 JP 352; (1970) 120 NLJ 362; (1970) 114 SJ 130; [1970] 1 WLR 562 HC QBD Touch to unarrested person answered with great force is unlawful assault on constable.

Fagan v Metropolitan Police Commissioner [1968] 3 All ER 442; (1968) 52 Cr App R 700; (1969) 133 JP 16; [1969] 1 QB 439; (1968) 112 SJ 800; [1968] 3 WLR 1120 HC QBD Uncriminal act became criminal once criminal intent formed so initially innocent act transformed into assault on constable.

G v Superintendent of Police, Stroud (1988) 86 Cr App R 92; [1987] Crim LR 269 HC QBD Short time-span in which constable had to make decision to arrest relevant in deciding reasonableness of arrest that breach of peace likely: here reasonable so assault was assault on constable in execution of duty.

Hollands v Abel [1956] Crim LR 336 HC QBD Police entering onto property to request that noise level be kept down were acting in the course of their duty.

Jones and Jones v Lloyd [1981] Crim LR 340 CA Police invited into house by guest of householder not trespassing so assault on them an assault on police in execution of their duty.

Jones v Kelsey (1987) 85 Cr App R 226; [1987] Crim LR 392; (1987) 151 JP 429 HC QBD Constable could arrest person wanted for breach of community service order though not in possession of warrant at time - assault on constable doing same was therefore assault on constable in execution of duty.

Kay v Hibbert [1977] Crim LR 226 HC QBD Was assault on constable in the exercise of his duty to strike constable after had told him to leave premises but within reasonable time it took him to do so.

Kenlin and another v Gardiner and another [1966] 3 All ER 931; [1967] Crim LR 39; (1967) 131 JP 91; (1965-66) 116 NLJ 1685; [1967] 2 QB 510; (1966) 110 SJ 848; [1967] 2 WLR 129 HC QBD Proportionate use of force following technical assault by constable legitimate self-defence.

Kerr v Director of Public Prosecutions [1995] Crim LR 394; (1994) 158 JP 1048; [1994] TLR 459 HC QBD Police officer not acting in course of duty where held person in erroneous belief that person had been arrested.

King v Gardner (1980) 71 Cr App R 13 HC QBD Police officer detaining person following radio message did not have reasonable suspicion to justify detention so not acting in course of duty when assaulted.

King v Hodges [1974] Crim LR 424 HC QBD Police officer was acting in course of his duty when prior to arresting appellant so as to prevent breach of the peace he applied reasonable force to seek to restrain her from committing breach.

Lamb v Director of Public Prosecutions (1990) 154 JP 381 HC QBD Trespassing police officer was nonetheless acting in course of duty when stayed in place to prevent expected breach of the peace.

Ludlow and others v Burgess (1982) 75 Cr App R 227; [1971] Crim LR 238 HC QBD Not assault on constable in execution of duty where person unlawfully detained by constable assaults same.

McArdle v Wallace [1964] Crim LR 467g; (1964) 108 SJ 483 HC QBD Constable not acting in course of duty where requested by son of owner to leave property had entered so subsequent assault by son on constable not assault on same in execution of his duty.

McBean v Parker [1983] Crim LR 399; (1983) 147 JP 205; [1983] TLR 85 HC QBD Person using reasonable force to resist (unexplained) search who assaulted second officer coming to aid of searching officer not guilty of assault on police officer in the execution of his duty.

McBride v Turnock [1964] Crim LR 456t; (1964) 108 SJ 336 HC QBD Person who struck constable in course of assault on another was guilty of assault on police officer in the execution of his duty.

McLorie v Oxford (1982) 75 Cr App R 137; [1982] Crim LR 603; [1982] QB 1290; [1983] RTR 265; (1982) 126 SJ 536; [1982] TLR 287; [1982] 3 WLR 423 HC QBD No post-arrest common law right of police to enter property and look for material evidence; is assault on police in execution of their duty to assault same while doing what is lawfully proper for them to do.

Mepstead v Director of Public Prosecutions [1996] Crim LR 111 HC QBD Police officer holding arm of person to whom was speaking but whom did not seek to arrest/detain was acting in execution of duty.

North v Pullen [1962] Crim LR 97t; (1962) 106 SJ 77 HC QBD Brief delay in effecting arrest did not mean police constable not acting in execution of his duty when was head-butted by offender.

Pedro v Diss [1981] 2 All ER 59; (1981) 72 Cr App R 193; [1981] Crim LR 236; (1981) 145 JP 445; (1981) 131 NLJ 448 HC QBD Constable detaining without advising why acts unlawfully so assault on constable not assault on same in execution of duty.

R v Coleman (Ian) (1975) 61 Cr App R 206 CA Custodial sentences necessary for those who assault police when latter trying to keep order.

R v D'Souza (E); R v D'Souza (C) [1992] Crim LR 119 HC QBD Assaults of police officers properly seeking to apprehend mental patient were assaults on same in execution of their duty.

R v Fennell [1970] 3 All ER 215; (1970) 54 Cr App R 451; [1970] Crim LR 581t; (1970) 134 JP 678; (1970) 120 NLJ 732; [1971] 1 QB 428; (1970) 114 SJ 651; [1970] 3 WLR 513 CA Is offence to assault constable effecting lawful arrest in mistaken belief that unlawful.

R v Knightsbridge Crown Court; ex parte Umeh [1979] Crim LR 727 HC QBD Assault on police officer forcibly removing accused from police station was assault on constable in execution of his duty.

R v McKenzie (Weston George) and Davis (Jennifer Dorcas) [1979] Crim LR 164 CrCt Invalidity of arrest meant assault on constable was not assault on same in execution of his duty.

R v Roff; R v Dowie [1976] RTR 7 CA Constable's forming opinion while defendant 'committing' offence includes short time thereafter so where officer arrested motorist immediately after crash he was acting in execution of his duty.

R v Waterfield and Lynn [1963] 3 All ER 659; (1964) 48 Cr App R 42; [1964] Crim LR 57t; (1964) 128 JP 48; (1963) 113 LJ 788; [1964] 1 QB 164; (1963) 107 SJ 833; [1963] 3 WLR 946 CCA Assault on constable wrongfully detaining vehicle not assault of same in execution of duty.

Riley v Director of Public Prosecutions (1990) 91 Cr App R 14; [1990] Crim LR 422; (1990) 154 JP 453 HC QBD Could not be guilty of assault on police officer in execution of duty where validity of arrest unproven.

Robson and another v Hallett [1967] 2 All ER 407; (1967) 51 Cr App R 307; [1967] Crim LR 293t; (1967) 131 JP 333; [1967] 2 QB 939; (1967) 111 SJ 254; [1967] 3 WLR 28 HC QBD Police have implied licence to enter garden in course of duty; once licence revoked by owner have reasonable time to go before become trespasser; if breach of peace in garden police can enter to stop it.

Robson and Robson v MallettHC QBD Constable told to leave house had to be given reasonable time to do so before was not acting in course of his duty.

Sanders v Director of Public Prosecutions [1988] Crim LR 605 CA Officer was acting in course of duty where assaulted when after stopping car under Road Traffic Act 1972, s 159, sought to stop driver driving off until had ascertained whether was stolen (of which had reasonable suspicion).

Squires v Botwright [1973] Crim LR 106; [1972] RTR 462 HC QBD That constable had blocked person from moving while conducted his inquiries did not mean had not been acting in course of duty.

Toohey v Woolwich Justices and another [1966] 2 All ER 429; [1967] 2 AC 1; (1966) 130 JP 326; (1965-66) 116 NLJ 894; [1966] 2 WLR 1442 HL Assault/aggravated assault (even on constable) to be tried summarily.

Townley v Rushworth [1964] Crim LR 590; (1963) 107 SJ 1004 HC QBD Person in respect of whom incomplete recommendation for committal to mental hospital made not guilty of assault where struck out at persons who entered his property seeking to forcibly remove him.

Weight v Long [1986] Crim LR 746 HC QBD Police officer seeking to speak to another in connection with crime/breach of the peace was acting in course of duty.

Whiteside v Gamble [1968] Crim LR 560 Sessions Person not guilty of assault on constable in execution of his duty where latter grossly insulted individual and then invited him to fight.

ASSAULT (assault with intent to rape)

R v P [1990] Crim LR 323 HC QBD Is no offence of assault with intent to rape.

R v Waite (Philip) [1988] Crim LR 434 CrCt Is no offence of assault with intent to rape.

ASSAULT (assault with intent to resist arrest)

R v Brightling [1991] Crim LR 364 CA On effect of belief that persons apprehending one are not police officers to guilt for assault with intent to resist arrest.

ASSAULT (assault with intent to rob)

R v King-Jones and Gladdy [1966] Crim LR 510; [1966] 1 WLR 1077 Assizes Entitled to acquittal on charge of assault with intent to rob if (possible) bona fide belief that were entitled to money and to use force in obtaining it.

ASSAULT (causing bodily harm)

Bolton v Crawley [1972] Crim LR 222 CA Assault occasioning actual bodily harm did not require mens rea so though had injected oneself with drugs could not claim did not possess mens rea for said offence.

Burrell v Harmer [1967] Crim LR 169 CA Tattooist guilty, upon tattoos administered to two boys becoming inflamed, of causing actual bodily harm to the boys.

Burrell v Harmer (1965-66) 116 NLJ 1658 HC QBD Tattooist not guilty, upon tattoos administered to two boys becoming inflamed, of causing actual bodily harm to the boys.

Director of Public Prosecutions v Khan [1990] Crim LR 321; (1989) 139 NLJ 1455 HC QBD Was occasioning actual bodily harm to place dangerous substance in machine used by public where (albeit that had not intended harm) next user was harmed by substance being ejected from machine.

R v Austin [1973] Crim LR 778 CA Person charged with causing grievous bodily harm with intent ought not (absent greater specificity as to events at issue) to have been convicted of assault occasioning actual bodily harm.

R v Barrett (Alan Gordon); R v Barrett (John Graham) (1981) 72 Cr App R 212; (1980) 124 SJ 542 CA Honest mistake of law defence unavailable once competent court has declared relevant law; test whether force used in self-defence is excessive is objective.

R v Brown and other appeals [1993] 2 All ER 75; [1994] 1 AC 212; (1993) 97 Cr App R 44; [1993] Crim LR 583; (1993) 157 JP 337; (1993) 143 NLJ 399; [1993] TLR 129; [1993] 2 WLR 556 HL Consensual homosexual sado-masochistic acts causing actual bodily harm are assaults occasioning actual bodily harm/unlawful woundings.

R v Chan-Fook [1994] 2 All ER 552; (1994) 99 Cr App R 147; [1994] Crim LR 432; [1993] TLR 582; [1994] 1 WLR 689 CA Psychiatric fears but not strong emotions are actual bodily harm but issue of psychiatric injury not for jury unless expert evidence.

R v Constanza [1997] Crim LR 576; [1997] TLR 177 CA 'Stalker' whose behaviour created fear of immediate violence (stalker living near victim) was guilty of assault.

R v Cowdell [1962] Crim LR 262t CA Inappropriate that person be convicted of unlawful wounding and assault on basis of same facts.

R v Gunstone; R v Hughes; R v Morse; R v Uffindell [1978] Crim LR 176 CA Nine/six months' imprisonment for unprovoked assault occasioning actual bodily harm.

R v Ireland [1997] 1 All ER 112 CA Making of silent telephone calls could (as here) constitute assault occasioning actual bodily harm contrary to the Offences against the Person Act 1861, s 47.

R v Ireland (Robert Matthew) [1997] 1 All ER 112; [1996] 2 Cr App R 426; [1997] Crim LR 434; [1997] 1 FLR 687; [1997] QB 114; (1996) 140 SJ LB 148; (1996) TLR 22/5/96; [1996] 3 WLR 650 CA Making telephone calls and then not speaking held to assault occasioning actual bodily harm.

R v Ireland; R v Burstow (1997) 147 NLJ 1273; [1997] TLR 412; [1997] 3 WLR 534 HL Could be guilty of assault as result of injury occasioned by way of silent telephone calls.

R v Jones (Kevin Edward); R v Mirrless (Neil Robert) (1977) 65 Cr App R 250 CA Must intend to and actually encourage assault to be guilty of assault occasioning actual bodily harm where did not physically partake in same.

R v Jones (Terence); R v Campbell (Michael); R v Smith (Lee); R v Nicholas (Victor); R v Blackwood (Winston); R v Muir (Ricky) (1986) 83 Cr App R 375 CA Is defence to assault that arose from rough play to which consented.

R v Kelbie [1996] Crim LR 802 CA On making of citizen's arrest as defence to charge of assault occasioning actual bodily harm.

R v McCready; R v Hurd (1978) 122 SJ 247 CA Could not plead guilty to common assault where were only charged with causing grievous bodily harm with intent.

R v Miller [1954] 2 All ER 529; (1954) 38 Cr App R 1; [1954] Crim LR 219; (1954) 11 JP 341; [1954] 2 QB 282; (1954) 98 SJ 62; [1954] 2 WLR 138 HC QBD Husband could not be guilty of raping wife absent separation agreement/order; assault for husband to use force in exercising right to marital sex.

R v Nash [1991] Crim LR 768; (1991) 155 JP 709; [1991] TLR 285 CA On recklessness as an element of mens rea for assault occasioning actual bodily harm.

R v Owino (Nimrod) [1996] 2 Cr App R 128; [1995] Crim LR 743 CA On force allowable in self-defence.

R v Parmenter [1991] 2 All ER 225; [1992] 1 AC 699 (also HL); (1991) 92 Cr App R 68; [1991] Crim LR 41; (1990) 154 JP 941; (1990) 140 NLJ 1231; (1990) 134 SJ 1368; [1990] TLR 564; [1991] 2 WLR 408 CA Foreseeability of some harm required for malicious wounding; intention to/realisation of risk of harm required for occasioning actual bodily harm.

R v Reigate Justices; ex parte Counsell (1984) 148 JP 193; [1983] TLR 794 HC QBD Kick in stomach which occasioned considerable pain but no bruising was 'actual bodily harm' for purpose of Offences against the Person Act 1861.

R v Roberts (Kenneth Joseph) (1972) 56 Cr App R 95; [1972] Crim LR 27; (1971) 115 SJ 809 CA Test whether threats lead to injury (girl jumping from car) was whether that reaction reasonably foreseeable result of what doing.

R v Savage [1991] 2 All ER 220; [1992] 1 AC 699 (also HL); (1990) 91 Cr App R 317; [1990] Crim LR 709; (1990) 154 JP 757; [1990] TLR 378; [1991] 2 WLR 418 CA Malicious wounding requires foreseeability of harm unlike occasioning actual bodily harm which does not even require recklessness.

R v Savage; R v Parmenter [1991] 4 All ER 698; [1992] 1 AC 699 (also CA); (1992) 94 Cr App R 193; [1992] Crim LR 288 (only Savage); (1991) 155 JP 935; (1991) 141 NLJ 1553; [1991] TLR 499; [1991] 3 WLR 914 HL Unlawful and malicious wounding/inflicting grievous bodily harm requires intent/actual foresight of harm, however slight; assault occasioning actual bodily harm requires assault and actual bodily harm but not intent to cause harm or recklessness that harm likely to be caused.

R v Spratt [1991] 2 All ER 210; (1990) 91 Cr App R 362; [1990] Crim LR 797; (1990) 154 JP 884; (1990) 134 SJ 860; [1990] TLR 369; [1990] 1 WLR 1073 CA If no actual intent/recklessness then no mens rea.

R v Taylor [1983] TLR 798 CA Schoolteacher who used excessive force when meting out corporal punishment to pupil found guilty of assault occasioning actual bodily harm.

R v White [1995] Crim LR 393 CA Substitution of verdict of guilt of causing grievous bodily harm (not causing same with intent) where because of post-traumatic stress disorder did not have requisite intent.

Reference by the Attorney-General under Section 36 of the Criminal Justice Act 1972 (No 6 of 1980) (1981) 73 Cr App R 63; [1981] Crim LR 553; (1981) 145 JP 429; (1981) 131 NLJ 781; [1981] QB 715; (1981) 125 SJ 426; [1981] 3 WLR 125 CA Is assault if intend and/or cause actual bodily harm even if victim consents.

Taylor v Granville [1978] Crim LR 482 CA On what constitutes assault occasioning actual bodily harm (blow to face was such).

ASSAULT (child)

R v Smith (David George) [1985] Crim LR 42 CA On relevance of intention to determination whether physical chastisement of child constituted assault occasioning actual bodily harm.

ASSAULT (general)

Albert v Lavin [1981] 1 All ER 628; [1982] AC 546 (also HL); (1981) 72 Cr App R 178; [1981] Crim LR 238; (1981) 145 JP 184; (1981) 131 NLJ 368; (1981) 125 SJ 114; [1981] 2 WLR 1070 HC QBD Unreasonable belief acting in self-defence not defence to assault charge.

Ansell v Swift [1987] Crim LR 194 CrCt May plead defence of self-defence where assaulted police officer following unlawful assault by the officer.

Attorney General's Reference [1981] 2 All ER 1057 CA Cannot consent to assault.

Connor v Chief Constable of Cambridgeshire [1984] TLR 230 HC QBD Exemplary damages for assault by police officer.

Director of Public Prosecutions v K (a minor) [1990] 1 All ER 331; (1990) 91 Cr App R 23; (1990) 154 JP 192; (1990) 134 SJ 636; [1990] 1 WLR 1067 HC QBD Recklessly placing dangerous substance in machine can ground conviction for causing actual bodily harm to later user of machine.

Director of Public Prosecutions v Taylor; Director of Public Prosecutions v Little [1992] 1 All ER 299; [1991] Crim LR 900/904; (1991) 155 JP 713; (1991) 141 NLJ 964; (1991) 141 NLJ 1038t; [1992] QB 645; [1992] 2 WLR 460 HC QBD Assault and battery separate offences; assaults and batteries triable summarily.

Ellis v Burton [1975] 1 All ER 395; [1975] Crim LR 32; (1975) 139 JP 199 HC QBD Cannot dismiss charge where plea of guilty as no hearing 'upon the merits'.

Gibbons v Harris (1956) 106 LJ ccr828 CyCt Binding over of plaintiff under recognisance by magistrates' court following assault did not preclude later tortious action in respect of said assault.

Hickman v O'Dwyer [1979] Crim LR 309 HC QBD Not assault on constable in course of his duty where constable assaulted while arresting noisy youth whose behaviour officer had no cause to believe would result in breach of the peace.

Jones v Lamond (1935) 79 SJ 859 CA Binding over by court of summary jurisdiction for assault did not constitute conviction.

Jones v Sherwood [1942] 1 KB 127; (1942) 106 JP 65; (1941) WN (I) 214 HC KBD Conviction for assault or battery bad as are two separate offences.

Poutney v Griffiths [1975] Crim LR 702; (1975) 125 NLJ 722 HL Conviction of mental nurse for assault on patient validly quashed as had been acting in on-duty capacity (Mental Health Act 1959, s 141 applied).

R v Ball (Simon Leonard John) (1990) 90 Cr App R 378; [1989] Crim LR 579 CA Bona fide belief that arrest unlawful/police using excessive force not defence to assault.

R v Bracknell Justices, ex parte Griffiths (1975) 125 NLJ 111t HC QBD Conviction of mental nurse for assault on patient quashed as had been acting in on duty-capacity (Mental Health Act 1959, s 141 applied).

R v Brown (Morton); ex parte Ainsworth (1910) 74 JP 53 HC KBD Home Secretary not liable in respect of alleged assault committed upon prisoner by means of force-feeding.

R v Brown and other appeals [1992] 2 All ER 552; (1992) 94 Cr App R 302; (1992) 156 JP 475; (1992) 142 NLJ 275; [1992] QB 491; (1992) 136 SJ LB 90; [1992] TLR 71; [1992] 2 WLR 441 CA Private, consensual sado-masochistic acts not causing permanent injury may constitute unlawful wounding/ assault causing actual bodily harm.

R v Donovan [1934] All ER 207; (1934-39) XXX Cox CC 187; (1934-36) 25 Cr App R 1; (1934) 98 JP 409; [1934] 2 KB 498; (1934) 78 LJ 149; (1934) 103 LJCL 683; (1935) 152 LTR 46; (1934) 78 SJ 601; (1933-34) L TLR 566 CCA On consent of 'victim' as defence to criminal charges.

R v Fagan [1968] Crim LR 560 HC QBD While may not have deliberately driven onto constable's foot, leaving car on foot once had was an assault.

R v Forman and Ford [1988] Crim LR 677 CrCt Police officer who does not act when other assaults prisoner is guilty of assault; where not proved which of two officers assaulted prisoner with whom were alone both must be acquitted (if one must have encouraged the other both are guilty).

R v Hatton [1925] All ER 396; (1926-30) XXVIII Cox CC 43; (1925) 89 JP 164; [1925] 2 KB 322; (1925) 60 LJ 705; [1925] 94 LJCL 863; (1925) 133 LTR 735; (1924-25) XLI TLR 637; (1925) WN (I) 199 CCA Interpretation of phrase 'wilfully assaults' in Children Act 1908, s 12(1).

R v Ireland; R v Burstow [1997] 2 Cr App R (S) 1273; (1997) 147 NLJ 1273; [1997] TLR 412; [1997] 3 WLR 534 HL Could be guilty of assault as result of injury occasioned by way of silent telephone calls.

R v Julien [1969] 2 All ER 856; (1969) 53 Cr App R 407; [1969] Crim LR 381t; (1969) 133 JP 489; (1969) 119 NLJ 390t; (1969) 113 SJ 342; [1969] 1 WLR 839 CA Person must show did not want to fight if seeks to raise self-defence.

R v Linzee (Robert Alexander Craig); R v O'Driscoll (Gerald) (1956) 40 Cr App R 177; (1957) 107 LJ 57 CMAC Was legitimate to look for corroboration of evidence of witness who possibly took part in crime of which accused charged.

R v Lynsey [1995] 3 All ER 654; [1995] 2 Cr App R 667; (1995) 159 JP 437 CA The term 'common assault' is to be construed in its everyday sense and its technical sense.

R v Mackie (Robert) [1973] Crim LR 54 CrCt Liability for injuries/for death suffered in course of escape from assault by child to whom assailant was in loco parentis.

R v Mark (Malcolm), Brown and Mark (Maureen) [1961] Crim LR 173 CCC Need not know are assaulting peace officer to be guilty of offence under Offences against the Person Act 1861, s 38: are not guilty if act in honest/reasonable/bona fide belief that person 'assaulted' committing breach of peace/a felony.

R v Miller [1954] 2 All ER 529; (1954) 38 Cr App R 1; [1954] Crim LR 219; [1954] 2 QB 282; (1954) 98 SJ 62; (1954) 118 JP 341; [1954] 2 WLR 138 HC QBD Husband could not be guilty of raping wife absent separation agreement/order; assault for husband to use force in exercising right to marital sex.

R v Newport (Salop) Justices; ex parte Wright (1928-29) XLV TLR 477 HC KBD Parents presumed to authorise headmaster to inflict reasonable corporal punishment on children when in his care.

R v Notman [1994] Crim LR 518 CA Actions must have been substantial cause of injury suffered to constitute assault; direction to convict of using threatening words/behaviour ought not to have been made where guilty plea to same rather than affray (offence charged) withdrawn.

R v O'Brien (1911-13) XXII Cox CC 374; (1911) 104 LTR 113; (1910-11) XXVII TLR 204 CCA Could properly be convicted of assault where charged with riot.

R v Parmenter (1991) 92 Cr App R 164 CA Leave to appeal granted on question of foreseeability as an element of malicious wounding/assault occasioning actual bodily harm.

R v Renshaw [1989] Crim LR 811 CA Complainant in assault case who sought not to give evidence ought not to have been prosecuted for contempt.

R v Sherriff [1969] Crim LR 260 CA Forcefully seeking to draw back is not an assault.

R v Venna [1975] 3 All ER 788; (1975) 61 Cr App R 310; [1975] Crim LR 701t; (1976) 140 JP 31; [1976] QB 421; (1975) 119 SJ 679; [1975] 3 WLR 737 CA Recklessness sufficient to sustain charge of assault.

R v Williams (Gladstone) (1984) 78 Cr App R 276; [1984] Crim LR 163 CA When pleading mistake as defence to assault reasonableness of belief relevant to deciding whether held but not to whether guilty/innocent.

R v Wilson (Alan Thomas) [1996] 2 Cr App R 241; [1996] Crim LR 573; [1997] QB 47; (1996) 140 SJ LB 93; (1996) TLR 5/3/96; [1996] 3 WLR 125 CA Successful appeal against assault conviction as appellant's branding of wife's buttocks had been done with her consent.

Reed v Wastie and another [1972] Crim LR 221t HC QBD Successful action against police officer for assault of arrestee after had been arrested.

Smith v Chief Superintendent, Woking Station (1983) 76 Cr App R 234; [1983] Crim LR 323 HC QBD Was assault to peer into flat of elderly spinster in manner calculated to cause her fear of immediate assault.

Vaughan v McKenzie [1968] 1 All ER 1154; [1968] Crim LR 265; (1968) 118 NLJ 204t; (1968) 112 SJ 212; [1968] 2 WLR 1133 HC QBD Not assault on bailiff in execution of duty where assault occurred when resident sought to impede bailiff's entry (bailiff in so entering was trespassing).

Young and others v Peck (1913-14) XXIII Cox CC 270; (1912-13) 107 LTR 857 HC KBD Persons in crowd from which eggs thrown but who had not themselves thrown eggs properly convicted of intimidation.

ASSAULT (ill-treatment of patient)

R v Holmes [1979] Crim LR 52 CrCt One-off assault of mental patient could be ill-treatment of same.

ATTEMPT (abortion)

R v Spicer [1955] Crim LR 772 Assizes Were guilty of attempted abortion where sought to produce miscarriage (though means whereby sought to do so bound to fail).

ATTEMPT (arson)

R v O'Toole (Michael) [1987] Crim LR 759 CA On requisite intent to be guilty of attempt (here attempted arson).

ATTEMPT (attempt to discharge firearm)

R v Jones (1901-02) XVIII TLR 156 Assizes Could not be convicted of attempting to discharge loaded revolver with intent to kill where pointed same at person and pulled trigger knowing gun had to jam (Offences against the Person Act 1861, s 14).

R v Linneker [1904-07] All ER 797; (1907-09) XXI Cox CC 196; (1906) 70 JP 293; [1906] 2 KB 99; [1906] 75 LJKB 385; (1906) XCIV LTR 856; (1905-06) 50 SJ 440; (1905-06) XXII TLR 495; (1905-06) 54 WR 494 CCR More than intent and possession necessary to establish attempt to discharge revolver.

ATTEMPT (attempt to incite perjury)

R v Cromack [1978] Crim LR 217 CA Successful appeal in light of jury misdirection against conviction for attempt to incite perjury.

ATTEMPT (attempt to obstruct/pervert the course of justice)

Ping-nam (Tsang) v R (1982) 74 Cr App R; [1982] Crim LR 46; (1981) 125 SJ 709; [1981] 1 WLR 1462 PC Could not charge accused with attempting to pervert course of justice rather than perjury so as to overcome evidential difficulties; could not seek upholding of convictions on completely different basis to that argued in lower courts.

R v Britton [1973] Crim LR 375; [1973] RTR 502 CA Valid conviction for attempting to defeat the course of justice by drinking alcohol so as to render the laboratory specimen provided unreliable.

R v Coxhead [1986] Crim LR 251; [1986] RTR 411 CA Is/is not discretion not to bring criminal proceedings in non-serious/serious cases: seriousness a matter for jury.

R v Greenberg (1918-21) XXVI Cox CC 466; (1919) 121 LTR 288; (1918-19) 63 SJ 553 CCA Attempting to get witness to change evidence/not give certain evidence is same common law misdemeanour.

R v Rowell [1978] 1 All ER 665; (1977) 65 Cr App R 174; [1977] Crim LR 681; (1978) 142 JP 181; (1977) 127 NLJ 662t; (1977) 121 SJ 790; [1978] 1 WLR 132 CA Person acting alone can attempt to pervert course of justice; false allegation could be attempt; attempt can be made up of one/series of actions.

R v Williams (1991) 92 Cr App R 158; [1991] Crim LR 205; (1991) 155 JP 365; [1990] TLR 669 CA Attempting to pervert the course of justice a substantive common law offence.

ATTEMPT (attempt to obtain by deception/false pretences)

Comer v Bloomfield (1971) 55 Cr App R 305; [1971] Crim LR 230; [1971] RTR 49 CA Letter of inquiry to insurance company (preliminary to unmade false claim) not attempted obtaining of property by deception.

R v Bunche (Jacques Emmanuel) (1993) 96 Cr App R 274; (1993) 157 JP 780; [1992] TLR 513 CA Could be convicted of attempting to obtain property by deception where sought passport using false name.

R v Ilyas (Mohammed) (1984) 78 Cr App R 17 CA Must have done everything preparatory to offence before guilty of attempt (and acts must be proximate to offence): merely obtaining insurance claim form could not support attempted obtaining of property by deception conviction.

R v Laitwood (John) (1910) 4 Cr App R 248; (1910) WN (I) 122 CCA Can be convicted of attempt to obtain by false pretences where did not manage attempt solely because were apprehended.

R v Light (Arthur Dennison) [1914-15] All ER 659; (1914-15) XXIV Cox CC 718; (1914-15) 11 Cr App R 111; [1915] 84 LJKB 865; (1915) 112 LTR 1144; (1914-15) 59 SJ 351; (1914-15) XXXI TLR 257; (1915) WN (I) 97 CCA Can be convicted of attempted obtaining of money by false pretences though victim knew pretences were false.

R v Punch (Samuel Adolphus David) (1927-28) 20 Cr App R 18 CCA On attempts; on attempting to obtain by false pretences.

R v Robinson [1914-17] All ER 101; (1914-15) XXIV Cox CC 726; (1914-15) 11 Cr App R 124; (1915) 79 JP 303; [1915] 2 KB 342; (1915) 50 LJ 159; [1915] 84 LJKB 1149; (1915-16) 113 LTR 379; (1914-15) 59 SJ 366; (1914-15) XXXI TLR 313; (1915) WN (I) 133 CCA Mere intention to commit crime could not sustain conviction for attempt to commit crime.

ATTEMPT (attempt to procure)

R v Saunders (Ernest) (1916-17) 12 Cr App R 56 CCA Attempt to obtain money by false pretences not punishable with hard labour.

R v Widdowson (Stanley) (1986) 82 Cr App R 314; [1986] Crim LR 233; [1986] RTR 124; (1986) 130 SJ 88 CA Not attempted obtaining services by deception where gave false personal details on hire purchase credit inquiry form.

ATTEMPT (attempt to procure)

R v Christian and another (1913-14) XXIII Cox CC 541; (1914) 78 JP 112 CCC Cannot be convicted of attempt to/conspiracy to/actual procuration where woman freely chooses to be at brothel.

ATTEMPT (attempt to procure act of gross indecency)

Chief Constable of Hampshire v Mace (1987) 84 Cr App R 40; [1986] Crim LR 752; (1986) 150 JP 470 HC QBD Can be charged with attempt to procure act of gross indecency.

R v Butters [1959] Crim LR 215 Sessions Was attempted gross indecency to write letter to another inviting him to commit act of gross indecency with writer.

R v Gammon (Dennis) (1959) 43 Cr App R 155; [1959] Crim LR 448t; (1959) 123 JP 410 CCA Is/is not attempted procuring of grossly indecent act to clearly seek grossly indecent act/to seek apparently innocent act though intending grossly immoral one; corroboration required of complainant's evidence in attempted procuring of grossly indecent act.

R v Miskell [1954] 1 All ER 137; (1953) 37 Cr App R 214; [1954] Crim LR 137; (1954) 118 JP 113; (1954) 104 LJ 41; (1954) 98 SJ 148 CMAC Attempt to procure act of gross indecency with male person inferred from circumstances.

R v Riley [1967] Crim LR 656 Assizes Person acquitted of attempt to procure act of gross indecency where at time of alleged offence was suffering from psychoneurosis which led him to want to get into trouble.

R v Spight [1986] Crim LR 817 CA On evidential responsibilities placed on defendant (regarding such issues as age and consent) in prosecution for attempting to procure grossly indecent act.

R v Wood [1957] Crim LR 54 Sessions Acts deemed to constitute attempt to procure act of gross indecency with another male.

ATTEMPT (attempt to procure drugs)

Kyprianou v Reynolds [1969] Crim LR 656; (1969) 113 SJ 563 HC QBD Intention to acquire drugs along with invitation to drug dealers to treat or make offer not enough to support conviction for attempted procurement of drugs.

ATTEMPT (attempt to procure woman to become prostitute)

R v Gold and Cohen (1907) 71 JP 360 CCC Can only be convicted of attempting to procure woman to become prostitute outside King's Dominions where woman concerned not already a prostitute (Criminal Law Amendment Act 1885, s 2(2)).

R v Morris-Lowe (Brian John) [1985] 1 All ER 400; (1985) 80 Cr App R 114; [1985] Crim LR 50; (1984) 128 SJ 872; [1984] TLR 595; [1985] 1 WLR 29 CA On what is meant by attempting to procure woman to become 'common' prostitute.

ATTEMPT (attempt to steal)

Davey and others v Lee [1967] 2 All ER 423; (1967) 51 Cr App R 303; [1967] Crim LR 357; (1967) 131 JP 327; [1968] 1 QB 366; (1967) 111 SJ 212; [1967] 3 WLR 105 HC QBD On what constitutes attempt.

R v Cooper and Miles [1979] Crim LR 42 CrCt On elements of attempt to steal.

ATTEMPT (attempt to supply drugs)

R v Tulloch (Wayne Andrew) (1986) 83 Cr App R 1; [1986] Crim LR 50 CA Could be convicted of attempt where sought to commit what thought was possible but was in fact impossible offence.

ATTEMPT (attempted false imprisonment)

R v Geddes [1996] Crim LR 894; (1996) TLR 15/7/96 CA Person who entered school with means of falsely imprisoning child, no more, was not guilty of attempted false imprisonment - had only committed preparatory acts.

ATTEMPT (attempted unlawful carnal knowledge of under-sixteen year old)

R v Collier [1960] Crim LR 204 Assizes Statutory defence open to accused when committed offence of having unlawful sex with under-sixteen year old also available where attempted offence.

ATTEMPT (burglary)

R v Bates (William) (1930-31) Cr App R 49 CCA For purposes of Prevention of Crimes Act 1871, s 20, attempted burglary is not a crime.

R v Boyle (George); R v Boyle (James) (1987) 84 Cr App R 270; [1987] Crim LR 111 CA Courts could look to pre-Criminal Attempts Act 1981 law to determine what constitutes an attempt.

Re Attorney General's References (Nos 1 and 2 of 1979) [1979] 3 All ER 143; (1979) 69 Cr App R 266; [1979] Crim LR 585; (1979) 143 JP 708; [1980] QB 180; (1979) 123 SJ 472; [1979] 3 WLR 577 CA Entering building with intent to steal (even if nothing worth stealing) is burglary/attempted burglary; guidelines on indictment of theft offences.

Scudder v Barrett (1979) 69 Cr App R 277; [1980] QB 195; [1979] 3 WLR 591 HC QBD Need not prove intention to steal particular objects on charge of attempted theft/burglary.

ATTEMPT (false imprisonment)

R v Geddes [1996] Crim LR 894; (1996) TLR 15/7/96 CA Person who entered school with means of falsely imprisoning child, no more, was not guilty of attempted false imprisonment - had only committed preparatory acts.

ATTEMPT (general)

Anderton v Ryan [1985] 2 All ER 355; [1985] AC 560 (also HL); (1985) 81 Cr App R 166; [1985] Crim LR 503; (1985) 149 JP 433; (1985) 135 NLJ 485; (1985) 135 NLJ 485; [1985] 2 WLR 968 HL Cannot be guilty of crime where believed was committing crime but was not.

Director of Public Prosecutions v Stonehouse [1977] 2 All ER 909; [1978] AC 55; (1977) 65 Cr App R 192 (also CCA); [1977] Crim LR 544; (1977) 141 JP 473; (1977) 127 NLJ 864; (1977) 121 SJ 491; [1977] 3 WLR 143 HL Guilty of obtaining property by deception where acts done abroad but property obtained by deception in England; doing all possible acts to obtain property by deception could sustain conviction for attempt thereof.

Haughton v Smith [1973] 3 All ER 1109; [1975] AC 476; (1974) 58 Cr App R 198; (1974) 138 JP 31; (1973) 123 NLJ 1112t; [1974] 2 WLR 1 HL Cannot be attempt to handle stolen goods unless goods handled are stolen goods.

Mieras v Rees [1975] Crim LR 224; (1975) 139 JP 549 HC QBD Cannot attempt to supply controlled drug (even if have requisite mens rea) where substance are supplying is not controlled drug as is no actus reus.

R v Baxter [1971] 2 All ER 359; [1971] Crim LR 281t; (1971) 135 JP 345; (1971) 121 NLJ 130t; [1972] 1 QB 1; (1971) 115 SJ 246; [1971] 2 WLR 1138 CA English courts had jurisdiction in attempted obtaining by deception case where person mailed false pools claims from Northern Ireland to Liverpool.

R v Bloxham (Bernard Conrad) (1942-44) 29 Cr App R 37 CCA Was no taking and carrying away/attempt at same so could not be convicted of larceny.

R v Campbell [1991] Crim LR 268 CA On what constitutes an attempt (no fixed rule).

R v Dunnington [1984] 1 All ER 676; (1984) 78 Cr App R 171; [1984] Crim LR 98; (1984) 148 JP 316; [1984] QB 472; (1983) 127 SJ 822; [1983] TLR 569; [1984] 2 WLR 125 CA Is attempt where acts if completed would be aiding and abetting even if principal act only attempt.

ATTEMPT (grievous bodily harm)

R v Fussell [1951] 2 All ER 761; (1951-52) 35 Cr App R 135; (1951) 115 JP 562; (1951) 101 LJ 582 CCA Could try attempted (taking and driving away) indictable offence summarily.

R v Griffin [1993] Crim LR 515 CA On respective roles of judge/jury in child abduction case; was possible to find attempted abduction where had arranged boat trip and went to school to request control of children in local authority care.

R v Ilyas (Mohammed) (1984) 78 Cr App R 17 CA Must have done everything preparatory to offence before guilty of attempt (and acts must be proximate to offence): merely obtaining insurance claim form could not support attempted obtaining of property by deception conviction.

R v Males [1961] 3 All ER 705; (1962) 46 Cr App R 35; [1962] Crim LR 46; (1961) 125 JP 647; [1962] 2 QB 500; (1961) 105 SJ 891 CCA Can be guilty of attempt though substantive offence committed.

R v Manchester Crown Court, ex parte Hill [1984] TLR 601 HC QBD Justices cannot convict person of attempted offence where are charged with complete offence.

R v Millard and Vernon [1987] Crim LR 393 CA On intent requirement under the Criminal Attempts Act 1981, s 1(1).

R v Mohan [1975] 2 All ER 193; (1975) 60 Cr App R 272; [1975] Crim LR 283t; (1975) 139 JP 523; (1975) 125 NLJ 186t; [1976] QB 1; [1975] RTR 337; (1975) 119 SJ 219; [1975] 2 WLR 859 CA Specific intent to commit offence essential element of attempt to commit crime.

R v Percy Dalton (London) Ltd; R v Dalton (Jack); R v Strong (Joseph) (1948-49) 33 Cr App R 102; [1949] 118 LJR 1626; (1949) LXV TLR 326 CCA Not/is attempt to commit crime to do an act which does not contribute/contributes towards commission of full offence.

R v Shivpuri [1986] 2 All ER 334; [1987] AC 1; (1986) 83 Cr App R 178; [1986] Crim LR 536; (1986) 150 JP 353; (1986) 136 NLJ 488; (1986) 130 SJ 392; [1986] 2 WLR 988 HL Attempt possible even if full offence impossible; need not know precise name/category of imported drug to sustain drug importation conviction.

R v Shivpuri (Pyare) [1985] 1 All ER 143; (1985) 80 Cr App R 241; [1985] Crim LR 43; [1985] QB 1029; (1985) 129 SJ 31; [1984] TLR 610; [1985] 2 WLR 29 CA Attempt possible even though full offence impossible.

R v Stonehouse (John Thomson) (1977) 65 Cr App R 192 (also HL) CA Guilty of obtaining property by deception where acts done abroad but property obtained by deception in England.

Webley v Buxton [1977] 2 All ER 595; (1977) 65 Cr App R 136; [1977] Crim LR 160; (1977) 141 JP 407; [1977] QB 481; [1977] RTR 193; (1977) 121 SJ 153; [1977] 2 WLR 766 HC QBD Can convict of attempted offence even if complete offence proved.

ATTEMPT (grievous bodily harm)

R v Pearman (Stephen Dennis) (1985) 80 Cr App R 259; [1984] Crim LR 675; [1985] RTR 39 CA That foresee consequences need not mean intended them.

ATTEMPT (gross indecency)

R v Lawson [1959] Crim LR 134 Sessions Acts alleged by prosecution (lewd conversation with boy) could not amount to attempt to commit act of gross indecency.

ATTEMPT (handling)

Anderton v Ryan [1985] 2 All ER 355; [1985] AC 560 (also HC QBD); (1985) 81 Cr App R 166; (1985) 149 JP 433; (1985) 135 NLJ 485; (1985) 129 SJ 362; [1985] Crim LR 503; [1985] 2 WLR 968 HL Cannot be guilty of crime where believed was committing crime but was not.

Anderton v Ryan [1985] 1 All ER 138; [1985] AC 560 (also HL); (1985) 80 Cr App R 235; [1984] Crim LR 483; (1984) 128 SJ 850; [1984] TLR 227; [1985] 2 WLR 23 HC QBD Could be guilty of attempted handling of stolen goods though not proved that goods in issue stolen.

Chief Constable of Greater Manchester Police v Ryan (1985) 149 JP 79 HC QBD On what constitutes offence of attempted handling.

Houghton v Smith [1973] 3 All ER 1109; [1975] AC 476; (1974) 58 Cr App R 198; (1974) 138 JP 31; (1973) 123 NLJ 112t; [1974] 2 WLR 1 HL Cannot be attempt to handle stolen goods unless goods handled are stolen goods.

R v Smith (RD) (1973) 117 SJ 429 CA Cannot be guilty of attempt to commit crime where did acts which if uninterrupted would not amount to criminal act.

R v Smith (Roger) [1974] Crim LR 305; (1974) 118 SJ 7; [1974] 2 WLR 1 HL On attempt; on attempted handling.

ATTEMPT (incitement of child to gross indecency)

R v Rowley [1991] 4 All ER 649; (1992) 94 Cr App R 95; [1991] Crim LR 785; (1992) 156 JP 319; (1991) 141 NLJ 1038t; (1991) 135 SJ LB 84; [1991] TLR 347; [1991] 1 WLR 1020 CA Act outraging public decency must outrage public decency in and of itself; preparatory acts to inciting gross indecency not attempted incitement of child to gross indecency.

ATTEMPT (infanticide)

R v Smith (KA) [1983] Crim LR 739 CrCt Could be convicted of attempted infanticide under Infanticide Act 1938.

ATTEMPT (larceny)

Carey v Martin [1954] Crim LR 139t HC QBD Was not attempted larceny to break shop skylight (with intent to enter) and then to run away.

R v Hawkey [1964] Crim LR 465 CCA Ought not to have been convicted of attempted larceny where evidence pointed equally towards guilt of lesser offence of attempted taking/driving away.

ATTEMPT (murder)

R v Bruzas (John) [1972] Crim LR 367 CrCt On whether provocation a defence to attempted murder; on whether is an offence of attempted manslaughter.

R v Campbell [1997] Crim LR 495 CA Cannot plead diminished responsibility as defence to attempted murder.

R v Gotts [1992] 1 All ER 832; [1992] 2 AC 412; (1992) 94 Cr App R 312; [1992] Crim LR 724; (1992) 156 JP 225; (1992) 142 NLJ 311; (1992) 136 SJ LB 89; [1992] TLR 77; [1992] 2 WLR 284 HL Duress not available as defence to charge of attempted murder.

R v Grimwood [1962] 3 All ER 285; (1962) 46 Cr App R 393; [1962] Crim LR 632t; (1962) 112 LJ 785; [1962] 2 QB 621; (1962) 106 SJ 613; [1962] 3 WLR 747 CCA DPP v Smith inapplicable to attempted murder; direction that if death a foreseeable consequenc of accused's actions, accused could be guilty of attempted murder, despite absence of intent to kill, a mistaken direction.

R v Jones (Kenneth) [1990] 3 All ER 886; (1990) 91 Cr App R 351; [1990] Crim LR 800; (1990) 154 JP 413; [1990] 1 WLR 1057 CA Pointing of loaded gun at person where gun cannot be fired may be attempted murder.

R v Loughlin [1959] Crim LR 518t CCA On necessary intent for attempted murder.

R v Morris [1977] Crim LR 231 CA Twelve years' imprisonment for attempted murder of burglary victim who could have recognised perpetrator of burglary-attempted murderer.

R v O'Brien (Michael) [1995] 2 Cr App R 649; [1995] Crim LR 734; (1995) 139 SJ LB 130; [1995] TLR 202 CA That knew principal might have intention to kill could sustain conviction of secondary party of attempted murder.

R v Pond [1984] Crim LR 164 CA Plea of guilty to wounding with intent to grievous bodily harm where charged with attempted murder (the two offences requiring different intent) not a defence to latter charge.

R v Pridmore (George Edward) (1912-13) 8 Cr App R 198; (1913) 77 JP 339; (1912-13) XXIX TLR 330 CCA On guilt of parties to common unlawful enterprise for attempted murder by one; on appropriate sentencing for same.

R v Sheldon (Leslie Maxwell) [1996] 2 Cr App R 50 CA Guilty verdict in respect of near-fourteen year old allowed stand despite non-direction as to doli incapax presumption.

R v Walker and Hayles [1990] Crim LR 44 CA On when intent to kill may be inferred.

R v White (1911-13) XXII Cox CC 325; [1910] 2 KB 125; (1910) 79 LJKB 854; (1909-10) 54 SJ 523; (1910) WN (I) 123 CCA Guilty of attempted murder where do one of series of non-lethal acts intended to cause death; liable to punishment for attempted murder under Offences Against the Person Act 1861, ss 11-15.

R v Whybrow (1951) 95 SJ 745 CCA On necessary intent in case of attempted murder.

ATTEMPT (rape)

Attorney General's Reference (No 1 of 1992) [1993] 2 All ER 190; (1993) 96 Cr App R 298; [1993] Crim LR 274; (1993) 157 JP 753; (1992) 136 SJ LB 304; [1992] TLR 528; [1993] 1 WLR 274 CA Prima facie case of attempted rape if necessary intent can be inferred and acts preparatory to rape have taken place.

R v Finney (1964) 108 SJ 260 CCA Attempted rape a misdemeanour.

R v Kelly [1992] Crim LR 181 CA Bringing complainant to suspect to see whether was assailant was permissible where all happened within minutes of offence; on what constitutes criminal attempt (here in context of attempted rape).

R v Khan and others [1990] 2 All ER 783; (1990) 91 Cr App R 29; [1990] Crim LR 519; (1990) 154 JP 805; (1994) 144 NLJ 863; (1990) 134 SJ 401; [1990] TLR 86; [1990] 1 WLR 813 CA Attempted rape possible even where man reckless as to whether consent given.

R v Lankford [1959] Crim LR 209t CCA Person who voluntarily desists from raping woman whom has assaulted may not be guilty of attempted rape.

R v Matthews [1981] Crim LR 325 CrCt Could be attempted rape where pinned person down with expressed intention of having non-consensual sex (albeit that penis was never erect/penetration never attempted).

ATTEMPT (rape per anum)

R v Gaston (Daniel) (1981) 73 Cr App R 164 CA Attempted rape per anum not an offence.

R v O'Sullivan and others [1981] Crim LR 406 CA No offence of attempted rape per anum.

ATTEMPT (suicide)

R v Mann (John William) (1914) 10 Cr App R 31; (1914) 49 LJ 99; (1913-14) 58 SJ 303 CCA Attempted suicide an attempted felony.

R v Spence (George) (1957) 41 Cr App R 80; [1957] Crim LR 188 CCA Is murder where attempted suicide results in death of another.

R v Wilson (Ernest) (1922-23) 17 Cr App R 130 CCA Leave to appeal against sentence for attempted suicide granted.

ATTEMPT (theft)

Partington v Williams (1976) 62 Cr App R 220; [1977] Crim LR 609; (1976) 126 NLJ 89t CA Could not be convicted of attempted offence where could not have committed complete offence.

Partington v Williams (1976) 120 SJ 80 HC QBD Could not be convicted of attempted offence where could not have committed complete offence.

R v Bayley and Easterbrook [1980] Crim LR 503 CA On necessary intent for attempted theft.

R v Gullefer [1990] 3 All ER 882; (1990) 91 Cr App R 356; [1987] Crim LR 195; [1990] 1 WLR 1063 CA Not attempted theft where leaped onto race track with intention of foiling race so that could recover money bet on (what would have turned out if succeeded to be void) race.

R v Hector (Joseph) (1978) 67 Cr App R 224; (1978) 128 NLJ 212t CA Not attempted theft to get into car with view to see if anything worth stealing therefrom.

R v Hussein [1978] Crim LR 219 CA Not attempted theft to open van door so as to look inside holdall and take anything of value that might be contained therein.

R v Husseyn (otherwise Hussein) (Ulus) (1978) 67 Cr App R 131 HL Given presence of intent to steal was attempted theft to open van door as prelude to taking holdall.

R v Marchant (Stephen); R v McCallister (Stephen) (1985) 80 Cr App R 361 CA Was attempt to take conveyance without authority even though did not use conveyance.

Scudder v Barrett (1979) 69 Cr App R 277; [1980] QB 195; [1979] 3 WLR 591 HC QBD Need not prove intention to steal particular objects on charge of attempted theft/burglary.

ATTEMPT (to obtain by deception/false pretences)

R v Dargue (Walter) (1910-11) 6 Cr App R 261 CCA Must show person parting with goods was induced by false pretences to do so.

R v Dunleavy (1909) 73 JP 56 CCA Attempted obtaining by false pretences conviction quashed where convict had not known that ring was seeling as gold ring actually made of brass.

R v Harris (Paul Andrew) (1976) 62 Cr App R 28; [1976] Crim LR 514 CA Giving fake identity and telling untrue story in bid to get hotel room was attempted obtaining of pecuniary advantage by deception not just preparatory steps.

AUCTION (conspiracy to effect auction)

R v Barnett and others [1951] 1 All ER 917; (1951-52) 35 Cr App R 37; (1951) 115 JP 305; [1951] 2 KB 425; (1951) 95 SJ 337; [1951] 1 TLR 899; (1951) WN (I) 214 CCA Conspiracy to effect offence under Auctions (Bidding Agreements) Act 1927 triable summarily.

AUCTION (general)

Allen v Simmons [1978] 3 All ER 662; [1978] Crim LR 362; (1979) 143 JP 105; (1978) 128 NLJ 512t; (1978) 122 SJ 470; [1978] 1 WLR 879 HC QBD Competitive bidding includes any form of competition for purchase.

Clements and another v Rydeheard [1978] 3 All ER 658; (1979) 143 JP 25 HC QBD Selective competitive bidding covered by Mock Auctions Act.

Lomas v Rydeheard (1975) 125 NLJ 262t HC QBD Failed appeal against conviction for participating in mock auction contrary to the Mock Auctions Act 1961.

R v Pollard (1984) 148 JP 679 CA On what constitutes competitive bidding for purposes of Mock Auctions Act 1961.

AVIATION (general)

R v Silvertop [1954] Crim LR 205 Magistrates Fine (imprisonment in default) for person who was drunk on board aeroplane/interfered with pilot of aeroplane.

R v Warburton-Pitt (1991) 92 Cr App R 136; [1991] Crim LR 434; [1990] TLR 521 CA Conviction for recklessly acting in manner likely to endanger aircraft (here microlight)/persons inside/other persons or property (under Air Navigation Order 1982) quashed as was inadequate specificity by prosecution as to nature of recklessness involved.

AVOIDING FARE (general)

Murphy v Verati [1967] 1 All ER 861; [1967] Crim LR 370; (1967) 111 SJ 254; [1967] 1 WLR 641 HC QBD Can avoid payment of fare of fellow-passenger after travelling.

BAIL (conspiracy to effect public mischief)

R v Foy; R v Noe; R v Kelly [1972] Crim LR 504t; (1972) 116 SJ 506 CA Valid withdrawal of question from jury whether agreement to indemnify bail was a conspiracy to effect public mischief.

BAIL (general)

Curtis: Motion for Bail (1965-66) 116 NLJ 612t HC QBD Police objections to bail that applicant might interfere with/seek to frighten witnesses not defeated simply because is no evidence of such behaviour on part of applicant/his colleagues.

Das (Lala Jairam) and others v RI (1945) 89 SJ 164; (1944-45) LXI TLR 245 PC Indian HC cannot grant bail to convict granted leave to appeal to PC but Provincial Government can stay execution of convict's sentence pending appeal.

Director of Public Prosecutions v Richards [1988] 3 All ER 406; (1989) 88 Cr App R 97; [1988] Crim LR 606; (1988) 152 JP 333; [1988] QB 701; (1988) 132 SJ 623; [1988] 3 WLR 153 HC QBD Can be arrested for leaving court building after surrendering to bail but not guilty of offence.

Ex parte Blyth [1944] 1 All ER 587; [1944] KB 532; [1944] 113 LJ 401; (1944) 171 LTR 283; (1944) 88 SJ 204; (1943-44) LX TLR 353 HC KBD HC KBD judge has no inherent jurisdiction to grant bail.

Ex parte Goswani [1967] Crim LR 234; (1965-66) 116 NLJ 1712t; (1967) 111 SJ 17 HC QBD Bail here not deemed unreasonable: that defendant cannot meet bail set does not per se mean it is unreasonable.

Ex parte L (1944-45) LXI TLR 180 HC KBD Granting of bail to convict not within remit of High Court judge.

Ex parte Speculand (1946) 110 JP 92; [1946] KB 48; [1946] 115 LJ 218; (1946) 174 LTR 334; (1946) 90 SJ 152; (1945-46) LXII TLR 32 HC KBD Jurisdiction of HC KBD judge in respect of bail prior to appeal.

Ex parte Thomas [1956] Crim LR 119 HC QBD Habeas corpus application made where bail excessive.

Ex parte Williams (Robert Franklin) [1970] Crim LR 102; (1969) 113 SJ 853 HC QBD Habeas corpus application as cover for bail application not approved of.

France v Dewsbury Magistrates' Court [1988] Crim LR 295; (1988) 152 JP 301 HC QBD Improper for later court to convict person for non-surrender to bail where justices present upon surrender indicated that one-day delay in surrender would be overlooked.

Murphy v Director of Public Prosecutions [1990] 2 All ER 390; (1990) 91 Cr App R 96; [1990] Crim LR 395; (1990) 154 JP 467; [1990] 1 WLR 601 HC QBD Failure of bailee to surrender a single summary offence if bail granted by police/magistrates' court but normally contempt before Crown Court.

R v Barking Justices; ex parte Shankshaft (1983) 147 JP 399 HC QBD Old and new factors to be taken into account at second bail application.

R v Blyth Juvenile Court; ex parte G [1991] Crim LR 693 HC QBD Judicial review not an appropriate route for seeking of bail; need not be enormous change in circumstances to merit further bail application.

R v Bournemouth Magistrates' Court; ex parte Cross, Griffin and Pamment (1989) 89 Cr App R 90 [1989] Crim LR 207; (1989) 153 JP 440 HC QBD On attaching conditions when granting bail to person charged with offence not punishable by imprisonment.

R v Bow Street Magistrates' Court; ex parte Hall and Otobo (1986) 136 NLJ 1111 CA Recognisance may remain valid despite change in bail conditions.

R v Boyle [1993] Crim LR 40 CA On correct procedure as regards dealing with bail absconder.

R v Brown (Isidore Edward) (1927-28) 20 Cr App R 94 CCA Bail application dismissed by CCA.

R v Calder Justices, ex parte Kennedy [1992] Crim LR 496; (1992) 156 JP 716; [1992] TLR 65 HC QBD Could apply for bail where had not been granted bail at earlier stage because of lack of information on which justices could make decision.

R v Central Criminal Court, ex parte Guney [1994] 2 All ER 423; [1995] 1 Cr App R 50; (1994) 138 SJ LB 58; [1994] TLR 55; [1994] 1 WLR 438 HC QBD Arraignment possible even if defendant not in custody.

R v Central Criminal Court; ex parte Porter [1992] Crim LR 121 HC QBD Improper attempt to vary bail conditions; disclosure of medical report obtained pursuant to Bail Act 1976, s 3(6A), usually a discretionary matter for trial judge/sometimes for other judge engaged in pre-trial review.

R v Charavanmuttu (Edward Vanniascheram) (1928-29) 21 Cr App R 184 CCA Bail granted in light of pending vacation.

R v Coe (Anthony William) (1969) 53 Cr App R 66; (1969) 133 JP 103; [1968] 1 WLR 1950 CA Bail post-committal for sentence very exceptional.

R v Crown Court at Leeds, ex parte Hussain and others [1995] 3 All ER 527 HC QBD High Court cannot undertake judicial review of matters relating to trial on indictment including legitimate arraignment; arraignment legitimate despite subsequent tendering of further evidence; no eligibility for bail arising from delay caused by action for judicial review.

R v Crown Court at Reading , ex parte Malik and another [1981] 1 All ER 249; (1981) 72 Cr App R 146; [1981] Crim LR 240; (1981) 145 JP 132; (1981) 131 NLJ 43; [1981] QB 451; (1981) 125 SJ 97; [1981] 2 WLR 473 HC QBD Crown Court judge may grant bail despite refusal of bail by High Court judge.

R v Crown Court at Warwick; ex parte Smalley (1987) 84 Cr App R 51; [1987] Crim LR 112; (1987) 131 SJ 257; [1984] TLR 163; [1987] 1 WLR 237 HC QBD Crown Court judge could estreat recognisance where bail originally set by justices but varied by High Court judge.

R v Crown Court at Wood Green, ex parte Howe [1992] 3 All ER 366; (1991) 93 Cr App R 213; [1991] Crim LR 694; (1991) 155 JP 652; [1991] TLR 123; [1992] 1 WLR 702 HC QBD Failure to provide defendant opens surety to estreatment unless applies for further time/instalment payments/discharge from or reduction of sum due under recognisance.

R v Croydon Crown Court; ex parte Cox [1997] 1 Cr App R 20 HC QBD On appropriate way in which to challenge bail condition.

R v Davidson (Joseph) (1927-28) 20 Cr App R 66 CCA Bail only exceptionally available where appealing to CCA.

R v Dover and East Kent Justices, ex parte Dean [1992] Crim LR 33; (1992) 156 JP 357; [1991] TLR 404 HC QBD Can apply for bail at second remand hearings where originally agreed to remand without making such application.

R v Edwards [1976] Crim LR 122t HC QBD Permission to emigrate a condition of bail.

R v Fitzgerald (Edward), Duke of Leinster (1922-23) 17 Cr App R 147 CCA Bail applications generally refused by CCA.

R v Fletcher (1949) 113 JP 365 CCA Refusal of bail properly preceded by evidence of previous convictions meriting denial of bail.

R v Garnham (William) (1910) 4 Cr App R 150 CCA Bail pending appeal unusual.

R v Garrett; ex parte De Dryver (1917) WN (I) 301 HC KBD Metropolitan police magistrate ought not to have remanded accused on bail for over eight days.

R v Gateshead Justices; ex parte Usher and another [1981] Crim LR 491 HC QBD Conviction for failure to surrender to custody quashed where inter alia persons on bail had only been seven minutes late in arriving at court.

R v Gordon (Edgar) (1911-12) 7 Cr App R 182 CCA Bail generally refused pending appeal.

R v Gott (John William) (1921-22) 16 Cr App R 86 CCA Bail consistently refused pending appeal to CCA.

R v Governor of Ashford Remand Centre; ex parte Harris [1984] Crim LR 618; [1984] TLR 314 HC QBD Magistrate did not act functus officio where added bail condition after finished speaking but before defendant left dock.

R v Governor of Brixton Prison and another, ex parte Walsh [1984] 1 All ER 344; [1984] Crim LR 676; [1984] QB 392; (1983) 127 SJ 841; [1983] TLR 632; [1984] 2 WLR 217 HC QBD Neither prison governor nor Home Secretary under duty to present persons on bail before court on date stated in remands; habeas corpus inappropriate in such a situation.

R v Governor of Brixton Prison and another, ex parte Walsh [1985] AC 154; (1984) 128 SJ 482; [1984] TLR 414 HL Neither prison governor nor Home Secretary under duty to present persons on bail before court on date stated in remands.

R v Governor of Haslar Prison and another; ex parte Egbe [1991] TLR 276 CA Pending decision on habeas corpus application of person against whom deportation order made, that person not to be granted bail.

R v Governor of Pentonville Prison; ex parte Gilliland [1984] Crim LR 229 HC QBD Increase in bail not revocation of original bail order; appeal against excessive bail is by way of summons to judge in chambers.

R v Gregory (William) (1927-28) 20 Cr App R 185 CCA Bail not generally granted by CCA.

R v Harding (William); R v Turner (Harry Holt); R v King (Frank William) (1931-32) 23 Cr App R 143 CCA Bail granted pending appeal where Christmas Vacation came between bail application and appeal hearing.

R v Horner (Frederick William) (1910) 4 Cr App R 189 CCA No bail where merely device to postpone appeal.

R v Howeson (John Henry Charles Ernest); R v Hardy (Louis) (1934-36) 25 Cr App R 167 CCA Pre-appeal bail refused absent special circumstances.

R v Inner London Crown Court; ex parte Springall and another (1987) 85 Cr App R 214; [1987] Crim LR 252 HC QBD Behaviour of surety/variations in bail that surety might not have welcomed were mitigating factors insofar as estreatment of recognisances concerned.

R v Isleworth Crown Court and D; ex parte Commissioners of Customs and Excise [1990] Crim LR 859 HC QBD That committal papers served/further sureties offered adequate change to merit new bail hearing; refusal of right to reply by Crown on new application was valid.

R v K [1978] 1 All ER 180; (1978) 66 Cr App R 183; (1978) 142 JP 108; (1977) 121 SJ 728; [1978] 1 WLR 139 CrCt That in local authority care/assessment centre after magistrates' conviction does not mean 'in custody' so no bail.

R v Klein (Arthur Jack) (1931-32) 23 Cr App R 173 CCA Not customary for CCA to grant bail pending appeal (and here was not granted despite occurrence of Easter Vacation between bail application and appeal).

R v Liverpool City Justices; ex parte Santos [1997] TLR 38 HC QBD Depends on individual case whether failure to surrender to bail can be excused where was due to mistake on part of defendant's solicitor.

R v Liverpool City Magistrates' Court, ex parte Director of Public Prosecutions [1992] 3 All ER 249; (1992) 95 Cr App R 222; [1992] Crim LR 294; (1992) 156 JP 634; (1991) 141 NLJ 1740t; [1993] QB 233; [1991] TLR 566; [1992] 3 WLR 20 HC QBD Single justice may decide if bail conditions to be altered but may not adjourn proceedings.

R v MacDonald (Michael) (1928-29) 21 Cr App R 26 CCA Bail granted by CCA.

R v Maidstone Crown Court; ex parte Jodka [1997] TLR 311 HC QBD Bail ended upon surrender.

R v Mansfield Justices, ex parte Sharkey; R v Same, ex parte Hunt; R v Same, ex parte Barron; R v Same, ex parte Fretwell; R v Same, ex parte Robinson; R v Same, ex parte Swatten; R v Same, ex parte Grove; R v Same, ex parte Fellows; R v Same, ex parte Anderson [1985] 1 All ER 193; [1985] Crim LR 148; (1985) 149 JP 129; [1985] QB 613; (1984) 128 SJ 872; [1984] TLR 559; [1984] 3 WLR 1328 HC QBD Justices could rely on local knowledge when attaching conditions to bail (here preventing miners from joining pickets).

R v McLean; ex parte Aikens and others (1975) 139 JP 261 HC QBD Summary trials of applicants allowed to proceed despite very rigorous bail conditions imposed by magistrate as though severe was no evidence of bias on magistrate's part.

R v Meyer (1908-09) XCIX LTR 202; (1907-08) XXIV TLR 620 CCA Substantive application necessary for bail by person granted leave to appeal who was not present and had previously been convicted.

R v Moles [1981] Crim LR 170; (1981) 131 NLJ 143 HC QBD Refusal in second bail application to hear whether change of circumstances since refusal of first application did not justify granting writ of habeas corpus.

R v Neville and others [1972] Crim LR 589t CA Bail granted on application for leave to appeal.

R v Newbery (Frederick); R v Elman (Burnett Leon) (1931-32) 23 Cr App R 66 CCA Bail granted in view of pending Long Vacation/tortuous nature of case.

R v Newcastle upon Tyne City Justices, ex parte Skinner [1987] 1 All ER 349; [1987] Crim LR 113; (1987) 151 JP 92; (1987) 131 SJ 194; [1987] 1 WLR 312 HC QBD Recognisance imposed when case stated should be means-related.

R v Nottingham Justices, ex parte Davies [1980] 2 All ER 775; (1980) 71 Cr App R 178; (1980) 144 JP 233; (1980) 130 NLJ 509; [1981] QB 38; (1980) 124 SJ 444; [1980] 3 WLR 15 HC QBD Magistrates cannot change own decision that exception to bail law applies absent fresh evidence.

R v O/C Depot battalion, RASC, Colchester, ex parte Elliott [1949] 1 All ER 373 HC KBD Means by which person over whom court has jurisdiction was brought into jurisdiction irrelevant; High Court may grant bail where undue delay in military case.

R v P [1980] Crim LR 796; (1980) 144 JP 39 CrCt Young person committed to custody following conviction can be granted bail pending appeal from magistrates to CrCt.

R v Pegg [1955] Crim LR 308 CCA Bail inappropriate for prisoner with bad criminal history and no apparent explanation for latest offence of which charged.

R v Phillips (1947) 111 JP 333; (1947) WN (I) 129 CCA Possibility of repeat offence by person charged with housebreaking renders giving bail to same inadvisable.

R v Phillips [1922] All ER 275; (1922-23) 67 SJ 64; (1921-22) XXXVIII TLR 897 HC KBD Alleged fugitive offender not entitled to bail while in remand.

R v Phillips (1921-25) XXVII Cox CC 332; (1922) 86 JP 188; (1923) 128 LTR 113; (1922) WN (I) 274 HC KBD Bail possible in extradition case at magistrate's discretion.

R v Phillips (Michael Patrick) (1946-48) 32 Cr App R 47 CCA Bail not favoured for alleged housebreakers where is possibility of further housebreaking pending trial.

R v Porter [1908-10] All ER 78; (1911-13) XXII Cox CC 295; (1909) 3 Cr App R 237; (1910) 74 JP 159; [1910] 1 KB 369; (1910) 79 LJKB 241; (1910) 102 LTR 255; (1909-10) XXVI TLR 200; (1910) WN (I) 5 CCA Bail indemnification agreement a criminal conspiracy.

R v Ridley (Frank) (1911-13) XXII Cox CC 127; (1909) 2 Cr App R 113; (1909) 100 LTR 944; (1908-09) XXV TLR 508 CCA Notice to prosecution required where seek post-conviction bail.

R v Secretary of State for the Home Department and another, ex parte Turkoglu [1987] 2 All ER 823; [1988] QB 398; (1987) 131 SJ 1186 CA Respective jurisdictions of High Court/Court of Appeal to grant bail.

R v Selkirk (Joseph) (1924-25) 18 Cr App R 172 CCA Bail granted by CCA where sentence short and time before appeal to be heard long.

R v Shah (Imdad) (1980) 144 JP 460 CA Bail inappropriate in appeals against short sentences: hearing of action should be hastened.

R v Sheffield Justices, ex parte Turner (1991) 93 Cr App R 181; [1991] Crim LR 529; [1991] 2 QB 472; [1990] TLR 728 HC QBD Bail mandatory where 70-day limit on custody prior to committal exceeded but once committal started could re-commit to custody (so habeas corpus application failed).

R v Singh (Harbax) [1979] 1 All ER 524; (1979) 68 Cr App R 108; (1979) 143 JP 214; [1979] QB 319; [1979] 2 WLR 100 CA Absconding from bail punishable per se summarily or as criminal contempt.

R v Slough Justices; ex parte Duncan and Embling (1983) 147 JP 1; [1982] TLR 406 HC QBD On exercise of discretion to refuse bail: here properly refused without hearing application as were no new facts since remanded in custody to justify application.

R v Southampton Justices, ex parte Green [1975] 2 All ER 1073; (1975) 139 JP 667; [1976] QB 11; (1975) 119 SJ 541; [1975] 3 WLR 277 CA Estreatment of recognisance not criminal cause or matter; forfeiture of recognisance for non-appearance not automatic - all circumstances to be considered.

R v Starkie (Richard William) (1932-34) 24 Cr App R 1; (1932) 76 SJ 780 CCA Long Vacation not an exceptional circumstance justifying bail.

R v Stewart (Alexander Davidson) (1931-32) 23 Cr App R 68 CCA Bail granted pending Long Vacation.

R v Thompson (Arthur) (1916-17) 12 Cr App R 278 CCA Bail pending appeal against conviction in gross indecency with male case.

R v Tottenham Magistrates' Court, ex parte Riccardi (1978) 66 Cr App R 150 HC QBD Valid forfeiture of recognisance.

R v Tower Bridge Magistrates' Court; ex parte Gilbert (1988) 152 JP 307 HC QBD Bail properly refused where at adjourned hearing new information available about person granted unconditional bail at original hearing.

R v Uxbridge Justices, ex parte Heward-Mills [1983] 1 All ER 530; [1983] Crim LR 165; (1983) 147 JP 225; (1982) 126 SJ 854; [1983] 1 WLR 56 HC QBD Surety may give evidence of means in trying to persuade magistrates that should not forfeit entire recognisance.

R v Vernege [1982] 1 All ER 403; (1982) 74 Cr App R 232; (1982) 126 SJ 117; [1982] 1 WLR 293 CA Granting of bail in murder cases.

R v Watton (Joseph) (1979) 68 Cr App R 293; [1979] Crim LR 246 CA Bail may only be granted pending appeal to CA if appeal likely to succeed/would have served entire sentence by time appeal heard.

R v Waxman (Isaac) (1930-31) Cr App R 81 CCA Bail granted in light of pending Vacation.

R v Welham [1960] 1 All ER 260; (1960) 44 Cr App R 79; [1960] Crim LR 190; (1960) 124 JP 156; (1960) 110 LJ 156; [1960] 2 QB 445; (1960) 104 SJ 108 CCA Intent when uttering forged document is to induce someone to act contrary to their interest/their duty; successful action for bail pending appeal.

R v Wharton [1955] Crim LR 565t CCA Serious criminals not to be granted bail unless is real doubt as to their guilt of offence charged.

R v Wirral District Magistrates Court; ex parte Meikle [1990] Crim LR 801; [1990] TLR 416 HC QBD Inapplicability of abuse of process doctrine to bail application (absent bad faith).

R v Wise (Philip) (1922-23) 17 Cr App R 17 CCA On granting of bail by CCA.

R v Woods [1990] Crim LR 275 CA On dealing with person who does not surrender to bail.

R v York Crown Court; ex parte Coleman and How (1988) 86 Cr App R 151; [1987] Crim LR 761 HC QBD Full estreatment of recognisances inappropriate where accused had surrendered to bail on morning of trial but thereafter absconded.

R v Zaman (Mohammed) (1975) 61 Cr App R 227; [1975] Crim LR 710; (1975) 125 NLJ 645; (1975) 119 SJ 657 CA Jurisdiction of CCA/trial judge to grant bail pending deportation.

Re A Solicitor (1901-02) 46 SJ 531 HC ChD Unprofessional behaviour for solicitor to be party to agreement whereby surety is indemnified against possible loss arising from bailing of another.

Re Bone (1995) 159 JP 111 HC QBD On permissible period of remand in custody when CrCt hearing appeal against granting of bail by justices.

Re Harris (1984) 148 JP 584 HC QBD Magistrate's remanding of person in custody immediately after granting bail (at which point person made remark to police officer) permissible.

Re Kray; Re Kray; Re Smith [1965] 1 All ER 710; [1965] Ch 736; (1965) 49 Cr App R 164; [1965] Crim LR 224t; (1965) 115 LJ 212; (1965) 109 SJ 176; [1965] 2 WLR 626 LC Lord Chancellor cannot hear bail applications/appeals.

Re Lyttleton (1945) 172 LTR 173 HC HC KBD On granting bail to convict.

Re Marshall [1994] Crim LR 915; (1995) 159 JP 688 HC QBD CrCt recorder not justice of peace within meaning of Bail Act 1976, s 7(4).

Re Sherman and Apps (1981) 72 Cr App R 266; [1981] Crim LR 335 HC QBD Accused must be charged/told will be prosecuted as soon as possible once evidence available; arrested person must be granted bail/brought before court as soon as possible.

Re Whitehouse [1951] 1 All ER 353; (1951-52) 35 Cr App R 8; (1951) 115 JP 125; [1951] 1 KB 673; (1951) 95 SJ 138; [1951] 1 TLR 405; (1951) WN (I) 75 HC KBD High Court bail available to person appealing against conviction by summary court.

Re Wright (WH) (1905-06) 50 SJ 707 HC VacCt Ought to have been service of bail summons on prosecutrix.

R v Kray; R v Kray; R v Smith [1965] Crim LR 223; (1965) 109 SJ 150 HC QBD Divisional Court could grant bail; judge in chambers considered to have jurisdiction to grant bail even if CCC in continuous session.

Schiavo v Anderton [1986] 3 All ER 10; (1986) 83 Cr App R 228; [1986] Crim LR 542; (1986) 150 JP 264; [1987] QB 20; (1970) 130 SJ 542; [1986] 3 WLR 176 HC QBD Magistrates can deal with failure to surrender for bail without formal charge; failure to appear before magistrates court triable by magistrates.

Walsh v Governor of Brixton Prison and another [1984] 2 All ER 609; (1985) 80 Cr App R 186 HL Home Secretary/prison governor not under absolute duty to produce prisoners on bail in court on dates specified in remands.

BAIL (habeas corpus)

R v Governor of Brixton Prison, ex parte Singh (Kirpal) Singh (Jit) [1969] Crim LR 436; (1969) 113 SJ 406 HC QBD Home Office custody order took precedence over justices' bail order.

BAIL (indemnity)

Consolidated Exploration and Finance Company v Musgrave [1900] 1 Ch 37; [1900] LXIX (1) LJ 11; (1899-1900) LXXXI LTR 747; (1899-1900) XVI TLR 13 HC ChD Indemnity for bail is an illegal contract.

BAIL (surety)

Cockhill v Davies (1943) 107 JP 130; [1943] 112 LJ 441; (1943) 169 LTR 78; (1942-43) LIX TLR 259; (1943) WN (I) 109 HC KBD Could appeal to quarter sessions against magistrate's decision that recognisance be forfeited.

R v Crown Court at Maidstone, ex parte Lever; R v Crown Court at Maidstone, ex parte Connell [1995] 2 All ER 35; [1996] 1 Cr App R 524; (1994) 144 NLJ 1661; [1995] 1 WLR 928 CA Recognisance forfeited on non-attendance of accused despite non-culpability of surety although judge may remit some/all recognisance.

R v Crown Court at Reading, ex parte Bello [1992] 3 All ER 353; (1991) 92 Cr App R 303; (1991) 155 JP 637; [1990] TLR 775 CA Duty of surety is to provide accused at trial and sentence.

R v Crown Court at Warwick; ex parte Smalley (1987) 84 Cr App R 51; [1987] Crim LR 112; (1987) 131 SJ 257; [1984] TLR 163; [1987] 1 WLR 237 HC QBD Crown Court judge could estreat recognisance where bail originally set by justices but varied by High Court judge.

R v Harrow Justices, ex parte Morris [1972] 3 All ER 494; [1972] Crim LR 636t; (1972) 136 JP 868; (1972) 116 SJ 765; [1973] QB 672; [1972] 3 WLR 697 HC QBD Justices cannot require money/security be given by surety before bail granted.

R v Horseferry Road Stipendiary Magistrate; ex parte Pearson [1976] Crim LR 304t; (1976) 140 JP 382; (1976) 126 NLJ 522t; (1976) 120 SJ 352; [1976] 1 WLR 511 HC QBD On forfeiture of surety's recognisance.

R v Inner London Crown Court; ex parte Springall and another (1987) 85 Cr App R 214; [1987] Crim LR 252 HC QBD Behaviour of surety/variations in bail that surety might not have welcomed were mitigating factors insofar as estreatment of recognisances concerned.

R v Maidstone County Court; ex parte Lever [1994] TLR 559 CA Forfeiture of substantial portion of recognisance merited where bailed individual absconded before trial.

R v Salford Stipendiary Magistrate; ex parte Monaghan and another [1984] TLR 465 HC QBD On extent of duty owed by surety.

R v Wells Street Magistrates' Court, ex parte Albanese [1981] 3 All ER 769; (1982) 74 Cr App R 180; [1981] Crim LR 771; (1982) 146 JP 177; [1982] QB 333; (1981) 125 SJ 638; [1981] 3 WLR 694 HC QBD On duties of surety: surety need not be informed of variation in bail conditions but ignorance of variation may justify remission of recognisance.

R v York Crown Court; ex parte Coleman and How (1988) 86 Cr App R 151; [1987] Crim LR 761 HC QBD Full estreatment of recognisances inappropriate where accused had surrendered to bail on morning of trial but thereafter absconded.

Re Attfield and another [1924] 93 LJCL 1064 HC KBD On liability of sureties for bail in action brought by writ of capias under Customs Laws Consolidation Act 1876.

BANK (general)

Re Green's Application (1975) 125 NLJ 530t CA On appropriate means of dealing with wife who had acted as surety for husband who did not appear for his committal.

BANK (general)

Bank of Credit and Commerce International (Overseas) Ltd (in liquidation) and others v Price Waterhouse and others, Abu Dhabi and others (third parties); Bank of England intervening [1997] TLR 336 HC ChD Criminal offence to disclose bank information in breach of the Banking Act 1987, s 82(1).

BANKRUPTCY (general)

Director of Public Prosecutions v Ashley [1955] Crim LR 565 Assizes Annulment of bankruptcy did not mean could not be prosecuted for bankruptcy offences.

Fisher v Raven; Raven v Fisher [1963] 2 All ER 389; [1964] AC 210; (1963) 47 Cr App R 174; [1963] Crim LR 503; (1963) 127 JP 382; (1963) 113 LJ 332; (1963) 107 SJ 373; [1963] 2 WLR 1137 HL Accepting money in return for promise of services/goods not obtaining credit contrary to Debtors Act 1869 or Bankruptcy Act 1914.

M Bulteel and Colmore v The Trustee in Bankruptcy of MP Parker and FT Bulteel (1915-16) XXXII TLR 661 HC ChD Charge deemed not to be fraudulent preference of trustees of marriage settlement over other creditors of bankrupt bank; on burden of establishing fraudulent preference under Bankruptcy Act 1914.

R v Baxter (1974) 124 NLJ 648t CA Inappropriate to fine bankrupt guilty of bankruptcy offence simply because bankrupt's spouse had funds available.

R v Boughton (1911-13) XXII Cox CC 599; (1912) 76 JP 51 CCC Must be a trader to be convicted as trader pawning goods.

R v Cain [1984] 2 All ER 737; [1985] AC 46; (1984) 79 Cr App R 298; [1984] Crim LR 679; (1985) 149 JP 73; (1984) 134 NLJ 886; (1984) 128 SJ 530; [1984] TLR 471; [1984] 3 WLR 393 HL Criminal bankruptcy order a 'sentence' aginst which no appeal unless challenging jurisdiction of court making order; judge determines at sentencing stage if conspiracy to commit crimes from which loss resulted.

R v Cannon (Terence Francis); R v James (Roy George) (1986) 82 Cr App R 286 CA Criminal bankruptcy order properly made where was clear evidence of connection between subjects of order and handling of stolen goods.

R v Dandridge (Arthur Ernest) (1930-31) Cr App R 156 CCA Failure to keep books under Bankruptcy Act 1914, s 158, as amended not 'excusable' though might be 'honest'.

R v Doubleday (William Donald) (1965) 49 Cr App R 62 CCA Is offence for bankrupt to set up in business under new name without revealing name under which found bankrupt.

R v Downing (Geoge) (1980) 71 Cr App R 316 CA Criminal bankruptcy order need not later be perfected by trial judge in court where perfection necessary.

R v Fisher [1963] 1 All ER 744; (1963) 107 SJ 177 CCA Accepting money in return for promise of services/goods is/is not obtaining credit contrary to Debtors Act 1869/Bankruptcy Act 1914.

R v Hartley [1972] 1 All ER 599; (1972) 56 Cr App R 189; [1972] Crim LR 309; [1972] 2 QB 1; (1972) 116 SJ 56; [1972] 2 WLR 101 CA Successive obtainings of credit by bankrupt can be aggregated in deciding if committed offence under Bankruptcy Act 1914.

R v Humphries (1903-04) 48 SJ 509 CCR Valid conviction of bankrupt under Debtors Act 1869, s 12, for unlawful removal of 'his' property.

R v Klein [1958] Crim LR 185 CCC On elements of offence of bankrupt fraudulently obtaining property on credit.

R v Lusty [1964] 1 All ER 960; [1964] Crim LR 396; (1964) 128 JP 334; (1964) 108 SJ 465; [1964] 1 WLR 606 CCA Prosecution must prove fraud under Bankruptcy Act 1914, s 154(5).

R v Miller [1977] 3 All ER 986; (1977) 65 Cr App R 79; [1977] Crim LR 562; (1977) 121 SJ 423; [1977] 1 WLR 1129 CA Defaulting on hire-purchase agreement not obtaining goods by credit.

R v Phillips (Alfred Samuel) (1921) 85 JP 120 CCC Elements of offence of bankrupt making exaggerated/untrue statements as to loss of estate (Bankruptcy Act 1914, s 157(1)(c)).

R v Pitchforth (Thomas Clarence) (1908) 1 Cr App R 249 CCA On absence of 'intent to defraud' defence under Debtors Act 1869, s 12.

R v Raeburn (Jack) (1982) 74 Cr App R 21 CA On making of criminal bankruptcy order.

R v Richman (Jacob) (1910) 4 Cr App R 233 CCA May be 'transfer' under Debtors Act 1869, s 13(2) though is no transfer as against creditors.

R v Riley (William James) (1988) 87 Cr App R 125; (1988) 152 JP 399 CA Criminal bankruptcy order possible where total loss occasioned by person convicted of dishonesty offences exceeds £15,000.

R v Salter [1968] 3 WLR 39 CA No intent necessary to be guilty of failing contrary to Bankruptcy Act 1914, s 157(1) (c) to satisfactorily explain loss of estate.

R v Saville (1980) 144 JP 209; (1980) 124 SJ 202 CA Valid variation of criminal bankruptcy order.

R v Vaccari [1958] 1 All ER 468; (1958) 42 Cr App R 85; [1958] Crim LR 261t; (1958) 122 JP 209; (1958) 108 LJ 168 CCA On gambling by bankrupt.

Re a Debtor (1908-09) XXV TLR 140 CA Married woman could be made bankrupt in respect of company which she owned but husband managed; interest in trust of surplus of assigned property was separate property.

Re Borovsky and Weinbaum; ex parte Salaman [1902] 2 KB 312; [1902] 71 LJCL 992; (1902-03) LXXXVII LTR 184 HC KBD On bankruptcy of fugitive offender.

Re Pascoe; ex parte Northumberland County Council v The Trustee (1944) 108 JP 126 CA On ordering payment of costs from after-acquired property of bankrupt.

Re Ross (a debtor) (1978) 122 SJ 680 CA On admissibility of debtor's affidavit where same did not attend for cross-examination.

Re Simon (Ida) [1909] 1 KB 201 CA Woman owning trade managed by husband is carrying on trade separate from same under Married Women's Property Act 1882, s 1(5).

Re Solomons; ex parte Solomons [1904] 73 LJCL 963 HC KBD On allowing inspection by debtor of records kept by trustee in bankruptcy.

Re Solomons; ex parte Solomons [1904] 73 LJCL 1029 CA On allowing inspection by debtor of records kept by trustee in bankruptcy.

Re Tabrisky (1947) 91 SJ 421 CA On suspending discharge from bankruptcy.

Rose v Buckett [1901] 2 KB 449; [1901] 70 LJK/QB 736; (1901) LXXXIV LTR 670; (1900-01) XVII TLR 544; (1901-02) 50 WR 8 CA Right of action for trespass/conversion did not pass to trustee upon plaintiff becoming bankrupt.

BANKRUPTCY (obtaining credit)

Fisher v Raven; Raven v Fisher [1963] 2 All ER 389; [1964] AC 210; (1963) 47 Cr App R 174; [1963] Crim LR 503; (1963) 127 JP 382; (1963) 113 LJ 332; (1963) 107 SJ 373; [1963] 2 WLR 1137 HL Accepting money in return for promise of services/goods not obtaining credit contrary to Debtors Act 1869 or Bankruptcy Act 1914.

Osborn v Barton (1950) 94 SJ 15; [1950] 66 (1) TLR 115 HC KBD Not obtaining credit in contravention of Bankruptcy Act 1914, s 155(a) for bankrupt to accept cheque and immediately send goods on foot thereof.

R v Armitage (John) (1909) 3 Cr App R 80; (1910) 74 JP 48 CCA Was adequate evidence of obtaining credit by fraud.

R v Brownlow (1910) 74 JP 240; (1909-10) XXVI TLR 345 CCA Must be intent to defraud to be guilty of obtaining credit under false pretences contrary to Debtors Act 1869, s 13(1).

R v Dawson; R v Wenlock [1960] 1 All ER 558; (1960) 44 Cr App R 87; [1960] Crim LR 358; (1960) 110 LJ 236; (1960) 104 SJ 191; [1960] 1 WLR 163 CCA Conspiracy charge unnecessary in light of substantive charges; bankruptcy examination inadmissible at trial for fraudulent conversion; where alternative counts should be convicted on one of which most certainly guilty; non-delivery post-sale not an obtaining of credit by fraud.

R v Edward Fitzgerald, Duke of Leinster (1921-25) XXVII Cox CC 574; (1922-23) 17 Cr App R 176; (1923) 87 JP 191; [1924] 1 KB 311; [1924] 93 LJCL 144; (1924) 130 LTR 318; (1923-24) 68 SJ 211; (1923-24) XL TLR 33; (1923) WN (I) 286 CCA Undischarged bankrupt must disclose is same where seeks credit of £10 or more.

R v Fisher [1963] 1 All ER 744; (1963) 107 SJ 177 CCA Accepting money in return for promise of services/goods is/is not obtaining credit contrary to Debtors Act 1869/Bankruptcy Act 1914.

R v Garlick (Frederick William) (1957) 41 Cr App R 141 CCA Obtaining credit by fraud convictions quashed where actus reus missing.

R v Godwin (Roger Wyatt) (1980) 71 Cr App R 97; [1980] Crim LR 426; (1980) 130 NLJ 473; (1980) 124 SJ 344 CA Was obtaining credit by bankrupt despite ostensible obtaining of same for wife's registered company.

R v Goodall (George Albert) (1959) 43 Cr App R 24; [1959] Crim LR 47 CCA Quashing of bankruptcy offence conviction where not satisfactorily proved whether credit obtained for self.

R v Hayat (Masood) (1976) 63 Cr App R 181; [1976] Crim LR 508t; (1976) 126 NLJ 568t CA On what constitutes 'obtaining credit' by bankrupt: must show 'obtaining' and 'credit'.

R v Ingram [1956] 2 All ER 639; (1956) 40 Cr App R 115; [1956] Crim LR 565; (1956) 120 JP 397; (1956) 106 LJ 442; [1956] 2 QB 424; (1956) 100 SJ 491; [1956] 3 WLR 309 CCA Taking advance payments on foot of promised services is obtaining credit by fraud.

R v Inman [1966] 3 All ER 414; (1966) 50 Cr App R 247; [1966] Crim LR 445t; (1966) 130 JP 415; [1967] 1 QB 140; (1966) 110 SJ 424; [1966] 3 WLR 567 CA Money transfer under hire-purchase contract not obtaining of credit; not duplicitous to charge fraudulent trading for certain purposes/with intent together but here former merely specified elements of latter.

R v Laker (Herbert William) (1949-50) 34 Cr App R 36 CCA Bankrupt's taking cheque from person for one purpose and using for another not obtaining credit by fraud contrary to Bankruptcy Act 1914, s 156(a).

R v Mitchell [1955] 3 All ER 263; (1955) 39 Cr App R 49; [1955] Crim LR 246; (1955) 119 JP 563; (1955) 105 LJ 682; (1955) 99 SJ 764; [1955] 1 WLR 1125 CCA Non-creation of debt meant no credit obtained so no obtaining thereof by fraud.

R v Pryce (Charles Lewis) (1949-50) 34 Cr App R 21 CCA Bankrupt's obtaining loan of money was obtaining credit as specified in Bankruptcy Act 1914, s 155(a)/Debtors Act 1869, s 13.

R v Steel (Alfred) (1910) 5 Cr App R 289 CCA On fraud amounting to false pretence justifying conviction for obtaining credit by fraud.

R v Thornton [1963] 1 All ER 170; (1963) 47 Cr App R 1; [1963] Crim LR 197; (1963) 127 JP 113; (1963) 113 LJ 90; [1964] 2 QB 176; [1963] 3 WLR 444 CCA Not guilty of fraudulently inducing signature to security where do not impose any liability on another party but can be guilty of obtaining credit by fraud.

R v Zeitlin (Leon) (1931-32) 23 Cr App R 163 CCA Bankrupt not guilty of obtaining credit where tells creditor of status as bankrupt within reasonable time before obtaining said credit.

BIGAMY (general)

R v Audley [1904-07] All ER 1180; (1907) 71 JP 101; [1907] 1 KB 383; (1906) 41 LJ 838; [1907] 76 LJKB 270; (1906-07) 51 SJ 146; (1906-07) XXIII TLR 211 CCR On format of indictment for bigamy.

R v Bayley (Harry) (1908) 1 Cr App R 86 CCA Husband's alleged belief in invalidity of earlier marriage not defence to his entering into later bigamous union.

R v Birtles (James) (1910-11) 6 Cr App R 177; (1911) 75 JP 288 CCA On adequacy of evidence to sustain prosecution for bigamy.

R v Connatty (1919) 83 JP 292 CCC Not guilty of bigamy if when enter 'bigamous' union genuinely believe original marriage to be void.

R v Dolman [1949] 1 All ER 813; (1948-49) 33 Cr App R 128 Assizes Defence to bigamy that at time of bigamous marriage held reasonable belief earlier marriage void as bigamous.

R v Faulkes (1902-03) XIX TLR 250 Assizes Re-marriage after spouse's seven-year absence justified even if absent through wilful desertion.

R v Gould [1968] 1 All ER 849; (1968) 52 Cr App R 152; [1968] Crim LR 212; (1968) 132 JP 209; (1968) 118 NLJ 85t; [1968] 2 QB 65; (1968) 112 SJ 69; [1968] 2 WLR 643 CA Honest belief in fact that if true would make marriage non-bigamous a defence to bigamy.

R v Hammer (1921-25) XXVII Cox CC 458; (1922-23) 17 Cr App R 142; (1923) 87 JP 194; [1923] 2 KB 786; (1923) 58 LJ 366; [1923] 92 LJCL 1045; (1923) 129 LTR 479; (1923-24) 68 SJ 121; (1922-23) XXXIX TLR 670; (1923) WN (I) 221 CCA Whether foreign Jewish marriage valid a question of fact.

R v King [1963] 3 All ER 561; (1964) 48 Cr App R 17; [1963] Crim LR 841; (1963) 113 LJ 752; (1963) 107 SJ 832; [1964] 1 QB 285; [1963] 3 WLR 892 CCA Honest belief first marriage invalid a defence to bigamy (but no facts supporting belief here).

R v Lamb [1934] All ER 540; (1934-39) XXX Cox CC 91; (1932-34) 24 Cr App R 145; (1934) 150 LTR 519; (1934) 78 SJ 279; (1933-34) L TLR 310 CCA Giving false name (with partner's knowledge) in certificate after notice does not preclude marriage being valid (and later marriage being bigamous).

R v Morrison [1938] 3 All ER 787; (1938-40) 27 Cr App R 1 CCA Must find valid first marriage to sustain bigamy charge.

R v Robinson [1938] 1 All ER 301; (1936-38) 26 Cr App R 129; (1938) 85 LJ 124 CCA Can be convicted of bigamy though second marriage invalid (apart from being bigamous).

R v Russell (Earl) [1901] AC 446; (1901-07) XX Cox CC 51; [1901] 70 LJK/QB 998; (1901-02) LXXXV LTR 253; (1900-01) XVII TLR 685; (1901) WN (I) 156 HL Can be tried for bigamy though second marriage outside Empire.

R v Sagoo [1975] 2 All ER 926; (1975) 61 Cr App R 191; [1975] Crim LR 448t; (1975) 139 JP 604; (1975) 125 NLJ 554t; [1975] QB 885; (1975) 119 SJ 543; [1975] 3 WLR 267 CA Date for testing if bigamy is date of allegedly bigamous marriage.

R v Shaw (1943-44) LX TLR 344 CCA Failed appeal against conviction for bigamy.

R v Singh (Sarwan) [1962] 3 All ER 612; [1963] Crim LR 269 Quarter Sessions Cannot ground bigamy prosecution in (possibly) polygamous first marriage.

R v Taylor [1950] 2 All ER 170; (1949-50) 34 Cr App R 138; [1950] 2 KB 368; (1950) 100 LJ 303; (1950) 94 SJ 458; [1950] 66 (1) TLR 1182; (1950) WN (I) 296 CCA Seven year's absence/unaware that wife alive defence (under Offences against the Person Act 1861, s 57) exists in bigamy prosecution.

R v Thomson (Peter) (1906) 70 JP 6 CCC On burden of proof on defence in bigamy prosecution once prosecution establish subsistence of two marriages.

R v Treanor (or McEvoy) [1939] 1 All ER 330; (1939-40) XXXI Cox CC 235; (1938-40) 27 Cr App R 35; (1939) 160 LTR 286; (1939) 83 SJ 219; (1938-39) LV TLR 348; (1939) WN (I) 29 CCA Seven year proviso regarding 'second marriage[s]' applies only to second marriage.

R v Wheat; R v Stocks [1921] All ER 602; (1918-21) XXVI Cox CC 717; (1920-21) 15 Cr App R 134; (1921) 85 JP 203; [1921] 2 KB 119; [1921] LJCL 583; (1921) 124 LTR 830; (1920-21) 65 SJ 554; (1920-21) XXXVII TLR 417; (1921) WN (I) 70 CCA Not defence to bigamy that genuinely thought were divorced from first wife.

BIRTH (concealment)

R v English (Alistair James Henry) (1968) 52 Cr App R 119 CA On appropriate sentence for concealment of birth in light of Criminal Justice Act 1961, s 3.

R v Kersey (Maud) (1907-09) XXI Cox CC 690 Assizes Murder/concealment of birth conviction not possible/possible on evidence though no dead body.

R v Rosenberg (1906) 70 JP 264 CCC On elements of offence of concealment of birth.

BLACKMAIL (demanding with menaces)

Hardie and Lane, Ltd v Chilton and others [1928] All ER 36 CA No conspiracy unless agreement between two/more persons to do something unlawful/lawful in an unlawful way; trade association sending letter in which seeks to resolve dispute by recipient of letter paying money not uttering letter demanding money with menaces contrary to Larceny Act 1916, s 29 (1) (i).

R v Bernhard [1938] 2 All ER 140; (1939-40) XXXI Cox CC 61; (1936-38) 26 Cr App R 137; (1938) 102 JP 282; [1938] 2 KB 264; (1938) 85 LJ 243; [1938] 107 LJCL 449; (1938) 82 SJ 257; (1937-38) LIV TLR 615; (1938) WN (I) 142 CCA On term 'claim of right' in Larceny Act 1916, s 1(1).

R v Boyle; R v Merchant [1914-15] All ER 553; (1914-15) XXIV Cox CC 406; (1914) 10 Cr App R 180; (1914) 78 JP 390; [1914] 83 LJKB 1801; (1914-15) 111 LTR 638; (1913-14) 58 SJ 673; (1913-14) XXX TLR 521; (1914) WN (I) 236 CCA Threatening to lambast company in newspaper unless demands met was demand for money with menaces; similar fact evidence admissible to rebut accident/mistake defence - to prove guilty intent.

R v Clear [1968] 1 All ER 74; (1968) 52 Cr App R 58; [1968] Crim LR 100t; (1968) 112 SJ 67; (1968) 132 JP 103; (1967) 117 NLJ 1217t; [1968] 1 QB 670; [1968] 2 WLR 122 CA Menace if words/conduct induce other's unwilling accession to demand; intent needed is intent to steal.

R v Collister (Thomas James); R v Warhurst (John) (1955) 39 Cr App R 100 CCA On what constitutes demanding money with menaces; on duty of prosecution to tell defence of prosecutor's record.

R v Denyer (1926-30) XXVIII Cox CC 153; (1925-26) 19 Cr App R 93; [1926] 2 KB 258; (1926) 61 LJ 363; [1926] 95 LJCL 699; (1926) 134 LTR 637; (1925-26) XLII TLR 452 CCA Properly convicted of demanding money with menaces contrary to Larceny Act 1916, s 29(1) (i) even though sought to protect trade interest.

R v Dymond [1920] All ER 259; (1918-21) XXVI Cox CC 621; (1920-21) 15 Cr App R 1; (1920) 84 JP 103; [1920] 2 KB 260; [1920] 89 LJCL 876; (1920) 123 LTR 336; (1919-20) 64 SJ 571; (1919-20) XXXVI TLR 421; (1920) WN (I) 130 CCA Must actually have (not just believe have) reasonable/probable cause for demand to defeat charge of demanding money with menaces.

R v Garwood [1987] 1 All ER 1032; (1987) 85 Cr App R 85; [1987] Crim LR 476; (1987) 131 SJ 357; [1987] 1 WLR 319 CA Not generally necessary for judge to explain word 'menaces' although could be desirable.

R v Hacker [1957] 1 All ER 608; (1957) 41 Cr App R 85; (1957) 121 JP 223; (1957) 101 SJ 210; [1957] 1 WLR 455 CCA Blackmail to be tried at assizes.

R v Harry [1974] Crim LR 32 CrCt On what is meant by demanding with 'menaces' in the Theft Act 1968, s 21(1).

R v Lambert [1972] Crim LR 422 CA On meaning of 'unwarranted' demand of money with menaces.

R v Lawrence and Pomroy [1972] Crim LR 645 CA On elements of demanding money with menaces.

R v Moran [1952] 1 All ER 803; (1952) 116 JP 216; (1952) 102 LJ 191 CCA On attempt to demand money with menaces.

R v Perfect [1914-17] All ER 407; (1915-17) XXV Cox CC 780; (1917-18) 117 LTR 416 CCA Wife's writing to third party claiming was father of her child and seeking money was uttering letter demanding money with menaces.

R v Studer [1914-15] All ER 607; (1915-17) XXV Cox CC 312; (1914-15) 11 Cr App R 307; [1916] 85 LJKB 1017; (1916) 114 LTR 424 CCA 'Demand' for money may take form of request.

Thorne v Motor Trade Association (1936-38) 26 Cr App R 51; (1937) 83 LJ 426 HL Not demanding money with menaces to write letter on behalf of trade association requiring payment if are not to be put on black list.

BLACKMAIL (general)

R v Bevans [1988] Crim LR 236; (1988) 132 SJ 90 CA Demanding injection of pain reliever at gun-point was blackmail.

R v Bevans (Ronald George Henry) (1988) 87 Cr App R 64 CA Demanding injection of morphine at gunpoint was demand made with view to gain for self within meaning of Theft Act 1968.

R v Harvey and others [1981] Crim LR 104 CA Threats to kill/injure/rape individual could not be used to buttress demand for debt to be paid.

R v Parkes [1973] Crim LR 358 CA On what is meant by demand 'with a view to gain' in the Theft Act 1968, s 21(1).

R v Stuart; R v Leonard; R v Maples; R v Tannen; R v Taylor (1927-28) 20 Cr App R 74; (1926-27) XLIII TLR 715 CCA On elements of offence of blackmail under Larceny Act 1916, s 29(2) (b).

R v Treacy [1970] 3 All ER 205; [1970] Crim LR 584t; (1970) 114 SJ 604; [1970] 3 WLR 592 CA Can be charged with blackmail though entirety of offence not in England.

R v Wyatt (John Thomas) (1921-22) 16 Cr App R 57; (1922) 86 JP 20; [1922] 91 LJCL 402; (1921-22) 66 SJ 143; (1921-22) XXXVIII TLR 118; (1921) WN (I) 355 CCA Meaning of 'threatens'/'to abstain' in Larceny Act 1916, s 31.

Treacy v Director of Public Prosecutions [1971] 1 All ER 110; [1971] AC 537; (1971) 55 Cr App R 113; [1972] Crim LR 590; (1971) 135 JP 112; (1971) 115 SJ 12; [1971] 2 WLR 112 HL Can be tried for blackmail only partly committed in England.

BLACKMAIL (uttering threatening letter)

R v Binney (1935) 79 SJ 419 CCA Conviction for uttering threatening letters quashed where were further threatening letters sent to victim after appellant imprisoned (so could not have sent them).

BLASPHEMY (blasphemous libel)

R v Boulter (1908) 72 JP 188 CCC On what constitutes blasphemous libel.

R v Lemon; R v Gay News Ltd [1979] 1 All ER 898; [1979] Crim LR 311; (1979) 143 JP 315; (1979) 129 (1) NLJ 218 HL Intention to publish blasphemy/not intention to blaspheme is mens rea for blasphemous libel.

R v Lemon; R v Gay News Ltd [1978] 3 All ER 175; (1978) 67 Cr App R 70; (1978) 142 JP 558; (1978) 128 NLJ 488t; [1979] QB 10; (1978) 122 SJ 295; [1978] 3 WLR 404 CA Blasphemy if insult/offend/vilify Christ/ianity even if do not intend same.

Whitehouse v Gay News Ltd; Whitehouse v Lemon [1979] AC 617; (1979) 68 Cr App R 381; (1979) 123 SJ 163; [1979] 2 WLR 281 HL Intention to publish blasphemy/not intention to blaspheme is mens rea for blasphemous libel.

BLASPHEMY (general)

R v Chief Metropolitan Stipendiary Magistrate, ex parte Choudhury [1991] 1 All ER 306; (1990) 91 Cr App R 393; [1990] Crim LR 711; (1990) 140 NLJ 702; [1991] 1 QB 429; [1990] TLR 294; [1990] 3 WLR 986 HC QBD Common law of blasphemy applies only to Christian religion; sedition involves attack against Sovereign/government not on different classes of citizen.

R v Gott (John William) (1921-22) 16 Cr App R 87 CCA On what constitutes blasphemy; may commit blasphemy both in writing and in speaking.

BREACH OF PEACE (general)

Davies v Griffiths (1934-39) XXX Cox CC 595; (1937) 101 JP 247; (1937) 157 LTR 23; (1936-37) LIII TLR 680 HC KBD Cannot be fined for conduct likely to cause breach of peace, can only be bound over/ordered to find sureties.

G v Superintendent of Police, Stroud (1988) 86 Cr App R 92; [1987] Crim LR 269 HC QBD Short time-span in which constable had to make decision to arrest relevant in deciding reasonableness of arrest that breach of peace likely: here reasonable so assault was assault on constable in execution of duty.

Joyce v Hertfordshire Constabulary (1985) 80 Cr App R 298 HC QBD If breach of peace occurring police officer may use reasonable force to stop it.

Lamb v Director of Public Prosecutions (1990) 154 JP 381 HC QBD Trespassing police officer was nonetheless acting in course of duty when stayed in place to prevent expected breach of the peace.

Lavin v Albert [1981] 3 All ER 878; [1982] AC 546 (also HC QBD); (1982) 74 Cr App R 150; (1982) 146 JP 78; (1981) 125 SJ 860; [1981] 3 WLR 955 HL Can restrain breach of peace (even by detention) though not police officer; mistaken belief that person detaining one as part of restraint of breach of peace not police officer not defence to assault.

Lewis and anr v Chief Constable of Greater Manchester (1991) 141 NLJ 1486i CA May arrest for breach of peace on anticipatory basis.

Maile v McDowell [1980] Crim LR 586 CA On what constitutes a breach of the peace (here in football crowd context).

McConnell v Chief Constable of the Greater Manchester Police [1990] 1 All ER 423; (1990) 91 Cr App R 88; (1990) 154 JP 325; (1990) 134 SJ 457; [1990] 1 WLR 364 CA Police may exercise power of arrest in private premises if likely breach of peace by persons inside.

Nicol and Selvanayagam v Director of Public Prosecutions [1996] Crim LR 318; [1995] TLR 607 HC QBD Criminal/non-criminal behaviour likely to provoke violence on part of others a breach of the peace.

North v Pullen [1962] Crim LR 97t; (1962) 106 SJ 77 HC QBD Brief delay in effecting arrest did not mean police constable not acting in execution of his duty when was head-butted by offender.

Percy v Director of Public Prosecutions [1995] 3 All ER 124; [1995] Crim LR 714; (1995) 159 JP 337; (1995) 139 SJ LB 34; [1994] TLR 644; [1995] 1 WLR 1382 HC QBD Civil trespass not a breach of peace unless violence a natural consequence of trespass; criminal standard of proof necessary to establish breach of peace.

Piddington v Bates; Robson and another v Ribton-Turner [1961] Crim LR 262; [1961] 1 WLR 162 HC QBD Valid for police to act to prevent anticipated breach of peace where anticipation of same is reasonable.

R v Gedge [1978] Crim LR 167; (1977) 127 NLJ 1174t CA Could be convicted of using words likely to occasion breach of the peace where employed words likely to aggravate existing breach of the peace.

R v Howell (Errol) (1981) 73 Cr App R 31; [1981] Crim LR 697; (1982) 146 JP 13; (1981) 131 NLJ 605; [1982] QB 416; (1981) 125 SJ 462; [1981] 3 WLR 501 CA On what constitutes a breach of the peace; on when can arrest for breach of the peace.

R v Little and Dunning, ex parte Wise (1910) 74 JP 7; (1909-10) 101 LTR 859; (1909-10) XXVI TLR 8 HC KBD Magistrate justified in circumstances in requiring person to enter recognisance to keep the peace though police no longer objected to person's leading proposed procession through streets.

R v Podger [1979] Crim LR 524 CrCt On extent of power of arrest in anticipation of breach of the peace.

Read v Jones and others (1983) 77 Cr App R 246; [1983] Crim LR 809; (1983) 147 JP 477; [1983] TLR 365 HC QBD Could be breach of peace by group though no member of public witnesses same.

Robson and another v Hallett [1967] 2 All ER 407; (1967) 51 Cr App R 307; (1967) 131 JP 333; [1967] 2 QB 939; (1967) 111 SJ 254; [1967] 3 WLR 28 HC QBD Police have implied licence to enter garden in course of duty; once licence revoked by owner have reasonable time to go before become trespasser; if breach of peace in garden police can enter to stop it.

Wise v Dunning [1900-03] All ER 727; (1901-07) XX Cox CC 121; [1902] 71 LJCL 165; (1901-02) 46 SJ 152; (1901-02) XVIII TLR 85; (1901-02) 50 WR 317 HC KBD Justices can bind over provocative public speaker to keep the peace/be of good behaviour.

BREACH OF PEACE (wilful obstruction)

R v Chief Constable of Devon and Cornwall; ex parte Central Electricity Generating Board [1981] 3 All ER 826; (1982) 146 JP 91; (1981) 125 SJ 745 CA Demonstrators guilty of criminal obstruction likely to give rise to breach of the peace.

BREACH OF SANCTIONS (general)

Attorney-General's Reference (No 2 of 1977) [1978] 2 All ER 646; [1978] Crim LR 495; (1978) 142 JP 403; (1978) 128 NLJ 112t; (1978) 122 SJ 78; [1978] 1 WLR 290 CA Rhodesian sanctions breached where individual sought individuals to take up employment/residence in Rhodesia.

R v Searle and KCS Products; R v Borjanovic [1996] Crim LR 58 CA Valid conviction for acting in breach of Order in Council adopted pursuant to United Nations resolution.

BROADCAST (general)

Director of Public Prosecutions v Waite [1997] Crim LR 123; (1996) TLR 17/5/96 HC QBD On when using radio scanner constitutes offence of unauthorised monitoring of broadcast contrary to the Wireless Telegraphy Act 1949, s 5(b)(i).

Paul v Ministry of Posts and Telecommunications [1973] Crim LR 322; (1973) 123 NLJ 250t; [1973] RTR 245 HC QBD Person using wireless to listen in on fire brigade emergency calls was committing offence under Wireless Telegraphy Act 1949, s 5.

Postmaster-General v Seager [1955] Crim LR 716 Magistrates Person with wireless that was not plugged in (and which claimed was never used) acquitted of unlicensed use of wireless.

R v Murray and others [1990] Crim LR 803; [1990] TLR 234; [1990] 1 WLR 1360 CA Marine etc Broadcasting (Offences) Act 1967 applies to pirate broadcasters who are not British subjects.

Rudd v Department of Trade and Industry [1986] Crim LR 455 CA Records/cassettes not (but speakers were) susceptible to forfeiture as wireless apparatus under the Wireless Telegraphy Act 1949.

Rudd v Department of Trade and Industry (1970) 130 SJ 504 HC QBD Records/cassettes not (but speakers were) susceptible to forfeiture as wireless apparatus under the Wireless Telegraphy Act 1949.

Rudd v Secretary of State for Trade and Industry (1987) 85 Cr App R 358; (1987) 131 SJ 805; [1987] 1 WLR 786 HL Only wireless telegraphy apparatus liable to forfeiture under Wireless Telegraphy Act 1949, s 14(3) - records/cassettes in use not 'apparatus'; on what constitutes 'use' of apparatus under Wireless Telegraphy Act 1949, s 14(3) as substituted.

Whiley v Director of Public Prosecutions [1995] Crim LR 39 HC QBD On what constitutes 'using' wireless (unlawfully) for purposes of the Wireless Telegraphy Act 1949, s 5(b)(i).

BROADCAST (incitement to use unlicensed radio)

Invicta Plastics Ltd and another v Clare [1976] Crim LR 131; [1976] RTR 251; (1976) 120 SJ 62 HC QBD Company (but not chairman) advertising for sale speed trap detectors properly convicted of incitement to use unlicensed apparatus for wireless telegraphy.

BROADCAST (unlicensed)

King v Bull (1934-39) XXX Cox CC 567; (1937) 81 SJ 219; (1937) WN (I) 76 HC KBD Conviction for unlicensed use of apparatus for wireless telegraphy.

R v Blake [1997] 1 All ER 963; [1997] 1 Cr App R 209; [1997] Crim LR 207; (1996) TLR 13/8/96; [1997] 1 WLR 1167 CA Unlicensed broadcasting an absolute offence.

CAUSING BODILY HARM WHEN IN CHARGE OF VEHICLE (general)

R v Cooke (Philip) [1971] Crim LR 44 Sessions On elements of offence of causing bodily harm by misconduct when in charge of a vehicle.

CHILD (abandonment)

R v Boulden [1957] Crim LR 182 Sessions Successful prosecution for abandonment/neglect of children: on what constitutes abandonment/neglect.

R v Boulden (Edward Ernest) (1957) 41 Cr App R 105; [1957] Crim LR 322 CCA On what constitutes 'abandonment' of child under Children and Young Persons Act 1933, s 1(1).

CHILD (assault)

R v Hatton [1925] All ER 396; (1926-30) XXVIII Cox CC 43; (1925) 89 JP 164; [1925] 2 KB 322; (1925) 60 LJ 705; [1925] 94 LJCL 863; (1925) 133 LTR 735; (1924-25) XLI TLR 637; (1925) WN (I) 199 CCA Interpretation of phrase 'wilfully assaults' in Children Act 1908, s 12(1).

CHILD (corporal punishment)

R v Ferguson (Robert) (1969) 53 Cr App R 637 CA In chastising their children immigrant parents must conform with British standards.

CHILD (cruelty)

Butler v Gregory (1901-02) XVIII TLR 370 HC KBD Father of illegitimate child who did not have care/custody of child nor had bastardy proceedings brought against him not father for purposes of Prevention of Cruelty to Children Act 1894, s 23.

Cornall v Cornall (1910) 74 JP 379 HC PDAD On what constitutes persistent cruelty for purposes of Summary Jurisdiction (Married Women) Act 1895, s 4.

Gollins v Gollins [1962] 2 All ER 366; (1962) 106 SJ 313 HC PDAD Absent desire to injure longterm failure to adequately maintain wife not cruelty.

R v Bowditch [1991] Crim LR 831 CA On burden of proof as regards proving cruelty to child under Children and Young Persons Act 1933.

R v Byers (Jessie) (1910) 4 Cr App R 5 CCA Manslaughter of child by means of cruel treatment - even though post-cruelty betterment in child's condition.

R v C and another [1990] TLR 344 CA Failed prosecution for cruelty to child where was inadequate evidence of guiltiness.

R v Chalker (Kate) (1910) 4 Cr App R 2 CCA Manslaughter of child by means of consistently cruel treatment.

R v Gibbins (David John) [1977] Crim LR 741 CrCt On elements of offence whereby 'expose[d]' child to unnecessary suffering/injury to health contrary to Children and Young Persons Act 1933, s 1(1).

R v Hale (1901-07) XX Cox CC 739; (1905) 69 JP 83; [1905] 1 KB 126; (1904-05) XCI LTR 839; (1904-05) 49 SJ 68; (1904-05) XXI TLR 70; (1904-05) 53 WR 400 CCR Child need not be present at trial concerning cruelty thereto unless evidence of child needed.

R v Perch (Edmund) (1908-09) XXV TLR 401 CCA Finding that were guilty of wilful neglect of children not affected by jury's rider that accused acted through ignorance.

R v Sheppard (James Martin) (1980) 70 Cr App R 210 CA Must be intentional neglect of child where charged with cruelty to child by reason of wilful neglect.

R v Young (Tara Moira Lisa) (1993) 97 Cr App R 280; (1993) 137 SJ LB 32; [1992] TLR 641 CA Where jury convinced overall that was cruelty (even though disagree on specific incidents) can convict of cruelty to children.

CHILD (general)

R v Birmingham Juvenile Court and others, ex parte S and another; R v Birmingham Juvenile Court and others, ex parte P and another [1984] 1 All ER 393; [1984] FLR 343; [1984] 1 WLR 618 HC QBD In renewing care order - unlike bail order - court looks to all the circumstances on each occasion; 28-day care order expires at start of twenty-eighth day.

R v West Malling Juvenile Court; ex parte K (1986) 150 JP 367; (1970) 130 SJ 650 HC QBD Case ought to have been adjourned where parent in care action given social worker/guardian ad litem reports containing unexpected material on day of hearing.

CHILD (neglect)

R v Boulden [1957] Crim LR 182 Sessions Successful prosecution for abandonment/neglect of children: on what constitutes abandonment/neglect.

R v Williams (John Owen) (1910) 4 Cr App R 89; (1909-10) XXVI TLR 290 CCA On what constitutes exposure/abandonment of child (Children Act 1908, s 12(1)).

CHILD (running away/leaving)

Pallin v Buckland (1911-13) XXII Cox CC 545; (1911) 75 JP 362 HC KBD Accused found as matter of fact not to have run away and left children.

CHILD (tobacco sale)

Hereford and Worcester County Council v T and S Stores plc [1994] TLR 549 HC QBD Valid acquittal of offence of selling cigarettes to under-age purchaser.

CHILD (wilful neglect)

R v Andrews (Paul) (1986) 82 Cr App R 148 CA Wilful neglect of child properly inferred from circumstantial evidence.

R v Connor (1907-09) XXI Cox CC 628; (1908) 72 JP 212; [1908] 2 KB 26; (1908) 43 LJ 283; [1908] 77 LJCL 527; (1908) XCVIII LTR 932; (1907-08) 52 SJ 444; (1907-08) XXIV TLR 483 CCR Father in desertion guilty of wilful neglect (failed to provide food/money).

R v S and M [1995] Crim LR 486 CA Could be found guilty of wilful neglect of child where did not seek medical attention for child because were reckless as to whether it was necessary.

CHILD-STEALING (conspiracy to steal child)

R v B [1984] Crim LR 352 CA Father who was immune from prosecution for child-stealing in respect of own child could nonetheless be charged with conspiracy to do same.

CHILD-STEALING (general)

R v Austin and others [1981] 1 All ER 374; (1981) 72 Cr App R 104; [1980] Crim LR 716; (1981) 145 JP 145; (1981) 131 NLJ 68 CA Person with right to possession of child exempt from child-stealing but not paid accessories.

R v Jones (William) (1911-13) XXII Cox CC 212; (1911) 75 JP 272 CCC Must prove accused intended to permanently withdraw child from parent to sustain conviction for stealing away child under fourteen.

R v Mears (William Colin John) [1975] Crim LR 155 CrCt Mere lifting of child against her will was sufficient to support conviction for child stealing.

R v Pryce [1972] Crim LR 307 CA On unlawful detention contrary to the Offences against the Person Act 1861, s 56.

R v Smith (1965) 115 LJ 628 CA Interpretation of Offences against the Person Act 1861, s 56 (detaining child by fraud with intention of permanently depriving father of child).

COMMON NUISANCE (general)

Toronto Railway Company v R (Attorney-General for England and Attorney-General for Canada, Interveners) [1917] AC 630; [1917] 86 LJPC 195; (1917-18) 117 LTR 579; (1917-18) XXXIV TLR 1; (1917) WN (I) 277 PC Interpretation of provisions of Ontario Criminal Code concerning common nuisance.

COMMUNICATING FALSE INFORMATION (general)

R v Webb [1995] TLR 350 CA On ingredients of offence of communicating false information (by bomb hoaxer): need merely state existence not location of supposed bomb.

COMPUTER (data protection)

Data Protection Registrar v Amnesty International [1995] Crim LR 633; [1994] TLR 597 HC QBD On what constitutes 'recklessness' for purposes of data protection offences of recklessly holding/disclosing data.

COMPUTER (failure to register as user)

Data Protection Registrar v Griffin [1993] TLR 115 HC QBD Accountant ought to have registered as data user under the Data Protection Act 1984 where used data provided by clients to prepare accounts for Inland Revenue on computer.

COMPUTER (general)

Attorney General's Reference (No 1 of 1991) [1992] 3 All ER 897; (1993) 157 JP 258; [1993] QB 94; (1992) 136 SJ LB 197; [1992] TLR 380; [1992] 3 WLR 432 CA Unauthorised access to data includes direct access from any computer.

Cox v Riley (1986) 83 Cr App R 54; [1986] Crim LR 460 HC QBD Was criminal damage to erase program from circuit card of computerised saw.

Director of Public Prosecutions v Bignall (1997) 161 JP 541; [1997] TLR 296 HC QBD Not offence under Computer Misuse Act 1990, s 1, for generally authorised person to access a programme for unauthorised reason.

R v Brown (1994) 99 Cr App R 69; [1994] QB 547; (1993) 137 SJ LB 151; [1993] TLR 321; [1994] 2 WLR 673 CA For there to be unlawful 'use' of data it must be employed for a purpose, not just accessed or retrieved.

R v Brown [1996] 1 All ER 545; [1996] 1 AC 543; [1996] 2 Cr App R 72; [1996] Crim LR 408; (1996) 146 NLJ 209; (1996) 140 SJ LB 66; (1996) TLR 9/2/96; [1996] 2 WLR 202 HL For there to be unlawful 'use' of data it must be employed for a purpose, not just accessed or retrieved.

R v Gold [1988] 2 All ER 186; (1988) 86 Cr App R 52; (1988) 152 JP 445; [1988] 2 WLR 984 HL Computer hacking not making of false instrument.

R v Gold; R v Schifreen [1987] 3 All ER 618; [1988] AC 1063; (1988) 87 Cr App R 257; [1988] Crim LR 437; (1988) 138 NLJ 117; (1988) 132 SJ 624 HL Hacking does not involve making/use of false device under Forgery and Counterfeiting Act 1981.

R v Gold; R v Schifreen [1987] Crim LR 762; [1987] QB 1116; (1987) 131 SJ 1247; [1987] 3 WLR 803 CA Hacking does not involve forgery or making/use of false device under Forgery and Counterfeiting Act 1981.

CONDONATION (general)

R v Bisset (1979) 123 SJ 718; [1980] 1 WLR 335 CMAC On what constitutes condonation of offence (no condonation here).

CONSPIRACY (auction)

R v Barnett and others [1951] 1 All ER 917; (1951-52) 35 Cr App R 37; (1951) 115 JP 305; [1951] 2 KB 425; (1951) 95 SJ 337; [1951] 1 TLR 899; (1951) WN (I) 214 CCA Conspiracy to effect offence under Auctions (Bidding Agreements) Act 1927 triable summarily.

CONSPIRACY (conspiracy to abduct)

R v Sherry; R v El Yamani [1993] Crim LR 536 CA Non-parent could be guilty of conspiracy with parent to abduct child of latter.

CONSPIRACY (conspiracy to breach toiletries regulations)

R v Weitzman and others (1948) 98 LJ 175 CCA Successful appeal against conviction for conspiracy to contravene toiletries regulations.

R v West and others (1948) 98 LJ 191 CCA Successful appeals against conviction for conspiracy to contravene toiletries regulations.

CONSPIRACY (conspiracy to cause explosion)

R v Coughlan (Martin); R v Young (Gerard Peter) (1976) 63 Cr App R 33; [1976] Crim LR 631 CA Within conspiracy to cause explosion can be sub-conspiracies to cause other explosions: can be charged separately for each; that acquitted of one does not mean cannot be convicted of other - autrefois convict plea unavailable in respect of various conspiracies charged.

CONSPIRACY (conspiracy to cheat/defraud)

Adams v R [1995] 2 Cr App R 295; [1995] Crim LR 561; (1995) 139 SJ LB 13; [1994] TLR 555; [1995] 1 WLR 52 PC Was conspiracy to defraud where director sought to conceal information so as to preclude recovery by company of undisclosed profits made by directors.

Attorney General's Reference (No 1 of 1982) [1983] 2 All ER 721; [1983] Crim LR 534; (1984) 148 JP 115; [1983] QB 751; (1983) 127 SJ 377; [1983] TLR 268; [1983] 3 WLR 72 CA If a tangential effect of conspiracy to perform act abroad is it causes economic/other loss in England then is not conspiracy to defraud.

Beechey v R (1915-17) XXV Cox CC 217; [1916] 85 LJPC 32; (1916) 114 LTR 1 PC Conspirator may be convicted as such though co-conspirator absent.

R v Allsop (Anthony Adward) (1977) 64 Cr App R 29; [1976] Crim LR 738t; (1976) 126 NLJ 937t; (1976) 120 SJ 635 CA Is fraud where make false statements likely to cause another economic loss (and do) though no loss intended.

R v Ayres (David Edward) (1984) 78 Cr App R 232 (also HL); [1984] Crim LR 165; (1984) 148 JP 458; (1984) 128 SJ 63; [1983] TLR 734 CA Appellant properly charged with conspiracy to defraud and not statutory conspiracy.

R v Cooke (Anthony); R v Sutcliffe (Kathleen) [1985] Crim LR 215 CA On appropriate charge where possessed article for cheating.

R v Fountain [1965] 2 All ER 671; (1965) 49 Cr App R 315; [1965] Crim LR 544; (1965) 129 JP 391; (1965) 115 LJ 498; [1966] 1 WLR 212 Assizes On common law cheating.

R v Grant [1986] Crim LR 235 CA Application of proviso so as to allow conviction for conspiracy to defraud.

R v Grosvenor (1914-15) XXIV Cox CC 468; (1914) 10 Cr App R 235; (1914-15) 111 LTR 1116 CCA Is conspiracy to defraud though acquired no money/made no false pretence; both parties liable to conviction for obtaining money by false pretences where obtain money following jointly executed false pretence; is false pretences by conduct where implicitly agree to making of false pretence.

R v Hollinshead (Peter Gordon); R v Dettlaff (Stefen); R v Griffiths (Kenneth David) [1985] 1 All ER 850; [1985] AC 975 (also HL); (1985) 80 Cr App R 285; [1985] Crim LR 301; (1985) 129 SJ 219; [1985] 2 WLR 761 CA Cannot be guilty of conspiracy to aid and abet offences so providing devices for another to deal in not criminal act.

R v Hollinshead and others [1985] 2 All ER 769; [1985] AC 975 (also CA); (1985) 81 Cr App R 365; [1985] Crim LR 653; (1985) 135 NLJ 631; (1985) 129 SJ 447; [1985] 3 WLR 159 HL Manufacturing/selling devices intended to cause loss to another is conspiracy to defraud.

R v James (Alan Michael); R v Ashford (John Phillip) (1986) 82 Cr App R 226; [1986] Crim LR 118 CA Where charged with common law and statutory conspiracy and trial judge directed acquittal on former and conviction for latter quashed on appeal was no alternative ground for conviction.

CONSPIRACY (conspiracy to cheat/defraud)

R v Landy and others [1981] 1 All ER 1172; (1981) 72 Cr App R 237; [1981] Crim LR 326; (1981) 125 SJ 80; [1981] 1 WLR 355 CA Actual dishonesty in accused's mind needed for conspiracy to defraud; guidelines on summings-up.

R v Levitz; R v Mbele; R v Vowell [1989] Crim LR 714; (1989) 133 SJ 818 CA On appropriate charge of conspiracy to defraud where persons charged improperly sought to use devices to render telephone calls to them cost-free.

R v Lloyd and others [1985] 2 All ER 661; (1985) 81 Cr App R 182; (1985) 149 JP 634; (1985) 135 NLJ 605; [1985] QB 829; [1985] 3 WLR 30 CA No intention of permanently depriving where borrow/lend unless return in worthless state; statutory not common law conspiracy where full offence would be substantive.

R v Lockhart (Arthur Norman) (1909) 2 Cr App R 308 CCA Small act treated as evidence of conspiracy to defraud.

R v McPherson and Watts [1985] Crim LR 508 CA Conspiracy conviction quashed where not left to jury to decide whether substantive offence if effected would have been indictable in United Kingdom.

R v Mendez [1990] Crim LR 397 CA On relevance of accused's good character to credibility of his testimony.

R v Moses and Ansbro [1991] Crim LR 617 CA Aiding illegal immigrants to receive work permits which would probably not otherwise have received was criminal conspiracy to defraud (albeit that none of the acts making up the conspiracy were themselves unlawful).

R v Moss; R v Ricardo; R v Ricardo; R v Van West [1965] Crim LR 368; (1965) 109 SJ 269 CCA Bankruptcy not of itself evidence of bad character.

R v Parker and Bulteel (1915-17) XXV Cox CC 145; (1916) 80 JP 271 CCC Banker by remaining open/carrying on business could be impliedly representing that is solvent.

R v Scott [1974] 2 All ER 204; [1974] Crim LR 243t; (1974) 138 JP 420; [1974] QB 733; (1974) 118 SJ 147; [1974] 2 WLR 379 CA Need not be agreement to defraud by deceit to sustain conviction for conspiracy to defraud.

R v Sinclair and others [1968] 3 All ER 241; (1968) 52 Cr App R 618; (1968) 132 JP 527; (1968) 118 NLJ 956; [1968] 1 WLR 1246 CA On what constitutes 'fraud' in conspiracy to cheat and defraud.

R v Smithson; R v Queenswood (Holdings) Ltd; R v Sinclair [1968] Crim LR 610; (1968) 112 SJ 703 CA On dishonesty as an element of fraud (accused charged with conspiracy to cheat/defraud).

R v Spicer [1970] Crim LR 695; (1970) 114 SJ 824 CA Conspiracy to defraud not an arrestable offence.

R v Tonner (Gordon Campbell); R v Rees (Wilfrid Haydn); R v Harding (William); R v Evans (Ronald) [1985] 1 All ER 807; (1985) 80 Cr App R 170; [1984] Crim LR 618; (1984) 128 SJ 702; [1984] TLR 429; [1985] 1 WLR 344 CA Can only be charged with statutory conspiracy where conspiracy was to commit substantive offence.

R v Walters (Terence); R v Tovey (George); R v Padfield (David Albert); R v Padfield (Colin John) (1979) 69 Cr App R 115; [1979] RTR 220 CA Was common law conspiracy to defraud where hired cars and then sold on with fake log books.

Reference by the Attorney-General under Section 36 of the Criminal Justice Act 1972 (No 1 of 1983) (1983) 77 Cr App R 9; [1984] Crim LR 570; [1985] QB 182; (1984) 128 SJ 596; [1984] TLR 424; [1984] 3 WLR 686 CA Cannot be charged in England with conspiracy to defraud where conspiracy to be effected abroad.

Scott v Metropolitan Police Commissioner [1974] 3 All ER 1032; [1975] AC 819; (1975) 60 Cr App R 124; [1975] Crim LR 94; (1975) 139 JP 121; (1974) 124 NLJ 1157t; (1974) 118 SJ 863; [1974] 3 WLR 741 HL Need not be agreement to defraud by deceit to sustain conviction for conspiracy to defraud.

Yu-Tsang (Wai) v R [1991] 4 All ER 664; [1992] 1 AC 269; (1992) 94 Cr App R 264; [1992] Crim LR 425; (1991) 135 SJ LB 164; [1991] TLR 451; [1991] 3 WLR 1006 PC Was conspiracy to defraud where intended to effect state of affairs that could deceive another into acting to his economic detriment even though that was not purpose of conspiracy.

CONSPIRACY (conspiracy to commit public nuisance)

R v Soul (Patricia June) (1980) 70 Cr App R 295; [1980] Crim LR 233 CA Valid conviction for conspiracy to commit public nuisance where intended but failed to bring about escape of person from mental hospital.

CONSPIRACY (conspiracy to contravene statute)

R v Jacobs (Phillip), Carr (Henry Simon) and Fairhurst (William Longton) [1944] 1 All ER 485; (1943-45) 30 Cr App R 1; [1944] KB 417; [1944] 113 LJ 433; (1944) 171 LTR 264; (1944) 88 SJ 188; (1943-44) LX TLR 288 CCA Conspiracy to breach of maximum price legislation did not require intent.

R v Pain; R v Jory; R v Hawkins [1986] Crim LR 168 CA Convictions quashed where prosecution brought out of time under Theft Act 1968, s 1(1)(b).

R v Sorsky (Issac), Bresler (Herman) and H Bresler and Sons, Ltd [1944] 2 All ER 333; (1943-45) 30 Cr App R 84 CCA Conspiracy to breach Limitation of Supplies (Miscellaneous) Order 1940 requires no mens rea.

CONSPIRACY (conspiracy to corrupt public morals)

Knuller (Publishing, Printing and Promotions) Ltd and others v Director of Public Prosecutions [1972] 2 All ER 898; [1973] AC 435; (1972) 56 Cr App R 633; [1975] Crim LR 704; (1972) 136 JP 728; (1972) 116 SJ 545; [1972] 3 WLR 143 HL Is offence of conspiracy to corrupt public morals and of conspiring to outrage public decency which advertisements by men seeking homosexual partners could violate.

R v Knuller (Publishing, Printing and Promotions) Ltd and others [1971] 3 All ER 314; (1971) 135 JP 569; [1972] 2 QB 179; (1971) 115 SJ 772; [1971] 3 WLR 633 CA Agreement to place advertisements seeking homosexual partners can be conspiracy to corrupt public morals.

R v Neville (Richard Clive); R v Anderson (James); R v Dennis (Felix); R v Oz Publications Ink Ltd (1972) 56 Cr App R 115; (1971) 115 SJ 847 CA Different meaning of obscene when used in Post Office Act 1953, s 11(1) (b) and Obscene Publications Act 1959, s 2. Expert evidence inadmissible in Obscene Publications Act prosecution to determine if work obscene; jury to receive proper direction on defence that publication causes aversion but is not obscene; look to individual articles in magazine but entirety of book to see if obscene.

R v Shaw [1961] 1 All ER 330; (1961) 111 LJ 137 CCA Is common law offence of conspiracy to corrupt public morals; can be prosecuted for same notwithstanding Obscene Publications Act 1959, s 2(4); publishing advertisements for prostitutes is living off earnings of prostitution; need not be intent to corrupt for publication to be obscene.

Shaw v Director of Public Prosecutions [1961] 2 All ER 446; [1962] AC 220; (1961) 45 Cr App R 113; [1961] Crim LR 468; (1961) 125 JP 437; (1961) 111 LJ 356; (1961) 105 SJ 421; [1961] 2 WLR 897 HL Test of obscenity is whether article would corrupt/deprave another (intent of author irrelevant); are living off earnings of prostitution if provide goods/services to prostitutes which would not if they were not prostitutes; agreement to publish obscene publication an agreement to corrupt public morals (even if never published), a common law misdemeanour.

CONSPIRACY (conspiracy to effect public mischief)

R v Foy; R v Noe; R v Kelly [1972] Crim LR 504t; (1972) 116 SJ 506 CA Valid withdrawal of question from jury whether agreement to indemnify bail was a conspiracy to effect public mischief.

R v Newland and others [1953] 2 All ER 1067; (1953) 37 Cr App R 154; (1953) 117 JP 573; (1953) 103 LJ 717; [1954] 1 QB 158; (1953) 97 SJ 782; [1953] 3 WLR 826 CCA On public mischief prosecutions.

R v Withers and others [1974] 1 All ER 101; (1974) 58 Cr App R 187; [1974] Crim LR 36t; (1974) 138 JP 123; (1973) 123 NLJ 1017t; [1974] QB 414; (1973) 117 SJ 834; [1974] 2 WLR 26 CA Public duty owed by bank can sustain conviction for conspiracy to effect public mischief; conspiracy to effect public mischief need not involve criminal or tortious acts/the state.

CONSPIRACY (conspiracy to import drugs)

Withers v Director of Public Prosecutions [1974] 3 All ER 984; [1975] AC 842; (1975) 60 Cr App
R 85; [1975] Crim LR 95; (1975) 139 JP 94; (1974) 124 NLJ 1157t; (1974) 118 SJ 862; [1974]
3 WLR 751 HL No offence of conspiracy to effect public mischief (though acts complained of
may fall within definition of other criminal offence).

CONSPIRACY (conspiracy to import drugs)

R v Ardacan and others (1972) 116 SJ 237 CA Could be conspiracy to illegally import cannabis
though relevant acts distant in time and proximity from time and place of importation.

CONSPIRACY (conspiracy to import prohibited goods)

R v Siracusa (Francesco); R v Di Carlo (Francesco); R v Monteleone (Filippo); R v Luciani
(Antonio) (1990) 90 Cr App R 340; [1989] Crim LR 712 CA Crux of conspiracy to import
prohibited goods is agreement to import prohibited goods concerned.

CONSPIRACY (conspiracy to intimidate)

R v Jones (John McKinsie); R v Tomlinson (Eric); R v Warren (Dennis Michael); R v O'Shea
(Kenneth Desmond Francis); R v Carpenter (John); R v Llywarch (John Elfyn) (1974) 59 Cr App
R 120 CA On what constitutes 'intimidation' under Conspiracy and Protection of Property Act
1875, s 7; on constituent elements of unlawful assembly and of affray.

CONSPIRACY (conspiracy to obstruct/pervert the course of justice)

R v Head and Head [1978] Crim LR 427 CA Was conspiracy to obstruct course of justice where
agreed to act as surety in return for future indemnity even though did not possess sum for which
stood surety.

Silcott v Commissioner of Police of the Metropolis (1996) TLR 9/7/96 CA On extent of public
policy immunity enjoyed by police in respect of actions for conspiracy to pervert the course of
justice/misfeasance in public office.

CONSPIRACY (conspiracy to obtain by deception/false pretences)

R v Bolton (Roger John Alexander) (1992) 94 Cr App R 74; [1992] Crim LR 57; (1992) 156 JP
138; [1991] TLR 323 CA Jury ought to have been allowed decide whether execution of securities
was in part purpose of conspiracy.

R v Dearlove (Terence David); R v Druker (David Didy) (1989) 88 Cr App R 279 CA Can
prosecute for conspiracy to obtain property by deception where deception is via contract that
contravenes Article 85(1)/EEC.

R v Kutas (Harry); R v Jerichower (James) (1922-23) 17 Cr App R 179; (1923) 87 JP 196; (1923)
58 LJ 510; (1923-24) XL TLR 51; (1923) WN (I) 287 CCA Conspiracy to obtain goods by fraud
a misdemeanour contrary to Larceny Act 1916, s 33(1).

R v Nanayakkara (Basil Chanrarahra); R v Khor (Teong Leng); R v Tan (Tang Loong) [1987] 1 All
ER 650; (1987) 84 Cr App R 125; (1987) 131 SJ 295; [1987] 1 WLR 265 CA 'Acceptance' of
a valuable security under Theft Act 1968, s 20(2) had same meaning as 'acceptance' in Bills of
Exchange Act 1882, s 17: giving valuable securities to bank not 'acceptance'.

CONSPIRACY (conspiracy to outrage public decency)

Knuller (Publishing, Printing and Promotions) Ltd and others v Director of Public Prosecutions
[1972] 2 All ER 898; [1973] AC 435; (1972) 56 Cr App R 633; [1975] Crim LR 704; (1972)
136 JP 728; (1972) 116 SJ 545; [1972] 3 WLR 143 HL Is offence of conspiracy to corrupt public
morals and of conspiring to outrage public decency which advertisements by men seeking
homosexual partners could violate.

CONSPIRACY (conspiracy to possess firearm)

R v Jones (Ivor Frank); R v Jones (Diane Jane); R v Blarick (John Lee); R v Jarman (Peter David); R v Chennells (Trevor Boyce) [1997] 1 Cr App R 46; [1997] Crim LR 510; (1996) 140 SJ LB 206; (1996) TLR 14/8/96; [1997] 2 WLR 792 CA On necessary intent for offence of conspiracy to possess firearms/ammunition with intent to enable another to thereby endanger life.

CONSPIRACY (conspiracy to prevent burial)

R v Hunter and others [1973] 3 All ER 286; (1973) 57 Cr App R 772; [1973] Crim LR 514t; (1973) 137 JP 774; (1973) 123 NLJ 544t; [1974] QB 95; (1973) 117 SJ 430; [1973] 3 WLR 374 CA Conspiracy to prevent burial if agree to conceal body and this prevents burial.

CONSPIRACY (conspiracy to procure)

R v Christian and another (1913-14) XXIII Cox CC 541; (1914) 78 JP 112 CCC Cannot be convicted of attempt to/conspiracy to/actual procuration where woman freely chooses to be at brothel.

CONSPIRACY (conspiracy to procure execution of valuable security)

R v Dhillon (IK) and Dhillon (GS) [1992] Crim LR 889 CA Method whereby mortgage advances made not a matter to be left to jury's own knowledge/experience.

CONSPIRACY (conspiracy to produce drug)

R v Harris (Kevin Arthur) (1979) 69 Cr App R 122 CA Was conspiracy to produce controlled drug where sought to manufacture amphetamine and used correct ingredients but failed because of lack of chemical knowledge.

R v McGowan [1990] Crim LR 399; [1990] TLR 68 CA Burden of proof stays on Crown for course of prosecution for conspiracy to produce controlled drug.

CONSPIRACY (conspiracy to receive)

R v Bradley [1970] Crim LR 171 CA Six years' imprisonment for airport baggage master guilty of conspiracy to receive stolen property/of receiving.

CONSPIRACY (conspiracy to rob)

R v King and King [1966] Crim LR 280t CCA Had to be definite agreement to rob before could (as here) be convicted of conspiracy to rob.

CONSPIRACY (conspiracy to steal)

R v Barnard (Philip Charles) (1980) 70 Cr App R 28; [1980] Crim LR 235; (1979) 123 SJ 803 CA Conviction quashed where evidence of conspiracy to rob admitted on charge of conspiracy to steal.

R v Duncalf and others [1979] 2 All ER 1116; (1979) 69 Cr App R 206; [1979] Crim LR 452; (1979) 143 JP 654; (1979) 129 (1) NLJ 492; (1979) 123 SJ 336; [1979] 1 WLR 918 CA Conspiracy to steal a statutory offence; conspiracy only to defraud a common law offence; no fixed rules regarding questions under Criminal Evidence Act on previous convictions.

R v Froggett [1965] 2 All ER 832; (1965) 49 Cr App R 334; [1965] Crim LR 489g; (1965) 129 JP 474; (1965) 115 LJ 513; [1966] 1 QB 152; (1965) 109 SJ 492; [1965] 3 WLR 602 CCA Party not principal in second (or first degree) to theft could be convicted of conspiracy to steal and receiving.

R v Hopkins; R v Kendrick [1997] Crim LR 359 CA On appropriation necessary to be guilty of conspiracy to steal.

R v Riley (Terence) (1984) 78 Cr App R 121; [1984] Crim LR 40; [1984] RTR 159 CA Could not disqualify person for facilitating commission of crime where allowed use of car on foot of conspiracy to steal.

CONSPIRACY (conspiracy to steal child)

R v Weymouth [1955] Crim LR 775 CCA Conspiracy conviction quashed where conspiracy could only be proved by reference to larceny (of which also convicted) which was in essence therefore the same offence.

CONSPIRACY (conspiracy to steal child)

R v B [1984] Crim LR 352 CA Father who was immune from prosecution for child-stealing in respect of own child could nonetheless be charged with conspiracy to do same.

CONSPIRACY (conspiracy to supply drug)

R v El Ghazal [1986] Crim LR 52 CA Were guilty of conspiracy to unlawfully supply cocaine where introduced one person to another knowing that one sought to meet the other so as to acquire cocaine.

R v Gill (Simon Imran) (1993) 97 Cr App R 215; (1993) 137 SJ LB 19; [1993] TLR 4 CA Offence to offer to supply drug transpires when offer made (irrespective of presence of conspiracy).

CONSPIRACY (general)

Board of Trade v Owen and another [1957] 1 All ER 411; [1957] AC 602; (1957) 41 Cr App R 11; [1957] Crim LR 244; (1957) 121 JP 177; (1957) 107 LJ 104; (1957) 101 SJ 186; [1957] 2 WLR 351 HL Conspiracy to fully commit crime abroad not indictable in England.

Chiu-Cheung (Yip) v R [1994] 2 All ER 924; [1995] 1 AC 111; (1994) 99 Cr App R 406; [1994] Crim LR 824; (1994) 144 NLJ 863; (1994) 138 SJ LB 146; [1994] TLR 335; [1994] 3 WLR 514 PC Undercover drug agent could be guilty of conspiracy to commit crime if had requisite intent so co-conspirators guilty of conspiracy; no general defence of superior orders, Crown of Executive fiat in English/Hong Kong law.

Churchill v Walton [1967] 1 All ER 497; [1967] 2 AC 224; (1967) 51 Cr App R 212; [1967] Crim LR 235t; (1967) 131 JP 277; (1967) 111 SJ 112; [1967] 2 WLR 682 HL Not conspiracy if agree to commit absolute offence not knowing are agreeing to unlawful act.

Conteh (Thomas) and Others v R [1956] AC 158; [1956] Crim LR 189; (1956) 100 SJ 72; [1956] 2 WLR 277 PC Must know that accusation was false to be convicted of conspiring to accuse person of crime.

Dharmasena (Kannangara Aratchige) v R [1951] AC 1; (1950) 94 SJ 565; [1950] 66 (2) TLR 365; (1950) WN (I) 391 PC Either all or neither party (where two persons charged) guilty of criminal conspiracy: re-trial of one conspirator demands re-trial of other.

Director of Public Prosecutions v Bhagwan [1970] 3 All ER 97; [1972] AC 60; (1970) 54 Cr App R 460; [1970] Crim LR 582; (1970) 134 JP 622; (1970) 114 SJ 683; [1970] 3 WLR 501 HL Not an offence to seek to do something the doing of which Parliament had aimed but failed to prohibit via statute.

Director of Public Prosecutions v Doot and others [1973] 1 All ER 940; [1973] AC 807; (1973) 57 Cr App R 600; [1973] Crim LR 292; (1973) 137 JP 375; (1973) 123 NLJ 370t; (1973) 117 SJ 266; [1973] 2 WLR 532 HL Conspiracy abroad to commit acts in England punishable in England if acts partly/completely done.

Director of Public Prosecutions v Nock; Director of Public Prosecutions v Alsford [1978] 2 All ER 655; [1978] AC 979 (also CA); (1978) 67 Cr App R 116 (also CA); [1978] Crim LR 483; (1978) 142 JP 414; (1978) 128 NLJ 759t; (1978) 122 SJ 417; [1978] 3 WLR 56 (also CA) HL Conspiracy to commit a crime only if planned conduct would result in crime.

Director of Public Prosecutions v Nock; Director of Public Prosecutions v Alsford [1978] AC 979 (also HL); (1978) 67 Cr App R 116 (also HL); (1978) 128 NLJ 264t; (1978) 122 SJ 128; [1978] 3 WLR 56 (also HL) CA Conspiracy to commit a crime though planned conduct would not result in crime.

Director of Public Prosecutions v Shannon [1974] 2 All ER 1009; [1975] AC 717; (1974) 59 Cr App R 250; [1974] Crim LR 177; (1974) 138 JP 587; [1974] 3 WLR 155 CA One conspirator's acquittal does not preclude other's conviction.

Director of Public Prosecutions v Shannon [1974] 2 All ER 1009; [1975] AC 717; (1974) 59 Cr App R 250; [1975] Crim LR 703; (1974) 138 JP 587; (1974) 118 SJ 515; [1974] 3 WLR 155 HL One conspirator's acquittal does not preclude other's conviction.

Farmer v Wilson (1899-1901) XIX Cox CC 502; (1900) 35 LJ 245; [1900] 69 LJCL 496; (1900) LXXXII LTR 566; (1899-1900) XVI TLR 309 HC QBD Was besetting of persons on board ship (irrespective of whether contract permitting persons to be there was legal or not).

Hardie and Lane, Ltd v Chilton and others [1928] All ER 36 CA No conspiracy unless agreement between two/more persons to do something unlawful/lawful in an unlawful way; trade association sending letter in which seeks to resolve dispute by recipient of letter paying money not uttering letter demanding money with menaces contrary to Larceny Act 1916, s 29 (1) (i).

Kamara and others v Director of Public Prosecutions [1973] 2 All ER 1242; [1974] AC 104; (1973) 57 Cr App R 880; [1974] Crim LR 39; (1973) 137 JP 714; (1973) 123 NLJ 700t; (1973) 117 SJ 581; [1973] 3 WLR 198 HL Unlawful assembly need not take place in public place; not all agreements to commit torts indictable conspiracies.

Lonrho Ltd and another v Shell Petroleum Co Ltd and another (1981) 125 SJ 255 CA Conspiracy to do unlawful act not actionable where (as here) was no intent to injure plaintiff.

R v Anderson (1985) 80 Cr App R 64; [1984] Crim LR 550; (1984) 128 SJ 660; [1984] TLR 364 CA Agreement to participate in conduct seeking to bring about criminal act was conspiracy even though had mental reservations about participation.

R v Anderson (William Ronald) [1986] AC 27; (1985) 81 Cr App R 253; [1985] Crim LR 650; (1985) 135 NLJ 727; (1985) 129 SJ 522; [1985] 3 WLR 268 HL On requisite intention to be guilty of statutory conspiracy.

R v Anthony [1965] 1 All ER 440; (1965) 49 Cr App R 104; [1965] Crim LR 160t; (1965) 129 JP 168; [1965] 2 QB 189; [1965] 2 WLR 748 CCA Can be accessory to felony of which principal not convicted/party to conspiracy though other conspirators unknown.

R v Ayres [1984] 1 All ER 619; [1984] AC 447; (1984) 78 Cr App R 232 (also CA); [1984] Crim LR 353; (1986) 150 JP 193; (1984) 128 SJ 151; [1984] TLR 80; [1984] 2 WLR 257 HL Common law/statutory conspiracy are distinct; attempt to obtain insurance money by deception is statutory conspiracy.

R v Barnett and others [1951] 1 All ER 917; (1951-52) 35 Cr App R 37; (1951) 115 JP 305; [1951] 2 KB 425; (1951) 95 SJ 337; [1951] 1 TLR 899; (1951) WN (I) 214 CCA Conspiracy to effect offence under Auctions (Bidding Agreements) Act 1927 triable summarily.

R v Bennett (William Anthony); R v Wilfred (Charles); R v West (Clyde Brierley) (1979) 68 Cr App R 168; [1979] Crim LR 454 CA On burden of proof where common law conspiracy charged.

R v Bhagwan [1970] 1 All ER 1129; [1970] Crim LR 275t; (1970) 120 NLJ 201t; (1970) 114 SJ 166; [1970] 2 WLR 837 CA No offence of conspiracy to evade immigration control.

R v Bishop and Grantway (1918-21) XXVI Cox CC 182; (1917-18) 13 Cr App R 42; (1918) 82 JP 79; [1918] 1 KB 310; [1918] 87 LJCL 440; (1918) 118 LTR 379; (1917-18) XXXIV TLR 139; (1917) WN (I) 383 CCA Conviction for conspiracy to avoid effects of Military Service Acts.

R v Blamires Transport Services, Ltd and another [1963] 3 All ER 170; (1963) 47 Cr App R 272; [1963] Crim LR 698; (1963) 127 JP 519; (1963) 113 LJ 594; (1963) 107 SJ 598; [1963] 3 WLR 496 CCA Conspiracy triable by indictment though substantive offence summary.

R v Bonsall and others [1985] Crim LR 151 CrCt Three months' imprisonment plus fine merited for striking miners guilty of offences under Public Order Act 1936, s 5/Conspiracy and Protection Act 1875, s 7.

R v Brailsford and another [1904-07] All ER 240; (1907-09) XXI Cox CC 16; (1905) 69 JP 370; [1905] 2 KB 730; [1906] 75 LJKB 64; (1905-06) XCIII LTR 401; (1904-05) 49 SJ 701; (1904-05) XXI TLR 727; (1905-06) 54 WR 283 HC KBD Combination to falsely obtain passport a conspiracy to effect public mischief.

R v Burns (James); R v Ralph (Michael Peter); R v Jackson (Stephen Ronald); R v Burns (Sidney) (1984) 79 Cr App R 173 CA Person could be prosecuted for conspiracy to commit offence though immune from prosecution for substantive offence.

R v Chrastny (No 1) [1992] 1 All ER 189; (1992) 94 Cr App R 283; (1991) 155 JP 850; [1991] TLR 135; [1991] 1 WLR 1381 CA Spouse conspiring with other spouse alone but knowing of other parties to conspiracy are guilty of conspiracy.

R v Churchill and others [1965] 2 All ER 793; [1965] Crim LR 545; (1965) 129 JP 387; (1965) 109 SJ 792; [1965] 1 WLR 1174 CCC Application for particulars of overt acts in conpiracy case refused if indictment/Crown opening statement meet that need.

R v Cooke [1986] 2 All ER 985; [1986] AC 909; (1986) 83 Cr App R 339; [1987] Crim LR 114; (1986) 150 JP 498; (1986) 136 NLJ 730; (1970) 130 SJ 572; [1986] 3 WLR 327 HL Statutory conspiracy with presence of fraud can be charged as common law conspiracy; no false accounting where no deception and no fraud.

R v Cooper and Compton [1947] 2 All ER 701; (1946-48) 32 Cr App R 102; (1947) 97 LJ 591; (1947) LXIII TLR 561 CCA On charging conspiracy with nearly same fact substantive offences.

R v Cox (Peter) [1968] 1 All ER 410; (1968) 52 Cr App R 106; [1968] Crim LR 163; (1968) 132 JP 162; (1968) 118 NLJ 109; (1967) 111 SJ 966; [1968] 1 WLR 88 CA No criminal conspiracy charge possible where conspiracy to be completely effected abroad.

R v Crane and others [1982] TLR 179 CA Later events cannot obviate offence of conspiracy.

R v Cruttenden, Doxsey, Jones and others [1968] Crim LR 213 Assizes Separate conspiracies to be charged in separate counts; on whether various acts amounted to misuse of public office by councillor.

R v Curr [1967] 1 All ER 478; (1967) 51 Cr App R 113; [1967] Crim LR 301; [1968] 2 QB 944; (1967) 111 SJ 152; [1967] 2 WLR 595 CA No soliciting/conspiracy if persons assisting in committing crime unaware what are doing is offence.

R v Dawson; R v Wenlock [1960] 1 All ER 558; (1960) 44 Cr App R 87; [1960] Crim LR 358; (1960) 110 LJ 236; (1960) 104 SJ 191; [1960] 1 WLR 163 CCA Conspiracy charge unnecessary in light of substantive charges; bankruptcy examination inadmissible at trial for fraudulent conversion; where alternative counts should be convicted on one of which most certainly guilty; non-delivery post-sale not an obtaining of credit by fraud.

R v Doyle [1963] Crim LR 37g CCA Conspiracy conviction quashed in respect of fourth conspirator whose three other alleged co-conspirators were acquitted.

R v Duguid (1907-09) XXI Cox CC 200; (1906) 70 JP 294; (1906) 41 LJ 335; [1906] 75 LJKB 470; (1906) XCIV LTR 887; (1905-06) 50 SJ 465; (1905-06) XXII TLR 506; (1906) WN (I) 100 CCR Was criminal conspiracy on part of person agreeing with mother to remove her child from lawful custody.

R v Evans (Ian) (1977) 64 Cr App R 237; [1977] Crim LR 223 CA Preliminary steps taken in England for carrying cannabis from Belguim to Canada was assisting in drugs offence contrary to Misuse of Drugs Act 1971, s 20.

R v Golechha (Ummed Chand); R v Choraria (Rajendra Kumar) [1989] 3 All ER 908; (1990) 90 Cr App R 241; [1990] Crim LR 865; (1989) 133 SJ 1001; [1989] 1 WLR 1050 CA Using forged bills of exchange to delay but not for all time avoid bank enforcing previous bills was not falsification with a view to gain contrary to Theft Act 1968, s 17.

R v Griffiths and others [1965] 2 All ER 448; [1965] Crim LR 364t; (1965) 129 JP 380; [1966] 1 QB 589; (1965) 109 SJ 312; [1965] 3 WLR 405 CCA Conspiracy to be charged separately from substantive offences; distinction between one collective conspiracy and several related conspiracies.

R v Hawkesley [1959] Crim LR 211 Sessions Taxi driver told by passengers that they wanted to be dropped off at certain place to commit offence there did not thereby become guilty of conspiracy to commit said offence.

R v Hickson (Isaac) (1921-22) 16 Cr App R 47 CCA Twelve months' hard labour for false pretences/conspiracy offences (reduced from three years' penal servitude as co-prisoners' sentences reduced).

R v Higgins (Frederick) (1919-20) 14 Cr App R 28 CCA Alleged conspirator can be convicted as conspirator with person/s unknown where alleged co-conspirator acquitted of charge.

R v Hillman (Israel) (1931-32) 23 Cr App R 53 CCA Generally where one of two defendants acquitted of conspiracy other willl also be acquitted.

R v Holmes and others [1980] 2 All ER 458; (1980) 144 JP 378; (1980) 130 NLJ 808; (1980) 124 SJ 575; [1980] 1 WLR 1055 CA If possibility of disparate verdicts for alleged conspirators trial judge can ask for dual conviction/acquittal.

R v Hornett [1975] RTR 256 CA Were guilty of uttering forged documents (forged international haulage permits) though those sought to defraud were in foreign jurisdiction.

R v Kerr (Neil) (1920-21) 15 Cr App R 165 CCA Liability of co-conspirator for act of another.

R v King and King [1966] Crim LR 280t CCA Had to be definite agreement to rob before could (as here) be convicted of conspiracy to rob.

R v Lunnon (Keith) (1989) 88 Cr App R 71; [1988] Crim LR 456 CA Guilty plea properly admitted to show were party to conspiracy.

R v McDonnell [1966] 1 All ER 193; (1966) 50 Cr App R 5; [1966] Crim LR 40; (1965-66) 116 NLJ 386; [1966] 1 QB 233; (1965) 109 SJ 919; [1965] 3 WLR 1138 Assizes Cannot be conspiracy between company and person with sole responsibility therefor; conspiracy charge need not include term 'with others unknown'.

R v Merrick (Francis Paul); R v Holmes (Brian William); R v Thornton (Pauline); R v Wood (Maurice) (1980) 71 Cr App R 130; [1980] Crim LR 427 CA Judge may at his discretion direct that co-conspiractors be convicted/acquitted together.

R v Meyrick (Kate Evelyn); R v Ribuffi (Luigi Achille) (1928-29) 21 Cr App R 94; (1928-29) XLV TLR 421 CCA Essence of conspiracy is that acts of accused be done in pursuance of criminal purpose held in common between them; sentences ran from date of conviction not date of appeal in light of bureaucratic delay in appeal.

R v Mitchell, Dyer, Lowry and Field [1964] Crim LR 297t CCA That other party to alleged conspiracy acquitted does not mean rôle played by him in same cannot be considered at later trial of 'co-conspirator'.

R v Mulligan [1990] Crim LR 427 CA Is an offence of conspiracy to cheat the Revenue; was intention to permanently deprive if intended to dispose of Inland Revenue's property as though it was own property.

R v O'Brien (Patrick Joseph) (1974) 59 Cr App R 222 CA Must be agreement between parties for there to be conspiracy.

R v Owen and another [1956] 3 All ER 432; (1956) 40 Cr App R 103; [1956] Crim LR 829; (1956) 120 JP 553; (1956) 106 LJ 666; [1957] 1 QB 174 (also CCC); (1956) 100 SJ (1956) 100 SJ 769; [1956] 3 WLR 739 CCA Cannot be convicted of conspiracy to do crime abroad unless crime indictable in England; was conspiracy to utter forged document as forged documents posted in London/objectives could have been achieved in London.

R v Owen and others [1956] Crim LR 550; [1957] 1 QB 174 (also CCA); (1956) 100 SJ 454; [1956] 3 WLR 252 CCC Cannot be convicted of conspiracy to do crime abroad unless crime indictable in England.

R v Plummer [1900-03] All ER 613; (1901-07) XX Cox CC 269; [1902] 2 KB 339; (1902) 37 LJ 333; [1902] 71 LJCL 805; (1902) LXXXVI LTR 836; (1901-02) 46 SJ 587; (1902) WN (I) 126; (1902-03) 51 WR 137 CCR Cannot be found guilty of conspiracy if 'co-conspirators' acquitted.

R v Porter [1908-10] All ER 78; (1911-13) XXII Cox CC 295; (1909) 3 Cr App R 237; (1910) 74 JP 159; [1910] 1 KB 369; (1910) 79 LJKB 241; (1910) 102 LTR 255; (1909-10) XXVI TLR 200; (1910) WN (I) 5 CCA Bail indemnification agreement a criminal conspiracy.

R v Potter and another [1953] 1 All ER 296; (1953) 117 JP 77 Assizes Elements of conspiracy.

R v Roberts (John Joseph) (1984) 78 Cr App R 41; [1985] Crim LR 218; [1983] TLR 267 CA Judge to decide whether one co-conspirator to be convicted and other acquitted.

R v Sansom and others [1991] 2 All ER 145; (1991) 92 Cr App R 115; [1991] 2 QB 130; (1990) 134 SJ 1300; [1990] TLR 624; [1991] 2 WLR 366 CA Extraterritorial conspiracy to commit criminal act in England a triable offence in England despite no act taking place there pursuant to conspiracy.

R v Secretary of State for the Home Department; ex parte Gilmore and another [1997] TLR 365 HC QBD Conspiracy to commit offence not an extraditable matter.

R v Shannahan (Thomas); R v Watts (James Wesley); R v Fay (Michael Augustus); R v Doot (Robert Leray); R v Loving (Jeffrey Richard) (1973) 57 Cr App R 13 CA On what constitutes conspiracy; on jurisdiction of courts in respect of conspiracies with foreign element.

R v Shaw [1961] 1 All ER 330; (1961) 111 LJ 137 CCA Is common law offence of conspiracy to corrupt public morals; can be prosecuted for same notwithstanding Obscene Publications Act 1959, s 2(4); publishing advertisements for prostitutes is living off earnings of prostitution; need not be intent to corrupt for publication to be obscene.

R v Simmonds and others [1967] 2 All ER 399; (1967) 131 JP 341; [1969] 1 QB 685; [1967] 3 WLR 367 CA No time limit on prosecution of common law conspiracy.

R v Spens (1992) 142 NLJ 528 CrCt Where prosecution offer no evidence/trial against fellow conspirator discontinued court could order indictment to be placed on file marked not to be proceeded with.

R v Thomson (1966) 50 Cr App R 1 Assizes On mens rea of conspiracy.

R v Tibbits and another [1900-03] All ER 896; [1902] 71 LJCL 4; (1901-02) 46 SJ 51; (1901-02) 50 WR 125 CCR Agreement to publish material prejudicing fair trial a criminal conspiracy to obstruct course of justice.

R v Tomsett [1985] Crim LR 369 CA Conspiracy conviction quashed where substantive offence if effected would not have been indictable in United Kingdom.

R v Walker [1962] Crim LR 458 CCA On what constitutes agreement for purposes of crime of conspiracy.

R v West; R v Northcott; R v Weitzman; R v White [1948] 1 All ER 718; (1946-48) 32 Cr App R 152; (1948) 112 JP 222; [1948] 1 KB 709; [1948] 117 LJR 1377; (1948) LXIV TLR 241; (1948) WN (I) 136 CCA Cannot be charged of different conspiracies in same count where conspiracies did not exist at same time in history.

R v Willetts and others (1906) 70 JP 127 CCC Is criminal conspiracy for two/more persons to seek to deny other of benefits of copyright through unauthorised printing/selling of music; certified copies of copyright register entries admissible to prove copyright ownership.

Reference by the Attorney-General under Section 36 of the Criminal Justice Act 1972 (No 1 of 1983) (1983) 77 Cr App R 9; [1984] Crim LR 570; [1985] QB 182; (1984) 128 SJ 596; [1984] TLR 424; [1984] 3 WLR 686 CA Cannot be charged in England with conspiracy to defraud where conspiracy to be effected abroad.

Shaw v Director of Public Prosecutions [1961] 2 All ER 446; [1962] AC 220; (1961) 45 Cr App R 113; [1961] Crim LR 468; (1961) 125 JP 437; (1961) 111 LJ 356; (1961) 105 SJ 421; [1961] 2 WLR 897 HL Is common law offence of conspiracy to corrupt public morals (how indictable); may be charged therewith notwithstanding Obscene Publications Act 1959, s 2(4); publishing advertisements by prostitutes is living on earnings of prostitution.

CONSPIRACY (husband and wife)

Mawji (Laila Jhina) and Another v R [1957] AC 126; [1957] 1 All ER 385; (1957) 41 Cr App R 69; [1957] Crim LR 185; (1957) 101 SJ 146; [1957] 2 WLR 277 PC Tanganyikan husband and wife could not be guilty of criminal conspiracy between them.

R v Lovick (Sylvia) [1993] Crim LR 890 CA Could be no conspiracy between only husband and wife.

CORPORATION (criminal insolvency)

R v Cole; R v Lees; R v Birch [1997] TLR 392 CA Acting as director of company of prohibited name an absolute offence.

CORPORATION (director)

R v Haulage (Stanley) [1964] Crim LR 221; (1964) 114 LJ 25 CrCt On when company will be criminally liable for criminal acts of director.

Re London and Globe Finance Corporation, Ltd [1900-03] All ER 891 HC ChD Official receiver authorised to prosecute company director, costs of prosecution payable from company assets.

CORPORATION (failure to keep books)

R v Dandridge (Arthur Ernest) (1930-31) Cr App R 156 CCA Failure to keep books under Bankruptcy Act 1914, s 158, as amended not 'excusable' though might be 'honest'.

CORPORATION (false accounting)

R v Mallett [1978] 3 All ER 10; (1978) 67 Cr App R 239; (1978) 142 JP 528; (1978) 128 NLJ 535t; (1978) 122 SJ 295; [1978] 1 WLR 820 CA Accounting document false in material particular though false element unconcerned with accounting.

CORPORATION (false business name)

Solicitor to the Board of Trade v Ernest (1918-21) XXVI Cox CC 600; [1920] 1 KB 816; [1920] 89 LJCL 766 HC KBD Giving false statement contrary to Registration of Business Names Act 1916, s 9, not a continuing offence.

CORPORATION (false prospectus)

R v Bishirgian; R v Howeson; R v Hardy [1936] 1 All ER 586; (1934-39) XXX Cox CC 379; (1934-36) 25 Cr App R 176; (1936) 81 LJ 260; (1936) 154 LTR 499; (1935-36) LII TLR 361; CCA Glossing of truth in prospectus rendered its publication a contravention of Larceny Act 1916, s 84.

R v Kylsant [1931] All ER 179; (1931-34) XXIX Cox CC 379; (1931-32) 23 Cr App R 83; [1932] 1 KB 442; (1932) 146 LTR 21; (1931) 75 SJ 815; (1931-32) XLVIII TLR 62 CCA May overall be false prospectus though individual statements therein are true.

CORPORATION (false statement)

R v Lawrence (James) (1909) 2 Cr App R 42 CCA Obtaining by false pretences by means of deceitful promotional pamphlet and postcard.

CORPORATION (fraudulent trading)

Director of Public Prosecutions v Schildkamp [1971] AC 1; (1970) 54 Cr App R 90; [1970] Crim LR 95; [1970] 2 WLR 279 HL Company must be in liquidation before can be prosecuted for fraudulent trading.

R v Buzalek and Schiffer [1991] Crim LR 115 CA Six and a half year delay in bringing case to trial not an abuse of process where case rested heavily on documentary evidence; on relevance of character to credibility; on when R v Ghosh direction as to dishonesty necessary.

R v Cox (Peter Nevill); R v Hodges (Graham David) (1982) 75 Cr App R 291; [1983] Crim LR 167 CA Must be element of dishonesty to sustain conviction for fraudulent trading.

R v Grantham (Paul Reginald George) (1984) 79 Cr App R 86; [1984] Crim LR 492; [1984] QB 675; [1984] TLR 180; [1984] 2 WLR 815 CA Was fraudulent trading where company director had intended to deceive another into providing credit.

R v Kemp (Peter David Glanville) (1988) 87 Cr App R 95; [1988] Crim LR 376; (1988) 152 JP 461; [1988] QB 645; (1988) 132 SJ 461; [1988] 2 WLR 975 CA Person carrying on business with intent of defrauding customers was guilty of fraudulent trading under Companies Act 1948, s 332 (as amended).

R v Lockwood [1986] Crim LR 243 CA What constitutes dishonesty is set out in R v Ghosh (1982).

R v Miles [1992] Crim LR 657 CA Interpretation of Companies Act 1985, s 458: party to carrying on of business engaged in fraudulent trading includes those controlling/managing, i.e., running same.

R v Redmond and Redmond [1984] Crim LR 292 CA Fraudulent trading conviction could be brought against company that was not winding-up in respect of acts committed before relevant statutory provision (Companies Act 1981, s 96) came into force.

R v Rollafson (1969) 53 Cr App R 389; [1969] Crim LR 314t; (1969) 119 NLJ 364t; (1969) 113 SJ 342; [1969] 1 WLR 815 CA Cannot be guilty of fraudulent trading offence under Companies Act 1948, s 332(3) where company concerned not being wound up.

R v Schildkamp (1969) 119 NLJ 1116t; (1969) 113 SJ 486; [1969] 1 WLR 818 CA Cannot be guilty of fraudulent trading offence under Companies Act 1948, s 332(3) where company concerned not being wound up.

R v Smith (Wallace Duncan) [1996] 2 Cr App R 1; [1996] Crim LR 329; (1996) 140 SJ LB 11 CA On meaning of 'creditor' in context of fraudulent trading; on imposition of confiscation order as regards disposal by way of gift.

R v Stansell and others [1959] Crim LR 779 CCC Valid that prosecution for fraudulent trading pursuant to the Companies Act 1948, s 334, be taken by the Board of Trade.

CORPORATION (general)

Dean v Hiesler [1942] 2 All ER 340 HC KBD Defence (General) Regulations 1939 penal so interpreted strictly: person not appointed company director could not be convicted as such thereunder.

Director of Public Prosecutions v Kent and Sussex Contractors, Ltd and another [1944] 1 All ER 119; [1944] KB 146; [1944] 113 LJ 88; (1945) 95 LJ 102; (1944) 170 LTR 41; (1944) 88 SJ 59; (1943-44) LX TLR 175 HC KBD Intentions of its servants are attributed to corporation.

Houghton-Le Touzel v Mecca, Ld [1950] 2 KB 612 HC KBD Liability of limited company under Sunday Observance Act 1781, s 1.

John Henshall (Quarries), Ltd v Harvey [1965] 1 All ER 725; [1965] Crim LR 235t; (1965) 129 JP 224; (1965) 115 LJ 230; [1965] 2 QB 233; [1965] 2 WLR 758 HC QBD Knowledge of responsible company officer of facts of offence necessary to prove company aided/abetted offence.

Moore v I Bresler, Ltd [1944] 2 All ER 515 HC KBD Company officers acting to defraud company are still its agents.

Orpen v Haymarket Capitol, Ltd and others [1931] All ER 360; (1931) 95 JP 199; (1931) 145 LTR 614 HC KBD Limited company guilty of offence under Sunday Observance Act 1780; common informer could seek penalties from company per se, not directors.

R v Daily Mirror Newspapers, Limited; R v Glover (Charles William) (1921-22) 16 Cr App R 131; (1922) 86 JP 151; [1922] 2 KB 530; (1922) 57 LJ 196; [1922] 91 LJCL 712; (1922) 127 LTR 218; (1921-22) 66 SJ 559; (1921-22) XXXVIII TLR 531 CCA Could not try limited company by indictment but might charge person for aiding and abetting limited company in criminal act.

R v Hamid (Richard) [1945] 2 All ER 456; (1943-45) 30 Cr App R 190; (1946) 110 JP 73; [1945] KB 540; [1946] 115 LJ 49; (1945) 173 LTR 250; (1945) 89 SJ 425; (1944-45) LXI TLR 522; (1945) WN (I) 172 CCA Prevention of Fraud (Investments) Act 1939 applied to unformed companies.

R v ICR Haulage, Ltd [1944] 1 All ER 691; (1943-45) 30 Cr App R 31; (1944) 108 JP 181; [1944] KB 550; [1944] 113 LJ 492; (1944) 171 LTR 180; (1943-44) LX TLR 399; (1944) WN (I) 135 CCA Whether fraud of agent was fraud of company depends on relationship/position: here was.

R v Moore [1956] Crim LR 264t CCA Successful appeal against conviction for inducing investment by false statement as evidence did not support conviction.

R v Redfern and Dunlop Ltd (Aircraft Division) [1993] Crim LR 43 CA On when company liable for criminal acts of person to whom has delegated authority; valid conviction for exporting goods to Iran (licence obtained without fully disclosing relevant facts was of no defence).

R v Robinson [1990] Crim LR 804 CA Failed appeal against conviction for fraudulent removal of company property ('asset-stripping').

R v Shacter (1960) 44 Cr App R 42; [1960] Crim LR 186t; (1960) 124 JP 108; (1960) 110 LJ 120; [1960] 2 QB 252; (1960) 104 SJ 90 CCA Auditor filling company office properly convicted as company officer within meaning of Larceny Act 1861, ss 83 and 84.

Re a Company [1979] Crim LR 650 CA Application of Companies Act 1948, s 441.

Re London United Investments plc [1992] Ch 578; (1992) 142 NLJ 87 CA Common law privilege against self-incrimination abrogated by Companies Act 1985 insofar as questioning of directors on matters of company fraud were concerned.

Stockdale v Coulson [1974] Crim LR 474 HC QBD Could not be convicted of failure to annex to annual return documents approved at annual general meeting when no such meeting had been held.

Taylor v McGirr [1986] Crim LR 544 HC QBD Offence under Act repealed before charges brought was properly charged under terms of repealed act.

Tesco Stores Ltd v Brent London Borough Council [1993] Crim LR 624; (1993) 137 SJ LB 93; [1993] TLR 80 HC QBD Company liable for sale of '18' certificate video to under-eighteen year old where sales clerk had reasonable cause for believing purchaser to be under eighteen.

CORPORATION (illegal insurance business)

R v Wilson [1997] 1 All ER 119 CA On elements of offence of carrying on illegal insurance business contrary to the Insurance Companies Act 1982.

CORPORATION (insider dealing)

R v Cross (John Morris) (1990) 91 Cr App R 115 CA Prosecution must prove insider dealing but accused must establish Company Securities (Insider Dealing) Act 1985, s 3 defence; material irregularity where accused questioned on document which had not seen and whose author not called.

R v Goodman (Ivor Michael) (1993) 97 Cr App R 210; [1992] Crim LR 676 CA Guilt of insider dealing justified disqualification of director.

R v Morrissey; R v Staines [1997] TLR 231 CA Disappointing that court was unable to apply European Court of Human Rights decision in insider dealing case.

Re an Inquiry under the Company Securities (Insider Dealing) Act 1985 [1988] AC 660; (1987) 137 NLJ 454 (CA); (1987) 137 NLJ 1181 (HL) [1988] 2 WLR 33 HL Journalist could (but here did not) have reasonable excuse for refusing to reveal source.

Re an Inquiry under the Company Securities (Insider Dealing) Act 1985 (1987) 137 NLJ 345 HC ChD Journalist had reasonable excuse for refusing to reveal source.

Reference by the Attorney-General under Section 36 of the Criminal Justice Act (No 1 of 1988) (1989) 88 Cr App R 191; [1989] Crim LR 134; (1988) 138 NLJ 304; (1988) 132 SJ 1754 CA On what it means to 'obtain' information (Company Securities (Insider Dealing) Act 1985, s 1).

Reference by the Attorney-General under Section 36 of the Criminal Justice Act (No 1 of 1988) [1989] AC 971; (1989) 89 Cr App R 60; [1989] Crim LR 647; (1989) 139 NLJ 541 HL On what it means to 'obtain' information (Company Securities (Insider Dealing) Act 1985, s 1).

CORPORATION (manslaughter)

R v HM Coroner for East Kent; ex parte Spooner and others; R v HM Coroner for East Kent; ex parte De Rohan and others (1989) 88 Cr App R 10; (1988) 152 JP 115 HC QBD Company could be guilty of manslaughter but inadequate case against directors here.

R v P and O European Ferries (Dover) Ltd (1991) 93 Cr App R 72; [1991] Crim LR 695 CCC Corporation can be guilty of manslaughter.

CORPORATION (mens rea)

Director of Public Prosecutions v Kent and Sussex Contractors, Ltd and another [1944] 1 All ER 119; [1944] KB 146; [1944] 113 LJ 88; (1945) 95 LJ 102; (1944) 170 LTR 41; (1944) 88 SJ 59; (1943-44) LX TLR 175 HC KBD Intentions of its servants are attributed to corporation.

CORPORATION (shares)

R v Findlater [1939] 1 All ER 82; (1939-40) XXXI Cox CC 217; (1938-40) 27 Cr App R 24; [1939] 1 KB 594; [1939] 108 LJCL 289; (1939) 160 LTR 182; (1939) 83 SJ 240; (1938-39) LV TLR 330 CCA Meaning of 'share'/'debenture' in Companies Act 1929, ss 356 (7) and 380 (1).

R v Russell (1953) 97 SJ 12; [1953] 1 WLR 77 CCA 'Recklessness' in Prevention of Fraud (Investments) Act 1939, s 12(1) includes forecasts that are negligent but not dishonest.

CORPSE (conspiracy to prevent burial)

R v Hunter and others [1973] 3 All ER 286; (1973) 57 Cr App R 772; [1973] Crim LR 514t; (1973) 137 JP 774; (1973) 123 NLJ 544t; [1974] QB 95; (1973) 117 SJ 430; [1973] 3 WLR 374 CA Conspiracy to prevent burial if agree to conceal body and this prevents burial.

CORPSE (prevention of burial)

R v Le Grand; R v Townsend; R v Cooper [1983] Crim LR 626 CrCt On elements of offence of preventing lawful/decent burial of corpse.

CORRUPTION (bribery)

Attorney General for Hong Kong v Reid and others [1994] 1 All ER 1; [1994] 1 AC 324; (1993) 143 NLJ 1569 PC Fiduciary receiving bribe holds in trust for principal and where bribe increases in value is accountable for bribe and increase. New Zealand Court of Appeal free to review Court of Appeal decisions.

Attorney-General of Ceylon v De Livera and another [1963] Crim LR 105; (1963) 113 LJ 8; (1962) 106 SJ 935; [1962] 3 WLR 1413 PC Person deemed to have acted in contravention of Ceylon Bribery Act 1954, s 14.

Attorney-General of Hong Kong v Chiu (Ip) and another [1980] AC 663; [1980] Crim LR 169; (1980) 124 SJ 47; [1980] 2 WLR 332 PC Accepting bribe in 'capacity' as public servant - meaning of 'capacity' in Prevention of Bribery Ordinance, s 4(2) (a); was not bribery where accepted HK$2000 so as not to plant evidence on/beat up person whom sought to bring to police station.

Attorney-General of Hong Kong v Pui-Yiu (Ho) [1981] 1 WLR 395; [1981] Crim LR 241; (1981) 125 SJ 198 PC On duty of prosecution in proving guilt of bribery under Prevention of Bribery Ordinance 1973.

Attorney-General v Goddard (1928-29) XLV TLR 609 HC KBD On recovery by (principal) Crown of bribes ('secret profits') paid to (its agent) Metropolitan Police officer.

Chee-Kwong (Cheung) v R; Attorney-General v Chee-Kwong (Cheung) [1979] Crim LR 788; (1979) 123 SJ 473; [1979] 1 WLR 1454 PC On determining appropriate sum payable as penalty following conviction of bribery offence under Hong Kong Prevention of Bribery Ordinance 1974 (as revised).

Commissioner of the Independent Commission against Corruption v Poh (Ch'ng) [1997] 1 WLR 1175 PC On nature of bribery offence caught by the Hong Kong Prevention of Bribery Ordinance 1987, s 9(1)(a).

Ming Pao Newspapers Ltd and others v Attorney-General of Hong Kong [1996] 3 WLR 272 PC On elements of offence of disclosing details of investigation being conducted under the Hong Kong Prevention of Bribery Ordinance.

R v Bateman and Linnecor [1955] Crim LR 108 Assizes Would not be guilty of corruption if money advanced by company to army officer was reasonable price for stolen property rather than bribe for future favours.

R v Carr [1956] 3 All ER 979; (1956) 40 Cr App R 188; (1957) 121 JP 58; [1957] Crim LR 113; (1957) 101 SJ 112 CMAC On bribery: was offence to accept bribe as inducement to do favour (favour need not actually be done).

R v Lindley [1957] Crim LR 321 Assizes On intent necessary for offence of bribery (here - allegedly - of company servants).

R v Mills (Leslie Ernest) (1979) 68 Cr App R 154; [1979] Crim LR 456; (1978) 128 NLJ 859t CA Is corruption to acept bribe though do not intend to do act paid for.

R v Whitaker (1914-15) XXIV Cox CC 472; (1915) 79 JP 28; [1915] 84 LJKB 225; (1915) 112 LTR 41 CCA Agreement to bribe regimental commander a misdemeanour.

Tak (Mok Wei) and another v R [1990] 2 AC 333; (1991) 92 Cr App R 209; [1991] Crim LR 614; (1990) 134 SJ 341; [1990] 2 WLR 897 PC Valid convictions for Crown servant's maintaining/ aiding and abetting in Crown servant's maintenance of standard of living beyond that possible on what was paid where could provide no other reasonable explanation.

CORRUPTION (general)

Director of Public Prosecutions v Holly; Director of Public Prosecutions v Manners [1977] 1 All ER 316; [1978] AC 43 (also CA); (1977) 64 Cr App R 143; [1977] Crim LR 289; (1977) 141 JP 143; (1977) 127 NLJ 190t; (1977) 121 SJ 103; [1977] 2 WLR 178 HL Officers of any body with public/statutory duties may be guilty of corruption.

Ex parte Caine and others (1922-23) XXXIX TLR 100 HC KBD Relief granted under Corrupt and Illegal Practices Act 1883, s 23, in respect of illegal payment of certain election expenses.

Morgan v Director of Public Prosecutions [1970] 3 All ER 1053; [1970] Crim LR 696; (1971) 135 JP 86; (1970) 120 NLJ 994t; (1970) 114 SJ 805 HC QBD Corrupt act in course of union business was corrupt act in course of employer's business.

Nicol v Fearby; Same v Robinson [1923] 92 LJCL 280 HC KBD On requirement that candidates to declare election expenses.

R v Andrews-Weatherfoil Ltd; R v Sporle; R v Day [1972] 1 All ER 65; (1972) 56 Cr App R 31; [1972] Crim LR 706t; (1972) 136 JP 128; (1971) 121 NLJ 930t (R v Sporle alone); (1971) 115 SJ 888; [1972] 1 WLR 118 CA Persons concerned must have authority to bind company before company criminally liable for actions of persons; on what constitutes 'reward' under Public Bodies Corrupt Practices Act 1889.

R v Barrett (George) [1976] 3 All ER 895; (1976) 63 Cr App R 174; [1976] Crim LR 576t; (1977) 141 JP 46; (1976) 126 NLJ 596t; (1976) 120 SJ 402; [1976] 1 WLR 946 CA Additional superintendant registrar of births/deaths/marriages can be guilty of corruption.

R v Braithwaite; R v Girdham [1983] 2 All ER 87; (1983) 77 Cr App R 34; [1983] Crim LR 468; (1983) 147 JP 301; (1983) 127 SJ 222; [1983] TLR 103; [1983] 1 WLR 385 CA Receipt of goods/services a consideration which raises presumption of corruption.

R v Calland [1967] Crim LR 236 Assizes On what constitutes corruption.

R v Carr-Briant [1943] 2 All ER 156; (1943) 107 JP 167; [1943] 112 LJ 581; (1944) 94 LJ 100; (1943) 169 LTR 175; (1943) WN (I) 134 CCA On burden of proof in prosecution under Prevention of Corruption Act 1916.

R v Dickinson and De Rable (1948) WN (I) 320 CCA On burden of proof in corruption trial pursuant to the Prevention of Corruption Act 1906.

R v Hailwood; R v Hailwood and Ackroyd Limited (1926-30) XXVIII Cox CC 489; (1927-28) 20 Cr App R 177 CCA; [1928] 2 KB 277; (1928) 97 LJCL 394; (1928) 138 LTR 495 CCA Corrupt practice conviction where unauthorised party entailed expense in advising public not to vote for the Conservative Party.

R v Hirst and McNamee (1977) 64 Cr App R 151 CCC Area gas board a public body for purposes of Prevention of Corruption Act 1916.

R v Jenkins; R v Evans-Jones (1923) 87 JP 115; (1922-23) 67 SJ 707; (1922-23) XXXIX TLR 458 CCA On trials for corruption pursuant to Prevention of Corruption Act 1916.

R v Joy and Emmony (1975) 60 Cr App R 133 CCC Gas Council is a public body for purposes of Prevention of Corruption Act 1916, s 2.

R v Manners; R v Holly [1976] 2 All ER 96; [1978] AC 43 (also HL); [1976] Crim LR 255t; (1976) 140 JP 364; (1976) 126 NLJ 137t; (1976) 120 SJ 96; [1976] 2 WLR 709 CA Officers of any body performing public/statutory duties for public are capable of corruption.

R v Millray Window Cleaning Co Ltd [1962] Crim LR 99 CCA On what constitutes corruption.

R v Newbould [1962] 1 All ER 693; (1962) 46 Cr App R 247; (1962) 126 JP 156; [1962] 2 QB 102; (1962) 106 SJ 244 HC QBD National Coal Board not public body under Prevention of Corruption Acts 1889 to 1916.

R v Parker (Leslie Charles) (1986) 82 Cr App R 69; [1985] Crim LR 589 CA Was corruption to accept reward for act after act done.

R v Raud [1989] Crim LR 809 CA Was jurisdiction for prosecution under Prevention of Corruption Act 1906 where foreign embassy official improperly taking money for passports part performed transaction outside Embassy.

R v Rowe, ex parte Mainwaring [1992] 4 All ER 821; [1992] 1 WLR 1059 CA Election pamphlet may be fraudulent even though true but must impede/prevent free voting to be undue influence.

R v Smith [1960] 1 All ER 256; (1960) 44 Cr App R 55; [1960] Crim LR 185t; (1960) 124 JP 137; (1960) 110 LJ 73; [1960] 2 QB 423; (1960) 104 SJ 69 CCA It is corruption to offer officer of public body something to enter into corrupt agreement even if no intention to cartry out deal.

R v Tweedie [1984] 2 All ER 136; (1984) 79 Cr App R 168; [1984] Crim LR 231; (1984) 148 JP 716; [1984] QB 729; (1984) 128 SJ 262; [1984] TLR 52; [1984] 2 WLR 608 CA Document containing false information intended to deceive must have been intended for third party.

R v Wellburn (Geoffrey Elliot); R v Nurdin (Frank Percival); R v Randel (David Arthur Charles) (1979) 69 Cr App R 254 CA Interpretation of term 'corruptly' in Prevention of Corruption Act 1916, s 2.

Re the Application of the Right Hon David Lloyd George (1932) 76 SJ 166 HC KBD Lloyd George had authorised excuse (illness/unintended inadvertence) for non-return of declaration of election expenses to constituency returning officer.

Sage v Eichholz [1918-19] All ER 424; (1918-21) XXVI Cox CC 432; (1919) 83 JP 170; [1919] 2 KB 171; [1919] 88 LJCL 816; (1919) 121 LTR 151; (1918-19) XXXV TLR 382; (1919) WN (I) 115 HC KBD Charge under Prevention of Corruption Act 1906, s 1(1) (3) does not require corruption/intention to corrupt to sustain conviction.

CORRUPTION (misbehaviour in public office)

R v Bowden (1995) 159 JP 502; [1996] 1 Cr App R 104; [1996] Crim LR 57; [1995] TLR 142; [1996] 1 WLR 98 CA Any person appointed to perform public duty can be guilty of misconduct in public office (need not be Crown officer/agent).

R v Dytham [1979] 3 All ER 641; (1979) 69 Cr App R 387; [1979] Crim LR 666; (1980) 144 JP 49; (1979) 129 (2) NLJ 836; [1979] QB 722; (1979) 123 SJ 621; [1979] 3 WLR 467 CA Negligent failure to perform public duty which is injurious to public interest is misconduct in public office.

R v Llewellyn-Jones [1967] 3 All ER 225; (1967) 51 Cr App R 204; [1967] Crim LR 293; [1968] 1 QB 429; [1967] 3 WLR 1298 CA Dishonest intent inferred from particulars stated.

R v South Worcestershire Magistrates, ex parte Lilley [1995] 4 All ER 186; [1996] 1 Cr App R 420; (1995) 139 SJ LB 67; [1995] TLR 106; [1995] 1 WLR 1595 HC QBD Justices must disqualify themselves from further part in a trial if they have heard and ruled on a public interest immunity contention by the prosecution.

COUNTERFEIT (general)

Horsey v Hutchings [1984] TLR 618 HC QBD On ingredients of offences under the Forgery and Counterfeiting Act 1981, ss 1 and 3.

R v Dickinson; ex parte Newman [1921] LJCL 140; (1919-20) XXXVI TLR 860 HC KBD Current gold coins were 'goods' liable to forfeiture under Defence of the Realm Regulations, regulation 48.

R v Heron (David); R v Storey (Peter Edwin); R v Thomas (Christopher Robin); R v Santi (George Henry) [1981] 3 All ER 641; (1981) 73 Cr App R 327; [1981] Crim LR 698; (1981) 131 NLJ 1008; (1981) 125 SJ 638; [1981] 1 WLR 1480 CA Mere intent to make coins sufficient intent for falsely making/counterfeiting money.

R v Heron and others [1982] 1 All ER 993; (1982) 75 Cr App R 7; [1982] Crim LR 430; (1982) 132 NLJ 437; (1982) 126 SJ 242; [1982] TLR 174; [1982] 1 WLR 451 HL No specific intent required to be guilty of counterfeiting: counterfeiting per se an offence.

R v Johnson (William) (1909) 3 Cr App R 168 CCA That whole party acting in concert merited inference person in guilty possession of counterfeit where other actually in possession of same.

R v Maltman (Peter) [1995] 1 Cr App R 239; [1995] Crim LR 144; [1994] TLR 352 CA Chromolin was a 'thing...for the purpose of making a counterfeit' (Forgery and Counterfeiting Act 1981, s 17(1)).

R v Rowlands (Elizabeth) (1909) 3 Cr App R 224 CCA Evidence of passing counterfeit was admissible to show scienter.

R v Selby [1971] 2 All ER 1324; (1971) 121 NLJ 296t; [1971] Crim LR 353; (1971) 115 SJ 484; [1971] 3 WLR 87 CA Any passing (save to police/authorities) of counterfeit known by person passing to resemble gold coins is offence.

R v Sunman [1995] Crim LR 569 CA On lawful excuse as a defence to offence of having custody of counterfeit note.

R v Walmsley (Jack Ronald); R v De Reya (Anthony); R v Jackson (Peter Michael) (1978) 67 Cr App R 30; [1978] Crim LR 287; (1978) 128 NLJ 163t; (1978) 122 SJ 127 CA Meaning of 'utter' in Coinage Offences Act 1936, s 5(1); was conspiracy to utter counterfeit to sell copies of old coins.

Selby v Director of Public Prosecutions [1971] 3 All ER 810; [1972] AC 515; (1972) 56 Cr App R 72; [1972] Crim LR 705t; (1971) 135 JP 619; (1971) 121 NLJ 953t; (1971) 115 SJ 948; [1971] 3 WLR 647 HL Guilty of uttering/putting off counterfeit if attempt to (or do) pass them off as genuine.

CRIMINAL CONVERSATION (general)

Lemm v Mitchell (1912) 81 LJPC 173; (1911-12) XXVIII TLR 282 PC Second action for criminal conversation was res judicata: plea that earlier judgment obviated by later legislation could only be proved on clearest of evidence that that was intended effect.

CRIMINAL INJURIES COMPENSATION (general)

Berkeley v Orchard [1975] Crim LR 225; (1975) 119 SJ 353 HC QBD Connection between possession conviction and injury suffered by another who accepted drug from possessor too tenuous to support criminal compensation award.

Ex parte Laine [1967] Crim LR 42t HC QBD Leave to move for certiorari granted to widow refused compensation after her husband (a police constable) violently killed in course of his duty.

R v Criminal Injuries Compensation Board and another, ex parte P and another [1995] 1 All ER 870; [1995] 2 FCR 553; (1994) 144 NLJ 674; (1994) 144 NLJ 760t; [1994] TLR 284; [1995] 1 WLR 845 CA Legality of executive action reviewable unless Parliament decides otherwise; non-retrospective application of revised criminal injuries compensation scheme rational.

R v Criminal Injuries Compensation Board ex parte Cook [1996] 2 All ER 144; [1995] TLR 704; [1996] 1 WLR 1037 CA Decision of Board to refuse compensation need deal only with principal issue(s) - oral appeal available if Board fails to do so.

R v Criminal Injuries Compensation Board, ex parte Clowes [1977] 3 All ER 854; (1977) 65 Cr App R 289; [1977] Crim LR 419; (1978) 142 JP 33; (1977) 127 NLJ 570t; (1977) 121 SJ 391; [1977] 1 WLR 1353 HC QBD Offence of damaging property not crime of violence as no injury/violence to another.

R v Criminal Injuries Compensation Board, ex parte Ince [1973] 3 All ER 808; [1973] Crim LR 624; (1973) 137 JP 869; (1973) 123 NLJ 747t; (1973) 117 SJ 616; [1973] 1 WLR 1334 CA That no offence to be committed did not mean 'attempted prevention of...offence' impossible; that death due to carelessness in going to aid did not mean not 'directly attributable' to attempted prevention.

R v Criminal Injuries Compensation Board, ex parte Ince [1973] Crim LR 110 HC QBD Police officer rushing to scene of crime on foot of radio message was engaged in 'attempted prevention of...offence'; death due to carelessness in going to scene of crime meant fault entirely attributable to officer.

R v Criminal Injuries Compensation Board, ex parte Lain [1967] 2 All ER 770; (1967) 111 SJ 331; [1967] 3 WLR 348 HC QBD may review Criminal Injuries Compensation Board's exercise of functions.

R v Criminal Injuries Compensation Board, ex parte Lawton [1972] 3 All ER 583; [1972] Crim LR 702; (1972) 136 JP 828; (1972) 116 SJ 901; [1972] 1 WLR 1589 HC QBD Damages available for injury while chasing person in detention being admitted to mental hospital.

R v Criminal Injuries Compensation Board, ex parte P [1994] 1 All ER 80; [1994] 2 FLR 861 CA Exclusion of victim from compensation to which later victims entitled not impugnable.

R v Criminal Injuries Compensation Board, ex parte P [1994] 1 All ER 80; [1993] 2 FLR 600 HC QBD Exclusion of victim from compensation to which later victims entitled not impugnable.

R v Criminal Injuries Compensation Board, ex parte S [1995] 2 FLR 615; (1995) 159 JP 637; (1995) 145 NLJ 489; [1995] TLR 219 HC QBD Criminal Injuries Compensation Board made error in refusing compensation on basis of delayed complaint in rape case as did not consider why delay had occurred.

R v Criminal Injuries Compensation Board, ex parte Schofield [1971] 2 All ER 1011; (1971) 135 JP 429; (1971) 121 NLJ 570t; [1971] Crim LR 355t; (1971) 115 SJ 367; [1971] 1 WLR 926 HC QBD Bystander may recover criminal injury compensation.

R v Criminal Injuries Compensation Board, ex parte Staten [1972] 1 All ER 1034; [1972] Crim LR 224t; (1972) 136 JP 311; (1972) 122 NLJ129t; (1972) 116 SJ 121; [1972] 1 WLR 569 HC QBD Whether husband/wife living together a matter of fact; 'living together' to be given ordinary non-legal meaning.

R v Criminal Injuries Compensation Board, ex parte Thompstone; R v Criminal Injuries Compensation Board, ex parte Crowe [1983] 1 All ER 936; [1983] Crim LR 325; (1983) 133 NLJ 375; (1983) 127 SJ 121; [1983] TLR 33; [1983] 1 WLR 422 HC QBD General character and way of life relevant to award of compensation.

R v Criminal Injuries Compensation Board, ex parte Tong [1977] 1 All ER 171; [1976] Crim LR 123; (1977) 141 JP 105; (1976) 126 NLJ 721t; (1976) 120 SJ 487; [1976] 1 WLR 1237 CA Award vests in victim instant Board makes it; Board subject to High Court review.

R v Criminal Injuries Compensation Board, ex parte Tong [1975] 3 All ER 678; (1976) 140 JP 41; (1975) 119 SJ 680; [1976] 1 WLR 47 HC QBD Board's decision to pay compensation not final until payment made.

R v Criminal Injuries Compensation Board, ex parte Warner and others [1985] 2 All ER 1069 HC QBD Suicide on railway not crime of violence: must be (threatened) infliction of force on victim.

R v Criminal Injuries Compensation Board, ex parte Warner and others [1986] 2 All ER 478 CA Test whether eligible for compensation is would reasonable man think act of which victim an act of violence.

R v Criminal Injuries Compensation Board, ex parte Webb and others (1986) 136 NLJ 536; [1987] QB 74; (1986) 130 SJ 468; [1986] 3 WLR 251 CA No compensation for train drivers where persons had thrown themselves/fallen in front of trains as crimes at issue not 'crimes of violence'.

R v Criminal Injuries Compensation Board, ex parte Webb and others (1985) 81 Cr App R 355; (1985) 135 NLJ 412; [1986] QB 184; (1985) 129 SJ 432; [1985] 3 WLR 618 HC QBD No compensation for train drivers where persons had thrown themselves/fallen in front of trains as crimes at issue not 'crimes of violence'.

R v Criminal Injuries Compensation Board; ex parte Barrett [1994] 1 FLR 587; [1993] TLR 617 HC QBD On appropriate method of compensating father/children where mother was murdered.

R v Criminal Injuries Compensation Board; ex parte C (RJ) [1978] Crim LR 220; (1978) 128 NLJ 211t; (1978) 122 SJ 95 HC QBD Criminal Injuries Compensation Board could not operate according to self-set guidelines which deprived it of jurisdiction it enjoyed under Criminal Injuries Compensation Scheme.

R v Criminal Injuries Compensation Board; ex parte Cummins [1992] TLR 9 HC QBD On need for reasoned decisions by Criminal Injuries Compensation Board.

R v Criminal Injuries Compensation Board; ex parte Gambles (1994) 144 NLJ 270; (1994) 138 SJ LB 23; [1994] TLR 5 HC QBD On awarding compensation to participant in affray.

R v Criminal Injuries Compensation Board; ex parte Johnson [1994] TLR 472 HC QBD On recoverability of criminal injuries compensation for psychiatric injury suffered by individual who discovered murdered friend.

R v Criminal Injuries Compensation Board; ex parte Lloyd (1981) 131 NLJ 91 HC QBD On whether/when reduction of criminal injuries compensation is merited in light of victim's conduct or way of life.

R v Criminal Injuries Compensation Board; ex parte McGuffie and another [1978] Crim LR 160; (1978) 142 JP 217; (1977) 121 SJ 816 HC QBD On deducting boarding-out allowances from amount payable under criminal injuries scheme to relatives who lost out on salaries through resigning to care for children after mother strangled.

R v Criminal Injuries Compensation Board; ex parte P (1993) 143 NLJ 655; [1995] TLR 305 HC QBD Unsuccessful action seeking (contrary to Criminal Injuries Compensation Board policy) an award of damages for sexual abuse prior to October 1, 1979.

R v Criminal Injuries Compensation Board; ex parte Parsons [1982] TLR 585 CA Train driver could seek criminal injuries compensation for nervous shock suffered who when performing his duty discovered headless body of suicide victim on track.

R v Criminal Injuries Compensation Board; ex parte Penny [1982] Crim LR 298; [1982] TLR 41 HC QBD No compensation for prison officer injured through act of carrying prisoner to cell so as to avoid breach of Prison Rules.

R v Criminal Injuries Compensation Board; ex parte Richardson [1974] Crim LR 99; (1973) 123 NLJ 1112; (1974) 118 SJ 184 HC QBD On relevant earnings figure on which to gauge criminal injuries compensation due to crime victim's widow.

R v Criminal Injuries Compensation Board; ex parte Thompstone; R v Criminal Injuries Compensation Board; ex parte Crowe (1984) 128 SJ 768; [1984] TLR 544; [1984] 1 WLR 1234 CA General character and way of life relevant to award of compensation.

R v Secretary of State for the Home Department ex parte Fire Brigades Union and others; R v Secretary of State for the Home Department, ex parte Bateman; R v Same, ex parte Howse [1995] 1 All ER; (1994) 144 NLJ 1587; [1994] TLR 573; [1993] TLR 259 HC QBD On when person whose conviction has been overturned is eligible for compensation under the Criminal Justice Act 1988, s 133.

R v Secretary of State for the Home Department, ex parte Fire Brigades Union and others [1995] 2 All ER 244; (1995) 145 NLJ 521; [1995] TLR 182 H'. Home Secretary's decision not to bring legislation into force but replace it by using prerogative powers a failure of duty to constantly review if legislation should be brought into force.

Re G (a ward) [1992] 2 FCR 713; [1993] 1 FLR 103 CA Issue estoppel/res judicata inapplicable to Criminal Injuries Compensation Board; compensation could be available to child sex abuse victim whose assailant was not convicted.

CRIMINAL RECORD (general)

R v Harris [1950] 2 All ER 816; (1949-50) 34 Cr App R 184; [1951] 1 KB 107 CCA Evidence of earlier conditional discharge not by way of conviction certificate but by witness who heard confession/ordering of conditional discharge in earlier case.

CURRENCY (general)

R v Harrison-Owen [1951] 2 All ER 726; (1951-52) 35 Cr App R 108 CCA No cross-examination upon previous convictions of party claiming automatism.

CURRENCY (general)

Freed v Director of Public Prosecutions (1969) 53 Cr App R 137; [1969] Crim LR 86t; (1968) 118 NLJ 1172t; (1968) 112 SJ 1020 HC QBD Meaning of 'gold coin'/'gold bullion' under Exchange Control Act 1947.

Pickett v Fesq (1949) 113 JP 528; (1950) 94 SJ 14 HC KBD Inappropriate that witting offender under Exchange Control Act 1947, s 22(1) be dealt with under Probation of Offenders Act 1947.

R v Thompson (Brian Ernest George); R v Thompson (Brian Albert); R v Woodiwiss (Colin Alex Norman) (1979) 69 Cr App R 22 CA Was permissible under Article 36/EEC to prohibit export of non-legal tender so as to prevent melting down abroad.

CUSTODY (general)

R v Birmingham Crown Court, ex parte Bell; R v Birmingham Crown Court, ex parte Brown and Francis (1997) 161 JP 345 HC QBD On relevant period to be considered when deciding whether prosecution (seeking extension of custody time limit) has acted with all due expedition.

DAMAGING/DESTROYING PROPERTY (arson)

R v Appleyard (Gordon Henry) (1985) 81 Cr App R 319; [1985] Crim LR 723 CA Managing director could be guilty of arson of company premises: that owned same did not mean had lawful excuse for acts.

R v Arthur (1968) 118 NLJ 301t; [1968] 2 WLR 533 Assizes Cannot be arson of property under Malicious Damage Act 1861, s 2, where 'person...therein' is alleged arsonist.

DAMAGING/DESTROYING PROPERTY (computer)

R v Whiteley (Nicholas Alan) (1991) 93 Cr App R 25; [1991] Crim LR 436; (1991) 155 JP 917; [1991] TLR 57 CA Was criminal damage for computer hacker to alter data on computer disks.

DAMAGING/DESTROYING PROPERTY (criminal damage)

A v R [1978] Crim LR 689 CrCt Spitting on police officer's raincoat was not criminal damage as no damage occurred.

Blake v Director of Public Prosecutions [1993] Crim LR 586 HC QBD Not lawful excuse to criminal damage charge (vicar writing anti-government policy graffiti on pillar) that had genuine belief were acting in accordance with what God wanted (and so law of England protected).

C (A) v Hume [1979] Crim LR 328; [1979] RTR 424 HC QBD Ingredients of taking vehicle without authority (mens rea particularly important as accused had just reached age of doli capax).

Chief Constable of Avon and Somerset Constabulary v Shimmen (1987) 84 Cr App R 7; [1986] Crim LR 800 HC QBD Was recklessness where recognised risk and took inadequate steps to prevent damage occurring.

Cox v Riley (1986) 83 Cr App R 54; [1986] Crim LR 460 HC QBD Was criminal damage to erase program from circuit card of computerised saw.

Croydon Rural District Council v Crowley and another (1911-13) XXII Cox CC 22; (1909) 73 JP 205; (1909) C LTR 441 HC KBD Failed claim of right in malicious damage action.

Elliott v C (a minor) [1983] 2 All ER; (1983) 77 Cr App R 103; [1983] Crim LR 616; (1983) 147 JP 425; (1983) 127 SJ 442; [1983] TLR 379; [1983] 1 WLR 939 HC QBD Can be guilty of damaging/destroying property though did not see danger if reasonable person would.

Hardman and others v The Chief Constable of Avon and Somerset Constabulary [1986] Crim LR 330 CrCt Graffti that would definitely be erased over time by rain and traffic was nonetheless criminal damage.

Heaven and another v Crutchley (1904) 68 JP 53 HC KBD Valid conviction for malicious damage with intent to destroy plants despite defence that had merely exercised right to roam over particular land to which claimed free access.

Jaggard v Dickinson [1980] 3 All ER 716; (1981) 72 Cr App R 33; [1980] Crim LR 717; (1980) 130 NLJ 907; [1981] QB 527; (1980) 124 SJ 847; [1981] 2 WLR 118 HC QBD Honest belief (even if result of self-induced intoxication) of lawful excuse to damage property a defence.

Lloyd v Director of Public Prosecutions [1992] 1 All ER 982; [1991] Crim LR 904; (1992) 156 JP 342; [1992] RTR 215; [1991] TLR 315 HC QBD Availability of civil remedies of no interest in criminal case save for deciding if that availability a defence to criminal charge.

M and another v Oxford [1981] RTR 246 HC QBD Test of guilt on criminal damage to property charge is subjective.

Miles v Hutchings (1901-07) XX Cox CC 555; [1903] 2 KB 714; [1903] 72 LJKB 775; (1903-04) LXXXIX LTR 420; (1903-04) 52 WR 284 HC KBD Not malicious injury to dog where injure in belief that must do so to protect own/master's property.

Morphitis v Salmon [1990] Crim LR 48; (1990) 154 JP 365 HC QBD On what constitutes 'damage' for purposes of Criminal Damage Act 1971.

R v Ashford and Smith [1988] Crim LR 682 CA Is objective test whether alleged criminal damage was done to protect property of another.

R v Asquith (Lee David); R v Webster (Andrew); R v Seamans (David Leigh); R v Warwick (Wayne Michael) [1995] 1 Cr App R 492 CA Could infer intent to endanger life from throwing stone over bridge at train/from purposely crashing into police cars.

R v Aylesbury Crown Court, ex parte Simons [1972] 3 All ER 574; (1972) 136 JP 870; (1972) 122 NLJ 728t; (1972) 116 SJ 745 HC QBD Offence of criminal damage to property but no intent to endanger life to be tried as arson.

R v Baker and another (1996) TLR 26/11/96 CA Child not 'property' for purposes of defence of lawful excuse to criminal damage under the Criminal Damage Act 1971, s 1(1).

R v Baker and Wilkins [1997] Crim LR 497 CA Defences of duress/lawful excuse deemed not to arise in this criminal damage case.

R v Briggs [1977] 1 All ER 475; (1976) 63 Cr App R 215; [1976] Crim LR 438t; (1977) 141 JP 155; (1976) 126 NLJ 521t; (1976) 120 SJ 352; [1977] 1 WLR 605 CA Reckless as to damage only if knew risk existed.

R v Buckingham (David) (1976) 63 Cr App R 159; [1977] Crim LR 674 CA Conditional/unconditional intention/allowance of other to use thing to damage property immediately/sometime in future means are guilty of offence under Criminal Damage Act 1971, s 3.

R v Caldwell [1981] 1 All ER 961; [1982] AC 341; (1981) 73 Cr App R 13; [1981] Crim LR 392; (1981) 145 JP 211; (1981) 131 NLJ 338; (1981) 125 SJ 239; [1981] 2 WLR 509 HL Definition of recklessness; self-induced intoxication irrelevant to recklessness.

R v Canterbury and St Augustine's Justices, ex parte Klisiak; R v Ramsgate Justices, ex parte Warren and others [1981] 2 All ER 129 HC QBD Magistrates must look to value of property in deciding if right to jury trial; substitution by prosecution of summary charge where non-prosecution of indictable charge not an abuse of process.

R v Dudley [1989] Crim LR 57 CA On what is meant by 'destruction or damage' in Criminal Damage Act 1971, s 1(2).

R v Dyer (Raymond); R v Harris (Anthony Thomas); R v Probert (Edward); R v Cox (Royston John); R v Dowling (Alan Kenneth); R v Smith (Maurice Charles); R v Bastin (Frederick Gerald) (1952) 36 Cr App R 155 CCA Not malicious damage to remove notice board unlawfully placed by parish council on common.

R v Fancy [1980] Crim LR 171 CrCt Failed criminal damage action against person transporting bucket of white paint/a roller and who had been whitewashing National Front slogans from walls.

R v Francis [1972] Crim LR 549t; (1972) 122 NLJ 655t; (1972) 116 SJ 632 CA Malicious damage committed between 9pm and 6am an arrestable offence; police officer not required to know offence arrestable before could enter premises to arrest for same.

R v Gatenby and others [1960] Crim LR 195 Assizes Notional as well as actual obstruction of railway prohibited by the Malicious Damage Act 1861, s 36.

R v Gittins [1982] Crim LR 584; [1982] RTR 363 CA On ingredients of offence of malicious damage under Malicious Damage Act 1861, s 36.

R v Haddock [1976] Crim LR 374t CA Could not on basis of same facts be convicted of damage to property and damage to property with intent to endanger life.

R v Hewitt (Mary) (1911-12) 7 Cr App R 219; (1912) 76 JP 360; (1911-12) XXVIII TLR 378 CCA Sum obtainable through sale of damaged remains non-deductible from value of property damaged maliciously.

R v Hill (James) (1909) 2 Cr App R 144 CCA Proper conviction for destroying/concealing trade books/papers contrary to Debtors Act 1869, s 11(9).

R v Hill (Valerie Mary); R v Hill (Jennifer) (1989) 89 Cr App R 74; [1989] Crim LR 136 CA Possession of article with intent to damage property: subjective test what was in accused's mind/objective test whether lawful excuse sustainable.

R v Joachim (Maud) (1911-12) 7 Cr App R 222; (1911-12) XXVIII TLR 380 CCA Where value of malicious damage done exceeeds £5 each party to concerted act guilty of offence under Malicious Damage Act 1861, s 51, though separate damage was not to the value of £5.

R v Lee [1965] Crim LR 554; (1965) 115 LJ 450 CrCt Evidence tending to show fire fixation prejudicial but admissible at prosecution for setting fire to house.

R v Lockhead [1955] Crim LR 573 Assizes Acquittal of charge of malicious prosecution where did not have necessary intent/where recklessness not established.

R v Merrick [1996] 1 Cr App R 130; [1995] Crim LR 802 CA Person removing electrical equipment for householder and who, in the process, left a live mains-connected cable temporarily exposed was guilty of criminal damage to property.

R v Mullins [1980] Crim LR 37 CA Test as to recklessness a subjective one.

R v Orpin [1980] 2 All ER 321; (1980) 70 Cr App R 306; [1980] Crim LR 304; (1980) 144 JP 428; (1980) 130 NLJ 471; (1980) 124 SJ 271; [1980] 1 WLR 1050 CA Damaging property with intent to endanger life a crime of specific intent so drunkenness relevant to intent.

R v Orpin (Michael John) [1979] Crim LR 722 CrCt Criminal damage not an offence of specific intent to which drunkenness a defence.

R v Parker [1977] 2 All ER 37; (1976) 63 Cr App R 211; [1977] Crim LR 102; (1977) 141 JP 274; (1977) 121 SJ 353; [1977] 1 WLR 600 CA 'Reckless' is deliberate closing of mind to obvious risk of damage.

R v Rutter (William) (1908) 1 Cr App R 174; (1909) 73 JP 12; (1908-09) XXV TLR 73 CCA On malice as an element of the offence of damage to property; on desirability of production of shorthand notes of proceedings upon appeal.

R v Salisbury Magistrates' Court; ex parte Mastin (1987) 84 Cr App R 248; [1986] Crim LR 545 HC QBD Prosecution could put forward maximum and minimum values of property with no readily determined value in criminal damage action.

R v Smith (David Raymond) [1974] 1 All ER 632; (1974) 58 Cr App R 320; [1974] Crim LR 101t; (1974) 138 JP 236; (1973) 123 NLJ 1090t; [1974] QB 354; (1973) 117 SJ 938; [1974] 2 WLR 20 CA No criminal damage to property if honestly believe property own as no mens rea; right of appeal on point of law does not require certificate.

R v Steer [1986] 3 All ER 611; (1987) 84 Cr App R 25; [1986] Crim LR 619; (1986) 136 NLJ 801; (1970) 130 SJ 541; [1986] 1 WLR 1286 CA Life must be endangered/threatened by damaged property for offence of damage to property with intent to endanger/threaten life.

R v Steer [1987] 2 All ER 833; [1988] AC 111; (1987) 85 Cr App R 352; [1987] Crim LR 684; (1987) 151 JP 793; (1987) 137 NLJ 640; (1987) 131 SJ 939; [1987] 3 WLR 205 HL Offence of damaging property with intent of endangering life requires that damaged property endanger life.

R v Stephenson [1979] 2 All ER 1198; (1979) 69 Cr App R 213; [1979] Crim LR 590; (1979) 143 JP 592; (1979) 129 (1) NLJ 612; (1979) QB 695; (1979) 123 SJ 403; [1979] 3 WLR 193 CA Recklessness a subjective test.

R v Webster and others; R v Warwick [1995] 2 All ER 168 CA Where charge of 'damage to property with intent to endanger life' danger must be from damaged property and not act of damaging.

R v Woolcock [1977] Crim LR 104 CrCt Person removing nails/corrugated iron that were blocking derelict shop was not guilty of criminal damage.

Roe v Kingerlee [1986] Crim LR 735 HC QBD Writing graffiti on wall using mud was criminal damage.

Sears v Broome [1986] Crim LR 461 CA Damage done when acting in self-defence cannot be criminal damage.

Stear v Scott [1992] RTR 226 HC QBD Valid conviction for criminal damage to clamp (that levered free from car with crowbar before throwing away) absent lawful excuse.

Webb v Stansfield [1966] Crim LR 449 Magistrates Forcing of quarter light on door of car obstructing right to use highway was valid step in enforcement of that right; absent damage to complainant smearing marmalade inside the car went unpunished.

Woodley v Woodley [1978] Crim LR 629 HC QBD Wife could be convicted of criminal damage of husband's property where husband was subject of exclusion order.

DAMAGING/DESTROYING PROPERTY (damaging ancient monuments)

R v Noble; R v King [1954] Crim LR 712 Magistrates Failed prosecution for damage to ancient monuments.

DEATH (certificate)

R v Ryan (1914-15) XXIV Cox CC 135; (1914) 10 Cr App R 4; (1914) 78 JP 192; (1914) 110 LTR 779; (1913-14) 58 SJ 251; (1913-14) XXX TLR 242 CCA 'Wilful' making of fake death certificates.

DECEPTION (accepting Bill of Exchange with intent to defraud)

R v Holden (Frank) (1911-12) 7 Cr App R 93; (1911-12) 56 SJ 188; (1911-12) XXVIII TLR 173 CCA Accepting of bill of exchange with intent to defraud.

DECEPTION (acting as auditor when disqualified)

Secretary of State for Trade and Industry v Hart [1982] 1 All ER 817; [1982] Crim LR 583; (1982) 132 NLJ 85; (1982) 126 SJ 172; [1982] 1 WLR 481 HC QBD Ignorance of law a defence to acting as auditor when disqualfied.

DECEPTION (acting as solicitor)

Beeston and Stapleford UDC and another v Smith (1949) 113 JP 160 HC KBD Valid conviction for acting as solicitor.

DECEPTION (attempt to obtain by deception/false pretences)

R v Ayres [1984] 1 All ER 619; [1984] AC 447; (1984) 78 Cr App R 232 (also CA); [1984] Crim LR 353; (1986) 150 JP 193; (1984) 128 SJ 151; [1984] TLR 80; [1984] 2 WLR 257 HL Common law/statutory conspiracy are distinct; attempt to obtain insurance money by deception is statutory conspiracy.

R v Bunche (Jacques Emmanuel) (1993) 96 Cr App R 274; (1993) 157 JP 780; [1992] TLR 513 CA Could be convicted of attempting to obtain property by deception where sought passport using false name.

R v Dargue (Walter) (1910-11) 6 Cr App R 261 CCA Must show person parting with goods was induced by false pretences to do so.

R v Dunleavy (1909) 73 JP 56 CCA Attempted obtaining by false pretences conviction quashed where convict had not known that ring was selling as gold ring actually made of brass.

DECEPTION (breach of trust)

R v Ilyas (Mohammed) (1984) 78 Cr App R 17 CA Must have done everything preparatory to offence before guilty of attempt (and acts must be proximate to offence): merely obtaining insurance claim form could not support attempted obtaining of property by deception conviction.

R v Laitwood (John) (1910) 4 Cr App R 248; (1910) WN (I) 122 CCA Can be convicted of attempt to obtain by false pretences where did not manage attempt solely because were apprehended.

R v Light (Arthur Dennison) [1914-15] All ER 659; (1914-15) XXIV Cox CC 718; (1914-15) 11 Cr App R 111; [1915] 84 LJKB 865; (1915) 112 LTR 1144; (1914-15) 59 SJ 351; (1914-15) XXXI TLR 257; (1915) WN (I) 97 CCA Can be convicted of attempted obtaining of money by false pretences though victim knew pretences were false.

R v Punch (Samuel Adolphus David) (1927-28) 20 Cr App R 18 CCA On attempts; on attempting to obtain by false pretences.

R v Robinson [1914-17] All ER 101; (1914-15) XXIV Cox CC 726; (1914-15) 11 Cr App R 124; (1915) 79 JP 303; [1915] 2 KB 342; (1915) 50 LJ 159; [1915] 84 LJKB 1149; (1915-16) 113 LTR 379; (1914-15) 59 SJ 366; (1914-15) XXXI TLR 313; (1915) WN (I) 133 CCA Mere intention to commit crime could not sustain conviction for attempt to commit crime.

R v Saunders (Ernest) (1916-17) 12 Cr App R 56 CCA Attempt to obtain money by false pretences not punishable with hard labour.

R v Widdowson (Stanley) (1986) 82 Cr App R 314; [1986] Crim LR 233; [1986] RTR 124; (1986) 130 SJ 88 CA Not attempted obtaining services by deception where gave false personal details on hire purchase credit inquiry form.

DECEPTION (breach of trust)

Cooray (Mahumarakalage Edward Andrew) v R [1953] AC 407; (1953) 97 SJ 314 PC To be convicted as agent having committed criminal breach of trust must act as agent by way of business.

DECEPTION (conspiracy to cheat/defraud)

Adams v R [1995] 2 Cr App R 295; [1995] Crim LR 561; (1995) 139 SJ LB 13; [1994] TLR 555; [1995] 1 WLR 52 PC Was conspiracy to defraud where director sought to conceal information so as to preclude recovery by company of undisclosed profits made by directors.

Attorney General's Reference (No 1 of 1982) [1983] 2 All ER 721; [1983] Crim LR 534; (1984) 148 JP 115; [1983] QB 751; (1983) 127 SJ 377; [1983] TLR 268; [1983] 3 WLR 72 CA If a tangential effect of conspiracy to perform act abroad is it causes economic/other loss in England then is not conspiracy to defraud.

Beechey v R (1915-17) XXV Cox CC 217; [1916] 85 LJPC 32; (1916) 114 LTR 1 PC Conspirator may be convicted as such though co-conspirator absent.

R v Allsop (Anthony Edward) (1977) 64 Cr App R 29; [1976] Crim LR 738t; (1976) 126 NLJ 937t; (1976) 120 SJ 635 CA Is fraud where make false statements likely to cause another economic loss (and do) though no loss intended.

R v Ayres (David Edward) (1984) 78 Cr App R 232 (also HL); [1984] Crim LR 165; (1984) 148 JP 458; (1984) 128 SJ 63; [1983] TLR 734 CA Appellant properly charged with conspiracy to defraud and not statutory conspiracy.

R v Cooke (Anthony); R v Sutcliffe (Kathleen) [1985] Crim LR 215 CA On appropriate charge where possessed article for cheating.

R v Grant [1986] Crim LR 235 CA Application of proviso so as to allow conviction for conspiracy to defraud.

R v Grosvenor (1914-15) XXIV Cox CC 468; (1914) 10 Cr App R 235; (1914-15) 111 LTR 1116 CCA Is conspiracy to defraud though acquired no money/made no false pretence; both parties liable to conviction for obtaining money by false pretences where obtain money following jointly executed false pretence; is false pretences by conduct where implicitly agree to making of false pretence.

R v Hollinshead (Peter Gordon); R v Dettlaff (Stefen); R v Griffiths (Kenneth David) [1985] 1 All ER 850; [1985] AC 975 (also HL); (1985) 80 Cr App R 285; [1985] Crim LR 301; (1985) 129 SJ 219; [1985] 2 WLR 761 CA Cannot be guilty of conspiracy to aid and abet offences so providing devices for another to deal in not criminal act.

R v Hollinshead and others [1985] 2 All ER 769; [1985] AC 975 (also CA); (1985) 81 Cr App R 365; [1985] Crim LR 653; (1985) 135 NLJ 631; (1985) 129 SJ 447; [1985] 3 WLR 159 HL Manufacturing/selling devices intended to cause loss to another is conspiracy to defraud.

R v James (Alan Michael); R v Ashford (John Phillip) (1986) 82 Cr App R 226; [1986] Crim LR 118 CA Where charged with common law and statutory conspiracy and trial judge directed acquittal on former and conviction for latter quashed on appeal was no alternative ground for conviction.

R v Landy and others [1981] 1 All ER 1172; (1981) 72 Cr App R 237; [1981] Crim LR 326; (1981) 125 SJ 80; [1981] 1 WLR 355 CA Actual dishonesty in accused's mind needed for conspiracy to defraud; guidelines on summings-up.

R v Levitz; R v Mbele; R v Vowell [1989] Crim LR 714; (1989) 133 SJ 818 CA On appropriate charge of conspiracy to defraud where persons charged improperly sought to use devices to render telephone calls to them cost-free.

R v Lloyd and others [1985] 2 All ER 661; (1985) 81 Cr App R 182; (1985) 149 JP 634; (1985) 135 NLJ 605; [1985] QB 829; [1985] 3 WLR 30 CA No intention of permanently depriving where borrow/lend unless return in worthless state; statutory not common law conspiracy where full offence would be substantive.

R v Lockhart (Arthur Norman) (1909) 2 Cr App R 308 CCA Small act treated as evidence of conspiracy to defraud.

R v McPherson and Watts [1985] Crim LR 508 CA Conspiracy conviction quashed where not left to jury to decide whether substantive offence if effected would have been indictable in United Kingdom.

R v Mendez [1990] Crim LR 397 CA On relevance of accused's good character to credibility of his testimony.

R v Moses and Ansbro [1991] Crim LR 617 CA Aiding illegal immigrants to receive work permits which would probably not otherwise have received was criminal conspiracy to defraud (albeit that none of the acts making up the conspiracy were themselves unlawful).

R v Moss; R v Ricardo; R v Ricardo; R v Van West [1965] Crim LR 368; (1965) 109 SJ 269 CCA Bankruptcy not of itself evidence of bad character.

R v Mulligan [1990] Crim LR 427 CA Is an offence of conspiracy to cheat the Revenue; was intention to permanently deprive if intended to dispose of Inland Revenue's property as though it was own property.

R v Scott [1974] 2 All ER 204; [1974] Crim LR 243t; (1974) 138 JP 420; [1974] QB 733; (1974) 118 SJ 147; [1974] 2 WLR 379 CA Need not be agreement to defraud by deceit to sustain conviction for conspiracy to defraud.

R v Seillon [1982] Crim LR 676 CA Offence of conspiracy to defraud creditor includes conspiracy to defraud likely possible creditors.

R v Sinclair and others [1968] 3 All ER 241; (1968) 52 Cr App R 618; (1968) 132 JP 527; (1968) 118 NLJ 956; [1968] 1 WLR 1246 CA On what constitutes 'fraud' in conspiracy to cheat and defraud.

R v Smithson; R v Queenswood (Holdings) Ltd; R v Sinclair [1968] Crim LR 610; (1968) 112 SJ 703 CA On dishonesty as an element of fraud (accused charged with conspiracy to cheat/defraud).

R v Spicer [1970] Crim LR 695; (1970) 114 SJ 824 CA Conspiracy to defraud not an arrestable offence.

R v Tonner (Gordon Campbell); R v Rees (Wilfrid Haydn); R v Harding (William); R v Evans (Ronald) [1985] 1 All ER 807; (1985) 80 Cr App R 170; [1984] Crim LR 618; (1984) 128 SJ 702; [1984] TLR 429; [1985] 1 WLR 344 CA Can only be charged with statutory conspiracy where conspiracy was to commit substantive offence.

R v Walters (Terence); R v Tovey (George); R v Padfield (David Albert); R v Padfield (Colin John) (1979) 69 Cr App R 115; [1979] RTR 220 CA Was common law conspiracy to defraud where hired cars and then sold on with fake log books.

Reference by the Attorney-General under Section 36 of the Criminal Justice Act 1972 (No 1 of 1983) (1983) 77 Cr App R 9; [1984] Crim LR 570; [1985] QB 182; (1984) 128 SJ 596; [1984] TLR 424; [1984] 3 WLR 686 CA Cannot be charged in England with conspiracy to defraud where conspiracy to be effected abroad.

Scott v Metropolitan Police Commissioner [1974] 3 All ER 1032; [1975] AC 819; (1975) 60 Cr App R 124; [1975] Crim LR 94; (1975) 139 JP 121; (1974) 124 NLJ 1157t; (1974) 118 SJ 863; [1974] 3 WLR 741 HL Need not be agreement to defraud by deceit to sustain conviction for conspiracy to defraud.

Yu-Tsang (Wai) v R [1991] 4 All ER 664; [1992] 1 AC 269; (1992) 94 Cr App R 264; [1992] Crim LR 425; (1991) 135 SJ LB 164; [1991] TLR 451; [1991] 3 WLR 1006 PC Was conspiracy to defraud where intended to effect state of affairs that could deceive another into acting to his economic detriment even though that was not purpose of conspiracy.

DECEPTION (conspiracy to obtain by deception/false pretences)

R v Bolton (Roger John Alexander) (1992) 94 Cr App R 74; [1992] Crim LR 57; (1992) 156 JP 138; [1991] TLR 323 CA Jury ought to have been allowed decide whether execution of securities was in part purpose of conspiracy.

R v Dearlove (Terence David); R v Druker (David Didy) (1989) 88 Cr App R 279 CA Can prosecute for conspiracy to obtain property by deception where deception is via contract that contravenes Article 85(1)/EEC.

R v Dhillon (IK) and Dhillon (GS) [1992] Crim LR 889 CA Method whereby mortgage advances made not a matter to be left to jury's own knowledge/experience.

R v Kutas (Harry); R v Jerichower (James) (1922-23) 17 Cr App R 179; (1923) 87 JP 196; (1923) 58 LJ 510; (1923-24) XL TLR 51; (1923) WN (I) 287 CCA Conspiracy to obtain goods by fraud a misdemeanour contrary to Larceny Act 1916, s 33(1).

R v Nanayakkara (Basil Chanrarahra); R v Khor (Teong Leng); R v Tan (Tang Loong) [1987] 1 All ER 650; (1987) 84 Cr App R 125; (1987) 131 SJ 295; [1987] 1 WLR 265 CA 'Acceptance' of a valuable security under Theft Act 1968, s 20(2) had same meaning as 'acceptance' in Bills of Exchange Act 1882, s 17: giving valuable securities to bank not 'acceptance'.

DECEPTION (false instrument)

R v Campbell (Mary Sylvia) (1985) 80 Cr App R 47; [1984] TLR 500 CA Was forgery to endorse cheque and so secure payment from bank which would not have made if knew of true circumstances.

R v Clarke (Ediakpo) [1985] AC 1037; (1985) 135 NLJ 632; [1985] 3 WLR 113 HL On elements of offence of making false statement to person lawfully acting in execution of Immigration Act 1971.

R v Donnelly (Ian David) (1984) 79 Cr App R 76; [1984] Crim LR 490; (1984) 128 SJ 514; [1984] TLR 322; [1984] 1 WLR 1017 CA Valuation certificate where was no jewellery to be valued was a forgery.

R v Gambling [1974] 3 All ER 479; (1975) 60 Cr App R 25; [1974] Crim LR 600t; (1974) 138 JP 749; (1974) 124 NLJ 696t; [1975] QB 207; (1974) 118 SJ 735; [1974] 3 WLR 558 CA Must not only prove that maker of false statement intended it to taken as genuine but that untrue statement a factor in it being accepted as true.

R v Garcia (Emilio) (1988) 87 Cr App R 175; [1988] Crim LR 115 CA Must be actual prejudice to be guilty of forging document to induce another to act/not to act to their or another's prejudice in belief that forged document genuine.

R v Hopley (Samuel) (1914-15) 11 Cr App R 248 CCA Inferring of intent to defraud from knowing use of forged instrument in course of bona fide claim.

R v Lack (Peter Andrew) (1987) 84 Cr App R 342 CA Documents allegedly emanating from company but actually made after liquidation of same were false for purposes of Forgery and Counterfeiting Act 1981.

R v Lawson (1901-07) XX Cox CC 812 CCR On who constitutes 'manager' of enterprise for purposes of Larceny Act 1861, s 84.

R v Mason (Reginald) (1914) 10 Cr App R 169; (1914-15) 111 LTR 336 CCA Forged deeds of later date than that of which accused charged with uttering admissible to prove guilty knowledge.

R v Matthews (Albert Edward) (1958) 42 Cr App R 93 CMAC Properly convicted of knowingly making false/fraudulent statement where signed one's name to blank form knowing another would complete it falsely.

R v Moore [1986] Crim LR 552 CA Withdrawal slip completed in name of non-existent person was a forgery; person guilty of obtaining property by deception where intended to retain cheque had dishonestly obtained.

R v Tobierre [1986] 1 All ER 346; (1986) 82 Cr App R 212; [1986] Crim LR 243; (1986) 130 SJ 35; [1986] 1 WLR 125 CA Mens rea for use of false instrument is that intended to induce other to accept forgery as genuine and to use to other's (or another's) detriment.

R v Utting (John Benjamin) (1988) 86 Cr App R 164; [1987] Crim LR 636; (1987) 131 SJ 1154; [1987] 1 WLR 1375 CA Successful appeal against conviction for making false instrument with intent of inducing another to act/not to act on belief that document genuine (Forgery and Counterfeiting Act 1981, s 1).

R v Warneford and Gibbs [1994] Crim LR 753; [1994] TLR 279 CA On what constitutes a 'false instrument' under the Forgery and Counterfeiting Act 1981, s 9(1).

Singh (Baljinder) v Hammond [1987] 1 WLR 283 HC QBD Could be convicted of making false statement to immigration officer though did so after date of entry and away from port of entry.

DECEPTION (false statement)

R v Cross [1987] Crim LR 43 CA Construction of document a matter for judge.

DECEPTION (forgery)

R v Buono [1970] Crim LR 154 CA Documents that were either hire purchase agreements/proposal forms were valuable securities.

R v Macer [1979] Crim LR 659 CMAC Was not forgery where signed cheque in different style to usual but nonetheless signed with correct (own) name.

R v Woods [1922] All ER 781; (1922) 57 LJ 174 CCA Need not provide real banknote for comparison in trial for possession of paper intended to pass as banknote - jury familiar with bank notes.

DECEPTION (fortune-telling)

Irwin v Barker (1924-25) 69 SJ 575/589 HC KBD Person who conducted spiritualist seance was guilty of offence of fortune-telling under the Vagrancy Act 1824, s 4.

DECEPTION (fraud)

King v Spencer (1901-07) XX Cox CC 692; (1904) 68 JP 530; (1904-05) XCI LTR 470 HC KBD Not per se criminal fraud to weigh goods and wrapper together where purchaser aware of same; evidence of trade custom admissible to establish if behaviour fraudulent.

DECEPTION (fraudulent appropriation)

Nelson v R [1902] AC 250; (1901-07) XX Cox CC 150; [1902] 71 LJPC 55; (1902) LXXXVI LTR 164 PC Prosecution failed as could not show bank had fraudulently appropriated funds by stopping payment from solvent account.

DECEPTION (fraudulent conversion)

R v Arthur [1967] Crim LR 298t; (1967) 111 SJ 434 CA Successful conviction of company director for fraudulent conversion of company funds for own use.

R v Banyard and Lacey [1958] Crim LR 49 CCC On what constitutes fraudulent conversion (here of cheque proceeds).

R v Bryce (Marshall Nicholas) (1956) 40 Cr App R 62; [1956] Crim LR 122 CCA On what constitutes fraudulent conversion.

R v Davies (1913) 77 JP 279; (1913) 48 LJ 138; [1913] 82 LJKB 471; (1912-13) 57 SJ 376; (1913) WN (I) 55 CCA Prosecution of club treasurer for fraudulent conversion did not require fiat of Attorney-General.

R v Davies [1954] 3 All ER 335; [1955] Crim LR 40; (1955) 119 JP 15; (1954) 104 LJ 744; [1955] 1 QB 71; (1954) 98 SJ 117/789; [1954] 3 WLR 664 CCA 'Public company' in Larceny Act 1916, s 20(1)(ii) includes company that is 'private' under Companies Act 1948, s 28.

R v Greenwood (Sidney Debenham) (1910) 5 Cr App R 113 CCA On time of formation of necessary intent for fraudulent conversion.

R v Grubb [1914-15] All ER 667; (1915-17) XXV Cox CC 77; (1914-15) 11 Cr App R 153; (1915) 79 JP 430; [1915] 2 KB 683; [1915] 84 LJKB 1744; (1915-16) 113 LTR 510; (1914-15) 59 SJ 547; (1914-15) XXXI TLR 429; (1915) WN (I) 208 CCA Meaning of 'entrusted'/'receipt' in context of fraudulent conversion (under Larceny Act 1901, s 1).

R v Hignett (1950) 94 SJ 149 CCA On ingredients of fraudulent conversion.

R v Inman and Mercury Self-Drive Ltd [1966] Crim LR 106 Assizes Not larceny/fraudulent conversion where manager of car dealing firm sold cars at less than price agreed with vendor: situation gave rise only to debts of a personal nature.

R v Laurens (Alfred) alias Lawson (Arthur) (1914-15) 11 Cr App R 215 CCA Promotion of company constituted 'purpose' under Larceny Act 1901, s 1(1) (a).

R v Lawson [1952] 1 All ER 804; (1952) 36 Cr App R 30; (1952) 116 JP 195; [1952] 1 TLR 889 Assizes On proper indictment for fraudulent conversion.

R v Lord (John) (1905) 69 JP 467 CCR Valid conviction for fraudulent conversion of property to own use where property at issue was employer's money.

R v Lyle (William Stacey) (1924-25) 18 Cr App R 59 CCA Fraudulent conversion commenced abroad and completed in UK can be prosecuted for in UK.

R v Lyon [1959] Crim LR 54 CCC Director of private company acquitted of fraudulent conversion of company property.

R v Maywhort [1955] 2 All ER 752; (1955) 39 Cr App R 107; (1955) 119 JP 473; (1955) 105 LJ 457; (1955) 99 SJ 510; [1955] 1 WLR 848 HC QBD Cannot be convicted of fraudulent conversion first revealed on oath.

R v Messer (1913-14) XXIII Cox CC 59; (1911-12) 7 Cr App R 49; (1912) 76 JP 124; [1913] 2 KB 421; [1913] 82 LJKB 913; (1912-13) 107 LTR 31; (1911-12) XXVIII TLR 69 CCA Taxi-cab driver liable in conversion for portion of earnings due but not given to owner of cab.

R v Morter (Alfred Ernest) (1927-28) 20 Cr App R 53 CCA Control of property following entrustment of same is essence of fraudulent conversion.

R v Noel (John Beauchamp) (1914) 10 Cr App R 255; (1914) WN (I) 318 CCA Conversion of money by person in whose name money intentionally deposited; application of Larceny Act 1861, s 85.

R v O'Brien (1911) 75 JP 392 CCC Defendant who kept deposit paid as security for honesty while employed by defendant not guilty/guilty of fraudulent conversion/obtaining money by false pretences.

R v Parsons [1964] Crim LR 824t CCA Valid conviction of estate agent for fraudulent conversion of deposit cheques.

R v Pilkington [1958] Crim LR 545 CCA Person guilty of taking house deposits for self was guilty of fraudulent conversion on persons who paid deposits.

R v Sheaf (Robert Ernest) (1925-26) 19 Cr App R 46; (1925) 89 JP 207; (1926) 134 LTR 127; (1925-26) XLII TLR 57 CCA Specificity in dates may be necessary to prove fraudulent conversion.

R v Smith (1924-25) 18 Cr App R 76; (1924) 88 JP 108; [1924] 2 KB 194; (1924) 59 LJ 404; [1924] 93 LJCL 1006; (1924) 131 LTR 28; (1924-25) 69 SJ 37; (1924) WN (I) 187 CCA Whether transaction at issue involves fraudulent conversion a question of fact for jury.

R v South (1907) 71 JP 191 CCC Failed prosecution for receiving money and fraudulently converting same to own use (Larceny Act 1901, s 1(1)(b)).

R v Stevens (Francis Joseph) (1932-34) 24 Cr App R 85 CCA Cannot be convicted of fraudulent conversion where charged with simple larceny.

R v Waller, Hutton and Artis [1960] Crim LR 759 CCC Alternate directors were directors for purposes of Larceny Act 1916, s 20(1)(ii).

R v Yule [1963] 2 All ER 780; (1963) 47 Cr App R 229; [1963] Crim LR 564; (1963) 127 JP 469; (1963) 113 LJ 465; [1964] 1 QB 5; (1963) 107 SJ 497; [1963] 3 WLR 285 CCA Solicitor paying fees intended for other into own account commits fraudulent conversion; indictment defective but as no embarrassment to defendant was allowed.

Rogers v Arnott [1960] 2 All ER 417; (1960) 44 Cr App R 195; (1960) 124 JP 349; (1960) 110 LJ 446; [1960] 2 QB 244; (1960) 104 SJ 508 HC QBD Bailee lawfully in possession who dishonestly offers it for sale is guilty of larceny (not attempt) though no sale.

DECEPTION (fraudulent debtor)

R v Humphris (1901-07) XX Cox CC 620; (1904) 68 JP 325; [1904] 2 KB 89; [1904] 73 LJCL 464; (1904) XC LTR 555; (1903-04) XX TLR 425; (1903-04) 52 WR 591 CCR Property of assignor passes to trusee when in possession of latter: properly convicted for absconding with assignor's property.

DECEPTION (fraudulent declaration on licence application)

Bloomfield v Williams [1970] Crim LR 292t; [1970] RTR 184 HC QBD Person who did not know that what were signing was false could not be guilty of false declaration.

DECEPTION (fraudulent inducement to invest)

R v Brown (Kevin) [1984] Crim LR 167; [1983] TLR 739 CA On whether conviction merited where different members of jury find accused guilty on different parts of the count.

DECEPTION (fraudulent misrepresentation)

Jewelowski v Propp [1944] 1 All ER 483; (1944) 171 LTR 234; (1943-44) LX TLR 559 HC KBD No duty to mitigate damages in fraudulent misrepresentation action.

DECEPTION (general)

R v Firth (Peter Stanley) (1990) 91 Cr App R 217; [1990] Crim LR 326; (1990) 154 JP 577 CA Could be guilty of evading liability by deception (under Theft Act 1978, s 2(1) (c)) before liability arose.

R v Hopley (Samuel) (1914-15) 11 Cr App R 248 CCA Inferring of intent to defraud from knowing use of forged instrument in course of bona fide claim.

DECEPTION (going equipped to cheat)

R v Corboz [1984] Crim LR 629; [1984] TLR 430 CA Doukas the relevant precedent in 'going equipped to cheat' cases.

DECEPTION (holy orders)

R v Else; R v Kemp (1964) 48 Cr App R 131; [1964] Crim LR 312t; (1964) 114 LJ 220; [1964] 2 QB 341; [1964] 2 WLR 648 CCA Intent to deceive necessary for offence of wilful pretence at being in Holy Orders (Marriage Act 1949, s 75(1) (d)).

DECEPTION (house-to-house collection)

Hankinson v Dowland [1974] Crim LR 539; (1974) 138 JP 795; (1974) 118 SJ 644 HC QBD On what constitutes an offence for purpose of House to House Collections Act 1939, s 11(1).

DECEPTION (immigration)

R v Gill [1976] 2 All ER 893; (1976) 140 JP 507; (1976) 120 SJ 316; [1977] 1 WLR 78 CA Immigrant's untruth to constable not false statement where constable not acting under Immigration Act.

DECEPTION (impersonation of police)

Turner v Shearer [1973] 1 All ER 397; (1973) 137 JP 191; (1972) 116 SJ 800; [1972] 1 WLR 1387 HC QBD Wearing uniform 'calculated to deceive' under Police Act 1964, s 52(2) means 'likely to deceive'.

DECEPTION (incitement to obtain property by deception/false pretences)

R v Shaw [1994] Crim LR 365 CA On mens rea of incitement to obtain property by deception.

DECEPTION (inducement to invest money)

Hughes v Trapnell; Trapnell v JR Berman, Ltd and another [1962] 3 All ER 616; (1963) 127 JP 1; (1962) 112 LJ 749; [1963] 1 QB 737; [1962] 3 WLR 1068 HC QBD Circulars not contrary to Prevention of Fraud (Investments) Act 1958, s 14 (1)(a) as only concerned with security not investment.

R v Bates and another [1952] 2 All ER 842; (1952) 36 Cr App R 175; (1952) 96 SJ 785; (1952) WN (I) 506 CCC 'Reckless' in Prevention of Fraud (Investments) Act 1939, s 12(1) has everyday meaning.

R v Clowes and another (No 2) [1994] 2 All ER 316 CCA Issue of legal relationship in investment scheme a matter of law; issue of dishonesty a matter of fact.

R v Delmayne [1969] 2 All ER 980; (1969) 53 Cr App R 392; [1969] Crim LR 485; (1969) 133 JP 458; (1969) 119 NLJ 676t; [1970] 2 QB 170; (1969) 113 SJ 605; [1969] 3 WLR 300 CA Pamphlets issued to mutual benefit society members was advertisement to public.

R v Mackinnon and others [1958] 3 All ER 657; (1959) 43 Cr App R 1; [1958] Crim LR 809; (1959) 123 JP 43; (1959) 109 LJ 8; [1959] 1 QB 150; (1958) 102 SJ 861 CCC For statement/forecast to be reckless must not matter to maker whether true/false.

R v Markus [1974] 3 All ER 705; [1976] AC 35 (also HL); [1974] Crim LR 603t; (1975) 139 JP 19; (1974) 118 SJ 809; [1974] 3 WLR 645 CA Can be guilty of inducing other 'to...offer to take part' and 'to take part...in' course of action and can be guilty of doing so in England even if did so from abroad.

R v Seelig and another [1991] 4 All ER 429; (1992) 94 Cr App R 17; (1991) 141 NLJ 638; [1992] 1 WLR 148 CA Evidence given/confession made to Department of Trade and Industry inspectors admissible in later criminal proceedings against person questioned.

Secretary of State for Trade v Markus [1975] 1 All ER 958; [1976] AC 35 (also CA); (1975) 61 Cr App R 58; [1975] Crim LR 716; (1975) 139 JP 301; (1975) 119 SJ 271; [1975] 2 WLR 708 HL Can be guilty of inducing other 'to...offer to take part' and 'to take part...in' course of action and can be guilty of doing so in England even if did so from abroad.

DECEPTION (insurance fraud)

R v Thompson (Graham Frederick) (1978) 66 Cr App R 130 CA Suspended nine months' imprisonment sentence for fraud on insurance company; forfeiture order quashed where money obtained by fraud repaid and property in respect of which claim made not in possession/control when arrested.

DECEPTION (making false statement)

Lawrence v MAFF [1992] Crim LR 874 HC QBD Offence of making false statement is complete when intended recipient receives it.

DECEPTION (obtaining by deception/false pretences)

Barrette v Le Syndicat Lyonnais du Klondyke (1906-07) XXIII TLR 532 PC Dismissal of appeal where allegedly fraudulent misrepresentations central to case were unproven.

Bogdal v Hall [1987] Crim LR 500 HC QBD On proving receipt of supplementary benefit in cases where alleged that obtained same by deception.

Comer v Bloomfield (1971) 55 Cr App R 305; [1971] Crim LR 230; [1971] RTR 49 CA Letter of inquiry to insurance company (preliminary to unmade false claim) not attempted obtaining of property by deception.

Coyne v Ward [1962] Crim LR 169t HC QBD Comparison of/contrast between larceny by trick and obtaining by false pretences.

Davies v Flackett [1972] Crim LR 708t; (1972) 122 NLJ 537t; [1973] RTR 8; (1972) 116 SJ 526 HC QBD Not obtaining property by deception where had exited pay-car park without paying when presented with sudden opportunity on leaving.

Director of Public Prosecutions v Ray [1973] 3 All ER 131; [1974] AC 370; (1974) 58 Cr App R 130; (1973) 137 JP 744; (1973) 117 SJ 663; [1973] 3 WLR 359 HL Person deciding not to pay only after ordering meal obtains pecuniary advantage by deception: regard to be had to all of behaviour in restaurant.

Director of Public Prosecutions v Stonehouse [1977] 2 All ER 909; [1978] AC 55; (1977) 65 Cr App R 192 (also CCA); [1977] Crim LR 544; (1977) 141 JP 473; (1977) 127 NLJ 864; (1977) 121 SJ 491; [1977] 3 WLR 143 HL Guilty of obtaining property by deception where acts done abroad but property obtained by deception in England; doing all possible acts to obtain property by deception could sustain conviction for attempt thereof.

Director of Public Prosecutions v Turner [1973] 3 All ER 124; [1974] AC 357; (1973) 57 Cr App R 932; [1974] Crim LR 186; (1973) 137 JP 736; (1973) 123 NLJ 747t; (1973) 117 SJ 664; [1973] 3 WLR 352 HL That evaded debt proved obtained pecuniary advantage even if not so.

Fisher v Raven; Raven v Fisher [1963] 2 All ER 389; [1964] AC 210; (1963) 47 Cr App R 174; [1963] Crim LR 503; (1963) 127 JP 382; (1963) 113 LJ 332; (1963) 107 SJ 373; [1963] 2 WLR 1137 HL Accepting money in return for promise of services/goods not obtaining credit contrary to Debtors Act 1869 or Bankruptcy Act 1914.

Gardiner v Fudge [1954] Crim LR 210 HC QBD 'Obtaining' under Larceny Act 1916, s 32 meant obtaining property in goods, not (as here) merely possession of same.

Guildford v Lockyer [1975] Crim LR 235; (1975) 119 SJ 353 HC QBD Was not obtaining pecuniary advantage by deception for person in restaurant to sample food served which had not ordered and then not to pay for same.

Halstead v Patel [1972] 2 All ER 147; (1972) 56 Cr App R 334; [1972] Crim LR 235t; (1972) 136 JP 465; (1972) 116 SJ 218; [1972] 1 WLR 661 HC QBD Unless repayment of actual notes/coins obtained intended is intention to permanently deprive; honest intention to replace with reasonable expectation that could replace did not displace dishonesty.

Hickmott v Curd [1971] 2 All ER 1399; (1971) 55 Cr App R 461; (1971) 135 JP 519; [1972] Crim LR 484t; (1971) 115 SJ 526; [1971] 1 WLR 1221 HC QBD Charge containing errors but true as to substance of offence and means whereby effected and not embarrassing to accused was valid.

Holder v McCarthy (1918-21) XXVI Cox CC 314; [1918] 2 KB 309; (1918) WN (I) 149 HC KBD Receipt of old age pension by means of false representation.

Hudson v Bishop Cavanagh (Commodities) Ltd [1982] Crim LR 114; (1981) 131 NLJ 1238 HC QBD Conviction merited for mailing circulars in violation of Prevention of Fraud (Investments) Act 1958, s 14(1) albeit that circulars mailed to particular persons who answered newspaper advertisement.

Levene v Pearcey [1976] Crim LR 63 HC QBD Conviction of taxi-driver for deliberately misleading passenger into thinking that had to take longer journey because normal route obstructed.

Metropolitan Police Commissioner v Charles [1976] 3 All ER 112; [1977] AC 177; (1976) 63 Cr App R 252; [1977] Crim LR 615; (1976) 140 JP 531; (1976) 126 NLJ 936t; (1976) 120 SJ 588; [1976] 3 WLR 431 HL Acceptance of cheque and cheque card where drawer has no money in bank is obtaining pecuniary advantage by deception.

R v Abdullah [1982] Crim LR 122 CrCt On establishing forgery of Barclaycard; on when using forged Barclaycard to obtain goods could be obtaining property by deception.

R v Adams [1993] Crim LR 525; [1994] RTR 220; [1993] TLR 32 CA Interpretation of driver declaration form (completed when hiring car) a matter of fact for jury.

R v Alexander [1981] Crim LR 183 CA Obtaining void/voidable insurance policy was obtaining pecuniary advantage by deception.

R v Andrews and Hedges [1981] Crim LR 106 CA Failed prosecution for inducing creditor to wait for payment.

R v Armitage (John) (1909) 3 Cr App R 80; (1910) 74 JP 48 CCA Was adequate evidence of obtaining credit by fraud.

R v Ashgar [1973] Crim LR 701 CA On elements of obtaining cheques by deception (as here).

R v Aston; R v Hadley [1970] 3 All ER 1045; (1971) 55 Cr App R 48; [1971] Crim LR 98t; (1970) 120 NLJ 1016t; (1970) 114 SJ 906; [1970] 1 WLR 1584 CA Deception must induce person affected to do/not to do something so that debt is evaded/put off.

R v Atwal (Harkindel) [1989] Crim LR 293 CrCt On precise nature of offences committed where fraudulently obtained credit cards which intended to use for fraudulent ends.

R v Bagley (George Arthur) (1922-23) 17 Cr App R 162 CCA Lodging is not a chattel, money or valuable security for purpose of Larceny Act 1916, s 32.

R v Ball (1951-52) 35 Cr App R 24; (1951) 115 JP 210; [1951] 2 KB 109; (1951) 101 LJ 665; (1951) 95 SJ 239; (1951) WN (I) 130 CCA Is obtaining by false pretences to obtain property from person who does not own same but can transfer property therein.

R v Banaster (Michael) (1979) 68 Cr App R 272; [1979] RTR 113 CA Was obtaining property by deception for mini-cab to be described as airport taxi and for driver to take 'correct' fare from passenger as though was required fare.

R v Bancroft (Basil) (1909) 3 Cr App R 16; (1909-10) XXVI TLR 10 CCA Obtaining money for advertisements in publication which did not have bona fide intention of publishing was obtaining money by false pretences.

R v Barker (Charles Reginald) (1910) 5 Cr App R 283 CCA Promises as to future conduct adequate to sustain conviction for obtaining by false pretences.

R v Baxter [1971] 2 All ER 359; [1971] Crim LR 281t; (1971) 135 JP 345; (1971) 121 NLJ 130t; [1972] 1 QB 1; (1971) 115 SJ 246; [1971] 2 WLR 1138 CA English courts had jurisdiction in attempted obtaining by deception case where person mailed false pools claims from Northern Ireland to Liverpool.

R v Bevan (David John) (1987) 84 Cr App R 143; [1987] Crim LR 129 CA Was obtaining pecuniary advantage by deception triable in England to use cheques abroad in respect of English bank account that was overdrawn.

R v Boothby (Edwin) (1932-34) 24 Cr App R 112 CCA False pretences conviction quashed where had been questioned at trial on alleged false pretence post-dating that with which charged.

R v Brownlow (1910) 74 JP 240; (1909-10) XXVI TLR 345 CCA Must be intent to defraud to be guilty of obtaining credit under false pretences contrary to Debtors Act 1869, s 13(1).

R v Button [1900-03] All ER 1648; (1899-1901) XIX Cox CC 568; (1900) 35 LJ 458; [1900] 69 LJCL 901; (1900-01) LXXXIII LTR 288; [1900] 2 QB 597; (1899-1900) 44 SJ 659; (1899-1900) XVI TLR 525; (1900) WN (I) 176; (1899-1900) 48 WR 703 CCR Was attempting to obtain goods by false pretences to deliberately enter prize race under false name and so receive false handicap.

R v Callender [1992] 3 All ER 51; (1992) 95 Cr App R 210; [1992] Crim LR 591; (1992) 156 JP 903; (1992) 142 NLJ 716; [1993] QB 303; (1992) 136 SJ LB 112; [1992] TLR 178; [1992] 3 WLR 501 CA For purposes of Theft Act contract to provide services an employment contract.

R v Carpenter (1911-13) XXII Cox CC 618; (1912) 76 JP 158 CCC On what constitutes intent to defraud.

R v Chapman (Horace William) (1910) 4 Cr App R 276; (1910) 74 JP 360; (1910) 45 LJ 341; (1910) WN (I) 131 CCA Rail ticket a chattel that could be obtained by false pretences.

R v Charles [1976] 1 All ER 659; [1976] Crim LR 196t; (1976) 140 JP 254; (1976) 126 NLJ 14t; (1976) 120 SJ 147; [1976] 1 WLR 248 CA Unauthorised drawing of cheque is obtaining pecuniary advantage by deception.

R v Charlesworth (Miriam) and Charlesworth (May otherwise Violet) (1910) 4 Cr App R 167 CCA Could disprove defence of innocent belief by reference to earlier false representations.

R v Christian and another (1913-14) XXIII Cox CC 541; (1914) 78 JP 112 CCC Cannot be convicted of attempt to/conspiracy to/actual procuration where woman freely chooses to be at brothel.

R v Christou [1972] Crim LR 653; (1971) 115 SJ 687 CA Drawing by cheque on account into which paid useless cheques was obtaining property by false pretences.

R v Clarke (Victor) [1996] Crim LR 824 CA On dishonesty as an element of obtaining pecuniary advantage by deception.

R v Clow (1978) 128 NLJ 1029t CA Failure to prove property obtained by way of false representation fatal to conviction for obtaining property by deception.

R v Clucas [1949] 2 All ER 40; (1948-49) 33 Cr App R 136; [1949] 2 KB 226; (1949) 99 LJ 275; [1949] 118 LJR 1571; (1949) LXV TLR 346; (1949) WN (I) 252 CCA Not obtaining by false pretences to place winning bets under false pretext.

R v Coady [1996] Crim LR 518 CA Obtaining must result from deception to be guilty of obtaining (property) by deception (unlike here where obtained petrol, then effected deception - told attendant to charge cost to onetime employer though was not authorised to do so).

R v Coffey [1987] Crim LR 498 CA On mental element of offence of obtaining property by deception.

R v Collins (1921-25) XXVII Cox CC 322; (1922-23) 17 Cr App R 42; (1923) 87 JP 60; (1923) 128 LTR 31; (1922-23) 67 SJ 367 CCA Non-substitution of conviction for obtaining money by false pretences for one of larceny.

R v Collis-Smith [1972] Crim LR 716 CA Where petrol put in car and then driver made false representation as to mode of payment there was no obtaining of property by deception.

R v Cooke [1997] Crim LR 436 CA On ramifications of Preddy decision for Theft Act offences.

R v Cooke [1986] 2 All ER 985; [1986] AC 909; (1986) 83 Cr App R 339; [1987] Crim LR 114; (1986) 150 JP 498; (1986) 136 NLJ 730; (1970) 130 SJ 572; [1986] 3 WLR 327 HL Statutory conspiracy with presence of fraud can be charged as common law conspiracy; no false accounting where no deception and no fraud.

R v Cosnett (1901-07) XX Cox CC 6; (1901) LXXXIV LTR 800; (1900-01) 45 SJ 538; (1900-01) XVII TLR 524; (1900-01) 49 WR 633 CCR Obtaining goods upon presentation of false cheque is obtaining goods (not credit) by false pretences.

R v Crick and another [1993] TLR 465 CA Could be guilty of obtaining property by deception by way of electronic transfer from one account to another.

R v Crook (Thomas William Ireland) (1910) 4 Cr App R 60 CCA Intent to defraud where attempted to sell item obtained by false pretence.

R v Cummings-John [1997] Crim LR 660 CA Mortgage fraudsters found guilty of obtaining services by deception under the Theft Act 1978, s 1(1).

R v Dalgleish [1963] Crim LR 350 Sessions Failed prosecution for procuring another to pay money to third party by paying cheque to former with intent to defraud (insufficient connection between original cheque payment and later payment to third party).

R v Dalton-Brockwell [1969] Crim LR 329 CA On proving that false pretence was in fact the/a cause of the obtaining where person charged with obtaining by false pretences.

R v Davies (Arthur) [1982] Crim LR 458 CA Was obtaining property by deception to present cheques to bank for payment after fraudulently induced cheque account holder to indorse cheque.

R v Dawson; R v Wenlock [1960] 1 All ER 558; (1960) 44 Cr App R 87; [1960] Crim LR 358; (1960) 110 LJ 236; (1960) 104 SJ 191; [1960] 1 WLR 163 CCA Conspiracy charge unnecessary in light of substantive charges; bankruptcy examination inadmissible at trial for fraudulent conversion; where alternative counts should be convicted on one of which most certainly guilty; non-delivery post-sale not an obtaining of credit by fraud.

R v Deller (Charles Avon) (1952) 36 Cr App R 184; (1952) 102 LJ 679 CCA Court could look to real and not apparent situation where alleged sale of car by false pretences was claimed to be one of loan on the security of the car.

R v Dent [1955] 2 All ER 806; (1955) 39 Cr App R 131; [1955] Crim LR 501; (1955) 119 JP 512; (1955) 105 LJ 473; [1955] 2 QB 590; [1955] 99 SJ 511; [1955] 3 WLR 297 CCA Statement about intended future conduct cannot be false pretence.

R v Doukas [1978] 1 All ER 1061; (1978) 66 Cr App R 228; [1978] Crim LR 177; (1978) 142 JP 254; (1978) 128 NLJ 34t; (1978) 122 SJ 30; [1978] 1 WLR 372 CA If hypothetical customer would not have agreed to fraud can be conviction for obtaining property by deception.

R v Dunleavey (Edward) (1908) 1 Cr App R 240 CCA Must prove guilty knowledge beyond reasonable doubt to sustain conviction for obtaining by false pretences.

R v Duru and others [1973] 3 All ER 715; (1974) 58 Cr App R 151; (1974) 118 SJ 7; [1974] 1 WLR 2 CA That cheques returned/money would eventually be returned/cheques paid to third party for benefit of another not defence to obtaining property by deception.

R v Eaton (1966) 50 Cr App R 189; [1966] Crim LR 333t; (1965-66) 116 NLJ 754; (1966) 110 SJ 329 CCA Person could not pass title in approbated property unless had met the requirements of the relevant approbation note.

R v Edwards [1978] Crim LR 49 CA Squatter who charged rent to another for portion of property could be guilty of (here attempted) obtaining of rent by deception.

R v Ellis (1911-13) XXII Cox CC 330; [1910] 2 KB 746; (1910) 102 LTR 922; (1909-10) XXVI TLR 535 CCA Evidence showing generally fraudulent character inadmissible in prosecution for obtaining by false pretences.

R v Ewing (Terence Patrick) (1977) 65 Cr App R 4 CA Advance rent/refundable deposit were debts/charges for purposes of Theft Act 1968, s 16.

R v Fazackerley [1973] 2 All ER 819; (1973) 57 Cr App R 578; [1973] Crim LR 368; (1973) 137 JP 590; (1973) 123 NLJ 369t; (1973) 117 SJ 303; [1973] 1 WLR 632 CA Need not be cancelling/forgiving of debts when invalid cheque presented to obtain advantage by deception.

R v Fisher (1911-13) XXII Cox CC 270; (1910) 74 JP 104; [1910] 1 KB 149; (1910) 79 LJKB 187; (1910) 102 LTR 111; (1909) WN (I) 252 CCA Evidence of earlier false pretences admissible at trial for false pretences if shows system of false pretences - not if simply shows fraudulent character.

R v Fisher [1963] 1 All ER 744; (1963) 107 SJ 177 CCA Accepting money in return for promise of services/goods is/is not obtaining credit contrary to Debtors Act 1869/Bankruptcy Act 1914.

R v Fisher (Edward) (1910) 5 Cr App R 102; (1910-11) 103 LTR 320 CCA On whether obtaining goods by virtue of fraud is larceny/obtaining by false pretences/conspiracy to defraud.

R v Fisher (Florence Sarah) (1921-22) 16 Cr App R 53; (1921) 56 LJ 448; [1922] 91 LJCL 145; (1921-22) 66 SJ 109; (1921) WN (I) 327 CCA Where acquitted of obtaining by false pretences contrary to Larceny Act 1916, s 44(3), could not be convicted of larceny CCA cannot substitute conviction with one in respect of which have been acquitted.

R v Fisher (George Samuel) (1975) 60 Cr App R 225; [1975] Crim LR 162t; (1975) 125 NLJ 68t CA Where cheque made out by 'victim' in favour of company prosecution must show company made false pretence and accused aided and abetted same to secure false pretences conviction of accused.

R v Garlick (Frederick William) (1957) 41 Cr App R 141 CCA Obtaining credit by fraud convictions quashed where actus reus missing.

R v Garrett, ex parte Sharf and others (1917) 81 JP 145 (also HC KBD) CA No appeal to CA from KBD decision that persons on vessel detained for search for contraband could in time of war be arrested for alleged obtaining of passport by false statement.

R v Garrett; ex parte Sharf and others (1917) 81 JP 145 (also CA); (1917) 116 LTR 82; (1916-17) XXXIII TLR 188 HC KBD Persons on vessel detained for search for contraband could in time of war be arrested for alleged obtaining of passport by false statement.

R v Gilmartin [1983] 1 All ER 829; (1983) 76 Cr App R 238; [1983] Crim LR 330; (1983) 147 JP 183; [1983] QB 953; (1983) 127 SJ 119; [1982] TLR 613; [1983] 2 WLR 547 CA Giving of postdated cheque implies that will be met for payment on/after date on cheque.

R v Governor of Brixton Prison; ex parte Sjoland and Metzler (1913) 77 JP 23; [1912] 3 KB 568; (1912) 47 LJ 648; [1913] 82 LJKB 5; (1912-13) XXIX TLR 10; (1912) WN (I) 237 HC KBD Parties to three card trick pretending to be winners so as to induce another to play are not obtaining money by false pretences.

R v Greenstein; R v Green [1976] 1 All ER 1; (1975) 61 Cr App R 296; [1975] Crim LR 714t; (1975) 119 SJ 742; [1975] 1 WLR 1353 CA Guilt of dishonesty a matter for jury.

R v Grosvenor (1914-15) XXIV Cox CC 468; (1914) 10 Cr App R 235; (1914-15) 111 LTR 1116 CCA Is conspiracy to defraud though acquired no money/made no false pretence; both parties liable to conviction for obtaining money by false pretences where obtain money following jointly executed false pretence; is false pretences by conduct where implicitly agree to making of false pretence.

R v Halai [1983] Crim LR 624 CA Case of obtaining services in connection with mortgage by deception.

R v Hamer [1954] Crim LR 209 Assizes Must be obtaining credit for self to be guilty of obtaining credit by false pretences.

R v Hamilton (1991) 92 Cr App R 54; [1990] Crim LR 806; (1991) 155 JP 264; [1990] TLR 583 CA Withdrawing money which withdrawer had paid into bank account by means of forged cheques was obtaining property by deception.

R v Harris (Paul Andrew) (1976) 62 Cr App R 28; [1976] Crim LR 514 CA Giving fake identity and telling untrue story in bid to get hotel room was attempted obtaining of pecuniary advantage by deception not just preparatory steps.

R v Hickson (Isaac) (1921-22) 16 Cr App R 47 CCA Twelve months' hard labour for false pretences/conspiracy offences (reduced from three years' penal servitude as co-prisoners' sentences reduced).

R v Hircock (William Roy) (1978) 67 Cr App R 278; [1979] Crim LR 184 CA Could be guilty of theft and obtaining property by deception in respect of same property.

R v Hurford; R v Williams [1963] 2 All ER 254; (1963) 47 Cr App R 141; [1963] Crim LR 432; (1963) 127 JP 374; (1963) 113 LJ 382; [1963] 2 QB 398; (1963) 107 SJ 275; [1963] 2 WLR 1038 CCA Forging signature on document that instigates eventual obtaining of property is obtaining property with forged instrument.

R v Ingram [1956] 2 All ER 639; (1956) 40 Cr App R 115; [1956] Crim LR 565; (1956) 120 JP 397; (1956) 106 LJ 442; [1956] 2 QB 424; (1956) 100 SJ 491; [1956] 3 WLR 309 CCA Taking advance payments on foot of promised services is obtaining credit by fraud.

R v Jakeman (1914-15) XXIV Cox CC 153; (1914) 10 Cr App R 38; (1914) 110 LTR 833 CCA Failed prosecution for obtaining cheque by false pretences where pigs sold were not own as claimed but delivered straight from farmers.

R v Jeff; R v Bassett [1967] Crim LR 46t; (1965-66) 116 NLJ 1489; (1967) 111 SJ 53 CA On whether false pretences conviction valid (here was) where part-based on representation alleged to be opinion.

R v Johl [1994] Crim LR 522 CA On what constitutes a valuable security: telegraphic transfer of funds is not (even if it was 'execution' of same could not be established).

R v Johnson [1963] 3 All ER 577; (1964) 48 Cr App R 25; (1963) 127 JP 556; (1963) 113 LJ 752; [1964] 2 QB 404; (1963) 107 SJ 1042; [1963] 3 WLR 1031 CCA Must prove unlawful intercourse/intention of same for procuring/attempted procuring of third party sex with under-21 year old.

R v Johnson (Violet) (1920-21) 15 Cr App R 55 CCA Nine months' imprisonment in second division for obtaining by false pretences of woman acting under influence of man with whom lived.

R v Johnson (William) (1910-11) 6 Cr App R 82 CCA Party to be jointly guilty of obtaining by false pretences must be clearly shown to have acted in concert.

R v Jones (Ivor) [1993] TLR 72 CA Milkman who consistently and determinedly overcharged for milk deliveries for years was guilty of obtaining property by deception.

R v Kassim [1991] 3 All ER 713; [1992] 1 AC 9; (1991) 93 Cr App R 391; (1992) 156 JP 157; (1991) 141 NLJ 1038t; (1991) 141 NLJ 1072; (1991) 135 SJ LB 101; [1991] TLR 351; [1991] 3 WLR 254 HL Execution of valuable security by deception requires acts be done to/regarding security, not just that its instructions be followed.

R v King and another [1987] 1 All ER 547; (1987) 84 Cr App R 357; [1987] Crim LR 398; (1987) 151 JP 559; [1987] QB 547; (1987) 131 SJ 325; [1987] 2 WLR 746 CA Deception must be core element of obtaining property before property obtained by deception.

R v King and others [1991] 3 All ER 705; (1991) 93 Cr App R 259; [1991] Crim LR 906; (1991) 141 NLJ 1071; [1992] QB 20; (1991) 135 SJ LB 76; [1991] 3 WLR 246 CA Clearing house automated payment system a valuable security executed when signed by bank officials.

R v Kovacs [1974] 1 All ER 1236; (1974) 58 Cr App R 412; [1974] Crim LR 183t; (1974) 138 JP 425; (1974) 124 NLJ 36t; (1974) 118 SJ 116; [1974] 1 WLR 370 CA Person deceived need not directly suffer loss to sustain conviction for obtaining pecuniary advantage by deception.

R v Kritz [1949] 2 All ER 406; [1950] 1 KB 82; [1949] 118 LJR 1535; (1949) LXV TLR 505; (1949) WN (I) 374 CCA R v Carpenter (1911) direction on intent to defraud was ideal direction.

R v Laker (Herbert William) (1949-50) 34 Cr App R 36 CCA Bankrupt's taking cheque from person for one purpose and using for another not obtaining credit by fraud contrary to Bankruptcy Act 1914, s 156(a).

R v Lambie [1981] 1 All ER 332; (1980) 71 Cr App R 350; [1980] Crim LR 725; (1980) 124 SJ 808; [1981] 1 WLR 78 CA Use of credit card over limit not false representation to shop assistant to obtain advantage by deception.

R v Lambie [1981] 2 All ER 776; [1982] AC 449; (1981) 73 Cr App R 294; [1981] Crim LR 712; (1981) 145 JP 364; (1980) 130 NLJ 908; (1981) 131 NLJ 725; (1981) 125 SJ 480; [1981] 3 WLR 88 HL Presentation of credit card not representation that had requisite credit standing.

R v Landow (Marks) (1913-14) XXIII Cox CC 457; (1913) 77 JP 364; (1913-14) 109 LTR 48; (1912-13) XXIX TLR 375 CCA Failed prosecution for attempt to procure wife to become brothel-prostitute outside Empire.

R v Lartey (Mensah) and Relevy [1996] 1 Cr App R 143; [1996] Crim LR 203 CA On elements of offence of procuring execution of valuable security by deception.

R v Laverty [1970] 3 All ER 432; (1970) 54 Cr App R 495; [1971] Crim LR 100; [1971] RTR 124; (1970) 134 JP 699 CA Prosecution must show that false representation induced purchaser's behaviour.

R v Lawrence (James) (1909) 2 Cr App R 42 CCA Obtaining by false pretences by means of deceitful promotional pamphlet and postcard.

R v Leach (William Robert) (1928-29) 21 Cr App R 44 CCA Falseness is the essence of obtaining by false pretences.

R v Lewis (Joseph George) (1976) 62 Cr App R 206; [1976] Crim LR 383t CA Gauging dishonesty for purposes of Theft Act 1968 a subjective test.

R v Lightfoot (Richard James) (1993) 97 Cr App R 24; [1993] Crim LR 137; (1993) 157 JP 265 CA Was dishonest intent to do what reasonable people would regard as dishonest.

R v Locker [1971] 2 All ER 875; (1971) 55 Cr App R 375; [1971] Crim LR 422t; (1971) 135 JP 437; (1971) 121 NLJ 319t; [1971] 2 QB 321; (1971) 115 SJ 346; [1971] 2 WLR 1302 CA On elements of offence of obtaining pecuniary advantage by deception.

R v Lurie [1951] 2 All ER 704; (1951-52) 35 Cr App R 113; (1951) 115 JP 551; (1951) 101 LJ 511; (1951) 95 SJ 580; [1951] 2 TLR 686 CCA Not obtaining where possess property but are obtaining for another.

R v Manjadria and another [1993] Crim LR 73 CA On proving execution of valuable security in context of mortgage fraud.

R v Marck (Henry William) (1928-29) 21 Cr App R 65 CCA Intent to defraud is an essential ingredient of obtaining by false pretences.

R v Matthews (Albert Edward) (1958) 42 Cr App R 93 CMAC Properly convicted of knowingly making false/fraudulent statement where signed one's name to blank form knowing another would complete it falsely.

R v Maytum-White (Leslie Percy) (1958) 42 Cr App R 165; [1957] Crim LR 806 CCA Was obtaining by false pretences to make out postdated cheque for tickets albeit in anticipation that money would be in bank when cheque presented.

R v McCall (Paul Richard) (1971) 55 Cr App R 175; [1971] Crim LR 237; (1971) 115 SJ 75 CA Is obtaining property by deception to secure loan on basis of false representation - intention to repay no defence.

R v McHugh (David) (1977) 64 Cr App R 92; [1977] Crim LR 174t; (1977) 127 NLJ 44t; [1977] RTR 1 CA Whether driving away from petrol station without paying for petrol was theft/obtaining pecuniary advantage by deception.

R v McNiff [1986] Crim LR 57 CA Tenancy of public house not an 'office' and even if was, application for same is not application for payment so falsehoods in tennacy application not obtaining pecuniary advantage by deception.

R v Melwani [1989] Crim LR 565 CA Matter for jury whether behaviour that could be described as dishonest was in fact dishonest.

R v Metcalfe [1963] Crim LR 502g CCA Evidence of bank manager as to previous dishonoured cheques of accused admissible where charged with obtaining goods by false pretences (using cheque that knew was likely to bounce).

R v Miller (Steven Henry) (1992) 95 Cr App R 421; [1992] Crim LR 744; [1993] RTR 6 CA Need only show that deceptions resulted in money being handed over (need not show deception at precise instant handed over money) to convict for obtaining property by deception.

R v Mitchell [1955] 3 All ER 263; (1955) 39 Cr App R 49; [1955] Crim LR 246; (1955) 119 JP 563; (1955) 105 LJ 682; (1955) 99 SJ 764; [1955] 1 WLR 1125 CCA Non-creation of debt meant no credit obtained so no obtaining thereof by fraud.

R v Mitchell [1993] Crim LR 788 CA On nature of offence of obtaining cheque by deception.

R v Moore [1986] Crim LR 552 CA Withdrawal slip completed in name of non-existent person was a forgery; person guilty of obtaining property by deception where intended to retain cheque had dishonestly obtained.

R v Moreton [1911-13] All ER 699; (1913-14) XXIII Cox CC 560; (1913-14) 109 LTR 417 CCA Obtaining goods under contract induced by (continuing) fraud is obtaining goods by false pretences.

R v Muirhead (James) (1908) 1 Cr App R 189; (1909) 73 JP 31; (1908-09) 53 SJ 164; (1908-09) XXV TLR 88 CCA Intent to defraud necessary to sustain conviction of obtaining credit by false pretences contrary to Debtors Act 1869, s 13(1).

R v Nathan (Nathaniel) and Harris (Edward) (1909) 2 Cr App R 35 CCA Fraudulent statements precluded defence of 'puffing' - on limits of praise.

DECEPTION (obtaining by deception/false pretences)

R v Naviede [1997] Crim LR 662 CA On whether (in light of Halai decision) credit facilities could be regarded as services.

R v Newton and Bennett (1913-14) XXIII Cox CC 609; (1913-14) 109 LTR 747 CCA Test of admissibility of evidence on value of property subject of false pretences claim.

R v Nordeng (Jarl) (1976) 62 Cr App R 123; [1976] Crim LR 194t; (1976) 126 NLJ 41t CA Is obtaining pecuniary advantage by deception to obtain services of hotel and have it charged to third party.

R v O'Connell (Michael John) (1992) 94 Cr App R 39; [1991] Crim LR 771; (1991) 135 SJ LB 53; [1991] TLR 284 CA That intended to repay money loaned under deception not a defence but was evidence of honesty.

R v Okanta [1997] Crim LR 451 CA Court would not submit conviction for furnishing false information instead of (quashed) obtaining property by deception conviction following on mortgage fraud.

R v Page [1971] 2 All ER 870; (1971) 55 Cr App R 184; [1971] Crim LR 425; (1971) 135 JP 376; [1971] 2 QB 330; (1971) 115 SJ 385; [1971] 2 WLR 1308 CA Can evade a debt which continues to exist despite evasion.

R v Paynter (1908) 1 Cr App R 253; (1908-09) XXV TLR 191 CCA Was obtaining by false pretences for fraudster to retain deposits of people whom tricked when they had not applied for return of same (as had been stipulated in dealings with them).

R v Plunkett [1973] Crim LR 367 CA Was obtaining pecuniary advantage by deception to seek to settle debts using false cheques.

R v Potger (Christopher Granville Louis) (1971) 55 Cr App R 42 CA On meaning of 'dishonestly' in Theft Act 1968, ss 15 and 16.

R v Potter and another [1958] 2 All ER 51; (1958) 122 JP 234; (1958) 42 Cr App R 168; [1958] Crim LR 472; [1958] 1 WLR 638 Assizes Where party sits driving test for another both are guilty of procuring with intent to defraud; in signing for licence former guilty of forgery; in seeking thereon latter uttering forged document.

R v Preddy; R v Slade [1995] Crim LR 564 CA Was obtaining property by deception (under Theft Act 1968, s 15(1)) to fraudulently obtain advances from building societies/other financial institutions by way of cheque/computer transfer.

R v Preddy; R v Slade; R v Dhillon [1996] 3 All ER 481; [1996] AC 815; [1996] 2 Cr App R 524; [1996] Crim LR 726; (1996) 146 NLJ 1057; (1996) 140 SJ LB 184; [1996] 3 WLR 255 HL Not obtaining property by deception (under Theft Act 1968, s 15(1)) to fraudulently obtain advances from building societies/other financial institutions by way of cheque/computer transfer.

R v Price (Ronald William) (1990) 90 Cr App R 409; [1990] Crim LR 200 CA R v Ghosh direction on dishonesty does not have to be given in every case in which dishonesty arises.

R v Rashid [1977] 2 All ER 237; (1977) 64 Cr App R 201; [1977] Crim LR 237; (1977) 141 JP 305; (1976) 120 SJ 856; [1977] 1 WLR 298 CA Intent to deceive not enough; intent to successfully deceive necessary to sustain obtaining property by deception charge.

R v Renton (Ralph) (1925-26) 19 Cr App R 33 CCA Must be intent to defraud for there to be obtaining by false pretences.

R v Rowland (Harry) (1911-13) XXII Cox CC 273; (1909) 3 Cr App R 277; (1910) 102 LTR 112; (1909-10) XXVI TLR 202 CCA Accused giving evidence for other accused can be questioned on own guilt; previous convictions involving fraud/dishonesty admissible in receiving prosecution where stolen property in accused's possession though not at time of arrest; can be convicted as habitual criminal though no evidence as to behaviour in half-year prior to conviction.

R v Royle [1971] 3 All ER 1359; (1972) 56 Cr App R 131; [1972] Crim LR42t; (1972) 136 JP 106; (1971) 121 NLJ 1026t; (1971) 115 SJ 910; [1971] 1 WLR 1764 CA Honest belief that hotel bills would be paid meant no dishonest intent; must be personally liable for debt to sustain conviction; that the debts might be discharged could be relevant to intent/dishonesty.

R v Rozeik [1996] 3 All ER 281; [1996] 1 Cr App R 260; [1996] Crim LR 271; (1995) 139 SJ LB 219; [1995] TLR 551; [1996] 1 WLR 159 CA Company not deceived where branch managers not deceived so person ought not to have been convicted of obtaining property (cheques from finance company) by deception.

R v Sagar (1914-15) XXIV Cox CC 500; (1915) 79 JP 32; [1914] 3 KB 1112; (1915) 112 LTR 135 CCA Admissibility of receipts for goods legitimately sold to accused admissible as defence evidence in obtaining money by false pretences charge.

R v Sanders [1918-23] All ER 141; (1918-21) XXVI Cox CC 390; [1919] 1 KB 550; [1919] 88 LJCL 982; (1919) 120 LTR 573 CCA Knowingly giving false warranty to induce payment of money was obtaining by false pretences.

R v Seely (Roger George) (1928-29) 21 Cr App R 18 CCA On falseness of words necessary to support obtaining by false pretences conviction.

R v Shortland [1996] 1 Cr App R 116; [1995] Crim LR 893; [1995] TLR 304 CA Could not presume that banking facilities would be subject of charge (and so that opening of accounts under false name was obtaining of services by deception).

R v Silverman [1987] Crim LR 574; (1987) 151 JP 657 CA On elements of offence of obtaining property by deception; records of police interviews are evidence of the facts contained therein.

R v Singh (Gurmit) [1965] 3 All ER 384; [1965] Crim LR 718; (1965) 129 JP 578; [1966] 2 WLR 88 Assizes On attempted committing of offence.

R v Skinner (Joseph Herbert) (1920-21) 15 Cr App R 114 CCA False signing of declaration without which could not have obtained money was false pretence.

R v Smith (1901-07) XX Cox CC 804; (1905) XCII LTR 208 CCR Acts subsequent to those with which charged admissible in false pretences prosecution if relevant (even if point to guilt of offence separate to that with which charged).

R v Smith (Albert William) (1914-15) 11 Cr App R 81 CCA Agreeing to pay rent in future in set amounts was obtaining credit for purpose of Bankruptcy and Deeds of Arrangement Act 1913.

R v Steel (Alfred) (1910) 5 Cr App R 289 CCA On fraud amounting to false pretence justifying conviction for obtaining credit by fraud.

R v Stoddart (1909) 73 JP 348; (1908-09) 53 SJ 578 CCA Is obtaining by false pretences in this jurisdiction to induce another by false pretences to mail money here to place abroad, there to be received by fraudster.

R v Stonehouse (John Thomson) (1977) 65 Cr App R 192 (also HL) CA Guilty of obtaining property by deception where acts done abroad but property obtained by deception in England.

R v Stones (George Kenneth) (1968) 52 Cr App R 36; [1967] Crim LR 708t; (1967) 117 NLJ 1112t; (1967) 111 SJ 832 CA Successful prosecution for causing cheque to be delivered for own use/benefit (Larceny Act 1916, s 32(1)).

R v Strong (1965-66) 116 NLJ 1573t CA Successful appeal against conviction for obtaining money by false pretences where never proved had made fraudulent misrepresentation of fact rather than false statement of intent/had been misdirection as to elements of offence.

R v Sullivan (John James) (1943-45) 30 Cr App R 132 CCA Valid conviction for obtaining property by false pretences though no evidence as to inducing effect of false pretences.

R v Talbott [1995] Crim LR 396 CA Valid conviction for obtaining property by deception (obtained housing benefit on foot of false statement).

R v Taylor (1900-01) 45 SJ 538; (1900-01) XVII TLR 523; (1900-01) 49 WR 671 CCR Society officer's deceit to obtain money ostensibly due to another member could be prosecuted for obtaining by false pretences.

R v Thompson (Harry) (1910) 5 Cr App R 9 CCA Was obtaining credit other than by false pretences to obtain goods without intending to pay for same.

R v Thompson (Michael) (1984) 79 Cr App R 191; [1984] Crim LR 427; (1984) 128 SJ 447; [1984] 1 WLR 962 CA Where monies telexed to English accounts on foot of computer fraudulently programmed abroad was obtaining property by deception in England; credit balance resulting from fraud not a chose in action.

R v Thornton [1963] 1 All ER 170; (1963) 47 Cr App R 1; [1963] Crim LR 197; (1963) 127 JP 113; (1963) 113 LJ 90; [1964] 2 QB 176; [1963] 3 WLR 444 CCA Not guilty of fraudulently inducing signature to security where do not impose any liability on another party but can be guilty of obtaining credit by fraud.

R v Tirado (Emilio) (1974) 59 Cr App R 80 CA Was obtaining property by deception in England to accept drafts from abroad and cash them in England.

R v Turner [1973] 2 All ER 828; (1973) 57 Cr App R 650; [1973] Crim LR 370t; (1973) 123 NLJ 494t; (1973) 117 SJ 303; [1973] 1 WLR 653 CA Giving worthless cheque for pre-existing debt not obtaining advantage by deception.

R v Waites [1982] Crim LR 369 CA Running up unauthorised overdraft by way of cheques was obtaining pecuniary advantage by deception.

R v Waterfall [1969] 3 All ER 1048; (1969) 53 Cr App R 597; [1970] Crim LR 34; (1970) 134 JP 1; [1970] 1 QB 148; (1969) 113 SJ 872; [1969] 3 WLR 947 CA Dishonest belief necessary for obtaining by deception.

R v Watkins [1976] 1 All ER 578; (1976) 140 JP 197 CrCt Granting of overdraft after false representation is obtaining pecuniary advantage by deception.

R v Weeks (Charles Frederick) (1927-28) 20 Cr App R 188 CCA Conviction for obtaining money by false pretences quashed where issue of character improperly raised.

R v Wilson (Alfred John) (1910-11) 6 Cr App R 207 CCA Sheer volume of accident claims was evidence were bogus.

R v Woolven (Jonathan Robert) (1983) 77 Cr App R 231; [1983] Crim LR 623; [1983] TLR 405 CA On inclusion of claim of right direction when directing jury on what dishonesty (in Theft Act 1968, s 2(1) (a)) means.

R v Wright [1960] Crim LR 366 CCA To be guilty of obtaining by false pretences must act with intention to defraud (must be dishonest).

R v Young; R v Kassim [1988] Crim LR 372; (1988) 152 JP 405 CA On what constitutes 'execution' of valuable security by deception (Theft Act 1968, s 20(2)).

Ray v Sempers [1973] 1 All ER 860; (1973) 57 Cr App R 324; [1973] Crim LR 182; (1973) 137 JP 329; (1973) 123 NLJ 16t; (1973) 117 SJ 124; [1973] 1 WLR 317 HC QBD Unless false representation cannot be deception.

Ray v Sempers [1974] Crim LR 181 HL Was obtaining pecuniary advantage by deception to enter restaurant with intention of paying for meal but to then change one's mind and dash off without paying.

Richardson v Skells [1976] Crim LR 448 CrCt Was obtaining pecuniary advantage by deception to secure free travel on train for another by virtue of the deception.

Smith v Koumourou [1979] Crim LR 116; [1979] RTR 355 HC QBD Was obtaining pecuniary advantage by deception where driver without excise licence displayed undated police receipt for earlier expired licence to avoid non-payment of duty being discovered and so avoid paying excise duty.

Tolfree v Florence (1970) 114 SJ 930 HC QBD Valid conviction for making false representation for the purpose of obtaining sickness benefit.

Wells v Smith [1914] 83 LJKB 1614; (1913-14) XXX TLR 623 HC KBD Person knowingly making false statement to another unaware of untruthfulness with intention of seeking latter to act on untruth cannot later plead that latter's agent knew was untruth as defence.

DECEPTION (possession of changed passport)

Chajutin v Whitehead [1938] 1 KB 506; (1938) 85 LJ 87; [1938] 107 LJCL 270 HC KBD Offence of possessing altered passport requires no mens rea, merely actus reus.

DECEPTION (pretending to be solicitor)

Carter v Butcher [1965] Crim LR 247g HC QBD Valid conviction for wilful pretence of being qualified to work as solicitor.

Law Society v United Services Bureau Limited (1934) 98 JP 33; (1933) 76 LJ 321; (1934) 103 LJCL 81; (1934) 150 LTR 159; (1933) 77 SJ 815; (1933) WN (I) 263 HC KBD Corporate body could not be guilty of wilfully pretending to be solicitor under Solicitors Act 1932, s 46.

DECEPTION (theft)

R v Hircock (William Roy) (1978) 67 Cr App R 278; [1979] Crim LR 184 CA Could be guilty of theft and obtaining property by deception in respect of same property.

DECEPTION (theft in breach of trust)

R v Pearlberg and O'Brien [1982] Crim LR 829 CrCt 100% shareholders could not be guilty of theft from companies of which were 100% shareholders.

DECEPTION (train/tram fare)

Bastable v Metcalfe (1906) 70 JP 343 HC KBD Getting off one tram and getting on another without buying new ticket (even though had not travelled full distance on first ticket) was a fare offence.

Hunt v Green (1907-09) XXI Cox CC 333; (1907) 71 JP 18; (1907) XCVI LTR 23 HC KBD Passenger need not be asked to deliver up ticket to contravene by-law concerning payment of fares.

Tuffley v Tate (1907-09) XXI Cox CC 337; (1907) 71 JP 21; (1907) XCVI LTR 24 HC KBD By-law requiring full fare where had no ticket was valid.

DECEPTION (unlawful obtaining of benefit)

Barrass v Reeve [1981] Crim LR 417 HC QBD Making of any false representation in connection with obtaining of benefit (albeit that lie not directed towards obtaining of money) was unlawful obtaining of benefit.

DECEPTION (unlicensed credit broker)

R v Marshall (Roy) (1990) 90 Cr App R 73 CA No distinction between unlicensed credit transactions initiated by customer/seller: only distinguish between regular/occasional transactions.

DECEPTION (unlicensed deposit-taking)

Attorney-General's Reference (No 1 of 1995) (B and F) [1996] 4 All ER 21; [1996] 2 Cr App R 320; [1996] Crim LR 575; (1996) TLR 30/1/96; [1996] 1 WLR 970 CA On mens rea necessary to suupport conviction of director for unlicensed acceptance of deposits.

DEFENCES (alibi)

Comptroller of Customs v Western Electric Co, Ltd [1965] 3 All ER 599; [1966] AC 367; (1965) 109 SJ 873; [1965] 3 WLR 1229 PC Making false customs entry an absolute offence; dispute over country of origin not one of 'whence...goods brought'; admission revealing no more than marks proves no more than marks.

R v Armstrong [1995] TLR 261 CA Prosecution ought (upon defendant's request) to have been required to read portion of prosecution witness statement that confirmed alibi notice of defendant.

R v Ashman [1954] Crim LR 382t CCA Conviction quashed where inter alia inadequate attention paid to alibi evidence.

R v Blick [1966] Crim LR 508t; (1966) 110 SJ 545 CCA Evidence from juror which aided in rebuttal of alibi defence proffered by accused was validly admitted.

R v Bonnick (Derek Denton) (1978) 66 Cr App R 266; [1978] Crim LR 246; (1977) 121 SJ 791 CA On when self-defence to go to jury: self-defence evidence may arise even where accused pleads alibi.

DEFENCES (alibi)

R v Brigden [1973] Crim LR 579 CA Alibi notice (consequent upon which no defence witnesses called) could be put in evidence against accused by prosecution.

R v Buck, Fowkes and Howland [1964] Crim LR 223t CCA Failed appeal on basis of non-direction that rejection of alibi was not admission that had committed offence.

R v Carnegie and Webber [1994] Crim LR 591 CA Second false alibi by second person did not destroy false alibi already given by another person.

R v Denney [1963] Crim LR 191t CCA Conviction quashed where was inadequate direction as to evidence necessary to support alibi defence/was improper questioning as to accused's association with criminals.

R v Field and Adams [1991] Crim LR 38; (1991) 155 JP 396 CA Was evidence in support of alibi for defence witness to state person was in certain place prior to time of offence when prosecution witness testifying had seen person elsewhere before and at time of offfence; prosecution could introduce alibi notice though might thereby oblige defendant to be called to support alibi.

R v Finch [1914-17] All ER 535; (1915-17) XXV Cox CC 537; [1916] 85 LJKB 1575; (1916-17) 115 LTR 458 CCA Conviction quashed for inadequate direction regarding possible alibi defence.

R v Froggatt (William) (1910) 4 Cr App R 115 CCA Rebuttal of alibi defence: evidence admissible.

R v Gibbs [1974] Crim LR 474 CrCt No need for notice of names/addresses of two persons giving 'alibi' evidence whereby alleged that one was driver/other was passenger at time accused supposed to be in car.

R v Harrigan [1957] Crim LR 52t CCA Admission of further evidence before CA pertaining to alibi defence.

R v Harron (Robert David George) [1996] 2 Cr App R 457 CA On adequacy of direction as to alibi defence where lies had been told.

R v Hassan [1970] 1 All ER 745; (1970) 54 Cr App R 56; [1970] Crim LR 151; (1969) 113 SJ 996; (1970) 134 JP 266; [1970] 1 QB 423; [1970] 2 WLR 82 CA Where charge continuing in time evidence specific in time/place not alibi evidence.

R v Irwin [1987] 2 All ER 1085; (1987) 131 SJ 357 CA Person not entitled in all situations to be consulted by counsel on calling of alibi witnesses.

R v Jacks [1991] Crim LR 611 CA Valid refusal to allow alibi evidence to be given where no alibi notice given.

R v Jackson and Robertson [1973] Crim LR 356 CrCt Notice of alibi required even where defendant is the only witness testifying to the alibi.

R v Johnson [1961] 3 All ER 969; (1962) 46 Cr App R 55; [1962] Crim LR 52; (1962) 126 JP 40; (1961) 111 LJ 838; (1961) 105 SJ 1108 CCA Burden of proving alibi/guilt on defence/always on prosecution.

R v Johnson (Aldin) [1995] 2 Cr App R 1; (1994) 158 JP 867; (1994) 138 SJ LB 78; [1994] TLR 162 CA Evidence supporting alibi defence must show were in different place at time of offence.

R v Jones (William) (1928-29) 21 Cr App R 27 CCA On defence of alibi.

R v Lewis [1973] Crim LR 576t CA Conviction quashed in light of criticism by judge of accused's purported alibi.

R v Lewis (Albert Roy) (1969) 133 JP 111; [1969] 2 QB 1; (1968) 112 SJ 904; [1969] 2 WLR 55 CA Scope and effect of Criminal Justice Act 1967, s 11 (alibi evidence) considered.

R v Liddle (Stanley) (1928-29) 21 Cr App R 3 CCA On defence of alibi.

R v Mack (John) (1908) 1 Cr App R 132 CCA Generally no re-trial where pleaded alibi but did not enter witness-box; Chairman's clear intimation at trial that accused had previously been convicted not sufficient to justify overturning conviction.

R v Millichamp (John) (1921-22) 16 Cr App R 83 CCA On need for caution regarding identification by single witness where alibi defence pleaded.

R v Musial [1956] Crim LR 843t CCA That alibi witness did not get to trial did not furnish good basis for appeal.

R v Patel (Sabhas); R v Javed (Shakeel Nawab); R v Hurree (Kamal); R v McCormick (Alan Paul) (1993) 97 Cr App R 294; [1993] Crim LR 291 CA Judge's exclusion of alibi statement from witness abroad somewhere not objectionable.

R v Pepper (Edwin) (1909) 2 Cr App R 38 CCA Alibi defence does not depend on number of witnesses for/against it.

R v Preece (Conrad) (1993) 96 Cr App R 264; [1992] TLR 557 CA General practice to direct jury that prosecution must disprove alibi.

R v Rossborough (Paul Anthony Patrick) (1985) 81 Cr App R 139; [1985] Crim LR 372; (1985) 149 JP 529 CA Alibi notice could be entered in evidence by prosecution as part of its case.

R v Rufino (Emilio) (1911-12) 7 Cr App R 47 CCA Alibi defence must go to jury.

R v Sullivan [1970] 2 All ER 681; (1970) 54 Cr App R 389; [1970] Crim LR 641; (1970) 134 JP 583; [1971] 1 QB 253; (1970) 114 SJ 664; [1970] 3 WLR 210 CA Alibi evidence admissible despite failure to notify particulars.

R v Witton (Edward) (1910-11) 6 Cr App R 149 CCA Conviction quashed where alibi established by means of fresh evidence upon appeal.

R v Young (Charles) and Young (Mark) [1979] Crim LR 651 CrCt Alibi notice not required where prosecution/defence alleging in context of road traffic offence that C/M was driving and M/C was aiding and abetting.

Thompson v Director of Public Prosecutions [1918-19] All ER 521; (1918) 53 LJ 62; (1918) 118 LTR 418; (1917-18) 62 SJ 266; (1918) WN (I) 21 HL Possession of powder puffs/lewd photographs showed offender and accused had same tendencies - admissible to rebut alibi.

DEFENCES (automatism)

Attorney General's Reference (No 2 of 1992) [1993] 4 All ER 683; (1993) 97 Cr App R 429; [1994] Crim LR 692; (1994) 158 JP 741; (1993) 143 NLJ 919; [1994] QB 91; [1993] RTR 337; (1993) 137 SJ LB 152; [1993] TLR 303; [1993] 3 WLR 982 CA 'Driving without awareness' not automatism as partial not total loss of control.

Bratty v Attorney-General for Northern Ireland [1961] 3 All ER 523; [1963] AC 386; (1962) 46 Cr App R 1; [1961] Crim LR 829; (1961) 111 LJ 692; [1961] 3 WLR 965 HL Jury rejection of insanity defence does not preclude acceptance of automatism defence if solid evidence thereof.

Moses v Winder [1980] Crim LR 232; [1981] RTR 37 HC QBD Failed attempt by diabetic to establish automatism defence to driving without due care and attention charge.

Police v Beaumont [1958] Crim LR 620 Magistrates Successful plea of automatism (consequent upon pneumonia) in careless driving prosecution.

R v Bailey (John Graham) (1983) 77 Cr App R 76; [1983] Crim LR 533; (1983) 147 JP 558; (1983) 127 SJ 425; [1983] TLR 181; [1983] 1 WLR 760 CA Self-induced automatism brought about other than by alcohol/unlawful drugs could be defence to crimes of basic intent.

R v Bingham [1991] Crim LR 433 CA Hyperglycaemia/hypoglycaemia resulting in automatism raises question of insanity as a defence/should generally lead to acquittal.

R v Budd [1962] Crim LR 49t; (1962) 112 LJ 105 CCA On proving/disproving automatism.

R v Burgess [1991] 2 All ER 769; (1991) 93 Cr App R 41; [1991] Crim LR 548; (1991) 141 NLJ 527; [1991] 2 QB 92; [1991] TLR 161; [1991] 2 WLR 1206 CA Passing disorder prompting violent behaviour and caused by internal factor comes within M'Naghten Rules and is not non-insane automatism.

R v Burns (Dafydd John) (1974) 58 Cr App R 364; [1975] Crim LR 155 CA On insanity vis-à-vis automatism.

R v Charlson [1955] 1 All ER 859; (1955) 39 Cr App R 37; [1955] Crim LR 316; (1955) 119 JP 283; (1955) 99 SJ 221; [1955] 1 WLR 317 HC QBD Cannot be unlawful and malicious grievous bodily harm where not acting consciously.

R v Dervish [1968] Crim LR 37t; (1967) 117 NLJ 1218t CA Failed attempt to establish defence of automatism to homicide charge.

R v Hennessy [1989] 2 All ER 9; (1989) 89 Cr App R 10; [1989] Crim LR 356; [1989] RTR 153; (1989) 133 SJ 263; [1989] 1 WLR 287 CA Mental state arising through hyperglycaemia falls within M'Naghten Rules/is not automatism.

R v Quick [1973] Crim LR 434t CA On what constitutes a 'disease of the mind' (in context of diabetic suffering hypoglycaemia after taking medically prescribed insulin).

R v Sell (1962) 106 SJ 355 CCA On onus of proof as regards establishing defence of automatism.

R v Smith (PR) [1989] Crim LR 734 CA Evidence of previous behaviour towards deceased admissible to defeat defence of automatism (based on alleged unlikelihood of behaviour if behaving as usually did).

R v Smith (Stanley) [1979] 3 All ER 605; (1979) 69 Cr App R 378; [1979] Crim LR 592; (1980) 144 JP 53; (1979) 129 (2) NLJ 835 (incomplete)/862; (1979) 123 SJ 602; [1979] 1 WLR 1445 CA Prison psychiatrists' reports not confidential/are admissible; jury requires expert help on automatism.

R v Stripp (David Peter) (1979) 69 Cr App R 318 CA Once ground for automatism established for jury prosecution must prove accused acted wilfully.

R v Sullivan [1983] 2 All ER 673; [1984] AC 156 (also CA); (1983) 77 Cr App R 176; [1983] Crim LR 740; (1984) 148 JP 207; (1983) 133 NLJ 699; (1983) 127 SJ 460; [1983] TLR 443; [1983] 3 WLR 123 HL Whatever cause or duration if accused did not know what was doing/that it was wrong, he is legally insane.

R v Sullivan [1983] 1 All ER 577; [1984] AC 156 (also HL); [1983] Crim LR 257; (1983) 133 NLJ 203; (1983) 127 SJ 120; [1982] TLR 627 [1983] 2 WLR 392 CA Epileptic suffering total loss of memory/understanding insane under M'Naghten Rules.

R v T [1990] Crim LR 256 CrCt Rape is an external factor that could thereafter cause one not to act with conscious mind/will.

Roberts v Ramsbottom (1980) 144 JP 89 HC QBD To succeed with defence of automatism must prove were totally unconscious at relevant time.

Wood v Director of Public Prosecutions (1989) 153 JP 20 HC QBD On admissibility of expert medical evidence that was fact/opinion (here on defence of automatism).

DEFENCES (battered woman syndrome)

R v Hobson [1997] TLR 338 CA Retrial ordered of woman convicted of murder but who may have suffered from 'battered woman's syndrome' (a mental disease only recognised after she had been convicted).

R v Thornton (No 2) [1996] 2 All ER 1023; [1996] 2 Cr App R 108; [1996] Crim LR 597; (1995) 145 NLJ 1888; (1996) 140 SJ LB 38; [1995] TLR 674; [1996] TLR 6/6/96; [1996] 1 WLR 1174 CA Battered woman syndrome relevant when determining if provocation.

DEFENCES (claim of right)

R v Hancock [1963] Crim LR 572 CCA Conviction quashed where claim of right defence not properly left to jury.

R v King-Jones and Gladdy [1966] Crim LR 510; [1966] 1 WLR 1077 Assizes Ought not to be convicted of assault with intent to rob where believed had right to money and to secure same by force if necessary.

R v Williams [1962] Crim LR 111 CCA May assert claim of right on behalf of third party.

DEFENCES (diminished responsibility)

R v Bastian [1958] 1 All ER 568; (1958) 42 Cr App R 75; [1958] Crim LR 391; (1958) 102 SJ 272; [1958] 1 WLR 413 CCC On diminished responsibility/insanity.

R v Bathurst [1968] 1 All ER 1175; (1968) 52 Cr App R 251; [1968] Crim LR 334; (1968) 118 NLJ 253t; [1968] 2 QB 99; (1968) 112 SJ 272; [1968] 2 WLR 1092 CA Remark on failure of person of diminished responsibility to give evidence unfair.

R v Bradshaw (Colin) (1986) 82 Cr App R 79; [1985] Crim LR 733 CA On admissibility of hearsay/direct evidence by doctor called in case where diminished responsibility pleaded.

R v Burgess [1965] Crim LR 726t CCA On determining presence of diminished responsibility.

R v Byrne [1960] 3 All ER 1; (1960) 44 Cr App R 246; [1960] Crim LR 763; (1960) 110 LJ 525; [1960] 2 QB 396; (1960) 104 SJ 645 CCA Abnormal failure to control mental urges directing physical acts was diminished responsibility.

R v Campbell [1997] Crim LR 495 CA Cannot plead diminished responsibility as defence to attempted murder.

R v Campbell (Colin Frederick) (1987) 84 Cr App R 255; [1987] Crim LR 257 CA Diminished responsibility not to be left to jury despite psychiatrist witness' suggestion of same as defence had not sought to rely on it as defence.

R v Campbell (Colin Frederick) [1997] 1 Cr App R 199; [1997] Crim LR 227 CA Re-trial ordered where in light of new psychiatric evidence (unavailable at trial) defence of diminished responsibility might have been successfully relied upon.

R v Cox [1968] 1 All ER 386; (1968) 118 NLJ 134; [1968] 1 WLR 308 CA If of diminished responsibility can plead guilty to manslaughter though charged with murder.

R v Din (Ahmed) [1962] 2 All ER 123; (1962) 46 Cr App R 269; [1962] Crim LR 482; (1962) 112 LJ 353; (1962) 106 SJ 329; [1962] 1 WLR 680 CCA Diminished responsibility to be carefully examined if raised; here whether existed a question of fact though medical evidence important.

R v Dix (Trevor Glyn John) (1982) 74 Cr App R 306; [1982] Crim LR 302 CA Medical evidence not legally/is practically necessary when pleading diminished responsibility defence.

R v Dunbar [1957] 2 All ER 737; (1957) 41 Cr App R 182; [1957] Crim LR 616; (1957) 121 JP 506; (1957) 107 LJ 505; [1958] 1 QB 1; (1957) 101 SJ 594 CCA On respective burdens of proof where diminished responsibility claimed.

R v Egan [1992] 4 All ER 470; (1992) 95 Cr App R 278; [1993] Crim LR 131; (1992) 142 NLJ 751; [1992] TLR 275 CA Intoxication not relevant when deciding whether there was diminished responsibility.

R v Fenton (Martin Charles) (1975) 61 Cr App R 261; [1975] Crim LR 712; (1975) 119 SJ 695 CA Self-induced intoxication not an abnormality of mind in which to ground diminished responsibility defence.

R v Gittens [1984] Crim LR 553; [1984] QB 698; (1984) 128 SJ 515; [1984] TLR 383; [1984] 3 WLR 327 CA On appropriate direction where combined effect of drink and drugs gave rise to automatism plea.

R v Gomez [1964] Crim LR 723 CCA Inadequate direction as to defence of diminished responsibility led to manslaughter verdict being substituted for murder verdict.

R v Grant [1960] Crim LR 424 Assizes On establishing diminished responsibility/insanity.

R v Inseal [1992] Crim LR 35 CA On alcoholism as basis for defence of diminished responsibility.

R v Jennion (Yvonne) [1962] 1 All ER 689; (1962) 46 Cr App R 212; [1962] Crim LR 384; (1962) 112 LJ 258; (1962) 106 SJ 224 CCA Jury must resolve conflicting expert (here medical) evidence.

R v King [1964] Crim LR 133g CCA Failed plea of diminished responsibility - on elements of same; no defence that were prompted to kill son by seeing him injured; on provocation as it applies to people of African origin.

R v Kiszko (Stefan Ivan) (1979) 68 Cr App R 62; [1979] Crim LR 465 CA Responsibilities of jury as regards considering evidence when diminished responsibility pleaded.

R v Latham [1965] Crim LR 434t; (1965) 115 LJ 403; (1965) 109 SJ 371 CCA Jury could legitimately reject defence of diminished responsibility despite contrary medical evidence.

R v Lloyd [1966] 1 All ER 107; (1966) 50 Cr App R 61; [1966] Crim LR 106; (1966) 130 JP 118; (1965-66) 116 NLJ 360; [1967] 1 QB 175; (1965) 109 SJ 955; [1966] 2 WLR 13 CA On diminished responsibility.

R v Matheson [1958] 2 All ER 87; (1957) 41 Cr App R 145; [1958] Crim LR 393t; (1958) 108 LJ 297; (1958) 102 SJ 309 CCA Diminished responsibility a matter for jury; where diminished responsibility one of several defences raised and manslaughter verdict returned judge to ask on which defence is based.

R v Mitchell [1995] Crim LR 506; [1994] TLR 618 CA Defence of diminished responsibility did not have to be considered by jury in precise sequence in which is set out in the Homicide Act 1957, s 2(1).

R v Nott (1959) 43 Cr App R 8; [1959] Crim LR 365 Assizes Prosecution may call evidence to rebut insanity by proving diminished responsibility.

R v Price [1962] 3 All ER 957; (1963) 47 Cr App R 21; [1963] Crim LR 117; (1963) 113 LJ 26; [1962] 3 WLR 1308 HC QBD Absent contrary statutory provision insanity not to be put to jury where raised by prosecution not defence.

R v Salt (1955) 105 LJ 266 HC QBD Is no verdict of diminished responsibility.

R v Sanders [1991] Crim LR 781; [1991] TLR 210 CA Person could in light of all the evidence be convicted of murder even though there was uncontroverted medical evidence for defence pointing to diminished responsibility of offender.

R v Sanderson (Lloyd) (1994) 98 Cr App R 325; [1993] Crim LR 857 CA Could ground diminished responsibility defence on paranoid psychosis.

R v Seers (John Samuel) (1984) 79 Cr App R 261; [1985] Crim LR 315; (1985) 149 JP 124; [1984] TLR 291 CA Direction in terms of partial insanity inappropriate where accused relying on depression to maintain diminished responsibility plea.

R v Simcox [1964] Crim LR 402t CCA On what having one's mental ability 'substantially impaired' involves.

R v Spriggs [1958] 1 All ER 300; [1958] Crim LR 190t; (1958) 108 LJ 90; [1958] 1 QB 270; (1958) 102 SJ 89 CCA Definition of terms in Homicide Act 1957, s 2(1) unnecessary when leaving diminished responsibility defence to jury.

R v Straw [1995] 1 All ER 187 CA Appeal based on diminished responsibility not available where plea deliberately not relied on in murder trial.

R v Tandy (Linda Mary) [1989] 1 All ER 267; (1988) 87 Cr App R 45; [1988] Crim LR 308; (1988) 152 JP 453; (1988) 132 SJ 90; [1989] 1 WLR 350 CA On ingredients of diminished responsibility.

R v Terry [1961] 2 All ER 569; (1961) 45 Cr App R 180; [1961] Crim LR 479t; (1961) 111 LJ 388; (1961) 105 SJ 445 CCA Diminished responsibility provisions of Homicide Act 1957 (s 2) to be explained to jury: not desirable that just given copy of medical evidence.

R v Vinagre (Orlando Jose Gonzales) (1979) 69 Cr App R 104 CA Must be clear evidence of mental imbalance where plead diminished responsibility.

R v Walden [1959] 3 All ER 203; [1959] Crim LR 845; (1959) 109 LJ 571; (1959) 103 SJ 875; [1959] 1 WLR 1008 CCA In diminished responsibility direction judge may both refer jury to Homicide Act 1957, s 2 and give general guidance.

Rose v R [1961] 1 All ER 859; (1961) 45 Cr App R 102; [1961] Crim LR 404; (1961) 105 SJ 253; [1961] 2 WLR 506 PC Mental abnormality not to be measured by reference to M'Naghten definition of insanity.

Walton v R [1978] 1 All ER 542; [1978] AC 788; (1978) 66 Cr App R 25; [1977] Crim LR 747; (1978) 142 JP 151; (1977) 127 NLJ 1050t; (1977) 121 SJ 728; [1977] 3 WLR 902 PC Jury may reject diminished responsibilty defence even if psychiatrist credits it in evidence.

DEFENCES (drug addiction)

R v Flatt [1996] Crim LR 576 CA Addiction to drugs not a characteristic (so reasonable person could not have that characteristic).

DEFENCES (drunkenness)

R v Allen [1988] Crim LR 698 CA Where know are drinking alcohol fact that are mistaken as to its strength does not render drinking of same involuntary.

R v Davies [1991] Crim LR 469 CA On relevance of drunkenness to intent.

DEFENCES (duress)

Abbott v R [1976] 3 All ER 140; [1977] AC 755; (1976) 63 Cr App R 241; [1976] Crim LR 563; (1976) 140 JP 567; (1976) 126 NLJ 888t; (1976) 120 SJ 538; [1976] 3 WLR 462 PC Duress not defence to party accused of murder as principal in first degree.

Barton v Armstrong and others [1975] 2 All ER 465; [1976] AC 104; [1975] 2 WLR 1050 PC Agreement made under duress/undue influence in same category as those where fraudulent misrepresentation.

Director of Public Prosecutions for Northern Ireland v Lynch [1975] 1 All ER 913; [1975] AC 653; (1975) 61 Cr App R 6; [1975] Crim LR 707; (1975) 139 JP 312; (1975) 125 NLJ 362t; (1975) 119 SJ 233; [1975] 2 WLR 641 HL Principal in second degree in murder case can plead duress.

Director of Public Prosecutions v Bell [1992] Crim LR 176; [1992] RTR 335 HC QBD Person with excess alcohol fleeing from dangerous scene in terror/not proven to have driven longer than necessary/ who did not cease being terrified while driving could rely on defence of duress.

Director of Public Prosecutions v Davis; Director of Public Prosecutions v Pittaway [1994] Crim LR 600 HC QBD On test when determining whether duress present (here in context of offence of driving with excess alcohol).

R v Ali [1995] Crim LR 303 CA Person cannot plead duress where voluntarily join in criminal offence with violent person who then threatens violence in order to get said person to commit criminal offence.

R v Bowen (Cecil) [1996] 4 All ER 837; [1996] 2 Cr App R 157; [1996] Crim LR 577; (1996) 146 NLJ 442; (1996) 140 SJ LB 100; (1996) TLR 19/3/96; [1997] 1 WLR 372 CA On determining presence of duress in case involving low-intelligence person.

R v Burke; R v Clarkson; R v Howe; R v Bannister [1986] Crim LR 331; (1986) 130 SJ 110 CA On duress as a defence to murder.

R v Burke; R v Howe; R v Bannister; R v Clarkson [1987] Crim LR 480; (1987) 131 SJ 258 HL On duress as a defence to murder.

R v Cole [1994] Crim LR 582 CA On elements of defences of duress by threats/of circumstances.

R v Conway [1988] 3 All ER 1025; (1989) 88 Cr App R159; [1989] Crim LR 74; (1988) 152 JP 649; [1989] QB 290; [1989] RTR 35; (1988) 132 SJ 1244; [1988] 3 WLR 1238 CA Necessity a defence to reckless driving if duress of circumstances present.

R v Gill [1963] 2 All ER 688; (1963) 127 JP 429; (1963) 113 LJ 434; [1963] 1 WLR 841 CCA Person relying on duress to place enough evidence before court to make it a real issue - is then for prosecution to defeat it.

R v Gill (1963) 107 SJ 416 HC QBD Person relying on duress to place enough evidence before court to make it a real issue - is then for prosecution to defeat it.

R v Gotts [1992] 1 All ER 832; [1992] 2 AC 412; (1992) 94 Cr App R 312; [1992] Crim LR 724; (1992) 156 JP 225; (1992) 142 NLJ 311; (1992) 136 SJ LB 89; [1992] TLR 77; [1992] 2 WLR 284 HL Duress not available as defence to charge of attempted murder.

R v Gotts [1991] 2 All ER 1; (1991) 92 Cr App R 269; [1991] Crim LR 366; (1991) 155 JP 700; (1991) 141 NLJ 129; [1991] 1 QB 660; [1991] TLR 41; [1991] 2 WLR 878 CA Duress not a defence to attempted murder.

R v Graham [1982] 1 All ER 801; (1982) 74 Cr App R 235; [1982] Crim LR 365; (1982) 146 JP 206; (1982) 132 NLJ 113; (1982) 126 SJ 117; [1982] 1 WLR 294 CA Duress tested by reference to person of reasonable self-control so voluntary taking of drink/drugs irrelevant.

R v Horne [1994] Crim LR 584 CA On test as to whether duress present; psychiatric evidence deemed inadmissible in determining whether appellant in instant case acted under duress.

R v Howe and another appeal [1987] 1 All ER 771; [1987] AC 417; (1987) 85 Cr App R 32; (1987) 151 JP 265; (1987) 137 NLJ 197; [1987] 2 WLR 568 HL Duress an objective defence not open to those charged with murder in first/second degree; accessory before fact using duress to get another to commit offence can be guilty of greater offence than other.

R v Howe and other appeals [1986] 1 All ER 833; (1986) 83 Cr App R 28; (1986) 150 JP 161; [1986] QB 626; [1986] 2 WLR 294 CA Duress open as defence to alleged aider and abettor not alleged principal; accessory before fact cannot be convicted of more serious crime than principal.

R v Hudson; R v Taylor [1971] 2 All ER 244; (1972) 56 Cr App R 1; [1971] Crim LR 357; (1971) 135 JP 407; [1971] 2 QB 202; (1971) 115 SJ 303; [1971] 2 WLR 1047 CA Need not be possible for threat to be immediately effected for duress to arise.

R v K (1984) 78 Cr App R 82; [1983] Crim LR 736; (1984) 148 JP 410; [1983] TLR 576 CA On duress as defence to contempt.

R v Pommell (Fitzroy Derek) [1995] 2 Cr App R 607; (1995) 145 NLJ 960; (1995) 139 SJ LB 178; [1995] TLR 296 CA Can plead necessity (duress of circumstance) to possession of firearms charge.

R v Rodger and another [1997] TLR 428 CA Duress of necessity could not arise from within oneself but had to emanate from another.

R v Sharp [1987] 3 All ER 103; (1987) 85 Cr App R 207; [1987] Crim LR 566; (1987) 151 JP 832; [1987] QB 853; (1987) 131 SJ 624; [1987] 3 WLR 1 CA Pressure by criminal group on person who voluntarily joined to commit crime not duress.

R v Shepherd (Martin Brian) (1988) 86 Cr App R 47; [1987] Crim LR 686 CA On availability of duress defence to person voluntarily involved in joint criminal enterprise.

R v Steane [1947] 1 All ER 813; (1946-48) 32 Cr App R 61; (1947) 111 JP 337; [1947] KB 997; [1947] 116 LJR 969; (1947) 177 LTR 122; (1947) 91 SJ 279; (1947) LXIII TLR 403; (1947) WN (I) 184 CCA Can only convict of assisting enemy if act done with criminal/not innocent (such as saving family) intent to assist.

Rossides v R [1957] Crim LR 813t PC Failed application for leave to appeal murder conviction on basis inter alia of duress.

DEFENCES (forgetfulness)

Director of Public Prosecutions v Gregson (1993) 96 Cr App R 240; (1993) 157 JP 201; (1992) 136 SJ LB 245; [1992] TLR 403 HC QBD That had good reason for knife some days previously and then forgot possession not good defence to possession of offensive weapon.

DEFENCES (hypoglycaemia)

R v Marison [1996] Crim LR 909 CA Diabetic who suffered hypoglycaemic attack while driving was legitimately found guilty of causing death by dangerous driving of other driver with whom collided following attack.

DEFENCES (insanity)

Attorney-General for Northern Ireland v Gallagher [1961] 3 All ER 299; [1963] AC 349; (1961) 45 Cr App R 316; [1961] Crim LR 717t; (1961) 111 LJ 532; [1961] 3 WLR 619 HL Rôle of HL upon appeal; mental disease occasioning violent behaviour in which unaware of type/quality/ wrongness of act required to sustain insanity defence.

Bratty v Attorney-General for Northern Ireland [1961] 3 All ER 523; [1963] AC 386; (1962) 46 Cr App R 1; [1961] Crim LR 829; (1961) 111 LJ 692; [1961] 3 WLR 965 HL Jury rejection of insanity defence does not preclude acceptance of automatism defence if solid evidence thereof.

Director of Public Prosecutions v H [1997] TLR 238 HC QBD Insanity not a defence to strict liability offence (here driving with excess alcohol).

Felstead v R [1914-15] All ER 41; [1914] AC 534; (1914) 10 Cr App R 129; (1914) 78 JP 313; (1914) 49 LJ 243; (1914-15) 111 LTR 218; (1913-14) XXX TLR 469; (1914) WN (I) 179 HL No right of appeal to CCA against finding of insanity.

R v Abramovitch [1911-13] All ER 1178; (1913-14) XXIII Cox CC 179; (1911-12) 7 Cr App R 145; (1912) 76 JP 287; (1912-13) 107 LTR 416 CCA Prosecution calling doctor to prove accused sane where defence raised insanity but called no evidence good practice.

R v Adams [1954] Crim LR 720t CCA Insane person who knew the difference between right and wrong could be convicted of offence he committed.

R v Alexander (1913-14) XXIII Cox CC 604; (1913-14) 109 LTR 745 CCA Insanity verdict may not be open to jury just because accused proved mentally deficient.

R v Atherley (1909) WN (I) 251 CCA No leave to appeal in petition where was pleaded that evidence of insanity might perhaps have been procured for trial had there been time.

R v Bastian [1958] 1 All ER 568; (1958) 42 Cr App R 75; [1958] Crim LR 391; (1958) 102 SJ 272; [1958] 1 WLR 413 CCC On diminished responsibility/insanity.

R v Burgess (Barry Douglas) (1991) 93 Cr App R 41 CA Judge properly decided that automatism relied upon in defence was insane automatism coming under M'Naghten Rules.

R v Burns (Dafydd John) (1974) 58 Cr App R 364; [1975] Crim LR 155 CA On insanity vis-à-vis automatism.

R v Casey (1947) 91 SJ 693; (1947) LXIII TLR 487; (1947) WN (I) 265 CCA Crown's calling prison-doctor as medical witness so that he might be cross-examined by defence seeking to establish accused's insanity is not good practice.

R v Clarke [1972] 1 All ER 219; (1972) 56 Cr App R 225; [1972] Crim LR 183t; (1972) 136 JP 184; (1972) 122 NLJ 10t; (1972) 116 SJ 56 CA M'Naghten rules require that person loses power of reasoning.

R v Codere (Georges) (1916-17) 12 Cr App R 21 CCA Consideration of M'Naghten Rules (especially term 'the nature and quality of the act').

R v Coelho (Alberto Oliviero) (1914) 10 Cr App R 210; (1913-14) XXX TLR 535 CCA Admissibility on appeal of medical evidence pre-dating offence; syphilitic neurasthenia not good ground for insanity plea as could distinguish right from wrong though could not control actions.

R v Dickie (Andrew Plummer) (1984) 79 Cr App R 213; [1984] Crim LR 497; (1984) 128 SJ 331; [1984] TLR 248; [1984] 1 WLR 1031 CA Exceptionally judge could raise insanity issue though neither prosecution/defence did so.

R v Dixon [1961] 3 All ER 460; (1961) 111 LJ 677; (1961) 105 SJ 208 HC QBD On insanity defence.

R v Duke [1961] 3 All ER 737; (1962) 46 Cr App R 42; [1961] Crim LR 833t; (1961) 111 LJ 725; (1961) 105 SJ 891 CCA Cannot appeal acquittal on ground that 'guilty of the act charged but insane at the time of commission' (Trial of Lunatics Act, 1883: s 2(1)).

R v F (1910) 74 JP 384 CCC On what constitutes idiot/imbecile female for purposes of Criminal Law Amendment Act 1885, s 5.

R v Flavell (Joseph Edward) (1925-26) 19 Cr App R 141 CCA M'Naghten Rules unvariable by CCA.

R v Fryer (1914-15) XXIV Cox CC 403 Assizes On appropriate jury direction where defence of insanity pleaded.

R v Governor of Stafford Prison; ex parte Emery [1908-10] All ER 843; (1911-13) XXII Cox CC 143; (1909) 73 JP 284; [1909] 2 KB 81; [1909] 78 LJKB 629; (1909) 100 LTR 993; (1908-09) XXV TLR 440; (1909) WN (I) 95 HC KBD Deaf mute found incapable of pleading properly committed as insane.

R v Grant [1960] Crim LR 424 Assizes On establishing diminished responsibility/insanity.

R v Green-Emmott (George Vereker) [1931] All ER 380; (1931-34) XXIX Cox CC 280; (1930-31) Cr App R 183; (1931) 144 LTR 671 CCA Certified lunatic cannot enter into recognisance.

R v Harding (Ethel) (1908-09) XXV TLR 139 CCA Jury verdict that accused guilty but had frenzied mind not insanity verdict; proper that opinion of coroner's jury after finding accused guilty of murder that accused was not responsible for actions properly excluded at trial.

R v Hay (1911-13) XXII Cox CC 268; (1911) 75 JP 480 CCC Accused who knew nature and quality of acts but because of sick mind could not resist murderous impulse was insane.

R v Hill (1942) 86 SJ 134 CCA Sadism does not constitute insanity.

R v Holmes [1953] 2 All ER 324; (1953) 37 Cr App R 61; (1953) 117 JP 346; (1953) 97 SJ 355; [1953] 1 WLR 686 CCA Medical evidence on insanity admissible.

R v Holt (Frederick Rothwell) (1920-21) 15 Cr App R 10 CCA Uncontrollable impulse as basis for insanity defence.

R v Horseferry Road Magistrates' Court; ex parte K [1996] 3 All ER 719; [1996] 2 Cr App R 574; [1997] Crim LR 129; [1997] QB 23; [1996] 3 WLR 68 HC QBD Insanity available as defence in summary trial.

R v Ireland (1911-13) XXII Cox CC 322; (1910) 102 LTR 608; (1910) WN (I) 35 CCA Party found guilty but insane can under Criminal Appeal Act 1907, s 3, appeal against that conviction.

R v MacDonald (James) (otherwise Murphy) (1908) 1 Cr App R 262 CCA That CCA refused leave to appeal did not preclude Crown exercising prerogative of mercy.

R v Jefferson (James) (1908) 1 Cr App R 95; (1907-08) XXIV TLR 877 CCA Jury decision that accused fit to plead mistaken per CCA: guilty but insane verdict substituted.

R v Jolly (1919) 83 JP 296 Assizes Where through disease of the mind one momentarily loses control over one's actions one can be found to have been insane when acted.

R v Kemp [1956] 3 All ER 249; (1956) 40 Cr App R 121; [1956] Crim LR 774; (1956) 120 JP 457; (1956) 106 LJ 538; [1957] 1 QB 399; (1956) 100 SJ 768; [1956] 3 WLR 724 HC QBD On insanity/M'Naghten's Case.

R v Larkins (1911-13) XXII Cox CC 598; (1911) 75 JP 320; (1910-11) XXVII TLR 438 CCA No appeal against pre-trial imposition of detention during His Majesty's pleasure.

R v MacHardy (1911-13) XXII Cox CC 614; (1911-12) XXVIII TLR 2 CCA Can under Criminal Appeal Act 1907, s 3, appeal against conviction of being guilty but insane.

R v Nott (1959) 43 Cr App R 8; [1959] Crim LR 365 Assizes Prosecution may call evidence to rebut insanity by proving diminished responsibility.

R v Perry (Henry) (1919-20) 14 Cr App R 48 CCA Epileptic must be suffering from epileptic seizure at time commits crime to support insanity verdict.

R v Price [1962] 3 All ER 957; (1963) 47 Cr App R 21; [1963] Crim LR 117; (1963) 113 LJ 26; [1962] 3 WLR 1308 HC QBD Absent contrary statutory provision insanity not to be put to jury where raised by prosecution not defence.

R v Quick; R v Paddison [1973] 3 All ER 347; (1973) 57 Cr App R 722; (1973) 137 JP 763; [1973] QB 910; (1973) 117 SJ 371; [1973] 3 WLR 26 CA Mental malfunction from external factor (not disease) raises automatism defence (not insanity).

R v Rivett (James Frank) (1949-50) 34 Cr App R 87 CCA Issue when insanity pleaded not just whether diseased mind meant not reasoning properly but also whether meant not responsible for what did.

R v Smith (1909-10) XXVI TLR 614 CCA To successfully plead insanity must show that when did act did not know what was doing or that what was doing was wrong.

R v Sullivan [1983] 2 All ER 673; [1984] AC 156 (also CA); (1983) 77 Cr App R 176; [1983] Crim LR 740; (1984) 148 JP 207; (1983) 133 NLJ 699; (1983) 127 SJ 460; [1983] TLR 443; [1983] 3 WLR 123 HL Whatever cause or duration if accused did not know what was doing/that it was wrong he is legally insane.

R v Sullivan [1983] 1 All ER 577; [1984] AC 156 (also HL); [1983] Crim LR 257; (1983) 133 NLJ 203; (1983) 127 SJ 120; [1982] TLR 627 [1983] 2 WLR 392 CA Epileptic suffering total loss of memory/understanding insane under M'Naghten Rules.

R v Thomas (Sharon) [1995] Crim LR 314 CA Issue of insanity though not raised by defence, can be (but here ought not to have been) left to jury.

R v True (1921-25) XXVII Cox CC 287; (1922) 127 LTR 561 CCA M'Naghten's Rules applied as originally stated.

R v Wilkinson [1955] Crim LR 575t CCA Refusal to consider adequacy of direction on provocation/insanity where those defences deemed by court not to arise.

R v Wilkinson [1954] Crim LR 144t CCA Failed appeal against finding that psychopathic frame of mind did not constitute insanity.

R v Windle [1952] 2 All ER 1; (1952) 36 Cr App R 85; (1952) 116 JP 365; (1952) 102 LJ 303; [1952] 2 QB 826; (1952) 96 SJ 379; [1952] 1 TLR 1344; (1952) WN (I) 283 CCA If claiming insanity must show that did not know what were doing was unlawful.

R v Winstanley (1924-25) 69 SJ 777 CCA That person behaved in cruel and lustful way did not entitle them to succeed on insanity defence.

S (otherwise U) v Attorney-General (1932) 146 LTR 144 HC PDAD Dismissal of legitimacy petition brought on behalf of mentally unsound person.

Sodeman v R [1936] 2 All ER 1138; (1936) 82 LJ 117; (1936) 80 SJ 532; (1936) WN (I) 190 PC M'Naghten Rules approved as stood.

DEFENCES (intoxication)

Broadhurst (Malcolm Stewart) v R [1964] 1 All ER 111; [1964] AC 441; (1964) 114 LJ 88; (1963) 107 SJ 1037; [1964] 2 WLR 38 PC Impact of drunkenness on intent.

Director of Public Prosecutions v Beard [1920] All ER 21; [1920] AC 479; (1918-21) XXVI Cox CC 573; (1919-20) 14 Cr App R 159; (1920) 84 JP 129 (also CCA); [1920] 89 LJCL 437; (1920) 55 LJ 116; (1920) 122 LTR 625; (1919-20) 64 SJ 340; (1919-20) XXXVI TLR 379; (1920) WN (I) 110 HL Cannot be guilty of murder if so drunk could not form necessary intent (are guilty of manslaughter); (temporary) insanity deriving from drink will sustain insanity defence.

Director of Public Prosecutions v Majewski [1976] 2 All ER 142; [1977] AC 443 (also CA); (1976) 62 Cr App R 262; [1976] Crim LR 374; (1976) 140 JP 315; (1976) 126 NLJ 542t; (1976) 120 SJ 299; [1976] 2 WLR 623 HL Self-induced intoxication no defence unless specific intent required.

Jaggard v Dickinson [1980] 3 All ER 716; (1981) 72 Cr App R 33; [1980] Crim LR 717; (1980) 130 NLJ 907; [1981] QB 527; (1980) 124 SJ 847; [1981] 2 WLR 118 HC QBD Honest belief (even if result of self-induced intoxication) of lawful excuse to damage property a defence.

Osgerby v Rushton [1968] 2 All ER 1196; (1968) 118 NLJ 613t; [1968] 2 QB 466; (1968) 112 SJ 519; [1968] 3 WLR 438 HC QBD Conviction possible under statutory provision about to be repealed.

R v Aitken; R v Bennett; R v Barson [1992] 1 WLR 1006 CMAC Drunkenness not defence to malicious wounding: test for malice is whether would have foreseen injury if had not been intoxicated; direction on unlawfulness of wounding unsatisfactory as excluded possibility of consent to actions that resulted in wounding.

R v Atkinson (John) [1985] Crim LR 314 CA On appropriate direction to jury as to effect of voluntary intoxication on drunkenness.

R v Beard (Arthur) (1919-20) 14 Cr App R 110; (1920) 84 JP 129 (also HL); (1919-20) XXXVI TLR 94 CCA On drunkenness as defence reducing murder to manslaughter; where force used in rape which results in death may be murder.

R v Bowden [1993] Crim LR 380 CA On intoxication and intent.

R v C [1992] Crim LR 642; (1992) 156 JP 649 CA Indecent assault an offence of basic intent so self-induced drunkenness not a defence thereto.

R v Caldwell [1981] 1 All ER 961; [1982] AC 341; (1981) 73 Cr App R 13; [1981] Crim LR 392; (1981) 145 JP 211; (1981) 131 NLJ 338; (1981) 125 SJ 239; [1981] 2 WLR 509 HL Definition of recklessness; self-induced intoxication irrelevant to recklessness.

R v Caldwell (James) (1980) 71 Cr App R 237; [1980] Crim LR 572 CA Self-induced drunkenness relevant to deciding whether were criminally reckless.

R v Cole (and others) [1993] Crim LR 300 CA On drunkenness as defence to causing grievous bodily harm with intent: issue is whether had requisite intent, not whether capable of forming same.

R v Davies (Leslie James) [1983] Crim LR 741 CrCt On consequences for intent of involuntary drunkenness.

R v Dodson [1973] Crim LR 518 CA On effect of drunkenness on intent in context of murder.

R v Eatch [1980] Crim LR 650 CrCt On ramifications of voluntary drunkenness vis-à-vis intent in rape (a crime of basic intent).

R v Foote [1964] Crim LR 405 CCA Once defence raises drunkenness as reasonable possible defence it is for the prosecution to prove accused had the necessary intent.

R v Fotheringham (William Bruce) (1989) 88 Cr App R 206; [1988] Crim LR 846 CA Self-induced intoxication not a defence to rape.

R v Galbraith (William Wallace) (1912-13) 8 Cr App R 101 CCA Drunkenness as defence to murder.

R v Gannon (Kevin) (1988) 87 Cr App R 254; [1988] RTR 49 CA Drunkenness precluded defence on basis of belief had lawful authority for unauthorised taking of conveyance.

R v Garlick (Clifford Patrick) (1981) 72 Cr App R 291; [1981] Crim LR 178 CA Drunkenness defence raises question whether had formed necessary intent.

R v Haden (Josiah) (1909) 2 Cr App R 148 CCA One's drunkenness can mitigate one's guilt; pre-trial custody relevant when determining sentence.

R v Hardie (Paul Deverall) (1985) 80 Cr App R 156; (1984) 128 SJ 851; [1984] TLR 511; [1985] 1 WLR 64 CA Self-induced drunkenness cannot be defence where recklessness alleged - taking of sedative drug need not raise same presumption.

R v Howell [1974] 2 All ER 806; (1974) 138 JP 483 CrCt Self-induced intoxication not a defence to manslaughter.

R v Inseal [1992] Crim LR 35 CA On alcoholism as basis for defence of diminished responsibility.

R v Kearon and Williamson [1955] Crim LR 183 Sessions Person could not be guilty of aiding and abetting offence where was too drunk to possess necessary intent.

R v Kingston [1994] 3 All ER 353; [1995] 2 AC 355; (1994) 99 Cr App R 286; [1994] Crim LR 846; (1994) 158 JP 717; (1994) 144 NLJ 1044; [1994] TLR 422; [1994] 3 WLR 519 HL Lack of moral blame does not negative intent (unless incapable of forming intent) but can mitigate sentence.

R v Kingston [1993] 4 All ER 373; (1993) 97 Cr App R 401; [1993] Crim LR 781; (1993) 157 JP 1171; (1993) 143 NLJ 724; [1994] QB 81; (1993) 137 SJ LB 144; [1993] TLR 262; [1993] 3 WLR 676 CA Involuntary intoxication precludes necessary intent.

R v Majewski [1975] 3 All ER 296; [1977] AC 443 (also HL); (1976) 62 Cr App R 5; [1975] Crim LR 570; (1975) 139 JP 760; (1975) 125 NLJ 698t; (1975) 119 SJ 560; [1975] 3 WLR 401 CA Self-induced intoxication not defence unless crime of specific intent/so drunk are temporarily insane.

R v Mason (Tom) (1912-13) 8 Cr App R 121 CCA Drunkenness as defence to murder; words of provocation/abuse plus spitting at accused could reduce murder to manslaughter.

R v McCarthy [1954] 2 All ER 262; (1954) 38 Cr App R 74; (1964) 128 JP 191; [1954] 2 QB 105; (1954) 98 SJ 356; [1954] 2 WLR 1044 CCA Drunkenness cannot support provocation plea nor is it defence to murder (unless so drunk cannot form necessary intent).

R v Meade (Thomas) (1909) 2 Cr App R 54; (1909) 73 JP 239; [1909] 1 KB 895; [1909] 78 LJKB 476; (1908-09) 53 SJ 378; (1908-09) XXV TLR 359; (1909) WN (I) 62 CCA That were drunk can reduce apparent murder to manslaughter.

R v O'Connor [1991] Crim LR 135 CA On relevance of drunkenness to intent.

R v O'Driscoll (John) (1977) 65 Cr App R 50; [1977] Crim LR 560 CA No defence of drunkenness available to act of basic intent (setting fire to room).

R v O'Grady [1987] 3 All ER 420; (1987) 85 Cr App R 315; [1987] Crim LR 706; (1987) 137 NLJ 565; [1987] QB 995; (1987) 131 SJ 887; [1987] 3 WLR 321 CA Self-defence unavailable as defence if excessive force because of self-induced intoxication.

R v Orpin (Michael John) [1979] Crim LR 722 CrCt Criminal damage not an offence of specific intent to which drunkenness a defence.

R v Pordage [1975] Crim LR 575 CA On appropriate direction to jury as to intent in case where possibly drunken person charged with wounding with intent.

R v Stubbs (Kevin John) (1989) 88 Cr App R 53 CA Must be very drunk before could plead guilty to unlawful wounding where charged with wounding to do grievous bodily harm.

R v Wardrope [1960] Crim LR 770 CCC On provocation/self defence/drunkenness as defences to murder.

R v Woods (Walter) (1982) 74 Cr App R 312; [1982] Crim LR 42 CA Self-induced drunkenness not defence to rape: 'relevant matters' in Sexual Offences (Amendment) Act 1976, s 1(2) means legally relevant.

R v Young [1984] 2 All ER 164; (1984) 78 Cr App R 288; [1984] Crim LR 363; (1984) 148 JP 492; (1984) 128 SJ 297; [1984] TLR 78; [1984] 1 WLR 654 CMAC Test whether knew or ought to have known was controlled drug is objective: self induced intoxication irrelevant to belief.

Williams v Director of Public Prosecutions (1992) 95 Cr App R 415; (1992) 156 JP 804; [1992] TLR 80 HC QBD Landing of block of flats to which was controlled access not a public place.

DEFENCES (lawful excuse)

Blake v Director of Public Prosecutions [1993] Crim LR 586 HC QBD Not lawful excuse to criminal damage charge (vicar writing anti-government policy graffiti on pillar) that had genuine belief were acting in accordance with what God wanted (and so law of England protected).

Brook v Ashton [1974] Crim LR 105 HC QBD Could not ground lawful excuse defence in mistake of law.

Godwin v Director of Public Prosecutions (1993) 96 Cr App R 244; (1993) 157 JP 197; [1992] TLR 406 HC QBD That explanation uncontroverted by prosecution did not mean had established lawful authority for possession of weapon.

Johnson v Director of Public Prosecutions [1994] Crim LR 673 HC QBD Failed attempt by squatter (who replaced existing locks with own lock) to plead lawful excuse to criminal damage (allegedly believed property in need of immediate protection): on deciding whether lawful excuse defence ought to be successful.

R v Baker and another (1996) TLR 26/11/96 CA Child not 'property' for purposes of defence of lawful excuse to criminal damage under the Criminal Damage Act 1971, s 1(1).

R v Cousins [1982] 2 All ER 115; (1982) 74 Cr App R 363; [1982] Crim LR 444; (1982) 146 JP 264; [1982] QB 526; (1982) 126 SJ 154; [1982] TLR 67; [1982] 2 WLR 621 CA Self-defence/ prevention of crime lawful excuse to threat to kill; jury direction on burden of proof if lawful excuse exists/absent.

R v Denton [1982] 1 All ER 65; (1982) 74 Cr App R 81; [1982] Crim LR 107; (1982) 146 JP 138; (1981) 125 SJ 746; [1981] 1 WLR 1446 CA Damage to own property not arson even if tainted with intent to commit fraud.

R v Smith (DR) (1973) 117 SJ 938 CA Bona fide belief that property accused damaged was his own property a valid defence to charge of criminal damage to property.

R v Sunman [1995] Crim LR 569 CA On lawful excuse as a defence to offence of having custody of counterfeit note.

DEFENCES (necessity)

Cichon v Director of Public Prosecutions [1994] Crim LR 918 HC QBD Could not plead defence of necessity to having unmuzzled pit bull terrier in public place (allegedly unmuzzled to prevent discomfort in coughing).

Director of Public Prosecutions v Jones [1990] RTR 33 HC QBD Person using car to escape attack by another could not succeed on defence of necessity insofar as entire journey was concerned.

R v Conway [1988] 3 All ER 1025; (1989) 88 Cr App R159; [1989] Crim LR 74; (1988) 152 JP 649; [1989] QB 290; [1989] RTR 35; (1988) 132 SJ 1244; [1988] 3 WLR 1238 CA Necessity a defence to reckless driving if duress of circumstances present.

R v Martin [1989] 1 All ER 652; (1989) 88 Cr App R 343; [1989] Crim LR 284; (1989) 153 JP 231; [1989] RTR 63; [1988] 1 WLR 655 CA Defence of necessity arises if objectively viewed person acted reasonably/proportionately to avoid death/serious injury threat.

R v Pommell (Fitzroy Derek) [1995] 2 Cr App R 607; (1995) 145 NLJ 960; (1995) 139 SJ LB 178; [1995] TLR 296 CA Can plead necessity (duress of circumstance) to possession of firearms charge.

R v Rodger and another [1997] TLR 428 CA Duress of necessity could not arise from within oneself but had to emanate from another.

DEFENCES (pre-menstrual syndrome)

R v Smith (Sandie) [1982] Crim LR 531 CA Pre-menstrual syndrome not a defence but is a relevant factor when sentencing.

DEFENCES (provocation)

Afonja v R [1955] Crim LR 783t PC No leave to appeal murder conviction on issue of provocation (claimed that deceased was member of political party that previously attacked meeting of party to which offender belonged).

Bedder v Director of Public Prosecutions [1954] 2 All ER 801; (1954) 38 Cr App R 133; [1954] Crim LR 721; (1954) 104 LJ 536; (1954) 98 SJ 556; [1954] 1 WLR 1119 HL Test provocation by reference to reasonable man who need not possess characteristics peculiar to accused.

Bharat, Son of Dorsamy v R [1959] 3 All ER 292; [1959] Crim LR 786; [1959] 3 WLR 406 PC Conviction quashed where assessors aiding judge misdirected by same on provocation.

Bullard (Joseph) v R [1961] 3 All ER 470; [1957] AC 635; (1957) 41 Cr App R 1; [1957] Crim LR 816; (1957) 121 JP 576; (1957) 101 SJ 797 PC Evidence that does not support self defence plea could support provocation plea; must be clear to jury from direction that burden of proving guilt rests with prosecution.

Chun-Chuen (Lee) alias Wing-Cheuk (Lee) v R [1963] 1 All ER 73; [1963] AC 220; [1963] Crim LR 114; (1963) 113 LJ 56; (1962) 106 SJ 1008; [1962] 3 WLR 1461 PC Can rely on defence of provocation even if intended to kill/cause grievous bodily harm.

Director of Public Prosecutions v Camplin [1978] 2 All ER 168; [1978] AC 705; (1978) 67 Cr App R 14; [1978] Crim LR 432; (1978) 142 JP 320; (1978) 128 NLJ 537t; (1978) 122 SJ 280; [1978] 2 WLR 679 HL 'Reasonable man' not just adult male; unusual characteristics of accused relevant to 'reasonable man' test.

Edwards v R [1973] 1 All ER 152; [1973] AC 648; (1973) 57 Cr App R 157; [1972] Crim LR 782; (1973) 137 JP 119; (1972) 122 NLJ 941t; (1972) 116 SJ 822; [1972] 3 WLR 893 PC Extreme reaction to blackmailer's conduct might constitute provocation.

Holmes v Director of Public Prosecutions [1946] 2 All ER 124; [1946] AC 588; (1945-46) 31 Cr App R 123; [1946] 115 LJ 417; (1946) 175 LTR 327; (1946) 90 SJ 441; (1945-46) LXII TLR 466; (1946) WN (I) 146 HL On provocation reducing murder to manslaughter.

Kau (Chan) alias Kai (Chan) v R [1955] 1 All ER 266; [1955] AC 206; [1955] Crim LR 187; (1955) 99 SJ 72; [1955] 2 WLR 192 PC Burden of (dis-) proof remains on prosecution where evidence points to provocation/self-defence.

Logan v R [1996] 4 All ER 190; [1996] AC 871; (1996) 140 SJ LB 93; [1996] 2 WLR 711 PC Words by themselves could constitute provocation under Belizean Criminal Code 1981 rev.

Mancini v Director of Public Prosecutions [1941] 3 All ER 272; [1942] AC 1; (1940-42) 28 Cr App R 65; (1941) 91 LJ 406; (1942) 92 LJ 52; [1942] 111 LJ 84; (1941) 165 LTR 353; (1941-42) LVIII TLR 25; (1941) WN (I) 212 HL Judge must refer to apparent provocation (if any) even if not argued; direction on manslaughter in murder cases only if manslaughter verdict a real possibility; no ideal summing-up; reasonable doubt as to provocation must reduce verdict from murder to manslaughter.

Mensah (Kwaku) v R [1946] AC 83; [1946] 115 LJ 20; (1946) 174 LTR 96; (1945-46) LXII TLR 83 PC In murder trial if provocation defence arises it must be left to jury.

Nameless Case (1962) 112 LJ 459 CCA On provocation as a defence to murder.

Parker (Frank) v R [1964] AC 1369; [1964] Crim LR 659t; (1964) 114 LJ 472; (1964) 108 SJ 459; [1964] 3 WLR 70 PC Provocation could reduce murder to manslaughter even if provoked intent to kill; accused bears burden of establishing provocation (on balance of probabilities).

Phillips (Glasford) v R [1969] 2 AC 130; (1969) 53 Cr App R 132; [1969] Crim LR 144; (1969) 113 SJ 14; [1969] 2 WLR 581 PC Test of provocation: did accused lose self-control/would reasonable man have done so (former/latter a question of fact/opinion for jury).

R v Acott [1997] 1 All ER 706; [1997] 2 Cr App R 94; [1997] 2 Cr App R (S) 290; [1997] Crim LR 514; (1997) 161 JP 368; (1997) 147 NLJ 290; (1997) 141 SJ LB 65; [1997] TLR 90; [1997] 1 WLR 306 HL On evidence necessary to support plea of provocation.

R v Acott (Brian Gordon) [1996] 4 All ER 443; [1996] 2 Cr App R 290; [1996] Crim LR 664; (1996) TLR 5/4/96 CA On evidence necessary to support plea of provocation.

R v Ahluwalia [1992] 4 All ER 889; (1993) 96 Cr App R 133; [1993] Crim LR 63; (1992) 142 NLJ 1159 CA Delayed action not fatal to provocation defence; mental, physical characteristics of accused may be taken into account when determining provocation.

R v Ali [1989] Crim LR 736 CA On pleading provocation as defence to murder.

R v Baillie (John Dickie Spellacie) [1995] 2 Cr App R 31 CA Issue of provocation ought to have gone to jury where accused claimed had been provoked into killing person by their threat to his son.

R v Birchall (1913-14) XXIII Cox CC 579; (1913-14) 109 LTR 478; (1912-13) XXIX TLR 711; (1913) WN (I) 260 CCA Baseless suspicion that deceased committed adultery with killer's wife did not merit manslaughter (and not murder) conviction.

R v Brown [1972] 2 All ER 1328; (1972) 56 Cr App R 564; [1972] Crim LR 506t; (1972) 122 NLJ 448t; [1972] 2 QB 229; (1972) 116 SJ 431; [1972] 3 WLR 11 CA Must consider nature of provocation and nature of retaliation when deciding whether provoked reasonable man would have behaved as accused behaved.

R v Bruzas (John) [1972] Crim LR 367 CrCt On whether provocation a defence to attempted murder; on whether is an offence of attempted manslaughter.

R v Burgess and McLean [1995] Crim LR 425 CA Manslaughter convictions substituted for murder convictions where defence of provocation ought to have been, but was not left to jury.

R v Cambridge [1994] 2 All ER 760; (1994) 99 Cr App R 142; [1994] Crim LR 690; (1994) 158 JP 799; (1994) 144 NLJ 267; [1994] TLR 77; [1994] 1 WLR 971 CA Real evidence of provocation requires that judge leave issue of provocation to jury.

R v Camplin [1978] 1 All ER 1236; (1978) 66 Cr App R 37; [1977] Crim LR 748; (1977) 127 NLJ 938t; [1978] QB 254; (1977) 121 SJ 676; [1977] 3 WLR 929 CA 'Reasonable man' where youth charged is person of youth's age.

R v Cascoe [1970] 2 All ER 833; (1970) 54 Cr App R 401; [1970] Crim LR 644; (1970) 134 JP 603 CA Proper direction on law/burden of proof necessary once provocation left to jury.

R v Clarke [1991] Crim LR 383 CA Entirety of accused's conduct relevant to jury determination whether acted under provocation.

R v Cobbett (1940) 84 SJ 539 CCA Manslaughter/fifteen years' conviction/penal servitude substituted for murder/death verdict/sentence where had been inadequate direction as to possible provocation.

R v Cocker [1989] Crim LR 740 CA Husband's agreeing to yet another of his ailing wife's requests to end her life could not plead that was provoked by persistence of her requests into killing her.

R v Cook [1982] Crim LR 670 CA Was misdirection for judge to indicate as expert evidence a doctor's non-medical opinion that person prosecuted for murder acted under provocation.

R v Cox (1995) 139 SJ LB 86 CA Counsel to tell judge if there is material on which provocation might be found so that judge might address the matter.

R v Crawford (1994) 138 SJ LB 60 CA On provocation: murder conviction reduced to manslaughter where provocation (of which there was evidence) not left to jury.

R v Cunningham [1958] 3 All ER 711; (1959) 43 Cr App R 79; [1959] Crim LR 126t; (1959) 123 JP 134; (1959) 109 LJ 57; [1959] 1 QB 288; (1959) 103 SJ 56 CCA On provocation: provocation only a defence to murder.

R v Davies [1975] 1 All ER 890; (1975) 60 Cr App R 253; [1975] Crim LR 231t; (1975) 139 JP 381; (1975) 125 NLJ 110t; [1975] QB 691; (1975) 119 SJ 202; [1975] 2 WLR 586 CA Jury may consider if words of non-victim might have constituted provocation.

R v Dhillon [1997] 2 Cr App R 104; [1997] Crim LR 295 CA On whether/when defence of provocation ought (as should have been here) to be left to jury.

R v Doughty (Stephen Clifford) (1986) 83 Cr App R 319; [1986] Crim LR 625 CA Provocation ought to have been left to jury where killing of baby by father prompted by baby's crying.

R v Dryden [1995] 4 All ER 987 CA Permanent characteristics like obseessive or eccentric behaviour relevant to issue of provocation.

R v Duffy [1949] 1 All ER 932; (1949) 99 LJ 203 CCA On direction regarding provocation in murder/manslaughter case.

R v Ellor [1920] All ER 475; (1918-21) XXVI Cox CC 680; (1920-21) 15 Cr App R 41; (1921) 85 JP 107; [1921] LJCL 218; (1921) 124 LTR 287; (1919-20) XXXVI TLR 840 CCA Statement understood to mean wife would commit adultery not provocation reducing wife's killing of her from murder to manslaughter.

R v Fairbrother (John James) (1908) 1 Cr App R 233 CCA Finding of provocation need not reduce offence with which charged from murder to manslaughter.

R v Fantle [1959] Crim LR 584 CCC On provocation as defence to murder.

R v Finley [1965] Crim LR 105t CCA Reduction of murder conviction to manslaughter where was evidence of provocation (man found at home another man with whom wife had been mixing).

R v Garner (Walter John) (1924-25) 18 Cr App R 125 CCA Twelve months' hard labour (not three years' penal servitude) for wounding with intent to murder where greatly provoked by wife (who refused to cease being prostitute).

R v Gauthier (Charles Eugene) (1942-44) 29 Cr App R 113 CCA On what constitutes provocation.

R v Gilbert (Raymond Sidney) (1978) 66 Cr App R 237 CA Provocation only to go to jury if there is evidence of provocation that caused accused to lose self-control.

R v Greening (1913-14) XXIII Cox CC 601; [1913] 3 KB 846; [1914] 83 LJKB 195; (1913-14) 109 LTR 720; (1912-13) XXIX TLR 732 CCA Person's killing of unmarried partner whom discovered in disreputable house was murder: adultery/manslaughter defence not open to unmarried couple.

R v Hall (1926-30) XXVIII Cox CC 567; (1928-29) 21 Cr App R 48; (1929) 140 LTR 142 CCA On what constitutes/on need to consider provocation.

R v Hodges [1962] Crim LR 385 CCA On establishing provocation.

R v Holmes (Leonard) [1946] 1 All ER 524; (1946) 96 LJ 218; (1946) 90 SJ 371; (1945-46) LXII TLR 342 CCA Confession of adultery held not to be provocation reducing murder to manslaughter as husband suspected same for some time/murder was protracted.

R v Humphreys [1995] 4 All ER 1008; [1996] Crim LR 431; (1995) 145 NLJ 1032 CA Abnormal immaturity or history of attention seeking relevant to issue of provocation; complex history of provocation requires careful explanation to jury by judge.

R v Ibrams (James David); R v Gregory (Ian David) (1982) 74 Cr App R 154 CA No provocation where planned to and did kill persistent tormentor as was no sudden, temporary loss of self-control.

R v Ives [1969] 3 All ER 470; (1969) 53 Cr App R 474; [1969] Crim LR 437; [1970] 1 QB 208; (1969) 113 SJ 467; [1969] 3 WLR 266 CA Intent of accused relevant when determining if provocation.

R v Johnson [1989] 2 All ER 839; (1989) 89 Cr App R 148; [1989] Crim LR 738; (1989) 153 JP 533; (1989) 139 NLJ 643; (1989) 133 SJ 596; [1989] 1 WLR 740 CA Self-induced provocation is possible and possibility ought to be left to jury.

R v Jones (1908) 72 JP 215 CCC Can be provocation by words such as to reduce murder to manslaughter.

R v King [1964] Crim LR 133g CCA Failed plea of diminished responsibility - on elements of same; no defence that were prompted to kill son by seeing him injured; on provocation as it applies to people of African origin.

R v Lesbini (1914-15) XXIV Cox CC 516; (1914-15) 11 Cr App R 7; [1914] 3 KB 1116; [1915] 84 LJKB 1102; (1915) 112 LTR 175; (1914) WN (I) 362 CCA Test for provocation is would reasonable man lose self-control (individual characteristics of accused irrelevant).

R v Letenock (Alexei) (1916-17) 12 Cr App R 221 CCA On aggravation of provocation through drunkenness.

R v Martindale [1966] 3 All ER 305; (1966) 50 Cr App R 273; [1966] Crim LR 621; (1965-66) 116 NLJ 1433; [1966] 1 WLR 1564 CMAC Provocation possible despite intent to kill/do grievous bodily harm if acts arose from sudden passion.

R v McCarthy (Michael Dennis) [1954] 2 All ER 262; (1954) 38 Cr App R 74; [1954] Crim LR 549; [1954] 2 QB 105; (1954) 98 SJ 356; [1954] 2 WLR 1044 CCA Drunkenness not provocation nor is it defence to murder (unless so drunk cannot form necessary intent).

R v McPherson [1957] Crim LR 618t CCA On burden of proof where issue of manslaughter by virtue of provocation left to jury.

R v Morhall [1995] 3 All ER 659; [1996] 1 AC 90; [1995] 2 Cr App R 502; [1995] Crim LR 890; (1995) 145 NLJ 1126; (1995) 139 SJ LB 175; [1995] TLR 431; [1995] 3 WLR 330 HL Glue-sniffing addiction relevant when determining gravity of provocation.

R v Morhall (1994) 98 Cr App R 108; [1993] Crim LR 957; (1993) 143 NLJ 1441; (1993) 137 SJ LB 189; [1993] TLR 459 CA Glue-sniffing addiction not relevant when determining whether had been provocation.

R v Newell [1989] Crim LR 906 CA On provocation as possible defence to murder.

R v Newell (Alan Lawrie Alastair) (1980) 71 Cr App R 331; [1980] Crim LR 576 CA Transitory characteristics of accused irrelevant to defence of provocation.

R v Nuttall [1956] Crim LR 125t CCA Unfaithfulness of wife did not per se constitute provocation reducing murder to manslaughter.

R v Palmer (1913-14) XXIII Cox CC 377; (1912-13) 8 Cr App R 207; (1913) 77 JP 340; [1913] 2 KB 29; [1913] 82 LJKB 531; (1913) 108 LTR 814; (1912-13) XXIX TLR 349; (1913) WN (I) 80 CCA Fiancée's confession of immoral life not sufficient provocation to merit manslaughter and not murder conviction where fiancé kills her in response.

R v Phillis (1915-16) XXXII TLR 414 CCA That cross language was spoken not provocation reducing murder to manslaughter.

R v Porritt [1961] 3 All ER 463; [1961] Crim LR 776t; (1961) 125 JP 605; (1961) 111 LJ 710; (1961) 105 SJ 991 CCA Provocation if seems an issue to be left to jury though prosecution want murder/not manslaughter conviction.

R v Prince [1941] 3 All ER 37; (1941-42) LVIII TLR 21 CCA Reasonable doubt in jury's minds whether act unintended/provoked merits acquittal of accused.

R v Raven [1982] Crim LR 51 CCC 'Reasonable man' endowed with peculiar characteristics of accused (mental age of child despite being twenty-two).

R v Richens [1993] 4 All ER 877; (1994) 98 Cr App R 43; [1993] Crim LR 384; [1992] TLR 560 CA Provocation requires sudden and temporary but not complete loss of control; judge must warn jury to consider alternatives to accused's lies tending to guilt.

R v Roberts [1990] Crim LR 122 CA Provocation decided by reference to reasonable man who has characteristics peculiar to defendant.

R v Robinson [1965] Crim LR 491t CCA Valid decision not to leave provocation to jury.

R v Rossiter [1994] 2 All ER 752; (1992) 95 Cr App R 326; (1992) 142 NLJ 824 CA Real evidence of provocation, however slim, requires that issue of provocation be left to jury.

R v Sawyer [1989] Crim LR 831 CA Judge could of own volition leave provocation as issue to jury if thought that facts merited it (did not merit it here).

R v Semini [1949] 1 All ER 233; (1948-49) 33 Cr App R 51; [1949] 1 KB 405; (1949) 99 LJ 34; [1949] 118 LJR 556; (1949) LXV TLR 91; (1949) WN (I) 28 CA Chance-medley doctrine no longer exists; test for provocation is that in Holmes v DPP.

R v Simon [1964] Crim LR 141t CCA Prosecution to disprove provocation.

R v Simpson [1957] Crim LR 815t CCC Nagging/threats by wife reduced her homicide by husband from murder to manslaughter on basis of provocation.

R v Simpson [1914-15] All ER 917; (1915-17) XXV Cox CC 269; (1914-15) 11 Cr App R 218; [1915] 84 LJKB 1893; (1916) 114 LTR 238; (1914-15) XXXI TLR 560 CCA Third party provocation prompting accused to kill victim did not reduce killing to manslaughter.

R v Stewart [1995] 4 All ER 999; [1995] Crim LR 66 CA If directing jury to consider provocation judge must mention evidence of provocation unless obvious.

R v Stewart (Benjamin James) [1996] 1 Cr App R 229; [1994] TLR 403 CA On appropriate direction as to provocation in context of murder.

R v Thornton [1992] 1 All ER 306; (1993) 96 Cr App R 112; [1992] Crim LR 53; (1991) 141 NLJ 1223 CA Provocation not present if murder on foot of history of domestic violence but no sudden loss of control.

R v Thornton (No 2) [1996] 2 All ER 1023; [1996] 2 Cr App R 108; [1996] Crim LR 597; (1995) 145 NLJ 1888; (1996) 140 SJ LB 38; [1995] TLR 674; [1996] TLR 6/6/96; [1996] 1 WLR 1174 CA Battered woman syndrome relevant when determining if provocation.

R v Truss (George William) (1909) 2 Cr App R 69 CCA Appeal on ground of provocation dismissed as was no evidence of serious provocation for what was serious unlawful wounding.

R v Twine [1967] Crim LR 710 CA On third party provocation as defence to murder.

R v Walker (Harold Raymond) (1969) 53 Cr App R 195; [1969] Crim LR 146; (1969) 119 NLJ 13t; (1969) 113 SJ 52; [1969] 1 WLR 311 CA On whether is necessary for the mode of resentment to bear a reasonable relationship to the provocation.

R v Wardrope [1960] Crim LR 770 CCC On provocation/self defence/drunkenness as defences to murder.

R v Whitfield (Melvyn Thomas) (1976) 63 Cr App R 39; [1976] Crim LR 443t; (1976) 126 NLJ 360t CA Provocation if conduct such that accused lost self-control and reasonable man would have done so.

R v Wilkinson [1955] Crim LR 575t CCA Refusal to consider adequacy of direction on provocation/insanity where those defences deemed by court not to arise.

R v Williams (Albert) [1968] Crim LR 678; (1968) 112 SJ 760 CA Objective test of provocation under Homicide Act 1957, s 3, unaffected by subjective test of intent in the Criminal Justice Act 1967, s 8.

R v Acott [1997] 1 All ER 706; [1997] 2 Cr App R 94; [1997] Crim LR 514; (1997) 161 JP 368; (1997) 147 NLJ 290; (1997) 141 SJ LB 65; [1997] TLR 90; [1997] 1 WLR 306 HL On evidence necessary to support plea of provocation.

Thuan (Luc Thiet) v R [1996] 2 All ER 1033; [1997] AC 131; [1996] 2 Cr App R 178; [1996] Crim LR 820; (1996) 146 NLJ 513; (1996) 140 SJ LB 107; (1996) TLR 2/4/96; [1996] 3 WLR 45 PC Provocation an objective test to which particular charcteristics of defendant have no relevance.

Vasquez v R; O'Neil v R [1994] 3 All ER 674; [1994] Crim LR 845; (1994) 138 SJ LB 161; [1994] 1 WLR 1304 PC Where evidence of provocation burden on prosecution to negative that suggestion.

DEFENCES (reasonable force)

R v Duffy [1966] 1 All ER 62; (1966) 50 Cr App R 68; [1966] Crim LR 108; (1966) 130 JP 137; (1965-66) 116 NLJ 360; [1967] 1 QB 63; (1966) 110 SJ 70; [1966] 2 WLR 229 CA Is defence that were using reasonable force to stop crime.

DEFENCES (self-defence)

Albert v Lavin [1981] 1 All ER 628; [1982] AC 546 (also HL); (1981) 72 Cr App R 178; [1981] Crim LR 238; (1981) 145 JP 184; (1981) 131 NLJ 368; (1981) 125 SJ 114; [1981] 2 WLR 1070 HC QBD Unreasonable belief acting in self-defence not defence to assault charge.

Ansell v Swift [1987] Crim LR 194 CrCt May plead defence of self-defence where assaulted police officer following unlawful assault by the officer.

Ashbee v Jayne [1966] Crim LR 49; (1965) 109 SJ 919 HC QBD That carried sand-filled sock for purpose of self-defence did not mean could not be offensive weapon.

Attorney-General's Reference (No 2 of 1983) [1984] 1 All ER 988; (1984) 78 Cr App R 183; [1984] Crim LR 289; (1985) 149 JP 104; [1984] QB 456; [1984] TLR 42; [1984] 2 WLR 465 CA Exceptionally preparation of petrol-bomb may be lawful where prepared as planned act of self-defence.

Beckford v R [1987] 3 All ER 425; [1988] AC 130; (1987) 85 Cr App R 378; [1988] Crim LR 116; (1987) 137 NLJ 591; (1987) 131 SJ 1122; [1987] 3 WLR 611 PC Self-defence plea grounded in mistake of fact to be judged on mistaken facts even if mistake unreasonable.

Blackburn v Bowering [1995] Crim LR 38; [1993] TLR 551; [1994] 1 WLR 1324 CA Person pleading self-defence to be judged on facts however perceived them (whether reasonably or unreasonably) to be; must be guilty of assault to be guilty of aggravated assault.

Bullard (Joseph) v R [1957] AC 635; (1957) 41 Cr App R 1; [1957] Crim LR 816; (1957) 121 JP 576; (1957) 101 SJ 797 PC Evidence that does not support self defence plea could support provocation plea; must be clear to jury from direction that burden of proving guilt rests with prosecution.

Director of Public Prosecutions v Walker (Leary) [1974] Crim LR 368; [1974] 1 WLR 1090 PC Where inter alia force far exceeded what was necessary for self-defence could not successfully plead self-defence.

Kau (Chan) alias Kai (Chan) v R [1955] 1 All ER 266; [1955] AC 206; [1955] Crim LR 187; (1955) 99 SJ 72; [1955] 2 WLR 192 PC Burden of (dis-) proof remains on prosecution where evidence points to provocation/self-defence.

Kenlin and another v Gardiner and another [1966] 3 All ER 931; [1967] Crim LR 39; (1967) 131 JP 91; (1965-66) 116 NLJ 1685; [1967] 2 QB 510; (1966) 110 SJ 848; [1967] 2 WLR 129 HC QBD Proportionate use of force following technical assault by constable legitimate self-defence.

Palmer v R [1971] 1 All ER 1077; [1971] AC 814; (1971) 55 Cr App R 223; [1972] Crim LR 649; (1971) 121 NLJ 152t; (1971) 115 SJ 265; [1971] 2 WLR 831 PC If self-defence fails because excessive force a manslaughter sentence need not always follow.

Plunkett v Matchell [1958] Crim LR 252 Magistrates Conviction (but absolute discharge) of security man guilty of assault in using security dog to attack trespasser in mistaken view that was necessary self-defence.

Priestnall v Cornish [1979] Crim LR 310 CA Attack on person backing away was not self-defence.

R v Abraham [1973] 3 All ER 694; (1973) 57 Cr App R 799; [1974] Crim LR 246; (1973) 137 JP 826; (1973) 117 SJ 663; [1973] 1 WLR 1270 CA Jury direction when self-defence raised.

R v Asbury [1986] Crim LR 258 CA On reasonableness of belief that were acting in self-defence to sustaining a plea of self-defence.

R v Bird [1985] 2 All ER 513; (1985) 81 Cr App R 110; [1985] Crim LR 388; (1985) 129 SJ 362; [1985] 1 WLR 816 CA Defendant need not show unwillingness to fight for self-defence but is preferable.

R v Bonnick (Derek Denton) (1978) 66 Cr App R 266; [1978] Crim LR 246; (1977) 121 SJ 791 CA On when self-defence to go to jury: self-defence evidence may arise even where accused pleads alibi.

R v Chisam (Colin) (1963) 47 Cr App R 130; [1963] Crim LR 353g; (1963) 113 LJ 580 CCA To successfully plead 'self-defence' of relative must have thought same to be in imminent danger and must have been reasonable - though not necessarily correct - to think so.

R v Clegg [1995] 1 All ER 334; [1995] 1 AC 482; [1995] 1 Cr App R 507; [1995] Crim LR 418; (1995) 145 NLJ 87; (1995) 139 SJ LB 48; [1995] TLR 18; [1995] 2 WLR 80 HL Self-defence plea cannot reduce culpable homicide from murder to manslaughter.

R v Corrigan [1985] Crim LR 388 CA May successfully plead self-defence though cause accidental injury/damage in course of self-defence.

R v Cousins [1982] 2 All ER 115; (1982) 74 Cr App R 363; [1982] Crim LR 444; (1982) 146 JP 264; [1982] QB 526; (1982) 126 SJ 154; [1982] TLR 67; [1982] 2 WLR 621 CA Self-defence/prevention of crime lawful excuse to threat to kill; jury direction on burden of proof if lawful excuse exists/absent.

R v Field [1972] Crim LR 435 CA Are not required to avoid certain streets where have lawful right to be simply because may encounter people antagonistic towards one there.

R v Fisher [1987] Crim LR 334 CA Person pleading self-defence entitled to have defence considered on basis of facts as he believed them to be.

R v Folley [1978] Crim LR 556 CA On establishing defence of self-defence.

R v Hassin [1963] Crim LR 852t CCA On self-defence as defence to murder.

R v Julien [1969] 2 All ER 856; (1969) 53 Cr App R 407; [1969] Crim LR 381t; (1969) 133 JP 489; (1969) 119 NLJ 390t; (1969) 113 SJ 342; [1969] 1 WLR 839 CA Person must show did not want to fight if seeks to raise self-defence.

R v Khan and Rakhman [1963] Crim LR 562t CCA Self-defence a defence to affray.

R v Lobell [1957] 1 All ER 734; (1957) 41 Cr App R 100; [1957] Crim LR 323; (1957) 121 JP 282; [1957] 1 QB 547; (1957) 101 SJ 268; [1957] 2 WLR 524 CCA Burden of proof rests on prosecution though self-defence raised; if in doubt as to whether self-defence acquittal required.

R v McInnes [1971] 3 All ER 295; (1971) 55 Cr App R 551; [1972] Crim LR 651; (1971) 121 NLJ 883; (1971) 115 SJ 655; [1971] 1 WLR 1600 CA Excessive force in self-defence can ground murder conviction; failure to retreat tends to reasonableness of self-defence.

R v O'Grady [1987] 3 All ER 420; (1987) 85 Cr App R 315; [1987] Crim LR 706; (1987) 137 NLJ 565; [1987] QB 995; (1987) 131 SJ 887; [1987] 3 WLR 321 CA Self-defence unavailable as defence if excessive force because of self-induced intoxication.

R v Oatridge (Gaynor) (1992) 94 Cr App R 367; [1992] Crim LR 205 CA On assessing whether accused acted in self-defence.

R v Owen (1964) 108 SJ 802 CCA On need for specific direction as to onus of proof as regards establishing self-defence where that defence raised.

R v Owino (Nimrod) [1996] 2 Cr App R 128; [1995] Crim LR 743 CA On force allowable in self-defence.

R v Rothwell and Barton [1993] Crim LR 626 CA That acted in self-defence/defence of another are defences to the statutory offences which replaced affray.

R v Shannon (James Russell) (1980) 71 Cr App R 192; [1980] Crim LR 438; (1980) 130 NLJ 606; (1980) 124 SJ 374 CA Whether was self-defence depends on whether accords to what one would expect in the circumstances.

R v Wardrope [1960] Crim LR 770 CCC On provocation/self defence/drunkenness as defences to murder.

R v Whyte [1987] 3 All ER 416; (1987) 85 Cr App R 283 CA Excessive force where immediate but expected danger not ground for self-defence.

Sears v Broome [1986] Crim LR 461 CA Damage done when acting in self-defence cannot be criminal damage.

DEFENCES (sleep)

Kay v Butterworth (1945) 173 LTR 191; (1945) 89 SJ 381; (1944-45) LXI TLR 452 HC KBD That driver of car was asleep and so unaware of offences not defence to charges of careless and dangerous driving.

Kay v Butterworth (1946) 110 JP 75 CA Person driving car while asleep was guilty of careless and dangerous driving.

DEFENCES (uncontrollable impulse)

Attorney-General for the State of South Australia v Brown [1960] 1 All ER 734; (1960) 44 Cr App R 100; [1960] Crim LR 425; (1960) 110 LJ 301; (1960) 104 SJ 268; [1960] 2 WLR 588 PC No defence of insanity by virtue of uncontrollable impulse.

R v Holt (Frederick Rothwell) (1920-21) 15 Cr App R 10 CCA Uncontrollable impulse as basis for insanity defence.

R v Jolly (1919) 83 JP 296 Assizes Where through disease of the mind one momentarily loses control over one's actions one can be found to have been insane when acted.

R v Quarmby (Fred) (1920-21) 15 Cr App R 163 CCA No defence of irresistible impulse in English law.

DEPORTATION (general)

Teame v Aberash and others; R v Secretary of State for the Home Department; ex parte Teame [1994] TLR 205 CA Deportation could continue notwithstanding that there was wardship/ residence order or proceedings in existence in relation to person it is sought to deport.

DESERTION (general)

Keslake v Board of Trade [1903] 2 KB 453 HC KBD Absent court order cannot make post-desertion deduction from seaman's wages.

DISHONESTY (abstracting electricity)

Martin v Marsh [1955] Crim LR 781t HC QBD Was larceny from the Electricity Authority to take money that had been deposited in an electrcity meter.

R v McCreadie (Malcolm); R v Tume (William John) (1993) 96 Cr App R 143; [1992] Crim LR 872; (1993) 157 JP 541; [1992] TLR 285 CA Proof that electricity abstracted without authority could support theft conviction - did not have to prove accused tampered with meter.

Swallow v Director of Public Prosecutions [1991] Crim LR 610 HC QBD Acquittal merited where husband or wife had abstracted electricity through interference with meter but was no real indication as to which had done so.

DISHONESTY (advertisement)

Denham v Scott (1983) 77 Cr App R 210; [1983] Crim LR 558; (1983) 147 JP 521; [1983] TLR 246 HC QBD Publication of 'no questions asked' reward advertisement contrary to Theft Act 1968, s 23, a strict liability offence - advertising manager who was unaware advertisement was therefore guilty of same.

Mirams v Our Dogs Publishing Company, Limited [1901] 2 KB 564; [1901] 70 LJK/QB 879; (1901-02) LXXXV LTR 6; (1900-01) XVII TLR 649; (1900-01) 49 WR 626 CA Larceny Act 1861, s 102 prohibition on advertising for stolen property on 'no questions asked' basis includes advertisements for stolen dogs.

Smith v Stevens (1928-29) XLV TLR 429 HC KBD Penalty plus costs for placing advertisement of reward for return of lost property on 'no questions asked' basis (Larceny Act 1861, s 102).

Wilkins v Gill; Major v Gill (1903-04) XX TLR 3 HC KBD Attorney-General's fiat necessary for bringing of action against certain publication for advertisement offering reward for return of stolen property on 'no questions asked' basis as publication at issue was newspaper under Larceny (Advertisements) Act 1870/Post Office Act 1870.

DISHONESTY (aggravated burglary)

R v Kelly (Ronnie Peter) (1993) 97 Cr App R 245; [1993] Crim LR 763; (1993) 157 JP 845; (1992) 136 SJ LB 324; [1992] TLR 578 CA Burglar must have weapon of offence as burglary takes place to be guilty of aggravated burglary.

R v O'Leary (Michael) (1986) 82 Cr App R 341; (1989) 153 JP 69 CA If are armed at moment of theft is aggravated burglary.

R v Stones (James) (1989) 89 Cr App R 26; (1988) 132 SJ 1670; [1989] 1 WLR 156 CA Was aggravated burglary where burglar in possession of knife though may not have intended to use same during burglary.

DISHONESTY (animus furandi)

R v Mortimer (1907-09) XXI Cox CC 677; (1908) 1 Cr App R 20; (1908) 72 JP 349 CCA On need for animus furandi.

DISHONESTY (appropriation)

Anderton v Wish (1981) 72 Cr App R 23; [1980] Crim LR 319/657 HC QBD Is appropriation to switch lower price tags to higher priced goods so as to pay lower price.

Attorney-General of Hong Kong v Nai-Keung (1988) 86 Cr App R 174; [1988] Crim LR 125; [1987] 1 WLR 1339 PC Export quotas were intangible property that could be dishonestly appropriated.

Broom v Crowther (1984) 148 JP 592; [1984] TLR 315 HC QBD Retaining stolen property after discover is stolen not per se appropriation of same.

Corcoran v Anderton (1980) 71 Cr App R 104; [1980] Crim LR 385 HC QBD Snatching handbag which dropped and ran off without was appropriation.

Edwards v Ddin [1976] 3 All ER 705; (1976) 63 Cr App R 218; [1976] Crim LR 580; (1977) 141 JP 27; [1976] (1976) 126 NLJ 718t; [1976] RTR 508; (1976) 120 SJ 587; [1976] 1 WLR 942 HC QBD Petrol from pump appropriated with assent of both parties when enters tank, not when payment made.

Man-Sin (Chan) v R [1988] 1 All ER 1; (1988) 86 Cr App R 303; [1988] Crim LR 319; (1988) 132 SJ 126; [1988] 1 WLR 196 PC Drawing/presenting/negotiating forged company cheques for self was dishonest appropriation.

R v Atakpu and another [1993] 4 All ER 215; (1994) 98 Cr App R 254; [1994] Crim LR 693; (1993) 143 NLJ 652; [1994] QB 69; [1994] RTR 23; [1993] TLR 162; [1993] 3 WLR 812 CA Goods once stolen by thief cannot then be stolen or appropriated by him.

R v Cahill [1993] Crim LR 141 CA On appropriation of property.

R v Caresana [1996] Crim LR 667 CA Deception involving letters of credit did not involve requisite appropriation to constitute theft; English courts would assume jurisdiction in deception case with international aspects where gist of offence/appropriation occurred within England and Wales.

R v Devall [1984] Crim LR 428 CA Successful appeals against convictions for 'second appropriation'.

R v Feely [1973] 1 All ER 341; (1973) 57 Cr App R 312; [1973] Crim LR 192t; (1973) 137 JP 157; (1973) 123 NLJ 15t; [1973] QB 530; (1973) 117 SJ 54; [1973] 2 WLR 201 CA Appropriation with intent to repay not dishonest - jury must decide whether honest.

R v Fritschy [1985] Crim LR 745 CA Non-interference with owner's rights meant could not be guilty of theft.

R v Gallasso (Lesley Caroline) (1994) 98 Cr App R 284; [1993] Crim LR 459 CA Whether taking of property amounted to appropriation decided objectively.

R v Gomez [1991] 3 All ER 394; (1991) 93 Cr App R 156; (1992) 156 JP 39; (1991) 141 NLJ 599; [1991] TLR 206; [1991] 1 WLR 1334 CA Possession of property on foot of unavoided voidable contract not appropriation/theft.

R v Gregory (John Paul) (1983) 77 Cr App R 41 CA Appropriation a continuing process/may involve several people: thus person who seems to be handling might properly be convicted of theft.

R v Hilton [1997] TLR 201 CA On necessary appropriation where are charged with theft of credit balance.

R v Holden [1991] Crim LR 478 CA On necessary dishonesty before one's appropriation of property constitutes theft.

R v Hopkins; R v Kendrick [1997] Crim LR 359 CA On appropriation necessary to be guilty of conspiracy to steal.

R v Lockley [1995] Crim LR 656 CA Appropriation is a continuing act.

R v McHugh (Eileen Cecilia); R v Tringham (Rodney Duncan) (1989) 88 Cr App R 385 CA On what constitutes 'appropriation'.

R v McIvor [1982] 1 All ER 491; (1982) 74 Cr App R 74; [1982] Crim LR 312; (1982) 146 JP 193; (1981) 131 NLJ 1310; (1982) 126 SJ 48; [1982] 1 WLR 409 CA Evidence of state of mind to be given such weight as jury think in deciding if appropriation dishonest.

R v McPherson and others [1973] Crim LR 191t; (1972) 122 NLJ 1133; (1973) 117 SJ 13 CA Was appropriation to place shop stock in bag with intention to avoid payment.

R v Monaghan [1979] Crim LR 673 CA Was adequate appropriation to ground theft conviction where dishonest cashier accepted money, did not ring it up on till, and placed it in till drawer with intention of later removing it for herself.

R v Morris [1983] 2 All ER 448; (1983) 77 Cr App R 164; [1983] Crim LR 559; [1983] QB 587; (1983) 127 SJ 205; [1983] TLR 170; [1983] 2 WLR 768 CA Theft possible even if appropriation originally with owner's consent and honest intent.

R v Morris; Anderton v Burnside [1983] 3 All ER 288; [1984] AC 320; (1983) 77 Cr App R 309; [1983] Crim LR 813; (1984) 148 JP 1; (1983) 127 SJ 713; [1983] TLR 598; [1983] 3 WLR 697 HL Dishonest appropriation occurs even if dishonest act follows appropriation.

R v Navvabi [1986] 3 All ER 102; (1986) 83 Cr App R 271; [1987] Crim LR 57; (1986) 150 JP 474; (1986) 136 NLJ 893; (1970) 130 SJ 681; [1986] 1 WLR 1311 CA Use of cheque card to guarantee cheque drawn on account without necessary funds not an assumption of bank's rights and so not appropriation.

R v Ngan [1997] TLR 407 CA Was not appropriation to send cheque (that drew on money mistakenly paid into account) to relative in Scotland but were guilty of theft where cheque presented for payment in England.

R v Philippou (Christakis) (1989) 89 Cr App R 290; [1989] Crim LR 559; [1989] Crim LR 585 CA Sole directors/shareholders using funds of company that soon after went into liquidation to buy flats abroad was appropriation of company funds.

R v Pitham (Charles Henry); R v Hehl (Brian Robert) (1977) 65 Cr App R 45; [1977] Crim LR 285 CA Any assumption of owner's rights constitutes appropriation.

R v Rader [1992] Crim LR 663 CA Is necessary degree of appropriation to sustain theft conviction where come by another's property with full consent of that other (no appropriation) and thereafter assume rights of owner (appropriation).

R v Roberts [1991] RTR 361 CA Conviction quashed where had been misdirection by judge as to jurisdiction (which depended on appropriation occurring in England).

R v Skipp [1975] Crim LR 114 CA On appropriation necessary to support conviction for theft.

R v Small (Adrian Anthony) (1988) 86 Cr App R 170; [1987] Crim LR 777; [1988] RTR 32 CA Whether was dishonest appropriation depended on whether dishonest by ordinary standards and whether accused would have understood it to be such.

R v Stringer (Neil Bancroft) (1992) 94 Cr App R 13 CA Signing false invoices was sufficient appropriation to support conviction for theft.

R v Stuart (1983) 147 JP 221; [1982] TLR 632 CA For there to be theft there must be dishonest intent at time of appropriation.

R v Wille (Bryan James) (1988) 86 Cr App R 296 CA Drawing and issuing of company cheques for self was appropriation under Theft Act 1968, s 3(1).

Stapylton v O'Callaghan [1973] 2 All ER 782; [1974] Crim LR 63; (1973) 137 JP 579 HC QBD Dishonest appropriation and intention of retention merits theft conviction.

DISHONESTY (asportation)

R v Davenport [1954] 1 All ER 602; (1954) 38 Cr App R 37; [1954] Crim LR 383; (1954) 118 JP 241; (1954) 98 SJ 217; [1954] 1 WLR 569 CCA Not liable for stealing money as no asportation but was liable for embezzlement.

R v Taylor (William) (1910-11) 6 Cr App R 12; (1911) 75 JP 126; [1911] 1 KB 674; (1911) 80 LJCL 311; (1910-11) XXVII TLR 108 CCA Was sufficient asportavit in attempted pickpocketing to support larceny conviction.

R v Turvey [1946] 2 All ER 60; (1945-46) 31 Cr App R 154; (1946) 110 JP 270; (1946) 96 LJ 304; (1946) 175 LTR 308; (1946) 90 SJ 395; (1945-46) LXII TLR 511; (1946) WN (I) 121 CCA No asportation (despite handing of goods being part of entrapment) so no larceny.

DISHONESTY (attempt)

Davey and others v Lee [1967] 2 All ER 423; (1967) 51 Cr App R 303; [1967] Crim LR 357; (1967) 131 JP 327; [1968] 1 QB 366; (1967) 111 SJ 212; [1967] 3 WLR 105 HC QBD On what constitutes attempt.

Partington v Williams (1976) 62 Cr App R 220; [1977] Crim LR 609; (1976) 126 NLJ 89t CA Could not be convicted of attempted offence where could not have committed complete offence.

Partington v Williams (1976) 120 SJ 80 HC QBD Could not be convicted of attempted offence where could not have committed complete offence.

DISHONESTY (attempted burglary)

R v Bates (William) (1930-31) Cr App R 49 CCA For purposes of Prevention of Crimes Act 1871, s 20, attempted burglary is not a crime.

R v Boyle (George); R v Boyle (James) (1987) 84 Cr App R 270; [1987] Crim LR 111 CA Courts could look to pre-Criminal Attempts Act 1981 law to determine what constitutes an attempt.

Scudder v Barrett (1979) 69 Cr App R 277; [1980] QB 195; [1979] 3 WLR 591 HC QBD Need not prove intention to steal particular objects on charge of attempted theft/burglary.

DISHONESTY (attempted larceny)

Carey v Martin [1954] Crim LR 139t HC QBD Was not attempted larceny to break shop skylight (with intent to enter) and then to run away.

R v Hawkey [1964] Crim LR 465 CCA Ought not to have been convicted of attempted larceny where evidence pointed equally towards guilt of lesser offence of attempted taking/driving away.

DISHONESTY (attempted theft)

R v Bayley and Easterbrook [1980] Crim LR 503 CA On necessary intent for attempted theft.

R v Cooper and Miles [1979] Crim LR 42 CrCt On elements of attempt to steal.

R v Easom [1971] 2 All ER 945; (1971) 55 Cr App R 410; [1972] Crim LR 487t; (1971) 135 JP 477; [1971] 2 QB 315; (1971) 115 SJ 485; [1971] 3 WLR 82 CA For theft/attempted theft must be intent to permanently deprive.

R v Gullefer [1990] 3 All ER 882; (1990) 91 Cr App R 356; [1987] Crim LR 195; [1990] 1 WLR 1063 CA Not attempted theft where leaped onto race track with intention of foiling race so that could recover money bet on (what would have turned out if succeded to be void) race.

R v Hector (Joseph) (1978) 67 Cr App R 224; (1978) 128 NLJ 212t CA Not attempted theft to get into car with view to see if anything worth stealing therefrom.

R v Hussein [1978] Crim LR 219 CA Not attempted theft to open van door so as to look inside holdall and take anything of value that might be contained therein.

R v Husseyn (otherwise Hussein) (Ulus) (1978) 67 Cr App R 131 HL Given presence of intent to steal was attempted theft to open van door as prelude to taking holdall.

Scudder v Barrett (1979) 69 Cr App R 277; [1980] QB 195; [1979] 3 WLR 591 HC QBD Need not prove intention to steal particular objects on charge of attempted theft/burglary.

DISHONESTY (breaking and entering)

R v Beacontree Justices; ex parte Mercer and others (1969) 119 NLJ 1166t HC QBD Persons refused summonses for inter alia alleged riotous assembly under Statute of Forcible Entry Act 1381 - statute not in force.

R v Brittain and others [1972] 1 All ER 353; (1972) 56 Cr App R 234; [1972] Crim LR 104t; (1972) 136 JP 198; (1971) 121 NLJ 1169t; [1972] 1 QB 357; [1972] 2 WLR 450 CA No intention to occupy premises needed to sustain forcible entry conviction.

R v Chandler [1911-13] All ER 428; (1913-14) XXIII Cox CC 330; [1913] 1 KB 125; (1912) 47 LJ 707; [1913] 82 LJKB 106; (1913) 108 LTR 352; (1912) WN (I) 276 CCA Shopbreaking conviction secured after entrapment valid.

DISHONESTY (burglary)

B and S v Leathley [1979] Crim LR 314 CrCt Freezer container was a building for purposes of Theft Act 1968, s 9.

Holloran v Haughton [1976] Crim LR 270; (1976) 140 JP 352; (1976) 120 SJ 116 HC QBD Sorting room in post office not a 'warehouse' for purposes of Vagrancy Act 1824, s 4.

Norfolk Constabulary v Seekings and Gould [1986] Crim LR 167 CrCt Unhitched articulated lorry trailer not a 'building' for purposes of Theft Act 1968, s 9.

R v Ayres [1956] Crim LR 129t/210t CCA Civil trespass not sufficient to support conviction for shopbreaking.

R v Boyle [1954] 2 All ER 721; (1954) 38 Cr App R 111; [1954] Crim LR 790; (1954) 118 JP 481; (1954) 104 LJ 488; [1954] 2 QB 292; (1954) 98 SJ 559; [1954] 3 WLR 364 CCA Can be guilty of housebreaking where trick one's entry into house.

R v Bozickovic [1978] Crim LR 686 CrCt Could not be guilty of burglary with intent to steal as entered building without knowing/to ascertain if there was anything worth stealing so did not have requisite intent.

R v Brodrick [1960] Crim LR 426 Sessions Person found in street with new dressing-gowns bearing shop name convicted of shopbreaking and larceny.

R v Brown [1985] Crim LR 212 CA Person whose body was half inside premises did 'enter' same for purposes of Theft Act 1968, s 9.

R v Clarke (Dennis Geoffrey) (1985) 80 Cr App R 344; [1985] Crim LR 209 CA Exceptionally police informer could rely on efforts to impede crime as defence; ought not to be convicted of aiding and abetting burglary where acquitted of burglary.

R v Collins [1972] 2 All ER 1105; (1972) 56 Cr App R 554; [1972] Crim LR 498; (1972) 136 JP 605; [1973] QB 100; (1972) 116 SJ 432; [1972] 3 WLR 243 CA Only enter premises as trespasser if know/reckless as to whether entering without permission.

R v Collins (Christopher) [1976] Crim LR 249 CCC Issue estoppel applied to preclude conviction for burglary following acquittal of rape charge arising from same occasion; failed autrefois acquit plea where charged with burglary after acquitted of rape charge arising from same occasion.

R v Godspeed (1911) 75 JP 232 CCA Person charged with burglary and receiving can be found guilty as accessory before the fact to both.

R v Gregory [1982] Crim LR 229 CA Person acting in 'handling' capacity could nonetheless be guilty of theft/burglary.

R v Hollis [1972] Crim LR 525 CA Person charged with offence under Theft Act 1968, s 9(1)(b) could not be convicted of offence under Theft Act 1968, s 9(1)(a).

R v Jones (John); R v Smith (Christopher) [1976] 3 All ER 54; (1976) 63 Cr App R 47; (1976) 140 JP 515; (1976) 120 SJ 299; [1976] 1 WLR 672 CA Trespass where exceed permission/reckless whether exceeding permission.

R v Kelly [1963] Crim LR 855g CCA Improper to allow jury return verdict of warehousebreaking with intent in respect of person charged with warehousebreaking and larceny (Larceny Act 1916, ss 26(1) and 27(2)).

R v Lackey [1954] Crim LR 57 Assizes Where something that has been secured is broken, that is a breaking.

R v Laing [1995] Crim LR 395 CA Could not be guilty of burglary where were not trespasser when entered building.

R v Loughlin (James) (1951-52) 35 Cr App R 69; (1951) 95 SJ 516 CCA Can be convicted of breaking and entering where discovered in possession of stolen property shortly after robbery of premises.

R v Lumsden [1951] 1 All ER 1101; (1951-52) 35 Cr App R 57; (1951) 115 JP 364; [1951] 2 KB 513; (1951) 101 LJ 275; (1951) 95 SJ 355; [1951] 1 TLR 987; (1951) WN (I) 257 CCA To be 'found...in' building with intent to steal contrary to Larceny Act 1916, s 28(4) must be firm evidence were actually in building.

R v Pearson (William David) (1910) 4 Cr App R 40; (1910) 74 JP 175 CCA Essence of feloniously entering dwelling-house in the night is the felonious intention.

R v Phillips (Michael Patrick) (1946-48) 32 Cr App R 47; (1947) 111 JP 333; (1947) WN (I) 129 CCA Possibility of repeat offence by person charged with housebreaking renders giving bail to same inadvisable.

R v Richards (George) (1924-25) 18 Cr App R 144 CCA Non-substitution by CCA of receiving conviction where acquitted of housebreaking.

R v Robinson and others [1970] 3 All ER 369; (1970) 54 Cr App R 441; [1970] Crim LR 645; (1970) 134 JP 668; [1971] 1 QB 156; (1970) 114 SJ 906; [1970] 3 WLR 1039 CA Barricading need not be use of force in retention.

R v Ryan [1996] Crim LR 320 CA Person who sought to enter building and was trapped mid-way in window-frame was guilty of burglary.

R v Starling; R v Calvey; R v Wright [1969] Crim LR 556; (1969) 113 SJ 584 CA Shopbreakers intending to steal goods which had been removed onto floor of store on previous night by fellow shopbreaker were guilty of larceny.

R v Tindale [1962] Crim LR 704 CCA Quashing of convictions to which pleaded guilty but which were unsupported by evidence; improper to impose consecutive sentences for offences arising from same facts.

R v Walkington [1979] 2 All ER 716; (1979) 68 Cr App R 427; [1979] Crim LR 526; (1979) 143 JP 542; (1979) 123 SJ 704; [1979] 1 WLR 1169 CA Burglary if trespass with intent to steal (even if nothing worth stealing); for jury to decide if area is 'part of building' from which public excluded.

R v Wheelhouse [1994] Crim LR 756 CA Could convict/acquit one/other co-accused jointly charged with burglary.

R v Whiting [1987] Crim LR 473 CA Could be convicted of burglary under s 9(1)(a) of the Theft Act 1968 though were charged under s 9(1)(b).

R v Williams and Woodley (1920) 84 JP 90; [1920] 89 LJCL 557; (1920) 123 LTR 270; (1919-20) 64 SJ 309 CCA Conviction allowed to stand notwithstanding inadvertent disclosure to jury of previous convictions of accused.

R v Wood (Ernest George) (1911-12) 7 Cr App R 56 CCA On housebreaking charge can infer felonious intent from circumstantial evidence.

Re Attorney General's References (Nos 1 and 2 of 1979) [1979] 3 All ER 143; (1979) 69 Cr App R 266; [1979] Crim LR 585; (1979) 143 JP 708; [1980] QB 180; (1979) 123 SJ 472; [1979] 3 WLR 577 CA Entering builiding with intent to steal (even if nothing worth stealing) is burglary/attempted burglary; guidelines on indictment of theft offences.

DISHONESTY (cheque)

R v Davis (Gary) (1989) 88 Cr App R 347 [1988] Crim LR 762 CA Cash given in exchange for uncashed cheque is the 'proceeds' of the cheque under Theft Act 1968, s 5(4); prosecution need not prove which of two cashed cheques (where only one should have been sent) was subject of theft.

DISHONESTY (claim of right)

Harris v Harrison [1963] Crim LR 497g; (1963) 107 SJ 397 HC QBD On claim of right as defence to embezzlement.

R v Bernhard [1938] 2 All ER 140; (1939-40) XXXI Cox CC 61; (1936-38) 26 Cr App R 137; (1938) 102 JP 282; [1938] 2 KB 264; (1938) 85 LJ 243; [1938] 107 LJCL 449; (1938) 82 SJ 257; (1937-38) LIV TLR 615; (1938) WN (I) 142 CCA On term 'claim of right' in Larceny Act 1916, s 1(1).

R v King-Jones and Gladdy [1966] Crim LR 510; [1966] 1 WLR 1077 Assizes Entitled to acquittal on charge of assault with intent to rob if (possible) bona fide belief that were entitled to money and to use force in obtaining it.

R v Woolven (Jonathan Robert) (1983) 77 Cr App R 231; [1983] Crim LR 623; [1983] TLR 405 CA On inclusion of claim of right direction when directing jury on what dishonesty (in Theft Act 1968, s 2(1)(a)) means.

DISHONESTY (conspiracy to rob)

R v King and King [1966] Crim LR 280t CCA Had to be definite agreement to rob before could (as here) be convicted of conspiracy to rob.

DISHONESTY (conspiracy to steal)

R v Barnard (Philip Charles) (1980) 70 Cr App R 28; [1980] Crim LR 235; (1979) 123 SJ 803 CA Conviction quashed where evidence of conspiracy to rob admitted on charge of conspiracy to steal.

R v Duncalf and others [1979] 2 All ER 1116; (1979) 69 Cr App R 206; [1979] Crim LR 452; (1979) 143 JP 654; (1979) 129 (1) NLJ 492; (1979) 123 SJ 336; [1979] 1 WLR 918 CA Conspiracy to steal a statutory offence; conspiracy only to defraud a common law offence; no fixed rules regarding questions under Criminal Evidence Act on previous convictions.

R v Froggett [1965] 2 All ER 832; (1965) 49 Cr App R 334; [1965] Crim LR 489g; [1966] 1 QB 152; (1965) 109 SJ 492; [1965] 3 WLR 602 CCA Party not principal in second (or first degree) to theft could be convicted of conspiracy to steal and receiving.

R v Hopkins; R v Kendrick [1997] Crim LR 359 CA On appropriation necessary to be guilty of conspiracy to steal.

R v Riley (Terence) (1984) 78 Cr App R 121; [1984] Crim LR 40; [1984] RTR 159 CA Could not disqualify person for facilitating commission of crime where allowed use of car on foot of conspiracy to steal.

R v Weymouth [1955] Crim LR 775 CCA Conspiracy conviction quashed where conspiracy could only be proved by reference to larceny (of which also convicted) which was in essence therefore the same offence.

DISHONESTY (fish)

Iremonger v Wynne [1957] Crim LR 624 HC QBD Parties acting jointly (one with light/one with gaff) were each guilty of aiding and abetting other in contravention of the Salmon and Fresh Water Fisheries Act 1923, s 1.

DISHONESTY (forcible detainer)

R v Mountford [1971] 2 All ER 81; (1971) 55 Cr App R 266; [1971] Crim LR 280t; (1971) 135 JP 250; (1971) 121 NLJ 177t; [1972] 1 QB 28; (1971) 115 SJ 302; [1971] 2 WLR 1106 CA Forcible detainer triable on indictment.

DISHONESTY (fraudulent conversion)

R v Bianchi [1958] Crim LR 813 Sessions Person charged with receiving money knowing it to have been obtained by fraudulent conversion might better have been charged with aiding and abetting fraudulent conversion/conspiracy.

R v Davenport [1954] 1 All ER 602; (1954) 38 Cr App R 37; [1954] Crim LR 383; (1954) 118 JP 241; (1954) 98 SJ 217; [1954] 1 WLR 569 CCA Not liable for stealing money as no asportation but was liable for embezzlement.

R v Davies (1913) 77 JP 279; (1913) 48 LJ 138; [1913] 82 LJKB 471; (1912-13) 57 SJ 376; (1913) WN (I) 55 CCA Prosecution of club treasurer for fraudulent conversion did not require fiat of Attorney-General.

R v Hignett (1950) 94 SJ 149 CCA On ingredients of fraudulent conversion.

R v Holmes (Percy) (1931-32) 23 Cr App R 46 CCA Twelve months in second division for fraudulent conversion by first time offender.

R v Lyle (William Stacey) (1924-25) 18 Cr App R 59 CCA Fraudulent conversion commenced abroad and completed in UK can be prosecuted for in UK.

R v Lyon [1959] Crim LR 54 CCC Director of private company acquitted of fraudulent conversion of company property.

R v Morris [1968] Crim LR 221; (1968) 118 NLJ 86t CA Must prove fraudulent conversion to sustain conviction for larceny by bailee.

R v Morter (Alfred Ernest) (1927-28) 20 Cr App R 53 CCA Control of property following entrustment of same is essence of fraudulent conversion.

R v Sheaf (Robert Ernest) (1925-26) 19 Cr App R 46; (1925) 89 JP 207; (1926) 134 LTR 127; (1925-26) XLII TLR 57 CCA Specificity in dates may be necessary to prove fraudulent conversion.

DISHONESTY (fraudulent misapplication)

R v Nicholson [1957] 1 All ER 67; (1956) 40 Cr App R 194; [1957] Crim LR 110; (1957) 107 LJ 43 (1957) 101 SJ 89; [1957] 1 WLR 146 CMAC Fraudulent misapplication of service bar takings was fraudulent misapplication of service property.

DISHONESTY (going equipped)

Minor v Director of Public Prosecutions (1988) 86 Cr App R 378; [1988] Crim LR 55; (1988) 152 JP 30 HC QBD Can be convicted of going equipped for theft where do act in preparation of an offence.

R v Bundy [1977] 2 All ER 382; (1977) 65 Cr App R 239; [1977] Crim LR 570; (1977) 141 JP 345; (1977) 127 NLJ 468t; [1977] RTR 357; (1977) 121 SJ 252; [1977] 1 WLR 914 CA Car could be place of abode but not when in transit.

R v Ellames [1974] 3 All ER 130; (1975) 60 Cr App R 7; [1974] Crim LR 554t; (1974) 138 JP 682; (1974) 124 NLJ 597t; (1974) 118 SJ 578; [1974] 1 WLR 1391 CA Article in possession must be for/in connection with future stealing.

R v Goodwin [1996] Crim LR 262 CA Person who successfully used Kenyan coins as substitutes for 50 pence pieces in gaming machines was guilty of going equipped for theft.

R v Hargreaves [1985] Crim LR 243 CA On required intention before are guilty of going equipped for theft.

R v Harrison [1970] Crim LR 415 CA Misdirection on 'going equipped for stealing' charge did not justify quashing of conviction on said charge.

R v Whiteside and Antoniou [1989] Crim LR 436 CA On necessary element of deception to sustain conviction for going equipped for cheating.

DISHONESTY (intoxication)

R v Foote [1964] Crim LR 405 CCA Once defence raises drunkenness as reasonable possible defence it is for the prosecution to prove accused had the necessary intent.

DISHONESTY (invito domino)

R v Miller (Keith Eric); R v Page (Terence Frank) (1965) 49 Cr App R 241; (1965) 115 LJ 402 CCA No larceny as no taking invito domino.

DISHONESTY (larceny)

Barnard v Roberts and Williams (1907) 71 JP 277; (1907) XCVI LTR 648; (1906-07) 51 SJ 411; (1906-07) XXIII TLR 439 HC KBD Laying night lines was not angling (and so not covered by Larceny Act 1861, s 25).

Billing v Pill [1953] 2 All ER 1061; (1953) 37 Cr App R 174; [1954] Crim LR 58; (1953) 117 JP 569; (1953) 103 LJ 719; [1954] 1 QB 71; (1953) 97 SJ 764; [1953] 3 WLR 758 HC QBD Temporary army hut was chattel which could be subject of larceny of fixture.

Buller and Co, Ltd v TJ Brooks, Ltd [1930] All ER 534; (1929-30) XLVI TLR 233 HC KBD Persons to whom stolen ring pawned could not be sued for its return by persons from whom title to goods originally derived but who did not own goods at time of pawning.

Digby v Heelan and others (1952) 102 LJ 287 HC QBD Failed larceny prosecution against bin-men who (contrary to council instructions) took scrap metal from third party's trash (no animus furandi).

Folkes v King [1922] 2 KB 348; (1923) 128 LTR 405 HC KBD Recovery of property from good faith purchaser who obtained same from agent who in turn obtained possession from principal by means of larceny by trick.

Harrison and Crossfield (Limited) v London and North-Western Railway Company (1917-18) 117 LTR 570; (1916-17) 61 SJ 647; (1916-17) XXXIII TLR 517 HC KBD Common carriers not liable in negligence for theft by employee of goods to be carried (despite accepting property in goods when prosecuting employee).

Hibbert v McKiernan [1948] 1 All ER 860; (1948) 112 JP 287; [1948] 2 KB 142; (1948) 98 LJ 245; [1948] 117 LJR 1521; (1948) LXIV TLR 256; (1948) WN (I) 169 HC KBD Larceny for trespasser to steal goods lost by another and found by trespasser on private land.

Hood v Smith [1933] All ER 706; (1934-39) XXX Cox CC 82; (1934) 98 JP 73; (1934) 150 LTR 477 HC KBD Entrapment of person charged with stealing postal packet in course of transmission by post.

Lacis v Cashmarts (1968) 112 SJ 1005; [1969] Crim LR 102t; [1969] 2 QB 400; [1969] 2 WLR 329 HC QBD In supermarket/cash and carry property passes when price paid: here authorised manager intended to pass property (albeit at unintended reduced price) so taking of property and carrying away not larceny.

Leicester and Co v Cherryman (1907) 71 JP 301; [1907] 76 LJKB 678; (1907) XCVI LTR 784; (1907) WN (I) 95 HC KBD Owners of goods could bring action in detinue against pawnbroker for stolen goods pawned with him despite court order for restitution of goods upon payment to him of amounts he advanced for the goods.

Martin v Marsh [1955] Crim LR 781t HC QBD Was larceny from the Electricity Authority to take money that had been deposited in an electrcity meter.

Martin v Puttick [1967] 1 All ER 899; [1967] Crim LR 241; (1967) 131 JP 286; [1968] 2 QB 82; (1967) 111 SJ 131; [1967] 2 WLR 1131 HC QBD No property passes to customer picking up supermarket items; such items not in manager's control/customer's possession so taking from store without paying (after manager sees goods) is larceny.

Martin v Puttick (1967) 51 Cr App R 272 CA No property passes to customer picking up supermarket items; such items not in manager's control/customer's possession so taking from store without paying (after manager sees goods) is larceny.

Mogan v Caldwell [1919] 88 LJCL 1141; (1918-19) XXXV TLR 381 HC KBD Shipowner enjoys property in untouched provisions given to seaman by shipmaster pursuant to Merchant Shipping Act 1906, s 25(1) but larceny of said goods unproven here.

Moynes v Cooper [1956] 1 All ER 450; (1956) 40 Cr App R 20; [1956] Crim LR 268; (1956) 120 JP 147; (1956) 106 LJ 138; [1956] 1 QB 439; (1956) 100 SJ 171; [1956] 2 WLR 562 HC QBD No taking unless animus furandi at moment of taking, not later.

R v Allan; R v Prentice [1963] Crim LR 118; (1963) 113 LJ 270; (1962) 106 SJ 960 CCA Person charged with larceny as servant could be convicted of simple larceny.

R v Ashman [1954] Crim LR 382t CCA Conviction quashed where inter alia inadequate attention paid to alibi evidence.

R v Ashworth (George Thomas) (1910-11) 6 Cr App R 112 CCA On joint indictment for stealing/receiving: one person not guilty of receiving unless property not always in exclusive possession of other.

R v Bagley (George Arthur) (1922-23) 17 Cr App R 162 CCA Lodging is not a chattel, money or valuable security for purpose of Larceny Act 1916, s 32.

R v Bergin [1969] Crim LR 328; (1969) 113 SJ 283 CA Absent fraudulent conversion of hire purchase car accused could not be guilty of larceny by bailee.

R v Bishirgian and others (1936) 154 LTR 499; (1935-36) LII TLR 361 CCA Non-mention of future commitments of business in prospectus for investment of same rendered it false in material particular contrary to Larceny Act 1861, s 84.

R v Bloom (Harry) (1910) 74 JP 183 CCA Person wearing ring of husband with whose wife had eloped must have been party to taking of ring or known ring belonged to husband to be guilty of larceny.

R v Bloxham (Bernard Conrad) (1942-44) 29 Cr App R 37 CCA Was no taking and carrying away/attempt at same so could not be convicted of larceny.

R v Boylan [1960] Crim LR 193 Sessions Not guilty of larceny of 10s note which was handed voluntarily to accused for another but not given by accused to that other.

R v Brockwell (1905) 69 JP 376 CCC Court cannot make restitution order in action arising under Larceny Act 1901.

R v Brodrick [1960] Crim LR 426 Sessions Person found in street with new dressing-gowns bearing shop name convicted of shopbreaking and larceny.

R v Bryant [1955] 2 All ER 406; (1955) 39 Cr App R 59; [1955] Crim LR 505; (1955) 105 LJ 346; (1955) 99 SJ 438; [1955] 1 WLR 715 CMAC Charge of common law larceny should not refer to Larceny Act 1916.

R v Bryant [1956] 1 All ER 340; [1956] Crim LR 200; (1956) 120 JP 103; (1956) 100 SJ 113; [1956] 1 WLR 133 CMAC On larceny by party under military law.

R v Christ [1951] 2 All ER 254; (1951) 115 JP 410; (1951) 95 SJ 531; [1951] 2 TLR 85; (1951) WN (I) 337 CCA On direction as to larceny/receiving.

R v Clay (1910) 74 JP 55 CCA Larceny conviction quashed where had been no evidence of felonious intent.

R v Clayton (Sam) (1920-21) 15 Cr App R 45 CCA Good faith belief that had right to money required quashing of larceny conviction.

R v Cockburn [1968] 1 All ER 466; (1968) 52 Cr App R 134; [1968] Crim LR 223; (1968) 112 SJ 91; (1968) 132 JP 166; (1968) 118 NLJ 182; [1968] 1 WLR 281 CA Not defence to larceny that intended to replace money taken (but is mitigating factor).

R v Collins (1921-25) XXVII Cox CC 322; (1923) 87 JP 60; (1923) 128 LTR 31; (1922-23) 67 SJ 367 CCA Non-substitution of conviction for obtaining money by false pretences for one of larceny.

R v Court [1954] Crim LR 622 CCA Adequate direction regarding possibility that certain witness might be accomplice.

R v Cuffin (1921-25) XXVII Cox CC 293; (1921-22) 16 Cr App R 179; (1922) 127 LTR 564 CCA On entrustment to company/company director.

R v Fenley (Charles) and others (1901-07) XX Cox CC 252 Assizes Cannot be found guilty of simple larceny where charged with compound larceny.

R v Fisher (Charles) [1969] Crim LR 20t; (1968) 118 NLJ 1102t; (1968) 112 SJ 905; [1969] 1 WLR 8 CA Could be charged as accessory after the fact to felony where offence existed when was allegedly committed but had been abolished by time charged.

R v Fisher (Edward) (1910) 5 Cr App R 102; (1910-11) 103 LTR 320 CCA On whether obtaining goods by virtue of fraud is larceny/obtaining by false pretences/conspiracy to defraud.

R v Fisher (Florence Sarah) (1921-22) 16 Cr App R 53; (1921) 56 LJ 448; [1922] 91 LJCL 145; (1921-22) 66 SJ 109; (1921) WN (I) 327 CCA Where acquitted of obtaining by false pretences contrary to Larceny Act 1916, s 44(3), could not be convicted of larceny CCA cannot substitute conviction with one in respect of which have been acquitted.

R v Frizzle [1966] Crim LR 221; (1966) 110 SJ 87 CCA On elements of larceny by finding (must believe upon finding object that owner can reasonably be discovered).

R v Gibbs (George Dennis) (1960) 44 Cr App R 77; [1960] Crim LR 197 CCA Cannot on same fact evidence be convicted of larceny of and taking and driving away motor vehicle.

R v Graham (Lawrence Brisco) (1912-13) 8 Cr App R 149 HC KBD Document could be valuable security for purposes of Larceny Act 1861, s 90 though could not be used for purpose which allegedly served.

R v Green and another (1914-15) XXIV Cox CC 41; (1914) 78 JP 224; (1914) 110 LTR 240; (1913-14) XXX TLR 170 CCA Presumption of coercion of wife by husband precluded her conviction for larceny.

R v Greenaway (William) (1908) 1 Cr App R 31; (1908) 72 JP 389; (1907-08) XXIV TLR 755 CCA On the elements of larceny.

R v Hampton (1914-15) XXIV Cox CC 722; [1915] 84 LJKB 1137; (1915-16) 113 LTR 378 CCA No larceny unless knowingly commit conversion.

R v Harding [1929] All ER 186; (1928-29) 21 Cr App R 166; (1930) 94 JP 55; (1930) 142 LTR 583; (1929) 73 SJ 863; (1929-30) XLVI TLR 105; (1929) WN (I) 262 CCA Domestic servant left alone in house may be named as owner of chattels in prosecution for larceny.

R v Harlow and Winstanley [1967] 1 All ER 683; (1967) 51 Cr App R 184; [1967] Crim LR 242; (1967) 131 JP 272; [1967] 2 QB 193; (1967) 111 SJ 93; [1967] 2 WLR 702 CA Not larceny to steal pipes from building under Larceny Act 1916, s 8(1).

R v Hawkins and others [1959] Crim LR 729 Assizes Deposition of witness absent through pregnancy read but portions on which defence counsel would have challenged witness omitted; on larceny by trick.

R v Hepburn [1961] Crim LR 621 CCA Test letter was a letter in the course of transmission by post for purposes of Post Office Act 1953, s 87(2)(b).

R v Hooley (Ernest Terah); R v Macdonald (John Angus); R v Wallis (William Alfred) (1921-22) 16 Cr App R 171; [1923] 92 LJCL 78; (1922) 127 LTR 228; (1921-22) XXXVIII TLR 724 CCA Jurisdiction for trying crime under Larceny Act 1916, s 84.

R v Hotine (1904) 68 JP 143 CCC Not offence under Larceny Act 1901 for employer to use money deposited with him by employees as security for their honesty to use such money so that it was unavailable to the employees when they quit their employment.

R v Howlett and Howlett [1968] Crim LR 222t; (1968) 118 NLJ 157t; (1968) 112 SJ 150 CA Convictions for larceny of mussels quashed where not proved that mussels were actally in another's 'possession' before were 'stolen'.

R v Hudson [1943] 1 All ER 642; (1942-44) 29 Cr App R 65; (1943) 107 JP 134; [1943] KB 458; (1944) 94 LJ 100; [1943] 112 LJ 332; (1943) 169 LTR 46; (1943) 87 SJ 237; (1942-43) LIX TLR 250; (1943) WN (I) 98 CCA Innocent taking succeeded by fraudulent appropriation was larceny.

R v Inman and Mercury Self-Drive Ltd [1966] Crim LR 106 Assizes Not larceny/fraudulent conversion where manager of car dealing firm sold cars at less than price agreed with vendor: situation gave rise only to debts of a personal nature.

R v James and another (1902) 37 LJ 76; (1901-02) 46 SJ 247; (1901-02) 50 WR 286 HC KBD Valid conviction of wife for larceny of husband's goods.

R v Joiner (Frederick) (1910) 4 Cr App R 64; (1910) 74 JP 200; (1909-10) XXVI TLR 265; (1910) WN (I) 43 CCA Must prove property at issue was stolen to support conviction for larceny.

R v Kelly [1963] Crim LR 855g CCA Improper to allow jury return verdict of warehousebreaking with intent in respect of person charged with warehousebreaking and larceny (Larceny Act 1916, ss 26(1) and 27(2)).

R v Kelson (Thomas Henry) (1909) 3 Cr App R 230 CCA Accused not explaining away supposed involvement with proceeds of theft presumed guilty of larceny.

R v Kidd and Walsh (1908) 72 JP 104 CCC Selling pirated music is not per se common law larceny.

R v Kindon (Thelma Daphne) (1957) 41 Cr App R 208; [1957] Crim LR 607 CCA Conversion of money obtained by way of tort was larceny.

R v King-Jones and Gladdy [1966] Crim LR 510; [1966] 1 WLR 1077 Assizes Ought not to be convicted of assault with intent to rob where believed had right to money and to secure same by force if necessary.

R v Kirkup (Johnson) (1949-50) 34 Cr App R 150 CCA Soldier accused of larceny of Government property from base ought properly to be dealt with under military law.

R v Knight (1909) 73 JP 15 CCA Failed prosecution for larceny of own goods from sheriff where goods had been seized by sheriff from accused in belief that were those of accused's wife.

R v Knight (Thomas) (1908) 1 Cr App R 186; (1908-09) 53 SJ 101 CCA Owner of goods cannot be guilty of larceny of same unless in possession of bailee.

R v Lackey [1954] Crim LR 57 Assizes Where something that has been secured is broken, that is a breaking.

R v Marcus (Jacob) (1922-23) 17 Cr App R 191 CCA On notion of recency in 'recent possession' doctrine.

R v Miles (Frederick) (1909) 3 Cr App R 13 CCA Could be tried under Prevention of Crimes Act 1871, s 7 though had already been tried/acquitted of larceny.

R v Millar and Page [1965] Crim LR 437t CCA Larceny convictions quashed where employer in attempt to catch criminals whom had been warned were trying to steal his property went further than merely facilitating the offence.

R v Mortimer (1907-09) XXI Cox CC 677; (1908) 1 Cr App R 20; (1908) 72 JP 349 CCA On need for animus furandi.

R v Neat [1900] 69 LJCL 118; (1899-1900) LXXXI LTR 680; (1899-1900) XVI TLR 109 HC QBD Conviction for theft of money of which prisoner was beneficial owner approved. (Larceny Act 1868, s 116(1)).

R v O'Driscoll [1967] 1 All ER 632; (1967) 51 Cr App R 84; [1967] Crim LR 303; (1967) 131 JP 207; (1967) 111 SJ 682; [1967] 3 WLR 1143 CA No larceny if owner retains possession; embezzlement conviction sustained though in reality act of larceny.

R v Oliver (John Simpson) (1909) 3 Cr App R 246 CCA Trustee cannot seek protection of Larceny Act 1861, s 85 where admitted misdemeanour before action thereunder began.

R v Parker (1969) 133 JP 343 CA One of two persons cannot be convicted of theft and the other not so where are jointly charged.

R v Parkin [1949] 2 All ER 651; (1949-50) 34 Cr App R 1; (1949) 113 JP 509; [1950] 1 KB 155; (1949) 99 LJ 581; (1949) LXV TLR 658; (1949) WN (I) 383 CCA Person climbing into building not 'found by night...in...building' contrary to Larceny Act 1916, s 28(4).

R v Parks [1966] Crim LR 559t CCA Successful appeal against larceny by finding conviction where jury not told that must have intent to steal at time of finding to be guilty of larceny by finding.

R v Parsons [1964] Crim LR 824t CCA Valid conviction of estate agent for fraudulent conversion of deposit cheques.

R v Richards (1911-13) XXII Cox CC 372; [1911] 1 KB 260; (1910) 45 LJ 790; (1911) 80 LJCL 174; (1911) 104 LTR 48 CCA Repairer removing fixtures in good condition guilty of larceny.

R v Rose [1956] Crim LR 198 Assizes Sale to third party of cars obtained on hire-purchase could be larceny; property transfer contract induced by fraud a valuable security for purposes of Larceny Act 1916, s 32(2).

R v Scranton (Archibald Frederick) (1920-21) 15 Cr App R 104 CCA Need not be breach of Larceny Act 1916, s 20(1)/larceny by bailee where do not pay person from whom bought goods which then pledged/sold to another.

R v Seymour [1954] 1 All ER 1006; [1954] Crim LR 475 (1954) 118 JP 311; (1954) 104 LJ 281; (1954) 98 SJ 288; [1954] 1 WLR 678 CCA Should be indicted for larceny and receiving where in possession of recently stolen property and allow jury decide of which are guilty.

R v Shacter (1960) 44 Cr App R 42; [1960] Crim LR 186t; (1960) 124 JP 108; (1960) 110 LJ 120; [1960] 2 QB 252; (1960) 104 SJ 90 CCA Auditor filling company office properly convicted as company officer within meaning of Larceny Act 1861, ss 83 and 84.

R v Singh; Billing v Pill [1989] Crim LR 724; [1953] 2 All ER 1061 HC QBD Hut bolted to concrete foundation was not attached to/forming part of realty so could be stolen.

R v Skujins [1956] Crim LR 266 Sessions Farm gate a part of the land and could not be stolen.

R v Smith [1918] 87 LJCL 676; (1918) 118 LTR 179 CCA On post-acquittal disclosure of convictions.

R v Smith [1962] 2 All ER 200; (1962) 46 Cr App R 277; [1962] Crim LR 388; (1962) 126 JP 333; (1962) 112 LJ 320; [1962] 2 QB 317; (1962) 106 SJ 265; [1962] 2 WLR 1145 CCA Cannot be receiving under Larceny Act 1916, s 33(1) if theft outside jurisdiction; can be guilty of larceny under Larceny Act 1916 s 33(4) regardless of whether convicted thereof elsewhere.

R v Smith (James Reginald) (1922-23) 17 Cr App R 133 CCA On substitution by CCA of larceny conviction for receiving conviction.

R v Starling; R v Calvey; R v Wright [1969] Crim LR 556; (1969) 113 SJ 584 CA Shopbreakers intending to steal goods which had been removed onto floor of store on previous night by fellow shopbreaker were guilty of larceny.

R v Stevens (Francis Joseph) (1932-34) 24 Cr App R 85 CCA Cannot be convicted of fraudulent conversion where charged with simple larceny.

R v Streeter (1899-1901) XIX Cox CC 570; (1900) 35 LJ 458; [1900] 69 LJCL 915; (1900-01) LXXXIII LTR 288; [1900] 2 QB 601; (1899-1900) 44 SJ 659; (1899-1900) XVI TLR 526; (1900) WN (I) 176; (1899-1900) 48 WR 702 CCR Not felony to receive goods stolen by wife from husband as her larceny not larceny at common law/under Larceny Act.

R v Sutton [1966] 1 All ER 571; (1966) 50 Cr App R 114; [1966] Crim LR 164; (1966) 130 JP 183; (1965-66) 116 NLJ 612; (1966) 110 SJ 51; [1966] 1 WLR 236 CCA Bailees giving goods on foot of forged document pass possession not property so is larceny by trick.

R v Taylor (William) (1910-11) 6 Cr App R 12; (1911) 75 JP 126; [1911] 1 KB 674; (1911) 80 LJCL 311; (1910-11) XXVII TLR 108 CCA Was sufficient asportavit in attempted pickpocketing to support larceny conviction.

R v Thompson [1965] Crim LR 553g CCA On whether/when to leave one or two charges to jury where person is charged with larceny and, alternatively, receiving.

R v Tideswell (1907-09) XXI Cox CC 10; (1905) 69 JP 318; [1905] 2 KB 273; (1905-06) XCIII LTR 111; (1904-05) XXI TLR 531 CCR Larceny where fraudulently agree to accept more of goods sold from bulk than contracted for.

R v Turvey [1946] 2 All ER 60; (1945-46) 31 Cr App R 154; (1946) 110 JP 270; (1946) 96 LJ 304; (1946) 175 LTR 308; (1946) 90 SJ 395; (1945-46) LXII TLR 511; (1946) WN (I) 121 CCA No asportation (despite handing of goods being part of entrapment) so no larceny.

R v Uxbridge Justices; ex parte Logan [1956] Crim LR 270 HC QBD Restitution of stolen property to rightful owner could be made by justices immediately upon conviction of thief.

R v White [1960] Crim LR 132; (1959) 103 SJ 814 CCA Was larceny to take drinks in public house after barman refused to sell same after-hours.

R v Williams and Hamilton-Walker [1959] Crim LR 727 CCC Failed prosecution for larceny of cars that were in possession of alleged offenders pursuant to hire-purchase agreement.

R v Williams; R v Williams (1953) 37 Cr App R 71; (1953) 117 JP 251; [1953] 1 QB 660; (1953) 97 SJ 318; [1953] 2 WLR 937 CCA Interpretation of Larceny Act 1916, s 1(1): 'fraudulently and without a claim of right'.

R v Woods [1968] 3 All ER 709; (1969) 133 JP 51; [1969] 1 QB 447; [1968] 3 WLR 1192 CA Cannot convict absent specific/implied charge: receiving not implied in charge of larceny; direction on implied charges to be irreproachable.

Rose v Matt [1951] 1 All ER 361; (1951-52) 35 Cr App R 1; (1951) 115 JP 122; [1951] 1 KB 810; (1951) 101 LJ 63; (1951) 95 SJ 62; [1951] 1 TLR 474; (1951) WN (I) 60 HC KBD Bailor depriving bailee of property (in which has special property) commits larceny.

Ruse v Read [1949] 1 All ER 398; (1948-49) 33 Cr App R 67; [1949] 1 KB 377; (1949) 99 LJ 77; (1949) LXV TLR 124; (1949) WN (I) 56 HC KBD Taking without dishonest intention followed by appropriation with dishonest intention is larceny.

Russell v Smith [1957] 2 All ER 796; (1957) 41 Cr App R 198; [1957] Crim LR 610; (1957) 121 JP 538; (1957) 107 LJ 570; [1958] 1 QB 27; (1957) 101 SJ 665 HC QBD Cannot possess something of which do not know: an innocent taking.

Smith v Dear (1901-07) XX Cox CC 458; (1903) 67 JP 244; (1903) LXXXVIII LTR 664 HC KBD Any person (not just owner) may prosecute for unlawful and wilful killing of house pigeon.

Stamp v United Dominions Trust (Commercial), Ltd [1967] 1 All ER 251; (1967) 131 JP 177; [1967] 1 QB 418; (1966) 110 SJ 906; [1967] 2 WLR 541 HC QBD Post-conviction restitution order for property in possession of third party permissible but exceptional.

Walters v Lunt and another [1951] 2 All ER 645; (1951-52) 35 Cr App R 94; (1951) 115 JP 512; (1951) 101 LJ 482; (1951) 95 SJ 625; (1951) WN (I) 472 HC KBD Child under eight cannot commit larceny so person acquiring 'stolen' items therefrom not receiving stolen property.

Waterfield v Murcutt (1927) 64 LJ ccr38 CyCt Damages plus interest to pawnbroker in action where sought return of goods pledged with him.

Wells v Hardy [1964] 1 All ER 953; [1964] Crim LR 405t; (1964) 128 JP 328; (1964) 114 LJ 440; (1964) 108 SJ 238; [1964] 2 WLR 958 HC QBD Construction of Larceny Act 1861, s 24 (unlawful and wilful taking of fish).

Whitehorn Brothers v Davison [1908-10] All ER 885; [1911] 1 KB 463 CA Person obtaining delivery of goods for re-sale by fraud guilty of obtaining by false pretences, not larceny by trick.

Williams and others v Phillips; Roberts and others v Phillips (1957) 41 Cr App R 5; (1957) 121 JP 163 HC QBD Dustmen convicted for larceny where sold refuse from dustbins.

Williams v Hallam (1942-43) LIX TLR 287 HC KBD Accused's agreeing to both charges being taken together meant that could not argue that could not be convicted and punished on both charges.

Williams v Phillips [1957] Crim LR 186t HC QBD Corporation refuse collectors guilty of larceny from corporation where took material from collected refuse.

DISHONESTY (larceny by agent)

R v Kane (1899-1901) XIX Cox CC 658; [1901] 1 KB 472; (1900) 35 LJ 712; [1901] 70 LJK/QB 143; (1901) LXXXIV LTR 240; (1900-01) XVII TLR 181 CCR Interpretation of larceny by agent provision (s 75) of Larceny Act 1861.

DISHONESTY (larceny by bailee)

R v Foster [1957] Crim LR 470 Sessions Failed prosecution for larceny as bailee where was inadequate evidence as to conversion necessary to sutain conviction.

R v Hastings [1958] Crim LR 128 CCA Successful appeal against conviction for larceny by bailee: on elements of offence of larceny by bailee.

R v Hastings [1957] Crim LR 612 CrCt Was evidence to go to jury as to possible larceny by bailee.

R v Morris [1968] Crim LR 221; (1968) 118 NLJ 86t CA Must prove fraudulent conversion to sustain conviction for larceny by bailee.

R v Rose (William) (1909) 2 Cr App R 265 CCA Valid conviction for larceny/larceny by bailee.

R v Scranton (Archibald Frederick) (1920-21) 15 Cr App R 104 CCA Need not be breach of Larceny Act 1916, s 20(1)/larceny by bailee where do not pay person from whom bought goods which then pledged/sold to another.

R v Wainwright (Clifford Walter) (1960) 44 Cr App R 190; [1960] Crim LR 494t CCA Was larceny by bailee for company representative who had been given company articles and told to sell at certain price to sell at own price and keep proceeds for self.

R v Wakeman (Robert) (1912-13) 8 Cr App R 18 CCA Fraudulent non-return of item loaned was larceny by bailee.

Thompson v Nixon [1965] 2 All ER 741; (1965) 49 Cr App R 324; [1965] Crim LR 438t; (1965) 129 JP 414; (1965) 115 LJ 545; [1966] 1 QB 103; (1965) 109 SJ 471; [1965] 3 WLR 501 HC QBD Person finding item and assuming possession thereof not a bailee.

DISHONESTY (larceny by finding)

McGregor v Benyon [1957] Crim LR 250 Magistrates Person could not be guilty of larceny by finding where was given (originally stolen) handbag by her daughter (who found the handbag).

McGregor v Benyon [1957] Crim LR 608 HC QBD Person could be guilty of larceny by finding where was given (originally stolen) handbag by her daughter (who found the handbag).

R v Whitaker; R v White (1914-15) XXIV Cox CC 472; (1915) 79 JP 28; [1915] 84 LJKB 225; (1915) 112 LTR 41; (1913-14) XXIII Cox CC 190; (1912) 76 JP 384; (1912-13) 107 LTR 528 CCA Failed prosecution for larceny by finding.

DISHONESTY (larceny by trick)

Coyne v Ward [1962] Crim LR 169t HC QBD Comparison of/contrast between larceny by trick and obtaining by false pretences.

Heap v Motorists' Advisory Agency, Ltd [1922] All ER 251; [1923] 92 LJCL 553; (1923) 129 LTR 146; (1922-23) XXXIX TLR 150 HC KBD Must be animus furandi for there to be larceny by trick.

Lake v Simmons [1927] All ER 49 HL Insurance policy effective as purported entrusting of goods to thief was larceny by trick.

R v Collins (Martin) (1922-23) 17 Cr App R 42 CCA On substitution by CCA of obtaining by false pretences conviction where accused charged with larceny by trick.

R v Edmundson (Harry) (1912-13) 8 Cr App R 107 CCA Keeping clothes sent pending payment but not paid for was larceny by trick.

R v Fisher (Edward) (1911-13) XXII Cox CC 340; (1910) 74 JP 427; (1909-10) XXVI TLR 589 CCA No larceny if property and possession thereof intentionally transferred.

R v Hilliard (1913-14) XXIII Cox CC 617; (1913) 48 LJ 659; [1914] 83 LJKB 439; (1913-14) 109 LTR 750 CCA On larceny by trick.

R v Jones (1910) 74 JP 168 CCA Conviction for larceny by trick quashed where was good ground for civil action for debt.

R v Jones (Alfred) (1910) 4 Cr App R 17; (1909-10) XXVI TLR 226 CCA Receiver of goods obtained where promised would but did not pay for same need not be guilty of larceny by trick.

R v Stephens (John) (1910) 4 Cr App R 52 CCA Was larceny by trick where provider of goods believed would be paid for same in cash though this point never stated.

DISHONESTY (larceny from the person)

R v Fenley (Charles) and others (1901-07) XX Cox CC 252 Assizes Cannot be found guilty of simple larceny where charged with compound larceny.

DISHONESTY (larceny in presence of husband)

R v Caroubi (1913-14) XXIII Cox CC 177; (1911-12) 7 Cr App R 149; (1912) 76 JP 262; (1912-13) 107 LTR 415 CCA Conviction of larceny by wife (in presence of husband) set aside for inadequate direction on collusion/coercion.

DISHONESTY (larceny of deer)

Threlkeld v Smith (1901-07) XX Cox CC 38; [1901] 2 KB 531; [1901] 70 LJK/QB 921; (1901-02) LXXXV LTR 275; (1900-01) XVII TLR 612; (1901-02) 50 WR 158 HC KBD Killing of deer outside place kept is killing deer lawfully come by (Larceny Act 1861, s 14) even though killer wrongly on third party's land.

DISHONESTY (larceny of fish)

Cain v Campbell [1978] Crim LR 292 CA Must intend to catch salmon to be guilty of offence under Salmon and Freshwater Fisheries Act 1975, s 19.

Davies v Jones and others (1901-02) 46 SJ 319 HC KBD No evidence that tenant did not enjoy right of fishing under lease so conviction for taking of fish quashed.

Leavett v Clark (1915) 79 JP 396; [1915] 3 KB 9; (1915) 50 LJ 253; [1915] 84 LJKB 2157; (1915-16) 113 LTR 424; (1914-15) XXXI TLR 424; (1915) WN (I) 211 HC KBD Taking of winkles was larceny of fish under Larceny Act 1861, s 24.

R v Mallison (William) (1901-07) XX Cox CC 204; (1902) LXXXVI LTR 600 CCR Was larceny from smack-owner for skipper of smack to sell fish caught at sea and take proceeds for self.

Stead v Tillotson and another (1899-1900) 44 SJ 212; (1899-1900) XVI TLR 170; (1899-1900) 48 WR 431 HC QBD Taking dying trout with improperly licensed instrument is crime under Salmon Fishery Act 1873, s 22.

DISHONESTY (larceny of fixture)

R v Cooper (Edward), Shea, and Stocks (1908) 1 Cr App R 88; (1907-08) XXIV TLR 867 CCA Though principal acquitted of common law larceny of fixtures could convict receiver for breach of Larceny Act 1861, s 59.

R v Molloy (John) (1920-21) 15 Cr App R 170; (1921) 85 JP 233; (1920-21) XXXVII TLR 611 CCA Consideration of Larceny Act 1916, s 8(1) (larceny of fixtures); cannot be convicted of common law larceny where charged with larceny of fixtures (contrary to Larceny Act 1916, s 8(1)).

R v Richards (George Henry) (1910-11) 6 Cr App R 21; (1911) 75 JP 144; (1910) WN (I) 268 CCA Application of larceny by trick to real property.

DISHONESTY (larceny of pigeon)

Cotterill v Penn [1935] All ER 204; (1934-39) XXX Cox CC 258; (1935) 99 JP 276; [1936] 1 KB 53; (1935) 79 LJ 432; [1936] 105 LJCL 1; (1935) 153 LTR 377; (1935) 79 SJ 383; (1934-35) LI TLR 459; (1935) WN (I) 107 HC KBD That mistook breed of bird did not relieve liability for intended killing of particular bird under Larceny Act 1861, s 23.

Farey v Welch (1926-30) XXVIII Cox CC 604; (1929) 93 JP 70; [1929] 1 KB 388; (1929) 67 LJ 145; (1929) 98 LJCL 318; (1929) 140 LTR 560; (1928-29) XLV TLR 277; (1929) WN (I) 32 HC KBD Failed conviction for larceny of pigeon where acted under honest mistaken belief that was taking own pigeon.

Horton v Gwynne [1921] All ER 497; (1918-21) XXVI Cox CC 744; (1921) 85 JP 210; [1921] 2 KB 661; [1921] LJCL 1151; (1921) 125 LTR 309; (1921) WN (I) 144 HC KBD No defence to killing house pigeon that thought it was wild pigeon.

Smith v Dear (1901-07) XX Cox CC 458; (1903) 67 JP 244; (1903) LXXXVIII LTR 664 HC KBD Any person (not just owner) may prosecute for unlawful and wilful killing of house pigeon.

DISHONESTY (misapplication of service property)

R v Tucker [1952] 2 All ER 1074; (1952) 96 SJ 866 CMAC Shortfall in mess funds and non-excuse by accused not proof that misapplied service property contrary to Army Act, s 17.

DISHONESTY (misappropriation)

Sargeant v Large [1954] Crim LR 213t HC QBD Successful prosecution for wrongful withholding/ misapplication of club property contrary to Industrial and Provident Societies Act 1893.

DISHONESTY (pawnbroker)

Levinson v Rees (1918-21) XXVI Cox CC 384 HC KBD Failed prosecution against pawnbroker for charging a profit.

DISHONESTY (possession of housebreaking implements)

R v Brown (Harry) (1968) 52 Cr App R 70; [1968] Crim LR 112t; (1967) 111 SJ 907 CA Instrument which aids in housebreaking but cannot be used for actual act of breaking and entering can be housebreaking implement.

R v Harris [1961] Crim LR 256 CCA On burden of proof in context of prosecution for possession of housebreaking implements by night.

R v Harris [1924] All ER 286; (1921-25) XXVII Cox CC 746; (1925) 89 JP 37; [1925] 94 LJCL 164; (1925) 132 LTR 672; (1924-25) XLI TLR 205 CCA Possessing housebreaking implements at night contrary to Larceny Act 1916, s 28 involves actual possession at night and upon arrest of implements.

R v Harris (Davis) (1924-25) 18 Cr App R 157; (1925) 60 LJ 11; (1925) WN (I) 8 CCA Must be in possession of housebreaking implements after 9pm to be guilty of Larceny Act 1916, s 28(2) offence.

R v Hatch (William Robert) (1932-34) 24 Cr App R 100 CCA Conviction quashed as evidence given that door marks made by implements at issue though accused told would not be charged with housebreaking.

R v Hodges (1957) 41 Cr App R 218; [1957] Crim LR 682 CCA Evidence of persons to whom showed keys/invited to join in break-in admissible to rebut lawful excuse defence to charge of possessing housebreaking implements by night.

R v Lester (John Edward); R v Byast (Trevor Humphrey) (1955) 39 Cr App R 157; [1955] Crim LR 648 CCA Conviction for possession of housebreaking implements at night for driver who had same on person and in car boot affirmed; conviction of passenger for same - where had no implements on person - quashed.

R v Mansfield [1975] Crim LR 101 CA Using documents to get job so that at some later time might steal was too tenuous a factual basis to support conviction.

R v Patterson [1962] 1 All ER 340; (1962) 46 Cr App R 106; [1962] Crim LR 167; (1962) 126 JP 126; (1962) 112 LJ 138; [1962] 2 QB 429; (1962) 106 SJ 156 CCA Burden on defendant to show why carrying implement at night once proven to be housebreaking implement.

R v Percival, Smith and Graham (1905) 69 JP 320 Sessions Stone/linen coated in treacle are housebreaking implements for purposes of Larceny Act 1861, s 58.

R v Seckree alias Ward (Edward) (1914-15) 11 Cr App R 245; (1916) 80 JP 16 CCA Burden of proof on prosecution to show guilty goal where accused shows had implements for innocent purpose.

R v Stevenson and Baldwin (1905) 69 JP 84 Sessions Person continuously observed from 5am to 7am (at which time attempted crime) could then be charged with possession of housebreaking implements without lawful excuse between 9pm and 6am.

R v Taylor (William) (1922-23) 17 Cr App R 109; (1923) 87 JP 104 CCA On need to show connection between possession of implement and committing of offence using instrument.

R v Ward (1915-17) XXV Cox CC 255; [1915] 3 KB 696; [1916] 85 LJKB 483; (1916) 114 LTR 192; (1915-16) 60 SJ 27; (1915) WN (I) 317 CCA Is lawful excuse to possession of housebreaking tools (contrary to Larceny Act 1861, s 58) that possess tools for trading purposes.

R v Webley (WA); R v Webley (PR) [1967] Crim LR 300; (1967) 111 SJ 111 CA On need for person to be aware of presence of housebreaking implements before can be convicted of possession of same.

DISHONESTY (possession of stolen property)

R v Bailey (John) (1917-18) 13 Cr App R 27 CCA On adequacy of possession of stolen property some months after larceny as evidence of shopbreaking.

DISHONESTY (receiving)

R v Goodwin (William) (1910) 4 Cr App R 196 CCA Once jury decides was mens rea only limited possession necessary to sustain receiving conviction.

DISHONESTY (recent possession)

R v Gordon (Nathan) (1909) 2 Cr App R 52 CCA Servant with guilty knowledge subject to recent possession doctrine.

R v Greatwood (1946) 96 LJ 431 CCA Doctrine of recent possession held not to apply where was three month gap between theft and possession.

R v Green (Isaac) (1908) 1 Cr App R 124 CCA Whether knew had stolen property in possession a matter for jury; slip as to previous conviction not picked up on by judge/jury does not merit quashing of conviction.

R v Hobbs and Geoffrey-Smith (1982) 132 NLJ 440 CA On the 'doctrine of recent possession'.

R v Marcus (Jacob) (1922-23) 17 Cr App R 191 CCA On notion of recency in 'recent posession' doctrine.

R v O'Brien Fallon (Matthew) (1963) 47 Cr App R 160; [1963] Crim LR 515; (1963) 107 SJ 398 CCA Robbery with violence conviction quashed for want of evidence but simple robbery conviction substituted in light of recent possession.

R v Smith (1984) 148 JP 215 CA On inferring guilt of theft from possession of recently stolen property.

R v Smith (William) [1983] TLR 692 CA On doctrine of recent possession.

DISHONESTY (restitution)

R v London County Justices; ex parte Dettmer and Co (1908) 72 JP 513 HC KBD Restitution of stolen property or of money made when sold but not both ought to have been ordered.

DISHONESTY (robbery)

R v Dawson [1976] Crim LR 692 CA Matter for jury whether shoving of another by offender in course of robbery in tandem with another constituted force.

R v Dawson (Anthony Mark); R v James (Anthony) (1977) 64 Cr App R 170 CA Only issue in charge of robbery is whether force employed so as to steal.

R v Desmond; R v Hall [1964] 3 All ER 587; (1965) 49 Cr App R 1; [1964] Crim LR 724; (1964) 128 JP 591; (1964) 114 LJ 773; (1964) 108 SJ 677; [1964] 3 WLR 1148 CCA Robbery not in presence of person if not physically present at scene; can be convicted for crime that is element of serious offence (simple larceny where charge is robbery with violence).

R v Donaghy and Marshall [1981] Crim LR 644 CrCt On elements of offence of robbery (on need for ongoing threat).

R v Fallon [1963] Crim LR 515; (1963) 107 SJ 398 CCA Robbery with violence conviction quashed for want of evidence but simple robbery conviction substituted in light of recent possession.

R v Foreman [1991] Crim LR 702 CA On evidential basis to support robbery or at least handling conviction.

R v Forrester [1992] Crim LR 793 CA Valid conviction for robbery of person who believing self to act honestly took property from another (whom believed to have wrongfully withheld his money) to use as bargaining counter for return of money/to sell on, returning any excess above amount withheld.

R v Guy (Christopher) (1991) 93 Cr App R 108; [1991] Crim LR 462; (1991) 155 JP 778; [1991] TLR 92 CA Could be convicted of possessing firearm during robbery though relevant statute only refers to theft as robbery is theft with threat/use of violence.

R v Hale (Robert Angus) (1979) 68 Cr App R 415; [1979] Crim LR 596 CA Appropriation under Theft Act 1968, s 1(1) a continuing act.

R v Harrison (James) (1930-31) Cr App R 82 CCA Any violence sufficient to support conviction for robbery with violence.

R v O'Brien Fallon (Matthew) (1963) 47 Cr App R 160; [1963] Crim LR 515; (1963) 107 SJ 398 CCA Recent possession doctrine did not apply to robbery with violence charge where was charged with others - possession could be evidence that participated in robbery but not that used violence.

R v Pollock and Divers [1966] 2 All ER 97; (1966) 50 Cr App R 149; [1966] Crim LR 285; (1966) 130 JP 287; (1965-66) 116 NLJ 556t; [1967] 2 QB 195; (1966) 110 SJ 212; [1966] 2 WLR 1145 CA Common law offence of robbery by threatening to accuse of sodomy covered by demanding money with menaces under Larceny Act 1916, s 29.

R v Skivington [1967] 1 All ER 483; (1967) 51 Cr App R 167; [1967] Crim LR 182t; (1967) 131 JP 265; [1968] 1 QB 167; (1967) 111 SJ 72; [1967] 2 WLR 665 CA Claim of right (absent honest belief that could enforce claim as did) a defence to robbery charge.

R v Turner and others (1975) 61 Cr App R 67; [1975] Crim LR 451t; (1975) 125 NLJ 333t; (1975) 125 NLJ 410; (1975) 119 SJ 422/575 CA Appropriate sentence for serious offences (should be proportional to sentence imposed for murder: life imprisonment); fifteen years' imprisonment appropriate for armed Post Office robbers, eighteen years for those with criminal reccord.

Smith v Desmond and another [1965] 1 All ER 976; [1965] AC 960; (1965) 49 Cr App R 246; [1965] Crim LR 315t; (1965) 129 JP 331; (1965) 115 LJ 297; (1965) 109 SJ 269; [1965] 2 WLR 894 HL Crime done in presence of persons if done in other room within their care/control.

DISHONESTY (shoplifting)

R v Jamieson (Ronald Hamilton) (1975) 60 Cr App R 318 CA Heavier sentence not merited simply because sought trial by jury; appropriate sentence for single act of shoplifting by depressed man.

DISHONESTY (stealing)

R v Poolman (John) (1909) 3 Cr App R 36 CCA Failure to explain possession of recently stolen property need not merit conviction for stealing and receiving.

DISHONESTY (taking)

Russell v Smith [1957] 2 All ER 796; (1957) 41 Cr App R 198; [1957] Crim LR 610; (1957) 121 JP 538; (1957) 107 LJ 570; [1958] 1 QB 27; (1957) 101 SJ 665 HC QBD Cannot possess something of which do not know: an innocent taking.

DISHONESTY (theft)

Anderton v Wish (1981) 72 Cr App R 23; [1980] Crim LR 319/657 HC QBD Is appropriation to switch lower price tags to higher priced goods so as to pay lower price.

Attorney General's Reference (No 1 of 1985) [1986] 2 All ER 219; (1986) 83 Cr App R 70; [1986] Crim LR 476; (1986) 150 JP 242; [1986] QB 491; (1986) 130 SJ 299; [1986] 2 WLR 733 CA Employer has no proprietary right in profits from private sales by employee on employer's premises.

Attorney General's Reference (No 2 of 1982) [1984] 2 All ER 216; (1984) 78 Cr App R 131; [1984] QB 624; (1984) 128 SJ 221; [1983] TLR 702; [1984] 2 WLR 447 CA Illegal acts by all shareholders and directors will be imputed to them, not company; where plead defendant and company one and same cannot plead company consented to appropriations.

Attorney-General of Hong Kong v Nai-Keung (1988) 86 Cr App R 174; [1988] Crim LR 125; [1987] 1 WLR 1339 PC Export quotas were intangible property that could be dishonestly appropriated.

Attorney-General's Reference (No 2 of 1983) [1985] Crim LR 241; (1984) 128 SJ 203 CA Person/two persons in total control of company could be guilty/jointly guilty of theft of company property.

Atwal v Massey [1971] 3 All ER 881; (1972) 56 Cr App R 6; [1972] Crim LR 37; (1972) 136 JP 35 HC QBD Test in handling cases is whether believed were stolen or was reckless as to that fact.

Boggeln v Williams [1978] 2 All ER 1060; (1978) 67 Cr App R 50; [1978] Crim LR 242; (1978) 142 JP 503; (1978) 128 NLJ 242t; (1978) 122 SJ 94; [1978] 1 WLR 873 HC QBD Reconnection of electricity supply without permission not unlawful where no dishonest intent.

Bremme v Dubery [1964] 1 All ER 193; [1964] Crim LR 47; (1964) 128 JP 148; (1963) 113 LJ 806; (1963) 107 SJ 911; [1964] 1 WLR 119 HC QBD Relevant period in which to form intent to avoid paying fare included all travel on railway including alightment at station.

135

Brightside and Carbrook (Sheffield) Co-operative Society Ltd v Phillips (1964) 108 SJ 53; [1964] 1 WLR 185 CA Can make non-specific claim of conversion.

Corcoran v Whent [1977] Crim LR 52 HC QBD Could not be guilty of theft of food where formed requisite intention after ate it.

Davidge v Bunnett [1984] Crim LR 297 HC QBD Cheques given by persons with whom shared house to meet gas bill owed collectively was property to be used as sought so long as gas bill was paid.

Davies v Leighton (1979) 68 Cr App R 4; [1978] Crim LR 575; (1978) 128 NLJ 913t; (1978) 122 SJ 641 HC QBD Property in supermarket goods did not pass to customer until had paid for same.

Director of Public Prosecutions v Huskinson (1988) 152 JP 582; [1988] Crim LR 620 HC QBD Person using partly for self, partly for landlord benefit cheque paid to him and intended for rent/rent arrears not guilty of theft.

Director of Public Prosecutions v Lavender [1994] Crim LR 297; [1993] TLR 315 HC QBD Was theft to remove doors from one council property and hang them in other property of same council.

Eddy v Niman (1981) 73 Cr App R 237; [1981] Crim LR 502 HC QBD Actus reus of shoplifting is that do acts incompatible with owner's rights over goods.

Edwards v Tombs [1983] Crim LR 43 HC QBD Turnstile meter was a record so operator of same who wrongfully allowed persons through it was guilty of falsifying record made for accounting purpose (Theft Act 1968, s 17(1)(a)).

French and another v Director of Public Prosecutions [1994] TLR 71 HC QBD Could convict/acquit of handling/theft where person charged with both.

Harris v Harrison [1963] Crim LR 497g; (1963) 107 SJ 397 HC QBD On claim of right as defence to embezzlement.

Heaton v Costello [1984] Crim LR 485 CA On whether/when theft of several items a single course of action.

Kaur (Dip) v Chief Constable for Hampshire [1981] 2 All ER 430; (1981) 72 Cr App R 359; [1981] Crim LR 259; (1981) 145 JP 313; (1981) 131 NLJ 366; (1981) 125 SJ 323; [1981] 1 WLR 578 HC QBD Lawful transfer of property where voidable not void contract of sale.

Lanier (Louis Edouard) v R [1914] AC 221; (1914-15) XXIV Cox CC 53; [1914] 83 LJPC 116; (1914) 110 LTR 326; (1913-14) XXX TLR 53 PC On what constitutes embezzlement under Seychelles Penal Code.

Lawrence v Commissioner of Police for the Metropolis [1971] 2 All ER 1253; [1972] AC 626; (1971) 55 Cr App R 471; [1972] Crim LR 667; (1971) 135 JP 481; (1971) 121 NLJ 594t; (1971) 115 SJ 565; [1971] 3 WLR 225 HL Issue of consent relevant to whether dishonesty not whether appropriation.

Lewis v Lethbridge [1987] Crim LR 59 HC QBD Non-payment contributions received for charity was not theft.

Low v Blease [1975] Crim LR 513; (1975) 119 SJ 695 HC QBD Trespasser who made telephone call not guilty of stealing property (electricity).

Machent v Quinn [1970] 2 All ER 255; [1970] Crim LR 414t; (1970) 134 JP 501; (1970) 120 NLJ 434t; (1970) 114 SJ 336 HC QBD Prosecution need not show all items in information stolen by accused but can only be sentenced for those proved.

Man-Sin (Chan) v R [1988] 1 All ER 1; (1988) 86 Cr App R 303; [1988] Crim LR 319; (1988) 132 SJ 126; [1988] 1 WLR 196 PC Drawing/presenting/negotiating forged company cheques for self was dishonest appropriation.

Minor v Director of Public Prosecutions (1988) 86 Cr App R 378; [1988] Crim LR 55; (1988) 152 JP 30 HC QBD Can be convicted of going equipped for theft where do act in preparation of an offence.

Moberly v Allsop (1992) 156 JP 514; [1991] TLR 576 HC QBD Ticket inspectors can hold passengers who do not show tickets; Theft Act 1978 can be applicable to rail-connected cases.

Noon v Smith [1964] 3 All ER 895; (1965) 49 Cr App R 55; [1965] Crim LR 41t; (1965) 129 JP 48; (1964) 114 LJ 859; (1964) 108 SJ 898; [1964] 1 WLR 1450 HC QBD Theft can be evidenced directly or by inference.

Owners of Cargo of City of Baroda v Hall Line, Limited (1925-26) XLII TLR 717 HC KBD
Carriers liable in damages where failed to show that theft of goods was not due to neglect of their
servants.

Oxford v Moss (1979) 68 Cr App R 183; [1979] Crim LR 119 HC QBD Was not obtaining
intangible University property (contrary to Theft Act 1968, s 1) for student to obtain proof copy
of examination paper before sitting examination.

Oxford v Peers (1981) 72 Cr App R 19 HC QBD Is appropriation to switch lower price tags from
lower priced goods to higher priced goods so as to pay lower price.

Paterson v Norris (1913-14) XXX TLR 393 HC KBD Boarding-house keeper owes duty of care to
keep door of premises closed.

Pilgrim v Rice-Smith and another [1977] 2 All ER 658; (1977) 65 Cr App R 142; [1977] Crim LR
371; (1977) 141 JP 427; (1977) 127 NLJ 516t; (1977) 121 SJ 333; [1977] 1 WLR 671 HC QBD
Fraud nullified contract of sale so taking of product was theft.

Powell v MacRae [1977] Crim LR 571 HC QBD Bribe accepted by employee did not belong to
employers so employee not guilty of theft of bribe.

R v Adams [1993] Crim LR 72 CA Appeal against theft conviction allowed where non-direction of
jury that appellant may have had 'good faith purchase' defence under Theft Act 1968, s 3(2).

R v Allen [1985] 1 All ER 148; (1984) 79 Cr App R 265; [1984] Crim LR 498; (1984) 128 SJ 660;
[1984] TLR 333; [1985] 1 WLR 50 CA 'Intent to avoid payment' must be intent to avoid
permanently.

R v Allen [1985] 2 All ER 641; [1985] AC 1029; (1985) 81 Cr App R 200; [1985] Crim LR 739;
(1985) 149 JP 587; (1985) 135 NLJ 603; (1985) 129 SJ 447; [1985] 3 WLR 107 HL 'Intent to
avoid payment' must be intent to avoid permanently.

R v Atakpu and another [1993] 4 All ER 215; (1994) 98 Cr App R 254; [1994] Crim LR 693;
(1993) 143 NLJ 652; [1994] QB 69; [1994] RTR 23; [1993] TLR 162; [1993] 3 WLR 812 CA
Goods once stolen by thief cannot then be stolen or appropriated by him.

R v Aziz [1993] Crim LR 708 CA On whether/when (as here) non-payment of taxi-fare and
departure from scene could be offence of making off without payment.

R v Barr [1978] Crim LR 244 CrCt On what is meant by public having 'access to a building in
order to view' in the Theft Act 1968, s 11.

R v Beck (Brian) [1985] 1 All ER 571; (1985) 80 Cr App R 355; (1985) 149 JP 260; (1984) 128
SJ 871; [1985] 1 WLR 22 CA Was procuring execution of valuable security to fraudulently use
travellers' cheques/credit card vouchers abroad (in respect of which last payment occurred in
England).

R v Benstead (Peter David); R v Taylor (Malcolm) (1982) 75 Cr App R 276; [1982] Crim LR 456;
(1982) 126 SJ 308; [1982] TLR 152 CA Obtaining of irrevocable letter of credit could ground
conviction for procuring execution of valuable security.

R v Bhachu (Harminder) (1977) 65 Cr App R 261 CA Cashier guilty of appropriation where
undercharged customer whom knew and who then left with goods.

R v Bonner and others [1970] 2 All ER 97; (1970) 54 Cr App R 257; [1970] Crim LR 299; (1970)
134 JP 429; (1970) 120 NLJ 224t; (1970) 114 SJ 188; [1970] 1 WLR 838 CA On theft of
property by one business partner from another.

R v Brewster (Robert George) (1979) 69 Cr App R 375; [1979] Crim LR 798 CA Was theft for
insurance broker to use insurance premiums for self.

R v Brooks (Edward George); R v Brooks (Julie Ann) (1983) 76 Cr App R 66; [1983] Crim LR
188; (1982) 126 SJ 855; [1982] TLR 489 CA Must move past point where payment to be made
before guilty of making off without payment (may be attempt if stopped beforehand).

R v Candy; R v Wise; R v Wise [1990] TLR 524 CA That received advice from counsel that what
were doing was not a criminal act was not a defence to said act.

R v Caresana [1996] Crim LR 667 CA Deception involving letters of credit did not involve requisite
appropriation to constitute theft; English courts would assume jurisdiction in deception case with
international aspects where gist of offence/appropriation occurred within England and Wales.

R v Clotworthy [1981] Crim LR 501; [1981] RTR 477 CA Defence that believed owner would have agreed to (apparently unauthorised) taking of conveyance ought to have been heard.

R v Clouden [1987] Crim LR 56 CA On what constitutes force necessary to ground conviction for robbery under Theft Act 1968, s 8.

R v Coles (Thomas) (1910) 5 Cr App R 36 CCA Cannot plead general deficiency where admit possession of missing money.

R v Cooper (Charles Thomas) (1909) 3 Cr App R 100 CCA Non-receipt of moneys justifies jury finding of embezzlement.

R v Cording and others [1983] Crim LR 175 CrCt Was not theft to re-sell records given by record companies as gifts to people in media industry with view to promotion of said records.

R v Davenport [1954] 1 All ER 602; (1954) 38 Cr App R 37; [1954] Crim LR 383; (1954) 118 JP 241; (1954) 98 SJ 217; [1954] 1 WLR 569 CCA Not liable for stealing money as no asportation but was liable for embezzlement.

R v Davies [1982] 1 All ER 513; (1982) 74 Cr App R 94 CA Indorsement of cheque absent knowledge of what indorsing not transfer of property; indorsee's lodging of cheque is false representation so payment obtained by deception.

R v Devall [1984] Crim LR 428 CA Successful appeals against convictions for 'second appropriation'.

R v Dolan (Joseph Daniel Philip) (1976) 62 Cr App R 36; [1976] Crim LR 145t; (1975) 125 NLJ 1066t CA Can be convicted of handling stolen goods and theft where handled goods after theft.

R v Doole [1985] Crim LR 450 CA Even had debiting of deposit account occurred on foot of appellant's wrongful instructions that would not have rendered appellant guilty of theft of credit balance.

R v Downes (Patrick Joseph) (1983) 77 Cr App R 260; [1983] Crim LR 819 CA Sale of sub-contractor's tax vouchers where vouchers would ultimately be returned to Inland Revenue was theft.

R v Dubar [1995] 1 All ER 781; [1995] 1 Cr App R 280; (1994) 138 SJ LB 104; [1994] 1 WLR 1484 CMAC Trial judge must direct jury to find obligation if they find relevant facts to have been proved.

R v Dunn; R v Derby [1984] Crim LR 367 CrCt Moving motor cycle to have a better look at it was not taking conveyance.

R v Durkin [1973] 2 All ER 872; (1973) 57 Cr App R 637; [1973] Crim LR 372t; (1973) 123 NLJ 392t; [1973] QB 786; (1973) 117 SJ 355; [1973] 2 WLR 741 CA Pictures loaned recurrently to gallery are intended for permanent public exhibition: taking of one is theft.

R v Easom [1971] 2 All ER 945; (1971) 55 Cr App R 410; [1972] Crim LR 487t; (1971) 135 JP 477; [1971] 2 QB 315; (1971) 115 SJ 485; [1971] 3 WLR 82 CA For theft/attempted theft must be intent to permanently deprive.

R v Falconer-Atlee (Joan Olive) (1974) 58 Cr App R 348 CA On what constitutes 'dishonesty' under Theft Act 1968.

R v Feely [1973] 1 All ER 341; (1973) 57 Cr App R 312; (1973) 137 JP 157; [1973] QB 530; [1973] 2 WLR 201 CA Appropriation with intent to repay not dishonest - jury must decide whether honest.

R v Fernandes (Roland Anthony Peter Francis) [1996] 1 Cr App R 175; [1995] TLR 235 CA On what constitutes intention permanently to deprive another of his rights in his property.

R v Folkes [1982] Crim LR 610 CA Shoplifter could be convicted of theft though shop employee with whom probably acted in collusion not convicted.

R v Fritschy [1985] Crim LR 745 CA Non-interference with owner's rights meant could not be guilty of theft.

R v Fynn [1970] Crim LR 118t CMAC Conviction quashed where was inadequate direction as to failure of prosecution to call evidence as to whether 'advances' of pay (which formed basis for theft charge) were generally permitted by the defendant's employer.

R v Garwood [1987] 1 All ER 1032; (1987) 85 Cr App R 85; [1987] Crim LR 476; (1987) 131 SJ 357; [1987] 1 WLR 319 CA Not generally necessary for judge to explain word 'menaces' although could be desirable.

R v Ghosh [1982] 2 All ER 689; (1982) 75 Cr App R 154; [1982] Crim LR 608; (1982) 146 JP 376; [1982] QB 1053; (1982) 126 SJ 429; [1982] TLR 196; [1982] 3 WLR 110 CA Dishonest act if reasonable man would think dishonest and accused realised reasonable man would so think.

R v Gilks [1972] 3 All ER 280; (1972) 56 Cr App R 734; [1972] Crim LR 585t; (1972) 136 JP 777; (1972) 122 NLJ 609t; (1972) 116 SJ 632; [1972] 1 WLR 1341 CA Money paid under mistake is 'property belonging to another' and keeping it theft.

R v Gomez [1993] 1 All ER 1; [1993] AC 442; (1993) 96 Cr App R 359; [1993] Crim LR 304; (1993) 157 JP 1; (1992) 142 NLJ 1719; (1993) 137 SJ LB 36; [1992] TLR 592; [1992] 3 WLR 1067 HL Taking of goods with consent where fraud/deception/misrepresentation is theft (even if also obtaining property by deception).

R v Gomez [1991] 3 All ER 394; (1991) 93 Cr App R 156; (1992) 156 JP 39; (1991) 141 NLJ 599; [1991] TLR 206; [1991] 1 WLR 1334 CA Possession of property on foot of unavoided voidable contract not appropriation/theft.

R v Gordon (Nathan) (1909) 2 Cr App R 52 CCA Servant with guilty knowledge subject to recent possession doctrine.

R v Governor of Pentonville Prison and another; ex parte Osman [1989] 3 All ER 701 HC QBD On determining locus of theft/false accounting.

R v Graham and others [1997] Crim LR 340 CA On ramifications of Preddy decision for Theft Act offences.

R v Graham and others [1997] Crim LR 358; (1996) 140 SJ LB 253; (1996) TLR 28/10/96 CA Can be guilty of theft of chose in action though destroy same in course of appropriation.

R v Greenhoff [1979] Crim LR 108 CrCt Did not have requisite intent for burglary with intent to steal where entered premises with intent to steal any worthwhile money found.

R v Gregory (John Paul) (1983) 77 Cr App R 41; [1982] Crim LR 229 CA Person acting in 'handling' capacity could nonetheless be guilty of theft/burglary.

R v Grimer [1982] Crim LR 674; (1982) 126 SJ 641 CA Identification of shoplifter from video tape by person who had known shoplifter for some years rightly admitted in evidence.

R v Hall [1972] 2 All ER 1009; (1972) 56 Cr App R 547; [1972] Crim LR 453t; (1972) 136 JP 593; (1972) 122 NLJ 450t; [1973] QB 126; (1972) 116 SJ 598; [1972] 3 WLR 381 CA Breach of contractual obligation involving money not theft if not under duty 'to retain and deal with [it]...in a particular way'.

R v Hallam and Blackburn [1995] Crim LR 323; [1994] TLR 306 CA On elements of theft.

R v Hammond [1982] Crim LR 611 CrCt Not making off without payment to tender cheque which knew would not be met.

R v Hargreaves [1985] Crim LR 243 CA On required intention before are guilty of going equipped for theft.

R v Hayes (John Allan) (1977) 64 Cr App R 82; [1977] Crim LR 691 CA Conviction of estate agent for theft following wrongful appropriation of deposit quashed in light of inadequate jury direction.

R v Hilton (1997) 161 JP 459; [1997] TLR 201 CA On elements of theft of property (where said property is a credit balance).

R v Hollis [1972] Crim LR 525 CA Person charged with offence under Theft Act 1968, s 9(1)(b) could not be convicted of offence under Theft Act 1968, s 9(1)(a).

R v Holt and another [1981] 2 All ER 854; (1981) 73 Cr App R 96; [1981] Crim LR 499; (1981) 145 JP 377; (1981) 125 SJ 373; [1981] 1 WLR 1000 CA Plan not to pay for restaurant meal involves intent to make permanent default on whole/part of existing liability.

R v Ingram [1975] Crim LR 457t CA On pleading defence of absent-mindedness (absence of mens rea) to charge (of theft).

R v Jamieson (Ronald Hamilton) (1975) 60 Cr App R 318 CA Heavier sentence not merited simply because sought trial by jury; appropriate sentence for single act of shoplifting by depressed man.

R v Johnstone; R v Comerford; R v Jalil [1982] Crim LR 454/607 CA Where intended that owner of property receive same albeit in roundabout way there was no intention to permanently deprive owner of property and so no theft.

R v Kell [1985] Crim LR 239 CA On belief that had permission to take property/absence of intention to permanently deprive as defences to theft.

R v Large [1978] Crim LR 222 CA On direction necessary from judge as to relevance of series of thefts that did not establish guilt of defendant but did explain trap set by police to catch thief.

R v Lawrence [1970] 3 All ER 933; (1971) 55 Cr App R 73; [1971] Crim LR 51t; (1971) 135 JP 144; [1971] 1 QB 373; (1970) 114 SJ 864; [1970] 3 WLR 1103 CA Consent obtained through dishonesty does not vitiate theft; on what constitutes theft.

R v Lawrence (1970) 120 NLJ 1066 HC QBD Consent obtained through dishonesty does not vitiate theft.

R v Levy and Sobell [1973] Crim LR 453 CA Roughly three weeks' imprisonment for solicitor guilty of aiding undischarged bankrupt in management of company; five years' imprisonment merited by estate agent guilty of theft of deposits of clients.

R v Lloyd and others [1985] 2 All ER 661; (1985) 81 Cr App R 182; [1985] Crim LR 518; (1985) 149 JP 634; (1985) 135 NLJ 605; [1985] QB 829; (1985) 129 SJ 431; [1985] 3 WLR 30 CA No intention of permanently depriving where borrow/lend unless return in worthless state; statutory not common law conspiracy where full offence would be substantive.

R v Mainwaring (Paul Rex Garfield); R v Madders (Peter Clive) (1982) 74 Cr App R 99 CA Issue for jury where was unlawful business by company not whether intra/ultra vires memorandum of association but whether honest/dishonest behaviour; misappropriation of money: Theft Act 1968, s 5(3) applied; warning necessary where two company directors prosecuted incriminated each other/exculpated self.

R v Marchant (Stephen); R v McCallister (Stephen) (1985) 80 Cr App R 361 CA Was attempt to take conveyance without authority even though did not use conveyance.

R v Matthews [1950] 1 All ER 137; (1950) 114 JP 73; (1950) 100 LJ 20; [1950] 66 (1) TLR 153 CCA Acquiring property without guilty intent, then appropriating it is stealing not receiving.

R v McDavitt [1981] Crim LR 843 CrCt Person who intended to leave restaurant without paying bill but who remained in restaurant (though refusing to pay bill) guilty/not guilty of attempted theft/theft.

R v McHugh (Christopher John Patrick) (1993) 97 Cr App R 335 CA Was theft where dealt with clients' proceeds in way that mixed their funds with own.

R v McHugh (David) (1977) 64 Cr App R 92; [1977] Crim LR 174t; (1977) 127 NLJ 44t; [1977] RTR 1 CA Whether driving away from petrol station without paying for petrol was theft/obtaining pecuniary advantage by deception.

R v McHugh (Eileen Cecilia); R v Tringham (Rodney Duncan) (1989) 88 Cr App R 385 CA On what constitutes 'appropriation'.

R v McIvor [1982] 1 All ER 491; (1982) 74 Cr App R 74; [1982] Crim LR 312; (1982) 146 JP 193; (1981) 131 NLJ 1310; (1982) 126 SJ 48; [1982] 1 WLR 409 CA Evidence of state of mind to be given such weight as jury think in deciding if appropriation dishonest.

R v McPherson and others [1973] Crim LR 191t; (1972) 122 NLJ 1133; (1973) 117 SJ 13 CA Was appropriation to place shop stock in bag with intention to avoid payment.

R v Meech and others [1973] 3 All ER 939; (1974) 58 Cr App R 74; [1973] Crim LR 771; (1974) 138 JP 6; [1974] QB 549; (1973) 117 SJ 713; [1973] 3 WLR 507 CA Taking of proceeds of cheque cashed from one who obtained cheque by fraud is taking 'property...belonging to' another.

R v Meredith [1973] Crim LR 253 CrCt Inappropriate to accuse car-owner of theft of own impounded car.

R v Miller [1976] Crim LR 147 CA Cannot be guilty of being carried in conveyance without authority unless conveyance is actually moved.

R v Miller (Steven Henry) (1992) 95 Cr App R 421; [1992] Crim LR 744; [1993] RTR 6 CA Need only show that deceptions resulted in money being handed over (need not show deception at precise instant handed over money) to convict for obtaining property by deception.

R v Molloy (1914-15) XXIV Cox CC 226; (1914) 78 JP 216; (1914) 49 LJ 182; (1914-15) 111 LTR 166 CCA Theft of lead piping not simple larceny but contravention of Larceny Act 1861, s 31.

R v Monaghan [1979] Crim LR 673 CA Was adequate appropriation to ground theft conviction where dishonest cashier accepted money, did not ring it up on till, and placed it in till drawer with intention of later removing it for herself.

R v Morris [1983] 2 All ER 448; (1983) 77 Cr App R 164; [1983] Crim LR 559; [1983] QB 587; (1983) 127 SJ 205; [1983] TLR 170; [1983] 2 WLR 768 CA Theft possible even if appropriation originally with owner's consent and honest intent.

R v Navvabi [1986] 3 All ER 102; (1986) 83 Cr App R 271; [1987] Crim LR 57; (1986) 150 JP 474; (1986) 136 NLJ 893; (1970) 130 SJ 681; [1986] 1 WLR 1311 CA Use of cheque card to guarantee cheque drawn on account without necessary funds not an assumption of bank's rights and so not appropriation.

R v Ngan [1997] TLR 407 CA Was not appropriation to send cheque (that drew on money mistakenly paid into account) to relative in Scotland but were guilty of theft where cheque presented for payment in England.

R v O'Driscoll [1967] 1 All ER 632; (1967) 51 Cr App R 84; [1967] Crim LR 303; (1967) 131 JP 207; (1967) 111 SJ 682; [1967] 3 WLR 1143 CA No larceny if owner retains possession; embezzlement conviction sustained though in reality act of larceny.

R v Ofori (Noble Julius); R v Tackie (Nazar) (No 2) (1994) 99 Cr App R 223 CCA Prosecution ought to have proven that cars from abroad had been stolen under relevant foreign law.

R v Parker (1969) 133 JP 343 CA One of two persons cannot be convicted of theft and the other not so where are jointly charged.

R v Pearce [1973] Crim LR 321 CA Taking away dinghy after placing it in trailer was taking a conveyance (even though dinghy per se was for use in water).

R v Pick [1982] Crim LR 238 CrCt On appropriate charge for person who allegedly wrongfully took gaming chips from casino roulette table.

R v Rader [1992] Crim LR 663 CA Is necessary degree of appropriation to sustain theft conviction where come by another's property with full consent of that other (no appropriation) and thereafter assume rights of owner (appropriation).

R v Rao [1972] Crim LR 451 CA That hoped at some stage to put back the money was taking was not a defence to theft.

R v Roberts [1991] RTR 361 CA Conviction quashed where had been misdirection by judge as to jurisdiction (which depended on appropriation occurring in England).

R v Robertson (Stanley) [1977] Crim LR 629 CrCt Insurance agent who did not fully account to insurance companies for premiiums he received was not guilty of theft.

R v Robinson [1977] Crim LR 173 CA Not theft where of view that had right to take money.

R v Sainthouse [1980] Crim LR 506 CA Handler could be guilty of theft.

R v Shadrokh-Cigari [1988] Crim LR 465 CA Valid conviction of guardian for theft where got child for whom acted as guardian to authorise issue of bankers' drafts in guardian's name in respect of money mistakenly paid into child's account.

R v Shelton [1986] Crim LR 637; (1986) 150 JP 380 CA On handling/theft.

R v Shuck [1992] Crim LR 209 CA On appropriation necessary for theft.

R v Skipp [1975] Crim LR 114 CA On appropriation necessary to support conviction for theft.

R v Small (Adrian Anthony) (1988) 86 Cr App R 170; [1987] Crim LR 777; [1988] RTR 32 CA Whether was dishonest appropriation depended on whether dishonest by ordinary standards and whether accused would have understood it to be such.

R v Smith (1984) 148 JP 215 CA On inferring guilt of theft from possession of recently stolen property.

R v Sobel [1986] Crim LR 261 CA Failed appeal against theft conviction arising from unpermitted part use of company cheque to settle personal debt.

R v Spencer [1979] Crim LR 538 CA Five years' (not life) imprisonment for offender with personality disorder guilty of arson and theft but not an unceasing public menace.

R v Staines (Linda Irene) (1975) 60 Cr App R 160; [1975] Crim LR 651 CA On meaning of 'deception' and 'reckless' in Theft Act 1968, s 15(4).

R v Stalham [1993] Crim LR 310 CA Keeping money mistakenly paid by employer into one's account was theft of a chose in action.

R v Stringer (Neil Bancroft) (1992) 94 Cr App R 13 CA Signing false invoices was sufficient appropriation to support conviction for theft.

R v Stringer and Banks [1991] Crim LR 639 CA Can appropriate by way of innocent agent.

R v Stuart (1983) 147 JP 221; [1982] TLR 632 CA For there to be theft there must be dishonest intent at time of appropriation.

R v Tillings and Tillings [1985] Crim LR 393; (1985) 135 NLJ 510 CrCt Is no offence of deception in procuring execution of will.

R v Tomlin [1954] 2 All ER; [1954] Crim LR 540; (1954) 118 JP 354; [1954] 2 QB 274; (1954) 98 SJ 374; [1954] 2 WLR 1140 CCA Can charge for embezzlement of aggregate amount where impossible to divide into individual amounts taken.

R v Turner (No 2) [1971] 2 All ER 441; (1971) 55 Cr App R 336; [1971] Crim LR 373; (1971) 135 JP 419; [1971] RTR 396; (1971) 115 SJ 405; [1971] 1 WLR 901 CA Possession or control an issue of fact; no theft if honest but mistaken belief that had right to property.

R v Velumyl [1989] Crim LR 299 CA Was dishonest intent (and so was theft) where was unauthorised taking of money from company safe.

R v Vernon [1962] Crim LR 35; (1962) 112 LJ 76 CCA Thief might not be accomplice of handler.

R v Wain (Peter) [1995] 2 Cr App R 660 CA On what constitute 'proceeds' for purpose of Theft Act 1968, s 5(3).

R v Walker [1984] Crim LR 112 CA Theft conviction quashed in light of inadequate direction as to burden of proof on prosecution (to show that property at issue did not belong to party who sold it at time).

R v Warner (1971) 55 Cr App R 93; [1971] Crim LR 114t; (1971) 135 JP 199; (1970) 120 NLJ 1113; (1970) 114 SJ 971 CA On elements of theft under Theft Act, s 1(1).

R v Wilkins [1975] 2 All ER 734; (1975) 60 Cr App R 300; [1975] Crim LR 343t; (1975) 139 JP 543; (1975) 125 NLJ 285t CA Evidence of theft/handling conviction where charged with handling relates to guilty knowledge only.

R v Wille (Bryan James) (1988) 86 Cr App R 296 CA Drawing and issuing of company cheques for self was appropriation under Theft Act 1968, s 3(1).

R v Williams (Jean-Jacques) [1980] Crim LR 589 CA Was theft where sold out-of-circulation Yugoslavian money to bureau de change on basis that was good currency.

R v Williams (Jean-Jacques) [1979] Crim LR 736 CrCt Was no deception but was theft where sold out-of-circulation Yugoslavian money to bureau de change on basis that was good currency.

R v Williams; R v Lamb [1995] Crim LR 77 CA Solicitor properly prosecuted under Theft Act 1968, s 5(3) for holding on to money of client.

R v Wills; R v Wills (Graham George) [1990] Crim LR 714; (1991) 92 Cr App R 297 CA Successful appeal against conviction for theft of debt (did not handle cheque in accordance with drawer's instructions).

R v Wiltshire [1976] Crim LR 458 CA Four years' imprisonment for stockbroker guilty of theft from clients.

R v Woodman [1974] 2 All ER 955; (1974) 59 Cr App R 200; [1974] Crim LR 441t; (1974) 138 JP 567; (1974) 124 NLJ 464t; [1974] QB 754; [1974] 2 WLR 821 CA Persons in control of property prima facie in control of materials there.

Re Attorney General's References (Nos 1 and 2 of 1979) [1979] 3 All ER 143; (1979) 69 Cr App R 266; [1979] Crim LR 585; (1979) 143 JP 708; [1980] QB 180; (1979) 123 SJ 472; [1979] 3 WLR 577 CA Entering building with intent to steal (even if nothing worth stealing) is burglary/attempted burglary; guidelines on indictment of theft offences.

Ryan and French v Director of Public Prosecutions [1994] Crim LR 457; (1994) 158 JP 485 HC QBD On charging theft and handling together as alternative charges.

Scottish Dyers and Cleaners (London), Ltd v Manheimer (1942) WN (I) 114 HC KBD Bailed goods stolen from bailees deemed not to be 'detained'.

Solomon v Metropolitan Police Commissioner [1982] Crim LR 606 CA Action in detinue/ conversion failed where person bringing action/property subject of action a thief/car bought from money made through theft.

Stapylton v O'Callaghan [1973] 2 All ER 782; [1974] Crim LR 63; (1973) 137 JP 579 HC QBD Dishonest appropriation and intention of retention merits theft conviction.

Troughton v The Metropolitan Police [1987] Crim LR 138 HC QBD Could not be guilty of making off without payment from taxi-driver to whom one's obligations had ceased when he went into breach of contract by not completing journey.

Wakeman v Farrar [1974] Crim LR 136 HC QBD Was theft to cash a benefits giro in lieu of which had already received equivalent payment in cash on promise that would return giro if it later arrived (as it did).

DISHONESTY (theft in breach of trust)

Leesh River Tea Co Ltd and others v British India Steam Navigation Co Ltd [1967] 2 QB 250; [1966] 3 WLR 642 CA Shipowners as bailees for reward of goods carried by them not liable for theft by stevedores who were not their agents/servants.

R v Bowler (Ronald Arthur) (1973) 57 Cr App R 275 CA On appropriate sentence for petty theft by employee.

R v Kohn (David James) (1979) 69 Cr App R 395; [1979] Crim LR 675 CA On various circumstances in which employee using company cheques for own ends was theft.

DISHONESTY (theft of valuable security)

R v Beck (Brian) [1985] 1 All ER 571; (1985) 80 Cr App R 355; (1985) 149 JP 260; (1984) 128 SJ 871; [1985] 1 WLR 22 CA Was procuring execution of valuable security to fraudulently use travellers' cheques/credit card vouchers abroad (in respect of which last payment occurred in England).

R v Graham (Lawrence Brisco) (1912-13) 8 Cr App R 149 HC KBD Document could be valuable security for purposes of Larceny Act 1861, s 90 though could not be used for purpose which allegedly served.

DISHONESTY (treasure trove)

R v Hancock [1990] 3 All ER 183; (1990) 90 Cr App R 422; [1990] Crim LR 125; [1990] 2 QB 242; [1990] 2 WLR 640 CA In prosecution for theft of treasure trove jury to decide whether beyond reasonable doubt that property is such; coroner's verdict to that effect unnecessary.

DISHONESTY (union official wilfully withholding moneys)

Best v Butler and another (1931-34) XXIX Cox CC 482 HC KBD Trade union officer's withholding trade union moneys a continuing offence.

DISHONESTY (unlawful possession)

Stowe v Marjoram (1911-13) XXII Cox CC 198; (1909) 73 JP 498; (1909-10) 101 LTR 569 HC KBD Conviction for unlawful possession of eggs.

DOCK OFFENCE (general)

Gray v Heathcote (1918) WN (I) 147 HC KBD Conviction for dumping of refuse (oil-water mixture) into dock.

DRUGS (assisting in offfence)

R v Ahmed [1990] Crim LR 648 CA Were guilty of assisting in/inducing drugs offence abroad by way of act in England: that principal offender unidentified/actual importer an innocent third party did not affect guilt.

DRUGS (attempt to procure)

Kyprianou v Reynolds [1969] Crim LR 656; (1969) 113 SJ 563 HC QBD Intention to acquire drugs along with invitation to drug dealers to treat or make offer not enough to support conviction for attempted procurement of drugs.

DRUGS (attempt to supply)

R v Tulloch (Wayne Andrew) (1986) 83 Cr App R 1; [1986] Crim LR 50 CA Could be convicted of attempt where sought to commit what thought was possible but was in fact impossible offence.

DRUGS (causing/permitting premises to be used)

R v Ashdown (Robert James); R v Howard (Leonard); R v Howard (Judith Mary); R v Stuart (Michael Adrian) (1974) 59 Cr App R 193 CA Is possible for co-tenant to commit offence of permitting other co-tenant to use premises for cannabis-smoking.

R v Campbell (Guy); R v Campbell (Shaun) [1982] Crim LR 595 CrCt Sons holding party in parents' house were not 'occupiers' of house.

R v Josephs (Ivan Dick); R v Christie (Ransford) (1977) 65 Cr App R 253; (1977) 127 NLJ 415t CA Could be convicted of managing premises for cannabis smoking where controlled but unlawfully possessed premises.

R v Mogford and others (1976) 63 Cr App R 168; [1970] Crim LR 401; (1970) 114 SJ 318; [1970] 1 WLR 988 Assizes Daughters occupying house while parents away were not 'occupiers' of premises who could be guilty of allowing same to be used for cannabis-smoking.

R v Niemira [1970] Crim LR 28 CA Public house licensee's conviction for management of premises used for cannabis-dealing quashed where did not actually know that trafficking taking place.

R v Richards [1967] Crim LR 589t; (1967) 111 SJ 634 CA Successful appeal against conviction for allowing premises to be used for cannabis-smoking where evidence admitted as to condition of one party on premises but no warning given as to the weak connection between that and the offence charged.

R v Tao [1976] 3 All ER 65; (1976) 63 Cr App R 163; [1976] Crim LR 516t; (1976) 140 JP 596; (1976) 126 NLJ 566t; [1977] QB 141; (1976) 120 SJ 420; [1976] 3 WLR 25 CA Need not be owner to be occupier.

R v Thomas (Keith Ian); R v Thomson (Peter William) (1976) 63 Cr App R 65 CA Offender normally must have mens rea to be guilty of 'knowingly' permitting premises to be used for cannabis-smoking.

Sweet v Parsley [1970] AC 132; (1969) 53 Cr App R 221; [1969] Crim LR 189t; (1969) 133 JP 188; (1969) 113 SJ 86; [1969] 2 WLR 470 HL Managing premises used for smoking cannabis (Dangerous Drugs Act 1965, s 5) not an absolute offence.

Yeandel and another v Fisher [1965] 3 All ER 158; [1965] Crim LR 548; (1965) 129 JP 546; (1965) 115 LJ 643; [1966] 1 QB 440; (1965) 109 SJ 593; [1965] 3 WLR 1002 HC QBD Management of premises in which cannabis used/sold an absolute offence.

DRUGS (conspiracy to import)

R v Ardacan and others (1972) 116 SJ 237 CA Could be conspiracy to illegally import cannabis though relevant acts distant in time and proximity from time and place of importation.

DRUGS (conspiracy to produce)

R v Harris (Kevin Arthur) (1979) 69 Cr App R 122 CA Was conspiracy to produce to controlled drug where sought to manufacture amphetamine and used correct ingredients but failed because of lack of chemical knowledge.

R v McGowan [1990] Crim LR 399; [1990] TLR 68 CA Burden of proof stays on Crown for course of prosecution for conspiracy to produce controlled drug.

DRUGS (conspiracy to supply)

R v El Ghazal [1986] Crim LR 52 CA Were guilty of conspiracy to unlawfully supply cocaine where introduced one person to another knowing that one sought to meet the other so as to acquire cocaine.

R v Gill (Simon Imran) (1993) 97 Cr App R 215; (1993) 137 SJ LB 19; [1993] TLR 4 CA Offence to offer to supply drug transpires when offer made (irrespective of presence of conspiracy).

DRUGS (cultivation/production)

R v Champ (Kathleen Angela Carol) (1981) 73 Cr App R 367; [1982] Crim LR 108 CA On charge of cultivating cannabis accused must show did not know plant concerned was cannabis.

R v Farr [1982] Crim LR 745 CA Person allowing premises to be used for production of controlled drug had to make positive contribution to manufacturing process to be guilty of producing controlled drug.

R v Harris (Kevin); R v Joseph Cox [1996] 1 Cr App R 369; [1996] Crim LR 36; [1995] TLR 455 CA On what constitutes 'production' of 'cannabis' under Misuse of Drugs Act 1971.

R v Russell (Peter Andrew) (1992) 94 Cr App R 351; [1992] Crim LR 362; [1991] TLR 609 CA Production of crack from cocaine hydrochloride was 'production' of controlled drug contrary to Misuse of Drugs Act 1971, s 4(2).

Taylor v Chief Constable of Kent (1981) 72 Cr App R 318; [1981] Crim LR 244; (1981) 125 SJ 219; [1981] 1 WLR 606 HC QBD Cultivation of cannabis under Misuse of Drugs Act 1971, s 6 amounted to cultivation of controlled drug under s 4 thereof.

DRUGS (general)

Farrow v Tunnicliffe [1976] Crim LR 126 HC QBD Could under Misuse of Drugs Act 1971 remove suspect offender thereunder to another place to conduct search there.

R v Atkinson [1976] Crim LR 307 CA Substantial error in search warrant rendered actions thereunder improper.

R v Buswell [1972] 1 All ER 75; [1972] Crim LR 30t; (1972) 136 JP 141; (1971) 121 NLJ 1026t; (1972) 116 SJ 36; [1972] 1 WLR 64 CA Possession of prescription drugs not unlawful when prescription ends.

R v Evans (Ian) (1977) 64 Cr App R 237; [1977] Crim LR 223 CA Preliminary steps taken in England for carrying cannabis from Belguim to Canada was assisting in drugs offence contrary to Misuse of Drugs Act 1971, s 20.

R v Geen [1982] Crim LR 604 CA Conviction quashed where jury not left with issue as to whether offender genuinely believed plain clothes police officer to be mugger; right to detain and search person under Misuse of Drugs Act 1971, s 23(2)(a) includes right to question.

R v Goodchild [1977] 2 All ER 163; (1977) 64 Cr App R 100; (1977) 141 JP 295; (1977) 127 NLJ 168t; (1977) 121 SJ 103; [1977] 1 WLR 473 CA 'Cannabis' must be part of the flowering or fruiting top of cannabis plant.

R v Graham (Christopher Bruce) (1978) 67 Cr App R 356 CA Conviction for cannabis possession merited as amount found was measurable.

R v Kence (1978) 128 NLJ 537t CA Fact that drugs being transported through (not to) United Kingdom a minor but nonetheless mitigating factor when sentencing for unlawful importation of controlled drugs.

R v Panayi (Michael); R v Karte (Klaas) (1988) 86 Cr App R 261; [1987] Crim LR 764 CA Cannot be guilty of commissioning offence outside UK unless offence was committed.

R v Russell (Peter Andrew) (1992) 94 Cr App R 351; [1992] Crim LR 362; [1991] TLR 609 CA Production of crack from cocaine hydrochloride was 'production' of controlled drug contrary to Misuse of Drugs Act 1971, s 4(2).

R v Souter [1971] 2 All ER 1151; (1971) 55 Cr App R 403; [1972] Crim LR 478t; (1971) 135 JP 458; (1971) 115 SJ 548; [1971] 1 WLR 1187 CA Must be knowingly allowing/closing one's eyes to deliberate use of premises for drug use to be 'permitting' it.

R v Storey (Stephanie); R v Anwar (Rashid) (1968) 52 Cr App R 334 CA Unsworn statement, which if true would be complete defence to charge, was only reaction to police accusation and did not mean was no case to answer.

R v Watts [1984] 2 All ER 380; (1984) 79 Cr App R 127; [1984] TLR 7; [1984] 1 WLR 757 CA Broadest meaning to be given to word 'amphetamine' in Misuse of Drugs Act 1971.

R v Young [1984] 2 All ER 164; (1984) 78 Cr App R 288; [1984] Crim LR 363; (1984) 148 JP 492; (1984) 128 SJ 297; [1984] TLR 78; [1984] 1 WLR 654 CMAC Test whether knew or ought to have known was controlled drug is objective: self induced intoxication irrelevant to belief.

Tarpy v Rickard [1980] Crim LR 375 HC QBD Could be convicted on basis of aggregate total of cannabis found at premises.

DRUGS (importation)

Attorney General's Reference (No 1 of 1981) [1982] 2 All ER 417; (1982) 75 Cr App R 45; [1982] Crim LR 512 (1981) 131 NLJ 504; [1982] QB 848; [1982] TLR 153 CA Fraudulent conduct not deceit before customs officer needed to ground importation of prohibited goods conviction.

Attorney-General v Brown [1921] 3 KB 29 CA Ejusdem generis interpretation of Customs Consolidation Act 1876, s 43.

Bruhn (Jacob) v R (on the prosecution of the opium farmer) [1909] AC 317; [1909] 78 LJPC 85; PC Master of steamship properly convicted for importing opium though unaware ship contained chandu.

R v Borro and Abdullah [1973] Crim LR 513 CA Facts gave court jurisdiction to try persons for conspiracy to evade restriction on importation of dangerous drug.

R v Ciappara (Simon) (1988) 87 Cr App R 316; [1988] Crim LR 172 CA Interception of parcel containing cocaine by Customs officers and substitution of baking powder for cocaine did not mean ultimate recipient of parcel was not guilty of importing cocaine.

R v Green (Harry Rodney) [1975] 3 All ER 1011; (1976) 62 Cr App R 74; [1976] Crim LR 47t; (1976) 140 JP 112; (1975) 125 NLJ 1117t; [1976] QB 985; (1975) 119 SJ 825; [1976] 2 WLR 57 CA Need not succeed in evading prohibition on importation to be guilty of evasion/attempted evasion.

R v Jakeman (Susan Lesley) (1983) 76 Cr App R 223; [1983] Crim LR 104; [1982] TLR 557 CA Change of intention after effecting of importation did not mitigate guilt in respect of same.

R v Karte (Klaas); R v Panayi (Michael) (1989) 88 Cr App R 267; [1989] Crim LR 210; (1988) 132 SJ 1697; [1989] 1 WLR 187 CA On mens rea of fraudulent evasion of prohibition on importation of controlled drug (Customs and Excise Management Act 1979, s 170(2)).

R v Mitchell [1992] Crim LR 594 CA Could be guilty of unlawful importation of drugs where knowingly retained drugs that were received unsolicited.

R v Morgan [1993] Crim LR 56 CA That accused acquainted with drug users/allowed them to take drugs at her house was admissible to prove connection with drugs world.

R v Neal (John Frederick); R v Cardwell (Michael Phillip); R v Cardwell (Anthony John); R v D'Antoni (Salvatore) (1983) 77 Cr App R 283; [1983] Crim LR 677; [1983] TLR 484 CA Could be convicted of evading prohibition on importation of dangerous drugs though not involved in actual importation.

R v Smith [1973] Crim LR 516 CA Goods were im/exported where passed through jurisdiction en route from one place to another without going through customs.

R v Suurmeijer [1991] Crim LR 773 CA Drugs importation conviction of car passenger quashed where was inadequate proof that passenger had known drugs being carried in car.

R v Wall [1974] 2 All ER 245; (1974) 59 Cr App R 58; [1974] Crim LR 665; (1974) 124 NLJ 271t; (1974) 118 SJ 241; [1974] 1 WLR 930 CA Steps abroad to assist in illegal importation could prove 'knowingly concerned' in act.

R v Watts (John Lackland); R v Stack (David Charles) (1980) 70 Cr App R 187; [1980] Crim LR 38 CA Must be actual intentional evasion of prohibition on importation of controlled drugs to be guilty of same: cannot presume by acts that must have done so in past.

DRUGS (incitement to supply)

R v Chelmsford Justices; ex parte JJ Amos [1973] Crim LR 437 HC QBD Attempt to incite supply of dangerous drug a common law offence (not offence under the Dangerous Drugs Act 1965).

DRUGS (offer to supply)

R v Goodard [1992] Crim LR 588 CA Offence of offering to supply controlled drug is complete once the offer is made.

R v Mitchell [1992] Crim LR 723 CA Was offence to offer to supply controlled drug (even though substance offered was not in fact a controlled drug).

DRUGS (possession)

Bocking v Roberts [1973] 3 All ER 962; (1978) 67 Cr App R 359; [1973] Crim LR 517; (1974) 138 JP 13; (1973) 123 NLJ 516t; [1974] QB 307; (1973) 117 SJ 581; [1973] 3 WLR 465 HC QBD Possession however small the quantity as long as enough to show not possession on earlier date.

Bong (Kwan Ping) and another v R [1979] AC 609; [1979] Crim LR 245; [1979] 2 WLR 433 PC Quashing of unauthorised possession of drugs conviction where jury possibly laboured under misapprehension as to burden of proof.

Chief Constable of Cheshire Constabulary v Hunt and others (1983) 147 JP 567 HC QBD Person who admits smoking cannabis must be in possession of same.

Director of Public Prosecutions v Brooks [1974] 2 All ER 840; [1974] AC 862; (1974) 59 Cr App R 185; [1974] Crim LR 364; (1974) 118 SJ 420; [1974] 2 WLR 899 PC Possession if in physical custody/control.

Hodder v Director of Public Prosecutions; Matthews v Director of Public Prosecutions [1990] Crim LR 261 HC QBD That had picked and frozen hallucinogenic mushrooms meant were in possession of 'product' containing controlled substance contrary to Misuse of Drugs Act 1971.

Lang v Evans (Inspector of Police) [1977] Crim LR 286 CrCt On what constitutes cannabis.

Lockyer v Gibb [1966] 2 All ER 653; [1966] Crim LR 504; (1966) 130 JP 306; (1965-66) 116 NLJ 1062; [1967] 2 QB 243; (1966) 110 SJ 507; [1966] 3 WLR 84 HC QBD Must know are in possession of item, otherwise possession an absolute offence.

Muir v Smith [1978] Crim LR 293; (1978) 128 NLJ 364t; (1978) 122 SJ 210 HC QBD Conviction quashed where charged with possessing cannabis resin but only possession of cannabis (and not that it was cannabis resin) proven.

R v Ashton-Rickardt [1977] Crim LR 424; (1978) 142 JP 90; (1977) 121 SJ 774; [1978] 1 WLR 37 CA Must prove person knew had possession of controlled substance to secure conviction for same.

R v Boyesen [1982] 2 All ER 161; [1982] AC 768; (1982) 75 Cr App R 51; [1982] Crim LR 596; (1982) 146 JP 217; (1982) 132 NLJ 609; (1982) 126 SJ 308; [1982] TLR 215; [1982] 2 WLR 882 HL Possession of any amount of controlled drug may ground possession conviction.

R v Boyesen (Peregrine) (1981) 72 Cr App R 43 CA Possession of trivial amount of controlled drug could not sustain possession conviction.

DRUGS (possession)

R v Carver [1978] 3 All ER 60; (1978) 67 Cr App R 352; (1978) 142 JP 620; (1978) 128 NLJ 635t; [1978] QB 472; (1978) 122 SJ 332; [1978] 2 WLR 872 CA No possession if amount of drug is so minute as to amount to nothing.

R v Cavendish [1961] 2 All ER 856; [1961] Crim LR 623; (1961) 125 JP 460; (1961) 111 LJ 469; [1961] 1 WLR 1083 CCA Must show arranged for delivery of goods or aware that they arrived took control over them: otherwise no possession.

R v Cunliffe (Kenneth John) [1986] Crim LR 547 CA Mushrooms that had been dried and contained Class A controlled drug were an unlawful 'preparation' under the Misuse of Drugs Act 1971, s 5(2).

R v Dempsey (Michael Bruce); R v Dempsey (Maureen Patricia) (1986) 82 Cr App R 291; [1986] Crim LR 171; (1986) 150 JP 213 CA Was possession where in good faith took controlled drug from person legally allowed use it; 'supply' of drug must benefit person taking possession and person passing same.

R v Downes [1984] Crim LR 552 CA Not possession with intent to supply where have joint possession of controlled drug but (unlike party with whom sharing possession) do not intend to supply same (though know of other party's intention to do so).

R v Dunbar [1982] 1 All ER 188; (1982) 74 Cr App R 88; [1982] Crim LR 45; (1981) 125 SJ 746; [1981] 1 WLR 1536 CA Possession of controlled drug by doctor who has made bona fide prescription thereof for self is lawful.

R v Ewens [1966] 2 All ER 470; [1966] Crim LR 440; (1965-66) 116 NLJ 921; [1967] 1 QB 322; (1966) 110 SJ 329/483; [1966] 2 WLR 1372 CA Burden of showing exempted from offence falls on accused.

R v Forde (James Thomas) (1985) 81 Cr App R 19; [1985] Crim LR 323; (1985) 149 JP 458 CA Obstruction of police searching for drugs before are warned as to why detained can nonetheless be offence where is obvious why are being detained.

R v Frederick [1969] 3 All ER 804; (1969) 53 Cr App R 455; [1969] Crim LR 370t; (1969) 133 JP 698; (1969) 119 NLJ 462t; (1969) 113 SJ 485; [1970] 1 WLR 107 CA Possession of unmeasurable amount of dangerous drug could sustain possession conviction.

R v Graham [1969] 2 All ER 1181; (1969) 133 JP 505; [1970] 1 WLR 113 CA Possession conviction possible if quantity of drug measurable (albeit by microscope).

R v Graham (Christopher Bruce) (1978) 67 Cr App R 356 CA Conviction for cannabis possession merited as amount found was measurable.

R v Graham (Christopher) [1969] Crim LR 192; (1969) 113 SJ 87 CA Were in possession of cannabis though amount possessed amounted only to a few milligrammes.

R v Greenfield (Evan) (1984) 78 Cr App R 179; [1983] Crim LR 397 CA On what is meant by 'intent to supply' under Misuse of Drugs Act 1971, s 5(3).

R v Greensmith [1983] 3 All ER 444; (1983) 77 Cr App R 202; [1983] Crim LR 798; (1984) 148 JP 270; (1983) 127 SJ 578; [1983] TLR 408; [1983] 1 WLR 1124 CA Broadest possible meaning to 'cocaine' in Misuse of Drugs Act.

R v Halpin [1996] Crim LR 112 CA Lifestyle evidence is not relevant to issue of whether or not were actually in possession of drug charged.

R v Healey; R v Comerford; R v Owens; R v Smith [1965] 1 All ER 365; (1965) 109 SJ 572; [1965] 1 WLR 1059 CCA Exceptionally can direct issue be decided adversely to accused: unusual in possession on receiving charge; preferable that guidance notes to jury be shown to counsel; need in possession cases to distinguish unlawful assistance/joint possession.

R v Hierowski [1978] Crim LR 563 CrCt Could not be convicted of possession of indivisible amounts of cannabis.

R v Hunt [1987] 1 All ER 1; [1987] AC 352; (1987) 84 Cr App R 163; [1987] Crim LR 263; (1986) 136 NLJ 1183; (1970) 130 SJ 984; [1986] 3 WLR 1115 HL Statute may place task of proving statutory defence on accused expressly/impliedly but court slow to find such an obligation.

R v Hunt [1986] 1 All ER 184; (1986) 82 Cr App R 244; [1986] Crim LR 172; (1986) 150 JP 83; [1986] QB 125; (1985) 129 SJ 889; [1986] 2 WLR 225 CA Burden of proof on defendant to show drugs fall within exception to prohibition.

R v Irving [1970] Crim LR 642 CA Accused not liable for possession of drug surreptitiously placed in bottle of tablets unbeknownst to him.

R v Jagger [1967] Crim LR 587t; (1967) 111 SJ 633 CA Conditional discharge for person guilty of unlawful possession of controlled substance as his personal doctor was aware of and acquiesced to his use of same.

R v Lewis (Gareth Edmund) (1988) 87 Cr App R 270; [1988] Crim LR 517 CA Intention to possess/that knew possessed dangerous substance could sustain conviction for possession of drugs: need not show that actually knew had control of drugs.

R v Littleford [1978] Crim LR 48 CrCt On what may ground reasonable suspicion that are in possession of drugs in car.

R v Lloyd [1992] Crim LR 361 CA On extent of posssession that must be proved to support conviction for burglary/handling.

R v Maginnis [1986] 2 All ER 110; (1986) 82 Cr App R 351; [1986] Crim LR 237; [1986] QB 618; (1986) 130 SJ 128; [1986] 2 WLR 767 CA Bailment relationship did not mean bailee supplying drugs when returning them to bailor.

R v Marriott [1971] 1 All ER 595; (1971) 55 Cr App R 82; [1971] Crim LR 172; (1971) 135 JP 165; (1971) 115 SJ 11; [1971] 1 WLR 187 CA Must prove accused had reason to know of drug traces on penknife to sustain possession conviction.

R v Martin and others (1956) 120 JP 255; [1956] 2 QB 272; [1956] 2 WLR 975 CCC Possession of drugs on aircaft not triable in England as offence not committed in England.

R v Martindale [1986] 3 All ER 25; (1987) 84 Cr App R 31; [1986] Crim LR 736; (1986) 150 JP 548; (1970) 130 SJ 613; [1986] 1 WLR 1042 CA Non-recollection of possession did not mean not in possession.

R v McMillan (Paul) (1977) 64 Cr App R 104; [1977] Crim LR 680; [1984] TLR 347 CA Conviction set aside as was inadequate jury direction on nature of cannabis plant portion accused possessed and whether could be 'leaf' for purpose of Misuse of Drugs Act 1971, s 37(1).

R v McNamara (James) (1988) 87 Cr App R 246; [1988] Crim LR 440; (1988) 152 JP 390; (1988) 132 SJ 300 CA That knew had control of box and knew something therein (which was dangerous drug) enough to support conviction for possession of dangerous drugs.

R v Middleton (Thomas Mansfield) (1922-23) 17 Cr App R 89 CCA Strict proof of possession needed in receiving prosecution.

R v Moore (Alan Jan) [1979] Crim LR 789 CrCt Intention to share cannabis cigarette rendered party liable to conviction for possession of cannabis with intent to supply same.

R v Peaston (Andrew Gordon) (1979) 69 Cr App R 203; [1979] Crim LR 183 CA Person sending for drug was deemed to be in possession when mail arrived at house in which had bed-sit though was unaware of its arrival.

R v Peevey (James Frederick) (1973) 57 Cr App R 554 CA If possessed any of the unauthorised drugs with which charged of possession are completely guilty of unauthorised possession.

R v Pragliola (James) and Pragliola (Antonio) [1977] Crim LR 612 CrCt On what constitutes unlawful 'possession' of controlled drug for purposes of Misuse of Drugs Act 1971, s 5.

R v Prevost (1965) 109 SJ 738 CCA Possession conviction quashed where had been inadequate direction as to elements of possession.

R v Rana [1969] Crim LR 597 CA Conviction for holding drugs for/on behalf of another quashed where agent convicted in respect of drugs held by principal.

R v Rourke [1956] Crim LR 326 Magistrates Doctor not guilty of aiding and abetting unlawful possession of drugs where prescribed heroin to patient who - unknown to him - was also obtaining same from another doctor.

R v Scott [1996] Crim LR 652; (1996) TLR 10/4/96 CA Evidence of possession of money/drugs equipment was admissible even though only issue at trial was possession.

R v Searle and others [1972] Crim LR 592; (1971) 115 SJ 739 CA On what constitutes 'joint possession' of drugs.

R v Sharp [1964] Crim LR 826g CCA Valid finding of joint possession on part of person apparently indirectly party to loading with stolen property of van owned by his wife.

R v Stevens (Robert) [1981] Crim LR 568 CA On meaning of word 'preparation' in Misuse of Drugs Act 1971, Schedule 2, Part I.

R v Storey [1968] Crim LR 387; (1968) 118 NLJ 373t; (1968) 112 SJ 417 CA Unsworn statement to police by flat occupier to effect that cannabis found therein belonged to another present there did not obviate presumption that she (the flat occupier) was in possession of the cannabis found there.

R v Tomblin [1964] Crim LR 780t CCA Person who took no part in opening stolen safe deemed not guilty of possession of same (though might well be guilty of joint possession of same).

R v Walker [1987] Crim LR 565 CA On what is meant by possession of a 'preparation' containing an unlawful substance contrary to the Misuse of Drugs Act 1971.

R v Webb [1979] Crim LR 462 CrCt On level of cannabis which there must be present before can be said to possess it.

R v Wells [1976] Crim LR 518 CA On extent of burden on prosecution to prove that substance at issue in possession of controlled drug case was in fact a controlled substance.

R v Worledge [1972] Crim LR 321 CA Three year probation order for university student guilty of possession (and party to supply) of drugs but who may have been stooge for others more seriously involved.

R v Wright (Brian Lloyd) (1976) 62 Cr App R 169; [1976] Crim LR 249t; (1975) 125 NLJ 1191t; (1975) 119 SJ 825 CA Not possession of controlled drug to take tin containing such drugs for another without knowing contents and immediately throw away when told to do so - even though then suspect something is wrong.

Searle v Randolph [1972] Crim LR 779 HC QBD Possession of cigarette end containing cannabis adequate to support cannabis possession conviction - did not have to prove accused knew cigarette end to contain cannabis.

Tansley v Painter [1969] Crim LR 139; (1968) 112 SJ 1005 HC QBD Evidence that had certain drug in urine sample not corroboration of possession of same.

Warner v Metropolitan Police Commissioner [1968] 2 All ER 356; [1969] 2 AC 256; (1968) 52 Cr App R 373; [1968] Crim LR 380t; (1968) 132 JP 378; (1968) 112 SJ 378; [1968] 2 WLR 1303 HL Possession not absolute offence: if no right to open parcel/ignorant of its contents, no possession.

DRUGS (possession with intent to supply)

R v Brown [1995] Crim LR 716 CA Evidence, inter alia, of money, scales, plastic bags were evidence of intent to supply on part of person charged with possession of cannabis with intent to supply.

R v Grant [1996] 1 Cr App R 73; [1995] Crim LR 715; [1995] TLR 147 CA Money found in possession of person charged with possession of drugs with intent to supply was relevant to determining whether dealt in drugs/had intent to supply.

R v Maginnis [1987] 1 All ER 907; [1987] AC 303; (1987) 85 Cr App R 127; [1987] Crim LR 564; (1987) 151 JP 537; (1987) 137 NLJ 244; (1987) 131 SJ 357; [1987] 2 WLR 765 HL Person temporarily holding drugs for other may be guilty of possession with intent to supply.

R v Richards [1997] Crim LR 499 CA On relevance of lifestyle evidence on charge of possessing drug with intent to supply.

DRUGS (procuring)

R v Miyagawa (Yasukichi) (1924-25) 18 Cr App R 4 CCA Guilty of procuring drugs contrary to Dangerous Drugs Act 1920 where had bill of lading to drugs in one country which intended to ship to another country.

DRUGS (supply)

Holmes v Chief Constable, Merseyside Police [1976] Crim LR 125; (1976) 126 NLJ 113t HC QBD On what constitutes 'supplying' controlled drug.

Mieras v Rees [1975] Crim LR 224; (1975) 139 JP 549 HC QBD Cannot attempt to supply controlled drug (even if have requisite mens rea) where substance are supplying is not controlled drug as is no actus reus.

R v Blake (Jason Joseph); R v Ronald O'Connor (1979) 68 Cr App R 1; [1979] Crim LR 464 CA Offer to supply controlled drug a broadly drawn offence.

R v Bradbury [1996] Crim LR 808 CA On ingredients of offence of permitting premises to be used for the supply of drugs.

R v Buckley (Leslie); R v Lane (David) (1979) 69 Cr App R 371; [1979] Crim LR 664 CA To 'supply' a drug under Misuse of Drugs Act 1971, s 37(1) also means to distribute same.

R v Connelly (1992) 156 JP 406 CA Can be charged with supplying controlled drug to person named in same indictment (but not same charge).

R v Delgado (Winston) [1984] 1 All ER 449; (1984) 78 Cr App R 175; [1984] Crim LR 169; (1984) 148 JP 431; (1984) 128 SJ 32; [1983] TLR 690; [1984] 1 WLR 89 CA Could be convicted of supplying dangerous drug where were storing (but had control of) large quantity of drug for friend.

R v Harris [1968] 2 All ER 49; (1968) 52 Cr App R 277; [1968] Crim LR 267; (1968) 132 JP 322; (1968) 118 NLJ 421; (1968) 112 SJ 272; [1968] 1 WLR 769 CA On 'supply' of drugs to others.

R v Hughes (Robert) (1985) 81 Cr App R 344 CA On what it means to be 'concerned in' the unlawful supply of drugs (Misuse of Drugs Act 1971, s 4).

R v King (Jeffery David) [1978] Crim LR 228 CrCt On what constitutes 'intention to supply' for purposes of Misuse of Drugs Act 1971, s 5(3).

R v Showers [1995] Crim LR 400 CA Need not intend to supply drug to be guilty of offering to supply same.

R v Taylor [1986] Crim LR 680 CrCt Offence of supplying controlled drug did not embrace bad faith handing over of prescription by medical practitioner.

R v X [1994] Crim LR 827 CA On what constitutes 'supply' of drugs.

DRUGS (trafficking)

Ali v R; Rasool v R [1992] 2 All ER 1; (1992) 136 SJ LB 62; [1992] 2 WLR 357 PC No separate offence of 'importing-cum-drug trafficking'; discretion of Director of Public Prosecutions to elect which sentence appropriate for accused a breach of separation of powers.

Chuan (Ong Ah) v Public Prosecutor; Cheng (Koh Chai) v Public Prosecutor [1981] AC 648; [1981] Crim LR 245; (1981) 131 NLJ 44; (1980) 124 SJ 757; [1980] 3 WLR 855 PC Carrying over two grammes of heroin in car raised constitutionally valid presumption that were trafficker.

Francis and Francis (a firm) v Central Criminal Court [1988] 3 All ER 775; (1989) 88 Cr App R 213; [1988] 3 WLR 989 HL Documents otherwise privileged not so if held with criminal intention of laundering drug trafficking proceeds.

Gaffoor v R (1991) 92 Cr App R 349; [1991] Crim LR 613 PC Proper inference from evidence that appellant a drug trafficker.

R v Central Criminal Court, ex parte Francis and Francis [1989] AC 346 (also HC QBD); [1989] Crim LR 444; (1988) 138 NLJ 316; (1988) 132 SJ 1592 HL Legal privilege attaches to client not solicitor - criminal intent of client vitiates privilege.

R v Central Criminal Court, ex parte Francis and Francis (a firm) [1988] 1 All ER 677; [1989] AC 346 (also HL); (1988) 87 Cr App R 104; [1988] Crim LR 305; (1988) 138 NLJ 14; (1988) 132 SJ 302; [1988] 2 WLR 627 HC QBD Police application for production of documents normally ex parte but subject must be allowed seek discharge/variation before effected; legal privilege attaches to client not solicitor - criminal intent of client vitiates privilege.

DRUGS (use)

R v Colle (Valerie Anne) (1992) 95 Cr App R 67; (1992) 156 JP 360; (1991) 135 SJ LB 125; [1991] TLR 410 CA Defendant must prove on balance of probabilities the statutory defence in Drug Trafficking Offences Act 1986, s 24(4) to assisting another with drug trafficking proceeds.

R v Uxbridge Magistrates' Court; ex parte Henry [1994] Crim LR 581; [1994] TLR 103 CA Customs and Excise authorities out of time in their application for continued detention of suspected drug trafficking money.

Re L (J); Re the Drug Trafficking Offences Act 1986 (Designated Countries and Territories) Order 1990 [1994] TLR 241 HC QBD On making of restraint order pursuant to the Drug Trafficking Offences Act 1986 (Designated Countries and Territories) Order 1990.

DRUGS (use)

R v Thomas [1976] Crim LR 517 CA Construction of effect of word 'knowingly' in the Misuse of Drugs Act 1971, s 8(d).

DURESS (general)

Director of Public Prosecutions v Bell [1992] Crim LR 176; [1992] RTR 335 HC QBD Person with excess alcohol fleeing from dangerous scene in terror/not proven to have driven longer than necessary/ who did not cease being terrified while driving could rely on defence of duress.

EDUCATION (general)

Fox v Burgess (1921-25) XXVII Cox CC 162; [1922] 1 KB 623 HC KBD Father properly convicted of not causing child to attend school where knowingly sent to school in such a state that was not admitted.

ELECTION OFFENCE (general)

Caldicott (Walter) v The Commissioners appointed to inquire into corrupt practices at the City of Worcester Parliamentary (1906) Election (The Director of Public Prosecutions intervening) (1907-09) XXI Cox CC 404 Assizes Absent evidence of prior agreement post-voting payment of voters not bribery; Election Commissioners not estopped from acting in relation to illegal practices by earlier decision of Election Petition Judges.

R v Taylor (1924) 59 LJ 482; (1924) WN (I) 246 CCA Valid conviction under the Municipal Corporations Act 1882, s 74, for delivering forged nomination paper to Returning Officer.

Re Berry and another [1978] Crim LR 357 CA Court not satisfied that election offence committed inadvertently and not in good faith.

Thompson v Dann and other (1994) 138 SJ LB 221 HC QBD Court not satisfied beyond reasonable doubt that personation (and not mere mistake) had occurred.

EMBRACERY (general)

R v Owen (Norman) (1976) 63 Cr App R 199 CA Offence of embracery no longer extant; generally custodial sentence appropriate for interference with administration of justice.

ENDANGERING SAFETY OF RAIL PASSENGERS (general)

R v Rayner [1973] Crim LR 67 CA Borstal training merited by seventeen year old guilty of endangering safety of rail passengers/obstructing the railway/burglary.

ENGINE SETTING (general)

R v Munks [1963] 3 All ER 757; (1964) 48 Cr App R 56; [1964] Crim LR 52; (1963) 107 SJ 874; (1964) 128 JP 77; (1963) 113 LJ 804; [1964] 1 QB 304; [1963] 3 WLR 952 CCA Use of two live wires to give person shock not 'engine' under Offences Against the Person Act 1861, s 31.

ENTRAPMENT (general)

Chiu-Cheung (Yip) v R [1994] 2 All ER 924; [1995] 1 AC 111; (1994) 99 Cr App R 406; [1994] Crim LR 824; (1994) 144 NLJ 863; (1994) 138 SJ LB 146; [1994] TLR 335; [1994] 3 WLR 514 PC Undercover drug agent could be guilty of conspiracy to commit crime if had requisite intent so co-conspirators guilty of conspiracy; no general defence of superior orders, Crown or Executive fiat in English/Hong Kong law.

London Borough of Ealing v Woolworths plc [1995] Crim LR 58 HC QBD Is no defence of entrapment; not improper for Trading Standards Officer to send young boy into store to buy '18's' video and then prosecute store for having sold it.

R v Chandler [1911-13] All ER 428; (1913-14) XXIII Cox CC 330; [1913] 1 KB 125; (1912) 47 LJ 707; [1913] 82 LJKB 106; (1913) 108 LTR 352; (1912) WN (I) 276 CCA Shopbreaking conviction secured after entrapment valid.

R v Farooq; R v Ramzan [1995] Crim LR 169 CA Entrapment is not a defence.

R v Gill and Ruana [1989] Crim LR 358 CA Remains substantive rule of law that entrapment no defence to offence.

R v Haghighat-Khou [1995] Crim LR 337 CA Valid decision on part of judge not to allow counsel suggest defendant had been victim of 'set-up' by police.

R v Harwood [1989] Crim LR 285 CA Continues to be substantive rule of law that entrapment is no defence.

R v Heuser (Henry) (1910-11) 6 Cr App R 76 CCA Police officers party to entrapment are not accomplices.

R v Jelen (Lawrence); R v Katz (Anthony) (1990) 90 Cr App R 456 CA Tape recording obtained via police entrapment was admissible.

R v Latif (Khalid); R v Shahzad (Mohammed Khalid) [1995] 1 Cr App R 270; [1994] Crim LR 750; (1994) 138 SJ LB 85; [1994] TLR 154 CA Was punishable fraudulent evasion of prohibition on importation of drugs though happened in course of entrapment; admission of informant's evidence appropriate.

R v Latif; R v Shahzad [1996] 1 All ER 353; [1996] 2 Cr App R 92; [1996] Crim LR 414; (1996) 146 NLJ 121; (1996) 140 SJ LB 39; (1996) TLR 23/1/96; [1996] 1 WLR 104 HL Prosecution on foot of entrapment an abuse of process where authorities act so unworthily or shamefully it is affront to public conscience for prosecution to proceed.

R v Mann; R v Dixon [1995] Crim LR 647 CA Undercover police officers did not act as agents provocateurs in either of two solicitation to murder cases and their evidence was validly admitted.

R v McCann (Edward) (1972) 56 Cr App R 359 CA On entrapment where already have evidence of conspiracy to commit offence.

R v Mealey (Jeremiah); R v Sheridan (Philip Michael) (1974) 124 NLJ 792; (1975) 60 Cr App R 59; [1974] Crim LR 710 CA Is no defence of entrapment; that acted with agent provocateur may count towards sentence; on police infiltrators vis-à-vis agents provocateurs.

R v Sang; R v Mangan [1979] 2 All ER 46; (1979) 68 Cr App R 240; [1979] Crim LR 389; (1979) 143 JP 352; (1979) 129 (1) NLJ 118t; (1979) 123 SJ 232; [1979] 2 WLR 439 CA Unless oppression/abuse of process judge cannot exclude prosecution evidence however got.

R v Turvey [1946] 2 All ER 60; (1945-46) 31 Cr App R 154; (1946) 110 JP 270; (1946) 96 LJ 304; (1946) 175 LTR 308; (1946) 90 SJ 395; (1945-46) LXII TLR 511; (1946) WN (I) 121 CCA No asportation (despite handling of goods being part of entrapment) so no larceny.

R v Willis (Christopher); R v Wertheimer (Henry Joseph David); R v Linford (Michael Kevin); R v Willis (John Michael); R v Westbrook (Simon Jeffrey Edney) (1979) 68 Cr App R 265 CA Is no defence of entrapment; evidence obtained by 'entrapment' properly admitted.

R v X [1994] Crim LR 827 CA On what constitutes 'supply' of drugs.

Sneddon v Stevenson [1967] 2 All ER 1277; [1967] Crim LR 476t; (1967) 131 JP 441; (1967) 111 SJ 515; [1967] 1 WLR 1051 HC QBD Not accomplice where police officer places self in position to facilitate offence if offence to be committed.

ENVIRONMENT (causing effluent to be discharged)

Wychavon District Council v National Rivers Authority [1993] Crim LR 766 HC QBD Positive act necessary to render council liable for 'causing' discharge of effluent which had somehow started somehow previously found not to be present.

ENVIRONMENT (control of pollution)

Durham County Council v Thomas Swan and Co [1995] Crim LR 319 HC QBD Barrels containing under 1% of starting volume were 'empty' for purposes of Control of Pollution Act 1974.

JB and M Motor Haulage Ltd v London Waste Regulation Authority [1990] TLR 746 HC QBD On necessary prerequisites before may convict individual of failing to furnish information contrary to the Control of Pollution Act 1974, s 93(3).

London Borough of Lambeth v Mullings [1990] Crim LR 426; [1990] TLR 33 HC QBD Service of pollution abatement notice via a letter box was adequate service of same.

Long v Brooke [1980] Crim LR 109 CrCt On what constitutes 'waste' (in context of offence of unlawfully depositing same) under Control of Pollution Act 1974, s 30.

National Rivers Authority v Wright Engineering Ltd [1994] Crim LR 453 CA 'Causation' of pollution a question of fact; foreseeability of some relevance in determining causation.

National Rivers Authority v Yorkshire Water Services [1994] Crim LR 451; [1993] TLR 589; [1994] TLR 592 HC QBD 'Causation' of pollution a question of fact (said 'causation' proved here).

R v Folkestone Magistrates' Court, ex parte Kibble [1993] Crim LR 704; [1993] TLR 103 HC QBD Could not be guilty of contravening provisions of the Control of Pollution Act 1974 after repealed/replaced by the Environmental Protection Act 1990.

Rankin v De Coster [1975] Crim LR 226 HC QBD Construction of Prevention of Oil Pollution Act 1971, s 2.

Southern Water Authority v Pegrum and Pegrum [1989] Crim LR 442 HC QBD Direction to convict in prosecution for causing pollution (pig effluent) to enter stream contrary to Control of Pollution Act 1974, s 31(1).

Thanet District Council v Kent County Council [1993] Crim LR 703 HC QBD On what constituted 'controlled waste' for purposes of the Control of Pollution Act 1974 (did not include seaweed).

Trent River Authority v FH Drabble and Sons Ltd [1970] Crim LR 106; (1969) 113 SJ 898 HC QBD Application of the Rivers (Prevention of Pollution) Act 1971, s 1(1).

ENVIRONMENT (depositing controlled waste)

Shanks and McEwan (Teesside) Ltd v The Environment Agency [1997] Crim LR 684; [1997] TLR 50 HC QBD On elements of offence of knowingly causing controlled waste to be deposited in breach of waste management licence.

ENVIRONMENT (depositing/leaving litter)

Vaughan v Biggs [1960] 2 All ER 473; [1960] Crim LR 561; (1960) 110 LJ 446; (1960) 104 SJ 508 HC QBD Depositing and leaving litter not a continuing offence.

ENVIRONMENT (destroying controlled waste)

Durham County Council v Peter Connors Industrial Services Ltd [1992] Crim LR 743 HC QBD Conviction for depositing controlled waste merited as failed to set up special defence that were advised by informed persons that were not acting unlawfully and had no cause to believe contrary.

ENVIRONMENT (discharge of oil)

Federal Steam Navigation Co Ltd v Department of Trade and Industry (1974) 59 Cr App R 131 HL Liability of master/owner of ship to prosecution under Oil in Navigable Waters Act 1955 (as amended).

ENVIRONMENT (disposal of waste)

Shanks and McEwan (Teeside) Ltd v The Environment Agency [1997] Crim LR 684; [1997] TLR 50 HC QBD On elements of offence of knowingly causing controlled waste to be deposited in breach of waste management licence.

ENVIRONMENT (litter)

Hills v Davies (1901-07) XX Cox CC 398 HC KBD Paper advertisement bills could be litter under Metropolitan Police Act 1839, s 60(3).

Westminster City Council v Riding [1995] TLR 448 HC QBD On what constitutes 'litter' for the purposes of the Environmental Protection Act 1990, s 87(1).

ENVIRONMENT (oil in navigable waters)

R v Federal Steam Navigation Co Ltd; R v Moran [1973] 3 All ER 849; (1974) 58 Cr App R 68; [1973] Crim LR 575t CA Owner and master can be guilty of unlawfully discharging oil.

ENVIRONMENT (pollution)

Cheshire County Council v Armstrong's Transport (Wigan) Ltd [1995] Crim LR 162 HC QBD On what constitutes 'waste'.

ESCAPE (aiding and abetting)

R v Moss (Robert Francis); R v Harte (Stephen Patrick) (1986) 82 Cr App R 116; [1985] Crim LR 659; (1986) 150 JP 26 CA On what constitutes a 'prison' under Prison Act 1952, s 39.

ESCAPE (assisting escape)

R v Abbott [1956] Crim LR 337t CCA Valid conviction for assisting prisoner (doing work outside prison) to escape.

ESCAPE (general)

R v Holden [1965] Crim LR 556; (1965) 115 LJ 450 CrCt Person who helped hospitalised prisoner escape not guilty of aiding a prisoner to escape from prison (contrary to Prison Act 1952, s 13 (as amended)).

ESCAPE (harbouring escapee)

Darch v Weight [1984] 2 All ER 245; (1984) 79 Cr App R 40; [1984] Crim LR 168; (1984) 148 JP 588; (1984) 128 SJ 315; [1983] TLR 715; [1984] 1 WLR 659 HC QBD Positive act necessary for harbouring to arise; harbouring by non-owner of property possible.

Nicoll v Catron (1985) 81 Cr App R 339; [1985] Crim LR 223; (1985) 149 JP 424 HC QBD Could not be guilty of harbouring escaped 'prisoner' where escapee had fled on way to remand centre.

ESCAPE (lawful custody)

Hans (William Francis) v R [1955] AC 378; [1955] Crim LR 373; (1955) 99 SJ 233; [1955] 2 WLR 700 PC Bermudan releasing sailor from custody of US naval patrol was guilty of releasing person from 'lawful custody'.

ESCAPE (military service)

R v Chiswell (Lawrence John Charles) (1930-31) Cr App R 67 CCA Committing crime to escape military service not normally a serious offence.

ESCAPE (prison)

Dillon v R [1982] 1 All ER 1017; [1982] AC 484; (1982) 74 Cr App R 274; [1982] Crim LR 438; (1982) 126 SJ 117; [1982] TLR 24; [1982] 2 WLR 538 PC Crown must prove lawfulness of detention when prosecuting for escape from lawful custody.

R v Frascati (Umberto) (1981) 73 Cr App R 28 CA Breach of prison an offence per se - that acquitted of offence for which were in custody not a defence.

R v Hinds (Alfred George) (1957) 41 Cr App R 143; [1957] Crim LR 465t CCA Is common law escape to leave prison in which held by walking out (as opposed to breaking out).

EVICTION/HARASSMENT (general)

Hooper v Eaglestone [1978] Crim LR 161 CA Was offence for person without site licence who nonetheless operated a caravan site on his land to seek to harass/evict caravan occupant from site by cutting off electricity (Caravan Sites Act 1968, s 3 applied).

R v Burke [1990] 2 All ER 385; [1991] 1 AC 135; (1990) 91 Cr App R 384; [1990] Crim LR 877; (1990) 154 JP 798; (1990) 140 NLJ 742; (1990) 134 SJ 1106 HL Acts that are not civil wrongs may be harassment if intended to secure tenant's departure.

EXPLOSIVES (conspiracy to cause explosion)

R v Coughlan (Martin); R v Young (Gerard Peter) (1976) 63 Cr App R 33 CA Within conspiracy to cause explosion can be sub-conspiracies to cause other explosions: can be charged separately for each; that acquitted of one does not mean cannot be convicted of other - autrefois convict plea unavailable in respect of various conspiracies charged.

EXPLOSIVES (general)

Attorney-General's Reference (No 2 of 1983) [1984] 1 All ER 988; (1984) 78 Cr App R 183; [1984] Crim LR 289; (1985) 149 JP 104; [1984] QB 456; [1984] TLR 42; [1984] 2 WLR 465 CA Exceptionally preparation of petrol-bomb may be lawful where prepared as planned act of self-defence.

R v Berry [1984] 2 All ER 296; (1985) 80 Cr App R 98; [1984] Crim LR 421; (1984) 128 SJ 399; [1984] TLR 192; [1984] 1 WLR 824 CA Jury cannot have regard to use of timers abroad when deciding whether 'lawful intent' behind making of timers in England.

R v Berry [1985] AC 246; [1985] Crim LR 102; (1985) 149 JP 276; (1984) 128 SJ 851; [1984] TLR 677; [1984] 3 WLR 1274 HL Offence of making explosive substance involves knowing that item of manufacture/ in possession/under control can trigger explosion and reasonably suspect manufactured item will not be used lawfully.

R v Berry (No 3) [1994] 2 All ER 913; (1994) 99 Cr App R 88; [1995] 1 WLR 7 CA Offence of making explosive substance involves knowing that item of manufacture/ in possession/under control can cause explosion.

R v Bouch [1982] 3 All ER 918; (1983) 76 Cr App R 11; [1982] Crim LR 675; [1983] QB 246; (1982) 126 SJ 511; [1982] TLR 392; [1982] 3 WLR 673 CA Petrol bomb an 'explosive substance' under Explosive Substances Act 1883.

R v Cain; R v Schollick [1975] 2 All ER 900; (1975) 61 Cr App R 186; (1975) 139 JP 598; (1975) 125 NLJ 553; [1976] QB 496; (1975) 119 SJ 422; [1975] 3 WLR 131 CA Attorney-General's duty under Explosive Substances Act is to consider generalities not minutiae of charge.

R v Howard [1993] Crim LR 213 CA On what constitutes an 'explosive substance' (petrol bomb is an explosive substance).

R v McCarthy (John Augustine) (1964) 48 Cr App R 111; [1964] 1 WLR 196 CCA On what constitutes aiding and abetting possession of an explosve substance.

R v McVitie [1960] 2 All ER 498; [1960] Crim LR 559; (1960) 124 JP 404; [1960] 2 QB 483; (1960) 104 SJ 510; [1960] 3 WLR 99 CCA Valid conviction for knowingly possessing explosives though term 'knowingly' not in indictment.

R v Wheatley [1979] 1 All ER 954; (1979) 68 Cr App R 287; (1979) 143 JP 376; (1978) 122 SJ 791; [1979] 1 WLR 144 CA 'Explosive' under Explosive Substances Act 1883 to be defined by reference to Explosives Act 1875.

EXPLOSIVES (possession)

R v Dacey [1939] 2 All ER 641; (1939-40) XXXI Cox CC 283; (1938-40) 27 Cr App R 86; (1939) 160 LTR 652; (1939) 83 SJ 480; (1938-39) LV TLR 670; (1939) WN (I) 166 CCA Circumstantial evidence suggesting knew what possessed placed burden on accused to disprove had knowledge.

R v Eadie (Elizabeth) (1922-23) 17 Cr App R 24 CCA Leave to appeal granted on prima facie basis in posession of explosives case.

R v Hallam [1957] 1 All ER 665; (1957) 41 Cr App R 111; [1957] Crim LR 247; (1957) 121 JP 255; (1957) 107 LJ 185; [1957] 1 QB 569; (1957) 101 SJ 268; [1957] 2 WLR 521 CCA Knowingly possessing explosives involves knowing have possession and know what possess is explosive.

R v Rutter and White [1959] Crim LR 288t CCA Conviction for unlawful possession of explosives quashed as was inadequate evidence of possession/control of same.

R v Stewart and Harris [1960] Crim LR 57t CCA Must possess explosive and know that what possess is explosive to be guilty of illegal possession of explosive.

EXTRADITION (general)

Armah v Government of Ghana and another [1966] 3 All ER 177; [1968] AC 192 (also CA); [1966] Crim LR 618t; [1967] Crim LR 240t; (1967) 131 JP 43; (1965-66) 116 NLJ 1204t; (1966) 110 SJ 890; [1966] 3 WLR 828 HL 'Strong and probable presumption' that accused committed offence to be given natural meaning; issues for appellate court are did magistrate apply correct test/was there a 'strong and probable presumption' accused committed offence.

Athanassiadis v Government of Greece [1969] 3 All ER 293; [1971] AC 282; (1969) 133 JP 577; [1969] 3 WLR 544 HL 'Months' in Anglo-Greek Extradition Treaty means calendar months; conviction for contumacy explained.

Atkinson v United States Government and others [1969] 3 All ER 1317; [1971] AC 197; [1970] Crim LR 30; (1970) 134 JP 29; (1969) 119 NLJ 1045t; (1969) 113 SJ 901; [1969] 3 WLR 1074 HL If sufficient evidence for committal magistrate must commit.

Attorney-General for the Dominion of Canada v Fedorenko [1911] AC 735; (1912) 81 LJPC 74; (1911-12) 105 LTR 343; (1910-11) XXVII TLR 541 PC Under 1886 Extradition Treaty with Russia person sought must be arrested after formally correct requisition presented.

Beese and another v Governor of Ashford Remand Centre and another [1973] 3 All ER 689; (1974) 138 JP 1; (1973) 123 NLJ 993t; (1973) 117 SJ 835; [1973] 1 WLR 1426 HL Judges' Rules inapplicable to foreign detectives; sufficiency of evidence.

Bennett v Horseferry Road Magistrates' Court and another [1993] 3 All ER 138; (1993) 143 NLJ 955; (1993) 137 SJ LB 159/172 HL Rule of law more important than public interest in punishment of crime; tacit extradition via deportation an abuse of process.

Cheng (Tzu-Tsai) v Governor of Pentonville Prison [1973] 2 All ER 204; [1973] AC 931; [1973] Crim LR 362; (1973) 137 JP 422; (1973) 117 SJ 527; [1973] 2 WLR 746 HL Political offence ground open only if political offence against requesting state.

De Demko v Home Secretary and others [1959] 1 All ER 341; [1959] AC 654; [1959] Crim LR 212t; (1959) 123 JP 156; (1959) 109 LJ 120; (1959) 103 SJ 130 HL CA has original/not appellate jurisdiction under Fugitive Offenders Act 1881, s 10.

Diamond v Minter and others [1941] 1 All ER 390; (1939-40) XXXI Cox CC 468; (1941) 105 JP 181; [1941] 1 KB 656; (1942) 92 LJ 52/59; [1941] 110 LJ 503; (1941) 164 LTR 362; (1941) 85 SJ 155; (1940-41) LVII TLR 332; (1941) WN (I) 58 HC KBD Can only arrest fugitive offender under Fugitive Offenders Act 1881 and if have indorsed/provisional warrant.

Dowse v Government of Sweden [1983] 2 All ER 123; [1983] 2 AC 464; (1983) 133 NLJ 537; [1983] TLR 280; [1983] 2 WLR 791 HL Affirmation certified by foreign judge as true is admissible evidence.

Ex parte Enahoro [1963] Crim LR 568; (1963) 107 SJ 397 HC QBD Habeas corpus application heard in person (where alleging that previous non-appearance had been contrived to ensure evidence presented in certain way.

Ex parte Johnston [1959] Crim LR 524t HC QBD Evidence not especially strong but did nonetheless justify committal for extradition.

Ex parte Le Gros (1913-14) XXX TLR 249; (1914) WN (I) 31 CA CA cannot grant rule nisi for habeas corpus where HC has refused same.

Ex parte Moser (1915-17) XXV Cox CC 69; [1915] 2 KB 698; [1915] 84 LJKB 1820; (1915-16) 113 LTR 496; (1914-15) XXXI TLR 384; (1915) WN (I) 169 HC KBD Extradition of 'fugitive offender' was valid.

Ex parte Moser (1914-15) XXXI TLR 438 HC KBD Extradition of 'fugitive offender' was valid.

Ex parte Orimolade [1963] Crim LR 110t HC QBD Fugitive offender seeking release encouraged to apply under the Fugitive Offenders Act 1881 and to make habeas corpus application.

Ex parte Shalom Schtraks (No 2) [1962] 3 All ER 849; [1963] Crim LR 111; [1964] 1 QB 191; [1962] 3 WLR 1435 HC QBD No habeas corpus writ where alleged evidence that committal obtained by fraud insufficiently probative.

Ex parte Singapore Republic Government (1977) 127 NLJ 962t HC QBD Failed appeal by Singaporean Government against magistrates' refusal to approve extradition application.

Ex parte Suidan [1966] Crim LR 445t; (1965-66) 116 NLJ 837t HC QBD Leave to seek habeas corpus but no bail for proposed extraditee who alleged the requesting warrant/deposition were seriously defective.

Ex parte Tarling (1979) 129 (1) NLJ 881t CA Habeas corpus application granted where delay in extradition case meant would be unjust/opressive to return proposed extraditee to requesting country.

Fernandez v Government of Singapore and others [1971] 2 All ER 691; (1971) 115 SJ 469; [1971] 1 WLR 987 HL Foreign affidavit admissible as evidence; need not prove on balance of probabilities for race/religion/nationality/politics clause to arise.

Government of Australia v Harrod [1975] 2 All ER 1; [1976] Crim LR 57; (1975) 139 JP 389; (1975) 119 SJ 371; [1975] 1 WLR 745 HL Question is would evidence warrant trial for offence in England; failure to supply party with transcript not breach of natural justice.

Government of Belgium v Postlethwaite and others [1988] AC 924 (also HC QBD); (1987) 137 NLJ 666; (1987) 131 SJ 1038; [1987] 3 WLR 365 HL On what constitutes satisfactory submission of evidence within time constraints imposed by the Anglo-Belgian Extradition Treaty.

Government of Canada and another v Aronson [1989] 2 All ER 1025; [1990] 1 AC 579; (1990) 90 Cr App R 199; (1989) 139 NLJ 1040; (1989) 133 SJ 1031; [1989] 3 WLR 436 HL Ingredients of Commonwealth country's offence must point to guilt of matching English offence.

Government of Denmark v Nielsen [1984] 2 All ER 81; [1984] AC 606; (1984) 79 Cr App R 1 (also HC QBD); (1984) 134 NLJ 657; (1984) 128 SJ 317; [1984] TLR 239; [1984] 2 WLR 737 HL Magistrate need only decide whether acts described would be offences under English law - foreign law irrelevant.

Government of the Federal Republic of Germany v Sotiriadis and another [1974] 1 All ER 692; [1975] AC 1; [1974] Crim LR 250; (1974) 138 JP 305; (1974) 124 NLJ 176t; (1974) 118 SJ 148; [1974] 2 WLR 253 HL Date of apprehension is date of arrest after requesting state requisition; sufficiency of evidence.

In the matter of Anderson [1994] Crim LR 594 HC QBD Failed habeas corpus application where claimed that because of delay/nature of offence involved it would be oppressive to return extraditee to Greece.

In the matter of Chetta (1996) TLR 11/7/96 HC QBD Improper for Home Secretary not to disclose reasons for issuing extradition warrant until after judicial review of decision sought.

In the matter of Evans [1994] Crim LR 593 HC QBD Magistrate not to examine law of requesting state beyond what is stated in extradition materials.

In the matter of McAngus [1994] Crim LR 602 HC QBD Person who showed counterfeit shirts to another with view to sale could be extradited on charge of going equipped to cheat.

In the matter of Nagdhi (David) [1989] Crim LR 825 HC QBD On relevance of order to proceed to validity of extradition proceedings; on determination (by magistrates) of issue of jurisdiction.

In the matter of Osbourne [1993] Crim LR 694 HC QBD Photocopied photograph properly admitted in evidence as was referred to as enclosure in requesting state's warrant.

In the matter of Wai Kit Lee; R v Metropolitan Stipendiary Magistrate; ex parte Wai Kit Lee [1993] Crim LR 696 HC QBD No power in extradition proceedings for court to request more evidence from requesting state; failed habeas corpus application where extraditee claimed undertakings by the Hong Kong government might not be honoured by the Chinese government after the hand-over.

Jennings v United States Government [1982] 3 All ER 104 (also HC QBD); [1983] 1 AC 624; (1982) 75 Cr App R 367; [1982] Crim LR 748; (1982) 146 JP 396; (1982) 132 NLJ 881; [1983] RTR 1 (also HC QBD); (1982) 126 SJ 659; [1982] TLR 424; [1982] 3 WLR 450 HL Causing death by reckless driving is manslaughter; character of offence for which sought determines if extradition possible.

Kakis v Government of the Republic of Cyprus and others [1978] 2 All ER 634; [1978] Crim LR 489; (1978) 142 JP 429; (1978) 122 SJ 400; [1978] 1 WLR 779 HL No extradition because of delay, death of alibi witness, reasonable belief would not be prosecuted for offence.

Kossekechatko and Others v Attorney-General for Trinidad [1932] AC 78; (1931-34) XXIX Cox CC 394; (1931) 72 LJ 386; (1932) 101 LJPC 17; (1932) 146 LTR 101; (1931) 75 SJ 741; (1931-32) XLVIII TLR 27 PC Non-compliance by magistrate with procedural requirements and absence of evidence that fugitives had committed offence in French territory (as required in French Extradition Treaty) meant no extradition.

Lee v Governor of Pentonville Prison and the Government of the United Sattes of America [1987] Crim LR 635 HC QBD Unauthenticated copy of authenticated copy of warrant inadmissible in evidence.

Liangsiriprasert v United States Government and another [1990] 2 All ER 866; [1991] 1 AC 225; (1991) 92 Cr App R 77; (1990) 134 SJ 1123; [1990] TLR 507; [1990] 3 WLR 606 PC Enticement into jurisdiction from where extradition possible not abuse of extradition process. Inchoate crimes - here conspiracy - entered into abroad/in Thailand to commit offence in England/Hong Kong triable in England/Hong Kong.

Metropolitan Police Commissioner v Hammond [1965] AC 810; [1964] Crim LR 589t; (1964) 114 LJ 488; (1964) 108 SJ 478; [1964] 3 WLR 1 HL Fugitive offender released as warrant not endorsed by (non-existent) police officer/magistrate had not properly considered case.

Morgan v Attorney-General [1990] TLR 515 PC Person convicted but not yet sentenced in the US could be extradited as 'convicted person'.

Oskar v Government of Australia and others [1988] 1 All ER 183; [1988] AC 366; (1988) 87 Cr App R 299; [1988] Crim LR 457; (1988) 132 SJ 52; [1988] 2 WLR 82 HL Secretary of State can authorise magistrate to proceed with extradition case despite a charge lying on file; original statements or single separate certificate identifying statements acceptable; 22-month delay did not mean return unjust or oppressive.

R v Ashford (Kent) Justices, ex parte Gilmore [1966] Crim LR 618 (1966) 110 SJ 709 HC QBD Court could not under the Backing of Warrants (Republic of Ireland) Act 1965 act on warrant issued in Jersey.

R v Aubrey-Fletcher, ex parte Ross-Munro [1968] 1 All ER 99; [1968] Crim LR 39t; (1968) 132 JP 109; (1967) 117 NLJ 1217t; [1968] 1 QB 620; (1967) 111 SJ 911; [1968] 2 WLR 23 HC QBD Trial if offences charged match those for which surrendered.

R v Bow Street Magistrates' Court and another; ex parte Allison [1997] TLR 291 HC QBD On what constitutes (as here) an 'urgent' extradition case for the purposes of the United States of America (Extradition) Order 1976.

R v Bow Street Magistrates' Court; ex parte Paloka [1995] TLR 597 HC QBD Need be no reference to limitation in materials presented as part of extradition request.

R v Bow Street Magistrates' Court; ex parte Van der Holst (1986) 83 Cr App R 114 HC QBD Admissibility of various pieces of evidence in extradition proceedings.

R v Bow Street Magistrates; ex parte Mackeson (1982) 75 Cr App R 24 CA Prohibition of committal proceedings where party had been subject of deportation by means of purported extradition.

R v Brixton Prison Governor and another, ex parte Enahoro [1963] 2 All ER 477; [1963] Crim LR 566; [1963] 2 QB 455; [1963] 2 WLR 1260 HC QBD Person will be released if over one month delay after committal unless Home Secretary convinces otherwise; Home Secretary free to/not to have fugitive returned to whence is fugitive.

R v Brixton Prison Governor, ex parte Atkinson [1969] 2 All ER 1146; [1969] Crim LR 487t; (1969) 133 JP 617; (1969) 113 SJ 690 HC QBD Post-arrest preferring of charges admissible; question of oppression not matter for court; presumption requesting state will respect extradition treaty despite contrary indications in affidavit.

R v Brixton Prison Governor; ex parte Atkinson [1970] Crim LR 661t HL Refusal of habeas corpus application arising in course of extradition proceedings.

R v Brixton Prison Governor, ex parte Kahan [1989] 2 All ER 368; [1989] QB 716; (1989) 133 SJ 121; [1989] 2 WLR 721 HC QBD Extradition to Fiji possible because Fiji a 'designated Commonwealth country' although outside Commonwealth.

R v Brixton Prison Governor, ex parte Kotronis [1969] 3 All ER 304; [1969] Crim LR 600; (1969) 133 JP 674; (1969) 119 NLJ 902t; (1969) 113 SJ 794; [1969] 3 WLR 528 HC QBD No extradition despite conviction certificate as conviction contrary to natural justice.

R v Brixton Prison Governor; ex parte McCheyne (1951) 95 SJ 353; [1951] 1 TLR 1155 HC KBD Fugitive discharged where return to country of crime would be unjust/oppressive/involve too severe a punishment (Fugitive Offenders Act 1881, s 10).

R v Brixton Prison Governor, ex parte Soblen [1962] 3 All ER 640; [1962] Crim LR 700t; (1962) 112 LJ 733; [1963] 2 QB 243 (also HC QBD); (1962) 106 SJ 736; [1962] 3 WLR 1154 CA Difference between deportation and extradition.

R v Brixton Prison Governor; ex parte Thompson [1970] Crim LR 281; (1970) 114 SJ 187 HC QBD Extradition order valid though granted by magistrate aware of proposed extraditee's criminal history.

R v Brixton Prison Governor; Re Anwera [1907] 76 LJKB 661 HC KBD Extradition allowed despite passing of five-year prescriptive period in requesting country as had not passed when extradition order made.

R v Chief Metropolitan Magistrate, ex parte Government of the Republic of Singapore; R v Governor of Pentonville Prison, ex parte Tarling (1980) 70 Cr App R 77; [1978] Crim LR 490 HL (also HC QBD) No extradition for crime which is not crime in England/in respect of which is no prima facie evidence prisoner committed offence.

R v Chief Metropolitan Magistrate; ex parte Government of Denmark (1984) 79 Cr App R 1; (1984) 148 JP 551; (1983) 127 SJ 377; [1983] TLR 348 HC QBD Magistrate need only decide whether acts described would be offences under English law - foreign law irrelevant.

R v Chief Metropolitan Stipendiary Magistrate, ex parte Secretary of State for the Home Department [1989] 1 All ER 151; [1988] Crim LR 835; (1988) 132 SJ 1430; [1988] 1 WLR 1204 HC QBD Offence arising out of tax evasion may be extraditable offence.

R v Chief Metropolitan Stipendiary Magistrate, ex parte Osman [1988] 3 All ER 173; [1988] Crim LR 681 HC QBD Court may award costs to extraditing state against habeas corpus applicant if application fails.

R v Cohen (1907) 71 JP 190 CCC Person could be tried on additional charges to those for which arrested and returned from colony.

R v Corrigan (1931-34) XXIX Cox CC 198; (1930-31) Cr App R 106; [1931] 1 KB 527; (1930) 70 LJ 317; (1931) 100 LJCL 55; (1931) 144 LTR 187; (1930-31) XLVII TLR 27; (1930) WN (I) 235 CCA Failed attempt to avoid prosecution for offences in Britain on basis that process of appellant's surrender to France for other offences had already commenced.

R v Davidson (John Pollitt) (1977) 64 Cr App R 209; [1977] Crim LR 219 CA On determining validity of extradition to Britain from another country.

R v Davies (David William Martin) (1983) 76 Cr App R 120 CA Conviction quashed where fugitive offender returning voluntarily pleaded guilty to non-extraditable offence.

R v Daye (1907-09) XXI Cox CC 659; (1908) 72 JP 269; [1908] 2 KB 333; [1908] 77 LJCL 659; (1908-09) XCIX LTR 165 HC KBD Bank required to release document deposited with them.

R v Director of Public Prosecutions and another; ex parte Thom [1996] Crim LR 116; (1995) 139 SJ LB 25; [1994] TLR 660 HC QBD Once Home Secretary issued order requiring extradition of person, neither Home Secretary/Director of Public Prosecutions could end the extradition process.

R v Dix (1901-02) XVIII TLR 231 HC KBD On need for offences to be offences according to law of requesting and extraditing state before extradition possible.

R v Godfrey [1922] All ER 266; (1921-25) XXVII Cox CC 338; (1922) 86 JP 219; [1923] 1 KB 24; [1923] 92 LJCL 205; (1923) 128 LTR 115; (1922-23) 67 SJ 147; (1922-23) XXXIX TLR 4; (1922) WN (I) 285 HC KBD Can be 'fugitive offender' though were never in and never left foreign country.

R v Government of Norway; ex parte Singh (Harmohan) (1981) 131 NLJ 367; (1981) 125 SJ 480 HC QBD On admissibility in extradition proceedings in England of statements by witnesses in Norway.

R v Governor of Ashford Remand Centre, ex parte Beese and another [1973] 3 All ER 250; [1973] Crim LR 524; (1973) 123 NLJ 611t; (1973) 117 SJ 545; [1973] 1 WLR 969 HC QBD Judges' Rules inapplicable to operations of foreign detectives in foreign states; sufficeiency of evidence.

R v Governor of Belmarsh Prison and another, ex parte Francis [1995] 3 All ER 634; (1995) 139 SJ LB 100; [1995] TLR 190; [1995] 1 WLR 1121 HC QBD Court will not interfere with magistrate's decision to commit where a reasonable magistrate properly directed in law would do likewise.

R v Governor of Belmarsh Prison and another, ex parte Martin [1995] 2 All ER 548; [1995] 1 WLR 412 HC QBD Telephone tapping to be an offence must involve UK public telephone communication person so US phone-taps by US agents were admissible evidence in extradition case.

R v Governor of Belmarsh Prison and another; ex parte Dunlayici (1996) TLR 2/8/96 HC QBD Dominant motive underlying commission of offence is fundamental determinant as to whether offence political.

R v Governor of Brixton Prison [1911] 2 KB 82 HC KBD Non-discharge of fugitive despite irregularities in requesting state's procedure.

R v Governor of Brixton Prison (1962) 106 SJ 856 HC ChD Writ of habeas corpus issued where inter alia affidavit concerning law of requesting country had not been authenticated.

R v Governor of Brixton Prison and another, ex parte Osman (No 4) [1992] 1 All ER 579; [1991] Crim LR 533; [1990] TLR 781 HC QBD Series of appplications on same grounds for habeas corpus permissible if fresh evidence but court may strike out vexatious applications; self-induced delay will not benefit applicant; court may look to previous applications.

R v Governor of Brixton Prison and another, ex parte Osman (No 4) [1990] TLR 748 HC QBD Public interest immunity also arises in habeas corpus applications.

R v Governor of Brixton Prison and another; ex parte Armah (No 2) [1967] Crim LR 175; (1966) 110 SJ 978 HC QBD Not unjust/oppressive to extradite party once court assured extraditee would not immediately be taken into protective custody on arrival in requesting state.

R v Governor of Brixton Prison and another; ex parte Enahoro (No 2) (1963) 107 SJ 357 HC QBD On procedure as regards extradition of person who has been detained for over thirty days after order for return of fugitive made: here procedure employed was valid.

R v Governor of Brixton Prison and another; ex parte Evans [1994] TLR 419 HL Accused could not bring forward evidence at extradition hearings.

R v Governor of Brixton Prison and another; ex parte Orimolade [1963] Crim LR 200; (1963) 107 SJ 37 HC QBD Two year delay between depositions being taken and then arriving from requesting country not unreasonable/oppressive delay.

R v Governor of Brixton Prison and another; ex parte Rush [1969] 1 All ER 316; [1969] Crim LR 197; (1969) 133 JP 153; (1969) 119 NLJ 177t; (1969) 113 SJ 106; [1969] 1 WLR 165 HC QBD Inadequate evidence to satisfy necessary conditions for extradition (Fugitive Offenders Act 1967, s 5) - conspiracy alleged would not be triable in England as was conspiracy to commit crime outside (requesting) jurisdiction.

R v Governor of Brixton Prison, ex parte Athanassiadis [1966] Crim LR 677t; (1966) 110 SJ 769 HC QBD Valid extradition to Greece where proposed extraditee had been convicted of obtaining property by false pretences from Dutch firm.

R v Governor of Brixton Prison, ex parte Bidwell [1936] 3 All ER 1; (1934-39) XXX Cox CC 462; (1936) 100 JP 458; [1937] 1 KB 305; [1937] 106 LJCL 599; (1936) 155 LTR 453; (1936) 80 SJ 876; (1936-37) LIII TLR 1; (1936) WN (I) 275 HC KBD On indorsement of warrants under Fugitive Offenders Act 1881, s 3.

R v Governor of Brixton Prison, ex parte Caldough [1961] 1 All ER 606; [1961] Crim LR 402; (1961) 125 JP 250; (1961) 111 LJ 239; (1961) 105 SJ 157; [1961] 1 WLR 464 HC QBD Foreign depositions admissible though fugitive's lawyer could not attend taking of depositions.

R v Governor of Brixton Prison, ex parte Gardner [1968] 1 All ER 636; [1968] Crim LR 109t; (1968) 132 JP 187; (1968) 118 NLJ 230; [1968] 2 QB 399; (1968) 112 SJ 153; [1968] 2 WLR 512 HC QBD Habeas corpus where offences on which sought not offences under English law.

R v Governor of Brixton Prison, ex parte Osman (No 1) [1992] 1 All ER 108; (1991) 93 Cr App R 202; [1992] Crim LR 741; [1991] 1 WLR 281 HC QBD Public interest immunity applies to criminal and civil proceedings; refusal to grant discovery at interlocutory stage estops relevant documents being raised in substantive application.

R v Governor of Brixton Prison, ex parte Osman (No 2) [1991] TLR 265 HC QBD Court would not guess as to ramifications of future change in sovereignty of requesting state upon fate of proposed extraditee.

R v Governor of Brixton Prison, ex parte Osman (No 3) [1992] 1 All ER 122; [1992] 1 WLR 36 HC QBD Court need not speculate on validity of specialty guarantee.

R v Governor of Brixton Prison, ex parte Osman (No 5); R v Secretary of State for the Home Department, ex parte Osman (No 2) [1992] TLR 565 HC QBD Home Secretary could commence return of extraditee who had made habeas corpus application if Home Secretary decided extradition request did not conform with the Administration of Justice Act 1960, s 14(2).

R v Governor of Brixton Prison, ex parte Percival (1907-09) XXI Cox CC 387; (1907) 71 JP 148; [1907] 1 KB 696; [1907] 76 LJCL 619; (1907) XCVI LTR 545; (1906-07) XXIII TLR 238 HC KBD On rendition of fugitive offenders within King's Dominions.

R v Governor of Brixton Prison, ex parte Perry [1923] All ER 182; (1921-25) XXVII Cox CC 597; [1924] 1 KB 455; (1923) 58 LJ 601; [1924] 93 LJCL 380; (1924) 130 LTR 731; (1923-24) 68 SJ 370; (1923-24) XL TLR 181; (1924) WN (I) 11 HC KBD No writ of habeas corpus where cause of complaint could be addressed by Secretary of State under Extradition Act 1870, s 11.

R v Governor of Brixton Prison, ex parte Sadri [1962] 3 All ER 747; [1962] Crim LR 835; (1962) 112 LJ 767; (1962) 106 SJ 836; [1962] 1 WLR 1304 HC QBD Habeas corpus writ issued as no admissible evidence of guilt; foreign affidavit defective as no indication how offences punishable.

R v Governor of Brixton Prison, ex parte Servini (1913-14) XXIII Cox CC 713; (1914) 78 JP 47; [1914] 1 KB 77; (1913) 48 LJ 661; [1914] 83 LJKB 212; (1913-14) 109 LTR 986; (1913-14) 58 SJ 68; (1913-14) XXX TLR 35; (1913) WN (I) 302 HC KBD Habeas corpus application refused though evidential irregularity proved.

R v Governor of Brixton Prison, ex parte Singh [1961] 2 All ER 565; [1961] Crim LR 617; [1962] 1 QB 211; [1961] 2 WLR 980 CCA Extradition in relation to crime allegedly committed ten years previously refused as return after delay would be unjust/oppressive.

R v Governor of Brixton Prison, ex parte Thompson (1911-13) XXII Cox CC 494; (1911) 75 JP 311; (1911) 80 LJCL 986; (1911-12) 105 LTR 66; (1910-11) XXVII TLR 350; (1911) WN (I) 81 HC KBD Procedural error in extradition process did not merit discharge of accused.

R v Governor of Brixton Prison; ex parte Bekar [1997] TLR 303 HC QBD Question as to whether warrant genuine regulated by the Extradition Act 1989, s 26.

R v Governor of Brixton Prison; ex parte Calberla (1907-09) XXI Cox CC 544; (1907) 71 JP 509; [1907] 2 KB 861; [1907] 76 LJKB 1117; (1908) XCVIII LTR 100; (1906-07) 51 SJ 721; (1906-07) XXIII TLR 737 HC KBD Extradition to complete sentence despite earlier release on basis of ill-health/passage of time.

R v Governor of Brixton Prison; ex parte Campbell [1956] Crim LR 624t HC QBD Discharge of propsed extraditee ordered where undue delay in seeking extradition prejudiced chances of fair trial.

R v Governor of Brixton Prison; ex parte Cook [1970] Crim LR 699; (1970) 120 NLJ 945t; (1970) 114 SJ HC QBD In the circumstances two year delay in extradition process justified discharging person sought by foreign state.

R v Governor of Brixton Prison; ex parte Enahoro [1963] Crim LR 199t; (1963) 113 LJ 498; (1963) 107 SJ 75 HC QBD Extradition for treasonable felony allowed.

R v Governor of Brixton Prison; ex parte Green [1955] Crim LR 110t HC QBD Extradition to Nigeria of person charged with theft/forgery of cheque ordered.

R v Governor of Brixton Prison; ex parte Hurwitz (1924-25) 69 SJ 727 HC QBD Failed habeas corpus application in extradition case: was sufficient evidence to justify extradition of applicant.

R v Governor of Brixton Prison; ex parte Lennon [1963] Crim LR 41t HC QBD Failed request for extradition of person for forgery; cheques not forgeries where drawn on imaginary bank.

R v Governor of Brixton Prison; ex parte Levin [1997] 3 All ER 289; [1997] 2 Cr App R (S) 990; (1997) 147 NLJ 990; (1997) 141 SJ LB 148; [1997] TLR 319; [1997] 3 WLR 117 HL Computer records of improper bank transfers (on foot of which proposed extraditee sought) were admissible.

R v Governor of Brixton Prison; ex parte Levin [1996] 4 All ER 350; [1997] 1 Cr App R 335; [1997] QB 65; (1996) 140 SJ LB 94; (1996) TLR 11/3/96; [1996] 3 WLR 657 HC QBD Computer print-outs admissible in evidence in extradition action (which was a criminal proceeding).

R v Governor of Brixton Prison; ex parte Mehmet (Mourat) [1962] 1 All ER 463; [1962] Crim LR 108t; (1962) 112 LJ 154; [1962] 2 QB 1; (1962) 106 SJ 196 HC QBD Discharge from custody where evidence such that no reasonable magistrate would have committed thereon.

R v Governor of Brixton Prison; ex parte Otchere [1963] Crim LR 43t HC QBD No extradition where requesting country's submission full of errors.

R v Governor of Brixton Prison; ex parte Penn (1952) 96 SJ 696 HC QBD Failed application by Indian authorities for extradition of alleged offender (application in grossly irregular form).

R v Governor of Brixton Prison; ex parte Savarkar [1908-10] All ER 603; [1910] 2 KB 1056; (1911) 80 LJCL 57; (1910-11) 103 LTR 473; (1909-10) 54 SJ 635; (1909-10) XXVI TLR 561 CA CA a court of first instance in 'trivial offence' fugitive offender cases; 'trivial offence' plea can be entered at same time seek habeas corpus; individual longtime resident in England ought really to be tried in England.

R v Governor of Brixton Prison; ex parte Savarkar (Vinayak Damodar) (1910) 74 JP 417; (1909-10) XXVI TLR 512 HC KBD Not unjust and oppressive to return fugitive offender to one of Her Majesty's dominions for trial by judges without jury.

R v Governor of Brixton Prison; ex parte Shure (1926-30) XXVIII Cox CC 126; [1926] 1 KB 127; [1926] 95 LJCL 361; (1926) 134 LTR 317; (1925) WN (I) 242 HC KBD On seeking of habeas corpus in extradition action.

R v Governor of Brixton Prison; ex parte Smyth; R v Robey; ex parte Same [1955] Crim LR 375 HC QBD Failed habeas corpus application by proposed extraditee who had been committed to prison following two adjournments to enable extraditee to obtain evidence from abroad (which failed to do).

R v Governor of Brixton Prison; ex parte Soblen [1962] Crim LR 700t; [1963] 2 QB 243 (also CA); (1962) 106 SJ 706 HC QBD Difference between deportation and extradition.

R v Governor of Brixton Prison; ex parte Stallmann [1911-13] All ER 385; (1913-14) XXIII Cox CC 192; (1913) 77 JP 5; [1912] 3 KB 424; [1913] 82 LJKB 8; (1912-13) 107 LTR 553; (1911-12) XXVIII TLR 572 HC KBD Extradition allowed despite party having been set at large on previous writ of habeas corpus.

R v Governor of Brixton Prison; ex parte Van der Auwera (1907-09) XXI Cox CC 446; (1907) 71 JP 226; [1907] 2 KB 157; (1907) XCVI LTR 821; (1906-07) XXIII TLR 415; (1907) WN (I) 88 HC KBD Valid extradition where proceedings begun/committal made within period prescribed but extradition delayed beyond period through serving of unconnected sentence in England.

R v Governor of Brixton Prison; ex parte Wells; R v Governor of Holloway Prison; ex parte Burns (1913-14) XXIII Cox CC 161; (1912) 76 JP 310; [1912] 2 KB 578; (1912) 81 LJKB 912; (1912-13) 107 LTR 408; (1911-12) XXVIII TLR 405 HC KBD Requisition required under Anglo-French Extradition Treaty from diplomatic agent of country to which fugitive belonged when allegedly committed offence.

R v Governor of Durham Prison; ex parte Carlisle [1979] Crim LR 175 HC QBD Failed appeal against extradition by alleged terrorist that offence for which sought in Ireland was a political offence.

R v Governor of Gloucester Prison, ex parte Miller [1979] 2 All ER 1103; (1979) 143 JP 651; (1978) 128 NLJ 1124t; (1979) 123 SJ 373; [1979] 1 WLR 537 HC QBD English legal/not procedural rules applicable in extradition cases.

R v Governor of HM Prison, Brixton, ex parte Minervini [1958] 3 All ER 318; [1958] Crim LR 808; (1958) 122 JP 473; (1958) 108 LJ 745; [1959] 1 QB 155; (1958) 102 SJ 777; [1958] 3 WLR 559 HC QBD Requesting government may be represented/heard at fugitive convict's habeas corpus application; 'territory' includes places within jurisdiction of state (such as ships).

R v Governor of Holloway Prison [1900-03] All ER 609 HC KBD Court cannot consider fresh evidence concerning extraditiion in habeas corpus application.

R v Governor of Holloway Prison, ex parte Siletti (1901-07) XX Cox CC 353; (1903) 67 JP 67; [1902] 71 LJCL 935; (1902-03) LXXXVII LTR 332; (1901-02) 46 SJ 686; (1902-03) 51 WR 191 HC KBD On making of habeas corpus orders in extradition cases.

R v Governor of Holloway Prison; ex parte Jennings [1982] Crim LR 590; (1982) 132 NLJ 488; [1983] RTR 1 (also HL); (1982) 126 SJ 413; [1982] TLR 210; [1982] 1 WLR 949 HC QBD Cannot extradite person for manslaughter where evidence suggests are guilty of death by reckless driving.

R v Governor of Pentonville Prison and another, ex parte Lee; R v Bow Street Metropolitan Stipendiary Magistrate, ex parte Lee [1993] 3 All ER 504; [1993] 1 WLR 1294 HC QBD Magistrate may examine evidence provided by requesting state, and circumstances at time of extradition; may not request further materials or decide on future events.

R v Governor of Pentonville Prison and another, ex parte Osman [1989] 3 All ER 701; (1990) 90 Cr App R 281; [1988] Crim LR 611; (1990) 134 SJ 458; [1990] 1 WLR 277 HC QBD Usually theft takes place where property appropriated; must be non-hearsay evidence that person a co-conspirator before evidence of other conspirator admissible against him; court in deciding if allegedly criminal document is privileged may look to document without requiring any action from party objecting to privilege.

R v Governor of Pentonville Prison and another; ex parte Cheng [1973] Crim LR 180; (1973) 117 SJ 146 HC QBD On political defence to extradition: covers only political offences between requesting state and proposed extraditee.

R v Governor of Pentonville Prison, ex parte Budlong and another [1980] 1 All ER 701; [1980] Crim LR 176; (1980) 144 JP 185; (1980) 130 NLJ 90; (1980) 124 SJ 220; [1980] 1 WLR 1110 HC QBD Extradition possible absent document specifying (alleged) offence; magistrates may look to evidence, not just documents before them; elements of foreign crime need not be identical to English crime so long as act criminal in England; political defence inapplicable; Treaty of Rome inapplicable to extradition.

R v Governor of Pentonville Prison, ex parte Chinoy [1992] 1 All ER 317 HC QBD That evidence unlawfully obtained not an abuse of process in magistrates' court; that evidence obtained in manner unlawful under foreign law does not require exclusion if lawful in English law; laundering of drug trafficking money an extraditable offence.

R v Governor of Pentonville Prison, ex parte Ecke (1981) 73 Cr App R 223; [1974] Crim LR 102; (1974) 118 SJ 168 HC QBD Individual already in custody can be apprehended on extradition warrant; could extradite individual for crimes not in existence when Anglo-German Extradition Treaty signed.

R v Governor of Pentonville Prison, ex parte Fernandez [1971] 2 All ER 24; [1971] Crim LR 235t; (1971) 115 SJ 188; [1971] 1 WLR 459 HC QBD Foreign evidence need not be given in legal proceedings to be admissible; must be real chance of prejudice for race/religion/nationality/politics clause to arise.

R v Governor of Pentonville Prison, ex parte Khubchandani (1980) 71 Cr App R 241; [1980] Crim LR 436; (1980) 124 SJ275 HC QBD Habeas corpus granted where extradition sought for 'offences' that were not offences under English law.

R v Governor of Pentonville Prison, ex parte Kirby [1979] 2 All ER 1094; (1979) 143 JP 641; [1979] 1 WLR 541 HC QBD Non-compliance with English evidence rules renders evidence inadmissible.

R v Governor of Pentonville Prison, ex parte Naghdi [1990] 1 All ER 257; [1990] 1 WLR 317 HC QBD Person whose extradition is sought need only be told of English approximations to charges faced abroad; court cannot commit for attempt where could not commit for full offence.

R v Governor of Pentonville Prison, ex parte Osman (No 3) [1990] 1 All ER 999; (1990) 91 Cr App R 409; [1990] 1 WLR 878 HC QBD Provisional warrant for arrest available if belief person in/on way to country and magistrate would issue warrant for similar offence within jurisdiction; unlawfulness of provisional warrant does not colour all later steps in case.

R v Governor of Pentonville Prison, ex parte Passingham and another [1982] 3 All ER 1012; [1982] Crim LR 592; [1983] QB 254; (1982) 126 SJ 784; [1982] TLR 346; [1982] 3 WLR 981 HC QBD Admissible evidence need not have been subject to perjury rules in the giving.

R v Governor of Pentonville Prison, ex parte Sinclair [1990] 2 All ER 789; [1990] Crim LR 584; [1990] 2 QB 112; [1992] TLR 38; [1990] 2 WLR 1248 HC QBD Delay irrelevant in extradition to US as extradition not part of prosecution in US; abuse of process doctrine does not apply to extradition of person convicted of extraditable crime.

R v Governor of Pentonville Prison, ex parte Sinclair (1991) 141 NLJ 530i; [1991] 2 WLR 1028 HL Extradition of individual convicted of offence while in United States and sentenced to imprisonment a decade previous to extradition proceedings.

R v Governor of Pentonville Prison, ex parte Singh [1981] 3 All ER 23; (1981) 73 Cr App R 216; (1981) 145 JP 476; [1981] 1 WLR 1031 HC QBD Evidence from third party state inadmissible; affirmation admissible as evidence; what is affirmation a subjective issue.

R v Governor of Pentonville Prison, ex parte Sotiriadis [1974] 1 All ER 504; [1974] Crim LR 44; (1973) 123 NLJ 1068t; (1973) 117 SJ 913 HC QBD Time limit for evidence expired; requesting state must produce sufficient evidence.

R v Governor of Pentonville Prison, ex parte Teja [1971] 2 All ER 11; (1971) 121 NLJ 82t; [1971] 2 QB 274; (1971) 115 SJ 305; [1971] 2 WLR 816 HC QBD Cannot claim no offence because of PC decision - matter for foreign law; political defence inapplicable despite case being subject of Indian Parliamentary debate; cannot plead delay if are responsible for it.

R v Governor of Pentonville Prison, ex parte Tzu-Tsai Cheng [1973] 1 All ER 935 HC QBD Political offence ground arises only if political offence in requesting state, not third state.

R v Governor of Pentonville Prison, ex parte Voets [1986] 2 All ER 630; [1986] Crim LR 465; (1986) 130 SJ 245; [1986] 1 WLR 470 HC QBD All relevant evidence admissible; evidence admitted for one purpose not to be excluded because inadmissible for other purpose.

R v Governor of Pentonville Prison; ex parte Carter [1984] TLR 456 HC QBD No need for corroboration of evidence of children admitted on affirmation at extradition hearings.

R v Governor of Pentonville Prison; ex parte Elliott [1975] Crim LR 516; (1975) 119 SJ 709 HC QBD On what constitutes a 'relevant offence' for which may be extradited under Fugitive Offenders Act 1967.

R v Governor of Pentonville Prison; ex parte Healy (1984) 128 SJ 498; [1984] TLR 303 HC QBD Extradition of Irish citizen from Ireland to the UK on foot of request by latter did not violate Article 48/EEC.

R v Governor of Pentonville Prison; ex parte Herbage (No 3) (1987) 84 Cr App R 149 HC QBD Habeas corpus application by fugitive awaiting extradition refused where was prima facie case that had committed non-time barred felony in United States punishable by over one year's imprisonment.

R v Governor of Pentonville Prison; ex parte Kakis (1978) 128 NLJ 139t; (1978) 122 SJ 96 HC QBD Failed action in which applicant sought to rely on political offence/delay grounds as bases justifying non-extradition.

R v Governor of Pentonville Prison; ex parte Khuschundani (1980) 130 NLJ 415 CA Non-extradition of person sought for offence which was not 'relevant' offence for purposes of Fugitive Offenders Act 1967.

R v Governor of Pentonville Prison; ex parte Mancini [1984] TLR 523 HC QBD Failed habeas corpus application by subject of habeas corpus proceedings requested for murder but extradited for manslaughter.

R v Governor of Pentonville Prison; ex parte Osman (No 2) (1989) 133 SJ 121 HC QBD On status/effect of Foreign Secretary's certificate that proposed extraditee(though apparently attached to the Liberian embassy) did not enjoy diplomatic immunity.

R v Governor of Pentonville Prison; ex parte Passingham and another [1983] Crim LR 678; (1983) 127 SJ 308 HL On 'affirmations' admissible under the Anglo-Swedish Extradition Treaty of 1983.

R v Governor of Pentonville Prison; ex parte Rodriguez [1984] TLR 674 HC QBD Interpretation of provision of evidence requirements under the Anglo-Portugese extradition treaty.

R v Governor of Risley Remand Centre; ex parte Marks [1984] Crim LR 238 HC QBD Unnecessary to prove conviction of person sought under warrant issued under the Backing of Warrants (Republic of Ireland Act) 1965 - warrant adequate evidence of conviction.

R v Horseferry Road Magistrates' Court and another, ex parte Bennett [1993] 2 All ER 474; [1993] Crim LR 200 HC QBD Circumstances by which defendant comes to be in jurisdiction cannot be abuse of process.

R v Kerr (Hugh Gilmour); R v Smith (Derrick Albert) (1976) 62 Cr App R 210; [1976] Crim LR 192t CA Quashing of firearms conviction on foot of extradition as was not extraditable offence.

R v Liverpool City Justices; ex parte Santos [1997] TLR 38 HC QBD Depends on individual case whether failure to surrender to bail can be excused where was due to mistake on part of defendant's solicitor.

R v Lord Mayor of Cardiff; ex parte Lewis (1921-25) XXVII Cox CC 327; (1922) 86 JP 207; [1922] 2 KB 777; [1923] 92 LJCL 28; (1923) 128 LTR 63; (1922) WN (I) 269 HC KBD Court can compel production of documents in extradition cases.

R v Metropolitan Police Commissioner [1955] Crim LR 309t HC QBD Magistrate's perusal of extradition materials in private was procedurally regular.

R v Metropolitan Police Commissioner; ex parte Hammond [1964] 1 All ER 821; [1964] Crim LR 293t; (1964) 128 JP 299; (1964) 114 LJ 272; [1964] 2 QB 385; (1964) 108 SJ 179; [1964] 2 WLR 777 HC QBD Fugitive offender released as warrant not endorsed by (non-existent) police officer.

R v Metropolitan Stipendiary Magistrate, ex parte Lee [1993] TLR 74 HC QBD Magistrate may examine evidence provided by requesting state, and circumstances at time of extradition; may not request further materials or decide on future events.

R v Morgan [1985] Crim LR 447/596 CA Person may be convicted for offence other than that for which warrant issued under Backing of Warrants (Republic of Ireland) Act 1965.

R v Morgan (Oliver) [1991] RTR 365 CA Dishonest appropriation conviction allowed despite possible misdirection by judge as to need for appropriation to take place in England; court could not try person for obtaining pecuniary advantage by deception where extradited on theft charge.

R v Phillips [1922] All ER 275; (1922-23) 67 SJ 64; (1921-22) XXXVIII TLR 897 HC KBD Alleged fugitive offender not entitled to bail while in remand.

R v Phillips (1921-25) XXVII Cox CC 332; (1922) 86 JP 188; (1923) 128 LTR 113; (1922) WN (I) 274 HC KBD Bail possible in extradition case at magistrate's discretion.

R v Plymouth Magistrates' Court and others, ex parte Driver [1985] 2 All ER 681 HC QBD Means by which person came into jurisdiction irrelevant.

R v Secretary of State for India in Council and others; ex parte Ezekiel [1941] 2 All ER 546; [1941] 2 KB 169; (1942) 92 LJ 53; [1942] 111 LJ 237 HC KBD Second World War no excuse for non-extradition to India; need not be avoiding arrest to be extradited; warrant need not refer to Fugitive Offenders Act 1881; depositions admissible though not apparently taken in pursuance of Fugitive Offenders Act 1881, s 29; affidavit of foreign legal expert not conclusive; barrister should not act as counsel and witness.

R v Secretary of State for India in Council and others; ex parte Ezekiel (1942) 92 LJ 45 HC KBD Admissibility of depositions not taken before magistrate.

R v Secretary of State for the Home Department, ex parte Kirkwood [1984] 2 All ER 390; (1984) 128 SJ 332 HC QBD Cannot stay Home Secretary order for surrender.

R v Secretary of State for the Home Department, ex parte Schmidt [1994] 2 All ER 784; [1995] 1 AC 339 (also HL) HC QBD High Court may only order discharge on grounds in Extradition Act 1989; decision of Secretary of State to seek extradition not open to residual review.

R v Secretary of State for the Home Department; ex parte Gilmore and another [1997] TLR 365 HC QBD Conspiracy to commit offence not an extraditable matter.

R v Secretary of State for the Home Department; ex parte Hill [1997] 2 All ER 638; [1997] 2 Cr App R (S) 525 HC QBD Could be extradited for crimes committed before requesting state became designated state under Extradition Act; could be extradited for offences that were offences under English law even where were not sought by requesting state for said offences.

R v Secretary of State for the Home Department; ex parte Launder [1997] 3 All ER 961; [1997] 2 Cr App R (S) 793; (1997) 147 NLJ 793; (1997) 141 SJ LB 123; [1997] TLR 283; [1997] 1 WLR 839 HL Extradition to Hong Kong allowed, Home Secretary having decided that hand-over to China would not result in proposed extraditee suffering unfair trial/injustice/oppression upon return.

R v Secretary of State for the Home Department; ex parte Launder (1996) TLR 28/10/96 HC QBD May usually challenge Home Secretary's decision to make extradition order.

R v Secretary of State for the Home Department; ex parte Patel [1994] TLR 73 HC QBD Successful application for judicial review of Home Office Minister's decision to allow extradition of man for offences he was said to have committed around a decade previously.

R v Secretary of State for the Home Office; ex parte Osman and In the Matter of Osman [1993] Crim LR 214 HC QBD Court would not invoke injustice/oppression grounds to intervene in extradition proceedings after Home Secretary had ordered extradition of person concerned.

R v Smith (1976) 126 NLJ 65t CA Possession of firearms not an offence for which could be extradited under Extradition Act 1870, schedule 1.

R v The Governor of Brixton Prison; ex parte Guerin (1906-07) 51 SJ 571 HC KBD Successful plea that were British-born subject and so not liable to extradition.

R v The Governor of Brixton Prison; ex parte Mehamed Ben Romdan (1912) 76 JP 391; [1912] 3 KB 190; (1912) 81 LJKB 1128; (1911-12) XXVIII TLR 530; (1912) WN (I) 208 HC KBD Discharge from custody required if not surrendered/conveyed away within two days of final committal by magistrate pending extradition warrant.

R v The Governor of Her Majesty's Prison at Holloway (1899-1900) XVI TLR 247 HC QBD Extradition to be ordered where depositions show alleged offence in respect of which extradition is possible.

R v Uxbridge Justices; ex parte Davies [1981] 1 WLR 1080 HC QBD Unlawful detention of extraditee for offence other than that for which extradited.

R v Vyner (1904) 68 JP 142 HC KBD HC can review exercise of magistrate's discretion not to extradite fugitive offender.

R v Zossenheim (1903-04) XX TLR 121 HC KBD On taking foreign depositions.

Re Anderson [1993] Crim LR 954 HC QBD On evidence admissible when determining whether proposed extraditee is in fact unlawfully at large.

Re Armah (Kwesi) [1966] 2 All ER 1006; [1966] Crim LR 446; (1966) 110 SJ 468; [1966] 3 WLR 23 HC QBD Extradition to Ghana possible; 'strong or probable presumption' of guilt requires prima facie case; injustice/oppression in return obviated by special guarantees of Ghanaian government; sworn statements admissible evidence.

Re Bartley [1994] TLR 420 HC QBD Authenticated copy of foreign conviction order adequate document for requesting state to submit.

Re Bluhm [1901] 1 KB 764; (1901) 36 LJ 160; [1901] 70 LJK/QB 472; (1900-01) 45 SJ 362; (1900-01) XVII TLR 358; (1900-01) 49 WR 464 HC KBD Non-discharge of fugitive where was sufficient evidence to justify detention.

Re Borovsky and Weinbaum; ex parte Salaman [1902] 2 KB 312; [1902] 71 LJCL 992; (1902-03) LXXXVII LTR 184 HC KBD On bankruptcy of fugitive offender.

Re Bruce Parkyn-Jackson [1988] Crim LR 834 HC QBD Could extradite to the United States wire fraudster who had received suspended sentence and was in breach of his probation.

Re Caborn-Waterfield [1960] 2 All ER 178; [1961] Crim LR 112; (1960) 124 JP 316; (1960) 110 LJ 350; [1960] 2 QB 498; (1960) 104 SJ 369; [1960] 2 WLR 792 HC QBD No extradition of person sought as an 'accused' though in fact a convict.

Re Clementson [1956] Crim LR 50t HC QBD Failed appeal against extradition for alleged embezzlement of £6 which claimed to have repaid before coming to England as student nurse.

Re De Demko (Baron Kalman) [1958] 3 All ER 360; [1959] Crim LR 53; (1958) 122 JP 477; (1958) 108 LJ 729; (1958) 102 SJ 827; [1958] 3 WLR 624 CA CA has original/has not appellate jurisdiction under Fugitive Offenders Act 1881.

Re Demetrious [1966] 2 All ER 998; [1966] Crim LR 335; (1966) 130 JP 337; (1965-66) 116 NLJ 1144; [1966] 2 QB 194; (1966) 110 SJ 249; [1966] 2 WLR 1066 HC QBD Extradition to Qatar allowed.

Re Drummond [1957] Crim LR 682t HC QBD Was not unjust/oppressive/unduly severe to order extradition of person to Kenya for alleged larceny/false accounting involving £200.

Re Espinosa [1986] Crim LR 684 HC QBD Florida state attorney's affidavit deposing to affidavits of proposed extraditee's accomplices rendered copies of said affidavits admissible in support of extradition request.

Re Evans [1994] 3 All ER 449; (1994) 144 NLJ 1095; (1994) 138 SJ LB 184; [1994] 1 WLR 1006 HL Magistrate not to examine law of requesting state beyond what is stated in extradition materials.

Re Farinha [1992] Crim LR 438; (1991) 141 NLJ 1594t; [1991] TLR 510 HC QBD On need for specificity in order to proceed in extradition case.

Re Farinha [1993] TLR 239 HC QBD On degree of specificity necessary in order to proceed in extradition case.

Re Government of India and Mubarak Ali Ahmed [1952] 1 All ER 1060; (1952) 96 SJ 296; [1952] 1 TLR 964; (1952) WN (I) 217 HC QBD Fugitive Offenders Act 1881 applied to India.

Re Henderson; Henderson v Secretary of State for Home Affairs and another [1950] 1 All ER 283; (1950) 94 SJ 48 CA Five year delay/change in means of trying charge abroad not oppression justifying non-extradition for serious charges.

Re Kirby [1976] Crim LR 569; (1976) 126 NLJ 766t; (1976) 120 SJ 571 HC QBD Interpretation of Fugitive Offenders Act 1967, s 11 (admissibility of authenticated material).

Re Kolczynski and others [1955] 1 All ER 31; (1955) 119 JP 68; (1955) 105 LJ 10; [1955] 1 QB 540; (1955) 99 SJ 61; [1955] 2 WLR 116 HC QBD Non-extradition where sought for political offence.

Re Malinowski and others [1987] Crim LR 324 HC QBD Could not seek persons under Backing of Warrants (Republic of Ireland Act) 1965 simply so that appeal against a conviction might be heard.

Re McFadden [1982] TLR 143 HC QBD Rule of specialty inapplicable to arrangements under the Backing of Warrants (Republic of Ireland) Act 1965 and the Irish equivalent.

Re Mullin [1993] Crim LR 390 HC QBD On proof of conviction for purposes of extradition (here US conviction adequately proved).

Re Nuland [1988] Crim LR 690 HC QBD Was reasonable cause for non-return within two months of committal of person sought in extradition case.

Re Oskar [1987] Crim LR 768 HC QBD Secretary of State can authorise magistrate to proceed with extradition case despite a charge lying on file; original statements or single separate certificate identifying statements acceptable; 22-month delay did not mean return unjust or oppressive.

Re Osman (No 5) [1992] Crim LR 46 HC QBD Specialty guarantee can only ever be on part of requesting state as it exists at moment of guarantee.

Re Parekh [1988] Crim LR 832 HC QBD On test for magistrate in deciding whether or not to commit subject of extradition request.

Re Postlethwaite and others [1987] Crim LR 569 HC QBD On what constitutes satisfactory submission of evidence within time constraints imposed by Anglo-Belgian Extradition Treaty.

Re Schmidt [1995] 1 AC 339; [1994] 3 WLR 228 HC QBD High Court may only order discharge on grounds in Extradition Act 1989; decision of Secretary of State to seek extradition not open to residual review.

Re Schmidt [1994] 3 All ER 65; [1996] 3 All ER 65; [1995] 1 AC 339; (1994) 144 NLJ 973; (1994) 138 SJ LB 160; [1994] TLR 361; [1994] 3 WLR 228 HL High Court may only order discharge on grounds in Extradition Act 1989; decision of Secretary of State to seek extradition not open to residual review.

Re Schtraks (Shalom) [1962] 2 All ER 176; [1962] Crim LR 474; (1962) 126 JP 277; (1962) 112 LJ 385; (1963) 113 LJ 41; [1963] 1 QB 55; (1962) 106 SJ 372; [1962] 2 WLR 976 HC QBD Israeli territory extends to territory in de facto control; political offence only if recognised as political when committed; magistrates' decision interfered with if no reasonable jury would have made same decision.

Re Shuter [1959] 2 All ER 782; [1959] Crim LR 656; (1959) 123 JP 459; (1959) 109 LJ 588; [1960] 2 QB 89; (1959) 103 SJ 636 HC QBD Must be expert evidence on local law on punishments available for offences on which sought.

Re Shuter (No 2) [1959] 3 All ER 481; [1959] Crim LR 844; (1959) 123 JP 534; (1959) 109 LJ 651; [1960] 1 QB 142; (1959) 103 SJ 855; [1959] 3 WLR 652 HC QBD Unless sufficient cause to explain over one-month committal to prison fugitive must be released.

Re Singh (Naranjan) [1961] 2 All ER 565; (1961) 111 LJ 390; (1961) 105 SJ 427 HC QBD Desirability of broad interpretation of non-return as unjust/oppressive clause of Fugitive Offenders Act 1881, s 10.

Re Soering [1988] Crim LR 307 HC QBD Non-disclosure of assurance by US Government to Secretary of State regarding use of death penalty in extradition case where subject of same sought for murder.

Re Tarling [1979] 1 All ER 981; (1979) 68 Cr App R 297; (1979) 143 JP 399; (1979) 129 (1) NLJ 117; [1979] 1 WLR 1417 HC QBD Fresh evidence at second habeas corpus hearing to be evidence unheard at first hearing and which could not previously have been obtained.

Rees v Secretary of State for the Home Department and another [1986] 2 All ER 321; [1986] AC 937; (1986) 83 Cr App R 128; (1986) 136 NLJ 490; (1986) 130 SJ 408; [1986] 2 WLR 1024 HL Depositions/statements from non-requesting state admissible; magistrate cannot consider whether evidence before court acceptable in requesting state; Home Secretary can issue second order while first order stands.

Royal Government of Greece v Brixton Prison Governor and others [1969] 3 All ER 1337; [1970] Crim LR 29t; [1971] AC 250; (1970) 134 JP 47; (1969) 119 NLJ 1045t; (1969) 113 SJ 901; [1969] 3 WLR 1107 HL If sufficient evidence for committal magistrate must commit.

R v Secretary of State for the Home Department; Ex parte Hill [1997] 2 All ER 638; (1997) 147 NLJ 525 HC QBD Could be extradited for crimes committed before requesting state became designated state under Extradition Act; could be extradited for offences that were offences under English law even where were not sought by requesting state for said offences.

R v Secretary of State for the Home Department; Ex parte Launder [1997] 3 All ER 961; (1997) 147 NLJ 793; (1997) 141 SJ LB 123; [1997] TLR 283; [1997] 1 WLR 839 HL Extradition to Hong Kong allowed, Home Secretary having decided that hand-over to China would not result in proposed extraditee suffering unfair trial/injustice/oppression upon return.

Schtraks v Government of Israel and others [1962] 3 All ER 529; [1964] AC 556; [1962] Crim LR 773t; (1962) 112 LJ 717; (1962) 106 SJ 833; [1962] 3 WLR 1013 HL Israeli territory includes areas of de facto control; habeas corpus hearing not akin to appeal/re-hearing; no precise definition of political offences - conjures idea of asylum; test in deciding if committal proper: would reasonable jury have done same?

Sinclair v Director of Public Prosecutions and another [1991] 2 All ER 366; (1991) 93 Cr App R 329; [1991] TLR 187 HL Magistrate cannot determine if extradition case an abuse of process; whether relevant extradition treaty complied with. 'Prosecution' in USA (Extradition) Order means beginning of criminal proceedings.

Sinclair v Government of the United States of America [1990] TLR 144 HC QBD Abuse of process doctrine inapplicable to extradition proceedings in which seeking extradition of already convicted person.

Suidan v Governor of Brixton Prison (1965-66) 116 NLJ 978 HC QBD Was sufficient evidence to justify extradition of applicant to West Germany for trial for larceny.

The United States of America v Gaynor and another [1905] AC 128; [1905] 74 LJPC 44; (1905) XCII LTR 276; (1904-05) XXI TLR 254 PC Habeas corpus writ on basis that no extraditable offence revealed invalid as determining whether was such offence was reason for detention.

Union of India v Narang (Manohar Lal) and another; Union of India v Narang (Omi Prakash) and another [1977] 2 All ER 348; [1978] AC 247; (1977) 64 Cr App R 259; (1977) 141 JP 361; [1977] 2 WLR 862 HC QBD If facts relevant to objection raised by fugitive show unjust/oppressive to return court must discharge from custody.

Union of India v Narang (Manohar Lal) and another; Union of India v Narang (Omi Prakash) and another [1977] 2 All ER 348; [1978] AC 247; (1977) 64 Cr App R 259; [1977] Crim LR 352; (1977) 141 JP 361; (1977) 127 NLJ 542t; (1977) 121 SJ 286; [1977] 2 WLR 862 HL If facts relevant to objection raised by fugitive show unjust/oppressive to return court must discharge from custody.

United States Government and others v McCaffery [1984] 2 All ER 570; (1985) 80 Cr App R 82; (1984) 128 SJ 448; [1984] TLR 389; [1984] 1 WLR 867 HL Extradition for state crimes possible under extradition treaty with federal government; magistrate need only decide whether acts described would be offences under English law.

United States Government v Atkinson [1969] 2 All ER 1151; [1969] Crim LR 487t; (1969) 133 JP 621 HC QBD Appeal by case stated from magistrates' courts in extradition cases; no autrefois convict possible between attempted armed robbery and aggravated burglary.

United States Government v Bowe [1989] 3 All ER 315; [1990] 1 AC 500; [1990] Crim LR 196; (1989) 133 SJ 1298; [1989] 3 WLR 1256 PC Conspiracy to commit drug offence an extraditable offence; no award of costs available in criminal cause or matter.

Ying-Lun (Cheung) v Government of Australia and another (1991) 92 Cr App R 199; [1991] Crim LR 629; (1990) 134 SJ 1227; [1990] 1 WLR 1497 PC Prima facie case against fugitive offender justified detention of same.

Zezza v Government of Italy and another [1982] 2 All ER 513; [1983] 1 AC 46; (1982) 75 Cr App R 338; [1982] Crim LR 749; (1982) 132 NLJ 663; (1982) 126 SJ 398; [1982] TLR 284; [1982] 2 WLR 1077 HL Person whose extradition sought to be treated as convict if facts justify it.

FALSE ACCOUNTING (general)

Attorney General's Reference (No 1 of 1980) [1981] 1 All ER 366; [1981] 1 WLR 34 CA Document made/required for accounting included documents for which accounting secondary purpose.

R v Cooke [1986] 2 All ER 985; [1986] AC 909; (1986) 83 Cr App R 339; [1987] Crim LR 114; (1986) 150 JP 498; (1986) 136 NLJ 730; (1970) 130 SJ 572; [1986] 3 WLR 327 HL Statutory conspiracy with presence of fraud can be charged as common law conspiracy; no false accounting where no deception and no fraud.

R v Eden (Thomas Henry) (1971) 55 Cr App R 193; [1971] Crim LR 416 CA Person may be guilty of false accounting though not guilty of theft.

R v Fowler [1956] Crim LR 330 Sessions On difference between intent to deceive/intent to defraud.

R v Golechha (Ummed Chand); R v Choraria (Rajendra Kumar) [1989] 3 All ER 908; (1990) 90 Cr App R 241; [1990] Crim LR 865; (1989) 133 SJ 1001; [1989] 1 WLR 1050 CA Using forged bills of exchange to delay but not for all time avoid bank enforcing previous bills was not falsification with a view to gain contrary to Theft Act 1968, s 17.

R v Governor of Pentonville Prison and another; ex parte Osman [1989] 3 All ER 701; (1990) 90 Cr App R 281; [1988] Crim LR 611; (1990) 134 SJ 458; [1990] 1 WLR 277 HL QBD Usually theft takes place where property appropriated; must be non-hearsay evidence that person a co-conspirator before evidence of other conspirator admissible against him; court in deciding if allegedly criminal document is privileged may look to document without requiring any action from party objecting to privilege.

R v Keatley [1980] Crim LR 505 CrCt On what constitutes false accounting.

R v Oliphant (1907-09) XXI Cox CC 192; (1905) 69 JP 230; [1905] 2 KB 67; (1905) 40 LJ 322; (1906) XCIV LTR 824; (1904-05) 49 SJ 460; (1904-05) XXI TLR 416; (1904-05) 53 WR 556 CCR Conviction for falsification of account in London though act resulting in falsification committed abroad.

R v Oliphant (1905) 69 JP 175 CCR Could not be tried in London for falsification of account where act resulting in falsification committed abroad.

R v Palin (1905) 69 JP 423; [1906] 1 KB 7; (1905) 40 LJ 788; [1906] 75 LJKB 15; (1905-06) XCIII LTR 673; (1905-06) XXII TLR 41; (1905) WN (I) 162; (1905-06) 54 WR 396 CCR Falsification of accounts by servant not offence under Falsification of Accounts Act 1875 as was not falsification of employer's accounts.

R v Shama [1990] 2 All ER 602; (1990) 91 Cr App R 138; [1990] Crim LR 411; (1990) 134 SJ 958; [1990] TLR 39; [1990] 1 WLR 661 CA Dishonest omission of material particulars in accounting document proves false accounting.

R v Wines [1953] 2 All ER 1497; (1953) 37 Cr App R 197; [1954] Crim LR 136; (1954) 118 JP 49; (1954) 98 SJ 14; [1954] 1 WLR 64 CCA Intending a deceit through falsifying accounts was sufficient intent to sustain accounts falsification charge.

Reference by the Attorney-General under Section 36 of the Criminal Justice Act 1972 (No 1 of 1980) (1981) 72 Cr App R 60; [1981] Crim LR 41; (1981) 145 JP 165; (1981) 131 NLJ 146; (1980) 124 SJ 881 CA Interpretation of term 'made or required' in Theft Act 1968, s 17(1) (a) (false accounting).

Wing (Lee Cheung) v R; Yau (Lam Man) v R (1992) 94 Cr App R 355; [1992] Crim LR 440 PC Employees faking withdrawal slips guilty of falsification with view to gain where had not intended to account to company for profits made.

FALSE IMPRISONMENT (attempt)

R v Geddes [1996] Crim LR 894; (1996) TLR 15/7/96 CA Person who entered school with means of falsely imprisoning child, no more, was not guilty of attempted false imprisonment - had only committed preparatory acts.

FALSE IMPRISONMENT (general)

R v Brewin [1976] Crim LR 742 CrCt On correct procedure as regards arrest of child (so that does not entail false imprisonment of same).

R v Hutchins [1988] Crim LR 379 CA On ingredients of false imprisonment/kidnapping: both may be committed through recklessness.

R v Rahman (Mohammed Moqbular) (1985) 81 Cr App R 349; [1985] Crim LR 596; (1985) 129 SJ 431 CA Parent's detention of child not false imprisonment unless unlawful/unreasonable parental behaviour.

FIREARMS (attempt to discharge)

R v Jones (1901-02) XVIII TLR 156 Assizes Could not be convicted of attempting to discharge loaded revolver with intent to kill where pointed same at person and pulled trigger knowing gun had to jam (Offences against the Person Act 1861, s 14).

R v Linneker [1904-07] All ER 797; (1907-09) XXI Cox CC 196; (1906) 70 JP 293; [1906] 2 KB 99; [1906] 75 LJKB 385; (1906) XCIV LTR 856; (1905-06) 50 SJ 440; (1905-06) XXII TLR 495; (1905-06) 54 WR 494 CCR More than intent and possession necessary to establish attempt to discharge revolver.

FIREARMS (carrying in public place)

R v Vann and Davis [1996] Crim LR 52 CA Offence of carrying firearm in public place an absolute offence.

FIREARMS (certificate)

Bennett v Brown (1980) 71 Cr App R 109 HC QBD Twentieth century Mauser 8mm rifle and Mauser pocket pistol were/nineteenth century Enfield .476 Mk 3 revolver were not/was antique firearm so firearms certificate was/was not required.

Broome v Walter [1989] Crim LR 725 HC QBD Silencer legitimately found not to be accessory (and so not to require separate certificate).

Burditt v Joslin [1981] 3 All ER 203; (1982) 146 JP 39 HC QBD Ownership but non-residency of property insufficient for application for firearms certifiate from chief police officer in area of residence.

Chief Constable of Essex v Germain (1992) 156 JP 109; [1991] TLR 185 HC QBD On exercise by Chief Constable of discretionary power to revoke shotgun certificate.

Creaser and another v Tunnicliffe [1978] 1 All ER 569; (1978) 66 Cr App R 66; [1977] Crim LR 746; (1978) 142 JP 245; (1977) 127 NLJ 638t; (1977) 121 SJ 775; [1977] 1 WLR 1493 HC QBD Altered firearm capable of firing original ammunition still required certificate.

Dabek v Chief Constable of Devon and Cornwall (1991) 155 JP 55; [1990] TLR 487 HC QBD Firearms certificate properly revoked where holder (although of good character) was married to person of dubious character.

Dickinson v Bainbridge (1921-25) XXVII Cox CC 143; (1922) 86 JP 8; [1922] 1 KB 423; [1922] 91 LJCL 329; (1921-22) 66 SJ 196; (1921-22) XXXVIII TLR 50; (1921) WN (I) 328 HC KBD Postmaster required to hold firearms certificate in respect of gun/ammunition unless being conveyed through mail/required by duty to possess same.

Kavanagh v Chief Constable of Devon and Cornwall [1974] 2 All ER 697; (1974) 138 JP 618; (1974) 124 NLJ 387t; (1974) 118 SJ 347 CA Court can consider all matters - even hearsay - in appeal against refusal to give firearms certificate.

R v Acton Crown Court, ex parte Varney [1984] Crim LR 683 CA Successful appeal against revocation by CrCt of firearms certificate following conviction for non-compliance with term of certificate.

R v Bull (Adrian William) (1994) 99 Cr App R 193; [1994] Crim LR 224; (1993) 137 SJ LB 202; [1993] TLR 464 CA Firearms dealer exemption from need for firearms certificate applied to place not person (so ought to have had certificate in respect of ammunition stored in unnotified place).

R v Burke (Robert) (1978) 67 Cr App R 220; [1978] Crim LR 431 CA Determining whether firearm an antique is question of fact for jury.

R v Howells [1977] 3 All ER 417; (1977) 65 Cr App R 86; [1977] Crim LR 354t; (1977) 141 JP 641; (1977) 127 NLJ 370t; [1977] QB 614; (1977) 121 SJ 154; [1977] 2 WLR 716 CA Absolute liability if no certificate yet possess firearm; mistaken belief an antique no defence.

R v Hucklebridge; Attorney General's Reference (No 3 of 1980) [1980] 3 All ER 273; (1980) 71 Cr App R 171; [1980] Crim LR 646; (1981) 145 JP 13; (1980) 130 NLJ 836; (1980) 124 SJ 592; [1980] 1 WLR 1284 CA Smooth-bore gun with barrel more than 24' long a shotgun so no firearms certificate required.

R v Wilson [1989] Crim LR 146 HC QBD Must be alteration of certificate upon exchange of particular firearm in respect of which certificate issued.

Spencer-Stewart v Chief Constable of Kent (1989) 89 Cr App R 307 HC QBD In revoking shot-gun certificate on basis that there is danger of breach of peace that danger must be connected to shotgun.

Wilson v Coombe (1989) 88 Cr App R 322; (1988) 132 SJ 1300; [1989] 1 WLR 78 HC QBD Possession of firearms certificates apply to particular gun not type of gun: valid conviction of dealer who exchanged certificate-holders' guns for different gun of same class.

Woodage v Moss [1974] 1 All ER 584; [1974] Crim LR 104; (1974) 138 JP 253; (1974) 118 SJ 204; [1974] 1 WLR 411 HC QBD Person carrying uncertificated firearm from party to dealer is in possession/not dealer's servant (as no payment/obligation to so act).

FIREARMS (conspiracy to possess)

R v Jones (Ivor Frank); R v Jones (Diane Jane); R v Blarick (John Lee); R v Jarman (Peter David); R v Chennells (Trevor Boyce) [1997] 1 Cr App R 46; [1997] Crim LR 510; (1996) 140 SJ LB 206; (1996) TLR 14/8/96; [1997] 2 WLR 792 CA On necessary intent for offence of conspiracy to possess firarms/ammunition with intent to enable another to thereby endanger life.

FIREARMS (general)

Ackers and others v Taylor [1974] 1 All ER 771; [1974] Crim LR 103; (1974) 138 JP 269; (1974) 124 NLJ 56t; (1974) 118 SJ 185; [1974] 1 WLR 405 HC QBD Any possible misuse of gun justifies revocation of licence.

Anderson v Miller and another (1977) 64 Cr App R 178; [1976] Crim LR 743; (1976) 126 NLJ 1091t; (1976) 120 SJ 735 HC QBD Shop a single unit so even place behind counter was place to which public had access for purpose of Firearms Act 1968, ss 19 and 57(4).

Bell v Director of Public Prosecutions of Jamaica and another [1985] 2 All ER 585; [1985] Crim LR 738 PC Jamaican Constitution right to trial in reasonable time does not require prejudice; reasonableness judged by reference to general practice/conditions.

Bryson v Gamage Limited (1907-09) XXI Cox CC 515; (1907) 71 JP 439; [1907] 2 KB 630; [1907] 76 LJKB 936; (1907-08) XCVII LTR 399; (1907) WN (I) 164 HC KBD 'Pistol' under Pistols Act 1903 includes spring pistols from which shot/bullets dischargeable.

Cafferata v Wilson; Reeve v Wilson [1936] 3 All ER 149; (1934-39) XXX Cox CC 475; (1936) 100 JP 489; (1936) 155 LTR 510; (1936) 80 SJ 856; (1936-37) LIII TLR 34 HC KBD Fake revolver that could be converted into real revolver a firearm.

Flack v Baldry [1988] 1 All ER 412; [1988] Crim LR 610; (1988) 152 JP 418; (1988) 132 SJ 89; [1988] 1 WLR 214 HC QBD Stun gun could be noxious thing but did not discharge anything so not prohibited weapon.

Grace v Director of Public Prosecutions [1989] Crim LR 365; (1989) 153 JP 491 HC QBD On proving that air-gun a lethal weapon (which it was).

Greenly v Lawrence [1949] 1 All ER 241; (1949) 113 JP 120; (1949) LXV TLR 86 HC KBD On appeal to quarter sessions against refusal of gun licence.

Matthews v Gray (1909) 73 JP 303; [1909] 2 KB 89; (1909) 44 LJ 233; [1909] 78 LJKB 545; (1908-09) XXV TLR 476; (1909) WN (I) 88 HC KBD On sale of pistol to party for use in own house.

Moore v Gooderham [1960] 3 All ER 575; (1960) 124 JP 513; (1960) 110 LJ 781; (1960) 104 SJ 1036 HC QBD Airgun a lethal weapon: direction to convict person of selling airgun/lethal weapon to under-seventeen year old contrary to Firearms Act 1937.

Morton v Chaney; Morton v Christopher [1960] 3 All ER 632; (1961) 125 JP 37; (1960) 110 LJ 797; (1960) 104 SJ 1035 HC QBD 'Sporting purposes' exemption to firearms possession does not apply to shooting rats.

Police v Lane [1957] Crim LR 542 Magistrates Harpoon gun a gun for purposes of the Gun Licence Act 1870.

R v Baker [1961] 3 All ER 703; (1962) 46 Cr App R 47; [1962] Crim LR 41; (1961) 125 JP 650; (1961) 111 LJ 772; [1962] 2 QB 530 CCA Can only convict under Firearms Act 1937 for an offence in schedule to Act; meaning of 'apprehension'.

R v Clarke [1986] 1 All ER 846; (1986) 82 Cr App R 308; [1986] Crim LR 334; (1986) 130 SJ 110; [1986] 1 WLR 209 CA Firearm without trigger capable of being firearm.

R v Formosa; R v Upton [1991] 1 All ER 131; (1991) 92 Cr App R (1991) 92 Cr App R 11; [1990] Crim LR 868; (1991) 155 JP 97; [1991] 2 QB 1; (1990) 134 SJ 1191; [1990] TLR 54; [1990] 3 WLR 1179 CA Object to be designed/adapted as prohibited weapon must be physically altered.

R v Freeman [1970] 2 All ER 413; (1970) 54 Cr App R 251; [1970] Crim LR 403; (1970) 134 JP 462; (1970) 114 SJ 336; [1970] 1 WLR 788 CA Starting-pistol is firearm.

R v Jobling [1981] Crim LR 625 CrCt On what constitutes an automatic weapon (Bren gun altered so that could not fire automatically was not automatic gun).

R v Kelt [1977] 3 All ER 1099; (1977) 65 Cr App R 74; [1977] Crim LR 558; (1978) 142 JP 60; (1977) 121 SJ 423; [1977] 1 WLR 1365 CA Firearm needs to be physically close/in immediate control but need not be carried to have it with one.

R v Pawlicki and another [1992] 3 All ER 902; (1992) 95 Cr App R 246; [1992] Crim LR 584; (1992) 136 SJ LB 104; [1992] TLR 153; [1992] 1 WLR 827 CA Ready accessibility to firearms enough to support conviction for having with intent to commit robbery.

R v Pommell (Fitzroy Derek) [1995] 2 Cr App R 607; (1995) 145 NLJ 960; (1995) 139 SJ LB 178; [1995] TLR 296 CA Can plead necessity (duress of circumstance) to possession of firearms charge.

R v Stubbings [1990] Crim LR 811; [1990] TLR 251 CA On what constitutes ammunition (primer cartridge was ammunition).

R v Thorpe (Stephen) (1987) 85 Cr App R 107; [1987] Crim LR 493; (1987) 131 SJ 325; [1987] 1 WLR 383 CA Weapon using carbon dioxide for propulsion not an air gun: was lethal weapon if could cause death.

R v Wakefield Crown Court; ex parte Wakefield [1978] Crim LR 164 CA On validity of decision of Chief Police Officer to apply certain policy to determination of applications for shotgun certificates.

Read v Donovan [1947] 1 All ER 37; (1947) 111 JP 46; [1947] KB 326; (1947) 97 LJ 9; [1947] 116 LJR 849; (1947) 176 LTR 124; (1947) 91 SJ 101; (1947) LXIII TLR 89; (1947) WN (I) 42 HC KBD Signal pistol a lethal weapon.

Richards v Curwen [1977] 3 All ER 426; (1977) 65 Cr App R 95; [1977] Crim LR 356; (1977) 141 JP 641; (1977) 127 NLJ 468t; (1977) 121 SJ 270; [1977] 1 WLR 747 HC QBD Whether firearm antique to be determined in each case - no set age.

Saint v Hockley (1924-25) 69 SJ 575; (1924-25) XLI TLR 555 HC KBD Once air gun specified by Secretary of State under Firearms Act 1920 to be a dangerous firearm it is a firearm for purposes of same: Webley Air Pistol not a firearm for which certificate necessary.

Sambasivam v Public Prosecutor, Federation of Malaya [1950] AC 458; [1950] 66 (2) TLR 254 PC Interpretation of Malayan Emergency Regulations pertaining to carrying firearms/possessing ammunition.

Staravia Ltd v Gordon [1973] Crim LR 298 CA Company per se was not registered firearms dealer so could not be guilty of carrying on business at place not entered in register.

Watson v Herman [1952] 2 All ER 70; (1952) 116 JP 395; (1952) 102 LJ 329; (1952) 96 SJ 413; (1952) WN (I) 308 HC QBD Telescopic sight not a firearm.

Watts v Seymour [1967] 1 All ER 1044; [1967] Crim LR 239t; (1967) 131 JP 309; [1967] 2 QB 647; (1967) 111 SJ 294; [1967] 2 WLR 1072 HC QBD Is an offence to sell firearm to under-aged party but not pass possession until later stage.

Zakos v R [1956] Crim LR 625t; (1956) 100 SJ 631 PC Interpretation of emergency regulations pertaining to carrying/discharging of firerarms in Cyprus.

FIREARMS (going about armed)

R v Meade (1902-03) XIX TLR 540 Assizes Two month's imprisonment for going about armed in public (contrary to statute of King Edward III) and for causing public nuisance for firing revolver in public street.

FIREARMS (imitation)

R v Debreli [1964] Crim LR 53; (1963) 107 SJ 894 CCA Gun with firing pin removed was an 'imitation firearm'.

R v Morris (Harold Lyndon); R v King (Kenneth) (1984) 79 Cr App R 104; [1984] Crim LR 422; (1985) 149 JP 60; [1984] TLR 179 CA In deciding whether imitation firearm looked like firearm must have regard to what looked like at moment of crime.

R v Titus and others [1971] Crim LR 279 CCC Water pistols containing ammonia were imitation firearms for puposes of Firearms Act 1968, s 18.

FIREARMS (possession)

Brown v Director of Public Prosecutions [1992] TLR 155 HC QBD Stun-gun a prohibited weapon though was not functioning properly.

Davies v Tomlinson (1980) 71 Cr App R 279 HC QBD Total sentences (even where consecutively imposed) measure by which gauge whether person sentenced to three or more years' imprisonment (and hence guilty of offence where possessed firearm).

Flack v Baldry (1988) 87 Cr App R 130; (1988) 138 NLJ 63; (1988) 132 SJ 334; [1988] 1 WLR 393 HL Electric stun gun 'discharged' noxious thing and was therefore a prohibited weapon.

Hall v Cotton and another [1986] 3 All ER 332; (1986) 83 Cr App R 257; [1987] QB 504; (1970) 130 SJ 785; [1986] 3 WLR 681 HC QBD Transfer of custodial and not proprietary possession transfers possession.

Heritage v Claxon (1941) 85 SJ 323 HC KBD Home Guard member in possession of uncertificated firearm/ammunition who was not acting in capacity as Home Guard member in possession of same was guilty of offence.

R v Bentham and others [1972] 3 All ER 271; (1972) 56 Cr App R 618; [1972] Crim LR 640; (1972) 136 JP 761; [1973] QB 357; (1972) 116 SJ 598; [1972] 3 WLR 398 CA Possession of firearms with intent even if intent not immediate/is conditional.

R v Bradish [1990] 1 All ER 460; (1990) 90 Cr App R 271; [1990] Crim LR 723; (1990) 154 JP 21; [1990] 1 QB 981; (1989) 133 SJ 1605; [1990] 2 WLR 223 CA Possession of prohibited weapon a strict liability offence.

R v East [1990] Crim LR 413 CA On elements of offence of possession of firearm with intent to endanger life.

R v Edgecombe [1963] Crim LR 574t CCA Valid conviction for possession of firearm with intent to endanger life.

R v El-Hakkaoui [1975] 2 All ER 146; (1975) 60 Cr App R 281; [1975] Crim LR 229; (1975) 139 JP 467; (1975) 119 SJ 186; [1975] 1 WLR 396 CA Intent to injure someone in England not necessary for possession conviction.

R v Georgiades (Michael) (1989) 89 Cr App R 206; [1989] Crim LR 574; (1989) 133 SJ 724; [1989] 1 WLR 759 CA Whether self-defence justified possesion of firearm ought to be left to jury.

R v Guy (Christopher) (1991) 93 Cr App R 108; [1991] Crim LR 462; (1991) 155 JP 778; [1991] TLR 92 CA Could be convicted of possessing firearm during robbery though relevant statute only refers to theft as robbery is theft with threat/use of violence.

R v Harrison [1996] 1 Cr App R 138; [1996] Crim LR 200 CA Need only prove that accused knowingly possessed firearm in public place for accused to be guilty of possessing same in public place.

R v Houghton [1982] Crim LR 112 CA On elements of offence of having firearm with intent to commit indictable offence.

R v Hussain [1981] 2 All ER 287; (1981) 72 Cr App R 143; [1981] Crim LR 251; (1981) 131 NLJ 70; (1981) 125 SJ 166; [1981] 1 WLR 416 CA Possession of firearm without certificate an absolute offence - no mens rea needed.

R v Jones [1995] 3 All ER 139; [1995] 1 Cr App R 262; [1995] Crim LR 416; (1995) 159 JP 94; [1995] QB 235; (1994) 138 SJ LB 194; [1994] TLR 488; [1995] 2 WLR 64 CA Firearm certificate not lawful authority for possession of firearm/ammunition in public place; defendant's mistaken belief to contrary not a reasonable excuse.

R v Norton (Rex) [1977] Crim LR 478 CrCt Not guilty of possession of firearm with intent to endanger life where only sought to endanger own life.

R v Nyberg (Simon); R v White (Alfred) (1922-23) 17 Cr App R 59 CCA White granted leave to appeal against conviction for riot; possession of firearms/shooting with intent to endanger life.

R v Pannell (Robin Masterman) (1983) 76 Cr App R 53; [1982] Crim LR 752; [1982] TLR 429 CA Was possession of prohibited weapon to have parts of automatic weapons in possession.

R v Smith (1976) 126 NLJ 65t CA Possession of firearms not an offence for which could be extradited under Extradition Act 1870, schedule 1.

R v Steele [1993] Crim LR 298 CA On mens rea for possession of firearms (without certificate).

R v Waller [1991] Crim LR 381 CA Possession of firearm without certificate an offence of strict liability.

Ross v Collins [1982] Crim LR 368 CA Holder of shotgun certificate not allowed possess loaded shotgun in public place; honest belief that not in public place unsuccessfuly pleaded in defence.

Sullivan v Earl of Caithness [1976] 1 All ER 844; (1976) 62 Cr App R 105; [1976] Crim LR 130; (1976) 140 JP 277; (1975) 125 NLJ 1220t; [1976] QB 966; (1976) 120 SJ 8; [1976] 2 WLR 361 HC QBD Control rather than custody can constitute possession.

Tartellin v Bowen [1947] 2 All ER 837; (1948) 112 JP 99; [1948] LXIV TLR 20; (1948) WN (I) 15 HC KBD Member of Armed Forces guilty of possession of firearm (privately purchased for self) without certificate.

Taylor v Mucklow [1973] Crim LR 750; (1973) 117 SJ 792 HC QBD That use of airgun was to protect one's property (in protection of which one may use some force) was not reasonable excuse for same.

FIREARMS (use with intent to resist arrest)

R v Pierre [1963] Crim LR 513 CCA Not necessary that person charged with using firearm to resist arrest know that what possessed is a firearm as defined in the Firerarms Act.

FORGERY (false instrument)

R v Gold [1988] 2 All ER 186; (1988) 86 Cr App R 52; (1988) 152 JP 445; [1988] 2 WLR 984 HL Computer hacking not making of false instrument.

FORGERY (general)

Attorney General's Reference (No 2 of 1980) [1981] 1 All ER 493; (1981) 72 Cr App R 64; [1981] Crim LR 43; (1981) 145 JP 169; (1981) 131 NLJ 292; (1981) 125 SJ 16; [1981] 1 WLR 148 CA Pre-trial forgery of evidence is forgery of document 'made evidence by law'.

Attorney-General of Hong Kong v Chiuk-Wah (Pat) and others [1971] 2 All ER 1460; [1971] AC 835; (1971) 55 Cr App R 342; (1971) 135 JP 507; (1971) 121 NLJ 273t; (1971) 115 SJ 348; [1971] 2 WLR 1381 PC National security stamp a valuable security; can be convicted of forgery though forgery not complete.

Holloway v Brown [1979] Crim LR 58; [1978] RTR 537 HC QBD Successful appeal against conviction for use of forged international road haulage permit.

Horsey v Hutchings [1984] TLR 618 HC QBD On ingredients of offences under the Forgery and Counterfeiting Act 1981, ss 1 and 3.

Hughes v Brook [1973] Crim LR 526 HC QBD Once justices decided item resembled a banknote they did not have to find it to be calculated to deceive to be guilty of forging banknote.

R v Barrass [1981] Crim LR 116 CA Six years' imprisonment merited by person guilty of various forgeries and of obtaining property on forged instrument and of theft.

R v Butler (1954) 38 Cr App R 57; [1954] Crim LR 379t CCA Completing pools coupons in false names was forgery/putting amounts down that signatories could not pay was not forgery.

R v Cade (1914-15) XXIV Cox CC 131; (1914) 10 Cr App R 23; (1914) 78 JP 240; [1914] 2 KB 209; (1914) 49 LJ 98; [1914] 83 LJKB 796; (1914) 110 LTR 624; (1913-14) 58 SJ 289; (1913-14) XXX TLR 289; (1914) WN (I) 48 CCA Forged letter to employer seeking money was a 'forged instrument' under Forgery Act 1913, s 7.

R v Campbell (Mary Sylvia) (1985) 80 Cr App R 47; [1984] Crim LR 683; [1984] TLR 500 CA Was forgery to endorse cheque and so secure payment from bank which would not have made if knew of true circumstances.

R v Clayton (Terence Edward) (1981) 72 Cr App R 135; [1981] Crim LR 186 CA Intent to deceive was adequate mens rea for forgery of excise licence (contrary to Vehicles (Excise) Act 1971, s 26(1)).

R v Dodge and Harris [1971] 2 All ER 1523; (1971) 55 Cr App R 440; (1971) 135 JP 523; [1972] 1 QB 416; (1971) 115 SJ 623; [1971] 3 WLR 366 CA Fake bonds not lying about bonds themselves are not false documents.

R v Donnelly (Ian David) (1984) 79 Cr App R 76; [1984] Crim LR 490; (1984) 128 SJ 514; [1984] TLR 322; [1984] 1 WLR 1017 CA Valuation certificate where was no jewellery to be valued was a forgery.

R v Douce [1972] Crim LR 105 CA Painting with signature (purporting thereby to be painting by particular painter) was forgery for purposes of the Forgery Act 1913.

R v Draper [1962] Crim LR 107 CCA Valid conviction for forger of will.

R v Etheridge (1899-1901) XIX Cox CC 676 Assizes Forgery of 'record' under means record of court of competent jurisdiction.

R v Gambling [1974] 3 All ER 479; (1975) 60 Cr App R 25; [1974] Crim LR 600t; (1974) 138 JP 749; (1974) 124 NLJ 696t; [1975] QB 207; (1974) 118 SJ 735; [1974] 3 WLR 558 CA Must not only prove that maker of false statement intended it to taken as genuine but that untrue statement a factor in it being accepted as true.

R v Garcia (Emilio) (1988) 87 Cr App R 175; [1988] Crim LR 115 CA Must be actual prejudice to be guilty of forging document to induce another to act/not to act to their or another's prejudice in belief that forged document genuine.

R v Garland [1960] Crim LR 129 Sessions Need not be intent to cause pecuniary loss to sustain conviction for forgery with intent to defraud.

R v Gold; R v Schifreen [1987] 3 All ER 618; [1988] AC 1063; (1988) 87 Cr App R 257; [1988] Crim LR 437; (1988) 138 NLJ 117; (1988) 132 SJ 624 HL Hacking does not involve making/use of false device under Forgery and Counterfeiting Act 1981.

R v Gold; R v Schifreen [1987] Crim LR 762; [1987] QB 1116; (1987) 131 SJ 1247; [1987] 3 WLR 803 CA Hacking does not involve forgery or making/use of false device under Forgery and Counterfeiting Act 1981.

R v Governor of Brixton Prison; ex parte Lennon [1963] Crim LR 41t HC QBD Failed request for extradition of person for forgery; cheques not forgeries where drawn on imaginary bank.

R v Hadjimitsis [1964] Crim LR 128 CCA Person who signed cheque using name by which commonly called was not guilty of forgery.

R v Hagan [1985] Crim LR 598 CA Intent for forgery under Forgery Act 1913, s 7, was intent to defraud which was present here even though intended use of money obtained by way of forgery was honest/not for self.

R v Harran [1969] Crim LR 662 CA To prove possession of forged ten-dollar bills in bag had to prove possessed the bag in knowledge that were forged notes inside.

R v Harris [1972] Crim LR 531 CA Document that did not lie about itself was not a forgery.

R v Hassard; R v Devereux [1970] 2 All ER 647; (1970) 54 Cr App R 295; [1970] Crim LR 226; (1970) 134 JP 510; (1970) 114 SJ 106; [1970] 1 WLR 1109 CA Cheque drawn on false account/signed with fake name a forgery.

R v Hemming (William) (1908) 1 Cr App R 34 CCA Refusal of handwriting evidence tending to show another forged letter at issue.

R v Hiscox (Brian John) (1979) 68 Cr App R 411 CA Tax exemption certificate which seemed to be signed by one person but was actually signed by another was consequently forgery.

R v Holden (1911-13) XXII Cox CC 727; (1912) 76 JP 143; [1912] 1 KB 483; (1912) 81 LJKB 327; (1912) 106 LTR 305 CCA Party accepting bill of exchange in name of his firm accepted in name of another for purposes of Forgery Act 1861, s 24.

R v Hopkins (William Edgar); R v Collins (Herbert James) (1957) 41 Cr App R 231; [1957] Crim LR 808t CCA Putting in/leaving out false/possible entry in cash book is/may not be forgery.

R v Hopley (Samuel) (1914-15) 11 Cr App R 248 CCA Inferring of intent to defraud from knowing use of forged instrument in course of bona fide claim.

R v Horner (1911-13) XXII Cox CC 13; (1910) 74 JP 216 CCC Must intend to deceive another to be convicted of uttering telegram knowing to be false (whether contents of telegram true or not does not matter).

R v Hornett [1975] RTR 256 CA Were guilty of uttering forged documents (forged international haulage permits) though those sought to defraud were in foreign jurisdiction.

R v Hurford; R v Williams [1963] 2 All ER 254; (1963) 47 Cr App R 141; [1963] Crim LR 432; (1963) 127 JP 374; (1963) 113 LJ 382; [1963] 2 QB 398; (1963) 107 SJ 275; [1963] 2 WLR 1038 CCA Forging signature on document that instigates eventual obtaining of property is obtaining property with forged instrument.

R v Hutchinson (Robert Hopwood Percy) (1911-12) 7 Cr App R 19 CCA Forgery Act 1861, s 38 considered.

R v Jeraj [1994] Crim LR 595 CA Untrue document verifying that had received letter of credit from non-existent bank which had been endorsed by bank for which appellant worked did constitute a forgery.

R v Lack (Peter Andrew) (1987) 84 Cr App R 342 CA Documents allegedly emanating from company but actually made after liquidation of same were false for purposes of Forgery and Counterfeiting Act 1981.

R v Lowden (1913-14) XXIII Cox CC 643; (1914) 78 JP 111; [1914] 1 KB 144; (1913) 48 LJ 689; [1914] 83 LJKB 114; (1913-14) 109 LTR 832; (1913-14) 58 SJ 157; (1913-14) XXX TLR 70; (1913) WN (I) 318 CCA Forged cancelled stamps were 'stamps' for purposes of Stamp Duties Management Act 1891, s 13.

R v Macrae [1994] Crim LR 363; (1995) 159 JP 359 CA Need not intend to cause another economic loss to be guilty of forging a licence.

R v McKenzie [1971] 1 All ER 729; [1972] Crim LR 655; (1971) 135 JP 26 Assizes Invalid recognisance could not be subject of forgery; recognisance invalid where imposed on person who would not be detained.

R v Moon [1967] 3 All ER 962; (1968) 52 Cr App R 12; [1967] Crim LR 709; (1967) 117 NLJ 1086t; (1967) 111 SJ 791; [1967] 1 WLR 1536 CA Intent to defraud not intent to deceive needed to sustain forgery conviction.

R v Moore [1986] Crim LR 552 CA Withdrawal slip completed in name of non-existent person was a forgery; person guilty of obtaining property by deception where intended to retain cheque had dishonestly obtained.

R v More [1987] 3 All ER 825; (1988) 86 Cr App R 234 (also CCA); [1988] Crim LR 176; (1987) 131 SJ 1550; [1987] 1 WLR 1578 HL Withdrawal form signed in account holder's name not a false instrument so no forgery.

R v More (Kevin Vincent) (1988) 86 Cr App R 234 (also HL) CA Withdrawal form signed in account holder's name a false instrument but not forgery.

R v Parker (1910) 74 JP 208 CCC On elements of forgery under Forgery Act 1861, s 38.

R v Potter and another [1958] 2 All ER 51; (1958) 122 JP 234; (1958) 42 Cr App R 168; [1958] Crim LR 472; [1958] 1 WLR 638 Assizes Where party sits driving test for another both are guilty of procuring with intent to defraud; in signing for licence former guilty of forgery; in seeking thereon latter uttering forged document.

R v Smith (Sydney Edward) (1919-20) 14 Cr App R 101; (1920) 84 JP 67 CCA Can be guilty of intent to defraud under Forgery Act 1913, s 7(a) though are legally entitled to whatever obtained.

R v Tobierre [1986] 1 All ER 346; (1986) 82 Cr App R 212; [1986] Crim LR 243; (1986) 130 SJ 35; [1986] 1 WLR 125 CA Mens rea for use of false instrument is that intended to induce other to accept forgery as genuine and to use to other's (or another's) detriment.

R v Torri (1982) 132 NLJ 348 CA Failed appeal against conviction for forging bill of exchange.

R v Utting (John Benjamin) (1988) 86 Cr App R 164; [1987] Crim LR 636; (1987) 131 SJ 1154; [1987] 1 WLR 1375 CA Successful appeal against conviction for making fasle instrument with intent of inducing another to act/not to act on belief that document genuine (Forgery and Counterfeiting Act 1981, s 1).

R v Warneford and Gibbs [1994] Crim LR 753; [1994] TLR 279 CA On what constitutes a 'false instrument' under the Forgery and Counterfeiting Act 1981, s 9(1).

R v Wells [1939] 2 All ER 169; (1938-40) 27 Cr App R 72; (1939) 87 LJ 268; (1939) 83 SJ 441 CCA Indorsement of deed with false date deemed forgery though at time of indorsement false date was of no consequence but was expected to later be of consequence.

R v Wuyts [1969] 2 All ER 799; (1969) 53 Cr App R 417; [1969] Crim LR 373t; (1969) 133 JP 492; (1969) 119 NLJ 389t; [1969] 2 QB 474; (1969) 113 SJ 324; [1969] 3 WLR 1 CA Possession of forged banknotes not offence when intend to give them to police.

Walker and another v Manchester and Liverpool District Banking Company Limited (1913) 108 LTR 728; (1912-13) 57 SJ 478 HC KBD Customer could recover amounts bank paid out on foot of forged cheques though customer had not checked pass-book when from time to time was returned to him.

FORGERY (possession of changed passport)

Chajutin v Whitehead [1938] 1 KB 506; (1938) 85 LJ 87; [1938] 107 LJCL 270 HC KBD Offence of possessing altered passport requires no mens rea, merely actus reus.

FORGERY (uttering)

R v Harris [1965] 3 All ER 206; (1965) 49 Cr App R 330; [1965] Crim LR 550; (1965) 129 JP 542; (1965) 115 LJ 661; [1966] 1 QB 184; (1965) 109 SJ 572; [1965] 3 WLR 1040 CCA On uttering of forgeries.

R v Owen and another [1956] 3 All ER 432; (1956) 40 Cr App R 103; [1956] Crim LR 829; (1956) 120 JP 553; (1956) 106 LJ 666; [1957] 1 QB 174 (also CCC); (1956) 100 SJ (1956) 100 SJ 769; [1956] 3 WLR 739 CCA Cannot be convicted of conspiracy to do crime abroad unless crime indictable in England; was conspiracy to utter forged document as forged documents posted in London/objectives could have been achieved in London.

R v Owen and others [1956] Crim LR 550; [1957] 1 QB 174 (also CCA); (1956) 100 SJ 454; [1956] 3 WLR 252 CCC Cannot be convicted of conspiracy to do crime abroad unless crime indictable in England.

R v Turner (Basil William Ivor) (1981) 72 Cr App R 117; [1980] Crim LR 797 CA Was forgery for police officer to forge document with intent to deceive (that intent was adequate malo animo).

R v Welham [1960] 1 All ER 260; (1960) 44 Cr App R 79; [1960] Crim LR 190; (1960) 124 JP 156; (1960) 110 LJ 156; [1960] 2 QB 445; (1960) 104 SJ 108 CCA Intent when uttering forged document is to induce someone to act contrary to their interest/their duty; successful action for bail pending appeal.

Welham v Director of Public Prosecutions [1960] 1 All ER 805; (1960) 44 Cr App R 124; [1960] Crim LR 423; (1960) 124 JP 280; (1960) 110 LJ 284; (1960) 104 SJ 308; [1960] 2 WLR 669 HL Can intend to defraud (and be guilty of uttering forged document) though do not intend to cause financial loss.

GRIEVOUS BODILY HARM (assault occasioning)

R v Austin [1973] Crim LR 778 CA Person charged with causing grievous bodily harm with intent ought not (absent greater specificity as to events at issue) to have been convicted of assault occasioning actual bodily harm.

R v Jones (Terence); R v Campbell (Michael); R v Smith (Lee); R v Nicholas (Victor); R v Blackwood (Winston); R v Muir (Ricky) (1986) 83 Cr App R 375 CA Is defence to assault that arose from rough play to which consented.

R v McCready; R v Hurd (1978) 122 SJ 247 CA Could not plead guilty to common assault where were only charged with causing grievous bodily harm with intent.

R v White [1995] Crim LR 393 CA Substitution of verdict of guilt of causing grievous bodily harm (not causing same with intent) where because of post-traumatic stress disorder did not have requisite intent.

GRIEVOUS BODILY HARM (attempt)

R v Pearman (Stephen Dennis) (1985) 80 Cr App R 259; [1984] Crim LR 675; [1985] RTR 39 CA That foresee consequences need not mean intended them.

GRIEVOUS BODILY HARM (causing with intent)

R v Cole (and others) [1993] Crim LR 300 CA On drunkenness as defence to causing grievous bodily harm with intent: issue is whether had requisite intent, not whether capable of forming same.

GRIEVOUS BODILY HARM (general)

Cartledge v Allen [1973] Crim LR 530 HC QBD Person who injured self in running away from others who had threatened him thereby suffered infliction of grievous bodily harm by those others.

R v Beech [1911-13] All ER 530; (1913-14) XXIII Cox CC 181; (1911-12) 7 Cr App R 197; (1912) 76 JP 287; (1912-13) 107 LTR 461 CCA Self-inflicted injuries directly resulting from threat of injury resulted in proper conviction for grievous bodily harm of party making threat.

R v Belfon [1976] 3 All ER 46; (1976) 63 Cr App R 59; [1976] Crim LR 449t; (1976) 140 JP 523; (1976) 120 SJ 329; [1976] 1 WLR 741 CA For grievous bodily harm must do acts with intent to cause same.

R v Brown and other appeals [1993] 2 All ER 75; [1994] 1 AC 212; (1993) 97 Cr App R 44; [1993] Crim LR 583; (1993) 157 JP 337; (1993) 143 NLJ 399; [1993] TLR 129; [1993] 2 WLR 556 HL Consensual homosexual sado-masochistic acts causing actual bodily harm are assaults occasioning actual bodily harm/unlawful woundings.

R v Burstow [1996] Crim LR 331 CrCt Offence of inflicting grievous bodily harm includes cases of psychiatric injury consequent upon non-physical injury.

R v Burstow (Andrew Christopher) [1997] 1 Cr App R 144; [1997] Crim LR 452; (1996) 140 SJ LB 194; (1996) TLR 30/7/96 CA Offence of inflicting grievous bodily harm includes cases of psychiatric injury consequent upon non-physical injury.

R v Chapin (Alice) (1911-13) XXII Cox CC 10; (1910) 74 JP 71 CCC Interference with loose ballot papers at bottom of box (a 'packet of ballot papers') an interference with box; need not be personal malice to sustain charge of maliciously inflicting grievous bodily harm.

R v Charlson [1955] 1 All ER 859; (1955) 39 Cr App R 37; [1955] Crim LR 316; (1955) 119 JP 283; (1955) 99 SJ 221; [1955] 1 WLR 317 HC QBD Cannot be unlawful and malicious grievous bodily harm where not acting consciously.

R v Field [1993] Crim LR 456; (1993) 157 JP 834; [1992] TLR 631 CA Cannot be found guilty of inflicting grievous bodily harm where charged with causing grievous bodily harm with intent.

R v Gibson (Turhan Clint); R v Gibson (Julie) (1985) 80 Cr App R 24; [1984] Crim LR 615 CA Could infer that both parents guilty of grievous bodily harm to baby where child harmed and was no explanation from/evidence pointing to either parent.

R v Grimshaw [1984] Crim LR 108 CA On foreseeability as an element of offence of inflicting grievous bodily harm contrary to Offences against the Person Act 1861, s 20.

R v Hilton, Critchley, Lythe and Greatrex [1956] Crim LR 122 Assizes On distinction between wounding with intent to cause grievous bodily harm and unlawful wounding.

R v Jenkins; R v Jenkins [1983] Crim LR 386 CA On what is meant by to 'inflict grievous bodily harm' in Theft Act 1968, s 9(1)(b) (as opposed to Offences against the Person Act 1861, s 20).

R v Jones and others [1987] Crim LR 123 CA Is defence to charge of inflicting grievous bodily harm that 'victim' consented to same or that genuinely believed victim consented.

R v Mandair [1994] 2 All ER 715; [1995] 1 AC 208; (1994) 99 Cr App R 250; [1994] Crim LR 666; (1994) 158 JP 685; (1994) 144 NLJ 708; (1994) 138 SJ LB 123; [1994] 2 WLR 700 HL Offence of 'causing' -not 'inflicting' - grievous bodily harm is known to law. House of Lords assumes full jurisdiction of Court of Appeal upon appeal therefrom. Restoration of conviction by House of Lords can only be set aside by Court of Appeal in reference from Home Secretary.

R v Mandair [1993] Crim LR 679 CA On difference between wounding and causing grievous bodily harm (under the Offences against the Person Act 1861, ss 18 and 20).

R v Metharam [1961] 3 All ER 200; [1961] Crim LR 616; (1961) 125 JP 578 CCA A misdirection to state intent to interfere with health/comfort can sustain charge of grievous bodily harm.

R v Monger [1973] Crim LR 301 CA On transferred malice.

R v Mowatt [1967] 3 All ER 47; [1967] Crim LR 591; (1967) 131 JP 463; (1967) 117 NLJ 860; [1968] 1 QB 421; (1967) 111 SJ 716; [1967] 3 WLR 1192 CA Definition of 'maliciously' in Offences Against the Person Act 1861 unnecessary in circumstances.

R v Palmer (Helen Claire) (1994) 15 Cr App R (S) 654 CA Fifteen months' imprisonment for mother guilty of inflicting grievous bodily harm on infant child.

R v Wilson (Clarence); R v Jenkins (Edward John) and another [1983] 3 All ER 448; [1984] AC 242; (1984) 148 JP 435; (1983) 127 SJ 712; [1983] TLR 595 HL If indictment includes allegation of other offence can be convicted of that offence.

GRIEVOUS BODILY HARM (incitement to cause)

R v Sirat (Mohammed) (1986) 83 Cr App R 41; [1986] Crim LR 245 CA Not an offence to incite another to agreeing with a further person that latter will cause grievous bodily harm to yet another person.

GRIEVOUS BODILY HARM (mens rea)

R v Cunningham [1981] 2 All ER 863; [1982] AC 566; (1981) 73 Cr App R 253; [1981] Crim LR 835; (1981) 145 JP 411; (1981) 131 NLJ 755; (1981) 125 SJ 512; [1981] 3 WLR 223 HL Intention to cause grievous bodily harm sufficient intent for murder.

R v Cunningham [1981] Crim LR 180 CA On whether intention to cause grievous bodily harm sufficient intent for murder.

Wing-Siu (Chan) and others v R [1985] AC 168; (1985) 80 Cr App R 117; [1984] Crim LR 549; (1984) 128 SJ 685; [1984] TLR 411; [1984] 3 WLR 677 PC Person guilty of murder/grievous bodily harm if proved that entered premises as part of unlawful common enterprise and had contemplated that serious bodily harm might result.

GRIEVOUS BODILY HARM (sado-masochism)

R v Brown and other appeals [1993] 2 All ER 75; [1994] 1 AC 212; (1993) 97 Cr App R 44; [1993] Crim LR 583; (1993) 157 JP 337; (1993) 143 NLJ 399; [1993] TLR 129; [1993] 2 WLR 556 HL Consensual homosexual sado-masochistic acts causing actual bodily harm are assaults occasioning actual bodily harm/unlawful woundings.

R v Brown and other appeals [1992] 2 All ER 552; (1992) 94 Cr App R 302; (1992) 156 JP 475; (1992) 142 NLJ 275; [1992] QB 491; (1992) 136 SJ LB 90; [1992] TLR 71; [1992] 2 WLR 441 CA Private, consensual sado-masochistic acts not causing permanent injury may constitute unlawful wounding/ assault causing actual bodily harm.

GRIEVOUS BODILY HARM (unlawfully and maliciously causing)

Ex parte Worth [1967] Crim LR 178t; (1965-66) 116 NLJ 1685 HC QBD Leave to seek order of mandamus against justices who dismissed information for unlawful/grievous bodily harm in case where victim tied up with rope that was set on fire - a thing any reasonable man would see involved chance of serious injury.

R v Lewis [1970] Crim LR 647 CA Were guilty of maliciously inflicting grievous bodily harm where caused person to leap in terror from window on foot of threats shouted to them from another room.

GROSS INDECENCY (attempt to procure)

R v Riley [1967] Crim LR 656 Assizes Person acquitted of attempt to procure act of gross indecency where at time of alleged offence was suffering from psychoneurosis which led him to want to get into trouble.

HABEAS CORPUS (bail)

R v Governor of Brixton Prison, ex parte Singh (Kirpal) and Singh (Jit) [1969] Crim LR 436; (1969) 113 SJ 406 HC QBD Home Office custody order took precedence over justices' bail order.

HABEAS CORPUS (general)

Armah v Government of Ghana and another [1966] 3 All ER 177; [1968] AC 192 (also CA); [1966] Crim LR 618t; [1967] Crim LR 240t; (1967) 131 JP 43; (1965-66) 116 NLJ 1204t; (1966) 110 SJ 890; [1966] 3 WLR 828 HL 'Strong and probable presumption' that accused committed offence to be given natural meaning; issues for appellate court are did magistrate apply correct test/was there a 'strong and probable presumption' accused committed offence.

Baker v Alford (1960) 104 SJ PC Failed habeas corpus application in which complained that extension of Colonial Prisoners Removal Act 1869 to Bahrain (and application of same) improper.

Budd v Anderson, Morrrison and Williamson [1943] 2 All ER 452; [1943] KB 642; (1943) WN (I) 150 HC KBD Technical error in detention order did not render it invalid.

Eleko (Eshugbayi) v Nigeria Government (Administration Officer) [1928] All ER 598; [1928] AC 459; (1928) 66 LJ 46; (1928) 97 LJPC 97; (1928) 139 LTR 527; (1928) 72 SJ 452; (1928) WN (I) 175 PC Each judge of High Court (and so Nigerian Supreme Court) has power to (and must) hear habeas corpus application regardless of whether already decided on by another judge.

Eleko (Eshugbayi) v Officer Administering the Government of Nigeria and Another [1931] AC 662; (1931) 100 LJPC 152; (1931) 145 LTR 297 PC Habeas corpus petition arising from deportation of party from one part of Nigerian Colony to another.

Eliezer v General Officer Commanding Palestine and Another [1947] AC 246 PC English habeas corpus rules apply in Palestine.

Ex parte Askew [1963] Crim LR 507t HC QBD Failed habeas corpus application on basis of error in warrant of committal.

Ex parte Budd [1941] 2 All ER 749; (1942) 92 LJ 51 HC KBD Wartime detention order procedurally valid.

Ex parte Chapple [1950] 66 (2) TLR 932 CA CA could not hear appeal from HC KBD decision in habeas corpus application as sprang from criminal cause/matter.

Ex parte Corke [1954] 2 All ER 440; [1954] Crim LR 544; (1954) 104 LJ 393; (1954) 98 SJ 406; [1954] 1 WLR 899 HC QBD Habeas corpus not to be used as guise for appeal against sentence.

Ex parte Docherty [1960] Crim LR 835t HC QBD Habeas corpus order in light of doubts as to identification evidence before magistrates.

Ex parte Enahoro [1963] Crim LR 568; (1963) 107 SJ 397 HC QBD Habeas corpus application heard in person (where alleging that previous non-appearance had been contrived to ensure evidence presented in certain way).

Ex parte Garrett [1954] Crim LR 621t HC QBD Costs ordered against medical health officer who (in good faith) wrongfully detained a mental health patient beyond period stated in detention order.

Ex parte Goswani [1967] Crim LR 234; (1965-66) 116 NLJ 1712t; (1967) 111 SJ 17 HC QBD Bail here not deemed unreasonable: that defendant cannot meet bail set does not per se mean it is unreasonable.

Ex parte Hastings [1960] Crim LR 61t HC QBD Corrective training merited by offences correctly described in notice containing one misdescribed offence.

Ex parte Hinds [1961] 1 All ER 707; (1961) 111 LJ 222; (1961) 105 SJ 180 HC QBD No habeas corpus for non-hearing by CA of point of law; where leave to appeal sought and only point of law deemed to be involved will be listed as point of law appeal.

Ex parte Hoswin (Hilda Margaret) (1916-17) XXXIII TLR 527 CA Habeas corpus rule nisi refused in respect of interned British subject whom Home Secretary had grounds to suspect of dubious connections.

Ex parte Lannoy (1941-42) LVIII TLR 207 HC KBD Detention of alien national was valid: costs of habeas corpus application refused.

Ex parte Lannoy (1941-42) LVIII TLR 350 CA Detention of alien national was valid: costs of habeas corpus application refused.

Ex parte Le Gros (1913-14) XXX TLR 249; (1914) WN (I) 31 CA CA cannot grant rule nisi for habeas corpus where HC has refused same.

Ex parte Moser (1915-17) XXV Cox CC 69; [1915] 2 KB 698; [1915] 84 LJKB 1820; (1915-16) 113 LTR 496; (1914-15) XXXI TLR 384; (1915) WN (I) 169 HC KBD Extradition of 'fugitive offender' was valid.

Ex parte Moser (1914-15) XXXI TLR 438 HC KBD Extradition of 'fugitive offender' was valid.

Ex parte O'Brien (1922-23) XXXIX TLR 413 HC KBD Failed habeas corpus application by person interned under regulations made pursuant to Restoration of Ireland Act 1920 which applicant claimed was rendered inoperable once Ireland secured independence.

Ex parte Shalom Schtraks (No 2) [1962] 3 All ER 849; [1963] Crim LR 111; [1964] 1 QB 191; [1962] 3 WLR 1435 HC QBD No habeas corpus writ where alleged evidence that committal obtained by fraud insufficiently probative.

Ex parte Suidan [1966] Crim LR 445t; (1965-66) 116 NLJ 837t HC QBD Leave to seek habeas corpus but no bail for proposed extraditee who alleged the requesting warrant/deposition were seriously defective.

Ex parte Thomas [1956] Crim LR 119 HC QBD Habeas corpus application made where bail excessive.

Ex parte Weber [1916] 1 AC 421; (1915-17) XXV Cox CC 258; (1916) 80 JP 249; (1916) 51 LJ 102; [1916] 85 LJKB 944; (1916) 114 LTR 214; (1915-16) XXXII TLR 312; (1916) WN (I) 83 HL German resident in England for fifteen years was nonetheless properly interned.

Ex parte Weber (1915-17) XXV Cox CC 137; (1916) 80 JP 14; [1916] 1 KB 280; [1916] 85 LJKB 217; (1915-16) 113 LTR 968; (1914-15) XXXI TLR 602 CA German resident in England for fifteen years was nonetheless properly interned.

Ex parte Williams (Robert Franklin) [1970] Crim LR 102; (1969) 113 SJ 853 HC QBD Habeas corpus application as cover for bail application not approved of.

Greene v Secretary of State for Home Affairs [1941] 3 All ER 388; [1942] AC 284; (1942) 92 LJ 51; [1942] 111 LJ 24; (1942) 166 LTR 24; (1941) 85 SJ 461 (also CA); (1941-42) LVIII TLR 53 HL Home Secretary's affidavit that valid detention under Defence (General) Regulations 1939, reg 18(b) being good on face meant no writ of habeas corpus would be issued.

In the matter of Anderson [1994] Crim LR 594 HC QBD Failed habeas corpus application where claimed that because of delay/nature of offence involved it would be oppressive to return extraditee to Greece.

In the matter of Crichton (Jean), an Infant (1935) 79 LJ 239; (1935) 79 SJ 181 HC KBD Child who had been left with school proprietress ordered to be returned to mother who could now look after child.

In the matter of Wai Kit Lee; R v Metropolitan Stipendiary Magistrate; ex parte Wai Kit Lee [1993] Crim LR 696 HC QBD No power in extradition proceedings for court to request more evidence from requesting state; failed habeas corpus application where extraditee claimed undertakings by the Hong Kong government might not be honoured by the Chinese government after the hand-over.

Phillip and others v Director of Public Prosecutions of Trinidad and Tobago and another; Phillip and others v Commissioner of Prisons and another [1992] 1 All ER 665; [1992] 1 AC 545; [1991] TLR 596; [1992] 2 WLR 211 PC Prima facie valid pardon requires immediate hearing of habeas corpus application.

R v Board of Control and others; ex parte Rutty [1956] 1 All ER 769; [1956] Crim LR 331; (1956) 106 LJ 234; [1956] 2 QB 109; [1956] 2 WLR 822 HC QBD Affidavit evidence admissible to test judicial finding; cannot under Mental Deficiency Act 1927, s 2 issue reception order unless person 'found neglected' - meaning thereof.

R v Bottrill, ex parte Kuchenmeister [1946] 1 All ER 635; [1947] KB 41; (1946) 96 LJ 232; (1946) 90 SJ 321; (1945-46) LXII TLR 374 HC KBD Enemy alien interned during wartime cannot seek writ of habeas corpus.

R v Bottrill; ex parte Kuchenmeister [1946] 2 All ER 434; [1946] 115 LJ 500; (1946) 175 LTR 232; (1945-46) LXII TLR 570; (1946) WN (I) 177 CA Enemy alien interned during wartime cannot seek writ of habeas corpus.

R v Brixton Prison Governor; ex parte Pitt-Rivers [1942] 1 All ER 207 HC KBD Detention order good on face/conforming with procedural requirements precluded writ of habeas corpus being issued.

R v Campbell [1959] 2 All ER 557; [1959] Crim LR 362; (1959) 123 JP 361 CrCt Habeas Corpus Act 1679, s 6 only applies if procedural terms therein complied with (not here but discretion exercised).

R v Campbell and others (1959) 103 SJ 434 CrCt CrCt could but did not make habeas corpus order in respect of prisoner whose trial was postponed but in its discretion ordered that case lie on file, not be proceeded with absent court order.

R v Chief Metropolitan Magistrate, ex parte Government of the Republic of Singapore; R v Governor of Pentonville Prison, ex parte Tarling (1980) 70 Cr App R 77; [1978] Crim LR 490 HL (also HC QBD) No extradition for crime which is not crime in England/in respect of which is no prima facie evidence prisoner committed offence.

R v Chief Metropolitan Stipendiary Magistrate, ex parte Osman [1988] 3 All ER 173; [1988] Crim LR 681 HC QBD Court may award costs to extraditing state against habeas corpus applicant if application fails.

R v Commandant of Knockaloe Camp; ex parte Forman (1917-18) 117 LTR 627; (1917-18) 62 SJ 35; (1917-18) XXXIV TLR 4 HC KBD Unregistered alien can be validly interned.

R v Commissioner of Police and another; ex parte Nalder [1947] 2 All ER 611; (1948) 112 JP 20; [1948] 1 KB 251; (1947) 97 LJ 621; [1948] 117 LJR 439; (1947) 91 SJ 614; (1947) LXIII TLR 591; (1947) WN (I) 295 HC KBD Valid sending of person to Ireland under Indictable Offences Act 1848/Petty Sessions (Ireland) Act 1851, not Fugitive Offenders Act 1881.

R v Commissioner of Police of the Metropolis; ex parte Nahar and another [1983] TLR 393 HC QBD Failed habeas corpus applications by persons being held in unsatisfactory but lawful detention in cells at magistrates' court after being remanded in custody.

R v Crown Court at Maidstone, ex parte Clark; R v Governor of Elmley Prison, ex parte Clark [1995] 3 All ER 513; [1995] 1 WLR 831 HC QBD Habeas corpus available (where no other remedy) if arraignment used as anything other than preparatory to trial.

R v Crown Court at Maidstone, ex parte Hollstein [1995] 3 All ER 503 HC QBD Court may review legitimacy of arraignment; remedy of habeas corpus available where arraignment not legitimate.

R v Earl of Crewe (1910) 102 LTR 760; (1909-10) XXVI TLR 192 HC KBD Seeking of habeas corpus writ regarding detention of person in Crown Protectorate failed for want of jurisdiction/procedural reasons.

R v Governor of Brixton Prison and another, ex parte Osman (No 4) [1990] TLR 748 HC QBD Public interest immunity also arises in habeas corpus applications.

R v Governor of Brixton Prison and another, ex parte Walsh [1984] 1 All ER 344; [1984] Crim LR 676; [1984] QB 392; (1983) 127 SJ 841; [1983] TLR 632; [1984] 2 WLR 217 HC QBD Neither prison governor nor Home Secretary under duty to present persons on bail before court on date stated in remands; habeas corpus inappropriate in such a situation.

R v Governor of Brixton Prison and another, ex parte Walsh [1985] AC 154; (1984) 128 SJ 482; [1984] TLR 414 HL Neither prison governor nor Home Secretary under duty to present persons on bail before court on date stated in remands.

R v Governor of Brixton Prison, ex parte Gardner [1968] 1 All ER 636; [1968] Crim LR 109t; (1968) 132 JP 187; (1968) 118 NLJ 230; [1968] 2 QB 399; (1968) 112 SJ 153; [1968] 2 WLR 512 HC QBD Habeas corpus where offences on which sought not offences under English law.

R v Governor of Brixton Prison, ex parte Osman (No 5); R v Secretary of State for the Home Department, ex parte Osman (No 2) [1992] TLR 565 HC QBD Home Secretary could commence return of extraditee who had made habeas corpus application if Home Secretary decided extradition request did not conform with the Administration of Justice Act 1960, s 14(2).

R v Governor of Brixton Prison, ex parte Perry [1923] All ER 182; (1921-25) XXVII Cox CC 597; [1924] 1 KB 455; (1923) 58 LJ 601; [1924] 93 LJCL 380; (1924) 130 LTR 731; (1923-24) 68 SJ 370; (1923-24) XL TLR 181; (1924) WN (I) 11 HC KBD No writ of habeas corpus where cause of complaint could be addressed by Secretary of State under Extradition Act 1870, s 11.

R v Governor of Brixton Prison, ex parte Sadri [1962] 3 All ER 747; [1962] Crim LR 835; (1962) 112 LJ 767; (1962) 106 SJ 836; [1962] 1 WLR 1304 HC QBD Habeas corpus writ issued as no admissible evidence of guilt; foreign affidavit defective as no indication how offences punishable.

R v Governor of Brixton Prison, ex parte Servini (1913-14) XXIII Cox CC 713; (1914) 78 JP 47; [1914] 1 KB 77; (1913) 48 LJ 661; [1914] 83 LJKB 212; (1913-14) 109 LTR 986; (1913-14) 58 SJ 68; (1913-14) XXX TLR 35; (1913) WN (I) 302 HC KBD Habeas corpus application refused though evidential irregularity proved.

R v Governor of Brixton Prison, ex parte Singh [1961] 2 All ER 565; [1961] Crim LR 617; [1962] 1 QB 211; [1961] 2 WLR 980 CCA Extradition in relation to crime allegedly committed ten years previously refused as return after delay would be unjust/oppressive.

R v Governor of Brixton Prison; ex parte Ahsan and others [1969] Crim LR 317; [1969] 2 WLR 618 HC QBD On burden of proof in respect of justifying detention of British subject-Commonwealth citizens.

R v Governor of Brixton Prison; ex parte Campbell [1956] Crim LR 624t HC QBD Discharge of proposed extraditee ordered where undue delay in seeking extradition prejudiced chances of fair trial.

R v Governor of Brixton Prison; ex parte Green [1955] Crim LR 110t HC QBD Extradition to Nigeria of person charged with theft/forgery of cheque ordered.

R v Governor of Brixton Prison; ex parte Hurwitz (1924-25) 69 SJ 727 HC QBD Failed habeas corpus application in extradition case: was sufficient evidence to justify extradition of applicant.

R v Governor of Brixton Prison; ex parte Mehmet (Mourat) [1962] 1 All ER 463; [1962] Crim LR 108t; (1962) 112 LJ 154; [1962] 2 QB 1; (1962) 106 SJ 196 HC QBD Discharge from custody where evidence such that no reasonable magistrate would have committed thereon.

R v Governor of Brixton Prison; ex parte Penn (1952) 96 SJ 696 HC QBD Failed application by Indian authorities for extradition of alleged offender (application in grossly irregular form).

R v Governor of Brixton Prison; ex parte Sarno (1916-17) 115 LTR 608; (1915-16) XXXII TLR 717 HC KBD Habeas corpus writ available where person properly held at time of application but unlawful Ececutive action is forthcoming.

R v Governor of Brixton Prison; ex parte Savarkar [1908-10] All ER 603; [1910] 2 KB 1056; (1911) 80 LJCL 57; (1910-11) 103 LTR 473; (1909-10) 54 SJ 635; (1909-10) XXVI TLR 561 CA CA a court of first instance in 'trivial offence' fugitive offender cases; 'trivial offence' plea can be entered at same time seek habeas corpus; individual longtime resident in England ought really to be tried in England.

R v Governor of Brixton Prison; ex parte Singleton (1965) 109 SJ 354 HC QBD Habeas corpus writ would not be issued with conditions.

R v Governor of Brixton Prison; ex parte Stallmann [1911-13] All ER 385; (1913-14) XXIII Cox CC 192; (1913) 77 JP 5; [1912] 3 KB 424; [1913] 82 LJKB 8; (1912-13) 107 LTR 553; (1911-12) XXVIII TLR 572 HC KBD Extradition allowed despite party having been set at large on previous writ of habeas corpus.

R v Governor of Brixton Prison; ex parte Gardner [1968] Crim LR 111t HC QBD Immediate re-arrest on new warrant following granting of habeas corpus writ was justified.

R v Governor of Brixton; ex parte Ahsen and others (1968) 112 SJ 422 HC QBD Successful application for habeas corpus writs by Pakistanis who illegally entered Britain and claimed were not interviewed by immigration authorities until after initial twenty-four hours passed.

R v Governor of Durham Prison; ex parte Handial Singh [1983] TLR 763 HC QBD Length of time for which may be detained under immigration legislation limited to time reasonable to effect deportation.

R v Governor of Haslar Prison and another; ex parte Egbe [1991] TLR 276 CA Pending decision on habeas corpus application of person against whom deportation order made, that person not to be granted bail.

R v Governor of HM Bedford Prison and others; ex parte Ames (1953) 97 SJ 282; (1953) 117 JP 237; [1953] 1 WLR 607 HC QBD Committal warrant after non-payment of maintenance could be made in defaultee's absence (but here invalid as did not take into account post-making of maintenance of order).

R v Governor of HM Prison, Brixton, ex parte Minervini [1958] 3 All ER 318; [1958] Crim LR 808; (1958) 122 JP 473; (1958) 108 LJ 745; [1959] 1 QB 155; (1958) 102 SJ 777; [1958] 3 WLR 559 HC QBD Requesting government may be represented/heard at fugitive convict's habeas corpus application; 'territory' includes places within jurisdiction of state (such as ships).

R v Governor of Holloway Prison [1900-03] All ER 609 HC KBD Court cannot consider fresh evidence concerning extradition in habeas corpus application.

R v Governor of Holloway Prison, ex parte Siletti (1901-07) XX Cox CC 353; (1903) 67 JP 67; [1902] 71 LJCL 935; (1902-03) LXXXVII LTR 332; (1901-02) 46 SJ 686; (1902-03) 51 WR 191 HC KBD On making of habeas corpus orders in extradition cases.

R v Governor of Maidstone Prison; ex parte Maguire (1925) 89 JP 89; [1925] 2 KB 265; (1925) 60 LJ 419; [1925] 94 LJCL 679; (1925) 133 LTR 710; (1924-25) 69 SJ 524/691; (1924-25) XLI TLR 456; (1925) WN (I) 119 HC KBD Northern Ireland prisoner validly transferred to English prison.

R v Governor of Pentonville Prison (1903) 67 JP 206 HC KBD Successful habeas corpus application where had been procedural irregularities in committal of prisoner.

R v Governor of Pentonville Prison and another; ex parte Azam; R v Secretary of State for Home Department; ex parte Khera; Same v Same; ex parte Sidhu (1973) 117 SJ 546; [1973] 2 WLR 949 CA Person about to be removed from jurisdiction as illegal entrant can seek review of that decision by way of habeas corpus application.

R v Governor of Pentonville Prison, ex parte Khubchandani (1980) 71 Cr App R 241; [1980] Crim LR 436; (1980) 124 SJ275 HC QBD Habeas corpus granted where extradition sought for 'offences' that were not offences under English law.

R v Governor of Pentonville Prison, ex parte Teja [1971] 2 All ER 11; (1971) 121 NLJ 82t; [1971] 2 QB 274; (1971) 115 SJ 305; [1971] 2 WLR 816 HC QBD Cannot claim no offence because of PC decision - matter for foreign law; political defence inapplicable despite case being subject of Indian Parliamentary debate; cannot plead delay if are responsible for it.

R v Governor of Pentonville Prison; ex parte Healy (1984) 128 SJ 498; [1984] TLR 303 HC QBD Extradition of Irish citizen from Ireland to the UK on foot of request by latter did not violate Article 48/EEC.

R v Governor of Pentonville Prison; ex parte Mancini [1984] TLR 523 HC QBD Failed habeas corpus application by subject of habeas corpus proceedings requested for murder but extradited for manslaughter.

R v Governor of Risley Remand Centre, ex parte Hassan (1976) 120 SJ 333; [1976] 1 WLR 971 HC QBD Failed application by alien detained under immigration law who failed to discharge onus of proof on him (considered) to show that he was unlawfully detained.

R v Governor of Wandsworth Prison; ex parte Silverman (1952) 96 SJ 853 HC QBD Failed application by person in preventive detention who sought habeas corpus writ.

R v Governor of Winchester Prison, ex parte Roddie and another; R v Crown Court at Southampton, ex parte Roddie and another [1991] 2 All ER 931; (1991) 93 Cr App R 190; [1991] Crim LR 619; (1991) 155 JP 676; [1991] TLR 67; [1991] 1 WLR 303 HC QBD Gravity of offence/shortness of extension did not justify extension of period of pre-committal custody.

R v Governor of Wormwood Scrubs Prison; ex parte Foy (1920) 84 JP 94; (1919-20) XXXVI TLR 432 HC KBD Internment under wartime internment provisions not unlawful though war had ended.

R v Governor of Wormwood Scrubs Prison; ex parte Boydell [1948] 2 KB 193; (1948) 98 LJ 133; (1948) LXIV TLR 184; (1948) WN (I) 100 HC KBD Illegal detention of ex-officer by army authorities for arrest and trial.

R v Halliday (Sir Frederick Loch) (1916) 80 JP 233 (also CA); (1916) 51 LJ 64; [1916] 85 LJKB 953 (also CA); (1915-16) XXXII TLR 245 HC KBD Provision for internment of naturalised British subject valid.

R v Halliday; ex parte Zadig [1914-17] All ER 496; [1917] AC 260; (1915-17) XXV Cox CC 278; (1917) 81 JP 237; [1917] 86 LJCL 1119; (1917) 116 LTR 417; (1916-17) 61 SJ 443; (1916-17) XXXIII TLR 336 HL Provision for internment of naturalised British subject valid.

R v Halliday; ex parte Zadig (1916) 80 JP 233 (also HC KBD); (1916) 51 LJ 102; [1916] 85 LJKB 953 (also HC KBD); (1916) 114 LTR 303; (1915-16) 60 SJ 290; (1915-16) XXXII TLR 300 CA Provision for internment of naturalised British subject valid.

R v Home Secretary, ex parte Budd [1942] 1 All ER 373; [1942] 111 LJ 475; (1942) 166 LTR 293; (1941-42) LVIII TLR 212 CA Legality of detention at issue - good faith behaviour of Home Secretary precluded inquiry into facts of detention; writ of habeas corpus did not preclude future detention.

R v Home Secretary, ex parte Eva Bressler (1924) 131 LTR 36 CA Refusal of habeas corpus application made by alien facing deportation pursuant to Aliens' Order 1920.

R v Home Secretary, ex parte O'Brien (1921-25) XXVII Cox CC 433; (1923) 87 JP 166; [1923] 2 KB 361; (1923) 58 LJ 223; [1923] 92 LJCL 797; (1923) 129 LTR 419; (1922-23) XXXIX TLR 487 CA Home Secretary could not order internment of person in Irish Free State; writ of habeas corpus against Home Secretary proper though person interned in Irish Free State.

R v Ipswich Justices; ex parte Edwards (1979) 143 JP 699 HC QBD Justices' improper admission of evidence irremediable through certiorari: habeas corpus application refused.

R v Iqbal [1979] 1 WLR 425 CA Failed habeas corpus application by person detained under the Immigration Act 1971.

R v Maidstone Crown Court; ex parte Clark; R v Governor of Elmley Prison; ex parte Clark (1995) 139 SJ LB 32 HC QBD Arraignment arrangements challengeable by way of habeas corpus application.

R v O/C Depot battalion, RASC, Colchester; ex parte Elliott [1949] 1 All ER 373; (1949) WN (I) 52 HC KBD Means by which person over whom court has jurisdiction was brought into jurisdiction irrelevant; High Court may grant bail where undue delay in military case.

R v Oldham Justices and another, ex parte Cawley and other applications [1996] 1 All ER 464; (1996) 146 NLJ 49; [1997] QB 1; [1996] 2 WLR 681 HC QBD Legality of detention is open to judicial review where reasons for detention not stated by magistrates.

R v Pinckney; ex parte Pinckney [1904-07] All ER 406; (1904) 68 JP 361; [1904] 2 KB 84; [1904] 73 LJCL 475; (1904) XC LTR 468; (1903-04) 48 SJ 328; (1903-04) XX TLR 363; (1904) WN (I) 68; (1903-04) 52 WR 338 CA Cannot issue writ of habeas corpus against person who at time of order is outside jurisdiction.

R v Richards; ex parte Fitzpatrick and Browne [1955] Crim LR 570t PC Warrants issued by Speaker of Australian lower House taken as conclusive that breach of privilege had occurred.

R v Secretary of State for Home Affairs; ex parte Budd [1942] 2 KB 14; (1942) 86 SJ 111 CA On reviewability of detention ordered by Home Secretary under emergency legislation.

R v Secretary of State for Home Affairs; ex parte Lees [1941] 1 KB 72 CA HC KBD not a court of appeal from detention order by Home Secretary: would not order same to produce reports on which grounded order.

R v Secretary of State for India in Council and others; ex parte Ezekiel [1941] 2 All ER 546; [1941] 2 KB 169; (1942) 92 LJ 53; [1942] 111 LJ 237 HC KBD Second World War no excuse for non-extradition to India; need not be avoiding arrest to be extradited; warrant need not refer to Fugitive Offenders Act 1881; depositions admissible though not apparently taken in pursuance of Fugitive Offenders Act 1881, s 29; affidavit of foreign legal expert not conclusive; barrister should not act as counsel and witness.

R v Secretary of State for the Home Department and another, ex parte Choudhary [1978] 1 WLR 1177 CA Failed habeas corpus application where Home Secretary had reasonable ground for detaining person whom believed to be unlawfully in country on foot of fraudulent entry.

R v Secretary of State for the Home Department, ex parte Cheblak [1991] 1 WLR 890 CA Failed application for writ of habeas corpus by person being detained prior to deportation.

R v Secretary of State for the Home Department, ex parte Hussain [1978] 1 WLR 700 CA Failed habeas corpus application where Secretary of State had reasonable basis on which to ground belief that applicant was illegally in country and so to be detained.

R v Secretary of State for the Home Department, ex parte Iqbal [1979] 1 All ER 675; [1979] QB 264; [1978] 3 WLR 884 HC QBD Court may look beyond material error in document justifying detention to see if legitimate.

R v Secretary of State for the Home Department, ex parte Muboyayi [1992] QB 244 CA Where basis of immigration-related action was challenge to administrative decision refusing entry court would not consider administrative decision in habeas corpus proceedings.

R v Secretary of State for the Home Department, ex parte Ram [1979] 1 WLR 148 HC QBD Successful habeas corpus application against detention of immigrant whose passport had been duly stamped (albeit by mistake) by immigration officer.

R v Secretary of State for the Home Department, ex parte Virk (Parmjeet Singh); R v Same, ex parte Taggar; R v Same, ex parte Virk (Satnam); R v Same, ex parte Singh [1995] TLR 512 HC QBD No restriction allowed on employment of person freed after habeas corpus application regarding detention pursuant to immigration legislation.

R v Secretary of State for the Home Department; ex parte Awa [1983] TLR 183 HC QBD Successful habeas corpus action by person being detained as illegal entrant into UK.

R v Secretary of State for the Home Department; ex parte D (1996) 140 SJ LB 119 HC QBD Failed application for writ of habeas corpus by person subject to restriction order who was recalled to hospital where was at time of recall already getting care.

R v Secretary of State for the Home Department; ex parte Rahman [1996] 4 All ER 945; (1996) TLR 19/7/96 HC QBD Hearsay evidence could be relied on in habeas corpus application in context of illegal immigration.

R v Secretary of the Board of Control and another; Re Dawson; ex parte Abdul Kayum (1948) 112 JP 453; (1949) LXV TLR 39 HC KBD Failed application for habeas corpus by mental institution detainee whose period of detention had been extended by general order.

R v Superintendant of Vine Street Police Station; ex parte Liebmann (1915-17) XXV Cox CC 179; (1916) 80 JP 49; [1916] 85 LJKB 210; (1915-16) 113 LTR 971; (1915-16) XXXII TLR 3; (1915) WN (I) 320 HC KBD German resident in England for twenty-seven years was nonetheless properly interned.

R v Superintendent of Chiswick Police Station; ex parte Sacksteder (1918) 53 LJ 96; (1918) 118 LTR 165 CA Wartime deportation order in respect of alien deemed valid.

R v The Board of Control Lunacy and Mental Deficiency for England and Wales - Ex parte Winterflood (1937-38) LIV TLR 698 CA Successful appeal against failed habeas corpus application in respect of detention of mental defective where had been procedural irregularity but was done bona fide.

R v The Board of Control; The Corporation of the County Borough of East Ham v Mordey; ex parte Winterflood (1937-38) LIV TLR 73 HC KBD Failed habeas corpus application in respect of detention of mental defective where had been procedural irregularity but was done bona fide.

R v The Commanding Officer of Morn Hill Camp, Winchester; ex parte Ferguson (1917) 81 JP 73; [1917] 1 KB 176; [1917] 86 LJCL 410; (1916-17) 115 LTR 927 HC KBD Habeas corpus application not means of testing writ of lower court.

R v The Earl of Crewe; ex parte Sekgome [1910] 2 KB 576; (1909-10) XXVI TLR 439 CA Valid detention of person in Crown Protectorate.

R v The Governor of Brixton Prison; ex parte Guerin (1906-07) 51 SJ 571 HC KBD Successful plea that were British-born subject and so not liable to extradition.

R v The Governor of Winson Green Prison, Birmingham; ex parte Trotter (1992) 94 Cr App R 29; (1991) 155 JP 671 HC QBD Detention justified despite abortion of committal proceedings.

R v The Home Secretary, ex parte L and another [1945] KB 7 HC KBD No habeas corps for enemy alien rendered stateless by enemy country in time of war.

R v Vyner (1904) 68 JP 142 HC KBD HC can review exercise of magistrate's discretion not to extradite fugitive offender.

Re Amand [1942] 1 All ER 480; [1942] 111 LJ 349; (1943) 93 LJ 85 (also HL); (1942) 166 LTR 292; (1942) 86 SJ 384 (also HL); (1941-42) LVIII TLR 198; (1942) WN (I) 93 CA No appeal to CA in criminal cause or matter (appeal from refusal of habeas corpus application).

Re Amand [1941] 110 LJ 524; (1942) 86 SJ 111; (1941-42) LVIII TLR 186 HC KBD Refusal of habeas corpus application by Dutchman resident in England who was arrested for not returning to service in Netherlands army in England.

Re Amand [1942] 111 LJ 338 HC KBD Refusal of habeas corpus application by Dutchman resident in England who was arrested for not returning to service in Netherlands army in England.

Re an Application for Habeas Corpus [1964] Crim LR 722t PC Failure to establish that British Guianan emergency regulations under which applicant's husband detained were invalid.

Re Bruce Parkyn-Jackson [1988] Crim LR 834 HC QBD Could extradite to the United States wire fraudster who had received suspended sentence and was in breach of his probation.

Re Caborn-Waterfield [1960] 2 All ER 178; [1961] Crim LR 112; (1960) 124 JP 316; (1960) 110 LJ 350; [1960] 2 QB 498; (1960) 104 SJ 369; [1960] 2 WLR 792 HC QBD No extradition of person sought as an 'accused' though in fact a convict.

Re Carroll [1930] All ER 189; (1930) 94 JP 245; [1931] 1 KB 104; (1930) 70 LJ 281; (1931) 100 LJCL 62; (1931) 144 LTR 154; (1930) 74 SJ 770; (1930-31) XLVII TLR 20; (1930) WN (I) 218 CA CA has no original jurisdiction in habeas corpus action but may order security of costs therein.

Re Featherstone (William Oswald) (1953) 37 Cr App R 146 HC QBD Habeas corpus writ generally unavailable to person serving sentence passed by competent court.

Re Greene (1941) WN (I) 110 HC KBD On hearing of habeas corpus applications in person.

Re H (TL) (1968) 118 NLJ 396t VacCt Exercise of habeas corpus powers where grandmother abducted child so as to prevent son-in-law whose marriage to daughter was breaking down from gaining access to child.

Re Harris (1984) 148 JP 584 HC QBD Magistrate's remanding of person in custody immediately after granting bail (at which point person made remark to police officer) permissible.

Re Hastings [1958] Crim LR 687; (1959) 123 JP 502 CA No appeal to CA from Divisional Court on criminal cause or matter so no appeal from failed habeas corpus application.

Re Hastings (No 2) [1958] 3 All ER 625; [1959] Crim LR 125; (1959) 123 JP 79; (1958) 108 LJ 813; [1959] 1 QB 358; (1958) 102 SJ 936; [1958] 3 WLR 768 HC QBD Cannot go from judge to judge within Division.

Re Hastings (No 2) [1959] 1 All ER 698; (1959) 43 Cr App R 47; (1959) 123 JP 266 HC ChD Cannot go from judge to judge/division to division of High Court seeking habeas corpus.

Re Hastings (No 3) [1959] Ch 368; [1959] Crim LR 361t; (1959) 109 LJ 249; (1959) 103 SJ 240 HC ChD Cannot in criminal case seek habeas corpus on same grounds/evidence before ChD judge after application refused by HC QBD judge.

Re Hastings (No 3) [1959] 3 All ER 221; [1959] Crim LR 584t; (1959) 109 LJ 586; (1959) 103 SJ 544; [1959] 1 WLR 807 CA No appeal to CA from ChD on criminal cause or matter.

Re Keenan and another [1971] 3 All ER 883; (1971) 121 NLJ 794t; [1972] 1 QB 533; (1971) 115 SJ 757; [1971] 3 WLR 844 CA Habeas corpus writs from English courts inapplicable in Ireland/Northern Ireland.

Re Kray; Re Kray; Re Smith [1965] 1 All ER 710; [1965] Ch 736; (1965) 49 Cr App R 164; [1965] Crim LR 224t; (1965) 115 LJ 212; (1965) 109 SJ 176; [1965] 2 WLR 626 LC Lord Chancellor cannot hear bail applications/appeals.

Re Lawlor (1978) 66 Cr App R 75 HC QBD Court can look to purpose of arrest when justices asked to back Irish warrant of arrest in England: here not bona fide so habeas corpus writ issued.

Re Lees [1941] 110 LJ 42; (1940) 84 SJ 539; (1940-41) LVII TLR 26 HC KBD Valid detention of alleged fascist under wartime legislation.

Re Lees (1941) 164 LTR 41; (1941) 85 SJ 9; (1940-41) LVII TLR 68 CA Valid detention of alleged fascist under wartime legislation.

Re Mohammed Javid's Application [1984] TLR 268 CA On importance attached by court to cases where appellants are in custody.

Re Mwenya [1959] 3 All ER 525; [1960] Crim LR 59; (1959) 109 LJ 702; [1960] 1 QB 241; (1959) 103 SJ 898; [1959] 3 WLR 767 CA Habeas corpus writ applies to all areas subjected by Crown; writ applies to actual/constructive custodian and ultimately Secretary of State.

Re Mwenya [1959] 3 All ER 525 (also CA); [1959] Crim LR 657t; [1960] 1 QB 241; (1959) 103 SJ 583; [1959] 3 WLR 509 HC QBD Habeas corpus writ applies to all areas subjected by Crown; writ applies to actual/constructive custodian and ultimately Secretary of State.

Re Ofili [1995] Crim LR 880 HC QBD Person unable to provide surety was covered by the custody time limit provisions of the Prosecution of Offences Act 1985, s 22.

Re Philpot [1960] 1 All ER 165; (1960) 44 Cr App R 49; (1960) 124 JP 124; (1960) 104 SJ 168 HC QBD Convict (or legal representatives) need not see Prison Commissioner's report before custodial sentence passed.

Re Raine (Nicola) [1982] TLR 234 HC QBD Where detention was originally non-consensual but later became consensual, writ of habeas corpus would not issue.

Re Shelmerdine and others (1941) 85 SJ 11 HC KBD Failed application for habeas corpus by persons alleging improperly held under wartime detention legislation; was no undue delay in hearing habeas corpus applications.

Re Soering [1988] Crim LR 307 HC QBD Non-disclosure of assurance by US Government to Secretary of State regarding use of death penalty in extradition case where subject of same sought for murder.

Re Tarling [1979] 1 All ER 981; (1979) 68 Cr App R 297; (1979) 143 JP 399; (1979) 129 (1) NLJ 117; [1979] 1 WLR 1417 HC QBD Fresh evidence at second habeas corpus hearing to be evidence unheard at first hearing and which could not previously have been obtained.

Re Walsh (On appeal from a Queen's Bench Divisional Court) (1985) 149 JP 175 HL Failed habeas corpus application where claimed Home Secretary/prison governor under absolute duty to produce remanded person in court on certain date.

Re Wring; Re Cook [1960] 1 All ER 536 HC QBD On habeas corpus hearings.

Re Yi-Ching (Ning) and others (1940) 84 SJ; (1939-40) LVI TLR 3 HC KBD Habeas corpus writ would not apply in respect of foreigner in foreign territory (leased by Britain); no writ of habeas corpus against Government Minister concerned as was only involved tangentially.

RI v Deshpande (Vimlabai) and another [1946] 115 LJ 71; (1945-46) LXII TLR 430; (1946) WN (I) 105 PC Can appeal direct to PC from Indian HC where object to release of person pursuant to habeas corpus application.

Schtraks v Government of Israel and others [1962] 3 All ER 529; [1964] AC 556; [1962] Crim LR 773t; (1962) 112 LJ 717; (1962) 106 SJ 833; [1962] 3 WLR 1013 HL Israeli territory includes areas of de facto control; habeas corpus hearing not akin to appeal/re-hearing; no precise definition of political offences - conjures idea of asylum; test in deciding if committal proper: would reasonable jury have done same?

Secretary of State for Home Affairs v O'Brien [1923] All ER 442; [1923] AC 603; (1923) 87 JP 174; (1923) 58 LJ 331; [1923] 92 LJCL 830; (1923) 129 LTR 577; (1922-23) 67 SJ 747; (1922-23) XXXIX TLR 638; (1923) WN (I) 217 HL Home Secretary cannot appeal habeas corpus writ (issued on appeal by CA) to HL.

The United States of America v Gaynor and another [1905] AC 128; [1905] 74 LJPC 44; (1905) XCII LTR 276; (1904-05) XXI TLR 254 PC Habeas corpus writ on basis that no extraditable offence revealed invalid as determining whether was such offence was reason for detention.

Tilonko v The Attorney-General of Natal (1906-07) XCV LTR 853; (1906-07) XXIII TLR 668 PC Leave to appeal in habeas corpus action refused where issue raised was settled by Act of Parliament.

Zabrovski v Palestine General Officer and Another [1947] 116 LJR 1053; (1947) 177 LTR 369 PC Habeas corpus relief if detained illegally and here though detained under emergency legislation was not illegal.

HANDLING (attempt)

Anderton v Ryan [1985] 2 All ER 355; [1985] AC 560 (also HC QBD); (1985) 81 Cr App R 166; (1985) 149 JP 433; (1985) 135 NLJ 485; (1985) 129 SJ 362; [1985] 2 WLR 968; [1985] Crim LR 503 HL Cannot be guilty of crime where believed was committing crime but was not.

Anderton v Ryan [1985] 1 All ER 138; [1985] AC 560 (also HL); (1985) 80 Cr App R 235; [1984] Crim LR 483; (1984) 128 SJ 850; [1984] TLR 227; [1985] 2 WLR 23 HC QBD Could be guilty of attempted handling of stolen goods though not proved that goods in issue stolen.

Chief Constable of Greater Manchester Police v Ryan (1985) 149 JP 79 HC QBD On what constitutes offence of attempted handling.

Haughton v Smith [1973] 3 All ER 1109; [1975] AC 476; (1974) 58 Cr App R 198; (1974) 138 JP 31; (1973) 123 NLJ 112t; [1974] 2 WLR 1 HL Cannot be attempt to handle stolen goods unless goods handled are stolen goods.

R v Smith (RD) (1973) 117 SJ 429 CA Cannot be guilty of attempt to commit crime where did acts which if uninterrupted would not amount to criminal act.

R v Smith (Roger) [1974] Crim LR 305; (1974) 118 SJ 7; [1974] 2 WLR 1 HL On attempt; on attempted handling.

HANDLING (conspiracy to receive)

R v Bradley [1970] Crim LR 171 CA Six years' imprisonment for airport baggage master guilty of conspiracy to receive stolen property/of receiving.

HANDLING (general)

Anderton v Ryan [1985] 2 All ER 355; (1985) 149 JP 433; (1985) 81 Cr App R 166; [1985] Crim LR 503; (1985) 149 JP 433; (1985) 129 SJ 362; (1985) 135 NLJ 485; (also HC QBD); [1985] 2 WLR 968 HL Cannot be guilty of crime where believed was committing crime but was not.

Attorney-General's Reference (No 1 of 1974) [1974] 2 All ER 899; (1974) 59 Cr App R 203; [1974] Crim LR 427t; (1974) 138 JP 570; (1974) 124 NLJ 483t; [1974] QB 744; (1974) 118 SJ 345; [1974] 2 WLR 891 CA Whether goods taken into police officer's possession a question of officer's intent and that is a matter for jury.

Attorney General's Reference (No 4 of 1979) [1981] 1 All ER 1193; (1980) 71 Cr App R 341; [1981] Crim LR 51; (1981) 145 JP 281; (1980) 130 NLJ 860; (1981) 125 SJ 355; [1981] 1 WLR 667 CA Cheque obtained by deception/bank balance 'goods' under Theft Act.

French and another v Director of Public Prosecutions [1994] TLR 71 HC QBD Could convict/ acquit of handling/theft where person charged with both.

Greater London Metropolitan Police Commissioner v Streeter and another (1980) 71 Cr App R 113; (1980) 130 NLJ 313 HC QBD Was not possession/control for security officer/police to mark/track stolen goods so accused could be convicted of handling.

Griffiths v Freeman; Jones v Freeman [1970] 1 All ER 1117; [1970] Crim LR 348; (1970) 114 SJ 263; [1970] 1 WLR 659 HC QBD Only one offence of handling: general information permissible but undesirable.

Haughton v Smith [1973] 3 All ER 1109; [1975] AC 476; (1974) 58 Cr App R 198; (1974) 138 JP 31; (1973) 123 NLJ 1112t; [1974] 2 WLR 1 HL Cannot be attempt to handle stolen goods unless goods handled are stolen goods.

R v Anderson [1978] Crim LR 223 CrCt On admissibility of evidence of other convictions as proof of guilt of handling.

R v Bellenie [1980] Crim LR 437 CA Quashing of handling conviction in light of jury misdirection as to whether suspicion that goods stolen was adequate basis for handling conviction.

R v Bloxham [1982] 1 All ER 582; [1983] 1 AC 109; (1982) 74 Cr App R 279; [1982] Crim LR 436; (1982) 146 JP 201; [1982] RTR 129; (1982) 126 SJ 154; [1982] 2 WLR 392 HL Buyer of goods not 'another person' for whom goods sold as is buying; buying of goods not disposal or realisation of goods by buyer.

R v Bloxham [1981] 2 All ER 647; (1981) 72 Cr App R 323; [1981] Crim LR 337; [1981] RTR 376; (1981) 125 SJ 198; [1982] TLR 75; [1981] 1 WLR 859 CA Can be undertaking/assisting in retention of goods for anyone benefiting from purchase of goods.

R v Bradley (Ivan) (1980) 70 Cr App R 200; [1980] Crim LR 173 CA Evidence of previous different handling inadmissible in later prosecution for receiving under Theft Act 1968, s 27(3) (a).

R v Brook [1993] Crim LR 455 CA On requisite mens rea for handling.

R v Brown [1969] 3 All ER 198; (1969) 53 Cr App R 527; [1969] Crim LR 489t; (1969) 133 JP 592; (1969) 119 NLJ 602t; [1970] 1 QB 105; (1969) 113 SJ 639; [1969] 3 WLR 370 CA Not revealing whereabouts of stolen goods not conclusive proof of retention thereof.

R v Cash [1985] 2 All ER 128; (1985) 80 Cr App R 314; [1985] Crim LR 311; [1985] QB 801; (1985) 129 SJ 268; [1985] 2 WLR 735 CA Words 'in the course of the stealing' irrelevant to charge of handling save where theft/possession very close in time.

R v Close [1977] Crim LR 107 CA Person could be convicted handling stolen goods despite acquittal of alleged thief of same.

R v Coleman [1986] Crim LR 56 CA On elements of handling.

R v Crispin [1971] Crim LR 229 CA On proximity to offence necessary to be guilty of attempt to handle stolen goods.

R v Dabek [1973] Crim LR 527 CA Person was guilty of handling where received goods from person guilty of obtaining them by deception.

R v Davis [1972] Crim LR 431 CA Evidence of handling after particular handling charge was validly admitted.

R v De Acetis [1982] TLR 21 CA Prosecution must still prove relevant goods to have been stolen even though person charged with handling same says that he believed the goods to be stolen.

R v Deakin [1972] 3 All ER 803; [1972] Crim LR 781; (1973) 137 JP 19; (1972) 116 SJ 944; [1972] 1 WLR 1618 CA Fence undertakes to realise goods for benefit of thief.

R v Dolan (Joseph Daniel Philip) (1976) 62 Cr App R 36; [1976] Crim LR 145t; (1975) 125 NLJ 1066t CA Can be convicted of handling stolen goods and theft where handled goods after theft.

R v Figures [1976] Crim LR 744 CrCt Handling of goods abroad not an offence in England.

R v Foreman [1991] Crim LR 702 CA On evidential basis to support robbery or at least handling conviction.

R v Forsyth [1997] 2 Cr App R 299; [1997] Crim LR 589 CA On theft of thing in action; on ramifications of Preddy decision for Theft Act offences.

R v Gould [1980] Crim LR 432 CA Newspaper advertisements ought to have been admitted where were relevant to determining alleged offender's state of mind regarding price of (possibly handled) goods.

R v Grainge [1984] Crim LR 493 CA On what is meant by 'believing' goods to have been stolen.

R v Grainge [1974] 1 All ER 928; (1974) 59 Cr App R 3; [1974] Crim LR 180t; (1974) 138 JP 275; (1974) 124 NLJ 56t; (1974) 118 SJ 116; [1974] 1 WLR 619 CA Accused must at least suspect but close eyes to possibility that goods were stolen.

R v Gregory [1972] 2 All ER 861; (1972) 136 JP 569 CA Necessary to name owner of common/indistinctive goods to sustain handling conviction.

R v Gregory [1982] Crim LR 229 CA Person acting in 'handling' capacity could nontheless be guilty of theft/burglary.

R v Hack (Alan Terence) [1978] Crim LR 359 CrCt Could infer guilty knowledge but not fact that goods were stolen from their peculiarly low price.

R v Hacker [1995] 1 All ER 45; [1995] 1 Cr App R 332; [1995] Crim LR 321; (1995) 159 JP 62; [1995] RTR 1; (1994) 144 NLJ 1625; (1994) 144 NLJ 1772t; (1994) 138 SJ LB 241; [1994] TLR 591; [1994] 1 WLR 1659 HL Certificate of previous handling conviction may list goods but may be excluded if too prejudicial.

R v Hall (Edward Leonard) (1985) 81 Cr App R 260; [1985] Crim LR 377; (1985) 135 NLJ 604; (1985) 129 SJ 283 CA On what it means to 'know or believe' that goods are stolen (Theft Act 1968, s 22(1)).

R v Kanwar [1982] 2 All ER 528; (1982) 75 Cr App R 87; [1982] Crim LR 532; (1982) 146 JP 283; (1982) 126 SJ 276; [1982] TLR 132; [1982] 1 WLR 845 CA Using stolen goods held by another not assisting in retention; assistance must be physical.

R v Lincoln [1980] Crim LR 575 CA On degree of awareness (that goods stolen) necessary to support handling conviction.

R v McCullum (Miriam Lavinia) (1973) 57 Cr App R 645; [1973] Crim LR 582; (1973) 117 SJ 525 CA Are guilty of handling stolen goods if knew/thought were carrying same though did not know what goods were.

R v McDonald (Lloyd George) (1980) 70 Cr App R 288; [1980] Crim LR 242 CA Jury could take that goods at issue were stolen from accused's admission as to circumstances of obtaining same.

R v Moys (Robert) (1984) 79 Cr App R 72; [1984] Crim LR 494; [1984] TLR 327 CA Subjective question whether accused knew/believed goods were stolen - merely suspecting goods were stolen could not ground handling conviction.

R v Nicklin [1977] 2 All ER 444; (1977) 64 Cr App R 205; [1977] Crim LR 221; (1977) 141 JP 391; (1976) 126 NLJ 1190t; (1977) 121 SJ 286; [1977] 1 WLR 403 CA Where indictment specific as to type of handling can only be convicted of that type of handling.

R v Ofori (Noble Julius); R v Tackie (Nazar) (No 2) (1994) 99 Cr App R 223 CCA Prosecution ought to have proven that cars from abroad had been stolen under relevant foreign law.

R v Overington [1978] Crim LR 692 CA On relevance of admission by accused that knew goods were stolen to determination whether goods subject of alleged handling were in fact stolen.

R v Park (James Chalmers) (1988) 87 Cr App R 164; [1988] Crim LR 238; (1989) 133 SJ 945 CA Goods subject of handling stolen goods prosecution must already have been stolen — mens rea is guilty knowledge at time goods handled.

R v Pethick [1980] Crim LR 242 CA That suspected goods were stolen was not sufficient to render one guilty of handling.

R v Pitchley (Abraham Joseph) (1973) 57 Cr App R 30; [1972] Crim LR 705 CA On what constitutes retention of goods contrary to Theft Act 1968, s 22: here paying money into Post Office was retention.

R v Porter [1976] Crim LR 58 CrCt Defendant's view that goods were stolen was not evidence that goods were stolen.

R v Powers and another [1990] Crim LR 586 CA On what constitutes 'recent' possession.

R v Reader (Alfred Raymond) (1978) 66 Cr App R 33 CA Accused must believe goods to have been stolen to be guilty of handling same.

R v Roberts (William) (1987) 84 Cr App R 117; [1986] Crim LR 122 CA R v Ghosh direction on dishonesty unnecessary where dishonesty not pleaded; jury need not find that handler of stolen goods acted dishonestly towards person who suffered loss.

R v Sainthouse [1980] Crim LR 506 CA Handler could be guilty of theft.

R v Sanders (William John) (1982) 75 Cr App R 84; [1982] Crim LR 695; [1982] TLR 116 CA Mere use of goods know were stolen insufficient to sustain conviction for handling by assisting in retention.

R v Shelton [1986] Crim LR 637; (1986) 150 JP 380 CA On handling/theft.

R v Sloggett [1972] Crim LR 594t; (1971) 115 SJ 655 CA On ingredients of offence of handling.

R v Smith [1973] 2 All ER 896; (1973) 57 Cr App R 666; [1973] Crim LR 508t; (1973) 137 JP 598; (1973) 123 NLJ 371t; [1973] 2 WLR 942 CA Cannot be convicted of handling stolen goods if goods handled are not stolen.

R v Stagg [1978] Crim LR 227 CA Whether accused had requisite knowledge/belief that goods were stolen to support handling conviction a subjective test.

R v Tamm [1973] Crim LR 115 CrCt On elements of offence of dishonest assistance in the realisation of stolen goods.

R v Wheeler (Stephen Godfrey) (1991) 92 Cr App R 279 CA Successful appeal against theft/ obtaining convictions that were good faith purchaser for value of relevant items.

R v Wilkins [1975] 2 All ER 734; (1975) 60 Cr App R 300; [1975] Crim LR 343t; (1975) 139 JP 543; (1975) 125 NLJ 285t CA Evidence of theft/handling conviction where charged with handling relates to guilty knowledge only.

R v Wood (William Douglas) (1987) 85 Cr App R 287; [1987] Crim LR 414; (1987) 131 SJ 840; [1987] 1 WLR 779 CA Evidence of earlier possession admissible in handling prosecution but not statements explaining same/description of how found.

Ryan and French v Director of Public Prosecutions [1994] Crim LR 457; (1994) 158 JP 485 HC QBD On charging theft and handling together as alternative charges.

Scott v Tilley (1937) 81 SJ 864 HC KBD Absent explanation by accused, finding that person had in his possession goods which were reasonable grounds to believe had been stolen meant accused guilty of offence under the Wolverhampton Corporation Act 1925, s 124(1).

HANDLING (incitement to receive)

R v McDonough (1963) 47 Cr App R 37; [1963] Crim LR 203; (1962) 106 SJ 961 CCA Could be guilty of incitement to receive stolen goods though at time of incitement the goods were not actually stolen.

HANDLING (possession)

Director of Public Prosecutions v Brooks [1974] 2 All ER 840; [1974] AC 862; (1974) 59 Cr App R 185; [1974] Crim LR 364; (1974) 118 SJ 420; [1974] 2 WLR 899 PC Possession if in physical custody/control.

Douglas Valley Finance Co, Ltd v S Hughes (Hirers), Ltd [1966] 3 All ER 214; (1965-66) 116 NLJ 1378; [1969] 1 QB 738; (1966) 110 SJ 980; [1967] 2 WLR 503 HC QBD Adverse possession not element of conversion: merely assertion of ownership/control contrary to other's rights of possession/control.

Lockyer v Gibb [1966] 2 All ER 653; [1966] Crim LR 504; (1966) 130 JP 306; (1965-66) 116 NLJ 1062; [1967] 2 QB 243; (1966) 110 SJ 507; [1966] 3 WLR 84 HC QBD Must know are in possession of item, otherwise possession an absolute offence.

R v Carver [1978] 3 All ER 60; (1978) 67 Cr App R 352; (1978) 142 JP 620; (1978) 128 NLJ 635t; [1978] QB 472; (1978) 122 SJ 332; [1978] 2 WLR 872 CA No possession if amount of drug is so minute as to amount to nothing.

R v Cavendish [1961] 2 All ER 856; [1961] Crim LR 623; (1961) 125 JP 460; (1961) 111 LJ 469; [1961] 1 WLR 1083 CCA Must show arranged for delivery of goods or aware that they arrived took control over them: otherwise no possession.

R v Goodwin (William) (1910) 4 Cr App R 196 CCA Once jury decides was mens rea only limited possession necessary to sustain receiving conviction.

R v Graham (Christopher Bruce) (1978) 67 Cr App R 356 CA Conviction for cannabis possession merited as amount found was measurable.

R v Lloyd [1992] Crim LR 361 CA On extent of possession that must be proved to support conviction for burglary/handling.

R v Scott (John) (1909) 2 Cr App R 215 CCA On possession of recently stolen property.

R v Smith (Richard) (1910) 5 Cr App R 77 CCA Matter for jury whether recent possession/whether possession adequately explained.

Warner v Metropolitan Police Commissioner [1968] 2 All ER 356; [1969] 2 AC 256; (1968) 52 Cr App R 373; [1968] Crim LR 380t; (1968) 132 JP 378; (1968) 112 SJ 378; [1968] 2 WLR 1303 HL Possession not absolute offence: if no right to open parcel/ignorant of its contents, no possession.

HANDLING (receiving)

Carter Patersons and Pickfords Carriers Limited v Wessel [1947] 2 All ER 280; (1947) 111 JP 474; [1947] KB 849; (1947) 97 LJ 373; (1947) 116 LJR 1370; (1947) 177 LTR 448; (1947) 91 SJ 446; (1947) LXIII TLR 517; (1947) WN (I) 216 HC KBD Aider and abettor, a principal in second degree, can be treated as principal in first degree; robber passing his stolen goods to receiver can himself be convicted as receiver.

Cohen and another v March [1951] 2 TLR 402 HC KBD Accused's lying as to when came into possession of goods is not per se evidence that goods were stolen.

D'Andrea v Woods [1953] 2 All ER 1028; (1953) 37 Cr App R 182; (1953) 117 JP 560; (1953) 103 LJ 687; (1953) 97 SJ 745; [1953] 1 WLR 1307 HC QBD Receipt of 'property' includes receipt of proceeds of theft/conversion.

Director of Public Prosecutions v Nieser [1958] 3 All ER 662; (1959) 43 Cr App R 35; [1959] Crim LR 128; (1959) 123 JP 105; (1959) 109 LJ 58; [1959] 1 QB 254; (1958) 102 SJ 955; [1958] 3 WLR 757 HC QBD Must know whether property obtained either by felony or misdemeanour to prove receiving.

Hawes v Edwards (1949) 113 JP 303; (1949) WN (I) 206 HC KBD Absent control did not have possession of goods so could not be convicted of receiving same.

Hobson v Impett (1957) 41 Cr App R 138; [1957] Crim LR 476 HC QBD Essence of receiving is that had control of stolen goods.

Police v Reilly [1955] Crim LR 651 Magistrates Person who acted as medium between thief and purchaser of stolen cycle, receiving commission for his services, was not a receiver.

Quinlan v Supermarket (Anthony Jackson) [1966] Crim LR 391g HC QBD Goods stolen by supermarket cashier and passed to packer did not pass into possession of customer who was not therefore guilty of receiving.

R v Alt [1972] Crim LR 552 CA Must know or believe property to be stolen when obtain it in order to be guilty of receiving.

R v Amott [1962] Crim LR 170 CCA Could validly be convicted of separate receiving where charged with joint receiving.

R v Ashworth (George Thomas) (1910-11) 6 Cr App R 112 CCA On joint indictment for stealing/receiving: one person not guilty of receiving unless property not always in exclusive possession of other.

R v Austin [1958] Crim LR 129t CCA Conviction for receiving quashed where despite not placing character in issue accused had been questioned about previous (unserious) income tax conviction as evidence of dishonesty.

R v Auton [1958] Crim LR 549 Sessions Adequate notice given of intention to prove previous conviction.

R v Aves [1950] 2 All ER 330; (1950) 114 JP 402; (1950) 100 LJ 374; (1950) 94 SJ 475; (1950) WN (I) 342 CCA If no/untrue explanation of being in possession of recently stolen goods can infer guilt of receiving.

R v Baines (Mary) (1899-1901) XIX Cox CC 524 (1900) 35 LJ 351; [1900] 69 LJCL 681; (1900) LXXXII LTR 724; (1899-1900) XVI TLR 413 CCR Coverture not defence to receiving - absent evidence of compulsion wife guilty of receiving.

R v Barrow (Albert) (1932-34) 24 Cr App R 141 CCA Possession of cheque received in payment for stolen goods not adequate evidence of possession to sustain charge of having received goods.

R v Batty (William) (1912) 76 JP 388; (1911-12) XXVIII TLR 485 CCA Receiving conviction quashed given tenuous connection between accused and crime.

R v Beetwell [1967] Crim LR 532t CA Receiving conviction quashed where had been no evidence to support same.

R v Berger (Edward) (1914-15) 11 Cr App R 72; [1915] 84 LJKB 541; (1914-15) XXXI TLR 159 CCA Not receiver if did not enjoy control over goods.

R v Bianchi [1958] Crim LR 813 Sessions Person charged with receiving money knowing it to have been obtained by fraudulent conversion might better have been charged with aiding and abetting fraudulent conversion/conspiracy.

R v Blake [1964] Crim LR 142t CCA Could be tried for breaking/stealing though were already convicted of receiving.

R v Booth (1946) 90 SJ 347 CCA On proving receiving.

R v Brooker [1956] Crim LR 489 CCA On possession necessary to be guilty of receiving.

R v Cavendish [1961] 2 All ER 856; [1961] Crim LR 623; (1961) 125 JP 460; (1961) 111 LJ 469; [1961] 1 WLR 1083 CCA Must show arranged for delivery of goods or aware that they arrived took control over them: otherwise no possession.

R v Christ [1951] 2 All ER 254; (1951) 115 JP 410; (1951) 95 SJ 531; [1951] 2 TLR 85; (1951) WN (I) 337 CCA On direction as to larceny/receiving.

R v Cooper (Edward), Shea, and Stocks (1908) 1 Cr App R 88; (1907-08) XXIV TLR 867 CCA Though principal acquitted of common law larceny of fixtures could convict receiver for breach of Larceny Act 1861, s 59.

R v Creamer [1918-19] All ER 222; (1918-21) XXVI Cox CC 393; (1919-20) 14 Cr App R 19; (1919) 83 JP 120; [1919] 1 KB 564; [1919] 88 LJCL 594; (1919) 120 LTR 575; (1918-19) XXXV TLR 281 CCA Absent proof that wife's taking husband's property was larceny recipient thereof could not be convicted of receiving.

R v Evans [1914-17] All ER 628; (1915-17) XXV Cox CC 342; [1916] 85 LJKB 1176; (1916) 114 LTR 616 CCA Conviction for receiving quashed as no evidence thereof.

R v Fallows (1949) LXV TLR 93; (1948) WN (I) 479 CCA That one's co-defendant pleads guilty to receiving is not evidence that one knew goods were stolen or that goods were in fact stolen.

R v Flatman (Arthur) (1912-13) 8 Cr App R 256 CCA Non-presumption of joint possession in receiving prosecution against two persons.

R v Foreman [1991] Crim LR 702 CA On evidential basis to support robbery or at least handling conviction.

R v Freedman (Sidney); R v Freedman (Woolf) (1930-31) Cr App R 133 CCA Must be in possession/control of stolen property to be convicted of receiving same; that intended to commit crime does not mean can be convicted of crime.

R v Froggett [1965] 2 All ER 832; (1965) 49 Cr App R 334; [1965] Crim LR 489g; [1966] 1 QB 152; (1965) 109 SJ 492; [1965] 3 WLR 602 CCA Party not principal in second (or first degree) to theft could be convicted of conspiracy to steal and receiving.

R v Fuschillo [1940] 2 All ER 489; (1938-40) 27 Cr App R 193 CCA Absent proof of theft circumstantial evidence may establish goods were stolen.

R v Garland and another (1911-13) XXII Cox CC 292; (1910) 74 JP 135; (1910) 102 LTR 254; (1909-10) XXVI TLR 130; (1909) WN (I) 252 CCA Can be convicted of misdemeanour of receiving where charged with same though evidence shows guilty of feloniously receiving.

R v Garside [1968] Crim LR 166t; (1967) 117 NLJ 1270t; (1967) 111 SJ 925 CA On proving previous 'possession' of stolen copper such as to indicate guilty knowledge on instant charge of receiving stolen copper.

R v Garth [1949] 1 All ER 773; (1949) 99 LJ 203; (1949) WN (I) 170 CCA Proper direction when summing-up in receiving case.

R v Gleed (Frederick) (1916-17) 12 Cr App R 32 CCA Essence of receiving is control of goods.

R v Goodspeed (Charles) (1910-11) 6 Cr App R 133; (1911) 75 JP 232; (1910-11) 55 SJ 273; (1910-11) XXVII TLR 255 CCA Accessory before burglary can be receiver thereafter; that did not carry out promise to aid and abet burglars was not countermanding of promise.

R v Goodwin (Thomas Henry) (1909) 3 Cr App R 276 CCA Could be charged as receiver (under Larceny Act 1861, s 91) but convicted as accessory under Accessories and Abettors Act 1861, ss 1 and 2.

R v Gordon (Nathan) (1909) 2 Cr App R 52 CCA Servant with guilty knowledge subject to recent possession doctrine.

R v Greatwood (1946) 96 LJ 431 CCA Doctrine of recent possession held not to apply where was three month gap between theft and possession.

R v Grinberg (1916-17) XXXIII TLR 428 CCA On burden of proof in receiving stolen property prosecution.

R v Harvard (Arthur James) (1914-15) 11 Cr App R 2 CCA Not sufficient to say that man reckless/careless as to origin of property has guilty knowledge.

R v Hayes and King [1964] Crim LR 542 CCA Where jury did not accept defence they could then infer that goods were stolen.

R v Head and another (1903) 67 JP 459 Sessions Evidence regarding stolen property taken after theft charged in indictment was inadmissible.

R v Head; R v Warrener (1961) 111 LJ 552 CCA On burden of proof in receiving case.

R v Healey; R v Comerford; R v Owens; R v Smith [1965] 1 All ER 365; (1965) 109 SJ 572; [1965] 1 WLR 1059 CCA Exceptionally can direct issue be decided adversely to accused: unusual in possession on receiving charge; preferable that guidance notes to jury be shown to counsel; need in possession cases to distinguish unlawful assistance/joint possession.

R v Hepworth; R v Fearnley [1955] 2 All ER 918; (1955) 119 JP 516; (1955) 105 LJ 489; (1955) 99 SJ 544 CCA Summing-up to include warning on burden of proof in receiving case where party found in possession soon after theft.

R v Herron [1963] Crim LR 575t CCA Untruths as regards one's possesssion of property could be evidence that property was stolen and one knew it.

R v Holmes (Thomas Charles) and Gregory (George) (1914-15) 11 Cr App R 130 CCA That bought goods cheaply need not mean had guilty knowledge; on possession by occupier of premises.

R v Johnson (Richard) (1910-11) 6 Cr App R 218; (1911) 75 JP 464; (1910-11) XXVII TLR 489 CCA Retention of property post-honest purchase discovery that was stolen not receiving.

R v King [1938] 2 All ER 662; (1938) 82 SJ 569 CCA Stolen property not in possesion of police when received by accused so did receive stolen property.

R v Lewis (Annie) (1910) 4 Cr App R 96 CCA Must be element of possession on accused's part to be convicted as receiver.

R v Lincoln (John Abraham) [1944] 1 All ER 604 CCA Defence not heard on offence for which convicted so conviction quashed; everything in indictment for which there is evidence must go to jury (though judge can state views).

R v Matthews [1950] 1 All ER 137; (1950) 114 JP 73; (1950) 100 LJ 20; [1950] 66 (1) TLR 153 CCA Acquiring property without guilty intent, then appropriating it is stealing not receiving.

R v Middleton (Thomas Mansfield) (1922-23) 17 Cr App R 89 CCA Strict proof of possession needed in receiving prosecution.

R v Misell (Daniel); R v Ringle (Judah); R v Errington (John) (1925-26) 19 Cr App R 109 CCA Meaning of 'obtained' in offence of receiving property obtained via misdemeanour (Larceny Act 1916, s 33).

R v Orris (James) (1908) 1 Cr App R 199; (1909) 73 JP 15 CCA Mere acquiesence to receipt of stolen property not sufficient to justify receiving conviction.

R v Payne (William) (1905) 69 JP 440 CCC Receiving goods stolen by married woman from her husband a common law misdemeanour.

R v Payne (William) (1909) 3 Cr App R 259; (1906) 70 JP 28; (1906) XCIV LTR 288; (1905-06) 50 SJ 112; (1905-06) XXII TLR 126; (1905-06) 54 WR 200 CCR Need not have exclusive possession to be a receiver; receiving goods stolen by married woman from her husband a common law misdemeanour.

R v Peach [1960] Crim LR 134; (1959) 103 SJ 814 CCA Was evidence of joint possession/control of stolen goods that joint tenant of room knew goods were stolen and did not seek to have other joint tenant remove them.

R v Poole and Blake [1959] Crim LR 45 Sessions On what constitutes being an accessory to receiving.

R v Poolman (John) (1909) 3 Cr App R 36 CCA Failure to explain possession of recently stolen property need not merit conviction for stealing and receiving.

R v Power (1918-21) XXVI Cox CC 399; (1919) 83 JP 124; [1919] 1 KB 572; (1919) 120 LTR 577; (1918-19) XXXV TLR 283; (1919) WN (I) 64 CCA CCA can consider defence evidence that incriminates defendant.

R v Pritchard (1913-14) XXIII Cox CC 682; (1913) 48 LJ 689; (1913-14) 109 LTR 911; (1913) WN (I) 338 CCA Absent agreement to receive wife's receiving did not mean husband guilty of receiving.

R v Purdie [1962] Crim LR 560g CCA On what constitutes possession in context of offence of receiving.

R v Reah [1968] 3 All ER 269; [1968] Crim LR 512; (1968) 112 SJ 599; [1968] 1 WLR 1508 CA Receiving provisions of Criminal Law Act 1967 not retrospective in effect.

R v Richards (George) (1924-25) 18 Cr App R 144 CCA Non-substitution by CCA of receiving conviction where acquitted of housebreaking.

R v Rowland (1910) 74 JP 144; [1910] 1 KB 458; (1910) 79 LJKB 327 CCA That pawned goods on day before arrest for receiving was sufficient element of possession; evidence of previous conviction for dishonesty offence admissible to prove guilty knowledge; co-prisoner testifying against another can be asked self-incriminatory questions.

R v Sbarra [1918-23] All ER 255; (1918-21) XXVI Cox CC 305; (1917-18) 13 Cr App R 118; (1918) 82 JP 171; [1918] 87 LJCL 1003; (1918-19) 119 LTR 89; (1917-18) XXXIV TLR 321; (1918) WN (I) 90 CCA Circumstantial evidence may establish that (knowingly) received goods that were in fact stolen.

R v Schama; R v Abramovitch [1914-15] All ER 204; (1914-15) XXIV Cox CC 591; (1914-15) 11 Cr App R 45; (1915) 79 JP 184; [1915] 84 LJKB 396; (1915) 112 LTR 480; (1914-15) 59 SJ 288; (1914-15) XXXI TLR 88 CCA Reasonable explanation offered after prosecution establishes possession of recently stolen goods merits acquittal on receiving charge.

R v Schweller (Joseph) (1924-25) 18 Cr App R 52 CCA Receiving goods in knowledge that seller obtained same by fraud/credit under false pretences not a crime.

R v Seymour [1954] 1 All ER 1006; [1954] Crim LR 475 (1954) 118 JP 311; (1954) 104 LJ 281; (1954) 98 SJ 288; [1954] 1 WLR 678 CCA Should be indicted for larceny and receiving where in possession of recently stolen property and allow jury decide of which are guilty.

R v Sharp [1964] Crim LR 826g CCA Valid finding of joint possession on part of person apparently indirectly party to loading with stolen property of van owned by his wife.

R v Shaw; R v Agard [1942] 2 All ER 342 CCA On meaning of 'possession'; convictions quashed as 'possession' unexplained; on division of trial into readily comprehensible parts where jury confronted with great number of counts.

R v Shears [1969] Crim LR 319 CA On possession as an element of receiving.

R v Smith [1962] 2 All ER 200; (1962) 46 Cr App R 277; [1962] Crim LR 388; (1962) 126 JP 333; (1962) 112 LJ 320; [1962] 2 QB 317; (1962) 106 SJ 265; [1962] 2 WLR 1145 CCA Cannot be receiving under Larceny Act 1916, s 33(1) if theft outside jurisdiction; can be guilty of larceny under Larceny Act 1916 s 33(4) regardless of whether convicted thereof elsewhere.

R v Smith (George) [1918] 87 LJCL 1023; (1918) WN (I) 209 CCA Relevant evidence in receiving trial includes what accused said when found in possession of goods.

R v Smith (George); R v Currier (Frank) (1917-18) XXXIV TLR 480 CCA Relevant evidence in receiving trial includes what accused said when found in possession of goods.

R v Smith (James Reginald) (1922-23) 17 Cr App R 133 CCA On substitution by CCA of larceny conviction for receiving conviction.

R v Smith (Richard) (1910) 5 Cr App R 77 CCA Matter for jury whether recent possession/whether possession adequately explained.

R v Snelling (Eve Nellie) (1940-42) 28 Cr App R 117; (1942) 86 SJ 134 CCA That suspected that goods supplied contrary to rationing legislation did not mean suspected were stolen; on appropriate punishment for breach of rationing laws.

R v South (1907) 71 JP 191 CCC Failed prosecution for receiving money and fraudulently converting same to own use (Larceny Act 1901, s 1(1)(b)).

R v Streeter (1899-1901) XIX Cox CC 570; (1900) 35 LJ 458; [1900] 69 LJCL 915; (1900-01) LXXXIII LTR 288; [1900] 2 QB 601; (1899-1900) 44 SJ 659; (1899-1900) XVI TLR 526; (1900) WN (I) 176; (1899-1900) 48 WR 702 CCR Not felony to receive goods stolen by wife from husband as her larceny not larceny at common law/under Larceny Act.

R v Tennet [1939] 1 All ER 86 CCA Receiver must know property not honestly obtained at moment receives it.

R v Thompson [1965] Crim LR 553g CCA On whether/when to leave one or two charges to jury where person is charged with larceny and, alternatively, receiving.

R v Tomblin [1964] Crim LR 780t CCA Person who took no part in opening stolen safe deemed not guilty of possession of same (though might well be guilty of joint possession of same).

R v Watson [1916-17] All ER 815; (1915-17) XXV Cox CC 470; (1916) 80 JP 391; [1916] 2 KB 385; (1916) 51 LJ 306; [1916] 85 LJKB 1142; (1916-17) 115 LTR 159; (1916) WN (I) 239 CCA Absent sole/joint possession/control of property could not be found guilty of receiving.

R v Watson (George) (1916-17) 12 Cr App R 62 CCA Cannot be convicted as accessory after fact where charged with receiving with guilty knowledge.

R v White (1913-14) XXIII Cox CC 190; (1912) 76 JP 384; (1912-13) 107 LTR 528 CCA Failed prosecution for larceny by finding.

R v Woods [1968] 3 All ER 709; (1969) 133 JP 51; [1969] 1 QB 447; [1968] 3 WLR 1192 CA Cannot convict absent specific/implied charge: receiving not implied in charge of larceny; direction on implied charges to be irreproachable.

R v Young and another [1953] 1 All ER 21; (1952) 36 Cr App R 200; (1953) 117 JP 42 CCA On proof of theft in receiving stolen property trial.

Walters v Lunt and another [1951] 2 All ER 645; (1951-52) 35 Cr App R 94; (1951) 115 JP 512; (1951) 101 LJ 482; (1951) 95 SJ 625; (1951) WN (I) 472 HC KBD Child under eight cannot commit larceny so person acquiring 'stolen' items therefrom not receiving stolen property.

HANDLING (recent possession)

R v Ball [1983] 2 All ER 1089; (1983) 77 Cr App R 131; [1983] 1 WLR 801 CA 'Recent possession' principle applies to handling by assisting in dealing with recently stolen goods.

R v Ball (Anthony); R v Winning [1983] Crim LR 546; (1983) 127 SJ 442; [1983] TLR 354 CA 'Recent possession' principle applies to handling by assisting in dealing with recently stolen goods.

R v Powers and another [1990] Crim LR 586 CA On what constitutes 'recent' possession.

R v Simmons [1986] Crim LR 397 CA On doctrine of 'recent possession'.

R v Wood (William Douglas) (1987) 85 Cr App R 287; [1987] Crim LR 414; (1987) 131 SJ 840; [1987] 1 WLR 779 CA Evidence of earlier possession admissible in handling prosecution but not statements explaining same/description of how found.

HARASSMENT (tenant)

R v Davidson-Acres [1980] Crim LR 50 CA Successful appeal against unlawful eviction prosecution where jury not left with possibility of finding that landlord believed tenants to have ceased to reside in flat.

R v Phekoo [1981] 3 All ER 84; (1981) 73 Cr App R 107; [1981] Crim LR 399; (1982) 146 JP 58 CA Crown must prove accused's intent to harass person he knew to be residential occupier; if claims did not know Crown must show belief not honest.

R v Yuthiwattana (Helen) (1985) 80 Cr App R 55; [1984] Crim LR 562; (1984) 128 SJ 661; [1984] TLR 391 CA Lock-out of tenant for one day and night could be harassment/was not unlawful eviction of occupier.

HIGHWAY (fire)

Hunton v Last [1965] Crim LR 433; (1965) 109 SJ 391 HC QBD Admission by defendant that were guilty of lighting fire within 50m of highway if lit further away with intention that should enter 50m perimeter.

HIJACK (general)

R v Membar (Moussa) and others [1983] Crim LR 618; [1983] TLR 399 CA On meaning/effect of Hijacking Act 1971, s 1(1).

HOMICIDE (attempted infanticide)

R v Smith (KA) [1983] Crim LR 739 CrCt Could be convicted of attempted infanticide under Infanticide Act 1938.

HOMICIDE (attempted murder)

R v Bruzas (John) [1972] Crim LR 367 CrCt On whether provocation a defence to attempted murder; on whether is an offence of attempted manslaughter.

R v Campbell [1997] Crim LR 495 CA Cannot plead diminished responsibility as defence to attempted murder.

R v Gotts [1992] 1 All ER 832; [1992] 2 AC 412; (1992) 94 Cr App R 312; [1992] Crim LR 724; (1992) 156 JP 225; (1992) 142 NLJ 311; (1992) 136 SJ LB 89; [1992] TLR 77; [1992] 2 WLR 284 HL Duress not available as defence to charge of attempted murder.

R v Grimwood [1962] 3 All ER 285; (1962) 46 Cr App R 393; [1962] Crim LR 632t; (1962) 112 LJ 785; [1962] 2 QB 621; (1962) 106 SJ 613; [1962] 3 WLR 747 CCA DPP v Smith inapplicable to attempted murder; direction that if death a foreseeable consequence of accused's actions accused could be guilty of attempted murder, despite absence of intent to kill, a mistaken direction.

R v Jones (Kenneth) [1990] 3 All ER 886; (1990) 91 Cr App R 351; [1990] Crim LR 800; (1990) 154 JP 413; [1990] 1 WLR 1057 CA Pointing of loaded gun at person where gun cannot be fired may be attempted murder.

R v Loughlin [1959] Crim LR 518t CCA On necessary intent for attempted murder.

R v Morris [1977] Crim LR 231 CA Twelve years' imprisonment for attempted murder of burglary victim who could have recognised perpetrator of burglary-attempted murderer.

R v O'Brien (Michael) [1995] 2 Cr App R 649; [1995] Crim LR 734; (1995) 139 SJ LB 130; [1995] TLR 202 CA That knew principal might have intention to kill could sustain conviction of secondary party of attempted murder.

R v Pond [1984] Crim LR 164 CA Plea of guilty to wounding with intent to grievous bodily harm where charged with attempted murder (the two offences requiring different intent) not a defence to latter charge.

R v Pridmore (George Edward) (1912-13) 8 Cr App R 198; (1913) 77 JP 339; (1912-13) XXIX TLR 330 CCA On guilt of parties to common unlawful enterprise for attempted murder by one; on appropriate sentencing for same.

R v Sheldon (Leslie Maxwell) [1996] 2 Cr App R 50 CA Guilty verdict in respect of near-fourteen year old allowed stand despite non-direction as to doli incapax presumption.

R v Walker and Hayles [1990] Crim LR 44 CA On when intent to kill may be inferred.

R v White (1911-13) XXII Cox CC 325; [1910] 2 KB 125; (1910) 79 LJKB 854; (1909-10) 54 SJ 523; (1910) WN (I) 123 CCA Guilty of attempted murder where do one of series of non-lethal acts intended to cause death; liable to punishment for attempted murder under Offences Against the Person Act 1861, ss 11-15.

R v Whybrow (1951) 95 SJ 745 CCA On necessary intent in case of attempted murder.

HOMICIDE (capital murder)

Director of Public Prosecutions v Smith [1960] 3 All ER 161; (1960) 44 Cr App R 261; [1960] Crim LR 765; (1960) 124 JP 473; (1960) 110 LJ 573; (1960) 104 SJ 683; [1960] 3 WLR 546 HL If objectively foreseeable result of voluntary unlawful act is grievous bodily harm then absent inability is presumed intended same.

Lamey v R (1996) 140 SJ LB 174; (1996) TLR 21/5/96; [1996] 1 WLR 902 PC On elements of offence of murder committed 'in the course or furtherance of an act of terrorism' under Offences against the Person Act 1864, s 2 (as amended).

R v Dobbing [1964] Crim LR 723t CCA Valid conviction for capital murder.

R v Duke [1961] Crim LR 833t; (1961) 111 LJ 725 CCA On form of verdict where offender is insane.

R v Grey [1963] Crim LR 44t CCA Valid conviction for capital murder despite alleged flaws in defence/summing up.

R v Jones [1959] 1 All ER 411; (1959) 43 Cr App R 94; [1959] Crim LR 291; (1959) 123 JP 164; (1959) 109 LJ 154; [1959] 1 QB 291; (1959) 103 SJ 133 CCA Post-theft murder done to escape discovery is murder in course of theft, hence capital murder.

R v Marwood [1959] Crim LR 784t CCA Valid conviction for capital murder (of police constable) on basis of confession.

R v Masters (1964) 48 Cr App R 303; [1964] Crim LR 534; (1964) 114 LJ 457; [1965] 1 QB 517; (1964) 108 SJ 465; [1964] 3 WLR 288 CCA Murder committed at moment when intent was intent to steal was capital murder.

R v Matheson [1958] 2 All ER 87; (1957) 41 Cr App R 145; [1958] Crim LR 393t; (1958) 108 LJ 297; (1958) 102 SJ 309 CCA Diminished responsibility a matter for jury; where diminished responsibility one of several defences raised and manslaughter verdict returned judge to ask on which defence is based.

R v Pankotai [1961] Crim LR 546t CCA Straightforward case of capital murder properly left to jury to decide.

R v Simcox [1964] Crim LR 402t CCA On what having one's mental ability 'substantially impaired' involves.

R v Smith [1960] 2 All ER 450; [1960] Crim LR 491t; (1960) 110 LJ 429; (1960) 104 SJ 510 CCA Is possible for person not to intend natural effects of acts though reasonable person would have foreseen them.

R v Spriggs [1958] 1 All ER 300; [1958] Crim LR 190t; (1958) 108 LJ 90; [1958] 1 QB 270; (1958) 102 SJ 89 CCA Definition of terms in Homicide Act 1957, s 2(1) unnecessary when leaving diminished responsibility defence to jury.

R v Stokes [1958] Crim LR 688 Assizes On meaning of 'in the course or...furtherance of theft' (as used in the Homicide Act 1957, s 5(1)).

R v Terry [1961] 2 All ER 569; (1961) 45 Cr App R 180; [1961] Crim LR 479t; (1961) 111 LJ 388; (1961) 105 SJ 445 CCA Diminished responsibility provisions of Homicide Act 1957 (s 2) to be explained to jury: not desirable that just given copy of medical evidence.

R v Vickers [1957] 2 All ER 741; (1957) 41 Cr App R 189; [1957] Crim LR 614; (1957) 121 JP 510; (1957) 107 LJ 473; [1957] 2 QB 664; (1957) 101 SJ 593; [1957] 3 WLR 326 CCA Implied malice doctrine remains post-/constructive malice extinguished by Homicide Act 1957, s 1(1).

R v Walden [1959] 3 All ER 203; [1959] Crim LR 845; (1959) 109 LJ 571; (1959) 103 SJ 875; [1959] 1 WLR 1008 CCA In diminished responsibility direction judge may both refer jury to Homicide Act 1957, s 2 and give general guidance.

HOMICIDE (constructive malice)

Moses (Andrew) v The State [1997] AC 53 PC On constructive malice.

HOMICIDE (general)

Attorney General's Reference (No 4 of 1980) [1981] 2 All ER 617; (1981) 73 Cr App R 40; [1981] Crim LR 493; (1981) 145 JP 394; (1981) 125 SJ 374; [1981] 1 WLR 705 CA Crown need not establish which act caused death where multiple acts capable of causing death.

Chun-Chuen (Lee) alias Wing-Cheuk (Lee) v R [1963] Crim LR 114; (1963) 113 LJ 56; (1962) 106 SJ 1008; [1962] 3 WLR 1461 PC Can rely on defence of provocation even if intended to kill/cause grieveous bodily harm.

Director of Public Prosecutions v Walker (Leary) [1974] Crim LR 368; [1974] 1 WLR 1090 PC Where inter alia force far exceeded what was necessary for self-defence could not successfully plead self-defence.

Mohan (Ramnath) and Another v R [1967] 2 All ER 58; [1967] 2 AC 187; [1967] Crim LR 356; (1967) 111 SJ 95; [1967] 2 WLR 676 PC Person present aiding and abetting in offence - though had not arranged to do so - guilty as principal in second degree (here of murder).

Phillips (Glasford) v R [1969] 2 AC 130; (1969) 53 Cr App R 132; [1969] Crim LR 144; (1969) 113 SJ 14; [1969] 2 WLR 581 PC Test of provocation: did accused lose self-control/would reasonable man have done so (former/latter a question of fact/opinion for jury).

R v Acott [1997] 1 All ER 706; [1997] 2 Cr App R 94; [1997] 2 Cr App R (S) 290; [1997] Crim LR 514; (1997) 161 JP 368; [1997] 2 Cr App R (S) 290; (1997) 141 SJ LB 65; [1997] TLR 90; [1997] 1 WLR 306 HL On evidence necessary to support plea of provocation.

R v Acott (Brian Gordon) [1996] 4 All ER 443; [1996] 2 Cr App R 290; [1996] Crim LR 664; (1996) TLR 5/4/96 CA On evidence necessary to support plea of provocation.

R v Blaue [1975] 3 All ER 446; (1975) 61 Cr App R 271; [1975] Crim LR 648; (1975) 125 NLJ 844t; (1975) 119 SJ 589 CA Person using violence on other must take victim as is.

R v Field [1972] Crim LR 435 CA Are not required to avoid certain streets where have lawful right to be simply because may encounter people antagonistic towards one there.

R v Gittens [1984] Crim LR 553; [1984] QB 698; (1984) 128 SJ 515; [1984] TLR 383; [1984] 3 WLR 327 CA On appropriate direction where combined effect of drink and drugs gave rise to automatism plea.

R v Malcherek; R v Steel [1981] 2 All ER 422; (1981) 73 Cr App R 173; [1981] Crim LR 401; (1981) 145 JP 329; (1981) 125 SJ 305; [1981] 1 WLR 690 CA Disconnection of life support machine does not break causation between inflicting of injury and death.

R v Mellor (Gavin Thomas) [1996] 2 Cr App R 245; [1996] Crim LR 743; (1996) TLR 29/2/96 CA On burden of proof on Crown as regards causation of death where death did not immediately follow on defendant's actions.

R v Pockett [1965] Crim LR 551; (1965) 109 SJ 594 CCA Failed appeal against capital murder conviction on basis that judge did not mention strain under which defendant had been functioning.

R v Spratt [1980] 2 All ER 269; [1980] Crim LR 372; (1980) 124 SJ 309; [1990] TLR 369; [1980] 1 WLR 554 CA Discredited evidence not affecting jury finding of unjustifiable/inexcusable homicide.

R v Twine [1967] Crim LR 710 CA On third party provocation as defence to murder.

R v Williams (Albert) [1968] Crim LR 678; (1968) 112 SJ 760 CA Objective test of provocation under Homicide Act 1957, s 3, unaffected by subjective test of intent in the Criminal Justice Act 1967, s 8.

HOMICIDE (incitement to murder)

R v Krause (1901-02) XVIII TLR 238 CCC Must show some form of communication to support charge of inciting another to murder contrary to Offences against the Person Act 1861, s 4.

R v Shephard [1918-19] All ER 374; (1918-21) XXVI Cox CC 483; (1919-20) 14 Cr App R 26; (1919) 83 JP 131; [1919] 2 KB 125; [1919] 88 LJCL 932; (1919) 121 LTR 393; (1918-19) XXXV TLR 366; (1919) WN (I) 108 CCA Person guilty of incitement to murder where advocate murdering baby after birth when baby as yet unborn.

HOMICIDE (incitement to solicit to murder)

R v Evans [1986] Crim LR 470 CA On whether inciting person to solicit murder equivalent to inciting person to conspire with another to murder.

HOMICIDE (infanticide)

R v O'Donoghue (1926-30) XXVIII Cox CC 461; (1927) 91 JP 199; (1927) 64 LJ 378; (1928) 97 LJCL 303; (1928) 138 LTR 240; (1927) WN (I) 289/297 CCA Verdict of infanticide unavailable as child not newborn/over one month old.

R v O'Donoghue (1927) 71 SJ 897 HC KBD Verdict of infanticide unavailable as child not newborn/over one month old.

HOMICIDE (intoxication)

R v McCarthy (Michael Dennis) (1954) 38 Cr App R 74; [1954] Crim LR 549; [1954] 2 WLR 1044 CCA Drunkenness not provocation nor is it defence to murder (unless so drunk cannot form necessary intent).

HOMICIDE (manslaughter)

Akerele v R [1943] 1 All ER 367; [1943] AC 255; [1943] 112 LJ 26; (1943) 168 LTR 102 PC Preparation of overly-strong medical solution not criminal negligence.

Attorney General's Reference (No 3 of 1994) [1997] 3 All ER 936; [1997] 2 Cr App R (S) 1185; (1997) 147 NLJ 1185; [1997] TLR 411; [1997] 3 WLR 421 HL Conviction for manslaughter of child may follow where deliberate injury to pregnant mother causes child to die after live birth but conviction for murder of child would not follow.

Attorney-General for Ceylon v Perera (Kumarasinghege Don John) [1953] AC 200; (1953) 97 SJ 78; [1953] 2 WLR 238 PC Murder reduced to manslaughter if were reacting proportionately to provocation.

Bullard (Joseph) v R [1957] AC 635; (1957) 41 Cr App R 1; [1957] Crim LR 816; (1957) 121 JP 576; (1957) 101 SJ 797 PC Evidence that does not support self defence plea could support provocation plea; must be clear to jury from direction that burden of proving guilt rests with prosecution.

Director of Public Prosecutions v Beard [1920] All ER 21; [1920] AC 479; (1918-21) XXVI Cox CC 573; (1919-20) 14 Cr App R 159; (1920) 84 JP 129 (also CCA); [1920] 89 LJCL 437; (1920) 55 LJ 116; (1920) 122 LTR 625; (1919-20) 64 SJ 340; (1919-20) XXXVI TLR 379; (1920) WN (I) 110 HL Cannot be guilty of murder if so drunk could not form necessary intent (are guilty of manslaughter); (temporary) insanity deriving from drink will sustain insanity defence.

Director of Public Prosecutions v Daley; Director of Public Prosecutions v McGhie [1980] AC 237; (1979) 69 Cr App R 39; [1979] Crim LR 182; (1978) 122 SJ 860; [1979] 2 WLR 239 PC On what constitutes manslaughter where death occurs in attempt to flee from assault.

Director of Public Prosecutions v Newbury; Director of Public Prosecutions v Jones [1976] 2 All ER 365; [1977] AC 500; (1976) 62 Cr App R 291; [1977] Crim LR 359; (1976) 140 JP 370; (1976) 126 NLJ 618t; (1976) 120 SJ 402; [1976] 2 WLR 918 HL Manslaughter if person un/knowingly does unlawful/dangerous act which causes death.

Jennings v United States Government [1982] 3 All ER 104 (also HC QBD); [1983] 1 AC 624; (1982) 75 Cr App R 367; [1982] Crim LR 748; (1982) 146 JP 396; (1982) 132 NLJ 881; [1983] RTR 1 (also HC QBD); (1982) 126 SJ 659; [1982] TLR 424; [1982] 3 WLR 450 HL Causing death by reckless driving is manslaughter; character of offence for which sought determines if extradition possible.

Kwan (Kong Cheuk) v R [1985] Crim LR 787; (1985) 129 SJ 504 PC Manslaughter by gross negligence conviction quashed in light of misdirection as to elements of same.

Mahadeo v R [1936] 2 All ER 813; (1936) 80 SJ 551; (1936) WN (I) 203 PC Absent malice unintended killing was manslaughter; evidence of accomplice needed corroboration; counsel for accessory could argue that no crime committed though accused pleaded guilty to charge.

Mohammed (Fazal) v The State (1990) 91 Cr App R 256; [1990] 2 AC 320; (1990) 134 SJ 401; [1990] 2 WLR 612 PC Child's evidence inadmissible where judge had not tested capacity of child; manslaughter conviction not possible where medical evidence showed fatal injury could not have been accidental.

Palmer v R [1971] 1 All ER 1077; [1971] AC 814; (1971) 55 Cr App R 223; [1972] Crim LR 649; (1971) 121 NLJ 152t; (1971) 115 SJ 265; [1971] 2 WLR 831 PC If self-defence fails because excessive force a manslaughter sentence need not always follow.

R v Adomako [1994] 3 All ER 79; [1995] 1 AC 171; (1994) 99 Cr App R 362; [1994] Crim LR 757; (1994) 158 JP 653; (1994) 144 NLJ 936; [1994] TLR 363; [1994] 3 WLR 288 HL Gross negligence of duty necessary for involuntary manslaughter - jury to find whether conduct so bad as to be criminal.

R v Anderson and Morris [1966] 2 All ER 644; (1966) 50 Cr App R 216; [1966] Crim LR 385t; (1966) 130 JP 318; [1966] 2 QB 110; (1966) 110 SJ 369; [1966] 2 WLR 1195 CCA Parties to joint action liable for all effects thereof except those caused by one party going further than agreed.

R v Armstrong [1989] Crim LR 149 CrCt Where not proved that heroin killed addict upon injection could not be manslaughter conviction of addict who supplied same (and anyway act of deceased in injecting self was novus actus interveniens relieving supplier of liability).

R v Aston (Roy Edward); R v Mason (Christine Janet) (1992) 94 Cr App R 180; [1991] Crim LR 701 CA Could not infer guilt of both parties charged of child's manslaughter where was no evidence to pointing to one over another.

R v Ball [1989] Crim LR 730 CA On relevance of state of mind to determination whether death resulting from accused's unlawful and dangerous act was manslaughter.

R v Beard (Arthur) (1919-20) 14 Cr App R 110; (1920) 84 JP 129 (also HL); (1919-20) XXXVI TLR 94 CCA On drunkenness as defence reducing murder to manslaughter; where force used in rape which results in death may be murder.

R v Betty (Carol) (1964) 48 Cr App R 6; [1964] Crim LR 132 CCA Where in course of concerted attack (in which was not intended to kill/cause grievous bodily harm) one party forms intent to kill and does (hence murder) other party to concert guilty only of manslaughter.

R v Blaub (1975) 139 JP 841 CA Was stabbing which caused murder even though was refusal (on religious grounds) of victim to accept blood transfusion which necessarily brought about death.

R v Bonnyman (Alexander Gordon) (1940-42) 28 Cr App R 131; (1942) 86 SJ 274 CCA On negligence necessary to sustain manslaughter conviction.

R v Boswell (and others) [1973] Crim LR 307 CA On elements of offence of (constructive) manslaughter.

R v Buck and Buck (1960) 44 Cr App R 213; [1960] Crim LR 760 Assizes Must be found guilty of (at least) manslaughter where death results from criminal abortion; person procuring criminal abortion that results in death is accessory before fact to manslaughter.

R v Burdee (1915-17) XXV Cox CC 598; (1916-17) 12 Cr App R 153; [1917] 86 LJCL 871; (1916-17) 115 LTR 904 CCA Anyone treating another medically must be competent and use reasonable skill: if not and death occurs is manslaughter.

R v Burgess and McLean [1995] Crim LR 425 CA Manslaughter convictions substituted for murder convictions where defence of provocation ought to have been, but was not left to jury.

R v Byers (Jessie) (1910) 4 Cr App R 5 CCA Manslaughter of child by means of cruel treatment - even though post-cruelty betterment in child's condition.

R v Cato and others [1976] 1 All ER 260; (1976) 62 Cr App R 41; [1976] Crim LR 59t; (1976) 140 JP 169; (1975) 125 NLJ 1066t; (1975) 119 SJ 775; [1976] 1 WLR 110 CA Consent of victim to unlawful act not defence/is relevant to question of recklessness/negligence; injection of drug an unlawful act from which manslaughter could spring; substance noxious if likely to cause injury when used; direct, intended injection of drug done 'maliciously'.

R v Chalker (Kate) (1910) 4 Cr App R 2 CCA Manslaughter of child by means of consistently cruel treatment.

R v Chattaway (William) and Chattaway (Ellen) (1922-23) 17 Cr App R 7 CCA Failure to assist person who could not assist self may be manslaughter if death results therefrom.

R v Church [1965] 2 All ER 72; (1965) 49 Cr App R 206; [1965] Crim LR 299t; (1965) 129 JP 366; (1965) 115 LJ 350; [1966] 1 QB 59; (1965) 109 SJ 371; [1965] 2 WLR 1220 CCA Unlawful act resulting in death plus mens rea that act would cause some harm necessary to sustain manslaughter conviction.

R v Clegg [1995] 1 All ER 334; [1995] 1 AC 482; [1995] 1 Cr App R 507; [1995] Crim LR 418; (1995) 145 NLJ 87; (1995) 139 SJ LB 48; [1995] TLR 18; [1995] 2 WLR 80 HL Self-defence plea cannot reduce culpable homicide from murder to manslaughter.

R v Cobbett (1940) 84 SJ 539 CCA Manslaughter/fifteen years' conviction/penal servitude substituted for murder/death verdict/sentence where had been inadequate direction as to possible provocation.

R v Creamer [1965] 3 All ER 257; (1965) 49 Cr App R 368; [1965] Crim LR 552; (1965) 129 JP 586; (1965) 115 LJ 676; [1966] 1 QB 72; (1965) 109 SJ 648; [1965] 3 WLR 583 CCA Involuntary manslaughter if un/intended/foreseen death flows from unlawful act likely to do injury; person seeking/arranging such act an accessory before fact to manslaughter.

R v Curley (James) (1909) 2 Cr App R CCA If well-grounded fear of violence from another moves person to do act which inadvertently causes their death other may be guilty of manslaughter though did no violent act.

R v Dalby [1982] 1 All ER 916; (1982) 74 Cr App R 348; [1982] Crim LR 439; (1982) 146 JP 392; (1982) 126 SJ 97; [1982] 1 WLR 425 CA For unlawful and dangerous act to be actus reus of manslaughter must be directed at victim and likely to cause immediate injury.

R v Dawson (Brian); R v Nolan (Stephen Thomas); R v Walmsley (Ian) (1985) 81 Cr App R 150; [1985] Crim LR 383; (1985) 149 JP 513 CA Is manslaughter if shock which caused in another results in physical harm and then death and reasonable man (without specialist medical knowledge) would have foreseen same.

R v Duffy [1949] 1 All ER 932; (1949) 99 LJ 203 CCA On direction regarding provocation in murder/manslaughter case.

R v Dyson [1908-10] All ER 736; (1907-09) XXI Cox CC 669; (1908) 72 JP 303; (1908-09) XCIX LTR 201; (1907-08) 52 SJ 535 CCA Cannot be convicted of manslaughter where death followed injury by more than year and a day.

R v Evens [1992] Crim LR 659 CA Failure to prove unlawful act on part of appellant that led to death of victim meant manslaughter conviction had to be quashed.

R v Fairbrother (John James) (1908) 1 Cr App R 233 CCA Finding of provocation need not reduce offence with which charged from murder to manslaughter.

R v Finley [1965] Crim LR 105t CCA Reduction of murder conviction to manslaughter where was evidence of provocation (man found at home another man with whom wife had been mixing).

R v Fisher [1987] Crim LR 334 CA Person pleading self-defence entitled to have defence considered on basis of facts as he believed them to be.

R v Garforth [1954] Crim LR 936 CCA Valid conviction for manslaughter where had assaulted another, causing injury which led to death.

R v Gault [1996] RTR 348 CA Slow running over of person with whom had tempestuous relationship properly found to be manslaughter: six years' imposed.

R v Gomez [1964] Crim LR 723 CCA Inadequate direction as to defence of diminished responsibility led to manslaughter verdict being substituted for murder verdict.

R v Goodfellow (Kevin) (1986) 83 Cr App R 23; [1986] Crim LR 468 CA Manslaughter where do unlawful act that reasonable person would foresee exposed some other to chance of harm.

R v Governor of Holloway Prison; ex parte Jennings [1982] Crim LR 590; (1982) 132 NLJ 488; [1983] RTR 1 (also HL); (1982) 126 SJ 413; [1982] TLR 210; [1982] 1 WLR 949 HC QBD Cannot extradite person for manslaughter where evidence suggests are guilty of death by reckless driving.

R v Gray (John Henry) (1916-17) 12 Cr App R 244 CCA Standing by when criminal act committed does not make one guilty of offence.

R v Gross (1913-14) XXIII Cox CC 455; (1913) 77 JP 352 CCC Manslaughter where inadvertently kill third party when fire at other party killing of whom would be manslaughter.

R v Gylee (Harold Burnett) (1908) 1 Cr App R 242 CCA Honest negligence did not preclude it being criminal negligence.

R v Hall (1918-21) XXVI Cox CC 525; (1920) 84 JP 56; (1920) 122 LTR 3 CCA Consideration of coroner's depositions.

R v Hayward (1907-09) XXI Cox CC 692 Assizes Absent proof of violence could convict accused where deceased died from fright resulting from accused's unlawful act.

R v HM Coroner for East Kent; ex parte Spooner and others; R v HM Coroner for East Kent; ex parte De Rohan and others (1989) 88 Cr App R 10; (1988) 152 JP 115 HC QBD Company could be guilty of manslaughter but inadequate case against directors here.

R v Holmes (Leonard) [1946] 1 All ER 524; (1946) 96 LJ 218; (1946) 90 SJ 371; (1945-46) LXII TLR 342 CCA Confession of adultery held not to be provocation reducing murder to manslaughter as husband suspected same for some time/murder was protracted.

R v Hosken [1974] Crim LR 48 CrCt Whether possess requisite mens rea for constructive manslaughter a subjective matter.

R v Howell [1974] 2 All ER 806; (1974) 138 JP 483 CrCt Self-induced intoxication not a defence to manslaughter.

R v Izod (1901-07) XX Cox CC 690 Assizes Must be criminally negligent to new-born child after born to sustain conviction for manslaughter of same through neglect.

R v Jackson (1936) 80 SJ 977 CCA On onus of proof on prosecution/defence respectively in murder/manslaughter cases.

R v Jennings [1990] Crim LR 588 CA Walking around with knife not an unlawful act on which could ground involuntary manslaughter conviction.

R v Jones (1908) 72 JP 215 CCC Can be provocation by words such as to reduce murder to manslaughter.

R v Jones (Ellen) (1899-1901) XIX Cox CC 678 Assizes Presumed to have means to support infant at time of neglect if had so before neglect and would not yet have exhausted same.

R v Lamb [1967] 2 All ER 1282; [1967] Crim LR 537t; (1967) 131 JP 456; (1967) 117 NLJ 834; [1967] 2 QB 981; (1967) 111 SJ 541; [1967] 3 WLR 888 CA Must consider accused's mind when criminal negligence alleged.

R v Lane (L); R v Lane (J) [1985] Crim LR 789 CA On what prosecution must prove in prosecution for manslaughter of child where both parents charged and nothing to prove was one rather than the other.

R v Large [1939] 1 All ER 753; (1939) 87 LJ 181; (1939) 83 SJ 155; (1938-39) LV TLR 470; (1939) WN (I) 73 CCA Careless act cannot support manslaughter conviction; preferably manslaughter to be indicted alone.

R v Le Brun [1991] 4 All ER 673; (1992) 94 Cr App R 101; (1991) 141 NLJ 1262; [1992] QB 61; [1991] TLR 358; [1991] 3 WLR 653 CA If act intended to cause serious harm later followed by connected act causing death can be guilty of manslaughter.

R v Lipman [1969] 3 All ER 410; (1969) 53 Cr App R 600; [1969] Crim LR 546t; (1969) 133 JP 712; (1969) 119 NLJ 768t; [1970] 1 QB 152; (1969) 113 SJ 670; [1969] 3 WLR 819 CA Once act unlawful no intent needed to support manslaughter where death; self-induced drunkenness no defence.

R v Mackie (Robert) (1973) 57 Cr App R 453; [1973] Crim LR 438 CA Liability for injuries/for death suffered in course of escape from assault; liability for same in respect of child to whom are in loco parentis; admission of evidence though prejudicial effect outweighed its probative value.

R v Mason (Tom) (1912-13) 8 Cr App R 121 CCA Drunkenness as defence to murder; words of provocation/abuse plus spitting at accused could reduce murder to manslaughter.

R v Matheson [1958] 2 All ER 87; (1957) 41 Cr App R 145; [1958] Crim LR 393t CCA Diminished responsibility a matter for jury; where diminished responsibility one of several defences raised and manslaughter verdict returned judge to ask on which defence is based.

R v Meade (Thomas) (1909) 2 Cr App R 54; (1909) 73 JP 239; [1909] 1 KB 895; [1909] 78 LJKB 476; (1908-09) 53 SJ 378; (1908-09) XXV TLR 359; (1909) WN (I) 62 CCA That were drunk can reduce apparent murder to manslaughter.

R v Millward (Frederick Thomas) (1931-32) 23 Cr App R 119 CCA That thought wife to have committed adultery did not mean were guilty only of manslaughter when killed her lover.

R v Mitchell [1983] 2 All ER 427; (1983) 76 Cr App R 293; [1983] Crim LR 549; [1983] QB 741; (1983) 127 SJ 305; [1983] TLR 132; [1983] 2 WLR 938 CA Can be manslaughter where accused's act indirectly caused victim's death.

R v Murtagh and Kennedy [1955] Crim LR 315 Assizes On elements of murder/manslaughter by way of knocking-down person with motor vehicle.

R v National Insurance Commissioner; ex parte Connor [1980] Crim LR 579 HC QBD Widow guilty of manslaughter of husband not entitled to state-provided widow's pension.

R v Nuttall [1956] Crim LR 125t CCA Unfaithfulness of wife did not per se constitute provocation reducing murder to manslaughter.

R v O'Driscoll (John) (1977) 65 Cr App R 50; [1977] Crim LR 560 CA No defence of drunkenness available to act of basic intent (setting fire to room).

R v Owen [1972] Crim LR 324 CA Thirty months' imprisonment for (pregnant) woman (who had often been struck by husband) guilty of manslaughter of husband (stabbing under provocation in quarrel).

R v Pagett [1983] Crim LR 393; [1983] TLR 76 CA On necessary causation for murder/ manslaughter (and on operation of novus actus interveniens in that context).

R v Palmer (1913-14) XXIII Cox CC 377; (1912-13) 8 Cr App R 207; (1913) 77 JP 340; [1913] 2 KB 29; [1913] 82 LJKB 531; (1913) 108 LTR 814; (1912-13) XXIX TLR 349; (1913) WN (I) 80 CCA Fiancée's confession of immoral life not sufficient provocation to merit manslaughter and not murder conviction where fiancé kills her in response.

R v Penfold (David); R v Penfold (William) (1980) 71 Cr App R 4; [1980] Crim LR 182 CA To be guilty of manslaughter in course of robbery must have arisen from planned common enterprise.

R v Perman (Sam) [1996] 1 Cr App R 24 CA Joint enterprise to terrify with gun insufficient to sustain manslaughter conviction.

R v Petters and Parfitt [1995] Crim LR 501 CA Must have common plan to hurt another (and communicate said intent to that other) to be guilty of joint enterprise.

R v Phillis (1915-16) XXXII TLR 414 CCA That cross language was spoken not provocation reducing murder to manslaughter.

R v Pike [1961] Crim LR 114 Assizes Conviction for manslaughter of man who was reckless as to whether mistress' inhalation of substance prior to sex would cause her death.

R v Pike [1961] Crim LR 547 CCA Failed appeal against conviction for manslaughter of man who was reckless as to whether mistress' inhalation of substance prior to sex would cause her death.

R v Pittwood (1902-03) XIX TLR 37 Assizes Manslaughter conviction appropriate where train gate-keeper negligently left gate open and person crossing line was killed.

R v Prentice and another; R v Adomako; R v Holloway [1993] 4 All ER 935; (1994) 98 Cr App R 262; [1994] Crim LR 598; (1993) 157 JP 1185; (1993) 143 NLJ 850; [1994] QB 302; (1993) 137 SJ LB 145; [1993] TLR 286; [1993] 3 WLR 927 CA Involuntary manslaughter by breach of duty if gross negligence - not recklessness - results in breach of duty and causes death.

R v Reid (Barry) (1976) 62 Cr App R 109; [1976] Crim LR 570 CA If people go about together with offensive weapons with intent of causing fear to another and one of them actually kills that other, fellow offenders are guilty of manslaughter if did not intend to kill/cause serious injury.

R v Richards (Jason); R v Stober (Ransford) (1993) 96 Cr App R 258 CA Crown could reject manslaughter pleas despite early willingness to do so and seek murder conviction instead.

R v Roberts [1942] 1 All ER 187; (1940-42) 28 Cr App R 102; (1943) 93 LJ 100; (1942) 86 SJ 98; (1941-42) LVIII TLR 138 CCA Style of summing-up a matter for trial judge; if manslaughter verdict possible in murder trial jury must be directed on point.

R v Saunders [1986] 3 All ER 327; (1986) 83 Cr App R 369; [1987] Crim LR 127; (1970) 130 SJ 553; [1986] 1 WLR 1163 CA Jury can return manslaughter verdict without giving not guilty to murder verdict.

R v Saunders [1987] 2 All ER 973; [1988] AC 148; (1987) 85 Cr App R 334; (1987) 137 NLJ 685; (1987) 131 SJ 1002; [1987] 3 WLR 355 HL Jury agreeing no murder but all elements of manslaughter can convict for manslaughter.

R v Scarlett (John) (1994) 98 Cr App R 290; [1994] Crim LR 288; (1993) 143 NLJ 1101; [1993] TLR 276 CA Where use of some force necessary must use force disproportionate to that required in circumstances as accused perceives them to be guilty of manslaughter.

R v Semini [1949] 1 All ER 233; (1948-49) 33 Cr App R 51; [1949] 1 KB 405; (1949) 99 LJ 34; [1949] 118 LJR 556; (1949) LXV TLR 91; (1949) WN (I) 28 CA Chance-medley doctrine no longer exists; test for provocation is that in Holmes v DPP.

R v Seymour [1983] 2 All ER 1058; [1983] 2 AC 493; (1983) 77 Cr App R 215; [1983] Crim LR 742; (1984) 148 JP 530; (1983) 133 NLJ 746; [1983] RTR 455; (1983) 127 SJ 522; [1983] TLR 525; [1983] 3 WLR 349 HL Direction to jury where manslaughter arising from reckless driving.

R v Simpson [1957] Crim LR 815t CCC Nagging/threats by wife reduced her homicide by husband from murder to manslaughter on basis of provocation.

R v Simpson [1914-15] All ER 917; (1915-17) XXV Cox CC 269; (1914-15) 11 Cr App R 218; [1915] 84 LJKB 1893; (1916) 114 LTR 238; (1914-15) XXXI TLR 560 CCA Third party provocation prompting accused to kill victim did not reduce killing to manslaughter.

R v Singh (Sharmpal) [1962] AC 188; [1962] Crim LR 165; (1962) 106 SJ 56; [1962] 2 WLR 238 PC Husband used unlawful force during sex but could be manslaughter as doubt whether intended to kill.

R v Slingsby (Simon) [1995] Crim LR 570 CrCt Death arising from sexual activities (normal intercourse/buggery/insertion of hand into vagina and rectum) all of which were consented to was not manslaughter.

R v Smith [1964] Crim LR 129 CCA On elements of being principal in second degree to/acting in concert towards homicide.

R v Smith [1979] Crim LR 251 CrCt Failed manslaughter prosecution of husband allegedly guilty of reckless disregard of wife (did not get doctor for sick wife who strongly disliked doctors and did not want one present).

R v Smith (Wesley) [1963] 3 All ER 597; (1963) 107 SJ 873; (1964) 128 JP 13; [1963] 1 WLR 1200 CCA Party to concerted act guilty of manslaughter by other as death foreseeable and knew killer had weapon (though party had no intent to kill/cause grievous bodily harm).

R v Stewart; R v Schofield [1995] 3 All ER 159; [1995] 1 Cr App R 441; [1995] Crim LR 420 CA Parties to joint enterprise resulting in death may be guilty of murder or manslaughter unless relevant act not committed in course of joint enterprise or other party to enterprise has a more specific intent.

R v Stone; R v Dobinson [1977] 2 All ER 341; (1977) 64 Cr App R 186; [1977] Crim LR 166; (1977) 141 JP 354; (1977) 127 NLJ 143t; [1977] QB 354; (1977) 121 SJ 83; [1977] 2 WLR 169 CA Reckless towards infirm person for whom have duty of care if indifferent to risk of injury or foresee risk but run the risk.

R v Walsh [1969] Crim LR 668 CA Four years' imprisonment for manslaughter arising from grossly negligent use of gun.

R v Watson [1989] 2 All ER 865; (1989) 89 Cr App R 211; [1989] Crim LR 733; (1989) 139 NLJ 866; (1989) 133 SJ 876; [1989] 1 WLR 684 CA Knowledge of burglar about victim is all knowledge acquired while in house.

R v Watson and Watson (1959) 43 Cr App R 111; [1959] Crim LR 785; (1959) 109 LJ 379 HC QBD Where husband and wife are living together wife can nonetheless be convicted of manslaughter of their child through neglect.

R v Williams and another [1992] 2 All ER 183; (1992) 95 Cr App R 1; [1992] Crim LR 198; [1991] TLR 466; [1992] 1 WLR 380 CA Evidence of joint enterprise concerning all defendants cannot secure conviction of remaining defendants if one defendant acquitted; for liability to arise action following threat must be reasonably foreseeable by assailant and (if death) reasonably recognisable that would have resulted in harm to victim; action disproportionate to threat is novus actus interveniens.

R v Woods (Sidney George) (1921) 85 JP 272 CCC Brother not acting in locus parenti guilty of manslaughter of brother whom struck in face and who died in consequence (as was in status lymphaticus - slight blow caused shock resulting in death).

Rolle v R [1965] 3 All ER 582; [1965] Crim LR 727; (1965-66) 116 NLJ 131; (1965) 109 SJ 813; [1965] 1 WLR 1341 PC Issue of manslaughter to be left to jury where appears accused lost self-control.

HOMICIDE (manslaughter, corporation)

R v P and O European Ferries (Dover) Ltd (1991) 93 Cr App R 72; [1991] Crim LR 695 CCC Corporation can be guilty of manslaughter.

HOMICIDE (motor manslaughter)

Andrews v Director of Public Prosecutions [1937] 2 All ER 552; [1937] AC 576; (1936-38) 26 Cr App R 34; (1937) 101 JP 386; (1937) 83 LJ 304; [1937] 106 LJCL 370; (1937) 81 SJ 497; (1936-37) LIII TLR 663; (1937) WN (I) 188 HL Can be convicted of reckless driving where negligence insufficient to sustain manslaughter charge in case where victim dies.

R v Andrews (1934-39) XXX Cox CC 576; (1937) 156 LTR 464 HL Death through negligent driving to be treated as death through any form of negligence: law of manslaughter remains the same.

R v Baldessare (Cyril) (1931-34) XXIX Cox CC 193; (1930-31) Cr App R 70; (1931) 144 LTR 185; (1930) WN (I) 193 CCA Passenger in recklessly driven car may be guilty of criminal negligence by driving.

R v Gault [1996] RTR 348 CA Slow running over of person with whom had tempestuous relationship properly found to be manslaughter: six years' imposed.

R v Stringer (1931-34) XXIX Cox CC 605; (1933) 97 JP 99; [1933] 1 KB 704; (1933) 75 LJ 96; (1933) 102 LJCL 206; (1933) 148 LTR 503; (1933) 77 SJ 65; (1932-33) XLIX TLR 189; (1933) WN (I) 28 CCA Could be tried together for manslaughter/dangerous driving and convicted of latter.

The Trial of Lord de Clifford (1936) 81 LJ 60 HL Failed prosecution of peer for manslaughter (following motor accident).

HOMICIDE (murder)

Abbott v R [1976] 3 All ER 140; [1977] AC 755; (1976) 63 Cr App R 241; [1976] Crim LR 563; (1976) 140 JP 567; (1976) 126 NLJ 888t; (1976) 120 SJ 538; [1976] 3 WLR 462 PC Duress not defence to party accused of murder as principal in first degree.

Afonja v R [1955] Crim LR 783t PC No leave to appeal murder conviction on issue of provocation (claimed that deceased was member of political party that previously attacked meeting of party to which offender belonged).

Attorney General's Reference (No 3 of 1994) [1996] 2 All ER 10; [1996] 1 Cr App R 351; [1996] Crim LR 268; [1996] 2 FLR 1; (1995) 145 NLJ 1777; [1996] QB 581; (1996) 140 SJ LB 20; [1995] TLR 625; [1996] 2 WLR 412 CA Murder or manslaughter arises if injury to a child in utero or its mother causes child to die after live birth; necessary intent is intent to kill or cause grievous bodily injury to mother.

Attorney General's Reference (No 3 of 1994) [1997] 3 All ER 936; [1997] 2 Cr App R (S) 1185; [1997] 2 Cr App R (S) 1185; [1997] 3 WLR 421 HL Conviction for manslaughter of child may follow where deliberate injury to pregnant mother causes child to die after live birth but conviction for murder of child would not follow.

Attorney-General for Ceylon v Perera (Kumarasinghege Don John) [1953] AC 200; (1953) 97 SJ 78; [1953] 2 WLR 238 PC Murder reduced to manslaughter if were reacting proportionately to provocation.

Attorney-General for the State of South Australia v Brown [1960] 1 All ER 734; (1960) 44 Cr App R 100; [1960] Crim LR 425; (1960) 110 LJ 301; (1960) 104 SJ 268; [1960] 2 WLR 588 PC No defence of insanity by virtue of uncontrollable impulse.

Bedder v Director of Public Prosecutions [1954] 2 All ER 801; (1954) 38 Cr App R 133; [1954] Crim LR 721; (1954) 104 LJ 536; (1954) 98 SJ 556; [1954] 1 WLR 1119 HL Test provocation by reference to reasonable man who need not possess characteristics peculiar to accused.

Bharat, Son of Dorsamy v R [1959] 3 All ER 292; [1959] Crim LR 786; [1959] 3 WLR 406 PC Conviction quashed where assessors aiding judge misdirected by same on provocation.

Bullard v R [1961] 3 All ER 470 PC Provocation if seems an issue to be left to jury though prosecution in murder case.

Director of Public Prosecutions for Northern Ireland v Lynch [1975] 1 All ER 913; [1975] AC 653; (1975) 61 Cr App R 6; [1975] Crim LR 707; (1975) 139 JP 312; (1975) 125 NLJ 362t; (1975) 119 SJ 233; [1975] 2 WLR 641 HL Principal in second degree in murder case can plead duress.

Director of Public Prosecutions v Beard [1920] All ER 21; [1920] AC 479; (1918-21) XXVI Cox CC 573; (1919-20) 14 Cr App R 159; (1920) 84 JP 129 (also CCA); [1920] 89 LJCL 437; (1920) 55 LJ 116; (1920) 122 LTR 625; (1919-20) 64 SJ 340; (1919-20) XXXVI TLR 379; (1920) WN (I) 110 HL Cannot be guilty of murder if so drunk could not form necessary intent (are guilty of manslaughter); (temporary) insanity deriving from drink will sustain insanity defence.

Director of Public Prosecutions v Camplin [1978] 2 All ER 168; [1978] AC 705; (1978) 67 Cr App R 14; [1978] Crim LR 432; (1978) 142 JP 320; (1978) 128 NLJ 537t; (1978) 122 SJ 280; [1978] 2 WLR 679 HL 'Reasonable man' not just adult male; unusual characteristics of accused relevant to 'reasonable man' test.

Director of Public Prosecutions v Daley; Director of Public Prosecutions v McGhie [1980] AC 237; (1979) 69 Cr App R 39; [1979] Crim LR 182; (1978) 122 SJ 860; [1979] 2 WLR 239 PC On what constitutes manslaughter where death occurs in attempt to flee from assault.

Farquharson (Philip) v R [1973] AC 786; [1973] Crim LR 305; (1973) 117 SJ 204; [1973] 2 WLR 596 PC Joint liability for murder under Bahamas Penal Code unaffected by common law.

Frankland v R; Moore v R [1987] AC 576; (1988) 86 Cr App R 116; [1988] Crim LR 117; (1987) 131 SJ 541; [1987] 2 WLR 1251 PC Objective test of intent in Manx murder case inappropriate.

Ghosh v RI (1924-25) XLI TLR 27 PC Where various persons shot at and killed another but could not be proved which shot was fatal each person was guilty of murder.

Holmes v Director of Public Prosecutions [1946] 2 All ER 124; [1946] AC 588; (1945-46) 31 Cr App R 123; [1946] 115 LJ 417; (1946) 175 LTR 327; (1946) 90 SJ 441; (1945-46) LXII TLR 466; (1946) WN (I) 146 HL On provocation reducing murder to manslaughter.

Hyam v Director of Public Prosecutions [1974] 2 All ER 41; [1975] AC 55; (1974) 59 Cr App R 91; [1974] Crim LR 365; (1974) 138 JP 374; (1974) 124 NLJ 320t; (1974) 118 SJ 311; [1974] 2 WLR 607 HL Intent for murder is intend to do acts which could (but need not be intended to) cause really serious bodily harm.

Kam-Kwok (Leung) v R (1985) 81 Cr App R 83; [1985] Crim LR 227 PC Conviction allowed stand despite gross misdirection on mental aspect of murder.

Knowles (Benjamin) v R [1930] AC 366; (1930) 69 LJ 217; (1930) 99 LJPC 108; (1929-30) XLVI TLR 276; (1930) WN (I) 66 PC On trial by jury in Ashanti; conviction quashed as possibility of manslaughter not considered where was possible finding.

Majara (Nkau) v R [1954] Crim LR 464; [1954] 2 WLR 771 PC On what constitutes being accessory after the fact in South Africa; headman's shortcomings in apprehension of ritual murderers which gave them chance to escape made him accessory after the fact to murder.

Mancini v Director of Public Prosecutions [1941] 3 All ER 272; [1942] AC 1; (1940-42) 28 Cr App R 65; (1941) 91 LJ 406; (1942) 92 LJ 52; [1942] 111 LJ 84; (1941) 165 LTR 353; (1941-42) LVIII TLR 25; (1941) WN (I) 212 HL Judge must refer to apparent provocation (if any) even if not argued; direction on manslaughter in murder cases only if manslaughter verdict a real possibility; no ideal summing-up; reasonable doubt as to provocation must reduce verdict from murder to manslaughter.

Mensah (Kwaku) v R [1946] AC 83; [1946] 115 LJ 20; (1946) 174 LTR 96; (1945-46) LXII TLR 83 PC In murder trial if provocation defence arises it must be left to jury.

Moey (Chung Kum) alias Ngar (Ah) v Public Prosecutor for Singapore [1967] 2 AC 173; (1967) 111 SJ 73; [1967] 2 WLR 657 PC Interpretation of Singaporean Penal Code provisions pertaining to murder.

Moses (Andrew) v The State [1997] AC 53 PC On constructive malice.

Muhandi v R [1957] Crim LR 814t PC Master of lion man guilty along with hirers of lion man of murder committed by him as master had enabled the commission of the offence.

Nkambule (Gideon) and Others v R [1950] AC 379 PC Once satisfied crime was committed can under Swaziland law convict accused thereof on accomplice's evidence.

R v Abramovitch [1911-13] All ER 1178; (1913-14) XXIII Cox CC 179; (1911-12) 7 Cr App R 145; (1912) 76 JP 287; (1912-13) 107 LTR 416 CCA Prosecution calling doctor to prove accused sane where defence raised insanity but called no evidence good practice.

R v Adams [1954] Crim LR 720t CCA Insane person who knew the difference between right and wrong could be convicted of offence he committed.

R v Alexander (1913-14) XXIII Cox CC 604; (1913-14) 109 LTR 745 CCA Insanity verdict may not be open to jury just because accused proved mentally deficient.

R v Ali [1989] Crim LR 736 CA On pleading provocation as defence to murder.

R v Appleby (William) (1940-42) 28 Cr App R 1 CCA Where is common design to use violence to resist arrest then where violence results in death all parties to common design guilty of murder.

R v Baillie (John Dickie Spellacie) [1995] 2 Cr App R 31 CA Issue of provocation ought to have gone to jury where accused claimed had been provoked into killing person by their threat to his son.

R v Baker [1994] Crim LR 444 CA Valid decision that alternative verdict of having caused grievous bodily harm with intent not be left to jury in case where accused charged with murder as part of joint enterprise (even though joint enterprise may have ended before killing).

R v Bamborough [1996] Crim LR 744 CA Party to joint enterprise who may have thought pistol was unloaded and to be used for pistol-whipping was guilty of murder where gun in fact loaded and used to kill.

R v Barr (Graham); R v Kenyon (James Stephen); R v Heacock (Anthony Peter) (1989) 88 Cr App R 362 CA Foreseeability of results of one's acts as an aid to jury in deciding whether was intent to kill/do grievous bodily harm.

R v Bathurst [1968] 1 All ER 1175; (1968) 52 Cr App R 251; [1968] Crim LR 334; (1968) 118 NLJ 253t; [1968] 2 QB 99; (1968) 112 SJ 272; [1968] 2 WLR 1092 CA Remark on failure of person of diminished responsibility to give evidence unfair.

R v Beard (Arthur) (1919-20) 14 Cr App R 110; (1920) 84 JP 129 (also HL); (1919-20) XXXVI TLR 94 CCA On drunkenness as defence reducing murder to manslaughter; where force used in rape which results in death may be murder.

R v Becerra (Antonio); R v Cooper (John David) (1976) 62 Cr App R 212 CA On means of dissociating self from common design.

R v Beer [1976] Crim LR 690t; (1976) 126 NLJ 791t CA Hyam direction rarely merited in murder cases (unmerited here).

R v Berry (David Donald) (1986) 83 Cr App R 7; [1986] Crim LR 394 CA History of relationship with victim inadmissible to establish motive in murder without motive or to establish intent when killing occurred.

R v Betts and Ridley (1931-34) XXIX Cox CC 259; (1930-31) Cr App R 148; (1931) 144 LTR 526 CCA Party to common design guilty of murder committed by other party thereto even if latter used more force/acted in way other than agreed.

R v Birchall (1913-14) XXIII Cox CC 579; (1913-14) 109 LTR 478; (1912-13) XXIX TLR 711; (1913) WN (I) 260 CCA Baseless suspicion that deceased committed adultery with killer's wife did not merit manslaughter (and not murder) conviction.

R v Blaub (1975) 139 JP 841 CA Was stabbing which caused murder even though was refusal (on religious grounds) of victim to accept blood transfusion which necessarily brought about death.

R v Brown [1972] 2 All ER 1328; (1972) 56 Cr App R 564; [1972] Crim LR 506t; (1972) 122 NLJ 448t; [1972] 2 QB 229; (1972) 116 SJ 431; [1972] 3 WLR 11 CA Must consider nature of provocation and nature of retaliation when deciding whether provoked reasonable man would have behaved as accused behaved.

R v Burgess and McLean [1995] Crim LR 425 CA Manslaughter convictions substituted for murder convictions where defence of provocation ought to have been, but was not left to jury.

R v Burke; R v Clarkson; R v Howe; R v Bannister [1986] Crim LR 331; (1986) 130 SJ 110 CA On duress as a defence to murder.

R v Burke; R v Howe; R v Bannister; R v Clarkson [1987] Crim LR 480; (1987) 131 SJ 258 HL On duress as a defence to murder.

R v Camplin [1978] 1 All ER 1236; (1978) 66 Cr App R 37; [1977] Crim LR 748; (1977) 127 NLJ 938t; [1978] QB 254; (1977) 121 SJ 676; [1977] 3 WLR 929 CA 'Reasonable man' where youth charged is person of youth's age.

R v Cascoe [1970] 2 All ER 833; (1970) 54 Cr App R 401; [1970] Crim LR 644; (1970) 134 JP 603 CA Proper direction on law/burden of proof necessary once provocation left to jury.

R v Cheshire [1991] 3 All ER 670; (1991) 93 Cr App R 251; [1991] Crim LR 709; (1991) 141 NLJ 743; (1991) 135 SJ LB 11; [1991] TLR 204; [1991] 1 WLR 844 CA Actions that are significant though not immediate cause of death could sustain conviction for murder.

R v Christ; Nkambule (Gideon) and Others v R [1951] 2 All ER 254; [1950] AC 379 PC Once satisfied crime was committed can under Swaziland law convict accused thereof on accomplice's evidence.

R v Clarke [1991] Crim LR 383 CA Entirety of accused's conduct relevant to jury determination whether acted under provocation.

R v Clegg [1995] 1 All ER 334; [1995] 1 AC 482; [1995] 1 Cr App R 507; [1995] Crim LR 418; (1995) 145 NLJ 87; (1995) 139 SJ LB 48; [1995] TLR 18; [1995] 2 WLR 80 HL Self-defence plea cannot reduce culpable homicide from murder to manslaughter.

R v Cobbett (1940) 84 SJ 539 CCA Manslaughter/fifteen years' conviction/penal servitude substituted for murder/death verdict/sentence where had been inadequate direction as to possible provocation.

R v Cocker [1989] Crim LR 740 CA Husband's agreeing to yet another of his ailing wife's requests to end her life could not plead that was provoked by persistence of her requests into killing her.

R v Conroy and Conroy [1954] Crim LR 141 Assizes Jointly tried parents found guilty of murder of newborn child.

R v Coulburn (Darren) (1988) 87 Cr App R 309 CA Doli incapax presumption of under-fourteen year old is rebuttable (here did not apply).

R v Croft [1944] 2 All ER 483; (1942-44) 29 Cr App R 169; [1944] KB 295; [1944] 113 LJ 308; (1944) 170 LTR 312; (1944) 88 SJ 152; (1943-44) LX TLR 226; (1944) WN (I) 46 CCA Mutual suicide agreement per se made survivor an accessory before the fact - to avoid conviction must show agreement was terminated.

R v Cunningham [1981] 2 All ER 863; [1982] AC 566; (1981) 73 Cr App R 253; [1981] Crim LR 835; (1981) 145 JP 411; (1981) 131 NLJ 755; (1981) 125 SJ 512; [1981] 3 WLR 223 HL Intention to cause grievous bodily harm sufficient intent for murder.

R v Cunningham [1981] Crim LR 180 CA On whether intention to cause grievous bodily harm sufficient intent for murder.

R v Davidson (Thomas Joseph) (1934-36) 25 Cr App R 21; (1934) 78 SJ 821 CCA On conviction for murder where is corpus delicti.

R v Dear [1996] Crim LR 595 CA Person could be convicted of murder where caused bleeding that led to death even though deceased may have been responsible for bleeding re-commencing/continuing.

R v Din (Ahmed) [1962] 2 All ER 123; (1962) 46 Cr App R 269; [1962] Crim LR 482; (1962) 112 LJ 353; (1962) 106 SJ 329; [1962] 1 WLR 680 CCA Diminished responsibility to be carefully examined if raised; here whether existed a question of fact though medical evidence important.

R v Dodson [1973] Crim LR 518 CA On effect of drunkenness on intent in context of murder.

R v Donnelly [1989] Crim LR 739 CA That appellant had been using gun as club did not have to mean (and here was not the case) that intended to fire it.

R v Doughty (Stephen Clifford) (1986) 83 Cr App R 319; [1986] Crim LR 625 CA Provocation ought to have been left to jury where killing of baby by father prompted by baby's crying.

R v Duffy [1949] 1 All ER 932; (1949) 99 LJ 203 CCA On direction regarding provocation in murder/manslaughter case.

R v Dyos (Martin) and others [1979] Crim LR 660 CCC Murder conviction unavailable where one of two blows probably caused death but was impossible to know whether single blow struck by defendant was causative blow.

R v Ellor [1920] All ER 475; (1918-21) XXVI Cox CC 680; (1920-21) 15 Cr App R 41; (1921) 85 JP 107; [1921] LJCL 218; (1921) 124 LTR 287; (1919-20) XXXVI TLR 840 CCA Statement understood to mean wife would commit adultery not provocation reducing wife's killing of her from murder to manslaughter.

R v Finlayson - Ex parte the Applicant (1940-41) LVII TLR 270 HC KBD Army officer charged with murder on the high seas to be tried before Court-martial.

R v Finley [1965] Crim LR 105t CCA Reduction of murder conviction to manslaughter where was evidence of provocation (man found at home another man with whom wife had been mixing).

R v Fletcher, Fletcher and Zimnowodski [1962] Crim LR 551t CCA On whether/when death arising from arson will be murder.

R v Giannetto [1996] Crim LR 722; (1996) 140 SJ LB 167; (1996) TLR 19/7/96 CA Jury to be satisfied that accused guilty as principal or as accessory where Crown allege was one or the other.

R v Gibbins (Walter) and Proctor (Edith Rose) (1917-18) 13 Cr App R 134; (1918) 82 JP 287 CCA On neglect of child as basis for conviction of murder of same.

R v Gomez [1964] Crim LR 723 CCA Inadequate direction as to defence of diminished responsibility led to manslaughter verdict being substituted for murder verdict.

R v Graham [1982] 1 All ER 801; (1982) 74 Cr App R 235; [1982] Crim LR 365; (1982) 146 JP 206; (1982) 132 NLJ 113; (1982) 126 SJ 117; [1982] 1 WLR 294 CA Duress tested by reference to person of reasonable self-control so voluntary taking of drink/drugs irrelevant.

R v Grant (Ian Arthur); R v Gilbert (Kenneth) (1954) 38 Cr App R 107; [1954] Crim LR 624t CCA Common design to use violence in commission of non-violent crime means common guilt of murder if death caused by violence.

R v Greening (1913-14) XXIII Cox CC 601; [1913] 3 KB 846; [1914] 83 LJKB 195; (1913-14) 109 LTR 720; (1912-13) XXIX TLR 732 CCA Person's killing of unmarried partner whom discovered in disreputable house was murder: adultery/manslaughter defence not open to unmarried couple.

R v Hancock and another [1986] 1 All ER 641; [1986] AC 455 (also HL); (1986) 82 Cr App R 264; [1986] Crim LR 180; (1986) 150 JP 33; (1985) 135 NLJ 1208; (1985) 129 SJ 793; [1985] 3 WLR 1014 CA Appropriate direction to jury where foreseeability an issue.

R v Hancock; R v Shankland [1986] AC 455 (also CA); (1986) 82 Cr App R 264; [1986] Crim LR 400; (1986) 150 JP 203; (1986) 136 NLJ 214; (1986) 130 SJ 184; [1986] 2 WLR 357 HL Appropriate direction to jury where foreseeability an issue.

R v Hobson [1997] TLR 338 CA Retrial ordered of woman convicted of murder but who may have suffered from 'battered woman's syndrome' (a mental disease only recognised after she had been convicted).

R v Holmes (Leonard) [1946] 1 All ER 524; (1946) 96 LJ 218; (1946) 90 SJ 371; (1945-46) LXII TLR 342 CCA Confession of adultery held not to be provocation reducing murder to manslaughter as husband suspected same for some time/murder was protracted.

R v Hopwood (Edward) (1912-13) 8 Cr App R 143 CCA Killing of another in course of apparent suicide attempt was murder.

R v Howe and another appeal [1987] 1 All ER 771; [1987] AC 417; (1987) 85 Cr App R 32; (1987) 151 JP 265; (1987) 137 NLJ 197; [1987] 2 WLR 568 HL Duress an objective defence not open to those charged with murder in first/second degree; accessory before fact using duress to get another to commit offence can be guilty of greater offence than other.

R v Humphreys [1995] 4 All ER 1008; [1996] Crim LR 431 CA Abnormal immaturity or history of attention seeking relevant to issue of provocation; complex history of provocation requires careful explanation to jury by judge.

R v Hyam [1973] 3 All ER 842; (1973) 57 Cr App R 824; [1973] Crim LR 633t; (1973) 123 NLJ 631t; [1974] QB 99; (1973) 117 SJ 543; [1973] 3 WLR 475 CA That death/grievous bodily harm foreseeable but unintended justified murder conviction.

R v Hyde and others [1990] 3 All ER 892; (1991) 92 Cr App R 131; [1991] Crim LR 133; (1991) 155 JP 430; [1991] 1 QB 134; (1990) 134 SJ 1190; [1990] 3 WLR 1115 CA Secondary party continuing in fight after realising principal may kill/seriously injure other is jointly guilty of murder if principal murders other.

R v Jackson (1936) 80 SJ 977 CCA On onus of proof on prosecution/defence respectively in murder/manslaughter cases.

R v Jarmain [1945] 2 All ER 613; (1945-46) 31 Cr App R 39; [1946] KB 74; (1946) 96 LJ 185; [1946] 115 LJ 205; (1946) 174 LTR 85; (1945) 89 SJ 497; (1945-46) LXII TLR 33; (1945) WN (I) 209 CCA Violent acts (such as using loaded revolver) in course of felony involving personal violence means guilty of murder if death results.

R v Jennion (Yvonne) [1962] 1 All ER 689; (1962) 46 Cr App R 212; [1962] Crim LR 384; (1962) 112 LJ 258; (1962) 106 SJ 224 CCA Jury must resolve conflicting expert (here medical) evidence.

R v Johnson [1989] 2 All ER 839; (1989) 89 Cr App R 148; [1989] Crim LR 738; (1989) 153 JP 533; (1989) 139 NLJ 643; (1989) 133 SJ 596; [1989] 1 WLR 740 CA Self-induced provocation is possible and possibility ought to be left to jury.

R v Jones (1908) 72 JP 215 CCC Can be provocation by words such as to reduce murder to manslaughter.

R v Jordan [1956] Crim LR 700t CCA Post-stabbing hospital treatment found to be cause of death so appellant not guilty of murder.

R v Kersey (Maud) (1907-09) XXI Cox CC 690 Assizes Murder/concealment of birth conviction not possible/possible on evidence though no dead body.

R v King [1964] Crim LR 133g CCA Failed plea of diminished responsibility - on elements of same; no defence that were prompted to kill son by seeing him injured; on provocation as it applies to people of African origin.

R v King [1963] 3 All ER 925; (1964) 48 Cr App R 141; [1965] 1 QB 443 (also CCA); (1964) 108 SJ 1048; [1964] 3 WLR 980 (also CCA) Assizes Death penalty does not make all murder capital murder; charge that murder done in course of theft dropped: no supporting facts; successive murders during one afternoon not done on different occasions.

R v Kopsch (Alfred Arthur) (1925-26) 19 Cr App R 50 CCA There is no defence of uncontrollable impulse.

R v Langham (KR); R v Langham (AD) (1972) 122 NLJ 402 CA Failed appeal against murder convictions on basis that trial judge had slept his way through portion of trial.

R v Lesbini (1914-15) XXIV Cox CC 516; (1914-15) 11 Cr App R 7; [1914] 3 KB 1116; [1915] 84 LJKB 1102; (1915) 112 LTR 175; (1914) WN (I) 362 CCA Test for provocation is would reasonable man lose self-control (individual characteristics of accused irrelevant).

R v Lipman [1969] 3 All ER 410; (1969) 53 Cr App R 600; [1969] Crim LR 546t; (1969) 133 JP 712; (1969) 119 NLJ 768t; [1970] 1 QB 152; (1969) 113 SJ 670; [1969] 3 WLR 819 CA Once act unlawful no intent needed to support manslaughter where death; self-induced drunkenness no defence.

R v Lovesey; R v Peterson [1969] 2 All ER 1077; (1969) 53 Cr App R 461; [1969] Crim LR 374t; (1969) 133 JP 571; (1969) 119 NLJ 485t; [1970] 1 QB 352; (1969) 113 SJ 445; [1969] 3 WLR 213 CA Joint offence and substantive offence separate offences; could not be convicted of murder if common design to rob did not include intent to kill/cause grievous bodily harm.

R v Martindale [1966] 3 All ER 305; (1966) 50 Cr App R 273; [1966] Crim LR 621; (1965-66) 116 NLJ 1433; (1966) 110 SJ 769; [1966] 1 WLR 1564 CMAC Provocation possible despite intent to kill/do grievous bodily harm if acts arose from sudden passion.

R v Mason (Tom) (1912-13) 8 Cr App R 121 CCA Drunkenness as defence to murder; words of provocation/abuse plus spitting at accused could reduce murder to manslaughter.

R v McCarthy (Michael Dennis) [1954] 2 All ER 262; (1954) 38 Cr App R 74; [1954] 2 QB 105; (1954) 98 SJ 356; [1954] 2 WLR 1044 CCA Drunkenness cannot support provocation plea nor is it defence to murder (unless so drunk cannot form necessary intent).

R v McCracken [1965] Crim LR 435g; (1965) 109 SJ 434 CCA Issue of criminal negligence did not always have to be left to jury at homicide trial where even slimmest possibility of such negligence existed.

R v McInnes [1971] 3 All ER 295; (1971) 55 Cr App R 551; [1972] Crim LR 651; (1971) 121 NLJ 883; (1971) 115 SJ 655; [1971] 1 WLR 1600 CA Excessive force in self-defence can ground murder conviction; failure to retreat tends to reasonableness of self-defence.

R v Meade (Thomas) (1909) 2 Cr App R 54; (1909) 73 JP 239; [1909] 1 KB 895; [1909] 78 LJKB 476; (1908-09) 53 SJ 378; (1908-09) XXV TLR 359; (1909) WN (I) 62 CCA That were drunk can reduce apparent murder to manslaughter.

R v Millward (Frederick Thomas) (1931-32) 23 Cr App R 119 CCA That thought wife to have committed adultery did not mean were guilty only of manslaughter when killed her lover.

R v Moloney [1985] 1 All ER 1025; [1985] AC 905; (1985) 81 Cr App R 93; [1985] Crim LR 378; (1985) 149 JP 369; (1985) 135 NLJ 315; (1985) 129 SJ 220; [1985] 2 WLR 648 HL Guidelines on requisite mental element for murder.

R v Moore and Dorn [1975] Crim LR 229 CA Mistake as to which of series of intended criminal acts caused death did not relieve of liability for murder.

R v Morhall [1995] 3 All ER 659; [1996] 1 AC 90; [1995] 2 Cr App R 502; [1995] Crim LR 890; (1995) 145 NLJ 1126; (1995) 139 SJ LB 175; [1995] TLR 431; [1995] 3 WLR 330 HL Glue-sniffing addiction relevant when determining gravity of provocation.

R v Murtagh and Kennedy [1955] Crim LR 315 Assizes On elements of murder/manslaughter by way of knocking-down person with motor vehicle.

R v Nedrick [1986] 3 All ER 1; (1986) 83 Cr App R 267; [1986] Crim LR 742; (1986) 150 JP 589; (1970) 130 SJ 572; [1986] 1 WLR 1025 CA Foresight is evidence of intent but does not constitute intent.

R v Newell [1989] Crim LR 906 CA On provocation as possible defence to murder.

R v Nuttall [1956] Crim LR 125t CCA Unfaithfulness of wife did not per se constitute provocation reducing murder to manslaughter.

R v O'Connell [1997] Crim LR 683 CA Sleeping drug not capable of causing injury giving rise to abnormality of mind such as to ground diminished responsibility defence under the Homicide Act 1957, s 3.

R v Onufrejczyk [1955] 1 All ER 247; (1955) 39 Cr App R 1; [1955] Crim LR 188; (1955) 105 LJ 73; [1955] 1 QB 388; (1955) 99 SJ 97; [1955] 2 WLR 273 CCA Where no body circumstantial evidence can establish occurrence of murder where no other rational explanation.

R v Page [1953] 2 All ER 1355; [1954] Crim LR 61; [1954] 1 QB 170; (1953) 97 SJ 799; [1953] 3 WLR 895 CMAC Subject to civil trial proviso court-martial may try offence committed anywhere if would be offence in England.

R v Pagett [1983] Crim LR 393; [1983] TLR 76 CA On necessary causation for murder/ manslaughter (and on operation of novus actus interveniens in that context).

R v Palmer (1913-14) XXIII Cox CC 377; (1912-13) 8 Cr App R 207; (1913) 77 JP 340; [1913] 2 KB 29; [1913] 82 LJKB 531; (1913) 108 LTR 814; (1912-13) XXIX TLR 349; (1913) WN (I) 80 CCA Fiancée's confession of immoral life not sufficient provocation to merit manslaughter and not murder conviction where fiancé kills her in response.

R v Petters and Parfitt [1995] Crim LR 501 CA Must have common plan to hurt another (and communicate said intent to that other) to be guilty of joint enterprise.

R v Phillis (1915-16) XXXII TLR 414 CCA That cross language was spoken not provocation reducing murder to manslaughter.

R v Porritt [1961] 3 All ER 463; [1961] Crim LR 776t; (1961) 125 JP 605; (1961) 111 LJ 710; (1961) 105 SJ 991 CCA Provocation if seems an issue to be left to jury though prosecution want murder/not manslaughter conviction.

R v Powell and Daniels [1996] 1 Cr App R 14; [1996] Crim LR 201; [1995] TLR 325 CA On necessary mens rea required of junior party charged of murder as part of joint enterprise.

R v Prince [1941] 3 All ER 37; (1941-42) LVIII TLR 21 CCA Reasonable doubt in jury's minds whether act unintended/provoked merits acquittal of accused.

R v Pritchard (1900-01) XVII TLR 310 Assizes Murder of new-born child: on what constitutes separate existence.

R v Raven [1982] Crim LR 51 CCC 'Reasonable man' endowed with peculiar characteristics of accused (mental age of child despite being twenty-two).

R v Richards (Jason); R v Stober (Ransford) (1993) 96 Cr App R 258 CA Crown could reject manslaughter pleas despite early willingness to do so and seek murder conviction instead.

R v Richens [1993] 4 All ER 877; (1994) 98 Cr App R 43; [1993] Crim LR 384; [1992] TLR 560 CA Provocation requires sudden and temporary but not complete loss of control; judge must warn jury to consider alternatives to accused's lies tending to guilt.

R v Roberts [1942] 1 All ER 187; (1940-42) 28 Cr App R 102; (1943) 93 LJ 100; (1942) 86 SJ 98; (1941-42) LVIII TLR 138 CCA Style of summing-up a matter for trial judge; if manslaughter verdict possible in murder trial jury must be directed on point.

R v Roberts [1993] 1 All ER 583; (1993) 96 Cr App R 291; [1993] Crim LR 302; (1993) 157 JP 583; (1992) 142 NLJ 1503 CA That person involved in joint unlawful enterprise guilty of murder by other party of general application; exceptionally judge may have to distinguish fleeting consideration from ongoing realisation of real risk.

R v Roberts [1990] Crim LR 122 CA Provocation decided by reference to reasonable man who has characteristics peculiar to defendant.

R v Robinson [1965] Crim LR 491t CCA Valid decision not to leave provocation to jury.

R v Rook [1993] 2 All ER 955; (1993) 97 Cr App R 327; [1993] Crim LR 698; (1993) 143 NLJ 238; [1993] TLR 87; [1993] 1 WLR 1005 CA Consequences of criminal enterprise need only be foreseeable, not intended, for accessory before fact to be liable; withdrawal from joint enterprise must be unequivocal before liability may be overcome.

R v Rowland (1947) 97 LJ 123; [1947] 116 LJR 331; (1947) 91 SJ 177; (1947) LXIII TLR 156; (1947) WN (I) 86 CCA Refusal to hear appeal at which appellant sought to call man who had after appellant's conviction confessed to crime for which appellant convicted.

R v Rubens (Mark) and Rubens (Morris) (1909) 2 Cr App R 163 CCA All parties to common design guilty of fatal act committed by one.

R v Sanders [1991] Crim LR 781; [1991] TLR 210 CA Person could in light of all the evidence be convicted of murder even though there was uncontroverted medical evidence for defence pointing to diminished responsibility of offender.

R v Sanderson (Lloyd) (1994) 98 Cr App R 325; [1993] Crim LR 857 CA Could ground diminished responsibility defence on paranoid psychosis.

R v Saunders [1986] 3 All ER 327; (1986) 83 Cr App R 369; [1987] Crim LR 127; (1970) 130 SJ 553; [1986] 1 WLR 1163 CA Jury can return manslaughter verdict without giving not guilty to murder verdict.

R v Saunders [1987] 2 All ER 973; [1988] AC 148; (1987) 85 Cr App R 334; (1987) 137 NLJ 685; (1987) 131 SJ 1002; [1987] 3 WLR 355 HL Jury agreeing no murder but all elements of manslaughter can convict for manslaughter.

R v Sawyer [1989] Crim LR 831 CA Judge could of own volition leave provocation as issue to jury if thought that facts merited it (did not merit it here).

R v Seddon (Frederick Henry) (1911-12) 7 Cr App R 207 CCA Case of murder based on cirmstantial evidence; can convict accused who gave evidence against co-accused though do not convict co-accused.

R v Semini [1949] 1 All ER 233; (1948-49) 33 Cr App R 51; [1949] 1 KB 405; (1949) 99 LJ 34; [1949] 118 LJR 556; (1949) LXV TLR 91; (1949) WN (I) 28 CA Chance-medley doctrine no longer exists; test for provocation is that in Holmes v DPP.

R v Sheehan; R v Moore [1975] 2 All ER 960; (1975) 60 Cr App R 308; [1975] Crim LR 339; (1975) 139 JP 636; (1975) 125 NLJ 333t; (1975) 119 SJ 271; [1975] 1 WLR 739 CA Issue for jury is if evidence - including self-induced intoxication - shows accused had intent to kill/do grievous bodily harm.

R v Sherriff and others (1901-07) XX Cox CC 334 Assizes Persons in unlawful possession of ferret ('animals kept in...state of confinement' under Larceny Act 1861, ss 21 and 22) guilty of murder where kill officer seeking to apprehend them.

R v Simpson [1914-15] All ER 917; (1915-17) XXV Cox CC 269; (1914-15) 11 Cr App R 218; [1915] 84 LJKB 1893; (1916) 114 LTR 238; (1914-15) XXXI TLR 560 CCA Third party provocation prompting accused to kill victim did not reduce killing to manslaughter.

R v Slack (Martin Andrew) (1989) 89 Cr App R 252; [1989] Crim LR 903; (1989) 139 NLJ 1075; [1989] QB 775; [1989] 3 WLR 513 CA To be guilty of murder committed in course of unlawful common enterprise must have at least implicitly consented to or taken part in causing serious harm to deceased.

R v Smith (1979) 123 SJ 602 CA Medical reports admissible in evidence to aid jury on question of automatism.

R v Smith [1962] Crim LR 43t CA Person properly convicted of murder where killing in course of pub brawl was part of common design.

R v Smith (PR) [1989] Crim LR 734 CA Evidence of previous behaviour towards deceased admissible to defeat defence of automatism (based on alleged unlikelihood of behaviour if behaving as usually did).

R v Spence (George) (1957) 41 Cr App R 80; [1957] Crim LR 188 CCA Is murder where attempted suicide results in death of another.

R v Stewart; R v Schofield [1995] 3 All ER 159; [1995] 1 Cr App R 441; [1995] Crim LR 420 CA Parties to joint enterprise resulting in death may be guilty of murder or manslaughter unless relevant act not committed in course of joint enterprise or other party to enterprise has a more specific intent.

R v Stone (1937) 81 SJ 735; (1936-37) LIII TLR 1046 CCA Strangulation in course of rape that unintentionally results in death is not analagous to death in course of procuring abortion: DPP v Beard principles applicable.

R v Tandy (Linda Mary) [1989] 1 All ER 267; (1988) 87 Cr App R 45; [1988] Crim LR 308; (1988) 152 JP 453; (1988) 132 SJ 90; [1989] 1 WLR 350 CA On ingredients of diminished responsibility.

R v Thomas [1949] 2 All ER 662; (1948-49) 33 Cr App R 200; [1950] 1 KB 26; (1949) 99 LJ 511; (1949) LXV TLR 586; (1949) WN (I) 379 CCA Person convicted of wounding with intent to murder cannot plead autrefois convict to charge of murder where victim later dies.

R v Thornton [1992] 1 All ER 306; (1993) 96 Cr App R 112; [1992] Crim LR 53; (1991) 141 NLJ 1223 CA Provocation not present if murder on foot of history of domestic violence but no sudden loss of control.

R v Thornton (No 2) [1996] 2 All ER 1023; [1996] 2 Cr App R 108; [1996] Crim LR 597; (1995) 145 NLJ 1888; (1996) 140 SJ LB 38; [1995] TLR 674; [1996] TLR 6/6/96; [1996] 1 WLR 1174 CA Battered woman syndrome relevant when determining if provocation.

R v Wakely; R v Symonds; R v Holly [1990] Crim LR 119 CA On degree of foreseeability of what transpired before party to joint enterprise guilty of act of another party thereto.

R v Wallace (William Herbert) (1931-32) 23 Cr App R 32; (1931) 75 SJ 459 CCA Murder conviction quashed where rested on suspicion.

R v Wallett [1968] 2 All ER 296; (1968) 52 Cr App R 271; [1968] Crim LR 271t; (1968) 132 JP 318; [1968] 2 QB 367; (1968) 112 SJ 232; [1968] 2 WLR 1199 CA On criminal intent (homicide prosecution).

R v Ward [1956] 1 All ER 565; [1956] Crim LR 203; (1956) 106 LJ 153; [1956] 1 QB 351; (1956) 100 SJ 112; [1956] 2 WLR 423 CCA Test of intention is what reasonable man would think.

R v Wardrope [1960] Crim LR 770 CCC On provocation/self defence/drunkenness as defences to murder.

R v Whiteway [1954] Crim LR 143t CCA Valid admission of evidence at murder trial by person whom accused was claimed to have raped; failed appeal against alibi direction as evidence in support of alibi irrelevant once jury accepted accused's confession (which they did).

R v Williamson (Anthony Colin); R v Ellerton (Stephen) (1978) 67 Cr App R 63; [1978] Crim LR 166; (1977) 127 NLJ 1177t CA On requisite intent for murder.

R v Woollin (Stephen Leslie) [1997] 1 Cr App R 97; [1997] Crim LR 519 CA On intent necessary for murder.

R v Xanthou; R v Attard [1962] 1 All ER 863 CCA On leave to appeal in non-capital murder cases.

Rose v R [1961] 1 All ER 859; (1961) 45 Cr App R 102; [1961] Crim LR 404; (1961) 105 SJ 253; [1961] 2 WLR 506 PC Mental abnormality not to be measured by reference to M'Naghten definition of insanity.

Sik-Chun (Lau) v R [1984] Crim LR 424 PC Inadequate direction as to common intent necessary for death resulting from common attack to be murder.

Sodeman v R [1936] 2 All ER 1138; (1936) 82 LJ 117; (1936) 80 SJ 532; (1936) WN (I) 190 PC M'Naghten Rules approved as stood.

Thabo Meli and others v R [1954] 1 All ER 373; [1954] Crim LR 217; (1954) 98 SJ 77; [1954] 1 WLR 228 PC Mistake as to which of series of intended criminal acts caued death did not relieve of liability for murder.

Thuan (Luc Thiet) v R [1996] 2 All ER 1033; [1997] AC 131; [1996] 2 Cr App R 178; [1996] Crim LR 820; (1996) 146 NLJ 513; (1996) 140 SJ LB 107; (1996) TLR 2/4/96; [1996] 3 WLR 45 PC Provocation an objective test to which particular characteristics of defendant have no relevance.

Walton v R [1978] 1 All ER 542; [1978] AC 788; (1978) 66 Cr App R 25; [1977] Crim LR 747; (1978) 142 JP 151; (1977) 127 NLJ 1050t; (1977) 121 SJ 728; [1977] 3 WLR 902 PC Jury may reject diminished responsibility defence even if psychiatrist credits it in evidence.

Wing-Siu (Chan) and others v R [1985] AC 168; (1985) 80 Cr App R 117; [1984] Crim LR 549; (1984) 128 SJ 685; [1984] TLR 411; [1984] 3 WLR 677 PC Person guilty of murder/grievous bodily harm if proved that entered premises as part of unlawful common enterprise and had contemplated that serious bodily harm might result.

Woolmington v Director of Public Prosecutions [1935] All ER 1; [1935] AC 462; (1934-39) XXX Cox CC 234; (1934-36) 25 Cr App R 72; (1935) 79 LJ 380; (1935) 153 LTR 232; (1934-35) LI TLR 446; (1935) 79 SJ 401 HL Crown must show accused's voluntary/malicious act caused death; accused may seek to disprove intent/malice; acquittal if Crown fails in duty/accused's story believed.

HOMICIDE (provocation)

Parker (Frank) v R [1964] AC 1369; [1964] Crim LR 659t; (1964) 114 LJ 472; (1964) 108 SJ 459; [1964] 3 WLR 70 PC Provocation could reduce murder to manslaughter even if provoked intent to kill; accused bears burden of establishing provocation (on balance of probabilities).

R v Walker [1969] Crim LR 146; (1969) 119 NLJ 13t; (1969) 113 SJ 52 CA On whether is necessary for the mode of resentment to bear a reasonable relationship to the provocation.

HOMICIDE (sending letter threatening to murder)

R v Solanke (Ladipo) [1969] 3 All ER 1383; (1970) 54 Cr App R 30; [1970] Crim LR 56; (1970) 134 JP 80; (1969) 113 SJ 834; [1970] 1 WLR 1 CA On what it means to 'maliciously' send a letter threatening to murder (Offences against the Person Act 1861, s 16).

R v Syme (John) (1910-11) 6 Cr App R 257; (1911) 75 JP 535; (1910-11) 55 SJ 704; (1910-11) XXVII TLR 562 CCA Need not intend threat to be convicted under Offences Against the Person Act 1861, s 16. of maliciously sending a letter threating to murder.

HOMICIDE (shooting with intent to murder)

R v Hufflett (Victor) (1920) 84 JP 24 CCC Person who fired revolver wide guilty of resisting/wilfully obstructing police officer in execution of his duty.

R v Short (William Leonard) (1931-32) 23 Cr App R 170 CCA On conviction on basis of common design.

HOMICIDE (soliciting murder)

R v Diamond (Charles) (1920) 84 JP 211 CCC On elements of offence of soliciting unknown individuals to murder contrary to the Offences against the Person Act 1861, s 4.

HOMICIDE (threat to kill)

R v Cousins [1982] 2 All ER 115; (1982) 74 Cr App R 363; [1982] Crim LR 444; (1982) 146 JP 264; [1982] QB 526; (1982) 126 SJ 154; [1982] TLR 67; [1982] 2 WLR 621 CA Self-defence/ prevention of crime lawful excuse to threat to kill; jury direction on burden of proof if lawful excuse exists/absent.

R v Ragg [1995] 4 All ER 155 CA Threat to kill not 'violent offence' under Criminal Justice Act 1991 unless intent of death or injury.

R v Tait (Stephen James) [1989] 3 All ER 682; (1990) 90 Cr App R 44; [1989] Crim LR 834; [1990] 1 QB 290; (1989) 133 SJ 849; [1989] 3 WLR 891 CA Foetus in utero not 'another person' whom can threaten to kill contrary to Offences against the Person Act 1861, s 16.

HOMICIDE (uncontrollable impulse)

R v Kopsch (Alfred Arthur) (1925-26) 19 Cr App R 50 CCA There is no defence of uncontrollable impulse.

HOMICIDE (unlawful killing)

R v Wolverhampton Coroner, ex parte McCurbin [1990] 2 All ER 759 CA Coroner's jury must be convinced beyond reasonable doubt of unlawful killing; otherwise death by misadventure on balance of probabilities.

HOUSING (general)

R v Mabbott [1987] Crim LR 826 CA On what constitutes boarding-house/house in multiple occupation (here for purposes of fire legislation prosecution).

ILL-TREATMENT OF PATIENT (general)

R v Newington (Susan) (1990) 91 Cr App R 247; [1990] Crim LR 593; (1990) 134 SJ 785 CA Ill-treatment and wilful neglect of patient not the same.

INCEST (general)

R v Ball (William Henry) and Ball (Edith Lillian) (1910-11) 6 Cr App R 49; (1911) 80 LJCL 691 (also HL); (1911) 104 LTR 48 CCA Enforcement of HL decision in DPP v Ball and another restoring incest conviction.

R v Edward (Harold) and Priestley (Blanche Annie) (1921-22) 16 Cr App R 143; (1922) 127 LTR 221 CCA Appeals against conviction under Punishment of Incest Act 1908 to be heard in camera.

R v Whitehouse [1977] 3 All ER 737; (1977) 65 Cr App R 33; [1977] Crim LR 689; (1978) 142 JP 45; (1977) 127 NLJ 369t; (1977) 121 SJ 171; [1977] QB 868; [1977] 2 WLR 925 CA Girl under 16 cannot aid and abet in incest; Court of Appeal may hear appeal that offence charged not an offence.

INCITEMENT (attempt to incite perjury)

R v Cromack [1978] Crim LR 217 CA Successful appeal in light of jury misdirection against conviction for attempt to incite perjury.

INCITEMENT (attempted incitement of child to gross indecency)

R v Rowley [1991] 4 All ER 649; (1992) 94 Cr App R 95; [1991] Crim LR 785; (1992) 156 JP 319; (1991) 141 NLJ 1038t; (1991) 135 SJ LB 84; [1991] TLR 347; [1991] 1 WLR 1020 CA Act outraging public decency must outrage public decency in and of itself; preparatory acts to inciting gross indecency not attempted incitement of child to gross indecency.

INCITEMENT (encouraging assassination)

R v Antonelli and Barberi (1906) 70 JP 4 CCC Valid conviction for inciting murder of sovereigns and rulers of Europe.

INCITEMENT (encouraging unlawful carnal knowledge of under-sixteen year old)

R v Chainey [1911-13] All ER 701; (1913-14) XXIII Cox CC 620; (1914) 78 JP 127; [1914] 1 KB 137; (1913) 48 LJ 673; [1914] 83 LJKB 306; (1913-14) 109 LTR 752; (1913-14) XXX TLR 51; (1913) WN (I) 318 CCA Criminal neglect of (under sixteen year old) child socialising with immoral persons did not mean guilty of causing/encouraging unlawful carnal knowledge of same.

R v Moon (Frederick); R v Moon (Emily) (1910) 4 Cr App R 171; [1910] 1 KB 818; (1910) 45 LJ 221; (1910) 79 LJKB 505 CCA Not offence under Children Act 1908, s 17 to encourage seduction of girl already seduced.

INCITEMENT (general)

R v Fitzmaurice [1983] 1 All ER 189; (1983) 76 Cr App R 17; [1982] Crim LR 677; (1982) 132 NLJ 814; [1983] QB 1083; (1982) 126 SJ 656; [1983] 2 WLR 227 CA Incitement to commit offence at common law only possible if offence possible.

R v Hendrickson and Turner [1977] Crim LR 356 CA Satisfactory evidence to justify conviction for incitement.

R v Whitehouse [1977] 3 All ER 737; (1977) 65 Cr App R 33; [1977] Crim LR 689; (1978) 142 JP 45; (1977) 127 NLJ 369t; (1977) 121 SJ 171; [1977] QB 868; [1977] 2 WLR 925 CA Girl under 16 cannot aid and abet in incest; Court of Appeal may hear appeal that offence charged not an offence.

INCITEMENT (incitement of gross indecency)

R v Bentley (1923) 87 JP 55; [1923] 1 KB 403; [1923] 92 LJCL 366; (1922-23) 67 SJ 279; (1922-23) XXXIX TLR 105; (1922) WN (I) 335 CCA Inciting criminal act details of which not arranged/inciting another to incite another to commit criminal act was punishable offence.

INCITEMENT (incitement to cause grievous bodily harm)

R v Sirat (Mohammed) (1986) 83 Cr App R 41; [1986] Crim LR 245 CA Not an offence to incite another to agreeing with a further person that latter will cause grievous bodily harm to yet another person.

INCITEMENT (incitement to commit summary offence)

R v Curr [1967] 1 All ER 478; (1967) 51 Cr App R 113; [1967] Crim LR 301; [1968] 2 QB 944; (1967) 111 SJ 152; [1967] 2 WLR 595 CA No soliciting/conspiracy if persons assisting in committing crime unaware what are doing is offence.

INCITEMENT (incitement to murder)

R v Krause (1901-02) XVIII TLR 238 CCC Must show some form of communication to support charge of inciting another to murder contrary to Offences against the Person Act 1861, s 4.

R v Shephard [1918-19] All ER 374; (1918-21) XXVI Cox CC 483; (1919-20) 14 Cr App R 26; (1919) 83 JP 131; [1919] 2 KB 125; [1919] 88 LJCL 932; (1919) 121 LTR 393; (1918-19) XXXV TLR 366; (1919) WN (I) 108 CCA Person guilty of incitement to murder where advocate murdering baby after birth when baby as yet unborn.

INCITEMENT (incitement to obtain by deception/false pretences)

R v Shaw [1994] Crim LR 365 CA On mens rea of incitement to obtain property by deception.

INCITEMENT (incitement to receive)

R v McDonough (1963) 47 Cr App R 37; [1963] Crim LR 203; (1962) 106 SJ 961 CCA Could be guilty of incitement to receive stolen goods though at time of incitement the goods were not actually stolen.

INCITEMENT (incitement to solicit to murder)

R v Evans [1986] Crim LR 470 CA On whether inciting person to solicit murder equivalent to inciting person to conspire with another to murder.

INCITEMENT (incitement to supply drugs)

R v Chelmsford Justices; ex parte JJ Amos [1973] Crim LR 437 HC QBD Attempt to incite supply of dangerous drug a common law offence (not offence under the Dangerous Drugs Act 1965).

INCITEMENT (incitement to use unlicensed radio)

Invicta Plastics Ltd and another v Clare [1976] Crim LR 131; [1976] RTR 251; (1976) 120 SJ 62 HC QBD Company (but not chairman) advertising for sale speed trap detectors properly convicted of incitement to use unlicensed apparatus for wireless telegraphy.

INDUCEMENT (inducement of unlawful act)

Davis v Thomas (1919-20) XXXVI TLR 39 HC ChD Persons inducing another to do something which is not unlawful for other to do are only responsible for what is done if secured same by unlawful means.

INTIMIDATION (general)

Director of Public Proseutions v Mills [1996] 3 WLR 1093 HC QBD Could be guilty of intimidation via the telephone.

R v Goult (Raymond Arthur) (1983) 76 Cr App R 140 CA On dealing with attempted intimidation of jury inside/outside court.

Shoukatallie v R [1961] 3 All ER 996 PC Judge's direction unsatisfactory but not so coercive as to merit quashing conviction.

Young and others v Peck (1913-14) XXIII Cox CC 270; (1912-13) 107 LTR 857 HC KBD Persons in crowd from which eggs thrown but who had not themselves thrown eggs properly convicted of intimidation.

INTOXICATION (drunk and disorderly)

Director of Public Prosecutions v Kitching [1990] Crim LR 394; (1990) 154 JP 293 HC QBD Police officer could arrest person for being drunk and disorderly in public place.

JOINT ENTERPRISE (attempted murder)

R v O'Brien (Michael) [1995] 2 Cr App R 649; [1995] Crim LR 734; (1995) 139 SJ LB 130; [1995] TLR 202 CA That knew principal might have intention to kill could sustain conviction of secondary party of attempted murder.

JOINT ENTERPRISE (general)

Chan Wing-Siu and others v R (1985) 80 Cr App R 117; (1984) 128 SJ 685; [1984] TLR 411 PC Secondary party guilty as principal of crime committed by primary offender in course of unlawful common enterprise where secondary party perceived risk of crime occurring.

Collins and Fox v Chief Constable of Merseyside [1988] Crim LR 247 HC QBD Where two parties jointly charged but not clear whether one or other acted independently or whether both acted jointly an acquittal is required.

King v R [1962] 1 All ER 816; [1962] AC 199; [1962] Crim LR 166; (1962) 106 SJ 56 PC Conviction quashed where jury's opinion if directed that two did not act in concert cannot be determined.

R v Anderson and Morris [1966] 2 All ER 644; (1966) 50 Cr App R 216; [1966] Crim LR 385t; (1966) 130 JP 318; [1966] 2 QB 110; (1966) 110 SJ 369; [1966] 2 WLR 1195 CCA Parties to joint action liable for all effects thereof except those caused by one party going further than agreed.

R v Appleby (William) (1940-42) 28 Cr App R 1 CCA Where is common design to use violence to resist arrest then where violence results in death all parties to common design guilty of murder.

R v Bamborough [1996] Crim LR 744 CA Party to joint enterprise who may have thought pistol was unloaded and to be used for pistol-whipping was guilty of murder where gun in fact loaded and used to kill.

R v Becerra (Antonio); R v Cooper (John David) (1976) 62 Cr App R 212 CA On means of dissociating self from common design.

R v Betts and Ridley (1931-34) XXIX Cox CC 259; (1930-31) Cr App R 148; (1931) 144 LTR 526 CCA Party to common design guilty of murder committed by other party thereto even if latter used more force/acted in way other than agreed.

R v Carberry [1994] Crim LR 446 CA Party to joint enterprise (knifing) that resulted in death of another could be guilty of manslaughter though had not used knife.

R v Clark; R v Sharp [1991] Crim LR 625 CA Evidence of other criminal damage committed on same occasion as arson and not genuinely separable from latter was properly admitted.

R v Fitzgerald [1992] Crim LR 660 CA On appropriate basis on which party/ies to alleged joint enterprise may be convicted.

R v Grant (Ian Arthur); R v Gilbert (Kenneth) (1954) 38 Cr App R 107; [1954] Crim LR 624t CCA Common design to use violence in commission of non-violent crime means common guilt of murder if death caused by violence.

R v Gray (David John); R v Liggins (William James); R v Riding (Mark); R v Rowlands (Catherine Mary) [1995] 2 Cr App R 100; [1995] Crim LR 45; (1994) 138 SJ LB 199; [1994] TLR 461 CA On admissibility of evidence of fellow parties to unlawful common enterprise against each other.

R v Grundy (Brian); R v Gerrard (Brian); R v Patterson (John) (1989) 89 Cr App R 333; [1989] Crim LR 502 CA Individual could be convicted of wounding with intent to cause grievous bodily harm where harm arose in course of joint unlawful enterprise though may not have involved accused at relevant moment.

R v Hyde and others [1990] 3 All ER 892; (1991) 92 Cr App R 131; [1991] Crim LR 133; (1991) 155 JP 430; [1991] 1 QB 134; (1990) 134 SJ 1190; [1990] 3 WLR 1115 CA Secondary party continuing in fight after realising principal may kill/seriously injure other is jointly guilty of murder if principal murders other.

R v Jubb; R v Rigby [1984] Crim LR 616 CA On when parties to joint enterprise (robbery) are liable for further offence (murder) committed by one party to joint enterprise in course of same.

R v Lovesey; R v Peterson [1969] 2 All ER 1077; (1969) 53 Cr App R 461; [1969] Crim LR 374t; (1969) 133 JP 571; (1969) 119 NLJ 485t; [1970] 1 QB 352; (1969) 113 SJ 445; [1969] 3 WLR 213 CA Joint offence and substantive offence separate offences; could not be convicted of murder if common design to rob did not include intent to kill/cause grievous bodily harm.

R v Mahmood (Asaf) [1994] Crim LR 368; [1995] RTR 48 CA Passenger jointly taking car without authority not guilty of joint enterprise when leaped along with driver from moving car which drove into pram killing child therein.

R v Maxwell [1994] Crim LR 848 CA Improper not to direct jury of availability of alternative verdicts in case involving joint enterprise.

R v Penfold (David); R v Penfold (William) (1980) 71 Cr App R 4; [1980] Crim LR 182 CA To be guilty of manslaughter in course of robbery must have arisen from planned common enterprise.

R v Petters and Parfitt [1995] Crim LR 501 CA Must have common plan to hurt another (and communicate said intent to that other) to be guilty of joint enterprise.

R v Pridmore (George Edward) (1912-13) 8 Cr App R 198; (1913) 77 JP 339; (1912-13) XXIX TLR 330 CCA On guilt of parties to common unlawful enterprise for attempted murder by one; on appropriate sentencing for same.

R v Roberts [1993] 1 All ER 583; (1993) 96 Cr App R 291; [1993] Crim LR 302; (1993) 157 JP 583; (1992) 142 NLJ 1503 CA That person involved in joint unlawful enterprise guilty of murder by other party of general application; exceptionally judge may have to distinguish fleeting consideration from ongoing realisation of real risk.

R v Rubens (Mark) and Rubens (Morris) (1909) 2 Cr App R 163 CCA All parties to common design guilty of fatal act committed by one.

R v Russell (Marion) and Russell (Andrew Louis) (1987) 85 Cr App R 388; [1987] Crim LR 494 CA Could infer that parents jointly responsible for administering drug where no proof one rather than another guilty/one did not interrupt ill-treatment of child by other.

R v Shepherd (Martin Brian) (1988) 86 Cr App R 47; [1987] Crim LR 686 CA On availability of duress defence to person voluntarily involved in joint criminal enterprise.

R v Short (William Leonard) (1931-32) 23 Cr App R 170 CCA On conviction on basis of common design.

R v Slack (Martin Andrew) (1989) 89 Cr App R 252; [1989] Crim LR 903; (1989) 139 NLJ 1075; [1989] QB 775; [1989] 3 WLR 513 CA To be guilty of murder committed in course of unlawful common enterprise must have at least implicitly consented to or taken part in causing serious harm to deceased.

R v Smith [1988] Crim LR 616 CA On mens rea necessary to be guilty of act undertaken as part of joint enterprise.

R v Smith [1962] Crim LR 43t CA Person properly convicted of murder where killing in course of pub brawl was part of common design.

R v Smith (Wesley) [1963] 3 All ER 597; (1963) 107 SJ 873; (1964) 128 JP 13; [1963] 1 WLR 1200 CCA Party to concerted act guilty of manslaughter by other as death foreseeable and knew killer had weapon (though party had no intent to kill/cause grievous bodily harm).

R v Wakely; R v Symonds; R v Holly [1990] Crim LR 119 CA On degree of foreseeability of what transpired before party to joint enterprise guilty of act of another party thereto.

R v Wan and Chan [1995] Crim LR 296 CA On liability of party to joint enterprise where another party goes further than was agreed.

R v Wheeelhouse [1994] Crim LR 756 CA Could convict/acquit one/other co-accused jointly charged with burglary.

R v Whitefield (Arthur Armour Mallie) (1984) 79 Cr App R 36; [1984] Crim LR 97 CA To extricate oneself from unlawful common enterprise must unequivocally explain to others that are not party to enterprise and will not help at all.

Scarsbrook v Mason (1961) 105 SJ 889 HC QBD Parties in car jointly/severally liable for negligent driving by driver.

JOINT ENTERPRISE (homicide)

R v Stewart; R v Schofield [1995] 3 All ER 159; [1995] 1 Cr App R 441; [1995] Crim LR 420 CA Parties to joint enterprise resulting in death may be guilty of murder or manslaughter unless relevant act not committed in course of joint enterprise or other party to enterprise has a more specific intent.

JOINT ENTERPRISE (husband and wife)

R v Hoar; R v Hoar [1982] Crim LR 606 CA On when may convict husband/wife for joint criminal enterprise.

JOINT ENTERPRISE (manslaughter)

R v Perman (Sam) [1996] 1 Cr App R 24 CA Joint enterprise to terrify with gun insufficient to sustain manslaughter conviction.

R v Smith [1964] Crim LR 129 CCA On elements of being principal in second degree to/acting in concert towards homicide.

JOINT ENTERPRISE (murder)

R v Powell and Daniels [1996] 1 Cr App R 14; [1996] Crim LR 201; [1995] TLR 325 CA On necessary mens rea required of junior party charged of murder as part of joint enterprise.

JOINT ENTERPRISE (possession of drugs)

R v Downes [1984] Crim LR 552 CA Not possession with intent to supply where have joint possession of controlled drug but (unlike party with whom sharing possession) do not intend to supply same (though know of other party's intention to do so).

R v Searle and others [1972] Crim LR 592; (1971) 115 SJ 739 CA On what constitutes 'joint possession' of drugs.

R v Sharp [1964] Crim LR 826g CCA Valid finding of joint possession on part of person apparently indirectly party to loading with stolen property of van owned by his wife.

R v Tomblin [1964] Crim LR 780t CCA Person who took no part in opening stolen safe deemed not guilty of possession of same (though might well be guilty of joint possession of same).

KEEPING UNCUSTOMED GOODS (general)

Sayce v Coupe [1952] 2 All ER 715; [1953] 1 QB 1 HC QBD Buying from unlicensed seller uncustomed tobacco using some/giving rest away is keeping uncustomed goods.

KIDNAP (general)

R v C [1991] 2 FLR 252; [1990] TLR 714 CA Conviction of father (who took own child outside jurisdiction without consent of mother-joint custodian) for child kidnapping (common law offence)/abduction quashed/upheld.

R v D [1984] 2 All ER 449; [1984] AC 778 (also CA); (1984) 79 Cr App R 313; [1984] Crim LR 558; [1984] FLR 847; (1984) 128 SJ 469; [1984] TLR 401; [1984] 3 WLR 186 HL Parent's taking/carrying away of child by force/fraud is kidnapping; parental kidnapping best dealt with as contempt.

R v D [1984] AC 778 (also HL); (1984) 78 Cr App R 219; [1984] Crim LR 103; [1984] FLR 300; (1984) 128 SJ 63; [1983] TLR 641; [1984] 2 WLR 112 CA Parent's taking/carrying away of own unmarried under-fourteen year old child by force/fraud is not kidnapping; parental kidnapping best dealt with as contempt.

R v Hale [1974] 1 All ER 1107; (1974) 59 Cr App R 1; (1974) 138 JP 294; [1974] QB 819; (1974) 118 SJ 548; [1974] 3 WLR 249 CrCt Absent force/fraud/lack of consent kidnapping impossible.

R v Henman [1987] Crim LR 333 CA Was not defence to kidnapping that committed act to protect kidnapped person from malign influence of religious sect to which latter belonged.

R v Hutchins [1988] Crim LR 379 CA On ingredients of false imprisonment/kidnapping: both may be committed through recklessness.

R v Reid [1972] 2 All ER 1350; (1972) 56 Cr App R 703; [1972] Crim LR 553t; (1972) 136 JP 624; (1972) 122 NLJ 634t; [1973] QB 299; [1972] 3 WLR 395 CA Husband may kidnap wife (even if two co-habiting); kidnapping complete if seize and carry away person.

R v Sherry; R v El Yamani [1993] Crim LR 536 CA Non-parent could be guilty of conspiracy with parent to abduct child of latter.

R v Wellard [1978] 3 All ER 161; (1978) 67 Cr App R 364; (1978) 142 JP 641; (1978) 128 NLJ 587t; (1978) 122 SJ 433; [1978] 1 WLR 921 CA False imprisonment sole requirement for kidnapping.

LANDLORD AND TENANT (unlawful eviction)

R v Blankley [1979] Crim LR 166/248 CrCt Contractual licensee not protected under the Rent Act 1965, s 30.

LARCENY (theft)

McErlaine v Jeffrey [1955] Crim LR 312 Sessions Conviction for theft of pedal cycle quashed as was inadequate evidence of intention to permanently deprive owner of same.

LOTTERY (general)

Dew v Director of Public Prosecutions (1920-21) XXXVII TLR 22 HC KBD Publication of draft ticket sale scheme to printers could sustain conviction under Lotteries Act 1823, s 41.

MENS REA (arson)

Attorney General's Reference (No 3 of 1992) [1994] 2 All ER 121; (1994) 98 Cr App R 383; [1994] Crim LR 348; (1993) 143 NLJ 1675; [1994] RTR 122; (1993) 137 SJ LB 278; [1993] TLR 576; [1994] 1 WLR 409 CA Intent to cause damage by fire and recklessness to endangerment of life establishes intent for attempted aggravated arson.

R v Sangha [1988] 2 All ER 385; (1988) 87 Cr App R 88; (1988) 152 JP 293; (1988) 132 SJ 191; [1988] 1 WLR 519 CA Mens rea for arson is that reasonable person would see risk of fire damaging property or endangering life.

MENS REA (assault)

R v Spratt [1991] 2 All ER 210; (1990) 91 Cr App R 362; [1990] Crim LR 797; (1990) 154 JP 884; (1990) 134 SJ 860; [1990] TLR 369; [1990] 1 WLR 1073 CA If no actual intent/recklessness then no mens rea.

R v Venna [1975] 3 All ER 788; (1975) 61 Cr App R 310; [1975] Crim LR 701t; (1976) 140 JP 31; [1976] QB 421; (1975) 119 SJ 679; [1975] 3 WLR 737 CA Recklessness sufficient to sustain charge of assault.

R v Williams (Gladstone) (1984) 78 Cr App R 276; [1984] Crim LR 163 CA When pleading mistake as defence to assault reasonableness of belief relevant to deciding whether held but not to whether guilty/innocent.

MENS REA (attempt)

R v Millard and Vernon [1987] Crim LR 393 CA On intent requirement under the Criminal Attempts Act 1981, s 1(1).

MENS REA (attempted murder)

R v Grimwood [1962] 3 All ER 285; (1962) 46 Cr App R 393; [1962] Crim LR 632t; (1962) 112 LJ 785; [1962] 2 QB 621; (1962) 106 SJ 613; [1962] 3 WLR 747 CCA DPP v Smith inapplicable to attempted murder; direction that if death a foreseeable consequence of accused's actions, accused could be guilty of attempted murder, despite absence of intent to kill, a mistaken direction.

R v Loughlin [1959] Crim LR 518t CCA On necessary intent for attempted murder.

MENS REA (breaking and entering)

R v Wood (Ernest George) (1911-12) 7 Cr App R 56 CCA On housebreaking charge can infer felonious intent from circumstantial evidence.

MENS REA (coercion)

R v Caroubi (1913-14) XXIII Cox CC 177; (1911-12) 7 Cr App R 149; (1912) 76 JP 262; (1912-13) 107 LTR 415 CCA Conviction of larceny by wife (in presence of husband) set aside for inadequate direction on collusion/coercion.

R v Ditta, Hussain and Kara [1988] Crim LR 42 CA 'Wife' could not plead defence of coercion under the Criminal Justice Act 1925 where she bona fide but nonetheless mistakenly believed she was married to coercer.

R v Smith (Mabel Adelaide) (1916-17) 12 Cr App R 42 CCA Presumption of coercion of wife by husband applies in respect of misdemeanours.

MENS REA (contempt)

R v Odhams Press Ltd and others; ex parte Attorney-General [1957] 1 QB 73; (1956) 100 SJ 819; [1956] 3 WLR 796 HC QBD Mens rea unnecessary for contempt - only counts towards punishment.

MENS REA (corporation)

Director of Public Prosecutions v Kent and Sussex Contractors, Ltd and another [1944] 1 All ER 119; [1944] KB 146; [1944] 113 LJ 88; (1945) 95 LJ 102; (1944) 170 LTR 41; (1944) 88 SJ 59; (1943-44) LX TLR 175 HC KBD Intentions of its servants are attributed to corporation.

R v ICR Haulage, Ltd [1944] 1 All ER 691; (1943-45) 30 Cr App R 31; (1944) 108 JP 181; [1944] KB 550; [1944] 113 LJ 492; (1944) 171 LTR 180; (1943-44) LX TLR 399; (1944) WN (I) 135 CCA Whether fraud of agent was fraud of company depends on relationship/position: here was.

MENS REA (doli incapax)

A v Director of Public Prosecutions [1997] 1 Cr App R 27; [1997] Crim LR 125 HC QBD On rebuttal of doli incapax presumption.

A v Director of Public Prosecutions [1992] Crim LR 34 HC QBD Successful appeal by eleven year old who rightly claimed that doli incapax presumption had not been rebutted in his regard.

A v Sharples [1991] TLR 244 HC QBD Not sufficient to rebut doli incapax presumption that child ran away after doing act that was subject of prosecution.

C v Director of Public Prosecutions [1995] 2 All ER 43; [1996] 1 AC 1 (also HC QBD); [1995] 2 Cr App R 166; [1995] Crim LR 801; [1995] 1 FLR 933; (1995) 159 JP 269; (1995) 145 NLJ 416; [1995] RTR 261; [1995] TLR 164; [1995] 2 WLR 383 HL On continuing presumption of doli incapax in respect of child aged between 10 and 14 and on rebuttal of said presumption.

C v Director of Public Prosecutions [1994] 3 All ER 190; [1996] 1 AC 1 (also HL); [1995] 1 Cr App R 118; [1994] Crim LR 523; (1994) 158 JP 389; [1994] RTR 341; (1994) 138 SJ LB 91; [1994] TLR 180; [1994] 3 WLR 888 HC QBD On demise of presumption of doli incapax in respect of child aged between 10 and 14.

Curry v Director of Public Prosecutions (1994) 144 NLJ 498 HC QBD Rebuttable doli incapax presumption in respect of ten to fourteen year olds not valid any more.

Director of Public Prosecutions v K and another (1997) 1 Cr App R 36; [1997] Crim LR 121 HC QBD Could be guilty of procuring rape by person aged between ten and fourteen in respect of whom the doli incapax presumption had not been rebutted.

Ex parte N [1959] Crim LR 523t HC QBD Physical bearing of party in court of (at best) very slight relevance to rebuttal of doli incapax presumption.

Ex parte N [1959] Crim LR 357t HC QBD Leave to appeal aginst finding that doli incapax presumption rebutted by fact that child well-dressed and apparently well reared.

F v Padwick [1959] Crim LR 439t HC QBD Presumption of doli incapax validly held to have been rebutted.

H (IP) v Chief Constable of South Wales [1987] Crim LR 42 HC QBD On evidence necessary to rebut doli incapax presumption in respect of child aged between ten and fourteen years of age.

L v Director of Public Prosecutions; T v Director of Public Prosecutions; W, H (G) and H (C) v Director of Public Prosecutions [1996] 2 Cr App R 501 HC QBD On rebuttal of doli incapax presumption.

R v B; R v A [1979] 3 All ER 460; (1979) 69 Cr App R 362; [1979] Crim LR 589; (1980) 144 JP 35; (1979) 123 SJ 487; [1979] 1 WLR 1185 CA Any evidence (including convictions) admissible to rebut criminal incapacity of 10-14 year old.

R v Coulburn (Darren) (1988) 87 Cr App R 309 CA Doli incapax presumption of under-fourteen year old is rebuttable (here did not apply).

R v Sheldon (Leslie Maxwell) [1996] 2 Cr App R 50 CA Guilty verdict in respect of near-fourteen year old allowed stand despite non-direction as to doli incapax presumption.

T v Director of Public Prosecutions; L v Director of Public Prosecutions; H and others v Director of Public Prosecutions [1997] Crim LR 127; (1996) TLR 31/5/96 HC QBD On rebuttal of presumption of doli incapax.

T v Director of Public Prosecutions [1989] Crim LR 498 HC QBD Doli incapax presumption rebutted.

W and another v Simpson [1967] Crim LR 360; (1967) 111 SJ 273 HC QBD Presumption of innocence in respect of under fourteen year old offenders rebutted here.

W v Director of Public Prosecutions [1996] Crim LR 320 HC QBD On rebutting the presumption of doli incapax (here not rebutted).

X v X [1958] Crim LR 805t HC QBD Failed appeal by child against rebuttal accepted in trial court of the doli incapax presumption.

MENS REA (drunkenness)

R v Davies [1991] Crim LR 469 CA On relevance of drunkenness to intent.

R v Lipman [1969] 3 All ER 410; (1969) 53 Cr App R 600; [1969] Crim LR 546t; (1969) 133 JP 712; (1969) 119 NLJ 768t; [1970] 1 QB 152; (1969) 113 SJ 670; [1969] 3 WLR 819 CA Once act unlawful no intent needed to support manslaughter where death; self-induced drunkeness no defence.

MENS REA (epilepsy)

R v Perry (Henry) (1919-20) 14 Cr App R 48 CCA Epileptic must be suffering from epileptic seizure at time commits crime to support insanity verdict.

MENS REA (firearms)

R v Steele [1993] Crim LR 298 CA On mens rea for possession of firearms (without certificate).

MENS REA (forgery)

R v Clayton (Terence Edward) (1981) 72 Cr App R 135; [1981] Crim LR 186 CA Intent to deceive was adequate mens rea for forgery of excise licence (contrary to Vehicles (Excise) Act 1971, s 26(1)).

R v Hagan [1985] Crim LR 598 CA Intent for forgery under Forgery Act 1913, s 7, was intent to defraud which was present here even though intended use of money obtained by way of forgery was honest/not for self.

MENS REA (general)

Aik (Lim Chin) v R [1963] 1 All ER 223; [1963] AC 160; [1963] Crim LR 122; (1962) 106 SJ 1028; [1963] 2 WLR 42 PC Ignorance of law a defence where no publication of law/where compliance order not served on subject thereof.

Arrowsmith v Jenkins [1963] 2 QB 561 HC QBD No mens rea required to be guilty of wilful obstruction of highway so long as have freely done acts causing/continuing obstruction.

Bolton v Crawley [1972] Crim LR 222 CA Assault occasioning actual bodily harm did not require mens rea so though had injected oneself with drugs could not claim did not possess mens rea for said offence.

Chilvers v Rayner (1984) 78 Cr App R 59; [1984] 1 WLR 328 HC QBD False hallmarking contrary to Hallmarking Act 1973, s 1 an absolute offence (no mens rea required).

Chivers v Hand (1915) 79 JP 88; [1915] 84 LJKB 304; (1915) 112 LTR 221 HC KBD Conviction of aider and abettor of (purchaser from) person breaching Sunday trading legislation quashed as requisite mens rea absent.

Jones v Brooks and another (1968) 112 SJ 745 HC QBD Pre-/post-actus reus expression of intention relevant evidence.

Mieras v Rees [1975] Crim LR 224; (1975) 139 JP 549 HC QBD Cannot attempt to supply controlled drug (even if have requisite mens rea) where substance are supplying is not controlled drug as is no actus reus.

R v Berry (No 3) [1994] 2 All ER 913; (1994) 99 Cr App R 88; [1995] 1 WLR 7 CA Offence of making explosive substance involves knowing that item of manufacture/ in possession/under control can cause explosion.

R v Bowden [1993] Crim LR 380 CA On intoxication and intent.

R v Cunningham [1981] Crim LR 180 CA On whether intention to cause grievous bodily harm sufficient intent for murder.

R v Davies (Willliam) (1912-13) 8 Cr App R 211; (1912-13) XXIX TLR 350 CCA No requirement on accused to show did not intend crime (of which intent an element).

R v Fitzpatrick (Norman) (1925-26) 19 Cr App R 91 CCA That accused was accessory after fact does not prove was principal/accessory before fact; accused may give account of own state of mind at pertinent time: mens rea a question of fact.

R v Hancock; R v Shankland [1986] AC 455 (also CA); (1986) 82 Cr App R 264; [1986] Crim LR 400; (1986) 150 JP 203; (1986) 136 NLJ 214; (1986) 130 SJ 184; [1986] 2 WLR 357 HL Appropriate direction to jury where foreseeability an issue.

R v Hussain [1981] 2 All ER 287; (1981) 72 Cr App R 143; [1981] Crim LR 251; (1981) 131 NLJ 70; (1981) 125 SJ 166; [1981] 1 WLR 416 CA Possession of firearm without certificate an absolute offence - no mens rea needed.

R v Miller [1982] 2 All ER 386; (1982) 75 Cr App R 109; [1982] Crim LR 526; (1982) 146 JP 243; [1982] QB 532; (1982) 126 SJ 327; [1982] TLR 123; [1982] 2 WLR 937 CA Usually actus reus/mens rea to coincide; absent statute omission does not generally raise criminal liability; reckless/intended omission after unintended act is criminal.

R v Miller (Geoffrey) [1983] TLR 404 CMAC On mens rea as an element of offences charged under the Army Act 1955, s 69.

R v Mohan [1975] 2 All ER 193; (1975) 60 Cr App R 272; [1975] Crim LR 283t; (1975) 139 JP 523; (1975) 125 NLJ 186t; [1976] QB 1; [1975] RTR 337; (1975) 119 SJ 219; [1975] 2 WLR 859 CA Specific intent to commit offence essential element of attempt to commit crime.

R v Murphy [1980] 2 All ER 325; (1980) 71 Cr App R 33; [1980] Crim LR 309; (1980) 144 JP 360; (1980) 130 NLJ 474; [1980] QB 434; [1980] RTR 145; (1980) 124 SJ 189; [1980] 2 WLR 743 CA Failure to drive with due care/attention or recklessness as to same is essence of reckless driving; mens rea is attitude leading to driving - need not show intent to take risk.

R v Nash [1991] Crim LR 768; (1991) 155 JP 709; [1991] TLR 285 CA On recklessness as an element of mens rea for assault occasioning actual bodily harm.

R v Nedrick [1986] 3 All ER 1; (1986) 83 Cr App R 267; [1986] Crim LR 742; (1986) 150 JP 589; (1970) 130 SJ 572; [1986] 1 WLR 1025 CA Foresight is evidence of intent but does not constitute intent.

R v Park (James Chalmers) (1988) 87 Cr App R 164; [1988] Crim LR 238; (1989) 133 SJ 945 CA Goods subject of handling stolen goods prosecution must already have been stolen - mens rea is guilty knowledge at time handle the goods.

R v Sorsky (Isaac), Bresler (Herman) and H Bresler and Sons, Ltd [1944] 2 All ER 333; (1943-45) 30 Cr App R 84 CCA Conspiracy to breach Limitation of Supplies (Miscellaneous) Order 1940 requires no mens rea.

R v Thomson (1966) 50 Cr App R 1 Assizes On mens rea of conspiracy.

R v Walker and Hayles [1990] Crim LR 44 CA On when intent to kill may be inferred.

R v Ward [1956] 1 All ER 565; [1956] Crim LR 203; (1956) 106 LJ 153; [1956] 1 QB 351; (1956) 100 SJ 112; [1956] 2 WLR 423 CCA Test of intention is what reasonable man would think.

R v Washer [1954] Crim LR 933 CMAC Intent irrelevant to offence of engaging in disgraceful conduct of indecent kind contrary to Army Act (unlike sister offence under Vagrancy Act 1824).

Sik-Chun (Lau) v R [1984] Crim LR 424 PC Inadequate direction as to common intent necessary for death resulting from common attack to be murder.

MENS REA (grievous bodily harm)

R v Pearman (Stephen Dennis) (1985) 80 Cr App R 259; [1984] Crim LR 675; [1985] RTR 39 CA That foresee consequences need not mean intended them.

MENS REA (handling)

R v Brook [1993] Crim LR 455 CA On requisite mens rea for handling.

R v Roberts (William) (1987) 84 Cr App R 117; [1986] Crim LR 122 CA R v Ghosh direction on dishonesty unnecessary where dishonesty not pleaded; jury need not find that handler of stolen goods acted dishonestly towards person who suffered loss.

MENS REA (homicide)

R v Stewart; R v Schofield [1995] 3 All ER 159; [1995] 1 Cr App R 441; [1995] Crim LR 420 CA Parties to joint enterprise resulting in death may be guilty of murder or manslaughter unless relevant act not committed in course of joint enterprise or other party to enterprise has a more specific intent.

Wing-Siu (Chan) and others v R [1985] AC 168; (1985) 80 Cr App R 117; [1984] Crim LR 549; (1984) 128 SJ 685; [1984] TLR 411; [1984] 3 WLR 677 PC Person guilty of murder/grievous bodily harm if proved that entered premises as part of unlawful common enterprise and had contemplated that serious bodily harm might result.

MENS REA (implied malice)

R v Vickers [1957] 2 All ER 741; (1957) 41 Cr App R 189; [1957] Crim LR 614; (1957) 121 JP 510; (1957) 107 LJ 473; [1957] 2 QB 664; (1957) 101 SJ 593; [1957] 3 WLR 326 CCA Implied malice doctrine remains post-/constructive malice extinguished by Homicide Act 1957, s 1(1).

MENS REA (importation of drugs)

R v Karte (Klaas); R v Panayi (Michael) (1989) 88 Cr App R 267; [1989] Crim LR 210; (1988) 132 SJ 1697; [1989] 1 WLR 187 CA On mens rea of fraudulent evasion of prohibition on importation of controlled drug (Customs and Excise Management Act 1979, s 170(2)).

MENS REA (incitement to obtain by deception/false pretences)

R v Shaw [1994] Crim LR 365 CA On mens rea of incitement to obtain property by deception.

MENS REA (intent to defraud)

R v Smith (Sydney Edward) (1919-20) 14 Cr App R 101; (1920) 84 JP 67 CCA Can be guilty of intent to defraud under Forgery Act 1913, s 7(a) though are legally entitled to whatever obtained.

MENS REA (intoxication)

Director of Public Prosecutions v Majewski [1976] 2 All ER 142; [1977] AC 443 (also CA); (1976) 62 Cr App R 262; [1976] Crim LR 374; (1976) 140 JP 315; (1976) 126 NLJ 542t; (1976) 120 SJ 299; [1976] 2 WLR 623 HL Self-induced intoxication no defence unless specific intent required.

R v Garlick (Clifford Patrick) (1981) 72 Cr App R 291; [1981] Crim LR 178 CA Drunkenness defence raises question whether had formed necessary intent.

R v O'Connor [1991] Crim LR 135 CA On relevance of drunkenness to intent.

MENS REA (larceny)

Ruse v Read [1949] 1 All ER 398; (1948-49) 33 Cr App R 67; [1949] 1 KB 377; (1949) 99 LJ 77; (1949) LXV TLR 124; (1949) WN (I) 56 HC KBD Taking without dishonest intention followed by appropriation with dishonest intention is larceny.

MENS REA (manslaughter)

Director of Public Prosecutions v Newbury; Director of Public Prosecutions v Jones [1976] 2 All ER 365; [1977] AC 500; (1976) 62 Cr App R 291; [1977] Crim LR 359; (1976) 140 JP 370; (1976) 126 NLJ 618t; (1976) 120 SJ 402; [1976] 2 WLR 918 HL Manslaughter if person un/knowingly does unlawful/dangerous act which causes death.

R v Church [1965] 2 All ER 72; (1965) 49 Cr App R 206; [1965] Crim LR 299t; (1965) 129 JP 366; (1965) 115 LJ 350; [1966] 1 QB 59; (1965) 109 SJ 371; [1965] 2 WLR 1220 CCA Unlawful act resulting in death plus mens rea that act would cause some harm necessary to sustain manslaughter conviction.

R v Lamb [1967] 2 All ER 1282; [1967] Crim LR 537t; (1967) 131 JP 456; (1967) 117 NLJ 834; [1967] 2 QB 981; (1967) 111 SJ 541; [1967] 3 WLR 888 CA Must consider accused's mind when criminal negligence alleged.

MENS REA (mistake)

Campbell v Edwards [1976] 1 All ER 785 CA Absent fraud/collusion mistaken non-speaking report by valuer cannot be set aside.

R v Williams [1987] 3 All ER 411 CA Person acting under mistake of fact to be judged in light of mistaken facts even if unreasonable mistake.

MENS REA (murder)

Attorney General's Reference (No 3 of 1994) [1996] 2 All ER 10; [1996] 1 Cr App R 351; [1996] Crim LR 268; [1996] 2 FLR 1; (1995) 145 NLJ 1777; [1996] QB 581; (1996) 140 SJ LB 20; [1995] TLR 625; [1996] 2 WLR 412 CA Murder or manslaughter arises if injury to a child in utero or its mother causes child to die after live birth; necessary intent is intent to kill or cause grievous bodily injury to mother.

Attorney General's Reference (No 3 of 1994) [1997] 3 All ER 936; [1997] 2 Cr App R (S) 1185; [1997] TLR 411; [1997] 3 WLR 421 HL Conviction for manslaughter of child may follow where deliberate injury to pregnant mother causes child to die after live birth but conviction for murder of child would not follow.

Frankland v R; Moore v R [1987] AC 576; (1988) 86 Cr App R 116; [1988] Crim LR 117; (1987) 131 SJ 541; [1987] 2 WLR 1251 PC Objective test of intent in Manx murder case inappropriate.

Hyam v Director of Public Prosecutions [1974] 2 All ER 41; [1975] AC 55; (1974) 59 Cr App R 91; [1974] Crim LR 365; (1974) 138 JP 374; (1974) 124 NLJ 320t; (1974) 118 SJ 311; [1974] 2 WLR 607 HL Intent for murder is intend to do acts which could (but need not be intended to) cause really serious bodily harm.

Kam-Kwok (Leung) v R (1985) 81 Cr App R 83; [1985] Crim LR 227 PC Conviction allowed stand despite gross misdirection on mental aspect of murder.

R v Barr (Graham); R v Kenyon (James Stephen); R v Heacock (Anthony Peter) (1989) 88 Cr App R 362 CA Foreseeability of results of one's acts an aid to jury in deciding whether was intent to kill/do grievous bodily harm.

R v Dodson [1973] Crim LR 518 CA On effect of drunkenness on intent in context of murder.

R v Donnelly [1989] Crim LR 739 CA That appellant had been using gun as club did not have to mean (and here was not the case) that intended to fire it.

R v Hancock and another [1986] 1 All ER 641; [1986] AC 455 (also HL); (1986) 82 Cr App R 264; [1986] Crim LR 180; (1986) 150 JP 33; (1985) 135 NLJ 1208; (1985) 129 SJ 793; [1985] 3 WLR 1014 CA Appropriate direction to jury where foreseeability an issue.

R v Moloney [1985] 1 All ER 1025; [1985] AC 905; (1985) 81 Cr App R 93; [1985] Crim LR 378; (1985) 149 JP 369; (1985) 135 NLJ 315; (1985) 129 SJ 220; [1985] 2 WLR 648 HL Guidelines on requisite mental element for murder.

R v Powell and Daniels [1996] 1 Cr App R 14; [1996] Crim LR 201; [1995] TLR 325 CA On necessary mens rea required of junior party charged of murder as part of joint enterprise.

R v Sheehan; R v Moore [1975] 2 All ER 960; (1975) 60 Cr App R 308; [1975] Crim LR 339; (1975) 139 JP 636; (1975) 125 NLJ 333t; (1975) 119 SJ 271; [1975] 1 WLR 739 CA Issue for jury is if evidence - including self-induced intoxication - shows accused had intent to kill/do grievous bodily harm.

R v Smith [1960] 2 All ER 450; [1960] Crim LR 491t; (1960) 110 LJ 429; (1960) 104 SJ 510 CCA Is possible for person not to intend natural effects of acts though reasonable person would have foreseen them.

MENS REA (offences against the person)

R v Wallett [1968] 2 All ER 296; (1968) 52 Cr App R 271; [1968] Crim LR 271t; (1968) 132 JP 318; [1968] 2 QB 367; (1968) 112 SJ 232; [1968] 2 WLR 1199 CA On criminal intent (homicide prosecution).

R v Ward [1956] 1 All ER 565; [1956] Crim LR 203; (1956) 106 LJ 153; [1956] 1 QB 351; (1956) 100 SJ 112; [1956] 2 WLR 423 CCA Test of intention is what reasonable man would think.

R v Williamson (Anthony Colin); R v Ellerton (Stephen) (1978) 67 Cr App R 63; [1978] Crim LR 166; (1977) 127 NLJ 1177t CA On requisite intent for murder.

R v Woollin (Stephen Leslie) [1997] 1 Cr App R 97; [1997] Crim LR 519 CA On intent necessary for murder.

MENS REA (offences against the person)

R v Wilson (Alan Thomas) [1996] 2 Cr App R 241; [1996] Crim LR 573; [1997] QB 47; (1996) 140 SJ LB 93; [1996] 3 WLR 125 CA Successful appeal against assault conviction as appellant's branding of wife's buttocks had been done with her consent.

MENS REA (rape)

Director of Public Prosecutions v Morgan; Director of Public Prosecutions v McDonald; Director of Public Prosecutions v McLarty; Director of Public Prosecutions v Parker [1975] 2 All ER 347; [1976] AC 182 (also CA); (1975) 61 Cr App R 136; [1975] Crim LR 717; (1975) 139 JP 476; (1975) 125 NLJ 530t; (1975) 119 SJ 319; [1975] 2 WLR 913 (also CA) HL Belief that woman consents means no rape as no mens rea.

R v Morgan and others [1975] 1 All ER 8; [1976] AC 182 (also HL); [1975] Crim LR 40t; (1974) 124 NLJ 987t; (1974) 118 SJ 809; [1975] 2 WLR 913 (also HL) CA Crown must objectively demonstrate absence of consent.

MENS REA (suicide)

Re Davis, decd [1968] 1 QB 72; [1967] 2 WLR 1089 CA Must intend to kill self to be guilty of suicide.

MENS REA (theft)

R v Fernandes (Roland Anthony Peter Francis) [1996] 1 Cr App R 175; [1995] TLR 235 CA On what constitutes intention permanently to deprive another of his rights in his property.

MENS REA (trespass)

Selvanayagam (Sinnasamy) v R [1951] AC 83 PC Principal/sole intent must have been to commit crime/harass another for entry onto other's land under ostensible claim of right to be criminal trespass.

MENS REA (wounding with intent)

R v Bryson [1985] Crim LR 669 CA On necessary intention to be guilty of wounding with intent.

MILITARY (condonation)

R v Durkin [1953] 3 WLR 479 CMAC Commanding officer's behaviour did not mean accused's offence condoned.

MILITARY (desertion)

Re Virdee (1980) 130 NLJ 313 HC QBD Article 48 of EEC Treaty (and rights of spouses pursuant thereto) did not preclude deserter from Indian army from being returned to military custody.

MILITARY (general)

R v Bland [1968] Crim LR 683t CMAC Dismissal of appeal against finding that had behaved to prejudice of good order/military discipline (fought with sergeant when 'drunk' - for purposes of Army Act 1955, s 43).

R v Hogan [1955] Crim LR 181t CCA Offences by soldiers involving military property ought not to be dealt with by civil courts.

MILITARY (military service)

Downsborough v Huddersfield Industrial Society, Ltd; Wadsworth v Huddersfield Industrial Society, Ltd; Ardron v Huddersfield Industrial Society, Ltd [1941] 3 All ER 434 HC KBD Dismissal of employees because were conscientious objectors not offence.

MILITARY (mutiny)

R v Grant, Davis, Riley and Topley [1957] 2 All ER 694; (1957) 41 Cr App R 173; [1957] Crim LR 542t; (1957) 101 SJ 594 CMAC Cannot commit mutiny alone.

MISPRISION OF FELONY (general)

R v Aberg [1948] 1 All ER 601; (1948) 112 JP 206; (1948) LXIV TLR 215 CCA Not misdirection not to refer to good character in summing-up; on concealment for benefit of person accused of misprision of felony.

R v King [1965] 1 All ER 1053; (1965) 49 Cr App R 140; [1965] Crim LR 237g; (1965) 129 JP 276; (1965) 115 LJ 280; (1965) 109 SJ 150/391; [1965] 1 WLR 706 CCA No misprision of felony if remaining silent after charge/exercising right against self-incrimination but if speaks lies can be active concealment.

R v Lucraft (Anthony Thomas) (1966) 50 Cr App R 296; [1966] Crim LR 678t; (1966) 110 SJ 759 CCA Right to non-disclosure on charge of misprision of felony did not arise as was no evidence that prisoner accessory after fact to robbery at issue.

R v Sykes [1961] 1 All ER 702; [1961] Crim LR 483; (1961) 111 LJ 189; [1961] 2 QB 9; (1961) 105 SJ 183; [1961] 2 WLR 392 CCA Misprision of felony a common law misdemeanour for which no maximum sentence (but restraint required).

R v Wilde, Ward, Wooley, Morrey and Copley [1960] Crim LR 116 Assizes Need not be advantage to defendant for there to be misprision of felony; agreement not to reveal offence a crime.

Sykes v Director of Public Prosecutions [1961] 3 All ER 33; [1962] AC 528; (1961) 45 Cr App R 230; [1961] Crim LR 715; (1961) 125 JP 523; (1961) 111 LJ 500; (1961) 105 SJ 566; [1961] 3 WLR 371 HL Misprision of felony an offence; need not be active concealment to establish offence.

NEWSPAPER PUBLISHER'S ADDRESS (general)

Attorney-General v Beauchamp [1920] 1 KB 650; (1919-20) XXXVI TLR 174; (1920) WN (I) 15 HC KBD Publisher liable for punishment under 2 and 3 Vict c12, s 2 for not publishing name/address of printer on newspaper.

OBSCENITY (general)

Darbo v Director of Public Prosecutions [1992] Crim LR 56; (1991) 141 NLJ 1004t; [1991] TLR 339 HC QBD Sexually explicit materials do not per se have to be obscene for purposes of Obscene Publications Act 1959, s 3.

R v Commissioner of Police for the Metropolis; ex parte Blackburn (1980) 130 NLJ 313 CA Refusal of order of mandamus requiring police commissioner to bring prosecution in obscenity cases.

R v Commissioner of Police of the Metropolis; ex parte Blackburn (1980) 130 NLJ 92 HC QBD Refusal of order of mandamus requiring police commissioner to bring prosecution in obscenity cases.

R v Commissioner of Police of the Metropolis; ex parte Blackburn and another (No 3) [1973] Crim LR 185; (1973) 137 JP 172; (1973) 117 SJ 57; [1973] 2 WLR 43 CA No mandamus directing police in conduct of their duties as regards obscene publications as not proven that such direction merited.

OBSCENITY (importation of obscene goods)

R v De Montalk (Geoffrey Wladislas Vaile Potocki) (1931-32) 23 Cr App R 182 CCA On elements of offence of publishing/uttering obscene libel.

R v Martin Secker and Warburg Ltd and others (1954) 38 Cr App R 124; (1954) 118 JP 438; (1954) 104 LJ 488; (1954) 98 SJ 577; [1954] 1 WLR 1138 CCC On what constitutes obscene libel: must be more than just objectionable/in poor taste.

R v Metropolitan Police Commissioner; ex parte Blackburn [1973] Crim LR 55 HC QBD No mandamus directing police in conduct of their duties as regards obscene publications as not proven that such direction merited.

R v Sumner (Matthew) [1977] Crim LR 362/614 CrCt On elements of defence of 'public good' to obscene publication prosecution; on what is meant by term 'deprave'.

Shaw v Director of Public Prosecutions [1961] 2 All ER 446; [1962] AC 220; (1961) 45 Cr App R 113; [1961] Crim LR 468; (1961) 125 JP 437; (1961) 111 LJ 356; (1961) 105 SJ 421; [1961] 2 WLR 897 HL Test of obscenity is whether article would corrupt/deprave another (intent of author irrelevant); are living off earnings of prostitution if provide goods/services to prostitutes which would not if they were not prostitutes; agreement to publish obscene publication an agreement to corrupt public morals (even if never published),a common law misdemeanour.

OBSCENITY (importation of obscene goods)

Henn and Darby v Director of Public Prosecutions [1981] AC 850; (1980) 71 Cr App R 44; (1980) 130 NLJ 389; (1980) 124 SJ 290; [1980] 2 WLR 597 HL Permissible prohibition of obscene goods under Article 36/EEC.

R v Henn; R v Derby [1978] 3 All ER 1190; (1979) 69 Cr App R 137; [1979] Crim LR 113; (1979) 143 JP 58; (1978) 128 NLJ 954t; (1978) 122 SJ 555; [1978] 1 WLR 1031 CA Total prohibition of certain type of goods permissible under Article 30/EEC; prohibition of obscene goods permissible under Article 36/EEC.

OBSCENITY (indecent photographs)

R v Fellows (Alban); R v Arnold (Stephen) [1997] 2 All ER 548; [1997] 1 Cr App R 244; [1997] Crim LR 524; (1996) TLR 3/10/96 CA Computer data whereby indecent pictures of children could be displayed on-screen was 'photograph' within meaning of Protection of Children Act 1978.

R v Graham-Kerr (John) (1989) 88 Cr App R 302; (1989) 153 JP 171; (1988) 132 SJ 1299; [1988] 1 WLR 1098 CA On elements of crime of taking indecent photographs of child contrary to Protection of Children Act 1978, s 1(1).

R v Owen (Charles William) (1988) 86 Cr App R 291; [1988] Crim LR 120; (1987) 131 SJ 1696; [1988] 1 WLR 134 CA Jury could have regard to age of child in photograph when deciding if photograph obscene: did not have to decide from intrinsic nature of photograph.

OBSCENITY (obscene libel)

R v Martin Secker and Warburg Ltd and others (1954) 38 Cr App R 124; (1954) 118 JP 438; (1954) 104 LJ 488; (1954) 98 SJ 577; [1954] 1 WLR 1138 CCC On what constitutes obscene libel: must be more than just objectionable/in poor taste.

OBSCENITY (obscene publication)

Attorney General's Reference (No 5 of 1980) [1980] 3 All ER 816; (1981) 72 Cr App R 71; [1981] Crim LR 45; (1981) 145 JP 110; (1980) 130 NLJ 1122; (1980) 124 SJ 827; [1981] 1 WLR 88 CA Video cassettes are articles capable of publication under Obscene Publications Act.

Attorney-General's Reference (No 2 of 1975) [1976] 2 All ER 753 (also CCC); [1976] Crim LR 444t; (1976) 62 Cr App R 255; (1976) 126 NLJ 366t; (1976) 120 SJ 315; [1976] 1 WLR 710 CA In deciding if obscene jury may only have regard to those people who would actually be exposed to publication of material.

Attorney-General's Reference (No 3 of 1977) [1978] 3 All ER 1166; (1978) 67 Cr App R 393; (1979) 143 JP 94; (1978) 122 SJ 641; [1978] 1 WLR 1123 CA 'Learning' justification in Obscene Publications Act does not include sex education; doubts on obscenity cannot be resolved by expert.

Burke v Copper [1962] 2 All ER 14; (1962) 126 JP 319; (1962) 106 SJ 451; [1962] 1 WLR 700 HC QBD Forfeiture in respect of all photographs: some could not be more obscene than others.

Chief Constable of Blackpool v Woodhall [1965] Crim LR 660 Magistrates On what is meant by publication for 'gain' under the Obscene Publications Acts 1959 and 1964.

Corbin v Whyte and another [1972] Crim LR 234t; (1972) 122 NLJ 196t HC QBD Not breach of Obscene Publications Act to make obscene publications available to those whose morals were already depraved.

Cox v Stinton [1951] 2 All ER 637; (1951) 115 JP 490; [1951] 2 KB 1021; (1951) 101 LJ 455; [1951] 2 TLR 728; (1951) WN (I) 497 HC KBD Negatives liable to seizure/destruction.

Director of Public Prosecutions v A and BC Chewing Gum, Ltd [1967] 2 All ER 504; [1967] Crim LR 419; (1967) 131 JP 373; [1968] 1 QB 159; (1967) 111 SJ 331; [1967] 3 WLR 493 HC QBD Expert evidence on effect not evidence on tendency to corrupt/deprave so admissible.

Director of Public Prosecutions v Jordan [1976] 3 All ER 775; [1977] AC 699 (also CA); (1977) 64 Cr App R 33; [1977] Crim LR 109; (1977) 141 JP 13; (1977) 127 NLJ 15t; (1976) 120 SJ 817; [1976] 3 WLR 887 HL No defence of public good that otherwise obscene publications of psychological relief to some individuals.

Director of Public Prosecutions v Whyte and another [1972] 3 All ER 12; [1972] AC 849; (1973) 57 Cr App R 74; [1972] Crim LR 556t; (1972) 136 JP 686; (1972) 122 NLJ 703t; (1972) 116 SJ 583; [1972] 3 WLR 410 HL Material obscene even if directed at the depraved; consequent sexual activity unnecessary to prove can deprave/corrupt.

Gold Star Publications Ltd v Director of Public Prosecutions [1981] 2 All ER 257; (1981) 73 Cr App R 141; [1981] Crim LR 633; (1981) 145 JP 289; (1981) 131 NLJ 525; (1981) 125 SJ 376; [1981] 1 WLR 732 HL Article held in England can be obscene publication though purely for export.

Gold Star Publications Ltd v Metropolitan Police Commissioner (1980) 71 Cr App R 185; (1980) 130 NLJ 508 HC QBD Article held in England can be obscene publication though purely for export.

John Calder (Publications), Ltd v Powell [1965] 1 All ER 159; [1965] Crim LR 111t; (1965) 129 JP 136; (1965) 115 LJ 90; [1965] 1 QB 509; (1965) 109 SJ 71; [1965] 2 WLR 138 HC QBD Obscene work need not concern sex; expert opinion that work for public good may be disregarded.

Kent County Council v Multi Media Marketing (Canterbury) Ltd and another [1995] TLR 263 HC QBD On what constitutes 'human sexual activity' for purposes of the Video Recordings Act 1984, s 2(2).

Kosmos Publications Ltd and another v DPP [1975] Crim LR 345 HC QBD On determining whether article is indecent or obscene.

Mella v Monahan [1961] Crim LR 175t HC QBD Failed prosecution of shop manager for offering for sale pornographic photographs left in shop window indicating what they were and how much they cost.

Morgan v Bowker [1963] 1 All ER 691; [1963] Crim LR 280; (1963) 127 JP 264; (1963) 113 LJ 302; [1964] 1 QB 507; (1963) 107 SJ 155; [1963] 2 WLR 860 HC QBD Justices hearing obscene publication forfeiture arguments may hear later action; type/carrying out of business part of circumstances in which materials found.

Olympia Press Ltd v Hollis and another [1974] 1 All ER 108; (1974) 59 Cr App R 28; [1973] Crim LR 757; (1974) 138 JP 100; (1973) 117 SJ 813; [1973] 1 WLR 1520 HC QBD Judges need not read entire publication to make decision; decide if obscene then if contrary to public good.

Paget Publications, Ltd v Watson [1952] 1 All ER 1256; (1952) 116 JP 320; (1952) 96 SJ 328; [1952] 1 TLR 1189; (1952) WN (I) 248 HC QBD May order entire publication destroyed even if only a portion thereof obscene.

Police v Fouldes [1954] Crim LR 868 Sessions Boccacio's 'The Decameron' deemed not to be obscene.

R v Adams [1980] 1 All ER 473; (1980) 70 Cr App R 149; [1980] Crim LR 53; (1980) 144 JP 69; [1980] QB 575; (1980) 124 SJ 527; [1980] 3 WLR 275 CA Warrant under Obscene Publications Act allows one entry; absent oppression/despite multiple entries conviction good.

R v Anderson and others [1971] 3 All ER 1152; [1972] Crim LR 40t; (1972) 136 JP 97; [1972] 1 QB 304; [1971] 3 WLR 939 CA If one element of article obscene, whole article is obscene; obscenity for jury not expert evidence; definition of 'obscene'.

R v Barker [1962] 1 All ER 748; (1962) 46 Cr App R 227; [1962] Crim LR 316; (1962) 126 JP 274; (1962) 112 LJ 238; (1962) 106 SJ 289 CA Questions for jury in obscene publications case; that did not know age of viewer/that viewer kept material to self irrelevant.

R v Barton [1976] Crim LR 514 CA Actor in obscene film could be guilty of abetting later publication of obscene film for gain.

R v Calder and Boyars Ltd [1968] 3 All ER 644; (1968) 52 Cr App R 706; [1968] Crim LR 614t; (1969) 133 JP 20; [1969] 1 QB 151; (1968) 112 SJ 688; [1968] 3 WLR 974 CA Procedure in obscene publications case; issue is whether would deprave/corrupt a significant proportion of readers - what is 'significant proportion' to be gauged by jury.

R v Clayton; R v Halsey [1962] 3 All ER 500; (1962) 46 Cr App R 450; [1962] Crim LR 705t; (1963) 127 JP 7; (1962) 112 LJ 719; [1963] 1 QB 163; (1962) 106 SJ 652; [1962] 3 WLR 815 CCA Publication must deprave/corrupt recipient to sustain obscene publication conviction.

R v De Marny [1904-07] All ER 923; (1907-09) XXI Cox CC 371; (1907) 71 JP 14 (also CCC); [1907] 1 KB 388; (1906) 41 LJ 838; [1907] 76 LJKB 210; (1907) XCVI LTR 159; (1906-07) 51 SJ 146; (1906-07) XXIII TLR 221; (1907) WN (I) 10 CCR Newspaper editor liable for causing/procuring publication/sale of obscene publications by accepting/printing advertisements for obscene materials.

R v Donnelly, Gallagher, Hayes and Mainchair Ltd [1980] Crim LR 723 CrCt Video films did not fall within terms of the Obscene Publications Act 1959.

R v Gradwell; ex parte Straker [1963] Crim LR 50t HC QBD On whether negatives could constitute articles for purposes of Obscene Publications Act 1959.

R v Love [1955] Crim LR 250t CCA Obscene publication conviction quashed where issue whether sole director of publishing company knew of obscene content of books not left to jury.

R v O'Sullivan (Paul Andrew) [1995] 1 Cr App R 455; (1994) 144 NLJ 635 CA On what constitutes an 'obscene' publication.

R v Penguin Books, Ltd [1961] Crim LR 176 CCC On obscenity: failed prosecution of Penguin Books for publishing 'Lady Chatterley's Lover' by DH Lawrence.

R v Reiter and others [1954] 1 All ER 741; (1954) 38 Cr App R 62; [1954] Crim LR 384; (1954) 118 JP 262; [1954] 2 QB 16; (1954) 98 SJ 235; [1954] 2 WLR 638 CCA Can only look to book alleged to be obscene - cannot compare with others.

R v Shaw [1961] 1 All ER 330; (1961) 111 LJ 137 CCA Is common law offence of conspiracy to corrupt public morals; can be prosecuted for same notwithstanding Obscene Publications Act 1959, s 2(4); publishing advertisements for prostitutes is living off earnings of prostitution; need not be intent to corrupt for publication to be obscene.

R v Skirving and another [1985] 2 All ER 705; [1985] Crim LR 317; [1985] QB 819 CA Expert evidence on tendency of allegedly obscene book to deprave/corrupt admissible.

R v Smyth (John) [1986] Crim LR 46 CrCt Trial of retailer of obscene videos where supplier had already been acquitted of offence under Obscene Publications Act 1959 was permissible.

R v Snaresbrook Crown Court; ex parte Commissioner of Police of the Metropolis [1984] TLR 206 HC QBD Could look to samples of material when seeking to determine whether entirety of said material was obscene.

R v Stamford [1972] 2 All ER 427; (1972) 56 Cr App R 398; [1972] Crim LR 374t; (1972) 136 JP 522; (1972) 122 NLJ 217t; [1972] 2 QB 391; (1972) 116 SJ 313; [1972] 2 WLR 1055 CA What is obscene/indecent is a matter exclusively for jury.

R v Staniforth; R v Jordan [1976] 2 All ER 714; [1977] AC 699 (also HL); [1976] Crim LR 446; (1976) 140 JP 483; (1976) 126 NLJ 522t; (1976) 120 SJ 266; [1976] 2 WLR 849 CA Otherwise obscene material must benefit general public to be justified; evidence must show particular (not all such) publications justified.

R v Stanley [1965] 1 All ER 1035; (1965) 49 Cr App R 175; [1965] Crim LR 239t; (1965) 129 JP 279; (1965) 115 LJ 265; [1965] 2 QB 327; (1965) 109 SJ 193; [1965] 2 WLR 917 CCA Something obscene is indecent (not vice versa) - can be convicted of either.

R v Straker [1965] Crim LR 239g CCA Objective test as to whether material sent by mail is 'indecent' (test is not to see whether material 'obscene').

R v Taylor (Alan) [1995] 1 Cr App R 131; [1994] Crim LR 527; (1994) 158 JP 317; (1994) 138 SJ LB 54; [1994] TLR 66 CA Developing obscene negatives into photographs was distributing obscene material.

R v Wells Street Stipendiary Magistrate; ex parte Golding [1979] Crim LR 254 HC QBD Court could not try common law offence (keeping disorderly house - showing obscene films) replaced by statutory offence (no transitory provisions made) albeit that summons received just before statute came into force.

Roandale Ltd v Metropolitan Police Commissioner [1979] Crim LR 254; (1979) 123 SJ 128 CA On police powers pursuant to seizure of (here a very large number of) items under Obscene Publications Act 1959, s 3.

Straker v Director of Public Prosecutions [1963] 1 All ER 697; [1963] Crim LR 279; (1963) 127 JP 260; (1963) 113 LJ 365; [1963] 1 QB 926; (1963) 107 SJ 156; [1963] 2 WLR 598 HC QBD Negatives cannot be obscene publication.

Thomson v Chain Libraries, Ltd [1954] 2 All ER 616; [1954] Crim LR 551t; (1954) 104 LJ 473; (1954) 98 SJ 473; [1954] 1 WLR 999 HC QBD Justices must themselves examine allegedly obscene publications to see if obscene.

OBSCENITY (obscene telephone call)

R v Johnson (Anthony Thomas) [1996] 2 Cr App R 434; [1996] Crim LR 828; (1996) 140 SJ LB 183; (1996) TLR 22/5/96; [1997] 1 WLR 367 CA Making obscene telephone calls to various persons could amount to public nuisance.

OBSCENITY (seizure/destruction of obscene publication)

Cox v Stinton [1951] 2 All ER 637; [1951] 2 KB 1021 HC KBD Negatives liable to seizure/destruction.

OBSCENITY (unlawful importation of obscene material)

R v Bow Street Stipendiary Magistrate and another; ex parte Noncyp (1989) 89 Cr App R 121; [1990] 1 QB 123; (1989) 133 SJ 1031 CA Obscenity in customs and excise condemnation proceedings was obscenity in terms of Obscene Publications Act 1959, s 1(1) - public good defence not available.

R v Bow Street Stipendiary Magistrate and another; ex parte Noncyp (1988) 132 SJ 1063 HC QBD Definition of obscenity in Obscene Publications Act 1959/public good defence under s 4 thereof did not require consideration in prosecution under the Customs Consolidation Act 1876, s 42.

OBSTRUCTING/PERVERTING THE COURSE OF JUSTICE (attempt to defeat)

R v Britton [1973] Crim LR 375; [1973] RTR 502 CA Valid conviction for attempting to defeat the course of justice by drinking alcohol so as to render the laboratory specimen provided unreliable.

OBSTRUCTING/PERVERTING THE COURSE OF JUSTICE (attempt to pervert)

Ping-nam (Tsang) v R (1982) 74 Cr App R; [1982] Crim LR 46; (1981) 125 SJ 709; [1981] 1 WLR 1462 PC Could not charge accused with attempting to pervert course of justice rather than perjury so as to overcome evidential difficulties; could not seek upholding of convictions on completely different basis to that argued in lower courts.

R v Coxhead [1986] Crim LR 251; [1986] RTR 411 CA Is/is not discretion not to bring criminal proceedings in non-serious/serious cases: seriousness a matter for jury.

R v Greenberg (1918-21) XXVI Cox CC 466; (1919) 121 LTR 288; (1918-19) 63 SJ 553 CCA Attempting to get witness to change evidence/not give certain evidence is same common law misdemeanour.

R v Machin [1980] 3 All ER 151; (1980) 71 Cr App R 166; [1980] Crim LR 376/585; (1981) 145 JP 21; (1980) 130 NLJ 473; [1980] RTR 233; (1980) 124 SJ 359; [1980] 1 WLR 763 CA Attempting to pervert course of justice covers acts intended to and in fact perverting course of justice.

R v Murray [1982] 2 All ER 225; (1982) 75 Cr App R 58; [1982] Crim LR 370; [1982] RTR 289; (1982) 126 SJ 227; [1982] TLR 93; [1982] 1 WLR 475 CA Attempting to pervert course of justice requires intent to do so and act which would tend to do so.

R v Rowell [1978] 1 All ER 665; (1977) 65 Cr App R 174; [1977] Crim LR 681; (1978) 142 JP 181; (1977) 127 NLJ 662t; (1977) 121 SJ 790; [1978] 1 WLR 132 CA Person acting alone can attempt to pervert course of justice; false allegation could be attempt; attempt can be made up of one/series of actions.

R v Williams (1991) 92 Cr App R 158; [1991] Crim LR 205; (1991) 155 JP 365; [1990] TLR 669 CA Attempting to pervert the course of justice a substantive common law offence.

OBSTRUCTING/PERVERTING THE COURSE OF JUSTICE (conspiracy)

R v Head and Head [1978] Crim LR 427 CA Was conspiracy to obstruct course of justice where agreed to act as surety in return for future indemnity even though did not possess sum for which stood surety.

Silcott v Commissioner of Police of the Metropolis (1996) TLR 9/7/96 CA On extent of public policy immunity enjoyed by police in respect of actions for conspiracy to pervert the course of justice/misfeasance in public office.

OBSTRUCTING/PERVERTING THE COURSE OF JUSTICE (conspiracy to intimidate)

R v Jones (John McKinsie); R v Tomlinson (Eric); R v Warren (Dennis Michael); R v O'Shea (Kenneth Desmond Francis); R v Carpenter (John); R v Llywarch (John Elfyn) (1974) 59 Cr App R 120 CA On what constitutes 'intimidation' under Conspiracy and Protection of Property Act 1875, s 7; on constituent elements of unlawful assembly and of affray.

OBSTRUCTING/PERVERTING THE COURSE OF JUSTICE (general)

Director of Public Prosecutions v Mills [1997] 2 Cr App R 6; [1996] Crim LR 746; [1997] QB 301; (1996) TLR 1/4/96 HC QBD Threatening witness by telephone was perverting the course of justice contrary to the Criminal Justice and Public Order Act 1994, s 51(1).

R v Ali [1993] Crim LR 396 CA Offer of bribery per se amounted to pressure (to withdraw charge).

R v Andrews [1973] 1 All ER 857; (1973) 57 Cr App R 254; [1973] Crim LR 117t; (1973) 137 JP 325; (1972) 122 NLJ 1133t; [1973] QB 422; [1973] RTR 508; (1973) 117 SJ 86; [1973] 2 WLR 116 CA Incitement to/actual production of untrue evidence is obstruction of justice.

R v Bains [1981] Crim LR 569 CCC Inducement of witness not to tell what knows to court.

R v Bassi [1985] Crim LR 671 CA Is act tending to pervert the course of justice for witness to agree not to appear in court in return for payment.

R v Firetto [1991] Crim LR 208 CA Conviction for doing acts tending and intended to pervert the course of justice: road traffic offender who tampered with blood specimen provided.

R v Gilroy (Lillian) and Lovett (Linda) [1984] Crim LR 560 CCC Was not perversion of justice to conceal from police evidence concerning person who was not actually guilty of crime concerned.

R v Kellett [1975] 3 All ER 466; (1975) 61 Cr App R 240; [1975] Crim LR 576t; (1976) 140 JP 1; (1975) 125 NLJ 698t; [1976] QB 372; (1975) 119 SJ 542; [1975] 3 WLR 713 CA Threatening witness to get them to change/withhold evidence is obstruction of justice.

R v Kellett [1974] Crim LR 552 CrCt Threatening to sue witness to get them to change/withhold evidence is obstruction of justice.

R v Kiffin [1994] Crim LR 449 CA Could be guilty of perverting course of justice where impeded police investigation into suspected criminal offence.

R v Purcy and others [1933] All ER 631; (1931-34) XXIX Cox CC 657; (1932-34) 24 Cr App R 70; (1933) 97 JP 153; (1933) 149 LTR 432; (1933) 77 SJ 421 CCA To sustain charge of obstructing coroner must show coroner under duty to hold inquest and party sought to obstruct same.

R v Selvage and another [1982] 1 All ER 96; (1981) 73 Cr App R 333; [1982] Crim LR 47; (1982) 146 JP 115; (1981) 131 NLJ 1008; [1982] QB 372; [1981] RTR 481; (1981) 125 SJ 708; [1981] 3 WLR 811 CA Cannot pervert course of justice if no case/investigation in progress.

R v Sharpe; R v Stringer [1938] 1 All ER; (1939-40) XXXI Cox CC 24; (1936-38) 26 Cr App R 122; (1938) 102 JP 113; (1938) 85 LJ 46; (1938) 82 SJ 158; (1938) WN (I) 29 CCA Need not be proceedings pending at time of conspiracy to obstruct for obstruction conviction to be sustained.

R v Smalley [1959] Crim LR 587 Assizes Police officer convicted of fabrication of evidence - 'evidence' to be given a wide interpretation.

R v Thomas; R v Ferguson [1979] 1 All ER 577; (1979) 68 Cr App R 275; (1979) 143 JP 219; (1978) 128 NLJ 1196t; [1979] QB 326; (1978) 122 SJ 791; [1979] 2 WLR 144 CA Anything done to help police suspect avoid arrest is obstruction of justice.

R v Toney; R v Ali (Tanveer) [1993] 2 All ER 409; (1993) 97 Cr App R 176; [1993] Crim LR 397; (1993) 157 JP 889; (1993) 143 NLJ 403; (1993) 137 SJ LB 46; [1992] TLR 608; [1993] 1 WLR 364 CA Interference with witness an obstruction of justice even if no inducement or threat.

OBSTRUCTING/PERVERTING THE COURSE OF JUSTICE (perverting)

R v Headley [1995] Crim LR 737; [1996] RTR 173; (1995) 139 SJ LB 67; [1995] TLR 78 CA Not perverting course of justice where passively allowed charges concerning brother but mistakenly naming defendant to be successfully prosecuted and sentence imposed.

R v Rafique and others [1993] 4 All ER 1; (1993) 97 Cr App R 395; [1993] Crim LR 761; (1993) 143 NLJ 581; [1993] QB 843; (1993) 137 SJ LB 119; [1993] TLR 220; [1993] 3 WLR 617 CA Perversion of justice may occur before criminal investigation begins.

R v Sinha [1995] Crim LR 68; [1994] TLR 392 CA Intention to mislead whatever court was adjudicating in whatever judicial proceedings might follow offence was adequate intention for offence of perverting the course of justice.

OBSTRUCTION (of fire brigade officer)

Sands v Director of Public Prosecutions [1990] Crim LR 585; (1991) 155 JP 28; [1990] TLR 240 HC QBD Fire brigade officer only has right to enter those premises on which is fire/is reasonably believed to be fire/is necessary to extinguish fire or safeguard place into which entering.

OBSTRUCTION OF HIGHWAY (general)

Abel v Stone (1970) 134 JP 237 HC QBD Wilful obstruction of highway a continuing offence so plea of autrefois acquit available.

Absalom v Martin (1973) 123 NLJ 946t; [1973] Crim LR 752 HC QBD Billposter's part-parking of van on pavement while putting up bill did not merit conviction for wilful obstruction of highway.

Attorney General v Gastonia Coaches Ltd (1976) 126 NLJ 1267t; [1977] RTR 219 HC ChD Obstruction of highway by coaches a public nuisance; smell/noise from premises of motor coach operator along with interference in access to private premises a private nuisance.

Baxter v Matthews [1958] Crim LR 263 Magistrates Valid conviction under Highway Act 1835, s 78, for negligent interruption of free passage of carriage on the highway.

OFFENCE UNDER STATUTORY ORDER (general)

Carey v Chief Constable of Avon and Somerset [1995] RTR 405 CA Removal by police of converted coach parked by kerb but not obstructing road-users was unlawful.

Dymond v Pearce and others [1972] 1 All ER 1142; (1972) 136 JP 397; (1972) 122 NLJ 58t; [1972] 1 QB 496; [1972] RTR 169; (1972) 116 SJ 62; [1972] 2 WLR 633 CA Obstruction of highway by parked vehicle a nuisance.

Dymond v Pearce and others [1971] RTR 417 Assizes Obstruction of highway by parked vehicle not a nuisance.

Ellis v Smith [1962] 3 All ER 954; [1963] Crim LR 128; (1963) 127 JP 51; (1963) 113 LJ 26; (1962) 106 SJ 1069; [1962] 1 WLR 1486 HC QBD Until relief (bus) driver assumes charge last (bus) driver is person in charge of vehicle.

Ende v Cassidy [1964] Crim LR 595t HC QBD Was prima facie good reason to believe that where motor vehicle guilty of obstructing free passage along highway owner of same responsible.

Evans v Barker (1971) 121 NLJ 457t; [1971] RTR 453 HC QBD On when parking of car in road not an obstruction but an unnecessary obstruction.

Gelberg v Miller [1961] 1 All ER 291; [1961] Crim LR 251; (1961) 125 JP 123; (1961) 111 LJ 172; (1961) 105 SJ 89; [1961] 1 WLR 153 HC QBD Valid arrest without warrant where wilful obstruction of highway/know of factual basis for arrest.

Hinde v Evans (1907-09) XXI Cox CC 331; (1906) 70 JP 548 HC KBD Cart was obstructing highway (even though person left in charge thereof).

Hudson and another v Bray (1917) 81 JP 105; [1917] 1 KB 520; (1917) CC Rep VI 14; [1917] 86 LJCL 576; (1917) 116 LTR 122; (1916-17) 61 SJ 234; (1916-17) XXXIII TLR 118 HC KBD No responsibility on occupier to draw attention of highway users to tree fallen across same during gale.

Mounsey v Campbell [1983] RTR 36 HC QBD Bumper to bumper parking by van driver occasioned unnecessary obstruction.

Nelmes v Rhys Howells Transport Ltd [1977] Crim LR 227 HC QBD On relevant factors to be considered in determining whether so used trailers as to cause unnecessary obstruction of highway.

Pitcher v Lockett [1966] Crim LR 283g HC QBD Valid conviction of hot dog salesman for obstruction of highway through manner in which parked van (from which sold hot dogs) on street.

R v Bartholomew (1907-09) XXI Cox CC 556; (1908) 72 JP 79; [1908] 1 KB 554; (1908) XCVIII LTR 284; (1907-08) 52 SJ 208; [1908] 77 LJCL 275; (1907-08) XXIV TLR 238; (1908) WN (I) 20 CCR Coffee stall on highway not common nuisance.

Solomon v Burbridge [1956] Crim LR 276t; (1956) 120 JP 231 HC QBD On elements of causing unnecessary obstruction (contrary to Motor Vehicles (Construction and Use) Regulations 1955, r 89) in way leave car parked.

The Police v O'Connor [1957] Crim LR 478 Sessions That large vehicle properly parked on road did not constitute unreasonable user adequate to support conviction for obstruction of road.

Wall v Williams [1966] Crim LR 50t HC QBD Taxi-driver who briefly blocked road in badly executed 'U-turn' could validly be found to have caused unnecessary obstruction.

Worth v Brooks [1959] Crim LR 855t HC QBD Parking on grass verge was causing of unnecessary obstruction contrary to the Motor Vehicles (Construction and Use) Regulations 1955, r89.

WR Anderson (Motors), Ltd v Hargreaves [1962] 1 All ER 129; [1962] Crim LR 115t; (1962) 126 JP 100; (1962) 112 LJ 154; [1962] 1 QB 425; (1961) 105 SJ 1127 HC QBD Not guilty of obstruction where park vehicles in parking place during operative hours, whatever intent.

OFFENCE UNDER STATUTORY ORDER (general)

R v Kakelo [1923] All ER 191; (1922-23) 17 Cr App R 150; (1923) 129 LTR 477; (1923-24) 68 SJ 41; (1922-23) XXXIX TLR 671; (1923) WN (I) 220 CCA Objection in trial for offence under statutory order that order not proved to be taken at trial.

R v Kakelo (1922-23) 17 Cr App R 149 CCA Leave to appeal in case where in trial for offence under statutory order same was not proved.

OFFENCE UNDER TEMPORARY STATUTE (general)

R v Wicks [1946] 2 All ER 529; (1946) 96 LJ 629; (1946) 175 LTR 427; (1946) 90 SJ 557; (1945-46) LXII TLR 674; (1946) WN (I) 205 CCA Can be punished for acts done contrary to temporary statute which lapses before prosecution/conviction.

Wicks v Director of Public Prosecutions [1947] 1 All ER 205; [1947] AC 362; (1946-48) 32 Cr App R 7; (1947) 97 LJ 65; [1947] 116 LJR 247; (1947) 176 LTR 150; (1947) LXIII TLR 6; (1947) WN (I) 30 HL Accused could be convicted under temporary statute despite its expiry.

OFFENCES AGAINST THE STATE (assisting the enemy)

R v Olsson (1914-15) XXXI TLR 559 CCA Conviction for obtaining information useful to enemy affirmed.

R v Steane [1947] 1 All ER 813; (1946-48) 32 Cr App R 61; (1947) 111 JP 337; [1947] KB 997; [1947] 116 LJR 969; (1947) 177 LTR 122; (1947) 91 SJ 279; (1947) LXIII TLR 403; (1947) WN (I) 184 CCA Can only convict of assisting enemy if act done with criminal/not innocent (such as saving family) intent to assist.

OFFENCES AGAINST THE STATE (communicating with the enemy)

Ex parte Dyson (1914-15) XXXI TLR 425 HC KBD Valid conviction of reporter for telegramming information jeopardising British forces (relevant regulation not ultra vires).

Fox v Spicer (1917) 116 LTR 86; (1916-17) XXXIII TLR 172 HC KBD Prosecution procedurally improper: information at issue was for publication in newspaper so proposed prosecution ought to have been referred to DPP.

R v M (1914-15) 11 Cr App R 207; (1915-16) XXXII TLR 1 CCA Regardless whether information true or not, if communicate with enemy to assist same are guilty of breach of Defence of the Realm (Consolidation) Regulations 1914, r18 and r48.

OFFENCES AGAINST THE STATE (coup d'état)

Liyanage and others v R [1966] 1 All ER 650 PC Retroactive legislation aimed at those involved in coup d'état void.

OFFENCES AGAINST THE STATE (diplomat)

R v B (A) (1939-40) XXXI Cox CC 462; [1941] 1 KB 455; (1941) 165 LTR 382 CCA Foreign embassy official liable under Official Secrets Acts 1911 and 1920.

R v Kent (Tyler Gatewood) (1940-42) 28 Cr App R 23; (1941) 85 SJ 315; (1940-41) LVII TLR 307 CCA Diplomatic privilege of embassy employee could be waived by Ambassador/foreign Government; Official Secrets Acts apply to diplomatic agents.

OFFENCES AGAINST THE STATE (internal security)

Poh (Teh Cheng) alias Meh (Char) v Public Prosecutor, Malaysia; Poh (Teh Cheng) alias Meh (Char) v Public Prosecutor, Malaysia [1980] AC 458; [1979] Crim LR 180; (1979) 129 (1) NLJ 18; (1979) 123 SJ 16; [1979] 2 WLR 623 PC Consideration of Malayisan emergency powers (possession of firearms/ammunition) legislation.

Public Prosecutor v Koi [1968] 1 All ER 419 PC Consorting with Indonesian soldiers not doing so with persons carrying arms contrary to Internal Security Act 1960.

OFFENCES AGAINST THE STATE (official secrets)

Adler v George [1964] 1 All ER 628; [1964] Crim LR 314t; (1964) 128 JP 251; (1964) 114 LJ 221; [1964] 2 QB 7; (1964) 108 SJ 119; [1964] 2 WLR 542 HC QBD '[I]n the vicinity of' in Official Secrets Act 1920, s 3 meant 'in or in the vicinity of'.

Chandler and others v Director of Public Prosecutions [1962] 3 All ER 142; [1964] AC 763; (1962) 46 Cr App R 347; [1962] Crim LR 634t; (1962) 112 LJ 552; (1962) 106 SJ 588; [1962] 3 WLR 694 HL Critique of defence policy inadmissible as defence to conspiring to enter prohibited place; definition of terms in Official Secrets Act 1911, s 1.

Lewis v Cattle [1938] 2 All ER 368; (1939-40) XXXI Cox CC 123; (1938) 102 JP 239; [1938] 2 KB 454; [1938] 107 LJCL 429; (1938) 82 SJ 376; (1937-38) LIV TLR 721; (1938) WN (I) 169 HC KBD Police officer a 'person holding office under His Majesty' within meaning of Official Secrets Act 1911, s 2.

Loat v Andrews (1986) 130 SJ 697 HC QBD Civilian working under police officer though employed by county council did come under the provisions of the Official Secrets Acts 1911 and 1920, ss 2 and 7 respectively.

Loat v James [1986] Crim LR 744; (1986) 150 JP 652 HC QBD Civilian working under police officer though employed by county council did come under the provisions of the Official Secrets Acts 1911 and 1920, ss 2 and 7 respectively.

R v Bettaney [1985] Crim LR 104 CA Quality of material taken not gauged by reference to purpose for which taken; jurors with previous dishonesty convictions legitimately asked by Crown to stand by.

R v Bingham [1973] 2 All ER 89; (1973) 57 Cr App R 439; [1973] Crim LR 309t; (1973) 137 JP 481; (1973) 123 NLJ 180t; [1973] QB 870; (1973) 117 SJ 265; [1973] 2 WLR 520 CA That may be transmitting information prejudicial to State intent for official secrets offence.

R v Chandler and others [1962] 2 All ER 314; (1962) 112 LJ 456; (1962) 106 SJ 331 CCA Once 'purpose' is to breach Official Secrets Act 1911 whether will jeopardise national security an objective issue; cannot challenge Crown prerogative regarding military matters.

R v Crisp and Homewood (1919) 83 JP 121 CCC Terms of tailoring contracts with War Office not official secrets the release of which was an offence.

R v Galvin [1987] 2 All ER 851; (1988) 86 Cr App R 85; [1987] Crim LR 700; [1987] QB 862; (1987) 131 SJ 657; [1987] 3 WLR 93 CA Under Official Secrets Act Crown must prove communicator of unauthorised information not authorised to do so.

R v Kent (Tyler Gatewood) (1940-42) 28 Cr App R 23; (1941) 85 SJ 315; (1940-41) LVII TLR 307 CCA Diplomatic privilege of embassy employee could be waived by Ambassador/foreign Government; Official Secrets Acts apply to diplomatic agents.

R v Loat [1985] Crim LR 154 CrCt Civilian employed by police force came within provisions of Official Secrets Act 1911.

R v Oakes [1959] 2 All ER 92; (1959) 43 Cr App R 114; [1959] Crim LR 456; (1959) 123 JP 290; (1959) 109 LJ 298; [1959] 2 QB 350; (1959) 103 SJ 373 CCA Is a separate offence of doing an act preparatory to committing an offence under the Official Secrets Act, 1911.

R v Parrott (George Charles) (1912-13) 8 Cr App R 186 CCA Meaning of 'enemy' in Official Secrets Act 1911, s 1.

R v Ponting [1985] Crim LR 318 CCC On meaning of terms 'duty' and 'interests of the state' under Official Secrets Act 1911, s 2(1).

R v Simington (1918-21) XXVI Cox CC 736; (1920-21) 15 Cr App R 97; (1921) 85 JP 179; [1921] 1 KB 451; [1921] LJCL 471; (1921) 125 LTR 128; (1920-21) XXXVII TLR 114; (1920) WN (I) 384 CCA Interpretation of Official Secrets Act 1911, s 2(1).

Stevenson v Fulton [1935] All ER 431; (1934-39) XXX Cox CC 293; (1935) 99 JP 423; [1936] 1 KB 320; (1936) 81 LJ 42; [1936] 105 LJCL 167; (1936) 154 LTR 162; (1935-36) LII TLR 89; (1936) 80 SJ 75; (1935) WN (I) 188 HC KBD Person using (rather than providing) accommodation address can be convicted for furnishing false information contrary to Official Secrets Act 1920, s 5(4).

OFFENCES AGAINST THE STATE (sedition)

Mattouk v Massad [1943] 2 All ER 517; (1943) 87 SJ 381; (1943) WN (I) 215 PC Does not matter whether intercourse with/without consent in seduction action as master suing for loss of services.

R v Aldred (1911-13) XXII Cox CC 1; (1910) 74 JP 55 CCC What constitutes seditious libel; test for seditious libel.

R v Arrowsmith [1975] 1 All ER 463; (1975) 60 Cr App R 211; [1975] Crim LR 161t; (1975) 139 JP 221; (1975) 125 NLJ 13t; [1975] QB 678; (1975) 119 SJ 165; [1975] 2 WLR 484 CA Seducing armed force members from allegiance a single offence with one of two intents - not duplicity if both intents mentioned; mistake that DPP will not prosecute not a defence to charge but may mitigate sentence.

R v Chief Metropolitan Stipendiary Magistrate, ex parte Choudhury [1991] 1 All ER 306; (1990) 91 Cr App R 393; [1990] Crim LR 711; [1991] 1 QB 429; [1990] TLR 294; [1990] 3 WLR 986 HC QBD Common law of blasphemy applies only to Christian religion; sedition involves attack against Sovereign/government not on different classes of citizen.

Wallace-Johnson v R [1940] 1 All ER 241; [1940] AC 231; (1940) 84 SJ 149; (1939-40) LVI TLR 215; (1940) WN (I) 5 PC Need not show seditious intent/subsequent incitement to violence to sustain charge of seditious writing.

OFFENCES AGAINST THE STATE (treason)

De Jager v Attorney-General of Natal [1904-07] All ER 1008; [1907] AC 326; (1907) XCVI LTR 857; (1906-07) XXIII TLR 516 PC Is treason for Crown subject to assist alien occupiers of Crown territory in which one resides.

Joyce v Director of Public Prosecutions [1946] 1 All ER 186; [1946] AC 347; (1945-46) 31 Cr App R 57; (1946) 96 LJ 94; [1946] 115 LJ 146; (1946) 174 LTR 206; (1945-46) LXII TLR 208; (1946) WN (I) 31 HL Person with British passport (albeit obtained by fraud) could be guilty of treason under Treason Act 1351; holding British passport (even one obtained by fraud) entitled bearer to normal rights/protection afforded bearers thereof.

R v Ahlers (1914-15) XXIV Cox CC 623; (1914-15) 11 Cr App R 63; (1915) 79 JP 255; [1915] 1 KB 616; [1915] 84 LJKB 901; (1915) 112 LTR 558; (1914-15) XXXI TLR 141 CCA High treason conviction quashed as inadequate direction to jury on necessary intent.

R v Casement [1916-17] All ER 214; (1915-17) XXV Cox CC 503; (1916-17) 12 Cr App R 99; [1917] 1 KB 98 (also HC KBD); (1916) 51 LJ 375; [1917] 86 LJCL 467 (also HC KBD); (1916-17) 115 LTR 277; (1915-16) 60 SJ 656; (1915-16) XXXII TLR 667 CCA Treason involves giving aid/comfort to King's enemies inside/outside realm; treason triable before HC KBD.

R v Casement (1915-17) XXV Cox CC 480; [1917] 1 KB 98 (also CCA); [1917] 86 LJCL 467 (also CCA); (1916-17) 115 LTR 267; (1915-16) XXXII TLR 601 HC KBD Treason involves giving aid/comfort to King's enemies inside/outside realm.

R v Joyce [1945] 2 All ER 673; (1946) 96 LJ 185; (1945) 173 LTR 377; (1945) 89 SJ 532; (1945-46) LXII TLR 57; (1945) WN (I) 220 CCA Person with British passport, though a foreigner, could be guilty of treason under Treason Act 1351; holding British passport (even one obtained by fraud) entitled bearer to normal rights/protection afforded bearers thereof.

R v Lynch [1900-03] All ER 688; (1901-07) XX Cox CC 468; (1903) 67 JP 41; [1903] 1 KB 444; (1903) 38 LJ 61; [1903] 72 LJKB 167; (1903) LXXXVIII LTR 26; (1902-03) XIX TLR 163; (1902-03) 51 WR 619 HC KBD Treason possible inside/outside Britain; cannot in time of war escape liability for treason by naturalisation as enemy national.

OFFENSIVE WEAPON (general)

Ashbee v Jayne [1966] Crim LR 49; (1965) 109 SJ 919 HC QBD That carried sand-filled sock for purpose of self-defence did not mean could not be offensive weapon.

Bates v Bulman [1979] 3 All ER 170; (1979) 68 Cr App R 21; [1979] Crim LR 531; (1979) 143 JP 750; (1979) 123 SJ 688; [1979] 1 WLR 1190 HC QBD Borrowing non-offensive item intending to use it offensively not crime of having offensive weapon with one.

Bryan v Mott (1976) 62 Cr App R 71; [1976] Crim LR 64t; (1975) 125 NLJ 1093t; (1975) 119 SJ 743 HC QBD Broken milk bottle was offensive weapon and carrying it about for purpose of committing suicide not reasonable excuse.

Davis v Alexander (1970) 54 Cr App R 398; [1972] Crim LR 595 HC QBD Prosecution need not prove accused carried weapon with intent to cause injury where is clearly offensive weapon.

Director of Public Prosecutions v Gregson (1993) 96 Cr App R 240; (1993) 157 JP 201; (1992) 136 SJ LB 245; [1992] TLR 403 HC QBD That had good reason for knife some days previously and then forgot possession not good defence to possession of offensive weapon.

Director of Public Prosecutions v Hynde [1997] TLR 398 HC QBD Court can take judicial notice of fact that butterfly knife an injurious weapon.

Evans v Hughes [1972] 3 All ER 412; (1972) 56 Cr App R 813; [1972] Crim LR 558; (1972) 136 JP 725; (1972) 122 NLJ 728t; (1972) 116 SJ 842; [1972] 1 WLR 1452 HC QBD Metal bar carried for self-defence reasons an offensive weapon; can only be reasonable excuse if immediate danger justifies carrying article.

Gibson v Wales [1983] 1 All ER 869; (1983) 76 Cr App R 60; [1983] Crim LR 113; (1983) 147 JP 143; (1983) 127 SJ 222; [1982] TLR 516; [1983] 1 WLR 393 HC QBD Flick-knife is an offensive weapon.

Harris v Director of Public Prosecutions; Fehmi v Director of Public Prosecutions [1993] 1 All ER 562; (1993) 96 Cr App R 235; (1993) 157 JP 205; (1952) 102 LJ 246; (1992) 136 SJ LB 228; [1992] TLR 405; [1993] 1 WLR 82 HC QBD Lock-knife not a 'folding pocketknife' and hence an offence to carry in public place.

M Potter Ltd v Customs and Excise Commissioners [1973] Crim LR 116 CA Gravity knife (a lock knife) was an offensive weapon.

McMahon and another v Dollard [1965] Crim LR 238t HC QBD Studded belt not per se an offensive weapon.

R v Allamby; R v Medford [1974] 3 All ER; (1974) 59 Cr App R 189; [1975] Crim LR 39; (1974) 138 JP 659; (1974) 118 SJ 830 [1974] 1 WLR 1494 CA At time/place in particulars must intend to use weapons offensively in future.

R v Butler [1988] Crim LR 695 CA Sword stick an offensive weapon per se.

R v Cugullere [1961] 2 All ER 343; (1961) 45 Cr App R 108; [1961] Crim LR 410; (1961) 125 JP 414; (1961) 111 LJ 322; (1961) 105 SJ 386 CCA Must 'knowingly' have offensive weapon/s in public place to be convicted of same under Prevention of Crime Act 1953, s 1(1).

R v Dayle [1973] 3 All ER 1151; (1974) 58 Cr App R 100; [1973] Crim LR 703t; (1974) 138 JP 65; [1974] 1 WLR 181 CA Intent to use non-offensive weapon to injure needed to sustain offensive weapon in public place charge.

R v Dayle (1973) 123 NLJ 748t HC QBD Person acquitted of unawful possession of offensive weapon ought to have been acquitted of assault occasioning bodily harm (using said weapon).

R v Edmonds and others [1963] 1 All ER 828; (1963) 47 Cr App R 114; (1963) 127 JP 283; (1963) 113 LJ 248; [1963] 2 QB 142; (1963) 107 SJ 196; [1963] 2 WLR 715 CCA If joint offensive weapons indictment must show common intent to injure; intent to 'frighten' undesirable terminology.

R v Flynn [1986] Crim LR 239 CA Jury must be satisfied in offensive weapon case either that item concerned was offensive per se or was intended to be used offensively.

R v Giles [1976] Crim LR 253 CrCt Holding of glass in hand after fight had ceased but with intent of using against another was not possession of offensive weapon.

R v Gipson [1963] Crim LR 281g CCA Shotgun not of itself an offensive weapon (must be intent to injure).

R v Jones (Keith Desmond) (1987) 85 Cr App R 259; (1987) 131 SJ 504; [1987] 1 WLR 692 CA On what constitutes being 'armed' with offensive weapon for purpose of Customs and Excise Management Act 1979, s 86.

R v McCogg [1982] Crim LR 685 CrCt Flick knife did not have to be offensive weapon.

R v McGuire and Page [1963] Crim LR 572 CCA Lawful object defence unavailable to person in possession of air pistol; successful appeal on basis of misdirection as to constructive possession.

R v McMahon [1961] Crim LR 622 CCA On what is meant by phrase 'for causing injury to the person' (Prevention of Crime Act 1953, s 1(4)).

R v Mehmed [1963] Crim LR 780t CCA Valid conviction for possession of offensive weapon in public place/acquittal of possessing same with intent to endanger life and of attempting to discharge same with intent to do grievous bodily harm.

R v Petrie [1961] 1 All ER 466; (1961) 45 Cr App R 73; [1961] Crim LR 264; (1961) 125 JP 198; (1961) 111 LJ 189; (1961) 105 SJ 131; [1961] 1 WLR 368 CCA Where offensive weapon not made/adapted but merely intended as such (here razor) burden on prosecution to prove that intent.

R v Powell [1963] Crim LR 511; (1963) 113 LJ 643 CCA Toy gun an offensive weapon where have intent to use it to cause injury (intent proved by fact that was in fact used to cause injury here).

R v Russell (Raymond) (1985) 81 Cr App R 315; [1985] Crim LR 231 CA Rarely credible but nonetheless possible defence that had so forgotten possession of offensive weapon as to be unaware it was there.

R v Simpson [1983] 3 All ER 789; (1984) 78 Cr App R 115; [1984] Crim LR 39 (1984) 148 JP 33; (1983) 127 SJ 748; [1983] TLR 638; [1983] 1 WLR 1494 CA Flick-knife is an offensive weapon.

R v Sparks [1965] Crim LR 113; (1964) 108 SJ 922 CCA Shotgun not an offensive weapon per se.

R v Williamson (Alan) (1978) 67 Cr App R 35; [1978] Crim LR 229; (1977) 127 NLJ 1205t; (1977) 121 SJ 812 CA Whether particular article an offensive weapon a question of fact for jury.

Smaje v Balmer [1965] 2 All ER 248; (1965) 129 JP 329 CrCt 'Dangerous or offensive weapon' under Larceny Act 1916, s 28(1) must be item fashioned to cause person injury.

Southwell v Chadwick (1987) 85 Cr App R 235 CA Machete knife and catapult not offensive weapons per se.

Wood v Commissioner of the Metropolis [1986] 2 All ER 570; (1986) 83 Cr App R 145; [1986] Crim LR 481; (1986) 150 JP 236; (1986) 130 SJ 446; [1986] 1 WLR 796 HC QBD Piece of glass instrument for offensive use, not offensive weapon; use of instrument for offensive purpose must be premeditated.

OFFENSIVE WEAPON (possession)

Bradley v Moss [1974] Crim LR 430 HC QBD Person who generally carried offensive weapons for general self-defence purposes did not have reasonable excuse to possession of same.

Copus v Director of Public Prosecutions [1989] Crim LR 577 HC QBD Rice flail an offensive weapon per se.

Evens v Wright [1964] Crim LR 466t HC QBD That weapons in car to protect one if attacked when carrying wages money did not furnish reasonable excuse to possession of the weapons when were not carrrying wages money.

Godwin v Director of Public Prosecutions (1993) 96 Cr App R 244; (1993) 157 JP 197; [1992] TLR 406 HC QBD That explanation uncontroverted by prosecution did not mean had established lawful authority for possession of weapon.

Harrison v Thornton (1979) 68 Cr App R 28; [1966] Crim LR 388t; (1966) 110 SJ 444 HC QBD Stone picked up and thrown in course of fight was offensive weapon.

Houghton v Chief Constable of Greater Manchester (1987) 84 Cr App R 319 CA Person wearing police truncheon as part of fancy dress had reasonable excuse for possessing what was an offensive weapon per se.

Knox v Anderton (1983) 76 Cr App R 156; [1983] Crim LR 114; (1983) 147 JP 340; [1982] TLR 565 HC QBD Landing in public flats was 'public place' within meaning of Prevention of Crime Act 1953, s 1(4).

Malnik v Director of Public Prosecutions [1989] Crim LR 451 HC QBD Defence of reasonable excuse unavailable to appellant convicted of possession of offensive weapon.

Ohlson v Hylton [1975] 2 All ER 490; [1975] Crim LR 292; (1975) 139 JP 531; (1975) 125 NLJ 261t; (1975) 119 SJ 255; [1975] 1 WLR 724 HC QBD Sudden use of non-offensive article as weapon not possession of offensive weapon.

OPPORTUNITY (general)

Patterson v Block [1984] TLR 398 HC QBD Failed appeal against conviction for possession of offensive weapon (lock-knife).

Pittard v Mahoney [1977] Crim LR 169 HC QBD Failed attempt to plead reasonable excuse (fear of attack) as defence to possession of offensive weapon.

R v Fleming (David Michael) [1989] Crim LR 71 CrCt Possession of carving knife with intention to injure self is not possession of offensive weapon.

R v Heffey [1981] Crim LR 111 CrCt Landing on block of flats not a 'public place' for purposes of Prevention of Crime Act 1953.

R v Humphreys [1977] Crim LR 225 CA Was not possession of offensive weapon to possess penknife for normal use (though end up using it to stab another in fight).

R v Jura [1954] 1 All ER 696; (1954) 38 Cr App R 53; [1954] Crim LR 378; (1954) 118 JP 260; (1954) 104 LJ 200; [1954] 1 QB 503; (1954) 98 SJ 198; [1954] 2 WLR 516 CCA Person in possession of air gun at shooting gallery has reasonable excuse to possess it (even if used unlawfully).

R v McCalla (Clevous Errol) (1988) 87 Cr App R 372; (1988) 152 JP 481 CA Cosh an offensive weapon: that had forgotten possession was not reasonable excuse excusing offence.

R v Peacock [1973] Crim LR 639 CA Was not defence to possession of offensive weapon that carried out of fear that might some day be attacked.

R v Rapier (Franklyn Joseph) (1980) 70 Cr App R 17; [1980] Crim LR 48 CA Term 'intimidate' seldom justified in possessing offensive weapon case (only if sought to cause injury by shock and so injury to individual).

R v Spanner, Poulter and Ward [1973] Crim LR 704 CA Though is matter for jury judge's finding that security guards had no reasonable excuse for always carrying truncheons was justified.

R v Whitman [1962] Crim LR 394 CCA On burden of proof as regards proving possession of 'offensive' weapon.

OPPORTUNITY (general)

R v Wood (1981) 131 NLJ 929 CA Failed appeal against manslaughter conviction where claimed evidence did not prove had opportunity to commit crime.

PAWNBROKER (general)

Allworthy and Walker v Clayton (1907-09) XXI Cox CC 352 HC KBD Pawnbroker could not be convicted of neglecting to deliver pledge where loss of same was in good faith.

PERJURY (attempt to incite perjury)

R v Cromack [1978] Crim LR 217 CA Successful appeal in light of jury misdirection against conviction for attempt to incite perjury.

PERJURY (general)

Appuhamy v R [1963] 1 All ER 762; [1963] AC 474; (1963) 113 LJ 233; (1963) 107 SJ 110; [1963] 2 WLR 375 PC When alleging perjury of elements of evidence must be precise enough to enable accused defend themself.

De Vries v National Westminster Bank Ltd and others [1984] TLR 531 HC QBD Perjury prosecution appropriate action against individual who swore/employed affidavit in knowledge that it was false.

Hargreaves v Bretherton and another [1958] 3 All ER 122 HC QBD Affected party cannot bring civil action against perjurer.

Kiu (Chang Hang) and others v Piggott and another [1908-10] All ER 1270; (1909) C LTR 310 PC Person to be heard in own defence before committal for contempt (for perjury).

R v Ashford (Kent) Justices, ex parte Richley [1955] 3 All ER 604; (1955) 105 LJ 760 CA Certiorari quashing proceedings need not issue when perjury discovered.

R v Ashford, Kent, Justices, ex parte Richley (No 2) [1956] Crim LR 48; [1956] 1 QB 167; [1955] 3 WLR 778 CA Certiorari quashing proceedings need not issue when perjury discovered.

R v Atkinson (Douglas Walter) (1932-34) 24 Cr App R 123 CCA Conviction quashed where was inadequate warning as to evidence from perjurer/accomplice.

R v Carroll (Deborah Louise); R v Perkins (Sean Daid); R v Dickerson (Andrea) (1994) 99 Cr App R 381; [1993] Crim LR 613 CA Must be evidence of more than one witness (or other buttressing evidence) to support conviction for perjury.

R v Castiglione and Porteous (1913-14) XXIII Cox CC 46; (1911-12) 7 Cr App R 233; (1912) 76 JP 351; (1912) 106 LTR 1023; (1911-12) XXVIII TLR 403 CCA False swearing of affidavit.

R v Crossley (1911-13) XXII Cox CC 40; (1909) 2 Cr App R 8; (1909) 73 JP 119; [1909] 1 KB 411; (1909) 44 LJ 48; [1909] 78 LJKB 299; (1909) C LTR 463; (1908-09) 53 SJ 214; (1908-09) XXV TLR 225; (1909) WN (I) 18 CCA Can be indicted for perjury before County Court judge hearing workmen's compensation action - is a judicial proceeding.

R v Crown Court at Wolverhampton, ex parte Crofts [1982] 3 All ER 702; [1983] RTR 389 HC QBD Superior court may quash Crown Court decision obtained by fraud unless raises prospect of double jeopardy.

R v Cummins (Patrick John); R v Perks (Lance Terence) (1987) 84 Cr App R 71 CA Convictions not quashed notwithstanding giving of perjured evidence against prisoners at trial.

R v Edwards (Maxine) [1996] 2 Cr App R 345; (1996) 140 SJ LB 43; (1996) TLR 31/1/96 CA Conviction quashed where evidence of police officers on which accused was convicted was seriously coloured by possibility of perjury on part of police officers.

R v Frickey and Frickey [1956] Crim LR 421 Sessions Was not perjury to falsely complete form indicating parents consented to marriage as document not mandated under Marriage Act 1949.

R v Gaskell (Mary Ann) (1913) 77 JP 112; (1912-13) XXIX TLR 108 CCA Conviction quashed where jury did not seem to understand that more than oath against oath required to sustain perjury conviction.

R v Hamid (Ahmed Youssef); R v Hamid (Beebee Nazmoon) (1979) 69 Cr App R 324 CA Perjury conviction cannot stand absent corroboration warning by judge unless jury would have made same decision anyway.

R v Hood-Barrs [1943] 1 All ER 665; (1942-44) 29 Cr App R 55; [1943] KB 455; (1944) 94 LJ 100; [1943] 112 LJ 420; (1943) 168 LTR 408; (1943) 87 SJ 220; (1942-43) LIX TLR 246; (1943) WN (I) 97 CCA Lie in income tax appeal heard by two Special Commissioners was perjury.

R v Hudson; R v Taylor [1971] 2 All ER 244; (1972) 56 Cr App R 1; [1971] Crim LR 357; (1971) 135 JP 407; [1971] 2 QB 202; (1971) 115 SJ 303; [1971] 2 WLR 1047 CA Need not be possible for threat to immediately effected for duress to arise.

R v Mailey [1957] Crim LR 328 Assizes Failed prosecution for perjury against farmer for making false claim when claiming subsidy under the Hill Framing and Livestock Rearing Acts 1946 to 1954.

R v Millward (1984) 78 Cr App R 263 CrCt That person accused of perjury believed what said was material not defence to perjury.

R v Millward (Neil Frederick) [1985] 1 All ER 859; (1985) 80 Cr App R 280; [1985] Crim LR 321; (1985) 149 JP 545; [1985] QB 519; (1985) 129 SJ 187; [1985] 2 WLR 532 CA On what has to be proved by prosecution to secure conviction for perjury.

R v O'Connor [1980] Crim LR 43 CA On proving perjury.

R v Parsons (Bruce and Alan) [1967] Crim LR 541 Assizes Committal to next assizes for trial for perjury at previous assizes (Perjury Act 1911, s 9).

R v Peach [1990] 2 All ER 966; (1990) 91 Cr App R 279; [1990] Crim LR 741; [1990] TLR 391; [1990] 1 WLR 976 CA Conviction for perjury may be supported by two witnesses to same falsity on same occasion.

R v Penn [1966] Crim LR 681t CA Perjury conviction quashed where falsehood had sprung from bona fide error.

R v Peters [1955] Crim LR 712 Sessions Was not perjury for divorced man to have self entered as 'bachelor' in marriage register.

R v Petricus (1903) 67 JP 378 CCC Might be possible for person who swore to document not knowing its contents to be untrue to be later convicted of perjury.

R v Plymouth Justices; ex parte W [1994] 1 FCR 80; [1993] 2 FLR 777 HC QBD Magistrates ought not to have adjourned contact hearing for rehearing by other magistrates simply because applicant committed perjury.

R v Rider [1986] Crim LR 626 CA On relevance of truth of statement to prosecution (and format of same) for perjury.

R v Shaw (James) (1911-13) XXII Cox CC 376; (1911) 75 JP 191; (1911) 104 LTR 112; (1910-11) XXVII TLR 181 CCA Could not be convicted of taking false oath before body not authorised to take oath.

R v Sweet-Escott (1971) 55 Cr App R 316 Assizes Could not be prosecuted for perjury on basis of false answers to cross-examination that ought not to have taken place.

R v Threlfall (1914-15) XXIV Cox CC 230; (1914-15) 111 LTR 168 CCA Single person may establish took oath but need more evidence to prove oath taken falsely.

R v Wheeler [1916-17] All ER 1111; (1915-17) XXV Cox CC 603; (1916-17) 12 Cr App R 159; (1917) 81 JP 75; [1917] 1 KB 283; [1917] 86 LJCL 40; (1917) 116 LTR 161; (1916-17) 61 SJ 100; (1916-17) XXXIII TLR 21; (1916) WN (I) 347 CCA Perjury if accused person giving post-conviction evidence in mitigation of sentence tells a lie.

R v Whelan [1997] Crim LR 353 CA (Unopposed) appeal against conviction allowed where was strong suggestion that police officers who gave evidence at trial may have perjured selves.

Samaratunga (Don Thomas) v R [1958] AC 424; [1958] Crim LR 548; (1958) 102 SJ 452 PC Must under Ceylon Criminal Code (s 440) be 'clear beyond doubt' for judge to pass contempt sentence summarily.

Sturrock v Director of Public Prosecutions; Subramaniam v R [1996] RTR 216; [1995] TLR 69; [1956] Crim LR 420; (1956) 100 SJ 316; [1956] 1 WLR 456 PC On sentencing for perjury pursuant to the Criminal Procedure Code of Ceylon, s 440.

PIRACY (general)

Re Piracy Jure Gentium [1934] All ER 506; [1934] AC 586; (1934) 78 SJ 585; (1934-35) LI TLR 12 PC Attempt to rob can sustain charge of piracy jure gentium - actual robbery unnecessary.

PUBLIC ORDER (breach of peace)

Wooster v Webb and Sussum [1936] LJNCCR 129 CyCt Nominal damages for demonstrators from whom police confiscated anti-war leaflets on basis that breach of the peace likely (though later proved to have no reasonable grounds for apprehending said breach of peace).

PUBLIC ORDER (busking)

De Cristofaro v British Transport Police [1997] Crim LR 124; (1996) TLR 7/5/96 HC QBD Valid conviction of busker for unlawfully soliciting for reward for playing of music in London Underground station.

PUBLIC ORDER (conspiracy to effect public mischief)

R v Newland and others [1953] 2 All ER 1067; (1953) 37 Cr App R 154; (1953) 117 JP 573; (1953) 103 LJ 717; [1954] 1 QB 158; (1953) 97 SJ 782; [1953] 3 WLR 826 CCA On public mischief prosecutions.

R v Withers and others [1974] 1 All ER 101; (1974) 58 Cr App R 187; [1974] Crim LR 36t; (1974) 138 JP 123; (1973) 123 NLJ 1017t; [1974] QB 414; (1973) 117 SJ 834; [1974] 2 WLR 26 CA Public duty owed by bank can sustain conviction for conspiracy to effect public mischief; conspiracy to effect public mischief need not involve criminal or tortious acts/the state.

PUBLIC ORDER (disorderly behaviour)

Chambers and Edwards v Director of Public Prosecutions [1995] Crim LR 896 HC QBD On what constitutes 'disorderly behaviour' for purposes of Public Order Act 1986, s 5(1).

Neale v E [1984] Crim LR 485 CA On meaning of word 'drunk' in Licensing Act 1872, s 12, as amended by the Criminal Justice Act 1967, s 91.

Neale v E (RMJ) (1985) 80 Cr App R 20; [1984] TLR 116 HC QBD Could not be convicted of disorderly behaviour while drunk where had actually been glue-sniffing.

PUBLIC ORDER (disturbing religious meeting)

R v Dinnick (1910) 74 JP 32; (1909-10) XXVI TLR 74 CCA Successful appeal against conviction for disturbing religious meeting (52 Geo III, c155, s 12).

PUBLIC ORDER (general)

Allen and others v Ireland (1984) 79 Cr App R 206; [1984] Crim LR 500; (1984) 148 JP 545; (1984) 128 SJ 482; [1984] TLR 212; [1984] 1 WLR 903 HC QBD Prima facie evidence of participation in threatening behaviour where were voluntarily present; prima facie case of identification as party to threatening behaviour where proceedings initiated against one as member of group.

Atkin v Director of Public Prosecutions (1989) 89 Cr App R 199; [1989] Crim LR 581; (1989) 153 JP 383 HC QBD Person against whom threatening words/behaviour directed must be physically present.

Cawley v Frost (1977) 64 Cr App R 20; [1976] Crim LR 747 (cf [1977] Crim LR 170); (1977) 141 JP 30; (1976) 126 NLJ 953t; (1976) 120 SJ 703; [1976] 1 WLR 1207 HC QBD Football ground a public place under terms of Public Order Act 1936. ss 5 and 9(1).

Cheeseman v Director of Public Prosecutions [1991] 3 All ER 54; (1991) 93 Cr App R 145; [1991] Crim LR 296; (1991) 155 JP 469; [1992] QB 83; [1990] TLR 690; [1991] 2 WLR 1105 HC QBD On-duty police officers policing public toilet were not 'passengers' before whom indecent exposure to their annoyance could constitute offence (Town Police Clauses Act 1847, s 28, as amended).

Cooper and others v Shield [1971] 2 All ER 917; [1971] Crim LR 365t; (1971) 135 JP 434; (1971) 121 NLJ 298t; [1971] 2 QB 334; (1971) 115 SJ 365; [1971] 2 WLR 1385 HC QBD Railway station platform not 'open space'.

Director of Public Prosecutions v Baillie [1995] Crim LR 426 HC QBD Passing on free information to travellers about possible upcoming festival that might be held in public place (contrary to police notice under Public Order Act 1986, s 14) was not public order offence.

Director of Public Prosecutions v Fidler and another (1992) 94 Cr App R 286; [1992] Crim LR 62; (1992) 156 JP 257; [1991] TLR 406; [1992] 1 WLR 91 HC QBD Absent threat to use force anti-abortionists verbally abusing persons outside clinic not guilty of public order offence; was prima facie case to answer by persons charged given membership of anti-abortion group and that had been outside premises being beset.

Director of Public Prosecutions v Orum [1988] 3 All ER 449; (1989) 88 Cr App R 261; [1988] Crim LR 848; (1989) 153 JP 85; (1988) 132 SJ 1637; [1989] 1 WLR 88 HC QBD Police officer may be person caused harassment/alarm/distress for purposes of Public Order Act but cannot arrest if not so affected and is only person present.

G v Superintendent of Police, Stroud (1988) 86 Cr App R 92; [1987] Crim LR 269 HC QBD Short time-span in which constable had to make decision to arrest relevant in deciding reasonableness of arrest that breach of peace likely: here reasonable so assault was assault on constable in execution of duty.

Grant v Taylor [1986] Crim LR 252 HC QBD On extent of power of arrest under Metropolitan Police Act 1839, s 54(13) for using insulting words or behaviour whereby breach of the peace may be occasioned.

Groom v Director of Public Prosecutions [1991] Crim LR 713 HC QBD On what suffices as a 'warning' before arrest under Public Order Act 1986, s 5(4).

Holman v Ward [1964] Crim LR 541g; (1964) 128 JP 397; (1964) 114 LJ 506; [1964] 2 QB 580; (1964) 108 SJ 380; [1964] 2 WLR 1313 HL QBD Interpretation of Public Order Act 1936, s 5.

Hudson v Chief Constable, Avon and Somerset Constabulary [1976] Crim LR 451 HC QBD Football match attendee who in his excitement fell forwards causing surge on terraces not guilty of using threatening behaviour whereby breach of the peace likely to be occasioned.

Jobson v Henderson (1899-1901) XIX Cox CC 477; (1900) LXXXII LTR 260 HC QBD Police district superintendant could lay information for offence of throwing stones at police.

Krumpa and Anderson v Director of Public Prosecutions [1989] Crim LR 295 HC QBD Have not been asked to leave land where are told that sometime in the future will be asked to leave.

Lawrenson v Oxford [1982] Crim LR 185 HC QBD Public house a 'public place' for purposes of Public Order Act 1936, s 5.

Maile v McDowell [1980] Crim LR 586 CA On what constitutes a breach of the peace (here in football crowd context).

Morrow, Greach and Thomas v Director of Public Prosecutions, Secretary of State for Health and Social Security, British Pregnancy Advisory Service [1994] Crim LR 58 HC QBD Disorderly behaviour conviction valid: reasonable conduct and reasonable force to prevent crime (allegedly illegal abortions) defences unsuccessful.

Nicholson v Gage (1985) 80 Cr App R 40 HC QBD Not offensive conduct conducive to breach of peace where had been in cubicle with door practically closed and had only been observed by police.

O'Moran and others v Director of Public Prosecutions; Whelan and others v Director of Public Prosecutions [1975] 1 All ER 473; (1975) 139 JP 245; (1975) 125 NLJ 18t; [1975] QB 864; (1975) 119 SJ 165; [1975] 2 WLR 413 HC QBD Identifying (items of) clothes can be uniform though not used as such; can prove uniform if historically used /persons charged intended to use as such.

Parkin v Norman; Valentine v Lilley [1982] 2 All ER 583; [1982] Crim LR 528; [1983] QB 92; (1982) 126 SJ 359; [1982] TLR 140; [1982] 3 WLR 523 HC QBD Whether behaviour intentionally insulting irrelevant in deciding if likely to cause breach of peace (for which must be actual/implied violence).

Parrish and others v Garfitt [1984] 1 WLR 911 HC QBD Group of football hooligans causing disturbance individually guilty of using threatening behaviour whereby breach of peace likely to be occasioned.

Poku (Kwasi) v Director of Public Prosecutions [1993] Crim LR 705; [1993] TLR 13 HC QBD Excessive use of seizure powers which prompted reaction from defendant that was subject of instant public order prosecution meant it was open to defendant to plead reasonable conduct defence.

Police v Reid (Lorna) [1987] Crim LR 702 Magistrates Assembly shouting at persons with whose politics did not agree so as to make them uneasy as entered building (but not to compel them not to do so) was not intimidation so police could not impose condition on the assembly.

R v Ball (Simon Leonard John) (1990) 90 Cr App R 378; [1989] Crim LR 579 CA Bona fide belief that arrest unlawful/police using excessive force not defence to assault.

R v Britton [1967] 1 All ER 486; (1967) 51 Cr App R 107; [1967] Crim LR 179t; (1967) 131 JP 235; [1967] 2 QB 51; (1966) 110 SJ 977; [1967] 2 WLR 537 CA Leaving racist leaflets in private porch not distribution to public/section thereof under Race Relations Act 1965, s 6.

R v Edwards (Llewellyn); R v Roberts (Eric) (1978) 67 Cr App R 228; [1978] Crim LR 564; (1978) 122 SJ 177 CA Not Public Order Act 1936 offence where insulting words could be heard across street but occurred on private property.

R v Hau (Va Kun) [1990] Crim LR 518 CA Cannot be guilty of using threatening words or behaviour in dwellinghouse.

R v Jordan and Tyndall [1963] Crim LR 125t CCA Valid conviction/imposition of deterrent sentences (despite being first time offence) for persons guilty of organising movement dedicated to use of force in achieving its political ends (Public Order Act 1936, s 2(1)(b)).

R v Lamb [1990] Crim LR 58 HC QBD Police officer justified in remaining on property had rightfully entered in anticipation of breach of the peace.

R v Oakwell [1978] Crim LR 168; (1977) 127 NLJ 1128t; (1978) 122 SJ 30 CA Failed appeal against conviction for using threatening behaviour likely to occasion breach of the peace where person so convicted had already been breaching the peace at relevant time.

R v Oakwell [1978] 1 All ER 1223; (1978) 66 Cr App R 174; (1978) 142 JP 259; [1978] 1 WLR 32 CA That facts fit two offences did not preclude conviction for one; fair summing-up required not replication of Crown's case.

Read v Jones and others (1983) 77 Cr App R 246; [1983] Crim LR 809; (1983) 147 JP 477; [1983] TLR 365 HC QBD Could be breach of peace by group though no member of public witnesses same.

Rogers v Wood [1968] Crim LR 274t HC QBD Not keeping premises open where sold refreshments through window of coffee bar to persons on the street.

Rukwira v Director of Public Prosecutions [1993] Crim LR 882; (1994) 158 JP 65; [1993] TLR 362 HC QBD Shared landing outside flat in block of flats not part of 'dwelling' for purposes of Public Order Act 1986.

Vernon v Paddon [1973] 3 All ER 302; [1974] Crim LR 51t; (1973) 137 JP 758; (1973) 117 SJ 416; [1973] 1 WLR 663 HC QBD Using 'threatening and insulting words and behaviour' a single offence.

Ward v Holman [1964] Crim LR 541g; (1964) 114 LJ 506; [1964] 2 QB 580; (1964) 108 SJ 380; [1964] 2 WLR 1313 HC QBD Interpretation of Public Order Act 1936, s 5.

Williams v Director of Public Prosecutions [1968] Crim LR 563; (1968) 112 SJ 599 HC QBD Passing out leaflets outside servicemen's club inviting them to desert was distributing insulting writing likely to occasion breach of the peace (contrary to the Public Order Act 1936, s 7).

Wilson v Skeock (1949) 113 JP 295; (1949) LXV TLR 418 HC KBD Public Order Act 1936 not for prosecution of neighbours who had been abusive towards each other but binding over was nonetheless valid exercise of justices' inherent powers/powers under Justices of the Peace Act 1360.

Winn v Director of Public Prosecutions (1992) 156 JP 881; (1992) 142 NLJ 527 HC QBD On four different ways of committing offence created by Public Order Act 1986, s 4 (likely provocation of violence through use of threatening/abusive words or behaviour).

PUBLIC ORDER (indecent behaviour in church)

Jones v Cotterall (1901-02) 46 SJ 396 HC KBD Non-interference with magistrates' decision of fact that person not guilty of indecent behaviour in church.

PUBLIC ORDER (indecent language)

Less v Parr [1967] Crim LR 481t HC QBD 'Bastard' not an indecent word; person not guilty of using indecent language in street where could not be heard in hearing of street.

Russon v Dutton (1911-13) XXII Cox CC 490; (1911) 75 JP 209; (1911) 104 LTR 601; (1910-11) XXVII TLR 197 HC KBD No conviction for indecent language uttered and heard within public house.

Wiggins v Field [1968] Crim LR 503; (1968) 112 SJ 656 HC QBD Ought never to have been prosecution for indecent language arising from public poetry recital involving line containing possibly indecent wording.

PUBLIC ORDER (insulting behaviour)

Brutus v Cozens [1972] 2 All ER 1297; [1973] AC 854; (1972) 56 Cr App R 799; [1973] Crim LR 56; (1972) 136 JP 636; (1972) 122 NLJ 681t; (1972) 116 SJ 647; [1972] 3 WLR 521 HL Behaviour causing affront/being rude need not be 'insulting behaviour' contrary to Public Order Act 1936, s 5 (as amended).

PUBLIC ORDER (obscene language)

Bryan v Robinson [1960] 2 All ER 173; [1960] Crim LR 489; (1960) 124 JP 310; (1960) 110 LJ 381; (1960) 104 SJ 389 HC QBD Hostess at refreshment house doorway seeking to entice custom not guilty of insulting behaviour.

Cozens v Brutus [1972] 2 All ER 1; (1972) 136 JP 390; (1972) 116 SJ 217; [1972] 1 WLR 484 HC QBD Behaviour causing affront is 'insulting behaviour'.

Masterson and another v Holden [1986] 3 All ER 39; (1986) 83 Cr App R 302; [1986] Crim LR 688; (1970) 130 SJ 592; [1986] 1 WLR 1017 HC QBD Overt homosexual behaviour in public street insulting albeit not directed at particular person/s.

PUBLIC ORDER (obscene language)

Hoogstraten v Goward [1967] Crim LR 590; (1967) 111 SJ 581 HC QBD Police officer could be passenger for purposes of prosecution under the Town Police Clauses Act 1847, s 28.

Myers v Garrett [1972] Crim LR 232 HC QBD Repeated use of word 'fucking' was obscene and persons had been annoyed by same so were guilty of using obscene language to annoyance of passengers.

Nicholson v Glasspool [1959] Crim LR 294t; (1959) 123 JP 229 HC QBD In prosecution for obscene language need not prove person actually annoyed if intention of accused was to annoy.

PUBLIC ORDER (procession)

Flockhart v Robertson [1950] 1 All ER 1091; [1950] 2 KB 498 HC KBD Guidance of procession which spontaneously formed rendered guilty of organising procession.

PUBLIC ORDER (public mischief)

R v Bassey (EIH) (1930-31) Cr App R 160; (1931) 75 SJ 121; (1930-31) XLVII TLR 222 CCA Public mischief to induce Benchers of Inn of Court to admit as student a person who ought not to be admitted.

R v Manley [1932] All ER 565; (1931-34) XXIX Cox CC 574; (1932-34) 24 Cr App R 25; (1933) 97 JP 6; [1933] 1 KB 529; (1933) 75 LJ 96; (1933) 102 LJCL 323; (1933) 148 LTR 335; (1933) 77 SJ 65; (1932-33) XLIX TLR 130; (1933) WN (I) 14 CCA Common law misdemeanour of public mischief still extant: making false statements to police about imagined crime is public mischief.

R v Young (Robert) (1943-45) 30 Cr App R 57 CCA On what constitutes public mischief.

PUBLIC ORDER (public nuisance)

Attorney General v Gastonia Coaches Ltd (1976) 126 NLJ 1267t; [1977] RTR 219 HC ChD Obstruction of highway by coaches a public nuisance; smell/noise from premises of motor coach operator along with interference in access to private premises a private nuisance.

Farmer v Long (1908) 72 JP 91 HC KBD Leaking drain a nuisance under Public Health (London) Act 1891, s 4.

Macfarlane v Gwalter [1958] 1 All ER 181; (1958) 122 JP 144; [1959] 2 QB 332; (1958) 102 SJ 123 CA Dangerous lighting grating a public nuisance for which occupier of adjoining building liable under Public Health Acts Amendment Act 1890, s 35(1).

Pontardawe Rural District Council v Moore-Gwyn [1929] 1 Ch 656; (1929) 93 JP 141; (1929) 67 LJ 203; (1929) 98 LJCh 242; (1929) 141 LTR 23; (1928-29) XLV TLR 276; (1929) WN (I) 67 HC ChD Landower not liable for damage occasioned through rock falling down slope where land has been subject to ordinary use.

R v Johnson (Anthony Thomas) [1996] 2 Cr App R 434; [1996] Crim LR 828; (1996) 140 SJ LB 183; (1996) TLR 22/5/96; [1997] 1 WLR 367 CA Making obscene telephone calls to various persons could amount to public nuisance.

R v Madden [1975] 3 All ER 155; (1975) 61 Cr App R 254; [1975] Crim LR 582t; (1975) 139 JP 685; (1975) 125 NLJ 772t; (1975) 119 SJ 657; [1975] 1 WLR 1379 CA Hoax bomb call affecting significant numbers of the public a public nuisance.

R v Norbury [1978] Crim LR 435 CrCt Was public nuisance to persistently make obscene telephone calls to women over protracted period.

R v Shorrock [1993] 3 All ER 917; (1994) 98 Cr App R 67; (1993) 143 NLJ 511; [1994] QB 279; [1993] TLR 128; [1993] 3 WLR 698 CA Responsibility for but not actual knowledge of public nuisance necessary for landowner to be guilty of public nuisance.

PUBLIC ORDER (threatening behaviour/words)

Allen and others v Ireland (1984) 79 Cr App R 206; [1984] Crim LR 500; (1984) 148 JP 545; (1984) 128 SJ 482; [1984] TLR 212; [1984] 1 WLR 903 HC QBD Prima facie evidence of participation in threatening behaviour where were voluntarily present; prima facie case of identification as party to threatening behaviour where proceedings initiated against one as member of group.

Atkin v Director of Public Prosecutions (1989) 89 Cr App R 199; [1989] Crim LR 581; (1989) 153 JP 383 HC QBD Person against whom threatening words/behaviour directed must be physically present.

Director of Public Prosecutions v Clarke and others (1992) 94 Cr App R 359; [1992] Crim LR 60; (1992) 156 JP 267; (1991) 135 SJ LB 135; [1991] TLR 407 HC QBD Where plead reasonable conduct as defence to public order charge reasonableness an objective issue and intent a subjective matter.

Holman v Ward [1964] Crim LR 541g; (1964) 128 JP 397; (1964) 114 LJ 506; [1964] 2 QB 580; (1964) 108 SJ 380; [1964] 2 WLR 1313 HC QBD Interpretation of Public Order Act 1936, s 5.

Jordan v Burgoyne [1963] 2 All ER 225; [1963] Crim LR 362t; (1963) 127 JP 368; (1963) 113 LJ 400; [1963] 2 QB 744; (1963) 107 SJ 338; [1963] 2 WLR 1045 HC QBD Audience are as found: if words provoke breach of peace by them is an offence.

Marsh v Arscott (1982) 75 Cr App R 211; [1982] Crim LR 827; [1982] TLR 121 HC QBD Shop car park was/was not public place when shop open/closed.

R v Ambrose (Peter Thomas) (1973) 57 Cr App R 538 CA Rude/objectionable words need not be insulting (and were not here).

R v Cushen and Spratley [1978] Crim LR 51 CA Three months' imprisonment for racially motivated threatening behaviour.

R v Hau (Va Kun) [1990] Crim LR 518 CA Cannot be guilty of using threatening words or behaviour in dwellinghouse.

R v Horseferry Road Metropolitan Stipendiary Magistrate, ex parte Siadatan [1991] 1 All ER 324; (1991) 92 Cr App R 257; [1990] Crim LR 598; (1990) 140 NLJ 704; [1991] 1 QB 260; [1990] TLR 298; [1990] 3 WLR 1006 HC QBD Offence only arises where writing would prompt immediate unlawful violence.

R v O'Brien [1993] Crim LR 71 CA Could plead guilty to threatening behaviour on charge of violent disorder without empanelling jury.

Simcock v Rhodes (1978) 66 Cr App R 192; [1977] Crim LR 751; (1977) 127 NLJ 1105t HC QBD Telling police officer to '**** off' was 'insulting' behaviour likely to cause breach of the peace.

Swanston v Director of Public Prosecutions (1997) 161 JP 203; [1997] TLR 37 HC QBD Person subjected to threatening/abusive/insulting words did not have to testify as to how received words for utterer of words to be convicted of using same.

PUBLIC ORDER (trespassory assembly)

Director of Public Prosecutions v Jones and another [1997] 2 All ER 119; (1997) 147 NLJ 162 HC QBD On elements of offence of trespassory assembly.

PUBLIC ORDER (unlawful assembly)

Burden v Rigler and another (1911) 75 JP 36; [1911] 1 KB 337; (1910-11) 103 LTR 758; (1910-11) XXVII TLR 140; (1910) WN (I) 279 HC KBD Public meeting held on highway not per se unlawful: legality depends on circumstances.

Kamara and others v Director of Public Prosecutions [1973] 2 All ER 1242; [1974] AC 104; (1973) 57 Cr App R 880; [1974] Crim LR 39; (1973) 137 JP 714; (1973) 123 NLJ 700t; (1973) 117 SJ 581; [1973] 3 WLR 198 HL Unlawful assembly need not take place in public place; not all agreements to commit torts indictable conspiracies.

R v Jones (John McKinsie); R v Tomlinson (Eric); R v Warren (Dennis Michael); R v O'Shea (Kenneth Desmond Francis); R v Carpenter (John); R v Llywarch (John Elfyn) (1974) 59 Cr App R 120 CA On what constitutes 'intimidation' under Conspiracy and Protection of Property Act 1875, s 7; on constituent elements of unlawful assembly and of affray.

PUBLIC ORDER (using indecent language)

Brabham v Wookey (1901-02) XVIII TLR 99 HC KBD Person using indecent language inside his house, heard by two officers outside but not proved to have annoyed passer-by could be convicted of offence of using indecent language contrary to Bristol Improvement Act 1840, s 77.

PUBLIC ORDER (violent disorder)

R v Mahroof (Abdul) (1989) 88 Cr App R 317; [1989] Crim LR 72 CA Could convict one person of violent disorder so long as involved two other persons (but procedural irregularity led to substitution of conviction for using threatening, abusive or insulting words).

R v McGuigan; R v Cameron [1991] Crim LR 719 CA On need for three or more parties to be party to violent disorder before offence can arise.

R v O'Brien [1993] Crim LR 71 CA Could plead guilty to threatening behaviour on charge of violent disorder without empanelling jury.

R v Worton [1990] Crim LR 124 CA Substitution of conviction of affray for one of violent disorder.

PUBLIC ORDER (watching/besetting premises)

Director of Public Prosecutions v Fidler and another (1992) 94 Cr App R 286; [1992] Crim LR 62; (1992) 156 JP 257; [1991] TLR 406; [1992] 1 WLR 91 HC QBD Absent threat to use force anti-abortionists verbally abusing persons outside clinic not guilty of public order offence; was prima facie case to answer by persons charged given membership of anti-abortion group and that had been outside premises being beset.

Hubbard and others v Pitt and others [1975] 3 All ER 1 CA Watching and besetting with view to securing certain behaviour might be nuisance.

R v Wall and others (1907-09) XXI Cox CC 401 Assizes Conviction for watching business place/place of residence.

RAPE (assault with intent to rape)

R v Waite (Philip) [1988] Crim LR 434 CrCt Is no offence of assault with intent to rape.

RECKLESSNESS (general)

Blakely and another v Director of Public Prosecutions [1991] Crim LR 763; [1991] RTR 405; [1991] TLR 288 HC QBD Recklessness an inappropriate consideration when deciding whether person had necessary mens rea to be guilty of procuring principal to commit offence.

Chief Constable of Avon and Somerset Constabulary v Shimmen (1987) 84 Cr App R 7; [1986] Crim LR 800 HC QBD Was recklessness where recognised risk and took inadequate steps to prevent damage occurring.

Flack v Hunt (1980) 70 Cr App R 51; [1980] Crim LR 44; (1979) 123 SJ 751 HC QBD Recklessness a subjective test: here unlawful wounding charge failed where no recklessness established.

Large v Mainprize [1989] Crim LR 213 HC QBD Interpretation of 'recklessness' in context of prosecution for breach of the Sea Fishing (Enforcement of Community Control Measures) Order 1985, reg 3.

R v B [1984] TLR 660 CA On definition of recklessness in the context of rape.

R v Bashir (Mohammed) (1983) 77 Cr App R 59; [1982] Crim LR 687 CA On proper direction regarding/on meaning of recklessness as to consent.

R v Belton (1976) 126 NLJ 467t CA On recklessness as an element of foreseeability.

R v Breckenridge (Ian) (1984) 79 Cr App R 244; [1984] Crim LR 174 CA Is rape by recklessness where were dismissive of need for consent.

R v Caldwell [1981] 1 All ER 961; [1982] AC 341; (1981) 73 Cr App R 13; [1981] Crim LR 392; (1981) 145 JP 211; (1981) 131 NLJ 338; (1981) 125 SJ 239; [1981] 2 WLR 509 HL Definition of recklessness; self-induced intoxication irrelevant to recklessness.

R v Caldwell (James) (1980) 71 Cr App R 237; [1980] Crim LR 572 CA Self-induced drunkenness relevant to deciding whether were criminally reckless.

R v Cato and others [1976] 1 All ER 260; (1976) 62 Cr App R 41; [1976] Crim LR 59t; (1976) 140 JP 169; (1975) 125 NLJ 1066t; (1975) 119 SJ 775; [1976] 1 WLR 110 CA Consent of victim to unlawful act not defence/is relevant to question of recklessness/negligence; injection of drug an unlawful act from which manslaughter could spring; substance noxious if likely to cause injury when used; direct, intended injection of drug done 'maliciously'.

R v Cullen [1993] Crim LR 936 CA On recklessness in the context of arson.

R v Hardie (Paul Deverall) (1985) 80 Cr App R 156; (1984) 128 SJ 851; [1984] TLR 511; [1985] 1 WLR 64 CA Self-induced drunkenness cannot be defence where recklessness alleged - taking of sedative drug need not raise same presumption.

R v Haughian (Anthony Edward); R v Pearson (Arthur Reginald) (1985) 80 Cr App R 334 CA Defence of mistaken belief must fail where jury finds was no consent to rape; adequate direction on recklessness.

R v Hutchins [1988] Crim LR 379 CA On ingredients of false imprisonment/kidnapping: both may be committed through recklessness.

R v Mullins [1980] Crim LR 37 CA Test as to recklessness a subjective one.

R v Parker [1977] 2 All ER 37; (1976) 63 Cr App R 211; [1977] Crim LR 102; (1977) 141 JP 274; (1977) 121 SJ 353; [1977] 1 WLR 600 CA 'Reckless' is deliberate closing of mind to obvious risk of damage.

R v Parsons [1993] Crim LR 792 CA On ingredients of offence of indecent assault: on recklessness as an element of the offence.

R v Pigg [1982] 2 All ER 591; (1982) 74 Cr App R 352; [1982] Crim LR 446; (1982) 146 JP 298; (1982) 126 SJ 344; [1982] TLR 60; [1982] 1 WLR 762 CA Foreman must openly state number of dissenting jurors; recklessness in rape if unbothered by consent in situation where possibly no consent; continuing with sex though aware possibly no consent.

R v Prentice and another; R v Adomako; R v Holloway [1993] 4 All ER 935; (1994) 98 Cr App R 262; [1994] Crim LR 598; (1993) 157 JP 1185; (1993) 143 NLJ 850; [1994] QB 302; (1993) 137 SJ LB 145; [1993] TLR 286; [1993] 3 WLR 927 CA Involuntary manslaughter by breach of duty if gross negligence - not recklessness - results in breach of duty and causes death.

R v R [1984] TLR 502 CA On characteristics of ordinary man where recklessness raised as an issue (here in context of being reckless as to danger to life created).

R v Reid [1992] 3 All ER 673; (1992) 95 Cr App R 391; [1992] Crim LR 814; (1994) 158 JP 517; [1992] RTR 341; (1992) 136 SJ LB 253; [1992] 1 WLR 793 HL Reckless driving occurs where accused disregards serious risk of injury to another/does not give that prospect consideration.

R v Reid [1991] Crim LR 269 CA On test for recklessness (Lawrence formula applied).

R v S (Satnam); R v S (Kewal) (1984) 78 Cr App R 149; [1985] Crim LR 236 CA Rape conviction quashed in absence of direction on rape/consent/recklessness as to consent.

R v Singh and Singh (1985) 149 JP 142 CA On recklessness in context of rape.

R v Stephenson [1979] 2 All ER 1198; (1979) 69 Cr App R 213; [1979] Crim LR 590; (1979) 143 JP 592; (1979) 129 (1) NLJ 612; [1979] QB 695; (1979) 123 SJ 403; [1979] 3 WLR 193 CA Recklessness a subjective test.

R v Taylor (Robert Peter) (1985) 80 Cr App R 327 CA Adequate direction on corroboration and recklessness: defence of honest mistake unlikely to succeed where jury conclude was no consent.

R v Thomas (Norman Livingstone) (1983) 77 Cr App R 63 CA On proper direction regarding recklessness as to consent.

R v Venna [1975] 3 All ER 788; (1975) 61 Cr App R 310; [1975] Crim LR 701t; (1976) 140 JP 31; [1976] QB 421; (1975) 119 SJ 679; [1975] 3 WLR 737 CA Recklessness sufficient to sustain charge of assault.

W v Dolbey (1989) 88 Cr App R 1; [1983] Crim LR 681 HC QBD No recklessness (where did not foresee any damage) so no malicious wounding.

RECOGNISANCE (arraignment)

R v Central Criminal Court, ex parte Guney [1995] 2 All ER; [1995] 2 Cr App R 350; (1995) 139 SJ LB 66; [1995] TLR 52; [1995] 1 WLR 576 CA Recognisance ends once defendant arraigned.

RECOGNISANCE (breach)

R v Green-Emmott (George Vereker) [1931] All ER 380; (1931-34) XXIX Cox CC 280; (1930-31) Cr App R 183; (1931) 144 LTR 671 CCA Certified lunatic cannot enter into recognisance.

R v Hibbert (John William) (1924-25) 18 Cr App R 36 CCA On breach of recognisance entered into before CCA.

R v McGregor (John) (1943-45) 30 Cr App R 155; (1945) 109 JP 136; [1946] 115 LJ 100 CCA On procedure where brought before court for breach of recognisance.

RECOGNISANCE (estreatment)

R v Ipswich Crown Court; ex parte Reddington [1981] Crim LR 618 HC QBD Successful appeal against estreatment of recognisance where had not inquired into means of surety/did not consider efforts made by surety to prevent bailed party absconding.

R v Southampton Justices, ex parte Green [1975] 2 All ER 1073; (1975) 139 JP 667; [1976] QB 11; (1975) 119 SJ 541; [1975] 3 WLR 277 CA Estreatment of recognisance not criminal cause or matter; forfeiture of recognisance for non-appearance not automatic - all circumstances to be considered.

R v York Crown Court; ex parte Coleman and How (1988) 86 Cr App R 151; [1987] Crim LR 761 HC QBD Full estreatment of recognisances inappropriate where accused had surrendered to bail on morning of trial but thereafter absconded.

RECOGNISANCE (forfeiture)

Cockhill v Davies (1943) 107 JP 130; [1943] 112 LJ 441; (1943) 169 LTR 78; (1942-43) LIX TLR 259; (1943) WN (I) 109 HC KBD Could appeal to quarter sessions against magistrate's decision that recognisance be forfeited.

R v Knightsbridge Crown Court; ex parte Newton [1980] Crim LR 715 CA Non-forfeiture of recognisance in light of circumstances despite failure of defendant bailed to appear in court.

R v Tottenham Magistrates' Court, ex parte Riccardi (1978) 66 Cr App R 150 HC QBD Valid forefiture of recognisance.

RECOGNISANCE (general)

Leyton Urban District Council v Wilkinson (1927) 91 JP 64; [1927] 1 KB 315; (1925-26) 70 SJ 1069; (1926-27) XLIII TLR 35; (1926) WN (I) 274 HC KBD Inadequacy of recognisance entered into personally by clerk of local authority.

Leyton Urban District Council v Wilkinson (1927) 137 LTR 10; (1927) 71 SJ 293; (1926-27) XLIII TLR 326 CA Inadequacy of recognisance entered into personally by clerk of local authority.

R v Bow Street Magistrates' Court; ex parte Hall and Otobo (1986) 136 NLJ 1111 CA Recognisance may remain valid despite change in bail conditions.

R v Central Criminal Court, ex parte Guney [1996] 2 All ER 705; [1996] AC 616; [1996] 2 Cr App R 352; [1996] Crim LR 896; (1996) 146 NLJ 716; (1996) 140 SJ LB 124; (1996) TLR 10/5/96; [1996] 2 WLR 675 HL Recognisance ends once defendant arraigned.

R v Central Criminal Court; ex parte Naraghi (Medhi) and Binji (Shirim) (1980) 2 Cr App R (S) 104 CA On procedure as regards estreatment of recognisance.

R v Chambers; ex parte Klitz [1919] 1 KB 638; [1919] 88 LJCL 688; (1918-19) XXXV TLR 328; (1919) WN (I) 95 HC KBD On jurisdiction of HC KBD in respect of recognisance entered into by party at Assizes.

R v Edgar (1913-14) XXIII Cox CC 558; (1913) 9 Cr App R 13; (1913) 77 JP 356; (1913-14) 109 LTR 416; (1912-13) 57 SJ 519; (1912-13) XXIX TLR 512 CCA Recognisance to be of good behaviour following misdemeanour to be of short/definite time.

R v Kettle and the London County Council (1901-07) XX Cox CC 753; [1905] 1 KB 212; (1905) XCII LTR 59; (1904-05) XXI TLR 151; (1904-05) 53 WR 364 HC KBD No need for fresh recognisance post-mandamus order to state case earlier refused to state even though surety has died.

R v McKenzie [1971] 1 All ER 729; (1971) 55 Cr App R 294; [1972] Crim LR 655; (1971) 135 JP 26 Assizes Invalid recognisance could not be subject of forgery; recognisance invalid where imposed on person who would not be detained.

R v Swindon Crown Court; ex parte Pawittar Singh [1983] TLR 728; [1984] 1 WLR 449 HC QBD Court could not order binding over of person not in any way party to action.

Sawyer v Bell [1962] Crim LR 390t HC QBD Abusive letters to bishops were defiance of recognisance to keep the peace and be of good behaviour.

RECOGNISANCE (insanity)

R v Green-Emmott (George Vereker) [1931] All ER 380; (1931-34) XXIX Cox CC 280; (1930-31) Cr App R 183; (1931) 144 LTR 671 CCA Certified lunatic cannot enter into recognisance.

RECOGNISANCE (surety)

Conlan v Oxford (1984) 79 Cr App R 157; (1984) 148 JP 97 HC QBD Magistrates can bind over juvenile under 17 to keep the peace on own recognisance or that of surety.

RENT (general)

Banks v Cope-Brown (1948) LXIV TLR 390 HC KBD Failed prosecution for charging extortionate rent contrary to Increase of Rent and Mortgage Interest (Restrictions) Act 1920.

Barker v Levinson [1951] 1 KB 342 HC KBD Landlord not liable for unlawful charging of rental premium by rent collector.

REVENUE (general)

R v Bradbury; R v Edlin [1956] 2 QB 262 HC QBD Offence of fraud on the Crown and the public an indictable common law offence.

R v Dealy (John Clark) [1995] 2 Cr App R 398; (1995) 139 SJ LB 14 CA On what constitutes 'evasion' of VAT under Value Added Tax Act 1983, s 39(1).

R v Hudson [1956] 1 All ER 814; [1956] Crim LR 333; (1956) 120 JP 216; (1956) 106 LJ 234; [1956] 2 QB 252; (1956) 100 SJ 284; [1956] 2 WLR 914 CCA Offence of fraud on the Crown and the public a common law misdemeanour.

R v Mavji [1987] 2 All ER 758; (1987) 84 Cr App R 34; [1987] Crim LR 39; (1987) 131 SJ 1121; [1987] 1 WLR 1388 CA Cheating public revenue involves serious/unusual fraudulent diversions of money from the revenue.

R v Redford (David) (1989) 89 Cr App R 1; [1989] Crim LR 152 CA Common law cheating of Revenue could be charged notwithstanding availability of statutory offences - inaction can justify conviction for same.

REWARD (general)

R v Silver (Sarah) (1948) LXIV TLR 502 CCA Only information not indictment required to have been brought within three years of offence under Finance (No 2) Act 1940, sch 9, para 2.

R v Squire [1963] Crim LR 700 CCA Stealing from company/defrauding Inland Revenue charges against company director werer not mutually exclusive.

REWARD (general)

R v Platt and Sines (1905) 69 JP 424 CCC Court could order that reward be paid to girl who assisted police constable in difficulty.

RIOT (general)

Kaufmann Brothers v Liverpool Corporation (1916) 80 JP 223; [1916] 85 LJKB 1127; (1916) 114 LTR 699; (1915-16) 60 SJ 446; (1915-16) XXXII TLR 402; (1916) WN (I) 155 HC KBD Public authority limitation did not apply in respect of action against same for compensation for riot damage.

R v Beach (William) and Morris (Arthur) (1909) 2 Cr App R 189 CCA Can convict two people for rioting with others.

R v Nyberg (Simon); R v White (Alfred) (1922-23) 17 Cr App R 59 CCA White granted leave to appeal against conviction for riot; possession of firearms/shooting with intent to endanger life.

R v O'Brien (1911-13) XXII Cox CC 374; (1910-11) 6 Cr App R; (1911) 75 JP 192; (1911) 104 LTR 113; (1910-11) 55 SJ 219; (1910-11) XXVII TLR 204 CCA Could properly be convicted of assault where charged with riot.

SALE OF POISON (general)

Oxford v Sangers, Ltd [1965] Crim LR 113g HC QBD Not unlawful for wholesalers of controlled poison to sell same to non-authorised retailer of poisons.

SEARCH AND SEIZURE (general)

Attorney-General of Jamaica v Williams and another [1997] 3 WLR 389 CA On issuing of search warrant: here search lawful though seizure had gone slightly further than warrant allowed.

Bayliss v Hill and another [1984] TLR 254 HC QBD On use of search warrants.

D'Souza v Director of Public Prosecutions [1992] 4 All ER 545; (1993) 96 Cr App R 278; (1992) 142 NLJ 1540; [1992] 1 WLR 1073 HL Police right of entry and search available only in course of chase.

Farrow v Tunnicliffe [1976] Crim LR 126 HC QBD Could under Misuse of Drugs Act 1971 remove suspect offender thereunder to another place to conduct search there.

Foster v Attard (1986) 83 Cr App R 214; [1986] Crim LR 627 HC QBD Once police had lawfully entered premises under one statutory power could exercise powers under other statute.

IRC v Rossminster Ltd (1979) 129 (2) NLJ 1260 HL Valid exercise of search and seizure powers by Inland Revenue.

Kynaston v Director of Public Prosecutions; Heron (Joseph) v Director of Public Prosecutions; Heron (Tracey) v Director of Public Prosecutions (1988) 87 Cr App R 200 HC QBD Was lawful entry of premises by police where knew offence committed, knew whom wanted to arrest, reasonably suspected were on premises and owner knew what police wanted.

Lindley v Rutter (1981) 72 Cr App R 1; [1980] Crim LR 729; (1980) 130 NLJ 906; [1981] QB 128; (1980) 124 SJ 792; [1980] 3 WLR 660 HC QBD Woman police officer forcibly removing woman detainee's brassiere not acting in course of duty so assault on same not assault on officer in execution of duty.

M v Metropolitan Police Commissioner [1979] Crim LR 53; (1978) 128 NLJ 759t CA On police retention until trial of money seized by police pursuant to search warrant.

McLorie v Oxford (1982) 75 Cr App R 137; [1982] Crim LR 603; [1982] QB 1290; [1983] RTR 265; (1982) 126 SJ 536; [1982] TLR 287; [1982] 3 WLR 423 HC QBD No post-arrest common law right of police to enter property and look for material evidence; is assault on police in execution of their duty to assault same while doing what is lawfully proper for them to do.

R v Atkinson [1976] Crim LR 307 CA Substantial error in search warrant rendered actions thereunder improper.

R v Badham [1987] Crim LR 202 CrCt On need for authorisation by police inspector of search and entry effected under Police and Criminal Evidence Act 1984.

R v Central Criminal Court and another; ex parte AJD Holdings and others [1992] TLR 76 HC QBD On need for care in applying for/effecting of search warrant.

R v Chief Constable of the Lancashire Constabulary, ex parte Parker and another [1993] 2 All ER 56; (1993) 97 Cr App R 90; [1993] Crim LR 204; [1993] QB 577; (1992) 136 SJ LB 136; [1992] TLR 177; [1993] 2 WLR 428 HC QBD Police must present original warrant and schedule upon search; may not retain unlawfully seized materials.

R v Eeet [1983] Crim LR 806 CrCt Search of prisoner to aid in identification of same was unlawful.

R v Hughes (Patrick Darren) (1994) 99 Cr App R 160; (1993) 137 SJ LB 260; [1993] TLR 564; [1994] 1 WLR 876 CA On what constitutes an 'intimate body search'.

R v Inland Revenue Commissioners; ex parte Rossminster Ltd and others (1979) 123 SJ 554 HC QBD Valid exercise of search and seizure powers by Inland Revenue.

R v Inland Revenue Commissioners; ex parte Rossminster Ltd and others [1980] Crim LR 111 CA Invalid exercise of search and seizure powers by Inland Revenue.

R v Justice of the Peace for Peterborough, ex parte Hicks and others [1978] 1 All ER 225; [1977] Crim LR 621; (1978) 142 JP 103; (1977) 121 SJ 605; [1977] 1 WLR 1371 HC QBD If clients could not prevent document being seized from solicitors' possession solicitor cannot.

R v Longman (John Barry) (1989) 88 Cr App R 148; [1988] Crim LR 534; [1988] 1 WLR 619 CA Entry and search under warrant may involve use of force/subterfuge; to 'produce' a warrant card (Police and Criminal Evidence Act 1984, s 16) means to make it available for occupier's inspection.

R v Richards (Colin David); R v Leeming (Paul) (1985) 81 Cr App R 125; [1985] Crim LR 368 CA Police can only enter premises under Criminal Law Act 1967, s 2 where seek to effect arrest.

R v South Western Magistrates' Court and the Commissioner of Police for the Metropolis; ex parte Cofie (1997) 161 JP 69; (1996) TLR 15/8/96; [1997] 1 WLR 885 HC QBD On need for specificity as regards place to be searched in police application for search warrant.

Reynolds v Commissioner of Police for the Metropolis (1985) 80 Cr App R 125; [1984] Crim LR 688; [1985] QB 881; (1984) 128 SJ 736; [1984] TLR 514; [1985] 2 WLR 93 CA Tort to obtain Forgery Act 1913 search warrant where do not reasonably believe subject of same has unlawful custody/possession of forgeries; police guilty of trespass to goods where took documents did not reasonably believe were forged.

Sargent v West [1964] Crim LR 412t HC QBD On what amounts to reasonable exercise of power of search/arrest under the Metropolitan Police Act 1839, s 66.

Slater v Commissioner of Police of the Metropolis (1996) TLR 23/1/96 HC QBD Police ought not to have retained seized money possession of which had not been declared to the Inland Revenue/Department of Social Security.

Taylor v Pritchard (1910) 45 LJ 392; (1909-10) XXVI TLR 496; (1910) WN (I) 147 HC KBD On powers of search of water bailiff under Salmon Fishery Act 1873, s 36.

Thomas v Sawkins (1934-39) XXX Cox CC 265; (1935) 99 JP 295; [1935] 2 KB 249; (1935) 79 LJ 415; (1935) 153 LTR 419; (1935) 79 SJ 478; (1934-35) LI TLR 514; (1935) WN (I) 109 HC KBD Police officer can enter/stay on premises where reasonable anticipation of offence/breach of peace.

Willey v Peace [1950] 2 All ER 724; (1950) 114 JP 502; [1951] 1 KB 94; (1950) 100 LJ 483; (1950) 94 SJ 597; [1950] 66 (2) TLR 450 HC KBD Police officer may under Metropolitan Police Act 1839, s 66 arrest anyone reasonably suspects of conveying stolen property.

SEXUAL OFFENCES (assault with intent to rape)

R v P [1990] Crim LR 323 HC QBD Is no offence of assault with intent to rape.

SEXUAL OFFENCES (association/conversation with prostitute)

R v Ptohopoulos (Chrisostomos) (1968) 52 Cr App R 47 CA Issue of fact whether talking to and being with prostitute constitutes being habitually in her company (Sexual Offences Act, s 30(2)).

SEXUAL OFFENCES (attempt to procure gross indecency)

Chief Constable of Hampshire v Mace (1987) 84 Cr App R 40; [1986] Crim LR 752; (1986) 150 JP 470 HC QBD Can be charged with attempt to procure act of gross indecency.

R v Butters [1959] Crim LR 215 Sessions Was attempted gross indecency to write letter to another inviting him to commit act of gross indecency with writer.

R v Gammon (Dennis) (1959) 43 Cr App R 155; [1959] Crim LR 448t; (1959) 123 JP 410 CCA Is/is not attempted procuring of grossly indecent act to clearly seek grossly indecent act/to seek apparently innocent act though intending grossly immoral one; corroboration required of complainant's evidence in atemptedprocuring of grossly indecent act.

R v Spight [1986] Crim LR 817 CA On evidential responsibilities placed on defendant (regarding such issues as age and consent) in prosecution for attempting to procure grossly indecent act.

R v Wood [1957] Crim LR 54 Sessions Acts deemed to constitute attempt to procure act of gross indecency with another male.

SEXUAL OFFENCES (attempt to procure woman to become prostitute)

R v Gold and Cohen (1907) 71 JP 360 CCC Can only be convicted of attempting to procure woman to be come prostitute outside King's Dominions where woman concerned not already a prostitute (Criminal Law Amendment Act 1885, s 2(2)).

R v Morris-Lowe (Brian John) [1985] 1 All ER 400; (1985) 80 Cr App R 114; [1985] Crim LR 50; (1984) 128 SJ 872; [1984] TLR 595; [1985] 1 WLR 29 CA On what is meant by attempting to procure woman to become 'common' prostitute.

SEXUAL OFFENCES (attempted gross indecency)

R v Lawson [1959] Crim LR 134 Sessions Acts alleged by prosecution (lewd conversation with boy) could not amount to attempt to commit act of gross indecency.

SEXUAL OFFENCES (attempted rape)

Attorney General's Reference (No 1 of 1992) [1993] 2 All ER 190; (1993) 96 Cr App R 298; [1993] Crim LR 274; (1993) 157 JP 753; (1992) 136 SJ LB 304; [1992] TLR 528; [1993] 1 WLR 274 CA Prima facie case of attempted rape if necessary intent can be inferred and acts preparatory to rape have taken place.

R v Finney (1964) 108 SJ 260 CCA Attempted rape a misdemeanour.

R v Kelly [1992] Crim LR 181 CA Bringing complainant to suspect to see whether was assailant was permissible where all happened within minutes of offence; on what constitutes criminal attempt (here in context of attempted rape).

R v Khan and others [1990] 2 All ER 783; (1990) 91 Cr App R 29; [1990] Crim LR 519; (1990) 154 JP 805; (1994) 144 NLJ 863; (1990) 134 SJ 401; [1990] TLR 86; [1990] 1 WLR 813 CA Attempted rape possible even where man reckless as to whether consent given.

R v Lankford [1959] Crim LR 209t CCA Person who voluntarily desists from raping woman whom has assaulted may not be guilty of attempted rape.

R v Matthews [1981] Crim LR 325 CrCt Could be attempted rape where pinned person down with expressed intention of having non-consensual sex (albeit that penis was never erect/penetration never attempted).

SEXUAL OFFENCES (attempted rape per anum)

R v Gaston (Daniel) (1981) 73 Cr App R 164 CA Attempted rape per anum not an offence.

R v O'Sullivan and others [1981] Crim LR 406 CA No offence of attempted rape per anum.

SEXUAL OFFENCES (attempted unlawul carnal knowledge of under-sixteen year old)

R v Collier [1960] Crim LR 204 Assizes Statutory defence open to accused when committed offence of having unlawful sex with under-sixteen year old also available where attempted offence.

SEXUAL OFFENCES (bestiality)

R v Bourne (Sydney Joseph) (1952) 36 Cr App R 125 CCA Consent irrelevant to bestiality charge.

SEXUAL OFFENCES (brothel)

Abbott and another v Smith [1964] 3 All ER 762; [1964] Crim LR 662; (1965) 129 JP 3; (1964) 114 LJ 738; [1965] 2 QB 662; [1965] 3 WLR 362 CrCt Brothel though premises let in separate rooms; management involves element of control: not present here.

Caldwell v Leech [1911-13] All ER 703; (1913-14) XXIII Cox CC 510; (1913) 77 JP 254; (1913-14) 109 LTR 188; (1912-13) XXIX TLR 457 HC KBD That have one prostitute in one's house cannot sustain conviction for keeping/managing brothel.

Donovan v Gavin [1965] 2 All ER 611; [1965] Crim LR 442; (1965) 129 JP 404; (1965) 115 LJ 418; [1965] 2 QB 648; (1965) 109 SJ 373; [1965] 3 WLR 352 HC QBD That rooms let separately to various prostitutes did not mean not brothel.

Durose v Wilson (1907-09) XXI Cox CC 421; (1907) 71 JP 263; (1907) XCVI LTR 645 HC KBD Porter properly convicted as wilful party to use of flats/portion thereof as brothel.

Gordon v Standen; Palace-Clark v Standen [1963] 3 All ER 627; (1964) 48 Cr App R 30; [1963] Crim LR 859t; (1963) 113 LJ 753; (1963) 107 SJ 811; (1964) 128 JP 28; [1964] 1 QB 294; [1963] 3 WLR 917 HC QBD Is brothel where only two women and one is occupier; woman can be convicted of assisting another in management of brothel.

Jones and Wood v Director of Public Prosecutions (1993) 96 Cr App R 130; (1992) 156 JP 866; [1992] TLR 271 HC QBD Need not control/manage premises to be successfully prosecuted for assisting in management of brothel.

Kelly v Purvis [1983] 1 All ER 525; (1983) 76 Cr App R 165; [1983] Crim LR 185; (1983) 147 JP 135; [1983] QB 663; (1983) 127 SJ 52; [1982] TLR 599; [1983] 2 WLR 299 HC QBD Provision of ordinary sex unnecessary to support charge of assisting in management of brothel.

Mattison v Johnson [1916-17] All ER 727; (1915-17) XXV Cox CC 373; (1916) 80 JP 243; [1916] 85 LJKB 741; (1916) 114 LTR 951; (1916) WN (I) 52 HC KBD Cannot permit own premises to be used as brothel where oneself is only prostitute using premises.

Moores v Director of Public Prosecutions [1991] 4 All ER 521; (1992) 94 Cr App R 173; [1992] Crim LR 49; (1992) 156 JP 113; [1992] QB 125; [1991] TLR 208; [1991] 3 WLR 549 HC QBD Public house to be disorderly house must be frequently disorderly - one disorderly occasion insufficient.

R v Berg (Alexander); R v Britt (Robert); R v Carré (Constance); R v Lummies (Bert) (1927-28) 20 Cr App R 38 CCA Meaning of 'disorderly house' at common law; admissibility in charge of keeping disorderly house of letters found therein referring to behaviour there.

R v Burnby (1901) 36 LJ 310; [1901] 70 LJK/QB 739; (1901-02) LXXXV LTR 168 HC KBD Permitting licensed premises to be used as brothel a continuing offence.

R v Korie [1966] 1 All ER 50; [1966] Crim LR 167; (1965-66) 116 NLJ 360 CrCt Evidence that women visiting premises are prostitutes admissible to show brothel though prejudicial to defence.

R v Quinn; R v Bloom [1961] 3 All ER 88; [1961] Crim LR 609; (1961) 125 JP 565; [1961] 3 WLR 611 CCA Can be disorderly house though persons attending not participating in indecent acts; film reconstruction of crimes inadmissible.

R v Tan and others [1983] 2 All ER 12; (1983) 76 Cr App R 300; [1983] Crim LR 404; (1983) 147 JP 257; [1983] QB 1053; (1983) 127 SJ 390; [1983] TLR 100; [1983] 3 WLR 361 CA Prostitute providing services openly but in own place on one-to-one basis guilty of keeping disorderly house; sex-changed male can still be 'man' living off prostitution.

Siviour v Napolitano [1930] All ER 626; (1931-34) XXIX Cox CC 236; (1931) 95 JP 72; [1931] 1 KB 636; (1931) 100 LJCL 151; (1931) 144 LTR 408; (1930-31) XLVII TLR 202; (1931) WN (I) 24 HC KBD On what constitutes being a 'lessee' of premises used for prostitution.

Stevens and Stevens v Christy (1987) 85 Cr App R 249; [1987] Crim LR 503; (1987) 151 JP 366 HC QBD Place could be brothel where was used by team of prostitutes albeit one at a time.

Strath v Foxon [1955] 3 All ER 398; (1955) 39 Cr App R 162; [1955] Crim LR 773; (1955) 119 JP 581; [1956] 1 QB 67; (1955) 99 SJ 799; [1955] 3 WLR 659 HC QBD Place being used by only one prostitute cannot be brothel.

Waroquiers v Marsden [1950] 1 All ER 93; (1950) 114 JP 78 HC KBD Keeping a brothel triable summarily under statute and indictable at common law.

Winter v Woolfe [1930] All ER 623; (1931-34) XXIX Cox CC 214; (1931) 95 JP 20; [1931] 1 KB 549; (1930) 70 LJ 410; (1931) 144 LTR 311; (1930-31) XLVII TLR 145; (1930) WN (I) 266 HC KBD Need/need not show illicit sex/ that women involved are prostitutes to sustain charge of permitting premises to be used as brothel.

Winter v Woolfe (1931) 100 LJCL 92 CCA Need/need not show illicit sex/ that women involved are prostitutes to sustain charge of permitting premises to be used as brothel.

SEXUAL OFFENCES (conspiracy to corrupt public morals)

Knuller (Publishing, Printing and Promotions) Ltd and others v Director of Public Prosecutions [1972] 2 All ER 898; [1973] AC 435; (1972) 56 Cr App R 633; [1975] Crim LR 704; (1972) 136 JP 728; (1972) 116 SJ 545; [1972] 3 WLR 143 HL Is offence of conspiracy to corrupt public morals and of conspiring to outrage public decency which advertisements by men seeking homosexual partners could violate.

R v Knuller (Publishing, Printing and Promotions) Ltd and others [1971] 3 All ER 314; (1971) 135 JP 569; [1972] 2 QB 179; (1971) 115 SJ 772; [1971] 3 WLR 633 CA Agreement to place advertisements seeking homosexual partners can be conspiracy to corrupt public morals.

R v Neville (Richard Clive); R v Anderson (James); R v Dennis (Felix); R v Oz Publications Ink Ltd (1972) 56 Cr App R 115; (1971) 115 SJ 847 CA Different meaning of obscene when used in Post Office Act 1953, s 11(1) (b) and Obscene Publications Act 1959, s 2. expert evidence inadmissible in Obscene Publications Act prosecution to determine if work obscene jury to receive proper direction on defence that publication causes aversion but is not obscene; look to individual articles in magazine but entirety of book to see if obscene.

SEXUAL OFFENCES (conspiracy to outrage public decency)

Knuller (Publishing, Printing and Promotions) Ltd and others v Director of Public Prosecutions [1972] 2 All ER 898; [1973] AC 435; (1972) 56 Cr App R 633; [1975] Crim LR 704; (1972) 136 JP 728; (1972) 116 SJ 545; [1972] 3 WLR 143 HL Is offence of conspiracy to corrupt public morals and of conspiring to outrage public decency which advertisements by men seeking homosexual partners could violate.

SEXUAL OFFENCES (corrupting public morals)

R v Keene and others [1972] Crim LR 526t; (1971) 121 NLJ 640 CA Was corrupting public morals for magazine to contain homosexual private advertisments.

SEXUAL OFFENCES (encouraging indecent assault on under-fourteen year old)

R v Drury (Alfred) (1975) 60 Cr App R 195; [1975] Crim LR 655 CA Was encouragement and intent to do so - conviction for encouraging indecent assault on girl under 14 therefore valid.

SEXUAL OFFENCES (encouraging unlawful carnal knowledge of under-sixteen year old)

R v Chainey [1911-13] All ER 701; (1913-14) XXIII Cox CC 620; (1914) 78 JP 127; [1914] 1 KB 137; (1913) 48 LJ 673; [1914] 83 LJKB 306; (1913-14) 109 LTR 752; (1913-14) XXX TLR 51; (1913) WN (I) 318 CCA Criminal neglect of (under sixteen year old) child socialising with immoral persons did not mean guilty of causing/encouraging unlawful carnal knowledge of same.

R v Moon (Frederick); R v Moon (Emily) (1910) 4 Cr App R 171; [1910] 1 KB 818; (1910) 45 LJ 221; (1910) 79 LJKB 505 CCA Not offence under Children Act 1908, s 17 to encourage seduction of girl already seduced.

SEXUAL OFFENCES (gross indecency)

Director of Public Prosecutions v Burgess [1970] 3 All ER 266; [1970] Crim LR 597t; (1970) 134 JP 646; (1970) 120 NLJ 661t and 946; [1971] 1 QB 432; (1970) 114 SJ 768; [1970] 3 WLR 805 HC QBD DPP must consent to gross indecency towards child prosecution; gross indecency towards child means gross indecency involving child.

R v Angel [1968] 2 All ER 607; (1968) 52 Cr App R 280; [1968] Crim LR 342t; (1968) 118 NLJ 277t; (1968) 112 SJ 310; [1968] 1 WLR 669 CA On consent of DPP to gross indecency proceedings.

R v Assistant Recorder of Kingston-upon-Hull, ex parte Morgan (1969) 133 JP 165; [1969] 2 WLR 246 HC QBD DPP's consent (pursuant to Sexual Offences Act 1967, s 8) unnecessary to bring prosecution for incitement of under-14 year old boy to act of gross indecency.

R v Cope (Charles William) (1921-22) 16 Cr App R 77; (1922) 86 JP 78; (1921-22) 66 SJ 406; (1921-22) XXXVIII TLR 243 CCA On letter as attempt to procure gross indecency contrary to Criminal Law Amendment Act 1885, s 11.

R v Francis (Colin Leslie) (1989) 88 Cr App R 127; [1988] Crim LR 528 CA Indecency with or towards children contrary to Indecency with Children Act 1960, s 1(1) requires that act be aimed at children and that accused pleased that children watching.

R v Ghik [1984] Crim LR 110 CCC Failed prosecution for act of gross indecency in public place where unproven that was real chance of being discovered by member of public where were performing act of gross indecency.

R v Hall [1963] 2 All ER 1075; (1963) 47 Cr App R 253; [1963] Crim LR 642; (1963) 127 JP 489; (1963) 113 LJ 578; [1964] 1 QB 273; (1963) 107 SJ 597; [1963] 3 WLR 482 CCA Can convict for gross indecency 'with' another though other did not consent.

R v Hornby and Peaple [1946] 2 All ER 487; (1946-48) 32 Cr App R 1; (1946) 110 JP 391; (1946) 175 LTR 518; (1945-46) LXII TLR 629 CCA Gross indecency possible though no physical touching.

R v Horwood [1969] 3 All ER 1156; (1969) 53 Cr App R 619; [1969] Crim LR 598; (1969) 113 SJ 895; (1970) 134 JP 23; [1970] 1 QB 133; [1969] 3 WLR 964 CA Evidence to be probative of offence - admission that homosexual not per se probative of gross indecency.

R v Hunt and another [1950] 2 All ER 291; (1949-50) 34 Cr App R 135; (1950) 114 JP 382 CCA Need not be physical touching for there to be gross indecency.

R v Pearce [1951] 1 All ER 493; (1951-52) 35 Cr App R 17; (1951) 115 JP 157; (1951) 95 SJ 239; [1951] 1 TLR 412; (1951) WN (I) 129 CCA Whn jointly charging two males with gross indecency can convict one and acquit the other.

R v Preece; R v Howells [1976] 2 All ER 690; (1976) 63 Cr App R 28; [1976] Crim LR 392t; (1976) 140 JP 450; (1976) 126 NLJ 338t; [1977] QB 370; (1976) 120 SJ 233; [1976] 2 WLR 749 CA Gross indecency 'with' another man requires consent of other.

R v Speck [1977] 2 All ER 859; (1977) 65 Cr App R 161; [1977] Crim LR 689; (1977) 141 JP 459; (1977) 127 NLJ 414t; (1977) 121 SJ 221 CA Passively allowing uninvited act to continue could be invitation to do act.

R v Thompson (1918-21) XXVI Cox CC 31; (1916-17) 12 Cr App R 261; (1917) 81 JP 266; [1917] 2 KB 630; (1917) 52 LJ 285; [1917] 86 LJCL 1321; (1917-18) 117 LTR 575; (1916-17) 61 SJ 647; (1916-17) XXXIII TLR 566; (1917) WN (I) 234 CCA Powder puffs/obscene photographs in accused's possession admissible on issue of identity.

R v Thompson (Arthur) (1916-17) 12 Cr App R 278 CCA Bail pending appeal against conviction in gross indecency with male case.

R v Twiss [1918-23] All ER 257; (1918-21) XXVI Cox CC 325; (1917-18) 13 Cr App R 177; (1919) 83 JP 23; [1918] 2 KB 853; [1919] 88 LJCL 20; (1918-19) 119 LTR 680; (1917-18) 62 SJ 752; (1918-19) XXXV TLR 3; (1918) WN (I) 300 CCA Finding powder puffs/photos of naked boys in accused's possession admissible as evidence of guilt; conviction allowed stand despite juror conversations with prosecution witnesses.

R v Warn [1968] 1 All ER 339; [1968] Crim LR 103t; (1967) 117 NLJ 1242t; [1968] 1 QB 718; (1967) 111 SJ 943; [1968] 2 WLR 131 CMAC Consent of DPP to gross indecency charge involving under-21 year old applies to court-martials.

R v Woods (1931-34) XXIX Cox CC 165; (1930-31) Cr App R 41; (1930) 143 LTR 311; (1929-30) XLVI TLR 401 CCA Acts complained of (letters written in guise of woman) too remote to constitute attempt to procure grossly indecent act.

Secretary of State for Defence v Warn [1970] AC 394; [1968] Crim LR 378; (1968) 112 SJ 461 HL Consent of DPP to gross indecency charge involving under-21 year old applies to court-martials.

Thompson v Director of Public Prosecutions [1918-19] All ER 521; (1918) 53 LJ 62; (1918) 118 LTR 418; (1917-18) 62 SJ 266; (1918) WN (I) 21 HL Possession of powder puffs/lewd photographs showed offender and accused had same tendencies - admissible to rebut alibi.

SEXUAL OFFENCES (harbouring prostitute)

Allen v Whitehead [1930] 1 KB 211; (1929) WN (I) 207 HC KBD Occupier liable for servant's knowingly suffering prostitutes to meet in former's refreshment house.

SEXUAL OFFENCES (importuning)

R v Gray (James Burns McWilliams) (1982) 74 Cr App R 324; [1982] Crim LR 176; (1981) 131 NLJ 1311 CA Importuning for gay sex is 'immoral purpose' within meaning of Sexual Offences Act 1956, s 32.

R v Tuck [1994] Crim LR 375 CA On what is meant by 'persistent' importuning.

SEXUAL OFFENCES (incest)

R v Dimes (Clifford) (1911-12) 7 Cr App R 43; (1912) 76 JP 47 CCA That jury did not find accused guilty of rape (but rather of incest) did not mean believed victim consented.

R v Gordon [1925] All ER 405; (1926-30) XXVIII Cox CC 41; (1925) 89 JP 156; (1925) 133 LTR 734; (1924-25) XLI TLR 611 CCA Where two parties charged with same incest one can be convicted though the other is acquitted.

R v Hemmings [1939] 1 All ER 417; (1939-40) XXXI Cox CC 240; (1938-40) 27 Cr App R 46; (1939) 87 LJ 122; (1939) 160 LTR 288; (1938-39) LV TLR 394; (1939) WN (I) 47 CCA Must be evidence of non-access by husband to prove stepfather was actual father of stepdaughter (and so capable of incest).

R v Tiso (Roland Leonard) (1990-91) 12 Cr App R (S) 122; [1990] Crim LR 607 CA Lengthy period between sex crimes towards children and investigation of/conviction for same need not be mitigating factor when sentencing.

SEXUAL OFFENCES (incitement of child to gross indecency)

R v Rowley [1991] 4 All ER 649; (1992) 94 Cr App R 95; [1991] Crim LR 785; (1992) 156 JP 319; (1991) 141 NLJ 1038t; (1991) 135 SJ LB 84; [1991] TLR 347; [1991] 1 WLR 1020 CA Act outraging public decency must outrage public decency in and of itself; preparatory acts to inciting gross indecency not attempted incitement of child to gross indecency.

SEXUAL OFFENCES (incitement of gross indecency)

R v Bentley (1923) 87 JP 55; [1923] 1 KB 403; [1923] 92 LJCL 366; (1922-23) 67 SJ 279; (1922-23) XXXIX TLR 105; (1922) WN (I) 335 CCA Inciting criminal act details of which not arranged/inciting another to incite another to commit criminal act was punishable offence.

SEXUAL OFFENCES (indecent assault)

Beal v Kelley [1951] 2 All ER 763; (1951-52) 35 Cr App R 128; (1951) 115 JP 566; (1951) 101 LJ 594; (1951) 95 SJ 685; [1951] 2 TLR 865; (1951) WN (I) 505 HC KBD Actual assault need not in itself be indecent to sustain indecent assault charge.

Director of Public Prosecutions v Rogers [1953] 2 All ER 644; (1953) 37 Cr App R 137; (1953) 117 JP 424; (1953) 97 SJ 541; [1953] 1 WLR 1017 HC QBD No coercion/violence in getting child to do indecent act meant no assault so could be no indecent assault.

Fairclough v Whipp [1951] 2 All ER 834; (1951) 115 JP 612; (1951) 95 SJ 699; [1951] 2 TLR 909; (1951) WN (I) 528 HC KBD Successfully asking girl to touch accused's exposed person not an assault (hence no indecent assault).

Fairclough v Whipp (1951-52) 35 Cr App R 138 CCA Successfully asking girl to touch accused's exposed person not an assault (hence no indecent assault).

Faulkner v Talbot [1981] 3 All ER 468; (1982) 74 Cr App R 1; [1981] Crim LR 705; (1981) 125 SJ 859; [1981] 1 WLR 1528 HC QBD Intentional touching of another absent consent/lawful excuse is assault; under-sixteen year old boy could not under Sexual Offences Act 1956, s 15(2) consent to act that absent consent was assault.

R v Bisp [1957] Crim LR 249 Sessions Consent of woman could be defence to indecent assault charge albeit that woman had been certified under the Lunacy Act 1890.

R v Boyea [1992] Crim LR 574; (1992) 156 JP 505; [1992] TLR 40 CA On victim's consent as (non-) defence to indecent assault where assault was 'likely' (ordinary meaning) to cause non-transient/-trifling injury (meaning of latter notions explained).

R v Burrows [1952] 1 All ER 58; (1951-52) 35 Cr App R 180; (1952) 116 JP 47; (1952) 96 SJ 122; [1952] 1 TLR 51; (1952) WN (I) 21 CCA Absent violent act cannot be indecent assault.

R v C [1992] Crim LR 642; (1992) 156 JP 649 CA Indecent assault an offence of basic intent so self-induced drunkenness not a defence thereto.

R v Carter [1956] Crim LR 772 Sessions On admissibility/effect of previous 'similar fact' evidence of homosexual encounters on instant charge of indecent assault of young boy.

R v Caswell [1984] Crim LR 111 CrCt On extent to which immunity of husband from liability for raping wife extends to sexual activities leading up to full intercourse.

R v Court [1987] 1 All ER 120; (1987) 84 Cr App R 210; [1987] Crim LR 134; [1987] QB 156; (1970) 130 SJ 859; [1986] 3 WLR 1029 CA Additional evidence of secret motive admissible in indecent assault case; secret motive cannot render indecent a situation which objectively is not indecent.

R v Court [1988] 2 All ER 221; [1989] AC 28; (1988) 87 Cr App R 144; [1988] Crim LR 537; (1988) 152 JP 422; (1988) 138 NLJ 128; (1988) 132 SJ 658; [1988] 2 WLR 1071 HL Intentional assault intended as indecent is indecent assault; any evidence showing intent admissible.

R v Culyer [1992] TLR 202 CA Did not have to be indecent intent to render one guilty of indecent assault where assault was per se indecent - intent for assault sufficed.

R v George [1956] Crim LR 52 Assizes Assault by way of attempted removal of shoe from girl (prompted by sexual motives) was not an indecent assault.

R v Gregg (1932) 74 LJ 424 CCA On need for corroboration (here present) in indecent assault case.

R v Hall (John Hamilton) (1988) 86 Cr App R 159; [1987] Crim LR 831 CA Woman is defective for purposes of Sexual Offences Act 1956, s 14(4) where compared to normal person suffers from seriously limited intelligence/social ability.

R v Hare [1933] All ER 550; (1934-39) XXX Cox CC 64; (1932-34) 24 Cr App R 108; (1934) 98 JP 49; [1934] 1 KB 354; (1933) 76 LJ 357; (1934) 103 LJCL 96; (1934) 150 LTR 279; (1933-34) L TLR 103 CCA Woman can be guilty of indecent assault on male under Offences Against the Person Act 1861, s 62.

R v Hart (Willie) (1914) 10 Cr App R 176 CCA Indecent assault conviction quashed where was some evidence of consent.

R v Killick (William John) (1924-25) 18 Cr App R 120 CCA Need for corroboration in indecent assault case where prosecutrix' case weak.

R v Kimber [1983] 3 All ER 316; (1983) 77 Cr App R 225; [1983] Crim LR 630; (1983) 133 NLJ 914; (1983) 127 SJ 578; [1983] TLR 388; [1983] 1 WLR 1118 CA Intent for indecent assault is intent to use violence without consent; reasonable belief of consent a valid defence.

R v Kowalski (Roy) (1988) 86 Cr App R 339; [1988] Crim LR 124; [1988] 1 FLR 447 CA Husband cannot rape wife per vaginam but can be guilty of indecent assault on her by reason of fellatio.

R v Laws (Ronald James) (1928-29) 21 Cr App R 45 CCA Improper that 'reasonable belief that girl over sixteen' defence open on charge of carnal knowledge but not indecent assault (Criminal Law Amendment Act 1922, s 2).

R v Lea [1977] Crim LR 489 CA Conditional discharge for man who could raise statutory defence to unlawful sex charge with under-sixteen year old but was found guilty of indecent assault on her.

R v Lee (John) (1911-12) 7 Cr App R 31 CCA On time lapse before prosecutrix' making of complaint.

R v Leeson (Maurice) (1968) 52 Cr App R 185; [1968] Crim LR 283; (1968) 112 SJ 151 CA Non-indecent physical assault coupled with suggestion of sexual intimacy was indecent assault.

R v Lynch [1993] Crim LR 868 CA Bona fide distress is capable of corroborating evidence of complainant; allowing presence of 'Victim Support' representative in witness box/erection of screen to shield witness were valid exercises of judge's discretion.

R v Mason (1969) 53 Cr App R 12; [1969] Crim LR 449 CA No assault by woman on boys so could not be guilty of indecent assault.

R v Mochan; R v Lathan; R v Micallef (1969) 113 SJ 773; [1969] 1 WLR 1331 Assizes Persons charged with rape could be convicted of indecent assault but not unlawful sex.

R v Murphy [1954] Crim LR 944t CCA Two years' imprisonment (maximum sentence) for indecent assault (court of opinion that maximum sentence inadequate).

R v Osborn [1963] Crim LR 193t; (1963) 107 SJ 117 CMAC Conviction for indecent assault quashed where grounded on inconsistent, uncorroborated evidence of teenage boy.

R v Parsons [1993] Crim LR 792 CA On ingredients of offence of indecent assault: on recklessness as an element of the offence.

R v Pratt [1984] Crim LR 41 CrCt Must prove (inter alia) indecent intention for offender to be guilty of indecent assault.

R v Sands [1958] Crim LR 256 CCA Indecent assault convictions quashed where trial judge told jury that evidence pointing to guilt of various similar offences was mutually corroborative.

R v Sargeant [1997] Crim LR 50; (1997) 161 JP 127; (1996) TLR 15/10/96 CA On what constitutes indecent assault (indecent contact not necessary).

R v Seaward [1973] Crim LR 642 CA Seven years' imprisonment merited by twenty-two year old guilty of burglary with intent to rape/of indecent assault.

R v Simmonite (1916-17) 12 Cr App R 142; (1917) 81 JP 80; [1916] 2 KB 821; [1917] 86 LJCL 15 CCA Could be convicted of indecent assault though charged with incest.

R v Sutton [1977] 3 All ER 476; (1978) 66 Cr App R 21; [1977] Crim LR 569; (1977) 141 JP 683; (1977) 127 NLJ 590t; (1977) 121 SJ 676; [1977] 1 WLR 1086 CA Non-indecent touching consented to by youth not indecent assault.

R v Thomas (Emrys) (1985) 81 Cr App R 331; [1985] Crim LR 677 CA Touching girl's skirt was assault but was not indecent assault.

R v Touhey (Peter) (1961) 45 Cr App R 23; [1960] Crim LR 843 CCA On availability of indecent assault conviction where defendant charged with rape.

R v Wood (Charles) (1919-20) 14 Cr App R 149; (1920) 84 JP 92; [1920] 89 LJCL 435; (1919-20) 64 SJ 409 CCA Seven months' hard labour (concurrent) for two convictions of indecent assault.

Williams v Gibbs [1958] Crim LR 127t HC QBD Drying of young girls after taking them for a paddle was not indecent assault.

SEXUAL OFFENCES (indecent assault on under-sixteen year old)

R v Maughan (Reginald) (1932-34) 24 Cr App R 130 CCA Not defence to charge of indecent assault on under-sixteen year old that genuinely believed was over sixteen.

SEXUAL OFFENCES (indecent behaviour)

R v Duke and Others (1909) 73 JP 88 Quarter Sessions On what constitutes riotous/indecent behaviour on part of prostitute for purposes of Vagrancy Act 1824, s 3.

SEXUAL OFFENCES (indecent exposure)

Cheeseman v Director of Public Prosecutions [1991] 3 All ER 54; (1991) 93 Cr App R 145; [1991] Crim LR 296; (1991) 155 JP 469; [1992] QB 83; [1990] TLR 690; [1991] 2 WLR 1105 HC QBD On-duty police officers policing public toilet were not 'passengers' before whom indecent exposure to their annoyance could constitute offence (Town Police Clauses Act 1847, s 28, as amended).

Evans v Ewels [1972] 2 All ER 22; (1972) 56 Cr App R 377; [1972] Crim LR 328; (1972) 136 JP 394; (1972) 116 SJ 274; [1972] 1 WLR 671 HC QBD Indecent exposure under Vagrancy Act means indecent exposure of penis.

Evens v Rogers [1956] Crim LR 496 HC QBD On appropriate means of prosecuting for indecent exposure.

Ford v Falcone [1971] 2 All ER 1138; [1971] Crim LR 373; (1971) 135 JP 451; (1971) 121 NLJ 642; (1971) 115 SJ 365; [1971] 1 WLR 809 HC QBD Indecent exposure may occur in private place.

Ford v Falcone (1971) 55 Cr App R 373 CA Indecent exposure may occur in private place.

Hunt v Director of Public Prosecutions [1990] Crim LR 812; (1990) 154 JP 762; [1990] TLR 402 HC QBD Witness need not have seen penis for justices to convict person of wilful/indecent exposure.

R v Washer [1954] Crim LR 933 CMAC Intent irrelevant to offence of engaging in disgraceful conduct of indecent kind contrary to Army Act (unlike sister offence under Vagrancy Act 1824).

SEXUAL OFFENCES (living on earnings of prostitution)

Attorney-General's Reference (No 2 of 1995) [1996] 3 All ER 860; [1997] 1 Cr App R 72; [1996] Crim LR 662 CA On what constitutes 'influencing' a prostitute for purposes of Sexual Offences Act 1956, s 31.

Calvert v Mayes [1954] 1 All ER 41; [1954] Crim LR 147; (1954) 118 JP 76; [1954] 1 QB 342; (1954) 98 SJ 13; [1954] 2 WLR 18 HC QBD Payment of money direct to accused rather than via prostitutes (over whom exercised some control) did not mean were not living off earnings of prostitution.

R v Ansell [1974] 3 All ER 568; (1975) 60 Cr App R 45; [1974] Crim LR 616t; (1974) 138 JP 781; (1974) 124 NLJ 768; [1975] QB 215; (1974) 118 SJ 715; [1974] 3 WLR 430 CA Man receiving payment directly from prostitute's clients guilty of living off earnings of prostitution.

R v Bell [1978] Crim LR 233 CA On proving that person is living off earnings of prostitution.

R v Calderhead (David Glen); R v Bidney (Harold) (1979) 68 Cr App R 37 CA Landlord charging inflated rent to woman knew was prostitute was living on earnings of prostitution.

R v Farrugia (Francis); R v Borg (Charles); R v Agius (Jean); R v Gauchi (Ronnie) (1979) 69 Cr App R 108; (1979) 129 (1) NLJ 566t CA Earnings made by escort agency manager/employee or mini-cab driver in anticipation of act of prostitution was living on earnings of prostitution.

R v Grant (Thomas) [1985] Crim LR 387 CA On Sexual Offences Act 1956, s 30(2).

R v McFarlane [1994] 2 All ER 283; (1994) 99 Cr App R 8; [1994] Crim LR 532; (1994) 158 JP 310; (1994) 144 NLJ 270; [1994] QB 419; (1994) 138 SJ LB 19; [1993] TLR 662; [1994] 2 WLR 494 CA 'Clipper' a prostitute because both offer sexual services for reward.

R v Pickford (Tom James) (1914) 10 Cr App R 269 CCA Prostitute need not be accomplice of man living on earnings of prostitution.

R v Shaw [1961] 1 All ER 330; (1961) 111 LJ 137 CCA Is common law offence of conspiracy to corrupt public morals; can be prosecuted for same notwithstanding Obscene Publications Act 1959, s 2(4); publishing advertisements for prostitutes is living off earnings of prostitution; need not be intent to corrupt for publication to be obscene.

R v Silver and others [1956] 1 All ER 716; (1956) 40 Cr App R 32; [1956] Crim LR 338; (1956) 120 JP 233; (1956) 100 SJ 228; [1956] 1 WLR 281 CCC Landlord's/estate agent's earnings from property rents where property rented by prostitutes not living off earnings off prostitution as rents from property are landlord's/agent's own earnings.

R v Stewart (John) (1986) 83 Cr App R 327; [1986] Crim LR 805 CA High rent not per se indication either way that are living on earnings of prostitution; corroboration warning in respect of accomplice to be clearly made.

R v Thomas [1957] 2 All ER 181; (1957) 41 Cr App R 117; [1957] Crim LR 255; (1957) 121 JP 338 CCC Matter for jury whether renting rooms at very high rates to prostitute is living on earnings of prostitution.

R v Thomas [1957] 2 All ER 342; (1957) 41 Cr App R 121; (1957) 107 LJ 315 CCA On living on earnings of prostitution.

R v Wilson (Donald Theodore) (1984) 78 Cr App R 247; [1984] Crim LR 173; [1983] TLR 653 CA On what constitutes 'living on' earnings of prostitution contrary to Sexual Offences Act 1956, s 30(1) (2).

Shaw v Director of Public Prosecutions [1961] 2 All ER 446; [1962] AC 220; (1961) 45 Cr App R 113; [1961] Crim LR 468; (1961) 125 JP 437; (1961) 111 LJ 356; (1961) 105 SJ 421; [1961] 2 WLR 897 HL Test of obscenity is whether article would corrupt/deprave another (intent of author irrelevant); are living off earnings of prostitution if provide goods/services to prostitutes which would not if they were not prostitutes; agreement to publish obscene publication an agreement to corrupt public morals (even if never published), a common law misdemeanour.

SEXUAL OFFENCES (marital rape)

R v C and another [1991] 1 All ER 755; (1990) 140 NLJ 1497 CrCt Husband may be guilty of raping wife regardless of living arrangements.

R v C and another [1991] Crim LR 60 CA Husband could be guilty of raping wife.

R v Caswell [1984] Crim LR 111 CrCt On extent to which immunity of husband from liability for raping wife extends to sexual activities leading up to full intercourse.

R v Clarke [1949] 2 All ER 448; (1948-49) 33 Cr App R 216; (1949) 99 LJ 441 Assizes Post-separation order rape of wife by husband possible.

R v J [1991] 1 All ER 759; (1991) 141 NLJ 17 CrCt Common law rule that husband cannot rape wife applies but cannot be extended.

R v Kowalski (Roy) (1988) 86 Cr App R 339; [1988] Crim LR 124; [1988] 1 FLR 447 CA Husband cannot rape wife per vaginam but can be guilty of indecent assault on her by reason of fellatio.

R v Miller [1954] 2 All ER 529; (1954) 38 Cr App R 1; [1954] Crim LR 219; [1954] 2 QB 282; (1954) 98 SJ 62; (1954) 118 JP 341; [1954] 2 WLR 138 HC QBD Husband could not be guilty of raping wife absent separation agreement/order; assault for husband to use force in exercising right to marital sex.

R v O'Brien [1974] 3 All ER 663; (1974) 138 JP 798 CrCt Husband capable of raping wife post-divorce decree nisi.

R v R [1991] 1 All ER 747 CrCt Wife may unilaterally withdraw implied consent to sexual intercourse with husband.

R v R [1991] 4 All ER 481; [1992] 1 AC 599 (also CA); (1992) 94 Cr App R 216; [1992] Crim LR 207; [1992] 1 FLR 217; (1991) 155 JP 989; (1991) 141 NLJ 1481; (1991) 135 SJ LB 181; [1991] TLR 468; [1991] 3 WLR 767 HL Husband can rape wife.

R v R (a husband) [1991] 2 All ER 257; [1992] 1 AC 599 (also HL); (1991) 93 Cr App R 1; [1991] Crim LR 475; (1991) 155 JP 373; (1991) 141 NLJ 383; [1991] TLR 139; [1991] 2 WLR 1065 CA Husband can rape wife.

SEXUAL OFFENCES (outraging public decency)

R v Gibson and another [1991] 1 All ER 439; (1990) 91 Cr App R 341; [1990] Crim LR 738; (1991) 155 JP 127; [1990] 2 QB 619; (1990) 134 SJ 1123; [1990] TLR 530; [1990] 3 WLR 595 CA Offence of outraging public decency does not require tendency to corrupt public morals/Need not intend to outrage public decency for culpability to arise/Need not draw special attention of public before culpability arises.

R v Lunderbech [1991] Crim LR 784 CA Police officers constitute members of public for purposes of witnessing acts outraging public decency; jury may infer from evidence that act likely to disgust/annoy though is no proof that anyone was disgusted/annoyed.

R v May (John) (1990) 91 Cr App R 157 [1990] Crim LR 415 CA Boys told to instruct teacher to do indecent performances were not partcipants to act so performances before them alone were acts outraging public decency.

R v Walker [1996] 1 Cr App R 111; (1995) 159 JP 509; (1995) 139 SJ LB 118; [1995] TLR 201; [1995] Crim LR 826 CA Offence of outraging public decency must be committed in public and must be possible for two or more persons to witness same.

SEXUAL OFFENCES (procuring sex with under twenty-one year old)

R v Johnson [1963] Crim LR 860 CCA On offence of procuring under twenty-one year old to have sex.

SEXUAL OFFENCES (procuring unlawful carnal connection)

R v Mackenzie (Elizabeth Smith); R v Higginson (George) (1910-11) 6 Cr App R 64; (1911) 75 JP 159; (1910-11) XXVII TLR 152 CCA On offence of procuring girl for unlawful carnal connection; on conviction of party having sex for aiding and abetting in unlawful carnal connection.

SEXUAL OFFENCES (procuring woman to become prostitute)

R v Brown (Raymond Andrew) (1985) 80 Cr App R 36; [1984] Crim LR 627; (1984) 128 SJ 736; [1984] TLR 457; [1984] 1 WLR 1211 CA On intent necessary for offence of procuring woman to become common prostitute: cannot procure woman whom already truly believe to be prostitute to become prostitute.

SEXUAL OFFENCES (prostitution)

Abbott and another v Smith [1964] 3 All ER 762; (1964) Crim LR 662; (1965) 129 JP 3; (1964) 114 LJ 738; [1965] 2 QB 662; [1965] 3 WLR 362 CrCt Brothel though premises let in separate rooms; management involves element of control not present here.

Behrendt v Burridge [1976] 3 All ER 285; (1976) 63 Cr App R 202; [1976] Crim LR 522; (1976) 140 JP 613; (1976) 126 NLJ 667t; (1976) 120 SJ 538; [1977] 1 WLR 29 HC QBD Passive behaviour may still be soliciting.

Carnill v Edwards and others [1953] 1 All ER 282; (1953) 117 JP 93; (1953) 97 SJ 98; [1953] 1 WLR 290 HC QBD Prostitutes committing indecent acts in car not 'wandering in a public highway'.

Crook v Edmondson [1966] 1 All ER 833; (1978) 66 Cr App R 90; [1966] Crim LR 227; (1966) 130 JP 191; [1966] 2 QB 81; (1966) 110 SJ 147; [1966] 2 WLR 672 HC QBD Not soliciting/ importuning for immoral purpose to seek sex with prostitute.

Director of Public Prosecutions v Bull [1994] 4 All ER 411; [1995] 1 Cr App R 413; [1994] Crim LR 762; (1994) 158 JP 1005; [1995] QB 88; [1994] TLR 314; [1994] 3 WLR 1196 HC QBD Male prostitute not a 'common prostitute'.

Ex parte Thompson-Schwab and Wingate [1956] Crim LR 126t HC ChD Injunction granted to restrain parties from using/permitting use of certain property for prostitution.

Mattison v Johnson [1916-17] All ER 727; (1915-17) XXV Cox CC 373; (1916) 80 JP 243; [1916] 85 LJKB 741; (1916) 114 LTR 951; (1916) WN (I) 52 HC KBD That sole tenant-occupier used premises for own acts of prostitution did not merit conviction for permitting premises to be used for habitual prostitution.

R v Broadfoot [1976] 3 All ER 753; (1977) 64 Cr App R 71; [1977] Crim LR 690; (1977) 141 JP 40 CA 'Procure' a common non-technical term; simply offering lots of money could be attempt to procure.

R v Clarke [1976] 2 All ER 696; (1976) 63 Cr App R 16; [1977] Crim LR 110; (1976) 140 JP 469 CA Presumption that man living with/habitually in company of prostitute knowingly living off her earnings.

R v De Munck [1918-19] All ER 499; (1918-21) XXVI Cox CC 302; (1917-18) 13 Cr App R 113; (1918) 82 JP 160; [1918] 1 KB 635; [1918] 87 LJCL 682; (1918-19) 119 LTR 88; (1917-18) 62 SJ 405; (1917-18) XXXIV TLR 305 CCA Prostitute includes women selling themselves into acts of common lewdness short of sex.

R v O [1983] Crim LR 401 CrCt Encouragement of and general assistance to prostitute by her lesbian cohabitee was not breach of Sexual Offences Act 1956, s 31.

R v Tan and others [1983] 2 All ER 12; (1983) 76 Cr App R 300; [1983] Crim LR 404; (1983) 147 JP 257; [1983] QB 1053; (1983) 127 SJ 390; [1983] TLR 100; [1983] 3 WLR 361 CA Prostitute providing services openly but in own place on one-to-one basis guilty of keeping disorderly house; sex-changed male can still be 'man' living off prostitution.

R v Webb [1963] 3 All ER 177; (1963) 47 Cr App R 265; [1963] Crim LR 644; (1963) 127 JP 516; (1963) 113 LJ 625; [1964] 1 QB 357; (1963) 107 SJ 597; [1963] 3 WLR 638 CCA Prostitution includes all acts where woman offers self as a participant in indecent acts.

Smith and another v Hughes and others [1960] 2 All ER 859; (1960) 124 JP 430; (1960) 104 SJ 606 HC QBD Soliciting from balcony/behind closed windows is soliciting 'in a street or public place'.

Thompson-Schwab and another v Costaki and another [1956] 1 All ER 652; [1956] Crim LR 274; (1956) 106 LJ 201; (1956) 100 SJ 246; [1956] 1 WLR 335 CA Use of neighbouring premises for prostitution a nuisance.

Webb v Commissioner of the Metropolitan Police [1963] Crim LR 708t HL No leave to appeal on point whether masturbation of men for payment was prostitution.

Weisz and another v Monahan [1962] 1 All ER 664; [1962] Crim LR 179t; (1962) 126 JP 184; (1962) 112 LJ 223; (1962) 106 SJ 114 HC QBD Soliciting involves physical presence and does not extend to window advertisements.

SEXUAL OFFENCES (rape)

Director of Public Prosecutions v Morgan; Director of Public Prosecutions v McDonald; Director of Public Prosecutions v McLarty; Director of Public Prosecutions v Parker [1975] 2 All ER 347; [1976] AC 182 (also CA); (1975) 61 Cr App R 136; [1975] Crim LR 717; (1975) 139 JP 476; (1975) 125 NLJ 530t; (1975) 119 SJ 319; [1975] 2 WLR 913 (also CA) HL Belief that woman consents means no rape as no mens rea.

Kaitamaki v R [1984] 2 All ER 435; [1985] AC 147; (1984) 79 Cr App R 251; [1984] Crim LR 564; (1984) 128 SJ 331; [1984] TLR 282; [1984] 3 WLR 137 PC Consented to complete penetration does not mean continuing sex cannot be rape.

Mattouk v Massad [1943] 2 All ER 517; (1943) 87 SJ 381; (1943) WN (I) 215 PC Does not matter whether intercourse with/without consent in seduction action as master suing for loss of services.

R v B [1984] TLR 660 CA On definition of recklessness in the context of rape.

R v Barnes [1994] Crim LR 691 CA Defence ought to have been allowed question rape complainant about her previous sexual experience (relevant to issue of whether there had been any sex between complainant and appellant) and her possession of vibrator (could not in any event be excluded).

R v Barton (Kevin John) (1987) 85 Cr App R 5; [1987] Crim LR 399; (1987) 131 SJ 74 CA Rape conviction proper despite exclusion of evidence of promiscuity - a discretionary matter for judge - where sought to raise consent defence.

R v Bashir (Mohammed) (1983) 77 Cr App R 59; [1982] Crim LR 687 CA On proper direction regarding/on meaning of recklessness as to consent.

R v Baxter [1977] Crim LR 686 CA Eight years' imprisonment for rape.

R v Birchall (Mark Christopher); R v Pollock (Ian Richard); R v Tatton (James Shaun) (1986) 82 Cr App R 208; [1986] Crim LR 119 CA Rape conviction set aside where no direction on corroboration.

R v Bradley (John Alfred) (1910) 4 Cr App R 225; (1910) 74 JP 247 CCA Conviction to be quashed if jury possibly believed consent not a defence to rape.

R v Breckenridge (Ian) (1984) 79 Cr App R 244; [1984] Crim LR 174 CA Is rape by recklessness where were dismissive of need for consent.

R v Chance (Terence Easton) (1988) 87 Cr App R 398; [1988] QB 932 CA On identifying accused in rape cases.

R v Clarkson and others [1971] 3 All ER 344; (1971) 55 Cr App R 445; [1972] Crim LR 586; (1971) 135 JP 533; (1971) 115 SJ 654; [1971] 1 WLR 1402 CMAC Intent to encourage and actual encouragement necessary where aiding and abetting rape.

R v Cogan; R v Leak [1975] 2 All ER 1059; (1975) 61 Cr App R 217; [1975] Crim LR 584t; (1975) 139 JP 608; (1975) 125 NLJ 623t; [1976] QB 217; (1975) 119 SJ 473; [1975] 3 WLR 316 CA Can be guilty of aiding/abetting rape even if principal acquitted of rape as believed consent.

R v Collins (Christopher) [1976] Crim LR 249 CCC Issue estoppel applied to preclude conviction for burglary following acquittal of rape charge arising from same occasion; failed autrefois acquit plea where charged with burglary after acquitted of rape charge arising from same occasion.

R v Cummings [1948] 1 All ER 551 CCA Early/not immediate complaint of rape sufficed to sustain conviction.

R v Dimes (Clifford) (1911-12) 7 Cr App R 43; (1912) 76 JP 47 CCA That jury did not find accused guilty of rape (but rather of incest) did not mean believed victim consented.

R v Eatch [1980] Crim LR 650 CrCt On ramifications of voluntary drunkenness vis-à-vis intent in rape (a crime of basic intent).

R v Elbekkay [1995] Crim LR 163 CA Sex obtained through impersonation of woman's boyfriend was rape as necessary consent to sex absent.

R v Ellis [1990] Crim LR 717 CA On admissibility of previous sexual history/post-sex practices of complainant.

R v Faulkner (James Charles) (1987) 9 Cr App R (S) 321 CA Seven years' imprisonment for rape of eight year old girl by man of low intelligence.

R v Fisher (Colin); R v Marshall (Christopher); R v Mitchell (George) (1969) 113 SJ 70; [1969] 2 WLR 452 Assizes Jury cannot convict accused of sex with under-sixteen year old girl where accused being tried for rape.

R v Fotheringham (William Bruce) (1989) 88 Cr App R 206; [1988] Crim LR 846 CA Self-induced intoxication not a defence to rape.

R v Gilligan [1987] Crim LR 501 CrCt Publication of name of (dead) rape victim allowed.

R v Ginson [1993] Crim LR 453 CA Denial of previous statement as to why had been delay in reporting of rape by complainant went to credit, not main issue.

R v Greatbanks [1959] Crim LR 450 CCC Where pleading consent as defence to rape it was permissible to call evidence showing that prosecutrix a woman of disreputable character.

R v Harling [1938] 1 All ER 307; (1936-38) 26 Cr App R 127 CCA Prosecution must demonstrate in any rape case that alleged victim did not consent.

R v Haughian (Anthony Edward); R v Pearson (Arthur Reginald) (1985) 80 Cr App R 334 CA Defence of mistaken belief must fail where jury finds was no consent to rape; adequate direction on recklessness.

R v Howard [1965] 3 All ER 684; (1966) 50 Cr App R 56; [1966] Crim LR 54; (1966) 130 JP 61; (1965-66) 116 NLJ 159; (1965) 109 SJ 920; [1966] 1 WLR 13 CA Rape of under-16 year old only if she physically resists or is incapable of deciding whether to consent/resist.

R v Howes (1996) TLR 15/4/96 CA On when cross-examination of rape complainant may be allowed.

R v Kitching (1928-29) XLV TLR 569 CCA Rape conviction quashed where was no proper bill for rape (and no alternative indecent assault indictment).

R v Krausz (Francis Leonard) (1973) 57 Cr App R 466; [1973] Crim LR 581 CA Defence witness called to prove prosecutrix a prostitute (as part of consent defence) can state general reasons why so believes.

R v Lang (Christopher Michael) (1976) 62 Cr App R 50; [1976] Crim LR 65t; (1975) 125 NLJ 1065t CA Circumstances in which took drink not relevant to issue of consent to later sex.

R v Larter and Castleton [1995] Crim LR 75 CA On consent in context of rape.

R v Linekar [1995] 3 All ER 69; [1995] 2 Cr App R 49; [1995] Crim LR 320; [1995] QB 250; (1994) 138 SJ LB 227; [1994] TLR 528; [1995] 2 WLR 237 CA Consent to sexual intercourse by prostitute not vitiated by non-payment and so no rape.

R v McFall [1994] Crim LR 226 CA In light of 'other relevant matters' (Sexual Offences (Amendment) Act 1976, s 1(2)) - that had kidnapped woman/behaved aggressively - indicated appellant knew complainant did not consent to sex.

R v Miller [1954] 2 All ER 529; (1954) 38 Cr App R 1; [1954] 2 WLR 138 Assizes Husband cannot be guilty of rape on unseparated wife; husband cannot use force to have sex with wife - if does is guilty of lesser offence than rape - here guilty of assault occasioning actual bodily harm where hysteria/nervousness arose from act of sex.

R v Mochan; R v Lathan; R v Micallef (1969) 113 SJ 773; [1969] 1 WLR 1331 Assizes Persons charged with rape could be convicted of indecent assault but not unlawful sex.

R v Morgan and others [1975] 1 All ER 8; [1976] AC 182 (also HL); [1975] Crim LR 40t; (1974) 124 NLJ 987t; (1974) 118 SJ 809; [1975] 2 WLR 913 (also HL) CA Crown must objectively demonstrate absence of consent.

R v Olugboja (Stephen Olumbini) [1981] 3 All ER 443; (1981) 73 Cr App R 344; [1981] Crim LR 717; (1982) 146 JP 82; (1981) 131 NLJ 781; [1982] QB 320; (1981) 125 SJ 587; [1981] 3 WLR 585 CA On what constitutes consent.

R v Pigg [1982] 2 All ER 591; (1982) 74 Cr App R 352; [1982] Crim LR 446; (1982) 146 JP 298; (1982) 126 SJ 344; [1982] TLR 60; [1982] 1 WLR 762 CA Foreman must openly state number of dissenting jurors; recklessness in rape if unbothered by consent in situation where possibly no consent; continuing with sex though aware possibly no consent.

R v Redguard [1991] Crim LR 213 CA Cross-examination on post-alleged rape sexual experience ought to have been allowed where was relevant to credibility of complainant/issue of consent.

R v Riley [1991] Crim LR 460 CA That woman had sex with another while child present ought to have been admitted as accused claimed had consensual sex, woman denying same saying emphasising denial by saying child was present and would never have sex with child present.

R v Roberts [1986] Crim LR 188 CA Existence of separation deed (without non-cohabitation/ molestation clause) meant wife's implied consent to sex with husband did not revive on expiry of non-molestation/ouster orders so husband was guilty of raping wife.

R v Rodley [1911-13] All ER 688; (1913-14) XXIII Cox CC 574; (1913) 77 JP 465; [1913] 3 KB 468; [1913] 82 LJKB 1070; (1913-14) 109 LTR 476; (1913-14) 58 SJ 51; (1912-13) XXIX TLR 700; (1913) WN (I) 240 CCA Inadmissibility of evidence of later sexual antics as irrelevant to charge of burglary with intent to commit rape.

R v S (Satnam); R v S (Kewal) (1984) 78 Cr App R 149; [1985] Crim LR 236 CA Rape conviction quashed in absence of direction on rape/consent/recklessness as to consent.

R v S (SM) [1992] Crim LR 310 CA On allowing questions of complainant as to previous sexual experience where is relevant to issue of consent (here ought to have been allowed).

R v Salman (Arthur) (1924-25) 18 Cr App R 50 CCA On consent as defence for rape; on need for corroboration of complainant where person accused of rape claims was consent.

R v Schaub; R v Cooper (Joey) [1994] Crim LR 531; (1994) 138 SJ LB 11; [1993] TLR 623 CA Screen blocking complainant from accused to be used only in exceptional circumstances.

R v Sharples [1990] Crim LR 198 CrCt Husband could not be guilty of raping wife (albeit that wife previously obtained non-molestation order against him).

R v Shaw [1991] Crim LR 301 CrCt Wife's obtaining family protection order was a withdrawal of her consent to sex with husband.

R v Shaw (Grenville); Attorney-General's Reference (No 28 of 1996) [1997] TLR 46 CA Was rape to force prostitute to have unprotected sex with accused when she wanted protected sex.

R v Singh and Singh (1985) 149 JP 142 CA On recklessness in context of rape.

R v Steele (Peter Edward George) (1977) 65 Cr App R 22; [1977] Crim LR 290 CA Husband could be guilty of raping wife where were living apart and had given undertaking not to molest wife.

R v Stone (1937) 81 SJ 735; (1936-37) LIII TLR 1046 CCA Strangulation in course of rape that unintentionally results in death is not analogous to death in course of procuring abortion: DPP v Beard principles applicable.

R v T [1990] Crim LR 256 CrCt Rape is an external factor that could thereafter cause one not to act with conscious mind/will.

R v Taylor (Robert Peter) (1985) 80 Cr App R 327 CA Adequate direction on corroboration and recklessness: defence of honest mistake unlikely to succeed where jury conclude was no consent.

R v Thomas (Norman Livingstone) (1983) 77 Cr App R 63 CA On proper direction regarding recklessness as to consent.

R v Touhey (Peter) (1961) 45 Cr App R 23; [1960] Crim LR 843 CCA On availability of indecent assault conviction where defendant charged with rape.

R v Valentine (Anthony) [1996] 2 Cr App R 213 CA Rape complaint admissible though not made at earliest possible opportunity.

R v Walker [1996] Crim LR 742 CA Rape conviction unsafe where inadequate attention paid to credibility of complainant who had previously retracted her allegation and then gone back on retraction.

R v Williams [1922] All ER 433; (1921-25) XXVII Cox CC 350; (1922-23) 17 Cr App R 56; (1923) 87 JP 67; [1923] 1 KB 340; (1923) 58 LJ 21; [1923] 92 LJCL 230; (1923) 128 LTR 128; (1922-23) 67 SJ 263; (1922-23) XXXIX TLR 131; (1923) WN (I) 7 CCA Consent obtained by fraud not real consent so act of sex is rape.

R v Wilson (Alan Thomas) [1996] 2 Cr App R 241; [1996] Crim LR 573; [1997] QB 47; (1996) 140 SJ LB 93; (1996) TLR 5/3/96; [1996] 3 WLR 125 CA Successful appeal against assault conviction as appellant's branding of wife's buttocks had been done with her consent.

R v Woods (Walter) (1982) 74 Cr App R 312; [1982] Crim LR 42 CA Self-induced drunkenness not defence to rape: 'relevant matters' in Sexual Offences (Amendment) Act 1976, s 1(2) means legally relevant.

SEXUAL OFFENCES (soliciting)

Burge v Director of Public Prosecutions [1962] 1 All ER 666; [1962] Crim LR 178t; (1962) 106 SJ 198 HC QBD On male soliciting (by advertisement).

Crook v Edmondson [1966] 1 All ER 833; (1978) 66 Cr App R 90; [1966] Crim LR 227; (1966) 130 JP 191; [1966] 2 QB 81; (1966) 110 SJ 147; [1966] 2 WLR 672 HC QBD Not soliciting/importuning for immoral purpose to seek sex with prostitute.

Dale v Smith [1967] 2 All ER 1133; [1967] Crim LR 372t; (1967) 131 JP 378; (1967) 111 SJ 330; [1967] 1 WLR 700 HC QBD Innocent word can be importuning in light of previous occurrence.

Darroch v Director of Public Prosecutions (1990) 91 Cr App R 378; [1990] Crim LR 814; (1990) 154 JP 844; [1990] TLR 368 HC QBD Persistent driving around 'red light' area was not persistent soliciting; single gesture to prostitute was soliciting but could not be persistent soliciting.

Horton v Mead [1911-13] All ER 954; (1913-14) XXIII Cox CC 279; (1913) 77 JP 129; [1913] 1 KB 154; (1912) 47 LJ 767; [1913] 82 LJKB 200; (1913) 108 LTR 156; (1912) WN (I) 304 HC KBD Man can be guilty of soliciting though no evidence that anyone conscious of/noticed acts of solicitation.

Paul v Director of Public Prosecutions (1990) 90 Cr App R 173; [1989] Crim LR 660 HC QBD Need not prove particular member of public suffered nuisance to convict person of kerb crawling.

Pul v Luton Justices; ex parte Crown Prosecution Service (1989) 153 JP 512 HC QBD Justices could rely on local knowledge of area in determining whether kerb crawling likely to cause nuisance in that area.

R v Burge [1961] Crim LR 412 Sessions Appeals Committee Placing card in shop window advertising one's availability for homosexual activities was soliciting.

R v Dickinson; ex parte Grandolini (1917) 81 JP 209; [1917] 86 LJCL 1040; (1917-18) 117 LTR 189; (1916-17) XXXIII TLR 347; (1917) WN (I) 166 HC KBD No right to trial by jury for rogue and vagabond charged with importuning male for immoral purposes.

R v Dodd (David) (1978) 66 Cr App R 87 CA Soliciting of girls of 14 by means of kerb crawling was soliciting for immoral purpose.

R v Ford [1978] 1 All ER 1129; (1978) 66 Cr App R 46; [1977] Crim LR 688; (1978) 142 JP 264; (1977) 127 NLJ 766t; (1977) 121 SJ 528; [1977] 1 WLR 1083 CA That act not criminal did not mean not immoral.

R v Kirkup [1993] 2 All ER 802; (1993) 96 Cr App R 352; [1993] Crim LR 777; (1993) 157 JP 825; (1992) 142 NLJ 1612; [1992] TLR 535; [1993] 1 WLR 774 CA Soliciting for immoral purposes means soliciting for sexual activity; immorality of that activity a matter for judge/jury/justices.

Smith and another v Hughes and others [1960] 2 All ER 859; [1960] Crim LR 709; (1960) 124 JP 430; (1960) 104 SJ 606; [1960] 1 WLR 830 HC QBD Soliciting from balcony/behind closed windows is soliciting 'in a street or public place'.

SEXUAL OFFENCES (stupefying woman with drug)

R v Shillingford [1968] Crim LR 282t; (1968) 112 SJ 170 CA Is single offence of administering drug to stupefy woman even though single administration enabled several men to have sex with woman.

R v Shillingford (Holly); R v Vanderwall (Rayonne Niel) (1968) 52 Cr App R 188; (1968) 132 JP 264; (1968) 118 NLJ 421; [1968] 1 WLR 566 CA Is single offence of administering drug to stupefy woman even though single administration enabled several men to have sex with woman.

SEXUAL OFFENCES (suffering unlawful carnal knowledge of under sixteen year old)

R v McPherson; R v Farrell; R v Kajal [1980] Crim LR 654 CrCt Construction of offence of inducing/knowingly suffering under sixteen year old girl to be on premises owned/occupied by offender for purposes of having sex with men (Sexual Offences Act 1956, s 26).

SEXUAL OFFENCES (unlawful carnal knowledge)

R v Balderstone (Ernest Victor) (1955) 39 Cr App R 97; [1955] Crim LR 499 CCA That mental defective had violated terms of licence from hospital did not mean was not certified mental defective when prisoner had carnal knowledge with her.

R v Cargill (1913-14) XXIII Cox CC 382; [1913] 82 LJKB 655; (1913) 108 LTR 816; (1912-13) XXIX TLR 382 CCA Accused could not later seek to counter prosecution's opening (unobjected) allegation of seduction as was irrelevant to charge of unlawful carnal knowledge.

R v Chapman (1912-13) XXIX TLR 117 Assizes Deposition before justices on misdemeanour charge admitted on later trial for related felony.

R v Harrison; R v Ward; R v Wallis; R v Gooding [1938] 3 All ER 134; (1939-40) XXXI Cox CC 98; (1936-38) 26 Cr App R 166; (1938) 82 SJ 436 CCA Defence need to show accused believed and had reasonable cause to so believe that girl/s aged over sixteen.

R v Marsh (Ronald William Frank) (1948-49) 33 Cr App R 185 CCA Evidence of previous confession of guilt/sentencing for indecent assault on child admissible in later charge for carnal knowledge of same child.

R v Mudge (William) (1908) 1 Cr App R 62 CCA Proper conviction of party for unlawful carnal knowledge where did not give evidence in own defence.

SEXUAL OFFENCES (unlawful carnal knowledge of mental defective)

Director of Public Prosecutions v Head [1958] 1 All ER 679; (1958) 108 LJ 200 HL Cannot be committed of unlawful carnal knowledge of 'defective' unlawfully detained as deficient.

R v Cook [1954] 1 All ER 60; (1954) 118 JP 71; [1954] 1 WLR 125 Assizes Sex with mental defective but did not procure it so not guilty under Mental Deficiency Act 1913, s 56(1)(a).

R v Head [1957] 3 All ER 426; (1957) 41 Cr App R 249; [1958] Crim LR 52t; (1957) 107 LJ 777; [1958] 1 QB 132; (1957) 101 SJ 887 CCA Cannot be unlawful carnal knowledge of 'defective' unlawfully detained as 'deficient'.

R v Hudson [1965] 1 All ER 721; (1965) 49 Cr App R 69; [1965] Crim LR 172; (1965) 129 JP 193; [1966] 1 QB 448; (1965) 109 SJ 49; [1965] 2 WLR 604 CCA Defence to sex with defective charge if accused shows (civil burden) did not know defective.

R v Ross (Andrew) (1927-28) 20 Cr App R 184 CCA Nine months' hard labour for carnal knowledge of mental defective in view of age/otherwise excellent character.

SEXUAL OFFENCES (unlawful carnal knowledge of under-sixteen year old)

R v Dumont (1930) 69 LJ 234 CCC Interpretation of the Criminal Law Amendment Act 1922, s 2 (defence for man of twenty-three years or under to first-time charge of unlawful carnal knowledge of under-sixteen year old that reasonably believed victim to be over sixteen).

SEXUAL OFFENCES (unlawful sex)

R v Banks [1916-17] All ER 356; (1915-17) XXV Cox CC 535; (1916) 80 JP 432; [1916] 2 KB 621; [1916] 85 LJKB 1657; (1916-17) 115 LTR 457; (1916) WN (I) 281 CCA Must show not that could but did believe girl over sixteen to raise defence on that ground.

R v Chapman [1958] 3 All ER 143; (1958) 42 Cr App R 257; [1958] Crim LR 623; (1958) 122 JP 462; (1958) 108 LJ 586; [1959] 1 QB 100; (1958) 102 SJ 621 CCA 'Unlawful' sex under Sexual Offences Act 1956 s 19(1) means sex outside marriage.

R v Chapman (1931-34) XXIX Cox CC 407; (1931-32) 23 Cr App R 63; (1931) 95 JP 205; [1931] 2 KB 606; (1931) 100 LJCL 562; (1932) 146 LTR 120; (1931) 75 SJ 660; (1930-31) XLVII TLR 620; (1931) WN (I) 203 CCA Proviso in Criminal Law Amendment Act 1922, s 2 extends reasonable belief that girl over sixteen defence to men who have not reached the age of twenty-four.

R v Crocker (William) (1922-23) 17 Cr App R 45 CCA Leave to appeal granted in unlawful carnal knowledge case where corroboration point arose.

R v Dharma (Chandra) (1905) 69 JP 39; (1905) 40 LJ 238 CCR Person who committed offence before extended prosecution period legislation received Royal Assent could be prosecuted within newly extended period.

R v Dharma (Chandra); R v Slater; R v Hutchinson; R v Court (1905) XCII LTR 700; (1904-05) 49 SJ 366; (1904-05) XXI TLR 353 CCR Extension by Prevention of Cruelty of Children Act 1904 to limitation on bringing prosecutions under Criminal Law Amendment Act 1885 operated retrospectively as did not create new offence.

R v Fisher (Colin); R v Marshall (Christopher); R v Mitchell (George) (1969) 113 SJ 70; [1969] 2 WLR 452 Assizes Jury cannot convict accused of sex with under-sixteen year old girl where accused being tried for rape.

R v Forde [1923] All ER 477; (1921-25) XXVII Cox CC 406; (1922-23) 17 Cr App R 99; (1923) 87 JP 76; [1923] 2 KB 400; [1923] 92 LJCL 501; (1923) 128 LTR 798; (1922-23) 67 SJ 539; (1922-23) XXXIX TLR 322; (1923) WN (I) 98 CCA Defence in proviso to Criminal Law Amendment Act 1922, s 2 (reasonable belief of under twenty-three year old facing first-time charge that girl over sixteen) not open in case of indecent assault.

R v Green [1971] Crim LR 299 CA Six months' detention for eighteen year old guilty of unlawful sex with fourteen year old whom believed to be sixteen.

R v Hewitt (1926-30) XXVIII Cox CC 101; (1926) 90 JP 68; (1926) 134 LTR 157; (1925-26) XLII TLR 216 CCA Previous assault on same girl admissible in unlawful carnal knowledge of under sixteen/over fourteen year old girl - time lapse since earlier assault reduces weight of evidence.

R v Jones (1973) 123 NLJ 787t CA On what is meant by 'unlawful sex' - intent to commit rape unnecessary.

R v Mochan; R v Lathan; R v Micallef (1969) 113 SJ 773;[1969] 1 WLR 1331 Assizes Persons charged with rape could be convicted of indecent assault but not unlawful sex.

R v Rider [1954] Crim LR 49; (1954) 118 JP 73 Assizes On what constitutes a charge when deciding whether accused to have benefit of first-time charge proviso in prosecution for having carnal knowledge of under-sixteen year old (Criminal Law Amendment Act 1922, s 2).

R v Wakeley [1918-19] All ER 1157; (1918-21) XXVI Cox CC 569; (1920) 84 JP 31; [1920] 1 KB 688; [1920] 89 LJCL 97; (1920) 122 LTR 623 CCA Prosecution began when information laid and information laid within six months of offence so prosecution in time.

Re Roberts (Thomas Price) (1967) 117 NLJ 1270 Assizes Non-committal on unlawful sex charge was justified.

SOLICITING (general)

Burge v Director of Public Prosecutions [1962] 1 All ER 666; [1962] Crim LR 178t; (1962) 106 SJ 198 HC QBD On male soliciting (by advertisement).

Crook v Edmondson [1966] 1 All ER 833; (1978) 66 Cr App R 90; [1966] Crim LR 227; (1966) 130 JP 191; [1966] 2 QB 81; (1966) 110 SJ 147; [1966] 2 WLR 672 HC QBD Soliciting by man of prostitute not soliciting for immoral purpose.

R v Burge [1961] Crim LR 412 Sessions Appeals Committee Placing card in shop window advertising one's availability for homosexual activities was soliciting.

R v Curr [1967] 1 All ER 478; (1967) 51 Cr App R 113; [1967] Crim LR 301; [1968] 2 QB 944; (1967) 111 SJ 152; [1967] 2 WLR 595 CA No soliciting/conspiracy if persons assisting in committing crime unaware what are doing is offence.

Smith and another v Hughes and others [1960] 2 All ER 859; (1960) 124 JP 430; (1960) 104 SJ 606 HC QBD Soliciting from balcony/behind closed windows is soliciting 'in a street or public place'.

SOLICITING (incitement to solicit to murder)

R v Evans [1986] Crim LR 470 CA On whether inciting person to solicit murder equivalent to inciting person to conspire with another to murder.

SOLICITING (soliciting for immoral purpose)

R v Dodd (David) (1978) 66 Cr App R 87 CA Soliciting of girls of 14 by means of kerb crawling was soliciting for immoral purpose.

STREET COLLECTIONS (general)

Meaden v Wood [1985] Crim LR 678 HC QBD On legislation pertaining to legitimate mode of effecting street collections.

STREET TRADING (general)

Stevenage Borough Council v Wright (1996) TLR 10/4/96 HC QBD On distinction between pedlar and street trader.

SUICIDE (aiding and abetting)

Attorney-General v Able and others [1984] 1 All ER 277; (1984) 78 Cr App R 197; [1984] Crim LR 35; [1984] QB 795; (1983) 127 SJ 731; [1983] TLR 294; [1983] 3 WLR 845 HC QBD Civil court will issue declaration on criminal law if declaration would not criminalise non-criminal behaviour; must know that giving euthanasia booklet to person considering suicide - which occurs imminently - to be assisting in suicide.

R v Reed (Nicholas) [1982] Crim LR 819 CA On what it means to 'procure' something (here suicide).

SUICIDE (attempted suicide)

R v Coroner for Inner West London; ex parte De Luca [1988] Crim LR 541 HC QBD Year and a day rule applies to suicide pacts/assisted suicides/suicide.

R v Mann (John William) (1914) 10 Cr App R 31; (1914) 49 LJ 99; (1913-14) 58 SJ 303 CCA Attempted suicide an attempted felony.

R v Spence (George) (1957) 41 Cr App R 80; [1957] Crim LR 188 CCA Is murder where attempted suicide results in death of another.

R v Wilson (Ernest) (1922-23) 17 Cr App R 130 CCA Leave to appeal against sentence for attempted suicide granted.

SUICIDE (general)

Ex parte Horwill [1956] Crim LR 551t HC QBD Fresh inquisition ordered into death of party previously found to have committed suicide.

R v Coroner for Inner West London; ex parte De Luca [1988] Crim LR 541 HC QBD Year and a day rule applies to suicide pacts/assisted suicides/suicide.

R v Croft [1944] 2 All ER 483; (1942-44) 29 Cr App R 169; [1944] KB 295 CCA Mutual suicide agreement per se made survivor an accessory before the fact - to avoid conviction must show agreement was terminated.

R v Hopwood (Edward) (1912-13) 8 Cr App R 143 CCA Killing of another in course of apparent suicide attempt was murder.

R v Williams (deceased) (1968) 118 NLJ 1174t; [1969] Crim LR 158t HC QBD On burden of proof as regards establishing suicide: is presumption against suicide.

Re Davis, decd [1968] 1 QB 72; [1967] 2 WLR 1089 CA Must intend to kill self to be guilty of suicide.

Rv Cardiff Coroner; ex parte Thomas (1970) 120 NLJ 661t HC QBD On need to prove suicide.

UNAUTHORISED THEATRE (general)

Lovelace v Director of Public Prosecutions [1954] Crim LR 944t HC QBD Successful appeal by theatre licensee against conviction for 'causing' play to be presented with unauthorised additions contrary to Theatres Act 1843, s 15.

UNLAWFUL DEPOSIT ON HIGHWAY (general)

Gatland and another v Metropolitan Police Commissioner [1968] Crim LR 275t; (1968) 112 SJ 336 HC QBD Failed appeal against acquittal of person charged with depositing vehicle on road without lawful authority/ excuse in such a way as to endanger another user of road.

UNLAWFULLY SOLICITING FOR REWARD (general)

De Cristofaro v British Transport Police [1997] Crim LR 124; (1996) TLR 7/5/96 HC QBD Valid conviction of busker for unlawfully soliciting for reward for playing of music in London Underground station.

UNSOLICITED PUBLICATIONS (general)

Director of Public Prosecutions v Beate Uhse (UK) Ltd and another [1974] 1 All ER 753; [1974] Crim LR 106; (1974) 138 JP 247; (1973) 123 NLJ 1112t; [1974] QB 158; (1974) 118 SJ 34; [1974] 2 WLR 50 HC QBD To send unsolicited non-explicit advertising material on sexual technique book an offence.

VACCINATION (general)

Langridge v Hobbs (1900-01) 45 SJ 260; (1900-01) XVII TLR 237; (1901) WN (I) 30 HC KBD Must bring non-vaccination action against parents of infant within twelve months of infant being six-months old.

Moore v Keyte (1901-02) XVIII TLR 396; (1901-02) 50 WR 457 HC KBD On bringing of vaccination prosecutions.

Over v Harwood (1899-1900) XVI TLR 163; (1899-1900) 48 WR 608 HC QBD On burden of proof where person charged with disobedience of order to have child vaccinated.

Pym v Wilsher (1901) 36 LJ 310; (1900-01) 45 SJ 578; (1900-01) XVII TLR 558; (1901) WN (I) 126; (1900-01) 49 WR 654 HC KBD Prosecution procedures under Vaccination Act 1898 did not apply to failure to vaccinate which occurred during lifetime of Vaccination Act 1867.

VAGRANCY (begging)

Gray v Chief Constable of Greater Manchester [1983] Crim LR 45 CrCt Street busker not guilty of begging/gathering alms contrary to Vagrancy Act 1824, s 3.

Mathers v Penfold [1914-15] All ER 891; (1914-15) XXIV Cox CC 642; (1915) 79 JP 225; [1915] 1 KB 515; (1915) 50 LJ 29; [1915] 84 LJKB 627; (1915) 112 LTR 726; (1914-15) 59 SJ 235; (1914-15) XXXI TLR 108; (1915) WN (I) 13 HC KBD Charity street-collector not 'begging' contrary to Vagrancy Act 1824, s 3.

R v Dalton [1982] Crim LR 375 Magistrates Single occasion of begging not offence of placing self in public place to beg/gather alms (Vagrancy Act 1824, s 3).

VAGRANCY (failure to maintain)

Nice v Lewisham Guardians (1921-25) XXVII Cox CC 606; [1924] 1 KB 618; (1924) 59 LJ 76; [1924] 93 LJCL 469; (1924) 131 LTR 22; (1923-24) XL TLR 270 HC KBD Not failure to maintain family where refused to work for less than union rates.

VAGRANCY (fortune-telling)

Barbanell v Naylor [1936] 3 All ER 66; (1937) 101 JP 13; (1936) 80 SJ 876 HC KBD Newspaper horoscope column did not contravene Vagrancy Act 1824, s 4.

Davis v Curry (1918-21) XXVI Cox CC 100; (1918) 82 JP 21; [1918] 1 KB 109; [1918] 87 LJCL 292; (1917-18) 117 LTR 716; (1917-18) XXXIV TLR 24 HC KBD Must be intention to deceive to be convicted of fortune-telling.

R v Marti [1981] Crim LR 109 CrCt On interrelationship between Fraudulent Mediums Act 1951, s 2(b) and Vagrancy Act 1824, s 4.

Stonehouse and another v Masson [1921] All ER 534; (1921-25) XXVII Cox CC 23; (1921) 85 JP 167; [1921] 2 KB 818; [1922] 91 LJCL 93; (1921) 125 LTR 463; (1920-21) XXXVII TLR 621; (1921) WN (I) 167 HC KBD No intent needed to be convicted for fortune-telling under Vagrancy Act 1824, s 4.

VAGRANCY (general)

Batty v Lee (1939-40) XXXI Cox CC 161; (1938) 102 JP 485; (1938) 82 SJ 871 HC KBD Prosecution ought to have been heard in action for leaving wife and child so were chargeable to public assistance committee (despite existence of maintenance order against husband being possible defence to charge).

Commissioner of Police of the Metropolis v Simeon [1982] 2 All ER 813; (1982) 75 Cr App R 359; (1982) 146 JP 286; [1982] 3 WLR 289 HL Repeal of Vagrancy Act did not affect pre-repeal based/instituted cases.

Cooper v Leeke (1968) 112 SJ 46 HC QBD Failed appeal against conviction for possession of various instruments with intent to commit felonious act (Vagrancy Act 1824, s 4).

Glynn and another v Simmonds [1952] 2 All ER 47; (1952) 116 JP 389; (1952) 102 LJ 318; (1952) 96 SJ 378; [1952] 1 TLR 1442; (1952) WN (I) 289 HC QBD Racecourse enclosure to which admission charged a public place under Vagrancy Act 1824, s 4.

Goodhew v Morton and Page [1962] 2 All ER 771; [1962] Crim LR 181; (1962) 126 JP 369; (1962) 106 SJ 78 HC QBD Yard so surrounded as to be 'inclosed yard': question of fact in each case.

Holloran v Haughton [1976] Crim LR 270; (1976) 140 JP 352; (1976) 120 SJ 116 HC QBD Sorting room in post office not a 'warehouse' for purposes of Vagrancy Act 1824, s 4.

Knott v Blackburn and another [1944] 1 All ER 116; (1944) 108 JP 19; [1944] KB 77; [1944] 113 LJ 154; (1944) 170 LTR 55; (1944) 88 SJ 60; (1943-44) LX TLR 92; (1943) WN (I) 253 HC KBD Fenced-in railway siding not an enclosed area for purposes of Vagrancy Act 1824, s 4.

Nakhla v R [1975] 2 All ER 138; [1976] AC 1; [1976] Crim LR 81; (1975) 139 JP 414; (1975) 119 SJ 286; [1975] 2 WLR 750 PC Being in place with felonious intent not 'frequenting'; must be continuous/repeated action of some sort.

Quatromini and another v Peck [1972] 3 All ER 521; [1972] Crim LR 596t; (1972) 136 JP 854; (1972) 122 NLJ 682t; (1972) 116 SJ 728; [1972] 1 WLR 1318 HC QBD Inclosed railway siding not a yard so not in enclosed yard for unlawful purpose.

R v Armstrong [1954] Crim LR 387 Sessions Place to rear of cinema where bins stored/ashes tipped was not an area for purpose of Vagrancy Act 1824, s 4.

R v Dickinson; ex parte Grandolini (1917) 81 JP 209; [1917] 86 LJCL 1040; (1917-18) 117 LTR 189; (1916-17) XXXIII TLR 347; (1917) WN (I) 166 HC KBD No right to trial by jury for rogue and vagabond charged with importuning male for immoral purposes.

R v Harris [1950] 2 All ER 816; (1949-50) 34 Cr App R 184; (1950) 114 JP 535; [1951] 1 KB 107; (1950) 100 LJ 539; (1950) 94 SJ 689; [1950] 66 (2) TLR 739; (1950) WN (I) 453 CCA Evidence of earlier conditional discharge not by way of conviction certificate but by witness who heard confession/ordering of conditional discharge in earlier case.

R v Silver and others [1956] 1 All ER 716; (1956) 40 Cr App R 32; [1956] Crim LR 338; (1956) 120 JP 233; (1956) 100 SJ 228; [1956] 1 WLR 281 CCC Landlord's/estate agent's earnings from property rents where property rented by prostitutes not living off earnings off prostitution as rents from property are landlord's/agent's own earnings.

VAGRANCY (habitual criminal)

R v Andrews [1938] 4 All ER 869; (1939-40) XXXI Cox CC 193; (1938-40) 27 Cr App R 12; (1939) 103 JP 11; (1939) 87 LJ 28; (1939) 160 LTR 181 CCA Person accused of being habitual criminal to be advised can call witnesses/ought to be represented by counsel.

R v Baggott (Isaiah) (1910) 4 Cr App R; (1910) 74 JP 213; (1909-10) XXVI TLR 266 CCA On when and what merits conviction as habitual criminal.

R v Brown (1913-14) XXIII Cox CC 615; (1914) 78 JP 79; (1913-14) 109 LTR 749; (1913-14) 58 SJ 69; (1913-14) XXX TLR 40; (1913) WN (I) 296 CCA Misdirection to say person who while avoiding arrest gained honest employment could be convicted as habitual criminal because was fugitive from justice.

R v Brummitt (Ernest) and Matthews (George) (1910) 4 Cr App R 192 CCA Can prove offences in (other than three necessary to sustain) prosecution as habitual criminal.

R v Condon (Wallace) (1910) 4 Cr App R 109 CCA Person could be convicted as habitual criminal though was not long out of prison.

R v Crowley; R v Sullivan (1914-15) XXIV Cox CC 13; (1913) 48 LJ 715; [1914] 83 LJKB 298; (1914) 110 LTR 127; (1913-14) XXX TLR 94; (1913) WN (I) 327 CCA Appropriate detention period for habitual criminal; earlier quashed conviction not to be mentioned in prosecution as habitual criminal.

R v Davis (1918-21) XXVI Cox CC 98; (1917-18) 13 Cr App R 10; [1917] 2 KB 855; [1918] 87 LJCL 119; (1917-18) 117 LTR 704; (1917-18) 62 SJ 55; (1917-18) XXXIV TLR 25; (1917) WN (I) 290 CCA Can be convicted as habitual criminal if prosecution prove previous conviction as such - regardless of post-conviction behaviour.

R v Dorrington (Mark) (1910) 5 Cr App R 119 (1910) 74 JP 392 CCA On differentiation in sentence between habitual criminal and non-habitual criminal who merits preventive detention.

R v Driscoll (1925) 89 JP 104; (1924-25) XLI TLR 425 CCA Burden of proving a person a habitual criminal always rests on prosecution.

R v Everitt (William George) (1910-11) 6 Cr App R 267; (1910-11) XXVII TLR 570 CCA On nature of evidence to prove are habitual criminal.

R v Foster (Henry) (1909) 3 Cr App R 173 CCA Valid conviction for habitual criminal where only six days between leaving prison and new arrest.

R v Fowler (George) (1912-13) XXIX TLR 422 CCA Habitual criminal conviction quashed where had not been given notice of offences to be relied on in proving habitual criminality.

R v Franklin (1909) 3 Cr App R 48; (1910) 74 JP 24; (1909-10) 54 SJ 217 CCA Constable can prove persistent criminality of offender by reference to police record even though not personally aware of all previous convictions of accused.

R v Hammersley (1918-21) XXVI Cox CC 552; (1919) 54 LJ 467; (1920) 122 LTR 383 CCA Conviction as habitual criminal quashed in light of complete consideration of accused's behaviour.

R v Harold Jones alias George Wright (1921-25) XXVII Cox CC 221; (1921-22) 16 Cr App R 124; (1922) 86 JP 123; (1922) 127 LTR 160; (1921-22) 66 SJ 489; (1922) WN (I) 100 CCA Cannot by reference to untried crime prove dishonest life of person accused of being habitual criminal.

R v Hayden (Lily) (1910-11) 6 Cr App R 213 CCA That have been honestly employed since last conviction not per se a defence to habitual criminal charge.

R v Hayes (Timothy) (1925-26) 19 Cr App R 157; (1926) 90 JP 190 CCA Honest work during last period of release not defence to charge of being habitual criminal.

R v Hayward (1926-30) XXVIII Cox CC 342; (1927) 137 LTR 64; (1926-27) XLIII TLR 356 CCA Three convictions to sustain habitual criminal charge must be rigorously proved - other offences not so rigorously.

R v Heard (1911-13) XXII Cox CC 725; (1911-12) 7 Cr App R 80; (1912) 76 JP 232; (1912) 106 LTR 304; (1911-12) XXVIII TLR 154 CCA That nine-month delay since last conviction/one of (over three) convictions mentioned was foreign did not preclude conviction as habitual criminal.

R v Jennings (George) (1910) 74 JP 245; (1909-10) XXVI TLR 339 CCA Habitual criminal still habitual criminal though spends small amount of time doing honest work.

R v Jones [1939] 1 All ER 181; (1939) 87 LJ 86 CCA Habitual criminal charge to be proved like any criminal charge: evidence that sought work may create reasonable doubt.

R v Jones (Thomas Robert) (1920-21) 15 Cr App R 20 CCA On when possible to convict party as habitual criminal.

R v Keane (James) and Watson (David) (1912-13) 8 Cr App R 12; (1912) WN (I) 205 CCA That have done honest work since last release from prison does not preclude finding that are habitual criminal.

R v Kelly (John) (1909) 3 Cr App R 248; (1909-10) XXVI TLR 196 CCA Accused's behaviour since most recent release from prison highly pertinent in deciding if habitual criminal.

R v Knight (James) (1928-29) 21 Cr App R 72 CCA Are not automatically habitual criminal just because were previously convicted as such.

R v Lavender (Herbert) (1927-28) 20 Cr App R 10 CCA That did honest work since last release not defence to charge of being habitual criminal.

R v Marshall (1910) 74 JP 381 CCA Habitual criminal conviction allowed stand though certain offences of which evidence had been given at trial had not been mentioned in notice of prosecution.

R v Martin (George) (1910) 5 Cr App R 31 CCA Need not be defence to habitual criminal charge that have been working since last release from prison.

R v Mitchell (1913-14) XXIII Cox CC 284; (1912) 76 JP 423; (1913) 108 LTR 224; (1911-12) XXVIII TLR 484 CCA That did not report to police after released from prison on licence not proof of dishonest/criminal lifestyle.

R v Mitchell (Charles) (1911-12) 7 Cr App R 283 CCA Non-reporting to police by convict on licence/that have many previous convictions not per se evidence of habitual criminality where long time between accused's release from prison and present habitual criminal charge.

R v Moran (James) (1910) 5 Cr App R 219 CCA 'Other grounds' specified in Prevention of Crime Act 1908, s 10, as evidence of habitual criminality are sole other grounds.

R v Morrison (Alexander) (1932) 101 LJCL 257 CCA Scottish convictions could sustain habitual criminal conviction.

R v Murray (1931-34) XXIX Cox CC 441; [1932] 1 KB 599; (1932) 73 LJ 153; (1932) 146 LTR 487; (1932) 76 SJ 166; (1931-32) XLVIII TLR 255; (1932) WN (I) 47 CCA Scottish conviction can be one of three to sustain habitual criminal conviction so long as offence exists in England.

R v Neilson (1913-14) XXIII Cox CC 685; (1913-14) 109 LTR 912; (1913-14) XXX TLR 125 CCA Conviction as habitual criminal quashed where accused not notified that evidence of being confederate of thieves would be given.

R v Nielsen (1914) 78 JP 158 CCA Habitual criminal conviction quashed where evidence on which had been secured had not been outlined in statutory notice of prosecution.

R v Norman (Charles Leslie) (1924) 88 JP 125; [1924] 2 KB 315; [1924] 93 LJCL 883; (1923-24) 68 SJ 814; (1923-24) XL TLR 693 CCA Person who was previously convicted as habitual criminal need not later be found such.

R v Raybould (Charles) (1909) 2 Cr App R 184; (1909) 73 JP 334; (1908-09) XXV TLR 581; (1909) WN (I) 118 CCA Invalid conviction as habitual criminal where previous criminality uncertain.

R v Rowland (Harry) (1911-13) XXII Cox CC 273; (1909) 3 Cr App R 277; (1910) 102 LTR 112; (1909-10) XXVI TLR 202 CCA Accused giving evidence for other accused can be questioned on own guilt; previous convictions involving fraud/dishonesty admissible in receiving prosecution where stolen property in accused's possession though not at time of arrest; can be convicted as habitual criminal though no evidence as to behaviour in half-year prior to conviction.

R v Smith (John) (1912-13) 8 Cr App R 151 CCA That have for better part of short interval been doing honest work does not preclude finding that are habitual criminal.

R v Stewart (Albert) (1910) 4 Cr App R 175; (1910) 74 JP 246 CCA On establishing accused is habitual criminal.

R v Stockdale (1915) WN (I) 86 CCA Habitual criminal conviction quashed in light of improper admission of matters not mentioned in notice (of assertion that were habitual criminal).

R v Summers (Peter) (1914) 10 Cr App R 11 CCA Can cite convictions (other than necessary three) as evidence of character.

R v Taylor (Edward) and Coney (Alfred) (1910) 5 Cr App R 168 CCA Early commencement of preventive detention where habitual criminal is young.

R v Triffitt [1938] 2 All ER 818; (1939-40) XXXI Cox CC 93; (1936-38) 26 Cr App R 169; (1938) 102 JP 388; (1938) 82 SJ 477; (1937-38) LIV TLR 1012; (1938) WN (I) 213 CCA On procedure when adding to substantive charge one of being a habitual criminal.

R v Turner [1908-10] All ER 1206; (1910) 74 JP 81; [1910] 1 KB 346; (1909) 44 LJ 780; (1910) 79 LJKB 176; (1910) 102 LTR 367; (1909-10) XXVI TLR 112 CCA On procedure/evidential procedure in prosecuting habitual criminal.

R v Turner; R v Waller (1909-10) 54 SJ 164 CCA On proving person to be habitual criminal.

R v Vale [1938] 3 All ER 355; (1939-40) XXXI Cox CC 138; (1936-38) 26 Cr App R 187; (1938) 102 JP 426; (1938) 86 LJ 26; (1937-38) LIV TLR 1014; (1938) WN (I) 272 CCA Trial of substantive offence and habitual criminal charge to be by same court but formal pleading to charge may be in different court.

R v Wallace (Arthur) (1928-29) 21 Cr App R 70 CCA Confession of being habitual criminal not to be accepted until offence explained to confessor.

R v Waller [1908-10] All ER 1215; (1910) 74 JP 81; [1910] 1 KB 364; (1910) 79 LJKB 184; (1910) 102 LTR 400; (1909-10) XXVI TLR 142 CCA On consent of DPP to/on notice to offender of habitual criminal charge.

R v Webber (1913-14) XXIII Cox CC 323; (1912) 76 JP 471; [1913] 1 KB 33; (1913) 108 LTR 349 CCA Notice of prosecution as habitual criminal not invalidated by reference therein to evidence on which prosecution based.

R v Webber (Charles) (1912-13) 8 Cr App R 59; [1913] 82 LJKB 108 CCA That prisoner does not explain behaviour since last release from prison does not per se justify finding is habitual criminal.

R v Westfall (Edward Ernest) (1921) 85 JP 116; (1920-21) XXXVII TLR 23 CCA Notice that would give evidence to prove accused 'professional pickpocket' adequate notice of habitual criminal charge.

R v Westwood (Frederick Charles) (1913) 77 JP 379; (1912-13) XXIX TLR 492 CCA Habitual criminal conviction affirmed though evidence at trial went beyond what stated in notice served.

R v White (Frederick) and Shelton (George) (1927-28) 20 Cr App R 61 CCA On relevant factors in trial of individual as habitual criminal.

R v Wilcock (John Joseph) (1921-22) 16 Cr App R 91; (1921-22) 66 SJ 335 CCA Admission by person accused as habitual criminal that was previously convicted as same tacit plea of guilt to charge.

R v Williams (Arthur) (1928-29) 21 Cr App R 121; (1929) 141 LTR 544 CCA Pre-habitual criminal trial confession of offence admissible in habitual criminal trial.

R v Williams (Frederick) (1912-13) 8 Cr App R 49 CCA Circumstances of instant crime with which charged justified finding was habitual criminal.

R v Wilson (1911-12) XXVIII TLR 561 CCA Inadequate notice of evidence to be served led to habitual criminal conviction being quashed; evidence on lifestyle not confined to lifestyle during time between release from prison and committal of offence.

R v Wilson (George) (1916-17) 12 Cr App R 95 CCA Person who refuses to give information about self since prison release can be found habitual criminal.

R v Wilson (John Henry); R v Marshall (Edward) (1912-13) 8 Cr App R 20 CCA On establishing that person a habitual criminal.

R v Young (1913-14) XXIII Cox CC 624; (1914) 78 JP 80; (1913-14) 109 LTR 753; (1913-14) 58 SJ 100; (1913-14) XXX TLR 69 CCA Must be leading criminal/dishonest life at time of arrest to sustain conviction; prosecution of person already convicted of offence to be closely monitored by court.

VAGRANCY (habitual drunk)

Eaton v Best [1908-10] All ER 651; (1911-13) XXII Cox CC 66; (1909) 73 JP 113; [1909] 1 KB 632; (1909) 44 LJ 63; [1909] 78 LJKB 425; (1909) C LTR 494; (1908-09) XXV TLR 244 HC KBD What constitutes 'habitual drunkard' (under Habitual Drunkards Act 1879, s 3).

Tayler v Tayler (1911-12) 56 SJ 573 HC PDAD On who constitutes a habitual drunkard for the purposes of the Habitual Drunkard Act 1879.

VAGRANCY (incorrigible rogue)

Director of Public Prosecutions v Blady (1911-13) XXII Cox CC 715; (1912) 76 JP 141; [1912] 2 KB 89; (1912) 81 LJKB 613; (1912) 106 LTR 302; (1911-12) XXVIII TLR 193 HC KBD Wife's evidence as prosecution witness could not be admitted under common law/Criminal Evidence Act 1898.

Moran and another v Jones [1911-13] All ER 309; (1911-13) XXII Cox CC 474; (1911) 75 JP 411; (1911) 104 LTR 921; (1910-11) XXVII TLR 421 HC KBD Must be found effecting the unlawful purpose on premises but need not be arrested therein.

R v Brown (Walter John) (1908) 1 Cr App R 85 CCA Can under Criminal Appeal Act 1907, s 20(2), appeal against sentence not conviction as incorrigible rogue.

R v Cadwell (Henry) (1927-28) 20 Cr App R 60 CCA Ought not to be prosecuted as incorrigible rogue simply because not enough evidence to convict of larceny.

R v Cope [1924] All ER 301; (1925) 89 JP 100; (1925) 60 LJ 324; [1925] 94 LJCL 662; (1925) 132 LTR 800; (1924-25) XLI TLR 418; (1925) WN (I) 108 CCA When person facing sentence as incorrigible rogue must be examination of case before him and in his hearing.

R v Evans (1915-17) XXV Cox CC 72; [1915] 2 KB 762; (1915-16) 113 LTR 508; (1914-15) XXXI TLR 410 CCA Quarter sessions could not convict party as incorrigible rogue, then sentence: conviction of summary court necessary.

R v Evans (Thomas) (1914-15) 11 Cr App R 178; (1915) 79 JP 415; (1915) 50 LJ 230; (1914-15) 59 SJ 496 CCA Do not become incorrigible rogue merely by virtue of two time conviction as rogue and vagabond: must be found to be such.

R v Evans; R v Connor (1914-15) XXIV Cox CC 138; (1914) 49 LJ 181; [1914] 83 LJKB 905; (1914) 110 LTR 780; (1913-14) XXX TLR 326 CCA Incorrigible rogue liable to three months' detention (not imprisonment) cannot claim trial by jury.

R v Herion (Albert); R v Jackson (John); R v Wilkin (Lewis) (1912-13) 8 Cr App R 99 [1913] 82 LJKB 82; (1912-13) 57 SJ 130; (1912-13) XXIX TLR 93; (1912) WN (I) 276 CCA Second offence under Vagrancy Act 1898 makes one incorrigible rogue under Vagrancy Act 1824, s 5 and so liable to flogging.

R v Johnson (1911-13) XXII Cox CC 43; (1909) 73 JP 135; [1909] 1 KB 439; (1909) 44 LJ 61; [1909] 78 LJKB 290; (1909) C LTR 464; (1908-09) XXV TLR 229; (1909) WN (I) 19 CCA Cannot be sentenced as incorrigible rogue absent prior sentence as rogue and vagabond.

R v Teesdale [1927] All ER 710; (1926-30) XXVIII Cox CC 438; (1927) 91 JP 184; (1928) 138 LTR 160 CCA Person may be incorrigible rogue though earlier conviction did not specifically state were rogue and vagabond.

R v Walters [1968] 3 All ER 863; (1969) 53 Cr App R 9; [1968] Crim LR 686; (1969) 133 JP 73; (1969) 119 NLJ 14; [1969] 1 QB 255; (1968) 112 SJ 801; [1968] 3 WLR 987 CA On Vagrancy Act, 1824 s 10 charge sentence to be imposed for being incorrigible rogue not for what did as such.

VAGRANCY (indecent behaviour)

R v Duke and Others (1909) 73 JP 88 Quarter Sessions On what constitutes riotous/indecent behaviour on part of prostitute for purposes of Vagrancy Act 1824, s 3.

VAGRANCY (living on earnings of prostitute)

Calvert v Mayes [1954] 1 All ER 41; [1954] Crim LR 147; (1954) 118 JP 76; [1954] 1 QB 342; (1954) 98 SJ 13; [1954] 2 WLR 18 HC QBD Payment of money direct to accused rather than via prostitutes (over whom exercised some control) did not mean were not living off earnings of prostitution.

R v Thomas [1957] 2 All ER 181 CCC Matter for jury whether renting rooms at very high rates to prostitute is living on earnings of prostitution.

R v Thomas [1957] 2 All ER 342 CCA On living on earnings of prostitution.

VAGRANCY (loitering with intent)

VAGRANCY (loitering with intent)

Bridge v Campbell (1947) 177 LTR 444; (1947) 91 SJ 459; (1947) LXIII TLR 470; (1947) WN (I) 223 HC KBD Loitering of suspected person with intent to commit felony an offence that can be committed from within motor-vehicle (Vagrancy Act 1824, s 4).

Clark v Taylor (1948) 112 JP 439; (1948) WN (I) 410 HC KBD On what constituted 'frequenting' a place for purpose of the Vagrancy Act 1824, s 4.

Cohen and another v Black [1942] 2 All ER 299; [1942] 111 LJ 573; (1943) 93 LJ 100; (1942) 86 SJ 210; (1941-42) LVIII TLR 306; (1942) WN (I) 119 HC KBD For loitering with intent arrest must be acts arousing suspicion preceding arrest; police officers' evidence could be pooled.

Cosh v Isherwood [1968] 1 All ER 383; (1968) 52 Cr App R 53; [1968] Crim LR 44t; (1968) 132 JP 149; (1967) 117 NLJ 1192t; (1967) 111 SJ 906; [1968] 1 WLR 48 HC QBD Acts showing suspected person must be separate from those showing loitering with intent but need not be different in kind.

Fitzgerald v Lyle [1972] Crim LR 125; (1970) 114 SJ 929 HC QBD On who (as here) constitues a suspected person who may be validly arrested for/charged with loitering with intent.

Hollyhomes (James) v Hind (Horace Percival) [1944] 2 All ER 8; (1944) 108 JP 190; [1944] KB 571; [1944] 113 LJ 285; (1944) 171 LTR 175; (1943-44) LX TLR 376; (1944) WN (I) 137 HC KBD Where house inside house loitering charge did not have to include phrase 'then in the occupation of...'.

Lyons v Owen [1963] Crim LR 123; (1962) 106 SJ 939 HC QBD Failed appeal against decision of justices that person keeping bank under surveillance not guilty of loitering with intent to commit felony.

Miles v Clovis and another (1979) 69 Cr App R 280; [1980] QB 195 HC QBD Need not prove intent to steal particular object at time of loitering to be guilty of loitering with intent under Vagrancy Act 1824, s 4.

Pyburn v Hudson [1950] 1 All ER 1006; (1950) 114 JP 287 HC KBD On sufficiency of evidence to sustain finding that were suspected person.

R v Clarke [1950] 1 KB 523 CCA Can if have previous convictions be 'suspected person' for purposes of Vagrancy Act 1824, s 4 even if police do not know of same when arresting suspect.

R v Goodwin (William) [1944] 1 All ER 506; (1943-45) 30 Cr App R 20; (1944) 108 JP 159; [1944] KB 518; [1944] 113 LJ 476; (1944) 171 LTR 14; (1944) 88 SJ 195; (1943-44) LX TLR 324; (1944) WN (I) 118 CCA On Prevention of Crimes Act 1871, ss 7(3), 20.

R v Johnson (George Thomas) [1945] 2 All ER 105; (1945) 109 JP 152; [1945] KB 419; [1945] 114 LJ 522; (1945) 173 LTR 47 CCA On duplicity in indictment; can be convicted of waiting to commit offence though have gone further than mere waiting.

R v Johnston (1945) WN (I) 114 CCA Attempt to commit crime did not preclude person who attempted to commit same from being convicted for waiting for opportunity to commit said crime contrary to the Prevention of Crimes Act 1871, s 7.

R v Pavitt (Arthur) (1910-11) 6 Cr App R 182; (1911) 75 JP 432 CCA Mere suspicion not enough to merit conviction for intending to commit crime contrary to Prevention of Crimes Act 1871, s 7(3).

R v Pryce (Timothy) [1979] Crim LR 737 CrCt On elements of offence of being suspected person loitering with intent.

R v Russell [1956] Crim LR 572 Magistrates Application of Vagrancy Act 1824, s 4.

R v West London Stipendiary Magistrate and another, ex parte Simeon [1982] 1 All ER 847; (1982) 74 Cr App R 331; [1982] Crim LR 698; (1982) 126 SJ 277; [1982] TLR 72; [1982] 1 WLR 705 HC QBD Vagrancy Act 1824, s 4 repeal means cannot prosecute for loitering with intent committed before repeal.

R v West London Stipendiary Magistrate, ex parte Simeon [1983] 1 AC 234; [1982] Crim LR 753; (1982) 132 NLJ 881; [1982] TLR 387 HL Vagrancy Act 1824, s 4 repeal did not mean could not prosecute for loitering with intent committed before repeal.

284

Rawlings v Smith [1938] 1 All ER 11; (1939-40) XXXI Cox CC 11; (1938) 102 JP 181; [1938] 1 KB 675; (1938) 85 LJ 46; [1938] 107 LJCL 151; (1938) 158 LTR 274; (1937) 81 SJ 1024; (1937-38) LIV TLR 255; (1938) WN (I) 15 HC KBD Need not be a suspected person on a day preceding loitering.

Woodward v Koessler [1958] 3 All ER 557; [1958] Crim LR 754; (1959) 123 JP 14; (1958) 108 LJ 793; (1958) 102 SJ 879 HC QBD Non-physical threats covered by term 'causing injury to the person' in Prevention of Crime Act 1953, s 1(1).

VAGRANCY (soliciting for immoral purposes)

R v Ford [1978] 1 All ER 1129; (1978) 66 Cr App R 46; [1977] Crim LR 688; (1978) 142 JP 264; (1977) 127 NLJ 766t; (1977) 121 SJ 528; [1977] 1 WLR 1083 CA That act not criminal did not mean not immoral.

VAGRANCY (suspected person)

Hartley v Ellnor [1916-17] All ER 260; (1918-21) XXVI Cox CC 10; (1917) 81 JP 201; [1917] 86 LJCL 938; (1917-18) 117 LTR 304 HC KBD To be rogue and vagabond must have been convicted/suspected person/reputed thief on a day before occurrence leading to arrest.

R v Clarke [1950] 1 All ER 546; (1949-50) 34 Cr App R 65; (1950) 114 JP 192; (1950) 100 LJ 107; (1950) 94 SJ 211; [1950] 66 (1) TLR 618; (1950) WN (I) 101 CCA Can be 'suspected person' though arresting officers do not know of earlier convictions when arresting.

R v Fairbairn (1948-49) 33 Cr App R 179; [1949] 2 KB 690; (1949) LXV TLR 559; (1949) WN (I) 327 CCA Admissibility of earlier conviction to prove person a 'suspected person' (Vagrancy Act 1824, s 4) at time of arrest.

VAGRANCY (wilful neglect)

Bannister v Sullivan (1901-07) XX Cox CC 685 HC KBD Can post-first conviction for running away leaving children be charged again if on leaving prison fail to remove children from workhouse.

Roberts v Regnart (1921-25) XXVII Cox CC 198; (1922) 86 JP 77; (1922) 126 LTR 667 HC KBD Husband guilty of wilful neglect of wife despite honest belief was no longer bound to maintain her.

VIOLENT DISORDER (general)

R v Rothwell and Barton [1993] Crim LR 626 CA That acted in self-defence/defence of another are defences to the statutory offences which replaced affray.

R v Turpin [1990] Crim LR 514; [1990] TLR 93 CA Need not acquit all co-accused of violent disorder where acquitting one of same; on relevance of guilty plea of one co-defendant to guilt/innocence of another.

WILFUL OBSTRUCTION OF CONSTABLE (general)

Bastable v Little [1904-07] All ER 1147; (1907-09) XXI Cox CC 354; (1907) 71 JP 52; [1907] 1 KB 59; (1906) 41 LJ 736; [1907] 76 LJKB 77; (1907) XCVI LTR 115; (1906-07) 51 SJ 49; (1906-07) XXIII TLR 38; (1906) WN (I) 196 HC KBD Person warning drivers of upcoming police speed trap not obstructing police in execution of duty.

Bennett v Bale [1986] Crim LR 404 HC QBD Must intend to obstruct and actually obstruct police officer to be guilty of obstruction of police officer.

Betts v Stevens [1908-10] All ER 1245; (1911-13) XXII Cox CC 187; (1909) 73 JP 486; [1910] 1 KB 1; (1909) 44 LJ 629; (1910) 79 LJKB 17; (1909-10) 101 LTR 564; (1909-10) XXVI TLR 5; (1909) WN (I) 200 HC KBD Person warning motorists of upcoming police speed trap were obstructing police in execution of their duty.

Coffin and another v Smith and another (1980) 71 Cr App R 221 HC QBD Was obstruction of police in execution of their duty to assault police constable in course of ejection from club/while standing on beat.

285

Dass and another v Rennie [1961] Crim LR 396t; (1961) 105 SJ 158 HC QBD Was obstruction of police officer in execution of his duty to ignore his request to cease throwing material from place which police could not approach without trespassing.

Davis v Lisle (1934-39) XXX Cox CC 412; (1936) 100 JP 280; [1936] 2 KB 434; [1936] 105 LJCL 593; (1936) 155 LTR 23; (1936) 80 SJ 409; (1935-36) LII TLR 475 HC KBD Not guilty of assault/obstruction of police in course of duty as had at material time requested police to leave property so police were trespassers.

Despard and others v Wilcox and others (1911-13) XXII Cox CC 258; (1910) 74 JP 115; (1910) 102 LTR 103; (1909-10) XXVI TLR 226 HC KBD Suffragettes blocking Downing Street despite police requests to disperse guilty of obstructing police in execution of their duty.

Dibble v Ingleton [1972] 1 All ER 275; (1972) 136 JP 155; (1971) 121 NLJ 1049t; [1972] RTR 161; (1972) 116 SJ 97; [1972] 2 WLR 163 HC QBD Act of obstruction need not be unlawful in itself to support obstruction conviction.

Duncan v Jones (1934-39) XXX Cox CC 279; (1935) 99 JP 399; [1936] 1 KB 218; (1935) 80 LJ 307; [1936] 105 LJCL 71; (1936) 154 LTR 110; (1935) 79 SJ 903; (1935-36) LII TLR 26 HC KBD Obstruction of police in execution of duty where sought to hold public meeting despite police prohibition.

Green v Director of Public Prosecutions [1991] Crim LR 782; (1991) 155 JP 816; (1991) 141 NLJ 783t; [1991] TLR 236 HC QBD Advice to person not to answer police questions could if given in certain fashion be obstruction of police in execution of their duty.

Green v Moore [1982] 1 All ER 428; (1982) 74 Cr App R 250; (1982) 146 JP 142; (1981) 131 NLJ 1265; [1982] QB 1044; [1982] 2 WLR 671 HC QBD Warning intended to enable lawbreaker to evade detection an obstruction of constable.

Hills v Ellis [1983] 1 All ER 667; (1983) 76 Cr App R 217; [1983] Crim LR 182; (1984) 148 JP 379; (1983) 133 NLJ 280; [1983] QB 680; (1982) 126 SJ 769; [1982] TLR 515; [1983] 2 WLR 234 HC QBD No lawful excuse for interfering with lawful arrest by police officer.

Hinchcliffe v Sheldon [1955] 3 All ER 406; [1955] Crim LR 189; (1956) 120 JP 13; (1955) 99 SJ 797; [1955] 1 WLR 1207 HC QBD Can be guilty of obstruction though not otherwise guilty of offence.

Johnson v Phillips [1975] 3 All ER 682; [1975] Crim LR 580; (1976) 140 JP 37; (1975) 125 NLJ 869t; [1976] RTR 170; (1975) 119 SJ 645; [1976] 1 WLR 65 HC QBD Is wilful obstruction to ignore police officer's instruction to ignore traffic regulations if necessary to protect life/property.

Kavanagh v Hiscock and another [1974] Crim LR 255 HC QBD Was obstruction of/assault on constable in execution of his duty for picketer to strike police officer seeking to form cordon to allow non-strikers cross picket line.

Ledger v Director of Public Prosecutions [1991] Crim LR 439 CA Total reaction to police making enquiries at house constituted wilful obstruction of police.

Lewis v Cox (1985) 80 Cr App R 1; [1984] Crim LR 756; (1984) 148 JP 601; [1985] QB 509; (1984) 128 SJ 596; [1984] TLR 441; [1984] 3 WLR 875 HC QBD Was wilful obstruction of police officer where repeatedly opened rear door of police vehicle to ask arrested friend where was being taken.

Liepins v Spearman [1985] Crim LR 229; [1986] RTR 24 HC QBD Passenger in/owner of car whose driver was found to be over limit did not have to be, but here was obstructing police in execution of their duty where sought to prevent car being removed to police station.

Lunt v Director of Public Prosecutions [1993] Crim LR 534 HC QBD Failure to admit police with right of entry could be obstruction of police.

Moore v Green [1983] 1 All ER 663; [1982] Crim LR 233; (1982) 126 SJ 79 HC QBD Warning by police officer of pending police investigation an obstruction of police in execution of their duty.

Moss and others v McLachlan (1985) 149 JP 167; [1984] TLR 672 HC QBD Police were acting in course of duty when stopped miners travelling towards another mine as had reasonable belief miners intended to commit breach of the peace.

Neal v Evans [1976] Crim LR 384; [1976] RTR 333; (1976) 120 SJ 354 HC QBD Person who drank more alcohol pending known arrival of police and so frustrated breath test was guilty of obstructing police officer in execution of duty.

Ostler v Elliott [1980] Crim LR 584 HC QBD Was not obstruction of (here plain clothes) policemen in conduct of their duty where resisted them in reasonable belief that were not policemen.

Pankhurst and another v Jarvis (1911-13) XXII Cox CC 228; (1910) 74 JP 64; (1909-10) 101 LTR 946; (1909-10) XXVI TLR 118 HC KBD Suffragettes insisting on admission to Palace of Westminster found guilty of obstructing police in execution of their duty.

Piddington v Bates; Robson and another v Ribton-Turner [1961] Crim LR 262; [1961] 1 WLR 162 HC QBD Valid for police to act to prevent anticipated breach of peace where anticipation of same is reasonable.

Plowden v Director of Public Prosecutions [1991] Crim LR 850 HC QBD Proper inference after finding that had been breach of peace that accused had been obstructing police officer who sought to prevent the breach of the peace.

R v Forde (1985) 81 Cr App R 19; [1985] Crim LR 323; (1985) 149 JP 458 CA Obstruction of police searching for drugs before are warned as to why detained can nonetheless be offence where is obvious why are being detained.

Rice v Connolly [1966] 2 All ER 649; [1966] Crim LR 389t; (1966) 130 JP 322; (1965-66) 116 NLJ 978; [1966] 2 QB 414; (1966) 110 SJ 371; [1966] 3 WLR 17 HC QBD Refusal to answer questions and escort police to station (absent arrest) not wilful obstruction.

Ricketts v Cox (1982) 74 Cr App R 298; [1982] Crim LR 184 HC QBD Extreme rudeness and lack of co-operation was obstruction of police in execution of their duty.

Smith v Reynolds and others; Smith v Hancock; Smith v Lowe [1986] Crim LR 559 HC QBD On elements of offence of aiding and abetting in obstruction of police officer.

Stunt v Bolton [1972] Crim LR 561; [1972] RTR 435; (1972) 116 SJ 803 HC QBD Passenger refusing to give ignition key to police officer seeking to make car safe after driver arrested was obstructing same in execution of duty.

Syce v Harrison [1980] Crim LR 649 (amended at [1981] Crim LR 110) HC QBD Not obstruction of police to refuse entry on foot of defective search warrant.

Tynan v Chief Constable of Liverpool [1965] 3 All ER 611; [1965] Crim LR 611; (1965) 115 LJ 610 CrCt Was obstruction of constable in execution of his duty strike committee chairman ordered that pickets continue after request by constable (who considered them to be an obstruction) that they stop.

Wershof v Commissioner of Police for the Metropolis [1978] 3 All ER 540; (1979) 143 JP 1; (1979) 68 Cr App R 82; [1978] Crim LR 424; (1978) 128 NLJ 486t; (1978) 122 SJ 279 HC QBD Arrest for wilful obstruction if obstruction likely to cause breach of peace/frustrate other arrest; officer acting in course of duty.

Willmott v Atack [1976] 3 All ER 794; (1976) 63 Cr App R 207; [1976] Crim LR 575; (1977) 141 JP 35; (1976) 126 NLJ 719t; [1977] QB 498; (1976) 120 SJ 587; [1976] 3 WLR 753 HC QBD Must intend obstructing act to obstruct for it to be unlawful obstruction of police officer.

WILFUL OBSTRUCTION OF OMNIBUS SERVANT (general)

Baker v Ellison (1914-15) XXIV Cox CC 208; (1914) 78 JP 244; [1914] 83 LJKB 1335 HC KBD Conviction for non-compliance with bus conductor's request.

WINDOW-CLEANING (general)

West Riding Cleaning Co Ltd v Jowett (1938) 86 LJ 293; (1938) 82 SJ 870 HC KBD Successful prosecution for unlawful window-cleaning contrary to the Town Police Clauses Act 1847, s 28.

WITCHCRAFT (general)

R v Duncan and others [1944] 2 All ER 220; (1943-45) 30 Cr App R 70; [1944] KB 713; [1944] 113 LJ 411; (1945) 95 LJ 102; (1944) 171 LTR 342; (1943-44) LX TLR 470; (1944) WN (I) 177 CCA Medium not allowed demonstrate powers in court; seance as pretence to exercise conjuration of spirits contrary to Witchcraft Act 1735, s 4.

R v Eugenie (1969) 113 SJ 586 CA Successful appeal against prosecution for witchcraft: on proving same.

R v Farrant [1973] Crim LR 241 CrCt Valid conviction for indecent behaviour in churchyard of man who performed nighttime churchyard magical ceremony in which sought to raise person from the dead.

WOUNDING (general)

C (JJ) v Eisenhower [1983] 3 All ER 230; (1984) 78 Cr App R 48; [1983] Crim LR 567; [1984] QB 331; (1983) 127 SJ 425; [1983] TLR 298; [1983] 3 WLR 537 HC QBD Internal rupture not a wound which must break the skin.

Flack v Hunt (1980) 70 Cr App R 51; [1980] Crim LR 44; (1979) 123 SJ 751 HC QBD Recklessness a subjective test: here unlawful wounding charge failed where no recklessness established.

R v Aitken; R v Bennett; R v Barson [1992] 1 WLR 1006 CMAC Drunkenness not defence to malicious wounding: test for malice is whether would have foreseen injury if had not been intoxicated; direction on unlawfulness of wounding unsatisfactory as excluded possibility of consent to actions that resulted in wounding.

R v Beasley (Dennis John) (1981) 73 Cr App R 44; [1981] Crim LR 635 CA Circumstances of case meant could not be convicted of common assault where charged with unlawful wounding.

R v Blain [1963] Crim LR 444t CMAC Successful appeal aginst conviction which Crown did not on appeal seek to support.

R v Bonnick (Derek Denton) (1978) 66 Cr App R 266; [1978] Crim LR 246; (1977) 121 SJ 791 CA On when self-defence to go to jury: self-defence evidence may arise even where accused pleads alibi.

R v Brown and other appeals [1993] 2 All ER 75; [1994] 1 AC 212; (1993) 97 Cr App R 44; [1993] Crim LR 583; (1993) 157 JP 337; (1993) 143 NLJ 399; [1993] TLR 129; [1993] 2 WLR 556 HL Consensual homosexual sado-masochistic acts causing actual bodily harm are assaults occasioning actual bodily harm/unlawful woundings.

R v Brown and other appeals [1992] 2 All ER 552; (1992) 94 Cr App R 302; (1992) 156 JP 475; (1992) 142 NLJ 275; [1992] QB 491; (1992) 136 SJ LB 90; [1992] TLR 71; [1992] 2 WLR 441 CA Private, consensual sado-masochistic acts not causing permanent injury may constitute unlawful wounding/ assault causing actual bodily harm.

R v Bryson [1985] Crim LR 669 CA On necessary intention to be guilty of wounding with intent.

R v Cowdell [1962] Crim LR 262t CA Inappropriate that person be convicted of inlawful wounding and assault on basis of same facts.

R v Dennis (Annie) (1905) 69 JP 256 CCC Woman who shot husband in mistaken belief that was burglar to be acquitted of wounding with intent to do grievous bodily harm if that belief was reasonable.

R v Foley [1959] Crim LR 286t CCA On necessary intent for offence of wounding with intent to murder.

R v Garner (Walter John) (1924-25) 18 Cr App R 125 CCA Twelve months' hard labour (not three years' penal servitude) for wounding with intent to murder where greatly provoked by wife (who refused to cease being prostitute).

R v Garratt [1977] Crim LR 687 CA Three years' imprisonment for serious unlawful wounding of another detainee at detention centre.

R v Grundy (Brian); R v Gerrard (Brian); R v Patterson (John) (1989) 89 Cr App R 333; [1989] Crim LR 502 CA Individual could be convicted of wounding with intent to cause grievous bodily harm where harm arose in course of joint unlawful enterprise though may not have involved accused at relevant moment.

R v Hilton, Critchley, Lythe and Greatrex [1956] Crim LR 122 Assizes On distinction between wounding with intent to cause grievous bodily harm and unlawful wounding.

R v Parmenter [1991] 2 All ER 225; [1992] 1 AC 699 (also HL); (1991) 92 Cr App R 68; [1991] Crim LR 41; (1990) 154 JP 941; (1990) 140 NLJ 1231; (1990) 134 SJ 1368; [1990] TLR 564; [1991] 2 WLR 408 CA Foreseeability of some harm required for malicious wounding; intention to/realisation of risk of harm required for occasioning actual bodily harm.

R v Parmenter (1991) 92 Cr App R 164 CA Leave to appeal granted on question of foreseeability as an element of malicious wounding/assault occasioning actual bodily harm.

R v Pearson [1994] Crim LR 534 CA On elements of offence of unlawful wounding.

R v Pond [1984] Crim LR 164 CA Plea of guilty to wounding with intent to grievous bodily harm where charged with attempted murder (the two offences requiring different intent) not a defence to latter charge.

R v Pordage [1975] Crim LR 575 CA On appropriate direction to jury as to intent in case where possibly drunken person charged with wounding with intent.

R v Rainbird [1989] Crim LR 505 CA Test as to whether wounding was malicious is a subjective test.

R v Rossi, Blythe and Dennis [1957] Crim LR 258t CCA Person charged with wounding with intent may be convicted of unlawful wounding.

R v Rushworth (Gary Alan) (1992) 95 Cr App R 252 CA Must intend physical harm/foresee risk of same before can be guilty of unlawful wounding.

R v Savage [1991] 2 All ER 220; [1992] 1 AC 699 (also HL); (1990) 91 Cr App R 317; [1990] Crim LR 709; (1990) 154 JP 757; [1990] TLR 378; [1991] 2 WLR 418 CA Malicious wounding requires foreseeability of harm unlike occasioning actual bodily harm which does not even require recklessness.

R v Savage; R v Parmenter [1991] 4 All ER 698; [1992] 1 AC 699 (also CA); (1992) 94 Cr App R 193; [1992] Crim LR 288 (only Savage); (1991) 155 JP 935; (1991) 141 NLJ 1553; [1991] TLR 499; [1991] 3 WLR 914 HL Unlawful and malicious wounding/inflicting grievous bodily harm requires intent/actual foresight of harm, however slight; assault occasioning actual bodily harm requires assault and actual bodily harm but not intent to cause harm or recklessness that harm likely to be caused.

R v Stubbs (Kevin John) (1989) 88 Cr App R 53 CA Must be very drunk before could plead guilty to unlawful wounding where charged with wounding to do grievous bodily harm.

R v Thomas [1949] 2 All ER 662; (1948-49) 33 Cr App R 200; [1950] 1 KB 26; (1949) 99 LJ 511; (1949) LXV TLR 586; (1949) WN (I) 379 CCA Person convicted of wounding with intent to murder cannot plead autrefois convict to charge of murder where victim later dies.

R v Truss (George William) (1909) 2 Cr App R 69 CCA Appeal on ground of provocation dismissed as was no evidence of serious provocation for what was serious unlawful wounding.

R v Whyte [1987] 3 All ER 416; (1987) 85 Cr App R 283 CA Excessive force where immediate but expected danger not ground for self-defence.

W v Dolbey (1989) 88 Cr App R 1; [1983] Crim LR 681 HC QBD No recklessness (where did not foresee any damage) so no malicious wounding.

ALPHABETICAL INDEX

A v Director of Public Prosecutions [1997] 1 Cr App R 27; [1997] Crim LR 125 HC QBD On rebuttal of doli incapax presumption.

A v Director of Public Prosecutions [1992] Crim LR 34 HC QBD Successful appeal by eleven year old who rightly claimed that doli incapax presumption had not been rebutted in his regard.

A v R [1978] Crim LR 689 CrCt Spitting on police officer's raincoat was not criminal damages as no damage occurred.

A v Sharples [1991] TLR 244 HC QBD Not sufficient to rebut doli incapax presumption that child ran away after doing act that was subject of prosecution.

Abbassy and another v Commissioner of Police of the Metropolis and others [1990] 1 All ER 193; (1990) 90 Cr App R 250; (1989) 139 NLJ 1266; [1990] RTR 164; [1990] 1 WLR 385 CA Police officer exercising power of arrest without warrant need not specify offence for which being arrested but can indicate general nature of offence.

Abbott and another v Smith [1964] 3 All ER 762; [1964] Crim LR 662; (1965) 129 JP 3; (1964) 114 LJ 738; [1965] 2 QB 662; [1965] 3 WLR 362 CrCt Brothel though premises let in separate rooms; management involves element of control: not present here.

Abbott v R [1976] 3 All ER 140; [1977] AC 755; (1976) 63 Cr App R 241; [1976] Crim LR 563; (1976) 140 JP 567; (1976) 126 NLJ 888t; (1976) 120 SJ 538; [1976] 3 WLR 462 PC Duress not defence to party accused of murder as principal in first degree.

Abbott, R v [1956] Crim LR 337t CCA Valid conviction for assisting prisoner (doing work outside prison) to escape.

Abdullah, R v [1982] Crim LR 122 CrCt On establishing forgery of Barclaycard; on when using forged Barclaycard to obtain goods could be obtaining property by deception.

Abel v Stone (1970) 134 JP 237 HC QBD Wilful obstruction of highway a continuing offence so plea of autrefois acquit available.

Abel, Hollands v [1956] Crim LR 336 HC QBD Police entering onto property to request that noise level be kept down were acting in the course of their duty.

Aberash and others, Teame v; R v Secretary of State for the Home Department; ex parte Teame [1994] TLR 205 CA Deportation could continue notwithstanding that there was wardship/residence order or proceedings in existence in relation to person it is sought to deport.

Aberg, R v [1948] 1 All ER 601; (1948) 112 JP 206; (1948) LXIV TLR 215 CCA Not misdirection not to refer to good character in summing-up; on concealment for benefit of person accused of misprision of felony.

Able and others, Attorney-General v [1984] 1 All ER 277; (1984) 78 Cr App R 197; [1984] Crim LR 35; [1984] QB 795; (1983) 127 SJ 731; [1983] TLR 294; [1983] 3 WLR 845 HC QBD Civil court will issue declaration on criminal law if declaration would not criminalise non-criminal behaviour; must know that giving euthanasia booklet to person considering suicide - which occurs imminently - to be assisting in suicide.

Abraham, R v [1973] 3 All ER 694; (1973) 57 Cr App R 799; [1974] Crim LR 246; (1973) 137 JP 826; (1973) 117 SJ 663; [1973] 1 WLR 1270 CA Jury direction when self-defence raised.

Abramovitch, R v [1911-13] All ER 1178; (1913-14) XXIII Cox CC 179; (1911-12) 7 Cr App R 145; (1912) 76 JP 287; (1912-13) 107 LTR 416 CCA Prosecution calling doctor to prove accused sane where defence raised insanity but called no evidence good practice.

Absalom v Martin (1973) 123 NLJ 946t; [1973] Crim LR 752 HC QBD Billposter's part-parking of van on pavement while putting up bill did not merit conviction for wilful obstruction of highway.

Akerele v R [1943] 1 All ER 367; [1943] AC 255; [1943] 112 LJ 26; (1943) 168 LTR 102 PC Preparation of overly-strong medical solution not criminal negligence.

Alan Helliwell and Sons (Bolton) Ltd, Cheshire County Council v [1991] Crim LR 210; (1991) 155 JP 425; [1990] TLR 766 HC QBD Transporting of animals while are unfit to travel a strict liability offence (Transport of Animals (Road and Rail) Order 1951).

Albert v Lavin [1981] 1 All ER 628; [1982] AC 546 (also HL); (1981) 72 Cr App R 178; [1981] Crim LR 238; (1981) 145 JP 184; (1981) 131 NLJ 368; (1981) 125 SJ 114; [1981] 2 WLR 1070 HC QBD Unreasonable belief acting in self-defence not defence to assault charge.

Albert, Lavin v [1981] 3 All ER 878; [1982] AC 546 (also HC QBD); (1982) 74 Cr App R 150; (1982) 146 JP 78; (1981) 125 SJ 860; [1981] 3 WLR 955 HL Can restrain breach of peace (even by detention) though not police officer; mistaken belief that person detaining one as part of restraint of breach of peace not police officer not defence to assault.

Alderson v Booth [1969] 2 All ER 271; (1969) 53 Cr App R 301; [1969] Crim LR 270t; (1969) 133 JP 346; (1969) 119 NLJ 225t; [1969] 2 QB 216; (1969) 113 SJ 268; [1969] 2 WLR 1252 HC QBD Any words clearly informing person that are under compulsion is valid arrest.

Aldred, R v (1911-13) XXII Cox CC 1; (1910) 74 JP 55 CCC What constitutes seditious libel; test for seditious libel.

Alexander v Tonkin [1979] Crim LR 248; (1979) 123 SJ 111 HC QBD On when fishing complete for purposes of Sea Fisheries Regulation Act 1966, s 11(2).

Alexander, Davis v (1970) 54 Cr App R 398; [1972] Crim LR 595 HC QBD Prosecution need not prove accused carried weapon with intent to cause injury where is clearly offensive weapon.

Alexander, R v (1913-14) XXIII Cox CC 604; (1913-14) 109 LTR 745 CCA Insanity verdict may not be open to jury just because accused proved mentally deficient.

Alexander, R v [1981] Crim LR 183 CA Obtaining void/voidable insurance policy was obtaining pecuniary advantage by deception.

Alexander, R v (1913-14) XXIII Cox CC 138; (1912) 76 JP 215; (1912-13) 107 LTR 240; (1911-12) XXVIII TLR 200 CCA Conviction quashed where trial judge actively encouraged accused to plead guilty to abduction charge.

Alford, Baker v (1960) 104 SJ PC Failed habeas corpus application in which complained that extension of Colonial Prisoners Removal Act 1869 to Bahrain (and application of same) improper.

Ali v R; Rasool v R [1992] 2 All ER 1; (1992) 136 SJ LB 62; [1992] 2 WLR 357 PC No separate offence of 'importing-cum-drug trafficking'; discretion of Director of Public Prosecutions to elect which sentence appropriate for accused a breach of separation of powers.

Ali, R v [1989] Crim LR 736 CA On pleading provocation as defence to murder.

Ali, R v [1995] Crim LR 303 CA Person cannot plead duress where voluntarily join in criminal offence with violent person who then threatens violence in order to get said person to commit criminal offence.

Ali, R v [1993] Crim LR 396 CA Offer of bribery per se amounted to pressure (to withdraw charge).

Allamby, R v; R v Medford [1974] 3 All ER; (1974) 59 Cr App R 189; [1975] Crim LR 39; (1974) 138 JP 659; (1974) 118 SJ 830 [1974] 1 WLR 1494 CA At time/place in particulars must intend to use weapons offensively in future.

Allan and others, R v [1963] 2 All ER 897; (1963) 47 Cr App R 243; (1963) 127 JP 511; (1963) 113 LJ 561; [1965] 1 QB 130; (1963) 107 SJ 596; [1963] 3 WLR 677 CCA Principal in second degree to affray must have physically encouraged affray.

Allan, R v; R v Prentice [1963] Crim LR 118; (1963) 113 LJ 270; (1962) 106 SJ 960 CCA Person charged with larceny as servant could be convicted of simple larceny.

Allen and others v Ireland (1984) 79 Cr App R 206; [1984] Crim LR 500; (1984) 148 JP 545; (1984) 128 SJ 482; [1984] TLR 212; [1984] 1 WLR 903 HC QBD Prima facie evidence of participation in threatening behaviour where were voluntarily present; prima facie case of identification as party to threatening behaviour where proceedings initiated against one as member of group.

Allen and others, R v [1963] Crim LR 561t CCA On what constitutes offence of affray.

Allen v Simmons [1978] 3 All ER 662; [1978] Crim LR 362; (1979) 143 JP 105; (1978) 128 NLJ 512t; (1978) 122 SJ 470; [1978] 1 WLR 879 HC QBD Competitive bidding includes any form of competition for purchase.

Allen v Whitehead [1930] 1 KB 211; (1929) WN (I) 207 HC KBD Occupier liable for servant's knowingly suffering prostitutes to meet in former's refreshment house.

Allen, Cartledge v [1973] Crim LR 530 HC QBD Person who injured self in running away from others who had threatened him thereby suffered infliction of grievous bodily harm by those others.

Allen, R v [1981] Crim LR 324; [1981] RTR 410 CA Police were trespassing once ordered by person (whom believed to have been in accident) to leave his property: arrest thereafter invalid.

Allen, R v [1985] 1 All ER 148; (1984) 79 Cr App R 265; [1984] Crim LR 498; (1984) 128 SJ 660; [1984] TLR 333; [1985] 1 WLR 50 CA 'Intent to avoid payment' must be intent to avoid permanently.

Allen, R v [1985] 2 All ER 641; [1985] AC 1029; (1985) 81 Cr App R 200; [1985] Crim LR 739; (1985) 149 JP 587; (1985) 135 NLJ 603; (1985) 129 SJ 447; [1985] 3 WLR 107 HL 'Intent to avoid payment' must be intent to avoid permanently.

Allen, R v [1988] Crim LR 698 CA Where know are drinking alcohol fact that are mistaken as to its strength does not render drinking of same involuntary.

Allsop (Anthony Adward), R v (1977) 64 Cr App R 29; [1976] Crim LR 738t; (1976) 126 NLJ 937t; (1976) 120 SJ 635 CA Is fraud where make false statements likely to cause another economic loss (and do) though no loss intended.

Allsop, Moberly v (1992) 156 JP 514; [1991] TLR 576 HC QBD Ticket inspectors can hold passengers who do not show tickets; Theft Act 1978 can be applicable to rail-connected cases.

Allworthy and Walker v Clayton (1907-09) XXI Cox CC 352 HC KBD Pawnbroker could not be convicted of neglecting to deliver pledge where loss of same was in good faith.

Allwright, R v [1991] TLR 107 CA On desirability of psychiatric report before sentencing for arson.

Alt, R v [1972] Crim LR 552 CA Must know or believe property to be stolen when obtain it in order to be guilty of receiving.

Ambrose (Peter Thomas), R v (1973) 57 Cr App R 538 CA Rude/objectionable words need not be insulting (and were not here).

Amnesty International, Data Protection Registrar v [1995] Crim LR 633; [1994] TLR 597 HC QBD On what constitutes 'recklessness' for purposes of data protection offences of recklessly holding/disclosing data.

Amott, R v [1962] Crim LR 170 CCA Could validly be convicted of separate receiving where charged with joint receiving.

Anderson (William Ronald), R v [1986] AC 27; (1985) 81 Cr App R 253; [1985] Crim LR 650; (1985) 135 NLJ 727; (1985) 129 SJ 522; [1985] 3 WLR 268 HL On requisite intention to be guilty of statutory conspiracy.

Anderson and Morris, R v [1966] 2 All ER 644; (1966) 50 Cr App R 216; [1966] Crim LR 385t; (1966) 130 JP 318; [1966] 2 QB 110; (1966) 110 SJ 369; [1966] 2 WLR 1195 CCA Parties to joint action liable for all effects thereof except those caused by one party going further than agreed.

Anderson and others, R v [1971] 3 All ER 1152; [1972] Crim LR 40t; (1972) 136 JP 97; [1972] 1 QB 304; [1971] 3 WLR 939 CA If one element of article obscene, whole article is obscene; obscenity for jury not expert evidence; definition of 'obscene'.

Anderson v Miller and another (1977) 64 Cr App R 178; [1976] Crim LR 743; (1976) 126 NLJ 1091t; (1976) 120 SJ 735 HC QBD Shop a single unit so even place behind counter was place to which public had access for purpose of Firearms Act 1968, ss 19 and 57(4).

Anderson, Morrrison and Williamson, Budd v [1943] 2 All ER 452; [1943] KB 642; (1943) WN (I) 150 HC KBD Technical error in detention order did not render it invalid.

Anderson, R v (1985) 80 Cr App R 64; [1984] Crim LR 550; (1984) 128 SJ 660; [1984] TLR 364 CA Agreement to participate in conduct seeking to bring about criminal act was conspiracy even though had mental reservations about participation.

Anderson, R v [1978] Crim LR 223 CrCt On admissibility of evidence of other convictions as proof of guilt of handling.

Anderton v Royle [1985] RTR 91 HC QBD Police station breath test results admissible though had not sought to adminsiter preliminary breath test upon stopping defendant on road.

Anderton v Ryan [1985] 2 All ER 355; [1985] AC 560 (also HC QBD); (1985) 81 Cr App R 166; [1985] Crim LR 503; (1985) 149 JP 433; (1985) 135 NLJ 485; (1985) 129 SJ 362; [1985] 2 WLR 968 HL Cannot be guilty of crime where believed was committing crime but was not.

Anderton v Ryan [1985] 1 All ER 138; [1985] AC 560 (also HL); (1985) 80 Cr App R 235; [1984] Crim LR 483; (1984) 128 SJ 850; [1984] TLR 227; [1985] 2 WLR 23 HC QBD Could be guilty of attempted handling of stolen goods though not proved that goods in issue stolen.

Anderton v Wish (1981) 72 Cr App R 23; [1980] Crim LR 319/657 HC QBD Is appropriation to switch lower price tags to higher priced goods so as to pay lower price.

Anderton, Corcoran v (1980) 71 Cr App R 104; [1980] Crim LR 385 HC QBD Snatching handbag which dropped and ran off without was appropriation.

Anderton, Knox v (1983) 76 Cr App R 156; [1983] Crim LR 114; (1983) 147 JP 340; [1982] TLR 565 HC QBD Landing in public flats was 'public place' within meaning of Prevention of Crime Act 1953, s 1(4).

Anderton, Schiavo v [1986] 3 All ER 10; (1986) 83 Cr App R 228; [1986] Crim LR 542; (1986) 150 JP 264; [1987] QB 20; (1970) 130 SJ 542; [1986] 3 WLR 176 HC QBD magistrates can deal with failure to surrender for bail without formal charge; failure to appear before magistrates court triable by magistrates.

Andrews (Paul), R v (1986) 82 Cr App R 148 CA Wilful neglect of child properly inferred from circumstantial evidence.

Andrews and Hedges, R v [1981] Crim LR 106 CA Failed prosecution for inducing creditor to wait for payment.

Andrews v Director of Public Prosecutions [1937] 2 All ER 552; [1937] AC 576; (1936-38) 26 Cr App R 34; (1937) 101 JP 386; (1937) 83 LJ 304; [1937] 106 LJCL 370; (1937) 81 SJ 497; (1936-37) LIII TLR 663; (1937) WN (I) 188 HL Can be convicted of reckless driving where negligence insufficient to sustain manslaughter charge in case where victim dies.

Andrews, Loat v (1970) 130 SJ 697 HC QBD Civilian working under police officer though employed by county council did come under the provisions of the Official Secrets Acts 1911 and 1920, ss 2 and 7 respectively.

Andrews, R v [1973] 1 All ER 857; (1973) 57 Cr App R 254; [1973] Crim LR 117t; (1973) 137 JP 325; (1972) 122 NLJ 1133t; [1973] QB 422; [1973] RTR 508; (1973) 117 SJ 86; [1973] 2 WLR 116 CA Incitement to/actual production of untrue evidence is obstruction of justice.

Andrews, R v [1938] 4 All ER 869; (1939-40) XXXI Cox CC 193; (1938-40) 27 Cr App R 12; (1939) 103 JP 11; (1939) 87 LJ 28; (1939) 160 LTR 181 CCA Person accused of being habitual criminal to be advised can call witnesses/ought to be represented by counsel.

Andrews, R v (1934-39) XXX Cox CC 576; (1937) 156 LTR 464 HL Death through negligent driving to be treated as death through any form of negligence: law of manslaughter remains the same.

Andrews, R v; R v Craig [1962] 3 All ER 961; (1963) 47 Cr App R 32; [1963] Crim LR 51; (1963) 127 JP 64; (1962) 106 SJ 1013; [1962] 1 WLR 1474 CCA On accessories after the fact.

Andrews-Weatherfoil Ltd, R v; R v Sporle; R v Day [1972] 1 All ER 65; (1972) 56 Cr App R 31; [1972] Crim LR 706t; (1972) 136 JP 128; (1971) 121 NLJ 930t (R v Sporle alone); (1971) 115 SJ 888; [1972] 1 WLR 118 CA Persons concerned must have authority to bind company before company criminally liable for actions of persons; on what constitutes 'reward' under Public Bodies Corrupt Practices Act 1889.

Aronson, Government of Canada and another v [1989] 2 All ER 1025; [1990] 1 AC 579; (1990) 90 Cr App R 199; (1989) 139 NLJ 1040; (1989) 133 SJ 1031; [1989] 3 WLR 436 HL Ingredients of Commonwealth country's offence must point to guilt of matching English offence.

Arrowsmith v Jenkins [1963] 2 QB 561 HC QBD No mens rea required to be guilty of wilful obstruction of highway so long as have freely done acts causing/continuing obstruction.

Arrowsmith, R v [1975] 1 All ER 463; (1975) 60 Cr App R 211; [1975] Crim LR 161t; (1975) 139 JP 221; (1975) 125 NLJ 13t; [1975] QB 678; (1975) 119 SJ 165; [1975] 2 WLR 484 CA Seducing armed force members from allegiance a single offence with one of two intents - not duplicity if both intents mentioned; mistake that DPP will not prosecute not a defence to charge but may mitigate sentence.

Arscott, Marsh v (1982) 75 Cr App R 211; [1982] Crim LR 827; [1982] TLR 121 HC QBD Shop car park was/was not public place when shop open/closed.

Arthur, R v (1968) 118 NLJ 301t; [1968] 2 WLR 533 Assizes Cannot be arson of property under Malicious Damage Act 1861, s 2, where 'person...therein' is alleged arsonist.

Arthur, R v [1967] Crim LR 298t; (1967) 111 SJ 434 CA Successful conviction of company director for fraudulent conversion of company funds for own use.

Arthur, R v [1968] Crim LR 114; [1968] 1 QB 810; (1967) 111 SJ 925 Assizes Maliciously setting fire to dwelling house where person inside meant person other than accused (Malicious Damage Act 1861, s 2).

Asbury, R v [1986] Crim LR 258 CA On reasonableness of belief that were acting in self-defence to sustaining a plea of self-defence.

Ash and another, Jenkins v (1926-30) XXVIII Cox CC 665; (1929) 93 JP 229; (1929) 141 LTR 591; (1928-29) XLV TLR 479 HC KBD Cruelty to rabbit (coursing/hunting exemptions inapplicable).

Ashbee v Jayne [1966] Crim LR 49; (1965) 109 SJ 919 HC QBD That carried sand-filled sock for purpose of self-defence did not mean could not be offensive weapon.

Ashdown (Robert James), R v; R v Howard (Leonard); R v Howard (Judith Mary); R v Stuart (Michael Adrian) (1974) 59 Cr App R 193 CA Is possible for co-tenant to commit offence of permitting other co-tenant to use premises for cannabis-smoking.

Ashford (Kent) Justices, ex parte Gilmore [1966] Crim LR 618, R v (1966) 110 SJ 709 HC QBD Court could not under the Backing of Warrants (Republic of Ireland) Act 1965 act on warrant issued in Jersey.

Ashford (Kent) Justices, ex parte Richley, R v [1955] 3 All ER 604; (1955) 105 LJ 760 CA Certiorari quashing proceedings need not issue when perjury discovered.

Ashford and Smith, R v [1988] Crim LR 682 CA Is objective test whether alleged criminal damage was done to protect property of another.

Ashford, Kent, Justices, ex parte Richley (No 2), R v [1956] Crim LR 48; [1956] 1 QB 167; [1955] 3 WLR 778 CA Certiorari quashing proceedings need not issue when perjury discovered.

Ashgar, R v [1973] Crim LR 701 CA On elements of obtaining cheques by deception (as here).

Ashley, Director of Public Prosecutions v [1955] Crim LR 565 Assizes Annulment of bankruptcy did not mean could not be prosecuted for bankruptcy offences.

Ashman, R v [1954] Crim LR 382t CCA Conviction quashed where inter alia inadequate attention paid to alibi evidence.

Ashton, Brook v [1974] Crim LR 105 HC QBD Could not ground lawful excuse defence in mistake of law.

Ashton-Rickardt, R v [1977] Crim LR 424; (1978) 142 JP 90; (1977) 121 SJ 774; [1978] 1 WLR 37 CA Must prove person knew had possession of controlled substance to secure conviction for same.

Ashworth (George Thomas), R v (1910-11) 6 Cr App R 112 CCA On joint indictment for stealing/receiving: one person not guilty of receiving unless property not always in exclusive possession of other.

Asquith (Lee David), R v; R v Webster (Andrew); R v Seamans (David Leigh); R v Warwick (Wayne Michael) [1995] 1 Cr App R 492 CA Could infer intent to endanger life from throwing stone over bridge at train/from purposely crashing into police cars.

Assistant Recorder of Kingston-upon-Hull, ex parte Morgan, R v (1969) 133 JP 165; [1969] 2 WLR 246 HC QBD DPP's consent (pursuant to Sexual Offences Act 1967, s 8) unnecessary to bring prosecution for incitement of under-14 year old boy to act of gross indecency.

Aston (Roy Edward), R v; R v Mason (Christine Janet) (1992) 94 Cr App R 180; [1991] Crim LR 701 CA Could not infer guilt of both parties charged of child's manslaughter where was no evidence to pointing to one over another.

Aston, R v; R v Hadley [1970] 3 All ER 1045; (1971) 55 Cr App R 48; [1971] Crim LR 98t; (1970) 120 NLJ 1016t; (1970) 114 SJ 906; [1970] 1 WLR 1584 CA Deception must induce person affected to do/not to do something so that debt is evaded/put off.

Atack, Willmott v [1976] 3 All ER 794; (1976) 63 Cr App R 207; [1976] Crim LR 575; (1977) 141 JP 35; (1976) 126 NLJ 719t; [1977] QB 498; (1976) 120 SJ 587; [1976] 3 WLR 753 HC QBD Must intend obstructing act to obstruct for it to be unlawful obstruction of police officer.

Atakpu and another, R v [1993] 4 All ER 215; (1994) 98 Cr App R 254; [1994] Crim LR 693; (1993) 143 NLJ 652; [1994] QB 69; [1994] RTR 23; [1993] TLR 162; [1993] 3 WLR 812 CA Goods once stolen by thief cannot then be stolen or appropriated by him.

Athanassiadis v Government of Greece [1969] 3 All ER 293; [1971] AC 282; (1969) 133 JP 577; [1969] 3 WLR 544 HL 'Months' in Anglo-Greek Extradition Treaty means calendar months; conviction for contumacy explained.

Atherley, R v (1909) WN (I) 251 CCA No leave to appeal in petition where was pleaded that evidence of insanity might perhaps have been procured for trial had there been time.

Atkin v Director of Public Prosecutions (1989) 89 Cr App R 199; [1989] Crim LR 581; (1989) 153 JP 383 HC QBD Person against whom threatening words/behaviour directed must be physically present.

Atkinson (Douglas Walter), R v (1932-34) 24 Cr App R 123 CCA Conviction quashed where was inadequate warning as to evidence from perjurer/accomplice.

Atkinson (John), R v [1985] Crim LR 314 CA On appropriate direction to jury as to effect of voluntary intoxication on drunkenness.

Atkinson v United States Government and others [1969] 3 All ER 1317; [1971] AC 197; [1970] Crim LR 30; (1970) 134 JP 29; (1969) 119 NLJ 1045t; (1969) 113 SJ 901; [1969] 3 WLR 1074 HL If sufficient evidence for committal magistrate must commit.

Atkinson, Burton v (1907-09) XXI Cox CC 575; (1908) 72 JP 198; (1908) XCVIII LTR 748; (1907-08) XXIV TLR 498 HC KBD Foxhound puppy not required to wear collar when on highway.

Atkinson, R v [1976] Crim LR 307 CA Substantial error in search warrant rendered actions thereunder improper.

Atkinson, United States Government v [1969] 2 All ER 1151; [1969] Crim LR 487t; (1969) 133 JP 621 HC QBD Appeal by case stated from magistrates' courts in extradition cases; no autrefois convict possible between attempted armed robbery and aggravated burglary.

Attard, Foster v (1986) 83 Cr App R 214; [1986] Crim LR 627 HC QBD Once police had lawfully entered premises under one statutory power could exercise powers under other statute.

Attorney General for Hong Kong v Reid and others [1994] 1 All ER 1; [1994] 1 AC 324; (1993) 143 NLJ 1569 PC Fiduciary receiving bribe holds in trust for principal and where bribe increases in value is accountable for bribe and increase. New Zealand Court of Appeal free to review Court of Appeal decisions.

Attorney General of Hong Kong, Gammon (Hong Kong) Ltd v [1984] 2 All ER 503; [1985] AC 1; (1985) 80 Cr App R 194; [1984] Crim LR 496; (1984) 128 SJ 549; [1984] TLR 308; [1984] 3 WLR 437 PC Strict liability in statutory offence permissible if statute concerned with public safety and strict liability furthers that goal.

Attorney General of Hong Kong, Man-in (Chan) v [1988] 1 All ER 1 PC Drawing, presenting and negotiating forged cheques appropriation and theft.

Attorney General v Gastonia Coaches Ltd (1976) 126 NLJ 1267t; [1977] RTR 219 HC ChD Obstruction of highway by coaches a public nuisance; smell/noise from premises of motor coach operator along with interference in access to private premises a private nuisance.

Attorney General's Reference [1981] 2 All ER 1057 CA Cannot consent to assault.

Attorney General's Reference (No 1 of 1980) [1981] 1 All ER 366; [1981] 1 WLR 34 CA Document made/required for accounting included documents for which accounting secondary purpose.

Attorney General's Reference (No 1 of 1981) [1982] 2 All ER 417; (1982) 75 Cr App R 45; [1982] Crim LR 512 (1981) 131 NLJ 504; [1982] QB 848; [1982] TLR 153 CA Fraudulent conduct not deceit before customs officer needed to ground importation of prohibited goods conviction.

Attorney General's Reference (No 1 of 1982) [1983] 2 All ER 721; [1983] Crim LR 534; (1984) 148 JP 115; [1983] QB 751; (1983) 127 SJ 377; [1983] TLR 268; [1983] 3 WLR 72 CA If a tangential effect of conspiracy to perform act abroad is it causes economic/other loss in England then is not conspiracy to defraud.

Attorney General's Reference (No 1 of 1985) [1986] 2 All ER 219; (1986) 83 Cr App R 70; [1986] Crim LR 476; (1986) 150 JP 242; [1986] QB 491; (1986) 130 SJ 299; [1986] 2 WLR 733 CA Employer has no proprietary right in profits from private sales by employee on employer's premises.

Attorney General's Reference (No 1 of 1991) [1992] 3 All ER 897; (1993) 157 JP 258; [1993] QB 94; (1992) 136 SJ LB 197; [1992] TLR 380; [1992] 3 WLR 432 CA Unauthorised access to data includes direct access from any computer.

Attorney General's Reference (No 1 of 1992) [1993] 2 All ER 190; (1993) 96 Cr App R 298; [1993] Crim LR 274; (1993) 157 JP 753; (1992) 136 SJ LB 304; [1992] TLR 528; [1993] 1 WLR 274 CA Prima facie case of attempted rape if necessary intent can be inferred and acts preparatory to rape have taken place.

Attorney General's Reference (No 2 of 1980) [1981] 1 All ER 493; (1981) 72 Cr App R 64; [1981] Crim LR 43; (1981) 145 JP 169; (1981) 131 NLJ 292; (1981) 125 SJ 16; [1981] 1 WLR 148 CA Pre-trial forgery of evidence is forgery of document 'made evidence by law'.

Attorney General's Reference (No 2 of 1982) [1984] 2 All ER 216; (1984) 78 Cr App R 131; [1984] QB 624; (1984) 128 SJ 221; [1983] TLR 702; [1984] 2 WLR 447 CA Illegal acts by all shareholders and directors will be imputed to them, not company; where plead defendant and company one and same cannot plead company consented to appropriations.

Attorney General's Reference (No 2 of 1992) [1993] 4 All ER 683; (1993) 97 Cr App R 429; [1994] Crim LR 692; (1994) 158 JP 741; (1993) 143 NLJ 919; [1994] QB 91; [1993] RTR 337; (1993) 137 SJ LB 152; [1993] TLR 303; [1993] 3 WLR 982 CA 'Driving without awareness' not automatism as partial not total loss of control.

Attorney General's Reference (No 3 of 1992) [1994] 2 All ER 121; (1994) 98 Cr App R 383; [1994] Crim LR 348; (1993) 143 NLJ 1675; [1994] RTR 122; (1993) 137 SJ LB 278; [1993] TLR 576; [1994] 1 WLR 409 CA Intent to cause damage by fire and recklessness to endangerment of life establishes intent for attempted aggravated arson.

Attorney General's Reference (No 3 of 1994) [1996] 2 All ER 10; [1996] 1 Cr App R 351; [1996] Crim LR 268; [1996] 2 FLR 1; (1995) 145 NLJ 1777; [1996] QB 581; (1996) 140 SJ LB 20; [1995] TLR 625; [1996] 2 WLR 412 CA Murder or manslaughter arises if injury to a child in utero or its mother causes child to die after live birth; necessary intent is intent to kill or cause grievous bodily injury to mother.

Attorney General's Reference (No 3 of 1994) [1997] 3 All ER 936; [1997] 2 Cr App R (S) 1185; (1997) 147 NLJ 1185; [1997] TLR 411; [1997] 3 WLR 421 HL Conviction for manslaughter of child may follow where deliberate injury to pregnant mother causes child to die after live birth but conviction for murder of child would not follow.

Attorney General's Reference (No 4 of 1979) [1981] 1 All ER 1193; (1980) 71 Cr App R 341; [1981] Crim LR 51; (1981) 145 JP 281; (1980) 130 NLJ 860; (1981) 125 SJ 355; [1981] 1 WLR 667 CA Cheque obtained by deception/bank balance 'goods' under Theft Act.

Attorney General's Reference (No 4 of 1980) [1981] 2 All ER 617; (1981) 73 Cr App R 40; [1981] Crim LR 493; (1981) 145 JP 394; (1981) 125 SJ 374; [1981] 1 WLR 705 CA Crown need not establish which act caused death where multiple acts capable of causing death.

Attorney General's Reference (No 5 of 1980) [1980] 3 All ER 816; (1981) 72 Cr App R 71; [1981] Crim LR 45; (1981) 145 JP 110; (1980) 130 NLJ 1122; (1980) 124 SJ 827; [1981] 1 WLR 88 CA Video cassettes are articles capable of publication under Obscene Publications Act.

Attorney-General and Registrar-General, Dinizulu v [1958] 3 All ER 555; (1958) 108 LJ 812; (1958) 102 SJ 879 HC QBD Marriage entry not struck from register as was ceremony though marriage was void.

Attorney-General for Ceylon v Perera (Kumarasinghege Don John) [1953] AC 200; (1953) 97 SJ 78; [1953] 2 WLR 238 PC Murder reduced to manslaughter if were reacting proportionately to provocation.

Attorney-General for Northern Ireland v Gallagher [1961] 3 All ER 299; [1963] AC 349; (1961) 45 Cr App R 316; [1961] Crim LR 717t; (1961) 111 LJ 532; [1961] 3 WLR 619 HL Rôle of HL upon appeal; mental disease occasioning violent behaviour in which unaware of type/quality/wrongness of act required to sustain insanity defence.

Attorney-General for Northern Ireland, Bratty v [1961] 3 All ER 523; [1963] AC 386; (1962) 46 Cr App R 1; [1961] Crim LR 829; (1961) 111 LJ 692; [1961] 3 WLR 965 HL Jury rejection of insanity defence does not preclude acceptance of automatism defence if solid evidence thereof.

Attorney-General for the Dominion of Canada v Fedorenko [1911] AC 735; (1912) 81 LJPC 74; (1911-12) 105 LTR 343; (1910-11) XXVII TLR 541 PC Under 1886 Extradition Treaty with Russia person sought must be arrested after formally correct requisition presented.

Attorney-General for the State of South Australia v Brown [1960] 1 All ER 734; (1960) 44 Cr App R 100; [1960] Crim LR 425; (1960) 110 LJ 301; (1960) 104 SJ 268; [1960] 2 WLR 588 PC No defence of insanity by virtue of uncontrollable impulse.

Attorney-General for Trinidad, Kossekechatko and Others v [1932] AC 78; (1931-34) XXIX Cox CC 394; (1931) 72 LJ 386; (1932) 101 LJPC 17; (1932) 146 LTR 101; (1931) 75 SJ 741; (1931-32) XLVIII TLR 27 PC Non-compliance by magistrate with procedural requirements and absence of evidence that fugitives had committed offence in French territory (as required in French Extradition Treaty) meant no extradition.

Attorney-General of Ceylon v De Livera and another [1963] Crim LR 105; (1963) 113 LJ 8; (1962) 106 SJ 935; [1962] 3 WLR 1413 PC Person deemed to have acted in contravention of Ceylon Bribery Act 1954, s 14.

Attorney-General of Hong Kong v Chiu (Ip) and another [1980] AC 663; [1980] Crim LR 169; (1980) 124 SJ 47; [1980] 2 WLR 332 PC Accepting bribe in 'capacity' as public servant - meaning of 'capacity' in Prevention of Bribery Ordinance, s 4(2) (a); was not bribery where accepted HK$2000 so as not to plant evidence on/beat up person whom sought to bring to police station.

Attorney-General of Hong Kong v Chiuk-Wah (Pat) and others [1971] 2 All ER 1460; [1971] AC 835; (1971) 55 Cr App R 342; (1971) 135 JP 507; (1971) 121 NLJ 273t; (1971) 115 SJ 348; [1971] 2 WLR 1381 PC National security stamp a valuable security; can be convicted of forgery though forgery not complete.

Attorney-General of Hong Kong v Nai-Keung (1988) 86 Cr App R 174; [1988] Crim LR 125; [1987] 1 WLR 1339 PC Export quotas were intangible property that could be dishonestly appropriated.

Attorney-General of Hong Kong v Pui-Yiu (Ho) [1981] 1 WLR 395; [1981] Crim LR 241; (1981) 125 SJ 198 PC On duty of prosecution in proving guilt of bribery under Prevention of Bribery Ordinance 1973.

Attorney-General of Hong Kong, Ming Pao Newspapers Ltd and others v [1996] 3 WLR 272 PC On elements of offence of disclosing details of investigation being conducted under the Hong Kong Prevention of Bribery Ordinance.

Attorney-General of Jamaica v Williams and another [1997] 3 WLR 389 CA On issuing of search warrant: here search lawful though seizure had gone slightly further than warrant allowed.

Attorney-General of Natal, De Jager v [1904-07] All ER 1008; [1907] AC 326; (1907) XCVI LTR 857; (1906-07) XXIII TLR 516 PC Is treason for Crown subject to assist alien occupiers of Crown territory in which one resides.

Attorney-General v Able and others [1984] 1 All ER 277; (1984) 78 Cr App R 197; [1984] Crim LR 35; [1984] QB 795; (1983) 127 SJ 731; [1983] TLR 294; [1983] 3 WLR 845 HC QBD Civil court will issue declaration on criminal law if declaration would not criminalise non-criminal behaviour; must know that giving euthanasia booklet to person considering suicide - which occurs imminently - to be assisting in suicide.

Attorney-General v Beauchamp [1920] 1 KB 650; (1919-20) XXXVI TLR 174; (1920) WN (I) 15 HC KBD Publisher liable for punishment under 2 and 3 Vict c12, s 2 for not publishing name/address of printer on newspaper.

Attorney-General v Brown [1921] 3 KB 29 CA Ejusdem generis interpretation of Customs Consolidation Act 1876, s 43.

Attorney-General v Goddard (1928-29) XLV TLR 609 HC KBD On recovery by (principal) Crown of bribes ('secret profits') paid to (its agent) Metropolitan Police officer.

Attorney-General's Reference (No 1 of 1974) [1974] 2 All ER 899; (1974) 59 Cr App R 203; [1974] Crim LR 427t; (1974) 138 JP 570; (1974) 124 NLJ 483t; [1974] QB 744; (1974) 118 SJ 345; [1974] 2 WLR 891 CA Whether goods taken into police officer's possession a question of officer's intent and that is a matter for jury.

Attorney-General's Reference (No 1 of 1975) [1975] 2 All ER 685; (1975) 61 Cr App R 118; [1975] Crim LR 449t; (1975) 139 JP 569; (1975) 125 NLJ 485t; [1975] QB 773; [1975] RTR 473; (1975) 119 SJ 373; [1975] 3 WLR 11 CA Covert act resulting in other unwittingly doing criminal act 'procured' criminal act.

Attorney-General's Reference (No 1 of 1995) (B and F) [1996] 4 All ER 21; [1996] 2 Cr App R 320; [1996] Crim LR 575; (1996) TLR 30/1/96; [1996] 1 WLR 970 CA On mens rea necessary to support conviction of director for unlicensed acceptance of deposits.

Attorney-General's Reference (No 2 of 1975) [1976] 2 All ER 753 (also CCC); [1976] Crim LR 444t; (1976) 62 Cr App R 255; (1976) 126 NLJ 366t; (1976) 120 SJ 315; [1976] 1 WLR 710 CA In deciding if obscene jury may only have regard to those people who would actually be exposed to publication of material.

Attorney-General's Reference (No 2 of 1977) [1978] 2 All ER 646; [1978] Crim LR 495; (1978) 142 JP 403; (1978) 128 NLJ 112t; (1978) 122 SJ 78; [1978] 1 WLR 290 CA Rhodesian sanctions breached where individual sought individuals to take up employment/residence in Rhodesia.

Attorney-General's Reference (No 2 of 1983) [1984] 1 All ER 988; (1984) 78 Cr App R 183; [1984] Crim LR 289; (1985) 149 JP 104; [1984] QB 456; [1984] TLR 42; [1984] 2 WLR 465 CA Exceptionally preparation of petrol-bomb may be lawful where prepared as planned act of self-defence.

Attorney-General's Reference (No 2 of 1983) [1985] Crim LR 241; (1984) 128 SJ 203 CA Person/two persons in total control of company could be guilty/jointly guilty of theft of company property.

Attorney-General's Reference (No 2 of 1995) [1996] 3 All ER 860; [1997] 1 Cr App R 72; [1996] Crim LR 662 CA On what constitutes 'influencing' a prostitute for purposes of Sexual Offences Act 1956, s 31.

Baker, R v [1994] Crim LR 444 CA Valid decision that alternative verdict of having caused grievous bodily harm with intent not be left to jury in case where accused charged with murder as part of joint enterprise (even though joint enterprise may have ended before killing).

Baker, Smith v [1972] Crim LR 25; [1971] RTR 350 HC QBD Not aiding and abetting in driving uninsured vehicle to sit in stolen car until no longer being driven and then run away when see police approaching.

Baker, Smith v (1961) 125 JP 53; (1960) 110 LJ 845; (1961) 105 SJ 17; [1961] 1 WLR 38 HC QBD Police officer can bring complaint under Dogs Act 1871, s 2.

Balderstone (Ernest Victor), R v (1955) 39 Cr App R 97; [1955] Crim LR 499 CCA That mental defective had violated terms of licence from hospital did not mean was not certified mental defective when prisoner had carnal knowledge with her.

Baldessare (Cyril), R v (1931-34) XXIX Cox CC 193; (1930-31) Cr App R 70; (1931) 144 LTR 185; (1930) WN (I) 193 CCA Passenger in recklessly driven car may be guilty of criminal negligence by driving.

Baldry, Flack v [1988] 1 All ER 412; [1988] Crim LR 610; (1988) 152 JP 418; (1988) 132 SJ 89; [1988] 1 WLR 214 HC QBD Stun gun could be noxious thing but did not discharge anything so not prohibited weapon.

Baldry, Flack v (1988) 87 Cr App R 130; (1988) 138 NLJ 63; (1988) 132 SJ 334; [1988] 1 WLR 393 HL Electric stun gun 'discharged' noxious thing and was therefore a prohibited weapon.

Bale, Bennett v [1986] Crim LR 404 HC QBD Must intend to obstruct and actually obstruct police officer to be guilty of obstruction of police officer.

Ball (Anthony), R v; R v Winning [1983] Crim LR 546; (1983) 127 SJ 442; [1983] TLR 354 CA 'Recent possession' principle applies to handling by assisting in dealing with recently stolen goods.

Ball (Simon Leonard John), R v (1990) 90 Cr App R 378; [1989] Crim LR 579 CA Bona fide belief that arrest unlawful/police using excessive force not defence to assault.

Ball (William Henry) and Ball (Edith Lillian), R v (1910-11) 6 Cr App R 49; (1911) 80 LJCL 691 (also HL); (1911) 104 LTR 48 CCA Enforcement of HL decision in DPP v Ball and another restoring incest conviction.

Ball, R v [1989] Crim LR 730 CA On relevance of state of mind to determination whether death resulting from accused's unlawful and dangerous act was manslaughter.

Ball, R v [1983] 2 All ER 1089; (1983) 77 Cr App R 131; [1983] 1 WLR 801 CA 'Recent possession' principle applies to handling by assisting in dealing with recently stolen goods.

Ball, R v (1951-52) 35 Cr App R 24; (1951) 115 JP 210; [1951] 2 KB 109; (1951) 101 LJ 665; (1951) 95 SJ 239; (1951) WN (I) 130 CCA Is obtaining by false pretences to obtain property from person who does not own same but can transfer property therein.

Balmer, Smaje v [1965] 2 All ER 248; (1965) 129 JP 329 CrCt 'Dangerous or offensive weapon' under Larceny Act 1916, s 28(1) must be item fashioned to cause person injury.

Bamborough, R v [1996] Crim LR 744 CA Party to joint enterprise who may have thought pistol was unloaded and to be used for pistol-whipping was guilty of murder where gun in fact loaded and used to kill.

Banaster (Michael), R v (1979) 68 Cr App R 272; [1979] RTR 113 CA Was obtaining property by deception for mini-cab to be described as airport taxi and for driver to take 'correct' fare from passenger as though was required fare.

Bancroft (Basil), R v (1909) 3 Cr App R 16; (1909-10) XXVI TLR 10 CCA Obtaining money for advertisements in publication which did not have bona fide intention of publishing was obtaining money by false pretences.

Bank of Credit and Commerce International (Overseas) Ltd (in liquidation) and others v Price Waterhouse and others, Abu Dhabi and others (third parties); Bank of England intervening [1997] TLR 336 HC ChD Criminal offence to disclose bank information in breach of the Banking Act 1987, s 82(1).

Banks v Cope-Brown (1948) LXIV TLR 390 HC KBD Failed prosecution for charging extortionate rent contrary to Increase of Rent and Mortgage Interest (Restrictions) Act 1920.

Barr, R v [1978] Crim LR 244 CrCt On what is meant by public having 'access to a building in order to view' in the Theft Act 1968, s 11.

Barrass v Reeve [1981] Crim LR 417 HC QBD Making of any false representation in connection with obtaining of benefit (albeit that lie not directed towards obtaining of money) was unlawful obtaining of benefit.

Barrass, R v [1981] Crim LR 116 CA Six years' imprisonment merited by person guilty of various forgeries and of obtaining property on forged instrument and of theft.

Barrett (Alan Gordon), R v; R v Barrett (John Graham) (1981) 72 Cr App R 212; (1980) 124 SJ 542 CA Honest mistake of law defence unavailable once competent court has declared relevant law; test whether force used in self-defence is excessive is objective.

Barrett (George), R v [1976] 3 All ER 895; (1976) 63 Cr App R 174; [1976] Crim LR 576t; (1977) 141 JP 46; (1976) 126 NLJ 596t; (1976) 120 SJ 402; [1976] 1 WLR 946 CA Additional superintendant registrar of births/deaths/marriages can be guilty of corruption.

Barrett, Scudder v (1979) 69 Cr App R 277; [1980] QB 195; [1979] 3 WLR 591 HC QBD Need not prove intention to steal particular objects on charge of attempted theft/burglary.

Barrett, Wiltshire v [1965] 2 All ER 271; [1965] Crim LR 295t; (1965) 129 JP 348; [1966] 1 QB 312; (1965) 109 SJ 274; [1965] 2 WLR 1195 CA Valid arrest if police officer has reasonable suspicion are committing road traffic offence/are released once discover innocent or no case.

Barrette v Le Syndicat Lyonnais du Klondyke (1906-07) XXIII TLR 532 PC Dismissal of appeal where allegedly fraudulent misrepresentations central to case were unproven.

Barrow (Albert), R v (1932-34) 24 Cr App R 141 CCA Possession of cheque received in payment for stolen goods not adequate evidence of possession to sustain charge of having received goods.

Barry, Crown Prosecution Service v (1989) 153 JP 557 HC QBD Procuring fight between dog and badger not an offence under Protection of Animals Act 1911 as badger not a domestic/captive animal as the 1911 Act requires.

Barry, Director of Public Prosecutions v [1989] Crim LR 645; (1989) 133 SJ 784 HC QBD Offence of procuring fighting of animal under Protection of Animals Act 1911, s 1(1)(c) included wild animals.

Bartholomew, R v (1907-09) XXI Cox CC 556; (1908) 72 JP 79; [1908] 1 KB 554; (1908) XCVIII LTR 284; (1907-08) 52 SJ 208; [1908] 77 LJCL 275; (1907-08) XXIV TLR 238; (1908) WN (I) 20 CCR Coffee stall on highway not common nuisance.

Barton (Kevin John), R v (1987) 85 Cr App R 5; [1987] Crim LR 399; (1987) 131 SJ 74 CA Rape conviction proper despite exclusion of evidence of promiscuity - a discretionary matter for judge - where sought to raise consent defence.

Barton v Armstrong and others [1975] 2 All ER 465; [1976] AC 104; [1975] 2 WLR 1050 PC Agreement made under duress/undue influence in same category as those where fraudulent misrepresentation.

Barton, Osborn v (1950) 94 SJ 15; [1950] 66 (1) TLR 115 HC KBD Not obtaining credit in contravention of Bankruptcy Act 1914, s 155(a) for bankrupt to accept cheque and immediately send goods on foot thereof.

Barton, R v [1976] Crim LR 514 CA Actor in obscene film could be guilty of abetting later publication of obscene film for gain.

Bashir (Mohammed), R v (1983) 77 Cr App R 59; [1982] Crim LR 687 CA On proper direction regarding/on meaning of recklessness as to consent.

Bassey (EIH), R v (1930-31) Cr App R 160; (1931) 75 SJ 121; (1930-31) XLVII TLR 222 CCA Public mischief to induce Benchers of Inn of Court to admit as student a person who ought not to be admitted.

Bassi, R v [1985] Crim LR 671 CA Is act tending to pervert the course of justice for witness to agree not to appear in court in return for payment.

Bastable v Little [1904-07] All ER 1147; (1907-09) XXI Cox CC 354; (1907) 71 JP 52; [1907] 1 KB 59; (1906) 41 LJ 736; [1907] 76 LJKB 77; (1907) XCVI LTR 115; (1906-07) 51 SJ 49; (1906-07) XXIII TLR 38; (1906) WN (I) 196 HC KBD Person warning drivers of upcoming police speed trap not obstructing police in execution of duty.

Bastable v Metcalfe (1906) 70 JP 343 HC KBD Getting off one tram and getting on another without buying new ticket (even though had not travelled full distance on first ticket) was a fare offence.

Bastian, R v [1958] 1 All ER 568; (1958) 42 Cr App R 75; [1958] Crim LR 391; (1958) 102 SJ 272; [1958] 1 WLR 413 CCC On diminished responsibility/insanity.

Bateman and Linnecor, R v [1955] Crim LR 108 Assizes Would not be guilty of corruption if money advanced by company to army officer was reasonable price for stolen property rather than bribe for future favours.

Bates (William), R v (1930-31) Cr App R 49 CCA For purposes of Prevention of Crimes Act 1871, s 20, attempted burglary is not a crime.

Bates and another, R v [1952] 2 All ER 842; (1952) 36 Cr App R 175; (1952) 96 SJ 785; (1952) WN (I) 506 CCC 'Reckless' in Prevention of Fraud (Investments) Act 1939, s 12(1) has everyday meaning.

Bates v Bulman [1979] 3 All ER 170; (1979) 68 Cr App R 21; [1979] Crim LR 531; (1979) 143 JP 750; (1979) 123 SJ 688; [1979] 1 WLR 1190 HC QBD Borrowing non-offensive item intending to use it offensively not crime of having offensive weapon with one.

Bates v Director of Public Prosecutions (1993) 157 JP 1004; [1993] TLR 118 HC QBD Having unmuzzled dangerous dog inside car in public place constituted offence of having unmuzzled dangerous dog in public place.

Bates, Piddington v; Robson and another v Ribton-Turner [1961] Crim LR 262; [1961] 1 WLR 162 HC QBD Valid for police to act to prevent anticipated breach of peace where anticipation of same is reasonable.

Bathurst, R v [1968] 1 All ER 1175; (1968) 52 Cr App R 251; [1968] Crim LR 334; (1968) 118 NLJ 253t; [1968] 2 QB 99; (1968) 112 SJ 272; [1968] 2 WLR 1092 CA Remark on failure of person of diminished responsibility to give evidence unfair.

Batty (William), R v (1912) 76 JP 388; (1911-12) XXVIII TLR 485 CCA Receiving conviction quashed given tenuous connection between accused and crime.

Batty v Lee (1939-40) XXXI Cox CC 161; (1938) 102 JP 485; (1938) 82 SJ 871 HC KBD Prosecution ought to have been heard in action for leaving wife and child so were chargeable to public assistance committee (despite existence of maintenance order against husband being possible defence to charge).

Baxter v Matthews [1958] Crim LR 263 Magistrates Valid conviction under Highway Act 1835, s 78, for negligent interruption of free passage of carriage on the highway.

Baxter, R v [1977] Crim LR 686 CA Eight years' imprisonment for rape.

Baxter, R v (1974) 124 NLJ 648t CA Inappropriate to fine bankrupt guilty of bankruptcy offence simply because bankrupt's spouse had funds available.

Baxter, R v [1971] 2 All ER 359; [1971] Crim LR 281t; (1971) 135 JP 345; (1971) 121 NLJ 130t; [1972] 1 QB 1; (1971) 115 SJ 246; [1971] 2 WLR 1138 CA English courts had jurisdiction in attempted obtaining by deception case where person mailed false pools claims from Northern Ireland to Liverpool.

Bayley (Harry), R v (1908) 1 Cr App R 86 CCA Husband's alleged belief in invalidity of earlier marriage not defence to his entering into later bigamous union.

Bayley and Easterbrook, R v [1980] Crim LR 503 CA On necessary intent for attempted theft.

Bayliss v Hill and another [1984] TLR 254 HC QBD On use of search warrants.

Beach (William) and Morris (Arthur), R v (1909) 2 Cr App R 189 CCA Can convict two people for rioting with others.

Beacontree Justices; ex parte Mercer and others, R v (1969) 119 NLJ 1166t HC QBD Persons refused summonses for inter alia alleged riotous assembly under Statute of Forcible Entry Act 1381 - statute not in force.

Beal v Kelley [1951] 2 All ER 763; (1951-52) 35 Cr App R 128; (1951) 115 JP 566; (1951) 101 LJ 594; (1951) 95 SJ 685; [1951] 2 TLR 865; (1951) WN (I) 505 HC KBD Actual assault need not in itself be indecent to sustain indecent assault charge.

Beard (Arthur), R v (1919-20) 14 Cr App R 110; (1920) 84 JP 129 (also HL); (1919-20) XXXVI TLR 94 CCA On drunkenness as defence reducing murder to manslaughter; where force used in rape which results in death may be murder.

Beard, Director of Public Prosecutions v [1920] All ER 21; [1920] AC 479; (1918-21) XXVI Cox CC 573; (1919-20) 14 Cr App R 159; (1920) 84 JP 129 (also CCA); [1920] 89 LJCL 437; (1920) 55 LJ 116; (1920) 122 LTR 625; (1919-20) 64 SJ 340; (1919-20) XXXVI TLR 379; (1920) WN (I) 110 HL Cannot be guilty of murder if so drunk could not form necessary intent (are guilty of manslaughter); (temporary) insanity deriving from drink will sustain insanity defence.

Beasley (Dennis John), R v (1981) 73 Cr App R 44; [1981] Crim LR 635 CA Circumstances of case meant could not be convicted of common assault where charged with unlawful wounding.

Beate Uhse (UK) Ltd and another, Director of Public Prosecutions v [1974] 1 All ER 753; [1974] Crim LR 106; (1974) 138 JP 247; (1973) 123 NLJ 1112t; [1974] QB 158; (1974) 118 SJ 34; [1974] 2 WLR 50 HC QBD To send unsolicited non-explicit advertising material on sexual technique book an offence.

Beauchamp, Attorney-General v [1920] 1 KB 650; (1919-20) XXXVI TLR 174; (1920) WN (I) 15 HC KBD Publisher liable for punishment under 2 and 3 Vict c12, s 2 for not publishing name/address of printer on newspaper.

Beaumont, Police v [1958] Crim LR 620 Magistrates Successful plea of automatism (consequent upon pneumonia) in careless driving prosecution.

Becerra (Antonio), R v; R v Cooper (John David) (1976) 62 Cr App R 212 CA On means of dissociating self from common design.

Beck (Brian), R v [1985] 1 All ER 571; (1985) 80 Cr App R 355; (1985) 149 JP 260; (1984) 128 SJ 871; [1985] 1 WLR 22 CA Was procuring execution of valuable security to fraudulently use travellers' cheques/credit card vouchers abroad (in respect of which last payment occurred in England).

Beckford (Junior), R v (1992) 94 Cr App R 43; [1991] Crim LR 918 CA Matter for determination in each case whether police search and entry powers post-arrest of person for drugs possession was justified.

Beckford v R [1987] 3 All ER 425; [1988] AC 130; (1987) 85 Cr App R 378; [1988] Crim LR 116; (1987) 137 NLJ 591; (1987) 131 SJ 1122; [1987] 3 WLR 611 PC Self-defence plea grounded in mistake of fact to be judged on mistaken facts even if mistake unreasonable.

Bedder v Director of Public Prosecutions [1954] 2 All ER 801; (1954) 38 Cr App R 133; [1954] Crim LR 721; (1954) 104 LJ 536; (1954) 98 SJ 556; [1954] 1 WLR 1119 HL Test provocation by reference to reasonable man who need not possess characteristics peculiar to accused.

Beech, R v [1911-13] All ER 530; (1913-14) XXIII Cox CC 181; (1911-12) 7 Cr App R 197; (1912) 76 JP 287; (1912-13) 107 LTR 461 CCA Self-inflicted injuries directly resulting from threat of injury resulted in proper conviction for grievous bodily harm of party making threat.

Beechey v R (1915-17) XXV Cox CC 217; [1916] 85 LJPC 32; (1916) 114 LTR 1 PC Conspirator may be convicted as such though co-conspirator absent.

Beer, R v [1976] Crim LR 690t; (1976) 126 NLJ 791t CA Hyam direction rarely merited in murder cases (unmerited here).

Beese and another v Governor of Ashford Remand Centre and another [1973] 3 All ER 689; (1974) 138 JP 1; (1973) 123 NLJ 993t; (1973) 117 SJ 835; [1973] 1 WLR 1426 HL Judges' Rules inapplicable to foreign detectives; sufficiency of evidence.

Beeston and Stapleford UDC and another v Smith (1949) 113 JP 160 HC KBD Valid conviction for acting as solicitor.

Beetwell, R v [1967] Crim LR 532t CA Receiving conviction quashed where had been no evidence to support same.

Behrendt v Burridge [1976] 3 All ER 285; (1976) 63 Cr App R 202; [1976] Crim LR 522; (1976) 140 JP 613; (1976) 126 NLJ 667t; (1976) 120 SJ 538; [1977] 1 WLR 29 HC QBD Passive behaviour may still be soliciting.

Belfon, R v [1976] 3 All ER 46; (1976) 63 Cr App R 59; [1976] Crim LR 449t; (1976) 140 JP 523; (1976) 120 SJ 329; [1976] 1 WLR 741 CA For grievous bodily harm must do acts with intent to cause same.

Bell v Director of Public Prosecutions of Jamaica and another [1985] 2 All ER 585; [1985] Crim LR 738 PC Jamaican Constitution right to trial in reasonable time does not require prejudice; reasonableness judged by reference to general practice/conditions.

Bell, Director of Public Prosecutions v [1992] Crim LR 176; [1992] RTR 335 HC QBD Person with excess alcohol fleeing from dangerous scene in terror/not proven to have driven longer than necessary/ who did not cease being terrified while driving could rely on defence of duress.

Bell, R v [1978] Crim LR 233 CA On proving that person is living off earnings of prostitution.

Bell, Sawyer v [1962] Crim LR 390t HC QBD Abusive letters to bishops were defiance of recognisance to keep the peace and be of good behaviour.

Bellenie, R v [1980] Crim LR 437 CA Quashing of handling conviction in light of jury misdirection as to whether suspicion that goods stolen was adequate basis for handling conviction.

Belton, R v (1976) 126 NLJ 467t CA On recklessness as an element of foreseeability.

Belville, Bond v [1963] Crim LR 103t HC QBD Valid dismissal of information in which had been alleged that hunt foxhounds had worried cattle.

Bennett (William Anthony), R v; R v Wilfred (Charles); R v West (Clyde Brierley) (1979) 68 Cr App R 168; [1979] Crim LR 454 CA On burden of proof where common law conspiracy charged.

Bennett v Bale [1986] Crim LR 404 HC QBD Must intend to obstruct and actually obstruct police officer to be guilty of obstruction of police officer.

Bennett v Brown (1980) 71 Cr App R 109 HC QBD Twentieth century Mauser 8mm rifle and Mauser pocket pistol were/nineteenth century Enfield .476 Mk 3 revolver were not/was antique firearm so firearms certificate was/was not required.

Bennett v Horseferry Road Magistrates' Court and another [1993] 3 All ER 138; (1993) 143 NLJ 955; (1993) 137 SJ LB 159/172 HL Rule of law more important than public interest in punishment of crime; tacit extradition via deportation an abuse of process.

Benstead (Peter David), R v; R v Taylor (Malcolm) (1982) 75 Cr App R 276; [1982] Crim LR 456; (1982) 126 SJ 308; [1982] TLR 152 CA Obtaining of irrevocable letter of credit could ground conviction for procuring execution of valuable security.

Bentham and others, R v [1972] 3 All ER 271; (1972) 56 Cr App R 618; [1972] Crim LR 640; (1972) 136 JP 761; [1973] QB 357; (1972) 116 SJ 598; [1972] 3 WLR 398 CA Possession of firearms with intent even if intent not immediate/is conditional.

Bentley v Brudzinski (1982) 75 Cr App R 217; [1982] Crim LR 825; [1982] TLR 122 HC QBD Unlawful arrest of person remaining with constable as volunteer meant assault on constable was not assault on constable in execution of duty.

Bentley v Mullen [1986] RTR 7 HC QBD Supervisor of learner driver convicted of aiding and abetting latter in not stopping after accident occurred.

Bentley, R v (1923) 87 JP 55; [1923] 1 KB 403; [1923] 92 LJCL 366; (1922-23) 67 SJ 279; (1922-23) XXXIX TLR 105; (1922) WN (I) 335 CCA Inciting criminal act details of which not arranged/inciting another to incite another to commit criminal act was punishable offence.

Benyon, McGregor v [1957] Crim LR 250 Magistrates Person could not be guilty of larceny by finding where was given (originally stolen) handbag by her daughter (who found the handbag).

Benyon, McGregor v [1957] Crim LR 608 HC QBD Person could be guilty of larceny by finding where was given (originally stolen) handbag by her daughter (who found the handbag).

Berg (Alexander), R v; R v Britt (Robert); R v Carré (Constance); R v Lummies (Bert) (1927-28) 20 Cr App R 38 CCA Meaning of 'disorderly house' at common law; admissibility in charge of keeping disorderly house of letters found therein referring to behaviour there.

Berger (Edward), R v (1914-15) 11 Cr App R 72; [1915] 84 LJKB 541; (1914-15) XXXI TLR 159 CCA Not receiver if did not enjoy control over goods.

Bergin, R v [1969] Crim LR 328; (1969) 113 SJ 283 CA Absent fraudulent conversion of hire purchase car accused could not be guilty of larceny by bailee.

Berkeley v Orchard [1975] Crim LR 225; (1975) 119 SJ 353 HC QBD Connection between possession conviction and injury suffered by another who accepted drug from possessor too tenuous to support criminal compensation award.

Bernhard, R v [1938] 2 All ER 140; (1939-40) XXXI Cox CC 61; (1936-38) 26 Cr App R 137; (1938) 102 JP 282; [1938] 2 KB 264; (1938) 85 LJ 243; [1938] 107 LJCL 449; (1938) 82 SJ 257; (1937-38) LIV TLR 615; (1938) WN (I) 142 CCA On term 'claim of right' in Larceny Act 1916, s 1(1).

Berry (David Donald), R v (1986) 83 Cr App R 7; [1986] Crim LR 394 CA History of relationship with victim inadmissible to establish motive in murder without motive or to establish intent when killing occurred.

Berry (No 3), R v [1994] 2 All ER 913; (1994) 99 Cr App R 88; [1995] 1 WLR 7 CA Offence of making explosive substance involves knowing that item of manufacture/ in possession/under control can cause explosion.

Berry, R v [1984] 2 All ER 296; (1985) 80 Cr App R 98; [1984] Crim LR 421; (1984) 128 SJ 399; [1984] TLR 192; [1984] 1 WLR 824 CA Jury cannot have regard to use of timers abroad when deciding whether 'lawful intent' behind making of timers in England.

Berry, R v [1985] AC 246; [1985] Crim LR 102; (1985) 149 JP 276; (1984) 128 SJ 851; [1984] TLR 677; [1984] 3 WLR 1274 HL Offence of making explosive substance involves knowing that item of manufacture/ in possession/under control can trigger explosion and reasonably suspect manufactured item will not be used lawfully.

Best v Butler and another (1931-34) XXIX Cox CC 482 HC KBD Trade union officer's withholding trade union moneys a continuing offence.

Best, Eaton v [1908-10] All ER 651; (1911-13) XXII Cox CC 66; (1909) 73 JP 113; [1909] 1 KB 632; (1909) 44 LJ 63; [1909] 78 LJKB 425; (1909) C LTR 494; (1908-09) XXV TLR 244 HC KBD What constitutes 'habitual drunkard' (under Habitual Drunkards Act 1879, s 3).

Bettaney, R v [1985] Crim LR 104 CA Quality of material taken not gauged by reference to purpose for which taken; jurors with previous dishonesty convictions legitimately asked by Crown to stand by.

Bettles, R v [1966] Crim LR 503t CCA Person was accessory before the fact if loaned car to another so that latter might commit a crime.

Betts and Ridley, R v (1931-34) XXIX Cox CC 259; (1930-31) Cr App R 148; (1931) 144 LTR 526 CCA Party to common design guilty of murder committed by other party thereto even if latter used more force/acted in way other than agreed.

Betts v Stevens [1908-10] All ER 1245; (1911-13) XXII Cox CC 187; (1909) 73 JP 486; [1910] 1 KB 1; (1909) 44 LJ 629; (1910) 79 LJKB 17; (1909-10) 101 LTR 564; (1909-10) XXVI TLR 5; (1909) WN (I) 200 HC KBD Person warning motorists of upcoming police speed trap were obstructing police in execution of their duty.

Betty (Carol), R v (1964) 48 Cr App R 6; [1964] Crim LR 132 CCA Where in course of concerted attack (in which was not intended to kill/cause grievous bodily harm) one party forms intent to kill and does (hence murder) other party to concert guilty only of manslaughter.

Bevan (David John), R v (1987) 84 Cr App R 143; [1987] Crim LR 129 CA Was obtaining pecuniary advantage by deception triable in England to use cheques abroad in respect of English bank account that was overdrawn.

Bevans, R v [1988] Crim LR 236; (1988) 132 SJ 90 CA Demanding injection of pain reliever at gun-point was blackmail.

Bezzina, R v; R v Codling; R v Elvin [1994] 3 All ER 964; (1994) 99 Cr App R 356; (1994) 158 JP 671; (1994) 138 SJ LB 11; [1993] TLR 629; [1994] 1 WLR 1057 CA Dangerous Dogs Act 1991, s 3(1) imposed strict liability on owners of dogs when latter are in public places and out of control.

Bhachu (Harminder), R v (1977) 65 Cr App R 261 CA Cashier guilty of appropriation where undercharged customer whom knew and who then left with goods.

Bishirgian, R v; R v Howeson; R v Hardy [1936] 1 All ER 586; (1934-39) XXX Cox CC 379; (1934-36) 25 Cr App R 176; (1936) 81 LJ 260; (1936) 154 LTR 499; (1935-36) LII TLR 361 CCA Glossing of truth in prospectus rendered its publication a contravention of Larceny Act 1916, s 84.

Bishop and Grantway, R v (1918-21) XXVI Cox CC 182; (1917-18) 13 Cr App R 42; (1918) 82 JP 79; [1918] 1 KB 310; [1918] 87 LJCL 440; (1918) 118 LTR 379; (1917-18) XXXIV TLR 139; (1917) WN (I) 383 CCA Conviction for conspiracy to avoid effects of Military Service Acts.

Bishop Cavanagh (Commodities) Ltd, Hudson v [1982] Crim LR 114; (1981) 131 NLJ 1238 HC QBD Conviction merited for mailing circulars in violation of Prevention of Fraud (Investments) Act 1958, s 14(1) albeit that circulars mailed to particular persons who answered newspaper advertisement.

Bishop, Seneviratne v [1978] RTR 92 HC QBD Invalid arrest where constable failed to examine crystals after some air blown into breathalyser (though bag not filled).

Bisp, R v [1957] Crim LR 249 Sessions Consent of woman could be defence to indecent assault charge albeit that woman had been certified under the Lunacy Act 1890.

Bisset, R v (1979) 123 SJ 718; [1980] 1 WLR 335 CMAC On what constitutes condonation of offence (no condonation here).

Black, Cohen and another v [1942] 2 All ER 299; [1942] 111 LJ 573; (1943) 93 LJ 100; (1942) 86 SJ 210; (1941-42) LVIII TLR 306; (1942) WN (I) 119 HC KBD For loitering with intent arrest must be acts arousing suspicion preceding arrest; police officers' evidence could be pooled.

Blackburn and another, Knott v [1944] 1 All ER 116; (1944) 108 JP 19; [1944] KB 77; [1944] 113 LJ 154; (1944) 170 LTR 55; (1944) 88 SJ 60; (1943-44) LX TLR 92; (1943) WN (I) 253 HC KBD Fenced-in railway siding not an enclosed area for purposes of Vagrancy Act 1824, s 4.

Blackburn v Bowering [1995] Crim LR 38; [1993] TLR 551; [1994] 1 WLR 1324 CA Person pleading self-defence to be judged on facts however perceived them (whether reasonably or unreasonably) to be; must be guilty of assault to be guilty of aggravated assault.

Blady, Director of Public Prosecutions v (1911-13) XXII Cox CC 715; (1912) 76 JP 141; [1912] 2 KB 89; (1912) 81 LJKB 613; (1912) 106 LTR 302; (1911-12) XXVIII TLR 193 HC KBD Wife's evidence as prosecution witness could not be admitted under common law/Criminal Evidence Act 1898.

Blain, R v [1963] Crim LR 444t CMAC Successful appeal against conviction which Crown did not on appeal seek to support.

Blake (Jason Joseph), R v; R v Ronald O'Connor (1979) 68 Cr App R 1; [1979] Crim LR 464 CA Offer to supply controlled drug a broadly drawn offence.

Blake v Director of Public Prosecutions [1993] Crim LR 586 HC QBD Not lawful excuse to criminal damage charge (vicar writing anti-government policy graffiti on pillar) that had genuine belief were acting in accordance with what God wanted (and so law of England protected).

Blake, R v [1964] Crim LR 142t CCA Could be tried for breaking/stealing though were already convicted of receiving.

Blake, R v [1997] 1 All ER 963; [1997] 1 Cr App R 209; [1997] Crim LR 207; (1996) TLR 13/8/96; [1997] 1 WLR 1167 CA Unlicensed broadcasting an absolute offence.

Blakely and another v Director of Public Prosecutions [1991] Crim LR 763; [1991] RTR 405; [1991] TLR 288 HC QBD Recklessness an inappropriate consideration when deciding whether person had necessary mens rea to be guilty of procuring principal to commit offence.

Blamires Transport Services, Ltd and another, R v [1963] 3 All ER 170; (1963) 47 Cr App R 272; [1963] Crim LR 698; (1963) 127 JP 519; (1963) 113 LJ 594; (1963) 107 SJ 598; [1963] 3 WLR 496 CCA Conspiracy triable by indictment though substantive offence summary.

Bland, R v [1988] Crim LR 41; (1987) 151 JP 857 CA Aiding and abetting requires some form of constructive action so mere knowledge that boyfriend a drug-dealer not enough to support aiding and abetting conviction.

Bland, R v [1968] Crim LR 683t CMAC Dismissal of appeal against finding that had behaved to prejudice of good order/military discipline (fought with sergeant when 'drunk' - for purposes of Army Act 1955, s 43).

Blankley, R v [1979] Crim LR 166/248 CrCt Contractual licensee not protected under the Rent Act 1965, s 30.

Blaub, R v (1975) 139 JP 841 CA Was stabbing which caused murder even though was refusal (on religious grounds) of victim to accept blood transfusion which necessarily brought about death.

Blaue, R v [1975] 3 All ER 446; (1975) 61 Cr App R 271; [1975] Crim LR 648; (1975) 125 NLJ 844t; (1975) 119 SJ 589 CA Person using violence on other must take victim as is.

Blease, Low v [1975] Crim LR 513; (1975) 119 SJ 695 HC QBD Trespasser who made telephone call not guilty of stealing property (electricity).

Blick, R v [1966] Crim LR 508t; (1966) 110 SJ 545 CCA Evidence from juror which aided in rebuttal of alibi defence proffered by accused was validly admitted.

Block, Michaels v (1917-18) XXXIV TLR 438 HC KBD On extent of power to arrest without warrant under Consolidated Defence of the Realm Regulations 1914, regulation 55.

Block, Patterson v [1984] TLR 398 HC QBD Failed appeal against conviction for possession of offensive weapon (lock-knife).

Bloom (Harry), R v (1910) 74 JP 183 CCA Person wearing ring of husband with whose wife had eloped must have been party to taking of ring or known ring belonged to husband to be guilty of larceny.

Bloomfield v Williams [1970] Crim LR 292t; [1970] RTR 184 HC QBD Person who did not know that what were signing was false could not be guilty of false declaration.

Bloomfield, Comer v (1971) 55 Cr App R 305; [1971] Crim LR 230; [1971] RTR 49 CA Letter of inquiry to insurance company (preliminary to unmade false claim) not attempted obtaining of property by deception.

Bloxham (Bernard Conrad), R v (1942-44) 29 Cr App R 37 CCA Was no taking and carrying away/attempt at same so could not be convicted of larceny.

Bloxham, R v [1982] 1 All ER 582; [1983] 1 AC 109; (1982) 74 Cr App R 279; [1982] Crim LR 436; (1982) 146 JP 201; [1982] RTR 129; (1982) 126 SJ 154; [1982] 2 WLR 392 HL Buyer of goods not 'another person' for whom goods sold as is buying; buying of goods not disposal or realisation of goods by buyer.

Bloxham, R v [1981] 2 All ER 647; (1981) 72 Cr App R 323; [1981] Crim LR 337; [1981] RTR 376; (1981) 125 SJ 198; [1982] TLR 75; [1981] 1 WLR 859 CA Can be undertaking/assisting in retention of goods for anyone benefiting from purchase of goods.

Blyth Juvenile Court; ex parte G, R v [1991] Crim LR 693 HC QBD Judicial review not an appropriate route for seeking of bail; need not be enormous change in circumstances to merit further bail application.

Board of Control and others; ex parte Rutty, R v [1956] 1 All ER 769; [1956] Crim LR 331; (1956) 106 LJ 234; [1956] 2 QB 109; [1956] 2 WLR 822 HC QBD Affidavit evidence admissible to test judicial finding; cannot under Mental Deficiency Act 1927, s 2 issue reception order unless person 'found neglected' - meaning thereof.

Board of Trade v Owen and another [1957] 1 All ER 411; [1957] AC 602; (1957) 41 Cr App R 11; [1957] Crim LR 244; (1957) 121 JP 177; (1957) 107 LJ 104; (1957) 101 SJ 186; [1957] 2 WLR 351 HL Conspiracy to fully commit crime abroad not indictable in England.

Board of Trade, Keslake v [1903] 2 KB 453 HC KBD Absent court order cannot make post-desertion deduction from seaman's wages.

Bocking v Roberts [1973] 3 All ER 962; (1978) 67 Cr App R 359; [1973] Crim LR 517; (1974) 138 JP 13; (1973) 123 NLJ 516t; [1974] QB 307; (1973) 117 SJ 581; [1973] 3 WLR 465 HC QBD Possession however small the quantity as long as enough to show not possession on earlier date.

Bodin (Leif Viktor) and Bodin (Dolores Patricia), R v [1979] Crim LR 176 CA No offence of inciting someone to become accessory before the fact to an offence (assault).

Bogdal v Hall [1987] Crim LR 500 HC QBD On proving receipt of supplementary benefit in cases where alleged that obtained same by deception.

Boggeln v Williams [1978] 2 All ER 1060; (1978) 67 Cr App R 50; [1978] Crim LR 242; (1978) 142 JP 503; (1978) 128 NLJ 242t; (1978) 122 SJ 94; [1978] 1 WLR 873 HC QBD Reconnection of electricity supply without permission not unlawful where no dishonest intent.

Bolton (Roger John Alexander), R v (1992) 94 Cr App R 74; [1992] Crim LR 57; (1992) 156 JP 138; [1991] TLR 323 CA Jury ought to have been allowed decide whether execution of securities was in part purpose of conspiracy.

Bolton v Crawley [1972] Crim LR 222 CA Assault occasioning actual bodily harm did not require mens rea so though had injected oneself with drugs could not claim did not possess mens rea for said offence.

Bolton, Stunt v [1972] Crim LR 561; [1972] RTR 435; (1972) 116 SJ 803 HC QBD Passenger refusing to give ignition key to police officer seeking to make car safe after driver arrested was obstructing same in execution of duty.

Bond v Belville [1963] Crim LR 103t HC QBD Valid dismissal of information in which had been alleged that hunt foxhounds had worried cattle.

Bong (Kwan Ping) and another v R [1979] AC 609; [1979] Crim LR 245; [1979] 2 WLR 433 PC Quashing of unauthorised possession of drugs conviction where jury possibly laboured under misapprehension as to burden of proof.

Bonner and others, R v [1970] 2 All ER 97; (1970) 54 Cr App R 257; [1970] Crim LR 299; (1970) 134 JP 429; (1970) 120 NLJ 224t; (1970) 114 SJ 188; [1970] 1 WLR 838 CA On theft of property by one business partner from another.

Bonnick (Derek Denton), R v (1978) 66 Cr App R 266; [1978] Crim LR 246; (1977) 121 SJ 791 CA On when self-defence to go to jury: self-defence evidence may arise even where accused pleads alibi.

Bonnyman (Alexander Gordon), R v (1940-42) 28 Cr App R 131; (1942) 86 SJ 274 CCA On negligence necessary to sustain manslaughter conviction.

Bonsall and others, R v [1985] Crim LR 151 CrCt Three months' imprisonment plus fine merited for striking miners guilty of offences under Public Order Act 1936, s 5/Conspiracy and Protection Act 1875, s 7.

Booth, Alderson v [1969] 2 All ER 271; (1969) 53 Cr App R 301; [1969] Crim LR 270t; (1969) 133 JP 346; (1969) 119 NLJ 225t; [1969] 2 QB 216; (1969) 113 SJ 268; [1969] 2 WLR 1252 HC QBD Any words clearly informing person that are under compulsion is valid arrest.

Booth, R v (1946) 90 SJ 347 CCA On proving receiving.

Boothby (Edwin), R v (1932-34) 24 Cr App R 112 CCA False pretences conviction quashed where had been questioned at trial on alleged false pretence post-dating that with which charged.

Borro and Abdullah, R v [1973] Crim LR 513 CA Facts gave court jurisdiction to try persons for conspiracy to evade restriction on importation of dangerous drug.

Boswell (and others), R v [1973] Crim LR 307 CA On elements of offence of (constructive) manslaughter.

Bottrill, ex parte Kuchenmeister, R v [1946] 1 All ER 635; [1947] KB 41; (1946) 96 LJ 232; (1946) 90 SJ 321; (1945-46) LXII TLR 374 HC KBD Enemy alien interned during wartime cannot seek writ of habeas corpus.

Bottrill; ex parte Kuchenmeister, R v [1946] 2 All ER 434; [1946] 115 LJ 500; (1946) 175 LTR 232; (1945-46) LXII TLR 570; (1946) WN (I) 177 CA Enemy alien interned during wartime cannot seek writ of habeas corpus.

Botwright, Squires v [1973] Crim LR 106; [1972] RTR 462 HC QBD That constable had blocked person from moving while conducted his inquiries did not mean had not been acting in course of duty.

Bouch, R v [1982] 3 All ER 918; (1983) 76 Cr App R 11; [1982] Crim LR 675; [1983] QB 246; (1982) 126 SJ 511; [1982] TLR 392; [1982] 3 WLR 673 CA Petrol bomb an 'explosive substance' under Explosive Substances Act 1883.

Boughton, R v (1911-13) XXII Cox CC 599; (1912) 76 JP 51 CCC Must be a trader to be convicted as trader pawning goods.

Boulden (Edward Ernest), R v (1957) 41 Cr App R 105; [1957] Crim LR 322 CCA On what constitutes 'abandonment' of child under Children and Young Persons Act 1933, s 1(1).

Boulden, R v [1957] Crim LR 182 Sessions Successful prosecution for abandonment/neglect of children: on what constitutes abandonment/neglect.

Boulter, R v (1908) 72 JP 188 CCC On what constitues blasphemous libel.

Bourne (Sydney Joseph), R v (1952) 36 Cr App R 125 CCA Consent irrelevant to bestiality charge.

Bourne, R v [1938] 3 All ER 615; [1939] 1 KB 687; (1938) 86 LJ 115; [1939] 108 LJCL 471 CCC On danger to life versus danger to health; on acts of abortionist versus those of surgeon.

Bournemouth Magistrates' Court; ex parte Cross, Griffin and Pamment (1989) 89 Cr App R 90, R v [1989] Crim LR 207; (1989) 153 JP 440 HC QBD On attaching conditions when granting bail to person charged with offence not punishable by imprisonment.

Bow Street Magistrates' Court and another; ex parte Allison, R v [1997] TLR 291 HC QBD On what constitutes (as here) an 'urgent' extradition case for the purposes of the United States of America (Extradition) Order 1976.

Bow Street Magistrates' Court; ex parte Hall and Otobo, R v (1986) 136 NLJ 1111 CA Recognisance may remain valid despite change in bail conditions.

Bow Street Magistrates' Court; ex parte Paloka, R v [1995] TLR 597 HC QBD Need be no reference to limitation in materials presented as part of extradition request.

Bow Street Magistrates' Court; ex parte Van der Holst, R v (1986) 83 Cr App R 114 HC QBD Admissibility of various pieces of evidence in extradition proceedings.

Bow Street Magistrates; ex parte Mackeson, R v (1982) 75 Cr App R 24 CA Prohibition of committal proceedings where party had been subject of deportation by means of purported extradition.

Bow Street Stipendiary Magistrate and another; ex parte Noncyp, R v (1989) 89 Cr App R 121; [1990] 1 QB 123; (1989) 133 SJ 1031 CA Obscenity in customs and excise condemnation proceedings was obscenity in terms of Obscene Publications Act 1959, s 1(1) - public good defence not available.

Bow Street Stipendiary Magistrate and another; ex parte Noncyp, R v (1988) 132 SJ 1063 HC QBD Definition of obscenity in Obscene Publications Act 1959/public good defence under s 4 thereof did not require consideration in prosecution under the Customs Consolidation Act 1876, s 42.

Bowden, R v (1995) 159 JP 502; [1996] 1 Cr App R 104; [1996] Crim LR 57; [1995] TLR 142; [1996] 1 WLR 98 CA Any person appointed to perform public duty can be guilty of misconduct in public office (need not be Crown officer/agent).

Bowden, R v [1993] Crim LR 380 CA On intoxication and intent.

Bowditch, R v [1991] Crim LR 831 CA On burden of proof as regards proving cruelty to child under Children and Young Persons Act 1933.

Bowe, United States Government v [1989] 3 All ER 315; [1990] 1 AC 500; [1990] Crim LR 196; (1989) 133 SJ 1298; [1989] 3 WLR 1256 PC Conspiracy to commit drug offence an extraditable offence; no award of costs available in criminal cause or matter.

Bowen (Cecil), R v [1996] 4 All ER 837; [1996] 2 Cr App R 157; [1996] Crim LR 577; (1996) 146 NLJ 442; (1996) 140 SJ LB 100; (1996) TLR 19/3/96; [1997] 1 WLR 372 CA On determining presence of duress in case involving low-intelligence person.

Bowen, Tartellin v [1947] 2 All ER 837; (1948) 112 JP 99; [1948] LXIV TLR 20; (1948) WN (I) 15 HC KBD Member of Armed Forces guilty of possession of firearm (privately purchased for self) without certificate.

Bowering, Blackburn v [1995] Crim LR 38; [1993] TLR 551; [1994] 1 WLR 1324 CA Person pleading self-defence to be judged on facts however perceived them (whether reasonably or unreasonably) to be; must be guilty of assault to be guilty of aggravated assault.

Bowker, Morgan v [1963] 1 All ER 691; [1963] Crim LR 280; (1963) 127 JP 264; (1963) 113 LJ 302; [1964] 1 QB 507; (1963) 107 SJ 155; [1963] 2 WLR 860 HC QBD Justices hearing obscene publication forfeiture arguments may hear later action; type/carrying out of business part of circumstances in which materials found.

ALPHABETICAL INDEX

Bowler (Ronald Arthur), R v (1973) 57 Cr App R 275 CA On appropriate sentence for petty theft by employee.

Bowley, Wills v [1982] 2 All ER 654; [1983] 1 AC 57; (1982) 75 Cr App R 164; [1982] 3 WLR 10 HC QBD Police have power of arrest where reasonably suspect crime committed in their sight.

Bowley, Wills v [1982] 2 All ER 654; [1983] 1 AC 57; (1982) 75 Cr App R 164; [1982] Crim LR 580; (1982) 146 JP 309; (1982) 126 SJ 411; [1982] TLR 286; [1982] 3 WLR 10 HL Police have power of arrest where reasonably suspect crime committed in their sight.

Bowyer v Morgan (1907-09) XXI Cox CC 203; (1906) 70 JP 252; (1906-07) XCV LTR 27; (1905-06) 50 SJ 377; (1905-06) XXII TLR 426 HC KBD Branding of sheep on nose with hot iron not cruelty.

Boyea, R v [1992] Crim LR 574; (1992) 156 JP 505; [1992] TLR 40 CA On victim's consent as (non-) defence to indecent assault where assault was 'likely' (ordinary meaning) to cause non-transient/-trifling injury (meaning of latter notions explained).

Boyesen (Peregrine), R v (1981) 72 Cr App R 43 CA Possession of trivial amount of controlled drug could not sustain possession conviction.

Boyesen, R v [1982] 2 All ER 161; [1982] AC 768; (1982) 75 Cr App R 51; [1982] Crim LR 596; (1982) 146 JP 217; (1982) 132 NLJ 609; (1982) 126 SJ 308; [1982] TLR 215; [1982] 2 WLR 882 HL Possession of any amount of controlled drug may ground possession conviction.

Boylan, R v [1960] Crim LR 193 Sessions Not guilty of larceny of 10s note which was handed voluntarily to accused for another but not given by accused to that other.

Boyle (George), R v; R v Boyle (James) (1987) 84 Cr App R 270; [1987] Crim LR 111 CA Courts could look to pre-Criminal Attempts Act 1981 law to determine what constitutes an attempt.

Boyle, R v [1993] Crim LR 40 CA On correct procedure as regards dealing with bail absconder.

Boyle, R v [1954] 2 All ER 721; (1954) 38 Cr App R 111; [1954] Crim LR 790; (1954) 118 JP 481; (1954) 104 LJ 488; [1954] 2 QB 292; (1954) 98 SJ 559; [1954] 3 WLR 364 CCA Can be guilty of housebreaking where trick one's entry into house.

Boyle, R v; R v Merchant [1914-15] All ER 553; (1914-15) XXIV Cox CC 406; (1914) 10 Cr App R 180; (1914) 78 JP 390; [1914] 3 KB 339; [1914] 83 LJKB 1801; (1914-15) 111 LTR 638; (1913-14) 58 SJ 673; (1913-14) XXX TLR 521; (1914) WN (1) 236 CCA Threatening to lambast company in newspaper unless demands met was demand for money with menaces; similar fact evidence admissible to rebut accident/mistake defence - to prove guilty intent.

Bozickovic, R v [1978] Crim LR 686 CrCt Could not be guilty of burglary with intent to steal as entered building without knowing/to ascertain if there was anything worth stealing so did not have requisite intent.

Brabham v Wookey (1901-02) XVIII TLR 99 HC KBD Person using indecent language inside his house, heard by two officers outside but not proved to have annoyed passer-by could be convicted of offence of using indecent language contrary to Bristol Improvement Act 1840, s 77.

Bracknell Justices, ex parte Griffiths, R v (1975) 125 NLJ 111t HC QBD Conviction of mental nurse for assault on patient quashed as had been acting in on duty-capacity (Mental Health Act 1959, s 141 applied).

Bradbury, R v [1996] Crim LR 808 CA On ingredients of offence of permitting premises to be used for the supply of drugs.

Bradbury, R v; R v Edlin [1956] 2 QB 262 HC QBD Offence of fraud on the Crown and the public an indictable common law offence.

Bradish, R v [1990] 1 All ER 460; (1990) 90 Cr App R 271; [1990] Crim LR 723; (1990) 154 JP 21; [1990] 1 QB 981; (1989) 133 SJ 1605; [1990] 2 WLR 223 CA Possession of prohibited weapon a strict liability offence.

Bradley (Ivan), R v (1980) 70 Cr App R 200; [1980] Crim LR 173 CA Evidence of previous different handling inadmissible in later prosecution for receiving under Theft Act 1968, s 27(3)(a).

Bradley (John Alfred), R v (1910) 4 Cr App R 225; (1910) 74 JP 247 CCA Conviction to be quashed if jury possibly believed consent not a defence to rape.

Brightling, R v [1991] Crim LR 364 CA On effect of belief that persons apprehending one are not police officers to guilt for assault with intent to resist arrest.

Brightside and Carbrook (Sheffield) Co-operative Society Ltd v Phillips (1964) 108 SJ 53; [1964] 1 WLR 185 CA Can make non-specific claim of conversion.

Brindley, R v; R v Long [1971] 2 All ER 698; (1971) 55 Cr App R 258; [1971] Crim LR 276t; (1971) 135 JP 357; (1971) 121 NLJ 178t; [1971] 2 QB 300; (1971) 115 SJ 285; [1971] 2 WLR 895 CA Need not show accused knew identity of offender to sustain charge of assisting them.

British India Steam Navigation Co Ltd, Leesh River Tea Co Ltd and others v [1967] 2 QB 250; [1966] 3 WLR 642 CA Shipowners as bailees for reward of goods carried by them not liable for theft by stevedores who were not their agents/servants.

British Transport Police, De Cristofaro v [1997] Crim LR 124; (1996) TLR 7/5/96 HC QBD Valid conviction of busker for unlawfully soliciting for reward for playing of music in London Underground station.

Brittain and others, R v [1972] 1 All ER 353; (1972) 56 Cr App R 234; [1972] Crim LR 104t; (1972) 136 JP 198; (1971) 121 NLJ 1169t; [1972] 1 QB 357; [1972] 2 WLR 450 CA No intention to occupy premises needed to sustain forcible entry conviction.

Britton, R v [1973] Crim LR 375; [1973] RTR 502 CA Valid conviction for attempting to defeat the course of justice by drinking alcohol so as to render the laboratory specimen provided unreliable.

Britton, R v [1967] 1 All ER 486; (1967) 51 Cr App R 107; [1967] Crim LR 179t; (1967) 131 JP 235; [1967] 2 QB 51; (1966) 110 SJ 977; [1967] 2 WLR 537 CA Leaving racist leaflets in private porch not distribution to public/section thereof under Race Relations Act 1965, s 6.

Brixton Prison Governor; ex parte Atkinson, R v [1970] Crim LR 661t HL Refusal of habeas corpus application arising in course of extradition proceedings.

Brixton Prison Governor; ex parte McCheyne, R v (1951) 95 SJ 353; [1951] 1 TLR 1155 HC KBD Fugitive discharged where return to country of crime would be unjust/oppressive/involve too severe a punishment (Fugitive Offenders Act 1881, s 10).

Brixton Prison Governor and another, ex parte Enahoro, R v [1963] 2 All ER 477; [1963] Crim LR 566; [1963] 2 QB 455; [1963] 2 WLR 1260 HC QBD Person will be released if over one month delay after committal unless Home Secretary convinces otherwise; Home Secretary free to/not to have fugitive returned to whence is fugitive.

Brixton Prison Governor and others, Royal Government of Greece v [1969] 3 All ER 1337; [1970] Crim LR 29t; [1971] AC 250; (1970) 134 JP 47; (1969) 119 NLJ 1045t; (1969) 113 SJ 901; [1969] 3 WLR 1107 HL If sufficient evidence for committal magistrate must commit.

Brixton Prison Governor, ex parte Atkinson, R v [1969] 2 All ER 1146; [1969] Crim LR 487t; (1969) 133 JP 617; (1969) 113 SJ 690 HC QBD Post-arrest preferring of charges admissible; question of oppression not matter for court; presumption requesting state will respect extradition treaty despite contrary indications in affidavit.

Brixton Prison Governor, ex parte Kahan, R v [1989] 2 All ER 368; [1989] QB 716; (1989) 133 SJ 121; [1989] 2 WLR 721 HC QBD Extradition to Fiji possible because Fiji a 'designated Commonwealth country' although outside Commonwealth.

Brixton Prison Governor, ex parte Kotronis, R v [1969] 3 All ER 304; [1969] Crim LR 600; (1969) 133 JP 674; (1969) 119 NLJ 902t; (1969) 113 SJ 794; [1969] 3 WLR 528 HC QBD No extradition despite conviction certificate as conviction contrary to natural justice.

Brixton Prison Governor, ex parte Soblen, R v [1962] 3 All ER 640; [1962] Crim LR 700t; (1962) 112 LJ 733; [1963] 2 QB 243 (also HC QBD); (1962) 106 SJ 736; [1962] 3 WLR 1154 CA Difference between deportation and extradition.

Brixton Prison Governor, R v; Re Anwera [1907] 76 LJKB 661 HC KBD Extradition allowed despite passing of five-year prescriptive period in requesting country as had not passed when extradition order made.

Brixton Prison Governor; ex parte Pitt-Rivers, R v [1942] 1 All ER 207 HC KBD Detention order good on face/conforming with procedural requirements precluded writ of habeas corpus being issued.

Brown, R v [1965] Crim LR 108; (1964) 108 SJ 921 CCA Must intend through disposal of property to aid thief to avoid arrest to be guilty as accessory after the fact.

Brown, R v [1996] 1 All ER 545; [1996] 1 AC 543; [1996] 2 Cr App R 72; [1996] Crim LR 408; (1996) 146 NLJ 209; (1996) 140 SJ LB 66; (1996) TLR 9/2/96; [1996] 2 WLR 202 HL For there to be unlawful 'use' of data it must be employed for a purpose, not just accessed or retrieved.

Brownlow, R v (1910) 74 JP 240; (1909-10) XXVI TLR 345 CCA Must be intent to defraud to be guilty of obtaining credit under false pretences contrary to Debtors Act 1869, s 13(1).

Brudzinski, Bentley v (1982) 75 Cr App R 217; [1982] Crim LR 825; [1982] TLR 122 HC QBD Unlawful arrest of person remaining with constable as volunteer meant assault on constable was not assault on constable in execution of duty.

Bruhn (Jacob) v R (on the prosecution of the opium farmer) [1909] AC 317; [1909] 78 LJPC 85 PC Master of steamship properly convicted for importing opium though unaware ship contained chandu.

Brummitt (Ernest) and Matthews (George), R v (1910) 4 Cr App R 192 CCA Can prove offences in (other than three necessary to sustain) prosecution as habitual criminal.

Brutus v Cozens [1972] 2 All ER 1297; [1973] AC 854; (1972) 56 Cr App R 799; [1973] Crim LR 56; (1972) 136 JP 636; (1972) 122 NLJ 681t; (1972) 116 SJ 647; [1972] 3 WLR 521 HL Behaviour causing affront/being rude need not be 'insulting behaviour' contrary to Public Order Act 1936, s 5 (as amended).

Brutus, Cozens v [1972] 2 All ER 1; (1972) 136 JP 390; (1972) 116 SJ 217; [1972] 1 WLR 484 HC QBD Behaviour causing affront is 'insulting behaviour'.

Bruzas (John), R v [1972] Crim LR 367 CrCt On whether provocation a defence to attempted murder; on whether is an offence of attempted manslaughter.

Bryan v Mott (1976) 62 Cr App R 71; [1976] Crim LR 64t; (1975) 125 NLJ 1093t; (1975) 119 SJ 743 HC QBD Broken milk bottle was offensive weapon and carrying it about for purpose of committing suicide not reasonable excuse.

Bryan v Robinson [1960] 2 All ER 173; [1960] Crim LR 489; (1960) 124 JP 310; (1960) 110 LJ 381; (1960) 104 SJ 389 HC QBD Hostess at refreshment house doorway seeking to entice custom not guilty of insulting behaviour.

Bryant, R v [1955] 2 All ER 406; (1955) 39 Cr App R 59; [1955] Crim LR 505; (1955) 105 LJ 346; (1955) 99 SJ 438; [1955] 1 WLR 715 CMAC Charge of common law larceny should not refer to Larceny Act 1916.

Bryant, R v [1956] 1 All ER 340; [1956] Crim LR 200; (1956) 120 JP 103; (1956) 100 SJ 113; [1956] 1 WLR 133 CMAC On larceny by party under military law.

Bryce (Marshall Nicholas), R v (1956) 40 Cr App R 62; [1956] Crim LR 122 CCA On what constitutes fraudulent conversion.

Bryson v Gamage Limited (1907-09) XXI Cox CC 515; (1907) 71 JP 439; [1907] 2 KB 630; [1907] 76 LJKB 936; (1907-08) XCVII LTR 399; (1907) WN (I) 164 HC KBD 'Pistol' under Pistols Act 1903 includes spring pistols from which shot/bullets dischargeable.

Bryson, R v [1985] Crim LR 669 CA On necessary intention to be guilty of wounding with intent.

Bubb, R v (1906) 70 JP 143 CCR Person charged with another (found guilty) as principal ought not to have been convicted as accessory after the fact.

Buck and Buck, R v (1960) 44 Cr App R 213; [1960] Crim LR 760 Assizes Must be found guilty of (at least) manslaughter where death results from criminal abortion; person procuring criminal abortion that results in death is accessory before fact to manslaughter.

Buck, Fowkes and Howland, R v [1964] Crim LR 223t CCA Failed appeal on basis of non-direction that rejection of alibi was not admission that had committed offence.

Buckett, Rose v [1901] 2 KB 449; [1901] 70 LJK/QB 736; (1901) LXXXIV LTR 670; (1900-01) XVII TLR 544; (1901-02) 50 WR 8 CA Right of action for trespass/conversion did not pass to trustee upon plaintiff becoming bankrupt.

Buckingham (David), R v (1976) 63 Cr App R 159; [1977] Crim LR 674 CA Conditional/ unconditional intention/allowance of other to use thing to damage property immediately/ sometime in future means are guilty of offence under Criminal Damage Act 1971, s 3.

Buckland, Pallin v (1911-13) XXII Cox CC 545; (1911) 75 JP 362 HC KBD Accused found as matter of fact not to have run away and left children.

Buckley (Leslie), R v; R v Lane (David) (1979) 69 Cr App R 371; [1979] Crim LR 664; CA To 'supply' a drug under Misuse of Drugs Act 1971, s 37(1) also means to distribute same.

Budd v Anderson, Morrrison and Williamson [1943] 2 All ER 452; [1943] KB 642; (1943) WN (I) 150 HC KBD Technical error in detention order did not render it invalid.

Budd, R v [1962] Crim LR 49t; (1962) 112 LJ 105 CCA On proving/disproving automatism.

Bull (Adrian William), R v (1994) 99 Cr App R 193; [1994] Crim LR 224; (1993) 137 SJ LB 202; [1993] TLR 464 CA Firearms dealer exemption from need for firearms certificate applied to place not person (so ought to have had certificate in respect of ammunition stored in unnotified place).

Bull, Director of Public Prosecutions v [1994] 4 All ER 411; [1995] 1 Cr App R 413; [1994] Crim LR 762; (1994) 158 JP 1005; [1995] QB 88; [1994] TLR 314; [1994] 3 WLR 1196 HC QBD Male prostitute not a 'common prostitute'.

Bull, King v (1934-39) XXX Cox CC 567; (1937) 81 SJ 219; (1937) WN (I) 76 HC KBD Conviction for unlicensed use of apparatus for wireless telegraphy.

Bullard (Joseph) v R [1961] 3 All ER 470; [1957] AC 635; (1957) 41 Cr App R 1; [1957] Crim LR 816; (1957) 121 JP 576; (1957) 101 SJ 797 PC Evidence that does not support self defence plea could support provocation plea; must be clear to jury from direction that burden of proving guilt rests with prosecution.

Buller and Co, Ltd v TJ Brooks, Ltd [1930] All ER 534; (1929-30) XLVI TLR 233 HC KBD Persons to whom stolen ring pawned could not be sued for its return by persons from whom title to goods originally derived but who did not own goods at time of pawning.

Bullock, R v [1955] 1 All ER 15; (1954) 38 Cr App R 151; [1955] Crim LR 179; (1955) 119 JP 65; (1955) 99 SJ 29; [1955] 1 WLR 1 CCA Jury question indicating believed general unlawful purpose existed justified non-explanation by judge when answering of general versus particular unlawful purpose distinction.

Bulman, Bates v [1979] 3 All ER 170; (1979) 68 Cr App R 21; [1979] Crim LR 531; (1979) 143 JP 750; (1979) 123 SJ 688; [1979] 1 WLR 1190 HC QBD Borrowing non-offensive item intending to use it offensively not crime of having offensive weapon with one.

Bulman, Nichols v [1985] RTR 236 HC QBD Invalid arrest meant obtaining blood/urine specimens impermissible.

Bunche (Jacques Emmanuel), R v (1993) 96 Cr App R 274; (1993) 157 JP 780; [1992] TLR 513 CA Could be convicted of attempting to obtain property by deception where sought passport using false name.

Bundy, R v [1977] 2 All ER 382; (1977) 65 Cr App R 239; [1977] Crim LR 570; (1977) 141 JP 345; (1977) 127 NLJ 468t; [1977] RTR 357; (1977) 121 SJ 252; [1977] 1 WLR 914 CA Car could be place of abode but not when in transit.

Bunnett, Davidge v [1984] Crim LR 297 HC QBD Cheques given by persons with whom shared house to meet gas bill owed collectively was property to be used as sought so long as gas bill was paid.

Bunyard v Hayes [1985] RTR 348; [1984] TLR 603 HC QBD Issue of lawfulness of arrest did not not affect culpability for failure to provide breath specimen.

Buono, R v [1970] Crim LR 154 CA Documents that were either hire purchase agreements/proposal forms were valuable securities.

Burbridge, Solomon v [1956] Crim LR 276t; (1956) 120 JP 231 HC QBD On elements of causing unnecessary obstruction (contrary to Motor Vehicles (Construction and Use) Regulations 1955, r89) in way leave car parked.

Burdee, R v (1915-17) XXV Cox CC 598; (1916-17) 12 Cr App R 153; [1917] 86 LJCL 871; (1916-17) 115 LTR 904 CCA Anyone treating another medically must be competent and use reasonable skill: if not and death occurs is manslaughter.

Burden v Rigler and another (1911) 75 JP 36; [1911] 1 KB 337; (1910-11) 103 LTR 758; (1910-11) XXVII TLR 140; (1910) WN (I) 279 HC KBD Public meeting held on highway not per se unlawful: legality depends on circumstances.

Burditt v Joslin [1981] 3 All ER 203; (1982) 146 JP 39 HC QBD Ownership but non-residency of property insufficient for application for firearms certifiate from chief police officer in area of residence.

Burge v Director of Public Prosecutions [1962] 1 All ER 666; [1962] Crim LR 178t; (1962) 106 SJ 198 HC QBD On male soliciting (by advertisement).

Burge, R v [1961] Crim LR 412 Sessions Appeals Committee Placing card in shop window advertising one's availability for homosexual activities was soliciting.

Burgess and McLean, R v [1995] Crim LR 425 CA Manslaughter convictions substituted for murder convictions where defence of provocation ought to have been, but was not left to jury.

Burgess, Director of Public Prosecutions v [1970] 3 All ER 266; [1970] Crim LR 597t; (1970) 134 JP 646; (1970) 120 NLJ 661t and 946; [1971] 1 QB 432; (1970) 114 SJ 768; [1970] 3 WLR 805 HC QBD DPP must consent to gross indecency towards child prosecution; gross indecency towards child means gross indecency involving child.

Burgess, Fox v (1921-25) XXVII Cox CC 162; [1922] 1 KB 623 HC KBD Father properly convicted of not causing child to attend school where knowingly sent to school in such a state that was not admitted.

Burgess, Ludlow and others v (1982) 75 Cr App R 227; [1971] Crim LR 238 HC QBD Not assault on constable in execution of duty where person unlawfully detained by constable assaults same.

Burgess, R v [1991] 2 All ER 769; (1991) 93 Cr App R 41; [1991] Crim LR 548; (1991) 141 NLJ 527; [1991] 2 QB 92; [1991] TLR 161; [1991] 2 WLR 1206 CA Passing disorder prompting violent behaviour and caused by internal factor comes within M'Naghten Rules and is not non-insane automatism.

Burgess, R v [1965] Crim LR 726t CCA On determining presence of diminished responsibility.

Burgoyne, Jordan v [1963] 2 All ER 225; [1963] Crim LR 362t; (1963) 127 JP 368; (1963) 113 LJ 400; [1963] 2 QB 744; (1963) 107 SJ 338; [1963] 2 WLR 1045 HC QBD Audience are as found: if words provoke breach of peace by them is an offence.

Burke (Robert), R v (1978) 67 Cr App R 220; [1978] Crim LR 431 CA Determining whether firearm an antique is question of fact for jury.

Burke v Copper [1962] 2 All ER 14; (1962) 126 JP 319; (1962) 106 SJ 451; [1962] 1 WLR 700 HC QBD Forfeiture in respect of all photographs: some could not be more obscene than others.

Burke, R v [1990] 2 All ER 385; [1991] 1 AC 135; (1990) 91 Cr App R 384; [1990] Crim LR 877; (1990) 154 JP 798; (1990) 140 NLJ 742; (1990) 134 SJ 1106 HL Acts that are not civil wrongs may be harassment if intended to secure tenant's departure.

Burke, R v; R v Clarkson; R v Howe; R v Bannister [1986] Crim LR 331; (1986) 130 SJ 110 CA On duress as a defence to murder.

Burke, R v; R v Howe; R v Bannister; R v Clarkson [1987] Crim LR 480; (1987) 131 SJ 258 HL On duress as a defence to murder.

Burnby, R v (1901) 36 LJ 310; [1901] 70 LJK/QB 739; (1901-02) LXXXV LTR 168 HC KBD Permitting licensed premises to be used as brothel a continuing offence.

Burns (Dafydd John), R v (1974) 58 Cr App R 364; [1975] Crim LR 155 CA On insanity vis-à-vis automatism.

Burns (James), R v; R v Ralph (Michael Peter); R v Jackson (Stephen Ronald); R v Burns (Sidney) (1984) 79 Cr App R 173 CA Person could be prosecuted for conspiracy to commit offence though immune from prosecution for substantive offence.

Burrell v Harmer [1967] Crim LR 169 CA Tattooist guilty, upon tattoos administered to two boys becoming inflamed, of causing actual bodily harm to the boys.

Burrell v Harmer (1965-66) 116 NLJ 1658 HC QBD Tattooist not guilty, upon tattoos administered to two boys becoming inflamed, of causing actual bodily harm to the boys.

Burridge, Behrendt v [1976] 3 All ER 285; (1976) 63 Cr App R 202; [1976] Crim LR 522; (1976) 140 JP 613; (1976) 126 NLJ 667t; (1976) 120 SJ 538; [1977] 1 WLR 29 HC QBD Passive behaviour may still be soliciting.

Burrows, R v [1952] 1 All ER 58; (1951-52) 35 Cr App R 180; (1952) 116 JP 47; (1952) 96 SJ 122; [1952] 1 TLR 51; (1952) WN (I) 21 CCA Absent violent act cannot be indecent assault.

Burstow (Andrew Christopher), R v [1997] 1 Cr App R 144; [1997] Crim LR 452; (1996) 140 SJ LB 194; (1996) TLR 30/7/96 CA Offence of inflicting grievous bodily harm includes cases of psychiatric injury consequent upon non-physical injury.

Burstow, R v [1996] Crim LR 331 CrCt Offence of inflicting grievous bodily harm includes cases of psychiatric injury consequent upon non-physical injury.

Burton v Atkinson (1907-09) XXI Cox CC 575; (1908) 72 JP 198; (1908) XCVIII LTR 748; (1907-08) XXIV TLR 498 HC KBD Foxhound puppy not required to wear collar when on highway.

Burton, Ellis v [1975] 1 All ER 395; [1975] Crim LR 32; (1975) 139 JP 199 HC QBD Cannot dismiss charge where plea of guilty as no hearing 'upon the merits'.

Buswell, R v [1972] 1 All ER 75; [1972] Crim LR 30t; (1972) 136 JP 141; (1971) 121 NLJ 1026t; (1972) 116 SJ 36; [1972] 1 WLR 64 CA Possession of prescription drugs not unlawful when prescription ends.

Butcher, Carter v [1965] Crim LR 247g HC QBD Valid conviction for wilful pretence of being qualified to work as solicitor.

Butler and another, Best v (1931-34) XXIX Cox CC 482 HC KBD Trade union officer's withholding trade union moneys a continuing offence.

Butler v Gregory (1901-02) XVIII TLR 370 HC KBD Father of illegitimate child who did not have care/custody of child nor had bastardy proceedings brought against him not father for purposes of Prevention of Cruelty to Children Act 1894, s 23.

Butler, R v [1988] Crim LR 695 CA Sword stick an offensive weapon per se.

Butler, R v (1954) 38 Cr App R 57; [1954] Crim LR 379t CCA Completing pools coupons in false names was forgery/putting amounts down that signatories could not pay was not forgery.

Butters, R v [1959] Crim LR 215 Sessions Was attempted gross indecency to write letter to another inviting him to commit act of gross indecency with writer.

Butterworth, Kay v (1945) 173 LTR 191; (1945) 89 SJ 381; (1944-45) LXI TLR 452 HC KBD That driver of car was asleep and so unaware of offences not defence to charges of careless and dangerous driving.

Butterworth, Kay v (1946) 110 JP 75 CA Person driving car while asleep was guilty of careless and dangerous driving.

Button v Director of Public Prosecutions; Swain v Director of Public Prosecutions [1965] 3 All ER 587; [1966] AC 591; (1966) 50 Cr App R 36; [1966] Crim LR 39; (1966) 130 JP 48; (1965-66) 116 NLJ 131; (1965) 109 SJ 872; [1965] 3 WLR 1131 HL Affray need not occur in public place to be affray.

Button, R v [1900-03] All ER 1648; (1899-1901) XIX Cox CC 568; (1900) 35 LJ 458; [1900] 69 LJCL 901; (1900-01) LXXXIII LTR 288; [1900] 2 QB 597; (1899-1900) 44 SJ 659; (1899-1900) XVI TLR 525; (1900) WN (I) 176; (1899-1900) 48 WR 703 CCR Was attempting to obtain goods by false pretences to deliberately enter prize race under false name and so receive false handicap.

Button, R v; R v Swain [1965] Crim LR 294t; (1965) 109 SJ 193; [1965] 2 WLR 992 CCA Affray occurs where fight between two or more persons in any place which puts fear into uninvolved third party.

Buxton, Webley v [1977] 2 All ER 595; (1977) 65 Cr App R 136; [1977] Crim LR 160; (1977) 141 JP 407; [1977] QB 481; [1977] RTR 193; (1977) 121 SJ 153; [1977] 2 WLR 766 HC QBD Can convict of attempted offence even if complete offence proved.

Cain, R v [1984] 2 All ER 737; [1985] AC 46; (1984) 79 Cr App R 298; [1984] Crim LR 679; (1985) 149 JP 73; (1984) 134 NLJ 886; (1984) 128 SJ 530; [1984] TLR 471; [1984] 3 WLR 393 HL Criminal bankruptcy order a 'sentence' against which no appeal unless challenging jurisdiction of court making order; judge determines at sentencing stage if conspiracy to commit crimes from which loss resulted.

Cain, R v; R v Schollick [1975] 2 All ER 900; (1975) 61 Cr App R 186; (1975) 139 JP 598; (1975) 125 NLJ 553; [1976] QB 496; (1975) 119 SJ 422; [1975] 3 WLR 131 CA Attorney-General's duty under Explosive Substances Act is to consider generalities not minutiae of charge.

Calder and Boyars Ltd, R v [1968] 3 All ER 644; (1968) 52 Cr App R 706; [1968] Crim LR 614t; (1969) 133 JP 20; [1969] 1 QB 151; (1968) 112 SJ 688; [1968] 3 WLR 974 CA Proecdure in obscene publications case; issue is whether would deprave/corrupt a significant proportion of readers - what is 'significant proportion' to be gauged by jury.

Calder Justices, ex parte Kennedy, R v [1992] Crim LR 496; (1992) 156 JP 716; [1992] TLR 65 HC QBD Could apply for bail where had not been granted bail at earlier stage because of lack of information on which justices could make decision.

Calderhead (David Glen), R v; R v Bidney (Harold) (1979) 68 Cr App R 37 CA Landlord charging inflated rent to woman knew was prostitute was living on earnings of prostitution.

Caldicott (Walter) v The Commissioners appointed to inquire into corrupt practices at the City of Worcester Parliamentary (1906) Election (The Director of Public Prosecutions intervening) (1907-09) XXI Cox CC 404 Assizes Absent evidence of prior agreement post-voting payment of voters not bribery; Election Commissioners not estopped from acting in relation to illegal practices by earlier decision of Election Petition Judges.

Caldwell (James), R v (1980) 71 Cr App R 237; [1980] Crim LR 572 CA Self-induced drunkenness relevant to deciding whether were criminally reckless.

Caldwell v Leech [1911-13] All ER 703; (1913-14) XXIII Cox CC 510; (1913) 77 JP 254; (1913-14) 109 LTR 188; (1912-13) XXIX TLR 457 HC KBD That have one prostitute in one's house cannot sustain conviction for keeping/managing brothel.

Caldwell, Mogan v [1919] 88 LJCL 1141; (1918-19) XXXV TLR 381 HC KBD Shipowner enjoys property in untouched provisions given to seaman by shipmaster pursuant to Merchant Shipping Act 1906, s 25(1) but larceny of said goods unproven here.

Caldwell, R v [1981] 1 All ER 961; [1982] AC 341; (1981) 73 Cr App R 13; [1981] Crim LR 392; (1981) 145 JP 211; (1981) 131 NLJ 338; (1981) 125 SJ 239; [1981] 2 WLR 509 HL Definition of recklessness; self-induced intoxication irrelevant to recklessness.

Calhaem, R v [1985] 2 All ER 266; (1985) 81 Cr App R 131; [1985] Crim LR 303; [1985] QB 808; (1985) 129 SJ 331; [1985] 2 WLR 826 CA 'Counsel' crime if advise or solicit other to act and does; need not be major reason for offence.

Calland, R v [1967] Crim LR 236 Assizes On what constitutes corruption.

Callender, R v [1992] 3 All ER 51; (1992) 95 Cr App R 210; [1992] Crim LR 591; (1992) 156 JP 903; (1992) 142 NLJ 716; [1993] QB 303; (1992) 136 SJ LB 112; [1992] TLR 178; [1992] 3 WLR 501 CA For purposes of Theft Act contract to provide services an employment contract.

Calvert v Mayes [1954] 1 All ER 41; [1954] Crim LR 147; (1954) 118 JP 76; [1954] 1 QB 342; (1954) 98 SJ 13; [1954] 2 WLR 18 HC QBD Payment of money direct to accused rather than via prostitutes (over whom exercised some control) did not mean were not living off earnings of prostitution.

Cambridge, R v [1994] 2 All ER 760; (1994) 99 Cr App R 142; [1994] Crim LR 690; (1994) 158 JP 799; (1994) 144 NLJ 267; [1994] TLR 77; [1994] 1 WLR 971 CA Real evidence of provocation requires that judge leave issue of provocation to jury.

Campbell (Colin Frederick), R v (1987) 84 Cr App R 255; [1987] Crim LR 257 CA Diminished responsibility not to be left to jury despite psychiatrist witness' suggestion of same as defence had not sought to rely on it as defence.

Campbell (Colin Frederick), R v [1997] 1 Cr App R 199; [1997] Crim LR 227 CA Re-trial ordered where in light of new psychiatric evidence (unavailable at trial) defence of diminished responsibility might have been successfully relied upon.

Campbell (Guy), R v; R v Campbell (Shaun) [1982] Crim LR 595 CrCt Sons holding party in parents' house were not 'occupiers' of house.

Campbell (Mary Sylvia), R v (1985) 80 Cr App R 47; [1984] Crim LR 683; [1984] TLR 500 CA Was forgery to endorse cheque and so secure payment from bank which would not have made if knew of true circumstances.

Campbell and others, R v (1959) 103 SJ 434 CrCt CrCt could but did not make habeas corpus order in respect of prisoner whose trial was postponed but in its discretion ordered that case lie on file, not be proceeded with absent court order.

Campbell v Edwards [1976] 1 All ER 785 CA Absent fraud/collusion mistaken non-speaking report by valuer cannot be set aside.

Campbell, Bridge v (1947) 177 LTR 444; (1947) 91 SJ 459; (1947) LXIII TLR 470; (1947) WN (I) 223 HC KBD Loitering of suspected person with intent to commit felony an offence that can be committed from within motor-vehicle (Vagrancy Act 1824, s 4).

Campbell, Cain v [1978] Crim LR 292 CA Must intend to catch salmon to be guilty of offence under Salmon and Freshwater Fisheries Act 1975, s 19.

Campbell, Mounsey v [1983] RTR 36 HC QBD Bumper to bumper parking by van driver occasioned unnecessary obstruction.

Campbell, R v [1997] Crim LR 495 CA Cannot plead diminished responsibility as defence to attempted murder.

Campbell, R v [1959] 2 All ER 557; [1959] Crim LR 362; (1959) 123 JP 361 CrCt Habeas Corpus Act 1679, s 6 only applies if procedural terms therein complied with (not here but discretion exercised).

Campbell, R v [1991] Crim LR 268 CA On what constitutes an attempt (no fixed rule).

Camplin, Director of Public Prosecutions v [1978] 2 All ER 168; [1978] AC 705; (1978) 67 Cr App R 14; [1978] Crim LR 432; (1978) 142 JP 320; (1978) 128 NLJ 537t; (1978) 122 SJ 280; [1978] 2 WLR 679 HL 'Reasonable man' not just adult male; unusual characteristics of accused relevant to 'reasonable man' test.

Camplin, R v [1978] 1 All ER 1236; (1978) 66 Cr App R 37; [1977] Crim LR 748; (1977) 127 NLJ 938t; [1978] QB 254; (1977) 121 SJ 676; [1977] 3 WLR 929 CA 'Reasonable man' where youth charged is person of youth's age.

Candy, R v; R v Wise; R v Wise [1990] TLR 524 CA That received advice from counsel that what were doing was not a criminal act was not a defence to said act.

Cannon (Terence Francis), R v; R v James (Roy George) (1986) 82 Cr App R 286 CA Criminal bankruptcy order properly made where was clear evidence of connection between subjects of order and handling of stolen goods.

Canterbury and St Augustine's Justices, ex parte Klisiak, R v; R v Ramsgate Justices, ex parte Warren and others [1981] 2 All ER 129 HC QBD Magistrates must look to value of property in deciding if right to jury trial; substitution by prosecution of summary charge where non-prosecution of indictable charge not an abuse of process.

Carberry, R v [1994] Crim LR 446 CA Party to joint enterprise (knifing) that resulted in death of another could be guilty of manslaughter though had not used knife.

Caresana, R v [1996] Crim LR 667 CA Deception involving letters of credit did not involve requisite appropriation to constitute theft; English courts would assume jurisdiction in deception case with international aspects where gist of offence/appropriation occurred within England and Wales.

Carey v Chief Constable of Avon and Somerset [1995] RTR 405 CA Removal by police of converted coach parked by kerb but not obstructing road-users was unlawful.

Carey v Martin [1954] Crim LR 139t HC QBD Was not attempted larceny to break shop skylight (with intent to enter) and then to run away.

Cargill, R v (1913-14) XXIII Cox CC 382; [1913] 82 LJKB 655; (1913) 108 LTR 816; (1912-13) XXIX TLR 382 CCA Accused could not later seek to counter prosecution's opening (unobjected) allegation of seduction as was irrelevant to charge of unlawful carnal knowledge.

Carmichael and Sons Ltd v Cottle [1971] Crim LR 45t; (1970) 120 NLJ 1040t; [1971] RTR 11; (1970) 114 SJ 867 HC QBD Persons hiring car to another could not be said to be using it/were not accessories before the fact to the car being used with threadbare tyres.

Carnegie and Webber, R v [1994] Crim LR 591 CA Second false alibi by second person did not destroy false alibi already given by another person.

Carnill v Edwards and others [1953] 1 All ER 282; (1953) 117 JP 93; (1953) 97 SJ 98; [1953] 1 WLR 290 HC QBD Prostitutes committing indecent acts in car not 'wandering in a public highway'.

Caroubi, R v (1913-14) XXIII Cox CC 177; (1911-12) 7 Cr App R 149; (1912) 76 JP 262; (1912-13) 107 LTR 415 CCA Conviction of larceny by wife (in presence of husband) set aside for inadequate direction on collusion/coercion.

Carpenter, R v (1911-13) XXII Cox CC 618; (1912) 76 JP 158 CCC On what constitutes intent to defraud.

Carr, R v [1956] 3 All ER 979; (1956) 40 Cr App R 188; (1957) 121 JP 58; [1957] Crim LR 113; (1957) 101 SJ 112 CMAC On bribery: was offence to accept bribe as inducement to do favour (favour need not actually be done).

Carr-Briant, R v [1943] 2 All ER 156; (1943) 107 JP 167; [1943] 112 LJ 581; (1944) 94 LJ 100; (1943) 169 LTR 175; (1943) WN (I) 134 CCA On burden of proof in prosecution under Prevention of Corruption Act 1916.

Carroll (Deborah Louise), R v; R v Perkins (Sean Daid); R v Dickerson (Andrea) (1994) 99 Cr App R 381; [1993] Crim LR 613 CA Must be evidence of more than one witness (or other buttressing evidence) to support conviction for perjury.

Carter Patersons and Pickfords Carriers Limited v Wessel [1947] 2 All ER 280; (1947) 111 JP 474; [1947] KB 849; (1947) 97 LJ 373; [1947] 116 LJR 1370; (1947) 177 LTR 448; (1947) 91 SJ 446; (1947) LXIII TLR 517; (1947) WN (I) 216 HC KBD Aider and abettor, a principal in second degree, can be treated as principal in first degree; robber passing his stolen goods to receiver can himself be convicted as receiver.

Carter v Butcher [1965] Crim LR 247g HC QBD Valid conviction for wilful pretence of being qualified to work as solicitor.

Carter v Richardson [1974] Crim LR 190; [1974] RTR 314 HC QBD Supervising driver validly convicted of aiding and abetting learner driver in offence of driving with excess alcohol.

Carter, R v [1956] Crim LR 772 Sessions On admissibility/effect of previous 'similar fact' evidence of homosexual encounters on instant charge of indecent assault of young boy.

Cartledge v Allen [1973] Crim LR 530 HC QBD Person who injured self in running away from others who had threatened him thereby suffered infliction of grievous bodily harm by those others.

Carver, R v [1978] 3 All ER 60; (1978) 67 Cr App R 352; (1978) 142 JP 620; (1978) 128 NLJ 635t; [1978] QB 472; (1978) 122 SJ 332; [1978] 2 WLR 872 CA No possession if amount of drug is so minute as to amount to nothing.

Cascoe, R v [1970] 2 All ER 833; (1970) 54 Cr App R 401; [1970] Crim LR 644; (1970) 134 JP 603 CA Proper direction on law/burden of proof necessary once provocation left to jury.

Casement, R v [1916-17] All ER 214; (1915-17) XXV Cox CC 503; (1916-17) 12 Cr App R 99; [1917] 1 KB 98 (also HC KBD); (1916) 51 LJ 375; [1917] 86 LJCL 467 (also HC KBD); (1916-17) 115 LTR 277; (1915-16) 60 SJ 656; (1915-16) XXXII TLR 667 CCA Treason involves giving aid/comfort to King's enemies inside/outside realm; treason triable before HC KBD.

Casement, R v (1915-17) XXV Cox CC 480; [1917] 1 KB 98 (also CCA); [1917] 86 LJCL 467 (also CCA); (1916-17) 115 LTR 267; (1915-16) XXXII TLR 601 HC KBD Treason involves giving aid/comfort to King's enemies inside/outside realm.

Casey, R v (1947) 91 SJ 693; (1947) LXIII TLR 487; (1947) WN (I) 265 CCA Crown's calling prison-doctor as medical witness so that he might be cross-examined by defence seeking to establish accused's insanity is not good practice.

Cash, R v [1985] 2 All ER 128; (1985) 80 Cr App R 314; [1985] Crim LR 311; [1985] QB 801; (1985) 129 SJ 268; [1985] 2 WLR 735 CA Words 'in the course of the stealing' irrelevant to charge of handling save where theft/possession very close in time.

Cashmarts, Lacis v (1968) 112 SJ 1005; [1969] Crim LR 102t; [1969] 2 QB 400; [1969] 2 WLR 329 HC QBD In supermarket/cash and carry property passes when price paid: here authorised manager intended to pass property (albeit at unintended reduced price) so taking of property and carrying away not larceny.

Cassidy, Ende v [1964] Crim LR 595t HC QBD Was prima facie good reason to believe that where motor vehicle guilty of obstructing free passage along highway owner of same responsible.

Castiglione and Porteous, R v (1913-14) XXIII Cox CC 46; (1911-12) 7 Cr App R 233; (1912) 76 JP 351; (1912) 106 LTR 1023; (1911-12) XXVIII TLR 403 CCA False swearing of affidavit.

Castorina v Chief Constable of Surrey (1988) 138 NLJ 180 CA On determining reasonableness of police arrest.

Caswell, R v [1984] Crim LR 111 CrCt On extent to which immunity of husband from liability for raping wife extends to sexual activities leading up to full intercourse.

Cato and others, R v [1976] 1 All ER 260; (1976) 62 Cr App R 41; [1976] Crim LR 59t; (1976) 140 JP 169; (1975) 125 NLJ 1066t; (1975) 119 SJ 775; [1976] 1 WLR 110 CA Consent of victim to unlawful act not defence/is relevant to question of recklessness/negligence; injection of drug an unlawful act from which manslaughter could spring; substance noxious if likely to cause injury when used; direct, intended injection of drug done 'maliciously'.

Catron, Nicoll v (1985) 81 Cr App R 339; [1985] Crim LR 223; (1985) 149 JP 424 HC QBD Could not be guilty of harbouring escaped 'prisoner' where escapee had fled on way to remand centre.

Cattle, Lewis v [1938] 2 All ER 368; (1939-40) XXXI Cox CC 123; (1938) 102 JP 239; [1938] 2 KB 454; [1938] 107 LJCL 429; (1938) 82 SJ 376; (1937-38) LIV TLR 721; (1938) WN (I) 169 HC KBD Police officer a 'person holding office under His Majesty' within meaning of Official Secrets Act 1911, s 2.

Cavendish, R v [1961] 2 All ER 856; [1961] Crim LR 623; (1961) 125 JP 460; (1961) 111 LJ 469; [1961] 1 WLR 1083 CCA Must show arranged for delivery of goods or aware that they arrived took control over them: otherwise no possession.

Cawley v Frost (1977) 64 Cr App R 20; [1976] Crim LR 747 (cf [1977] Crim LR 170); (1977) 141 JP 30; (1976) 126 NLJ 953t; (1976) 120 SJ 703; [1976] 1 WLR 1207 HC QBD Football ground a public place under terms of Public Order Act 1936. ss 5 and 9(1).

Central Criminal Court and another; ex parte AJD Holdings and others, R v [1992] TLR 76 HC QBD On need for care in applying for/effecting of search warrant.

Central Criminal Court, ex parte Francis and Francis (a firm), R v [1988] 1 All ER 677; [1989] AC 346 (also HL); (1988) 87 Cr App R 104; [1988] Crim LR 305; (1988) 138 NLJ 14; (1988) 132 SJ 302; [1988] 2 WLR 627 HC QBD Police application for production of documents normally ex parte but subject must be allowed seek discharge/variation before effected; legal privilege attaches to client not solicitor - criminal intent of client vitiates privilege.

Central Criminal Court, ex parte Francis and Francis, R v [1989] AC 346 (also HC QBD); [1989] Crim LR 444; (1988) 138 NLJ 316; (1988) 132 SJ 1592 HL Legal privilege attaches to client not solicitor - criminal intent of client vitiates privilege.

Central Criminal Court, ex parte Guney, R v [1995] 2 All ER; [1995] 2 Cr App R 350; (1995) 139 SJ LB 66; [1995] TLR 52; [1995] 1 WLR 576 CA Recognisance ends once defendant arraigned.

Central Criminal Court, ex parte Guney, R v [1994] 2 All ER 423; [1995] 1 Cr App R 50; (1994) 138 SJ LB 58; [1994] TLR 55; [1994] 1 WLR 438 HC QBD Arraignment possible even if defendant not in custody.

Central Criminal Court, ex parte Guney, R v [1996] 2 All ER 705; [1996] AC 616; [1996] 2 Cr App R 352; [1996] Crim LR 896; (1996) 146 NLJ 716; (1996) 140 SJ LB 124; (1996) TLR 10/5/96; [1996] 2 WLR 675 HL Recognisance ends once defendant arraigned.

Central Criminal Court, Francis and Francis (a firm) v [1988] 3 All ER 775; (1989) 88 Cr App R 213; [1988] 3 WLR 989 HL Documents otherwise privileged not so if held with criminal intention of laundering drug trafficking proceeds.

Central Criminal Court; ex parte Naraghi (Medhi) and Binji (Shirim), R v (1980) 2 Cr App R (S) 104 CA On procedure as regards estreatment of recognisance.

Central Criminal Court; ex parte Porter, R v [1992] Crim LR 121 HC QBD Improper attempt to vary bail conditions; disclosure of medical report obtained pursuant to Bail Act 1976, s 3(6A), usually a discretionary matter for trial judge/sometimes for other judge engaged in pre-trial review.

Chadwick, Southwell v (1987) 85 Cr App R 235 CA Machete knife and catapult not offensive weapons per se.

Chain Libraries, Ltd, Thomson v [1954] 2 All ER 616; [1954] Crim LR 551t; (1954) 104 LJ 473; (1954) 98 SJ 473; [1954] 1 WLR 999 HC QBD Justices must themselves examine allegedly obscene publications to see if obscene.

Chainey, R v [1911-13] All ER 701; (1913-14) XXIII Cox CC 620; (1914) 78 JP 127; [1914] 1 KB 137; (1913) 48 LJ 673; [1914] 83 LJKB 306; (1913-14) 109 LTR 752; (1913-14) XXX TLR 51; (1913) WN (I) 318 CCA Criminal neglect of (under sixteen year old) child socialising with immoral persons did not mean guilty of causing/encouraging unlawful carnal knowledge of same.

Chajutin v Whitehead [1938] 1 KB 506; (1938) 85 LJ 87; [1938] 107 LJCL 270 HC KBD Offence of possessing altered passport requires no mens rea, merely actus reus.

Chalker (Kate), R v (1910) 4 Cr App R 2 CCA Manslaughter of child by means of consistently cruel treatment.

Challans, Potter v (1911-13) XXII Cox CC 302; (1910) 74 JP 114; (1910) 102 LTR 325 HC KBD Prosecution failed to discharge burden of proof.

Chambers and Edwards v Director of Public Prosecutions [1995] Crim LR 896 HC QBD On what constitutes 'disorderly behaviour' for purposes of Public Order Act 1986, s 5(1).

Chambers; ex parte Klitz, R v [1919] 1 KB 638; [1919] 88 LJCL 688; (1918-19) XXXV TLR 328; (1919) WN (I) 95 HC KBD On jurisdiction of HC KBD in respect of recognisance entered into by party at Assizes.

Champ (Kathleen Angela Carol), R v (1981) 73 Cr App R 367; [1982] Crim LR 108 CA On charge of cultivating cannabis accused must show did not know plant concerned was cannabis.

Champion v Maughan and another [1984] Crim LR 291; (1984) 128 SJ 220; [1983] TLR 755 HC QBD Placing fixed engine in tidal waters an absolute offence under Salmon and Freshwater Fisheries Act 1975, s 6(1)(a).

Chan Wing-Siu and others v R (1985) 80 Cr App R 117; (1984) 128 SJ 685; [1984] TLR 411 PC Secondary party guilty as principal of crime committed by primary offender in course of unlawful common enterprise where secondary party perceived risk of crime occurring.

Chan-Fook, R v [1994] 2 All ER 552; (1994) 99 Cr App R 147; [1994] Crim LR 432; [1993] TLR 582; [1994] 1 WLR 689 CA Psychiatric fears but not strong emotions are actual bodily harm but issue of psychiatric injury not for jury unless expert evidence.

Chance (Terence Easton), R v (1988) 87 Cr App R 398; [1988] QB 932 CA On identifying accused in rape cases.

Chandler and others v Director of Public Prosecutions [1962] 3 All ER 142; [1964] AC 763; (1962) 46 Cr App R 347; [1962] Crim LR 634t; (1962) 112 LJ 552; (1962) 106 SJ 588; [1962] 3 WLR 694 HL Critique of defence policy inadmissible as defence to conspiring to enter prohibited place; definition of terms in Official Secrets Act 1911, s 1.

Chandler and others, R v [1962] 2 All ER 314; (1962) 112 LJ 456; (1962) 106 SJ 331 CCA Once 'purpose' is to breach Official Secrets Act 1911 whether will jeopardise national security an objective issue; cannot challenge Crown prerogative regarding military matters.

Chandler, R v [1911-13] All ER 428; (1913-14) XXIII Cox CC 330; [1913] 1 KB 125; (1912) 47 LJ 707; [1913] 82 LJKB 106; (1913) 108 LTR 352; (1912) WN (I) 276 CCA Shopbreaking conviction secured after entrapment valid.

Chaney, Morton v; Morton v Christopher [1960] 3 All ER 632; (1961) 125 JP 37; (1960) 110 LJ 797; (1960) 104 SJ 1035 HC QBD 'Sporting purposes' exemption to firearms possession does not apply to shooting rats.

Chapin (Alice), R v (1911-13) XXII Cox CC 10; (1910) 74 JP 71 CCC Interference with loose ballot papers at bottom of box (a 'packet of ballot papers') an interference with box; need not be personal malice to sustain charge of maliciously inflicting grievous bodily harm.

Chapman v Director of Public Prosecutions (1989) 89 Cr App R 190; [1988] Crim LR 843; (1989) 153 JP 27 HC QBD Conviction quashed where absence of evidence that entry onto premises to effect arrest was reasonable.

Chapman, R v [1958] 3 All ER 143; (1958) 42 Cr App R 257; [1958] Crim LR 623; (1958) 122 JP 462; (1958) 108 LJ 586; [1959] 1 QB 100; (1958) 102 SJ 621 CCA 'Unlawful' sex under Sexual Offences Act 1956 s 19(1) means sex outside marriage.

Chapman, R v (1931-34) XXIX Cox CC 407; (1931-32) 23 Cr App R 63; (1931) 95 JP 205; [1931] 2 KB 606; (1931) 100 LJCL 562; (1932) 146 LTR 120; (1931) 75 SJ 660; (1930-31) XLVII TLR 620; (1931) WN (1) 203 CCA Proviso in Criminal Law Amendment Act 1922, s 2 extends reasonable belief that girl over sixteen defence to men who have not reached the age of twenty-four.

Chapman (Horace William), R v (1910) 4 Cr App R 276; (1910) 74 JP 360; (1910) 45 LJ 341; (1910) WN (I) 131 CCA Rail ticket a chattel that could be obtained by false pretences.

Chapman, R v (1912-13) XXIX TLR 117 Assizes Deposition before justices on misdemeanour charge admitted on later trial for related felony.

Charavanmuttu (Edward Vanniascheram), R v (1928-29) 21 Cr App R 184 CCA Bail granted in light of pending vacation.

Charles, Metropolitan Police Commissioner v [1976] 3 All ER 112; [1977] AC 177; (1976) 63 Cr App R 252; [1977] Crim LR 615; (1976) 140 JP 531; (1976) 126 NLJ 936t; (1976) 120 SJ 588; [1976] 3 WLR 431 HL Acceptance of cheque and cheque card where drawer has no money in bank is obtaining pecuniary advantage by deception.

Charles, R v [1976] 1 All ER 659; [1976] Crim LR 196t; (1976) 140 JP 254; (1976) 126 NLJ 14t; (1976) 120 SJ 147; [1976] 1 WLR 248 CA Unauthorised drawing of cheque is obtaining pecuniary advantage by deception.

Charlesworth (Miriam) and Charlesworth (May otherwise Violet), R v (1910) 4 Cr App R 167 CCA Could disprove defence of innocent belief by reference to earlier false representations.

Charlson, R v [1955] 1 All ER 859; (1955) 39 Cr App R 37; [1955] Crim LR 316; (1955) 119 JP 283; (1955) 99 SJ 221; [1955] 1 WLR 317 HC QBD Cannot be unlawful and malicious grievous bodily harm where not acting consciously.

Chattaway (William) and Chattaway (Ellen), R v (1922-23) 17 Cr App R 7 CCA Failure to assist person who could not assist self may be manslaughter if death results therefrom.

Chee-Kwong (Cheung) v R; Attorney-General v Chee-Kwong (Cheung) [1979] Crim LR 788; (1979) 123 SJ 473; [1979] 1 WLR 1454 PC On determining appropriate sum payable as penalty following conviction of bribery offence under Hong Kong Prevention of Bribery Ordinance 1974 (as revised).

Cheeseman v Director of Public Prosecutions [1991] 3 All ER 54; (1991) 93 Cr App R 145; [1991] Crim LR 296; (1991) 155 JP 469; [1992] QB 83; [1990] TLR 690; [1991] 2 WLR 1105 HC QBD On-duty police officers policing public toilet were not 'passengers' before whom indecent exposure to their annoyance could constitute offence (Town Police Clauses Act 1847, s 28, as amended).

Chelmsford Justices; ex parte JJ Amos, R v [1973] Crim LR 437 HC QBD Attempt to incite supply of dangerous drug a common law offence (not offence under the Dangerous Drugs Act 1965).

Cheng (Tzu-Tsai) v Governor of Pentonville Prison [1973] 2 All ER 204; [1973] AC 931; [1973] Crim LR 362; (1973) 137 JP 422; (1973) 117 SJ 527; [1973] 2 WLR 746 HL Political offence ground open only if political offence against requesting state.

Cherryman, Leicester and Co v (1907) 71 JP 301; [1907] 76 LJKB 678; (1907) XCVI LTR 784; (1907) WN (I) 95 HC KBD Owners of goods could bring action in detinue against pawnbroker for stolen goods pawned with him despite court order for restitution of goods upon payment to him of amounts he advanced for the goods.

Cheshire County Council v Alan Helliwell and Sons (Bolton) Ltd [1991] Crim LR 210; (1991) 155 JP 425; [1990] TLR 766 HC QBD Transporting of animals while are unfit to travel a strict liability offence (Transport of Animals (Road and Rail) Order 1951).

Cheshire County Council v Armstrong's Transport (Wigan) Ltd [1995] Crim LR 162 HC QBD On what constitutes 'waste'.

Cheshire, R v [1991] 3 All ER 670; (1991) 93 Cr App R 251; [1991] Crim LR 709; (1991) 141 NLJ 743; (1991) 135 SJ LB 11; [1991] TLR 204; [1991] 1 WLR 844 CA Actions that are significant though not immediate cause of death could sustain conviction for murder.

Chief Constable for Hampshire, Kaur (Dip) v [1981] 2 All ER 430; (1981) 72 Cr App R 359; [1981] Crim LR 259; (1981) 145 JP 313; (1981) 131 NLJ 366; (1981) 125 SJ 323; [1981] 1 WLR 578 HC QBD Lawful transfer of property where voidable not void contract of sale.

Chief Constable for Northern Ireland, McKee v [1985] 1 All ER 1; (1984) 128 SJ 836; [1984] TLR 662; [1984] 1 WLR 1358 HL Necessary state of mind to justify constable's arresting suspected terrorist under emergency legislation could be grounded solely on superior's orders.

Chief Constable of Avon and Somerset Constabulary v Shimmen (1987) 84 Cr App R 7; [1986] Crim LR 800 HC QBD Was recklessness where recognised risk and took inadequate steps to prevent damage occurring.

Chief Constable of Avon and Somerset, Carey v [1995] RTR 405 CA Removal by police of converted coach parked by kerb but not obstructing road-users was unlawful.

Chief Constable of Blackpool v Woodhall [1965] Crim LR 660 Magistrates On what is meant by publication for 'gain' under the Obscene Publications Acts 1959 and 1964.

Chief Constable of Cambridgeshire, Connor v [1984] TLR 230 HC QBD Exemplary damages for assault by police officer.

Chief Constable of Cheshire Constabulary v Hunt and others (1983) 147 JP 567 HC QBD Person who admits smoking cannabis must be in possession of same.

Chief Constable of Devon and Cornwall, Dabek v (1991) 155 JP 55; [1990] TLR 487 HC QBD Firearms certificate properly revoked where holder (although of good character) was married to person of dubious character.

Chief Constable of Devon and Cornwall, Kavanagh v [1974] 2 All ER 697; (1974) 138 JP 618; (1974) 124 NLJ 387t; (1974) 118 SJ 347 CA Court can consider all matters - even hearsay - in appeal against refusal to give firearms certificate.

Chief Constable of Devon and Cornwall; ex parte Central Electricity Generating Board, R v [1981] 3 All ER 826; (1982) 146 JP 91; (1981) 125 SJ 745 CA Demonstrators guilty of criminal obstruction likely to give rise to breach of the peace.

Chief Constable of Essex v Germain (1992) 156 JP 109; [1991] TLR 185 HC QBD On exercise by Chief Constable of discretionary power to revoke shotgun certificate.

Chief Constable of Greater Manchester Police v Ryan (1985) 149 JP 79 HC QBD On what constitutes offence of attempted handling.

Chief Constable of Greater Manchester, Gray v [1983] Crim LR 45 CrCt Street busker not guilty of begging/gathering alms contrary to Vagrancy Act 1824, s 3.

Chief Constable of Greater Manchester, Houghton v (1987) 84 Cr App R 319 CA Person wearing police truncheon as part of fancy dress had reasonable excuse for possessing what was an offensive weapon per se.

Chief Constable of Greater Manchester, Lewis and anr v (1991) 141 NLJ 1486i CA May arrest for breach of peace on anticipatory basis.

Chrastny (No 1), R v [1992] 1 All ER 189; (1992) 94 Cr App R 283; (1991) 155 JP 850; [1991] TLR 135; [1991] 1 WLR 1381 CA Spouse conspiring with other spouse alone but knowing of other parties to conspiracy are guilty of conspiracy.

Christ, R v [1951] 2 All ER 254; (1951) 115 JP 410; (1951) 95 SJ 531; [1951] 2 TLR 85; (1951) WN (I) 337 CCA On direction as to larceny/receiving.

Christ, R v; Nkambule (Gideon) and Others v R [1951] 2 All ER 254; [1950] AC 379 PC Once satisfied crime was committed can under Swaziland law convict accused thereof on accomplice's evidence.

Christian and another, R v (1913-14) XXIII Cox CC 541; (1914) 78 JP 112 CCC Cannot be convicted of attempt to/conspiracy to/actual procuration where woman freely chooses to be at brothel.

Christou, R v [1972] Crim LR 653; (1971) 115 SJ 687 CA Drawing by cheque on account into which paid useless cheques was obtaining property by false pretences.

Christy, Stevens and Stevens v (1987) 85 Cr App R 249; [1987] Crim LR 503; (1987) 151 JP 366 HC QBD Place could be brothel where was used by team of prostitutes albeit one at a time.

Chuan (Ong Ah) v Public Prosecutor; Cheng (Koh Chai) v Public Prosecutor [1981] AC 648; [1981] Crim LR 245; (1981) 131 NLJ 44; (1980) 124 SJ 757; [1980] 3 WLR 855 PC Carrying over two grammes of heroin in car raised constitutionally valid presumption that were trafficker.

Chun-Chuen (Lee) alias Wing-Cheuk (Lee) v R [1963] 1 All ER 73; [1963] AC 220; [1963] Crim LR 114; (1963) 113 LJ 56; (1962) 106 SJ 1008; [1962] 3 WLR 1461 PC Can rely on defence of provocation even if intended to kill/cause grievous bodily harm.

Church, Flack v (1918) 82 JP 59; (1917-18) XXXIV TLR 32 HC KBD Can be convicted twice under Dog Licences Act 1867, s 8, for non-possession of licence on different days of same year.

Church, R v [1965] 2 All ER 72; (1965) 49 Cr App R 206; [1965] Crim LR 299t; (1965) 129 JP 366; (1965) 115 LJ 350; [1966] 1 QB 59; (1965) 109 SJ 371; [1965] 2 WLR 1220 CCA Unlawful act resulting in death plus mens rea that act would cause some harm necessary to sustain manslaughter conviction.

Churchill and others, R v [1965] 2 All ER 793; [1965] Crim LR 545; (1965) 129 JP 387; (1965) 109 SJ 792; [1965] 1 WLR 1174 CCC Application for particulars of overt acts in conpiracy case refused if indictment/Crown opening statement meet that need.

Churchill v Walton [1967] 1 All ER 497; [1967] 2 AC 224; (1967) 51 Cr App R 212; [1967] Crim LR 235t; (1967) 131 JP 277; (1967) 111 SJ 112; [1967] 2 WLR 682 HL Not conspiracy if agree to commit absolute offence not knowing are agreeing to unlawful act.

Churchill, R v [1989] Crim LR 226 CA Were entitled to resist unlawful force of police who upon appellant's arrest for burglary sought to forcibly/wrongfully take appellant's car keys.

Ciappara (Simon), R v (1988) 87 Cr App R 316; [1988] Crim LR 172 CA Interception of parcel containing cocaine by Customs officers and substitution of baking powder for cocaine did not mean ultimate recipient of parcel was not guilty of importing cocaine.

Cichon v Director of Public Prosecutions [1994] Crim LR 918 HC QBD Could not plead defence of necessity to having unmuzzled pit bull terrier in public place (allegedly unmuzzled to prevent discomfort in coughing).

Clare, Invicta Plastics Ltd and another v [1976] Crim LR 131; [1976] RTR 251; (1976) 120 SJ 62 HC QBD Company (but not chairman) advertising for sale speed trap detectors properly convicted of incitement to use unlicensed apparatus for wireless telegraphy.

Clark and others, R v (1963) 47 Cr App R 203; [1963] Crim LR 839 Assizes Bar was a public place.

Clark v Taylor (1948) 112 JP 439; (1948) WN (I) 410 HC KBD On what constituted 'frequenting' a place for purpose of the Vagrancy Act 1824, s 4.

Clark, Leavett v (1915) 79 JP 396; [1915] 3 KB 9; (1915) 50 LJ 253; [1915] 84 LJKB 2157; (1915-16) 113 LTR 424; (1914-15) XXXI TLR 424; (1915) WN (I) 211 HC KBD Taking of winkles was larceny of fish under Larceny Act 1861, s 24.

Clark, R v; R v Sharp [1991] Crim LR 625 CA Evidence of other criminal damage committed on same occasion as arson and not genuinely separable from latter was properly admitted.

Clark, Wilson v [1984] TLR 716 HC QBD On validity of arrest effected pursuant to the Immigration Act 1971.

Clarke (Dennis Geoffrey), R v (1985) 80 Cr App R 344; [1985] Crim LR 209 CA Exceptionally police informer could rely on efforts to impede crime as defence; ought not to be convicted of aiding and abetting burglary where acquitted of burglary.

Clarke (Ediakpo), R v [1985] AC 1037; (1985) 135 NLJ 632; [1985] 3 WLR 113 HL On elements of offence of making false statement to person lawfully acting in execution of Immigration Act 1971.

Clarke (Victor), R v [1996] Crim LR 824 CA On dishonesty as an element of obtaining pecuniary advantage by deception.

Clarke and others, Director of Public Prosecutions v (1992) 94 Cr App R 359; [1992] Crim LR 60; (1992) 156 JP 267; (1991) 135 SJ LB 135; [1991] TLR 407 HC QBD Where plead reasonable conduct as defence to public order charge reasonableness an objective issue and intent a subjective matter.

Clarke, R v [1991] Crim LR 383 CA Entirety of accused's conduct relevant to jury determination whether acted under provocation.

Clarke, R v [1986] 1 All ER 846; (1986) 82 Cr App R 308; [1986] Crim LR 334; (1986) 130 SJ 110; [1986] 1 WLR 209 CA Firearm without trigger capable of being firearm.

Clarke, R v [1950] 1 All ER 546; (1949-50) 34 Cr App R 65; (1950) 114 JP 192; (1950) 100 LJ 107; (1950) 94 SJ 211; [1950] 66 (1) TLR 618; (1950) WN (I) 101 CCA Can be 'suspected person' though arresting officers do not know of earlier convictions when arresting.

Clarke, R v [1976] 2 All ER 696; (1976) 63 Cr App R 16; [1977] Crim LR 110; (1976) 140 JP 469 CA Presumption that man living with/habitually in company of prostitute knowingly living off her earnings.

Clarke, R v [1972] 1 All ER 219; (1972) 56 Cr App R 225; [1972] Crim LR 183t; (1972) 136 JP 184; (1972) 122 NLJ 10t; (1972) 116 SJ 56 CA M'Naghten rules require that person loses power of reasoning.

Clarke, R v [1949] 2 All ER 448; (1948-49) 33 Cr App R 216; (1949) 99 LJ 441 Assizes Post-separation order rape of wife by husband possible.

Clarke, R v [1950] 1 KB 523 CCA Can if have previous convictions be 'suspected person' for purposes of Vagrancy Act 1824, s 4 even if police do not know of same when arresting suspect.

Clarkson and others, R v [1971] 3 All ER 344; (1971) 55 Cr App R 445; [1972] Crim LR 586; (1971) 135 JP 533; (1971) 115 SJ 654; [1971] 1 WLR 1402 CMAC Intent to encourage and actual encouragement necessary where aiding and abetting rape.

Claxon, Heritage v (1941) 85 SJ 323 HC KBD Home Guard member in possession of uncertificated firearm/ammunition who was not acting in capacity as Home Guard member in possession of same was guilty of offence.

Clay, R v (1910) 74 JP 55 CCA Larceny conviction quashed where had been no evidence of felonious intent.

Clayton (Sam), R v (1920-21) 15 Cr App R 45 CCA Good faith belief that had right to money required quashing of larceny conviction.

Clayton (Terence Edward), R v (1981) 72 Cr App R 135; [1981] Crim LR 186 CA Intent to deceive was adequate mens rea for forgery of excise licence (contrary to Vehicles (Excise) Act 1971, s 26(1)).

Clayton v Pearse (1903-04) 52 WR 495 HC KBD That had power to regulate nets meant had power to prohibit nets entirely.

Clayton, Allworthy and Walker v (1907-09) XXI Cox CC 352 HC KBD Pawnbroker could not be convicted of neglecting to deliver pledge where loss of same was in good faith.

Coffin and another v Smith and another (1980) 71 Cr App R 221 HC QBD Was obstruction of police in execution of their duty to assault police constable in course of ejection from club/while standing on beat.

Coffin and another v Smith and another; R v Coates (1980) 71 Cr App R 221; [1971] Crim LR 370; [1971] RTR 74 CA Conviction quashed where validity of arrest/proper functioning of breathalyser not left to jury.

Cogan, R v; R v Leak [1975] 2 All ER 1059; (1975) 61 Cr App R 217; [1975] Crim LR 584t; (1975) 139 JP 608; (1975) 125 NLJ 623t; [1976] QB 217; (1975) 119 SJ 473; [1975] 3 WLR 316 CA Can be guilty of aiding/abetting rape even if principal acquitted of rape as believed consent.

Coggan, Crawford v [1964] Crim LR 292t HC QBD Person charged with custody/control of dog has onus of proving are not in his custody/control; on elements of being a 'keeper' of a dog.

Cohen and another v Black [1942] 2 All ER 299; [1942] 111 LJ 573; (1943) 93 LJ 100; (1942) 86 SJ 210; (1941-42) LVIII TLR 306; (1942) WN (I) 119 HC KBD For loitering with intent arrest must be acts arousing suspicion preceding arrest; police officers' evidence could be pooled.

Cohen and another v March [1951] 2 TLR 402 HC KBD Accused's lying as to when came into possession of goods is not per se evidence that goods were stolen.

Cohen, R v (1907) 71 JP 190 CCC Person could be tried on additional charges to those for which arrested and returned from colony.

Cole (and others), R v [1993] Crim LR 300 CA On drunkenness as defence to causing grievous bodily harm with intent: issue is whether had requisite intent, not whether capable of forming same.

Cole, R v [1994] Crim LR 582 CA On elements of defences of duress by threats/of circumstances.

Cole, R v; R v Lees; R v Birch [1997] TLR 392 CA Acting as director of company of prohibited name an absolute offence.

Coleman (Ian), R v (1975) 61 Cr App R 206 CA Custodial sentences necessary for those who assault police when latter trying to keep order.

Coleman, R v [1986] Crim LR 56 CA On elements of handling.

Coles (Thomas), R v (1910) 5 Cr App R 36 CCA Cannot plead general deficiency where admit possession of missing money.

Coles, R v [1994] Crim LR 820 CA On recklessness in the context of arson; psychological evidence rightly excluded where went to matters that could be properly assessed by jury absent expert evidence.

Colle (Valerie Anne), R v (1992) 95 Cr App R 67; (1992) 156 JP 360; (1991) 135 SJ LB 125; [1991] TLR 410 CA Defendant must prove on balance of probabilities the statutory defence in Drug Trafficking Offences Act 1986, s 24(4) to assisting another with drug trafficking proceeds.

Collier, R v [1960] Crim LR 204 Assizes Statutory defence open to accused when committed offence of having unlawful sex with under-sixteen year old also available where attempted offence.

Collins (Christopher), R v [1976] Crim LR 249 CCC Issue estoppel applied to preclude conviction for burglary following acquittal of rape charge arising from same occasion; failed autrefois acquit plea where charged with burglary after acquitted of rape charge arising from same occasion.

Collins and Fox v Chief Constable of Merseyside [1988] Crim LR 247 HC QBD Where two parties jointly charged but not clear whether one or other acted independently or whether both acted jointly an acquittal is required.

Collins, R v [1972] 2 All ER 1105; (1972) 56 Cr App R 554; [1972] Crim LR 498; (1972) 136 JP 605; [1973] QB 100; (1972) 116 SJ 432; [1972] 3 WLR 243 CA Only enter premises as trespasser if know/reckless as to whether entering without permission.

Collins, R v (1921-25) XXVII Cox CC 322; (1922-23) 17 Cr App R 42; (1923) 87 JP 60; (1923) 128 LTR 31; (1922-23) 67 SJ 367 CCA Non-substitution of conviction for obtaining money by false pretences for one of larceny.

Collins, Ross v [1982] Crim LR 368 CA Holder of shotgun certificate not allowed possess loaded shotgun in public place; honest belief that not in public place unsuccessfully pleaded in defence.

Collis-Smith, R v [1972] Crim LR 716 CA Where petrol put in car and then driver made false representation as to mode of payment there was no obtaining of property by deception.

Collister (Thomas James), R v; R v Warhurst (John) (1955) 39 Cr App R 100 CCA On what constitutes demanding money with menaces; on duty of prosecution to tell defence of prosecutor's record.

Colville-Hyde, R v [1956] Crim LR 117 Assizes On necessary elements of offence of abduction.

Comer v Bloomfield (1971) 55 Cr App R 305; [1971] Crim LR 230; [1971] RTR 49 CA Letter of inquiry to insurance company (preliminary to unmade false claim) not attempted obtaining of property by deception.

Commandant of Knockaloe Camp; ex parte Forman, R v (1917-18) 117 LTR 627; (1917-18) 62 SJ 35; (1917-18) XXXIV TLR 4 HC KBD Unregistered alien can be validly interned.

Commissioner of Police and another; ex parte Nalder, R v [1947] 2 All ER 611; (1948) 112 JP 20; [1948] 1 KB 251; (1947) 97 LJ 621; [1948] 117 LJR 439; (1947) 91 SJ 614; (1947) LXIII TLR 591; (1947) WN (I) 295 HC KBD Valid sending of person to Ireland under Indictable Offences Act 1848/Petty Sessions (Ireland) Act 1851, not Fugitive Offenders Act 1881.

Commissioner of Police for the Metropolis, Lawrence v [1971] 2 All ER 1253; [1972] AC 626; (1971) 55 Cr App R 471; [1972] Crim LR 667; (1971) 135 JP 481; (1971) 121 NLJ 594t; (1971) 115 SJ 565; [1971] 3 WLR 225 HL Issue of consent relevant to whether dishonesty not whether appropriation.

Commissioner of Police for the Metropolis, Reynolds v (1985) 80 Cr App R 125; [1984] Crim LR 688; [1985] QB 881; (1984) 128 SJ 736; [1984] TLR 514; [1985] 2 WLR 93 CA Tort to obtain Forgery Act 1913 search warrant where do not reasonably believe subject of same has unlawful custody/possession of forgeries; police guilty of trespass to goods where took documents did not reasonably believe were forged.

Commissioner of Police for the Metropolis, Reynolds v [1982] Crim LR 600; [1982] TLR 274 CA £12,000 damages merited in serious case of wrongful arrest/false imprisonment.

Commissioner of Police for the Metropolis, Wershof v [1978] 3 All ER 540; (1979) 143 JP 1; (1979) 68 Cr App R 82; [1978] Crim LR 424; (1978) 128 NLJ 486t; (1978) 122 SJ 279 HC QBD Arrest for wilful obstruction if obstruction likely to cause breach of peace/frustrate other arrest; officer acting in course of duty.

Commissioner of Police for the Metropolis; ex parte Blackburn, R v (1980) 130 NLJ 313 CA Refusal of order of mandamus requiring police commissioner to bring prosecution in obscenity cases.

Commissioner of Police of the Metropolis and others, Abbassy and another v [1990] 1 All ER 193; (1990) 90 Cr App R 250; (1989) 139 NLJ 1266; [1990] RTR 164; [1990] 1 WLR 385 CA Police officer exercising power of arrest without warrant need not specify offence for which being arrested but can indicate general nature of offence.

Commissioner of Police of the Metropolis v Simeon [1982] 2 All ER 813; (1982) 75 Cr App R 359; (1982) 146 JP 286; [1982] 3 WLR 289 HL Repeal of Vagrancy Act did not affect pre-repeal based/instituted cases.

Commissioner of Police of the Metropolis, Silcott v (1996) TLR 9/7/96 CA On extent of public policy immunity enjoyed by police in respect of actions for conspiracy to pervert the course of justice/misfeasance in public office.

Commissioner of Police of the Metropolis, Slater v (1996) TLR 23/1/96 HC QBD Police ought not to have retained seized money possession of which had not been declared to the Inland Revenue/Department of Social Security.

Commissioner of Police of the Metropolis; ex parte Blackburn and another (No 3), R v [1973] Crim LR 185; (1973) 137 JP 172; (1973) 117 SJ 57; [1973] 2 WLR 43 CA No mandamus directing police in conduct of their duties as regards obscene publications as not proven that such direction merited.

Conway, R v [1988] 3 All ER 1025; (1989) 88 Cr App R159; [1989] Crim LR 74; (1988) 152 JP 649; [1989] QB 290; [1989] RTR 35; (1988) 132 SJ 1244; [1988] 3 WLR 1238 CA Necessity a defence to reckless driving if duress of circumstances present.

Cook, R v [1982] Crim LR 670 CA Was misdirection for judge to indicate as expert evidence a doctor's non-medical opinion that person prosecuted for murder acted under provocation.

Cook, R v [1954] 1 All ER 60; (1954) 118 JP 71; [1954] 1 WLR 125 Assizes Sex with mental defective but did not procure it so not guilty under Mental Deficiency Act 1913, s 56(1)(a).

Cooke (Anthony), R v; R v Sutcliffe (Kathleen) [1985] Crim LR 215 CA On appropriate charge where possessed article for cheating.

Cooke (Philip), R v [1971] Crim LR 44 Sessions On elements of offence of causing bodily harm by misconduct when in charge of a vehicle.

Cooke, R v [1997] Crim LR 436 CA On ramifications of Preddy decision for Theft Act offences.

Cooke, R v [1986] 2 All ER 985; [1986] AC 909; (1986) 83 Cr App R 339; [1987] Crim LR 114; (1986) 150 JP 498; (1986) 136 NLJ 730; (1970) 130 SJ 572; [1986] 3 WLR 327 HL Statutory conspiracy with presence of fraud can be charged as common law conspiracy; no false accounting where no deception and no fraud.

Coombe, Wilson v (1989) 88 Cr App R 322; (1988) 132 SJ 1300; [1989] 1 WLR 78 HC QBD Possession of firearms certificates apply to particular gun not type of gun: valid conviction of dealer who exchanged certificate-holders' guns for different gun of same class.

Cooper (Charles Thomas), R v (1909) 3 Cr App R 100 CCA Non-receipt of moneys justifies jury finding of embezzlement.

Cooper (Edward), Shea, and Stocks, R v (1908) 1 Cr App R 88; (1907-08) XXIV TLR 867 CCA Though principal acquitted of common law larceny of fixtures could convict receiver for breach of Larceny Act 1861, s 59.

Cooper (G), R v; R v Cooper (Y) [1991] Crim LR 524 CA On difference between criminal damage to property with fire (arson) and without fire (criminal damage).

Cooper and Compton, R v [1947] 2 All ER 701; (1946-48) 32 Cr App R 102; (1947) 97 LJ 591; (1947) LXIII TLR 561 CCA On charging conspiracy with nearly same fact substantive offences.

Cooper and Miles, R v [1979] Crim LR 42 CrCt On elements of attempt to steal.

Cooper and others v Shield [1971] 2 All ER 917; [1971] Crim LR 365t; (1971) 135 JP 434; (1971) 121 NLJ 298t; [1971] 2 QB 334; (1971) 115 SJ 365; [1971] 2 WLR 1385 HC QBD Railway station platform not 'open space'.

Cooper v Leeke (1968) 112 SJ 46 HC QBD Failed appeal against conviction for possession of various instruments with intent to commit felonious act (Vagrancy Act 1824, s 4).

Cooper, Moynes v [1956] 1 All ER 450; (1956) 40 Cr App R 20; [1956] Crim LR 268; (1956) 120 JP 147; (1956) 106 LJ 138; [1956] 1 QB 439; (1956) 100 SJ 171; [1956] 2 WLR 562 HC QBD No taking unless animus furandi at moment of taking, not later.

Cooray (Mahumarakalage Edward Andrew) v R [1953] AC 407; (1953) 97 SJ 314 PC To be convicted as agent having committed criminal breach of trust must act as agent by way of business.

Cope (Charles William), R v (1921-22) 16 Cr App R 77; (1922) 86 JP 78; (1921-22) 66 SJ 406; (1921-22) XXXVIII TLR 243 CCA On letter as attempt to procure gross indecency contrary to Criminal Law Amendment Act 1885, s 11.

Cope, R v [1924] All ER 301; (1925) 89 JP 100; (1925) 60 LJ 324; [1925] 94 LJCL 662; (1925) 132 LTR 800; (1924-25) XLI TLR 418; (1925) WN (I) 108 CCA When person facing sentence as incorrigible rogue must be examination of case before him and in his hearing.

Cope-Brown, Banks v (1948) LXIV TLR 390 HC KBD Failed prosecution for charging extortionate rent contrary to Increase of Rent and Mortgage Interest (Restrictions) Act 1920.

Copper, Burke v [1962] 2 All ER 14; (1962) 126 JP 319; (1962) 106 SJ 451; [1962] 1 WLR 700 HC QBD Forfeiture in respect of all photographs: some could not be more obscene than others.

Copus v Director of Public Prosecutions [1989] Crim LR 577 HC QBD Rice flail an offensive weapon per se.

Coulson, Stockdale v [1974] Crim LR 474 HC QBD Could not be convicted of failure to annex to annual return documents approved at annual general meeting when no such meeting had been held.

Coupe, Sayce v [1952] 2 All ER 715; [1953] 1 QB 1 HC QBD Buying from unlicensed seller uncustomed tobacco using some/giving rest away is keeping uncustomed goods.

Court, R v [1954] Crim LR 622 CCA Adequate direction regarding possibility that certain witness might be accomplice.

Court, R v [1987] 1 All ER 120; (1987) 84 Cr App R 210; [1987] Crim LR 134; [1987] QB 156; (1970) 130 SJ 859; [1986] 3 WLR 1029 CA Additional evidence of secret motive admissible in indecent assault case; secret motive cannot render indecent a situation which objectively is not indecent.

Court, R v [1988] 2 All ER 221; [1989] AC 28; (1988) 87 Cr App R 144; [1988] Crim LR 537; (1988) 152 JP 422; (1988) 138 NLJ 128; (1988) 132 SJ 658; [1988] 2 WLR 1071 HL Intentional assault intended as indecent is indecent assault; any evidence showing intent admissible.

Cousins, R v [1982] 2 All ER 115; (1982) 74 Cr App R 363; [1982] Crim LR 444; (1982) 146 JP 264; [1982] QB 526; (1982) 126 SJ 154; [1982] TLR 67; [1982] 2 WLR 621 CA Self-defence/prevention of crime lawful excuse to threat to kill; jury direction on burden of proof if lawful excuse exists/absent.

Cowdell, R v [1962] Crim LR 262t CA Inappropriate that person be convicted of unlawful wounding and assault on basis of same facts.

Cowper, Workman v [1961] Crim LR 394; (1961) 125 JP 254; (1961) 111 LJ 190; [1961] 2 QB 143; (1961) 105 SJ 130; [1961] 2 WLR 386 HC QBD Test for criminality in killing of dog running wild on land.

Cox (Peter Nevill), R v; R v Hodges (Graham David) (1982) 75 Cr App R 291; [1983] Crim LR 167 CA Must be element of dishonesty to sustain conviction for fraudulent trading.

Cox (Peter), R v [1968] 1 All ER 410; (1968) 52 Cr App R 106; [1968] Crim LR 163; (1968) 132 JP 162; (1968) 118 NLJ 109; (1967) 111 SJ 966; [1968] 1 WLR 88 CA No criminal conspiracy charge possible where conspiracy to be completely effected abroad.

Cox v Army Council [1962] Crim LR 459; (1962) 112 LJ 256; (1962) 106 SJ 305; [1962] 2 WLR 950 HL Proper that army sergeant be convicted under Army Act 1955 of driving without due care and attention in Germany.

Cox v Riley (1986) 83 Cr App R 54; [1986] Crim LR 460 HC QBD Was criminal damage to erase program from circuit card of computerised saw.

Cox v Stinton [1951] 2 All ER 637; (1951) 115 JP 490; [1951] 2 KB 1021; (1951) 101 LJ 455; [1951] 2 TLR 728; (1951) WN (I) 497 HC KBD Negatives liable to seizure/destruction.

Cox, Lewis v (1985) 80 Cr App R 1; [1984] Crim LR 756; (1984) 148 JP 601; [1985] QB 509; (1984) 128 SJ 596; [1984] TLR 441; [1984] 3 WLR 875 HC QBD Was wilful obstruction of police officer where repeatedly opened rear door of police vehicle to ask arrested friend where was being taken.

Cox, R v (1995) 139 SJ LB 86 CA Counsel to tell judge if there is material on which provocation might be found so that judge might address the matter.

Cox, R v (1962) 112 LJ 41; (1962) 106 SJ 17; [1962] 2 WLR 126 CMAC Proper that army sergeant be convicted under Army Act 1955 of driving without due care and attention in Germany.

Cox, R v [1968] 1 All ER 386; (1968) 118 NLJ 134; [1968] 1 WLR 308 CA If of diminished responsibility can plead guilty to manslaughter though charged with murder.

Cox, Ricketts v (1982) 74 Cr App R 298; [1982] Crim LR 184 HC QBD Extreme rudeness and lack of co-operation was obstruction of police in execution of their duty.

Cox, Swales v [1981] 1 All ER 1115; (1981) 72 Cr App R 171; [1981] Crim LR 235; (1981) 131 NLJ 372; [1981] QB 849; (1981) 125 SJ 133; [1981] 2 WLR 814 HC QBD Police may enter place using any necessary force to effect arrest.

Coxhead, R v [1986] Crim LR 251; [1986] RTR 411 CA Is/is not discretion not to bring criminal proceedings in non-serious/serious cases: seriousness a matter for jury.

Coyne v Ward [1962] Crim LR 169t HC QBD Comparison of/contrast between larceny by trick and obtaining by false pretences.

Cozens v Brutus [1972] 2 All ER 1; (1972) 136 JP 390; (1972) 116 SJ 217; [1972] 1 WLR 484 HC QBD Behaviour causing affront is 'insulting behaviour'.

Cozens, Brutus v [1972] 2 All ER 1297; [1973] AC 854; (1972) 56 Cr App R 799; [1973] Crim LR 56; (1972) 136 JP 636; (1972) 122 NLJ 681t; (1972) 116 SJ 647; [1972] 3 WLR 521 HL Behaviour causing affront/being rude need not be 'insulting behaviour' contrary to Public Order Act 1936, s 5 (as amended).

Craigen, Thielbar v (1907-09) XXI Cox CC 44; (1905) 69 JP 421; (1905-06) XCIII LTR 600; (1904-05) XXI TLR 745 HC KBD Creating situation in which lion could savage pony was unlawful cruelty to pony.

Crane and others, R v [1982] TLR 179 CA Later events cannot obviate offence of conspiracy.

Crawford v Coggan [1964] Crim LR 292t HC QBD Person charged with custody/control of dog has onus of proving are not in his custody/control; on elements of being a 'keeper' of a dog.

Crawford, R v (1994) 138 SJ LB 60 CA On provocation: murder conviction reduced to manslaughter where provocation (of which there was evidence) not left to jury.

Crawley, Bolton v [1972] Crim LR 222 CA Assault occasioning actual bodily harm did not require mens rea so though had injected oneself with drugs could not claim did not possess mens rea for said offence.

Creamer, R v [1918-19] All ER 222; (1918-21) XXVI Cox CC 393; (1919-20) 14 Cr App R 19; (1919) 83 JP 120; [1919] 1 KB 564; [1919] 88 LJCL 594; (1919) 120 LTR 575; (1918-19) XXXV TLR 281 CCA Absent proof that wife's taking husband's property was larceny recipient thereof could not be convicted of receiving.

Creamer, R v [1965] 3 All ER 257; (1965) 49 Cr App R 368; [1965] Crim LR 552; (1965) 49 Cr App R 368; (1965) 115 LJ 676; [1966] 1 QB 72; (1965) 109 SJ 648; [1965] 3 WLR 583 CCA Involuntary manslaughter if un/intended/foreseen death flows from unlawful act likely to do injury; person seeking/arranging such act an accessory before fact to manslaughter.

Creaser and another v Tunnicliffe [1978] 1 All ER 569; (1978) 66 Cr App R 66; [1977] Crim LR 746; (1978) 142 JP 245; (1977) 127 NLJ 638t; (1977) 121 SJ 775; [1977] 1 WLR 1493 HC QBD Altered firearm capable of firing original ammunition still required certificate.

Cresswell v Sirl (1948) 112 JP 69; [1948] 1 KB 241; (1947) 97 LJ 648; [1948] 117 LJR 654; (1947) 91 SJ 653; (1947) LXIII TLR 620 CA On test of criminal liability for shooting of trespassing dog.

Crick and another, R v [1993] TLR 465 CA Could be guilty of obtaining property by deception by way of electronic transfer from one account to another.

Criminal Injuries Compensation Board and another, ex parte P and another, R v [1995] 1 All ER 870; [1995] 2 FCR 553; (1994) 144 NLJ 674; (1994) 144 NLJ 760t; [1994] TLR 284; [1995] 1 WLR 845 CA Legality of executive action reviewable unless Parliament decides otherwise; non-retrospective application of revised criminal injuries compensation scheme rational.

Criminal Injuries Compensation Board ex parte Cook, R v [1996] 2 All ER 144; [1995] TLR 704; [1996] 1 WLR 1037 CA Decision of Board to refuse compensation need deal only with principal issue(s) - oral appeal available if Board fails to do so.

Criminal Injuries Compensation Board, ex parte Clowes, R v [1977] 3 All ER 854; (1977) 65 Cr App R 289; [1977] Crim LR 419; (1978) 142 JP 33; (1977) 127 NLJ 570t; (1977) 121 SJ 391; [1977] 1 WLR 1353 HC QBD Offence of damaging property not crime violence as no injury/violence to another.

Criminal Injuries Compensation Board, ex parte Ince, R v [1973] 3 All ER 808; [1973] Crim LR 624; (1973) 137 JP 869; (1973) 123 NLJ 747t; (1973) 117 SJ 616; [1973] 1 WLR 1334 CA That no offence to be committed did not mean 'attempted prevention of...offence' impossible; that death due to carelessness in going to aid did not mean not 'directly attributable' to attempted prevention.

Criminal Injuries Compensation Board, ex parte Ince, R v [1973] Crim LR 110 HC QBD Police officer rushing to scene of crime on foot of radio message was engaged in 'attempted prevention of...offence'; death due to carelessness in going to scene of crime meant fault entirely attributable to officer.

Curry, Davis v (1918-21) XXVI Cox CC 100; (1918) 82 JP 21; [1918] 1 KB 109; [1918] 87 LJCL 292; (1917-18) 117 LTR 716; (1917-18) XXXIV TLR 24 HC KBD Must be intention to deceive to be convicted of fortune-telling.

Curtis: Motion for Bail (1965-66) 116 NLJ 612t HC QBD Police objections to bail that applicant might interfere with/seek to frighten witnesses not defeated simply because is no evidence of such behaviour on part of applicant/his colleagues.

Curwen, Richards v [1977] 3 All ER 426; (1977) 65 Cr App R 95; [1977] Crim LR 356; (1977) 141 JP 641; (1977) 127 NLJ 468t; (1977) 121 SJ 270; [1977] 1 WLR 747 HC QBD Whether firearm antique to be determined in each case - no set age.

Cushen and Spratley, R v [1978] Crim LR 51 CA Three months' imprisonment for racially motivated threatening behaviout.

Customs and Excise Commissioners, M Potter Ltd v [1973] Crim LR 116 CA Gravity knife (a lock knife) was an offensive weapon.

D'Andrea v Woods [1953] 2 All ER 1028; (1953) 37 Cr App R 182; (1953) 117 JP 560; (1953) 103 LJ 687; (1953) 97 SJ 745; [1953] 1 WLR 1307 HC QBD Receipt of 'property' includes receipt of proceeds of theft/conversion.

D'Souza (E), R v; R v D'Souza (C) [1992] Crim LR 119 HC QBD Assaults of police officers properly seeking to apprehend mental patient were assaults on same in execution of their duty.

D'Souza v Director of Public Prosecutions [1992] 4 All ER 545; (1993) 96 Cr App R 278; (1992) 142 NLJ 1540; [1992] 1 WLR 1073 HL Police right of entry and search available only in course of chase.

D, R v [1984] 2 All ER 449; [1984] AC 778 (also CA); (1984) 79 Cr App R 313; [1984] Crim LR 558; [1984] FLR 847; (1984) 128 SJ 469; [1984] TLR 401; [1984] 3 WLR 186 HL Parent's taking/carrying away of child by force/fraud is kidnapping; parental kidnapping best dealt with as contempt.

D, R v [1984] AC 778 (also HL); (1984) 78 Cr App R 219; [1984] Crim LR 103; [1984] FLR 300; (1984) 128 SJ 63; [1983] TLR 641; [1984] 2 WLR 112 CA Parent's taking/carrying away of own unmarried under-fourteen year old child by force/fraud is not kidnapping; parental kidnapping best dealt with as contempt.

Da Costa Small v Kirkpatrick (1979) 68 Cr App R 186; [1979] Crim LR 41 HC QBD Unlawful arrest on warrant as warrant not physically in police officer's possession when effected arrest.

Da Costa Small v Kirkpatrick (1978) 128 NLJ 1125t CA Unlawful arrest on warrant as warrant not physically in police officer's possession when effected arrest.

Dabek v Chief Constable of Devon and Cornwall (1991) 155 JP 55; [1990] TLR 487 HC QBD Firearms certificate properly revoked where holder (although of good character) was married to person of dubious character.

Dabek, R v [1973] Crim LR 527 CA Person was guilty of handling where received goods from person guilty of obtaining them by deception.

Dacey, R v [1939] 2 All ER 641; (1939-40) XXXI Cox CC 283; (1938-40) 27 Cr App R 86; (1939) 160 LTR 652; (1939) 83 SJ 480; (1938-39) LV TLR 670; (1939) WN (I) 166 CCA Circumstantial evidence suggesting knew what possessed placed burden on accused to disprove had knowledge.

Daily Mirror Newspapers, Limited, R v; R v Glover (Charles William) (1921-22) 16 Cr App R 131; (1922) 86 JP 151; [1922] 2 KB 530; (1922) 57 LJ 196; [1922] 91 LJCL 712; (1922) 127 LTR 218; (1921-22) 66 SJ 559; (1921-22) XXXVIII TLR 531 CCA Could not try limited company by indictment but might charge person for aiding and abetting limited company in criminal act.

Dalby, R v [1982] 1 All ER 916; (1982) 74 Cr App R 348; [1982] Crim LR 439; (1982) 146 JP 392; (1982) 126 SJ 97; [1982] 1 WLR 425 CA For unlawful and dangerous act to be actus reus of manslaughter must be directed at victim and likely to cause immediate injury.

Dale v Smith [1967] 2 All ER 1133; [1967] Crim LR 372t; (1967) 131 JP 378; (1967) 111 SJ 330; [1967] 1 WLR 700 HC QBD Innocent word can be importuning in light of previous occurrence.

Daley, Director of Public Prosecutions v; Director of Public Prosecutions v McGhie [1980] AC 237; (1979) 69 Cr App R 39; [1979] Crim LR 182; (1978) 122 SJ 860; [1979] 2 WLR 239 PC On what constitutes manslaughter where death occurs in attempt to flee from assault.

Dalgleish, R v [1963] Crim LR 350 Sessions Failed prosecution for procuring another to pay money to third party by paying cheque to former with intent to defraud (insufficient connection between original cheque payment and later payment to third party).

Dalton and Stevens, Lee v [1954] Crim LR 206 HC QBD Persons who allowed poultry to wander freely by day over unfenced/uncultivated land entitled to protection of Dogs (Protection of Livestock) Act 1953.

Dalton, R v [1982] Crim LR 375 Magistrates Single occasion of begging not offence of placing self in public place to beg/gather alms (Vagrancy Act 1824, s 3).

Dalton-Brockwell, R v [1969] Crim LR 329 CA On proving that false pretence was in fact the/a cause of the obtaining where person charged with obtaining by false pretences.

Dandridge (Arthur Ernest), R v (1930-31) Cr App R 156 CCA Failure to keep books under Bankruptcy Act 1914, s 158, as amended not 'excusable' though might be 'honest'.

Daniel v Morrison (1980) 70 Cr App R 142; [1980] Crim LR 181 HC QBD No constraints imposed on power of detention under Metropolitan Police Act 1839, s 66 once reasonable suspicion of offences outlined therein.

Dann and other, Thompson v (1994) 138 SJ LB 221 HC QBD Court not satisfied beyond reasonable doubt that personation (and not mere mistake) had occurred.

Darbo v Director of Public Prosecutions [1992] Crim LR 56; (1991) 141 NLJ 1004t; [1991] TLR 339 HC QBD Sexually explicit materials do not per se have to be obscene for purposes of Obscene Publications Act 1959, s 3.

Darch v Weight [1984] 2 All ER 245; (1984) 79 Cr App R 40; [1984] Crim LR 168; (1984) 148 JP 588; (1984) 128 SJ 315; [1983] TLR 715; [1984] 1 WLR 659 HC QBD Positive act necessary for harbouring to arise; harbouring by non-owner of property possible.

Dargue (Walter), R v (1910-11) 6 Cr App R 261 CCA Must show person parting with goods was induced by false pretences to do so.

Darroch v Director of Public Prosecutions (1990) 91 Cr App R 378; [1990] Crim LR 814; (1990) 154 JP 844; [1990] TLR 368 HC QBD Persistent driving around 'red light' area was not persistent soliciting; single gesture to prostitute was soliciting but could not be persistent soliciting.

Das (Lala Jairam) and others v RI (1945) 89 SJ 164; (1944-45) LXI TLR 245 PC Indian HC cannot grant bail to convict granted leave to appeal to PC but Provincial Government can stay execution of convict's sentence pending appeal.

Dass and another v Rennie [1961] Crim LR 396t; (1961) 105 SJ 158 HC QBD Was obstruction of police officer in execution of his duty to ignore his request to cease throwing material from place which police could not approach without trespassing.

Data Protection Registrar v Amnesty International [1995] Crim LR 633; [1994] TLR 597 HC QBD On what constitutes 'recklessness' for purposes of data protection offences of recklessly holding/ disclosing data.

Data Protection Registrar v Griffin [1993] TLR 115 HC QBD Accountant ought to have registered as data user under the Data Protection Act 1984 where used data provided by clients to prepare accounts for Inland Revenue on computer.

Davenport, R v [1954] 1 All ER 602; (1954) 38 Cr App R 37; [1954] Crim LR 383; (1954) 118 JP 241; (1954) 98 SJ 217; [1954] 1 WLR 569 CCA Not liable for stealing money as no asportation but was liable for embezzlement.

Davey and others v Lee [1967] 2 All ER 423; (1967) 51 Cr App R 303; [1967] Crim LR 357; (1967) 131 JP 327; [1968] 1 QB 366; (1967) 111 SJ 212; [1967] 3 WLR 105 HC QBD On what constitutes attempt.

Davidge v Bunnett [1984] Crim LR 297 HC QBD Cheques given by persons with whom shared house to meet gas bill owed collectively was property to be used as sought so long as gas bill was paid.

Davies, R v [1954] 3 All ER 335; [1955] Crim LR 40; (1955) 119 JP 15; (1954) 104 LJ 744; [1955] 1 QB 71; (1954) 98 SJ 117/789; [1954] 3 WLR 664 CCA 'Public company' in Larceny Act 1916, s 20(1)(ii) includes company that is 'private' under Companies Act 1948, s 28.

Davies, Turner and Co Ld v Brodie [1954] 1 WLR 1364 HC QBD Accused not guilty of aiding and abetting (road traffic) offence where principal had given misleading good faith explanation of facts and accused had taken reasonable precautions.

Davis, Gary, R v (1989) 88 Cr App R 347, [1988] Crim LR 762 CA Cash given in exchange for uncashed cheque is the 'proceeds' of the cheque under Theft Act 1968, s 5(4); prosecution need not prove which of two cashed cheques (where only one should have been sent) was subject of theft.

Davis v Alexander (1970) 54 Cr App R 398; [1972] Crim LR 595 HC QBD Prosecution need not prove accused carried weapon with intent to cause injury where is clearly offensive weapon.

Davis v Curry (1918-21) XXVI Cox CC 100; (1918) 82 JP 21; [1918] 1 KB 109; [1918] 87 LJCL 292; (1917-18) 117 LTR 716; (1917-18) XXXIV TLR 24 HC KBD Must be intention to deceive to be convicted of fortune-telling.

Davis v Lisle (1934-39) XXX Cox CC 412; (1936) 100 JP 280; [1936] 2 KB 434; [1936] 105 LJCL 593; (1936) 155 LTR 23; (1936) 80 SJ 409; (1935-36) LII TLR 475 HC KBD Not guilty of assault/obstruction of police in course of duty as had at material time requested police to leave property so police were trespassers.

Davis v Thomas (1919-20) XXXVI TLR 39 HC ChD Persons inducing another to do something which is not unlawful for other to do are only responsible for what is done if secured same by unlawful means.

Davis, Director of Public Prosecutions v; Director of Public Prosecutions v Pittaway [1994] Crim LR 600 HC QBD On test when determining whether duress present (here in context of offence of driving with excess alcohol).

Davis, R v [1977] Crim LR 542 CA Successful appeal by person convicted of aiding and abetting burglary where person charged as burglar was acquitted.

Davis, R v [1972] Crim LR 431 CA Evidence of handling after particular handling charge was validly admitted.

Davis, R v (1968) 52 Cr App R 227 Assizes Must be person apart from accused in house to be guilty of arson under the Malicious Damage Act 1861, s 2.

Davis, R v (1918-21) XXVI Cox CC 98; (1917-18) 13 Cr App R 10; [1917] 2 KB 855; [1918] 87 LJCL 119; (1917-18) 117 LTR 704; (1917-18) 62 SJ 55; (1917-18) XXXIV TLR 25; (1917) WN (I) 290 CCA Can be convicted as habitual criminal if prosecution prove previous conviction as such - regardless of post-conviction behaviour.

Davison, R v [1992] Crim LR 31 CA On elements of offence of affray.

Davison, Whitehorn Brothers v [1908-10] All ER 885; [1911] 1 KB 463 CA Person obtaining delivery of goods for re-sale by fraud guilty of obtaining by false pretences, not larceny by trick.

Dawes v Director of Public Prosecutions [1995] 1 Cr App R 65; [1994] Crim LR 604; [1994] RTR 209; [1994] TLR 112 HC QBD Valid arrest for aggravated driving.

Dawson (Anthony Mark), R v; R v James (Anthony) (1977) 64 Cr App R 170 CA Only issue in charge of robbery is whether force employed so as to steal.

Dawson (Brian), R v; R v Nolan (Stephen Thomas); R v Walmsley (Ian) (1985) 81 Cr App R 150; [1985] Crim LR 383; (1985) 149 JP 513 CA Is manslaughter if shock which cause in another results in physical harm and then death and reasonable man (without specialist medical knowledge) would have foreseen same.

Dawson, R v [1976] Crim LR 692 CA Matter for jury whether shoving of another by offender in course of robbery in tandem with another constituted force.

Dawson, R v; R v Wenlock [1960] 1 All ER 558; (1960) 44 Cr App R 87; [1960] Crim LR 358; (1960) 110 LJ 236; (1960) 104 SJ 191; [1960] 1 WLR 163 CCA Conspiracy charge unnecessary in light of substantive charges; bankruptcy examination inadmissible at trial for fraudulent conversion; where alternative counts should be convicted on one of which most certainly guilty; non-delivery post-sale not an obtaining of credit by fraud.

Daye, R v (1907-09) XXI Cox CC 659; (1908) 72 JP 269; [1908] 2 KB 333; [1908] 77 LJCL 659; (1908-09) XCIX LTR 165 HC KBD Bank required to release document deposited with them.

Dayle, R v [1973] 3 All ER 1151; (1974) 58 Cr App R 100; [1973] Crim LR 703t; (1974) 138 JP 65; [1974] 1 WLR 181 CA Intent to use non-offensive weapon to injure needed to sustain offensive weapon in public place charge.

Dayle, R v (1973) 123 NLJ 748t HC QBD Person acquitted of unawful possession of offensive weapon ought to have been acquitted of assault occasioning bodily harm (using said weapon).

Ddin, Edwards v [1976] 3 All ER 705; (1976) 63 Cr App R 218; [1976] Crim LR 580; (1977) 141 JP 27; [1976] (1976) 126 NLJ 718t; [1976] RTR 508; (1976) 120 SJ 587; [1976] 1 WLR 942 HC QBD Petrol from pump appropriated with assent of both parties when enters tank, not when payment made.

De Acetis, R v [1982] TLR 21 CA Prosecution must still prove relevant goods to have been stolen even though person charged with handling same says that he believed the goods to be stolen.

De Coster, Rankin v [1975] Crim LR 226 HC QBD Construction of Prevention of Oil Pollution Act 1971, s 2.

De Cristofaro v British Transport Police [1997] Crim LR 124; (1996) TLR 7/5/96 HC QBD Valid conviction of busker for unlawfully soliciting for reward for playing of music in London Underground station.

De Demko v Home Secretary and others [1959] 1 All ER 341; [1959] AC 654; [1959] Crim LR 212t; (1959) 123 JP 156; (1959) 109 LJ 120; (1959) 103 SJ 130 HL CA has original/not appellate jurisdiction under Fugitive Offenders Act 1881, s 10.

De Jager v Attorney-General of Natal [1904-07] All ER 1008; [1907] AC 326; (1907) XCVI LTR 857; (1906-07) XXIII TLR 516 PC Is treason for Crown subject to assist alien occupiers of Crown territory in which one resides.

De Livera and another, Attorney-General of Ceylon v [1963] Crim LR 105; (1963) 113 LJ 8; (1962) 106 SJ 935; [1962] 3 WLR 1413 PC Person deemed to have acted in contravention of Ceylon Bribery Act 1954, s 14.

De Marny, R v [1904-07] All ER 923; (1907-09) XXI Cox CC 371; (1907) 71 JP 14 (also CCC); [1907] 1 KB 388; (1906) 41 LJ 838; [1907] 76 LJKB 210; (1907) XCVI LTR 159; (1906-07) 51 SJ 146; (1906-07) XXIII TLR 221; (1907) WN (I) 10 CCR Newspaper editor liable for causing/procuring publication/sale of obscene publications by accepting/printing advertisements for obscene materials.

De Montalk (Geoffrey Wladislas Vaile Potocki), R v (1931-32) 23 Cr App R 182 CCA On elements of offence of publishing/uttering obscene libel.

De Munck, R v [1918-19] All ER 499; (1918-21) XXVI Cox CC 302; (1917-18) 13 Cr App R 113; (1918) 82 JP 160; [1918] 1 KB 635; [1918] 87 LJCL 682; (1918-19) 119 LTR 88; (1917-18) 62 SJ 405; (1917-18) XXXIV TLR 305 CCA Prostitute includes women selling themselves into acts of common lewdness short of sex.

De Vries v National Westminster Bank Ltd and others [1984] TLR 531 HC QBD Perjury prosecution appropriate action against individual who swore/employed affidavit in knowledge that it was false.

Deakin, R v [1972] 3 All ER 803; [1972] Crim LR 781; (1973) 137 JP 19; (1972) 116 SJ 944; [1972] 1 WLR 1618 CA Fence undertakes to realise goods for benefit of thief.

Dealy (John Clark), R v [1995] 2 Cr App R 398; (1995) 139 SJ LB 14 CA On what constitutes 'evasion' of VAT under Value Added Tax Act 1983, s 39(1).

Dean v Hiesler [1942] 2 All ER 340 HC KBD Defence (General) Regulations 1939 penal so interpreted strictly: person not appointed company director could not be convicted as such thereunder.

Dear, R v [1996] Crim LR 595 CA Person could be convicted of murder where caused bleeding that led to death even though deceased may have been responsible for bleeding re-commencing/continuing.

Dear, Smith v (1901-07) XX Cox CC 458; (1903) 67 JP 244; (1903) LXXXVIII LTR 664 HC KBD Any person (not just owner) may prosecute for unlawful and wilful killing of house pigeon.

Dearlove (Terence David), R v; R v Druker (David Didy) (1989) 88 Cr App R 279 CA Can prosecute for conspiracy to obtain property by deception where deception is via contract that contravenes Article 85(1)/EEC.

Debreli, R v [1964] Crim LR 53; (1963) 107 SJ 894 CCA Gun with firing pin removed was an 'imitation firearm'.

Dee v Yorke (1914) 78 JP 359; (1913-14) XXX TLR 552 HC KBD Whether treatment of animal was cruelty a question of fact for justices.

Delgado (Winston), R v [1984] 1 All ER 449; (1984) 78 Cr App R 175; [1984] Crim LR 169; (1984) 148 JP 431; (1984) 128 SJ 32; [1983] TLR 690; [1984] 1 WLR 89 CA Could be convicted of supplying dangerous drug where were storing (but had control of) large quantity of drug for friend.

Deller (Charles Avon), R v (1952) 36 Cr App R 184; (1952) 102 LJ 679 CCA Court could look to real and not apparent situation where alleged sale of car by false pretences was claimed to be one of loan on the security of the car.

Delmayne, R v [1969] 2 All ER 980; (1969) 53 Cr App R 392; [1969] Crim LR 485; (1969) 133 JP 458; (1969) 119 NLJ 676t; [1970] 2 QB 170; (1969) 113 SJ 605; [1969] 3 WLR 300 CA Pamphlets issued to mutual benefit society members was advertisement to public.

Dempsey (Michael Bruce), R v; R v Dempsey (Maureen Patricia) (1986) 82 Cr App R 291; [1986] Crim LR 171; (1986) 150 JP 213 CA Was possession where in good faith took controlled drug from person legally allowed use it; 'supply' of drug must benefit person taking possession and person passing same.

Denham v Scott (1983) 77 Cr App R 210; [1983] Crim LR 558; (1983) 147 JP 521; [1983] TLR 246 HC QBD Publication of 'no questions asked' reward advertisement contrary to Theft Act 1968, s 23, a strict liability offence - advertising manager who was unaware advertisement was therefore guilty of same.

Denney, R v [1963] Crim LR 191t CCA Conviction quashed where was inadequate direction as to evidence necessary to support alibi defence/was improper questioning as to accused's association with criminals.

Dennis (Annie), R v (1905) 69 JP 256 CCC Woman who shot husband in mistaken belief that was burglar to be acquitted of wounding with intent to do grievous bodily harm if that belief was reasonable.

Dent, R v [1955] 2 All ER 806; (1955) 39 Cr App R 131; [1955] Crim LR 501; (1955) 119 JP 512; (1955) 105 LJ 473; [1955] 2 QB 590; (1955) 99 SJ 511; [1955] 3 WLR 297 CCA Statement about intended future condct cannot be false pretence.

Denton, R v [1982] 1 All ER 65; (1982) 74 Cr App R 81; [1982] Crim LR 107; (1982) 146 JP 138; (1981) 125 SJ 746; [1981] 1 WLR 1446 CA Damage to own property not arson even if tainted with intent to commit fraud.

Denyer, R v (1926-30) XXVIII Cox CC 153; (1925-26) 19 Cr App R 93; [1926] 2 KB 258; (1926) 61 LJ 363; [1926] 95 LJCL 699; (1926) 134 LTR 637; (1925-26) XLII TLR 452 CCA Properly convicted of demanding money with menaces contrary to Larceny Act 1916, s 29(1) (i) even though sought to protect trade interest.

Department of Trade and Industry, Federal Steam Navigation Co Ltd v (1974) 59 Cr App R 131 HL Liability of master/owner of ship to prosecution under Oil in Navigable Waters Act 1955 (as amended).

Department of Trade and Industry, Rudd v [1986] Crim LR 455 CA Records/cassettes not (but speakers were) susceptible to forfeiture as wireless apparatus under the Wireless Telegraphy Act 1949.

Department of Trade and Industry, Rudd v (1970) 130 SJ 504 HC QBD Records/cassettes not (but speakers were) susceptible to forfeiture as wireless apparatus under the Wireless Telegraphy Act 1949.

Dervish, R v [1968] Crim LR 37t; (1967) 117 NLJ 1218t CA Failed attempt to establish defence of automatism to homicide charge.

Deshpande (Vimlabai) and another, RI v [1946] 115 LJ 71; (1945-46) LXII TLR 430; (1946) WN (I) 105 PC Can appeal direct to PC from Indian HC where object to release of person pursuant to habeas corpus application.

Desmond and another, Smith v [1965] 1 All ER 976; [1965] AC 960; (1965) 49 Cr App R 246; [1965] Crim LR 315t; (1965) 129 JP 331; (1965) 115 LJ 297; (1965) 109 SJ 269; [1965] 2 WLR 894 HL Crime done in presence of persons if done in other room within their care/control.

Desmond, R v; R v Hall [1964] 3 All ER 587; (1965) 49 Cr App R 1; [1964] Crim LR 724; (1964) 128 JP 591; (1964) 114 LJ 773; (1964) 108 SJ 677; [1964] 3 WLR 1148 CCA Robbery not in presence of person if not physically present at scene; can be convicted for crime that is element of serious offence (simple larceny where charge is robbery with violence).

Despard and others v Wilcox and others (1911-13) XXII Cox CC 258; (1910) 74 JP 115; (1910) 102 LTR 103; (1909-10) XXVI TLR 226 HC KBD Suffragettes blocking Downing Street despite police requests to disperse guilty of obstructing police in execution of their duty.

Devall, R v [1984] Crim LR 428 CA Successful appeals against convictions for 'second appropriation'.

Dew v Director of Public Prosecutions (1920-21) XXXVII TLR 22 HC KBD Publication of draft ticket sale scheme to printers could sustain conviction under Lotteries Act 1823, s 41.

Dewsbury Magistrates' Court, France v [1988] Crim LR 295; (1988) 152 JP 301 HC QBD Improper for later court to convict person for non-surrender to bail where justices present upon surrender indicated that one-day delay in surrender would be overlooked.

Dharma (Chandra), R v (1905) 69 JP 39; (1905) 40 LJ 238 CCR Person who committed offence before extended prosecution period legislation received Royal Assent could be prosecuted within newly extended period.

Dharma (Chandra), R v; R v Slater; R v Hutchinson; R v Court (1905) XCII LTR 700; (1904-05) 49 SJ 366; (1904-05) XXI TLR 353 CCR Extension by Prevention of Cruelty of Children Act 1904 to limitation on bringing prosecutions under Criminal Law Amendment Act 1885 operated retrospectively as did not create new offence.

Dharmasena (Kannangara Aratchige) v R [1951] AC 1; (1950) 94 SJ 565; [1950] 66 (2) TLR 365; (1950) WN (I) 391 PC Either all or neither party (where two persons charged) guilty of criminal conspiracy: re-trial of one conspirator demands re-trial of other.

Dhillon (IK) and Dhillon (GS), R v [1992] Crim LR 889 CA Method whereby mortgage advances made not a matter to be left to jury's own knowledge/experience.

Dhillon, R v [1997] 2 Cr App R 104; [1997] Crim LR 295 CA On whether/when defence of provocation ought (as should have been here) to be left to jury.

Diamond (Charles), R v (1920) 84 JP 211 CCC On elements of offence of soliciting unknown individuals to murder contrary to the Offences against the Person Act 1861, s 4.

Diamond v Minter and others [1941] 1 All ER 390; (1939-40) XXXI Cox CC 468; (1941) 105 JP 181; [1941] 1 KB 656; (1942) 92 LJ 52/59; [1941] 110 LJ 503; (1941) 164 LTR 362; (1941) 85 SJ 155; (1940-41) LVII TLR 332; (1941) WN (I) 58 HC KBD Can only arrest fugitive offender under Fugitive Offenders Act 1881 and if have indorsed/provisional warrant.

Dibble v Ingleton [1972] 1 All ER 275; (1972) 136 JP 155; (1971) 121 NLJ 1049t; [1972] RTR 161; (1972) 116 SJ 97; [1972] 2 WLR 163 HC QBD Act of obstruction need not be unlawful in itself to support obstruction conviction.

Dick (Surujpaul called) v R [1958] 3 All ER 300; (1958) 42 Cr App R 266; [1958] Crim LR 806; (1958) 108 LJ 681; (1958) 102 SJ 757 PC Cannot be convicted accessory before fact when principals acquitted of substantive offence.

Dickie (Andrew Plummer), R v (1984) 79 Cr App R 213; [1984] Crim LR 497; (1984) 128 SJ 331; [1984] TLR 248; [1984] 1 WLR 1031 CA Exceptionally judge could raise insanity issue though neither prosecution/defence did so.

Director of Public Prosecutions of Trinidad and Tobago and another, Phillip and others v; Phillip and others v Commissioner of Prisons and another [1992] 1 All ER 665; [1992] 1 AC 545; [1991] TLR 596; [1992] 2 WLR 211 PC Prima facie valid pardon requires immediate hearing of habeas corpus application.

Director of Public Prosecutions v A and BC Chewing Gum, Ltd [1967] 2 All ER 504; [1967] Crim LR 419; (1967) 131 JP 373; [1968] 1 QB 159; (1967) 111 SJ 331; [1967] 3 WLR 493 HC QBD Expert evidence on effect not evidence on tendency to corrupt/deprave so admissible.

Director of Public Prosecutions v Ashley [1955] Crim LR 565 Assizes Annulment of bankruptcy did not mean could not be prosecuted for bankruptcy offences.

Director of Public Prosecutions v Baillie [1995] Crim LR 426 HC QBD Passing on free information to travellers about possible upcoming festival that might be held in public place (contrary to police notice under Public Order Act 1986, s 14) was not public order offence.

Director of Public Prosecutions v Barry [1989] Crim LR 645; (1989) 133 SJ 784 HC QBD Offence of procuring fighting of animal under Protection of Animals Act 1911, s 1(1)(c) included wild animals.

Director of Public Prosecutions v Beard [1920] All ER 21; [1920] AC 479; (1918-21) XXVI Cox CC 573; (1919-20) 14 Cr App R 159; (1920) 84 JP 129 (also CCA); [1920] 89 LJCL 437; (1920) 55 LJ 116; (1920) 122 LTR 625; (1919-20) 64 SJ 340; (1919-20) XXXVI TLR 379; (1920) WN (I) 110 HL Cannot be guilty of murder if so drunk could not form necessary intent (are guilty of manslaughter); (temporary) insanity deriving from drink will sustain insanity defence.

Director of Public Prosecutions v Beate Uhse (UK) Ltd and another [1974] 1 All ER 753; [1974] Crim LR 106; (1974) 138 JP 247; (1973) 123 NLJ 1112t; [1974] QB 158; (1974) 118 SJ 34; [1974] 2 WLR 50 HC QBD To send unsolicited non-explicit advertising material on sexual technique book an offence.

Director of Public Prosecutions v Bell [1992] Crim LR 176; [1992] RTR 335 HC QBD Person with excess alcohol fleeing from dangerous scene in terror/not proven to have driven longer than necessary/ who did not cease being terrified while driving could rely on defence of duress.

Director of Public Prosecutions v Bhagwan [1970] 3 All ER 97; [1972] AC 60; (1970) 54 Cr App R 460; [1970] Crim LR 582; (1970) 134 JP 622; (1970) 114 SJ 683; [1970] 3 WLR 501 HL Not an offence to seek to do something the doing of which Parliament had aimed but failed to prohibit via statute.

Director of Public Prosecutions v Bignall (1997) 161 JP 541; [1997] TLR 296 HC QBD Not offence under Computer Misuse Act 1990, s 1, for generally authorised person to access a programme for unauthorised reason.

Director of Public Prosecutions v Blady (1911-13) XXII Cox CC 715; (1912) 76 JP 141; [1912] 2 KB 89; (1912) 81 LJKB 613; (1912) 106 LTR 302; (1911-12) XXVIII TLR 193 HC KBD Wife's evidence as prosecution witness could not be admitted under common law/Criminal Evidence Act 1898.

Director of Public Prosecutions v Brooks [1974] 2 All ER 840; [1974] AC 862; (1974) 59 Cr App R 185; [1974] Crim LR 364; (1974) 118 SJ 420; [1974] 2 WLR 899 PC Possession if in physical custody/control.

Director of Public Prosecutions v Bull [1994] 4 All ER 411; [1995] 1 Cr App R 413; [1994] Crim LR 762; (1994) 158 JP 1005; [1995] QB 88; [1994] TLR 314; [1994] 3 WLR 1196 HC QBD Male prostitute not a 'common prostitute'.

Director of Public Prosecutions v Burgess [1970] 3 All ER 266; [1970] Crim LR 597t; (1970) 134 JP 646; (1970) 120 NLJ 661t and 946; [1971] 1 QB 432; (1970) 114 SJ 768; [1970] 3 WLR 805 HC QBD DPP must consent to gross indecency towards child prosecution; gross indecency towards child means gross indecency involving child.

Director of Public Prosecutions v Camplin [1978] 2 All ER 168; [1978] AC 705; (1978) 67 Cr App R 14; [1978] Crim LR 432; (1978) 142 JP 320; (1978) 128 NLJ 537t; (1978) 122 SJ 280; [1978] 2 WLR 679 HL 'Reasonable man' not just adult male; unusual characteristics of accused relevant to 'reasonable man' test.

Director of Public Prosecutions v K and another (1997) 1 Cr App R 36; [1997] Crim LR 121 HC QBD Could be guilty of procuring rape by person aged between ten and fourteen in respect of whom the doli incapax presumption had not been rebutted.

Director of Public Prosecutions v Kellet [1994] Crim LR 916; (1994) 158 JP 1138; [1994] TLR 399 HC QBD That had been drunk was no excuse for letting unmuzzled/untethered dangerous dog wander into public place.

Director of Public Prosecutions v Kent and Sussex Contractors, Ltd and another [1944] 1 All ER 119; [1944] KB 146; [1944] 113 LJ 88; (1945) 95 LJ 102; (1944) 170 LTR 41; (1944) 88 SJ 59; (1943-44) LX TLR 175 HC KBD Intentions of its servants are attributed to corporation.

Director of Public Prosecutions v Khan [1990] Crim LR 321; (1989) 139 NLJ 1455 HC QBD Was occasioning actual bodily harm to place dangerous substance in machine used by public where (albeit that had not intended harm) next user was harmed by substance being ejected from machine.

Director of Public Prosecutions v Kitching [1990] Crim LR 394; (1990) 154 JP 293 HC QBD Police officer could arrest person for being drunk and disorderly in public place.

Director of Public Prosecutions v Lavender [1994] Crim LR 297; [1993] TLR 315 HC QBD Was theft to remove doors from one council property and hang them in other property of same council.

Director of Public Prosecutions v Majewski [1976] 2 All ER 142; [1977] AC 443 (also CA); (1976) 62 Cr App R 262; [1976] Crim LR 374; (1976) 140 JP 315; (1976) 126 NLJ 542t; (1976) 120 SJ 299; [1976] 2 WLR 623 HL Self-induced intoxication no defence unless specific intent required.

Director of Public Prosecutions v Mills [1997] 2 Cr App R 6; [1996] Crim LR 746; [1997] QB 301; (1996) TLR 1/4/96 HC QBD Threatening witness by telephone was perverting the course of justice contrary to the Criminal Justice and Public Order Act 1994, s 51(1).

Director of Public Prosecutions v Morgan; Director of Public Prosecutions v McDonald; Director of Public Prosecutions v McLarty; Director of Public Prosecutions v Parker [1975] 2 All ER 347; [1976] AC 182 (also CA); (1975) 61 Cr App R 136; [1975] Crim LR 717; (1975) 139 JP 476; (1975) 125 NLJ 530t; (1975) 119 SJ 319; [1975] 2 WLR 913 (also CA) HL Belief that woman consents means no rape as no mens rea.

Director of Public Prosecutions v Newbury; Director of Public Prosecutions v Jones [1976] 2 All ER 365; [1977] AC 500; (1976) 62 Cr App R 291; [1977] Crim LR 359; (1976) 140 JP 370; (1976) 126 NLJ 618t; (1976) 120 SJ 402; [1976] 2 WLR 918 HL Manslaughter if person un/knowingly does unlawful/dangerous act which causes death.

Director of Public Prosecutions v Nieser [1958] 3 All ER 662; (1959) 43 Cr App R 35; [1959] Crim LR 128; (1959) 123 JP 105; (1959) 109 LJ 58; [1959] 1 QB 254; (1958) 102 SJ 955; [1958] 3 WLR 757 HC QBD Must know whether property obtained either by felony or misdemeanour to prove receiving.

Director of Public Prosecutions v Nock; Director of Public Prosecutions v Alsford [1978] 2 All ER 655; [1978] AC 979 (also CA); (1978) 67 Cr App R 116 (also CA); [1978] Crim LR 483; (1978) 142 JP 414; (1978) 128 NLJ 759t; (1978) 122 SJ 417; [1978] 3 WLR 56 (also CA) HL Conspiracy to commit a crime only if planned conduct would result in crime.

Director of Public Prosecutions v Nock; Director of Public Prosecutions v Alsford [1978] AC 979 (also HL); (1978) 67 Cr App R 116 (also HL); (1978) 128 NLJ 264t; (1978) 122 SJ 128; [1978] 3 WLR 56 (also HL) CA Conspiracy to commit a crime though planned conduct would not result in crime.

Director of Public Prosecutions v Orum [1988] 3 All ER 449; (1989) 88 Cr App R 261; [1988] Crim LR 848; (1989) 153 JP 85; (1988) 132 SJ 1637; [1989] 1 WLR 88 HC QBD Police officer may be person caused harrassment/alarm/distress for purposes of Public Order Act but cannot arrest if not so affected and is only person present.

Director of Public Prosecutions v Ray [1973] 3 All ER 131; [1974] AC 370; (1974) 58 Cr App R 130; (1973) 137 JP 744; (1973) 117 SJ 663; [1973] 3 WLR 359 HL Person deciding not to pay only after ordering meal obtains pecuniary advantage by deception: regard to be had to all of behaviour in restaurant.

Director of Public Prosecutions v Richards [1988] 3 All ER 406; (1989) 88 Cr App R 97; [1988] Crim LR 606; (1988) 152 JP 333; [1988] QB 701; (1988) 132 SJ 623; [1988] 3 WLR 153 HC QBD Can be arrested for leaving court building after surrendering to bail but not guilty of offence.

Director of Public Prosecutions v Rogers [1953] 2 All ER 644; (1953) 37 Cr App R 137; (1953) 117 JP 424; (1953) 97 SJ 541; [1953] 1 WLR 1017 HC QBD No coercion/violence in getting child to do indecent act meant no assault so could be no indecent assault.

Director of Public Prosecutions v Schildkamp [1971] AC 1; (1970) 54 Cr App R 90; [1970] Crim LR 95; [1970] 2 WLR 279 HL Company must be in liquidation before can be prosecuted for fraudulent trading.

Director of Public Prosecutions v Shannon [1974] 2 All ER 1009; [1975] AC 717; (1974) 59 Cr App R 250; [1974] Crim LR 177; (1974) 138 JP 587; [1974] 3 WLR 155 CA One conspirator's acquittal does not preclude other's conviction.

Director of Public Prosecutions v Shannon [1974] 2 All ER 1009; [1975] AC 717; (1974) 59 Cr App R 250; [1975] Crim LR 703; (1974) 138 JP 587; (1974) 118 SJ 515; [1974] 3 WLR 155 HL One conspirator's acquittal does not preclude other's conviction.

Director of Public Prosecutions v Smith [1960] 3 All ER 161; (1960) 44 Cr App R 261; [1960] Crim LR 765; (1960) 124 JP 473; (1960) 110 LJ 573; (1960) 104 SJ 683; [1960] 3 WLR 546 HL If objectively foreseeable result of vouluntary unlawful act is grievous bodily harm then absent inability is presumed intended same.

Director of Public Prosecutions v Stonehouse [1977] 2 All ER 909; [1978] AC 55; (1977) 65 Cr App R 192 (also CCA); [1977] Crim LR 544; (1977) 141 JP 473; (1977) 127 NLJ 864; (1977) 121 SJ 491; [1977] 3 WLR 143 HL Guilty of obtaining property by deception where acts done abroad but property obtained by deception in England; doing all possible acts to obtain property by deception could sustain conviction for attempt thereof.

Director of Public Prosecutions v Taylor; Director of Public Prosecutions v Little [1992] 1 All ER 299; [1991] Crim LR 900/904; (1991) 155 JP 713; (1991) 141 NLJ 964; (1991) 141 NLJ 1038t; [1992] QB 645; [1992] 2 WLR 460 HC QBD Assault and battery separate offences; assaults and batteries triable summarily.

Director of Public Prosecutions v Turner [1973] 3 All ER 124; [1974] AC 357; (1973) 57 Cr App R 932; [1974] Crim LR 186; (1973) 137 JP 736; (1973) 123 NLJ 747t; (1973) 117 SJ 664; [1973] 3 WLR 352 HL That evaded debt proved obtained pecuniary advantage even if not so.

Director of Public Prosecutions v Waite [1997] Crim LR 123; (1996) TLR 17/5/96 HC QBD On when using radio scanner constitutes offence of unauthorised monitoring of broadcast contrary to the Wireless Telegraphy Act 1949, s 5(b)(i).

Director of Public Prosecutions v Walker (Leary) [1974] Crim LR 368; [1974] 1 WLR 1090 PC Where inter alia force far exceeded what was necessary for self-defence could not successfully plead self-defence.

Director of Public Prosecutions v Whyte and another [1972] 3 All ER 12; [1972] AC 849; (1973) 57 Cr App R 74; [1972] Crim LR 556t; (1972) 136 JP 686; (1972) 122 NLJ 703t; (1972) 116 SJ 583; [1972] 3 WLR 410 HL Material obscene even if directed at the depraved; consequent sexual activity unnecessary to prove can deprave/corrupt.

Director of Public Prosecutions, A v [1997] 1 Cr App R 27; [1997] Crim LR 125 HC QBD On rebuttal of doli incapax presumption.

Director of Public Prosecutions, A v [1992] Crim LR 34 HC QBD Successful appeal by eleven year old who rightly claimed that doli incapax presumption had not been rebutted in his regard.

Director of Public Prosecutions, Ackroyds Air Travel, Ltd v [1950] 1 All ER 933; (1950) 114 JP 251 HC KBD Conviction for aiding and abetting unlawful carrying of passengers for hire/reward (Civil Aviation Act 1946, s 23(1)).

Director of Public Prosecutions, Andrews v [1937] 2 All ER 552; [1937] AC 576; (1936-38) 26 Cr App R 34; (1937) 101 JP 386; (1937) 83 LJ 304; [1937] 106 LJCL 370; (1937) 81 SJ 497; (1936-37) LIII TLR 663; (1937) WN (I) 188 HL Can be convicted of reckless driving where negligence insufficient to sustain manslaughter charge in case where victim dies.

Director of Public Prosecutions, Atkin v (1989) 89 Cr App R 199; [1989] Crim LR 581; (1989) 153 JP 383 HC QBD Person against whom threatening words/behaviour directed must be physically present.

Director of Public Prosecutions, Bates v (1993) 157 JP 1004; [1993] TLR 118 HC QBD Having unmuzzled dangerous dog inside car in public place constituted offence of having unmuzzled dangerous dog in public place.

Director of Public Prosecutions, Bedder v [1954] 2 All ER 801; (1954) 38 Cr App R 133; [1954] Crim LR 721; (1954) 104 LJ 536; (1954) 98 SJ 556; [1954] 1 WLR 1119 HL Test provocation by reference to reasonable man who need not possess characteristics peculiar to accused.

Director of Public Prosecutions, Blake v [1993] Crim LR 586 HC QBD Not lawful excuse to criminal damage charge (vicar writing anti-government policy graffiti on pillar) that had genuine belief were acting in accordance with what God wanted (and so law of England protected).

Director of Public Prosecutions, Blakely and another v [1991] Crim LR 763; [1991] RTR 405; [1991] TLR 288 HC QBD Recklessness an inappropriate consideration when deciding whether person had necessary mens rea to be guilty of procuring principal to commit offence.

Director of Public Prosecutions, Brown v [1992] TLR 155 HC QBD Stun-gun a prohibited weapon though was not functioning properly.

Director of Public Prosecutions, Burge v [1962] 1 All ER 666; [1962] Crim LR 178t; (1962) 106 SJ 198 HC QBD On male soliciting (by advertisement).

Director of Public Prosecutions, Button v; Swain v Director of Public Prosecutions [1965] 3 All ER 587; [1966] AC 591; (1966) 50 Cr App R 36; [1966] Crim LR 39; (1966) 130 JP 48; (1965-66) 116 NLJ 131; (1965) 109 SJ 872; [1965] 3 WLR 1131 HL Affray need not occur in public place to be affray.

Director of Public Prosecutions, C v [1995] 2 All ER 43; [1996] 1 AC 1 (also HC QBD); [1995] 2 Cr App R 166; [1995] Crim LR 801; [1995] 1 FLR 933; (1995) 159 JP 269; (1995) 145 NLJ 416; [1995] RTR 261; [1995] TLR 164; [1995] 2 WLR 383 HL On continuing presumption of doli incapax in respect of child aged between 10 and 14 and on rebuttal of said presumption.

Director of Public Prosecutions, C v [1994] 3 All ER 190; [1996] 1 AC 1 (also HL); [1995] 1 Cr App R 118; [1994] Crim LR 523; (1994) 158 JP 389; [1994] RTR 341; (1994) 138 SJ LB 91; [1994] TLR 180; [1994] 3 WLR 888 HC QBD On demise of presumption of doli incapax in respect of child aged between 10 and 14.

Director of Public Prosecutions, Chambers and Edwards v [1995] Crim LR 896 HC QBD On what constitutes 'disorderly behaviour' for purposes of Public Order Act 1986, s 5(1).

Director of Public Prosecutions, Chandler and others v [1962] 3 All ER 142; [1964] AC 763; (1962) 46 Cr App R 347; [1962] Crim LR 634t; (1962) 112 LJ 552; (1962) 106 SJ 588; [1962] 3 WLR 694 HL Critique of defence policy inadmissible as defence to conspiring to enter prohibited place; definition of terms in Official Secrets Act 1911, s 1.

Director of Public Prosecutions, Chapman v (1989) 89 Cr App R 190; [1988] Crim LR 843; (1989) 153 JP 27 HC QBD Conviction quashed where absence of evidence that entry onto premises to effect arrest was reasonable.

Director of Public Prosecutions, Cheeseman v [1991] 3 All ER 54; (1991) 93 Cr App R 145; [1991] Crim LR 296; (1991) 155 JP 469; [1992] QB 83; [1990] TLR 690; [1991] 2 WLR 1105 HC QBD On-duty police officers policing public toilet were not 'passengers' before whom indecent exposure to their annoyance could constitute offence (Town Police Clauses Act 1847, s 28, as amended).

Director of Public Prosecutions, Cichon v [1994] Crim LR 918 HC QBD Could not plead defence of necessity to having unmuzzled pit bull terrier in public place (allegedly unmuzzled to prevent discomfort in coughing).

Director of Public Prosecutions, Cobb v (1992) 156 JP 746 HC QBD On what constitutes (must be proved to establish) offence of affray.

Director of Public Prosecutions, Copus v [1989] Crim LR 577 HC QBD Rice flail an offensive weapon per se.

Director of Public Prosecutions, Curry v (1994) 144 NLJ 498 HC QBD Rebuttable doli incapax presumption in respect of ten to fourteen year olds not valid any more.

Director of Public Prosecutions, D'Souza v [1992] 4 All ER 545; (1993) 96 Cr App R 278; (1992) 142 NLJ 1540; [1992] 1 WLR 1073 HL Police right of entry and search available only in course of chase.

Director of Public Prosecutions, Darbo v [1992] Crim LR 56; (1991) 141 NLJ 1004t; [1991] TLR 339 HC QBD Sexually explicit materials do not per se have to be obscene for purposes of Obscene Publications Act 1959, s 3.

Director of Public Prosecutions, Darroch v (1990) 91 Cr App R 378; [1990] Crim LR 814; (1990) 154 JP 844; [1990] TLR 368 HC QBD Persistent driving around 'red light' area was not persistent soliciting; single gesture to prostitute was soliciting but could not be persistent soliciting.

Director of Public Prosecutions, Davies v [1954] 1 All ER 507; [1954] AC 378; [1954] Crim LR 305; (1954) 118 JP 222; (1954) 104 LJ 152; [1954] 2 WLR 343 HL Must be corroboration warning regarding accomplice's evidence; accomplice to be same must be party to crime charged.

Director of Public Prosecutions, Dawes v [1995] 1 Cr App R 65; [1994] Crim LR 604; [1994] RTR 209; [1994] TLR 112 HC QBD Valid arrest for aggravated driving.

Director of Public Prosecutions, Dew v (1920-21) XXXVII TLR 22 HC KBD Publication of draft ticket sale scheme to printers could sustain conviction under Lotteries Act 1823, s 41.

Director of Public Prosecutions, Edwards v (1993) 97 Cr App R 301; [1993] Crim LR 854; [1993] TLR 184 HC QBD Was not valid arrest for obstruction of police officer in execution of duty where arrestee aided person in turn arrested by officer under false pretext.

Director of Public Prosecutions, Fellowes v [1993] Crim LR 523; (1993) 157 JP 936; [1993] TLR 38 HC QBD Garden path not a 'public place' for purposes of Dangerous Dogs Act 1991.

Director of Public Prosecutions, Freed v (1969) 53 Cr App R 137; [1969] Crim LR 86t; (1968) 118 NLJ 1172t; (1968) 112 SJ 1020 HC QBD Meaning of 'gold coin'/'gold bullion' under Exchange Control Act 1947.

Director of Public Prosecutions, French and another v [1994] TLR 71 HC QBD Could convict/ acquit of handling/theft where person charged with both.

Director of Public Prosecutions, G v [1989] Crim LR 150 HC QBD On pre-requisites necessary for arrest to be valid under Town Police Clauses Act 1847, s 29/Police and Criminal Evidence Act 1984, s 25(3)).

Director of Public Prosecutions, Godwin v (1993) 96 Cr App R 244; (1993) 157 JP 197; [1992] TLR 406 HC QBD That explanation uncontroverted by prosecution did not mean had established lawful authority for possession of weapon.

Director of Public Prosecutions, Gold Star Publications Ltd v [1981] 2 All ER 257; (1981) 73 Cr App R 141; [1981] Crim LR 633; (1981) 145 JP 289; (1981) 131 NLJ 525; (1981) 125 SJ 376; [1981] 1 WLR 732 HL Article held in England can be obscene publication though purely for export.

Director of Public Prosecutions, Grace v [1989] Crim LR 365; (1989) 153 JP 491 HC QBD On proving that air-gun a lethal wepon (which it was).

Director of Public Prosecutions, Green v [1991] Crim LR 782; (1991) 155 JP 816; (1991) 141 NLJ 783t; [1991] TLR 236 HC QBD Advice to person not to answer police questions could if given in certain fashion be obstruction of police in execution of their duty.

Director of Public Prosecutions, Greener v (1996) TLR 15/2/96 HC QBD Could commit offence under Dangerous Dogs Act 1991 by omission.

Director of Public Prosecutions, Groom v [1991] Crim LR 713 HC QBD On what suffices as a 'warning' before arrest under Public Order Act 1986, s 5(4).

Director of Public Prosecutions, Harris v; Fehmi v Director of Public Prosecutions [1993] 1 All ER 562; (1993) 96 Cr App R 235; (1993) 157 JP 205; (1952) 102 LJ 246; (1992) 136 SJ LB 228; [1992] TLR 405; [1993] 1 WLR 82 HC QBD Lock-knife not a 'folding pocketknife' and hence an offence to carry in public place.

Director of Public Prosecutions, Henn and Darby v [1981] AC 850; (1980) 71 Cr App R 44; (1980) 130 NLJ 389; (1980) 124 SJ 290; [1980] 2 WLR 597 HL Permissible prohibition of obscene goods under Article 36/EEC.

Director of Public Prosecutions, Hodder v; Matthews v Director of Public Prosecutions [1990] Crim LR 261 HC QBD That had picked and frozen hallucinogenic mushrooms meant were in possession of 'product' containing controlled substance contrary to Misuse of Drugs Act 1971.

Director of Public Prosecutions, Holmes v [1946] 2 All ER 124; [1946] AC 588; (1945-46) 31 Cr App R 123; [1946] 115 LJ 417; (1946) 175 LTR 327; (1946) 90 SJ 441; (1945-46) LXII TLR 466; (1946) WN (I) 146 HL On provocation reducing murder to manslaughter.

Director of Public Prosecutions, Hunt v [1990] Crim LR 812; (1990) 154 JP 762; [1990] TLR 402 HC QBD Witness need not have seen penis for justices to convict person of wilful/indecent exposure.

Director of Public Prosecutions, Hyam v [1974] 2 All ER 41; [1975] AC 55; (1974) 59 Cr App R 91; [1974] Crim LR 365; (1974) 138 JP 374; (1974) 124 NLJ 320t; (1974) 118 SJ 311; [1974] 2 WLR 607 HL Intent for murder is intend to do acts which could (but need not be intended to) cause really serious bodily harm.

Director of Public Prosecutions, Johnson v [1994] Crim LR 673 HC QBD Failed attempt by squatter (who replaced existing locks with own lock) to plead lawful excuse to criminal damage (allegedly believed property in need of immediate protection): on deciding whether lawful excuse defence ought to be successful.

Director of Public Prosecutions, Jones and Wood v (1993) 96 Cr App R 130; (1992) 156 JP 866; [1992] TLR 271 HC QBD Need not control/manage premises to be successfully prosecuted for assisting in management of brothel.

Director of Public Prosecutions, Joyce v [1946] 1 All ER 186; [1946] AC 347; (1945-46) 31 Cr App R 57; (1946) 96 LJ 94; [1946] 115 LJ 146; (1946) 174 LTR 206; (1945-46) LXII TLR 208; (1946) WN (I) 31 HL Person with British passport (albeit obtained by fraud) could be guilty of treason under Treason Act 1351; holding British passport (even one obtained by fraud) entitled bearer to normal rights/protection afforded bearers thereof.

Director of Public Prosecutions, Kamara and others v [1973] 2 All ER 1242; [1974] AC 104; (1973) 57 Cr App R 880; [1974] Crim LR 39; (1973) 137 JP 714; (1973) 123 NLJ 700t; (1973) 117 SJ 581; [1973] 3 WLR 198 HL Unlawful assembly need not take place in public place; not all agreements to commit torts indictable conspiracies.

Director of Public Prosecutions, Kerr v [1995] Crim LR 394; (1994) 158 JP 1048; [1994] TLR 459 HC QBD Police officer not acting in course of duty where held person in erroneous belief that person had been arrested.

Director of Public Prosecutions, Knuller (Publishing, Printing and Promotions) Ltd and others v [1972] 2 All ER 898; [1973] AC 435; (1972) 56 Cr App R 633; [1975] Crim LR 704; (1972) 136 JP 728; (1972) 116 SJ 545; [1972] 3 WLR 143 HL Is offence of conspiracy to corrupt public morals and of conspiring to outrage public decency which advertisements by men seeking homosexual partners could violate.

Director of Public Prosecutions, Krumpa and Anderson v [1989] Crim LR 295 HC QBD Have not been asked to leave land where are told that sometime in the future will be asked to leave.

Director of Public Prosecutions, Kynaston v; Heron (Joseph) v Director of Public Prosecutions; Heron (Tracey) v Director of Public Prosecutions (1988) 87 Cr App R 200 HC QBD Was lawful entry of premises by police where knew offence committed, knew whom wanted to arrest, reasonably suspected were on premises and owner knew what police wanted.

Director of Public Prosecutions, L v; T v Director of Public Prosecutions; W, H (G) and H (C) v Director of Public Prosecutions [1996] 2 Cr App R 501 HC QBD On rebuttal of doli incapax presumption.

Director of Public Prosecutions, Lamb v (1990) 154 JP 381 HC QBD Trespassing police officer was nonetheless acting in course of duty when stayed in place to prevent expected breach of the peace.

Director of Public Prosecutions, Plowden v [1991] Crim LR 850 HC QBD Proper inference after finding that had been breach of peace that accused had been obstructing police officer who sought to prevent the breach of the peace.

Director of Public Prosecutions, Poku (Kwasi) v [1993] Crim LR 705; [1993] TLR 13 HC QBD Excessive use of seizure powers which prompted reaction from defendant that was subject of instant public order prosecution meant it was open to defendant to plead reasonable conduct defence.

Director of Public Prosecutions, Rafiq v (1997) 161 JP 412 HC QBD That dog bit person absent previous indication of inclination to bite could of itself be basis for reasonable apprehension of injury.

Director of Public Prosecutions, Riley v (1990) 91 Cr App R 14; [1990] Crim LR 422; (1990) 154 JP 453 HC QBD Could not be guilty of assault on police officer in execution of duty where validity of arrest unproven.

Director of Public Prosecutions, Rukwira v [1993] Crim LR 882; (1994) 158 JP 65; [1993] TLR 362 HC QBD Shared landing outside flat in block of flats not part of 'dwelling' for purposes of Public Order Act 1986.

Director of Public Prosecutions, Ryan and French v [1994] Crim LR 457; (1994) 158 JP 485 HC QBD On charging theft and handling together as alternative charges.

Director of Public Prosecutions, Sanders v [1988] Crim LR 605 CA Officer was acting in course of duty where assaulted when after stopping car under Road Traffic Act 1972, s 159, sought to stop driver driving off until had ascertained whether was stolen (of which had reasonable suspicion).

Director of Public Prosecutions, Sands v [1990] Crim LR 585; (1991) 155 JP 28; [1990] TLR 240 HC QBD Fire brigade officer only has right to enter those premises on which is fire/is reasonably believed to be fire/is necessary to extinguish fire or safeguard place into which entering.

Director of Public Prosecutions, Secretary of State for Health and Social Security, British Pregnancy Advisory Service, Morrow, Greach and Thomas v [1994] Crim LR 58 HC QBD Disorderly behaviour conviction valid: reasonable conduct and reasonable force to prevent crime (allegedly illegal abortions) defences unsuccessful.

Director of Public Prosecutions, Selby v [1971] 3 All ER 810; [1972] AC 515; (1972) 56 Cr App R 72; [1972] Crim LR 705t; (1971) 135 JP 619; (1971) 121 NLJ 953t; (1971) 115 SJ 948; [1971] 3 WLR 647 HL Guilty of uttering/putting off counterfeit if attempt to (or do) pass them off as genuine.

Director of Public Prosecutions, Shaw v [1961] 2 All ER 446; [1962] AC 220; (1961) 45 Cr App R 113; [1961] Crim LR 468; (1961) 125 JP 437; (1961) 111 LJ 356; (1961) 105 SJ 421; [1961] 2 WLR 897 HL Test of obscenity is whether article would corrupt/deprave another (intent of author irrelevant); are living off earnings of prostitution if provide goods/services to prostitutes which would not if they were not prostitutes; agreement to publish obscene publication an agreement to corrupt public morals (even if never published),a common law misdemeanour.

Director of Public Prosecutions, Straker v [1963] 1 All ER 697; [1963] Crim LR 279; (1963) 127 JP 260; (1963) 113 LJ 365; [1963] 1 QB 926; (1963) 107 SJ 156; [1963] 2 WLR 598 HC QBD Negatives cannot be obscene publication.

Director of Public Prosecutions, Sturrock v; Subramaniam v R [1996] RTR 216; [1995] TLR 69; [1956] Crim LR 420; (1956) 100 SJ 316; [1956] 1 WLR 456 PC On sentencing for perjury pursuant to the Criminal Procedure Code of Ceylon, s 440.

Director of Public Prosecutions, Swallow v [1991] Crim LR 610 HC QBD Acquittal merited where husband or wife had abstracted electricity through interference with meter but was no real indication as to which had done so.

Director of Public Prosecutions, Swanston v (1997) 161 JP 203; [1997] TLR 37 HC QBD Person subjected to threatening/abusive/insulting words did not have to testify as to how received words for utterer of words to be convicted of using same.

Director of Public Prosecutions, Sykes v [1961] 3 All ER 33; [1962] AC 528; (1961) 45 Cr App R 230; [1961] Crim LR 715; (1961) 125 JP 523; (1961) 111 LJ 500; (1961) 105 SJ 566; [1961] 3 WLR 371 HL Misprision of felony an offence; need not be active concealment to establish offence.

Director of Public Prosecutions, T v [1989] Crim LR 498 HC QBD Doli incapax presumption rebutted.

Director of Public Prosecutions, Taylor v [1973] 2 All ER 1108; [1974] Crim LR 98; [1973] AC 964; (1973) 57 Cr App R 915; (1973) 137 JP 608; (1973) 123 NLJ 746t; (1973) 117 SJ 544; [1973] 3 WLR 140 HL May be guilty of affray even if only person fighting unlawfully to terror of others.

Director of Public Prosecutions, Thompson v [1918-19] All ER 521; (1918) 53 LJ 62; (1918) 118 LTR 418; (1917-18) 62 SJ 266; (1918) WN (I) 21 HL Possession of powder puffs/lewd photographs showed offender and accused had same tendencies - admissible to rebut alibi.

Director of Public Prosecutions, Treacy v [1971] 1 All ER 110; [1971] AC 537; (1971) 55 Cr App R 113; [1972] Crim LR 590; (1971) 135 JP 112; (1971) 115 SJ 12; [1971] 2 WLR 112 HL Can be tried for blackmail only partly committed in England.

Director of Public Prosecutions, W v [1996] Crim LR 320 HC QBD On rebutting the presumption of doli incapax (here not rebutted).

Director of Public Prosecutions, Welham v [1960] 1 All ER 805; (1960) 44 Cr App R 124; [1960] Crim LR 423; (1960) 124 JP 280; (1960) 110 LJ 284; (1960) 104 SJ 308; [1960] 2 WLR 669 HL Can intend to defraud (and be guilty of uttering forged document) though do not intend to cause financial loss.

Director of Public Prosecutions, Whiley v [1995] Crim LR 39 HC QBD On what constitutes 'using' wireless (unlawfully) for purposes of the Wireless Telegraphy Act 1949, s 5(b)(i).

Director of Public Prosecutions, Wicks v [1947] 1 All ER 205; [1947] AC 362; (1946-48) 32 Cr App R 7; (1947) 97 LJ 65; [1947] 116 LJR 247; (1947) 176 LTR 150; (1947) LXIII TLR 6; (1947) WN (I) 30 HL Accused could be convicted under temporary statute despite its expiry.

Director of Public Prosecutions, Williams v (1992) 95 Cr App R 415; (1992) 156 JP 804; [1992] TLR 80 HC QBD Landing of block of flats to which was controlled access not a public place.

Director of Public Prosecutions, Williams v [1968] Crim LR 563; (1968) 112 SJ 599 HC QBD Passing out leaflets outside servicemen's club inviting them to desert was distributing insulting writing likely to occasion breach of the peace (contrary to the Public Order Act 1936, s 7).

Director of Public Prosecutions, Winder and others v (1996) TLR 13/8/96 CA Running after hunt with intent of interfering with same an offence under the Criminal Justice and Public Order Act 1994, s 68.

Director of Public Prosecutions, Winn v (1992) 156 JP 881; (1992) 142 NLJ 527 HC QBD On four different ways of committing offence created by Public Order Act 1986, s 4 (likely provocation of violence through use of threatening/abusive words or behaviour).

Director of Public Prosecutions, Withers v [1974] 3 All ER 984; [1975] AC 842; (1975) 60 Cr App R 85; [1975] Crim LR 95; (1975) 139 JP 94; (1974) 124 NLJ 1157t; (1974) 118 SJ 862; [1974] 3 WLR 751 HL No offence of conspiracy to effect public mischief (though acts complained of may fall within definition of other criminal offence).

Director of Public Prosecutions, Wood v (1989) 153 JP 20 HC QBD On admissibility of expert medical evidence that was fact/opinion (here on defence of automatism).

Director of Public Prosecutions, Woolmington v [1935] All ER 1; [1935] AC 462; (1934-39) XXX Cox CC 234; (1934-36) 25 Cr App R 72; (1935) 79 LJ 380; (1935) 153 LTR 232; (1934-35) LI TLR 446; (1935) 79 SJ 401 HL Crown must show accused's voluntary/malicious act caused death; accused may seek to disprove intent/malice; acquittal if Crown fails in duty/accused's story believed.

Director of Public Prosecutions v Jones and another [1997] 2 All ER 119; (1997) 147 NLJ 162 HC QBD On elements of offence of trespassory assembly.

Director of Public Proseutions v Mills [1996] 3 WLR 1093 HC QBD Could be guilty of intimidation via the telephone.

Diss, Pedro v [1981] 2 All ER 59; (1981) 72 Cr App R 193; [1981] Crim LR 236; (1981) 145 JP 445; (1981) 131 NLJ 448 HC QBD Constable detaining without advising why acts unlawfully so assault on constable not assault on same in execution of duty.

Ditta, Hussain and Kara, R v [1988] Crim LR 42 CA 'Wife' could not plead defence of coercion under the Criminal Justice Act 1925 where she bona fide but nonetheless mistakenly believed she was married to coercer.

Dix (Trevor Glyn John), R v (1982) 74 Cr App R 306; [1982] Crim LR 302 CA Medical evidence not legally/is practically necessary when pleading diminished responsibility defence.

Dix, R v (1901-02) XVIII TLR 231 HC KBD On need for offences to be offences according to law of requesting and extraditing state before extradition possible.

Dixon, R v [1980] RTR 17 CA Valid arrest where arrested as unfit through drink to drive but police indicated would not be charged with same and was later charged with driving with excess alcohol.

Dixon, R v [1993] Crim LR 579 CA On elements of offence of affray.

Dixon, R v [1961] 3 All ER 460; (1961) 111 LJ 677; (1961) 105 SJ 208 HC QBD On insanity defence.

Dobbing, R v [1964] Crim LR 723t CCA Valid conviction for capital murder.

Dodd (David), R v (1978) 66 Cr App R 87 CA Soliciting of girls of 14 by means of kerb crawling was soliciting for immoral purpose.

Dodge and Harris, R v [1971] 2 All ER 1523; (1971) 55 Cr App R 440; (1971) 135 JP 523; [1972] 1 QB 416; (1971) 115 SJ 623; [1971] 3 WLR 366 CA Fake bonds not lying about bonds themselves are not false documents.

Dodson, R v [1973] Crim LR 518 CA On effect of drunkenness on intent in context of murder.

Dolan (Joseph Daniel Philip), R v (1976) 62 Cr App R 36; [1976] Crim LR 145t; (1975) 125 NLJ 1066t CA Can be convicted of handling stolen goods and theft where handled goods after theft.

Dolbey, Kelly v [1984] RTR 67 HC QBD Arrest of driver after failed to inflate bag but crystals afforded negative reading was valid (though crystals later found at station to give positive reading): appellant properly convicted inter alia of failure to give specimen.

Dolbey, W v (1989) 88 Cr App R 1; [1983] Crim LR 681 HC QBD No recklessness (where did not foresee any damage) so no malicious wounding.

Dollard, McMahon and another v [1965] Crim LR 238t HC QBD Studded belt not per se an offensive weapon.

Dolman, R v [1949] 1 All ER 813; (1948-49) 33 Cr App R 128 Assizes Defence to bigamy that at time of bigamous marriage held reasonable belief earlier marriage void as bigamous.

Donaghy and Marshall, R v [1981] Crim LR 644 CrCt On elements of offence of robbery (on need for ongoing threat).

Donald (John Thomas), R v; R v Donald (Lesley) (1986) 83 Cr App R 49; [1986] Crim LR 535; (1986) 130 SJ 284 CA Could be convicted of assisting an offender who had not at time of assistance been convicted/admitted arrestable offence where was evidence had participated in same.

Dones, R v [1987] Crim LR 682 CCC Squirting ammonia at another was not 'administering a noxious thing' contrary to Offences against the Person Act 1861, s 24.

Donnelly (Ian David), R v (1984) 79 Cr App R 76; [1984] Crim LR 490; (1984) 128 SJ 514; [1984] TLR 322; [1984] 1 WLR 1017 CA Valuation certificate where was no jewellery to be valued was a forgery.

Donnelly v Jackman [1970] 1 All ER 987; (1970) 54 Cr App R 229; [1970] Crim LR 219; (1970) 134 JP 352; (1970) 120 NLJ 362; (1970) 114 SJ 130; [1970] 1 WLR 562 HC QBD Touch to unarrested person answered with great force is unlawful assault on constable.

Donnelly, Gallagher, Hayes and Mainchair Ltd, R v [1980] Crim LR 723 CrCt Video films did not fall within terms of the Obscene Publications Act 1959.

Donnelly, R v [1989] Crim LR 739 CA That appellant had been using gun as club did not have to mean (and here was not the case) that intended to fire it.

Donovan v Gavin [1965] 2 All ER 611; [1965] Crim LR 442; (1965) 129 JP 404; (1965) 115 LJ 418; [1965] 2 QB 648; (1965) 109 SJ 373; [1965] 3 WLR 352 HC QBD That rooms let separately to various prostitutes did not mean not brothel.

Donovan, R v [1934] All ER 207; (1934-39) XXX Cox CC 187; (1934-36) 25 Cr App R 1; (1934) 98 JP 409; [1934] 2 KB 498; (1934) 78 LJ 149; (1934) 103 LJCL 683; (1935) 152 LTR 46; (1934) 78 SJ 601; (1933-34) L TLR 566 CCA On consent of 'victim' as defence to criminal charges.

Donovan, Read v [1947] 1 All ER 37; (1947) 111 JP 46; [1947] KB 326; (1947) 97 LJ 9; [1947] 116 LJR 849; (1947) 176 LTR 124; (1947) 91 SJ 101; (1947) LXIII TLR 89; (1947) WN (I) 42 HC KBD Signal pistol a lethal weapon.

Doole, R v [1985] Crim LR 450 CA Even had debiting of deposit account occurred on foot of appellant's wrongful instructions that would not have rendered appellant guilty of theft of credit balance.

Doot and others, Director of Public Prosecutions v [1973] 1 All ER 940; [1973] AC 807; (1973) 57 Cr App R 600; [1973] Crim LR 292; (1973) 137 JP 375; (1973) 123 NLJ 370t; (1973) 117 SJ 266; [1973] 2 WLR 532 HL Conspiracy abroad to commit acts in England punishable in England if acts partly/completely done.

Dorrington (Mark) (1910) 5 Cr App R 119, R v (1910) 74 JP 392 CCA On differentiation in sentence between habitual criminal and non-habitual criminal who merits preventive detention.

Doubleday (William Donald), R v (1965) 49 Cr App R 62 CCA Is offence for bankrupt to set up in business under new name without revealing name under which found bankrupt.

Douce, R v [1972] Crim LR 105 CA Painting with signature (purporting thereby to be painting by particular painter) was forgery for purposes of the Forgery Act 1913.

Doughty (Stephen Clifford), R v (1986) 83 Cr App R 319; [1986] Crim LR 625 CA Provocation ought to have been left to jury where killing of baby by father prompted by baby's crying.

Douglas Valley Finance Co, Ltd v S Hughes (Hirers), Ltd [1966] 3 All ER 214; (1965-66) 116 NLJ 1378; [1969] 1 QB 738; (1966) 110 SJ 980; [1967] 2 WLR 503 HC QBD Adverse possession not element of conversion: merely assertion of ownership/control contrary to other's rights of possession/control.

Doukas, R v [1978] 1 All ER 1061; (1978) 66 Cr App R 228; [1978] Crim LR 177; (1978) 142 JP 254; (1978) 128 NLJ 34t; (1978) 122 SJ 30; [1978] 1 WLR 372 CA If hypothetical customer would not have agreed to fraud can be conviction for obtaining property by deception.

Dover and East Kent Justices, ex parte Dean, R v [1992] Crim LR 33; (1992) 156 JP 357; [1991] TLR 404 HC QBD Can apply for bail at second remand hearings where originally agreed to remand without making such application.

Dowland, Hankinson v [1974] Crim LR 539; (1974) 138 JP 795; (1974) 118 SJ 644 HC QBD On what constitutes an offence for purpose of House to House Collections Act 1939, s 11(1).

Downes (Patrick Joseph), R v (1983) 77 Cr App R 260; [1983] Crim LR 819 CA Sale of sub-contractor's tax vouchers where vouchers would ultimately be returned to Inland Revenue was theft.

Downes, R v [1984] Crim LR 552 CA Not possession with intent to supply where have joint possession of controlled drug but (unlike party with whom sharing possession) do not intend to supply same (though know of other party's intention to do so).

Downing (Geoge), R v (1980) 71 Cr App R 316 CA Criminal bankruptcy order need not later be perfected by trial judge in court where perfection necessary.

Downsborough v Huddersfield Industrial Society, Ltd; Wadsworth v Huddersfield Industrial Society, Ltd; Ardron v Huddersfield Industrial Society, Ltd [1941] 3 All ER 434 HC KBD Dismissal of employees because were conscientious objectors not offence.

Dunbar, R v [1982] 1 All ER 188; (1982) 74 Cr App R 88; [1982] Crim LR 45; (1981) 125 SJ 746; [1981] 1 WLR 1536 CA Possession of controlled drug by doctor who has made bona fide prescription thereof for self is lawful.

Dunbar, R v [1957] 2 All ER 737; (1957) 41 Cr App R 182; [1957] Crim LR 616; (1957) 121 JP 506; (1957) 107 LJ 505; [1958] 1 QB 1; (1957) 101 SJ 594 CCA On respective burdens of proof where diminished responsibility claimed.

Duncalf and others, R v [1979] 2 All ER 1116; (1979) 69 Cr App R 206; [1979] Crim LR 452; (1979) 143 JP 654; (1979) 129 (1) NLJ 492; (1979) 123 SJ 336; [1979] 1 WLR 918 CA Conspiracy to steal a statutory offence; conspiracy only to defraud a common law offence; no fixed rules regarding questions under Criminal Evidence Act on previous convictions.

Duncan and others, R v [1944] 2 All ER 220; (1943-45) 30 Cr App R 70; [1944] KB 713; [1944] 113 LJ 411; (1945) 95 LJ 102; (1944) 171 LTR 342; (1943-44) LX TLR 470; (1944) WN (I) 177 CCA Medium not allowed demonstrate powers in court; seance as pretence to exercise conjuration of spirits contrary to Witchcraft Act 1735, s 4.

Duncan v Jones (1934-39) XXX Cox CC 279; (1935) 99 JP 399; [1936] 1 KB 218; (1935) 80 LJ 307; [1936] 105 LJCL 71; (1936) 154 LTR 110; (1935) 79 SJ 903; (1935-36) LII TLR 26 HC KBD Obstruction of police in execution of duty where sought to hold public meeting despite police prohibition.

Dunleavey (Edward), R v (1908) 1 Cr App R 240 CCA Must prove guilty knowledge beyond reasonable doubt to sustain conviction for obtaining by false pretences.

Dunleavy, R v (1909) 73 JP 56 CCA Attempted obtaining by false pretences conviction quashed where convict had not known that ring was selling as gold ring actually made of brass.

Dunn, R v; R v Derby [1984] Crim LR 367 CrCt Moving motor cycle to have a better look at it was not taking conveyance.

Dunning, Wise v [1900-03] All ER 727; (1901-07) XX Cox CC 121; [1902] 71 LJCL 165; (1901-02) 46 SJ 152; (1901-02) XVIII TLR 85; (1901-02) 50 WR 317 HC KBD Justices can bind over provocative public speaker to keep the peace/be of good behaviour.

Dunnington, R v [1984] 1 All ER 676; (1984) 78 Cr App R 171; [1984] Crim LR 98; (1984) 148 JP 316; [1984] QB 472; (1983) 127 SJ 822; [1983] TLR 569; [1984] 2 WLR 125 CA Is attempt where acts if completed would be aiding and abetting even if principal act only attempt.

Durham County Council v Peter Connors Industrial Services Ltd [1992] Crim LR 743 HC QBD Conviction for depositing controlled waste merited as failed to set up special defence that were advised by informed persons that were not acting unlawfully and had no cause to believe contrary.

Durham County Council v Thomas Swan and Co [1995] Crim LR 319 HC QBD Barrels containing under 1% of starting volume were 'empty' for purposes of Control of Pollution Act 1974.

Durkin, R v [1973] 2 All ER 872; (1973) 57 Cr App R 637; [1973] Crim LR 372t; (1973) 123 NLJ 392t; [1973] QB 786; (1973) 117 SJ 355; [1973] 2 WLR 741 CA Pictures loaned recurrently to gallery are intended for permanent public exhibition: taking of one is theft.

Durkin, R v [1953] 3 WLR 479 CMAC Commanding officer's behaviour did not mean accused's offence condoned.

Durose v Wilson (1907-09) XXI Cox CC 421; (1907) 71 JP 263; (1907) XCVI LTR 645 HC KBD Porter properly convicted as wilful party to use of flats/portion thereof as brothel.

Duru and others, R v [1973] 3 All ER 715; (1974) 58 Cr App R 151; (1974) 118 SJ 7; [1974] 1 WLR 2 CA That cheques returned/money would eventually be returned/cheques paid to third party for benefit of another not defence to obtaining property by deception.

Dutton, Russon v (1911-13) XXII Cox CC 490; (1911) 75 JP 209; (1911) 104 LTR 601; (1910-11) XXVII TLR 197 HC KBD No conviction for indecent language uttered and heard within public house.

Dyer (Raymond), R v; R v Harris (Anthony Thomas); R v Probert (Edward); R v Cox (Royston John); R v Dowling (Alan Kenneth); R v Smith (Maurice Charles); R v Bastin (Frederick Gerald) (1952) 36 Cr App R 155 CCA Not malicious damage to remove notice board unlawfully placed by parish council on common.

Dymock and another, R v; R v Moger and another (1900-01) 45 SJ 597; (1900-01) XVII TLR 593; (1900-01) 49 WR 618 HC KBD Dog-owner need not be given choice of properly controlling dog before justices order its destruction; on format of dog destruction order.

Dymond v Pearce and others [1972] 1 All ER 1142; (1972) 136 JP 397; (1972) 122 NLJ 58t; [1972] 1 QB 496; [1972] RTR 169; (1972) 116 SJ 62; [1972] 2 WLR 633 CA Obstruction of highway by parked vehicle a nuisance.

Dymond v Pearce and others [1971] RTR 417 Assizes Obstruction of highway by parked vehicle not a nuisance.

Dymond, R v [1920] All ER 259; (1918-21) XXVI Cox CC 621; (1920-21) 15 Cr App R 1; (1920) 84 JP 103; [1920] 2 KB 260; [1920] 89 LJCL 876; (1920) 123 LTR 336; (1919-20) 64 SJ 571; (1919-20) XXXVI TLR 421; (1920) WN (I) 130 CCA Must actually have (not just believe have) reasonable/probable cause for demand to defeat charge of demanding money with menaces.

Dyos (Martin) and others, R v [1979] Crim LR 660 CCC Murder conviction unavailable where one of two blows probably caused death but was impossible to know whether single blow struck by defendant was causative blow.

Dyson, R v [1908-10] All ER 736; (1907-09) XXI Cox CC 669; (1908) 72 JP 303; (1908-09) XCIX LTR 201; (1907-08) 52 SJ 535 CCA Cannot be convicted of manslaughter where death followed injury by more than year and a day.

Dytham, R v [1979] 3 All ER 641; (1979) 69 Cr App R 387; [1979] Crim LR 666; (1980) 144 JP 49; (1979) 129 (2) NLJ 836; [1979] QB 722; (1979) 123 SJ 621; [1979] 3 WLR 467 CA Negligent failure to perform public duty which is injurious to public interest is misconduct in public office.

E (RMJ), Neale v (1985) 80 Cr App R 20; [1984] TLR 116 HC QBD Could not be convicted of disorderly behaviour while drunk where had actually been glue-sniffing.

E, Neale v [1984] Crim LR 485 CA On meaning of word 'drunk' in Licensing Act 1872, s 12, as amended by the Criminal Justice Act 1967, s 91.

Eadie (Elizabeth), R v (1922-23) 17 Cr App R 24 CCA Leave to appeal granted on prima facie basis in possession of explosives case.

Eaglestone, Hooper v [1978] Crim LR 161 CA Was offence for person without site licence who nonetheless operated a caravan site on his land to seek to harass/evict caravan occupant from site by cutting off electricity (Caravan Sites Act 1968, s 3 applied).

Earl of Caithness, Sullivan v [1976] 1 All ER 844; (1976) 62 Cr App R 105; [1976] Crim LR 130; (1976) 140 JP 277; (1975) 125 NLJ 1220t; [1976] QB 966; (1976) 120 SJ 8; [1976] 2 WLR 361 HC QBD Control rather than custody can constitute possession.

Earl of Crewe, R v (1910) 102 LTR 760; (1909-10) XXVI TLR 192 HC KBD Seeking of habeas corpus writ regarding detention of person in Crown Protectorate failed for want of jurisdiction/procedural reasons.

Easom, R v [1971] 2 All ER 945; (1971) 55 Cr App R 410; [1972] Crim LR 487t; (1971) 135 JP 477; [1971] 2 QB 315; (1971) 115 SJ 485; [1971] 3 WLR 82 CA For theft/attempted theft must be intent to permanently deprive.

East, R v [1990] Crim LR 413 CA On elements of offence of possession of firearm with intent to endanger life.

Eatch, R v [1980] Crim LR 650 CrCt On ramifications of voluntary drunkenness vis-à-vis intent in rape (a crime of basic intent).

Eaton v Best [1908-10] All ER 651; (1911-13) XXII Cox CC 66; (1909) 73 JP 113; [1909] 1 KB 632; (1909) 44 LJ 63; [1909] 78 LJKB 425; (1909) C LTR 494; (1908-09) XXV TLR 244 HC KBD What constitutes 'habitual drunkard' (under Habitual Drunkards Act 1879, s 3).

Eaton, R v (1966) 50 Cr App R 189; [1966] Crim LR 333t; (1965-66) 116 NLJ 754; (1966) 110 SJ 329 CCA Person could not pass title in approbated property unless had met the rquirements of the relevant approbation note.

Eddy v Niman (1981) 73 Cr App R 237; [1981] Crim LR 502 HC QBD Actus reus of shoplifting is that do acts incompatible with owner's rights over goods.

Eden (Thomas Henry), R v (1971) 55 Cr App R 193; [1971] Crim LR 416 CA Person may be guilty of false accounting though not guilty of theft.

Edgar v Spain (1899-1901) XIX Cox CC 719; (1901) LXXXIV LTR 631 HC KBD Interpretation of animal 'brought...for' slaughter clause of Cruelty to Animals Act 1849, s 8.

Edgar, R v (1913-14) XXIII Cox CC 558; (1913) 9 Cr App R 13; (1913) 77 JP 356; (1913-14) 109 LTR 416; (1912-13) 57 SJ 519; (1912-13) XXIX TLR 512 CCA Recognisance to be of good behaviour following misdemeanour to be of short/definite time.

Edgecombe, R v [1963] Crim LR 574t CCA Valid conviction for possession of firearm with intent to endanger life.

Edmonds and others, R v [1963] 1 All ER 828; (1963) 47 Cr App R 114; (1963) 127 JP 283; (1963) 113 LJ 248; [1963] 2 QB 142; (1963) 107 SJ 196; [1963] 2 WLR 715 CCA If joint offensive weapons indictment must show common intent to injure; intent to 'frighten' undesirable terminology.

Edmondson, Crook v [1966] 1 All ER 833; (1978) 66 Cr App R 90; [1966] Crim LR 227; (1966) 130 JP 191; [1966] 2 QB 81; (1966) 110 SJ 147; [1966] 2 WLR 672 HC QBD Not soliciting/importuning for immoral purpose to seek sex with prostitute.

Edmundson (Harry), R v (1912-13) 8 Cr App R 107 CCA Keeping clothes sent pending payment but not paid for was larceny by trick.

Edward (Harold) and Priestley (Blanche Annie), R v (1921-22) 16 Cr App R 143; (1922) 127 LTR 221 CCA Appeals against conviction under Punishment of Incest Act 1908 to be heard in camera.

Edward Fitzgerald, Duke of Leinster, R v (1921-25) XXVII Cox CC 574; (1922-23) 17 Cr App R 176; (1923) 87 JP 191; [1924] 1 KB 311; [1924] 93 LJCL 144; (1924) 130 LTR 318; (1923-24) 68 SJ 211; (1923-24) XL TLR 33; (1923) WN (I) 286 CCA Undischarged bankrupt must disclose is same where seeks credit of £10 or more.

Edwards (Llewellyn), R v; R v Roberts (Eric) (1978) 67 Cr App R 228; [1978] Crim LR 564; (1978) 122 SJ 177 CA Not Public Order Act 1936 offence where insulting words could be heard across street but occurred on private property.

Edwards (Maxine), R v [1996] 2 Cr App R 345; (1996) 140 SJ LB 43; (1996) TLR 31/1/96 CA Conviction quashed where evidence of police officers on which accused was convicted was seriously coloured by possibility of perjury on part of police officers.

Edwards and others, Carnill v [1953] 1 All ER 282; (1953) 117 JP 93; (1953) 97 SJ 98; [1953] 1 WLR 290 HC QBD Prostitutes committing indecent acts in car not 'wandering in a public highway'.

Edwards v Ddin [1976] 3 All ER 705; (1976) 63 Cr App R 218; [1976] Crim LR 580; (1977) 141 JP 27; [1976] (1976) 126 NLJ 718t; [1976] RTR 508; (1976) 120 SJ 587; [1976] 1 WLR 942 HC QBD Petrol from pump appropriated with assent of both parties when enters tank, not when payment made.

Edwards v Director of Public Prosecutions (1993) 97 Cr App R 301; [1993] Crim LR 854; [1993] TLR 184 HC QBD Was not valid arrest for obstruction of police officer in execution of duty where arrestee aided person in turn arrested by officer under false pretext.

Edwards v Morgan [1967] Crim LR 40t HC QBD Unless bailiff on duty exercising special responsibility under the Salmon and Freshwater Fisheries Act 1923 (for which must produce warrant) he is a constable and attack on same (as here) is attack on bailiff in execution of his duty.

Edwards v R [1973] 1 All ER 152; [1973] AC 648; (1973) 57 Cr App R 157; [1972] Crim LR 782; (1973) 137 JP 119; (1972) 122 NLJ 941t; (1972) 116 SJ 822; [1972] 3 WLR 893 PC Extreme reaction to blackmailer's conduct might constitute provocation.

Edwards v Tombs [1983] Crim LR 43 HC QBD Turnstile meter was a record so operator of same who wrongfully allowed persons through it was guilty of falsifying record made for accounting purpose (Theft Act 1968, s 17(1)(a)).

Edwards, Campbell v [1976] 1 All ER 785 CA Absent fraud/collusion mistaken non-speaking report by valuer cannot be set aside.

Edwards, Hawes v (1949) 113 JP 303; (1949) WN (I) 206 HC KBD Absent control did not have possession of goods so could not be convicted of receiving same.

Edwards, R v [1976] Crim LR 122t HC QBD Permission to emigrate a condition of bail.

Edwards, R v [1978] Crim LR 49 CA Squatter who charged rent to another for portion of property could be guilty of (here attempted) obtaining of rent by deception.

Eeet, R v [1983] Crim LR 806 CrCt Search of prisoner to aid in identification of same was unlawful.

Egan and others, McArdle v [1933] All ER 611; (1934-39) XXX Cox CC 67; (1934) 98 JP 103; (1934) 150 LTR 412 CA Reasonable and probable cause to suspect person of felony justifies arrest without warrant: question whether had such cause a matter for judge.

Egan v Floyde (1910) 74 JP 223 HC KBD Failed prosecution for not having licence in respect of farm-dog seen in pursuit of rabbits but not encouraged by owner to do same.

Egan, R v [1992] 4 All ER 470; (1992) 95 Cr App R 278; [1993] Crim LR 131; (1992) 142 NLJ 751; [1992] TLR 275 CA Intoxication not relevant when deciding whether there was diminished responsibility.

Eichholz, Sage v [1918-19] All ER 424; (1918-21) XXVI Cox CC 432; (1919) 83 JP 170; [1919] 2 KB 171; [1919] 88 LJCL 816; (1919) 121 LTR 151; (1918-19) XXXV TLR 382; (1919) WN (I) 115 HC KBD Charge under Prevention of Corruption Act 1906, s 1(1) (3) does not require corruption/intention to corrupt to sustain conviction.

Eisenhower, C (JJ) v [1983] 3 All ER 230; (1984) 78 Cr App R 48; [1983] Crim LR 567; [1984] QB 331; (1983) 127 SJ 425; [1983] TLR 298; [1983] 3 WLR 537 HC QBD Internal rupture not a wound which must break the skin.

El Ghazal, R v [1986] Crim LR 52 CA Were guilty of conspiracy to unlawfully supply cocaine where introduced one person to another knowing that one sought to meet the other so as to acquire cocaine.

El-Hakkaoui, R v [1975] 2 All ER 146; (1975) 60 Cr App R 281; [1975] Crim LR 229; (1975) 139 JP 467; (1975) 119 SJ 186; [1975] 1 WLR 396 CA Intent to injure someone in England not necessary for possession conviction.

Elbekkay, R v [1995] Crim LR 163 CA Sex obtained through impersonation of woman's boyfriend was rape as necessary consent to sex absent.

Eleko (Eshugbayi) v Nigeria Government (Administration Officer) [1928] All ER 598; [1928] AC 459; (1928) 66 LJ 46; (1928) 97 LJPC 97; (1928) 139 LTR 527; (1928) 72 SJ 452; (1928) WN (I) 175 PC Each judge of High Court (and so Nigerian Supreme Court) has power to (and must) hear habeas corpus application regardless of whether already decided on by another judge.

Eleko (Eshugbayi) v Officer Administering the Government of Nigeria and Another [1931] AC 662; (1931) 100 LJPC 152; (1931) 145 LTR 297 PC Habeas corpus petition arising from deportation of party from one part of Nigerian Colony to another.

Elias and others v Pasmore and others [1934] All ER 380; (1934) 98 JP 92; [1934] 2 KB 164; (1934) 77 LJ 94; (1934) 103 LJCL 223; (1934) 150 LTR 438; (1934) 78 SJ 104; (1933-34) L TLR 196; (1934) WN (I) 30 HC KBD Can search arrestee/take property relevant to crime; property seized may be retained until charges concluded; unlawful seizure of documents overlooked where are evidence of crime.

Eliezer v General Officer Commanding Palestine and Another [1947] AC 246 PC English habeas corpus rules apply in Palestine.

Ellames, R v [1974] 3 All ER 130; (1975) 60 Cr App R 7; [1974] Crim LR 554t; (1974) 138 JP 682; (1974) 124 NLJ 597t; (1974) 118 SJ 578; [1974] 1 WLR 1391 CA Article in possession must be for/in connection with future stealing.

Elliott v C (a minor) [1983] 2 All ER; (1983) 77 Cr App R 103; [1983] Crim LR 616; (1983) 147 JP 425; (1983) 127 SJ 442; [1983] TLR 379; [1983] 1 WLR 939 HC QBD Can be guilty of damaging/destroying property though did not see danger if reasonable person would.

Elliott, Ostler v [1980] Crim LR 584 HC QBD Was not obstruction of (here plain clothes) policemen in conduct of their duty where resisted them in reasonable belief that were not policemen.

Evans v Ewels [1972] 2 All ER 22; (1972) 56 Cr App R 377; [1972] Crim LR 328; (1972) 136 JP 394; (1972) 116 SJ 274; [1972] 1 WLR 671 HC QBD Indecent exposure under Vagrancy Act means indecent exposure of penis.

Evans v Hughes [1972] 3 All ER 412; (1972) 56 Cr App R 813; [1972] Crim LR 558; (1972) 136 JP 725; (1972) 122 NLJ 728t; (1972) 116 SJ 842; [1972] 1 WLR 1452 HC QBD Metal bar carried for self-defence reasons an offensive weapon; can only be reasonable excuse if immediate danger justifies carrying article.

Evans v Macklen [1976] Crim LR 120 HC QBD Person in respect of whom warrant for arrest for sentencing purposes had been issued could be arrested by police officer without warrant.

Evans, Barnard v (1926-30) XXVIII Cox CC 69; (1925) 89 JP 165; [1925] 2 KB 794; [1925] 94 LJCL 932; (1925) 133 LTR 829; (1924-25) XLI TLR 682; (1925) WN (I) 234 HC KBD Conviction merited for unwarranted shooting and injuring of trespassing dog.

Evans, Hinde v (1907-09) XXI Cox CC 331; (1906) 70 JP 548 HC KBD Cart was obstructing highway (even though person left in charge thereof).

Evans, Jones v [1978] Crim LR 230 CA Conviction for poaching rabbits.

Evans, Neal v [1976] Crim LR 384; [1976] RTR 333; (1976) 120 SJ 354 HC QBD Person who drank more alcohol pending known arrival of police and so frustrated breath test was guilty of obstructing police officer in execution of duty.

Evans, R v [1914-17] All ER 628; (1915-17) XXV Cox CC 342; [1916] 85 LJKB 1176; (1916) 114 LTR 616 CCA Conviction for receiving quashed as no evidence thereof.

Evans, R v (1915-17) XXV Cox CC 72; [1915] 2 KB 762; (1915-16) 113 LTR 508; (1914-15) XXXI TLR 410 CCA Quarter sessions could not convict party as incorrigible rogue, then sentence: conviction of summary court necessary.

Evans, R v [1986] Crim LR 470 CA On whether inciting person to solicit murder equivalent to inciting person to conspire with another to murder.

Evans, R v; R v Connor (1914-15) XXIV Cox CC 138; (1914) 49 LJ 181; [1914] 83 LJKB 905; (1914) 110 LTR 780; (1913-14) XXX TLR 326 CCA Incorrigible rogue liable to three months' detention (not imprisonment) cannot claim trial by jury.

Evans, Ross v [1959] Crim LR 582; (1959) 123 JP 320; (1959) 109 LJ 418; [1959] 2 QB 79; (1959) 103 SJ 393; [1959] 2 WLR 699 HC QBD Dog not 'at large' when was attached to lead.

Evens v Rogers [1956] Crim LR 496 HC QBD On appropriate means of prosecuting for indecent exposure.

Evens v Wright [1964] Crim LR 466t HC QBD That weapons in car to protect one if attacked when carrying wages money did not furnish reasonable excuse to possession of the weapons when were not carrrying wages money.

Evens, R v [1992] Crim LR 659 CA Failure to prove unlawful act on part of appellant that led to death of victim meant manslaughter conviction had to be quashed.

Everett and W and FC Bonham and Son Ltd, Robinson v [1988] Crim LR 699 HC QBD Rehearing ordered of prosecution for possession of dead wild bird.

Everitt (William George), R v (1910-11) 6 Cr App R 267; (1910-11) XXVII TLR 570 CCA On nature of evidence to prove are habitual criminal.

Ewels, Evans v [1972] 2 All ER 22; (1972) 56 Cr App R 377; [1972] Crim LR 328; (1972) 136 JP 394; (1972) 116 SJ 274; [1972] 1 WLR 671 HC QBD Indecent exposure under Vagrancy Act means indecent exposure of penis.

Ewens, R v [1966] 2 All ER 470; [1966] Crim LR 440; (1965-66) 116 NLJ 921; [1967] 1 QB 322; (1966) 110 SJ 329/483; [1966] 2 WLR 1372 CA Burden of showing exempted from offence falls on accused.

Ewing (Terence Patrick), R v (1977) 65 Cr App R 4 CA Advance rent/refundable deposit were debts/charges for purposes of Theft Act 1968, s 16.

Ex parte Askew [1963] Crim LR 507t HC QBD Failed habeas corpus application on basis of error in warrant of committal.

Ex parte N [1959] Crim LR 523t HC QBD Physical bearing of party in court of (at best) very slight relevance to rebuttal of doli incapax presumption.

Ex parte N [1959] Crim LR 357t HC QBD Leave to appeal against finding that doli incapax presumption rebutted by fact that child well-dressed and apparently well reared.

Ex parte O'Brien (1922-23) XXXIX TLR 413 HC KBD Failed habeas corpus application by person interned under regulations made pursuant to Restoration of Ireland Act 1920 which applicant claimed was rendered inoperable once Ireland secured independence.

Ex parte Orimolade [1963] Crim LR 110t HC QBD Fugitive offender seeking release encouraged to apply under the Fugitive Offenders Act 1881 and to make habeas corpus application.

Ex parte Shalom Schtraks (No 2) [1962] 3 All ER 849; [1963] Crim LR 111; [1964] 1 QB 191; [1962] 3 WLR 1435 HC QBD No habeas corpus writ where alleged evidence that committal obtained by fraud insufficiently probative.

Ex parte Singapore Republic Government (1977) 127 NLJ 962t HC QBD Failed appeal by Singaporean Government against magistrates' refusal to approve extradition application.

Ex parte Speculand (1946) 110 JP 92; [1946] KB 48; [1946] 115 LJ 218; (1946) 174 LTR 334; (1946) 90 SJ 152; (1945-46) LXII TLR 32 HC KBD Jurisdiction of HC KBD judge in respect of bail prior to appeal.

Ex parte Speculand [1946] KB 48 HC KBD Jurisdiction of HC KBD judge in respect of bail prior to appeal.

Ex parte Suidan [1966] Crim LR 445t; (1965-66) 116 NLJ 837t HC QBD Leave to seek habeas corpus but no bail for proposed extraditee who alleged the requesting warrant/deposition were seriously defective.

Ex parte Tarling (1979) 129 (1) NLJ 881t CA Habeas corpus application granted where delay in extradition case meant would be unjust/oppressive to return proposed extraditee to requesting country.

Ex parte Thomas [1956] Crim LR 119 HC QBD Habeas corpus application made where bail excessive.

Ex parte Thompson-Schwab and Wingate [1956] Crim LR 126t HC ChD Injunction granted to restrain parties from using/permitting use of certain property for prostitution.

Ex parte Weber [1916] 1 AC 421; (1915-17) XXV Cox CC 258; (1916) 80 JP 249; (1916) 51 LJ 102; [1916] 85 LJKB 944; (1916) 114 LTR 214; (1915-16) XXXII TLR 312; (1916) WN (I) 83 HL German resident in England for fifteen years was nonetheless properly interned.

Ex parte Weber (1915-17) XXV Cox CC 137; (1916) 80 JP 14; [1916] 1 KB 280; [1916] 85 LJKB 217; (1915-16) 113 LTR 968; (1914-15) XXXI TLR 602 CA German resident in England for fifteen years was nonetheless properly interned.

Ex parte Williams (Robert Franklin) [1970] Crim LR 102; (1969) 113 SJ 853 HC QBD Habeas corpus application as cover for bail application not approved of.

Ex parte Worth [1967] Crim LR 178t; (1965-66) 116 NLJ 1685 HC QBD Leave to seek order of mandamus against justices who dismissed information for unlawful/grievous bodily harm in case where victim tied up with rope that was set on fire - a thing any reasonable man would see involved chance of serious injury.

F v Padwick [1959] Crim LR 439t HC QBD Presumption of doli incapax validly held to have been rebutted.

F, R v (1910) 74 JP 384 CCC On what constitutes idiot/imbecile female for purposes of Criminal Law Amendment Act 1885, s 5.

Fagan v Metropolitan Police Commissioner [1968] 3 All ER 442; (1968) 52 Cr App R 700; (1969) 133 JP 16; [1969] 1 QB 439; (1968) 112 SJ 800; [1968] 3 WLR 1120 HC QBD Uncriminal act became criminal once criminal intent formed so initially innocent act transformed into assault on constable.

Fagan, R v [1968] Crim LR 560 HC QBD While may not have deliberately driven onto constable's foot, leaving car on foot once had was an assault.

Fairbairn, R v (1948-49) 33 Cr App R 179; [1949] 2 KB 690; (1949) LXV TLR 559; (1949) WN (I) 327 CCA Admissibility of earlier conviction to prove person a 'suspected person' (Vagrancy Act 1824, s 4) at time of arrest.

Fairbrother (John James), R v (1908) 1 Cr App R 233 CCA Finding of provocation need not reduce offence with which charged from murder to manslaughter.

Fairclough v Whipp [1951] 2 All ER 834; (1951) 115 JP 612; (1951) 95 SJ 699; [1951] 2 TLR 909; (1951) WN (I) 528 HC KBD Successfully asking girl to touch accused's exposed person not an assault (hence no indecent assault).

Fairclough v Whipp (1951-52) 35 Cr App R 138 CCA Successfully asking girl to touch accused's exposed person not an assault (hence no indecent assault).

Falcone, Ford v [1971] 2 All ER 1138; [1971] Crim LR 373; (1971) 135 JP 451; (1971) 121 NLJ 642; (1971) 115 SJ 365; [1971] 1 WLR 809 HC QBD Indecent exposure may occur in private place.

Falcone, Ford v (1971) 55 Cr App R 373 CA Indecent exposure may occur in private place.

Falconer-Atlee (Joan Olive), R v (1974) 58 Cr App R 348 CA On what constitutes 'dishonesty' under Theft Act 1968.

Fallon, R v [1993] Crim LR 591 CA On requirement that evidence of accomplice be corroborated.

Fallows, R v (1949) LXV TLR 93; (1948) WN (I) 479 CCA That one's co-defendant pleads guilty to receiving is not evidence that one knew goods were stolen or that goods were in fact stolen.

Fancy, R v [1980] Crim LR 171 CrCt Failed criminal damage action against person transporting bucket of white paint/a roller and who had been whitewashing National Front slogans from walls.

Fantle, R v [1959] Crim LR 584 CCC On provocation as defence to murder.

Farey v Welch (1926-30) XXVIII Cox CC 604; (1929) 93 JP 70; [1929] 1 KB 388; (1929) 67 LJ 145; (1929) 98 LJCL 318; (1929) 140 LTR 560; (1928-29) XLV TLR 277; (1929) WN (I) 32 HC KBD Failed conviction for larceny of pigeon where acted under honest mistaken belief that was taking own pigeon.

Farid (Mohamed), R v (1943-45) 30 Cr App R 168; (1945) 173 LTR 68 CCA Corroboration warning necessary where evidence given against accused of involvement in other offences to which witness is accomplice (though not accomplice to offence charged).

Farmer v Long (1908) 72 JP 91 HC KBD Leaking drain a nuisance under Public Health (London) Act 1891, s 4.

Farmer v Wilson (1899-1901) XIX Cox CC 502; (1900) 35 LJ 245; [1900] 69 LJCL 496; (1900) LXXXII LTR 566; (1899-1900) XVI TLR 309 HC QBD Was besetting of persons on board ship (irrespective of whether contract permitting persons to be there was legal or not).

Farmill (C), R v; R v Gladman; R v Firth; R v Wood [1982] Crim LR 38 CrCt On elements of offence of affray (need for third party to be put in terror).

Farooq, R v; R v Ramzan [1995] Crim LR 169 CA Entrapment is not a defence.

Farquharson (Philip) v R [1973] AC 786; [1973] Crim LR 305; (1973) 117 SJ 204; [1973] 2 WLR 596 PC Joint liability for murder under Bahamas Penal Code unaffected by common law.

Farr, R v [1982] Crim LR 745 CA Person allowing premises to be used for production of controlled drug had to make positive contribution to manufacturing process to be guilty of producing controlled drug.

Farrant, R v [1973] Crim LR 241 CrCt Valid conviction for indecent behaviour in churchyard of man who performed nighttime churchyard magical ceremony in which sought to raise person from the dead.

Farrar, Wakeman v [1974] Crim LR 136 HC QBD Was theft to cash a benefits giro in lieu of which had already received equivalent payment in cash on promise that would return giro if it later arrived (as it did).

Farrow v Tunnicliffe [1976] Crim LR 126 HC QBD Could under Misuse of Drugs Act 1971 remove suspect offender thereunder to another place to conduct search there.

Farrugia (Francis), R v; R v Borg (Charles); R v Agius (Jean); R v Gauchi (Ronnie) (1979) 69 Cr App R 108; (1979) 129 (1) NLJ 566t CA Earnings made by escort agency manager/employee or mini-cab driver in anticipation of act of prostitution was living on earnings of prostitution.

Faulkes, R v (1902-03) XIX TLR 250 Assizes Re-marriage after spouse's seven-year absence justified even if absent through wilful desertion.

Faulkner (James Charles), R v (1987) 9 Cr App R (S) 321 CA Seven years' imprisonment for rape of eight year old girl by man of low intelligence.

Faulkner v Talbot [1981] 3 All ER 468; (1982) 74 Cr App R 1; [1981] Crim LR 705; (1981) 125 SJ 859; [1981] 1 WLR 1528 HC QBD Intentional touching of another absent consent/lawful excuse is assault; under-sixteen year old boy could not under Sexual Offences Act 1956, s 15(2) consent to act that absent consent was assault.

Faulkner v Willetts [1982] Crim LR 453; [1982] RTR 159 HC QBD Valid arrest where constable's entry into house appeared from evidence not to be trespass.

Fazackerley, R v [1973] 2 All ER 819; (1973) 57 Cr App R 578; [1973] Crim LR 368; (1973) 137 JP 590; (1973) 123 NLJ 369t; (1973) 117 SJ 303; [1973] 1 WLR 632 CA Need not be cancelling/forgiving of debts when invalid cheque presented to obtain advantage by deception.

Fearby, Nicol v; Same v Robinson [1923] 92 LJCL 280 HC KBD On requirement that candidates to declare election expenses.

Federal Government of Germany and another, Scmidt v [1994] 3 All ER 65 HL High Court has statutory but no common law jurisdiction to intervene in extradition case.

Federal Steam Navigation Co Ltd v Department of Trade and Industry (1974) 59 Cr App R 131 HL Liability of master/owner of ship to prosecution under Oil in Navigable Waters Act 1955 (as amended).

Federal Steam Navigation Co Ltd, R v; R v Moran [1973] 3 All ER 849; (1974) 58 Cr App R 68; [1973] Crim LR 575t CA Owner and master can be guilty of unlawfully discharging oil.

Fedorenko, Attorney-General for the Dominion of Canada v [1911] AC 735; (1912) 81 LJPC 74; (1911-12) 105 LTR 343; (1910-11) XXVII TLR 541 PC Under 1886 Extradition Treaty with Russia person sought must be arrested after formally correct requisition presented.

Feely, R v [1973] 1 All ER 341; (1973) 57 Cr App R 312; [1973] Crim LR 192t; (1973) 137 JP 157; (1973) 123 NLJ 15t; [1973] QB 530; (1973) 117 SJ 54; [1973] 2 WLR 201 CA Appropriation with intent to repay not dishonest - jury must decide whether honest.

Felix v Thomas [1966] 3 All ER 21; [1967] AC 292; (1965-66) 116 NLJ 1173; (1966) 110 SJ 528; [1966] 3 WLR 902 PC Person could be arrested on suspicion of having stolen goods 'in any [public/private] place'.

Fellowes v Director of Public Prosecutions [1993] Crim LR 523; (1993) 157 JP 936; [1993] TLR 38 HC QBD Garden path not a 'public place' for purposes of Dangerous Dogs Act 1991.

Fellows (Alban), R v; R v Arnold (Stephen) [1997] 2 All ER 548; [1997] 1 Cr App R 244; [1997] Crim LR 524; (1996) TLR 3/10/96 CA Computer data whereby indecent pictures of children could be displayed on-screen was 'photograph' within meaning of Protection of Children Act 1978.

Felstead v R [1914-15] All ER 41; [1914] AC 534; (1914) 10 Cr App R 129; (1914) 78 JP 313; (1914) 49 LJ 243; (1914-15) 111 LTR 218; (1913-14) XXX TLR 469; (1914) WN (I) 179 HL No right of appeal to CCA against finding of insanity.

Fenley (Charles) and others, R v (1901-07) XX Cox CC 252 Assizes Cannot be found guilty of simple larceny where charged with compound larceny.

Fennell, R v [1970] 3 All ER 215; (1970) 54 Cr App R 451; [1970] Crim LR 581t; (1970) 134 JP 678; (1970) 120 NLJ 732; [1971] 1 QB 428; (1970) 114 SJ 651; [1970] 3 WLR 513 CA Is offence to assault constable effecting lawful arrest in mistaken belief that unlawful.

Fenton (Martin Charles), R v (1975) 61 Cr App R 261; [1975] Crim LR 712; (1975) 119 SJ 695 CA Self-induced intoxication not an abnormality of mind in which to ground diminished responsibility defence.

Fisher (Edward), R v (1910) 5 Cr App R 102; (1910-11) 103 LTR 320 CCA On whether obtaining goods by virtue of fraud is larceny/obtaining by false pretences/conspiracy to defraud.

Fisher (Florence Sarah), R v (1921-22) 16 Cr App R 53; (1921) 56 LJ 448; [1922] 91 LJCL 145; (1921-22) 66 SJ 109; (1921) WN (I) 327 CCA Where acquitted of obtaining by false pretences contrary to Larceny Act 1916, s 44(3), could not be convicted of larceny CCA cannot substitute conviction with one in respect of which have been acquitted.

Fisher (George Samuel), R v (1975) 60 Cr App R 225; [1975] Crim LR 162t; (1975) 125 NLJ 68t CA Where cheque made out by 'victim' in favour of company prosecution must show company made false pretence and accused aided and abetted same to secure false pretences conviction of accused.

Fisher v Raven; Raven v Fisher [1963] 2 All ER 389; [1964] AC 210; (1963) 47 Cr App R 174; [1963] Crim LR 503; (1963) 127 JP 382; (1963) 113 LJ 332; (1963) 107 SJ 373; [1963] 2 WLR 1137 HL Accepting money in return for promise of services/goods not obtaining credit contrary to Debtors Act 1869 or Bankruptcy Act 1914.

Fisher, R v (1911-13) XXII Cox CC 270; (1910) 74 JP 104; [1910] 1 KB 149; (1910) 79 LJKB 187; (1910) 102 LTR 111; (1909) WN (I) 252 CCA Evidence of earlier false pretences admissible at trial for false pretences if shows system of false pretences - not if simply shows fraudulent character.

Fisher, R v [1987] Crim LR 334 CA Person pleading self-defence entitled to have defence considered on basis of facts as he believed them to be.

Fisher, R v [1963] 1 All ER 744; (1963) 107 SJ 177 CCA Accepting money in return for promise of services/goods is/is not obtaining credit contrary to Debtors Act 1869/Bankruptcy Act 1914.

Fisher, Yeandel and another v [1965] 3 All ER 158; [1965] Crim LR 548; (1965) 129 JP 546; (1965) 115 LJ 643; [1966] 1 QB 440; (1965) 109 SJ 593; [1965] 3 WLR 1002 HC QBD Management of premises in which cannabis used/sold an absolute offence.

Fitzaucher, R v [1956] Crim LR 118 Assizes Was case to answer where fire caused either by accused or intruder and prosecution possessed of evidence proving fire not caused by intruder.

Fitzgerald (Edward), Duke of Leinster, R v (1922-23) 17 Cr App R 147 CCA Bail applications generally refused by CCA.

Fitzgerald v Lyle [1972] Crim LR 125; (1970) 114 SJ 929 HC QBD On who (as here) constitutes a suspected person who may be validly arrested for/charged with loitering with intent.

Fitzgerald, R v [1992] Crim LR 660 CA On appropriate basis on which party/ies to alleged joint enterprise may be convicted.

Fitzmaurice, R v [1983] 1 All ER 189; (1983) 76 Cr App R 17; [1982] Crim LR 677; (1982) 132 NLJ 814; [1983] QB 1083; (1982) 126 SJ 656; [1983] 2 WLR 227 CA Incitement to commit offence at common law only possible if offence possible.

Fitzpatrick (Norman), R v (1925-26) 19 Cr App R 91 CCA That accused was accessory after fact does not prove was principal/accessory before fact; accused may give account of own state of mind at pertinent time: mens rea a question of fact.

Flack v Baldry [1988] 1 All ER 412; [1988] Crim LR 610; (1988) 152 JP 418; (1988) 132 SJ 89; [1988] 1 WLR 214 HC QBD Stun gun could be noxious thing but did not discharge anything so not prohibited weapon.

Flack v Baldry (1988) 87 Cr App R 130; (1988) 138 NLJ 63; (1988) 132 SJ 334; [1988] 1 WLR 393 HL Electric stun gun 'discharged' noxious thing and was therefore a prohibited weapon.

Flack v Church (1918) 82 JP 59; (1917-18) XXXIV TLR 32 HC KBD Can be convicted twice under Dog Licences Act 1867, s 8, for non-possession of licence on different days of same year.

Flack v Hunt (1980) 70 Cr App R 51; [1980] Crim LR 44; (1979) 123 SJ 751 HC QBD Recklessness a subjective test: here unlawful wounding charge failed where no recklessness established.

Flackett, Davies v [1972] Crim LR 708t; (1972) 122 NLJ 537t; [1973] RTR 8; (1972) 116 SJ 526 HC QBD Not obtaining property by deception where had exited pay-car park without paying when presented with sudden opportunity on leaving.

Forde, R v [1923] All ER 477; (1921-25) XXVII Cox CC 406; (1922-23) 17 Cr App R 99; (1923) 87 JP 76; [1923] 2 KB 400; [1923] 92 LJCL 501; (1923) 128 LTR 798; (1922-23) 67 SJ 539; (1922-23) XXXIX TLR 322; (1923) WN (I) 98 CCA Defence in proviso to Criminal Law Amendment Act 1922, s 2 (reasonable belief of under twenty-three year old facing first-time charge that girl over sixteen) not open in case of indecent assault.

Foreman, R v [1991] Crim LR 702 CA On evidential basis to support robbery or at least handling conviction.

Forman and Ford, R v [1988] Crim LR 677 CrCt Police officer who does not act when other assaults prisoner is guilty of assault; where not proved which of two officers assaulted prisoner with whom were alone both must be acquitted (if one must have encouraged the other both are guilty).

Formosa, R v; R v Upton [1991] 1 All ER 131; (1991) 92 Cr App R (1991) 92 Cr App R 11; [1990] Crim LR 868; (1991) 155 JP 97; [1991] 2 QB 1; (1990) 134 SJ 1191; [1990] TLR 54; [1990] 3 WLR 1179 CA Object to be designed/adapted as prohibited weapon must be physically altered.

Forrester, R v [1992] Crim LR 793 CA Valid conviction for robbery of person who believing self to act honestly took property from another (whom believed to have wrongfully withheld his money) to use as bargaining counter for return of money/to sell on, returning any excess above amount withheld.

Forsyth, R v [1997] 2 Cr App R 299; [1997] Crim LR 589 CA On theft of thing in action; on ramifications of Preddy decision for Theft Act offences.

Foster (Henry), R v (1909) 3 Cr App R 173 CCA Valid conviction for habitual criminal where only six days between leaving prison and new arrest.

Foster v Attard (1986) 83 Cr App R 214; [1986] Crim LR 627 HC QBD Once police had lawfully entered premises under one statutory power could exercise powers under other statute.

Foster, R v [1957] Crim LR 470 Sessions Failed prosecution for larceny as bailee where was inadequate evidence as to conversion necessary to sutain conviction.

Fotheringham (William Bruce), R v (1989) 88 Cr App R 206; [1988] Crim LR 846 CA Self-induced intoxication not a defence to rape.

Fouldes, Police v [1954] Crim LR 868 Sessions Boccaccio's 'The Decameron' deemed not to be obscene.

Fountain, R v [1965] 2 All ER 671; (1965) 49 Cr App R 315; [1965] Crim LR 544; (1965) 129 JP 391; (1965) 115 LJ 498; [1966] 1 WLR 212 Assizes On common law cheating.

Fowler (George), R v (1912-13) XXIX TLR 422 CCA Habitual criminal conviction quashed where had not been given notice of offences to be relied on in proving habitual criminality.

Fowler, R v [1956] Crim LR 330 Sessions On difference between intent to deceive/intent to defraud.

Fox v Burgess (1921-25) XXVII Cox CC 162; [1922] 1 KB 623 HC KBD Father properly convicted of not causing child to attend school where knowingly sent to school in such a state that was not admitted.

Fox v Chief Constable of Gwent [1985] 1 All ER 230; [1984] Crim LR 567; [1984] RTR 402; (1985) 129 SJ 49; [1984] TLR 406; [1985] 1 WLR 33 HC QBD Breath specimen admissible though obtained on foot of unlawful arrest.

Fox v Chief Constable of Gwent [1986] Crim LR 59; (1985) 129 SJ 757 HL Breath specimen admissible though obtained on foot of unlawful arrest.

Fox v Spicer (1917) 116 LTR 86; (1916-17) XXXIII TLR 172 HC KBD Prosecution procedurally improper: information at issue was for publication in newspaper so proposed prosecution ought to have been referred to DPP.

Fox, White v (1931-32) XLVIII TLR 641 HC KBD Deer hind not a domestic animal so hunting of same not breach of Protection of Animals Act 1911.

Foxon, Strath v [1955] 3 All ER 398; (1955) 39 Cr App R 162; [1955] Crim LR 773; (1955) 119 JP 581; [1956] 1 QB 67; (1955) 99 SJ 799; [1955] 3 WLR 659 HC QBD Place being used by only one prostitute cannot be brothel.

Foy, R v; R v Noe; R v Kelly [1972] Crim LR 504t; (1972) 116 SJ 506 CA Valid withdrawal of question from jury whether agreement to indemnify bail was a conspiracy to effect public mischief.

France v Dewsbury Magistrates' Court [1988] Crim LR 295; (1988) 152 JP 301 HC QBD Improper for later court to convict person for non-surrender to bail where justices present upon surrender indicated that one-day delay in surrender would be overlooked.

Francis (Colin Leslie), R v (1989) 88 Cr App R 127; [1988] Crim LR 528 CA Indecency with or towards children contrary to Indecency with Children Act 1960, s 1(1) requires that act be aimed at children and that accused pleased that children watching.

Francis and Francis (a firm) v Central Criminal Court [1988] 3 All ER 775; (1989) 88 Cr App R 213; [1988] 3 WLR 989 HL Documents otherwise privileged not so if held with criminal intention of laundering drug trafficking proceeds.

Francis, R v [1972] Crim LR 549t; (1972) 122 NLJ 655t; (1972) 116 SJ 632 CA Malicious damage committed between 9pm and 6am an arrestable offence; police officer not required to know offence arrestable before could enter premises to arrest for same.

Frankland v R; Moore v R [1987] AC 576; (1988) 86 Cr App R 116; [1988] Crim LR 117; (1987) 131 SJ 541; [1987] 2 WLR 1251 PC Objective test of intent in Manx murder case inappropriate.

Franklin, R v (1909) 3 Cr App R 48; (1910) 74 JP 24; (1909-10) 54 SJ 217 CCA Constable can prove persistent criminality of offender by reference to police record even though not personally aware of all previous convictions of accused.

Frascati (Umberto), R v (1981) 73 Cr App R 28 CA Breach of prison an offence per se - that acquitted of offence for which were in custody not a defence.

Frederick, R v [1969] 3 All ER 804; (1969) 53 Cr App R 455; [1969] Crim LR 370t; (1969) 133 JP 698; (1969) 119 NLJ 462t; (1969) 113 SJ 485; [1970] 1 WLR 107 CA Possession of unmeasurable amount of dangerous drug could sustain possession conviction.

Freed v Director of Public Prosecutions (1969) 53 Cr App R 137; [1969] Crim LR 86t; (1968) 118 NLJ 1172t; (1968) 112 SJ 1020 HC QBD Meaning of 'gold coin'/'gold bullion' under Exchange Control Act 1947.

Freedman (Sidney), R v; R v Freedman (Woolf) (1930-31) Cr App R 133 CCA Must be in possession/control of stolen property to be convicted of receiving same; that intended to commit crime does not mean can be convicted of crime.

Freeman, Griffiths v; Jones v Freeman [1970] 1 All ER 1117; [1970] Crim LR 348; (1970) 114 SJ 263; [1970] 1 WLR 659 HC QBD Only one offence of handling: general information permissible but undesirable.

Freeman, R v [1970] 2 All ER 413; (1970) 54 Cr App R 251; [1970] Crim LR 403; (1970) 134 JP 462; (1970) 114 SJ 336; [1970] 1 WLR 788 CA Starting-pistol is firearm.

French and another v Director of Public Prosecutions [1994] TLR 71 HC QBD Could convict/acquit of handling/theft where person charged with both.

French v Hoggett (1967) 111 SJ 906; [1968] 1 WLR 94 HC QBD Sale of alcohol absent licence an absolute offence.

Frickey and Frickey, R v [1956] Crim LR 421 Sessions Was not perjury to falsely complete form indicating parents consented to marriage as document not mandated under Marriage Act 1949.

Friend v Brehout (1913-14) 58 SJ 741; (1914) WN (I) 283 HC KBD Bye-law prohibiting trawling in particular bay to safeguard crab-fishing in bay was valid.

Fritschy, R v [1985] Crim LR 745 CA Non-interference with owner's rights meant could not be guilty of theft.

Frizzle, R v [1966] Crim LR 221; (1966) 110 SJ 87 CCA On elements of larceny by finding (must believe upon finding object that owner can reasonably be discovered).

Froggatt (William), R v (1910) 4 Cr App R 115 CCA Rebuttal of alibi defence: evidence admissible.

Froggett, R v [1965] 2 All ER 832; (1965) 49 Cr App R 334; [1965] Crim LR 489g; (1965) 129 JP 474; (1965) 115 LJ 513; [1966] 1 QB 152; (1965) 109 SJ 492; [1965] 3 WLR 602 CCA Party not principal in second (or first degree) to theft could be convicted of conspiracy to steal and receiving.

Frost, Cawley v (1977) 64 Cr App R 20; [1976] Crim LR 747 (cf [1977] Crim LR 170); (1977) 141 JP 30; (1976) 126 NLJ 953t; (1976) 120 SJ 703; [1976] 1 WLR 1207 HC QBD Football ground a public place under terms of Public Order Act 1936. ss 5 and 9(1).

Fryer, R v (1914-15) XXIV Cox CC 403 Assizes On appropriate jury direction where defence of insanity pleaded.

Fudge, Gardiner v [1954] Crim LR 210 HC QBD 'Obtaining' under Larceny Act 1916, s 32 meant obtaining property in goods, not (as here) merely possession of same.

Fulton, Stevenson v [1935] All ER 431; (1934-39) XXX Cox CC 293; (1935) 99 JP 423; [1936] 1 KB 320; (1936) 81 LJ 42; [1936] 105 LJCL 167; (1936) 154 LTR 162; (1935-36) LII TLR 89; (1936) 80 SJ 75; (1935) WN (I) 188 HC KBD Person using (rather than providing) accommodation address can be convicted for furnishing false information contrary to Official Secrets Act 1920, s 5(4).

Fuschillo, R v [1940] 2 All ER 489; (1938-40) 27 Cr App R 193 CCA Absent proof of theft circumstantial evidence may establish goods were stolen.

Fussell, R v [1951] 2 All ER 761; (1951-52) 35 Cr App R 135; (1951) 115 JP 562; (1951) 101 LJ 582 CCA Could try attempted (taking and driving away) indictable offence summarily.

Fynn, R v [1970] Crim LR 118t CMAC Conviction quashed where was inadequate direction as to failure of prosecution to call evidence as to whether 'advances' of pay (which formed basis for theft charge) were generally permitted by the defendant's employer.

G v Director of Public Prosecutions [1989] Crim LR 150 HC QBD On pre-requisites necessary for arrest to be valid under Town Police Clauses Act 1847, s 29/Police and Criminal Evidence Act 1984, s 25(3)).

G v Superintendent of Police, Stroud (1988) 86 Cr App R 92; [1987] Crim LR 269 HC QBD Short time-span in which constable had to make decision to arrest relevant in deciding reasonableness of arrest that breach of peace likely: here reasonable so assault was assault on constable in execution of duty.

Gaffoor v R (1991) 92 Cr App R 349; [1991] Crim LR 613 PC Proper inference from evidence that appellant a drug trafficker.

Gage, Nicholson v (1985) 80 Cr App R 40 HC QBD Not offensive conduct conducive to breach of peace where had been in cubicle with door practically closed and had only been observed by police.

Galbraith (William Wallace), R v (1912-13) 8 Cr App R 101 CCA Drunkenness as defence to murder.

Gallagher, Attorney-General for Northern Ireland v [1961] 3 All ER 299; [1963] AC 349; (1961) 45 Cr App R 316; [1961] Crim LR 717t; (1961) 111 LJ 532; [1961] 3 WLR 619 HL Rôle of HL upon appeal; mental disease occasioning violent behaviour in which unaware of type/quality/wrongness of act required to sustain insanity defence.

Gallasso (Lesley Caroline), R v (1994) 98 Cr App R 284; [1993] Crim LR 459 CA Whether taking of property amounted to appropriation decided objectively.

Galvin, R v [1987] 2 All ER 851; (1988) 86 Cr App R 85; [1987] Crim LR 700; [1987] QB 862; (1987) 131 SJ 657; [1987] 3 WLR 93 CA Under Official Secrets Act Crown must prove communicator of unauthorised information not authorised to do so.

Gamage Limited, Bryson v (1907-09) XXI Cox CC 515; (1907) 71 JP 439; [1907] 2 KB 630; [1907] 76 LJKB 936; (1907-08) XCVII LTR 399; (1907) WN (I) 164 HC KBD 'Pistol' under Pistols Act 1903 includes spring pistols from which shot/bullets dischargeable.

Gamble, National Coal Board v [1958] 3 All ER 203; (1958) 42 Cr App R 240; [1958] Crim LR 682; (1958) 122 JP 453; (1958) 108 LJ 617; [1959] 1 QB 11; (1958) 102 SJ 621; [1958] 3 WLR 434 HC QBD Aiding and abetting where seller of unascertained goods completed sale despite knowing at weighing (passing) of property that conveyance of that weight an offence.

Gamble, Whiteside v [1968] Crim LR 560 Sessions Person not guilty of assault on constable in execution of his duty where latter grossly insulted individual and then invited him to fight.

Giles, R v [1976] Crim LR 253 CrCt Holding of glass in hand after fight had ceased but with intent of using against another was not possession of offensive weapon.

Gilks, R v [1972] 3 All ER 280; (1972) 56 Cr App R 734; [1972] Crim LR 585t; (1972) 136 JP 777; (1972) 122 NLJ 609t; (1972) 116 SJ 632; [1972] 1 WLR 1341 CA Money paid under mistake is 'property belonging to another' and keeping it theft.

Gill (Simon Imran), R v (1993) 97 Cr App R 215; (1993) 137 SJ LB 19; [1993] TLR 4 CA Offence to offer to supply drug transpires when offer made (irrespective of presence of conspiracy).

Gill and Ruana, R v [1989] Crim LR 358 CA Remains substantive rule of law that entrapment no defence to offence.

Gill, R v [1976] 2 All ER 893; (1976) 140 JP 507; (1976) 120 SJ 316; [1977] 1 WLR 78 CA Immigrant's untruth to constable not false statement where constable not acting under Immigration Act.

Gill, R v [1963] 2 All ER 688; (1963) 127 JP 429; (1963) 113 LJ 434; [1963] 1 WLR 841 CCA Person relying on duress to place enough evidence before court to make it a real issue - is then for prosecution to defeat it.

Gill, R v (1963) 107 SJ 416 HC QBD Person relying on duress to place enough evidence before court to make it a real issue - is then for prosecution to defeat it.

Gill, Wilkins v; Major v Gill (1903-04) XX TLR 3 HC KBD Attorney-General's fiat necessary for bringing of action against certain publication for advertisement offering reward for return of stolen property on 'no questions asked' basis as publication at issue was newspaper under Larceny (Advertisements) Act 1870/Post Office Act 1870.

Gillard (Simon Paul), R v (1988) 87 Cr App R 189; [1988] Crim LR 531 CA On what it means to 'administer' noxious thing under Offences against the Person Act 1861, s 24 (includes spraying CS gas from spray can into face).

Gilligan, R v [1987] Crim LR 501 CrCt Publication of name of (dead) rape victim allowed.

Gilmartin, R v [1983] 1 All ER 829; (1983) 76 Cr App R 238; [1983] Crim LR 330; (1983) 147 JP 183; [1983] QB 953; (1983) 127 SJ 119; [1982] TLR 613; [1983] 2 WLR 547 CA Giving of postdated cheque implies that will be met for payment on/after date on cheque.

Gilroy (Lillian) and Lovett (Linda), R v [1984] Crim LR 560 CCC Was not perversion of justice to conceal from police evidence concerning person who was not actually guilty of crime concerned.

Ginson, R v [1993] Crim LR 453 CA Denial of previous statement as to why had been delay in reporting of rape by complainant went to credit, not main issue.

Gipson, R v [1963] Crim LR 281g CCA Shotgun not of itself an offensive weapon (must be intent to injure).

Gittens, R v [1984] Crim LR 553; [1984] QB 698; (1984) 128 SJ 515; [1984] TLR 383; [1984] 3 WLR 327 CA On appropriate direction where combined effect of drink and drugs gave rise to automatism plea.

Gittins, R v [1982] Crim LR 584; [1982] RTR 363 CA On ingredients of offence of malicious damage under Malicious Damage Act 1861, s 36.

Glasspool, Nicholson v [1959] Crim LR 294t; (1959) 123 JP 229 HC QBD In prosecution for obscene language need not prove person actually annoyed if intention of accused was to annoy.

Gledhill, Hobson v [1978] Crim LR 45; (1978) 142 JP 250; (1977) 127 NLJ 1105; (1977) 121 SJ 757; [1978] 1 WLR 215 HC QBD Construction of Guard Dogs Act 1975, s 1(1).

Gleed (Frederick), R v (1916-17) 12 Cr App R 32 CCA Essence of receiving is control of goods.

Glynn and another v Simmonds [1952] 2 All ER 47; (1952) 116 JP 389; (1952) 102 LJ 318; (1952) 96 SJ 378; [1952] 1 TLR 1442; (1952) WN (I) 289 HC QBD Racecourse enclosure to which admission charged a public place under Vagrancy Act 1824, s 4.

Goddard, Attorney-General v (1928-29) XLV TLR 609 HC KBD On recovery by (principal) Crown of bribes ('secret profits') paid to (its agent) Metropolitan Police officer.

Godfrey, R v [1922] All ER 266; (1921-25) XXVII Cox CC 338; (1922) 86 JP 219; [1923] 1 KB 24; [1923] 92 LJCL 205; (1923) 128 LTR 115; (1922-23) 67 SJ 147; (1922-23) XXXIX TLR 4; (1922) WN (I) 285 HC KBD Can be 'fugitive offender' though were never in and never left foreign country.

Godwin (Roger Wyatt), R v (1980) 71 Cr App R 97; [1980] Crim LR 426; (1980) 130 NLJ 473; (1980) 124 SJ 344 CA Was obtaining credit by bankrupt despite ostensible obtaining of same for wife's registered company.

Godwin v Director of Public Prosecutions (1993) 96 Cr App R 244; (1993) 157 JP 197; [1992] TLR 406 HC QBD That explanation uncontroverted by prosecution did not mean had established lawful authority for possession of weapon.

Godwin, Director of Public Prosecutions v (1992) 156 JP 643; [1991] RTR 303 HC QBD Evidence as to excess alcohol in defendant's breath validly excluded on basis that obtained on foot of unlawful arrest.

Gold and Cohen, R v (1907) 71 JP 360 CCC Can only be convicted of attempting to procure woman to be come prostitute outside King's Dominions where woman concerned not already a prostitute (Criminal Law Amendment Act 1885, s 2(2)).

Gold Star Publications Ltd v Director of Public Prosecutions [1981] 2 All ER 257; (1981) 73 Cr App R 141; [1981] Crim LR 633; (1981) 145 JP 289; (1981) 131 NLJ 525; (1981) 125 SJ 376; [1981] 1 WLR 732 HL Article held in England can be obscene publication though purely for export.

Gold Star Publications Ltd v Metropolitan Police Commissioner (1980) 71 Cr App R 185; (1980) 130 NLJ 508 HC QBD Article held in England can be obscene publication though purely for export.

Gold, R v [1988] 2 All ER 186; (1988) 86 Cr App R 52; (1988) 152 JP 445; [1988] 2 WLR 984 HL Computer hacking not making of false instrument.

Gold, R v; R v Schifreen [1987] 3 All ER 618; [1988] AC 1063; (1988) 87 Cr App R 257; [1988] Crim LR 437; (1988) 138 NLJ 117; (1988) 132 SJ 624 HL Hacking does not involve making/use of false device under Forgery and Counterfeiting Act 1981.

Gold, R v; R v Schifreen [1987] Crim LR 762; [1987] QB 1116; (1987) 131 SJ 1247; [1987] 3 WLR 803 CA Hacking does not involve forgery or making/use of false device under Forgery and Counterfeiting Act 1981.

Golechha (Ummed Chand), R v; R v Choraria (Rajendra Kumar) [1989] 3 All ER 908; (1990) 90 Cr App R 241; [1990] Crim LR 865; (1989) 133 SJ 1001; [1989] 1 WLR 1050 CA Using forged bills of exchange to delay but not for all time avoid bank enforcing previous bills was not falsification with a view to gain contrary to Theft Act 1968, s 17.

Gollins v Gollins [1962] 2 All ER 366; (1962) 106 SJ 313 HC PDAD Absent desire to injure longterm failure to adequately maintain wife not cruelty.

Gomez, R v [1993] 1 All ER 1; [1993] AC 442; (1993) 96 Cr App R 359; [1993] Crim LR 304; (1993) 157 JP 1; (1992) 142 NLJ 1719; (1993) 137 SJ LB 36; [1992] TLR 592; [1992] 3 WLR 1067 HL Taking of goods with consent where fraud/deception/misrepresentation is theft (even if also obtaining property by deception).

Gomez, R v [1991] 3 All ER 394; (1991) 93 Cr App R 156; (1992) 156 JP 39; (1991) 141 NLJ 599; [1991] TLR 206; [1991] 1 WLR 1334 CA Possession of property on foot of unavoided viodable contract not appropriation/theft.

Gomez, R v [1964] Crim LR 723 CCA Inadequate direction as to defence of diminished responsibility led to manslaughter verdict being substituted for murder verdict.

Gommo, R v [1964] Crim LR 469 CCA That passenger had been sitting next to driver who was disqualified was not per se evidence that knew of disqualification (and so was guilty of aiding and abetting offence of driving while disqualified).

Goodall (George Albert), R v (1959) 43 Cr App R 24; [1959] Crim LR 47 CCA Quashing of bankruptcy offence conviction where not satisfactorily proved whether credit obtained for self.

Governor of Pentonville Prison, ex parte Singh, R v [1981] 3 All ER 23; (1981) 73 Cr App R 216; (1981) 145 JP 476; [1981] 1 WLR 1031 HC QBD Evidence from third party state inadmissible; affirmation admissible as evidence; what is affirmation a subjective issue.

Governor of Pentonville Prison, ex parte Sotiriadis, R v [1974] 1 All ER 504; [1974] Crim LR 44; (1973) 123 NLJ 1068t; (1973) 117 SJ 913 HC QBD Time limit for evidence expired; requesting state must produce sufficient evidence.

Governor of Pentonville Prison, ex parte Teja, R v [1971] 2 All ER 11; (1971) 121 NLJ 82t; [1971] 2 QB 274; (1971) 115 SJ 305; [1971] 2 WLR 816 HC QBD Cannot claim no offence because of PC decision - matter for foreign law; political defence inapplicable despite case being subject of Indian Parliamentary debate; cannot plead delay if are responsible for it.

Governor of Pentonville Prison, ex parte Tzu-Tsai Cheng, R v [1973] 1 All ER 935 HC QBD Political offence ground arises only if political offence in requesting state, not third state.

Governor of Pentonville Prison, ex parte Voets, R v [1986] 2 All ER 630; [1986] Crim LR 465; (1986) 130 SJ 245; [1986] 1 WLR 470 HC QBD All relevant evidence admissible; evidence admitted for one purpose not to be excluded because inadmissible for other purpose.

Governor of Pentonville Prison, R v (1903) 67 JP 206 HC KBD Successful habeas corpus application where had been procedural irregularities in committal of prisoner.

Governor of Pentonville Prison; ex parte Carter, R v [1984] TLR 456 HC QBD No need for corroboration of evidence of children admitted on affirmation at extradition hearings.

Governor of Pentonville Prison; ex parte Elliott, R v [1975] Crim LR 516; (1975) 119 SJ 709 HC QBD On what constitutes a 'relevant offence' for which may be extradited under Fugitive Offenders Act 1967.

Governor of Pentonville Prison; ex parte Gilliland, R v [1984] Crim LR 229 HC QBD Increase in bail not revocation of original bail order; appeal against excessive bail is by way of summons to judge in chambers.

Governor of Pentonville Prison; ex parte Healy, R v (1984) 128 SJ 498; [1984] TLR 303 HC QBD Extradition of Irish citizen from Ireland to the UK on foot of request by latter did not violate Article 48/EEC.

Governor of Pentonville Prison; ex parte Herbage (No 3), R v (1987) 84 Cr App R 149 HC QBD Habeas corpus application by fugitive awaiting extradition refused where was prima facie case that had committed non-time barred felony in United States punishable by over one year's imprisonment.

Governor of Pentonville Prison; ex parte Kakis, R v (1978) 128 NLJ 139t; (1978) 122 SJ 96 HC QBD Failed action in which applicant sought to rely on political offence/delay grounds as bases justifying non-extradition.

Governor of Pentonville Prison; ex parte Khuschundani, R v (1980) 130 NLJ 415 CA Non-extradition of person sought for offence which was not 'relevant' offence for purposes of Fugitive Offenders Act 1967.

Governor of Pentonville Prison; ex parte Mancini, R v [1984] TLR 523 HC QBD Failed habeas corpus application by subject of habeas corpus proceedings requested for murder but extradited for manslaughter.

Governor of Pentonville Prison; ex parte Osman (No 2), R v (1989) 133 SJ 121 HC QBD On status/effect of Foreign Secretary's certificate that proposed extraditee(though apparently attached to the Liberian embassy) did not enjoy diplomatic immunity.

Governor of Pentonville Prison; ex parte Passingham and another, R v [1983] Crim LR 678; (1983) 127 SJ 308 HL On 'affirmations' admissible under the Anglo-Swedish Extradition Treaty of 1983.

Governor of Pentonville Prison; ex parte Rodriguez, R v [1984] TLR 674 HC QBD Interpretation of provision of evidence requirements under the Anglo-Portugese extradition treaty.

Governor of Risley Remand Centre, ex parte Hassan, R v (1976) 120 SJ 333; [1976] 1 WLR 971 HC QBD Failed application by alien detained under immigration law who failed to discharge onus of proof on him (considered) to show that he was unlawfully detained.

Governor of Risley Remand Centre; ex parte Marks, R v [1984] Crim LR 238 HC QBD Unnecessary to prove conviction of person sought under warrant issued under the Backing of Warrants (Republic of Ireland Act) 1965 - warrant adequate evidence of conviction.

Governor of Stafford Prison; ex parte Emery, R v [1908-10] All ER 843; (1911-13) XXII Cox CC 143; (1909) 73 JP 284; [1909] 2 KB 81; [1909] 78 LJKB 629; (1909) 100 LTR 993; (1908-09) XXV TLR 440; (1909) WN (I) 95 HC KBD Deaf mute found incapable of pleading properly committed as insane.

Governor of Wandsworth Prison; ex parte Silverman, R v (1952) 96 SJ 853 HC QBD Failed application by person in preventive detention who sought habeas corpus writ.

Governor of Winchester Prison, ex parte Roddie and another, R v; R v Crown Court at Southampton, ex parte Roddie and another [1991] 2 All ER 931; (1991) 93 Cr App R 190; [1991] Crim LR 619; (1991) 155 JP 676; [1991] TLR 67; [1991] 1 WLR 303 HC QBD Gravity of offence/shortness of extension did not justify extension of period of pre-committal custody.

Governor of Wormwood Scrubs Prison Prison; ex parte Foy, R v (1920) 84 JP 94; (1919-20) XXXVI TLR 432 HC KBD Internment under wartime internment provisions not unlawful though war had ended.

Governor of Wormwood Scrubs Prison; ex parte Boydell, R v [1948] 2 KB 193; (1948) 98 LJ 133; (1948) LXIV TLR 184; (1948) WN (I) 100 HC KBD Illegal detention of ex-officer by army authorities for arrest and trial.

Goward, Hoogstraten v [1967] Crim LR 590; (1967) 111 SJ 581 HC QBD Police officer could be passenger for purposes of prosecution under the Town Police Clauses Act 1847, s 28.

Grace v Director of Public Prosecutions [1989] Crim LR 365; (1989) 153 JP 491 HC QBD On proving that air-gun a lethal wepon (which it was).

Gradwell; ex parte Straker, R v [1963] Crim LR 50t HC QBD On whether negatives could constitute articles for purposes of Obscene Publications Act 1959.

Graham (Christopher Bruce), R v (1978) 67 Cr App R 356 CA Conviction for cannabis possession merited as amount found was measurable.

Graham (Christopher), R v [1969] Crim LR 192; (1969) 113 SJ 87 CA Were in possession of cannabis though amount possessed amounted only to a few milligrammes.

Graham (Lawrence Brisco), R v (1912-13) 8 Cr App R 149 HC KBD Document could be valuable security for purposes of Larceny Act 1861, s 90 though could not be used for purpose which allegedly served.

Graham and others, R v [1997] Crim LR 340 CA On ramifications of Preddy decision for Theft Act offences.

Graham and others, R v [1997] Crim LR 358; (1996) 140 SJ LB 253; (1996) TLR 28/10/96 CA Can be guilty of theft of chose in action though destroy same in course of appropriation.

Graham, R v [1982] 1 All ER 801; (1982) 74 Cr App R 235; [1982] Crim LR 365; (1982) 146 JP 206; (1982) 132 NLJ 113; (1982) 126 SJ 117; [1982] 1 WLR 294 CA Duress tested by reference to person of reasonable self-control so voluntary taking of drink/drugs irrelevant.

Graham, R v [1969] 2 All ER 1181; (1969) 133 JP 505; [1970] 1 WLR 113 CA Possession conviction possible if quantity of drug measurable (albeit by microscope).

Graham-Kerr (John), R v (1989) 88 Cr App R 302; (1989) 153 JP 171; (1988) 132 SJ 1299; [1988] 1 WLR 1098 CA On elements of crime of taking indecent photographs of child contrary to Protection of Children Act 1978, s 1(1).

Grainge, R v [1984] Crim LR 493 CA On what is meant by 'believing' goods to have been stolen.

Grainge, R v [1974] 1 All ER 928; (1974) 59 Cr App R 3; [1974] Crim LR 180t; (1974) 138 JP 275; (1974) 124 NLJ 56t; (1974) 118 SJ 116; [1974] 1 WLR 619 CA Accused must at least suspect but close eyes to possibility that goods were stolen.

Grant (Ian Arthur), R v; R v Gilbert (Kenneth) (1954) 38 Cr App R 107; [1954] Crim LR 624t CCA Common design to use violence in commission of non-violent crime means common guilt of murder if death caused by violence.

Grant (Thomas), R v [1985] Crim LR 387 CA On Sexual Offences Act 1956, s 30(2).

Grant v Gorman [1979] Crim LR 669 (amended at [1980] Crim LR 184); [1980] RTR 119 HC QBD Valid arrest where warned that failure to provide specimen would result in arrest and refused specimen (though arrested for assault on constable who sought to effect arrest upon failure).

Grant v Taylor [1986] Crim LR 252 HC QBD On extent of power of arrest under Metropolitan Police Act 1839, s 54(13) for using insulting words or behaviour whereby breach of the peace may be occasioned.

Grant, Davis, Riley and Topley, R v [1957] 2 All ER 694; (1957) 41 Cr App R 173; [1957] Crim LR 542t; (1957) 101 SJ 594 CMAC Cannot commit mutiny alone.

Grant, R v [1996] 1 Cr App R 73; [1995] Crim LR 715; [1995] TLR 147 CA Money found in possession of person charged with possession of drugs with intent to supply was relevant to determining whether dealt in drugs/had intent to supply.

Grant, R v [1986] Crim LR 235 CA Application of proviso so as to allow conviction for conspiracy to defraud.

Grant, R v [1980] Crim LR 245; [1980] RTR 280 CA Arrest valid where clear from circumstances - though not specifically told - why arrested.

Grant, R v [1960] Crim LR 424 Assizes On establisihing diminished responsibility/insanity.

Grantham (Paul Reginald George), R v (1984) 79 Cr App R 86; [1984] Crim LR 492; [1984] QB 675; [1984] TLR 180; [1984] 2 WLR 815 CA Was fraudulent trading where company director had intended to deceive another into providing credit.

Granville, Taylor v [1978] Crim LR 482 CA On what constitutes assault occasioning actual bodily harm (blow to face was such).

Gray (David John), R v; R v Liggins (William James); R v Riding (Mark); R v Rowlands (Catherine Mary) [1995] 2 Cr App R 100; [1995] Crim LR 45; (1994) 138 SJ LB 199; [1994] TLR 461 CA On admissibility of evidence of fellow parties to unlawful common enterprise against each other.

Gray (James Burns McWilliams), R v (1982) 74 Cr App R 324; [1982] Crim LR 176 (1981) 131 NLJ 1311 CA Importuning for gay sex is 'immoral purpose' within meaning of Sexual Offences Act 1956, s 32.

Gray (John Henry), R v (1916-17) 12 Cr App R 244 CCA Standing by when criminal act committed does not make one guilty of offence.

Gray v Chief Constable of Greater Manchester [1983] Crim LR 45 CrCt Street busker not guilty of begging/gathering alms contrary to Vagrancy Act 1824, s 3.

Gray v Heathcote (1918) WN (I) 147 HC KBD Conviction for dumping of refuse (oil-water mixture) into dock.

Gray, Hooker v (1907-09) XXI Cox CC 437; (1907) 71 JP 337; (1907) XCVI LTR 706; (1906-07) XXIII TLR 472 HC KBD Party severely wounding cat, allowing to crawl away, then later killing it not guilty of cruelty.

Gray, Matthews v (1909) 73 JP 303; [1909] 2 KB 89; (1909) 44 LJ 233; [1909] 78 LJKB 545; (1908-09) XXV TLR 476; (1909) WN (I) 88 HC KBD On sale of pistol to party for use in own house.

Great Western Railway Company, Ormiston v [1917] 86 LJCL 759; (1917) 116 LTR 479; (1916-17) XXXIII TLR 171 HC KBD Railway company servant cannot arrest passenger for travelling without proper fare unless passenger refuses to show ticket and disclose name and address but what servant says in course of arrest can only be slanderous if is special damage.

Greatbanks, R v [1959] Crim LR 450 CCC Where pleading consent as defence to rape it was permissible to call evidence showing that prosecutrix a woman of disreputable character.

Greater London Metropolitan Police Commissioner v Streeter and another (1980) 71 Cr App R 113; (1980) 130 NLJ 313 HC QBD Was not possession/control for security officer/police to mark/track stolen goods so accused could be convicted of handling.

Greatwood, R v (1946) 96 LJ 431 CCA Doctrine of recent possession held not to apply where was three month gap between theft and possession.

Green (Harry Rodney), R v [1975] 3 All ER 1011; (1976) 62 Cr App R 74; [1976] Crim LR 47t; (1976) 140 JP 112; (1975) 125 NLJ 1117t; [1976] QB 985; (1975) 119 SJ 825; [1976] 2 WLR 57 CA Need not succeed in evading prohibition on importation to be guilty of evasion/attempted evasion.

Green (Isaac), R v (1908) 1 Cr App R 124 CCA Whether knew had stolen property in possession a matter for jury; slip as to previous conviction not picked up on by judge/jury does not merit quashing of conviction.

Green and another, R v (1914-15) XXIV Cox CC 41; (1914) 78 JP 224; (1914) 110 LTR 240; (1913-14) XXX TLR 170 CCA Presumption of coercion of wife by husband precluded her conviction for larceny.

Green v Cross (1910) 74 JP 357; (1910-11) 103 LTR 279; (1909-10) XXVI TLR 507 HC KBD Person unnecessarily leaving two-hour delay in releasing injured dog from vermin-trap could be guilty of cruelty.

Green v Director of Public Prosecutions [1991] Crim LR 782; (1991) 155 JP 816; (1991) 141 NLJ 783t; [1991] TLR 236 HC QBD Advice to person not to answer police questions could if given in certain fashion be obstruction of police in execution of their duty.

Green v Moore [1982] 1 All ER 428; (1982) 74 Cr App R 250; (1982) 146 JP 142; (1981) 131 NLJ 1265; [1982] QB 1044; [1982] 2 WLR 671 HC QBD Warning intended to enable lawbreaker to evade detection an obstruction of constable.

Green, Hunt v (1907-09) XXI Cox CC 333; (1907) 71 JP 18; (1907) XCVI LTR 23 HC KBD Passenger need not be asked to deliver up ticket to contravene by-law concerning payment of fares.

Green, Moore v [1983] 1 All ER 663; [1982] Crim LR 233; (1982) 126 SJ 79 HC QBD Warning by police offficer of pending police investigation an obstruction of police in execution of their duty.

Green, R v [1971] Crim LR 299 CA Six months' detention for eighteen year old guilty of unlawful sex with fourteen year old whom believed to be sixteen.

Green-Emmott (George Vereker), R v [1931] All ER 380; (1931-34) XXIX Cox CC 280; (1930-31) Cr App R 183; (1931) 144 LTR 671 CCA Certified lunatic cannot enter into recognisance.

Greenaway (William), R v (1908) 1 Cr App R 31; (1908) 72 JP 389; (1907-08) XXIV TLR 755 CCA On the elements of larceny.

Greenberg, R v (1918-21) XXVI Cox CC 466; (1919) 121 LTR 288; (1918-19) 63 SJ 553 CCA Attempting to get witness to change evidence/not give certain evidence is same common law misdemeanour.

Greene v Secretary of State for Home Affairs [1941] 3 All ER 388; [1942] AC 284; (1942) 92 LJ 51; [1942] 111 LJ 24; (1942) 166 LTR 24; (1941) 85 SJ 461 (also CA); (1941-42) LVIII TLR 53 HL Home Secretary's affidavit that valid detention under Defence (General) Regulations 1939, reg 18(b) being good on face meant no writ of habeas corpus would be issued.

Greener v Director of Public Prosecutions (1996) TLR 15/2/96 HC QBD Could commit offence under Dangerous Dogs Act 1991 by omission.

Greenfield (Evan), R v (1984) 78 Cr App R 179; [1983] Crim LR 397 CA On what is meant by 'intent to supply' under Misuse of Drugs Act 1971, s 5(3).

Greenhoff, R v [1979] Crim LR 108 CrCt Did not have requisite intent for burglary with intent to steal where entered premises with intent to steal any worthwhile money found.

Greening, R v (1913-14) XXIII Cox CC 601; [1913] 3 KB 846; [1914] 83 LJKB 195; (1913-14) 109 LTR 720; (1912-13) XXIX TLR 732 CCA Person's killing of unmarried partner whom discovered in disreputable house was murder: adultery/manslaughter defence not open to unmarried couple.

Greenly v Lawrence [1949] 1 All ER 241; (1949) 113 JP 120; (1949) LXV TLR 86 HC KBD On appeal to quarter sessions against refusal of gun licence.

Greensmith, R v [1983] 3 All ER 444; (1983) 77 Cr App R 202; [1983] Crim LR 798; (1984) 148 JP 270; (1983) 127 SJ 578; [1983] TLR 408; [1983] 1 WLR 1124 CA Broadest possible meaning to 'cocaine' in Misuse of Drugs Act.

Greenstein, R v; R v Green [1976] 1 All ER 1; (1975) 61 Cr App R 296; [1975] Crim LR 714t; (1975) 119 SJ 742; [1975] 1 WLR 1353 CA Guilt of dishonesty a matter for jury.

Greenwood (Sidney Debenham), R v (1910) 5 Cr App R 113 CCA On time of formation of necessary intent for fraudulent conversion.

Greenwood v Backhouse (1901-07) XX Cox CC 196; (1902) LXXXVI LTR 566 HC KBD Prosecution for cruelty to animals failed as no proof of guilty knowledge.

Gregg, R v (1932) 74 LJ 424 CCA On need for corroboration (here present) in indecent assault case.

Gregory (William), R v (1927-28) 20 Cr App R 185 CCA Bail not generally granted by CCA.

Gregory, Butler v (1901-02) XVIII TLR 370 HC KBD Father of illegitimate child who did not have care/custody of child nor had bastardy proceedings brought against him not father for purposes of Prevention of Cruelty to Children Act 1894, s 23.

Gregory, R v [1972] 2 All ER 861; (1972) 136 JP 569 CA Necessary to name owner of common/indistinctive goods to sustain handling conviction.

Gregory (John Paul), R v (1983) 77 Cr App R 41; [1982] Crim LR 229 CA Person acting in 'handling' capacity could nonetheless be guilty of theft/burglary.

Gregson, Director of Public Prosecutions v (1993) 96 Cr App R 240; (1993) 157 JP 201; (1992) 136 SJ LB 245; [1992] TLR 403 HC QBD That had good reason for knife some days previously and then forgot possession not good defence to possession of offensive weapon.

Grey, R v [1963] Crim LR 44t CCA Valid conviction for capital murder despite alleged flaws in defence/summing up.

Griffin, Data Protection Registrar v [1993] TLR 115 HC QBD Accountant ought to have registered as data user under the Data Protection Act 1984 where used data provided by clients to prepare accounts for Inland Revenue on computer.

Griffin, R v [1993] Crim LR 515 CA On respective roles of judge/jury in child abduction case; was possible to find attempted abduction where had arranged boat trip and went to school to request control of children in local authority care.

Griffin, Wimperis v [1973] Crim LR 533 HC QBD Arrest under Road Trfafic Act 1960 not rendered improper by virtue of immediately prior request for breath specimen under the Road Safety Act 1967.

Griffiths and others, R v [1965] 2 All ER 448; [1965] Crim LR 364t; (1965) 129 JP 380; [1966] 1 QB 589; (1965) 109 SJ 312; [1965] 3 WLR 405 CCA Conspiracy to be charged separately from substantive offences; distinction between one collective conspiracy and several related conspiracies.

Griffiths v Freeman; Jones v Freeman [1970] 1 All ER 1117; [1970] Crim LR 348; (1970) 114 SJ 263; [1970] 1 WLR 659 HC QBD Only one offence of handling: general information permissible but undesirable.

Griffiths, Davies v (1934-39) XXX Cox CC 595; (1937) 101 JP 247; (1937) 157 LTR 23; (1936-37) LIII TLR 680 HC KBD Cannot be fined for conduct likely to cause breach of peace, can only be bound over/ordered to find sureties.

Griffiths, Poutney v [1975] Crim LR 702; (1975) 125 NLJ 722 HL Conviction of mental nurse for assault on patient validly quashed as had been acting in on duty-capacity (Mental Health Act 1959, s 141 applied).

Grimer, R v [1982] Crim LR 674; (1982) 126 SJ 641 CA Identification of shoplifter from video tape by person who had known shoplifter for some years rightly admitted in evidence.

Grimshaw, R v [1984] Crim LR 108 CA On foreseeability as an element of offence of inflicting grievous bodily harm contrary to Offences against the Person Act 1861, s 20.

Grimwood, R v [1962] 3 All ER 285; (1962) 46 Cr App R 393; [1962] Crim LR 632t; (1962) 112 LJ 785; [1962] 2 QB 621; (1962) 106 SJ 613; [1962] 3 WLR 747 CCA DPP v Smith inapplicable to attempted murder; direction that if death a forseeable consequence of accused's actions accused could be guilty of attempted murder, despite absence of intent to kill, a mistaken direction.

Grinberg, R v (1916-17) XXXIII TLR 428 CCA On burden of proof in receiving stolen property prosecution.

Groom v Director of Public Prosecutions [1991] Crim LR 713 HC QBD On what suffices as a 'warning' before arrest under Public Order Act 1986, s 5(4).

Gross, R v (1913-14) XXIII Cox CC 455; (1913) 77 JP 352 CCC Manslaughter where inadvertently kill third party when fire at other party killing of whom would be manslaughter.

Grosvenor, R v (1914-15) XXIV Cox CC 468; (1914) 10 Cr App R 235; (1914-15) 111 LTR 1116 CCA Is conspiracy to defraud though acquired no money/made no false pretence; both parties liable to conviction for obtaining money by false pretences where obtain money following jointly executed false pretence; is false pretences by conduct where implicitly agree to making of false pretence.

Grubb, R v [1914-15] All ER 667; (1915-17) XXV Cox CC 77; (1914-15) 11 Cr App R 153; (1915) 79 JP 430; [1915] 2 KB 683; [1915] 84 LJKB 1744; (1915-16) 113 LTR 510; (1914-15) 59 SJ 547; (1914-15) XXXI TLR 429; (1915) WN (I) 208 CCA Meaning of 'entrusted'/'receipt' in context of fraudulent conversion (under Larceny Act 1901, s 1).

Grundy (Brian), R v; R v Gerrard (Brian); R v Patterson (John) (1989) 89 Cr App R 333; [1989] Crim LR 502 CA Individual could be convicted of wounding with intent to cause grievous bodily harm where harm arose in course of joint unlawful enterprise though may not have involved accused at relevant moment.

Grundy, R v [1977] Crim LR 543 CA Jury ought to have been allowed consider defence by person who originally urged offence that he had expressly communicated withdrawal from same prior to it being committed.

Guildford v Lockyer [1975] Crim LR 235; (1975) 119 SJ 353 HC QBD Was not obtaining pecuniary advantage by deception for person in restaurant to sample food served which had not ordered and then not to pay for same.

Gullefer, R v [1990] 3 All ER 882; (1990) 91 Cr App R 356; [1987] Crim LR 195; [1990] 1 WLR 1063 CA Not attempted theft where leaped onto race track with intention of foiling race so that could recover money bet on (what would have turned out if succeded to be void) race.

Gunstone, R v; Rv v Hughes; R v Morse; R v Uffindell [1978] Crim LR 176 CA Nine/six months' imprisonment for unprovoked assault occasioning actual bodily harm.

Guy (Christopher), R v (1991) 93 Cr App R 108; [1991] Crim LR 462; (1991) 155 JP 778; [1991] TLR 92 CA Could be convicted of possessing firearm during robbery though relevant statute only refers to theft as robbery is theft with threat/use of violence.

Gwalter, Macfarlane v [1958] 1 All ER 181; (1958) 122 JP 144; [1959] 2 QB 332; (1958) 102 SJ 123 CA Dangerous lighting grating a public nuisance for which occupier of adjoining building liable under Public Health Acts Amendment Act 1890, s 35(1).

Gwyn-Jones v Sutherland [1982] RTR 102 HC QBD Conviction quashed as arrest for second failure to provide breath specimen invalid in that it took place not near where driving but outside hospital to which admitted and promptly released.

Gwynne, Horton v [1921] All ER 497; (1918-21) XXVI Cox CC 744; (1921) 85 JP 210; [1921] 2 KB 661; [1921] LJCL 1151; (1921) 125 LTR 309; (1921) WN (I) 144 HC KBD No defence to killing house pigeon that thought it was wild pigeon.

Gylee (Harold Burnett), R v (1908) 1 Cr App R 242 CCA Honest negligence did not preclude it being criminal negligence.

H (IP) v Chief Constable of South Wales [1987] Crim LR 42 HC QBD On evidence necessary to rebut doli incapax presumption in respect of child aged between ten and fourteen years of age.

H, Director of Public Prosecutions v [1997] TLR 238 HC QBD Insanity not a defence to strict liability offence (here driving with excess alcohol).

Hack (Alan Terence), R v [1978] Crim LR 359 CrCt Could infer guilty knowledge but not fact that goods were stolen from their peculiarly low price.

Hacker, R v [1957] 1 All ER 608; (1957) 41 Cr App R 85; (1957) 121 JP 223; (1957) 101 SJ 210; [1957] 1 WLR 455 CCA Blackmail to be tried at assizes.

Hacker, R v [1995] 1 All ER 45; [1995] 1 Cr App R 332; [1995] Crim LR 321; (1995) 159 JP 62; [1995] RTR 1; (1994) 144 NLJ 1625; (1994) 144 NLJ 1772t; (1994) 138 SJ LB 241; [1994] TLR 591; [1994] 1 WLR 1659 HL Certificate of previous handling conviction may list goods but may be excluded if too prejudicial.

Haddock, R v [1976] Crim LR 374t CA Could not on basis of same facts be convicted of damage to property and damage to property with intent to endanger life.

Haden (Josiah), R v (1909) 2 Cr App R 148 CCA One's drunkenness can mitigate one's guilt; pre-trial custody relevant when determining sentence.

Hadjimitsis, R v [1964] Crim LR 128 CCA Person who signed cheque using name by which commonly called was not guilty of forgery.

Hagan, R v [1985] Crim LR 598 CA Intent for forgery under Forgery Act 1913, s 7, was intent to defraud which was present here even though intended use of money obtained by way of forgery was honest/not for self.

Haghighat-Khou, R v [1995] Crim LR 337 CA Valid decision on part of judge not to allow counsel suggest defendant had been victim of 'set-up' by police.

Hailwood, R v; R v Hailwood and Ackroyd Limited (1926-30) XXVIII Cox CC 489; (1927-28) 20 Cr App R 177 CCA; [1928] 2 KB 277; (1928) 97 LJCL 394; (1928) 138 LTR 495 CCA Corrupt practice conviction where unauthorised party entailed expense in advising public not to vote for the Conservative Party.

Halai, R v [1983] Crim LR 624 CA Case of obtaining services in connection with mortgage by deception.

Hale (Robert Angus), R v (1979) 68 Cr App R 415; [1979] Crim LR 596 CA Appropriation under Theft Act 1968, s 1(1) a continuing act.

Hale, R v (1901-07) XX Cox CC 739; (1905) 69 JP 83; [1905] 1 KB 126; (1904-05) XCI LTR 839; (1904-05) 49 SJ 68; (1904-05) XXI TLR 70; (1904-05) 53 WR 400 CCR Child need not be present at trial concerning cruelty thereto unless evidence of child needed.

Hale, R v [1974] 1 All ER 1107; (1974) 59 Cr App R 1; (1974) 138 JP 294; [1974] QB 819; (1974) 118 SJ 548; [1974] 3 WLR 249 CrCt Absent force/fraud/lack of consent kidnapping impossible.

Hall (Edward Leonard), R v (1985) 81 Cr App R 260; [1985] Crim LR 377; (1985) 135 NLJ 604; (1985) 129 SJ 283 CA On what it means to 'know or believe' that goods are stolen (Theft Act 1968, s 22(1)).

Hall (John Hamilton), R v (1988) 86 Cr App R 159; [1987] Crim LR 831 CA Woman is defective for purposes of Sexual Offences Act 1956, s 14(4) where compared to normal person suffers from seriously limited intelligence/social ability.

Hall Line, Limited, Owners of Cargo of City of Baroda v (1925-26) XLII TLR 717 HC KBD Carriers liable in damages where failed to show that theft of goods was not due to neglect of their servants.

Hall v Cotton and another [1986] 3 All ER 332; (1986) 83 Cr App R 257; [1987] QB 504; (1970) 130 SJ 785; [1986] 3 WLR 681 HC QBD Transfer of custodial and not proprietary possession transfers possession.

Hall, Bogdal v [1987] Crim LR 500 HC QBD On proving receipt of supplementary benefit in cases where alleged that obtained same by deception.

Hall, R v [1972] 2 All ER 1009; (1972) 56 Cr App R 547; [1972] Crim LR 453t; (1972) 136 JP 593; (1972) 122 NLJ 450t; [1973] QB 126; (1972) 116 SJ 598; [1972] 3 WLR 381 CA Breach of contractual obligation involving money not theft if not under duty 'to retain and deal with [it]...in a particular way'.

Hall, R v [1963] 2 All ER 1075; (1963) 47 Cr App R 253; [1963] Crim LR 642; (1963) 127 JP 489; (1963) 113 LJ 578; [1964] 1 QB 273; (1963) 107 SJ 597; [1963] 3 WLR 482 CCA Can convict for gross indecency 'with' another though other did not consent.

Hall, R v (1918-21) XXVI Cox CC 525; (1920) 84 JP 56; (1920) 122 LTR 3 CCA Consideration of coroner's depositions.

Hall, R v (1926-30) XXVIII Cox CC 567; (1928-29) 21 Cr App R 48; (1929) 140 LTR 142 CCA On what constitutes/on need to consider provocation.

Hallam and Blackburn, R v [1995] Crim LR 323; [1994] TLR 306 CA On elements of theft.

Hallam, R v [1957] 1 All ER 665; (1957) 41 Cr App R 111; [1957] Crim LR 247; (1957) 121 JP 255; (1957) 107 LJ 185; [1957] 1 QB 569; (1957) 101 SJ 268; [1957] 2 WLR 521 CCA Knowingly possessing explosives involves knowing have possession and know what possess is explosive.

Hallam, Williams v (1942-43) LIX TLR 287 HC KBD Accused's agreeing to both charges being taken together meant that could not argue that could not be convicted and punished on both charges.

Hallett, Robson and another v [1967] 2 All ER 407; (1967) 51 Cr App R 307; [1967] Crim LR 293t; (1967) 131 JP 333; [1967] 2 QB 939; (1967) 111 SJ 254; [1967] 3 WLR 28 HC QBD Police have implied licence to enter garden in course of duty; once licence revoked by owner have reasonable time to go before become trespasser; if breach of peace in garden police can enter to stop it.

Halliday (Sir Frederick Loch), R v (1916) 80 JP 233 (also CA); (1916) 51 LJ 64; [1916] 85 LJKB 953 (also CA); (1915-16) XXXII TLR 245 HC KBD Provision for internment of naturalised British subject valid.

Halliday; ex parte Zadig, R v [1917] AC 260; [1914-17] All ER 496; (1915-17) XXV Cox CC 278; (1917) 81 JP 237; [1917] 86 LJCL 1119; (1917) 116 LTR 417; (1916-17) 61 SJ 443; (1916-17) XXXIII TLR 336 HL Provision for internment of naturalised British subject valid.

Halliday; ex parte Zadig, R v (1916) 80 JP 233 (also HC KBD); (1916) 51 LJ 102; [1916] 85 LJKB 953 (also HC KBD); (1916) 114 LTR 303; (1915-16) 60 SJ 290; (1915-16) XXXII TLR 300 CA Provision for internment of naturalised British subject valid.

Halpin, R v [1996] Crim LR 112 CA Lifestyle evidence is not relevant to issue of whether or not were actually in possession of drug charged.

Halstead v Patel [1972] 2 All ER 147; (1972) 56 Cr App R 334; [1972] Crim LR 235t; (1972) 136 JP 465; (1972) 116 SJ 218; [1972] 1 WLR 661 HC QBD Unless repayment of actual notes/coins obtained intended is intention to permanently deprive; honest intention to replace with reasonable expectation that could replace did not displace dishonesty.

Hamer, R v [1954] Crim LR 209 Assizes Must be obtaining credit for self to be guilty of obtaining credit by false pretences.

Hamid (Ahmed Youssef), R v; R v Hamid (Beebee Nazmoon) (1979) 69 Cr App R 324 CA Perjury conviction cannot stand absent corroboration warning by judge unless jury would have made same decision anyway.

Hamid (Richard), R v [1945] 2 All ER 456; (1943-45) 30 Cr App R 190; (1946) 110 JP 73; [1945] KB 540; [1946] 115 LJ 49; (1945) 173 LTR 250; (1945) 89 SJ 425; (1944-45) LXI TLR 522; (1945) WN (I) 172 CCA Prevention of Fraud (Investments) Act 1939 applied to unformed companies.

Hamilton, R v (1991) 92 Cr App R 54; [1990] Crim LR 806; (1991) 155 JP 264; [1990] TLR 583 CA Withdrawing money which withdrawer had paid into bank account by means of forged cheques was obtaining property by deception.

Hamilton, R v [1970] Crim LR 400 Sessions Certificate of indictment granted that person committed for sentence who failed to appear might be arrested.

Hammer, R v (1921-25) XXVII Cox CC 458; (1922-23) 17 Cr App R 142; (1923) 87 JP 194; [1923] 2 KB 786; (1923) 58 LJ 366; [1923] 92 LJCL 1045; (1923) 129 LTR 479; (1923-24) 68 SJ 121; (1922-23) XXXIX TLR 670; (1923) WN (I) 221 CCA Whether foreign Jewish marriage valid a question of fact.

Hammersley, R v (1918-21) XXVI Cox CC 552; (1919) 54 LJ 467; (1920) 122 LTR 383 CCA Conviction as habitual criminal quashed in light of complete consideration of accused's behaviour.

Hammond, Metropolitan Police Commissioner v [1965] AC 810; [1964] Crim LR 589t; (1964) 114 LJ 488; (1964) 108 SJ 478; [1964] 3 WLR 1 HL Fugitive offender released as warrant not endorsed by (non-existent) police officer/magistrate had not properly considered case.

Hammond, R v [1982] Crim LR 611 CrCt Not making off without payment to tender cheque which knew would not be met.

Hammond, Singh (Baljinder) v [1987] 1 WLR 283 HC QBD Could be convicted of making false statement to immigration officer though did so after date of entry and away from port of entry.

Hampson (Thomas), R v (1914-15) 11 Cr App R 75 CCA That tried to avoid being arrested did not prove guilty of offence charged.

Hampton, R v (1914-15) XXIV Cox CC 722; [1915] 84 LJKB 1137; (1915-16) 113 LTR 378 CCA No larceny unless knowingly commit conversion.

Hancock and another, R v [1986] 1 All ER 641; [1986] AC 455 (also HL); (1986) 82 Cr App R 264; [1986] Crim LR 180; (1986) 150 JP 33; (1985) 135 NLJ 1208; (1985) 129 SJ 793; [1985] 3 WLR 1014 CA Appropriate direction to jury where foreseeability an issue.

Hancock and Tuttle, Director of Public Prosecutions v [1995] Crim LR 139 HC QBD Officer making arrest under the Public Order Act 1986, s 5(4) must be the same officer who administered warning required under that section to offender.

Hancock, R v [1990] 3 All ER 183; (1990) 90 Cr App R 422; [1990] Crim LR 125; [1990] 2 QB 242; [1990] 2 WLR 640 CA In prosecution for theft of treasure trove jury to decide whether beyond reasonable doubt that property is such; coroner's verdict to that effect unnecessary.

Hancock, R v [1963] Crim LR 572 CCA Conviction quashed where claim of right defence not properly left to jury.

Hancock, R v; R v Shankland [1986] AC 455 (also CA); (1986) 82 Cr App R 264; [1986] Crim LR 400; (1986) 150 JP 203; (1986) 136 NLJ 214; (1986) 130 SJ 184; [1986] 2 WLR 357 HL Appropriate direction to jury where foreseeability an issue.

Hand, Chivers v (1915) 79 JP 88; [1915] 84 LJKB 304; (1915) 112 LTR 221 HC KBD Conviction of aider and abettor of (purchaser from) person breaching Sunday trading legislation quashed as requisite mens rea absent.

Hankinson v Dowland [1974] Crim LR 539; (1974) 138 JP 795; (1974) 118 SJ 644 HC QBD On what constitutes an offence for purpose of House to House Collections Act 1939, s 11(1).

Hans (William Francis) v R [1955] AC 378; [1955] Crim LR 373; (1955) 99 SJ 233; [1955] 2 WLR 700 PC Bermudan releasing sailor from custody of US naval patrol was guilty of releasing person from 'lawful custody'.

Hardie (Paul Deverall), R v (1985) 80 Cr App R 156; (1984) 128 SJ 851; [1984] TLR 511; [1985] 1 WLR 64 CA Self-induced drunkenness cannot be defence where recklessness alleged - taking of sedative drug need not raise same presumption.

Hardie and Lane, Ltd v Chilton and others [1928] All ER 36 CA No conspiracy unless agreement between two/more persons to do something unlawful/lawful in an unlawful way; trade association sending letter in which seeks to resolve dispute by recipient of letter paying money not uttering letter demanding money with menaces contrary to Larceny Act 1916, s 29 (1) (i).

Harding (Ethel), R v (1908-09) XXV TLR 139 CCA Jury verdict that accused guilty but had frenzied mind not insanity verdict; proper that opinion of coroner's jury after finding accused guilty of murder that accused was not responsible for actions properly excluded at trial.

Harding (William), R v; R v Turner (Harry Holt); R v King (Frank William) (1931-32) 23 Cr App R 143 CCA Bail granted pending appeal where Christmas Vacation came between bail application and appeal hearing.

Harding, R v [1929] All ER 186; (1928-29) 21 Cr App R 166; (1930) 94 JP 55; (1930) 142 LTR 583; (1929) 73 SJ 863; (1929-30) XLVI TLR 105; (1929) WN (I) 262 CCA Domestic servant left alone in house may be named as owner of chattels in prosecution for larceny.

Hardman and others v The Chief Constable of Avon and Somerset Constabulary [1986] Crim LR 330 CrCt Graffiti that would definitely be erased over time by rain and traffic was nonetheless criminal damage.

Hardy, Wells v [1964] 1 All ER 953; [1964] Crim LR 405t; (1964) 128 JP 328; (1964) 114 LJ 440; (1964) 108 SJ 238; [1964] 2 WLR 958 HC QBD Construction of Larceny Act 1861, s 24 (unlawful and wilful taking of fish).

Hare, R v [1933] All ER 550; (1934-39) XXX Cox CC 64; (1932-34) 24 Cr App R 108; (1934) 98 JP 49; [1934] 1 KB 354; (1933) 76 LJ 357; (1934) 103 LJCL 96; (1934) 150 LTR 279; (1933-34) L TLR 103 CCA Woman can be guilty of indecent assault on male under Offences Against the Person Act 1861, s 62.

Hargreaves v Bretherton and another [1958] 3 All ER 122 HC QBD Affected party cannot bring civil action against perjurer.

Hargreaves, R v [1985] Crim LR 243 CA On required intention before are guilty of going equipped for theft.

Hargreaves, WR Anderson (Motors), Ltd v [1962] 1 All ER 129; [1962] Crim LR 115t; (1962) 126 JP 100; (1962) 112 LJ 154; [1962] 1 QB 425; (1961) 105 SJ 1127 HC QBD Not guilty of obstruction where park vehicles in parking place during operative hours, whatever intent.

Haringey Magistrates' Court; ex parte Cragg, R v (1997) 161 JP 61; (1996) TLR 4/11/96 HC QBD Immediate re-seizure of dog and bringing of new dangerous dogs charge following acquittal of same owner on same charge was improper.

Harling, R v [1938] 1 All ER 307; (1936-38) 26 Cr App R 127 CCA Prosecution must demonstrate in any rape case that alleged victim did not consent.

Harlow and Winstanley, R v [1967] 1 All ER 683; (1967) 51 Cr App R 184; [1967] Crim LR 242; (1967) 131 JP 272; [1967] 2 QB 193; (1967) 111 SJ 93; [1967] 2 WLR 702 CA Not larceny to steal pipes from building under Larceny Act 1916, s 8(1).

Harmer, Burrell v [1967] Crim LR 169 CA Tattooist guilty, upon tattoos administered to two boys becoming inflamed, of causing actual bodily harm to the boys.

Harmer, Burrell v (1965-66) 116 NLJ 1658 HC QBD Tattooist not guilty, upon tattoos administered to two boys becoming inflamed, of causing actual bodily harm to the boys.

Harran, R v [1969] Crim LR 662 CA To prove possession of forged ten-dollar bills in bag had to prove possessed the bag in knowledge that were forged notes inside.

Harrigan, R v [1957] Crim LR 52t CCA Admission of further evidence before CA pertaining to alibi defence.

Harris (Davis), R v (1924-25) 18 Cr App R 157; (1925) 60 LJ 11; (1925) WN (I) 8 CCA Must be in possession of housebreaking implements after 9pm to be guilty of Larceny Act 1916, s 28(2) offence.

Harris (Kevin Arthur), R v (1979) 69 Cr App R 122 CA Was conspiracy to produce to controlled drug where sought to manufacture amphetamine and used correct ingredients but failed because of lack of chemical knowledge.

Harris (Kevin), R v; R v Joseph Cox [1996] 1 Cr App R 369; [1996] Crim LR 36; [1995] TLR 455 CA On what constitutes 'production' of 'cannabis' under Misuse of Drugs Act 1971.

Harris (Paul Andrew), R v (1976) 62 Cr App R 28; [1976] Crim LR 514 CA Giving fake identity and telling untrue story in bid to get hotel room was attempted obtaining of pecuniary advantage by deception not just preparatory steps.

Harris v Director of Public Prosecutions; Fehmi v Director of Public Prosecutions [1993] 1 All ER 562; (1993) 96 Cr App R 235; (1993) 157 JP 205; (1952) 102 LJ 246; (1992) 136 SJ LB 228; [1992] TLR 405; [1993] 1 WLR 82 HC QBD Lock-knife not a 'folding pocketknife' and hence an offence to carry in public place.

Harris v Harrison [1963] Crim LR 497g; (1963) 107 SJ 397 HC QBD On claim of right as defence to embezzlement.

Harris v Lucas (1919) 83 JP 208; [1919] 88 LJCL 1082; (1918-19) XXXV TLR 486; (1919) WN (I) 147 HC KBD On deciding whether birds 'recently taken' for purposes of Wild Birds Protection Act 1880, s 1.

Harris, Gibbons v (1956) 106 LJ CCR 828 CyCt Binding over of plaintiff under recognisance by magistrates' court following assault did not preclude later tortious action in respect of said assault.

Harris, R v [1950] 2 All ER 816; (1949-50) 34 Cr App R 184; (1950) 114 JP 535; [1951] 1 KB 107; (1950) 100 LJ 539; (1950) 94 SJ 689; [1950] 66 (2) TLR 739; (1950) WN (I) 453 CCA Evidence of earlier conditional discharge not by way of conviction certificate but by witness who heard confession/ordering of conditional discharge in earlier case.

Harris, R v [1972] Crim LR 531 CA Document that did not lie about itself was not a forgery.

Harris, R v [1968] 2 All ER 49; (1968) 52 Cr App R 277; [1968] Crim LR 267; (1968) 132 JP 322; (1968) 118 NLJ 421; (1968) 112 SJ 272; [1968] 1 WLR 769 CA On 'supply' of drugs to others.

Harris, R v [1961] Crim LR 256 CCA On burden of proof in context of prosecution for possession of housebreaking implements by night.

Harris, R v [1924] All ER 286; (1921-25) XXVII Cox CC 746; (1925) 89 JP 37; [1925] 94 LJCL 164; (1925) 132 LTR 672; (1924-25) XLI TLR 205 CCA Possessing housebreaking implements at night contrary to Larceny Act 1916, s 28 involves actual possession at night and upon arrest of implements.

Harris, R v [1965] 3 All ER 206; (1965) 49 Cr App R 330; [1965] Crim LR 550; (1965) 129 JP 542; (1965) 115 LJ 661; [1966] 1 QB 184; (1965) 109 SJ 572; [1965] 3 WLR 1040 CCA On uttering of forgeries.

Harrison (James), R v (1930-31) Cr App R 82 CCA Any violence sufficient to support conviction for robbery with violence.

Harrison and Crossfield (Limited) v London and North-Western Railway Company (1917-18) 117 LTR 570; (1916-17) 61 SJ 647; (1916-17) XXXIII TLR 517 HC KBD Common carriers not liable in negligence for theft by employee of goods to be carried (despite accepting property in goods when prosecuting employee).

Harrison v Thornton (1979) 68 Cr App R 28; [1966] Crim LR 388t; (1966) 110 SJ 444 HC QBD Stone picked up and thrown in course of fight was offensive weapon.

Harrison, Harris v [1963] Crim LR 497g; (1963) 107 SJ 397 HC QBD On claim of right as defence to embezzlement.

Harrison, R v [1996] 1 Cr App R 138; [1996] Crim LR 200 CA Need only prove that accused knowingly possessed firearm in public place for accused to be guilty of possessing same in public place.

Harrison, R v [1970] Crim LR 415 CA Misdirection on 'going equipped for stealing' charge did not justify quashing of conviction on said charge.

Harrison, R v; R v Ward; R v Wallis; R v Gooding [1938] 3 All ER 134; (1939-40) XXXI Cox CC 98; (1936-38) 26 Cr App R 166; (1938) 82 SJ 436 CCA Defence need to show accused believed and had reasonable cause to so believe that girl/s aged over sixteen.

Harrison, Syce v [1980] Crim LR 649 (amended at [1981] Crim LR 110) HC QBD Not obstruction of police to refuse entry on foot of defective search warrant.

Harrison-Owen, R v [1951] 2 All ER 726; (1951-52) 35 Cr App R 108 CCA No cross-examination upon previous convictions of party claiming automatism.

Harrod, Government of Australia v [1975] 2 All ER 1; [1976] Crim LR 57; (1975) 139 JP 389; (1975) 119 SJ 371; [1975] 1 WLR 745 HL Question is would evidence warrant trial for offence in England; failure to supply party with transcript not breach of natural justice.

Harron (Robert David George), R v [1996] 2 Cr App R 457 CA On adequacy of direction as to alibi defence where lies had been told.

Harrow Justices, ex parte Morris, R v [1972] 3 All ER 494; [1972] Crim LR 636t; (1972) 136 JP 868; (1972) 116 SJ 765; [1973] QB 672; [1972] 3 WLR 697 HC QBD Justices cannot require money/security be given by surety before bail granted.

Harry, R v [1974] Crim LR 32 CrCt On what is meant by demanding with 'menaces' in the Theft Act 1968, s 21(1).

Hart (Willie), R v (1914) 10 Cr App R 176 CCA Indecent assault conviction quashed where was some evidence of consent.

Hart v Chief Constable of Kent [1983] Crim LR 117; [1983] RTR 484; [1982] TLR 549 HC QBD Person whom police began but failed to physically restrain outside house was arrested outside house; police could without permission lawfully enter house in pursuit of escaped arrestee.

Hart, Secretary of State for Trade and Industry v [1982] 1 All ER 817; [1982] Crim LR 583; (1982) 132 NLJ 85; (1982) 126 SJ 172; [1982] 1 WLR 481 HC QBD Ignorance of law a defence to acting as auditor when disqualfied.

Hartley v Ellnor [1916-17] All ER 260; (1918-21) XXVI Cox CC 10; (1917) 81 JP 201; [1917] 86 LJCL 938; (1917-18) 117 LTR 304 HC KBD To be rogue and vagabond must have been convicted/suspected person/reputed thief on a day before occurrence leading to arrest.

Hartley, R v [1972] 1 All ER 599; (1972) 56 Cr App R 189; [1972] Crim LR 309; [1972] 2 QB 1; (1972) 116 SJ 56; [1972] 2 WLR 101 CA Successive obtainings of credit by bankrupt can be aggregated in deciding if committed offence under Bankruptcy Act 1914.

Harvard (Arthur James), R v (1914-15) 11 Cr App R 2 CCA Not sufficient to say that man reckless/careless as to origin of property has guilty knowledge.

Harvey and others, R v [1981] Crim LR 104 CA Threats to kill/injure/rape individual could not be used to buttress demand for debt to be paid.

Harvey, John Henshall (Quarries), Ltd v [1965] 1 All ER 725; [1965] Crim LR 235t; (1965) 129 JP 224; (1965) 115 LJ 230; [1965] 2 QB 233; [1965] 2 WLR 758 HC QBD Knowledge of responsible company officer of facts of offence necessary to prove company aided/abetted offence.

Harwood, Over v (1899-1900) XVI TLR 163; (1899-1900) 48 WR 608 HC QBD On burden of proof where person charged with disobedience of order to have child vaccinated.

Harwood, R v [1989] Crim LR 285 CA Continues to be substantive rule of law that entrapment is no defence.

Hassan, R v [1970] 1 All ER 745; (1970) 54 Cr App R 56; [1970] Crim LR 151; (1969) 113 SJ 996; (1970) 134 JP 266; [1970] 1 QB 423; [1970] 2 WLR 82 CA Where charge continuing in time evidence specific in time/place not alibi evidence.

Hassard, R v; R v Devereux [1970] 2 All ER 647; (1970) 54 Cr App R 295; [1970] Crim LR 226; (1970) 134 JP 510; (1970) 114 SJ 106; [1970] 1 WLR 1109 CA Cheque drawn on false account/signed with fake name a forgery.

Hassin, R v [1963] Crim LR 852t CCA On self-defence as defence to murder.

Hastings, R v [1958] Crim LR 128 CCA Successful appeal against conviction for larceny by bailee: on elements of offence of larceny by bailee.

Hastings, R v [1957] Crim LR 612 CrCt Was evidence to go to jury as to possible larceny by bailee.

Hatch (William Robert), R v (1932-34) 24 Cr App R 100 CCA Conviction quashed as evidence given that door marks made by implements at issue though accused told would not be charged with housebreaking.

Hatton (Francis), R v (1978) 67 Cr App R 216; [1978] Crim LR 95 CA Was valid arrest where arrest for second offence had taken place while already under arrest for intial offence.

Hatton, R v [1925] All ER 396; (1926-30) XXVIII Cox CC 43; (1925) 89 JP 164; [1925] 2 KB 322; (1925) 60 LJ 705; [1925] 94 LJCL 863; (1925) 133 LTR 735; (1924-25) XLI TLR 637; (1925) WN (I) 199 CCA Interpretation of phrase 'wilfully assaults' in Children Act 1908, s 12(1).

Hau (Va Kun), R v [1990] Crim LR 518 CA Cannot be guilty of using threatening words or behaviour in dwellinghouse.

Haughian (Anthony Edward), R v; R v Pearson (Arthur Reginald) (1985) 80 Cr App R 334 CA Defence of mistaken belief must fail where jury finds was no consent to rape; adequate direction on recklessness.

Haughton v Smith [1973] 3 All ER 1109; [1975] AC 476; (1974) 58 Cr App R 198; (1974) 138 JP 31; (1973) 123 NLJ 1112t; [1974] 2 WLR 1 HL Cannot be attempt to handle stolen goods unless goods handled are stolen goods.

Haughton, Holloran v [1976] Crim LR 270; (1976) 140 JP 352; (1976) 120 SJ 116 HC QBD Sorting room in post office not a 'warehouse' for purposes of Vagrancy Act 1824, s 4.

Haulage (Stanley), R v [1964] Crim LR 221; (1964) 114 LJ 25 CrCt On when company will be criminally liable for criminal acts of director.

Hawes v Edwards (1949) 113 JP 303; (1949) WN (I) 206 HC KBD Absent control did not have possession of goods so could not be convicted of receiving same.

Hawkesley, R v [1959] Crim LR 211 Sessions Taxi driver told by passengers that they wanted to be dropped off at certain place to commit offence there did not thereby become guilty of conspiracy to commit said offence.

Hawkey, R v [1964] Crim LR 465 CCA Ought not to have been convicted of attempted larceny where evidence pointed equally towards guilt of lesser offence of attempted taking/driving away.

Hawkins and others, R v [1959] Crim LR 729 Assizes Deposition of witness absent through pregnancy read but portions on which defence counsel would have challenged witness omitted; on larceny by trick.

Hawkins v Wilson [1957] Crim LR 320 Magistrates Caravan not a building for purposes of Malicious Damage Act 1861, s 6.

Hawkins, Director of Public Prosecutions v [1988] 3 All ER 673; (1989) 88 Cr App R 166; [1988] Crim LR 741; (1988) 152 JP 518; (1988) 132 SJ 1460; [1988] 1 WLR 1166 HC QBD Is assault on officer in course of duty where person attacks officer who fails to say why arresting either immediately or when reasonably practicable.

Hay, R v (1911-13) XXII Cox CC 268; (1911) 75 JP 480 CCC Accused who knew nature and quality of acts but because of sick mind could not resist murderous impulse was insane.

Hayat (Masood), R v (1976) 63 Cr App R 181; [1976] Crim LR 508t; (1976) 126 NLJ 568 CA On what constitutes 'obtaining credit' by bankrupt: must show 'obtaining' and 'credit'.

Hayden (Lily), R v (1910-11) 6 Cr App R 213 CCA That have been honestly employed since last conviction not per se a defence to habitual criminal charge.

Hayes (Timothy), R v (1925-26) 19 Cr App R 157; (1926) 90 JP 190 CCA Honest work during last period of release not defence to charge of being habitual criminal.

Hayes and King, R v [1964] Crim LR 542 CCA Where jury did not accept defence they could then infer that goods were stolen.

Hayes, Bunyard v [1985] RTR 348; [1984] TLR 603 HC QBD Issue of lawfulness of arrest did not not affect culpability for failure to provide breath specimen.

Hayes (John Allan), R v (1977) 64 Cr App R 82; [1977] Crim LR 691 CA Conviction of estate agent for theft following wrongful appropriation of deposit quashed in light of inadequate jury direction.

Haymarket Capitol, Ltd and others, Orpen v [1931] All ER 360; (1931) 95 JP 199; (1931) 145 LTR 614 HC KBD Limited company guilty of offence under Sunday Observance Act 1780; common informer could seek penalties from company per se, not directors.

Hayward, R v (1926-30) XXVIII Cox CC 342; (1927) 137 LTR 64; (1926-27) XLIII TLR 356 CCA Three convictions to sustain habitual criminal charge must be rigorously proved - other offences not so rigorously.

Hayward, R v (1907-09) XXI Cox CC 692 Assizes Absent proof of violence could convict accused where deceased died from fright resulting from accused's unlawful act.

Head and another, R v (1903) 67 JP 459 Sessions Evidence regarding stolen property taken after theft charged in indictment was inadmissible.

Head and Head, R v [1978] Crim LR 427 CA Was conspiracy to obstruct course of justice where agreed to act as surety in return for future indemnity even though did not possess sum for which stood surety.

Head, Director of Public Prosecutions v [1958] 1 All ER 679; (1958) 108 LJ 200 HL Cannot be committed of unlawful carnal knowledge of 'defective' unlawfully detained as deficient.

Head, R v [1957] 3 All ER 426; (1957) 41 Cr App R 249; [1958] Crim LR 52t; (1957) 107 LJ 777; [1958] 1 QB 132; (1957) 101 SJ 887 CCA Cannot be unlawful carnal knowledge of 'defective' unlawfully detained as 'deficient'.

Head, R v; R v Warrener (1961) 111 LJ 552 CCA On burden of proof in receiving case.

Headley, R v [1995] Crim LR 737; [1996] RTR 173; (1995) 139 SJ LB 67; [1995] TLR 78 CA Not perverting course of justice where passively allowed charges concerning brother but mistakenly naming defendant to be successfully prosecuted and sentence imposed.

Healey, R v; R v Comerford; R v Owens; R v Smith [1965] 1 All ER 365; (1965) 109 SJ 572; [1965] 1 WLR 1059 CCA Exceptionally can direct issue be decided adversely to accused: unusual in possession on receiving charge; preferable that guidance notes to jury be shown to counsel; need in possession cases to distinguish unlawful assistance/joint possession.

Heap v Motorists' Advisory Agency, Ltd [1922] All ER 251; [1923] 92 LJCL 553; (1923) 129 LTR 146; (1922-23) XXXIX TLR 150 HC KBD Must be animus furandi for there to be larceny by trick.

Heard, R v (1911-13) XXII Cox CC 725; (1911-12) 7 Cr App R 80; (1912) 76 JP 232; (1912) 106 LTR 304; (1911-12) XXVIII TLR 154 CCA That nine-month delay since last conviction/one of (over three) convictions mentioned was foreign did not preclude conviction as habitual criminal.

Heathcote, Gray v (1918) WN (I) 147 HC KBD Conviction for dumping of refuse (oil-water mixture) into dock.

Heaton v Costello [1984] Crim LR 485 CA On whether/when theft of several items a single course of action.

Heaven and another v Crutchley (1904) 68 JP 53 HC KBD Valid conviction for malicious damage with intent to destroy plants despite defence that had merely exercised right to roam over particular land to which claimed free access.

Hector (Joseph), R v (1978) 67 Cr App R 224; (1978) 128 NLJ 212t CA Not attempted theft to get into car with view to see if anything worth stealing therefrom.

Heelan and others, Digby v (1952) 102 LJ 287 HC QBD Failed larceny prosecution against bin-men who (contrary to council instructions) took scrap metal from third party's trash (no animus furandi).

Heffey, R v [1981] Crim LR 111 CrCt Landing on block of flats not a 'public place' for purposes of Prevention of Crime Act 1953.

Hemming (William), R v (1908) 1 Cr App R 34 CCA Refusal of handwriting evidence tending to show another forged letter at issue.

Hemmings, R v [1939] 1 All ER 417; (1939-40) XXXI Cox CC 240; (1938-40) 27 Cr App R 46; (1939) 87 LJ 122; (1939) 160 LTR 288; (1938-39) LV TLR 394; (1939) WN (I) 47 CCA Must be evidence of non-access by husband to prove stepfather was actual father of stepdaughter (and so capable of incest).

Henderson, Jobson v (1899-1901) XIX Cox CC 477; (1900) LXXXII LTR 260 HC QBD Police district superintendant could lay information for offence of throwing stones at police.

Hendrickson and Turner, R v [1977] Crim LR 356 CA Satisfactory evidence to justify conviction for incitement.

Henman, R v [1987] Crim LR 333 CA Was not defence to kidnapping that committed act to protect kidnapped person from malign influence of religious sect to which latter belonged.

Henn and Darby v Director of Public Prosecutions [1981] AC 850; (1980) 71 Cr App R 44; (1980) 130 NLJ 389; (1980) 124 SJ 290; [1980] 2 WLR 597 HL Permissible prohibition of obscene goods under Article 36/EEC.

Henn, R v; R v Derby [1978] 3 All ER 1190; (1979) 69 Cr App R 137; [1979] Crim LR 113; (1979) 143 JP 58; (1978) 128 NLJ 954t; (1978) 122 SJ 555; [1978] 1 WLR 1031 CA Total prohibition of certain type of goods permissible under Article 30/EEC; prohibition of obscene goods permissible under Article 36/EEC.

Hennessy, R v [1989] 2 All ER 9; (1989) 89 Cr App R 10; [1989] Crim LR 356; [1989] RTR 153; (1989) 133 SJ 263; [1989] 1 WLR 287 CA Mental state arising through hyperglycaemia falls within M'Naghten Rules/is not automatism.

Hepburn, R v [1961] Crim LR 621 CCA Test letter was a letter in the course of transmission by post for purposes of Post Office Act 1953, s 87(2)(b).

Hepworth, R v; R v Fearnley [1955] 2 All ER 918; (1955) 119 JP 516; (1955) 105 LJ 489; (1955) 99 SJ 544 CCA Summing-up to include warning on burden of proof in receiving case where party found in possession soon after theft.

Hereford and Worcester County Council v T and S Stores plc [1994] TLR 549 HC QBD Valid acquittal of offence of selling cigarettes to under-age purchaser.

Herion (Albert), R v; R v Jackson (John); R v Wilkin (Lewis) (1912-13) 8 Cr App R 99 [1913] 82 LJKB 82; (1912-13) 57 SJ 130; (1912-13) XXIX TLR 93; (1912) WN (I) 276 CCA Second offence under Vagrancy Act 1898 makes one incorrigible rogue under Vagrancy Act 1824, s 5 and so liable to flogging.

Heritage v Claxon (1941) 85 SJ 323 HC KBD Home Guard member in possession of uncertificated firearm/ammunition who was not acting in capacity as Home Guard member in possession of same was guilty of offence.

Heritage, Rhodes v (1951) 115 JP 303; (1951) 101 LJ 219; (1951) 95 SJ 255; [1951] 1 TLR 802; (1951) WN (I) 221 HC KBD Court of summary jurisdiction could not, pursuant to Dogs Act 1871, s 2, order dog to be destroyed.

Herman, Watson v [1952] 2 All ER 70; (1952) 116 JP 395; (1952) 102 LJ 329; (1952) 96 SJ 413; (1952) WN (I) 308 HC QBD Telescopic sight not a firearm.

Heron (David), R v; R v Storey (Peter Edwin); R v Thomas (Christopher Robin); R v Santi (George Henry) [1981] 3 All ER 641; (1981) 73 Cr App R 327; [1981] Crim LR 698; (1981) 131 NLJ 1008; (1981) 125 SJ 638; [1981] 1 WLR 1480 CA Mere intent to make coins sufficient intent for falsely making/counterfeiting money.

Heron and others, R v [1982] 1 All ER 993; (1982) 75 Cr App R 7; [1982] Crim LR 430; (1982) 132 NLJ 437; (1982) 126 SJ 242; [1982] TLR 174; [1982] 1 WLR 451 HL No specific intent required to be guilty of counterfeiting: counterfeiting per se an offence.

Herron, R v [1963] Crim LR 575t CCA Untruths as regards one's possesssion of property could be evidence that property was stolen and one knew it.

Hertfordshire Constabulary, Joyce v (1985) 80 Cr App R 298 HC QBD If breach of peace occurring police officer may use reasonable force to stop it.

Heuser (Henry), R v (1910-11) 6 Cr App R 76 CCA Police officers party to entrapment are not accomplices.

Hewitt (Mary), R v (1911-12) 7 Cr App R 219; (1912) 76 JP 360; (1911-12) XXVIII TLR 378 CCA Sum obtainable through sale of damaged remains non-deductible from value of property damaged maliciously.

Hewitt, R v (1926-30) XXVIII Cox CC 101; (1926) 90 JP 68; (1926) 134 LTR 157; (1925-26) XLII TLR 216 CCA Previous assault on same girl admissible in unlawful carnal knowledge of under sixteen/over fourteen year old girl - time lapse since earlier assault reduces weight of evidence.

Hibbert (John William), R v (1924-25) 18 Cr App R 36 CCA On breach of recognisance entered into before CCA.

Hibbert v McKiernan [1948] 1 All ER 860; (1948) 112 JP 287; [1948] 2 KB 142; (1948) 98 LJ 245; [1948] 117 LJR 1521; (1948) LXIV TLR 256; (1948) WN (I) 169 HC KBD Larceny for trespasser to steal goods lost by another and found by trespasser on private land.

Hibbert, Kay v [1977] Crim LR 226 HC QBD Was assault on constable in the exercise of his duty to strike constable after had told him to leave premises but within reasonable time it took him to do so.

Hickman v O'Dwyer [1979] Crim LR 309 HC QBD Not assault on constable in course of his duty where constable assaulted while arresting noisy youth whose behaviour officer had no cause to believe would result in breach of the peace.

Hickmott v Curd [1971] 2 All ER 1399; (1971) 55 Cr App R 461; (1971) 135 JP 519; [1972] Crim LR 484t; (1971) 115 SJ 526; [1971] 1 WLR 1221 HC QBD Charge containing errors but true as to substance of offence and means whereby effected and not embarrassing to accused was valid.

Hickson (Isaac), R v (1921-22) 16 Cr App R 47 CCA Twelve months' hard labour for false pretences/conspiracy offences (reduced from three years' penal servitude as co-prisoners' sentences reduced).

Hierowski, R v [1978] Crim LR 563 CrCt Could not be convicted of possession of indivisible amounts of cannabis.

Hiesler, Dean v [1942] 2 All ER 340 HC KBD Defence (General) Regulations 1939 penal so interpreted strictly: person not appointed company director could not be convicted as such thereunder.

Higgins (Frederick), R v (1919-20) 14 Cr App R 28 CCA Alleged conspirator can be convicted as conspirator with person/s unknown where alleged co-conspirator acquitted of charge.

Hignett, R v (1950) 94 SJ 149 CCA On ingredients of fraudulent conversion.

Hill (Frederick Philip), R v (1985) 81 Cr App R 206; [1985] Crim LR 384 CA Must look to overall intent of accused in deciding if accused acted with intent to injure - keeping person awake need not mean intent to injure.

Hill (James), R v (1909) 2 Cr App R 144 CCA Proper conviction for destroying/concealing trade books/papers contrary to Debtors Act 1869, s 11(9).

Hill (Valerie Mary), R v; R v Hill (Jennifer) (1989) 89 Cr App R 74; [1989] Crim LR 136 CA Possession of article with intent to damage property: subjective test what was in accused's mind/objective test whether lawful excuse sustainable.

Hill and another, Bayliss v [1984] TLR 254 HC QBD On use of search warrants.

Hill, R v (1986) 83 Cr App R 386; [1986] Crim LR 815 HL Test of criminality where charged with administering noxious thing is whether intended to harm victim's health.

Hill, R v (1942) 86 SJ 134 CCA Sadism does not constitute insanity.

Hilliard, R v (1913-14) XXIII Cox CC 617; (1913) 48 LJ 659; [1914] 83 LJKB 439; (1913-14) 109 LTR 750 CCA On larceny by trick.

Hillman (Israel), R v (1931-32) 23 Cr App R 53 CCA Generally where one of two defendants acquitted of conspiracy other will also be acquitted.

Hills v Davies (1901-07) XX Cox CC 398 HC KBD Paper advertisement bills could be litter under Metropolitan Police Act 1839, s 60(3).

Hills v Ellis [1983] 1 All ER 667; (1983) 76 Cr App R 217; [1983] Crim LR 182; (1984) 148 JP 379; (1983) 133 NLJ 280; [1983] QB 680; (1982) 126 SJ 769; [1982] TLR 515; [1983] 2 WLR 234 HC QBD No lawful excuse for interfering with lawful arrest by police officer.

Hilton (John James), R v (1925-26) 19 Cr App R 29 CCA Interpretation of Children Act 1908, s 12(1).

Hilton, Critchley, Lythe and Greatrex, R v [1956] Crim LR 122 Assizes On distinction between wounding with intent to cause grievous bodily harm and unlawful wounding.

Hilton, R v (1997) 161 JP 459; [1997] TLR 201 CA On elements of theft of property (where said property is a credit balance).

Hinchcliffe v Sheldon [1955] 3 All ER 406; [1955] Crim LR 189; (1956) 120 JP 13; (1955) 99 SJ 797; [1955] 1 WLR 1207 HC QBD Can be guilty of obstruction though not otherwise guilty of offence.

Hind (Horace Percival), Hollyhomes (James) v [1944] 2 All ER 8; (1944) 108 JP 190; [1944] KB 571; [1944] 113 LJ 285; (1944) 171 LTR 175; (1943-44) LX TLR 376; (1944) WN (I) 137 HC KBD Where house inside house loitering charge did not have to include phrase 'then in the occupation of...'.

Hinde v Evans (1907-09) XXI Cox CC 331; (1906) 70 JP 548 HC KBD Cart was obstructing highway (even though person left in charge thereof).

Hinds (Alfred George), R v (1957) 41 Cr App R 143; [1957] Crim LR 465t CCA Is common law escape to leave prison in which held by walking out (as opposed to breaking out).

Hircock (William Roy), R v (1978) 67 Cr App R 278; [1979] Crim LR 184 CA Could be guilty of theft and obtaining property by deception in respect of same property.

Holden, R v (1911-13) XXII Cox CC 727; (1912) 76 JP 143; [1912] 1 KB 483; (1912) 81 LJKB 327; (1912) 106 LTR 305 CCA Party accepting bill of exchange in name of his firm accepted in name of another for purposes of Forgery Act 1861, s 24.

Holden, R v [1965] Crim LR 556; (1965) 115 LJ 450 CrCt Person who helped hospitalised prisoner escape not guilty of aiding a prisoner to escape from prison (contrary to Prison Act 1952, s 13 (as amended)).

Holder v McCarthy (1918-21) XXVI Cox CC 314; [1918] 2 KB 309; (1918) WN (I) 149 HC KBD Receipt of old age pension by means of false representation.

Holgate-Mohammed v Duke [1984] 1 All ER 1054; [1984] AC 437; (1984) 79 Cr App R 120; [1984] Crim LR 418; (1984) 134 NLJ 523; (1984) 128 SJ 244; [1984] TLR 196; [1984] 2 WLR 660 HL Valid arrest by police officer where effected in honest belief that arrestee more likely to answer questions truthfully at police station.

Hollands v Abel [1956] Crim LR 336 HC QBD Police entering onto property to request that noise level be kept down were acting in the course of their duty.

Holley, R v [1963] 1 All ER 106; (1963) 47 Cr App R 13; [1962] Crim LR 829g; (1963) 127 JP 71; (1963) 113 LJ 57/139; (1963) 107 SJ 116; [1963] 1 WLR 199 CCA Absent coercion by husband wife helping him in felony guilty as accessory after the fact.

Hollin, Erskine v [1971] Crim LR 243t; (1971) 121 NLJ 154t; [1971] RTR 199; (1971) 115 SJ 207 HC QBD Improper to arrest person and then wait for breathalyser to be brought to scene.

Hollinshead (Peter Gordon), R v; R v Dettlaff (Stefen); R v Griffiths (Kenneth David) [1985] 1 All ER 850; [1985] AC 975 (also HL); (1985) 80 Cr App R 285; [1985] Crim LR 301; (1985) 129 SJ 219; [1985] 2 WLR 761 CA Cannot be guilty of conspiracy to aid and abet offences so providing devices for another to deal in not criminal act.

Hollinshead and others, R v [1985] 2 All ER 769; [1985] AC 975 (also CA); (1985) 81 Cr App R 365; [1985] Crim LR 653; (1985) 135 NLJ 631; (1985) 129 SJ 447; [1985] 3 WLR 159 HL Manufacturing/selling devices intended to cause loss to another is conspiracy to defraud.

Hollis and another, Olympia Press Ltd v [1974] 1 All ER 108; (1974) 59 Cr App R 28; [1973] Crim LR 757; (1974) 138 JP 100; (1973) 117 SJ 813; [1973] 1 WLR 1520 HC QBD Judges need not read entire publication to make decision; decide if obscene then if contrary to public good.

Hollis v Young (1908) 72 JP 199; (1908) XCVIII LTR 751; (1907-08) XXIV TLR 500 HC KBD State and colour of birds plus supporting evidence of witness could have grounded conviction for possession of recently taken wild birds contrary to Wild Birds Protection Act 1880, s 3.

Hollis, R v [1972] Crim LR 525 CA Person charged with offence under Theft Act 1968, s 9(1)(b) could not be convicted of offence under Theft Act 1968, s 9(1)(a).

Holloran v Haughton [1976] Crim LR 270; (1976) 140 JP 352; (1976) 120 SJ 116 HC QBD Sorting room in post office not a 'warehouse' for purposes of Vagrancy Act 1824, s 4.

Holloway v Brown [1979] Crim LR 58; [1978] RTR 537 HC QBD Successful appeal against conviction for use of forged international road haulage permit.

Holly, Director of Public Prosecutions v; Director of Public Prosecutions v Manners [1977] 1 All ER 316; [1978] AC 43 (also CA); (1977) 64 Cr App R 143; [1977] Crim LR 289; (1977) 141 JP 143; (1977) 127 NLJ 190t; (1977) 121 SJ 103; [1977] 2 WLR 178 HL Officers of any body with public/statutory duties may be guilty of corruption.

Hollyhomes (James) v Hind (Horace Percival) [1944] 2 All ER 8; (1944) 108 JP 190; [1944] KB 571; [1944] 113 LJ 285; (1944) 171 LTR 175; (1943-44) LX TLR 376; (1944) WN (I) 137 HC KBD Where house inside house loitering charge did not have to include phrase 'then in the occupation of...'.

Holman, Ward v [1964] Crim LR 541g; (1964) 128 JP 397; (1964) 114 LJ 506; [1964] 2 QB 580; (1964) 108 SJ 380; [1964] 2 WLR 1313 HC QBD Interpretation of Public Order Act 1936, s 5.

Holmes (Leonard), R v [1946] 1 All ER 524; (1946) 96 LJ 218; (1946) 90 SJ 371; (1945-46) LXII TLR 342 CCA Confession of adultery held not to be provocation reducing murder to manslaughter as husband suspected same for some time/murder was protracted.

Holmes (Percy), R v (1931-32) 23 Cr App R 46 CCA Twelve months in second division for fraudulent conversion by first time offender.

Holmes (Thomas Charles) and Gregory (George), R v (1914-15) 11 Cr App R 130 CCA That bought goods cheaply need not mean had guilty knowledge; on possession by occupier of premises.

Holmes and others, R v [1980] 2 All ER 458; (1980) 144 JP 378; (1980) 130 NLJ 808; (1980) 124 SJ 575; [1980] 1 WLR 1055 CA If possibility of disparate verdicts for alleged conspirators trial judge can ask for dual conviction/acquittal.

Holmes v Chief Constable, Merseyside Police [1976] Crim LR 125; (1976) 126 NLJ 113t HC QBD On what constitutes 'supplying' controlled drug.

Holmes v Director of Public Prosecutions [1946] 2 All ER 124; [1946] AC 588; (1945-46) 31 Cr App R 123; [1946] 115 LJ 417; (1946) 175 LTR 327; (1946) 90 SJ 441; (1945-46) LXII TLR 466; (1946) WN (I) 146 HL On provocation reducing murder to manslaughter.

Holmes, ex parte Sherman and another, R v [1981] 2 All ER 612; (1981) 145 JP 337 HC QBD Requirement of charge as soon as possible after arrest is mandatory and cannot be qualified; 48 hours normal time for bringing before magistrate.

Holmes, R v [1953] 2 All ER 324; (1953) 37 Cr App R 61; (1953) 117 JP 346; (1953) 97 SJ 355; [1953] 1 WLR 686 CCA Medical evidence on insanity admissible.

Holmes, R v [1979] Crim LR 52 CrCt One-off assault of mental patient could be ill-treatment of same.

Holt (Frederick Rothwell), R v (1920-21) 15 Cr App R 10 CCA Uncontrollable impulse as basis for insanity defence.

Holt and another, R v [1981] 2 All ER 854; (1981) 73 Cr App R 96; [1981] Crim LR 499; (1981) 145 JP 377; (1981) 125 SJ 373; [1981] 1 WLR 1000 CA Plan not to pay for restaurant meal involves intent to make permanent default on whole/part of existing liability.

Home Secretary and others, De Demko v [1959] 1 All ER 341; [1959] AC 654; [1959] Crim LR 212t; (1959) 123 JP 156; (1959) 109 LJ 120; (1959) 103 SJ 130 HL CA has original/not appellate jurisdiction under Fugitive Offenders Act 1881, s 10.

Home Secretary, ex parte Budd, R v [1942] 1 All ER 373; [1942] 111 LJ 475; (1942) 166 LTR 293; (1941-42) LVIII TLR 212 CA Legality of detention at issue - good faith behaviour of Home Secretary precluded inquiry into facts of detention; writ of habeas corpus did not preclude future detention.

Home Secretary, ex parte Eva Bressler, R v (1924) 131 LTR 36 CA Refusal of habeas corpus application made by alien facing deportation pursuant to Aliens' Order 1920.

Home Secretary, ex parte O'Brien, R v (1921-25) XXVII Cox CC 433; (1923) 87 JP 166; [1923] 2 KB 361; (1923) 58 LJ 223; [1923] 92 LJCL 797; (1923) 129 LTR 419; (1922-23) XXXIX TLR 487 CA Home Secretary could not order internment of person in Irish Free State; writ of habeas corpus against Home Secretary proper though person interned in Irish Free State.

Homolka v Osmond [1939] 1 All ER 154 HC KBD Accessory before the fact to misdemeanour is considered akin to principal offender.

Hood v Smith [1933] All ER 706; (1934-39) XXX Cox CC 82; (1934) 98 JP 73; (1934) 150 LTR 477 HC KBD Entrapment of person charged with stealing postal packet in course of transmission by post.

Hood-Barrs, R v [1943] 1 All ER 665; (1942-44) 29 Cr App R 55; [1943] KB 455; (1944) 94 LJ 100; [1943] 112 LJ 420; (1943) 168 LTR 408; (1943) 87 SJ 220; (1942-43) LIX TLR 246; (1943) WN (I) 97 CCA Lie in income tax appeal heard by two Special Commissioners was perjury.

Hoogstraten v Goward [1967] Crim LR 590; (1967) 111 SJ 581 HC QBD Police officer could be passenger for purposes of prosecution under the Town Police Clauses Act 1847, s 28.

Hooker v Gray (1907-09) XXI Cox CC 437; (1907) 71 JP 337; (1907) XCVI LTR 706; (1906-07) XXIII TLR 472 HC KBD Party severely wounding cat, allowing to crawl away, then later killing it not guilty of cruelty.

Hooley (Ernest Terah), R v; R v Macdonald (John Angus); R v Wallis (William Alfred) (1921-22) 16 Cr App R 171; [1923] 92 LJCL 78; (1922) 127 LTR 228; (1921-22) XXXVIII TLR 724 CCA Jurisdiction for trying crime under Larceny Act 1916, s 84.

Hooper v Eaglestone [1978] Crim LR 161 CA Was offence for person without site licence who nonetheless operated a caravan site on his land to seek to harass/evict caravan occupant from site by cutting off electricity (Caravan Sites Act 1968, s 3 applied).

Hopkins (William Edgar), R v; R v Collins (Herbert James) (1957) 41 Cr App R 231; [1957] Crim LR 808t CCA Putting in/leaving out false/possible entry in cash book is/may not be forgery.

Hopkins and another; ex parte Lovejoy, R v (1911) 75 JP 341 HC KBD Issue of fact for magistrate whether bird recently taken.

Hopkins, R v; R v Kendrick [1997] Crim LR 359 CA On appropriation necessary to be guilty of conspiracy to steal.

Hopley (Samuel), R v (1914-15) 11 Cr App R 248 CCA Inferring of intent to defraud from knowing use of forged instrument in course of bona fide claim.

Hopwood (Edward), R v (1912-13) 8 Cr App R 143 CCA Killing of another in course of apparent suicide attempt was murder.

Hornby and Peaple, R v [1946] 2 All ER 487; (1946-48) 32 Cr App R 1; (1946) 110 JP 391; (1946) 175 LTR 518; (1945-46) LXII TLR 629 CCA Gross indecency possible though no physical touching.

Horne, R v [1994] Crim LR 584 CA On test as to whether duress present; psychiatric evidence deemed inadmissible in determining whether appellant in instant case acted under duress.

Horner (Frederick William), R v (1910) 4 Cr App R 189 CCA No bail where merely device to postpone appeal.

Horner, R v (1911-13) XXII Cox CC 13; (1910) 74 JP 216 CCC Must intend to deceive another to be convicted of uttering telegram knowing to be false (whether contents of telegram true or not does not matter).

Hornett, R v [1975] RTR 256 CA Were guilty of uttering forged documents (forged international haulage permits) though those sought to defraud were in foreign jurisdiction.

Horseferry Road Magistrates' Court and another, Bennett v [1993] 3 All ER 138; (1993) 143 NLJ 955; (1993) 137 SJ LB 159/172 HL Rule of law more important than public interest in punishment of crime; tacit extradition via deportation an abuse of process.

Horseferry Road Magistrates' Court and another, ex parte Bennett, R v [1993] 2 All ER 474; [1993] Crim LR 200 HC QBD Circumstances by which defendant comes to be in jurisdiction cannot be abuse of process.

Horseferry Road Magistrates' Court, ex parte Bennett (No 2), R v [1995] 1 Cr App R 147 HC QBD Arrests to be effected in strict accordance with procedure.

Horseferry Road Magistrates' Court; ex parte K, R v [1996] 3 All ER 719; [1996] 2 Cr App R 574; [1997] Crim LR 129; [1997] QB 23; [1996] 3 WLR 68 HC QBD Insanity available as defence in summary trial.

Horseferry Road Metropolitan Stipendiary Magistrate, ex parte Siadatan, R v [1991] 1 All ER 324; (1991) 92 Cr App R 257; [1990] Crim LR 598; (1990) 140 NLJ 704; [1991] 1 QB 260; [1990] TLR 298; [1990] 3 WLR 1006 HC QBD Offence only arises where writing would prompt immediate unlawful violence.

Horseferry Road Stipendiary Magistrate; ex parte Pearson, R v [1976] Crim LR 304t; (1976) 140 JP 382; (1976) 126 NLJ 522t; (1976) 120 SJ 352; [1976] 1 WLR 511 HC QBD On forfeiture of surety's recognisance.

Horsey v Hutchings [1984] TLR 618 HC QBD On ingredients of offences under the Forgery and Counterfeiting Act 1981, ss 1 and 3.

Horton v Gwynne [1921] All ER 497; (1918-21) XXVI Cox CC 744; (1921) 85 JP 210; [1921] 2 KB 661; [1921] LJCL 1151; (1921) 125 LTR 309; (1921) WN (I) 144 HC KBD No defence to killing house pigeon that thought it was wild pigeon.

Horton v Mead [1911-13] All ER 954; (1913-14) XXIII Cox CC 279; (1913) 77 JP 129; [1913] 1 KB 154; (1912) 47 LJ 767; [1913] 82 LJKB 200; (1913) 108 LTR 156; (1912) WN (I) 304 HC KBD Man can be guilty of soliciting though no evidence that anyone conscious of/noticed acts of solicitation.

Horwood, R v [1969] 3 All ER 1156; (1969) 53 Cr App R 619; [1969] Crim LR 598; (1969) 113 SJ 895; (1970) 134 JP 23; [1970] 1 QB 133; [1969] 3 WLR 964 CA Evidence to be probative of offence - admission that homosexual not per se probative of gross indecency.

Hosken, R v [1974] Crim LR 48 CrCt Whether possess requisite mens rea for constructive manslaughter a subjective matter.

Hotine, R v (1904) 68 JP 143 CCC Not offence under Larceny Act 1901 for employer to use money deposited with him by employees as security for their honesty to use such money so that it was unavailable to the employees when they quit their employment.

Houghton v Chief Constable of Greater Manchester (1987) 84 Cr App R 319 CA Person wearing police truncheon as part of fancy dress had reasonable excuse for possessing what was an offensive weapon per se.

Houghton, R v [1982] Crim LR 112 CA On elements of offence of having firearm with intent to commit indictable offence.

Houghton-Le Touzel v Mecca, Ld [1950] 2 KB 612 HC KBD Liability of limited company under Sunday Observance Act 1781, s 1.

Howard, R v [1965] 3 All ER 684; (1966) 50 Cr App R 56; [1966] Crim LR 54; (1966) 130 JP 61; (1965-66) 116 NLJ 159; (1965) 109 SJ 920; [1966] 1 WLR 13 CA Rape of under-16 year old only if she physically resists or is incapable of deciding whether to consent/resist.

Howard, R v [1993] Crim LR 213 CA On what constitutes an 'explosive substance' (petrol bomb is an explosive substance).

Howe and another appeal, R v [1987] 1 All ER 771; [1987] AC 417; (1987) 85 Cr App R 32; (1987) 151 JP 265; (1987) 137 NLJ 197; [1987] 2 WLR 568 HL Duress an objective defence not open to those charged with murder in first/second degree; accessory before fact using duress to get another to commit offence can be guilty of greater offence than other.

Howe and other appeals, R v [1986] 1 All ER 833; (1986) 83 Cr App R 28; (1986) 150 JP 161; [1986] QB 626; [1986] 2 WLR 294 CA Duress open as defence to alleged aider and abettor not alleged principal; accessory before fact cannot be convicted of more serious crime than principal.

Howell (Errol), R v (1981) 73 Cr App R 31; [1981] Crim LR 697; (1982) 146 JP 13; (1981) 131 NLJ 605; [1982] QB 416; (1981) 125 SJ 462; [1981] 3 WLR 501 CA On what constitutes a breach of the peace; on when can arrest for breach of the peace.

Howell, R v [1974] 2 All ER 806; (1974) 138 JP 483 CrCt Self-induced intoxication not a defence to manslaughter.

Howells, R v [1977] 3 All ER 417; (1977) 65 Cr App R 86; [1977] Crim LR 354t; (1977) 141 JP 641; (1977) 127 NLJ 370t; [1977] QB 614; (1977) 121 SJ 154; [1977] 2 WLR 716 CA Absolute liability if no certificate yet possess firearm; mistaken belief an antique no defence.

Howes, R v (1996) TLR 15/4/96 CA On when cross-examination of rape complainant may be allowed.

Howeson (John Henry Charles Ernest), R v; R v Hardy (Louis) (1934-36) 25 Cr App R 167 CCA Pre-appeal bail refused absent special circumstances.

Howlett and Howlett, R v [1968] Crim LR 222t; (1968) 118 NLJ 157t; (1968) 112 SJ 150 CA Convitions for larceny of mussels quashed where not proved that mussels were actally in another's 'possession' before were 'stolen'.

Hoyle, Reynolds v [1975] Crim LR 527; (1975) 125 NLJ 800t HC QBD Successful prosecution for unlawful conveyancing by unqualified person.

Hubbard and others v Pitt and others [1975] 3 All ER 1 CA Watching and besetting with view to securing certain behaviour might be nuisance.

Hughes, Robinson v [1987] Crim LR 644 HC QBD On elements of offence of laying poison for wild birds in breach of Wildlife and Countryside Act 1981, s 5(1)(a).

Hume, C (A) v [1979] Crim LR 328; [1979] RTR 424 HC QBD Ingredients of taking vehicle without authority (mens rea particularly important as accused had just reached age of doli capax).

Humphreys and Turner, R v [1965] 3 All ER 689; [1966] Crim LR 98; (1966) 130 JP 45; (1965-66) 116 NLJ 159 CrCt Person can be convicted of aiding and abetting in crime of which principal offender acquitted.

Humphreys, R v [1977] Crim LR 225 CA Was not possession of offensive weapon to possess penknife for normal use (though end up using it to stab another in fight).

Humphreys, R v [1995] 4 All ER 1008; [1996] Crim LR 431; (1995) 145 NLJ 1032 CA Abnormal immaturity or history of attention seeking relevant to issue of provocation; complex history of provocation requires careful explanation to jury by judge.

Humphries, R v (1903-04) 48 SJ 509 CCR Valid conviction of bankrupt under Debtors Act 1869, s 12, for unlawful removal of 'his' property.

Humphris, R v (1901-07) XX Cox CC 620; (1904) 68 JP 325; [1904] 2 KB 89; [1904] 73 LJCL 464; (1904) XC LTR 555; (1903-04) XX TLR 425; (1903-04) 52 WR 591 CCR Property of assignor passes to trusee when in possession of latter: properly convicted for absconding with assignor's property.

Hunt (Anthony Gerald), R v (1978) 66 Cr App R 105; [1977] Crim LR 740 CA Using objective test could not defend arson with plea of lawful excuse (that set fire to premises to highlight that fire alarm system defective).

Hunt and another, R v [1950] 2 All ER 291; (1949-50) 34 Cr App R 135; (1950) 114 JP 382 CCA Need not be physical touching for there to be gross indecency.

Hunt and others, Chief Constable of Cheshire Constabulary v (1983) 147 JP 567 HC QBD Person who admits smoking cannabis must be in possession of same.

Hunt v Director of Public Prosecutions [1990] Crim LR 812; (1990) 154 JP 762; [1990] TLR 402 HC QBD Witness need not have seen penis for justices to convict person of wilful/indecent exposure.

Hunt v Green (1907-09) XXI Cox CC 333; (1907) 71 JP 18; (1907) XCVI LTR 23 HC KBD Passenger need not be asked to deliver up ticket to contravene by-law concerning payment of fares.

Hunt, Flack v (1980) 70 Cr App R 51; [1980] Crim LR 44; (1979) 123 SJ 751 HC QBD Recklessness a subjective test: here unlawful wounding charge failed where no recklessness established.

Hunt, R v [1987] 1 All ER 1; [1987] AC 352; (1987) 84 Cr App R 163; [1987] Crim LR 263; (1986) 136 NLJ 1183; (1970) 130 SJ 984; [1986] 3 WLR 1115 HL Statute may place task of proving statutory defence on accused expressly/impliedly but court slow to find such an obligation.

Hunt, R v [1986] 1 All ER 184; (1986) 82 Cr App R 244; [1986] Crim LR 172; (1986) 150 JP 83; [1986] QB 125; (1985) 129 SJ 889; [1986] 2 WLR 225 CA Burden of proof on defendant to show drugs fall within exception to prohibition.

Hunter and others, R v [1973] 3 All ER 286; (1973) 57 Cr App R 772; [1973] Crim LR 514t; (1973) 137 JP 774; (1973) 123 NLJ 544t; [1974] QB 95; (1973) 117 SJ 430; [1973] 3 WLR 374 CA Conspiracy to prevent burial if agree to conceal body and this prevents burial.

Hunton v Last [1965] Crim LR 433; (1965) 109 SJ 391 HC QBD Admission by defendant that were guilty of lighting fire within 50m of highway if lit further away with intention that should enter 50m perimeter.

Hurford, R v; R v Williams [1963] 2 All ER 254; (1963) 47 Cr App R 141; [1963] Crim LR 432; (1963) 127 JP 374; (1963) 113 LJ 382; [1963] 2 QB 398; (1963) 107 SJ 275; [1963] 2 WLR 1038 CCA Forging signature on document that instigates eventual obtaining of property is obtaining property with forged instrument.

Huskinson, Director of Public Prosecutions v (1988) 152 JP 582; [1988] Crim LR 620 HC QBD Person using partly for self, partly for landlord benefit cheque paid to him and intended for rent/rent arrears not guilty of theft.

Hussain, R v [1981] 2 All ER 287; (1981) 72 Cr App R 143; [1981] Crim LR 251; (1981) 131 NLJ 70; (1981) 125 SJ 166; [1981] 1 WLR 416 CA Possession of firearm without certificate an absolute offence - no mens rea needed.

Hussein, R v [1978] Crim LR 219 CA Not attempted theft to open van door so as to look inside holdall and take anything of value that might be contained therein.

Husseyn (otherwise Hussein) (Ulus), R v (1978) 67 Cr App R 131 HL Given presence of intent to steal was attempted theft to open van door as prelude to taking holdall.

Hutchings, Horsey v [1984] TLR 618 HC QBD On ingredients of offences under the Forgery and Counterfeiting Act 1981, ss 1 and 3.

Hutchings, Miles v (1901-07) XX Cox CC 555; [1903] 2 KB 714; [1903] 72 LJKB 775; (1903-04) LXXXIX LTR 420; (1903-04) 52 WR 284 HC KBD Not malicious injury to dog where injure in belief that must do so to protect own/master's property.

Hutchins, R v [1988] Crim LR 379 CA On ingredients of false imprisonment/kidnapping: both may be committed through recklessness.

Hutchinson (Robert Hopwood Percy), R v (1911-12) 7 Cr App R 19 CCA Forgery Act 1861, s 38 considered.

Hyam v Director of Public Prosecutions [1974] 2 All ER 41; [1975] AC 55; (1974) 59 Cr App R 91; [1974] Crim LR 365; (1974) 138 JP 374; (1974) 124 NLJ 320t; (1974) 118 SJ 311; [1974] 2 WLR 607 HL Intent for murder is intend to do acts which could (but need not be intended to) cause really serious bodily harm.

Hyam, R v [1973] 3 All ER 842; (1973) 57 Cr App R 824; [1973] Crim LR 633t; (1973) 123 NLJ 631t; [1974] QB 99; (1973) 117 SJ 543; [1973] 3 WLR 475 CA That death/grievous bodily harm foreseeable but unintended justified murder conviction.

Hyde and others, R v [1990] 3 All ER 892; (1991) 92 Cr App R 131; [1991] Crim LR 133; (1991) 155 JP 430; [1991] 1 QB 134; (1990) 134 SJ 1190; [1990] 3 WLR 1115 CA Secondary party continuing in fight after realising principal may kill/seriously injure other is jointly guilty of murder if principal murders other.

Hyde, R v [1954] Crim LR 540 CMAC Conviction affirmed though related conviction of another not confirmed.

Hylton, Ohlson v [1975] 2 All ER 490; [1975] Crim LR 292; (1975) 139 JP 531; (1975) 125 NLJ 261t; (1975) 119 SJ 255; [1975] 1 WLR 724 HC QBD Sudden use of non-offensive article as weapon not possession of offensive weapon.

Hynde, Director of Public Prosecutions v [1997] TLR 398 HC QBD Court can take judicial notice of fact that butterfly knife an injurious weapon.

I Bresler, Ltd, Moore v [1944] 2 All ER 515 HC KBD Company officers acting to defraud company are still its agents.

Ibrams (James David), R v; R v Gregory (Ian David) (1982) 74 Cr App R 154 CA No provocation where planned to and did kill persistent tormentor as was no sudden, temporary loss of self-control.

ICR Haulage, Ltd, R v [1944] 1 All ER 691; (1943-45) 30 Cr App R 31; (1944) 108 JP 181; [1944] KB 550; [1944] 113 LJ 492; (1944) 171 LTR 180; (1943-44) LX TLR 399; (1944) WN (I) 135 CCA Whether fraud of agent was fraud of company depends on relationship/position: here was.

Ilyas (Mohammed), R v (1984) 78 Cr App R 17 CA Must have done everything preparatory to offence before guilty of attempt (and acts must be proximate to offence): merely obtaining insurance claim form could not support attempted obtaining of property by deception conviction.

Impett, Hobson v (1957) 41 Cr App R 138; [1957] Crim LR 476 HC QBD Essence of receiving is that had control of stolen goods.

In the matter of an aplication for a warrant of further detention [1988] Crim LR 296 Magistrates Interpretation of Police and Criminal Evidence Act 1984, s 42.

In the matter of Anderson [1994] Crim LR 594 HC QBD Failed habeas corpus application where claimed that because of delay/nature of offence involved it would be oppressive to return extraditee to Greece.

In the matter of Chetta (1996) TLR 11/7/96 HC QBD Improper for Home Secretary not to disclose reasons for issuing extradition warrant until after judicial review of decision sought.

In the matter of Crichton (Jean), an Infant (1935) 79 LJ 239; (1935) 79 SJ 181 HC KBD Child who had been left with school proprietress ordered to be returned to mother who could now look after child.

In the matter of Evans [1994] Crim LR 593 HC QBD Magistrate not to examine law of requesting state beyond what is stated in extradition materials.

In the matter of McAngus [1994] Crim LR 602 HC QBD Person who showed counterfeit shirts to another with view to sale could be extradited on charge of going equipped to cheat.

In the matter of Nagdhi (David) [1989] Crim LR 825 HC QBD On relevance of order to proceed to validity of extradition proceedings; on determination (by magistrates) of issue of jurisdiction.

In the matter of Osbourne [1993] Crim LR 694 HC QBD Photocopied photograph properly admitted in evidence as was referred to as enclosure in requesting state's warrant.

In the matter of Wai Kit Lee; R v Metropolitan Stipendiary Magistrate; ex parte Wai Kit Lee [1993] Crim LR 696 HC QBD No power in extradition proceedings for court to request more evidence from requesting state; failed habeas corpus application where extraditee claimed undertakings by the Hong Kong government might not be honoured by the Chinese government after the hand-over.

Ingleton, Dibble v [1972] 1 All ER 275; (1972) 136 JP 155; (1971) 121 NLJ 1049t; [1972] RTR 161; (1972) 116 SJ 97; [1972] 2 WLR 163 HC QBD Act of obstruction need not be unlawful in itself to support obstruction conviction.

Ingram, R v [1956] 2 All ER 639; (1956) 40 Cr App R 115; [1956] Crim LR 565; (1956) 120 JP 397; (1956) 106 LJ 442; [1956] 2 QB 424; (1956) 100 SJ 491; [1956] 3 WLR 309 CCA Taking advance payments on foot of promised services is obtaining credit by fraud.

Ingram, R v [1975] Crim LR 457t CA On pleading defence of absent-mindedness (absence of mens rea) to charge (of theft).

Inland Revenue Commissioners; ex parte Rossminster Ltd and others, R v (1979) 123 SJ 554 HC QBD Valid exercise of search and seizure powers by Inland Revenue.

Inland Revenue Commissioners; ex parte Rossminster Ltd and others, R v [1980] Crim LR 111 CA Invalid exercise of search and seizure powers by Inland Revenue.

Inman and Mercury Self-Drive Ltd, R v [1966] Crim LR 106 Assizes Not larceny/fraudulent conversion where manager of car dealing firm sold cars at less than price agreed with vendor: situation gave rise only to debts of a personal nature.

Inman, R v [1966] 3 All ER 414; (1966) 50 Cr App R 247; [1966] Crim LR 445t; (1966) 130 JP 415; [1967] 1 QB 140; (1966) 110 SJ 424; [1966] 3 WLR 567 CA Money transfer under hire-purchase contract not obtaining of credit; not duplicitous to charge fraudulent trading for certain purposes/with intent together but here former merely specified elements of latter.

Inner London Crown Court; ex parte Springall and another, R v (1987) 85 Cr App R 214; [1987] Crim LR 252 HC QBD Behaviour of surety/variations in bail that surety might not have welcomed were mitigating factors insofar as estreatment of recognisances concerned.

Inseal, R v [1992] Crim LR 35 CA On alcoholism as basis for defence of diminished responsibility.

Invicta Plastics Ltd and another v Clare [1976] Crim LR 131; [1976] RTR 251; (1976) 120 SJ 62 HC QBD Company (but not chairman) advertising for sale speed trap detectors properly convicted of incitement to use unlicensed apparatus for wireless telegraphy.

Inwood, R v [1973] 2 All ER 645; (1973) 57 Cr App R 529; [1973] Crim LR 290; (1973) 137 JP 559; (1973) 123 NLJ 249t; (1973) 117 SJ 303; [1973] 1 WLR 647 CA Unless made clear to person that under arrest police cannot use force in restraining them.

Ipswich Crown Court; ex parte Reddington, R v [1981] Crim LR 618 HC QBD Successful appeal against estreatment of recognisance where had not inquired into means of surety/did not consider efforts made by surety to prevent bailed party absconding.

Ipswich Justices; ex parte Edwards, R v (1979) 143 JP 699 HC QBD Justices' improper admission of evidence irremediable through certiorari: habeas corpus application refused.

Iqbal, R v [1979] 1 WLR 425 CA Failed habeas corpus application by person detained under the Immigration Act 1971.

IRC v Rossminster Ltd (1979) 129 (2) NLJ 1260 HL Valid exercise of search and seizure powers by Inland Revenue.

Ireland (Robert Matthew), R v [1997] 1 All ER 112; [1996] 2 Cr App R 426; [1997] Crim LR 434; [1997] 1 FLR 687; [1997] QB 114; (1996) 140 SJ LB 148; (1996) TLR 22/5/96; [1996] 3 WLR 650 CA Making telephone calls and then not speaking here held to be assault occasioning actual bodily harm.

Ireland, Allen and others v (1984) 79 Cr App R 206; [1984] Crim LR 500; (1984) 148 JP 545; (1984) 128 SJ 482; [1984] TLR 212; [1984] 1 WLR 903 HC QBD Prima facie evidence of participation in threatening behaviour where were voluntarily present; prima facie case of identification as party to threatening behaviour where proceedings initiated against one as member of group.

Ireland, R v (1911-13) XXII Cox CC 322; (1910) 102 LTR 608; (1910) WN (I) 35 CCA Party found guilty but insane can under Criminal Appeal Act 1907, s 3, appeal against that conviction.

Ireland, R v [1997] 1 All ER 112 CA Making of silent telephone calls could (as here) constitute assault occasioning actual bodily harm contrary to the Offences against the Person Act 1861, s 47.

Ireland, R v; R v Burstow [1997] 2 Cr App R (S) 1273; (1997) 147 NLJ 1273; [1997] TLR 412; [1997] 3 WLR 534 HL Could be guilty of assault as result of injury occasioned by way of silent telephone calls.

Iremonger v Wynne [1957] Crim LR 624 HC QBD Parties acting jointly (one with light/one with gaff) were each guilty of aiding and abetting other in contravention of the Salmon and Fresh Water Fisheries Act 1923, s 1.

Irving, R v [1970] Crim LR 642 CA Accused not liable for possession of drug surreptitiously placed in bottle of tablets unbeknownst to him.

Irwin v Barker (1924-25) 69 SJ 575/589 HC KBD Person who conducted spiritualist seance was guilty of offence of fortune-telling under the Vagrancy Act 1824, s 4.

Irwin, R v [1987] 2 All ER 1085; (1987) 131 SJ 357 CA Person not entitled in all situations to be consulted by counsel on calling of alibi witnesses.

Isaacs v Keech (1926-30) XXVIII Cox CC 22; (1925) 89 JP 189; [1925] 2 KB 354; [1925] 94 LJCL 676; (1925) 133 LTR 347; (1924-25) XLI TLR 432; (1925) WN (I) 109 HC KBD Police officer can under Town Police Clauses Act 1847, s 28 arrest anyone whom genuinely believes guilty of inter alia importuning for prostitution.

Isaacs, R v [1994] Crim LR 517 HC QBD Test as to what constitutes 'unnecessary suffering' to animal is objective.

Isherwood, Cosh v [1968] 1 All ER 383; (1968) 52 Cr App R 53; [1968] Crim LR 44t; (1968) 132 JP 149; (1967) 117 NLJ 1192t; (1967) 111 SJ 906; [1968] 1 WLR 48 HC QBD Acts showing suspected person must be separate from those showing loitering with intent but need not be different in kind.

Isleworth Crown Court and D; ex parte Commissioners of Customs and Excise, R v [1990] Crim LR 859 HC QBD That committal papers served/further sureties offered adequate change to merit new bail hearing; refusal of right to reply by Crown on new application was valid.

Ivens, Whiting v (1915-17) XXV Cox CC 128; (1915) 79 JP 457; [1915] 84 LJKB 1878; (1915-16) 113 LTR 869; (1914-15) XXXI TLR 492 HC KBD Case against owner ought not to have been dismissed where was prima facie case of cruelty to animal.

Ives, R v [1969] 3 All ER 470; (1969) 53 Cr App R 474; [1969] Crim LR 437; [1970] 1 QB 208; (1969) 113 SJ 467; [1969] 3 WLR 266 CA Intent of accused relevant when determining if provocation.

Izod, R v (1901-07) XX Cox CC 690 Assizes Must be criminally negligent to new-born child after born to sustain conviction for manslaughter of same through neglect.

Jayne, Ashbee v [1966] Crim LR 49; (1965) 109 SJ 919 HC QBD That carried sand-filled sock for purpose of self-defence did not mean could not be offensive weapon.

JB and M Motor Haulage Ltd v London Waste Regulation Authority [1990] TLR 746 HC QBD On necessary prerequisites before may convict individual of failing to furnish information contrary to the Control of Pollution Act 1974, s 93(3).

Jeff, R v; R v Bassett [1967] Crim LR 46t; (1965-66) 116 NLJ 1489; (1967) 111 SJ 53 CA On whether false pretences conviction valid (here was) where part-based on representation alleged to be opinion.

Jefferson (James), R v (1908) 1 Cr App R 95; (1907-08) XXIV TLR 877 CCA Jury decision that accused fit to plead mistaken per CCA: guilty but insane verdict substituted.

Jeffrey, McErlaine v [1955] Crim LR 312 Sessions Conviction for theft of pedal cycle quashed as was inadequate evidence of intention to permanently deprive owner of same.

Jelen (Lawrence), R v; R v Katz (Anthony) (1990) 90 Cr App R 456 CA Tape recording obtained via police entrapment was admissible.

Jenkins v Ash and another (1926-30) XXVIII Cox CC 665; (1929) 93 JP 229; (1929) 141 LTR 591; (1928-29) XLV TLR 479 HC KBD Cruelty to rabbit (coursing/hunting exemptions inapplicable).

Jenkins, Arrowsmith v [1963] 2 QB 561 HC QBD No mens rea required to be guilty of wilful obstruction of highway so long as have freely done acts causing/continuing obstruction.

Jenkins, R v; R v Evans-Jones (1923) 87 JP 115; (1922-23) 67 SJ 707; (1922-23) XXXIX TLR 458 CCA On trials for corruption pursuant to Prevention of Corruption Act 1916.

Jenkins, R v; R v Jenkins [1983] Crim LR 386 CA On what is meant by to 'inflict grievous bodily harm' in Theft Act 1968, s 9(1)(b) (as opposed to Offences against the Person Act 1861, s 20).

Jenner, Smith v [1968] Crim LR 99t; (1967) 117 NLJ 1296t; (1968) 112 SJ 52 HC QBD Successful appeal by driving instructor against conviction for aiding and abetting learner driver in unlicensed driving of car.

Jennings (George), R v (1910) 74 JP 245; (1909-10) XXVI TLR 339 CCA Habitual criminal still habitual criminal though spends small amount of time doing honest work.

Jennings v United States Government [1982] 3 All ER 104 (also HC QBD); [1983] 1 AC 624; (1982) 75 Cr App R 367; [1982] Crim LR 748; (1982) 146 JP 396; (1982) 132 NLJ 881; [1983] RTR 1 (also HC QBD); (1982) 126 SJ 659; [1982] TLR 424; [1982] 3 WLR 450 HL Causing death by reckless driving is manslaughter; character of offence for which sought determines if extradition possible.

Jennings, R v [1990] Crim LR 588 CA Walking around with knife not an unlawful act on which could ground involuntary manslaughter conviction.

Jennion (Yvonne), R v [1962] 1 All ER 689; (1962) 46 Cr App R 212; [1962] Crim LR 384; (1962) 112 LJ 258; (1962) 106 SJ 224 CCA Jury must resolve conflicting expert (here medical) evidence.

Jeraj, R v [1994] Crim LR 595 CA Untrue document verifying that had received letter of credit from non-existent bank which had been endorsed by bank for which appellant worked did constitute a forgery.

Jewelowski v Propp [1944] 1 All ER 483; (1944) 171 LTR 234; (1943-44) LX TLR 559 HC KBD No duty to mitigate damages in fraudulent misrepresentation action.

JF Alford Transport Ltd, R v; R v Alford; R v Paynes [1997] 2 Cr App R 326; (1997) 141 SJ LB 73; [1997] TLR 176 CA Failure to prove intention on part of company/its management to do what knew to be aiding and abetting tachograph offence merited quashing of convicion for same.

Jipps v Lord and another [1982] TLR 277 CA On determining whether mechanically propelled boat used in pursuit of wild bird for purpose of killing same.

Joachim (Maud), R v (1911-12) 7 Cr App R 222; (1911-12) XXVIII TLR 380 CCA Where value of malicious damage done exceeeds £5 each party to concerted act guilty of offence under Malicious Damage Act 1861, s 51, though separate damage was not to the value of £5.

Jobling, R v [1981] Crim LR 625 CrCt On what constitutes an automatic weapon (Bren gun altered so that could not fire automatically was not automatic gun).

Johnson, R v (1911-13) XXII Cox CC 43; (1909) 73 JP 135; [1909] 1 KB 439; (1909) 44 LJ 61; [1909] 78 LJKB 290; (1909) C LTR 464; (1908-09) XXV TLR 229; (1909) WN (I) 19 CCA Cannot be sentenced as incorrigible rogue absent prior sentence as rogue and vagabond.

Johnson, R v [1989] 2 All ER 839; (1989) 89 Cr App R 148; [1989] Crim LR 738; (1989) 153 JP 533; (1989) 139 NLJ 643; (1989) 133 SJ 596; [1989] 1 WLR 740 CA Self-induced provocation is possible and possibility ought to be left to jury.

Johnson, R v [1963] 3 All ER 577; (1964) 48 Cr App R 25; (1963) 127 JP 556; (1963) 113 LJ 752; [1964] 2 QB 404; (1963) 107 SJ 1042; [1963] 3 WLR 1031 CCA Must prove unlawful intercourse/intention of same for procuring/attempted procuring of third party sex with under-21 year old.

Johnson, R v [1961] 3 All ER 969; (1962) 46 Cr App R 55; [1962] Crim LR 52; (1962) 126 JP 40; (1961) 111 LJ 838; (1961) 105 SJ 1108 CCA Burden of proving alibi/guilt on defence/always on prosecution.

Johnson, R v [1963] Crim LR 860 CCA On offence of procuring under twenty-one year old to have sex.

Johnston, R v (1945) WN (I) 114 CCA Attempt to commit crime did not preclude person who attempted to commit same from being convicted for waiting for opportunity to commit said crime contrary to the Prevention of Crimes Act 1871, s 7.

Johnstone, R v; R v Comerford; R v Jalil [1982] Crim LR 454/607 CA Where intended that owner of property receive same albeit in roundabout way there was no intention to permanently deprive owner of property and so no theft.

Joiner (Frederick), R v (1910) 4 Cr App R 64; (1910) 74 JP 200; (1909-10) XXVI TLR 265; (1910) WN (I) 43 CCA Must prove property at issue was stolen to support conviction for larceny.

Jolly, R v (1919) 83 JP 296 Assizes Where through disease of the mind one momentarily loses control over one's actions one can be found to have been insane when acted.

Jones (Alfred), R v (1910) 4 Cr App R 17; (1909-10) XXVI TLR 226 CCA Receiver of goods obtained where promised would but did not pay for same need not be guilty of larceny by trick.

Jones (Ellen), R v (1899-1901) XIX Cox CC 678 Assizes Presumed to have means to support infant at time of neglect if had so before neglect and would not yet have exhausted same.

Jones (Harold) alias George Wright, R v (1921-25) XXVII Cox CC 221; (1921-22) 16 Cr App R 124; (1922) 86 JP 123; (1922) 127 LTR 160; (1921-22) 66 SJ 489; (1922) WN (I) 100 CCA Cannot by reference to untried crime prove dishonest life of person accused of being habitual criminal.

Jones (Ivor Frank), R v; R v Jones (Diane Jane); R v Blarick (John Lee); R v Jarman (Peter David); R v Chennells (Trevor Boyce) [1997] 1 Cr App R 46; [1997] Crim LR 510; (1996) 140 SJ LB 206; (1996) TLR 14/8/96; [1997] 2 WLR 792 CA On necessary intent for offence of conspiracy to possess firearms/ammunition with intent to enable another to thereby endanger life.

Jones (Ivor), R v [1993] TLR 72 CA Milkman who consistently and determinedly overcharged for milk deliveries for years was guilty of obtaining property by deception.

Jones (James William), R v [1973] Crim LR 621 CrCt Was not taking child out of possession of parents (contrary to Sexual Offences Act 1956, s 20) to seek to bring girls for walk, aim being to indecently assault them.

Jones (John McKinsie), R v; R v Tomlinson (Eric); R v Warren (Dennis Michael); R v O'Shea (Kenneth Desmond Francis); R v Carpenter (John); R v Llywarch (John Elfyn) (1974) 59 Cr App R 120 CA On what constitutes 'intimidation' under Conspiracy and Protection of Property Act 1875, s 7; on constituent elements of unlawful assembly and of affray.

Jones (John), R v; R v Smith (Christopher) [1976] 3 All ER 54; (1976) 63 Cr App R 47; (1976) 140 JP 515; (1976) 120 SJ 299; [1976] 1 WLR 672 CA Trespass where exceed permission/ reckless whether exceeding permission.

Jones (Keith Desmond), R v (1987) 85 Cr App R 259; (1987) 131 SJ 504; [1987] 1 WLR 692 CA On what constitutes being 'armed' with offensive weapon for purpose of Customs and Excise Management Act 1979, s 86.

Jowett, West Riding Cleaning Co Ltd v (1938) 86 LJ 293; (1938) 82 SJ 870 HC KBD Successful prosecution for unlawful window-cleaning contrary to the Town Police Clauses Act 1847, s 28.

Joy and Emmony, R v (1975) 60 Cr App R 133 CCC Gas Council is a public body for purposes of Prevention of Corruption Act 1916, s 2.

Joyce v Director of Public Prosecutions [1946] 1 All ER 186; [1946] AC 347; (1945-46) 31 Cr App R 57; (1946) 96 LJ 94; [1946] 115 LJ 146; (1946) 174 LTR 206; (1945-46) LXII TLR 208; (1946) WN (I) 31 HL Person with British passport (albeit obtained by fraud) could be guilty of treason under Treason Act 1351; holding British passport (even one obtained by fraud) entitled bearer to normal rights/protection afforded bearers thereof.

Joyce v Hertfordshire Constabulary (1985) 80 Cr App R 298 HC QBD If breach of peace occurring police officer may use reasonable force to stop it.

Joyce, R v [1945] 2 All ER 673; (1946) 96 LJ 185; (1945) 173 LTR 377; (1945) 89 SJ 532; (1945-46) LXII TLR 57; (1945) WN (I) 220 CCA Person with British passport, though a foreigner, could be guilty of treason under Treason Act 1351; holding British passport (even one obtained by fraud) entitled bearer to normal rights/protection afforded bearers thereof.

Jubb, R v; R v Rigby [1984] Crim LR 616 CA On when parties to joint enterprise (robbery) are liable for further offence (murder) committed by one party to joint enterprise in course of same.

Julien, R v [1969] 2 All ER 856; (1969) 53 Cr App R 407; [1969] Crim LR 381t; (1969) 133 JP 489; (1969) 119 NLJ 390t; (1969) 113 SJ 342; [1969] 1 WLR 839 CA Person must show did not want to fight if seeks to raise self-defence.

Jura, R v [1954] 1 All ER 696; (1954) 38 Cr App R 53; [1954] Crim LR 378; (1954) 118 JP 260; (1954) 104 LJ 200; [1954] 1 QB 503; (1954) 98 SJ 198; [1954] 2 WLR 516 CCA Person in possession of air gun at shooting gallery has reasonable excuse to possess it (even if used unlawfully).

Justice of the Peace for Peterborough, ex parte Hicks and others, R v [1978] 1 All ER 225; [1977] Crim LR 621; (1978) 142 JP 103; (1977) 121 SJ 605; [1977] 1 WLR 1371 HC QBD If clients could not prevent document being seized from solicitors' possession solicitor cannot.

K (a minor), Director of Public Prosecutions v [1990] 1 All ER 331; (1990) 91 Cr App R 23; (1990) 154 JP 192; (1990) 134 SJ 636; [1990] 1 WLR 1067 HC QBD Recklessly placing dangerous substance in machine can ground conviction for causing actual bodily harm to later user of machine.

K and another, Director of Public Prosecutions v (1997) 1 Cr App R 36; [1997] Crim LR 121 HC QBD Could be guilty of procuring rape by person aged between ten and fourteen in respect of whom the doli incapax presumption had not been rebutted.

K, R v [1978] 1 All ER 180; (1978) 66 Cr App R 183; (1978) 142 JP 108; (1977) 121 SJ 728; [1978] 1 WLR 139 CrCt That in local authority care/assessment centre after magistrates' conviction does not mean 'in custody' so no bail.

K, R v (1984) 78 Cr App R 82; [1983] Crim LR 736; (1984) 148 JP 410; [1983] TLR 576 CA On duress as defence to contempt.

Kaitamaki v R [1984] 2 All ER 435; [1985] AC 147; (1984) 79 Cr App R 251; [1984] Crim LR 564; (1984) 128 SJ 331; [1984] TLR 282; [1984] 3 WLR 137 PC Consented to complete penetration does not mean continuing sex cannot be rape.

Kakelo, R v [1923] All ER 191; (1922-23) 17 Cr App R 150; (1923) 129 LTR 477; (1923-24) 68 SJ 41; (1922-23) XXXIX TLR 671; (1923) WN (I) 220 CCA Objection in trial for offence under statutory order that order not proved to be taken at trial.

Kakelo, R v (1922-23) 17 Cr App R 149 CCA Leave to appeal in case where in trial for offence under statutory order same was not proved.

Kakis v Government of the Republic of Cyprus and others [1978] 2 All ER 634; [1978] Crim LR 489; (1978) 142 JP 429; (1978) 122 SJ 400; [1978] 1 WLR 779 HL No extradition because of delay, death of alibi witness, reasonable belief would not be prosecuted for offence.

Kam-Kwok (Leung) v R (1985) 81 Cr App R 83; [1985] Crim LR 227 PC Conviction allowed stand despite gross misdirection on mental aspect of murder.

Keddle v Payn [1964] 1 All ER 189; [1964] Crim LR 39; (1964) 128 JP 144; (1964) 114 LJ 25; (1963) 107 SJ 911; [1964] 1 WLR 262 HC QBD Dog could simultaneously be dangerous and not ferocious.

Keech, Isaacs v (1926-30) XXVIII Cox CC 22; (1925) 89 JP 189; [1925] 2 KB 354; [1925] 94 LJCL 676; (1925) 133 LTR 347; (1924-25) XLI TLR 432; (1925) WN (I) 109 HC KBD Police officer can under Town Police Clauses Act 1847, s 28 arrest anyone whom genuinely believes guilty of inter alia importuning for prostitution.

Keene and others, R v [1972] Crim LR 526t; (1971) 121 NLJ 640 CA Was corrupting public morals for magazine to contain homosexual private advertisments.

Kelbie, R v [1996] Crim LR 802 CA On making of citizen's arrest as defence to charge of assault occasioning actual bodily harm.

Kell, R v [1985] Crim LR 239 CA On belief that had permission to take property/absence of intention to permanently deprive as defences to theft.

Kellet, Director of Public Prosecutions v [1994] Crim LR 916; (1994) 158 JP 1138; [1994] TLR 399 HC QBD That had been drunk was no excuse for letting unmuzzled/untethered dangerous dog wander into public place.

Kellett, R v [1975] 3 All ER 466; (1975) 61 Cr App R 240; [1975] Crim LR 576t; (1976) 140 JP 1; (1975) 125 NLJ 698t; [1976] QB 372; (1975) 119 SJ 542; [1975] 3 WLR 713 CA Threatening witness to get them to change/withhold evidence is obstruction of justice.

Kellett, R v [1974] Crim LR 552 CrCt Threatening to sue witness to get them to change/withhold evidence is obstruction of justice.

Kelley, Beal v [1951] 2 All ER 763; (1951-52) 35 Cr App R 128; (1951) 115 JP 566; (1951) 101 LJ 594; (1951) 95 SJ 685; [1951] 2 TLR 865; (1951) WN (I) 505 HC KBD Actual assault need not in itself be indecent to sustain indecent assault charge.

Kelly (John), R v (1909) 3 Cr App R 248; (1909-10) XXVI TLR 196 CCA Accused's behaviour since most recent release from prison highly pertinent in deciding if habitual criminal.

Kelly v Dolbey [1984] RTR 67 HC QBD Arrest of driver after failed to inflate bag but crystals afforded negative reading was valid (though crystals later found at station to give positive reading): appellant properly convicted inter alia of failure to give specimen.

Kelly v Purvis [1983] 1 All ER 525; (1983) 76 Cr App R 165; [1983] Crim LR 185; (1983) 147 JP 135; [1983] QB 663; (1983) 127 SJ 52; [1982] TLR 599; [1983] 2 WLR 299 HC QBD Provision of ordinary sex unnecessary to support charge of assisting in management of brothel.

Kelly (Ronnie Peter), R v (1993) 97 Cr App R 245; [1993] Crim LR 763; (1993) 157 JP 845; (1992) 136 SJ LB 324; [1992] TLR 578 CA Burglar must have weapon of offence as burglary takes place to be guilty of aggravated burglary.

Kelly, R v [1992] Crim LR 181 CA Bringing complainant to suspect to see whether was assailant was permissible where all happened within minutes of offence; on what constitutes criminal attempt (here in context of attempted rape).

Kelly, R v [1963] Crim LR 855g CCA Improper to allow jury return verdict of warehousebreaking with intent in respect of person charged with warehousebreaking and larceny (Larceny Act 1916, ss 26(1) and 27(2)).

Kelsey, Jones v (1987) 85 Cr App R 226; [1987] Crim LR 392; (1987) 151 JP 429 HC QBD Constable could arrest person wanted for breach of community service order though not in possession of warrant at time - assault on constable doing same was therefore assault on constable in execution of duty.

Kelson (Thomas Henry), R v (1909) 3 Cr App R 230 CCA Accused not explaining away supposed involvement with proceeds of theft presumed guilty of larceny.

Kelt, R v [1977] 3 All ER 1099; (1977) 65 Cr App R 74; [1977] Crim LR 558; (1978) 142 JP 60; (1977) 121 SJ 423; [1977] 1 WLR 1365 CA Firearm needs to be physically close/in immediate control but need not be carried to have it with one.

Kemp (Peter David Glanville), R v (1988) 87 Cr App R 95; [1988] Crim LR 376; (1988) 152 JP 461; [1988] QB 645; (1988) 132 SJ 461; [1988] 2 WLR 975 CA Person carrying on business with intent of defrauding customers was guilty of fraudulent trading under Companies Act 1948, s 332 (as amended).

Kemp, R v [1968] Crim LR 32t CA Must be guilty of endeavouring to aid another to evade justice to be guilty as accessory after the fact.

Kemp, R v [1956] 3 All ER 249; (1956) 40 Cr App R 121; [1956] Crim LR 774; (1956) 120 JP 457; (1956) 106 LJ 538; [1957] 1 QB 399; (1956) 100 SJ 768; [1956] 3 WLR 724 HC QBD On insanity/M'Naghten's Case.

Kence, R v (1978) 128 NLJ 537t CA Fact that drugs being transported through (not to) United Kingdom a minor but nonetheless mitigating factor when sentencing for unlawful importation of controlled drugs.

Kenlin and another v Gardiner and another [1966] 3 All ER 931; [1967] Crim LR 39; (1967) 131 JP 91; (1965-66) 116 NLJ 1685; [1967] 2 QB 510; (1966) 110 SJ 848; [1967] 2 WLR 129 HC QBD Proportionate use of force following technical assault by constable legitimate self-defence.

Kent (Tyler Gatewood), R v (1940-42) 28 Cr App R 23; (1941) 85 SJ 315; (1940-41) LVII TLR 307 CCA Diplomatic privilege of embassy employee could be waived by Ambassador/foreign Government; Official Secrets Acts apply to diplomatic agents.

Kent and Sussex Contractors, Ltd and another, Director of Public Prosecutions v [1944] 1 All ER 119; [1944] KB 146; [1944] 113 LJ 88; [1945] 95 LJ 102; (1944) 170 LTR 41; (1944) 88 SJ 59; (1943-44) LX TLR 175 HC KBD Intentions of its servants are attributed to corporation.

Kent County Council v Multi Media Marketing (Canterbury) Ltd and another [1995] TLR 263 HC QBD On what constitutes 'human sexual activity' for purposes of the Video Recordings Act 1984, s 2(2).

Kent County Council, Thanet District Council v [1993] Crim LR 703 HC QBD On what constituted 'controlled waste' for purposes of the Control of Pollution Act 1974 (did not include seaweed).

Kenworthy, Robinson v [1982] TLR 257 HC QBD On determining whether bird a 'wild bird' for purposes of the Protection of Birds Act 1954, s 1.

Kerr (Hugh Gilmour), R v; R v Smith (Derrick Albert) (1976) 62 Cr App R 210; [1976] Crim LR 192t CA Quashing of firearms conviction on foot of extradition as was not extraditable offence.

Kerr (Neil), R v (1920-21) 15 Cr App R 165 CCA Liability of co-conspirator for act of another.

Kerr v Director of Public Prosecutions [1995] Crim LR 394; (1994) 158 JP 1048; [1994] TLR 459 HC QBD Police officer not acting in course of duty where held person in erroneous belief that person had been arrested.

Kersey (Maud), R v (1907-09) XXI Cox CC 690 Assizes Murder/concealment of birth conviction not possible/possible on evidence though no dead body.

Keslake v Board of Trade [1903] 2 KB 453 HC KBD Absent court order cannot make post-desertion deduction from seaman's wages.

Kettle and the London County Council, R v (1901-07) XX Cox CC 753; [1905] 1 KB 212; (1905) XCII LTR 59; (1904-05) XXI TLR 151; (1904-05) 53 WR 364 HC KBD No need for fresh recognisance post-mandamus order to state case earlier refused to state even though surety has died.

Keyte, Moore v (1901-02) XVIII TLR 396; (1901-02) 50 WR 457 HC KBD On bringing of vaccination prosecutions.

Khan and others, R v [1990] 2 All ER 783; (1990) 91 Cr App R 29; [1990] Crim LR 519; (1990) 154 JP 805; (1994) 144 NLJ 863; (1990) 134 SJ 401; [1990] TLR 86; [1990] 1 WLR 813 CA Attempted rape possible even where man reckless as to whether consent given.

Khan and Rakhman, R v [1963] Crim LR 562t CCA Self-defence a defence to affray.

Khan, Director of Public Prosecutions v [1990] Crim LR 321; (1989) 139 NLJ 1455 HC QBD Was occasioning actual bodily harm to place dangerous substance in machine used by public where (albeit that had not intended harm) next user was harmed by substance being ejected from machine.

Kidd and Walsh, R v (1908) 72 JP 104 CCC Selling pirated music is not per se common law larceny.

Kiffin, R v [1994] Crim LR 449 CA Could be guilty of perverting course of justice where impeded police investigation into suspected criminal offence.

Killick (William John), R v (1924-25) 18 Cr App R 120 CCA Need for corroboration in indecent assault case where prosecutrix' case weak.

Kimber, R v [1983] 3 All ER 316; (1983) 77 Cr App R 225; [1983] Crim LR 630; (1983) 133 NLJ 914; (1983) 127 SJ 578; [1983] TLR 388; [1983] 1 WLR 1118 CA Intent for indecent assault is intent to use violence without consent; reasonable belief of consent a valid defence.

Kindon (Thelma Daphne), R v (1957) 41 Cr App R 208; [1957] Crim LR 607 CCA Conversion of money obtained by way of tort was larceny.

King (Jeffery David), R v [1978] Crim LR 228 CrCt On what constitutes 'intention to supply' for purposes of Misuse of Drugs Act 1971, s 5(3).

King and another, R v [1987] 1 All ER 547; (1987) 84 Cr App R 357; [1987] Crim LR 398; (1987) 151 JP 559; [1987] QB 547; (1987) 131 SJ 325; [1987] 2 WLR 746 CA Deception must be core element of obtaining property before property obtained by deception.

King and King, R v [1966] Crim LR 280t CCA Had to be definite agreement to rob before could (as here) be convicted of conspiracy to rob.

King and others, R v [1991] 3 All ER 705; (1991) 93 Cr App R 259; [1991] Crim LR 906; (1991) 141 NLJ 1071; [1992] QB 20; (1991) 135 SJ LB 76; [1991] 3 WLR 246 CA Clearing house automated payment system a valuable security executed when signed by bank officials.

King v Bull (1934-39) XXX Cox CC 567; (1937) 81 SJ 219; (1937) WN (I) 76 HC KBD Conviction for unlicensed use of apparatus for wireless telegraphy.

King v Gardner (1980) 71 Cr App R 13 HC QBD Police officer detaining person following radio message did not have reasonable suspicion to justify detention so not acting in course of duty when assaulted.

King v Hodges [1974] Crim LR 424 HC QBD Police officer was acting in course of his duty when prior to arresting appellant so as to prevent breach of the peace he applied reasonable force to seek to restrain her from committing breach.

King v R [1962] 1 All ER 816; [1962] AC 199; [1962] Crim LR 166; (1962) 106 SJ 56 PC Conviction quashed where jury's opinion if directed that two did not act in concert cannot be determined.

King v Spencer (1901-07) XX Cox CC 692; (1904) 68 JP 530; (1904-05) XCI LTR 470 HC KBD Not per se criminal fraud to weigh goods and wrapper together where purchaser aware of same; evidence of trade custom admissible to establish if behaviour fraudulent.

King, Folkes v [1922] 2 KB 348; (1923) 128 LTR 405 HC KBD Recovery of property from good faith purchaser who obtained same from agent who in turn obtained possession from principal by means of larceny by trick.

King, R v [1964] Crim LR 133g CCA Failed plea of diminished responsibility - on elements of same; no defence that were prompted to kill son by seeing him injured; on provocation as it applies to people of African origin.

King, R v [1963] 3 All ER 561; (1964) 48 Cr App R 17; [1963] Crim LR 841; (1963) 113 LJ 752; (1963) 107 SJ 832; [1964] 1 QB 285; [1963] 3 WLR 892 CCA Honest belief first marriage invalid a defence to bigamy (but no facts supporting belief here).

King, R v [1963] 3 All ER 925; (1964) 48 Cr App R 141; [1965] 1 QB 443 (also CCA); (1964) 108 SJ 1048; [1964] 3 WLR 980 (also CCA) Assizes Death penalty does not make all murder capital murder; charge that murder done in course of theft dropped: no supporting facts; successive murders during one afternoon not done on different occasions.

King, R v [1965] 1 All ER 1053; (1965) 49 Cr App R 140; [1965] Crim LR 237g; (1965) 129 JP 276; (1965) 115 LJ 280; (1965) 109 SJ 150/391; [1965] 1 WLR 706 CCA No misprision of felony if remaining silent after charge/exercising right against self-incrimination but if speaks lies can be active concealment.

King, R v [1938] 2 All ER 662; (1938) 82 SJ 569 CCA Stolen property not in possession of police when received by accused so did receive stolen property.

King-Jones and Gladdy, R v [1966] Crim LR 510; [1966] 1 WLR 1077 Assizes Ought not to be convicted of assault with intent to rob where believed had right to money and to secure same by force if necessary.

Kingerlee, Roe v [1986] Crim LR 735 HC QBD Writing graffiti on wall using mud was criminal damage.

Kingston, R v [1994] 3 All ER 353; [1995] 2 AC 355; (1994) 99 Cr App R 286; [1994] Crim LR 846; (1994) 158 JP 717; (1994) 144 NLJ 1044; [1994] TLR 422; [1994] 3 WLR 519 HL Lack of moral blame does not negative intent (unless incapable of forming intent) but can mitigate sentence.

Kingston, R v [1993] 4 All ER 373; (1993) 97 Cr App R 401; [1993] Crim LR 781; (1993) 157 JP 1171; (1993) 143 NLJ 724; [1994] QB 81; (1993) 137 SJ LB 144; [1993] TLR 262; [1993] 3 WLR 676 CA Involuntary intoxication precludes necessary intent.

Kirkland v Robinson [1987] Crim LR 643 CA Possession of live birds contrary to Wildlife and Countryside Act 1981, s 1(2)(a), a strict liability offence.

Kirkpatrick, Da Costa Small v (1979) 68 Cr App R 186; [1979] Crim LR 41 HC QBD Unlawful arrest on warrant as warrant not physically in police officer's possession when effected arrest.

Kirkpatrick, Da Costa Small v (1978) 128 NLJ 1125t CA Unlawful arrest on warrant as warrant not physically in police officer's possession when effected arrest.

Kirkup (Johnson), R v (1949-50) 34 Cr App R 150 CCA Soldier accused of larceny of Government property from base ought properly to be dealt with under military law.

Kirkup, R v [1993] 2 All ER 802; (1993) 96 Cr App R 352; [1993] Crim LR 777; (1993) 157 JP 825; (1992) 142 NLJ 1612; [1992] TLR 535; [1993] 1 WLR 774 CA Soliciting for immoral purposes means soliciting for sexual activity; immorality of that activity a matter for judge/jury/justices.

Kiszko (Stefan Ivan), R v (1979) 68 Cr App R 62; [1979] Crim LR 465 CA Responsibilities of jury as regards considering evidence when diminished responsibility pleaded.

Kitching, Director of Public Prosecutions v [1990] Crim LR 394; (1990) 154 JP 293 HC QBD Police officer could arrest person for being drunk and disorderly in public place.

Kitching, R v (1928-29) XLV TLR 569 CCA Rape conviction quashed where was no proper bill for rape (and no alternative indecent assault indictment).

Kite v Napp [1982] TLR 294 HC QBD That dog bit people with bags a characteristic of that dog for purposes of the Animals Act 1971, s 2(2)(b).

Kiu (Chang Hang) and others v Piggott and another [1908-10] All ER 1270; (1909) C LTR 310 PC Person to be heard in own defence before committal for contempt (for perjury).

Klein (Arthur Jack), R v (1931-32) 23 Cr App R 173 CCA Not customary for CCA to grant bail pending appeal (and here was not granted despite occurrence of Easter Vacation between bail application and appeal).

Klein, R v [1958] Crim LR 185 CCC On elements of offence of bankrupt fraudulently obtaining property on credit.

Knight (James), R v (1928-29) 21 Cr App R 72 CCA Are not automatically habitual criminal just because were previously convicted as such.

Knight (Thomas), R v (1908) 1 Cr App R 186; (1908-09) 53 SJ 101 CCA Owner of goods cannot be guilty of larceny of same unless in possession of bailee.

Knight v Taylor [1979] Crim LR 318; [1979] RTR 304 HC QBD Where two constables acting together one could request breath specimen and other could arrest upon failure to provide same.

Knight, R v (1909) 73 JP 15 CCA Failed prosecution for larceny of own goods from sheriff where goods had been seized by sheriff from accused in belief that were those of accused's wife.

Knightsbridge Crown Court, ex parte Dunne, R v; Brock v Director of Public Prosecutions [1993] Crim LR 853; (1994) 158 JP 213; (1993) 143 NLJ 1479; [1993] TLR 418 HC QBD On determining what constitutes 'type' of dog 'known as the pit bull terrier' (Dangerous Dogs Act 1991, s 1).

Knightsbridge Crown Court; ex parte Newton, R v [1980] Crim LR 715 CA Non-forfeiture of recognisance in light of circumstances despite failure of defendant bailed to appear in court.

Knightsbridge Crown Court; ex parte Umeh, R v [1979] Crim LR 727 HC QBD Assault on police officer forcibly removing accused from police station was assault on constable in execution of his duty.

Knott v Blackburn and another [1944] 1 All ER 116; (1944) 108 JP 19; [1944] KB 77; [1944] 113 LJ 154; (1944) 170 LTR 55; (1944) 88 SJ 60; (1943-44) LX TLR 92; (1943) WN (I) 253 HC KBD Fenced-in railway siding not an enclosed area for purposes of Vagrancy Act 1824, s 4.

Knowlden (Derek James), R v; R v Knowlden (Harold) (1983) 77 Cr App R 94 CA Appropriate direction where defendant gives evidence detrimental to co-accused.

Knowles (Benjamin) v R [1930] AC 366; (1930) 69 LJ 217; (1930) 99 LJPC 108; (1929-30) XLVI TLR 276; (1930) WN (I) 66 PC On trial by jury in Ashanti; conviction quashed as possibility of manslaughter not considered where was possible finding.

Knox v Anderton (1983) 76 Cr App R 156; [1983] Crim LR 114; (1983) 147 JP 340; [1982] TLR 565 HC QBD Landing in public flats was 'public place' within meaning of Prevention of Crime Act 1953, s 1(4).

Knuller (Publishing, Printing and Promotions) Ltd and others v Director of Public Prosecutions [1972] 2 All ER 898; [1973] AC 435; (1972) 56 Cr App R 633; [1975] Crim LR 704; (1972) 136 JP 728; (1972) 116 SJ 545; [1972] 3 WLR 143 HL Is offence of conspiracy to corrupt public morals and of conspiring to outrage public decency which advertisements by men seeking homosexual partners could violate.

Knuller (Publishing, Printing and Promotions) Ltd and others, R v [1971] 3 All ER 314; (1971) 135 JP 569; [1972] 2 QB 179; (1971) 115 SJ 772; [1971] 3 WLR 633 CA Agreement to place advertisements seeking homosexual partners can be conspiracy to corrupt public morals.

Koessler, Woodward v [1958] 3 All ER 557; [1958] Crim LR 754; (1959) 123 JP 14; (1958) 108 LJ 793; (1958) 102 SJ 879 HC QBD Non-physical threats covered by term 'causing injury to the person' in Prevention of Crime Act 1953, s 1(1).

Kohn (David James), R v (1979) 69 Cr App R 395; [1979] Crim LR 675 CA On various circumstances in which employee using company cheques for own ends was theft.

Koi, Public Prosecutor v [1968] 1 All ER 419 PC Consorting with Indonesian soldiers not doing so with persons carrying arms contrary to Internal Security Act 1960.

Kopsch (Alfred Arthur), R v (1925-26) 19 Cr App R 50 CCA There is no defence of uncontrollable impulse.

Korie, R v [1966] 1 All ER 50; [1966] Crim LR 167; (1965-66) 116 NLJ 360 CrCt Evidence that women visiting premises are prostitutes admissible to show brothel though prejudicial to defence.

Kosmos Publications Ltd and another v DPP [1975] Crim LR 345 HC QBD On determining whether article is indecent or obscene.

Kossekechatko and Others v Attorney-General for Trinidad [1932] AC 78; (1931-34) XXIX Cox CC 394; (1931) 72 LJ 386; (1932) 101 LJPC 17; (1932) 146 LTR 101; (1931) 75 SJ 741; (1931-32) XLVIII TLR 27 PC Non-compliance by magistrate with procedural requirements and absence of evidence that fugitives had committed offence in French territory (as required in French Extradition Treaty) meant no extradition.

Koumourou, Smith v [1979] Crim LR 116; [1979] RTR 355 HC QBD Was obtaining pecuniary advantage by deception where driver without excise licence displayed undated police receipt for earlier expired licence to avoid non-payment of duty being discovered and so avoid paying excise duty.

Kovacs, R v [1974] 1 All ER 1236; (1974) 58 Cr App R 412; [1974] Crim LR 183t; (1974) 138 JP 425; (1974) 124 NLJ 36t; (1974) 118 SJ 116; [1974] 1 WLR 370 CA Person deceived need not directly suffer loss to sustain conviction for obtaining pecuniary advantage by deception.

Kowalski (Roy), R v (1988) 86 Cr App R 339; [1988] Crim LR 124; [1988] 1 FLR 447 CA Husband cannot rape wife per vaginam but can be guilty of indecent assault on her by reason of fellatio.

Krause, R v (1901-02) XVIII TLR 238 CCC Must show some form of communication to support charge of inciting another to murder contrary to Offences against the Person Act 1861, s 4.

Krausz (Francis Leonard), R v (1973) 57 Cr App R 466; [1973] Crim LR 581 CA Defence witness called to prove prosecutrix a prostitute (as part of consent defence) can state general reasons why so believes.

Kritz, R v [1949] 2 All ER 406; [1950] 1 KB 82; [1949] 118 LJR 1535; (1949) LXV TLR 505; (1949) WN (I) 374 CCA R v Carpenter (1911) direction on intent to defraud was ideal direction.

Krumpa and Anderson v Director of Public Prosecutions [1989] Crim LR 295 HC QBD Have not been asked to leave land where are told that sometime in the future will be asked to leave.

Kulynycz, R v [1970] 3 All ER 881; (1971) 55 Cr App R 34; [1970] Crim LR 693; (1971) 135 JP 82; (1970) 120 NLJ 945t; (1970) 114 SJ 785 CA Unlawfulness of arrest does not colour everything thereafter; arrest unlawful if not informed of basis for arrest.

Kutas (Harry), R v; R v Jerichower (James) (1922-23) 17 Cr App R 179; (1923) 87 JP 196; (1923) 58 LJ 510; (1923-24) XL TLR 51; (1923) WN (I) 287 CCA Conspiracy to obtain goods by fraud a misdemeanour contrary to Larceny Act 1916, s 33(1).

Kwan (Kong Cheuk) v R [1985] Crim LR 787; (1985) 129 SJ 504 PC Manslaughter by gross negligence conviction quashed in light of misdirection as to elements of same.

Kylsant, R v [1931] All ER 179; (1931-34) XXIX Cox CC 379; (1931-32) 23 Cr App R 83; [1932] 1 KB 442; (1932) 146 LTR 21; (1931) 75 SJ 815; (1931-32) XLVIII TLR 62 CCA May overall be false prosepctus though individual statements therein are true.

Kynaston v Director of Public Prosecutions; Heron (Joseph) v Director of Public Prosecutions; Heron (Tracey) v Director of Public Prosecutions (1988) 87 Cr App R 200 HC QBD Was lawful entry of premises by police where knew offence committed, knew whom wanted to arrest, reasonably suspected were on premises and owner knew what police wanted.

Kyprianou v Reynolds [1969] Crim LR 656; (1969) 113 SJ 563 HC QBD Intention to acquire drugs along with invitation to drug dealers to treat or make offer not enough to support conviction for attempted procurement of drugs.

L v Director of Public Prosecutions; T v Director of Public Prosecutions; W, H (G) and H (C) v Director of Public Prosecutions [1996] 2 Cr App R 501 HC QBD On rebuttal of doli incapax presumption.

Lacis v Cashmarts (1968) 112 SJ 1005; [1969] Crim LR 102t; [1969] 2 QB 400; [1969] 2 WLR 329 HC QBD In supermarket/cash and carry property passes when price paid: here authorised manager intended to pass property (albeit at unintended reduced price) so taking of property and carrying away not larceny.

Lack (Peter Andrew), R v (1987) 84 Cr App R 342 CA Documents allegedly emanating from company but actually made after liquidation of same were false for purposes of Forgery and Counterfeiting Act 1981.

Lackey, R v [1954] Crim LR 57 Assizes Where something that has been secured is broken, that is a breaking.

Laing, R v [1995] Crim LR 395 CA Could not be guilty of burglary where were not trespasser when entered building.

Laitwood (John), R v (1910) 4 Cr App R 248; (1910) WN (I) 122 CCA Can be convicted of attempt to obtain by false pretences where did not manage attempt solely because were apprehended.

Lake v Simmons [1927] All ER 49 HL Insurance policy effective as purported entrusting of goods to thief was larceny by trick.

Laker (Herbert William), R v (1949-50) 34 Cr App R 36 CCA Bankrupt's taking cheque from person for one purpose and using for another not obtaining credit by fraud contrary to Bankruptcy Act 1914, s 156(a).

Lamb v Director of Public Prosecutions (1990) 154 JP 381 HC QBD Trespassing police officer was nonetheless acting in course of duty when stayed in place to prevent expected breach of the peace.

Lamb v Gorham (1971) 115 SJ 831 HC QBD Valid finding by justices on basis of single incident that dog was dangerous dog.

Lamb, R v [1990] Crim LR 58 HC QBD Police officer justified in remaining on property had rightfully entered in anticipation of breach of the peace.

Lamb, R v [1967] 2 All ER 1282; [1967] Crim LR 537t; (1967) 131 JP 456; (1967) 117 NLJ 834; [1967] 2 QB 981; (1967) 111 SJ 541; [1967] 3 WLR 888 CA Must consider accused's mind when criminal negligence alleged.

Lamb, R v [1934] All ER 540; (1934-39) XXX Cox CC 91; (1932-34) 24 Cr App R 145; (1934) 150 LTR 519; (1934) 78 SJ 279; (1933-34) L TLR 310 CCA Giving false name (with partner's knowledge) in certificate after notice does not preclude marriage being valid (and later marriage being bigamous).

Lambert, R v [1972] Crim LR 422 CA On meaning of 'unwarranted' demand of money with menaces.

Lambie, R v [1981] 1 All ER 332; (1980) 71 Cr App R 350; [1980] Crim LR 725; (1980) 124 SJ 808; [1981] 1 WLR 78 CA Use of credit card over limit not false representation to shop assistant to obtain advantage by deception.

Lambie, R v [1981] 2 All ER 776; [1982] AC 449; (1981) 73 Cr App R 294; [1981] Crim LR 712; (1981) 145 JP 364; (1980) 130 NLJ 908; (1981) 131 NLJ 725; (1981) 125 SJ 480; [1981] 3 WLR 88 HL Presentation of credit card not representation that had requisite credit standing.

Lamey v R (1996) 140 SJ LB 174; (1996) TLR 21/5/96; [1996] 1 WLR 902 PC On elements of offence of murder committed 'in the course or furtherance of an act of terrorism' under Offences against the Person Act 1864, s 2 (as amended).

Lamond, Jones v (1935) 79 SJ 859 CA Binding over by court of summary jurisdiction for assault did not constitute conviction.

Lancaster v Whalley [1957] Crim LR 245 Magistrates Sucessful prosecution for non-possession of dog licence.

Landow (Marks), R v (1913-14) XXIII Cox CC 457; (1913) 77 JP 364; (1913-14) 109 LTR 48; (1912-13) XXIX TLR 375 CCA Failed prosecution for attempt to procure wife to become brothel-prostitute outside Empire.

Landy and others, R v [1981] 1 All ER 1172; (1981) 72 Cr App R 237; [1981] Crim LR 326; (1981) 125 SJ 80; [1981] 1 WLR 355 CA Actual dishonesty in accused's mind needed for conspiracy to defraud; guidelines on summings-up.

Lane (L), R v; R v Lane (J) [1985] Crim LR 789 CA On what prosecution must prove in prosecution for manslaughter of child where both parents charged and nothing to prove was one rather than the other.

Lane, Police v [1957] Crim LR 542 Magistrates Harpoon gun a gun for purposes of the Gun Licence Act 1870.

Lang (Christopher Michael), R v (1976) 62 Cr App R 50; [1976] Crim LR 65t; (1975) 125 NLJ 1065t CA Circumstances in which took drink not relevant to issue of consent to later sex.

Lang v Evans (Inspector of Police) [1977] Crim LR 286 CrCt On what constitutes cannabis.

Langham (KR), R v; R v Langham (AD) (1972) 122 NLJ 402 CA Failed appeal against murder convictions on basis that trial judge had slept his way through portion of trial.

Langridge v Hobbs (1900-01) 45 SJ 260; (1900-01) XVII TLR 237; (1901) WN (I) 30 HC KBD Must bring non-vaccination action against parents of infant within twelve months of infant being six-months old.

Lanier (Louis Edouard) v R [1914] AC 221; (1914-15) XXIV Cox CC 53; [1914] 83 LJPC 116; (1914) 110 LTR 326; (1913-14) XXX TLR 53 PC On what constitutes embezzlement under Seychelles Penal Code.

Lankford, R v [1959] Crim LR 209t CCA Person who voluntarily desists from raping woman whom has assaulted may not be guilty of attempted rape.

Large v Mainprize [1989] Crim LR 213 HC QBD Interpretation of 'recklessness' in context of prosecution for breach of the Sea Fishing (Enforcement of Community Control Measures) Order 1985, reg3.

Large, R v [1978] Crim LR 222 CA On direction necessary from judge as to relevance of series of thefts that did not establish guilt of defendant but did explain trap set by police to catch thief.

Large, R v [1939] 1 All ER 753; (1939) 87 LJ 181; (1939) 83 SJ 155; (1938-39) LV TLR 470; (1939) WN (I) 73 CCA Careless act cannot support manslaughter conviction; preferably manslaughter to be indicted alone.

Large, Sargeant v [1954] Crim LR 213t HC QBD Successful prosecution for wrongful withholding/misapplication of club property contrary to Industrial and Provident Societies Act 1893.

Larkins, R v (1911-13) XXII Cox CC 598; (1911) 75 JP 320; (1910-11) XXVII TLR 438 CCA No appeal against pre-trial imposition of detention during His Majesty's pleasure.

Larter and Castleton, R v [1995] Crim LR 75 CA On consent in context of rape.

Lartey (Mensah) and Relevy, R v [1996] 1 Cr App R 143; [1996] Crim LR 203 CA On elements of offence of procuring execution of valuable security by deception.

Last, Hunton v [1965] Crim LR 433; (1965) 109 SJ 391 HC QBD Admission by defendant that were guilty of lighting fire within 50m of highway if lit further away with intention that should enter 50m perimeter.

Latham, R v [1965] Crim LR 434t; (1965) 115 LJ 403; (1965) 109 SJ 371 CCA Jury could legitimately reject defence of diminished responsibility despite contrary medical evidence.

Latif (Khalid), R v; R v Shahzad (Mohammed Khalid) [1995] 1 Cr App R 270; [1994] Crim LR 750; (1994) 138 SJ LB 85; [1994] TLR 154 CA Was punishable fraudulent evasion of prohibition on importation of drugs though happened in course of entrapment; admission of informant's evidence appropriate.

Latif, R v; R v Shahzad [1996] 1 All ER 353; [1996] 2 Cr App R 92; [1996] Crim LR 414; (1996) 146 NLJ 121; (1996) 140 SJ LB 39; (1996) TLR 23/1/96; [1996] 1 WLR 104 HL Prosecution on foot of entrapment an abuse of process where authorities act so unworthily or shamefully it is affront to public conscience for prosecution to proceed.

Laurens (Alfred) alias Lawson (Arthur), R v (1914-15) 11 Cr App R 215 CCA Promotion of company constituted 'purpose' under Larceny Act 1901, s 1(1) (a).

Lavender (Herbert), R v (1927-28) 20 Cr App R 10 CCA That did honest work since last release not defence to charge of being habitual criminal.

Lavender, Director of Public Prosecutions v [1994] Crim LR 297; [1993] TLR 315 HC QBD Was theft to remove doors from one council property and hang them in other property of same council.

Laverty, R v [1970] 3 All ER 432; (1970) 54 Cr App R 495; [1971] Crim LR 100; [1971] RTR 124; (1970) 134 JP 699 CA Prosecution must show that false representation induced purchaser's behaviour.

Lavin v Albert [1981] 3 All ER 878; [1982] AC 546 (also HC QBD); (1982) 74 Cr App R 150; (1982) 146 JP 78; (1981) 125 SJ 860; [1981] 3 WLR 955 HL Can restrain breach of peace (even by detention) though not police officer; mistaken belief that person detaining one as part of restraint of breach of peace not police officer not defence to assault.

Lavin, Albert v [1981] 1 All ER 628; [1982] AC 546 (also HL); (1981) 72 Cr App R 178; [1981] Crim LR 238; (1981) 145 JP 184; (1981) 131 NLJ 368; (1981) 125 SJ 114; [1981] 2 WLR 1070 HC QBD Unreasonable belief acting in self-defence not defence to assault charge.

Law Society v United Services Bureau Limited (1934) 98 JP 33; (1933) 76 LJ 321; (1934) 103 LJCL 81; (1934) 150 LTR 159; (1933) 77 SJ 815; (1933) WN (I) 263 HC KBD Corporate body could not be guilty of wilfully pretending to be solicitor under Solicitors Act 1932, s 46.

Lawrence (James), R v (1909) 2 Cr App R 42 CCA Obtaining by false pretences by means of deceitful promotional pamphlet and postcard.

Lawrence and Pomroy, R v [1972] Crim LR 645 CA On elements of demanding money with menaces.

Lawrence and Stearns, Saqui v (1911) 80 LJCL 451 (also HC KBD) CA Porter who admitted burglars to house and was later given share of spoils a principal in second degree/guilty of theft.

Lawrence and Stearns, Saqui v (1911) 80 LJCL 451 (also CA) HC KBD Porter who admitted burglars to house and was later given share of spoils an accessory before the fact.

Lee (Robert Paul), R v [1996] 2 Cr App R 266; (1996) 140 SJ LB 38; [1995] TLR 715 CA Child's video-link evidence to court was valid as defendant charged with arson (being reckless as to threat to life) had threatened the child.

Lee v Dalton and Stevens [1954] Crim LR 206 HC QBD Persons who allowed poultry to wander freely by day over unfenced/uncultivated land entitled to protection of Dogs (Protection of Livestock) Act 1953.

Lee v Governor of Pentonville Prison and the Government of the United Sattes of America [1987] Crim LR 635 HC QBD Unauthenticated copy of authenticated copy of warrant inadmissible in evidence.

Lee, Batty v (1939-40) XXXI Cox CC 161; (1938) 102 JP 485; (1938) 82 SJ 871 HC KBD Prosecution ought to have been heard in action for leaving wife and child so were chargeable to public assistance committee (despite existence of maintenance order against husband being possible defence to charge).

Lee, Davey and others v [1967] 2 All ER 423; (1967) 51 Cr App R 303; [1967] Crim LR 357; (1967) 131 JP 327; [1968] 1 QB 366; (1967) 111 SJ 212; [1967] 3 WLR 105 HC QBD On what constitutes attempt.

Lee, R v [1965] Crim LR 554; (1965) 115 LJ 450 CrCt Evidence tending to show fire fixation prejudicial but admissible at prosecution for setting fire to house.

Leech, Caldwell v [1911-13] All ER 703; (1913-14) XXIII Cox CC 510; (1913) 77 JP 254; (1913-14) 109 LTR 188; (1912-13) XXIX TLR 457 HC KBD That have one prostitute in one's house cannot sustain conviction for keeping/managing brothel.

Leeke, Cooper v (1968) 112 SJ 46 HC QBD Failed appeal against conviction for possession of various instruments with intent to commit felonious act (Vagrancy Act 1824, s 4).

Leeson (Maurice), R v (1968) 52 Cr App R 185; [1968] Crim LR 283; (1968) 112 SJ 151 CA Non-indecent physical assault in tandem with suggestion of sexual intimacy was indecent assault.

Leicester and Co v Cherryman (1907) 71 JP 301; [1907] 76 LJKB 678; (1907) XCVI LTR 784; (1907) WN (I) 95 HC KBD Owners of goods could bring action in detinue against pawnbroker for stolen goods pawned with him despite court order for restitution of goods upon payment to him of amounts he advanced for the goods.

Leicester Justices, Workman v [1964] Crim LR 39 39 HC QBD Justices had no jurisdiction to hear dangerous dog-owner complaint against person who came into possession of dog post-summons/pre-hearing.

Leicester Justices; ex parte Workman, R v [1964] Crim LR 455t; (1964) 108 SJ 358; [1964] 1 WLR 707 HC QBD Person against whom dangerous dog order to be made is owner at date of proceedings.

Leighton, Davies v (1979) 68 Cr App R 4; [1978] Crim LR 575; (1978) 128 NLJ 913t; (1978) 122 SJ 641 HC QBD Property in supermarket goods did not pass to customer until had paid for same.

Lemm v Mitchell (1912) 81 LJPC 173; (1911-12) XXVIII TLR 282 PC Second action for criminal conversation was res judicata: plea that earlier judgment obviated by later legislation could only be proved on clearest of evidence that that was intended effect.

Lemon, R v; R v Gay News Ltd [1979] 1 All ER 898; [1979] Crim LR 311; (1979) 143 JP 315; (1979) 129 (1) NLJ 218 HL Intention to publish blasphemy/not intention to blaspheme is mens rea for blasphemous libel.

Lemon, R v; R v Gay News Ltd [1978] 3 All ER 175; (1978) 67 Cr App R 70; (1978) 142 JP 558; (1978) 128 NLJ 488t; [1979] QB 10; (1978) 122 SJ 295; [1978] 3 WLR 404 CA Blasphemy if insult/offend/vilify Christ/ianity even if do not intend same.

Lesbini, R v (1914-15) XXIV Cox CC 516; (1914-15) 11 Cr App R 7; [1914] 3 KB 1116; [1915] 84 LJKB 1102; (1915) 112 LTR 175; (1914) WN (I) 362 CCA Test for provocation is would reasonable man lose self-control (individual charcteristics of accused irrelevant).

Less v Parr [1967] Crim LR 481t HC QBD 'Bastard' not an indecent word; person not guilty of using indecent language in street where could not be heard in hearing of street.

Lester (John Edward), R v; R v Byast (Trevor Humphrey) (1955) 39 Cr App R 157; [1955] Crim LR 648 CCA Conviction for possession of housebreaking implements at night for driver who had same on person and in car boot affirmed; conviction of passenger for same - where had no implements on person - quashed.

Letenock (Alexei), R v (1916-17) 12 Cr App R 221 CCA On aggravation of provocation through drunkenness.

Lethbridge, Lewis v [1987] Crim LR 59 HC QBD Non-payment contributions received for charity was not theft.

Levene v Pearcey [1976] Crim LR 63 HC QBD Conviction of taxi-driver for deliberately misleading passenger into thinking that had to take longer journey because normal route obstructed.

Levinson v Rees (1918-21) XXVI Cox CC 384 HC KBD Failed prosecution against pawnbroker for charging a profit.

Levinson, Barker v [1951] 1 KB 342 HC KBD Landlord not liable for unlawful charging of rental premium by rent collector.

Levitz, R v; R v Mbele; R v Vowell [1989] Crim LR 714; (1989) 133 SJ 818 CA On appropriate charge of conspiracy to defraud where persons charged improperly sought to use devices to render telephone calls to them cost-free.

Levy (Beatrice), R v [1911-13] All ER 222; (1911-13) XXII Cox CC 702; (1911-12) 7 Cr App R 61; (1912) 76 JP 123; [1912] 1 KB 158; (1911) 46 LJ 753; [1912] 81 LJKB 264; (1912) 106 LTR 192; (1911-12) 56 SJ 143; (1911-12) XXVIII TLR 93; (1911) WN (I) 239 CCA On what constitutes being an accessory after the fact.

Levy and Sobell, R v [1973] Crim LR 453 CA Roughly three weeks' imprisonment for solicitor guilty of aiding undischarged bankrupt in management of company; five years' imprisonment merited by estate agent guilty of theft of deposits of clients.

Lewis (Albert Roy), R v (1969) 133 JP 111; [1969] 2 QB 1; (1968) 112 SJ 904; [1969] 2 WLR 55 CA Scope and effect of Criminal Justice Act 1967, s 11 (alibi evidence) considered.

Lewis (Annie), R v (1910) 4 Cr App R 96 CCA Must be element of possession on accused's part to be convicted as receiver.

Lewis (Gareth Edmund), R v (1988) 87 Cr App R 270; [1988] Crim LR 517 CA Intention to possess/that knew possessed dangerous substance could sustain conviction for possession of drugs: need not show that actually knew had control of drugs.

Lewis (Joseph George), R v (1976) 62 Cr App R 206; [1976] Crim LR 383t CA Gauging dishonesty for purposes of Theft Act 1968 a subjective test.

Lewis and another v Chief Constable of the South Wales Constabulary [1991] 1 All ER 206 CA Arrest unlawful for non-advice of basis is lawful once arrestee advised of basis of arrest.

Lewis and anr v Chief Constable of Greater Manchester (1991) 141 NLJ 1486i CA May arrest for breach of peace on anticipatory basis.

Lewis v Cattle [1938] 2 All ER 368; (1939-40) XXXI Cox CC 123; (1938) 102 JP 239; [1938] 2 KB 454; [1938] 107 LJCL 429; (1938) 82 SJ 376; (1937-38) LIV TLR 721; (1938) WN (I) 169 HC KBD Police officer a 'person holding office under His Majesty' within meaning of Official Secrets Act 1911, s 2.

Lewis v Cox (1985) 80 Cr App R 1; [1984] Crim LR 756; (1984) 148 JP 601; [1985] QB 509; (1984) 128 SJ 596; [1984] TLR 441; [1984] 3 WLR 875 HC QBD Was wilful obstruction of police officer where repeatedly opened rear door of police vehicle to ask arrested friend where was being taken.

Lewis v Lethbridge [1987] Crim LR 59 HC QBD Non-payment contributions received for charity was not theft.

Lewis, R v [1973] Crim LR 576t CA Conviction quashed in light of criticism by judge of accused's purported alibi.

Lewis, R v [1970] Crim LR 647 CA Were guilty of maliciously inflicting grievous bodily harm where caused person to leap in terror from window on foot of threats shouted to them from another room.

Lewisham Guardians, Nice v (1921-25) XXVII Cox CC 606; [1924] 1 KB 618; (1924) 59 LJ 76; [1924] 93 LJCL 469; (1924) 131 LTR 22; (1923-24) XL TLR 270 HC KBD Not failure to maintain family where refused to work for less than union rates.

Leyton Urban District Council v Wilkinson (1927) 91 JP 64; [1927] 1 KB 315; (1925-26) 70 SJ 1069; (1926-27) XLIII TLR 35; (1926) WN (I) 274 HC KBD Inadequacy of recognisance entered into personally by clerk of local authority.

Leyton Urban District Council v Wilkinson (1927) 137 LTR 10; (1927) 71 SJ 293; (1926-27) XLIII TLR 326 CA Inadequacy of recognisance entered into personally by clerk of local authority.

Liangsiriprasert v United States Government and another [1990] 2 All ER 866; [1991] 1 AC 225; (1991) 92 Cr App R 77; (1990) 134 SJ 1123; [1990] TLR 507; [1990] 3 WLR 606 PC Enticement into jurisdiction from where extradition possible not abuse of extradition process. Inchoate crimes - here conspiracy - entered into abroad/in Thailand to commit offence in England/Hong Kong triable in England/Hong Kong.

Liddle (Stanley), R v (1928-29) 21 Cr App R 3 CCA On defence of alibi.

Liepins v Spearman [1985] Crim LR 229; [1986] RTR 24 HC QBD Passenger in/owner of car whose driver was found to be over limit did not have to be, but here was obstructing police in execution of their duty where sought to prevent car being removed to police station.

Light (Arthur Dennison), R v [1914-15] All ER 659; (1914-15) XXIV Cox CC 718; (1914-15) 11 Cr App R 111; [1915] 84 LJKB 865; (1915) 112 LTR 1144; (1914-15) 59 SJ 351; (1914-15) XXXI TLR 257; (1915) WN (I) 97 CCA Can be convicted of attempted obtaining of money by false pretences though victim knew pretences were false.

Lightfoot (Richard James), R v (1993) 97 Cr App R 24; [1993] Crim LR 137; (1993) 157 JP 265 CA Was dishonest intent to do what reasonable people would regard as dishonest.

Lincoln (John Abraham), R v [1944] 1 All ER 604 CCA Defence not heard on offence for which convicted so conviction quashed; everything in indictment for which there is evidence must go to jury (though judge can state views).

Lincoln, R v [1980] Crim LR 575 CA On degree of awareness (that goods stolen) necessary to support handling conviction.

Lindley v Rutter (1981) 72 Cr App R 1; [1980] Crim LR 729; (1980) 130 NLJ 906; [1981] QB 128; (1980) 124 SJ 792; [1980] 3 WLR 660 HC QBD Woman police officer forcibly removing woman detainee's brassiere not acting in course of duty so assault on same not assault on officer in execution of duty.

Lindley, R v [1957] Crim LR 321 Assizes On intent necessary for offence of bribery (here - allegedly - of company servants).

Lindop, Thomas v (1950) 94 SJ 371; (1950) WN (I) 227 HC KBD On what it means to aid and abet an offence.

Linekar, R v [1995] 3 All ER 69; [1995] 2 Cr App R 49; [1995] Crim LR 320; [1995] QB 250; (1994) 138 SJ LB 227; [1994] TLR 528; [1995] 2 WLR 237 CA Consent to sexual intercourse by prostitute not vitiated by non-payment and so no rape.

Lines, R v (1901-07) XX Cox CC 142; [1902] 1 KB 199; [1902] 71 LJCL 125; (1901-02) LXXXV LTR 790; (1901-02) 46 SJ 138; (1901-02) XVIII TLR 176; (1901) WN (I) 251; (1901-02) 50 WR 303 CCR Could not be indicted for misdemeanour of night-poaching unless were twice previously charged with night-poaching by self.

Linneker, R v [1904-07] All ER 797; (1907-09) XXI Cox CC 196; (1906) 70 JP 293; [1906] 2 KB 99; [1906] 75 LJKB 385; (1906) XCIV LTR 856; (1905-06) 50 SJ 440; (1905-06) XXII TLR 495; (1905-06) 54 WR 494 CCR More than intent and possession necessary to establish attempt to discharge revolver.

Linzee (Robert Alexander Craig), R v; R v O'Driscoll (Gerald) (1956) 40 Cr App R 177; (1957) 107 LJ 57 CMAC Was legitimate to look for corroboration of evidence of witness who possibly took part in crime of which accused charged.

Lipman, R v [1969] 3 All ER 410; (1969) 53 Cr App R 600; [1969] Crim LR 546t; (1969) 133 JP 712; (1969) 119 NLJ 768t; [1970] 1 QB 152; (1969) 113 SJ 670; [1969] 3 WLR 819 CA Once act unlawful no intent needed to support manslaughter where death; self-induced drunkeness no defence.

Lisle, Davis v (1934-39) XXX Cox CC 412; (1936) 100 JP 280; [1936] 2 KB 434; [1936] 105 LJCL 593; (1936) 155 LTR 23; (1936) 80 SJ 409; (1935-36) LII TLR 475 HC KBD Not guilty of assault/obstruction of police in course of duty as had at material time requested police to leave property so police were trespassers.

Little and Dunning, ex parte Wise, R v (1910) 74 JP 7; (1909-10) 101 LTR 859; (1909-10) XXVI TLR 8 HC KBD Magistrate justified in circumstances in requiring person to enter recognisance to keep the peace though police no longer objected to person's leading proposed procession through streets.

Little, Bastable v [1904-07] All ER 1147; (1907-09) XXI Cox CC 354; (1907) 71 JP 52; [1907] 1 KB 59; (1906) 41 LJ 736; [1907] 76 LJKB 77; (1907) XCVI LTR 115; (1906-07) 51 SJ 49; (1906-07) XXIII TLR 38; (1906) WN (I) 196 HC KBD Person warning drivers of upcoming police speed trap not obstructing police in execution of duty.

Littleford, R v [1978] Crim LR 48 CrCt On what may ground reasonable suspicion that are in possession of drugs in car.

Liverpool City Justices; ex parte Santos, R v [1997] TLR 38 HC QBD Depends on individual case whether failure to surrender to bail can be excused where was due to mistake on part of defendant's solicitor.

Liverpool City Magistrates' Court, ex parte Director of Public Prosecutions, R v [1992] 3 All ER 249; (1992) 95 Cr App R 222; [1992] Crim LR 294; (1992) 156 JP 634; (1991) 141 NLJ 1740t; [1993] QB 233; [1991] TLR 566; [1992] 3 WLR 20 HC QBD Single justice may decide if bail conditions to be altered but may not adjourn proceedings.

Liverpool Corporation, Kaufmann Brothers v (1916) 80 JP 223; [1916] 85 LJKB 1127; (1916) 114 LTR 699; (1915-16) 60 SJ 446; (1915-16) XXXII TLR 402; (1916) WN (I) 155 HC KBD Public authority limitation did not apply in respect of action against same for compensation for riot damage.

Liyanage and others v R [1966] 1 All ER 650 PC Retroactive legislation aimed at those involved in coup d'état void.

Llewellyn-Jones, R v [1967] 3 All ER 225; (1967) 51 Cr App R 204; [1967] Crim LR 293; [1968] 1 QB 429; [1967] 3 WLR 1298 CA Dishonest intent inferred from particulars stated.

Lloyd and others, R v [1985] 2 All ER 661; (1985) 81 Cr App R 182; [1985] Crim LR 518; (1985) 149 JP 634; (1985) 135 NLJ 605; [1985] QB 829; (1985) 129 SJ 431; [1985] 3 WLR 30 CA No intention of permanently depriving where borrow/lend unless return in worthless state; statutory not common law conspiracy where full offence would be substantive.

Lloyd v Director of Public Prosecutions [1992] 1 All ER 982; [1991] Crim LR 904; (1992) 156 JP 342; [1992] RTR 215; [1991] TLR 315 HC QBD Availability of civil remedies of no interest in criminal case save for deciding if that availability a defence to criminal charge.

Lloyd, Jones and Jones v [1981] Crim LR 340 CA Police invited into house by guest of householder not trespassing so assault on them an assault on police in execution of their duty.

Lloyd, R v [1992] Crim LR 361 CA On extent of possession that must be proved to support conviction for burglary/handling.

Lloyd, R v [1966] 1 All ER 107; (1966) 50 Cr App R 61; [1966] Crim LR 106; (1966) 130 JP 118; (1965-66) 116 NLJ 360; [1967] 1 QB 175; (1965) 109 SJ 955; [1966] 2 WLR 13 CA On diminished responsibility.

Loat v Andrews (1970) 130 SJ 697 HC QBD Civilian working under police officer though employed by county council did come under the provisions of the Official Secrets Acts 1911 and 1920, ss 2 and 7 respectively.

Loat v James [1986] Crim LR 744; (1986) 150 JP 652 HC QBD Civilian working under police officer though employed by county council did come under the provisions of the Official Secrets Acts 1911 and 1920, ss 2 and 7 respectively.

Long, Farmer v (1908) 72 JP 91 HC KBD Leaking drain a nuisance under Public Health (London) Act 1891, s 4.

Long, Weight v [1986] Crim LR 746 HC QBD Police officer seeking to speak to another in connection with crime/breach of the peace was acting in course of duty.

Longman (John Barry), R v (1989) 88 Cr App R 148; [1988] Crim LR 534; [1988] 1 WLR 619 CA Entry and search under warrant may involve use of force/subterfuge; to 'produce' a warrant card (Police and Criminal Evidence Act 1984, s 16) means to make it available for occupier's inspection.

Lonrho Ltd and another v Shell Petroleum Co Ltd and another (1981) 125 SJ 255 CA Conspiracy to do unlawful act not actionable where (as here) was no intent to injure plaintiff.

Lord (John), R v (1905) 69 JP 467 CCR Valid conviction for fraudulent conversion of property to own use where property at issue was employer's money.

Lord and another, Jipps v [1982] TLR 277 CA On determining whether mechanically propelled boat used in pursuit of wild bird for purpose of killing same.

Lord Mayor of Cardiff; ex parte Lewis, R v (1921-25) XXVII Cox CC 327; (1922) 86 JP 207; [1922] 2 KB 777; [1923] 92 LJCL 28; (1923) 128 LTR 63; (1922) WN (I) 269 HC KBD Court can compel production of documents in extradition cases.

Loughlin (James), R v (1951-52) 35 Cr App R 69; (1951) 95 SJ 516 CCA Can be convicted of breaking and entering where discovered in possession of stolen property shortly after robbery of premises.

Loughlin, R v [1959] Crim LR 518t CCA On necessary intent for attempted murder.

Love, R v [1955] Crim LR 250t CCA Obscene publication conviction quashed where issue whether sole director of publishing company knew of obscene content of books not left to jury.

Lovelace v Director of Public Prosecutions [1954] Crim LR 944t HC QBD Successful appeal by theatre licensee against conviction for 'causing' play to be presented with unauthorised additions contrary to Theatres Act 1843, s 15.

Lovesey, R v; R v Peterson [1969] 2 All ER 1077; (1969) 53 Cr App R 461; [1969] Crim LR 374t; (1969) 133 JP 571; (1969) 119 NLJ 485t; [1970] 1 QB 352; (1969) 113 SJ 445; [1969] 3 WLR 213 CA Joint offence and substantive offence separate offences; could not be convicted of murder if common design to rob did not include intent to kill/cause grievous bodily harm.

Lovick (Sylvia), R v [1993] Crim LR 890 CA Could be no conspiracy between only husband and wife.

Low v Blease [1975] Crim LR 513; (1975) 119 SJ 695 HC QBD Trespasser who made telephone call not guilty of stealing property (electricity).

Lowden, R v (1913-14) XXIII Cox CC 643; (1914) 78 JP 111; [1914] 1 KB 144; (1913) 48 LJ 689; [1914] 83 LJKB 114; (1913-14) 109 LTR 832; (1913-14) 58 SJ 157; (1913-14) XXX TLR 70; (1913) WN (I) 318 CCA Forged cancelled stamps were 'stamps' for purposes of Stamp Duties Management Act 1891, s 13.

Lowe, R v; R v Lowe (JD) [1973] 1 All ER 805; (1973) 57 Cr App R 365; [1973] Crim LR 238; (1973) 137 JP 334; (1973) 123 NLJ 107t; [1973] QB 702; (1973) 117 SJ 144; [1973] 2 WLR 481; [1986] Crim LR 49 CrCt Arrest unlawful where person not told why arrested and arresting officers considered accused to have been arrested for different offences.

Lucas, Harris v (1919) 83 JP 208; [1919] 88 LJCL 1082; (1918-19) XXXV TLR 486; (1919) WN (I) 147 HC KBD On deciding whether birds 'recently taken' for purposes of Wild Birds Protection Act 1880, s 1.

Lucraft (Anthony Thomas), R v (1966) 50 Cr App R 296; [1966] Crim LR 678t; (1966) 110 SJ 759 CCA Right to non-disclosure on charge of misprision of felony did not arise as was no evidence that prisoner accessory after fact to robbery at issue.

Ludlow and others v Burgess (1982) 75 Cr App R 227; [1971] Crim LR 238 HC QBD Not assault on constable in execution of duty where person unlawfully detained by constable assaults same.

Lumley, R v (1911-13) XXII Cox CC 635; (1912) 76 JP 208 CCC Abortionist guilty of murder/manslaughter if did/did not (nor could not reasonably) consider that death or grievous bodily harm would result from actions.

Lumsden, R v [1951] 1 All ER 1101; (1951-52) 35 Cr App R 57; (1951) 115 JP 364; [1951] 2 KB 513; (1951) 101 LJ 275; (1951) 95 SJ 355; [1951] 1 TLR 987; (1951) WN (I) 257 CCA To be 'found...in' building with intent to steal contrary to Larceny Act 1916, s 28(4) must be firm evidence were actually in building.

Lunderbech, R v [1991] Crim LR 784 CA Police officers constitute members of public for purposes of witnessing acts outraging public decency; jury may infer from evidence that act likely to disgust/annoy though is no proof that anyone was disgusted/annoyed.

Lunnon (Keith), R v (1989) 88 Cr App R 71; [1988] Crim LR 456 CA Guilty plea properly admitted to show were party to conspiracy.

Lunt and another, Walters v [1951] 2 All ER 645; (1951-52) 35 Cr App R 94; (1951) 115 JP 512; (1951) 101 LJ 482; (1951) 95 SJ 625; (1951) WN (I) 472 HC KBD Child under eight cannot commit larceny so person acquiring 'stolen' items therefrom not receiving stolen property.

Lunt v Director of Public Prosecutions [1993] Crim LR 534 HC QBD Failure to admit police with right of entry could be obstruction of police.

Lurie, R v [1951] 2 All ER 704; (1951-52) 35 Cr App R 113; (1951) 115 JP 551; (1951) 101 LJ 511; (1951) 95 SJ 580; [1951] 2 TLR 686 CCA Not obtaining where possess property but are obtaining for another.

Lusty, R v [1964] 1 All ER 960; [1964] Crim LR 396; (1964) 128 JP 334; (1964) 108 SJ 465; [1964] 1 WLR 606 CCA Prosecution must prove fraud under Bankruptcy Act 1914, s 154(5).

Luton Justices; ex parte Crown Prosecution Service, Pul v (1989) 153 JP 512 HC QBD Justices coud rely on local knowledge of area in determining whether kerb crawling likely to cause nuisance in that area.

Lyle (William Stacey), R v (1924-25) 18 Cr App R 59 CCA Fraudulent conversion commenced abroad and completed in UK can be prosecuted for in UK.

Lyle, Fitzgerald v [1972] Crim LR 125; (1970) 114 SJ 929 HC QBD On who (as here) constitutes a suspected person who may be validly arrested for/charged with loitering with intent.

Lynch, Director of Public Prosecutions for Northern Ireland v [1975] 1 All ER 913; [1975] AC 653; (1975) 61 Cr App R 6; [1975] Crim LR 707; (1975) 139 JP 312; (1975) 125 NLJ 362t; (1975) 119 SJ 233; [1975] 2 WLR 641 HL Principal in second degree in murder case can plead duress.

Lynch, R v [1993] Crim LR 868 CA Bona fide distress is capable of corroborating evidence of complainant; allowing presence of 'Victim Support' representative in witness box/erection of screen to shield witness were valid exercises of judge's discretion.

Lynch, R v [1900-03] All ER 688; (1901-07) XX Cox CC 468; (1903) 67 JP 41; [1903] 1 KB 444; (1903) 38 LJ 61; [1903] 72 LJKB 167; (1903) LXXXVIII LTR 26; (1902-03) XIX TLR 163; (1902-03) 51 WR 619 HC KBD Treason possible inside/outside Britain; cannot in time of war escape liability for treason by naturalisation as enemy national.

Lynsey, R v [1995] 3 All ER 654; [1995] 2 Cr App R 667; (1995) 159 JP 437 CA The term 'common assault' is to be construed in its everyday sense and its technical sense.

Lyon, R v [1959] Crim LR 54 CCC Director of private company acquitted of fraudulent conversion of company property.

Lyons v Owen [1963] Crim LR 123; (1962) 106 SJ 939 HC QBD Failed appeal against decision of justices that person keeping bank under surveillance not guilty of loitering with intent to commit felony.

M and another v Oxford [1981] RTR 246 HC QBD Test of guilt on criminal damage to property charge is subjective.

M Bulteel and Colmore v The Trustee in Bankruptcy of MP Parker and FT Bulteel (1915-16) XXXII TLR 661 HC ChD Charge deemed not to be fraudulent preference of trustees of marriage settlement over other creditors of bankrupt bank; on burden of establishing fraudulent preference under Bankruptcy Act 1914.

M Potter Ltd v Customs and Excise Commissioners [1973] Crim LR 116 CA Gravity knife (a lock knife) was an offensive weapon.

M v Metropolitan Police Commissioner [1979] Crim LR 53; (1978) 128 NLJ 759t CA On police retention until trial of money seized by police pursuant to search warrant.

M, R v (1914-15) 11 Cr App R 207; (1915-16) XXXII TLR 1 CCA Regardless whether information true or not, if communicate with enemy to assist same are guilty of breach of Defence of the Realm (Consolidation) Regulations 1914, r18 and r48.

Mabbott, R v [1987] Crim LR 826 CA On what constitutes boarding-house/house in multiple occupation (here for purposes of fire legislation prosecution).

MacDonald (otherwise Murphy James), R v (1908) 1 Cr App R 262 CCA That CCA refused leave to appeal did not preclude Crown exercising prerogative of mercy.

MacDonald (Michael), R v (1928-29) 21 Cr App R 26 CCA Bail granted by CCA.

MacDonald (Michael), R v (1928-29) 21 Cr App R 33 CCA Grave doubt whether accused's admission could corroborate accomplice's evidence.

Mace, Chief Constable of Hampshire v (1987) 84 Cr App R 40; [1986] Crim LR 752; (1986) 150 JP 470 HC QBD Can be charged with attempt to procure act of gross indecency.

Macer, R v [1979] Crim LR 659 CMAC Was not forgery where signed cheque in different style to usual but nonetheless signed with correct (own) name.

Macfarlane v Gwalter [1958] 1 All ER 181; (1958) 122 JP 144; [1959] 2 QB 332; (1958) 102 SJ 123 CA Dangerous lighting grating a public nuisance for which occupier of adjoining building liable under Public Health Acts Amendment Act 1890, s 35(1).

MacHardy, R v (1911-13) XXII Cox CC 614; (1911-12) XXVIII TLR 2 CCA Can under Criminal Appeal Act 1907, s 3, appeal against conviction of being guilty but insane.

Machent v Quinn [1970] 2 All ER 255; [1970] Crim LR 414t; (1970) 134 JP 501; (1970) 120 NLJ 434t; (1970) 114 SJ 336 HC QBD Prosecution need not show all items in information stolen by accused but can only be sentenced for those proved.

Machin, R v [1980] 3 All ER 151; (1980) 71 Cr App R 166; [1980] Crim LR 376/585; (1981) 145 JP 21; (1980) 130 NLJ 473; [1980] RTR 233; (1980) 124 SJ 359; [1980] 1 WLR 763 CA Attempting to pervert course of justice covers acts intended to and in fact perverting course of justice.

Mack (John), R v (1908) 1 Cr App R 132 CCA Generally no re-trial where pleaded alibi but did not enter witness-box; Chairman's clear intimation at trial that accused had previously been convicted not sufficient to justify overturning conviction.

Mackenzie (Elizabeth Smith), R v; R v Higginson (George) (1910-11) 6 Cr App R 64; (1911) 75 JP 159; (1910-11) XXVII TLR 152 CCA On offence of procuring girl for unlawful carnal connection; on conviction of party having sex for aiding and abetting in unlawful carnal connection.

Mackie (Robert), R v (1973) 57 Cr App R 453; [1973] Crim LR 438 CA Liability for injuries/for death suffered in course of escape from assault; liability for same in respect of child to whom are in loco parentis; admission of evidence though prejudicial effect outweighed its probative value.

Mackie (Robert), R v [1973] Crim LR 54 CrCt Liability for injuries/for death suffered in course of escape from assault by child to whom assailant was in loco parentis.

Mackinnon and others, R v [1958] 3 All ER 657; (1959) 43 Cr App R 1; [1958] Crim LR 809; (1959) 123 JP 43; (1959) 109 LJ 8; [1959] 1 QB 150; (1958) 102 SJ 861 CCC For statement/forecast to be reckless must not matter to maker whether true/false.

Macklen, Evans v [1976] Crim LR 120 HC QBD Person in respect of whom warrant for arrest for sentencing purposes had been issued could be arrested by police officer without warrant.

MacRae, Powell v [1977] Crim LR 571 HC QBD Bribe accepted by employee did not belong to employers so employee not guilty of theft of bribe.

Macrae, R v [1994] Crim LR 363; (1995) 159 JP 359 CA Need not intend to cause another economic loss to be guilty of forging a licence.

Madden, R v [1975] 3 All ER 155; (1975) 61 Cr App R 254; [1975] Crim LR 582t; (1975) 139 JP 685; (1975) 125 NLJ 772t; (1975) 119 SJ 657; [1975] 1 WLR 1379 CA Hoax bomb call affecting significant numbers of the public a public nuisance.

MAFF, Lawrence v [1992] Crim LR 874 HC QBD Offence of making false statement is complete when intended recipient receives it.

Maginnis, R v [1987] 1 All ER 907; [1987] AC 303; (1987) 85 Cr App R 127; [1987] Crim LR 564; (1987) 151 JP 537; (1987) 137 NLJ 244; (1987) 131 SJ 357; [1987] 2 WLR 765 HL Person temporarily holding drugs for other may be guilty of possession with intent to supply.

Maginnis, R v [1986] 2 All ER 110; (1986) 82 Cr App R 351; [1986] Crim LR 237; [1986] QB 618; (1986) 130 SJ 128; [1986] 2 WLR 767 CA Bailment relationship did not mean bailee supplying drugs when returning them to bailor.

Mahadeo v R [1936] 2 All ER 813; (1936) 80 SJ 551; (1936) WN (I) 203 PC Absent malice unintended killing was manslaughter; evidence of accomplice needed corroboration; counsel for accessory could argue that no crime committed though accused pleaded guilty to charge.

Mahmood (Asaf), R v [1994] Crim LR 368; [1995] RTR 48 CA Passenger jointly taking car without authority not guilty of joint enterprise when leaped along with driver from moving car which drove into pram killing child therein.

Mahoney, Pittard v [1977] Crim LR 169 HC QBD Failed attempt to plead reasonable excuse (fear of attack) as defence to possession of offensive weapon.

Mahroof (Abdul), R v (1989) 88 Cr App R 317; [1989] Crim LR 72 CA Could convict one person of violent disorder so long as involved two other persons (but procedural irregularity led to substitution of conviction for using threatening, abusive or insulting words).

Maidstone County Court; ex parte Lever, R v [1994] TLR 559 CA Forfeiture of substantial portion of recognisance merited where bailed individual absconded before trial.

Maidstone Crown Court; ex parte Clark, R v; R v Governor of Elmley Prison; ex parte Clark (1995) 139 SJ LB 32 HC QBD Arraignment arrangements challengeable by way of habeas corpus application.

Maidstone Crown Court; ex parte Jodka, R v [1997] TLR 311 HC QBD Bail ended upon surrender.

Maile v McDowell [1980] Crim LR 586 CA On what constitutes a breach of the peace (here in football crowd context).

Mailey, R v [1957] Crim LR 328 Assizes Failed prosecution for perjury against farmer for making false claim whenn claiming subsidy under the Hill Framing and Livestock Rearing Acts 1946 to 1954.

Mainprize, Large v [1989] Crim LR 213 HC QBD Interpretation of 'recklessness' in context of prosecution for breach of the Sea Fishing (Enforcement of Community Control Measures) Order 1985, reg3.

Mainwaring (Paul Rex Garfield), R v; R v Madders (Peter Clive) (1982) 74 Cr App R 99 CA Issue for jury where was unlawful business by company not whether intra/ultra vires memorandum of association but whether honest/dishonest behaviour; misappropriation of money: Theft Act 1968, s 5(3) applied; warning necessary where two company directors prosecuted incriminated each other/exculpated self.

Majara (Nkau) v R [1954] Crim LR 464; [1954] 2 WLR 771 PC On what constitutes being accessory after the fact in South Africa; headman's shortcomings in apprehension of ritual murderers which gave them chance to escape made him accessory after the fact to murder.

Majewski, Director of Public Prosecutions v [1976] 2 All ER 142; [1977] AC 443 (also CA); (1976) 62 Cr App R 262; [1976] Crim LR 374; (1976) 140 JP 315; (1976) 126 NLJ 542t; (1976) 120 SJ 299; [1976] 2 WLR 623 HL Self-induced intoxication no defence unless specific intent required.

Majewski, R v [1975] 3 All ER 296; [1977] AC 443 (also HL); (1976) 62 Cr App R 5; [1975] Crim LR 570; (1975) 139 JP 760; (1975) 125 NLJ 698t; (1975) 119 SJ 560; [1975] 3 WLR 401 CA Self-induced intoxication not defence unless crime of specific intent/so drunk are temporarily insane.

Malcherek, R v; R v Steel [1981] 2 All ER 422; (1981) 73 Cr App R 173; [1981] Crim LR 401; (1981) 145 JP 329; (1981) 125 SJ 305; [1981] 1 WLR 690 CA Disconnection of life support machine does not break causation between inflicting of injury and death.

Males, R v [1961] 3 All ER 705; (1962) 46 Cr App R 35; [1962] Crim LR 46; (1961) 125 JP 647; [1962] 2 QB 500; (1961) 105 SJ 891 CCA Can be guilty of attempt though substantive offence committed.

Mallett, R v [1978] 3 All ER 10; (1978) 67 Cr App R 239; (1978) 142 JP 528; (1978) 128 NLJ 535t; (1978) 122 SJ 295; [1978] 1 WLR 820 CA Accounting document false in material particular though false element unconcerned with accounting.

Mallison (William), R v (1901-07) XX Cox CC 204; (1902) LXXXVI LTR 600 CCR Was larceny from smack-owner for skipper of smack to sell fish caught at sea and take proceeds for self.

Malnik v Director of Public Prosecutions [1989] Crim LR 451 HC QBD Defence of reasonable excuse unavailable to appellant convicted of possession of offensive weapon.

Maltman (Peter), R v [1995] 1 Cr App R 239; [1995] Crim LR 144; [1994] TLR 352 CA Chromolin was a 'thing...for the purpose of making a counterfeit' (Forgery and Counterfeiting Act 1981, s 17(1)).

Man-Sin (Chan) v R [1988] 1 All ER 1; (1988) 86 Cr App R 303; [1988] Crim LR 319; (1988) 132 SJ 126; [1988] 1 WLR 196 PC Drawing/presenting/negotiating forged company cheques for self was dishonest appropriation.

Manchester and Liverpool District Banking Company Limited, Walker and another v (1913) 108 LTR 728; (1912-13) 57 SJ 478 HC KBD Customer could recover amounts bank paid out on foot of forged cheques though customer had not checked pass-book when from time to time was returned to him.

Manchester Crown Court, ex parte Hill, R v [1984] TLR 601 HC QBD Justices cannot convict person of attempted offence where are charged with complete offence.

Mancini v Director of Public Prosecutions [1941] 3 All ER 272; [1942] AC 1; (1940-42) 28 Cr App R 65; (1941) 91 LJ 406; (1942) 92 LJ 52; [1942] 111 LJ 84; (1941) 165 LTR 353; (1941-42) LVIII TLR 25; (1941) WN (I) 212 HL Judge must refer to apparent provocation (if any) even if not argued; direction on manslaughter in murder cases only if manslaughter verdict a real possibility; no ideal summing-up; reasonable doubt as to provocation must reduce verdict from murder to manslaughter.

Mandair, R v [1994] 2 All ER 715; [1995] 1 AC 208; (1994) 99 Cr App R 250; [1994] Crim LR 666; (1994) 158 JP 685; (1994) 144 NLJ 708; (1994) 138 SJ LB 123; [1994] 2 WLR 700 HL Offence of 'causing' -not 'inflicting' - grievous bodily harm is known to law. House of Lords assumes full jurisdiction of Court of Appeal upon appeal therefrom. Restoration of conviction by House of Lords can only be set aside by Court of Appeal in reference from Home Secretary.

Mandair, R v [1993] Crim LR 679 CA On difference between wounding and causing grievous bodily harm (under the Offences against the Person Act 1861, ss 18 and 20).

Manheimer, Scottish Dyers and Cleaners (London), Ltd v (1942) WN (I) 114 HC KBD Bailed goods stolen from bailees deemed not to be 'detained'.

Manjadria and another, R v [1993] Crim LR 73 CA On proving execution of valuable security in context of mortgage fraud.

Manley, R v [1932] All ER 565; (1931-34) XXIX Cox CC 574; (1932-34) 24 Cr App R 25; (1933) 97 JP 6; [1933] 1 KB 529; (1933) 75 LJ 96; (1933) 102 LJCL 323; (1933) 148 LTR 335; (1933) 77 SJ 65; (1932-33) XLIX TLR 130; (1933) WN (I) 14 CCA Common law misdemeanour of public mischief still extant: making false statements to police about imagined crime is public mischief.

Mann (John William), R v (1914) 10 Cr App R 31; (1914) 49 LJ 99; (1913-14) 58 SJ 303 CCA Attempted suicide an attempted felony.

Mann, R v; R v Dixon [1995] Crim LR 647 CA Undercover police officers did not act as agents provocateurs in either of two solicitation to murder cases and their evidence was validly admitted.

Manners, R v; R v Holly [1976] 2 All ER 96; [1978] AC 43 (also HL); [1976] Crim LR 255t; (1976) 140 JP 364; (1976) 126 NLJ 137t; (1976) 120 SJ 96; [1976] 2 WLR 709 CA Officers of any body performing public/statutory duties for public are capable of corruption.

Mannion, Snook v [1982] Crim LR 601; [1982] RTR 321; [1982] TLR 158 HC QBD Defendant saying 'fuck off' to police on his property found not to be thereby revoking implied licence of police to enter thereon so his arrest was valid.

Mansfield Justices, ex parte Sharkey, R v; R v Same, ex parte Hunt; R v Same, ex parte Barron; R v Same, ex parte Fretwell; R v Same, ex parte Robinson; R v Same, ex parte Swatten; R v Same, ex parte Grove; R v Same, ex parte Fellows; R v Same, ex parte Anderson [1985] 1 All ER 193; [1985] Crim LR 148; (1985) 149 JP 129; [1985] QB 613; (1984) 128 SJ 872; [1984] TLR 559; [1984] 3 WLR 1328 HC QBD Justices could rely on local knowledge when attaching conditions to bail (here preventing miners from joining pickets).

Mansfield, R v [1975] Crim LR 101 CA Using documents to get job so that at some later time might steal was too tenuous a factual basis to support conviction.

Mapstone and others, R v [1963] 3 All ER 930; [1964] Crim LR 291; (1964) 128 JP 94; [1964] 1 WLR 439 Assizes On affray.

March, Cohen and another v [1951] 2 TLR 402 HC KBD Accused's lying as to when came into possession of goods is not per se evidence that goods were stolen.

Marchant (Stephen), R v; R v McCallister (Stephen) (1985) 80 Cr App R 361 CA Was attempt to take conveyance without authority even though did not use conveyance.

Marck (Henry William), R v (1928-29) 21 Cr App R 65 CCA Intent to defraud is an essential ingredient of obtaining by false pretences.

Marcus (Jacob), R v (1922-23) 17 Cr App R 191 CCA On notion of recency in 'recent possession' doctrine.

Marcus, R v [1981] 2 All ER 833; (1981) 73 Cr App R 49; [1981] Crim LR 490; (1981) 145 JP 380; (1981) 131 NLJ 504; (1981) 125 SJ 396; [1981] 1 WLR 774 CA Quantity and quality relevant in deciding if substance noxious; 'noxious' does not only apply to bodily health injury.

Marison, R v [1996] Crim LR 909 CA Diabetic who suffered hypoglycaemic attack while driving was legitimately found guilty of causing death by dangerous driving of other driver with whom collided following attack.

Marjoram, Stowe v (1911-13) XXII Cox CC 198; (1909) 73 JP 498; (1909-10) 101 LTR 569 HC KBD Conviction for unlawful possession of eggs.

Mark (Malcolm), Brown and Mark (Maureen), R v [1961] Crim LR 173 CCC Need not know are assaulting peace officer to be guilty of offence under Offences against the Person Act 1861, s 38: are not guilty if act in honest/reasonable/bona fide belief that person 'assaulted' committing breach of peace/a felony.

Markus, R v [1974] 3 All ER 705; [1976] AC 35 (also HL); [1974] Crim LR 603t; (1975) 139 JP 19; (1974) 118 SJ 809; [1974] 3 WLR 645 CA Can be guilty of inducing other 'to...offer to take part' and 'to take part...in' course of action and can be guilty of doing so in England even if did so from abroad.

Markus, Secretary of State for Trade v [1975] 1 All ER 958; [1976] AC 35 (also CA); (1975) 61 Cr App R 58; [1975] Crim LR 716; (1975) 139 JP 301; (1975) 119 SJ 271; [1975] 2 WLR 708 HL Can be guilty of inducing other 'to...offer to take part' and 'to take part...in' course of action and can be guilty of doing so in England even if did so from abroad.

Marlow, R v (1965) 49 Cr App R 49; [1965] Crim LR 35 CCC 'Noxious thing'/'poison' in Offences against the Person Act 1861, ss 58 and 59 not confined to abortifacients.

Marriott, R v [1971] 1 All ER 595; (1971) 55 Cr App R 82; [1971] Crim LR 172; (1971) 135 JP 165; (1971) 115 SJ 11; [1971] 1 WLR 187 CA Must prove accused had reason to know of drug traces on penknife to sustain possession conviction.

Marsden, Waroquiers v [1950] 1 All ER 93; (1950) 114 JP 78 HC KBD Keeping a brothel triable summarily under statute and indictable at common law.

Marsh (Ronald William Frank), R v (1948-49) 33 Cr App R 185 CCA Evidence of previous confession of guilt/sentencing for indecent assault on child admissible in later charge for carnal knowledge of same child.

Marsh v Arscott (1982) 75 Cr App R 211; [1982] Crim LR 827; [1982] TLR 121 HC QBD Shop car park was/was not public place when shop open/closed.

Marsh, Martin v [1955] Crim LR 781t HC QBD Was larceny from the Electricity Authority to take money that had been deposited in an electrcity meter.

Marshall (Roy), R v (1990) 90 Cr App R 73 CA No distinction between unlicensed credit transactions initiated by customer/seller: only distinguish between regular/occasional transactions.

Marshall, R v (1910) 74 JP 381 CCA Habitual criminal conviction allowed stand though certain offences of which evidence had been given at trial had not been mentioned in notice of prosecution.

Marti, R v [1981] Crim LR 109 CrCt On interrelationship between Fraudulent Mediums Act 1951, s 2(b) and Vagrancy Act 1824, s 4.

Martin (Francis Augustus), R v (1910) 5 Cr App R 4 CCA Co-prisoner's evidence against party did not render former accomplice.

Martin (George), R v (1910) 5 Cr App R 31 CCA Need not be defence to habitual criminal charge that have been working since last release from prison.

Martin and others, R v (1956) 120 JP 255; [1956] 2 QB 272; [1956] 2 WLR 975 CCC Possession of drugs on aircaft not triable in England as offence not committed in England.

Martin Secker and Warburg Ltd and others, R v (1954) 38 Cr App R 124; (1954) 118 JP 438; (1954) 104 LJ 488; (1954) 98 SJ 577; [1954] 1 WLR 1138 CCC On what constitutes obscene libel: must be more than just objectionable/in poor taste.

Martin v Marsh [1955] Crim LR 781t HC QBD Was larceny from the Electricity Authority to take money that had been deposited in an electrcity meter.

Martin v Puttick [1967] 1 All ER 899; [1967] Crim LR 241; (1967) 131 JP 286; [1968] 2 QB 82; (1967) 111 SJ 131; [1967] 2 WLR 1131 HC QBD No property passes to customer picking up supermarket items; such items not in manager's control/customer's possession so taking from store without paying (after manager sees goods) is larceny.

Martin v Puttick (1967) 51 Cr App R 272 CA No property passes to customer picking up supermarket items; such items not in manager's control/customer's possession so taking from store without paying (after manager sees goods) is larceny.

Martin, Absalom v (1973) 123 NLJ 946t; [1973] Crim LR 752 HC QBD Billposter's part-parking of van on pavement while putting up bill did not merit conviction for wilful obstruction of highway.

Martin, Carey v [1954] Crim LR 139t HC QBD Was not attempted larceny to break shop skylight (with intent to enter) and then to run away.

Martin, R v [1989] 1 All ER 652; (1989) 88 Cr App R 343; [1989] Crim LR 284; (1989) 153 JP 231; [1989] RTR 63; [1988] 1 WLR 655 CA Defence of necessity arises if objectively viewed person acted reasonably/proportionately to avoid death/serious injury threat.

Martindale, R v [1986] 3 All ER 25; (1987) 84 Cr App R 31; [1986] Crim LR 736; (1986) 150 JP 548; (1970) 130 SJ 613; [1986] 1 WLR 1042 CA Non-recollection of possession did not mean not in possession.

Martindale, R v [1966] 3 All ER 305; (1966) 50 Cr App R 273; [1966] Crim LR 621; (1965-66) 116 NLJ 1433; (1966) 110 SJ 769; [1966] 1 WLR 1564 CMAC Provocation possible despite intent to kill/do grievous bodily harm if acts arose from sudden passion.

Marwood, R v [1959] Crim LR 784t CCA Valid conviction for capital murder (of police constable) on basis of confession.

Mason (Reginald), R v (1914) 10 Cr App R 169; (1914-15) 111 LTR 336 CCA Forged deeds of later date than that of which accused charged with uttering admissible to prove guilty knowledge.

Mason (Tom), R v (1912-13) 8 Cr App R 121 CCA Drunkenness as defence to murder; words of provocation/abuse plus spitting at accused could reduce murder to manslaughter.

Mason, R v (1969) 53 Cr App R 12; [1969] Crim LR 449 CA No assault by woman on boys so could not be guilty of indecent assault.

Mason, Scarsbrook v (1961) 105 SJ 889 HC QBD Parties in car jointly/severally liable for negligent driving by driver.

Massad, Mattouk v [1943] 2 All ER 517; (1943) 87 SJ 381; (1943) WN (I) 215 PC Does not matter whether intercourse with/without consent in seduction action as master suing for loss of services.

Massey, Atwal v [1971] 3 All ER 881; (1972) 56 Cr App R 6; [1972] Crim LR 37; (1972) 136 JP 35 HC QBD Test in handling cases is whether believed were stolen or was reckless as to that fact.

Masson, Stonehouse and another v [1921] All ER 534; (1921-25) XXVII Cox CC 23; (1921) 85 JP 167; [1921] 2 KB 818; [1922] 91 LJCL 93; (1921) 125 LTR 463; (1920-21) XXXVII TLR 621; (1921) WN (I) 167 HC KBD No intent needed to be convicted for fortune-telling under Vagrancy Act 1824, s 4.

Masters, R v (1964) 48 Cr App R 303; [1964] Crim LR 534; (1964) 114 LJ 457; [1965] 1 QB 517; (1964) 108 SJ 465; [1964] 3 WLR 288 CCA Murder committed at moment when intent was intent to steal was capital murder.

Masterson and another v Holden [1986] 3 All ER 39; (1986) 83 Cr App R 302; [1986] Crim LR 688; (1970) 130 SJ 592; [1986] 1 WLR 1017 HC QBD Overt homosexual behaviour in public street insulting albeit not directed at particular person/s.

Matchell, Plunkett v [1958] Crim LR 252 Magistrates Conviction (but absolute discharge) of security man guilty of assault in using security dog to attack trespasser in mistaken view that was necessary self-defence.

Mathers v Penfold [1914-15] All ER 891; (1914-15) XXIV Cox CC 642; (1915) 79 JP 225; [1915] 1 KB 515; (1915) 50 LJ 29; [1915] 84 LJKB 627; (1915) 112 LTR 726; (1914-15) 59 SJ 235; (1914-15) XXXI TLR 108; (1915) WN (I) 13 HC KBD Charity street-collector not 'begging' contrary to Vagrancy Act 1824, s 3.

Matheson, R v [1958] 2 All ER 87; (1957) 41 Cr App R 145; [1958] Crim LR 393t; (1958) 108 LJ 297; (1958) 102 SJ 309 CCA Diminished responsibility a matter for jury; where diminished responsibility one of several defences raised and manslaughter verdict returned judge to ask on which defence is based.

Matt, Rose v [1951] 1 All ER 361; (1951-52) 35 Cr App R 1; (1951) 115 JP 122; [1951] 1 KB 810; (1951) 101 LJ 63; (1951) 95 SJ 62; [1951] 1 TLR 474; (1951) WN (I) 60 HC KBD Bailor depriving bailee of property (in which has special property) commits larceny.

Matthew O'Brien Fallon, R v (1963) 47 Cr App R 160 CCA Recent possession doctrine did not apply to robbery with violence charge where was charged with others - possession could be evidence that participated in robbery but not that used violence.

Matthews (Albert Edward), R v (1958) 42 Cr App R 93 CMAC Properly convicted of knowingly making false/fraudulent statement where signed one's name to blank form knowing another would complete it falsely.

Matthews v Gray (1909) 73 JP 303; [1909] 2 KB 89; (1909) 44 LJ 233; [1909] 78 LJKB 545; (1908-09) XXV TLR 476; (1909) WN (I) 88 HC KBD On sale of pistol to party for use in own house.

Matthews, Baxter v [1958] Crim LR 263 Magistrates Valid conviction under Highway Act 1835, s 78, for negligent interruption of free passage of carriage on the highway.

Matthews, R v [1981] Crim LR 325 CrCt Could be attempted rape where pinned person down with expressed intention of having non-consensual sex (albeit that penis was never erect/penetration never attempted).

Matthews, R v [1950] 1 All ER 137; (1950) 114 JP 73; (1950) 100 LJ 20; [1950] 66 (1) TLR 153 CCA Acquiring property without guilty intent, then appropriating it is stealing not receiving.

Matthews, Ware and another v (1981) 131 NLJ 830 HC QBD Successful action for damages for arrest without reasonable cause for alleged unlawful taking of car.

Mattison v Johnson [1916-17] All ER 727; (1915-17) XXV Cox CC 373; (1916) 80 JP 243; [1916] 85 LJKB 741; (1916) 114 LTR 951; (1916) WN (I) 52 HC KBD Cannot permit own premises to be used as brothel where oneself is only prostitute using premises.

Mattison v Johnson [1916-17] All ER 727; (1915-17) XXV Cox CC 373; (1916) 80 JP 243; [1916] 85 LJKB 741; (1916) 114 LTR 951; (1916) WN (I) 52 HC KBD That sole tenant-occupier used premises for own acts of prostitution did not merit conviction for permitting premises to be used for habitual prostitution.

Mattouk v Massad [1943] 2 All ER 517; (1943) 87 SJ 381; (1943) WN (I) 215 PC Does not matter whether intercourse with/without consent in seduction action as master suing for loss of services.

Maughan (Reginald), R v (1932-34) 24 Cr App R 130 CCA Not defence to charge of indecent assault on under-sixteen year old that genuinely believed was over sixteen.

Maughan and another, Champion v [1984] Crim LR 291; (1984) 128 SJ 220; [1983] TLR 755 HC QBD Placing fixed engine in tidal waters an absolute offence under Salmon and Freshwater Fisheries Act 1975, s 6(1)(a).

Mavji, R v [1987] 2 All ER 758; (1987) 84 Cr App R 34; [1987] Crim LR 39; (1987) 131 SJ 1121; [1987] 1 WLR 1388 CA Cheating public revenue involves serious/unusual fraudulent diversions of money from the revenue.

Mawji (Laila Jhina) and Another v R [1957] AC 126; [1957] 1 All ER 385; (1957) 41 Cr App R 69; [1957] Crim LR 185; (1957) 101 SJ 146; [1957] 2 WLR 277 PC Tanganyikan husband and wife could not be guilty of criminal conspiracy between them.

Maxwell (James Charles), R v (1979) 68 Cr App R 128; (1979) 143 JP 77; [1978] 1 WLR 1363 HL May be accomplice if anticipate limited number of crimes but unaware of precise crime in which assisting.

Maxwell, Director of Public Prosecutions for Northern Ireland v [1978] 3 All ER 1140; (1979) 68 Cr App R 128 (also CCA/NI); [1979] Crim LR 40; (1979) 143 JP 63 (also CCA/NI); (1978) 122 SJ 758; [1978] 1 WLR 1350 HL May be accomplice if anticipate limited number of crimes but unaware of precise crime in which assisting.

Maxwell, R v [1994] Crim LR 848 CA Improper not to direct jury of availability of alternative verdicts in case involving joint enterprise.

May (John) (1990) 91 Cr App R 157, R v [1990] Crim LR 415 CA Boys told to instruct teacher to do indecent performances were not participants to act so performances before them alone were acts outraging public decency.

Mayer, R v [1975] RTR 411 CA Person arrested after provided breath test specimen did not have to be told why as was apparent from circumstances.

Mayes, Calvert v [1954] 1 All ER 41; [1954] Crim LR 147; (1954) 118 JP 76; [1954] 1 QB 342; (1954) 98 SJ 13; [1954] 2 WLR 18 HC QBD Payment of money direct to accused rather than via prostitutes (over whom exercised some control) did not mean were not living off earnings of prostitution.

Maytum-White (Leslie Percy), R v (1958) 42 Cr App R 165; [1957] Crim LR 806 CCA Was obtaining by false pretences to make out postdated cheque for tickets albeit in anticipation that money would be in bank when cheque presented.

Maywhort, R v [1955] 2 All ER 752; (1955) 39 Cr App R 107; (1955) 119 JP 473; (1955) 105 LJ 457; (1955) 99 SJ 510; [1955] 1 WLR 848 HC QBD Cannot be convicted of fraudulent conversion first revealed on oath.

McArdle v Egan and others [1933] All ER 611; (1934-39) XXX Cox CC 67; (1934) 98 JP 103; (1934) 150 LTR 412 CA Reasonable and probable cause to suspect person of felony justifies arrest without warrant: question whether had such cause a matter for judge.

McArdle v Wallace [1964] Crim LR 467g; (1964) 108 SJ 483 HC QBD Constable not acting in course of duty where requested by son of owner to leave property had entered so subsequent assault by son on constable not assault on same in execution of his duty.

McBean v Parker [1983] Crim LR 399; (1983) 147 JP 205; [1983] TLR 85 HC QBD Person using reasonable force to resist (unexplained) search who assaulted second officer coming to aid of searching officer not guilty of assault on police officer in the execution of his duty.

McBride v Turnock [1964] Crim LR 456t; (1964) 108 SJ 336 HC QBD Person who struck constable in course of assault on another was guilty of assault on police officer in the execution of his duty.

McCaffery, United States Government and others v [1984] 2 All ER 570; (1985) 80 Cr App R 82; (1984) 128 SJ 448; [1984] TLR 389; [1984] 1 WLR 867 HL Extradition for state crimes possible under extradition treaty with federal government; magistrate need only decide whether acts described would be offences under English law.

McCall (Paul Richard), R v (1971) 55 Cr App R 175; [1971] Crim LR 237; (1971) 115 SJ 75 CA Is obtaining property by deception to secure loan on basis of false representation - intention to repay no defence.

McCalla (Clevous Errol), R v (1988) 87 Cr App R 372; (1988) 152 JP 481 CA Cosh an offensive weapon: that had forgotten possession was not reasonable excuse excusing offence.

McCann (Edward), R v (1972) 56 Cr App R 359 CA On entrapment where already have evidence of conspiracy to committ offence.

McCarrick v Oxford and another [1982] Crim LR 750; [1983] RTR 117 CA Constable's refusing to visit home of person (whom arrested on suspicion of driving while disqualified) and there see letter stating disqualification suspended pending appeal did not render arrest invalid.

McCarthy, Holder v (1918-21) XXVI Cox CC 314; [1918] 2 KB 309; (1918) WN (I) 149 HC KBD Receipt of old age pension by means of false representation.

McCarthy, R v [1954] 2 All ER 262; (1954) 38 Cr App R 74; (1964) 128 JP 191; [1954] 2 QB 105; (1954) 98 SJ 356; [1954] 2 WLR 1044 CCA Drunkenness not provocation nor is it defence to murder (unless so drunk cannot form necessary intent).

McCarthy, R v [1964] 1 All ER 95; (1964) 48 Cr App R 111; [1964] Crim LR 225; (1964) 114 LJ 74; (1964) 108 SJ 17; [1964] 1 WLR 196 CCA On elements necessary to establish guilt of aiding and abetting offence (here of possession of explosive substance).

McCarthy, R v [1996] Crim LR 818 CA Police evidence validly admitted even though obtained after police stopped and searched car without informing persons therein that police suspected drugs being carried in car.

McCogg, R v [1982] Crim LR 685 CrCt Flick knife did not have to be offensive weapon.

McConnell v Chief Constable of the Greater Manchester Police [1990] 1 All ER 423; (1990) 91 Cr App R 88; (1990) 154 JP 325; (1990) 134 SJ 457; [1990] 1 WLR 364 CA Police may exercise power of arrest in private premises if likely breach of peace by persons inside.

McCracken, R v [1965] Crim LR 435g; (1965) 109 SJ 434 CCA Issue of criminal negligence did not always have to be left to jury at homicide trial where even slimmest possibility of such negligence existed.

McCreadie (Malcolm), R v; R v Tume (William John) (1993) 96 Cr App R 143; [1992] Crim LR 872; (1993) 157 JP 541; [1992] TLR 285 CA Proof that electricity abstracted without authority could support theft conviction - did not have to prove accused tampered with meter.

McCready, R v; R v Hurd (1978) 122 SJ 247 CA Could not plead guilty to common assault where were only charged with causing grievous bodily harm with intent.

McCullum (Miriam Lavinia), R v (1973) 57 Cr App R 645; [1973] Crim LR 582; (1973) 117 SJ 525 CA Are guilty of handling stolen goods if knew/thought were carrying same though did not know what goods were.

McDavitt, R v [1981] Crim LR 843 CrCt Person who intended to leave restaurant without paying bill but who remained in restaurant (though refusing to pay bill) guilty/not guilty of attempted theft/theft.

McDonald (Lloyd George), R v (1980) 70 Cr App R 288; [1980] Crim LR 242 CA Jury could take that goods at issue were stolen from accused's admission as to circumstances of obtaining same.

McDonnell, R v [1966] 1 All ER 193; (1966) 50 Cr App R 5; [1966] Crim LR 40; (1965-66) 116 NLJ 386; [1966] 1 QB 233; (1965) 109 SJ 919; [1965] 3 WLR 1138 Assizes Cannot be conspiracy between company and person with sole responsibility therefor; conspiracy charge need not include term 'with others unknown'.

McDonough, R v (1963) 47 Cr App R 37; [1963] Crim LR 203; (1962) 106 SJ 961 CCA Could be guilty of incitement to receive stolen goods though at time of incitement the goods were not actually stolen.

McDowell, Maile v [1980] Crim LR 586 CA On what constitutes a breach of the peace (here in football crowd context).

McErlaine v Jeffrey [1955] Crim LR 312 Sessions Conviction for theft of pedal cycle quashed as was inadequate evidence of intention to permanently deprive owner of same.

McFall, R v [1994] Crim LR 226 CA In light of 'other relevant matters' (Sexual Offences (Amendment) Act 1976, s 1(2)) - that had kidnapped woman/behaved aggressively - indicated appellant knew complainant did not consent to sex.

McFarlane, R v [1994] 2 All ER 283; (1994) 99 Cr App R 8; [1994] Crim LR 532; (1994) 158 JP 310; (1994) 144 NLJ 270; [1994] QB 419; (1994) 138 SJ LB 19; [1993] TLR 662; [1994] 2 WLR 494 CA 'Clipper' a prostitute because both offer sexual services for reward.

McGirr, Taylor v [1986] Crim LR 544 HC QBD Offence under Act repealed before charges brought was properly charged under terms of repealed act.

McGlassons Ltd, Birkett v [1957] Crim LR 197t; (1957) 101 SJ 149 HC QBD Failed prosecution for sale of salmon during close season.

McGowan, R v [1990] Crim LR 399; [1990] TLR 68 CA Burden of proof stays on Crown for course of prosecution for conspiracy to produce controlled drug.

McGregor (John), R v (1943-45) 30 Cr App R 155; (1945) 109 JP 136; [1946] 115 LJ 100 CCA On procedure where brought before court for breach of recognisance.

McGregor v Benyon [1957] Crim LR 250 Magistrates Person could not be guilty of larceny by finding where was given (originally stolen) handbag by her daughter (who found the handbag).

McGregor v Benyon [1957] Crim LR 608 HC QBD Person could be guilty of larceny by finding where was given (originally stolen) handbag by her daughter (who found the handbag).

McGuigan, R v; R v Cameron [1991] Crim LR 719 CA On need for three or more parties to be party to violent disorder before offence can arise.

McGuire and Page, R v [1963] Crim LR 572 CCA Lawful object defence unavailable to person in possession of air pistol; successful appeal on basis of misdirection as to constructive possession.

McHugh (Christopher John Patrick), R v (1993) 97 Cr App R 335 CA Was theft where dealt with clients' proceeds in way that mixed their funds with own.

McHugh (David), R v (1977) 64 Cr App R 92; [1977] Crim LR 174t; (1977) 127 NLJ 44t; [1977] RTR 1 CA Whether driving away from petrol station without paying for petrol was theft/obtaining pecuniary advantage by deception.

McHugh (Eileen Cecilia), R v; R v Tringham (Rodney Duncan) (1989) 88 Cr App R 385 CA On what constitutes 'appropriation'.

McInnes, R v [1971] 3 All ER 295; (1971) 55 Cr App R 551; [1972] Crim LR 651; (1971) 121 NLJ 883; (1971) 115 SJ 655; [1971] 1 WLR 1600 CA Excessive force in self-defence can ground murder conviction; failure to retreat tends to reasonableness of self-defence.

McIvor, R v [1982] 1 All ER 491; (1982) 74 Cr App R 74; [1982] Crim LR 312; (1982) 146 JP 193; (1981) 131 NLJ 1310; (1982) 126 SJ 48; [1982] 1 WLR 409 CA Evidence of state of mind to be given such weight as jury think in deciding if appropriation dishonest.

McKee v Chief Constable for Northern Ireland [1985] 1 All ER 1; (1984) 128 SJ 836; [1984] TLR 662; [1984] 1 WLR 1358 HL Necessary state of mind to justify constable's arresting suspected terrorist under emergency legislation could be grounded solely on superior's orders.

McKenzie (Weston George) and Davis (Jennifer Dorcas), R v [1979] Crim LR 164 CrCt Invalidity of arrest meant assault on constable was not assault on same in execution of his duty.

McKenzie, R v [1971] 1 All ER 729; (1971) 55 Cr App R 294; [1972] Crim LR 655; (1971) 135 JP 26 Assizes Invalid recognisance could not be subject of forgery; recognisance invalid where imposed on person who would not be detained.

McKenzie, Vaughan v [1968] 1 All ER 1154; [1968] Crim LR 265; (1968) 118 NLJ 204t; (1968) 112 SJ 212; [1968] 2 WLR 1133 HC QBD Not assault on bailiff in execution of duty where assault occurred when resident sought to impede bailiff's entry (bailiff in so entering was trespassing).

McKiernan, Hibbert v [1948] 1 All ER 860; (1948) 112 JP 287; [1948] 2 KB 142; (1948) 98 LJ 245; [1948] 117 LJR 1521; (1948) LXIV TLR 256; (1948) WN (I) 169 HC KBD Larceny for trespasser to steal goods lost by another and found by trespasser on private land.

McLachlan, Moss and others v (1985) 149 JP 167; [1984] TLR 672 HC QBD Police were acting in course of duty when stopped miners travelling towards another mine as had reasonable belief miners intended to commit breach of the peace.

McLean; ex parte Aikens and others, R v (1975) 139 JP 261 HC QBD Summary trials of applicants allowed proceed despite very rigorous bail conditions imposed by magistrate as though severe was no evidence of bias on magistrate's part.

McLorie v Oxford (1982) 75 Cr App R 137; [1982] Crim LR 603; [1982] QB 1290; [1983] RTR 265; (1982) 126 SJ 536; [1982] TLR 287; [1982] 3 WLR 423 HC QBD No post-arrest common law right of police to enter property and look for material evidence; is assault on police in execution of their duty to assault same while doing what is lawfully proper for them to do.

McMahon and another v Dollard [1965] Crim LR 238t HC QBD Studded belt not per se an offensive weapon.

McMahon, R v [1961] Crim LR 622 CCA On what is meant by phrase 'for causing injury to the person' (Prevention of Crime Act 1953, s 1(4)).

McMillan (Paul), R v (1977) 64 Cr App R 104; [1977] Crim LR 680; [1984] TLR 347 CA Conviction set aside as was inadequate jury direction on nature of cannabis plant portion accused possessed and whether could be 'leaf' for purpose of Misuse of Drugs Act 1971, s 37(1).

McNamara (James), R v (1988) 87 Cr App R 246; [1988] Crim LR 440; (1988) 152 JP 390; (1988) 132 SJ 300 CA That knew had control of box and knew something therein (which was dangerous drug) enough to support conviction for possession of dangerous drugs.

McNiff, R v [1986] Crim LR 57 CA Tenancy of public house not an 'office' and even if was, application for same is not application for payment so falsehoods in tenancy application not obtaining pecuniary advantage by deception.

McPherson and others, R v [1973] Crim LR 191t; (1972) 122 NLJ 1133; (1973) 117 SJ 13 CA Was appropriation to place shop stock in bag with intention to avoid payment.

McPherson and Watts, R v [1985] Crim LR 508 CA Conspiracy conviction quashed where not left to jury to decide whether substantive offence if effected would have been indictable in United Kingdom.

McPherson, R v [1957] Crim LR 618t CCA On burden of proof where issue of manslaughter by virtue of provocation left to jury.

McPherson, R v; R v Farrell; R v Kajal [1980] Crim LR 654 CrCt Construction of offence of inducing/knowingly suffering under sixteen year old girl to be on premises owned/occupied by offender for purposes of having sex with men (Sexual Offences Act 1956, s 26).

McVitie, R v [1960] 2 All ER 498; [1960] Crim LR 559; (1960) 124 JP 404; [1960] 2 QB 483; (1960) 104 SJ 510; [1960] 3 WLR 99 CCA Valid conviction for knowingly possessing explosives though term 'knowingly' not in indictment.

Mead, Horton v [1911-13] All ER 954; (1913-14) XXIII Cox CC 279; (1913) 77 JP 129; [1913] 1 KB 154; (1912) 47 LJ 767; [1913] 82 LJKB 200; (1913) 108 LTR 156; (1912) WN (I) 304 HC KBD Man can be guilty of soliciting though no evidence that anyone conscious of/noticed acts of solicitation.

Mead, R v (1909) 73 JP 239; [1909] 1 KB 895; (1908-09) 53 SJ 378; (1908-09) XXV TLR 359 CCA On drunkenness as defence to murder/reason for manslaughter verdict.

Meade (Thomas), R v (1909) 2 Cr App R 54; [1909] 78 LJKB 476; (1909) WN (I) 62 CCA That were drunk can reduce apparent murder to manslaughter.

Meade, R v (1902-03) XIX TLR 540 Assizes Two months' imprisonment for going about armed in public (contrary to statute of King Edward III) and for causing public nuisance for firing revolver in public street.

Meaden v Wood [1985] Crim LR 678 HC QBD On legislation pertaining to legitimate mode of effecting street collections.

Meakin, Waters v (1915-17) XXV Cox CC 432; (1916) 80 JP 276; [1916] 2 KB 111; [1916] 85 LJKB 1378; (1916-17) 115 LTR 110; (1915-16) XXXII TLR 480; (1916) WN (I) 197 HC KBD Cruelty to rabbit conviction avoided by way of statutory protection afforded coursing meetings (Protection of Animals Act 1911, s 1(3) (b)).

ALPHABETICAL INDEX

Metropolitan Police Commissioner v Charles [1976] 3 All ER 112; [1977] AC 177; (1976) 63 Cr
App R 252; [1977] Crim LR 615; (1976) 140 JP 531; (1976) 126 NLJ 936t; (1976) 120 SJ 588;
[1976] 3 WLR 431 HL Acceptance of cheque and cheque card where drawer has no money in
bank is obtaining pecuniary advantage by deception.

Metropolitan Police Commissioner v Hammond [1965] AC 810; [1964] Crim LR 589t; (1964) 114
LJ 488; (1964) 108 SJ 478; [1964] 3 WLR 1 HL Fugitive offender released as warrant not
endorsed by (non-existent) police officer/magistrate had not properly considered case.

Metropolitan Police Commissioner, Fagan v [1968] 3 All ER 442; (1968) 52 Cr App R 700; (1969)
133 JP 16; [1969] 1 QB 439; (1968) 112 SJ 800; [1968] 3 WLR 1120 HC QBD Uncriminal act
became criminal once criminal intent formed so initially innocent act transformed into assault on
constable.

Metropolitan Police Commissioner, Gatland and another v [1968] Crim LR 275t; (1968) 112 SJ
336 HC QBD Failed appeal against acquittal of person charged with depositing vehicle on road
without lawful authority/ excuse in such a way as to endanger another user of road.

Metropolitan Police Commissioner, Gold Star Publications Ltd v (1980) 71 Cr App R 185; (1980)
130 NLJ 508 HC QBD Article held in England can be obscene publication though purely for
export.

Metropolitan Police Commissioner, M v [1979] Crim LR 53; (1978) 128 NLJ 759t CA On police
retention until trial of money seized by police pursuant to search warrant.

Metropolitan Police Commissioner, R v [1955] Crim LR 309t HC QBD Magistrate's perusal of
extradition materials in private was procedurally regular.

Metropolitan Police Commissioner, Roandale Ltd v [1979] Crim LR 254; (1979) 123 SJ 128 CA
On police powers pursuant to seizure of (here a very large number of) items under Obscene
Publications Act 1959, s 3.

Metropolitan Police Commissioner, Scott v [1974] 3 All ER 1032; [1975] AC 819; (1975) 60 Cr
App R 124; [1975] Crim LR 94; (1975) 139 JP 121; (1974) 124 NLJ 1157t; (1974) 118 SJ 863;
[1974] 3 WLR 741 HL Need not be agreement to defraud by deceit to sustain conviction for
conspiracy to defraud.

Metropolitan Police Commissioner, Solomon v [1982] Crim LR 606 CA Action in detinue/
conversion failed where person bringing action/property subject of action a thief/car bought from
money made through theft.

Metropolitan Police Commissioner, Warner v [1968] 2 All ER 356; [1969] 2 AC 256; (1968) 52
Cr App R 373; [1968] Crim LR 380t; (1968) 132 JP 378; (1968) 112 SJ 378; [1968] 2 WLR
1303 HL Possession not absolute offence: if no right to open parcel/ignorant of its contents, no
possession.

Metropolitan Police Commissioner; ex parte Blackburn, R v [1973] Crim LR 55 HC QBD No
mandamus directing police in conduct of their duties as regards obscene publications as not
proven that such direction merited.

Metropolitan Police Commissioner; ex parte Hammond, R v [1964] 1 All ER 821; [1964] Crim LR
293t; (1964) 128 JP 299; (1964) 114 LJ 272; [1964] 2 QB 385; (1964) 108 SJ 179; [1964] 2
WLR 777 HC QBD Fugitive offender released as warrant not endorsed by (non-existent) police
officer.

Metropolitan Stipendiary Magistrate, ex parte Lee, R v [1993] TLR 74 HC QBD Magistrate may
examine evidence provided by requesting state, and circumstances at time of extradition; may not
request further materials or decide on future events.

Meyer, R v (1908-09) XCIX LTR 202; (1907-08) XXIV TLR 620 CCA Substantive application
necessary for bail by person granted leave to appeal who was not present and had previously been
convicted.

Meyrick (Kate Evelyn), R v; R v Ribuffi (Luigi Achille) (1928-29) 21 Cr App R 94; (1928-29) XLV
TLR 421 CCA Essence of conspiracy is that acts of accused be done in pursuance of criminal
purpose held in common between them; sentences ran from date of conviction not date of appeal
in light of bureaucratic delay in appeal.

Michaels v Block (1917-18) XXXIV TLR 438 HC KBD On extent of power to arrest without warrant under Consolidated Defence of the Realm Regulations 1914, regulation 55.

Middleton (Thomas Mansfield), R v (1922-23) 17 Cr App R 89 CCA Strict proof of possession needed in receiving prosecution.

Mieras v Rees [1975] Crim LR 224; (1975) 139 JP 549 HC QBD Cannot attempt to supply controlled drug (even if have requisite mens rea) where substance are supplying is not controlled drug as is no actus reus.

Miles (Frederick), R v (1909) 3 Cr App R 13 CCA Could be tried under Prevention of Crimes Act 1871, s 7 though had already been tried/acquitted of larceny.

Miles v Clovis and another (1979) 69 Cr App R 280; [1980] QB 195 HC QBD Need not prove intent to steal particular object at time of loitering to be guilty of loitering with intent under Vagrancy Act 1824, s 4.

Miles v Hutchings (1901-07) XX Cox CC 555; [1903] 2 KB 714; [1903] 72 LJKB 775; (1903-04) LXXXIX LTR 420; (1903-04) 52 WR 284 HC KBD Not malicious injury to dog where injure in belief that must do so to protect own/master's property.

Miles, R v [1992] Crim LR 657 CA Interpretation of Companies Act 1985, s 458: party to carrying on of business engaged in fraudulent trading includes those controlling/managing, i.e., running same.

Millar and Page, R v [1965] Crim LR 437t CCA Larceny convictions quashed where employer in attempt to catch criminals whom had been warned trying to steal his property went further than merely facilitating the offence.

Millard and Vernon, R v [1987] Crim LR 393 CA On intent requirement under the Criminal Attempts Act 1981, s 1(1).

Miller (Geoffrey), R v [1983] TLR 404 CMAC On mens rea as an element of offences charged under the Army Act 1955, s 69.

Miller (Keith Eric), R v; R v Page (Terence Frank) (1965) 49 Cr App R 241; (1965) 115 LJ 402 CCA No larceny as no taking invito domino.

Miller (Steven Henry), R v (1992) 95 Cr App R 421; [1992] Crim LR 744; [1993] RTR 6 CA Need only show that deceptions resulted in money being handed over (need not show deception at precise instant handed over money) to convict for obtaining property by deception.

Miller and another, Anderson v (1977) 64 Cr App R 178; [1976] Crim LR 743; (1976) 126 NLJ 1091t; (1976) 120 SJ 735 HC QBD Shop a single unit so even place behind counter was place to which public had access for purpose of Firearms Act 1968, ss 19 and 57(4).

Miller, Gelberg v [1961] 1 All ER 291; [1961] Crim LR 251; (1961) 125 JP 123; (1961) 111 LJ 172; (1961) 105 SJ 89; [1961] 1 WLR 153 HC QBD Valid arrest without warrant where wilful obstruction of highway/know of factual basis for arrest.

Miller, R v [1954] 2 All ER 529; (1954) 38 Cr App R 1; [1954] Crim LR 219; (1954) 118 JP 341; [1954] 2 QB 282; (1954) 98 SJ 62; [1954] 2 WLR 138 HC QBD Husband could not be guilty of raping wife absent separation agreement/order; assault for husband to use force in exercising right to marital sex.

Miller, R v [1983] 1 All ER 978; [1983] 2 AC 161; (1983) 77 Cr App R 17; [1983] Crim LR 466; (1983) 133 NLJ 450; (1983) 127 SJ 223; [1983] TLR 192; [1983] 2 WLR 539 HL Actus reus of arson includes accidental starting of fire with intended/recklessness as to destruction/damage of property coupled with failure to put out fire/stop it damaging property.

Miller, R v [1982] 2 All ER 386; (1982) 75 Cr App R 109; [1982] Crim LR 526; (1982) 146 JP 243; [1982] QB 532; (1982) 126 SJ 327; [1982] TLR 123; [1982] 2 WLR 937 CA Usually actus reus/mens rea to coincide; absent statute omission does not generally raise criminal liability; reckless/intended omission after unintended act is criminal.

Miller, R v [1977] 3 All ER 986; (1977) 65 Cr App R 79; [1977] Crim LR 562; (1977) 121 SJ 423; [1977] 1 WLR 1129 CA Defaulting on hire-purchase agreement not obtaining goods by credit.

Miller, R v [1976] Crim LR 147 CA Cannot be guilty of being carried in conveyance without authority unless conveyance is actually moved.

Miller, RSPCA v [1994] Crim LR 516; [1994] TLR 131 HC QBD Whether have 'custody' of animal depends on particular facts of each case (holding leash of another's dog did not place it in leash-holder's custody).

Millichamp (John), R v (1921-22) 16 Cr App R 83 CCA On need for caution regarding identification by single witness where alibi defence pleaded.

Millray Window Cleaning Co Ltd, R v [1962] Crim LR 99 CCA On what constitutes corruption.

Mills (Leslie Ernest), R v (1979) 68 Cr App R 154; [1979] Crim LR 456; (1978) 128 NLJ 859t CA Is corruption to acept bribe though do not intend to do act paid for.

Mills, Director of Public Prosecutions v [1997] 2 Cr App R 6; [1996] Crim LR 746; [1997] QB 301; (1996) TLR 1/4/96 HC QBD Threatening witness by telephone was perverting the course of justice contrary to the Criminal Justice and Public Order Act 1994, s 51(1).

Mills, Director of Public Proseutions v [1996] 3 WLR 1093 HC QBD Could be guilty of intimidation via the telephone.

Mills, R v [1963] 1 All ER 202; (1963) 47 Cr App R 49; [1963] Crim LR 181; (1963) 127 JP 176; (1963) 113 LJ 90; [1963] 1 QB 522; (1963) 107 SJ 38; [1963] 2 WLR 137 CCA Meaning of 'procuring' instruments to effect abortion (Offences Against the Person Act 1861, s 59).

Millward (Frederick Thomas), R v (1931-32) 23 Cr App R 119 CCA That thought wife to have committed adultery did not mean were guilty only of manslaughter when killed her lover.

Millward (Neil Frederick), R v [1985] 1 All ER 859; (1985) 80 Cr App R 280; [1985] Crim LR 321; (1985) 149 JP 545; [1985] QB 519; (1985) 129 SJ 187; [1985] 2 WLR 532 CA On what has to be proved by prosecution to secure conviction for perjury.

Millward, R v (1984) 78 Cr App R 263 CrCt That person accused of perjury believed what said was material not defence to perjury.

Ming Pao Newspapers Ltd and others v Attorney-General of Hong Kong [1996] 3 WLR 272 PC On elements of offence of disclosing details of investigation being conducted under the Hong Kong Prevention of Bribery Ordinance.

Ministry of Defence, Murray v [1988] 2 All ER 521; (1988) 138 NLJ 164; (1988) 132 SJ 852; [1988] 1 WLR 692 HL Arrest can begin before formal words of arrest spoken; formal words usually to be said at moment of arrest.

Ministry of Posts and Telecommunications, Paul v [1973] Crim LR 322; (1973) 123 NLJ 250t; [1973] RTR 245 HC QBD Person using wireless to listen in on fire brigade emergency calls was committing offence under Wireless Telegraphy Act 1949, s 5.

Minor v Director of Public Prosecutions (1988) 86 Cr App R 378; [1988] Crim LR 55; (1988) 152 JP 30 HC QBD Can be convicted of going equipped for theft where do act in preparation of an offence.

Minter and others, Diamond v [1941] 1 All ER 390; (1939-40) XXXI Cox CC 468; (1941) 105 JP 181; [1941] 1 KB 656; (1942) 92 LJ 52/59; [1941] 110 LJ 503; (1941) 164 LTR 362; (1941) 85 SJ 155; (1940-41) LVII TLR 332; (1941) WN (I) 58 HC KBD Can only arrest fugitive offender under Fugitive Offenders Act 1881 and if have indorsed/provisional warrant.

Minton, Pope v [1954] Crim LR 711 HC QBD That person not at scene of offence when was perpetrated did not mean could not be accessory before the fact.

Mirams v Our Dogs Publishing Company, Limited [1901] 2 KB 564; [1901] 70 LJK/QB 879; (1901-02) LXXXV LTR 6; (1900-01) XVII TLR 649; (1900-01) 49 WR 626 CA Larceny Act 1861, s 102 prohibition on advertising for stolen property on 'no questions asked' basis includes advertisements for stolen dogs.

Misell (Daniel), R v; R v Ringle (Judah); R v Errington (John) (1925-26) 19 Cr App R 109 CCA Meaning of 'obtained' in offence of receiving property obtained via misdemeanour (Larceny Act 1916, s 33).

Miskell, R v [1954] 1 All ER 137; (1953) 37 Cr App R 214; [1954] Crim LR 137; (1954) 118 JP 113; (1954) 104 LJ 41; (1954) 98 SJ 148 CMAC Attempt to procure act of gross indecency with male person inferred from circumstances.

Mohammed-Holgate v Duke [1983] 3 All ER 526; (1984) 78 Cr App R 65; [1983] Crim LR 734; [1984] QB 209; (1983) 127 SJ 616; [1983] TLR 502; [1983] 3 WLR 598 CA Reasonable belief person committed offence justifies police arrest in hope will get more information during detention period.

Mohan (Ramnath) and Another v R [1967] 2 All ER 58; [1967] 2 AC 187; [1967] Crim LR 356; (1967) 111 SJ 95; [1967] 2 WLR 676 PC Person present aiding and abetting in offence - though had not arranged to do so - guilty as principal in second degree (here of murder).

Mohan, R v [1975] 2 All ER 193; (1975) 60 Cr App R 272; [1975] Crim LR 283t; (1975) 139 JP 523; (1975) 125 NLJ 186t; [1976] QB 1; [1975] RTR 337; (1975) 119 SJ 219; [1975] 2 WLR 859 CA Specific intent to commit offence essential element of attempt to commit crime.

Moles, R v [1981] Crim LR 170; (1981) 131 NLJ 143 HC QBD Refusal in second bail application to hear whether change of circumstances since refusal of first application did not justify granting writ of habeas corpus.

Molloy (John), R v (1920-21) 15 Cr App R 170; (1921) 85 JP 233; (1920-21) XXXVII TLR 611 CCA Consideration of Larceny Act 1916, s 8(1) (larceny of fixtures); cannot be convicted of common law larceny where charged with larceny of fixtures (contrary to Larceny Act 1916, s 8(1)).

Molloy, R v (1914-15) XXIV Cox CC 226; (1914) 78 JP 216; (1914) 49 LJ 182; (1914-15) 111 LTR 166 CCA Theft of lead piping not simple larceny but contravention of Larceny Act 1861, s 31.

Moloney, R v [1985] 1 All ER 1025; [1985] AC 905; (1985) 81 Cr App R 93; [1985] Crim LR 378; (1985) 149 JP 369; (1985) 135 NLJ 315; (1985) 129 SJ 220; [1985] 2 WLR 648 HL Guidelines on requisite mental element for murder.

Monaghan, R v [1979] Crim LR 673 CA Was adequate appropriation to ground theft conviction where dishonest cashier accepted money, did not ring it up on till, and placed it in till drawer with intention of later removing it for herself.

Monahan, Mella v [1961] Crim LR 175t HC QBD Failed prosecution of shop manager for offering for sale pornographic photographs left in shop window indicating what they were and how much they cost.

Monahan, Weisz and another v [1962] 1 All ER 664; [1962] Crim LR 179t; (1962) 126 JP 184; (1962) 112 LJ 223; (1962) 106 SJ 114 HC QBD Soliciting involves physical presence and does not extend to window advertisements.

Monger, R v [1973] Crim LR 301 CA On transferred malice.

Moon (Frederick), R v; R v Moon (Emily) (1910) 4 Cr App R 171; [1910] 1 KB 818; (1910) 45 LJ 221; (1910) 79 LJKB 505 CCA Not offence under Children Act 1908, s 17 to encourage seduction of girl already seduced.

Moon, R v [1967] 3 All ER 962; (1968) 52 Cr App R 12; [1967] Crim LR 709; (1967) 117 NLJ 1086t; (1967) 111 SJ 791; [1967] 1 WLR 1536 CA Intent to defraud not intent to deceive needed to sustain forgery conviction.

Moore (Alan Jan), R v [1979] Crim LR 789 CrCt Intention to share cannabis cigarette rendered party liable to conviction for possession of cannabis with intent to supply same.

Moore and Dorn, R v [1975] Crim LR 229 CA Mistake as to which of series of intended criminal acts caused death did not relieve of liability for murder.

Moore v Gooderham [1960] 3 All ER 575; (1960) 124 JP 513; (1960) 110 LJ 781; (1960) 104 SJ 1036 HC QBD Airgun a lethal weapon: direction to convict person of selling airgun/lethal weapon to under-seventeen year old contrary to Firearms Act 1937.

Moore v Green [1983] 1 All ER 663; [1982] Crim LR 233; (1982) 126 SJ 79 HC QBD Warning by police officer of pending police investigation an obstruction of police in execution of their duty.

Moore v I Bresler, Ltd [1944] 2 All ER 515 HC KBD Company officers acting to defraud company are still its agents.

Moore v Keyte (1901-02) XVIII TLR 396; (1901-02) 50 WR 457 HC KBD On bringing of vaccination prosecutions.

Morgan, Bowyer v (1907-09) XXI Cox CC 203; (1906) 70 JP 252; (1906-07) XCV LTR 27; (1905-06) 50 SJ 377; (1905-06) XXII TLR 426 HC KBD Branding of sheep on nose with hot iron not cruelty.

Morgan, Director of Public Prosecutions v; Director of Public Prosecutions v McDonald; Director of Public Prosecutions v McLarty; Director of Public Prosecutions v Parker [1975] 2 All ER 347; [1976] AC 182 (also CA); (1975) 61 Cr App R 136; [1975] Crim LR 717; (1975) 139 JP 476; (1975) 125 NLJ 530t; (1975) 119 SJ 319; [1975] 2 WLR 913 (also CA) HL Belief that woman consents means no rape as no mens rea.

Morgan, Edwards v [1967] Crim LR 40t HC QBD Unless bailiff on duty exercising special responsibility under the Salmon and Freshwater Fisheries Act 1923 (for which must produce warrant) he is a constable and attack on same (as here) is attack on bailiff in execution of his duty.

Morgan, R v [1972] 1 All ER 348; (1972) 56 Cr App R 181; [1972] Crim LR 96t; (1972) 136 JP 160; (1971) 121 NLJ 1098; (1972) 116 SJ 76; [1972] 2 WLR 123 CA Need to set out offence of principal offender when charging assistant.

Morgan, R v [1961] Crim LR 538t CCA Overnight detention of all persons arrested late at night was not good police practice.

Morgan, R v [1985] Crim LR 447/596 CA Person may be convicted for offence other than that for which warrant issued under Backing of Warrants (Republic of Ireland) Act 1965.

Morgan, R v [1993] Crim LR 56 CA That accused acquainted with drug users/allowed them to take drugs at her house was admissible to prove connection with drugs world.

Morhall, R v [1995] 3 All ER 659; [1996] 1 AC 90; [1995] 2 Cr App R 502; [1995] Crim LR 890; (1995) 145 NLJ 1126; (1995) 139 SJ LB 175; [1995] TLR 431; [1995] 3 WLR 330 HL Glue-sniffing addiction relevant when determining gravity of provocation.

Morhall, R v (1994) 98 Cr App R 108; [1993] Crim LR 957; (1993) 143 NLJ 1441; (1993) 137 SJ LB 189; [1993] TLR 459 CA Glue-sniffing addiction not relevant when determining whether had been provocation.

Morphitis v Salmon [1990] Crim LR 48; (1990) 154 JP 365 HC QBD On what constitutes 'damage' for purposes of Criminal Damage Act 1971.

Morris (Harold Lyndon), R v; R v King (Kenneth) (1984) 79 Cr App R 104; [1984] Crim LR 422; (1985) 149 JP 60; [1984] TLR 179 CA In deciding whether imitation firearm looked like firearm must have regard to what looked like at moment of crime.

Morris and others, R v (1963) 47 Cr App R 202; [1963] Crim LR 838 Assizes Dance hall was a public place.

Morris v Tolman [1922] All ER 182; (1921-25) XXVII Cox CC 345; (1922) 86 JP 221; [1923] 1 KB 166; [1923] 92 LJCL 215; (1923) 128 LTR 118; (1922-23) 67 SJ 169; (1922-23) XXXIX TLR 39 HC KBD Can be convicted as aider and abettor though principal acquitted (but not with respect to using vehicle for unlicensed purpose).

Morris, R v [1983] 2 All ER 448; (1983) 77 Cr App R 164; [1983] Crim LR 559; [1983] QB 587; (1983) 127 SJ 205; [1983] TLR 170; [1983] 2 WLR 768 CA Theft possible even if appropriation originally with owner's consent and honest intent.

Morris, R v [1977] Crim LR 231 CA Twelve years' imprisonment for attempted murder of burglary victim who could have recognised perpetrator of burglary-attempted murderer.

Morris, R v [1968] Crim LR 221; (1968) 118 NLJ 86t CA Must prove fraudulent conversion to sustain conviction for larceny by bailee.

Morris, R v; Anderton v Burnside [1983] 3 All ER 288; [1984] AC 320; (1983) 77 Cr App R 309; [1983] Crim LR 813; (1984) 148 JP 1; (1983) 127 SJ 713; [1983] TLR 598; [1983] 3 WLR 697 HL Dishonest appropriation occurs even if dishonest act follows appropriation.

Morris-Lowe (Brian John), R v [1985] 1 All ER 400; (1985) 80 Cr App R 114; [1985] Crim LR 50; (1984) 128 SJ 872; [1984] TLR 595; [1985] 1 WLR 29 CA On what is meant by attempting to procure woman to become 'common' prostitute.

Morrison (Alexander), R v (1932) 101 LJCL 257 CCA Scottish convictions could sustain habitual criminal conviction.

Morrison, Daniel v (1980) 70 Cr App R 142; [1980] Crim LR 181 HC QBD No constraints imposed on power of detention under Metropolitan Police Act 1839, s 66 once reasonable suspicion of offences outlined therein.

Morrison, R v [1938] 3 All ER 787; (1938-40) 27 Cr App R 1 CCA Must find valid first marriage to sustain bigamy charge.

Morrissey, R v; R v Staines [1997] TLR 231 CA Disappointing that court was unable to apply European Court of Human Rights decision in insider dealing case.

Morrow, Greach and Thomas v Director of Public Prosecutions, Secretary of State for Health and Social Security, British Pregnancy Advisory Service [1994] Crim LR 58 HC QBD Disorderly behaviour conviction valid: reasonable conduct and reasonable force to prevent crime (allegedly illegal abortions) defences unsuccessful.

Morter (Alfred Ernest), R v (1927-28) 20 Cr App R 53 CCA Control of property following entrustment of same is essence of fraudulent conversion.

Mortimer, R v (1907-09) XXI Cox CC 677; (1908) 1 Cr App R 20; (1908) 72 JP 349 CCA On need for animus furandi.

Morton and Page, Goodhew v [1962] 2 All ER 771; [1962] Crim LR 181; (1962) 126 JP 369; (1962) 106 SJ 78 HC QBD Yard so surrounded as to be 'inclosed yard': question of fact in each case.

Morton v Chaney; Morton v Christopher [1960] 3 All ER 632; (1961) 125 JP 37; (1960) 110 LJ 797; (1960) 104 SJ 1035 HC QBD 'Sporting purposes' exemption to firearms possession does not apply to shooting rats.

Moses (Andrew) v The State [1997] AC 53 PC On constructive malice.

Moses and Ansbro, R v [1991] Crim LR 617 CA Aiding illegal immigrants to receive work permits which would probably not otherwise have received was criminal conspiracy to defraud (albeit that none of the acts making up the conspiracy were themselves unlawful).

Moses v Raywood (1911) 80 LJCL 823 HC KBD Salmon net need not have been placed in water to be guilty of offence of using net to catch salmon contrary to Salmon Fishery Act 1865, s 36.

Moses v Winder [1980] Crim LR 232; [1981] RTR 37 HC QBD Failed attempt by diabetic to establish automatism defence to driving without due care and attention charge.

Moss (Robert Francis), R v; R v Harte (Stephen Patrick) (1986) 82 Cr App R 116; [1985] Crim LR 659; (1986) 150 JP 26 CA On what constitutes a 'prison' under Prison Act 1952, s 39.

Moss and others v McLachlan (1985) 149 JP 167; [1984] TLR 672 HC QBD Police were acting in course of duty when stopped miners travelling towards another mine as had reasonable belief miners intended to commit breach of the peace.

Moss, Bradley v [1974] Crim LR 430 HC QBD Person who generally carried offensive weapons for general self-defence purposes did not have reasonable excuse to possession of same.

Moss, Oxford v (1979) 68 Cr App R 183; [1979] Crim LR 119 HC QBD Was not obtaining intangible University property (contrary to Theft Act 1968, s 1) for student to obtain proof copy of examination paper before sitting examination.

Moss, R v; R v Ricardo; R v Ricardo; R v Van West [1965] Crim LR 368; (1965) 109 SJ 269 CCA Bankruptcy not of itself evidence of bad character.

Moss, Woodage v [1974] 1 All ER 584; [1974] Crim LR 104; (1974) 138 JP 253; (1974) 118 SJ 204; [1974] 1 WLR 411 HC QBD Person carrying uncertificated firearm from party to dealer is in possession/not dealer's servant (as no payment/obligation to so act).

Motor Trade Association, Thorne v (1936-38) 26 Cr App R 51; (1937) 83 LJ 426 HL Not demanding money with menaces to write letter on behalf of trade association requiring payment if are not to be put on black list.

Motorists' Advisory Agency, Ltd, Heap v [1922] All ER 251; [1923] 92 LJCL 553; (1923) 129 LTR 146; (1922-23) XXXIX TLR 150 HC KBD Must be animus furandi for there to be larceny by trick.

Mott, Bryan v (1976) 62 Cr App R 71; [1976] Crim LR 64t; (1975) 125 NLJ 1093t; (1975) 119 SJ 743 HC QBD Broken milk bottle was offensive weapon and carrying it about for purpose of committing suicide not reasonable excuse.

Mounsey v Campbell [1983] RTR 36 HC QBD Bumper to bumper parking by van driver occasioned unnecessary obstruction.

Mountford, R v [1971] 2 All ER 81; (1971) 55 Cr App R 266; [1971] Crim LR 280t; (1971) 135 JP 250; (1971) 121 NLJ 177t; [1972] 1 QB 28; (1971) 115 SJ 302; [1971] 2 WLR 1106 CA Forcible detainer triable on indictment.

Mowatt, R v [1967] 3 All ER 47; [1967] Crim LR 591; (1967) 131 JP 463; (1967) 117 NLJ 860; [1968] 1 QB 421; (1967) 111 SJ 716; [1967] 3 WLR 1192 CA Definition of 'maliciously' in Offences Against the Person Act 1861 unnecessary in circumstances.

Moynes v Cooper [1956] 1 All ER 450; (1956) 40 Cr App R 20; [1956] Crim LR 268; (1956) 120 JP 147; (1956) 106 LJ 138; [1956] 1 QB 439; (1956) 100 SJ 171; [1956] 2 WLR 562 HC QBD No taking unless animus furandi at moment of taking, not later.

Moys (Robert), R v (1984) 79 Cr App R 72; [1984] Crim LR 494; [1984] TLR 327 CA Subjective question whether accused knew/believed goods were stolen - merely suspecting goods were stolen could not ground handling conviction.

Mucklow, Taylor v [1973] Crim LR 750; (1973) 117 SJ 792 HC QBD That use of airgun was to protect one's property (in protection of which one may use some force) was not reasonable excuse for same.

Mudge (William), R v (1908) 1 Cr App R 62 CCA Proper conviction of party for unlawful carnal knowledge where did not give evidence in own defence.

Muhandi v R [1957] Crim LR 814t PC Master of lion man guilty along with hirers of lion man of murder committed by him as master had enabled the commission of the offence.

Muir v Smith [1978] Crim LR 293; (1978) 128 NLJ 364t; (1978) 122 SJ 210 HC QBD Conviction quashed where charged with possessing cannabis resin but only possession of cannabis (and not that it was cannabis resin) proven.

Muirhead (James), R v (1908) 1 Cr App R 189; (1909) 73 JP 31; (1908-09) 53 SJ 164; (1908-09) XXV TLR 88 CCA Intent to defraud necessary to sustain conviction of obtaining credit by false pretences contrary to Debtors Act 1869, s 13(1).

Mullen, Bentley v [1986] RTR 7 HC QBD Supervisor of learner driver convicted of aiding and abetting latter in not stopping after accident occurred.

Mulligan, R v [1990] Crim LR 427 CA Is an offence of conspiracy to cheat the Revenue; was intention to permanently deprive if intended to dispose of Inland Revenue's property as though it was own property.

Mullings, London Borough of Lambeth v [1990] Crim LR 426; [1990] TLR 33 HC QBD Service of pollution abatement notice via a letter box was adequate service of same.

Mullins, R v [1980] Crim LR 37 CA Test as to recklessness a subjective one.

Multi Media Marketing (Canterbury) Ltd and another, Kent County Council v [1995] TLR 263 HC QBD On what constitutes 'human sexual activity' for purposes of the Video Recordings Act 1984, s 2(2).

Munks, R v [1963] 3 All ER 757; (1964) 48 Cr App R 56; [1964] Crim LR 52; (1963) 107 SJ 874; (1964) 128 JP 77; (1963) 113 LJ 804; [1964] 1 QB 304; [1963] 3 WLR 952 CCA Use of two live wires to give person shock not 'engine' under Offences Against the Person Act 1861, s 31.

Murcutt, Waterfield v (1927) 64 LJ ccr38 CyCt Damages plus interest to pawnbroker in action where sought return of goods pledged with him.

Murphy v Director of Public Prosecutions [1990] 2 All ER 390; (1990) 91 Cr App R 96; [1990] Crim LR 395; (1990) 154 JP 467; [1990] 1 WLR 601 HC QBD Failure of bailiff to surrender a single summary offence if bail granted by police/magistrates' court but normally contempt before Crown Court.

Murphy v Verati [1967] 1 All ER 861; [1967] Crim LR 370; (1967) 111 SJ 254; [1967] 1 WLR 641 HC QBD Can avoid payment of fare of fellow-passenger after travelling.

Murphy, R v [1954] Crim LR 944t CCA Two years' imprisonment (maximum sentence) for indecent assault (court of opinion that maximum sentence inadequate).

Murphy, R v [1980] 2 All ER 325; (1980) 71 Cr App R 33; [1980] Crim LR 309; (1980) 144 JP 360; (1980) 130 NLJ 474; [1980] QB 434; [1980] RTR 145; (1980) 124 SJ 189; [1980] 2 WLR 743 CA Failure to drive with due care/attention or recklessness as to same is essence of reckless driving; mens rea is attitude leading to driving - need not show intent to take risk.

Murray and others, R v [1990] Crim LR 803; [1990] TLR 234; [1990] 1 WLR 1360 CA Marine etc Broadcasting (Offences) Act 1967 applies to pirate broadcasters who are not British subjects.

Murray v Ministry of Defence [1988] 2 All ER 521; (1988) 138 NLJ 164; (1988) 132 SJ 852; [1988] 1 WLR 692 HL Arrest can begin before formal words of arrest spoken; formal words usually to be said at moment of arrest.

Murray, R v [1982] 2 All ER 225; (1982) 75 Cr App R 58; [1982] Crim LR 370; [1982] RTR 289; (1982) 126 SJ 227; [1982] TLR 93; [1982] 1 WLR 475 CA Attempting to pervert course of justice requires intent to do so and act which would tend to do so.

Murray, R v (1931-34) XXIX Cox CC 441; [1932] 1 KB 599; (1932) 73 LJ 153; (1932) 146 LTR 487; (1932) 76 SJ 166; (1931-32) XLVIII TLR 255; (1932) WN (I) 47 CCA Scottish conviction can be one of three to sustain habitual criminal conviction so long as offence exists in England.

Murtagh and Kennedy, R v [1955] Crim LR 315 Assizes On elements of murder/manslaughter by way of knocking-down person with motor vehicle.

Musgrave, Consolidated Exploration and Finance Company v [1900] 1 Ch 37; [1900] LXIX (1) LJ 11; (1899-1900) LXXXI LTR 747; (1899-1900) XVI TLR 13 HC ChD Indemnity for bail is an illegal contract.

Musial, R v [1956] Crim LR 843t CCA That alibi witness did not get to trial did not furnish good basis for appeal.

Myers v Garrett [1972] Crim LR 232 HC QBD Repeated use of word 'fucking' was obscene and persons had been annoyed by same so were guilty of using obscene language to annoyance of passengers.

Nai-Keung, Attorney-General of Hong Kong v (1988) 86 Cr App R 174; [1988] Crim LR 125; [1987] 1 WLR 1339 PC Export quotas were intangible property that could be dishonestly appropriated.

Nakhla v R [1975] 2 All ER 138; [1976] AC 1; [1976] Crim LR 81; (1975) 139 JP 414; (1975) 119 SJ 286; [1975] 2 WLR 750 PC Being in place with felonious intent not 'frequenting'; must be continuous/repeated action of some sort.

Nameless Case (1962) 112 LJ 459 CCA On provocation as a defence to murder.

Nanayakkara (Basil Chanrarahra), R v; R v Khor (Teong Leng); R v Tan (Tang Loong) [1987] 1 All ER 650; (1987) 84 Cr App R 125; (1987) 131 SJ 295; [1987] 1 WLR 265 CA 'Acceptance' of a valuable security under Theft Act 1968, s 20(2) had same meaning as 'acceptance' in Bills of Exchange Act 1882, s 17: giving valuable securities to bank not 'acceptance'.

Napolitano, Siviour v [1930] All ER 626; (1931-34) XXIX Cox CC 236; (1931) 95 JP 72; [1931] 1 KB 636; (1931) 100 LJCL 151; (1931) 144 LTR 408; (1930-31) XLVII TLR 202; (1931) WN (I) 24 HC KBD On what constitutes being a 'lessee' of premises used for prostitution.

Napp, Kite v [1982] TLR 294 HC QBD That dog bit people with bags a characteristic of that dog for purposes of the Animals Act 1971, s 2(2)(b).

Narang (Manohar Lal) and another, Union of India v; Union of India v Narang (Omi Prakash) and another [1977] 2 All ER 348; [1978] AC 247; (1977) 64 Cr App R 259; (1977) 141 JP 361; [1977] 2 WLR 862 HC QBD If facts relevant to objection raised by fugitive show unjust/oppressive to return court must discharge from custody.

Narang (Manohar Lal) and another, Union of India v; Union of India v Narang (Omi Prakash) and another [1977] 2 All ER 348; [1978] AC 247; (1977) 64 Cr App R 259; [1977] Crim LR 352; (1977) 141 JP 361; (1977) 127 NLJ 542t; (1977) 121 SJ 286; [1977] 2 WLR 862 HL If facts relevant to objection raised by fugitive show unjust/oppressive to return court must discharge from custody.

Nash, R v [1991] Crim LR 768; (1991) 155 JP 709; [1991] TLR 285 CA On recklessness as an element of mens rea for assault occasioning actual bodily harm.

Nathan (Nathaniel) and Harris (Edward), R v (1909) 2 Cr App R 35 CCA Fraudulent statements precluded defence of 'puffing' - on limits of praise.

National Coal Board v Gamble [1958] 3 All ER 203; (1958) 42 Cr App R 240; [1958] Crim LR 682; (1958) 122 JP 453; (1958) 108 LJ 617; [1959] 1 QB 11; (1958) 102 SJ 621; [1958] 3 WLR 434 HC QBD Aiding and abetting where seller of unascertained goods completed sale despite knowing at weighing (passing) of property that conveyance of that weight an offence.

National Insurance Commissioner; ex parte Connor, R v [1980] Crim LR 579 HC QBD Widow guilty of manslaughter of husband not entitled to state-provided widow's pension.

National Rivers Authority v Wright Engineering Ltd [1994] Crim LR 453 CA 'Causation' of pollution a question of fact; foreseeabilty of some relevance in determining causation.

National Rivers Authority v Yorkshire Water Services [1994] Crim LR 451; [1993] TLR 589; [1994] TLR 592 HC QBD 'Causation' of pollution a question of fact (said 'causation' proved here).

National Rivers Authority, Wychavon District Council v [1993] Crim LR 766 HC QBD Positive act necessary to render council liable for 'causing' discharge of effluent which had somehow started/somehow previously found not to be present.

National Westminster Bank Ltd and others, De Vries v [1984] TLR 531 HC QBD Perjury prosecution appropriate action against individual who swore/employed affidavit in knowledge that it was false.

Naviede, R v [1997] Crim LR 662 CA On whether (in light of Halai decision) credit facilities could be regarded as services.

Navvabi, R v [1986] 3 All ER 102; (1986) 83 Cr App R 271; [1987] Crim LR 57; (1986) 150 JP 474; (1986) 136 NLJ 893; (1970) 130 SJ 681; [1986] 1 WLR 1311 CA Use of cheque card to guarantee cheque drawn on account without necessary funds not an assumption of bank's rights and so not appropriation.

Nawrot and Shaler v Director of Public Prosecutions [1988] Crim LR 107 HC QBD No offence of abusing constable and Justices of the Peace Act 1361 does not provide basis for arrest for such an offence.

Naylor (Angela), R v [1979] Crim LR 532 CrCt On extent of power of police to relieve person in custody of her property.

Naylor, Barbanell v [1936] 3 All ER 66; (1937) 101 JP 13; (1936) 80 SJ 876 HC KBD Newspaper horoscope column did not contravene Vagrancy Act 1824, s 4.

Neal (John Frederick), R v; R v Cardwell (Michael Phillip); R v Cardwell (Anthony John); R v D'Antoni (Salvatore) (1983) 77 Cr App R 283; [1983] Crim LR 677; [1983] TLR 484 CA Could be convicted of evading prohibition on importation of dangerous drugs though not involved in actual importation.

Neal v Evans [1976] Crim LR 384; [1976] RTR 333; (1976) 120 SJ 354 HC QBD Person who drank more alcohol pending known arrival of police and so frustrated breath test was guilty of obstructing police officer in execution of duty.

Neale v E [1984] Crim LR 485 CA On meaning of word 'drunk' in Licensing Act 1872, s 12, as amended by the Criminal Justice Act 1967, s 91.

Neale v E (RMJ) (1985) 80 Cr App R 20; [1984] TLR 116 HC QBD Could not be convicted of disorderly behaviour while drunk where had actually been glue-sniffing.

Neat, R v [1900] 69 LJCL 118; (1899-1900) LXXXI LTR 680; (1899-1900) XVI TLR 109 HC QBD Conviction for theft of money of which prisoner was beneficial owner approved. (Larceny Act 1868, s 116(1)).

Nedrick, R v [1986] 3 All ER 1; (1986) 83 Cr App R 267; [1986] Crim LR 742; (1986) 150 JP 589; (1970) 130 SJ 572; [1986] 1 WLR 1025 CA Foresight is evidence of intent but does not constitute intent.

Needham, Johnson v (1911-13) XXII Cox CC 63; (1909) 73 JP 117; [1909] 1 KB 626; (1909) C LTR 493; (1908-09) XXV TLR 245; (1909) WN (I) 26 HC KBD Ill-treatment/abuse/torture of animals are separate offences.

Noble, R v; R v King [1954] Crim LR 712 Magistrates Failed prosecution for damage to ancient monuments.

Nock, Director of Public Prosecutions v; Director of Public Prosecutions v Alsford [1978] 2 All ER 655; [1978] AC 979 (also CA); (1978) 67 Cr App R 116 (also CA); [1978] Crim LR 483; (1978) 142 JP 414; (1978) 128 NLJ 759t; (1978) 122 SJ 417; [1978] 3 WLR 56 (also CA) HL Conspiracy to commit a crime only if planned conduct would result in crime.

Nock, Director of Public Prosecutions v; Director of Public Prosecutions v Alsford [1978] AC 979 (also HL); (1978) 67 Cr App R 116 (also HL); (1978) 128 NLJ 264t; (1978) 122 SJ 128; [1978] 3 WLR 56 (also HL) CA Conspiracy to commit a crime though planned conduct would not result in crime.

Noel (John Beauchamp), R v (1914) 10 Cr App R 255; (1914) WN (I) 318 CCA Conversion of money by person in whose name money intentionally deposited; application of Larceny Act 1861, s 85.

Noon v Smith [1964] 3 All ER 895; (1965) 49 Cr App R 55; [1965] Crim LR 41t; (1965) 129 JP 48; (1964) 114 LJ 859; (1964) 108 SJ 898; [1964] 1 WLR 1450 HC QBD Theft can be evidenced directly or by inference.

Norbury, R v [1978] Crim LR 435 CrCt Was public nuisance to persistently make obscene telephone calls to women over protracted period.

Nordeng (Jarl), R v (1976) 62 Cr App R 123; [1976] Crim LR 194t; (1976) 126 NLJ 41t CA Is obtaining pecuniary advantage by deception to obtain services of hotel and have it charged to third party.

Norfolk Constabulary v Seekings and Gould [1986] Crim LR 167 CrCt Unhitched articulated lorry trailer not a 'building' for purposes of Theft Act 1968, s 9.

Norman (Charles Leslie), R v (1924) 88 JP 125; [1924] 2 KB 315; (1924) 93 LJCL 883; (1923-24) 68 SJ 814; (1923-24) XL TLR 693 CCA Person who was previously convicted as habitual criminal need not later be found such.

Norman, Parkin v; Valentine v Lilley [1982] 2 All ER 583; [1982] Crim LR 528; [1983] QB 92; (1982) 126 SJ 359; [1982] TLR 140; [1982] 3 WLR 523 HC QBD Whether behaviour intentionally insulting irrelevant in deciding if likely to cause breach of peace (for which must be actual/implied violence).

Norris, Paterson v (1913-14) XXX TLR 393 HC KBD Boarding-house keeper owes duty of care to keep door of premises closed.

North Staffordshire Railway Company v Waters (1914-15) XXIV Cox CC 27; (1914) 78 JP 116; (1914) 110 LTR 237 HC KBD Failed prosecution against railway company for cruel transport of animals.

North v Pullen [1962] Crim LR 97t; (1962) 106 SJ 77 HC QBD Brief delay in effecting arrest did not mean police constable not acting in execution of his duty when was head-butted by offender.

Norton (Rex), R v [1977] Crim LR 478 CrCt Not guilty of possession of firearm with intent to endanger life where only sought to endanger own life.

Notman, R v [1994] Crim LR 518 CA Actions must have been substantial cause of injury suffered to constitute assault; direction to convict of using threatening words/behaviour ought not to have been made where guilty plea to same rather than affray (offence charged) withdrawn.

Nott, R v (1959) 43 Cr App R 8; [1959] Crim LR 365 Assizes Prosecution may call evidence to rebut insanity by proving diminished responsibility.

Nottingham Justices, ex parte Davies, R v [1980] 2 All ER 775; (1980) 71 Cr App R 178; (1980) 144 JP 233; (1980) 130 NLJ 509; [1981] QB 38; (1980) 124 SJ 444; [1980] 3 WLR 15 HC QBD Magistrates cannot change own decision that exception to bail law applies absent fresh evidence.

Nottingham Justices; ex parte Fraser, R v [1995] TLR 279 HC QBD On relevant factors when justices deciding whether to issue warrant for arrest of defence witness.

Nuttall, R v [1956] Crim LR 125t CCA Unfaithfulness of wife did not per se constitute provocation reducing murder to manslaughter.

Nyberg (Simon), R v; R v White (Alfred) (1922-23) 17 Cr App R 59 CCA White granted leave to appeal against conviction for riot; possession of firearms/shooting with intent to endanger life.

Nye v Niblett and others (1918-21) XXVI Cox CC 113; (1918) 82 JP 57; [1918] 1 KB 23; [1918] 87 LJCL 590; (1917-18) 117 LTR 722; (1917) WN (I) 314 HC KBD Need not show particular animal kept for domestic purpose if such animals normally so kept to sustain conviction under Malicious Damage Act 1861, s 41.

O'Brien (Michael), R v [1995] 2 Cr App R 649; [1995] Crim LR 734; (1995) 139 SJ LB 130; [1995] TLR 202 CA That knew principal might have intention to kill could sustain conviction of secondary party of attempted murder.

O'Brien (Patrick Joseph), R v (1974) 59 Cr App R 222 CA Must be agreement between parties for there to be conspiracy.

O'Brien Fallon (Matthew), R v (1963) 47 Cr App R 160; [1963] Crim LR 515; (1963) 107 SJ 398 CCA Robbery with violence conviction quashed for want of evidence but simple robbery conviction substituted in light of recent possession.

O'Brien, R v [1993] Crim LR 71 CA Could plead guilty to threatening behaviour on charge of violent disorder without empanelling jury.

O'Brien, R v [1974] 3 All ER 663; (1974) 138 JP 798 CrCt Husband capable of raping wife post-divorce decree nisi.

O'Brien, R v (1911) 75 JP 392 CCC Defendant who kept deposit paid as security for honesty while employed by defendant not guilty/guilty of fraudulent coversion/obtaining money by false pretences.

O'Brien, R v (1911-13) XXII Cox CC 374; (1910-11) 6 Cr App R; (1911) 75 JP 192; (1911) 104 LTR 113; (1910-11) 55 SJ 219; (1910-11) XXVII TLR 204 CCA Could properly be convicted of assault where charged with riot.

O'Brien, Secretary of State for Home Affairs v [1923] All ER 442; [1923] AC 603; (1923) 87 JP 174; (1923) 58 LJ 331; [1923] 92 LJCL 830; (1923) 129 LTR 577; (1922-23) 67 SJ 747; (1922-23) XXXIX TLR 638; (1923) WN (I) 217 HL Home Secretary cannot appeal habeas corpus writ (issued on appeal by CA) to HL.

O'Callaghan, Stapylton v [1973] 2 All ER 782; [1974] Crim LR 63; (1973) 137 JP 579 HC QBD Dishonest appropriation and intention of retention merits theft conviction.

O'Connell (Michael John), R v (1992) 94 Cr App R 39; [1991] Crim LR 771; (1991) 135 SJ LB 53; [1991] TLR 284 CA That intended to repay money loaned under deception not a defence but was evidence of honesty.

O'Connell, R v [1997] Crim LR 683 CA Sleeping drug not capable of causing injury giving rise to abnormality of mind such as to ground diminished responsibility defence under the Homicide Act 1957, s 3.

O'Connor, R v [1991] Crim LR 135 CA On relevance of drunkenness to intent.

O'Connor, R v [1980] Crim LR 43 CA On proving perjury.

O'Connor, The Police v [1957] Crim LR 478 Sessions That large vehicle properly parked on road did not constitute unreasonable user adequate to support conviction for obstruction of road.

O'Donoghue, R v (1926-30) XXVIII Cox CC 461; (1927) 91 JP 199; (1927) 64 LJ 378; (1928) 97 LJCL 303; (1928) 138 LTR 240; (1927) WN (I) 289/297 CCA Verdict of infanticide unavailable as child not newborn/over one month old.

O'Donoghue, R v (1927) 71 SJ 897 HC KBD Verdict of infanticide unavailable as child not newborn/over one month old.

O'Driscoll (John), R v (1977) 65 Cr App R 50; [1977] Crim LR 560 CA No defence of drunkenness available to act of basic intent (setting fire to room).

O'Driscoll, R v [1967] 1 All ER 632; (1967) 51 Cr App R 84; [1967] Crim LR 303; (1967) 131 JP 207; (1967) 111 SJ 682; [1967] 3 WLR 1143 CA No larceny if owner retains possession; embezzlement conviction sustained though in reality act of larceny.

Oskar v Government of Australia and others [1988] 1 All ER 183; [1988] AC 366; (1988) 87 Cr App R 299; [1988] Crim LR 457; (1988) 132 SJ 52; [1988] 2 WLR 82 HL Secretary of State can authorise magistrate to proceed with extradition case despite a charge lying on file; original statements or single separate certificate identifying statements acceptable; 22-month delay did not mean return unjust or oppressive.

Osmond, Homolka v [1939] 1 All ER 154 HC KBD Accessory before the fact to misdemeanour is considered akin to principal offender.

Ostler v Elliott [1980] Crim LR 584 HC QBD Was not obstruction of (here plain clothes) policemen in conduct of their duty where resisted them in reasonable belief that were not policemen.

Our Dogs Publishing Company, Limited, Mirams v [1901] 2 KB 564; [1901] 70 LJK/QB 879; (1901-02) LXXXV LTR 6; (1900-01) XVII TLR 649; (1900-01) 49 WR 626 CA Larceny Act 1861, s 102 prohibition on advertising for stolen property on 'no questions asked' basis includes advertisements for stolen dogs.

Over v Harwood (1899-1900) XVI TLR 163; (1899-1900) 48 WR 608 HC QBD On burden of proof where person charged with disobedience of order to have child vaccinated.

Overington, R v [1978] Crim LR 692 CA On relevance of admission by accused that knew goods were stolen to determination whether goods subject of alleged handling were in fact stolen.

Owen (Charles William), R v (1988) 86 Cr App R 291; [1988] Crim LR 120; (1987) 131 SJ 1696; [1988] 1 WLR 134 CA Jury could have regard to age of child in photograph when deciding if photograph obscene: did not have to decide from intrinsic nature of photograph.

Owen (Norman), R v (1976) 63 Cr App R 199 CA Offence of embracery no longer extant; generally custodial sentence appropriate for interference with administration of justice.

Owen and another, Board of Trade v [1957] 1 All ER 411; [1957] AC 602; (1957) 41 Cr App R 11; [1957] Crim LR 244; (1957) 121 JP 177; (1957) 107 LJ 104; (1957) 101 SJ 186; [1957] 2 WLR 351 HL Conspiracy to fully commit crime abroad not indictable in England.

Owen and another, R v [1956] 3 All ER 432; (1956) 40 Cr App R 103; [1956] Crim LR 829; (1956) 120 JP 553; (1956) 106 LJ 666; [1957] 1 QB 174 (also CCC); (1956) 100 SJ (1956) 100 SJ 769; [1956] 3 WLR 739 CCA Cannot be convicted of conspiracy to do crime abroad unless crime indictable in England; was conspiracy to utter forged document as forged documents posted in London/objectives could have been achieved in London.

Owen and others, R v [1956] Crim LR 550; [1957] 1 QB 174 (also CCA); (1956) 100 SJ 454; [1956] 3 WLR 252 CCC Cannot be convicted of conspiracy to do crime abroad unless crime indictable in England.

Owen, Lyons v [1963] Crim LR 123; (1962) 106 SJ 939 HC QBD Failed appeal against decision of justices that person keeping bank under surveillance not guilty of loitering with intent to commit felony.

Owen, R v [1972] Crim LR 324 CA Thirty months' imprisonment for (pregnant) woman (who had often been struck by husband) guilty of manslaughter of husband (stabbing under provocation in quarrel).

Owen, R v (1964) 108 SJ 802 CCA On need for specific direction as to onus of proof as regards establishing self-defence where that defence raised.

Owino (Nimrod), R v [1996] 2 Cr App R 128; [1995] Crim LR 743 CA On force allowable in self-defence.

Owners of Cargo of City of Baroda v Hall Line, Limited (1925-26) XLII TLR 717 HC KBD Carriers liable in damages where failed to show that theft of goods was not due to neglect of their servants.

Oxford and another, McCarrick v [1982] Crim LR 750; [1983] RTR 117 CA Constable's refusing to visit home of person (whom arrested on suspicion of driving while disqualified) and there see letter stating disqualification suspended pending appeal did not render arrest invalid.

Oxford v Moss (1979) 68 Cr App R 183; [1979] Crim LR 119 HC QBD Was not obtaining intangible University property (contrary to Theft Act 1968, s 1) for student to obtain proof copy of examination paper before sitting examination.

Oxford v Peers (1981) 72 Cr App R 19 HC QBD Is appropriation to switch lower price tags from lower priced goods to higher priced goods so as to pay lower price.

Oxford v Sangers, Ltd [1965] Crim LR 113g HC QBD Not unlawful for wholesalers of controlled poison to sell same to non-authorised retailer of poisons.

Oxford, Conlan v (1984) 79 Cr App R 157; (1984) 148 JP 97 HC QBD Magistrates can bind over juvenile under 17 to keep the peace on own recognisance or that of surety.

Oxford, Lawrenson v [1982] Crim LR 185 HC QBD Public house a 'public place' for purposes of Public Order Act 1936, s 5.

Oxford, M and another v [1981] RTR 246 HC QBD Test of guilt on criminal damage to property charge is subjective.

Oxford, McLorie v (1982) 75 Cr App R 137; [1982] Crim LR 603; [1982] QB 1290; [1983] RTR 265; (1982) 126 SJ 536; [1982] TLR 287; [1982] 3 WLR 423 HC QBD No post-arrest common law right of police to enter property and look for material evidence; is assault on police in execution of their duty to assault same while doing what is lawfully proper for them to do.

P and O European Ferries (Dover) Ltd, R v (1991) 93 Cr App R 72; [1991] Crim LR 695 CCC Corporation can be guilty of manslaughter.

P, R v [1980] Crim LR 796; (1980) 144 JP 39 CrCt Young person committed to custody following conviction can be granted bail pending appeal from magistrates to CrCt.

P, R v [1990] Crim LR 323 HC QBD Is no offence of assault with intent to rape.

Paddon, Vernon v [1973] 3 All ER 302; [1974] Crim LR 51t; (1973) 137 JP 758; (1973) 117 SJ 416; [1973] 1 WLR 663 HC QBD Using 'threatening and insulting words and behaviour' a single offence.

Padwick, F v [1959] Crim LR 439t HC QBD Presumption of doli incapax validly held to have been rebutted.

Page, R v [1953] 2 All ER 1355; [1954] Crim LR 61; [1954] 1 QB 170; (1953) 97 SJ 799; [1953] 3 WLR 895 CMAC Subject to civil trial proviso court-martial may try offence committed anywhere if would be offence in England.

Page, R v [1971] 2 All ER 870; (1971) 55 Cr App R 184; [1971] Crim LR 425; (1971) 135 JP 376; [1971] 2 QB 330; (1971) 115 SJ 385; [1971] 2 WLR 1308 CA Can evade a debt which continues to exist despite evasion.

Paget Publications, Ltd v Watson [1952] 1 All ER 1256; (1952) 116 JP 320; (1952) 96 SJ 328; [1952] 1 TLR 1189; (1952) WN (I) 248 HC QBD May order entire publication destroyed even if only a portion thereof obscene.

Pagett, R v [1983] Crim LR 393; [1983] TLR 76 CA On necessary causation for murder/manslaughter (and on operation of novus actus interveniens in that context).

Pain, R v; R v Jory; R v Hawkins [1986] Crim LR 168 CA Convictions quashed where prosecution brought out of time under Theft Act 1968, s 1(1)(b).

Painter, Tansley v [1969] Crim LR 139; (1968) 112 SJ 1005 HC QBD Evidence that had certain drug in urine sample not corroboration of possession of same.

Palestine General Officer and Another, Zabrovski v [1947] 116 LJR 1053; (1947) 177 LTR 369 PC Habeas corpus relief if detained illegally and here though detained under emergency legislation was not illegal.

Palin, R v (1905) 69 JP 423; [1906] 1 KB 7; (1905) 40 LJ 788; [1906] 75 LJKB 15; (1905-06) XCIII LTR 673; (1905-06) XXII TLR 41; (1905) WN (I) 162; (1905-06) 54 WR 396 CCR Falsification of accounts by servant not offence under Falsification of Accounts Act 1875 as was not falsification of employer's accounts.

Pallin v Buckland (1911-13) XXII Cox CC 545; (1911) 75 JP 362 HC KBD Accused found as matter of fact not to have run away and left children.

Palmer (Helen Claire), R v (1994) 15 Cr App R (S) 654 CA Fifteen months' imprisonment for mother guilty of inflicting grievous bodily harm on infant child.

Palmer v R [1971] 1 All ER 1077; [1971] AC 814; (1971) 55 Cr App R 223; [1972] Crim LR 649; (1971) 121 NLJ 152t; (1971) 115 SJ 265; [1971] 2 WLR 831 PC If self-defence fails because excessive force a manslaughter sentence need not always follow.

Palmer, R v (1913-14) XXIII Cox CC 377; (1912-13) 8 Cr App R 207; (1913) 77 JP 340; [1913] 2 KB 29; [1913] 82 LJKB 531; (1913) 108 LTR 814; (1912-13) XXIX TLR 349; (1913) WN (I) 80 CCA Fiancée's confession of immoral life not sufficient provocation to merit manslaughter and not murder conviction where fiancé kills her in response.

Panayi (Michael), R v; R v Karte (Klaas) (1988) 86 Cr App R 261; [1987] Crim LR 764 CA Cannot be guilty of commissioning offence outside UK unless offence was committed.

Pankhurst and another v Jarvis (1911-13) XXII Cox CC 228; (1910) 74 JP 64; (1909-10) 101 LTR 946; (1909-10) XXVI TLR 118 HC KBD Suffragettes insisting on admission to Palace of Westminster found guilty of obstructing police in execution of their duty.

Pankotai, R v [1961] Crim LR 546t CCA Straightforward case of capital murder properly left to jury to decide.

Pannell (Robin Masterman), R v (1983) 76 Cr App R 53; [1982] Crim LR 752; [1982] TLR 429 CA Was possession of prohibited weapon to have parts of automatic weapons in possession.

Pardoe, R v [1963] Crim LR 263g CCA Successful appeal aginst conviction (despite guilty plea) as accessory after the fact to factory-breaking where facts did not merit conviction for same.

Park (James Chalmers), R v (1988) 87 Cr App R 164; [1988] Crim LR 238; (1989) 133 SJ 945 CA Goods subject of handling stolen goods prosecution must already have been stolen - mens rea is guilty knowledge at time handle the goods.

Parker (Frank) v R [1964] AC 1369; [1964] Crim LR 659t; (1964) 114 LJ 472; (1964) 108 SJ 459; [1964] 3 WLR 70 PC Provocation could reduce murder to manslaughter even if provoked intent to kill; accused bears burden of establishing provocation (on balance of probabilities).

Parker (Leslie Charles), R v (1986) 82 Cr App R 69; [1985] Crim LR 589 CA Was corruption to accept reward for act after act done.

Parker and Bulteel, R v (1915-17) XXV Cox CC 145; (1916) 80 JP 271 CCC Banker by remaining open/carrying on business could be impliedly representing that is solvent.

Parker, McBean v [1983] Crim LR 399; (1983) 147 JP 205; [1983] TLR 85 HC QBD Person using reasonable force to resist (unexplained) search who assaulted second officer coming to aid of searching officer not guilty of assault on police officer in the execution of his duty.

Parker, R v [1977] 2 All ER 37; (1976) 63 Cr App R 211; [1977] Crim LR 102; (1977) 141 JP 274; (1977) 121 SJ 353; [1977] 1 WLR 600 CA 'Reckless' is deliberate closing of mind to obvious risk of damage.

Parker, R v (1969) 133 JP 343 CA One of two persons cannot be convicted of theft and the other not so where are jointly charged.

Parker, R v [1993] Crim LR 856 CA Unnecessary to prove that life actually endangered (merely had to prove recklessness to same) to be guilty of arson.

Parker, R v (1910) 74 JP 208 CCC On elements of forgery under Forgery Act 1861, s 38.

Parkes, R v [1973] Crim LR 358 CA On what is meant by demand 'with a view to gain' in the Theft Act 1968, s 21(1).

Parkin v Norman; Valentine v Lilley [1982] 2 All ER 583; [1982] Crim LR 528; [1983] QB 92; (1982) 126 SJ 359; [1982] TLR 140; [1982] 3 WLR 523 HC QBD Whether behaviour intentionally insulting irrelevant in deciding if likely to cause breach of peace (for which must be actual/implied violence).

Parkin, R v [1949] 2 All ER 651; (1949-50) 34 Cr App R 1; (1949) 113 JP 509; [1950] 1 KB 155; (1949) 99 LJ 581; (1949) LXV TLR 658; (1949) WN (I) 383 CCA Person climbing into building not 'found by night...in...building' contrary to Larceny Act 1916, s 28(4).

Parks, R v [1966] Crim LR 559t CCA Successful appeal against larceny by finding conviction where jury not told that must have intent to steal at time of finding to be guilty of larceny by finding.

Parmenter, R v [1991] 2 All ER 225; [1992] 1 AC 699 (also HL); (1991) 92 Cr App R 68; [1991] Crim LR 41; (1990) 154 JP 941; (1990) 140 NLJ 1231; (1990) 134 SJ 1368; [1990] TLR 564; [1991] 2 WLR 408 CA Foreseeability of some harm required for malicious wounding; intention to/realisation of risk of harm required for occasioning actual bodily harm.

Parmenter, R v (1991) 92 Cr App R 164 CA Leave to appeal granted on question of foreseeability as an element of malicious wounding/assault occasioning actual bodily harm.

Parr, Less v [1967] Crim LR 481t HC QBD 'Bastard' not an indecent word; person not guilty of using indecent language in street where could not be heard in hearing of street.

Parrish and others v Garfitt [1984] 1 WLR 911 HC QBD Group of football hooligans causing disturbance individually guilty of using threatening behaviour whereby breach of peace likely to be occasioned.

Parrott (George Charles), R v (1912-13) 8 Cr App R 186 CCA Meaning of 'enemy' in Official Secrets Act 1911, s 1.

Parsley, Sweet v [1970] AC 132; (1969) 53 Cr App R 221; [1969] Crim LR 189t; (1969) 133 JP 188; (1969) 113 SJ 86; [1969] 2 WLR 470 HL Managing premises used for smoking cannabis (Dangerous Drugs Act 1965, s 5) not an absolute offence.

Parsonage, Nicholas v [1987] RTR 199 HC QBD Police were acting in course of duty (and arrest was valid) where in course of conversation indicated offence for which would be arrested if failed to give name and address.

Parsons (Bruce and Alan), R v [1967] Crim LR 541 Assizes Committal to next assizes for trial for perjury at previous assizes (Perjury Act 1911, s 9).

Parsons, R v [1993] Crim LR 792 CA On ingredients of offence of indecent assault: on recklessness as an element of the offence.

Parsons, R v [1964] Crim LR 824t CCA Valid conviction of estate agent for fraudulent conversion of deposit cheques.

Partington v Williams (1976) 62 Cr App R 220; [1977] Crim LR 609; (1976) 126 NLJ 89t CA Could not be convicted of attempted offence where could not have committed complete offence.

Partington v Williams (1976) 120 SJ 80 HC QBD Could not be convicted of attempted offence where could not have committed complete offence.

Partridge v Crittenden [1968] Crim LR 325t; (1968) 118 NLJ 374t; (1968) 112 SJ 582; [1968] 1 WLR 1204 HC QBD Classified sales advertisement an invitation to treat not an offer for sale (so not guilty of offering to sell protected live wild bird).

Pasmore and others, Elias and others v [1934] All ER 380; (1934) 98 JP 92; [1934] 2 KB 164; (1934) 77 LJ 94; (1934) 103 LJCL 223; (1934) 150 LTR 438; (1934) 78 SJ 104; (1933-34) L TLR 196; (1934) WN (I) 30 HC KBD Can search arrestee/take property relevant to crime; property seized may be retained until charges concluded; unlawful seizure of documents overlooked where are evidence of crime.

Patel (Sabhas), R v; R v Javed (Shakeel Nawab); R v Hurree (Kamal); R v McCormick (Alan Paul) (1993) 97 Cr App R 294; [1993] Crim LR 291 CA Judge's exclusion of alibi statement from witness abroad somewhere not objectionable.

Patel v Comptroller of Customs [1965] 3 All ER 593; [1966] AC 356; [1965] Crim LR 728; (1965-66) 116 NLJ 102; (1965) 109 SJ 832; [1965] 3 WLR 1221 PC Making false customs entry an absolute offence; burden of proving false rests on prosecution; dispute over country of origin not one of 'whence...goods brought'.

Patel, Halstead v [1972] 2 All ER 147; (1972) 56 Cr App R 334; [1972] Crim LR 235t; (1972) 136 JP 465; (1972) 116 SJ 218; [1972] 1 WLR 661 HC QBD Unless repayment of actual notes/coins obtained intended is intention to permanently deprive; honest intention to replace with reasonable expectation that could replace did not displace dishonesty.

Patel, R v [1970] Crim LR 274 CA Person must know that other in possession of a dangerous drug before can be guilty of aiding and abetting in possession of same.

Paterson v Norris (1913-14) XXX TLR 393 HC KBD Boarding-house keeper owes duty of care to keep door of premises closed.

Pearcey, Levene v [1976] Crim LR 63 HC QBD Conviction of taxi-driver for deliberately misleading passenger into thinking that had to take longer journey because normal route obstructed.

Pearlberg and O'Brien, R v [1982] Crim LR 829 CrCt 100% shareholders could not be guilty of theft from companies of which were 100% shareholders.

Pearman (Stephen Dennis), R v (1985) 80 Cr App R 259; [1984] Crim LR 675; [1985] RTR 39 CA That foresee consequences need not mean intended them.

Pearse, Clayton v (1903-04) 52 WR 495 HC KBD That had power to regulate nets meant had power to prohibit nets entirely.

Pearson (William David), R v (1910) 4 Cr App R 40; (1910) 74 JP 175 CCA Essence of feloniously entering dwelling-house in the night is the felonious intention.

Pearson, R v [1994] Crim LR 534 CA On elements of offence of unlawful wounding.

Peaston (Andrew Gordon), R v (1979) 69 Cr App R 203; [1979] Crim LR 183 CA Person sending for drug was deemed to be in possession when mail arrived at house in which had bed-sit though was unaware of its arrival.

Peck, Quatromini and another v [1972] 3 All ER 521; [1972] Crim LR 596t; (1972) 136 JP 854; (1972) 122 NLJ 682t; (1972) 116 SJ 728; [1972] 1 WLR 1318 HC QBD Inclosed railway siding not a yard so not in enclosed yard for unlawful purpose.

Peck, Young and others v (1913-14) XXIII Cox CC 270; (1912-13) 107 LTR 857 HC KBD Persons in crowd from which eggs thrown but who had not themselves thrown eggs properly convicted of intimidation.

Pedro v Diss [1981] 2 All ER 59; (1981) 72 Cr App R 193; [1981] Crim LR 236; (1981) 145 JP 445; (1981) 131 NLJ 448 HC QBD Constable detaining without advising why acts unlawfully so assault on constable not assault on same in execution of duty.

Peers, Oxford v (1981) 72 Cr App R 19 HC QBD Is appropriation to switch lower price tags from lower priced goods to higher priced goods so as to pay lower price.

Peevey (James Frederick), R v (1973) 57 Cr App R 554 CA If possessed any of the unauthorised drugs with which charged of possession are completely guilty of unauthorised possession.

Pegg, R v [1955] Crim LR 308 CCA Bail inappropriate for prisoner with bad criminal history and no apparent explanation for latest offence of which charged.

Pegrum and Pegrum, Southern Water Authority v [1989] Crim LR 442 HC QBD Direction to convict in prosecution for causing pollution (pig effluent) to enter stream contrary to Control of Pollution Act 1974, s 31(1).

Penfold (David), R v; R v Penfold (William) (1980) 71 Cr App R 4; [1980] Crim LR 182 CA To be guilty of manslaughter in course of robbery must have arisen from planned common enterprise.

Penfold, Mathers v [1914-15] All ER 891; (1914-15) XXIV Cox CC 642; (1915) 79 JP 225; [1915] 1 KB 515; (1915) 50 LJ 29; [1915] 84 LJKB 627; (1915) 112 LTR 726; (1914-15) 59 SJ 235; (1914-15) XXXI TLR 108; (1915) WN (I) 13 HC KBD Charity street-collector not 'begging' contrary to Vagrancy Act 1824, s 3.

Penguin Books, Ltd, R v [1961] Crim LR 176 CCC On obscenity: failed prosecution of Penguin Books for publishing 'Lady Chatterley's Lover' by DH Lawrence.

Penn, Cotterill v [1935] All ER 204; (1934-39) XXX Cox CC 258; (1935) 99 JP 276; [1936] 1 KB 53; (1935) 79 LJ 432; [1936] 105 LJCL 1; (1935) 153 LTR 377; (1935) 79 SJ 383; (1934-35) LI TLR 459; (1935) WN (I) 107 HC KBD That mistook breed of bird did not relieve liability for intended killing of particular bird under Larceny Act 1861, s 23.

Penn, R v [1966] Crim LR 681t CA Perjury conviction quashed where falsehood had sprung from bona fide error.

Pepper (Edwin), R v (1909) 2 Cr App R 38 CCA Alibi defence does not depend on number of witnesses for/against it.

Perch (Edmund), R v (1908-09) XXV TLR 401 CCA Finding that were guilty of wilful neglect of children not affected by jury's rider that accused acted through ignorance.

Percival v Stanton [1954] Crim LR 308; (1954) 98 SJ 114 HC QBD Net not a 'fixed engine' as was not fixed/secured by anchors.

Phillips, Brightside and Carbrook (Sheffield) Co-operative Society Ltd v (1964) 108 SJ 53; [1964] 1 WLR 185 CA Can make non-specific claim of conversion.

Phillips, Johnson v [1975] 3 All ER 682; [1975] Crim LR 580; (1976) 140 JP 37; (1975) 125 NLJ 869t; [1976] RTR 170; (1975) 119 SJ 645; [1976] 1 WLR 65 HC QBD Is wilful obstruction to ignore police officer's instruction to ignore traffic regulations if necessary to protect life/property.

Phillips (Michael Patrick), R v (1946-48) 32 Cr App R 47; (1947) 111 JP 333; (1947) WN (I) 129 CCA Possibility of repeat offence by person charged with housebreaking renders giving bail to same inadvisable.

Phillips, R v [1922] All ER 275; (1922-23) 67 SJ 64; (1921-22) XXXVIII TLR 897 HC KBD Alleged fugitive offender not entitled to bail while in remand.

Phillips, R v (1921-25) XXVII Cox CC 332; (1922) 86 JP 188; (1923) 128 LTR 113; (1922) WN (I) 274 HC KBD Bail possible in extradition case at magistrate's discretion.

Phillips, Williams and others v; Roberts and others v Phillips (1957) 41 Cr App R 5; (1957) 121 JP 163 HC QBD Dustmen convicted for larceny where sold refuse from dustbins.

Phillips, Williams v [1957] Crim LR 186t HC QBD Corporation refuse collectors guilty of larceny from corporation where took material from collected refuse.

Phillis, R v (1915-16) XXXII TLR 414 CCA That cross language was spoken not provocation reducing murder to manslaughter.

Pick, R v [1982] Crim LR 238 CrCt On appropriate charge for person who allegedly wrongfully took gaming chips from casino roulette table.

Pickersgill, Rodgers v (1910) 74 JP 324; (1909-10) 54 SJ 564; (1909-10) XXVI TLR 493 HC KBD On what constitutes hunting of animals (so that Wild Animals in Captivity Act 1900, s 4 does not apply and are not guilty of cruelty).

Pickett v Fesq (1949) 113 JP 528; (1950) 94 SJ 14 HC KBD Inappropriate that witting offender under Exchange Control Act 1947, s 22(1) be dealt with under Probation of Offenders Act 1947.

Pickford (Tom James), R v (1914) 10 Cr App R 269 CCA Prostitute need not be accomplice of man living on earnings of prostitution.

Piddington v Bates; Robson and another v Ribton-Turner [1961] Crim LR 262; [1961] 1 WLR 162 HC QBD Valid for police to act to prevent anticipated breach of peace where anticipation of same is reasonable.

Pierre, R v [1963] Crim LR 513 CCA Not necessary that person charged with using firearm to resist arrest know that what possessed is a firearm as defined in the Firearms Act.

Pigg, R v [1982] 2 All ER 591; (1982) 74 Cr App R 352; [1982] Crim LR 446; (1982) 146 JP 298; (1982) 126 SJ 344; [1982] TLR 60; [1982] 1 WLR 762 CA Foreman must openly state number of dissenting jurors; recklessness in rape if unbothered by consent in situation where possibly no consent; continuing with sex though aware possibly no consent.

Piggott and another, Kiu (Chang Hang) and others v [1908-10] All ER 1270; (1909) C LTR 310 PC Person to be heard in own defence before committal for contempt (for perjury).

Pike, R v [1961] Crim LR 114 Assizes Conviction for manslaughter of man who was reckless as to whether mistress' inhalation of substance prior to sex would cause her death.

Pike, R v [1961] Crim LR 547 CCA Failed appeal against conviction for manslaughter of man who was reckless as to whether mistress' inhalation of substance prior to sex would cause her death.

Pilgrim v Rice-Smith and another [1977] 2 All ER 658; (1977) 65 Cr App R 142; [1977] Crim LR 371; (1977) 141 JP 427; (1977) 127 NLJ 516t; (1977) 121 SJ 333; [1977] 1 WLR 671 HC QBD Fraud nullified contract of sale so taking of product was theft.

Pilkington, R v [1958] Crim LR 545 CCA Person guilty of taking house deposits for self was guilty of fraudulent conversion on persons who paid deposits.

Pill, Billing v [1953] 2 All ER 1061; (1953) 37 Cr App R 174; [1954] Crim LR 58; (1953) 117 JP 569; (1953) 103 LJ 719; [1954] 1 QB 71; (1953) 97 SJ 764; [1953] 3 WLR 758 HC QBD Temporary army hut was chattel which could be subject of larceny of fixture.

Porter, R v [1976] Crim LR 58 CrCt Defendant's view that goods were stolen was not evidence that goods were stolen.

Postlethwaite and others, Government of Belgium v [1988] AC 924 (also HC QBD); (1987) 137 NLJ 666; (1987) 131 SJ 1038; [1987] 3 WLR 365 HL On what constitutes satisfactory submission of evidence within time constraints imposed by the Anglo-Belgian Extradition Treaty.

Postmaster-General v Seager [1955] Crim LR 716 Magistrates Person with wireless that was not plugged in (and which claimed was never used) acquitted of unlicensed use of wireless.

Potger (Christopher Granville Louis), R v (1971) 55 Cr App R 42 CA On meaning of 'dishonestly' in Theft Act 1968, ss 15 and 16.

Potter and another, R v [1953] 1 All ER 296; (1953) 117 JP 77 Assizes Elements of conspiracy.

Potter and another, R v [1958] 2 All ER 51; (1958) 122 JP 234; (1958) 42 Cr App R 168; [1958] Crim LR 472; [1958] 1 WLR 638 Assizes Where party sits driving test for another both are guilty of procuring with intent to defraud; in signing for licence former guilty of forgery; in seeking thereon latter uttering forged document.

Potter v Challans (1911-13) XXII Cox CC 302; (1910) 74 JP 114; (1910) 102 LTR 325 HC KBD Prosecution failed to discharge burden of proof.

Poultry World, Ltd v Conder [1957] Crim LR 803t HC QBD Cannot be guilty of aiding/abetting offence unless know facts making up offence or are wilfully blind as to same.

Poutney v Griffiths [1975] Crim LR 702; (1975) 125 NLJ 722 HL Conviction of mental nurse for assault on patient validly quashed as had been acting in on-duty capacity (Mental Health Act 1959, s 141 applied).

Powell and Daniels, R v [1996] 1 Cr App R 14; [1996] Crim LR 201; [1995] TLR 325 CA On necessary mens rea required of junior party charged of murder as part of joint enterprise.

Powell v MacRae [1977] Crim LR 571 HC QBD Bribe accepted by employee did not belong to employers so employee not guilty of theft of bribe.

Powell, John Calder (Publications), Ltd v [1965] 1 All ER 159; [1965] Crim LR 111t; (1965) 129 JP 136; (1965) 115 LJ 90; [1965] 1 QB 509; (1965) 109 SJ 71; [1965] 2 WLR 138 HC QBD Obscene work need not concern sex; expert opinion that work for public good may be disregarded.

Powell, R v [1956] Crim LR 255 CCA On necessary attributes of accessory after the fact.

Powell, R v [1963] Crim LR 511; (1963) 113 LJ 643 CCA Toy gun an offensive weapon where have intent to use it to cause injury (intent proved by fact that was in fact usedv to cause injury here).

Powell, R v (1914-15) XXIV Cox CC 229; (1915) 79 JP 272 CCC Need not intend to forever deprive parent of child to be convicted of child abduction.

Power, R v (1918-21) XXVI Cox CC 399; (1919) 83 JP 124; [1919] 1 KB 572; (1919) 120 LTR 577; (1918-19) XXXV TLR 283; (1919) WN (I) 64 CCA CCA can consider defence evidence that incriminates defendant.

Powers and another, R v [1990] Crim LR 586 CA On what constitutes 'recent' possession.

Pragliola (James) and Pragliola (Antonio), R v [1977] Crim LR 612 CrCt On what constitutes unlawful 'possession' of controlled drug for purposes of Misuse of Drugs Act 1971, s 5.

Pratt, R v [1984] Crim LR 41 CrCt Must prove (inter alia) indecent intention for offender to be guilty of indecent assault.

Preddy, R v; R v Slade [1995] Crim LR 564 CA Was obtaining property by deception (under Theft Act 1968, s 15(1)) to fraudulently obtain advances from building societies/other financial institutions by way of cheque/computer transfer.

Preddy, R v; R v Slade; R v Dhillon [1996] 3 All ER 481; [1996] AC 815; [1996] 2 Cr App R 524; [1996] Crim LR 726; (1996) 146 NLJ 1057; (1996) 140 SJ LB 184; [1996] 3 WLR 255 HL Not obtaining property by deception (under Theft Act 1968, s 15(1)) to fraudulently obtain advances from building societies/other financial institutions by way of cheque/computer transfer.

Preece (Conrad), R v (1993) 96 Cr App R 264; [1992] TLR 557 CA General practice to direct jury that prosecution must disprove alibi.

Preece, R v; R v Howells [1976] 2 All ER 690; (1976) 63 Cr App R 28; [1976] Crim LR 392t; (1976) 140 JP 450; (1976) 126 NLJ 338t; [1977] QB 370; (1976) 120 SJ 233; [1976] 2 WLR 749 CA Gross indecency 'with' another man requires consent of other.

Prentice and another, R v; R v Adomako; R v Holloway [1993] 4 All ER 935; (1994) 98 Cr App R 262; [1994] Crim LR 598; (1993) 157 JP 1185; (1993) 143 NLJ 850; [1994] QB 302; (1993) 137 SJ LB 145; [1993] TLR 286; [1993] 3 WLR 927 CA Involuntary manslaughter by breach of duty if gross negligence - not recklessness - results in breach of duty and causes death.

Prevost, R v (1965) 109 SJ 738 CCA Possession conviction quashed where had been inadequate direction as to elements of possession.

Price (Ronald William), R v (1990) 90 Cr App R 409; [1990] Crim LR 200 CA R v Ghosh direction on dishonesty does not have to be given in every case in which dishonesty arises.

Price Waterhouse and others, Abu Dhabi and others (third parties); Bank of England intervening, Bank of Credit and Commerce International (Overseas) Ltd (in liquidation) and others v [1997] TLR 336 HC ChD Criminal offence to disclose bank information in breach of the Banking Act 1987, s 82(1).

Price, R v [1968] Crim LR 329t; (1968) 112 SJ 330 CA On warning to be given as to evidence of accomplice (here to offence of using instrument with intent to procure miscarriage).

Price, R v [1962] 3 All ER 957; (1963) 47 Cr App R 21; [1963] Crim LR 117; (1963) 113 LJ 26; [1962] 3 WLR 1308 HC QBD Absent contrary statutory provision insanity not to be put to jury where raised by prosecution not defence.

Pridmore (George Edward), R v (1912-13) 8 Cr App R 198; (1913) 77 JP 339; (1912-13) XXIX TLR 330 CCA On guilt of parties to common unlawful enterprise for attempted murder by one; on appropriate sentencing for same.

Priestnall v Cornish [1979] Crim LR 310 CA Attack on person backing away was not self-defence.

Prince, R v [1941] 3 All ER 37; (1941-42) LVIII TLR 21 CCA Reasonable doubt in jury's minds whether act unintended/provoked merits acquittal of accused.

Pritchard, R v (1913-14) XXIII Cox CC 682; (1913) 48 LJ 689; (1913-14) 109 LTR 911; (1913) WN (I) 338 CCA Absent agreement to receive wife's receiving did not mean husband guilty of receiving.

Pritchard, R v (1900-01) XVII TLR 310 Assizes Murder of new-born child: on what constitutes separate existence.

Pritchard, Taylor v (1910) 45 LJ 392; (1909-10) XXVI TLR 496; (1910) WN (I) 147 HC KBD On powers of search of water bailiff under Salmon Fishery Act 1873, s 36.

Propp, Jewelowski v [1944] 1 All ER 483; (1944) 171 LTR 234; (1943-44) LX TLR 559 HC KBD No duty to mitigte damages in fraudulent misrepresentation action.

Pryce (Charles Lewis), R v (1949-50) 34 Cr App R 21 CCA Bankrupt's obtaining loan of money was obtaining credit as specified in Bankruptcy Act 1914, s 155(a)/Debtors Act 1869, s 13.

Pryce (Timothy), R v [1979] Crim LR 737 CrCt On elements of offence of being suspected person loitering with intent.

Pryce, R v [1972] Crim LR 307 CA On unlawful detention contrary to the Offences against the Person Act 1861, s 56.

Ptohopoulos (Chrisostomos), R v (1968) 52 Cr App R 47 CA Issue of fact whether talking to and being with prostitute constitutes being habitually in her company (Sexual Offences Act, s 30(2)).

Public Prosecutor for Singapore, Moey (Chung Kum) alias Ngar (Ah) v [1967] 2 AC 173; (1967) 111 SJ 73; [1967] 2 WLR 657 PC Interpretation of Singaporean Penal Code provisions pertaining to murder.

Public Prosecutor v Koi [1968] 1 All ER 419 PC Consorting with Indonesian soldiers not doing so with persons carrying arms contrary to Internal Security Act 1960.

Public Prosecutor, Chuan (Ong Ah) v; Cheng (Koh Chai) v Public Prosecutor [1981] AC 648; [1981] Crim LR 245; (1981) 131 NLJ 44; (1980) 124 SJ 757; [1980] 3 WLR 855 PC Carrying over two grammes of heroin in car raised constitutionally valid presumption that were trafficker.

R, Beechey v (1915-17) XXV Cox CC 217; [1916] 85 LJPC 32; (1916) 114 LTR 1 PC Conspirator may be convicted as such though co-conspirator absent.

R, Bharat, Son of Dorsamy v [1959] 3 All ER 292; [1959] Crim LR 786; [1959] 3 WLR 406 PC Conviction quashed where assessors aiding judge misdirected by same on provocation.

R, Bong (Kwan Ping) and another v [1979] AC 609; [1979] Crim LR 245; [1979] 2 WLR 433 PC Quashing of unauthorised possession of drugs conviction where jury possibly laboured under misapprehension as to burden of proof.

R, Broadhurst (Malcolm Stewart) v [1964] 1 All ER 111; [1964] AC 441; (1964) 114 LJ 88; (1963) 107 SJ 1037; [1964] 2 WLR 38 PC Impact of drunkenness on intent.

R, Bullard (Joseph) v [1957] AC 635; (1957) 41 Cr App R 1; [1957] Crim LR 816; (1957) 121 JP 576; (1957) 101 SJ 797 PC Evidence that does not support self defence plea could support provocation plea; must be clear to jury from direction that burden of proving guilt rests with prosecution.

R, Bullard v [1961] 3 All ER 470 PC Provocation if seems an issue to be left to jury though prosecution in murder case.

R, Chan Wing-Siu and others v (1985) 80 Cr App R 117; (1984) 128 SJ 685; [1984] TLR 411 PC Secondary party guilty as principal of crime committed by primary offender in course of unlawful common enterprise where secondary party perceived risk of crime occurring.

R, Chee-Kwong (Cheung) v; Attorney-General v Chee-Kwong (Cheung) [1979] Crim LR 788; (1979) 123 SJ 473; [1979] 1 WLR 1454 PC On determining appropriate sum payable as penalty following conviction of bribery offence under Hong Kong Prevention of Bribery Ordinance 1974 (as revised).

R, Chiu-cheung (Yip) v [1994] 2 All ER 924; [1995] 1 AC 111; (1994) 99 Cr App R 406; [1994] Crim LR 824; (1994) 144 NLJ 863; (1994) 138 SJ LB 146; [1994] TLR 335; [1994] 3 WLR 514 PC No general defence of superior orders, Crown or Executive fiat in English/Hong Kong law.

R, Chiu-Cheung (Yip) v [1994] 2 All ER 924; [1995] 1 AC 111; (1994) 99 Cr App R 406; [1994] Crim LR 824; (1994) 144 NLJ 863; (1994) 138 SJ LB 146; [1994] TLR 335; [1994] 3 WLR 514 PC Undercover drug agent could be guilty of conspiracy to commit crime if had requisite intent so co-conspirators guilty of conspiracy; no general defence of superior orders, Crown or Executive fiat in English/Hong Kong law.

R, Chun-Chuen (Lee) alias Wing-Cheuk (Lee) v [1963] Crim LR 114; (1963) 113 LJ 56; (1962) 106 SJ 1008; [1962] 3 WLR 1461 PC Can rely on defence of provocation even if intended to kill/cause grievous bodily harm.

R, Conteh (Thomas) and Others v [1956] AC 158; [1956] Crim LR 189; (1956) 100 SJ 72; [1956] 2 WLR 277 PC Must know that accusation was false to be convicted of conspiring to accuse person of crime.

R, Cooray (Mahumarakalage Edward Andrew) v [1953] AC 407; (1953) 97 SJ 314 PC To be convicted as agent having committed criminal breach of trust must act as agent by way of business.

R, Dharmasena (Kannangara Aratchige) v [1951] AC 1; (1950) 94 SJ 565; [1950] 66 (2) TLR 365; (1950) WN (I) 391 PC Either all or neither party (where two persons charged) guilty of criminal conspiracy: re-trial of one conspirator demands re-trial of other.

R, Dick (Surujpaul called) v [1958] 3 All ER 300; (1958) 42 Cr App R 266; [1958] Crim LR 806; (1958) 108 LJ 681; (1958) 102 SJ 757 PC Cannot be convicted accessory before fact when principals acquitted of substantive offence.

R, Dillon v [1982] 1 All ER 1017; [1982] AC 484; (1982) 74 Cr App R 274; [1982] Crim LR 438; (1982) 126 SJ 117; [1982] TLR 24; [1982] 2 WLR 538 PC Crown must prove lawfulness of detention when prosecuting for escape from lawful custody.

R, Edwards v [1973] 1 All ER 152; [1973] AC 648; (1973) 57 Cr App R 157; [1972] Crim LR 782; (1973) 137 JP 119; (1972) 122 NLJ 941t; (1972) 116 SJ 822; [1972] 3 WLR 893 PC Extreme reaction to blackmailer's conduct might constitute provocation.

R, Thabo Meli and others v [1954] 1 All ER 373; [1954] Crim LR 217; (1954) 98 SJ 77; [1954] 1 WLR 228 PC Mistake as to which of series of intended criminal acts caused death did not relieve of liability for murder.

R, Thambiah v [1966] AC 37; [1965] 3 All ER 661; [1965] Crim LR 721; (1965-66) 116 NLJ 131; (1965) 109 SJ 832; [1966] 2 WLR 81 PC Person helping other to prepare for commission of crimes can be guilty of abetting them when done; admission anytime between beginning and ending of investigation is inadmissible.

R, Thuan (Luc Thiet) v [1996] 2 All ER 1033; [1997] AC 131; [1996] 2 Cr App R 178; [1996] Crim LR 820; (1996) 146 NLJ 513; (1996) 140 SJ LB 107; (1996) TLR 2/4/96; [1996] 3 WLR 45 PC Provocation an objective test to which particular characteristics of defendant have no relevance.

R, Vasquez v; O'Neil v R [1994] 3 All ER 674; [1994] Crim LR 845; (1994) 138 SJ LB 161; [1994] 1 WLR 1304 PC Where evidence of provocation burden on prosecution to negative that suggestion.

R, Wallace-Johnson v [1940] 1 All ER 241; [1940] AC 231; (1940) 84 SJ 149; (1939-40) LVI TLR 215; (1940) WN (I) 5 PC Need not show seditious intent/subsequent incitement to violence to sustain charge of seditious writing.

R, Walton v [1978] 1 All ER 542; [1978] AC 788; (1978) 66 Cr App R 25; [1977] Crim LR 747; (1978) 142 JP 151; (1977) 127 NLJ 1050t; (1977) 121 SJ 728; [1977] 3 WLR 902 PC Jury may reject diminished responsibilty defence even if psychiatrist credits it in evidence.

R, Wing (Lee Cheung) v; Yau (Lam Man) v R (1992) 94 Cr App R 355; [1992] Crim LR 440 PC Employees faking withdrawal slips guilty of falsification with view to gain where had not intended to account to company for profits made.

R, Wing-Siu (Chan) and others v [1985] AC 168; (1985) 80 Cr App R 117; [1984] Crim LR 549; (1984) 128 SJ 685; [1984] TLR 411; [1984] 3 WLR 677 PC Person guilty of murder/grievous bodily harm if proved that entered premises as part of unlawful common enterprise and had contemplated that serious bodily harm might result.

R, Yu-Tsang (Wai) v [1991] 4 All ER 664; [1992] 1 AC 269; (1992) 94 Cr App R 264; [1992] Crim LR 425; (1991) 135 SJ LB 164; [1991] TLR 451; [1991] 3 WLR 1006 PC Was conspiracy to defraud where intended to effect state of affairs that could deceive another into acting to his economic detriment even though that was not purpose of conspiracy.

R, Zakos v [1956] Crim LR 625t; (1956) 100 SJ 631 PC Interpretation of emergency regulations pertaining to carrying/discharging of firearms in Cyprus.

Rader, R v [1992] Crim LR 663 CA Is necessary degree of appropriation to sustain theft conviction where come by another's property with full consent of that other (no appropriation) and thereafter assume rights of owner (appropriation).

Raeburn (Jack), R v (1982) 74 Cr App R 21 CA On making of criminal bankruptcy order.

Rafiq v Director of Public Prosecutions (1997) 161 JP 412 HC QBD That dog bit person absent previous indication of inclination to bite could of itself be basis for reasonable apprehension of injury.

Rafique and others, R v [1993] 4 All ER 1; (1993) 97 Cr App R 395; [1993] Crim LR 761; (1993) 143 NLJ 581; [1993] QB 843; (1993) 137 SJ LB 119; [1993] TLR 220; [1993] 3 WLR 617 CA Perversion of justice may occur before criminal investigation begins.

Ragg, R v [1995] 4 All ER 155 CA Threat to kill not 'violent offence' under Criminal Justice Act 1991 unless intent of death or injury.

Rahman (Mohammed Moqbular), R v (1985) 81 Cr App R 349; [1985] Crim LR 596; (1985) 129 SJ 431 CA Parent's detention of child not false imprisonment unless unlawful/unreasonable parental behaviour.

Rainbird, R v [1989] Crim LR 505 CA Test as to whether wounding was malicious is a subjective test.

Ramsbottom, Roberts v (1980) 144 JP 89 HC QBD To succeed with defence of automatism must prove were totally unconscious at relevant time.

Rana, R v [1969] Crim LR 597 CA Conviction for holding drugs for/on behalf of another quashed where agent convicted in respect of drugs held by principal.

Randolph, Searle v [1972] Crim LR 779 HC QBD Possession of cigarette end containing cannabis adequate to support cannabis possession conviction - did not have to prove accused knew cigarette end to contain cannabis.

Rankin v De Coster [1975] Crim LR 226 HC QBD Construction of Prevention of Oil Pollution Act 1971, s 2.

Rao, R v [1972] Crim LR 451 CA That hoped at some stage to put back the money was taking was not a defence to theft.

Rapier (Franklyn Joseph), R v (1980) 70 Cr App R 17; [1980] Crim LR 48 CA Term 'intimidate' seldom justified in possessing offensive weapon case (only if sought to cause injury by shock and so injury to individual).

Rashid, R v [1977] 2 All ER 237; (1977) 64 Cr App R 201; [1977] Crim LR 237; (1977) 141 JP 305; (1976) 120 SJ 856; [1977] 1 WLR 298 CA Intent to deceive not enough; intent to successfully deceive necessary to sustain obtaining property by deception charge.

Raud, R v [1989] Crim LR 809 CA Was jurisdiction for prosecution under Prevention of Corruption Act 1906 where foreign embassy official improperly taking money for passports part performed transaction outside Embassy.

Raven (Alfred John) and Dellow (Mabel Nelly), R v (1920) 84 JP 139 CCC Failed bigamy prosecution where first (foreign) marriage not proved to court's satisfaction.

Raven, Fisher v; Raven v Fisher [1963] 2 All ER 389; [1964] AC 210; (1963) 47 Cr App R 174; [1963] Crim LR 503; (1963) 127 JP 382; (1963) 113 LJ 332; (1963) 107 SJ 373; [1963] 2 WLR 1137 HL Accepting money in return for promise of services/goods not obtaining credit contrary to Debtors Act 1869 or Bankruptcy Act 1914.

Raven, R v [1982] Crim LR 51 CCC 'Reasonable man' endowed with peculiar characteristics of accused (mental age of child despite being twenty-two).

Rawlings v Smith [1938] 1 All ER 11; (1939-40) XXXI Cox CC 11; (1938) 102 JP 181; [1938] 1 KB 675; (1938) 85 LJ 46; [1938] 107 LJCL 151; (1938) 158 LTR 274; (1937) 81 SJ 1024; (1937-38) LIV TLR 255; (1938) WN (I) 15 HC KBD Need not be a suspected person on a day preceding loitering.

Rawlings, R v [1994] Crim LR 433 CA Whether person in charge of dog ought to have been left to jury where was looking after dog for another and was out shopping when dog got out.

Rawson and another (Justices); ex parte Morley, R v (1909-10) 101 LTR 463 HC KBD One of four convictions for cruelty (to horses) allowed stand where procedural irregularity required quashing of other three.

Ray v Sempers [1973] 1 All ER 860; (1973) 57 Cr App R 324; [1973] Crim LR 182; (1973) 137 JP 329; (1973) 123 NLJ 16t; (1973) 117 SJ 124; [1973] 1 WLR 317 HC QBD Unless false representation cannot be deception.

Ray v Sempers [1974] Crim LR 181 HL Was obtaining pecuniary advantage by deception to enter restaurant with intention of paying for meal but to then change one's mind and dash off without paying.

Ray, Director of Public Prosecutions v [1973] 3 All ER 131; [1974] AC 370; (1974) 58 Cr App R 130; (1973) 137 JP 744; (1973) 117 SJ 663; [1973] 3 WLR 359 HL Person deciding not to pay only after ordering meal obtains pecuniary advantage by deception: regard to be had to all of behaviour in restaurant.

Raybould (Charles), R v (1909) 2 Cr App R 184; (1909) 73 JP 334; (1908-09) XXV TLR 581; (1909) WN (I) 118 CCA Invalid conviction as habitual criminal where previous criminality uncertain.

Rayner, Chilvers v (1984) 78 Cr App R 59; [1984] 1 WLR 328 HC QBD False hallmarking contrary to Hallmarking Act 1973, s 1 an absolute offence (no mens rea required).

Rayner, R v [1973] Crim LR 67 CA Borstal training merited by seventeen year old guilty of endangering safety of rail passengers/obstructing the railway/burglary.

Raywood, Moses v (1911) 80 LJCL 823 HC KBD Salmon net need not have been placed in water to be guilty of offence of using net to catch salmon contrary to Salmon Fishery Act 1865, s 36.

Re Solomons; ex parte Solomons [1904] 73 LJCL 1029 CA On allowing inspection by debtor of records kept by trustee in bankruptcy.

Re Tabrisky (1947) 91 SJ 421 CA On suspending discharge from bankruptcy.

Re Tarling [1979] 1 All ER 981; (1979) 68 Cr App R 297; (1979) 143 JP 399; (1979) 129 (1) NLJ 117; [1979] 1 WLR 1417 HC QBD Fresh evidence at second habeas corpus hearing to be evidence unheard at first hearing and which could not previously have been obtained.

Re the Application of the Right Hon David Lloyd George (1932) 76 SJ 166 HC KBD Lloyd George had authorised excuse (illness/unintended inadvertence) for non-return of declaration of election expenses to constitutency returning officer.

Re Virdee (1980) 130 NLJ 313 HC QBD Article 48 of EEC Treaty (and rights of spouses pursuant thereto) did not preclude deserter from Indian army from being returned to military custody.

Re Walsh (On appeal from a Queen's Bench Divisional Court) (1985) 149 JP 175 HL Failed habeas corpus application where claimed Home Secretary/prison governor under absolute duty to produce remanded person in court on certain date.

Re Whitehouse [1951] 1 All ER 353; (1951-52) 35 Cr App R 8; (1951) 115 JP 125; [1951] 1 KB 673; (1951) 95 SJ 138; [1951] 1 TLR 405; (1951) WN (I) 75 HC KBD High Court bail available to person appealing against conviction by summary court.

Re Wright (WH) (1905-06) 50 SJ 707 HC VacCt Ought to have been service of bail summons on prosecutrix.

Re Wring; Re Cook [1960] 1 All ER 536 HC QBD On habeas corpus hearings.

Re Yi-Ching (Ning) and others (1940) 84 SJ; (1939-40) LVI TLR 3 HC KBD Habeas corpus writ would not apply in respect of foreigner in foreign territory (leased by Britain); no writ of habeas corpus against Government Minister concerned as was only involved tangentially.

Read v Donovan [1947] 1 All ER 37; (1947) 111 JP 46; [1947] KB 326; (1947) 97 LJ 9; [1947] 116 LJR 849; (1947) 176 LTR 124; (1947) 91 SJ 101; (1947) LXIII TLR 89; (1947) WN (I) 42 HC KBD Signal pistol a lethal weapon.

Read v Jones and others (1983) 77 Cr App R 246; [1983] Crim LR 809; (1983) 147 JP 477; [1983] TLR 365 HC QBD Could be breach of peace by group though no member of public witnesses same.

Read, Ruse v [1949] 1 All ER 398; (1948-49) 33 Cr App R 67; [1949] 1 KB 377; (1949) 99 LJ 77; (1949) LXV TLR 124; (1949) WN (I) 56 HC KBD Taking without dishonest intention followed by appropriation with dishonest intention is larceny.

Reader (Alfred Raymond), R v (1978) 66 Cr App R 33 CA Accused must believe goods to have been stolen to be guilty of handling same.

Reah, R v [1968] 3 All ER 269; [1968] Crim LR 512; (1968) 112 SJ 599; [1968] 1 WLR 1508 CA Receiving provisions of Criminal Law Act 1967 not retrospective in effect.

Redfern and Dunlop Ltd (Aircraft Division), R v [1993] Crim LR 43 CA On when company liable for criminal acts of person to whom has delegated authority; valid conviction for exporting goods to Iran (licence obtained without fully disclosing relevant facts was of no defence).

Redford (David), R v (1989) 89 Cr App R 1; [1989] Crim LR 152 CA Common law cheating of Revenue could be charged notwithstanding availability of statutory offences - inaction can justify conviction for same.

Redguard, R v [1991] Crim LR 213 CA Cross-examination on post-alleged rape sexual experience ought to have been allowed where was relevant to credibility of complainant/issue of consent.

Redman, R v [1994] Crim LR 914 CA Legal issues to be resolved before speeches delivered so that all lawyers address jury on same basis.

Redmond and Redmond, R v [1984] Crim LR 292 CA Fraudulent trading conviction could be brought against company that was not winding-up in respect of acts committed before relevant statutory provision (Companies Act 1981, s 96) came into force.

Reed (Nicholas), R v [1982] Crim LR 819 CA On what it means to 'procure' something (here suicide).

Reid, R v [1992] 3 All ER 673; (1992) 95 Cr App R 391; [1992] Crim LR 814; (1994) 158 JP 517; [1992] RTR 341; (1992) 136 SJ LB 253; [1992] 1 WLR 793 HL Reckless driving occurs where accused disregards serious risk of injury to another/does not give that prospect consideration.

Reid, R v [1991] Crim LR 269 CA On test for recklessness (Lawrence formula applied).

Reigate Justices; ex parte Counsell, R v (1984) 148 JP 193; [1983] TLR 794 HC QBD Kick in stomach which occasioned considerable pain but no bruising was 'actual bodily harm' for purpose of Offences against the Person Act 1861.

Reilly, Police v [1955] Crim LR 651 Magistrates Person who acted as medium between thief and purchaser of stolen cycle, receiving commission for his services, was not a receiver.

Reiter and others, R v [1954] 1 All ER 741; (1954) 38 Cr App R 62; [1954] Crim LR 384; (1954) 118 JP 262; [1954] 2 QB 16; (1954) 98 SJ 235; [1954] 2 WLR 638 CCA Can only look to book alleged to be obscene - cannot compare with others.

Rennie, Dass and another v [1961] Crim LR 396t; (1961) 105 SJ 158 HC QBD Was obstruction of police officer in execution of his duty to ignore his request to cease throwing material from place which police could not approach without trespassing.

Renshaw, R v [1989] Crim LR 811 CA Complainant in assault case who sought not to give evidence ought not to have been prosecuted for contempt.

Renton (Ralph), R v (1925-26) 19 Cr App R 33 CCA Must be intent to defraud for there to be obtaining by false pretences.

Revuelta, R v [1959] Crim LR 777t CCA Successful appeal against conviction for being accessory after the fact to stealing.

Rey (Frederick Brian), R v (1978) 67 Cr App R 244; [1978] RTR 413 CA Valid arrest for failure to provide specimen where had provided same but in inadequate amount.

Reynolds and others, Smith v; Smith v Hancock; Smith v Lowe [1986] Crim LR 559 HC QBD On elements of offence of aiding and abetting in obstruction of police officer.

Reynolds v Commissioner of Police for the Metropolis (1985) 80 Cr App R 125; [1984] Crim LR 688; [1985] QB 881; (1984) 128 SJ 736; [1984] TLR 514; [1985] 2 WLR 93 CA Tort to obtain Forgery Act 1913 search warrant where do not reasonably believe subject of same has unlawful custody/possession of forgeries; police guilty of trespass to goods where took documents did not reasonably believe were forged.

Reynolds v Commissioner of Police for the Metropolis [1982] Crim LR 600; [1982] TLR 274 CA £12,000 damages merited in serious case of wrongful arrest/false imprisonment.

Reynolds v Hoyle [1975] Crim LR 527; (1975) 125 NLJ 800t HC QBD Successful prosecution for unlawful conveyancing by unqualified person.

Reynolds, Kyprianou v [1969] Crim LR 656; (1969) 113 SJ 563 HC QBD Intention to acquire drugs along with invitation to drug dealers to treat or make offer not enough to support conviction for attempted procurement of drugs.

Rhodes v Heritage (1951) 115 JP 303; (1951) 101 LJ 219; (1951) 95 SJ 255; [1951] 1 TLR 802; (1951) WN (I) 221 HC KBD Court of summary jurisdiction could not, pursuant to Dogs Act 1871, s 2, order dog to be destroyed.

Rhodes, Simcock v (1978) 66 Cr App R 192; [1977] Crim LR 751; (1977) 127 NLJ 1105t HC QBD Telling police officer to '**** off' was 'insulting' behaviour likely to cause breach of the peace.

Rhys Howells Transport Ltd, Nelmes v [1977] Crim LR 227 HC QBD On relevant factors to be considered in determining whether so used trailers as to cause unnecessary obstruction of highway.

RI v Deshpande (Vimlabai) and another [1946] 115 LJ 71; (1945-46) LXII TLR 430; (1946) WN (I) 105 PC Can appeal direct to PC from Indian HC where object to release of person pursuant to habeas corpus application.

RI, Das (Lala Jairam) and others v (1945) 89 SJ 164; (1944-45) LXI TLR 245 PC Indian HC cannot grant bail to convict granted leave to appeal to PC but Provincial Government can stay execution of convict's sentence pending appeal.

RI, Ghosh v (1924-25) XLI TLR 27 PC Where various persons shot at and killed another but could not be proved which shot was fatal each person was guilty of murder.

Rice v Connolly [1966] 2 All ER 649; [1966] Crim LR 389t; (1966) 130 JP 322; (1965-66) 116 NLJ 978; [1966] 2 QB 414; (1966) 110 SJ 371; [1966] 3 WLR 17 HC QBD Refusal to answer questions and escort police to station (absent arrest) not wilful obstruction.

Rice-Smith and another, Pilgrim v [1977] 2 All ER 658; (1977) 65 Cr App R 142; [1977] Crim LR 371; (1977) 141 JP 427; (1977) 127 NLJ 516t; (1977) 121 SJ 333; [1977] 1 WLR 671 HC QBD Fraud nullified contract of sale so taking of product was theft.

Richards (Colin David), R v; R v Leeming (Paul) (1985) 81 Cr App R 125; [1985] Crim LR 368 CA Police can only enter premises under Criminal Law Act 1967, s 2 where seek to effect arrest.

Richards (George Henry), R v (1910-11) 6 Cr App R 21; (1911) 75 JP 144; (1910) WN (I) 268 CCA Application of larceny by trick to real property.

Richards (George), R v (1924-25) 18 Cr App R 144 CCA Non-substitution by CCA of receiving conviction where acquitted of housebreaking.

Richards (Isabelle), R v [1973] 3 All ER 1088; [1974] Crim LR 96; (1974) 138 JP 68; [1974] QB 776; (1973) 117 SJ 852; [1973] 3 WLR 888 CA Person some distance from action not an abettor.

Richards (Jason), R v; R v Stober (Ransford) (1993) 96 Cr App R 258 CA Crown could reject manslaughter pleas despite early willingness to do so and seek murder conviction instead.

Richards v Curwen [1977] 3 All ER 426; (1977) 65 Cr App R 95; [1977] Crim LR 356; (1977) 141 JP 641; (1977) 127 NLJ 468t; (1977) 121 SJ 270; [1977] 1 WLR 747 HC QBD Whether firearm antique to be determined in each case - no set age.

Richards, Director of Public Prosecutions v [1988] 3 All ER 406; (1989) 88 Cr App R 97; [1988] Crim LR 606; (1988) 152 JP 333; [1988] QB 701; (1988) 132 SJ 623; [1988] 3 WLR 153 HC QBD Can be arrested for leaving court building after surrendering to bail but not guilty of offence.

Richards, R v (1911-13) XXII Cox CC 372; [1911] 1 KB 260; (1910) 45 LJ 790; (1911) 80 LJCL 174; (1911) 104 LTR 48 CCA Repairer removing fixtures in good condition guilty of larceny.

Richards, R v [1997] Crim LR 499 CA On relevance of lifestyle evidence on charge of possessing drug with intent to supply.

Richards, R v [1967] Crim LR 589t; (1967) 111 SJ 634 CA Successful appeal against conviction for allowing premises to be used for cannabis-smoking where evidence admitted as to condition of one party on premises but no warning given as to the weak connection between that and the offence charged.

Richards, Williams v [1971] Crim LR 41t; (1907) 71 JP 222; [1907] 2 KB 88; (1907) 42 LJ 249; [1907] 76 LJKB 589; (1907) XCVI LTR 644; (1970) 114 SJ 864; (1906-07) XXIII TLR 423; (1907) WN (I) 90 HC KBD That dog has killed sheep shows is dangerous for purposes of Dogs Act 1871, s 2.

Richards; ex parte Fitzpatrick and Browne, R v [1955] Crim LR 570t PC Warrants issued by Speaker of Australian lower House taken as conclusive that breach of privilege had occurred.

Richardson v Skells [1976] Crim LR 448 CrCt Was obtaining pecuniary advantage by deception to secure free travel on train for another by virtue of the deception.

Richardson, Carter v [1974] Crim LR 190; [1974] RTR 314 HC QBD Supervising driver validly convicted of aiding and abetting learner driver in offence of driving with excess alcohol.

Richens, R v [1993] 4 All ER 877; (1994) 98 Cr App R 43; [1993] Crim LR 384; [1992] TLR 560 CA Provocation requires sudden and temporary but not complete loss of control; judge must warn jury to consider alternatives to accused's lies tending to guilt.

Richman (Jacob), R v (1910) 4 Cr App R 233 CCA May be 'transfer' under Debtors Act 1869, s 13(2) though is no transfer as against creditors.

Rickard, Tarpy v [1980] Crim LR 375 HC QBD Could be convicted on basis of aggregate total of cannabis found at premises.

Ricketts v Cox (1982) 74 Cr App R 298; [1982] Crim LR 184 HC QBD Extreme rudeness and lack of co-operation was obstruction of police in execution of their duty.

Rider, R v [1986] Crim LR 626 CA On relevance of truth of statement to prosecution (and format of same) for perjury.

Rider, R v [1954] Crim LR 49; (1954) 118 JP 73 Assizes On what constitutes a charge when deciding whether accused to have benefit of first-time charge proviso in prosecution for having carnal knowledge of under-sixteen year old (Criminal Law Amendment Act 1922, s 2).

Riding, Westminster City Council v [1995] TLR 448 HC QBD On what constitutes 'litter' for the purposes of the Environmental Protection Act 1990, s 87(1).

Ridley (Frank), R v (1911-13) XXII Cox CC 127; (1909) 2 Cr App R 113; (1909) 100 LTR 944; (1908-09) XXV TLR 508 CCA Notice to prosecution required where seek post-conviction bail.

Rigler and another, Burden v (1911) 75 JP 36; [1911] 1 KB 337; (1910-11) 103 LTR 758; (1910-11) XXVII TLR 140; (1910) WN (I) 279 HC KBD Public meeting held on highway not per se unlawful: legality depends on circumstances.

Riley (Terence), R v (1984) 78 Cr App R 121; [1984] Crim LR 40; [1984] RTR 159 CA Could not disqualify person for facilitating commission of crime where allowed use of car on foot of conspiracy to steal.

Riley (William James), R v (1988) 87 Cr App R 125; (1988) 152 JP 399 CA Criminal bankruptcy order possible where total loss occasioned by person convicted of dishonesty offences exceeds £15,000.

Riley v Director of Public Prosecutions (1990) 91 Cr App R 14; [1990] Crim LR 422; (1990) 154 JP 453 HC QBD Could not be guilty of assault on police officer in execution of duty where validity of arrest unproven.

Riley, Cox v (1986) 83 Cr App R 54; [1986] Crim LR 460 HC QBD Was criminal damage to erase program from circuit card of computerised saw.

Riley, R v [1991] Crim LR 460 CA That woman had sex with another while child present ought to have been admitted as accused claimed had consensual sex, woman denying same saying emphasising denial by saying child was present and would never have sex with child present.

Riley, R v [1967] Crim LR 656 Assizes Person acquitted of attempt to procure act of gross indecency where at time of alleged offence was suffering from psychoneurosis which led him to want to get into trouble.

Rivett (James Frank), R v (1949-50) 34 Cr App R 87 CCA Issue when insanity pleaded not just whether diseased mind meant not reasoning properly but also whether meant not responsible for what did.

Roandale Ltd v Metropolitan Police Commissioner [1979] Crim LR 254; (1979) 123 SJ 128 CA On police powers pursuant to seizure of (here a very large number of) items under Obscene Publications Act 1959, s 3.

Roberts (John Joseph), R v (1984) 78 Cr App R 41; [1985] Crim LR 218; [1983] TLR 267 CA Judge to decide whether one co-conspirator to be convicted and other acquitted.

Roberts (Kenneth Joseph), R v (1972) 56 Cr App R 95; [1972] Crim LR 27; (1971) 115 SJ 809 CA Test whether threats lead to injury (girl jumping from car) was whether that reaction reasonably foreseeable result of what doing.

Roberts (William), R v (1987) 84 Cr App R 117; [1986] Crim LR 122 CA R v Ghosh direction on dishonesty unnecessary where dishonesty not pleaded; jury need not find that handler of stolen goods acted dishonestly towards person who suffered loss.

Roberts and another, Ledwith and another v [1936] 3 All ER 570; (1934-39) XXX Cox CC 500; (1937) 101 JP 23; [1937] 1 KB 232; [1937] 106 LJCL 20; (1936) 155 LTR 602; (1936) 80 SJ 912; (1936-37) LIII TLR 21; (1936) WN (I) 281 CA On arrest without warrant of 'suspected person or reputed thief'/'loose, idle or disorderly person' under Vagrancy Act 1824, ss 4, 6/Liverpool Corporation Act 1921, s 513.

Roberts and Williams, Barnard v (1907) 71 JP 277; (1907) XCVI LTR 648; (1906-07) 51 SJ 411; (1906-07) XXIII TLR 439 HC KBD Laying night lines was not angling (and so not covered by Larceny Act 1861, s 25).

Roberts v Jones [1969] Crim LR 90; (1968) 112 SJ 884 HC QBD Arrest of person in charge of motor car justified subsequent request that arrestee take breath test.

Roberts v Ramsbottom (1980) 144 JP 89 HC QBD To succeed with defence of automatism must prove were totally unconscious at relevant time.

Roberts v Regnart (1921-25) XXVII Cox CC 198; (1922) 86 JP 77; (1922) 126 LTR 667 HC KBD Husband guity of wilful neglect of wife despite honest belief was no longer bound to maintain her.

Roberts, Bocking v [1973] 3 All ER 962; (1978) 67 Cr App R 359; [1973] Crim LR 517; (1974) 138 JP 13; (1973) 123 NLJ 516t; [1974] QB 307; (1973) 117 SJ 581; [1973] 3 WLR 465 HC QBD Possession however small the quantity as long as enough to show not possession on earlier date.

Roberts, R v [1986] Crim LR 188 CA Existence of separation deed (without non-cohabitation/molestation clause) meant wife's implied consent to sex with husband did not revive on expiry of non-molestation/ouster orders so husband was guilty of raping wife.

Roberts, R v [1942] 1 All ER 187; (1940-42) 28 Cr App R 102; (1943) 93 LJ 100; (1942) 86 SJ 98; (1941-42) LVIII TLR 138 CCA Style of summing-up a matter for trial judge; if manslaughter verdict possible in murder trial jury must be directed on point.

Roberts, R v [1993] 1 All ER 583; (1993) 96 Cr App R 291; [1993] Crim LR 302; (1993) 157 JP 583; (1992) 142 NLJ 1503 CA That person involved in joint unlawful enterprise guilty of murder by other party of general application; exceptionally judge may have to distinguish fleeting consideration from ongoing realisation of real risk.

Roberts, R v [1991] RTR 361 CA Conviction quashed where had been misdirection by judge as to jurisdiction (which depended on appropriation occurring in England).

Roberts, R v [1990] Crim LR 122 CA Provocation decided by reference to reasonable man who has characteristics peculiar to defendant.

Robertson (Stanley), R v [1977] Crim LR 629 CrCt Insurance agent who did not fully account to insurance companies for premiums he received was not guilty of theft.

Robertson, Flockhart v [1950] 1 All ER 1091; [1950] 2 KB 498 HC KBD Guidance of procession which spontaneously formed rendered guilty of organising procession.

Robinson and others, R v [1970] 3 All ER 369; (1970) 54 Cr App R 441; [1970] Crim LR 645; (1970) 134 JP 668; [1971] 1 QB 156; (1970) 114 SJ 906; [1970] 3 WLR 1039 CA Barricading need not be use of force in retention.

Robinson v Everett and W and FC Bonham and Son Ltd [1988] Crim LR 699 HC QBD Rehearing ordered of prosecution for possession of dead wild bird.

Robinson v Hughes [1987] Crim LR 644 HC QBD On elements of offence of laying poison for wild birds in breach of Wildlife and Countryside Act 1981, s 5(1)(a).

Robinson v Kenworthy [1982] TLR 257 HC QBD On determining whether bird a 'wild bird' for purposes of the Protection of Birds Act 1954, s 1.

Robinson, Bryan v [1960] 2 All ER 173; [1960] Crim LR 489; (1960) 124 JP 310; (1960) 110 LJ 381; (1960) 104 SJ 389 HC QBD Hostess at refreshment house doorway seeking to entice custom not guilty of insulting behaviour.

Robinson, Kirkland v [1987] Crim LR 643 CA Possession of live birds contrary to Wildlife and Countryside Act 1981, s 1(2)(a), a strict liability offence.

Robinson, R v [1990] Crim LR 804 CA Failed appeal against conviction for fraudulent removal of company property ('asset-stripping').

Robinson, R v [1977] Crim LR 173 CA Not theft where of view that had right to take money.

Robinson, R v [1965] Crim LR 491t CCA Valid decision not to leave provocation to jury.

Robinson, R v [1938] 1 All ER 301; (1936-38) 26 Cr App R 129; (1938) 85 LJ 124 CCA Can be convicted of bigamy though second marriage invalid (apart from being bigamous).

Robinson, R v [1914-17] All ER 101; (1914-15) XXIV Cox CC 726; (1914-15) 11 Cr App R 124; (1915) 79 JP 303; [1915] 2 KB 342; (1915) 50 LJ 159; [1915] 84 LJKB 1149; (1915-16) 113 LTR 379; (1914-15) 59 SJ 366; (1914-15) XXXI TLR 313; (1915) WN (I) 133 CCA Mere intention to commit crime could not sustain conviction for attempt to commit crime.

Robinson, R v [1993] Crim LR 581 CA Mere words, albeit threateningly delivered, did not amount to affray.

Robson and another v Hallett [1967] 2 All ER 407; (1967) 51 Cr App R 307; [1967] Crim LR 293t; (1967) 131 JP 333; [1967] 2 QB 939; (1967) 111 SJ 254; [1967] 3 WLR 28 HC QBD Police have implied licence to enter garden in course of duty; once licence revoked by owner have reasonable time to go before become trespasser; if breach of peace in garden police can enter to stop it.

Robson, Tuck v [1970] Crim LR 273t HC QBD On what constitutes 'aiding and abetting' offence.

Rodger and another, R v [1997] TLR 428 CA Duress of necessity could not arise from within oneself but had to emanate from another.

Rodgers v Pickersgill (1910) 74 JP 324; (1909-10) 54 SJ 564; (1909-10) XXVI TLR 493 HC KBD On what constitutes hunting of animals (so that Wild Animals in Captivity Act 1900, s 4 does not apply and are not guilty of cruelty).

Rodley, R v [1911-13] All ER 688; (1913-14) XXIII Cox CC 574; (1913) 77 JP 465; [1913] 3 KB 468; [1913] 82 LJKB 1070; (1913-14) 109 LTR 476; (1913-14) 58 SJ 51; (1912-13) XXIX TLR 700; (1913) WN (I) 240 CCA Inadmissibility of evidence of later sexual antics as irrelevant to charge of burglary with intent to commit rape.

Roe v Kingerlee [1986] Crim LR 735 HC QBD Writing graffiti on wall using mud was criminal damage.

Roff, R v; R v Dowie [1976] RTR 7 CA Constable's forming opinion while defendant 'committing' offence includes short time thereafter so where officer arrested motorist immediately after crash he was acting in execution of his duty.

Rogers v Arnott [1960] 2 All ER 417; (1960) 44 Cr App R 195; (1960) 124 JP 349; (1960) 110 LJ 446; [1960] 2 QB 244; (1960) 104 SJ 508 HC QBD Bailee lawfully in possession who dishonestly offers it for sale is guilty of larceny (not attempt) though no sale.

Rogers v Wood [1968] Crim LR 274t HC QBD Not keeping premises open where sold refreshments through window of coffee bar to persons on the street.

Rogers, Director of Public Prosecutions v [1953] 2 All ER 644; (1953) 37 Cr App R 137; (1953) 117 JP 424; (1953) 97 SJ 541; [1953] 1 WLR 1017 HC QBD No coercion/violence in getting child to do indecent act meant no assault so could be no indecent assault.

Rogers, Evens v [1956] Crim LR 496 HC QBD On appropriate means of prosecuting for indecent exposure.

Rogers, Steele v (1912) 76 JP 150; (1911-12) XXVIII TLR 198 HC KBD Cruelty to stranded whale that would have been washed away with tide not offence under Wild Animals in Captivity Protection Act 1900.

Rollafson, R v (1969) 53 Cr App R 389; [1969] Crim LR 314t; (1969) 119 NLJ 364t; (1969) 113 SJ 342; [1969] 1 WLR 815 CA Cannot be guilty of fraudulent trading offence under Companies Act 1948, s 332(3) where company concerned not being wound up.

Rolle v R [1965] 3 All ER 582; [1965] Crim LR 727; (1965-66) 116 NLJ 131; (1965) 109 SJ 813; [1965] 1 WLR 1341 PC Issue of manslaughter to be left to jury where appears accused lost self-control.

Rook, R v [1993] 2 All ER 955; (1993) 97 Cr App R 327; [1993] Crim LR 698; (1993) 143 NLJ 238; [1993] TLR 87; [1993] 1 WLR 1005 CA Consequences of criminal enterprise need only be foreseeable, not intended, for accessory before fact to be liable; withdrawal from joint enterprise must be unequivocal before liability may be overcome.

Rose (Malcolm Joel), R v (1962) 46 Cr App R 103; [1962] Crim LR 252 CCA Not accessory after the fact to larceny where went to place stolen goods kept with view to purchasing same.

Rose (William), R v (1909) 2 Cr App R 265 CCA Valid conviction for larceny/larceny by bailee.

Rose v Buckett [1901] 2 KB 449; [1901] 70 LJK/QB 736; (1901) LXXXIV LTR 670; (1900-01) XVII TLR 544; (1901-02) 50 WR 8 CA Right of action for trespass/conversion did not pass to trustee upon plaintiff becoming bankrupt.

Rose v Matt [1951] 1 All ER 361; (1951-52) 35 Cr App R 1; (1951) 115 JP 122; [1951] 1 KB 810; (1951) 101 LJ 63; (1951) 95 SJ 62; [1951] 1 TLR 474; (1951) WN (I) 60 HC KBD Bailor depriving bailee of property (in which has special property) commits larceny.

Rose v R [1961] 1 All ER 859; (1961) 45 Cr App R 102; [1961] Crim LR 404; (1961) 105 SJ 253; [1961] 2 WLR 506 PC Mental abnormality not to be measured by reference to M'Naghten definition of insanity.

Rose, R v [1956] Crim LR 198 Assizes Sale to third party of cars obtained on hire-purchase could be larceny; property transfer contract induced by fraud a valuable security for purposes of Larceny Act 1916, s 32(2).

Rosenberg, R v (1906) 70 JP 264 CCC On elements of offence of concealment of birth.

Ross (Andrew), R v (1927-28) 20 Cr App R 184 CCA Nine months' hard labour for carnal knowledge of mental defective in view of age/otherwise excellent character.

Ross and another, Ryan v (1963) 113 LJ 383 HC QBD On elements of offence of possessing instrument used for taking salmon/trout with intent of committing fisheries offence.

Ross v Collins [1982] Crim LR 368 CA Holder of shotgun certificate not allowed possess loaded shotgun in public place; honest belief that not in public place unsuccessfully pleaded in defence.

Ross v Evans [1959] Crim LR 582; (1959) 123 JP 320; (1959) 109 LJ 418; [1959] 2 QB 79; (1959) 103 SJ 393; [1959] 2 WLR 699 HC QBD Dog not 'at large' when was attached to lead.

Rossborough (Paul Anthony Patrick), R v (1985) 81 Cr App R 139; [1985] Crim LR 372; (1985) 149 JP 529 CA Alibi notice could be entered in evidence by prosecution as part of its case.

Rossi, Blythe and Dennis, R v [1957] Crim LR 258t CCA Person charged with wounding with intent may be convicted of unlawful wounding.

Rossides v R [1957] Crim LR 813t PC Failed application for leave to appeal murder conviction on basis inter alia of duress.

Rossiter, R v [1994] 2 All ER 752; (1992) 95 Cr App R 326; (1992) 142 NLJ 824 CA Real evidence of provocation, however slim, requires that issue of provocation be left to jury.

Rossminster Ltd, IRC v (1979) 129 (2) NLJ 1260 HL Valid exercise of search and seizure powers by Inland Revenue.

Rothwell and Barton, R v [1993] Crim LR 626 CA That acted in self-defence/defence of another are defences to the statutory offences which replaced affray.

Rourke, R v [1956] Crim LR 326 Magistrates Doctor not guilty of aiding and abetting unlawful possession of drugs where prescribed heroin to patient who - unknown to him - was also obtaining same from another doctor.

Rowe, ex parte Mainwaring, R v [1992] 4 All ER 821; [1992] 1 WLR 1059 CA Election pamphlet may be fraudulent even though true but must impede/prevent free voting to be undue influence.

Rowell, R v [1978] 1 All ER 665; (1977) 65 Cr App R 174; [1977] Crim LR 681; (1978) 142 JP 181; (1977) 127 NLJ 662t; (1977) 121 SJ 790; [1978] 1 WLR 132 CA Person acting alone can attempt to pervert course of justice; false allegation could be attempt; attempt can be made up of one/series of actions.

Rowland (Harry), R v (1911-13) XXII Cox CC 273; (1909) 3 Cr App R 277; (1910) 102 LTR 112; (1909-10) XXVI TLR 202 CCA Accused giving evidence for other accused can be questioned on own guilt; previous convictions involving fraud/dishonesty admissible in receiving prosecution where stolen property in accused's possession though not at time of arrest; can be convicted as habitual criminal though no evidence as to behaviour in half-year prior to conviction.

Rowland, R v (1947) 97 LJ 123; [1947] 116 LJR 331; (1947) 91 SJ 177; (1947) LXIII TLR 156; (1947) WN (I) 86 CCA Refusal to hear appeal at which appellant sought to call man who had after appellant's conviction confessed to crime for which appellant convicted.

Rowland, R v (1910) 74 JP 144; [1910] 1 KB 458; (1910) 79 LJKB 327 CCA That pawned goods on day before arrest for receiving was sufficient element of possession; evidence of previous conviction for dishonesty offence admissible to prove guilty knowledge; co-prisoner testifying against another can be asked self-incriminatory questions.

Rowlands (Elizabeth), R v (1909) 3 Cr App R 224 CCA Evidence of passing counterfeit was admissible to show scienter.

Rowley, R v [1948] 1 All ER 570; (1946-48) 32 Cr App R 147; (1948) 112 JP 207 CCA Cannot plead guilty to being accessory after the fact until principal convicted.

Rowley, R v [1991] 4 All ER 649; (1992) 94 Cr App R 95; [1991] Crim LR 785; (1992) 156 JP 319; (1991) 141 NLJ 1038t; (1991) 135 SJ LB 84; [1991] TLR 347; [1991] 1 WLR 1020 CA Act outraging public decency must outrage public decency in and of itself; preparatory acts to inciting gross indecency not attempted incitement of child to gross indecency.

Royal Government of Greece v Brixton Prison Governor and others [1969] 3 All ER 1337; [1970] Crim LR 29t; [1971] AC 250; (1970) 134 JP 47; (1969) 119 NLJ 1045t; (1969) 113 SJ 901; [1969] 3 WLR 1107 HL If sufficient evidence for committal magistrate must commit.

Royle, Anderton v [1985] RTR 91 HC QBD Police station breath test results admissible though had not sought to administer preliminary breath test upon stopping defendant on road.

Royle, R v [1971] 3 All ER 1359; (1972) 56 Cr App R 131; [1972] Crim LR42t; (1972) 136 JP 106; (1971) 121 NLJ 1026t; (1971) 115 SJ 910; [1971] 1 WLR 1764 CA Honest belief that hotel bills would be paid meant no dishonest intent; must be personally liable for debt to sustain conviction; that the debts might be discharged could be relevant to intent/dishonesty.

Rozeik, R v [1996] 3 All ER 281; [1996] 1 Cr App R 260; [1996] Crim LR 271; (1995) 139 SJ LB 219; [1995] TLR 551; [1996] 1 WLR 159 CA Company not deceived where branch managers not deceived so person ought not to have been convicted of obtaining property (cheques from finance company) by deception.

RSPCA v Miller [1994] Crim LR 516; [1994] TLR 131 HC QBD Whether have 'custody' of animal depends on particular facts of each case (holding leash of another's dog did not place it in leash-holder's custody).

RSPCA, Peterssen v [1993] Crim LR 852 HC QBD On elements of offence of causing unreasonable suffering to animal (here conviction upheld for causing unreasonable suffering to sheep).

Rubens (Mark) and Rubens (Morris), R v (1909) 2 Cr App R 163 CCA All parties to common design guilty of fatal act committed by one.

Rudd v Department of Trade and Industry [1986] Crim LR 455 CA Records/cassettes not (but speakers were) susceptible to forfeiture as wireless apparatus under the Wireless Telegraphy Act 1949.

Rudd v Department of Trade and Industry (1970) 130 SJ 504 HC QBD Records/cassettes not (but speakers were) susceptible to forfeiture as wireless apparatus under the Wireless Telegraphy Act 1949.

Rudd v Secretary of State for Trade and Industry (1987) 85 Cr App R 358; (1987) 131 SJ 805; [1987] 1 WLR 786 HL Only wireless telegraphy apparatus liable to forfeiture under Wireless Telegraphy Act 1949, s 14(3) - records/cassettes in use not 'apparatus'; on what constitutes 'use' of apparatus under Wireless Telegraphy Act 1949, s 14(3) as substituted.

Rudd, R v (1948) LXIV TLR 240 CCA On effect of evidence of co-defendant; on extent of need for corroboration warning in respect of accomplice's evidence.

Rufino (Emilio), R v (1911-12) 7 Cr App R 47 CCA Alibi defence must go to jury.

Rukwira v Director of Public Prosecutions [1993] Crim LR 882; (1994) 158 JP 65; [1993] TLR 362 HC QBD Shared landing outside flat in block of flats not part of 'dwelling' for purposes of Public Order Act 1986.

Ruse v Read [1949] 1 All ER 398; (1948-49) 33 Cr App R 67; [1949] 1 KB 377; (1949) 99 LJ 77; (1949) LXV TLR 124; (1949) WN (I) 56 HC KBD Taking without dishonest intention followed by appropriation with dishonest intention is larceny.

Rushton, Osgerby v [1968] 2 All ER 1196; (1968) 118 NLJ 613t; [1968] 2 QB 466; (1968) 112 SJ 519; [1968] 3 WLR 438 HC QBD Conviction possible under statutory provision about to be repealed.

Rushworth (Gary Alan), R v (1992) 95 Cr App R 252 CA Must intend physical harm/foresee risk of same before can be guilty of unlawful wounding.

Rushworth, Townley v [1964] Crim LR 590; (1963) 107 SJ 1004 HC QBD Person in respect of whom incomplete recommendation for committal to mental hospital made not guilty of assault where struck out at persons who entered his property seeking to forcibly remove him.

Russell (Earl), R v [1901] AC 446; (1901-07) XX Cox CC 51; [1901] 70 LJK/QB 998; (1901-02) LXXXV LTR 253; (1900-01) XVII TLR 685; (1901) WN (I) 156 HL Can be tried for bigamy though second marriage outside Empire.

Russell (Marion) and Russell (Andrew Louis), R v (1987) 85 Cr App R 388; [1987] Crim LR 494 CA Could infer that parents jointly responsible for administering drug where no proof one rather than another guilty/one did not interrupt ill-treatment of child by other.

Russell (Peter Andrew), R v (1992) 94 Cr App R 351; [1992] Crim LR 362; [1991] TLR 609 CA Production of crack from cocaine hydrochloride was 'production' of controlled drug contrary to Misuse of Drugs Act 1971, s 4(2).

Russell (Raymond), R v (1985) 81 Cr App R 315; [1985] Crim LR 231 CA Rarely credible but nonetheless possible defence that had so forgotten possession of offensive weapon as to be unaware it was there.

Russell v Smith [1957] 2 All ER 796; (1957) 41 Cr App R 198; [1957] Crim LR 610; (1957) 121 JP 538; (1957) 107 LJ 570; [1958] 1 QB 27; (1957) 101 SJ 665 HC QBD Cannot possess something of which do not know: an innocent taking.

Russell, R v [1956] Crim LR 572 Magistrates Application of Vagrancy Act 1824, s 4.

Russell, R v (1953) 97 SJ 12; [1953] 1 WLR 77 CCA 'Recklessness' in Prevention of Fraud (Investments) Act 1939, s 12(1) includes forecasts that are negligent but not dishonest.

Russon v Dutton (1911-13) XXII Cox CC 490; (1911) 75 JP 209; (1911) 104 LTR 601; (1910-11) XXVII TLR 197 HC KBD No conviction for indecent language uttered and heard within public house.

Rutter (William), R v (1908) 1 Cr App R 174; (1909) 73 JP 12; (1908-09) XXV TLR 73 CCA On malice as an element of the offence of damage to property; on desirability of production of shorthand notes of proceedings upon appeal.

Rutter and White, R v [1959] Crim LR 288t CCA Conviction for unlawful possession of explosives quashed as was inadequate evidence of possession/control of same.

Rutter, Lindley v (1981) 72 Cr App R 1; [1980] Crim LR 729; (1980) 130 NLJ 906; [1981] QB 128; (1980) 124 SJ 792; [1980] 3 WLR 660 HC QBD Woman police officer forcibly removing woman detainee's brassiere not acting in course of duty so assault on same not assault on officer in execution of duty.

Ryan and French v Director of Public Prosecutions [1994] Crim LR 457; (1994) 158 JP 485 HC QBD On charging theft and handling together as alternative charges.

Ryan v Ross and another (1963) 113 LJ 383 HC QBD On elements of offence of possessing instrument used for taking salmon/trout with intent of committing fisheries offence.

Ryan, Anderton v [1985] 2 All ER 355; [1985] AC 560 (also HC QBD); (1985) 81 Cr App R 166; [1985] Crim LR 503; (1985) 149 JP 433; (1985) 135 NLJ 485; (1985) 129 SJ 362; [1985] 2 WLR 968 HL Cannot be guilty of crime where believed was committing crime but was not.

Ryan, Anderton v [1985] 1 All ER 138; [1985] AC 560 (also HL); (1985) 80 Cr App R 235; [1984] Crim LR 483; (1984) 128 SJ 850; [1984] TLR 227; [1985] 2 WLR 23 HC QBD Could be guilty of attempted handling of stolen goods though not proved that goods in issue stolen.

Ryan, Chief Constable of Greater Manchester Police v (1985) 149 JP 79 HC QBD On what constitutes offence of attempted handling.

Ryan, R v (1914-15) XXIV Cox CC 135; (1914) 10 Cr App R 4; (1914) 78 JP 192; (1914) 110 LTR 779; (1913-14) 58 SJ 251; (1913-14) XXX TLR 242 CCA 'Wilful' making of fake death certificates.

Ryan, R v [1996] Crim LR 320 CA Person who sought to enter building and was trapped mid-way in window-frame was guilty of burglary.

Rydeheard, Clements and another v [1978] 3 All ER 658; (1979) 143 JP 25 HC QBD Selective competitive bidding covered by Mock Auctions Act.

Savage, R v; R v Parmenter [1991] 4 All ER 698; [1992] 1 AC 699 (also CA); (1992) 94 Cr App R 193; [1992] Crim LR 288 (only Savage); (1991) 155 JP 935; (1991) 141 NLJ 1553; [1991] TLR 499; [1991] 3 WLR 914 HL Unlawful and malicious wounding/inflicting grievous bodily harm requires intent/actual foresight of harm, however slight; assault occasioning actual bodily harm requires assault and actual bodily harm but not intent to cause harm or recklessness that harm likely to be caused.

Saville, R v (1980) 144 JP 209; (1980) 124 SJ 202 CA Valid variation of criminal bankruptcy order.

Sawkins, Thomas v (1934-39) XXX Cox CC 265; (1935) 99 JP 295; [1935] 2 KB 249; (1935) 79 LJ 415; (1935) 153 LTR 419; (1935) 79 SJ 478; (1934-35) LI TLR 514; (1935) WN (I) 109 HC KBD Police officer can enter/stay on premises where reasonable anticipation of offence/ breach of peace.

Sawyer v Bell [1962] Crim LR 390t HC QBD Abusive letters to bishops were defiance of recognisance to keep the peace and be of good behaviour.

Sawyer, R v [1989] Crim LR 831 CA Judge could of own volition leave provocation as issue to jury if thought that facts merited it (did not merit it here).

Sayce v Coupe [1952] 2 All ER 715; [1953] 1 QB 1 HC QBD Buying from unlicensed seller uncustomed tobacco using some/giving rest away is keeping uncustomed goods.

Sbarra, R v [1918-23] All ER 255; (1918-21) XXVI Cox CC 305; (1917-18) 13 Cr App R 118; (1918) 82 JP 171; [1918] 87 LJCL 1003; (1918-19) 119 LTR 89; (1917-18) XXXIV TLR 321; (1918) WN (I) 90 CCA Circumstantial evidence may establish that (knowingly) received goods that were in fact stolen.

Scarlett (John), R v (1994) 98 Cr App R 290; [1994] Crim LR 288; (1993) 143 NLJ 1101; [1993] TLR 276 CA Where use of some force necessary must use force disproportionate to that required in circumstances as accused perceives them to be guilty of manslaughter.

Scarrow (Terence Roland), R v; R v Brown (Douglas Stephen); R v Attlesey (William) (1968) 52 Cr App R 591 CA On what constitutes affray; can be convicted of affray though those charged fought with others not each other.

Scarsbrook v Mason (1961) 105 SJ 889 HC QBD Parties in car jointly/severally liable for negligent driving by driver.

Schama, R v; R v Abramovitch [1914-15] All ER 204; (1914-15) XXIV Cox CC 591; (1914-15) 11 Cr App R 45; (1915) 79 JP 184; [1915] 84 LJKB 396; (1915) 112 LTR 480; (1914-15) 59 SJ 288; (1914-15) XXXI TLR 88 CCA Reasonable explanation offered after prosecution establishes possession of recently stolen goods merits acquittal on receiving charge.

Schaub, R v; R v Cooper (Joey) [1994] Crim LR 531; (1994) 138 SJ LB 11; [1993] TLR 623 CA Screen blocking complainant from accused to be used only in exceptional circumstances.

Schiavo v Anderton [1986] 3 All ER 10; (1986) 83 Cr App R 228; [1986] Crim LR 542; (1986) 150 JP 264; [1987] QB 20; (1970) 130 SJ 542; [1986] 3 WLR 176 HC QBD magistrates can deal with failure to surrender for bail without formal charge; failure to appear before magistrates court triable by magistrates.

Schildkamp, Director of Public Prosecutions v [1971] AC 1; (1970) 54 Cr App R 90; [1970] Crim LR 95; [1970] 2 WLR 279 HL Company must be in liquidation before can be prosecuted for fraudulent trading.

Schildkamp, R v (1969) 119 NLJ 1116t; (1969) 113 SJ 486; [1969] 1 WLR 818 CA Cannot be guilty of fraudulent trading offence under Companies Act 1948, s 332(3) where company concerned not being wound up.

Schtraks v Government of Israel and others [1962] 3 All ER 529; [1964] AC 556; [1962] Crim LR 773t; (1962) 112 LJ 717; (1962) 106 SJ 833; [1962] 3 WLR 1013 HL Israeli territory includes areas of de facto control; habeas corpus hearing not akin to appeal/re-hearing; no precise definition of political offences - conjures idea of asylum; test in deciding if committal proper: would reasonable jury have done same?

Schweller (Joseph), R v (1924-25) 18 Cr App R 52 CCA Receiving goods in knowledge that seller obtained same by fraud/credit under false pretences not a crime.

Scott (John), R v (1909) 2 Cr App R 215 CCA On possession of recently stolen property.

Scott v Metropolitan Police Commissioner [1974] 3 All ER 1032; [1975] AC 819; (1975) 60 Cr App R 124; [1975] Crim LR 94; (1975) 139 JP 121; (1974) 124 NLJ 1157t; (1974) 118 SJ 863; [1974] 3 WLR 741 HL Need not be agreement to defraud by deceit to sustain conviction for conspiracy to defraud.

Scott v Tilley (1937) 81 SJ 864 HC KBD Absent explanation by accused, finding that person had in his possession goods which were reasonable grounds to believe had been stolen meant accused guilty of offence under the Wolverhampton Corporation Act 1925, s 124(1).

Scott, Denham v (1983) 77 Cr App R 210; [1983] Crim LR 558; (1983) 147 JP 521; [1983] TLR 246 HC QBD Publication of 'no questions asked' reward advertisement contrary to Theft Act 1968, s 23, a strict liability offence - advertising manager who was unaware advertisement was therefore guilty of same.

Scott, R v [1974] 2 All ER 204; [1974] Crim LR 243t; (1974) 138 JP 420; [1974] QB 733; (1974) 118 SJ 147; [1974] 2 WLR 379 CA Need not be agreement to defraud by deceit to sustain conviction for conspiracy to defraud.

Scott, R v [1996] Crim LR 652; (1996) TLR 10/4/96 CA Evidence of possession of money/drugs equipment was admissible even though only issue at trial was possession.

Scott, Stear v [1992] RTR 226 HC QBD Valid conviction for criminal damage to clamp (that levered free from car with crowbar before throwing away) absent lawful excuse.

Scottish Dyers and Cleaners (London), Ltd v Manheimer (1942) WN (I) 114 HC KBD Bailed goods stolen from bailees deemed not to be 'detained'.

Scranton (Archibald Frederick), R v (1920-21) 15 Cr App R 104 CCA Need not be breach of Larceny Act 1916, s 20(1)/larceny by bailee where do not pay person from whom bought goods which then pledged/sold to another.

Scudder v Barrett (1979) 69 Cr App R 277; [1980] QB 195; [1979] 3 WLR 591 HC QBD Need not prove intention to steal particular objects on charge of attempted theft/burglary.

Seager, Postmaster-General v [1955] Crim LR 716 Magistrates Person with wireless that was not plugged in (and which claimed was never used) acquitted of unlicensed use of wireless.

Searle and KCS Products, R v; R v Borjanovic [1996] Crim LR 58 CA Valid conviction for acting in breach of Order in Council adopted pursuant to United Nations resolution.

Searle and others, R v [1972] Crim LR 592; (1971) 115 SJ 739 CA On what constitutes 'joint possession' of drugs.

Searle v Randolph [1972] Crim LR 779 HC QBD Possession of cigarette end containing cannabis adequate to support cannabis possession conviction - did not have to prove accused knew cigarette end to contain cannabis.

Sears v Broome [1986] Crim LR 461 CA Damage done when acting in self-defence cannot be criminal damage.

Seaward, R v [1973] Crim LR 642 CA Seven years' imprisonment merited by twenty-two year old guilty of burglary with intent to rape/of indecent assault.

Seckree alias Ward (Edward), R v (1914-15) 11 Cr App R 245; (1916) 80 JP 16 CCA Burden of proof on prosecution to show guilty goal where accused shows had implements for innocent purpose.

Secretary of State for Defence v Warn [1970] AC 394; [1968] Crim LR 378; (1968) 112 SJ 461 HL Consent of DPP to grosss indecency charge involving under-21 year old applies to court-martials.

Secretary of State for Home Affairs v O'Brien [1923] All ER 442; [1923] AC 603; (1923) 87 JP 174; (1923) 58 LJ 331; [1923] 92 LJCL 830; (1923) 129 LTR 577; (1922-23) 67 SJ 747; (1922-23) XXXIX TLR 638; (1923) WN (I) 217 HL Home Secretary cannot appeal habeas corpus writ (issued on appeal by CA) to HL.

Secretary of State for Home Affairs, Greene v [1941] 3 All ER 388; [1942] AC 284; (1942) 92 LJ 51; [1942] 111 LJ 24; (1942) 166 LTR 24; (1941) 85 SJ 461 (also CA); (1941-42) LVIII TLR 53 HL Home Secretary's affidavit that valid detention under Defence (General) Regulations 1939, reg 18(b) being good on face meant no writ of habeas corpus would be issued.

Secretary of State for Home Affairs; ex parte Budd, R v [1942] 2 KB 14; (1942) 86 SJ 111 CA On reviewability of detention ordered by Home Secretary under emergency legislation.

Secretary of State for Home Affairs; ex parte Lees, R v [1941] 1 KB 72 CA HC KBD not a court of appeal from detention order by Home Secretary: would not order same to produce reports on which grounded order.

Secretary of State for India in Council and others; ex parte Ezekiel, R v [1941] 2 All ER 546; [1941] 2 KB 169; (1942) 92 LJ 53; [1942] 111 LJ 237 HC KBD Second World War no excuse for non-extradition to India; need not be avoiding arrest to be extradited; warrant need not refer to Fugitive Offenders Act 1881; depositions admissible though not apparently taken in pursuance of Fugitive Offenders Act 1881, s 29; affidavit of foreign legal expert not conclusive; barrister should not act as counsel and witness.

Secretary of State for India in Council and others; ex parte Ezekiel, R v (1942) 92 LJ 45 HC KBD Admissibility of depositions not taken before magistrate.

Secretary of State for the Home Department and another, ex parte Choudhary, R v [1978] 1 WLR 1177 CA Failed habeas corpus application where Home Secretary had reasonable ground for detaining person whom believed to be unlawfully in country on foot of fraudulent entry.

Secretary of State for the Home Department and another, ex parte Turkoglu, R v [1987] 2 All ER 823; [1988] QB 398; (1987) 131 SJ 1186 CA Respective jurisdictions of High Court/Court of Appeal to grant bail.

Secretary of State for the Home Department and another, Rees v [1986] 2 All ER 321; [1986] AC 937; (1986) 83 Cr App R 128; (1986) 136 NLJ 490; (1986) 130 SJ 408; [1986] 2 WLR 1024 HL Depositions/statements from non-requesting state admissible; magistrate cannot consider whether evidence before court acceptable in requesting state; Home Secretary can issue second order while first order stands.

Secretary of State for the Home Department ex parte Fire Brigades Union and others, R v; R v Secretary of State for the Home Department, ex parte Bateman; R v Same, ex parte Howse [1995] 1 All ER; (1994) 144 NLJ 1587; [1994] TLR 573; [1993] TLR 259 HC QBD On when person whose conviction has been overturned is eligible for compensation under the Criminal Justice Act 1988, s 133.

Secretary of State for the Home Department, ex parte Cheblak, R v [1991] 1 WLR 890 CA Failed application for writ of habeas corpus by person being detained prior to deportation.

Secretary of State for the Home Department, ex parte Fire Brigades Union and others, R v [1995] 2 All ER 244; (1995) 145 NLJ 521; [1995] TLR 182 HL Home Secretary's decision not to bring legislation into force but replace it by using prerogative powers a failure of duty to constantly review if legislation should be brought into force.

Secretary of State for the Home Department, ex parte Hussain, R v [1978] 1 WLR 700 CA Failed habeas corpus application where Secretary of State had reasonable basis on which to ground belief that applicant was illegally in country and so to be detained.

Secretary of State for the Home Department, ex parte Iqbal, R v [1979] 1 All ER 675; [1979] QB 264; [1978] 3 WLR 884 HC QBD Court may look beyond material error in document justifying detention to see if legitimate.

Secretary of State for the Home Department, ex parte Kirkwood, R v [1984] 2 All ER 390; (1984) 128 SJ 332 HC QBD Cannot stay Home Secretary order for surrender.

Secretary of State for the Home Department, ex parte Muboyayi, R v [1992] QB 244 CA Where basis of immigration-related action was challenge to administrative decision refusing entry court would not consider administrative decision in habeas corpus proceedings.

Secretary of State for the Home Department, ex parte Ram, R v [1979] 1 WLR 148 HC QBD Successful habeas corpus application against detention of immigrant whose passport had been duly stamped (albeit by mistake) by immigration officer.

Secretary of State for the Home Department, ex parte Schmidt, R v [1994] 2 All ER 784; [1995] 1 AC 339 (also HL) HC QBD High Court may only order discharge on grounds in Extradition Act 1989; decision of Secretary of State to seek extradition not open to residual review.

Secretary of State for the Home Department, ex parte Virk (Parmjeet Singh), R v; R v Same, ex parte Taggar; R v Same, ex parte Virk (Satnam); R v Same, ex parte Singh [1995] TLR 512 HC QBD No restriction allowed on employment of person freed after habeas corpus application regarding detention pursuant to immigration legislation.

Secretary of State for the Home Department; ex parte Awa, R v [1983] TLR 183 HC QBD Successful habeas corpus action by person being detained as illegal entrant into UK.

Secretary of State for the Home Department; ex parte D, R v (1996) 140 SJ LB 119 HC QBD Failed application for writ of habeas corpus by person subject to restriction order who was recalled to hospital where was at time of recall already getting care.

Secretary of State for the Home Department; ex parte Gilmore and another, R v [1997] TLR 365 HC QBD Conspiracy to commit offence not an extraditable matter.

Secretary of State for the Home Department; ex parte Hill, R v [1997] 2 All ER 638; [1997] 2 Cr App R (S) 525 HC QBD Could be extradited for crimes committed before requesting state became designated state under Extradition Act; could be extradited for offences that were offences under English law even where were not sought by requesting state for said offences.

Secretary of State for the Home Department; ex parte Launder, R v [1997] 3 All ER 961; [1997] 2 Cr App R (S) 793; (1997) 147 NLJ 793; (1997) 141 SJ LB 123; [1997] TLR 283; [1997] 1 WLR 839 HL Extradition to Hong Kong allowed, Home Secretary having decided that hand-over to China would not result in proposed extraditee suffering unfair trial/injustice/oppression upon return.

Secretary of State for the Home Department; ex parte Launder, R v (1996) TLR 28/10/96 HC QBD May usually challenge Home Secretary's decision to make extradition order.

Secretary of State for the Home Department; ex parte Patel, R v [1994] TLR 73 HC QBD Successful application for judicial review of Home Office Minister's decision to allow extradition of man for offences he was said to have committed around a decade previously.

Secretary of State for the Home Department; ex parte Rahman, R v [1996] 4 All ER 945; (1996) TLR 19/7/96 HC QBD Hearsay evidence could be relied on in habeas corpus application in context of illegal immigration.

Secretary of State for the Home Office; ex parte Osman and In the Matter of Osman, R v [1993] Crim LR 214 HC QBD Court would not invoke injustice/oppression grounds to intervene in extradition proceedings after Home Secretary had ordered extradition of person concerned.

Secretary of State for Trade and Industry v Hart [1982] 1 All ER 817; [1982] Crim LR 583; (1982) 132 NLJ 85; (1982) 126 SJ 172; [1982] 1 WLR 481 HC QBD Ignorance of law a defence to acting as auditor when disqualified.

Secretary of State for Trade and Industry, Rudd v (1987) 85 Cr App R 358; (1987) 131 SJ 805; [1987] 1 WLR 786 HL Only wireless telegraphy apparatus liable to forfeiture under Wireless Telegraphy Act 1949, s 14(3) - records/cassettes in use not 'apparatus'; on what constitutes 'use' of apparatus under Wireless Telegraphy Act 1949, s 14(3) as substituted.

Secretary of State for Trade v Markus [1975] 1 All ER 958; [1976] AC 35 (also CA); (1975) 61 Cr App R 58; [1975] Crim LR 716; (1975) 139 JP 301; (1975) 119 SJ 271; [1975] 2 WLR 708 HL Can be guilty of inducing other 'to...offer to take part' and 'to take part...in' course of action and can be guilty of doing so in England even if did so from abroad.

Secretary of the Board of Control and another, R v; Re Dawson; ex parte Abdul Kayum (1948) 112 JP 453; (1949) LXV TLR 39 HC KBD Failed application for habeas corpus by mental institution detainee whose period of detention had been extended by general order.

Seddon (Frederick Henry), R v (1911-12) 7 Cr App R 207 CCA Case of murder based on circumstantial evidence; can convict accused who gave evidence against co-accused though do not convict co-accused.

Seekings and Gould, Norfolk Constabulary v [1986] Crim LR 167 CrCt Unhitched articulated lorry trailer not a 'building' for purposes of Theft Act 1968, s 9.

Seelig and another, R v [1991] 4 All ER 429; (1992) 94 Cr App R 17; (1991) 141 NLJ 638; [1992] 1 WLR 148 CA Evidence given/confession made to Department of Trade and Industry inspectors admissible in later criminal proceedings against person questioned.

Shah (Imdad), R v (1980) 144 JP 460 CA Bail inappropriate in appeals against short sentences: hearing of action should be hastened.

Shama, R v [1990] 2 All ER 602; (1990) 91 Cr App R 138; [1990] Crim LR 411; (1990) 134 SJ 958; [1990] TLR 39; [1990] 1 WLR 661 CA Dishonest omission of material particulars in accounting document proves false accounting.

Shanks and McEwan (Teeside) Ltd v The Environment Agency [1997] Crim LR 684; [1997] TLR 50 HC QBD On elements of offence of knowingly causing controlled waste to be deposited in breach of waste management licence.

Shannahan (Thomas), R v; R v Watts (James Wesley); R v Fay (Michael Augustus); R v Doot (Robert Leray); R v Loving (Jeffrey Richard) (1973) 57 Cr App R 13 CA On what constitutes conspiracy; on jurisdiction of courts in respect of conspiracies with foreign element.

Shannon (James Russell), R v (1980) 71 Cr App R 192; [1980] Crim LR 438; (1980) 130 NLJ 606; (1980) 124 SJ 374 CA Whether was self-defence depends on whether accords to what one would expect in the circumstances.

Shannon, Director of Public Prosecutions v [1974] 2 All ER 1009; [1975] AC 717; (1974) 59 Cr App R 250; [1974] Crim LR 177; (1974) 138 JP 587; [1974] 3 WLR 155 CA One conspirator's acquittal does not preclude other's conviction.

Shannon, Director of Public Prosecutions v [1974] 2 All ER 1009; [1975] AC 717; (1974) 59 Cr App R 250; [1975] Crim LR 703; (1974) 138 JP 587; (1974) 118 SJ 515; [1974] 3 WLR 155 HL One conspirator's acquittal does not preclude other's conviction.

Sharp and another, R v [1957] 1 All ER 577; (1957) 41 Cr App R 86; (1957) 121 JP 227; (1957) 107 LJ 169; [1957] 1 QB 552; (1957) 101 SJ 230; [1957] 2 WLR 472 CCA Fight where one acting in self-defence not affray; that would terrify reasonable person adequate proof of terror.

Sharp, R v [1987] 3 All ER 103; (1987) 85 Cr App R 207; [1987] Crim LR 566; (1987) 151 JP 832; [1987] QB 853; (1987) 131 SJ 624; [1987] 3 WLR 1 CA Pressure by criminal group on person who voluntarily joined to commit crime not duress.

Sharp, R v [1964] Crim LR 826g CCA Valid finding of joint possession on part of person apparently indirectly party to loading with stolen property of van owned by his wife.

Sharpe v Perry [1979] RTR 235 HC QBD Need not be roadside breath test when arresting person for being in charge of motor vehicle on road while unfit to drink (Road Traffic ct 1972, s 5(5)).

Sharpe, R v; R v Stringer [1938] 1 All ER; (1939-40) XXXI Cox CC 24; (1936-38) 26 Cr App R 122; (1938) 102 JP 113; (1938) 85 LJ 46; (1938) 82 SJ 158; (1938) WN (I) 29 CCA Need not be proceedings pending at time of conspiracy to obstruct for obstruction conviction to be sustained.

Sharples, A v [1991] TLR 244 HC QBD Not sufficient to rebut doli incapax presumption that child ran away after doing act that was subject of prosecution.

Sharples, R v [1990] Crim LR 198 CrCt Husband could not be guilty of raping wife (albeit that wife previously obtained non-molestation order against him).

Shaw (Grenville), R v; Attorney-General's Reference (No 28 of 1996) [1997] TLR 46 CA Was rape to force prostitute to have unprotected sex with accused when she wanted protected sex.

Shaw (James), R v (1911-13) XXII Cox CC 376; (1911) 75 JP 191; (1911) 104 LTR 112; (1910-11) XXVII TLR 181 CCA Could not be convicted of taking false oath before body not authorised to take oath.

Shaw v Director of Public Prosecutions [1961] 2 All ER 446; [1962] AC 220; (1961) 45 Cr App R 113; [1961] Crim LR 468; (1961) 125 JP 437; (1961) 111 LJ 356; (1961) 105 SJ 421; [1961] 2 WLR 897 HL Test of obscenity is whether article would corrupt/deprave another (intent of author irrelevant); are living off earnings of prostitution if provide goods/services to prostitutes which would not if they were not prostitutes; agreement to publish obscene publication an agreement to corrupt public morals (even if never published),a common law misdemeanour.

Shaw, R v (1943-44) LX TLR 344 CCA Failed appeal against conviction for bigamy.

Shaw, R v [1994] Crim LR 365 CA On mens rea of incitement to obtain property by deception.

Shaw, R v [1991] Crim LR 301 CrCt Wife's obtaining family protection order was a withdrawal of her consent to sex with husband.

Simington, R v (1918-21) XXVI Cox CC 736; (1920-21) 15 Cr App R 97; (1921) 85 JP 179; [1921] 1 KB 451; [1921] LJCL 471; (1921) 125 LTR 128; (1920-21) XXXVII TLR 114; (1920) WN (I) 384 CCA Interpretation of Official Secrets Act 1911, s 2(1).

Simmonds and others, R v [1967] 2 All ER 399; (1967) 131 JP 341; [1969] 1 QB 685; [1967] 3 WLR 367 CA No time limit on prosecution of common law conspiracy.

Simmonds, Glynn and another v [1952] 2 All ER 47; (1952) 116 JP 389; (1952) 102 LJ 318; (1952) 96 SJ 378; [1952] 1 TLR 1442; (1952) WN (I) 289 HC QBD Racecourse enclosure to which admission charged a public place under Vagrancy Act 1824, s 4.

Simmonite, R v (1916-17) 12 Cr App R 142; (1917) 81 JP 80; [1916] 2 KB 821; [1917] 86 LJCL 15 CCA Could be convicted of indecent assault though charged with incest.

Simmons, Allen v [1978] 3 All ER 662; [1978] Crim LR 362; (1979) 143 JP 105; (1978) 128 NLJ 512t; (1978) 122 SJ 470; [1978] 1 WLR 879 HC QBD Competitive bidding includes any form of competition for purchase.

Simmons, Lake v [1927] All ER 49 HL Insurance policy effective as purported entrusting of goods to thief was larceny by trick.

Simmons, R v [1986] Crim LR 397 CA On doctrine of 'recent possession'.

Simon, R v [1964] Crim LR 141t CCA Prosecution to disprove provocation.

Simpson, R v [1983] 3 All ER 789; (1984) 78 Cr App R 115; [1984] Crim LR 39 (1984) 148 JP 33; (1983) 127 SJ 748; [1983] TLR 638; [1983] 1 WLR 1494 CA Flick-knife is an offensive weapon.

Simpson, R v [1957] Crim LR 815t CCC Nagging/threats by wife reduced her homicide by husband from murder to manslaughter on basis of provocation.

Simpson, R v [1914-15] All ER 917; (1915-17) XXV Cox CC 269; (1914-15) 11 Cr App R 218; [1915] 84 LJKB 1893; (1916) 114 LTR 238; (1914-15) XXXI TLR 560 CCA Third party provocation prompting accused to kill victim did not reduce killing to manslaughter.

Simpson, W and another v [1967] Crim LR 360; (1967) 111 SJ 273 HC QBD Presumption of innocence in respect of under-fourteen year old offenders rebutted here.

Sinclair and others, R v [1968] 3 All ER 241; (1968) 52 Cr App R 618; (1968) 132 JP 527; (1968) 118 NLJ 956; [1968] 1 WLR 1246 CA On what constitutes 'fraud' in conspiracy to cheat and defraud.

Sinclair v Director of Public Prosecutions and another [1991] 2 All ER 366; (1991) 93 Cr App R 329; [1991] TLR 187 HL Magistrate cannot determine if extradition case an abuse of process; whether relevant extradition treaty complied with. 'Prosecution' in USA (Extradition) Order means beginning of criminal proceedings.

Sinclair v Government of the United States of America [1990] TLR 144 HC QBD Abuse of process doctrine inapplicable to extradition proceedings in which seeking extradition of already convicted person.

Singh (Baljinder) v Hammond [1987] 1 WLR 283 HC QBD Could be convicted of making false statement to immigration officer though did so after date of entry and away from port of entry.

Singh (Gurmit), R v [1965] 3 All ER 384; [1965] Crim LR 718; (1965) 129 JP 578; [1966] 2 WLR 88 Assizes On attempted committing of offence.

Singh (Harbax), R v [1979] 1 All ER 524; (1979) 68 Cr App R 108; (1979) 143 JP 214; [1979] QB 319; [1979] 2 WLR 100 CA Absconding from bail punishable per se summarily or as criminal contempt.

Singh (Sarwan), R v [1962] 3 All ER 612; [1963] Crim LR 269 Quarter Sessions Cannot ground bigamy prosecution in (possibly) polygamous first marriage.

Singh (Sharmpal), R v [1962] AC 188; [1962] Crim LR 165; (1962) 106 SJ 56; [1962] 2 WLR 238 PC Husband used unlawful force during sex but could be manslaughter as doubt whether intended to kill.

Singh and Singh, R v (1985) 149 JP 142 CA On recklessness in context of rape.

Singh, R v; Billling v Pill [1989] Crim LR 724; [1953] 2 All ER 1061 HC QBD Hut bolted to concrete foundation was not attached to/forming part of realty so could be stolen.

Smith (Albert William), R v (1914-15) 11 Cr App R 81 CCA Agreeing to pay rent in future in set amounts was obtaining credit for purpose of Bankruptcy and Deeds of Arrangement Act 1913.

Smith (David George), R v [1985] Crim LR 42 CA On relevance of intention to determination whether physical chastisement of child constituted assault occasioning actual bodily harm.

Smith (David Raymond), R v [1974] 1 All ER 632; (1974) 58 Cr App R 320; [1974] Crim LR 101t; (1974) 138 JP 236; (1973) 123 NLJ 1090t; [1974] QB 354; (1973) 117 SJ 938; [1974] 2 WLR 20 CA No criminal damage to property if honestly believe property own as no mens rea; right of appeal on point of law does not require certificate.

Smith (George), R v [1918] 87 LJCL 1023; (1918) WN (I) 209 CCA Relevant evidence in receiving trial includes what accused said when found in possession of goods.

Smith (George), R v; R v Currier (Frank) (1917-18) XXXIV TLR 480 CCA Relevant evidence in receiving trial includes what accused said when found in possession of goods.

Smith (James Reginald), R v (1922-23) 17 Cr App R 133 CCA On substitution by CCA of larceny conviction for receiving conviction.

Smith (John), R v [1974] 1 All ER 376; (1974) 58 Cr App R 106; (1974) 138 JP 175; (1973) 123 NLJ 723t; (1973) 117 SJ 774; [1973] 1 WLR 1510 CA Absence of good faith by doctor in decision-making may be found by jury absent expert evidence.

Smith (John), R v (1912-13) 8 Cr App R 151 CCA That have for better part of short interval been doing honest work does not preclude finding that are habitual criminal.

Smith (KA), R v [1983] Crim LR 739 CrCt Could be convicted of attempted infanticide under Infanticide Act 1938.

Smith (Mabel Adelaide), R v (1916-17) 12 Cr App R 42 CCA Presumption of coercion of wife by husband applies in respect of misdemeanours.

Smith (No 3), R v [1968] Crim LR 375t CA On effect of verdict of being not guilty of office breaking but guilty as accessory before the fact.

Smith (PR), R v [1989] Crim LR 734 CA Evidence of previous behaviour towards deceased admissible to defeat defence of automatism (based on alleged unlikelihood of behaviour if behaving as usually did).

Smith (RD), R v (1973) 117 SJ 429 CA Cannot be guilty of attempt to commit crime where did acts which if uninterrupted would not amount to criminal act.

Smith (Richard), R v (1910) 5 Cr App R 77 CCA Matter for jury whether recent possession/whether possession adequately explained.

Smith (Roger), R v [1974] Crim LR 305; (1974) 118 SJ 7; [1974] 2 WLR 1 HL On attempt; on attempted handling.

Smith (Sandie), R v [1982] Crim LR 531 CA Pre-menstrual syndrome not a defence but is a relevant factor when sentencing.

Smith (Stanley), R v [1979] 3 All ER 605; (1979) 69 Cr App R 378; [1979] Crim LR 592; (1980) 144 JP 53; (1979) 129 (2) NLJ 835 (incomplete)/862; (1979) 123 SJ 602; [1979] 1 WLR 1445 CA Prison psychiatrists' reports not confidential/are admissible; jury requires expert help on automatism.

Smith (Sydney Edward), R v (1919-20) 14 Cr App R 101; (1920) 84 JP 67 CCA Can be guilty of intent to defraud under Forgery Act 1913, s 7(a) though are legally entitled to whatever obtained.

Smith (Wallace Duncan), R v [1996] 2 Cr App R 1; [1996] Crim LR 329; (1996) 140 SJ LB 11 CA On meaning of 'creditor' in context of fraudulent trading; on imposition of confiscation order as regards disposal by way of gift.

Smith (Wesley), R v [1963] 3 All ER 597; (1963) 107 SJ 873; (1964) 128 JP 13; [1963] 1 WLR 1200 CCA Party to concerted act guilty of manslaughter by other as death foreseeable and knew killer had weapon (though party had no intent to kill/cause grievous bodily harm).

Smith (William), R v [1983] TLR 692 CA On doctrine of recent possession.

Smith and another v Hughes and others [1960] 2 All ER 859; (1960) 124 JP 430; (1960) 104 SJ 606 HC QBD Soliciting from balcony/behind closed windows is soliciting 'in a street or public place'.

Smith and another, Coffin and another v (1980) 71 Cr App R 221 HC QBD Was obstruction of police in execution of their duty to assault police constable in course of ejection from club/while standing on beat.

Smith and another, Coffin and another v; R v Coates (1980) 71 Cr App R 221; [1971] Crim LR 370; [1971] RTR 74 CA Conviction quashed where validity of arrest/proper functioning of breathalyser not left to jury.

Smith v Baker [1972] Crim LR 25; [1971] RTR 350 HC QBD Not aiding and abetting in driving uninsured vehicle to sit in stolen car until no longer being driven and then run away when see police approaching.

Smith v Baker (1961) 125 JP 53; (1960) 110 LJ 845; (1961) 105 SJ 17; [1961] 1 WLR 38 HC QBD Police officer can bring complaint under Dogs Act 1871, s 2.

Smith v Chief Superintendant, Woking Station (1983) 76 Cr App R 234; [1983] Crim LR 323 HC QBD Was assault to peer into flat of elderly spinster in manner calculated to cause her fear of immediate assault.

Smith v Dear (1901-07) XX Cox CC 458; (1903) 67 JP 244; (1903) LXXXVIII LTR 664 HC KBD Any person (not just owner) may prosecute for unlawful and wilful killing of house pigeon.

Smith v Desmond and another [1965] 1 All ER 976; [1965] AC 960; (1965) 49 Cr App R 246; [1965] Crim LR 315t; (1965) 129 JP 331; (1965) 115 LJ 297; (1965) 109 SJ 269; [1965] 2 WLR 894 HL Crime done in presence of persons if done in other room within their care/control.

Smith v Hughes [1960] Crim LR 709; [1960] 1 WLR 830 HC QBD Soliciting from behind windows or from balcony was soliciting in street contrary to Street Offences Act 1959, s 1(1).

Smith v Jenner [1968] Crim LR 99t; (1967) 117 NLJ 1296t; (1968) 112 SJ 52 HC QBD Successful appeal by driving instructor against conviction for aiding and abetting learner driver in unlicensed driving of car.

Smith v Koumourou [1979] Crim LR 116; [1979] RTR 355 HC QBD Was obtaining pecuniary advantage by deception where driver without excise licence displayed undated police receipt for earlier expired licence to avoid non-payment of duty being discovered and so avoid paying excise duty.

Smith v Reynolds and others; Smith v Hancock; Smith v Lowe [1986] Crim LR 559 HC QBD On elements of offence of aiding and abetting in obstruction of police officer.

Smith v Stevens (1928-29) XLV TLR 429 HC KBD Penalty plus costs for placing advertisement of reward for return of lost property on 'no questions asked' basis (Larceny Act 1861, s 102).

Smith, Abbott and another v [1964] 3 All ER 762; [1964] Crim LR 662; (1965) 129 JP 3; (1964) 114 LJ 738; [1965] 2 QB 662; [1965] 3 WLR 362 CrCt Brothel though premises let in separate rooms; management involves element of control: not present here.

Smith, Beeston and Stapleford UDC and another v (1949) 113 JP 160 HC KBD Valid conviction for acting as solicitor.

Smith, Dale v [1967] 2 All ER 1133; [1967] Crim LR 372t; (1967) 131 JP 378; (1967) 111 SJ 330; [1967] 1 WLR 700 HC QBD Innocent word can be importuning in light of previous occurrence.

Smith, Director of Public Prosecutions v [1960] 3 All ER 161; (1960) 44 Cr App R 261; [1960] Crim LR 765; (1960) 124 JP 473; (1960) 110 LJ 573; (1960) 104 SJ 683; [1960] 3 WLR 546 HL If objectively foreseeable result of vouluntary unlawful act is grievous bodily harm then absent inability is presumed intended same.

Smith, Ellis v [1962] 3 All ER 954; [1963] Crim LR 128; (1963) 127 JP 51; (1963) 113 LJ 26; (1962) 106 SJ 1069; [1962] 1 WLR 1486 HC QBD Until relief (bus) driver assumes charge last (bus) driver is person in charge of vehicle.

Smith, Haughton v [1973] 3 All ER 1109; [1975] AC 476; (1974) 58 Cr App R 198; (1974) 138 JP 31; (1973) 123 NLJ 1112t; [1974] 2 WLR 1 HL Cannot be attempt to handle stolen goods unless goods handled are stolen goods.

Smith, Hood v [1933] All ER 706; (1934-39) XXX Cox CC 82; (1934) 98 JP 73; (1934) 150 LTR 477 HC KBD Entrapment of person charged with stealing postal packet in course of transmission by post.

Smith, Muir v [1978] Crim LR 293; (1978) 128 NLJ 364t; (1978) 122 SJ 210 HC QBD Conviction quashed where charged with possessing cannabis resin but only possession of cannabis (and not that it was cannabis resin) proven.

Smith, Noon v [1964] 3 All ER 895; (1965) 49 Cr App R 55; [1965] Crim LR 41t; (1965) 129 JP 48; (1964) 114 LJ 859; (1964) 108 SJ 898; [1964] 1 WLR 1450 HC QBD Theft can be evidenced directly or by inference.

Smith, R v (1901-07) XX Cox CC 804; (1905) XCII LTR 208 CCR Acts subsequent to those with which charged admissible in false pretences prosecution if relevant (even if point to guilt of offence separate to that with which charged).

Smith, R v (1984) 148 JP 215 CA On inferring guilt of theft from possession of recently stolen property.

Smith, R v (1976) 126 NLJ 65t CA Possession of firearms not an offence for which could be extradited under Extradition Act 1870, schedule 1.

Smith, R v [1918] 87 LJCL 676; (1918) 118 LTR 179 CCA On post-acquittal disclosure of convictions.

Smith, R v [1988] Crim LR 616 CA On mens rea necessary to be guilty of act undertaken as part of joint enterprise.

Smith, R v [1964] Crim LR 129 CCA On elements of being principal in second degree to/acting in concert towards homicide.

Smith, R v [1979] Crim LR 251 CrCt Failed manslaughter prosecution of husband allegedly guilty of reckless disregard of wife (did not get doctor for sick wife who strongly disliked doctors and did not want one present).

Smith, R v [1973] Crim LR 700t CA On general need for medical evidence to support conviction of doctor for unlawful procuring of miscarriage.

Smith, R v [1973] 2 All ER 896; (1973) 57 Cr App R 666; [1973] Crim LR 508t; (1973) 137 JP 598; (1973) 123 NLJ 371t; [1973] 2 WLR 942 CA Cannot be convicted of handling stolen goods if goods handled are not stolen.

Smith, R v [1962] 2 All ER 200; (1962) 46 Cr App R 277; [1962] Crim LR 388; (1962) 126 JP 333; (1962) 112 LJ 320; [1962] 2 QB 317; (1962) 106 SJ 265; [1962] 2 WLR 1145 CCA Cannot be receiving under Larceny Act 1916, s 33(1) if theft outside jurisdiction; can be guilty of larceny under Larceny Act 1916 s 33(4) regardless of whether convicted thereof elsewhere.

Smith, R v [1960] 1 All ER 256; (1960) 44 Cr App R 55; [1960] Crim LR 185t; (1960) 124 JP 137; (1960) 110 LJ 73; [1960] 2 QB 423; (1960) 104 SJ 69 CCA It is corruption to offer officer of public body something to enter into corrupt agreement even if no intention to carry out deal.

Smith, R v (1909-10) XXVI TLR 614 CCA To successfully plead insanity must show that when did act did not know what was doing or that what was doing was wrong.

Smith, R v [1960] 2 All ER 450; [1960] Crim LR 491t; (1960) 110 LJ 429; (1960) 104 SJ 510 CCA Is possible for person not to intend natural effects of acts though reasonable person would have foreseen them.

Smith, R v (1924-25) 18 Cr App R 76; (1924) 88 JP 108; [1924] 2 KB 194; (1924) 59 LJ 404; [1924] 93 LJCL 1006; (1924) 131 LTR 28; (1924-25) 69 SJ 37; (1924) WN (I) 187 CCA Whether transaction at issue involves fraudulent conversion a question of fact for jury.

Smith, R v [1962] Crim LR 43t CA Person properly convicted of murder where killing in course of pub brawl was part of common design.

Smith, R v [1973] Crim LR 516 CA Goods were im/exported where passed through jurisdiction en route from one place to another without going through customs.

Smith, R v (1965) 115 LJ 628 CA Interpretation of Offences against the Person Act 1861, s 56 (detaining child by fraud with intention of permanently depriving father of child).

Smith, Rawlings v [1938] 1 All ER 11; (1939-40) XXXI Cox CC 11; (1938) 102 JP 181; [1938] 1 KB 675; (1938) 85 LJ 46; [1938] 107 LJCL 151; (1938) 158 LTR 274; (1937) 81 SJ 1024; (1937-38) LIV TLR 255; (1938) WN (I) 15 HC KBD Need not be a suspected person on a day preceding loitering.

Soul (Patricia June), R v (1980) 70 Cr App R 295; [1980] Crim LR 233 CA Valid conviction for conspiracy to commit public nuisance where intended but failed to bring about escape of person from mental hospital.

Souter, R v [1971] 2 All ER 1151; (1971) 55 Cr App R 403; [1972] Crim LR 478t; (1971) 135 JP 458; (1971) 115 SJ 548; [1971] 1 WLR 1187 CA Must be knowingly allowing/closing one's eyes to deliberate use of premises for drug use to be 'permitting' it.

South Western Magistrates' Court and the Commissioner of Police for the Metropolis; ex parte Cofie, R v (1997) 161 JP 69; (1996) TLR 15/8/96; [1997] 1 WLR 885 HC QBD On need for specificity as regards place to be searched in police application for search warrant.

South Worcestershire Magistrates, ex parte Lilley, R v [1995] 4 All ER 186; [1996] 1 Cr App R 420; (1995) 139 SJ LB 67; [1995] TLR 106; [1995] 1 WLR 1595 HC QBD Justices must disqualify themselves from further part in a trial if they have heard and ruled on a public interest immunity contention by the prosecution.

South, R v (1907) 71 JP 191 CCC Failed prosecution for receiving money and fraudulently converting same to own use (Larceny Act 1901, s 1(1)(b)).

Southampton Justices, ex parte Green, R v [1975] 2 All ER 1073; (1975) 139 JP 667; [1976] QB 11; (1975) 119 SJ 541; [1975] 3 WLR 277 CA Estreatment of recognisance not criminal cause or matter; forfeiture of recognisance for non-appearance not automatic - all circumstances to be considered.

Southern Water Authority v Pegrum and Pegrum [1989] Crim LR 442 HC QBD Direction to convict in prosecution for causing pollution (pig effluent) to enter stream contrary to Control of Pollution Act 1974, s 31(1).

Southern Water Authority v The Nature Conservancy Council [1991] Crim LR 769 HC QBD On who is an 'occupier' of land for purposes of Wildlife and Countryside Act 1981, s 28(1)(b).

Southwell v Chadwick (1987) 85 Cr App R 235 CA Machete knife and catapult not offensive weapons per se.

Spain, Edgar v (1899-1901) XIX Cox CC 719; (1901) LXXXIV LTR 631 HC KBD Interpretation of animal 'brought...for' slaughter clause of Cruelty to Animals Act 1849, s 8.

Spanner, Poulter and Ward, R v [1973] Crim LR 704 CA Though is matter for jury judge's finding that security guards had no reasonable excuse for always carrying truncheons was justified.

Sparks, R v [1965] Crim LR 113; (1964) 108 SJ 922 CCA Shotgun not an offensive weapon per se.

Spearman, Liepins v [1985] Crim LR 229; [1986] RTR 24 HC QBD Passenger in/owner of car whose driver was found to be over limit did not have to be, but here was obstructing police in execution of their duty where sought to prevent car being removed to police station.

Speck, R v [1977] 2 All ER 859; (1977) 65 Cr App R 161; [1977] Crim LR 689; (1977) 141 JP 459; (1977) 127 NLJ 414t; (1977) 121 SJ 221 CA Passively allowing uninvited act to continue could be invitation to do act.

Spence (George), R v (1957) 41 Cr App R 80; [1957] Crim LR 188 CCA Is murder where attempted suicide results in death of another.

Spencer, King v (1901-07) XX Cox CC 692; (1904) 68 JP 530; (1904-05) XCI LTR 470 HC KBD Not per se criminal fraud to weigh goods and wrapper together where purchaser aware of same; evidence of trade custom admissible to establish if behaviour fraudulent.

Spencer, R v [1979] Crim LR 538 CA Five years' (not life) imprisonment for offender with personality disorder guilty of arson and theft but not an unceasing public menace.

Spencer-Stewart v Chief Constable of Kent (1989) 89 Cr App R 307 HC QBD In revoking shot gun certificate on basis that there is danger of breach of peace that danger must be connected to shotgun.

Spens, R v (1992) 142 NLJ 528 CrCt Where prosecution offer no evidence/trial against fellow conspirator discontinued court could order indictment to be placed on file marked not to be proceeded with.

Spicer, Fox v (1917) 116 LTR 86; (1916-17) XXXIII TLR 172 HC KBD Prosecution procedurally improper: information at issue was for publication in newspaper so proposed prosecution ought to have been referred to DPP.

Spicer, R v (1955) 39 Cr App R 189; [1955] Crim LR 772 Assizes Could be convicted for procuring miscarriage where sought so to do though means used could not be successful.

Spicer, R v [1970] Crim LR 695; (1970) 114 SJ 824 CA Conspiracy to defraud not an arrestable offence.

Spight, R v [1986] Crim LR 817 CA On evidential responsibilities placed on defendant (regarding such issues as age and consent) in prosecution for attempting to procure grossly indecent act.

Spinks, R v [1982] 1 ALL ER 587; (1982) 74 Cr App R 263; [1982] Crim LR 231 CA That accused's out-of-court statements not be used against co-accused applies where alleged offender and person charged with assisting him tried together.

Spratt, R v [1980] 2 All ER 269; [1980] Crim LR 372; (1980) 124 SJ 309; [1990] TLR 369; [1980] 1 WLR 554 CA Discredited evidence not affecting jury finding of unjustifiable/inexcusable homicide.

Spratt, R v [1991] 2 All ER 210; (1990) 91 Cr App R 362; [1990] Crim LR 797; (1990) 154 JP 884; (1990) 134 SJ 860; [1990] TLR 369; [1990] 1 WLR 1073 CA If no actual intent/recklessness then no mens rea.

Spriggs, R v [1958] 1 All ER 300; [1958] Crim LR 190t; (1958) 108 LJ 90; [1958] 1 QB 270; (1958) 102 SJ 89 CCA Definition of terms in Homicide Act 1957, s 2(1) unnecessary when leaving diminshed responsibility defence to jury.

Squire, R v [1963] Crim LR 700 CCA Stealing from company/defrauding Inland Revenue charges against company director werer not mutually exclusive.

Squires v Botwright [1973] Crim LR 106; [1972] RTR 462 HC QBD That constable had blocked person from moving while conducted his inquiries did not mean had not been acting in course of duty.

St Margaret's Trust, Ltd and others, R v [1958] 2 All ER 289; (1958) 102 SJ 349 CCA Hire-purchaser breach of Hire-Purchase and Credit Sale Agreements (Control) Order 1956 an absolute offence.

Stagg, R v [1978] Crim LR 227 CA Whether accused had requisite knowledge/belief that goods were stolen to support handling conviction a subjective test.

Staines (Linda Irene), R v (1975) 60 Cr App R 160; [1975] Crim LR 651 CA On meaning of 'deception' and 'reckless' in Theft Act 1968, s 15(4).

Stalham, R v [1993] Crim LR 310 CA Keeping money mistakenly paid by employer into one's account was theft of a chose in action.

Stamford, R v [1972] 2 All ER 427; (1972) 56 Cr App R 398; [1972] Crim LR 374t; (1972) 136 JP 522; (1972) 122 NLJ 217t; [1972] 2 QB 391; (1972) 116 SJ 313; [1972] 2 WLR 1055 CA What is obscene/indecent is a matter exclusively for jury.

Stamp v United Dominions Trust (Commercial), Ltd [1967] 1 All ER 251; (1967) 131 JP 177; [1967] 1 QB 418; (1966) 110 SJ 906; [1967] 2 WLR 541 HC QBD Post-conviction restitution order for property in possession of third party permissible but exceptional.

Standen, Gordon v; Palace-Clark v Standen [1963] 3 All ER 627; (1964) 48 Cr App R 30; [1963] Crim LR 859t; (1963) 113 LJ 753; (1963) 107 SJ 811; (1964) 128 JP 28; [1964] 1 QB 294; [1963] 3 WLR 917 HC QBD Is brothel where only two women and one is occupier; woman can be convicted of assisting another in management of brothel.

Staniforth, R v; R v Jordan [1976] 2 All ER 714; [1977] AC 699 (also HL); [1976] Crim LR 446; (1976) 140 JP 483; (1976) 126 NLJ 522t; (1976) 120 SJ 266; [1976] 2 WLR 849 CA Otherwise obscene material must benefit general public to be justified; evidence must show particular (not all such) publications justified.

Stanley, R v [1965] 1 All ER 1035; (1965) 49 Cr App R 175; [1965] Crim LR 239t; (1965) 129 JP 279; (1965) 115 LJ 265; [1965] 2 QB 327; (1965) 109 SJ 193; [1965] 2 WLR 917 CCA Something obscene is indecent (not vice versa) - can be convicted of either.

Stansell and others, R v [1959] Crim LR 779 CCC Valid that prosecution for fraudulent trading pursuant to the Companies Act 1948, s 334, be taken by the Board of Trade.

Stansfield, Webb v [1966] Crim LR 449 Magistrates Forcing of quarter light on door of car obstructing right to use highway was valid step in enforcement of that right; absent damage to complainant smearing marmalade inside the car went unpunished.

Stanton (D) and Sons Ltd v Webber [1972] Crim LR 544; [1973] RTR 86; (1972) 116 SJ 666 HC QBD On what knowledge was necessary to prove employer guilty aiding/abetting worker-driver in unlicensed driving.

Stanton, Percival v [1954] Crim LR 308; (1954) 98 SJ 114 HC QBD Net not a 'fixed engine' as was not fixed/secured by anchors.

Stapylton v O'Callaghan [1973] 2 All ER 782; [1974] Crim LR 63; (1973) 137 JP 579 HC QBD Dishonest appropriation and intention of retention merits theft conviction.

Staravia Ltd v Gordon [1973] Crim LR 298 CA Company per se was not registered firearms dealer so could not be guilty of carrying on business at place not entered in register.

Starkie (Richard William), R v (1932-34) 24 Cr App R 1; (1932) 76 SJ 780 CCA Long Vacation not an exceptional circumstance justifying bail.

Starkie, R v (1921-22) 16 Cr App R 61; (1922) 86 JP 74; [1922] 2 KB 275; [1922] 91 LJCL 663; (1921-22) 66 SJ 300; (1921-22) XXXVIII TLR 181; (1922) WN (I) 10 CCA Admissibility of evidence pertaining to alternative counts in criminal abortion charge.

Starling v Brooks [1956] Crim LR 480t HC QBD Successful prosecution for confinement of budgerigars in small cages.

Starling, R v; R v Calvey; R v Wright [1969] Crim LR 556; (1969) 113 SJ 584 CA Shopbreakers intending to steal goods which had been removed onto floor of store on previous night by fellow shopbreaker were guilty of larceny.

Stead v Tillotson and another (1899-1900) 44 SJ 212; (1899-1900) XVI TLR 170; (1899-1900) 48 WR 431 HC QBD Taking dying trout with improperly licensed instrument is crime under Salmon Fishery Act 1873, s 22.

Steane, R v [1947] 1 All ER 813; (1946-48) 32 Cr App R 61; (1947) 111 JP 337; [1947] KB 997; [1947] 116 LJR 969; (1947) 177 LTR 122; (1947) 91 SJ 279; (1947) LXIII TLR 403; (1947) WN (I) 184 CCA Can only convict of assisting enemy if act done with criminal/not innocent (such as saving family) intent to assist.

Stear v Scott [1992] RTR 226 HC QBD Valid conviction for criminal damage to clamp (that levered free from car with crowbar before throwing away) absent lawful excuse.

Steel (Alfred), R v (1910) 5 Cr App R 289 CCA On fraud amounting to false pretence justifying conviction for obtaining credit by fraud.

Steele (Peter Edward George), R v (1977) 65 Cr App R 22; [1977] Crim LR 290 CA Husband could be guilty of raping wife where were living apart and had given undertaking not to molest wife.

Steele v Rogers (1912) 76 JP 150; (1911-12) XXVIII TLR 198 HC KBD Cruelty to stranded whale that would have been washed away with tide not offence under Wild Animals in Captivity Protection Act 1900.

Steele, R v [1993] Crim LR 298 CA On mens rea for possession of firearms (without certificate).

Steer, R v [1986] 3 All ER 611; (1987) 84 Cr App R 25; [1986] Crim LR 619; (1986) 136 NLJ 801; (1970) 130 SJ 541; [1986] 1 WLR 1286 CA Life must be endangered/threatened by damaged property for offence of damage to property with intent to endanger/threaten life.

Steer, R v [1987] 2 All ER 833; [1988] AC 111; (1987) 85 Cr App R 352; [1987] Crim LR 684; (1987) 151 JP 793; (1987) 137 NLJ 640; (1987) 131 SJ 939; [1987] 3 WLR 205 HL Offence of damaging property with intent of endangering life requires that damaged property endanger life.

Stephens (John), R v (1910) 4 Cr App R 52 CCA Was larceny by trick where provider of goods believed would be paid for same in cash though this point never stated.

Stephenson, R v [1979] 2 All ER 1198; (1979) 69 Cr App R 213; [1979] Crim LR 590; (1979) 143 JP 592; (1979) 129 (1) NLJ 612; [1979] QB 695; (1979) 123 SJ 403; [1979] 3 WLR 193 CA Recklessness a subjective test.

Stevenage Borough Council v Wright (1996) TLR 10/4/96 HC QBD On distinction between pedlar and street trader.

Stevens (Francis Joseph), R v (1932-34) 24 Cr App R 85 CCA Cannot be convicted of fraudulent conversion where charged with simple larceny.

Stevens (Robert), R v [1981] Crim LR 568 CA On meaning of word 'preparation' in Misuse of Drugs Act 1971, Schedule 2, Part I.

Stevens and Stevens v Christy (1987) 85 Cr App R 249; [1987] Crim LR 503; (1987) 151 JP 366 HC QBD Place could be brothel where was used by team of prostitutes albeit one at a time.

Stevens, Betts v [1908-10] All ER 1245; (1911-13) XXII Cox CC 187; (1909) 73 JP 486; [1910] 1 KB 1; (1909) 44 LJ 629; (1910) 79 LJKB 17; (1909-10) 101 LTR 564; (1909-10) XXVI TLR 5; (1909) WN (I) 200 HC KBD Person warning motorists of upcoming police speed trap were obstructing police in execution of their duty.

Stevens, Smith v (1928-29) XLV TLR 429 HC KBD Penalty plus costs for placing advertisement of reward for return of lost property on 'no questions asked' basis (Larceny Act 1861, s 102).

Stevenson and Baldwin, R v (1905) 69 JP 84 Sessions Person continuously observed from 5am to 7am (at which time attempted crime) could then be charged with possession of housebreaking implements without lawful excuse between 9pm and 6am.

Stevenson v Aubrook and others [1941] 2 All ER 476; (1941) 91 LJ 254 HC KBD Arrest under Vagrancy Act 1824, s 6 for offence not actually committed an unlawful arrest.

Stevenson v Fulton [1935] All ER 431; (1934-39) XXX Cox CC 293; (1935) 99 JP 423; [1936] 1 KB 320; (1936) 81 LJ 42; [1936] 105 LJCL 167; (1936) 154 LTR 162; (1935-36) LII TLR 89; (1936) 80 SJ 75; (1935) WN (I) 188 HC KBD Person using (rather than providing) accommodation address can be convicted for furnishing false information contrary to Official Secrets Act 1920, s 5(4).

Stevenson, Sneddon v [1967] 2 All ER 1277; [1967] Crim LR 476t; (1967) 131 JP 441; (1967) 111 SJ 515; [1967] 1 WLR 1051 HC QBD Not accomplice where police officer places self in position to facilitate offence if offence to be committed.

Stewart (Albert), R v (1910) 4 Cr App R 175; (1910) 74 JP 246 CCA On establishing accused is habitual criminal.

Stewart (Alexander Davidson), R v (1931-32) 23 Cr App R 68 CCA Bail granted pending Long Vacation.

Stewart (Benjamin James), R v [1996] 1 Cr App R 229; [1994] TLR 403 CA On appropriate direction as to provocation in context of murder.

Stewart (John), R v (1986) 83 Cr App R 327; [1986] Crim LR 805 CA High rent not per se indication either way that are living on earnings of prostitution; corroboration warning in respect of accomplice to be clearly made.

Stewart and Harris, R v [1960] Crim LR 57t CCA Must possess explosive and know that what possess is explosive to be guilty of illegal possession of explosive.

Stewart, R v [1995] 4 All ER 999; [1995] Crim LR 66 CA If directing jury to consider provocation judge must mention evidence of provocation unless obvious.

Stewart, R v; R v Schofield [1995] 3 All ER 159; [1995] 1 Cr App R 441; [1995] Crim LR 420 CA Parties to joint enterprise resulting in death may be guilty of murder or manslaughter unless relevant act not committed in course of joint enterprise or other party to enterprise has a more specific intent.

Stinton, Cox v [1951] 2 All ER 637; (1951) 115 JP 490; [1951] 2 KB 1021; (1951) 101 LJ 455; [1951] 2 TLR 728; (1951) WN (I) 497 HC KBD Negatives liable to seizure/destruction.

Stockdale v Coulson [1974] Crim LR 474 HC QBD Could not be convicted of failure to annex to annual return documents approved at annual general meeting when no such meeting had been held.

Stockdale, R v (1915) WN (I) 86 CCA Habitual criminal conviction quashed in light of improper admission of matters not mentioned in notice (of assertion that were habitual criminal).

Stoddart, R v (1909) 73 JP 348; (1908-09) 53 SJ 578 CCA Is obtaining by false pretences in this jurisdiction to induce another by false pretences to mail money here to place abroad, there to be received by fraudster.

Stokes, R v [1958] Crim LR 688 Assizes On meaning of 'in the course or...furtherance of theft' (as used in the Homicide Act 1957, s 5(1)).

Stone, Abel v (1970) 134 JP 237 HC QBD Wilful obstruction of highway a continuing offence so plea of autrefois acquit available.

Stone, R v (1937) 81 SJ 735; (1936-37) LIII TLR 1046 CCA Strangulation in course of rape that unintentionally results in death is not analagous to death in course of procuring abortion: DPP v Beard principles applicable.

Stone, R v; R v Dobinson [1977] 2 All ER 341; (1977) 64 Cr App R 186; [1977] Crim LR 166; (1977) 141 JP 354; (1977) 127 NLJ 143t; [1977] QB 354; (1977) 121 SJ 83; [1977] 2 WLR 169 CA Reckless towards infirm person for whom have duty of care if indifferent to risk of injury or foresee risk but run the risk.

Stonehouse (John Thomson), R v (1977) 65 Cr App R 192 (also HL) CA Guilty of obtaining property by deception where acts done abroad but property obtained by deception in England.

Stonehouse and another v Masson [1921] All ER 534; (1921-25) XXVII Cox CC 23; (1921) 85 JP 167; [1921] 2 KB 818; [1922] 91 LJCL 93; (1921) 125 LTR 463; (1920-21) XXXVII TLR 621; (1921) WN (I) 167 HC KBD No intent needed to be convicted for fortune-telling under Vagrancy Act 1824, s 4.

Stonehouse, Director of Public Prosecutions v [1977] 2 All ER 909; [1978] AC 55; (1977) 65 Cr App R 192 (also CCA); [1977] Crim LR 544; (1977) 141 JP 473; (1977) 127 NLJ 864; (1977) 121 SJ 491; [1977] 3 WLR 143 HL Guilty of obtaining property by deception where acts done abroad but property obtained by deception in England; doing all possible acts to obtain property by deception could sustain conviction for attempt thereof.

Stones (George Kenneth), R v (1968) 52 Cr App R 36; [1967] Crim LR 708t; (1967) 117 NLJ 1112t; (1967) 111 SJ 832 CA Successful prosecution for causing cheque to be delivered for own use/benefit (Larceny Act 1916, s 32(1)).

Stones (James), R v (1989) 89 Cr App R 26; (1988) 132 SJ 1670; [1989] 1 WLR 156 CA Was aggravated burglary where burglar in possession of knife though may not have intended to use same during burglary.

Storey (Stephanie), R v; R v Anwar (Rashid) (1968) 52 Cr App R 334 CA Unsworn statement, which if true would be complete defence to charge, was only reaction to police accusation and did not mean was no case to answer.

Storey, R v [1968] Crim LR 387; (1968) 118 NLJ 373t; (1968) 112 SJ 417 CA Unsworn statement to police by flat occupier to effect that cannabis found therein belonged to another present there did not obviate presumption that she (the flat occupier) was in possession of the cannabis found there.

Stowe v Marjoram (1911-13) XXII Cox CC 198; (1909) 73 JP 498; (1909-10) 101 LTR 569 HC KBD Conviction for unlawful possession of eggs.

Straker v Director of Public Prosecutions [1963] 1 All ER 697; [1963] Crim LR 279; (1963) 127 JP 260; (1963) 113 LJ 365; [1963] 1 QB 926; (1963) 107 SJ 156; [1963] 2 WLR 598 HC QBD Negatives cannot be obscene publication.

Straker, R v [1965] Crim LR 239g CCA Objective test as to whether material sent by mail is 'indecent' (test is not to see whether material 'obscene').

Strath v Foxon [1955] 3 All ER 398; (1955) 39 Cr App R 162; [1955] Crim LR 773; (1955) 119 JP 581; [1956] 1 QB 67; (1955) 99 SJ 799; [1955] 3 WLR 659 HC QBD Place being used by only one prostitute cannot be brothel.

Straw, R v [1995] 1 All ER 187 CA Appeal based on diminished responsibility not available where plea deliberately not relied on in murder trial.

Streeter and another, Greater London Metropolitan Police Commissioner v (1980) 71 Cr App R 113; (1980) 130 NLJ 313 HC QBD Was not possession/control for security officer/police to mark/track stolen goods so accused could be convicted of handling.

Sullivan, R v [1970] 2 All ER 681; (1970) 54 Cr App R 389; [1970] Crim LR 641; (1970) 134 JP 583; [1971] 1 QB 253; (1970) 114 SJ 664; [1970] 3 WLR 210 CA Alibi evidence admissible despite failure to notify particulars.

Sullivan, R v [1977] Crim LR 751 CA Conviction for failure to provide specimen quashed where arresting police officer had not told offender at time of arrest of reason for arrest.

Summers (Peter), R v (1914) 10 Cr App R 11 CCA Can cite convictions (other than necessary three) as evidence of character.

Summers (Stanley George), R v (1972) 56 Cr App R 604; [1972] Crim LR 635 CA On what constitutes an affray.

Sumner (Matthew), R v [1977] Crim LR 362/614 CrCt On elements of defence of 'public good' to obscene publication prosecution; on what is meant by term 'deprave'.

Sunman, R v [1995] Crim LR 569 CA On lawful excuse as a defence to offence of having custody of counterfeit note.

Superintendant of Vine Street Police Station; ex parte Liebmann, R v (1915-17) XXV Cox CC 179; (1916) 80 JP 49; [1916] 85 LJKB 210; (1915-16) 113 LTR 971; (1915-16) XXXII TLR 3; (1915) WN (I) 320 HC KBD German resident in England for twenty-seven years was nonetheless properly interned.

Superintendent of Chiswick Police Station; ex parte Sacksteder, R v (1918) 53 LJ 96; (1918) 118 LTR 165 CA Wartime deportation order in respect of alien deemed valid.

Superintendent of Police, Stroud, G v (1988) 86 Cr App R 92; [1987] Crim LR 269 HC QBD Short time-span in which constable had to make decision to arrest relevant in deciding reasonableness of arrest that breach of peace likely: here reasonable so assault was assault on constable in execution of duty.

Supermarket (Anthony Jackson), Quinlan v [1966] Crim LR 391g HC QBD Goods stolen by supermarket cashier and passed to packer did not pass into possession of customer who was not therefore guilty of receiving.

Surujpaul called Dick v R [1958] 3 All ER 300 PC Cannot be convicted accessory before fact when principals acquitted of substantive offence.

Sutherland, Gwyn-Jones v [1982] RTR 102 HC QBD Conviction quashed as arrest for second failure to provide breath specimen invalid in that it took place not near where driving but outside hospital to which admitted and promptly released.

Sutton, R v [1977] 3 All ER 476; (1978) 66 Cr App R 21; [1977] Crim LR 569; (1977) 141 JP 683; (1977) 127 NLJ 590t; (1977) 121 SJ 676; [1977] 1 WLR 1086 CA Non-indecent touching consented to by youth not indecent assault.

Sutton, R v [1966] 1 All ER 571; (1966) 50 Cr App R 114; [1966] Crim LR 164; (1966) 130 JP 183; (1965-66) 116 NLJ 612; (1966) 110 SJ 51; [1966] 1 WLR 236 CCA Bailees giving goods on foot of forged document pass possession not property so is larceny by trick.

Suurmeijer, R v [1991] Crim LR 773 CA Drugs importation conviction of car passenger quashed where was inadequate proof that passenger had known drugs being carried in car.

Swain, Siddiqui v [1979] Crim LR 318; [1979] RTR 454 HC QBD Invalid arrest as no proof that policeman suspected driver had alcohol in body: arrest per se not evidence of suspicion.

Swales v Cox [1981] 1 All ER 1115; (1981) 72 Cr App R 171; [1981] Crim LR 235; (1981) 131 NLJ 372; [1981] QB 849; (1981) 125 SJ 133; [1981] 2 WLR 814 HC QBD Police may enter place using any necessary force to effect arrest.

Swallow v Director of Public Prosecutions [1991] Crim LR 610 HC QBD Acquittal merited where husband or wife had abstracted electricity through interference with meter but was no real indication as to which had done so.

Swanston v Director of Public Prosecutions (1997) 161 JP 203; [1997] TLR 37 HC QBD Person subjected to threatening/abusive/insulting words did not have to testify as to how received words for utterer of words to be convicted of using same.

Tansley v Painter [1969] Crim LR 139; (1968) 112 SJ 1005 HC QBD Evidence that had certain drug in urine sample not corroboration of possession of same.

Tao, R v [1976] 3 All ER 65; (1976) 63 Cr App R 163; [1976] Crim LR 516t; (1976) 140 JP 596; (1976) 126 NLJ 566t; [1977] QB 141; (1976) 120 SJ 420; [1976] 3 WLR 25 CA Need not be owner to be occupier.

Tarpy v Rickard [1980] Crim LR 375 HC QBD Could be convicted on basis of aggregate total of cannabis found at premises.

Tartellin v Bowen [1947] 2 All ER 837; (1948) 112 JP 99; [1948] LXIV TLR 20; (1948) WN (I) 15 HC KBD Member of Armed Forces guilty of possession of firearm (privately purchased for self) without certificate.

Tate, Tuffley v (1907-09) XXI Cox CC 337; (1907) 71 JP 21; (1907) XCVI LTR 24 HC KBD By-law requiring full fare where had no ticket was valid.

Tayler v Tayler (1911-12) 56 SJ 573 HC PDAD On who constitutes a habitual drunkard for the purposes of the Habitual Drunkard Act 1879.

Taylor (Alan), R v [1995] 1 Cr App R 131; [1994] Crim LR 527; (1994) 158 JP 317; (1994) 138 SJ LB 54; [1994] TLR 66 CA Developing obscene negatives into photographs was distributing obscene material.

Taylor (Edward) and Coney (Alfred), R v (1910) 5 Cr App R 168 CCA Early commencement of preventive detention where habitual criminal is young.

Taylor (Robert Peter), R v (1985) 80 Cr App R 327 CA Adequate direction on corroboration and recklessness: defence of honest mistake unlikely to succeed where jury conclude was no consent.

Taylor (Vincent), R v [1973] 1 All ER 78; (1973) 57 Cr App R 122; [1972] Crim LR 772t; (1973) 137 JP 91; (1972) 122 NLJ 918t; (1972) 116 SJ 800; [1972] 3 WLR 961 CA One person fighting unlawfully may be guilty of affray; if two charged with affray and one acquitted other may be convicted.

Taylor (William), R v (1922-23) 17 Cr App R 109; (1923) 87 JP 104 CCA On need to show connection between possession of implement and committing of offence using instrument.

Taylor v Chief Constable of Kent (1981) 72 Cr App R 318; [1981] Crim LR 244; (1981) 125 SJ 219; [1981] 1 WLR 606 HC QBD Cultivation of cannabis under Misuse of Drugs Act 1971, s 6 amounted to cultivation of controlled drug under s 4 thereof.

Taylor v Director of Public Prosecutions [1973] 2 All ER 1108; [1974] Crim LR 98; [1973] AC 964; (1973) 57 Cr App R 915; (1973) 137 JP 608; (1973) 123 NLJ 746t; (1973) 117 SJ 544; [1973] 3 WLR 140 HL May be guilty of affray even if only person fighting unlawfully to terror of others.

Taylor v Granville [1978] Crim LR 482 CA On what constitutes assault occasioning actual bodily harm (blow to face was such).

Taylor v McGirr [1986] Crim LR 544 HC QBD Offence under Act repealed before charges brought was properly charged under terms of repealed act.

Taylor v Mucklow [1973] Crim LR 750; (1973) 117 SJ 792 HC QBD That use of airgun was to protect one's property (in protection of which one may use some force) was not reasonable excuse for same.

Taylor v Pritchard (1910) 45 LJ 392; (1909-10) XXVI TLR 496; (1910) WN (I) 147 HC KBD On powers of search of water bailiff under Salmon Fishery Act 1873, s 36.

Taylor, Ackers and others v [1974] 1 All ER 771; [1974] Crim LR 103; (1974) 138 JP 269; (1974) 124 NLJ 56t; (1974) 118 SJ 185; [1974] 1 WLR 405 HC QBD Any possible misuse of gun justifies revocation of licence.

Taylor, Clark v (1948) 112 JP 439; (1948) WN (I) 410 HC KBD On what constituted 'frequenting' a place for purpose of the Vagrancy Act 1824, s 4.

Taylor, Director of Public Prosecutions v; Director of Public Prosecutions v Little [1992] 1 All ER 299; [1991] Crim LR 900/904; (1991) 155 JP 713; (1991) 141 NLJ 964; (1991) 141 NLJ 1038t; [1992] QB 645; [1992] 2 WLR 460 HC QBD Assault and battery separate offences; assaults and batteries triable summarily.

Thompson (Arthur), R v (1916-17) 12 Cr App R 278 CCA Bail pending appeal against conviction in gross indecency with male case.

Thompson (Brian Ernest George), R v; R v Thompson (Brian Albert); R v Woodiwiss (Colin Alex Norman) (1979) 69 Cr App R 22 CA Was permissible under Article 36/EEC to prohibit export of non-legal tender so as to prevent melting down abroad.

Thompson (Graham Frederick), R v (1978) 66 Cr App R 130 CA Suspended nine months' imprisonment sentence for fraud on insurance company; forfeiture order quashed where money obtained by fraud repaid and property in respect of which claim made not in possession/control when arrested.

Thompson (Harry), R v (1910) 5 Cr App R 9 CCA Was obtaining credit other than by false pretences to obtain goods without intending to pay for same.

Thompson (Michael), R v (1984) 79 Cr App R 191; [1984] Crim LR 427; (1984) 128 SJ 447; [1984] 1 WLR 962 CA Where monies telexed to English accounts on foot of computer fraudulently programmed abroad was obtaining property by deception in England; credit balance resulting from fraud not a chose in action.

Thompson v Dann and other (1994) 138 SJ LB 221 HC QBD Court not satisfied beyond reasonable doubt that personation (and not mere mistake) had occurred.

Thompson v Director of Public Prosecutions [1918-19] All ER 521; (1918) 53 LJ 62; (1918) 118 LTR 418; (1917-18) 62 SJ 266; (1918) WN (I) 21 HL Possession of powder puffs/lewd photographs showed offender and accused had same tendencies - admissible to rebut alibi.

Thompson v Nixon [1965] 2 All ER 741; (1965) 49 Cr App R 324; [1965] Crim LR 438t; (1965) 129 JP 414; (1965) 115 LJ 545; [1966] 1 QB 103; (1965) 109 SJ 471; [1965] 3 WLR 501 HC QBD Person finding item and assuming possession thereof not a bailee.

Thompson, R v (1918-21) XXVI Cox CC 31; (1916-17) 12 Cr App R 261; (1917) 81 JP 266; [1917] 2 KB 630; (1917) 52 LJ 285; [1917] 86 LJCL 1321; (1917-18) 117 LTR 575; (1916-17) 61 SJ 647; (1916-17) XXXIII TLR 566; (1917) WN (I) 234 CCA Powder puffs/obscene photographs in accused's possession admissible on issue of identity.

Thompson, R v [1965] Crim LR 553g CCA On whether/when to leave one or two charges to jury where person is charged with larceny and, alternatively, receiving.

Thompson-Schwab and another v Costaki and another [1956] 1 All ER 652; [1956] Crim LR 274; (1956) 106 LJ 201; (1956) 100 SJ 246; [1956] 1 WLR 335 CA Use of neighbouring premises for prostitution anuisance.

Thomson (Peter), R v (1906) 70 JP 6 CCC On burden of proof on defence in bigamy prosecution once prosecution establish subsistence of two marriages.

Thomson v Chain Libraries, Ltd [1954] 2 All ER 616; [1954] Crim LR 551t; (1954) 104 LJ 473; (1954) 98 SJ 473; [1954] 1 WLR 999 HC QBD Justices must themselves examine allegedly obscene publications to see if obscene.

Thomson, R v (1966) 50 Cr App R 1 Assizes On mens rea of conspiracy.

Thorley, R v [1962] Crim LR 696 CCA On what it takes to be (unlike here) an accessory after the fact.

Thorne v Motor Trade Association (1936-38) 26 Cr App R 51; (1937) 83 LJ 426 HL Not demanding money with menaces to write letter on behalf of trade association requiring payment if are not to be put on black list.

Thornton (No 2), R v [1996] 2 All ER 1023; [1996] 2 Cr App R 108; [1996] Crim LR 597; (1995) 145 NLJ 1888; (1996) 140 SJ LB 38; [1995] TLR 674; [1996] TLR 6/6/96; [1996] 1 WLR 1174 CA Battered woman syndrome relevant when determining if provocation.

Thornton v Mitchell [1940] 1 All ER 339; (1940) 104 JP 108; (1940) 162 LTR 296; (1940) 84 SJ 257; (1939-40) LVI TLR 296; (1940) WN (I) 52 HC KBD Only driver can be guilty of driving without due care and attention; no conviction for aiding and abetting where principal acquitted of offence.

Thornton, Harrison v (1979) 68 Cr App R 28; [1966] Crim LR 388t; (1966) 110 SJ 444 HC QBD Stone picked up and thrown in course of fight was offensive weapon.

Thornton, R v [1992] 1 All ER 306; (1993) 96 Cr App R 112; [1992] Crim LR 53; (1991) 141 NLJ 1223 CA Provocation not present if murder on foot of history of domestic violence but no sudden loss of control.

Thornton, R v [1963] 1 All ER 170; (1963) 47 Cr App R 1; [1963] Crim LR 197; (1963) 127 JP 113; (1963) 113 LJ 90; [1964] 2 QB 176; [1963] 3 WLR 444 CCA Not guilty of fraudulently inducing signature to security where do not impose any liability on another party but can be guilty of obtaining credit by fraud.

Thorpe (Stephen), R v (1987) 85 Cr App R 107; [1987] Crim LR 493; (1987) 131 SJ 325; [1987] 1 WLR 383 CA Weapon using carbon dioxide for propulsion not an air gun: was lethal weapon if could cause death.

Threlfall, R v (1914-15) XXIV Cox CC 230; (1914-15) 111 LTR 168 CCA Single person may establish took oath but need more evidence to prove oath taken falsely.

Threlkeld v Smith (1901-07) XX Cox CC 38; [1901] 2 KB 531; [1901] 70 LJK/QB 921; (1901-02) LXXXV LTR 275; (1900-01) XVII TLR 612; (1901-02) 50 WR 158 HC KBD Killing of deer outside place kept is killing deer lawfully come by (Larceny Act 1861, s 14) even though killer wrongly on third party's land.

Thuan (Luc Thiet) v R [1996] 2 All ER 1033; [1997] AC 131; [1996] 2 Cr App R 178; [1996] Crim LR 820; (1996) 146 NLJ 513; (1996) 140 SJ LB 107; (1996) TLR 2/4/96; [1996] 3 WLR 45 PC Provocation an objective test to which particular characteristics of defendant have no relevance.

Tibbits and another, R v [1900-03] All ER 896; [1902] 71 LJCL 4; (1901-02) 46 SJ 51; (1901-02) 50 WR 125 CCR Agreement to publish material prejudicing fair trial a criminal conspiracy to obstruct course of justice.

Tideswell, R v (1907-09) XXI Cox CC 10; (1905) 69 JP 318; [1905] 2 KB 273; (1905-06) XCIII LTR 111; (1904-05) XXI TLR 531 CCR Larceny where fraudulently agree to accept more of goods sold from bulk than contracted for.

Tilley, Scott v (1937) 81 SJ 864 HC KBD Absent explanation by accused, finding that person had in his possession goods which were reasonable grounds to believe had been stolen meant accused guilty of offence under the Wolverhampton Corporation Act 1925, s 124(1).

Tillings and Tillings, R v [1985] Crim LR 393; (1985) 135 NLJ 510 CrCt Is no offence of deception in procuring execution of will.

Tillotson and another, Stead v (1899-1900) 44 SJ 212; (1899-1900) XVI TLR 170; (1899-1900) 48 WR 431 HC QBD Taking dying trout with improperly licensed instrument is crime under Salmon Fishery Act 1873, s 22.

Tilonko v The Atorney-General of Natal (1906-07) XCV LTR 853; (1906-07) XXIII TLR 668 PC Leave to appeal in habeas corpus action refused where issue raised was settled by Act of Parliament.

Timmis (David), R v [1976] Crim LR 129 CrCt Person who ran away after breath test could be guilty of escape from arrest.

Tims v John Lewis and Co, Ltd [1951] 1 All ER 814; (1951) 115 JP 265; [1951] 2 KB 459; (1951) 101 LJ 203; (1951) 95 SJ 268; [1951] 1 TLR 719; (1951) WN (I) 188 CA Upon arrest must be taken to police officer/justice of the peace forthwith.

Tindale, R v [1962] Crim LR 704 CCA Quashing of convictions to which pleaded guilty but which were unsupported by evidence; improper to impose consecutive sentences for offences arising from same facts.

Tirado (Emilio), R v (1974) 59 Cr App R 80 CA Was obtaining property by deception in England to accept drafts from abroad and cash them in England.

Tiso (Roland Leonard), R v (1990-91) 12 Cr App R (S) 122; [1990] Crim LR 607 CA Lengthy period between sex crimes towards children and investigation of/conviction for same need not be mitigating factor when sentencing.

Titus and others, R v [1971] Crim LR 279 CCC Water pistols containing ammonia were imitation firearms for puposes of Firearms Act 1968, s 18.

TJ Brooks, Ltd, Buller and Co, Ltd v [1930] All ER 534; (1929-30) XLVI TLR 233 HC KBD Persons to whom stolen ring pawned could not be sued for its return by persons from whom title to goods originally derived but who did not own goods at time of pawning.

Tobierre, R v [1986] 1 All ER 346; (1986) 82 Cr App R 212; [1986] Crim LR 243; (1986) 130 SJ 35; [1986] 1 WLR 125 CA Mens rea for use of false instrument is that intended to induce other to accept forgery as genuine and to use to other's (or another's) detriment.

Tolfree v Florence (1970) 114 SJ 930 HC QBD Valid conviction for making false representation for the purpose of obtaining sickness benefit.

Tolman, Morris v [1922] All ER 182; (1921-25) XXVII Cox CC 345; (1922) 86 JP 221; [1923] 1 KB 166; [1923] 92 LJCL 215; (1923) 128 LTR 118; (1922-23) 67 SJ 169; (1922-23) XXXIX TLR 39 HC KBD Can be convicted as aider and abettor though principal acquitted (but not with respect to using vehicle for unlicensed purpose).

Tomblin, R v [1964] Crim LR 780t CCA Person who took no part in opening stolen safe deemed not guilty of possession of same (though might well be guilty of joint possession of same).

Tombs, Edwards v [1983] Crim LR 43 HC QBD Turnstile meter was a record so operator of same who wrongfully allowed persons through it was guilty of falsifying record made for accounting purpose (Theft Act 1968, s 17(1)(a)).

Tomlin, R v [1954] 2 All ER; [1954] Crim LR 540; (1954) 118 JP 354; [1954] 2 QB 274; (1954) 98 SJ 374; [1954] 2 WLR 1140 CCA Can charge for embezzlement of aggregate amount where impossible to divide into individual amounts taken.

Tomlinson, Davies v (1980) 71 Cr App R 279 HC QBD Total sentences (even where consecutively imposed) measure by which gauge whether person sentenced to three or more years' imprisonment (and hence guilty of offence where possessed firearm).

Tomsett, R v [1985] Crim LR 369 CA Conspiracy conviction quashed where substantive offence if effected would not have been indictable in United Kingdom.

Toney, R v; R v Ali (Tanveer) [1993] 2 All ER 409; (1993) 97 Cr App R 176; [1993] Crim LR 397; (1993) 157 JP 889; (1993) 143 NLJ 403; (1993) 137 SJ LB 46; [1992] TLR 608; [1993] 1 WLR 364 CA Interference with witness an obstruction of justice even if no inducement or threat.

Tonkin, Alexander v [1979] Crim LR 248; (1979) 123 SJ 111 HC QBD On when fishing complete for purposes of Sea Fisheries Regulation Act 1966, s 11(2).

Tonner (Gordon Campbell), R v; R v Rees (Wilfrid Haydn); R v Harding (William); R v Evans (Ronald) [1985] 1 All ER 807; (1985) 80 Cr App R 170; [1984] Crim LR 618; (1984) 128 SJ 702; [1984] TLR 429; [1985] 1 WLR 344 CA Can only be charged with statutory conspiracy where conspiracy was to commit substantive offence.

Toohey v Woolwich Justices and another [1966] 2 All ER 429; [1967] 2 AC 1; (1966) 130 JP 326; (1965-66) 116 NLJ 894; [1966] 2 WLR 1442 HL Assault/aggravated assault (even on constable) to be tried summarily.

Toronto Railway Company v R (Attorney-General for England and Attorney-General for Canada, Interveners) [1917] AC 630; [1917] 86 LJPC 195; (1917-18) 117 LTR 579; (1917-18) XXXIV TLR 1; (1917) WN (I) 277 PC Interpretation of provisions of Ontario Criminal Code concerning common nuisance.

Torri, R v (1982) 132 NLJ 348 CA Failed appeal against conviction for forging bill of exchange.

Tottenham Magistrates' Court, ex parte Riccardi, R v (1978) 66 Cr App R 150 HC QBD Valid forefiture of recognisance.

Touhey (Peter), R v (1961) 45 Cr App R 23; [1960] Crim LR 843 CCA On availability of indecent assault conviction where defendant charged with rape.

Tower Bridge Magistrates' Court; ex parte Gilbert, R v (1988) 152 JP 307 HC QBD Bail properly refused where at adjourned hearing new information available about person granted unconditional bail at original hearing.

Townley v Rushworth [1964] Crim LR 590; (1963) 107 SJ 1004 HC QBD Person in respect of whom incomplete recommendation for committal to mental hospital made not guilty of assault where struck out at persons who entered his property seeking to forcibly remove him.

Trapnell, Hughes v; Trapnell v JR Berman, Ltd and another [1962] 3 All ER 616; (1963) 127 JP 1; (1962) 112 LJ 749; [1963] 1 QB 737; [1962] 3 WLR 1068 HC QBD Circulars not contrary to Prevention of Fraud (Investments) Act 1958, s 14 (1)(a) as only concerned with security not investment.

Treacy v Director of Public Prosecutions [1971] 1 All ER 110; [1971] AC 537; (1971) 55 Cr App R 113; [1972] Crim LR 590; (1971) 135 JP 112; (1971) 115 SJ 12; [1971] 2 WLR 112 HL Can be tried for blackmail only partly committed in England.

Treacy, R v [1970] 3 All ER 205; [1970] Crim LR 584t; (1970) 114 SJ 604; [1970] 3 WLR 592 CA Can be charged with blackmail though entirety of offence not in England.

Treanor (or McEvoy), R v [1939] 1 All ER 330; (1939-40) XXXI Cox CC 235; (1938-40) 27 Cr App R 35; (1939) 160 LTR 286; (1939) 83 SJ 219; (1938-39) LV TLR 348; (1939) WN (I) 29 CCA Seven year proviso regarding 'second marriage[s]' applies only to second marriage.

Trent River Authority v FH Drabble and Sons Ltd [1970] Crim LR 106; (1969) 113 SJ 898 HC QBD Application of the Rivers (Prevention of Pollution) Act 1971, s 1(1).

Triffitt, R v [1938] 2 All ER 818; (1939-40) XXXI Cox CC 93; (1936-38) 26 Cr App R 169; (1938) 102 JP 388; (1938) 82 SJ 477; (1937-38) LIV TLR 1012; (1938) WN (I) 213 CCA On procedure when adding to substantive charge one of being a habitual criminal.

Troughton v The Metropolitan Police [1987] Crim LR 138 HC QBD Could not be guilty of making off without payment from taxi-driver to whom one's obligations had ceased when he went into breach of contract by not completing journey.

True, R v (1921-25) XXVII Cox CC 287; (1922) 127 LTR 561 CCA M'Naghten's Rules applied as originally stated.

Truss (George William), R v (1909) 2 Cr App R 69 CCA Appeal on ground of provocation dismissed as was no evidence of serious provocation for what was serious unlawful wounding.

Tuck v Robson [1970] Crim LR 273t HC QBD On what constitutes 'aiding and abetting' offence.

Tuck, R v [1994] Crim LR 375 CA On what is meant by 'persistent' importuning.

Tucker, R v [1952] 2 All ER 1074; (1952) 96 SJ 866 CMAC Shortfall in mess funds and non-excuse by accused not proof that misapplied service property contrary to Army Act, s 17.

Tuffley v Tate (1907-09) XXI Cox CC 337; (1907) 71 JP 21; (1907) XCVI LTR 24 HC KBD By-law requiring full fare where had no ticket was valid.

Tulloch (Wayne Andrew), R v (1986) 83 Cr App R 1; [1986] Crim LR 50 CA Could be convicted of attempt where sought to commit what thought was possible but was in fact impossible offence.

Tunnicliffe, Creaser and another v [1978] 1 All ER 569; (1978) 66 Cr App R 66; [1977] Crim LR 746; (1978) 142 JP 245; (1977) 127 NLJ 638t; (1977) 121 SJ 775; [1977] 1 WLR 1493 HC QBD Altered firearm capable of firing original ammunition still required certificate.

Tunnicliffe, Farrow v [1976] Crim LR 126 HC QBD Could under Misuse of Drugs Act 1971 remove suspect offender thereunder to another place to conduct search there.

Turner (No 2), R v [1971] 2 All ER 441; (1971) 55 Cr App R 336; [1971] Crim LR 373; (1971) 135 JP 419; [1971] RTR 396; (1971) 115 SJ 405; [1971] 1 WLR 901 CA Possession or control an issue of fact; no theft if honest but mistaken belief that had right to property.

Turner (Basil William Ivor), R v (1981) 72 Cr App R 117; [1980] Crim LR 797 CA Was forgery for police officer to forge document with intent to deceive (that intent was adequate malo animo).

Turner (William), R v (1910) 4 Cr App R 203 CCA Person guilty of causing person to take noxious drug to procure miscarriage contrary to Offences Against the Person Act 1861, s 58, could be guilty of supplying same under s 59 of 1861 Act.

Turner and others, R v (1975) 61 Cr App R 67; [1975] Crim LR 451t; (1975) 125 NLJ 333t; (1975) 125 NLJ 410; (1975) 119 SJ 422/575 CA Appropriate sentence for serious offences (should be proportional to sentence imposed for murder: life imprisonment); fifteen years' imprisonment appropriate for armed Post Office robbers, eighteen years for those with criminal reccord.

Turner v Shearer [1973] 1 All ER 397; (1973) 137 JP 191; (1972) 116 SJ 800; [1972] 1 WLR 1387 HC QBD Wearing uniform 'calculated to deceive' under Police Act 1964, s 52(2) means 'likely to deceive'.

Turner, Director of Public Prosecutions v [1973] 3 All ER 124; [1974] AC 357; (1973) 57 Cr App R 932; [1974] Crim LR 186; (1973) 137 JP 736; (1973) 123 NLJ 747t; (1973) 117 SJ 664; [1973] 3 WLR 352 HL That evaded debt proved obtained pecuniary advantage even if not so.

Turner, R v [1973] 2 All ER 828; (1973) 57 Cr App R 650; [1973] Crim LR 370t; (1973) 123 NLJ 494t; (1973) 117 SJ 303; [1973] 1 WLR 653 CA Giving worthless cheque for pre-existing debt not obtaining advantage by deception.

Turner, R v [1908-10] All ER 1206; (1910) 74 JP 81; [1910] 1 KB 346; (1909) 44 LJ 780; (1910) 79 LJKB 176; (1910) 102 LTR 367; (1909-10) XXVI TLR 112 CCA On procedure/evidential procedure in prosecuting habitual criminal.

Turner, R v; R v Waller (1909-10) 54 SJ 164 CCA On proving person to be habitual criminal.

Turnock, McBride v [1964] Crim LR 456t; (1964) 108 SJ 336 HC QBD Person who struck constable in course of assault on another was guilty of assault on police officer in the execution of his duty.

Turpin, R v [1990] Crim LR 514; [1990] TLR 93 CA Need not acquit all co-accused of violent disorder where acquitting one of same; on relevance of guilty plea of one co-defendant to guilt/innocence of another.

Turvey, R v [1946] 2 All ER 60; (1945-46) 31 Cr App R 154; (1946) 110 JP 270; (1946) 96 LJ 304; (1946) 175 LTR 308; (1946) 90 SJ 395; (1945-46) LXII TLR 511; (1946) WN (I) 121 CCA No asportation (despite handing of goods being part of entrapment) so no larceny.

Tweedie, R v [1984] 2 All ER 136; (1984) 79 Cr App R 168; [1984] Crim LR 231; (1984) 148 JP 716; [1984] QB 729; (1984) 128 SJ 262; [1984] TLR 52; [1984] 2 WLR 608 CA Document containing false information intended to deceive must have been intended for third party.

Twine, R v [1967] Crim LR 710 CA On third party provocation as defence to murder.

Twiss, R v [1918-23] All ER 257; (1918-21) XXVI Cox CC 325; (1917-18) 13 Cr App R 177; (1919) 83 JP 23; [1918] 2 KB 853; [1919] 88 LJCL 20; (1918-19) 119 LTR 680; (1917-18) 62 SJ 752; (1918-19) XXXV TLR 3; (1918) WN (I) 300 CCA Finding powder puffs/photos of naked boys in accused's possession admissible as evidence of guilt; conviction allowed stand despite juror conversations with prosecution witnesses.

Tynan v Chief Constable of Liverpool [1965] 3 All ER 611; [1965] Crim LR 611; (1965) 115 LJ 610 CrCt Was obstruction of constable in execution of his duty strike committee chairman ordered that pickets continue after request by constable (who considered them to be an obstruction) that they stop.

Union of India v Narang (Manohar Lal) and another; Union of India v Narang (Omi Prakash) and another [1977] 2 All ER 348; [1978] AC 247; (1977) 64 Cr App R 259; (1977) 141 JP 361; [1977] 2 WLR 862 HC QBD If facts relevant to objection raised by fugitive show unjust/ oppressive to return court must discharge from custody.

Union of India v Narang (Manohar Lal) and another; Union of India v Narang (Omi Prakash) and another [1977] 2 All ER 348; [1978] AC 247; (1977) 64 Cr App R 259; [1977] Crim LR 352; (1977) 141 JP 361; (1977) 127 NLJ 542t; (1977) 121 SJ 286; [1977] 2 WLR 862 HL If facts relevant to objection raised by fugitive show unjust/oppressive to return court must discharge from custody.

United Dominions Trust (Commercial), Ltd, Stamp v [1967] 1 All ER 251; (1967) 131 JP 177; [1967] 1 QB 418; (1966) 110 SJ 906; [1967] 2 WLR 541 HC QBD Post-conviction restitution order for property in possession of third party permissible but exceptional.

United Services Bureau Limited, Law Society v (1934) 98 JP 33; (1933) 76 LJ 321; (1934) 103 LJCL 81; (1934) 150 LTR 159; (1933) 77 SJ 815; (1933) WN (I) 263 HC KBD Corporate body could not be guilty of wilfully pretending to be solicitor under Solicitors Act 1932, s 46.

United States Government and another, Liangsiriprasert v [1990] 2 All ER 866; [1991] 1 AC 225; (1991) 92 Cr App R 77; (1990) 134 SJ 1123; [1990] TLR 507; [1990] 3 WLR 606 PC Enticement into jurisdiction from where extradition possible not abuse of extradition process. Inchoate crimes - here conspiracy - entered into abroad/in Thailand to commit offence in England/Hong Kong triable in England/Hong Kong.

United States Government and others v McCaffery [1984] 2 All ER 570; (1985) 80 Cr App R 82; (1984) 128 SJ 448; [1984] TLR 389; [1984] 1 WLR 867 HL Extradition for state crimes possible under extradition treaty with federal government; magistrate need only decide whether acts described would be offences under English law.

United States Government and others, Atkinson v [1969] 3 All ER 1317; [1971] AC 197; [1970] Crim LR 30; (1970) 134 JP 29; (1969) 119 NLJ 1045t; (1969) 113 SJ 901; [1969] 3 WLR 1074 HL If sufficient evidence for committal magistrate must commit.

United States Government v Atkinson [1969] 2 All ER 1151; [1969] Crim LR 487t; (1969) 133 JP 621 HC QBD Appeal by case stated from magistrates' courts in extradition cases; no autrefois convict possible between attempted armed robbery and aggravated burglary.

United States Government v Bowe [1989] 3 All ER 315; [1990] 1 AC 500; [1990] Crim LR 196; (1989) 133 SJ 1298; [1989] 3 WLR 1256 PC Conspiracy to commit drug offence an extraditable offence; no award of costs available in criminal cause or matter.

United States Government, Jennings v [1982] 3 All ER 104 (also HC QBD); [1983] 1 AC 624; (1982) 75 Cr App R 367; [1982] Crim LR 748; (1982) 146 JP 396; (1982) 132 NLJ 881; [1983] RTR 1 (also HC QBD); (1982) 126 SJ 659; [1982] TLR 424; [1982] 3 WLR 450 HL Causing death by reckless driving is manslaughter; character of offence for which sought determines if extradition possible.

Utting (John Benjamin), R v (1988) 86 Cr App R 164; [1987] Crim LR 636; (1987) 131 SJ 1154; [1987] 1 WLR 1375 CA Successful appeal against conviction for making false instrument with intent of inducing another to act/not to act on belief that document genuine (Forgery and Counterfeiting Act 1981, s 1).

Uxbridge Justices, ex parte Heward-Mills, R v [1983] 1 All ER 530; [1983] Crim LR 165; (1983) 147 JP 225; (1982) 126 SJ 854; [1983] 1 WLR 56 HC QBD Surety may give evidence of means in trying to persuade magistrates that should not forfeit entire recognisance.

Uxbridge Justices; ex parte Davies, R v [1981] 1 WLR 1080 HC QBD Unlawful detention of extraditee for offence other than that for which extradited.

Uxbridge Justices; ex parte Logan, R v [1956] Crim LR 270 HC QBD Restitution of stolen property to rightful owner could be made by justices immediately upon conviction of thief.

Uxbridge Magistrates' Court; ex parte Henry, R v [1994] Crim LR 581; [1994] TLR 103 CA Customs and Excise authorities out of time in their application for continued detention of suspected drug trafficking money.

Vaccari, R v [1958] 1 All ER 468; (1958) 42 Cr App R 85; [1958] Crim LR 261t; (1958) 122 JP 209; (1958) 108 LJ 168 CCA On gambling by bankrupt.

Vale, R v [1938] 3 All ER 355; (1939-40) XXXI Cox CC 138; (1936-38) 26 Cr App R 187; (1938) 102 JP 426; (1938) 86 LJ 26; (1937-38) LIV TLR 1014; (1938) WN (I) 272 CCA Trial of substantive offence and habitual criminal charge to be by same court but formal pleading to charge may be in different court.

Valentine (Anthony), R v [1996] 2 Cr App R 213 CA Rape complaint admissible though not made at earliest possible opportunity.

Vann and Davis, R v [1996] Crim LR 52 CA Offence of carrying firearm in public place an absolute offence.

Vasey and Lally, R v (1905) 69 JP 455; [1905] 2 KB 748; (1905) 40 LJ 750; [1906] 75 LJKB 19; (1905-06) 50 SJ 14; (1905-06) XXII TLR 1; (1905) WN (I) 150; (1905-06) 54 WR 218 CCR On poisoning of fish in salmon river.

Vasquez v R; O'Neil v R [1994] 3 All ER 674; [1994] Crim LR 845; (1994) 138 SJ LB 161; [1994] 1 WLR 1304 PC Where evidence of provocation burden on prosecution to negative that suggestion.

Vaughan v Biggs [1960] 2 All ER 473; [1960] Crim LR 561; (1960) 110 LJ 446; (1960) 104 SJ 508 HC QBD Depositing and leaving litter not a continuing offence.

Wallace (William Herbert), R v (1931-32) 23 Cr App R 32; (1931) 75 SJ 459 CCA Murder conviction quashed where rested on suspicion.

Wallace, McArdle v [1964] Crim LR 467g; (1964) 108 SJ 483 HC QBD Constable not acting in course of duty where requested by son of owner to leave property had entered so subsequent assault by son on constable not assault on same in execution of his duty.

Wallace-Johnson v R [1940] 1 All ER 241; [1940] AC 231; (1940) 84 SJ 149; (1939-40) LVI TLR 215; (1940) WN (I) 5 PC Need not show seditious intent/subsequent incitement to violence to sustain charge of seditious writing.

Waller, Hutton and Artis, R v [1960] Crim LR 759 CCC Alternate directors were directors for purposes of Larceny Act 1916, s 20(1)(ii).

Waller, R v [1908-10] All ER 1215; (1910) 74 JP 81; [1910] 1 KB 364; (1910) 79 LJKB 184; (1910) 102 LTR 400; (1909-10) XXVI TLR 142 CCA On consent of DPP to/on notice to offender of habitual criminal charge.

Waller, R v [1991] Crim LR 381 CA Possession of firearm without certificate an offence of strict liability.

Wallett, R v [1968] 2 All ER 296; (1968) 52 Cr App R 271; [1968] Crim LR 271t; (1968) 132 JP 318; [1968] 2 QB 367; (1968) 112 SJ 232; [1968] 2 WLR 1199 CA On criminal intent (homicide prosecution).

Walmsley (Jack Ronald), R v; R v De Reya (Anthony); R v Jackson (Peter Michael) (1978) 67 Cr App R 30; [1978] Crim LR 287; (1978) 128 NLJ 163t; (1978) 122 SJ 127 CA Meaning of 'utter' in Coinage Offences Act 1936, s 5(1); was conspiracy to utter counterfeit to sell copies of old coins.

Walsh v Governor of Brixton Prison and another [1984] 2 All ER 609; (1985) 80 Cr App R 186 HL Home Secretary/prison governor not under absolute duty to produce prisoners on bail in court on dates specified in remands.

Walsh, R v [1969] Crim LR 668 CA Four years' imprisonment for manslaughter arising from grossly negligent use of gun.

Walter, Broome v [1989] Crim LR 725 HC QBD Silencer legitimately found not to be accessory (and so not to require separate certificate).

Walters (Terence), R v; R v Tovey (George); R v Padfield (David Albert); R v Padfield (Colin John) (1979) 69 Cr App R 115; [1979] RTR 220 CA Was common law conspiracy to defraud where hired cars and then sold on with fake log books.

Walters v Lunt and another [1951] 2 All ER 645; (1951-52) 35 Cr App R 94; (1951) 115 JP 512; (1951) 101 LJ 482; (1951) 95 SJ 625; (1951) WN (I) 472 HC KBD Child under eight cannot commit larceny so person acquiring 'stolen' items therefrom not receiving stolen property.

Walters, R v [1968] 3 All ER 863; (1969) 53 Cr App R 9; [1968] Crim LR 686; (1969) 133 JP 73; (1969) 119 NLJ 14; [1969] 1 QB 255; (1968) 112 SJ 801; [1968] 3 WLR 987 CA On Vagrancy Act, 1824 s 10 charge sentence to be imposed for being incorrigible rogue not for what did as such.

Walton Street Justices, ex parte Crothers, R v [1992] Crim LR 875; (1993) 157 JP 171; (1992) 136 SJ LB 221; [1992] TLR 323 HC QBD Person has been prosecuted for an offence for purposes of Dogs Act 1991 if prosecution started but discontinued; person ought to be afforded chance to be heard before destruction of property ordered.

Walton v R [1978] 1 All ER 542; [1978] AC 788; (1978) 66 Cr App R 25; [1977] Crim LR 747; (1978) 142 JP 151; (1977) 127 NLJ 1050t; (1977) 121 SJ 728; [1977] 3 WLR 902 PC Jury may reject diminished responsibility defence even if psychiatrist credits it in evidence.

Walton, Churchill v [1967] 1 All ER 497; [1967] 2 AC 224; (1967) 51 Cr App R 212; [1967] Crim LR 235t; (1967) 131 JP 277; (1967) 111 SJ 112; [1967] 2 WLR 682 HL Not conspiracy if agree to commit absolute offence not knowing are agreeing to unlawful act.

Wan and Chan, R v [1995] Crim LR 296 CA On liability of party to joint enterprise where another party goes further than was agreed.

Warburton-Pitt, R v (1991) 92 Cr App R 136; [1991] Crim LR 434; [1990] TLR 521 CA Conviction for recklessly acting in manner likely to endanger aircraft (here microlight)/persons inside/other persons or property (under Air Navigation Order 1982) quashed as was inadequate specificity by prosecution as to nature of recklessness involved.

Ward v Holman [1964] Crim LR 541g; (1964) 128 JP 397; (1964) 114 LJ 506; [1964] 2 QB 580; (1964) 108 SJ 380; [1964] 2 WLR 1313 HC QBD Interpretation of Public Order Act 1936, s 5.

Ward, Coyne v [1962] Crim LR 169t HC QBD Comparison of/contrast between larceny by trick and obtaining by false pretences.

Ward, R v [1956] 1 All ER 565; [1956] Crim LR 203; (1956) 106 LJ 153; [1956] 1 QB 351; (1956) 100 SJ 112; [1956] 2 WLR 423 CCA Test of intention is what reasonable man would think.

Ward, R v (1915-17) XXV Cox CC 255; [1915] 3 KB 696; [1916] 85 LJKB 483; (1916) 114 LTR 192; (1915-16) 60 SJ 27; (1915) WN (I) 317 CCA Is lawful excuse to possession of housebreaking tools (contrary to Larceny Act 1861, s 58) that possess tools for trading purposes.

Wardrope, R v [1960] Crim LR 770 CCC On provocation/self defence/drunkenness as defences to murder.

Ware and another v Matthews (1981) 131 NLJ 830 HC QBD Successful action for damages for arrest without reasonable cause for alleged unlawful taking of car.

Warn, R v [1968] 1 All ER 339; [1968] Crim LR 103t; (1967) 117 NLJ 1242t; [1968] 1 QB 718; (1967) 111 SJ 943; [1968] 2 WLR 131 CMAC Consent of DPP to gross indecency charge involving under-21 year old applies to court-martials.

Warn, Secretary of State for Defence v [1970] AC 394; [1968] Crim LR 378; (1968) 112 SJ 461 HL Consent of DPP to gross indecency charge involving under-21 year old applies to court-martials.

Warneford and Gibbs, R v [1994] Crim LR 753; [1994] TLR 279 CA On what constitutes a 'false instrument' under the Forgery and Counterfeiting Act 1981, s 9(1).

Warner v Metropolitan Police Commissioner [1968] 2 All ER 356; [1969] 2 AC 256; (1968) 52 Cr App R 373; [1968] Crim LR 380t; (1968) 132 JP 378; (1968) 112 SJ 378; [1968] 2 WLR 1303 HL Possession not absolute offence: if no right to open parcel/ignorant of its contents, no possession.

Warner, R v (1971) 55 Cr App R 93; [1971] Crim LR 114t; (1971) 135 JP 199; (1970) 120 NLJ 1113; (1970) 114 SJ 971 CA On elements of theft under Theft Act, s 1(1).

Waroquiers v Marsden [1950] 1 All ER 93; (1950) 114 JP 78 HC KBD Keeping a brothel triable summarily under statute and indictable at common law.

Washer, R v [1954] Crim LR 933 CMAC Intent irrelevant to offence of engaging in disgraceful conduct of indecent kind contrary to Army Act (unlike sister offence under Vagrancy Act 1824).

Wastie and another, Reed v [1972] Crim LR 221t HC QBD Successful action against police officer for assault of arrestee after had been arrested.

Waterfall, R v [1969] 3 All ER 1048; (1969) 53 Cr App R 597; [1970] Crim LR 34; (1970) 134 JP 1; [1970] 1 QB 148; (1969) 113 SJ 872; [1969] 3 WLR 947 CA Dishonest belief necessary for obtaining by deception.

Waterfield and Lynn, R v [1963] 3 All ER 659; (1964) 48 Cr App R 42; [1964] Crim LR 57t; (1964) 128 JP 48; (1963) 113 LJ 788; [1964] 1 QB 164; (1963) 107 SJ 833; [1963] 3 WLR 946 CCA Assault on constable wrongfully detaining vehicle not assault of same in execution of duty.

Waterfield v Murcutt (1927) 64 LJ ccr38 CyCt Damages plus interest to pawnbroker in action where sought return of goods pledged with him.

Waters v Braithwaite (1914-15) XXIV Cox CC 34; (1914) 78 JP 124; (1914) 110 LTR 266; (1913-14) XXX TLR 107 HC KBD Custom not defence to cruelty to animals charge.

Waters v Meakin (1915-17) XXV Cox CC 432; (1916) 80 JP 276; [1916] 2 KB 111; [1916] 85 LJKB 1378; (1916-17) 115 LTR 110; (1915-16) XXXII TLR 480; (1916) WN (I) 197 HC KBD Cruelty to rabbit conviction avoided by way of statutory protection afforded coursing meetings (Protection of Animals Act 1911, s 1(3) (b)).

Waters, North Staffordshire Railway Company v (1914-15) XXIV Cox CC 27; (1914) 78 JP 116; (1914) 110 LTR 237 HC KBD Failed prosecution against railway company for cruel transport of animals.

Watkins, R v [1976] 1 All ER 578; (1976) 140 JP 197 CrCt Granting of overdraft after false representation is obtaining pecuniary advantage by deception.

Watson (George), R v (1916-17) 12 Cr App R 62 CCA Cannot be convicted as accessory after fact where charged with receiving with guilty knowledge.

Watson and Watson, R v (1959) 43 Cr App R 111; [1959] Crim LR 785; (1959) 109 LJ 379 HC QBD Where husband and wife are living together wife can nonetheless be convicted of manslaughter of their child through neglect.

Watson v Herman [1952] 2 All ER 70; (1952) 116 JP 395; (1952) 102 LJ 329; (1952) 96 SJ 413; (1952) WN (I) 308 HC QBD Telescopic sight not a firearm.

Watson v Jones [1939] LJNCCR 9 CyCt On who is 'owner' of dog for purposes of Dogs Act 1906, s 1(1).

Watson, Paget Publications, Ltd v [1952] 1 All ER 1256; (1952) 116 JP 320; (1952) 96 SJ 328; [1952] 1 TLR 1189; (1952) WN (I) 248 HC QBD May order entire publication destroyed even if only a portion thereof obscene.

Watson, R v [1989] 2 All ER 865; (1989) 89 Cr App R 211; [1989] Crim LR 733; (1989) 139 NLJ 866; (1989) 133 SJ 876; [1989] 1 WLR 684 CA Knowledge of burglar about victim is all knowledge acquired while in house.

Watson, R v (1915-16) XXXII TLR 580 CCA Cannot be convicted as accessory after the fact where are only charged as being principal.

Watson, R v [1916-17] All ER 815; (1915-17) XXV Cox CC 470; (1916) 80 JP 391; [1916] 2 KB 385; (1916) 51 LJ 306; (1916-17) 115 LTR 159; [1916] 85 LJKB 1142; (1916) WN (I) 239 CCA Absent sole/joint possession/control of property could not be found guilty of receiving.

Watton (Joseph), R v (1979) 68 Cr App R 293; [1979] Crim LR 246 CA Bail may only be granted pending appeal to CA if appeal likely to succeed/would have served entire sentence by time appeal heard.

Watts (John Lackland), R v; R v Stack (David Charles) (1980) 70 Cr App R 187; [1980] Crim LR 38 CA Must be actual intentional evasion of prohibition on importation of controlled drugs to be guilty of same: cannot presume by acts that must have done so in past.

Watts v Seymour [1967] 1 All ER 1044; [1967] Crim LR 239t; (1967) 131 JP 309; [1967] 2 QB 647; (1967) 111 SJ 294; [1967] 2 WLR 1072 HC QBD Is an offence to sell firearm to under-aged party but not pass possession until later stage.

Watts, Flower v (1910) 45 LJ 391; (1909-10) XXVI TLR 495; (1910) WN (I) 146 HC KBD Possession in London of live larks lawfully caught in another place guilty of offence.

Watts, R v [1984] 2 All ER 380; (1984) 79 Cr App R 127; [1984] TLR 7; [1984] 1 WLR 757 CA Broadest meaning to be given to word 'amphetamine' in Misuse of Drugs Act 1971.

Waxman (Isaac), R v (1930-31) Cr App R 81 CCA Bail granted in light of pending Vacation.

Way, R v [1970] Crim LR 469; (1970) 120 NLJ 481; [1970] RTR 348; (1970) 114 SJ 418 CMAC That person's breath smelt of alcohol was not per se evidence that driving ability was impaired.

Weatherall, R v [1968] Crim LR 115 CCC Failed prosecution for administration of noxious thing (portion of sleeping tablet in tea) with intent to injure, aggrieve, annoy as insufficient proof of intent and thing administered not shown to be noxious.

Webb and Sussum, Wooster v [1936] LJNCCR 129 CyCt Nominal damages for demonstrators from whom police confiscated anti-war leaflets on basis that breach of the peace likely (though later proved to have no freasonable grounds for apprehending said breach of peace).

Webb v Commissioner of the Metropolitan Police [1963] Crim LR 708t HL No leave to appeal on point whether masturbation of men for payment was prostitution.

Webb v Stansfield [1966] Crim LR 449 Magistrates Forcing of quarter light on door of car obstructing right to use highway was valid step in enforcement of that right; absent damage to complainant smearing marmalade inside the car went unpunished.

Webb, R v [1954] Crim LR 49 Sessions Person found guilty of arson on basis inter alia of police dog identification evidence.

Webb, R v [1963] 3 All ER 177; (1963) 47 Cr App R 265; [1963] Crim LR 644; (1963) 127 JP 516; (1963) 113 LJ 625; [1964] 1 QB 357; (1963) 107 SJ 597; [1963] 3 WLR 638 CCA Prostitution includes all acts where woman offers self as a participant in indecent acts.

Webb, R v [1979] Crim LR 462 CrCt On level of cannabis which there must be present before can be said to possess it.

Webb, R v [1995] TLR 350 CA On ingredients of offence of communicating false information (by bomb hoaxer): need merely state existence not location of supposed bomb.

Webber (Charles), R v (1912-13) 8 Cr App R 59; [1913] 82 LJKB 108 CCA That prisoner does not explain behaviour since last release from prison does not per se justify finding is habitual criminal.

Webber, R v (1913-14) XXIII Cox CC 323; (1912) 76 JP 471; [1913] 1 KB 33; (1913) 108 LTR 349 CCA Notice of prosecution as habitual criminal not invalidated by reference therein to evidence on which prosecution based.

Webber, Stanton (D) and Sons Ltd v [1972] Crim LR 544; [1973] RTR 86; (1972) 116 SJ 666 HC QBD On what knowledge was necessary to prove employer guilty aiding/abetting worker-driver in unlicensed driving.

Webley (WA), R v; R v Webley (PR) [1967] Crim LR 300; (1967) 111 SJ 111 CA On need for person to be aware of presence of housebreaking implements before can be convicted of possession of same.

Webley v Buxton [1977] 2 All ER 595; (1977) 65 Cr App R 136; [1977] Crim LR 160; (1977) 141 JP 407; [1977] QB 481; [1977] RTR 193; (1977) 121 SJ 153; [1977] 2 WLR 766 HC QBD Can convict of attempted offence even if complete offence proved.

Webster and others, R v; R v Warwick [1995] 2 All ER 168 CA Where charge of 'damage to property with intent to endanger life' danger must be from damaged property and not act of damaging.

Wedderburn and others v The Duke of Atholl and others; The Duke of Atholl and others v The Glover Incorporation of Perth and others (1899-1900) XVI TLR 413 HL Was offence to use 'toot-and-haul' nets for salmon fishing on River Tay.

Weeks (Charles Frederick), R v (1927-28) 20 Cr App R 188 CCA Conviction for obtaining money by false pretences quashed where issue of character improperly raised.

Weight v Long [1986] Crim LR 746 HC QBD Police officer seeking to speak to another in connection with crime/breach of the peace was acting in course of duty.

Weight, Darch v [1984] 2 All ER 245; (1984) 79 Cr App R 40; [1984] Crim LR 168; (1984) 148 JP 588; (1984) 128 SJ 315; [1983] TLR 715; [1984] 1 WLR 659 HC QBD Positive act necessary for harbouring to arise; harbouring by non-owner of property possible.

Weisz and another v Monahan [1962] 1 All ER 664; [1962] Crim LR 179t; (1962) 126 JP 184; (1962) 112 LJ 223; (1962) 106 SJ 114 HC QBD Soliciting involves physical presence and does not extend to window advertisements.

Weitzman and others, R v (1948) 98 LJ 175 CCA Successful appeal against conviction for conspiracy to contravene toiletries regulations.

Welch, Farey v (1926-30) XXVIII Cox CC 604; (1929) 93 JP 70; [1929] 1 KB 388; (1929) 67 LJ 145; (1929) 98 LJCL 318; (1929) 140 LTR 560; (1928-29) XLV TLR 277; (1929) WN (I) 32 HC KBD Failed conviction for larceny of pigeon where acted under honest mistaken belief that was taking own pigeon.

Welham v Director of Public Prosecutions [1960] 1 All ER 805; (1960) 44 Cr App R 124; [1960] Crim LR 423; (1960) 124 JP 280; (1960) 110 LJ 284; (1960) 104 SJ 308; [1960] 2 WLR 669 HL Can intend to defraud (and be guilty of uttering forged document) though do not intend to cause financial loss.

Welham, R v [1960] 1 All ER 260; (1960) 44 Cr App R 79; [1960] Crim LR 190; (1960) 124 JP 156; (1960) 110 LJ 156; [1960] 2 QB 445; (1960) 104 SJ 108 CCA Intent when uttering forged document is to induce someone to act contrary to their interest/their duty; successful action for bail pending appeal.

Whelan, R v [1997] Crim LR 353 CA (Unopposed) appeal against conviction allowed where was strong suggestion that police officers who gave evidence at trial may have perjured selves.

Whent, Corcoran v [1977] Crim LR 52 HC QBD Could not be guilty of theft of food where formed requisite intention after ate it.

Whiley v Director of Public Prosecutions [1995] Crim LR 39 HC QBD On what constitutes 'using' wireless (unlawfully) for purposes of the Wireless Telegraphy Act 1949, s 5(b)(i).

Whipp, Fairclough v [1951] 2 All ER 834; (1951) 115 JP 612; (1951) 95 SJ 699; [1951] 2 TLR 909; (1951) WN (I) 528 HC KBD Successfully asking girl to touch accused's exposed person not an assault (hence no indecent assault).

Whipp, Fairclough v (1951-52) 35 Cr App R 138 CCA Successfully asking girl to touch accused's exposed person not an assault (hence no indecent assault).

Whitaker, R v (1914-15) XXIV Cox CC 472; (1915) 79 JP 28; [1915] 84 LJKB 225; (1915) 112 LTR 41 CCA Agreement to bribe regimental commander a misdemeanour.

Whitaker, R v; R v White (1914-15) XXIV Cox CC 472; (1915) 79 JP 28; [1915] 84 LJKB 225; (1915) 112 LTR 41; (1913-14) XXIII Cox CC 190; (1912) 76 JP 384; (1912-13) 107 LTR 528 CCA Failed prosecution for larceny by finding.

White (Frederick) and Shelton (George), R v (1927-28) 20 Cr App R 61 CCA On relevant factors in trial of individual as habitual criminal.

White v Fox (1931-32) XLVIII TLR 641 HC KBD Deer hind not a domestic animal so hunting of same not breach of Protection of Animals Act 1911.

White, R v (1913-14) XXIII Cox CC 190; (1912) 76 JP 384; (1912-13) 107 LTR 528 CCA Failed prosecution for larceny by finding.

White, R v (1911-13) XXII Cox CC 325; [1910] 2 KB 125; (1910) 79 LJKB 854; (1909-10) 54 SJ 523; (1910) WN (I) 123 CCA Guilty of attempted murder where do one of series of non-lethal acts intended to cause death; liable to punishment for attempted murder under Offences Against the Person Act 1861, ss 11-15.

White, R v [1960] Crim LR 132; (1959) 103 SJ 814 CCA Was larceny to take drinks in public house after barman refused to sell same after-hours.

White, R v [1995] Crim LR 393 CA Substitution of verdict of guilt of causing grievous bodily harm (not causing same with intent) where because of post-traumatic stress disorder did not have requisite intent.

Whitefield (Arthur Armour Mallie), R v (1984) 79 Cr App R 36; [1984] Crim LR 97 CA To extricate oneself from unlawful common enterprise must unequivocally explain to others that are not party to enterprise and will not help at all.

Whitehead, Allen v [1930] 1 KB 211; (1929) WN (I) 207 HC KBD Occupier liable for servant's knowingly suffering prostitutes to meet in former's refreshment house.

Whitehead, Chajutin v [1938] 1 KB 506; (1938) 85 LJ 87; [1938] 107 LJCL 270 HC KBD Offence of possessing altered passport requires no mens rea, merely actus reus.

Whitehorn Brothers v Davison [1908-10] All ER 885; [1911] 1 KB 463 CA Person obtaining delivery of goods for re-sale by fraud guilty of obtaining by false pretences, not larceny by trick.

Whitehouse v Gay News Ltd; Whitehouse v Lemon [1979] AC 617; (1979) 68 Cr App R 381; (1979) 123 SJ 163; [1979] 2 WLR 281 HL Intention to publish blasphemy/not intention to blaspheme is mens rea for blasphemous libel.

Whitehouse, R v [1977] 3 All ER 737; (1977) 65 Cr App R 33; [1977] Crim LR 689; (1978) 142 JP 45; (1977) 127 NLJ 369t; (1977) 121 SJ 171; [1977] QB 868; [1977] 2 WLR 925 CA Girl under 16 cannot aid and abet in incest; Court of Appeal may hear appeal that offence charged not an offence.

Whiteley (Nicholas Alan), R v (1991) 93 Cr App R 25; [1991] Crim LR 436; (1991) 155 JP 917; [1991] TLR 57 CA Was criminal damage for computer hacker to alter data on computer disks.

Whiteside and Antoniou, R v [1989] Crim LR 436 CA On necessary element of deception to sustain conviction for going equipped for cheating.

Whiteside v Gamble [1968] Crim LR 560 Sessions Person not guilty of assault on constable in execution of his duty where latter grossly insulted individual and then invited him to fight.

Whiteway, R v [1954] Crim LR 143t CCA Valid admission of evidence at murder trial by person whom accused was claimed to have raped; failed appeal against alibi direction as evidence in support of alibi irrelevant once jury accepted accused's confession (which they did).

Whitfield (Melvyn Thomas), R v (1976) 63 Cr App R 39; [1976] Crim LR 443t; (1976) 126 NLJ 360t CA Provocation if conduct such that accused lost self-control and reasonable man would have done so.

Whiting v Ivens (1915-17) XXV Cox CC 128; (1915) 79 JP 457; [1915] 84 LJKB 1878; (1915-16) 113 LTR 869; (1914-15) XXXI TLR 492 HC KBD Case against owner ought not to have been dismissed where was prima facie case of cruelty to animal.

Whiting, R v [1987] Crim LR 473 CA Could be convicted of burglary under s 9(1)(a) of the Theft Act 1968 though were charged under s 9(1)(b).

Whitman, R v [1962] Crim LR 394 CCA On burden of proof as regards proving possession of 'offensive' weapon.

Whybrow, R v (1951) 95 SJ 745 CCA On necessary intent in case of attempted murder.

Whyte and another, Corbin v [1972] Crim LR 234t; (1972) 122 NLJ 196t HC QBD Not breach of Obscene Publications Act to make obscene publications available to those whose morals were already depraved.

Whyte and another, Director of Public Prosecutions v [1972] 3 All ER 12; [1972] AC 849; (1973) 57 Cr App R 74; [1972] Crim LR 556t; (1972) 136 JP 686; (1972) 122 NLJ 703t; (1972) 116 SJ 583; [1972] 3 WLR 410 HL Material obscene even if directed at the depraved; consequent sexual activity unnecessary to prove can deprave/corrupt.

Whyte, R v [1987] 3 All ER 416; (1987) 85 Cr App R 283 CA Excessive force where immediate but expected danger not ground for self-defence.

Wicks v Director of Public Prosecutions [1947] 1 All ER 205; [1947] AC 362; (1946-48) 32 Cr App R 7; (1947) 97 LJ 65; [1947] 116 LJR 247; (1947) 176 LTR 150; (1947) LXIII TLR 6; (1947) WN (I) 30 HL Accused could be convicted under temporary statute despite its expiry.

Wicks, R v [1946] 2 All ER 529; (1946) 96 LJ 629; (1946) 175 LTR 427; (1946) 90 SJ 557; (1945-46) LXII TLR 674; (1946) WN (I) 205 CCA Can be punished for acts done contrary to temporary statute which lapses before prosecution/conviction.

Widdowson (Stanley), R v (1986) 82 Cr App R 314; [1986] Crim LR 233; [1986] RTR 124; (1986) 130 SJ 88 CA Not attempted obtaining services by deception where gave false personal details on hire purchase credit inquiry form.

Wiggins v Field [1968] Crim LR 503; (1968) 112 SJ 656 HC QBD Ought never to have been prosecution for indecent language arising from public poetry recital involving line containing possibly indecent wording.

Wilcock (John Joseph), R v (1921-22) 16 Cr App R 91; (1921-22) 66 SJ 335 CCA Admission by person accused as habitual criminal that was previously convicted as same tacit plea of guilt to charge.

Wilcox and others, Despard and others v (1911-13) XXII Cox CC 258; (1910) 74 JP 115; (1910) 102 LTR 103; (1909-10) XXVI TLR 226 HC KBD Suffragettes blocking Downing Street despite police requests to disperse guilty of obstructing police in execution of their duty.

Wilde, Ward, Wooley, Morrey and Copley, R v [1960] Crim LR 116 Assizes Need not be advantage to defendant for there to be misprision of felony; agreement not to reveal offence a crime.

Wilkins v Gill; Major v Gill (1903-04) XX TLR 3 HC KBD Attorney-General's fiat necessary for bringing of action against certain publication for advertisement offering reward for return of stolen property on 'no questions asked' basis as publication at issue was newspaper under Larceny (Advertisements) Act 1870/Post Office Act 1870.

Wilkins, R v [1975] 2 All ER 734; (1975) 60 Cr App R 300; [1975] Crim LR 343t; (1975) 139 JP 543; (1975) 125 NLJ 285t CA Evidence of theft/handling conviction where charged with handling relates to guilty knowledge only.

Wilkinson, Leyton Urban District Council v (1927) 91 JP 64; [1927] 1 KB 315; (1925-26) 70 SJ 1069; (1926-27) XLIII TLR 35; (1926) WN (I) 274 HC KBD Inadequacy of recognisance entered into personally by clerk of local authority.

Wilkinson, Leyton Urban District Council v (1927) 137 LTR 10; (1927) 71 SJ 293; (1926-27) XLIII TLR 326 CA Inadequacy of recognisance entered into personally by clerk of local authority.

Wilkinson, R v [1955] Crim LR 575t CCA Refusal to consider adequacy of direction on provocation/insanity where those defences deemed by court not to arise.

Wilkinson, R v [1954] Crim LR 144t CCA Failed appeal against finding that psychopathic frame of mind did not constitute insanity.

Wille (Bryan James), R v (1988) 86 Cr App R 296 CA Drawing and issuing of company cheques for self was appropriation under Theft Act 1968, s 3(1).

Willetts and others, R v (1906) 70 JP 127 CCC Is criminal conspiracy for two/more persons to seek to deny other of benefits of copyright through unauthorised printing/selling of music; certified copies of copyright register entries admissible to prove copyright ownership.

Willetts, Faulkner v [1982] Crim LR 453; [1982] RTR 159 HC QBD Valid arrest where constable's entry into house appeared from evidence not to be trespass.

Willey v Peace [1950] 2 All ER 724; (1950) 114 JP 502; [1951] 1 KB 94; (1950) 100 LJ 483; (1950) 94 SJ 597; [1950] 66 (2) TLR 450 HC KBD Police officer may under Metropolitan Police Act 1839, s 66 arrest anyone reasonably suspects of conveying stolen property.

Williams (Albert), R v [1968] Crim LR 678; (1968) 112 SJ 760 CA Objective test of provocation under Homicide Act 1957, s 3, unaffected by subjective test of intent in the Criminal Justice Act 1967, s 8.

Williams (Arthur), R v (1928-29) 21 Cr App R 121; (1929) 141 LTR 544 CCA Pre-habitual criminal trial confession of offence admissible in habitual criminal trial.

Williams (deceased), R v (1968) 118 NLJ 1174t; [1969] Crim LR 158t HC QBD On burden of proof as regards establishing suicide: is presumption against suicide.

Williams (Frederick), R v (1912-13) 8 Cr App R 49 CCA Circumstances of instant crime with which charged justified finding was habitual criminal.

Williams (Gladstone), R v (1984) 78 Cr App R 276; [1984] Crim LR 163 CA When pleading mistake as defence to assault reasonableness of belief relevant to deciding whether held but not to whether guilty/innocent.

Williams (Jean-Jacques), R v [1980] Crim LR 589 CA Was theft where sold out-of-circulation Yugoslavian money to bureau de change on basis that was good currency.

Williams (Jean-Jacques), R v [1979] Crim LR 736 CrCt Was no deception but was theft where sold out-of-circulation Yugoslavian money to bureau de change on basis that was good currency.

Williams (John Owen), R v (1910) 4 Cr App R 89; (1909-10) XXVI TLR 290 CCA On what constitutes exposure/abandonment of child (Children Act 1908, s 12(1)).

Williams and another, Attorney-General of Jamaica v [1997] 3 WLR 389 CA On issuing of search warrant: here search lawful though seizure had gone slightly further than warrant allowed.

Williams and another, R v [1992] 2 All ER 183; (1992) 95 Cr App R 1; [1992] Crim LR 198; [1991] TLR 466; [1992] 1 WLR 380 CA Evidence of joint enterprise concerning all defendants cannot secure conviction of remaining defendants if one defendant acquitted; for liability to arise action following threat must be reasonably foreseeable by assailant and (if death) reasonably recognisable that would have resulted in harm to victim; action disproportionate to threat is novus actus interveniens.

Williams and Hamilton-Walker, R v [1959] Crim LR 727 CCC Failed prosecution for larceny of cars that were in possession of alleged offenders pursuant to hire-purchase agreement.

Williams and others v Phillips; Roberts and others v Phillips (1957) 41 Cr App R 5; (1957) 121 JP 163 HC QBD Dustmen convicted for larceny where sold refuse from dustbins.

Williams and Woodley, R v (1920) 84 JP 90; [1920] 89 LJCL 557; (1920) 123 LTR 270; (1919-20) 64 SJ 309 CCA Conviction allowed stand notwithstanding inadvertent disclosure to jury of previous convictions of accused.

Williams v Director of Public Prosecutions (1992) 95 Cr App R 415; (1992) 156 JP 804; [1992] TLR 80 HC QBD Landing of block of flats to which was controlled access not a public place.

Williams v Director of Public Prosecutions [1968] Crim LR 563; (1968) 112 SJ 599 HC QBD Passing out leaflets outside servicemen's club inviting them to desert was distributing insulting writing likely to occasion breach of the peace (contrary to the Public Order Act 1936, s 7).

Williams v Gibbs [1958] Crim LR 127t HC QBD Drying of young girls after taking them for a paddle was not indecent assault.

Williams v Hallam (1942-43) LIX TLR 287 HC KBD Accused's agreeing to both charges being taken together meant that could not argue that could not be convicted and punished on both charges.

Williams v Phillips [1957] Crim LR 186t HC QBD Corporation refuse collectors guilty of larceny from corporation where took material from collected refuse.

Williams v Richards [1971] Crim LR 41t; (1907) 71 JP 222; [1907] 2 KB 88; (1907) 42 LJ 249; [1907] 76 LJKB 589; (1907) XCVI LTR 644; (1970) 114 SJ 864; (1906-07) XXIII TLR 423; (1907) WN (I) 90 HC KBD That dog has killed sheep shows is dangerous for purposes of Dogs Act 1871, s 2.

Williams, Bloomfield v [1970] Crim LR 292t; [1970] RTR 184 HC QBD Person who did not know that what were signing was false could not be guilty of false declaration.

Williams, Boggeln v [1978] 2 All ER 1060; (1978) 67 Cr App R 50; [1978] Crim LR 242; (1978) 142 JP 503; (1978) 128 NLJ 242t; (1978) 122 SJ 94; [1978] 1 WLR 873 HC QBD Reconnection of electricity supply without permission not unlawful where no dishonest intent.

Williams, Partington v (1976) 62 Cr App R 220; [1977] Crim LR 609; (1976) 126 NLJ 89t CA Could not be convicted of attempted offence where could not have committed complete offence.

Williams, Partington v (1976) 120 SJ 80 HC QBD Could not be convicted of attempted offence where could not have committed complete offence.

Williams, R v [1987] 3 All ER 411 CA Person acting under mistake of fact to be judged in light of mistaken facts even if unreasonable mistake.

Williams, R v (1991) 92 Cr App R 158; [1991] Crim LR 205; (1991) 155 JP 365; [1990] TLR 669 CA Attempting to pervert the course of justice a substantive common law offence.

Williams, R v [1962] Crim LR 111 CCA May assert claim of right on behalf of third party.

Williams, R v [1922] All ER 433; (1921-25) XXVII Cox CC 350; (1922-23) 17 Cr App R 56; (1923) 87 JP 67; [1923] 1 KB 340; (1923) 58 LJ 21; [1923] 92 LJCL 230; (1923) 128 LTR 128; (1922-23) 67 SJ 263; (1922-23) XXXIX TLR 131; (1923) WN (I) 7 CCA Consent obtained by fraud not real consent so act of sex is rape.

Williams, R v; R v Lamb [1995] Crim LR 77 CA Solicitor properly prosecuted under Theft Act 1968, s 5(3) for holding on to money of client.

Williams, R v; R v Williams (1953) 37 Cr App R 71; (1953) 117 JP 251; [1953] 1 QB 660; (1953) 97 SJ 318; [1953] 2 WLR 937 CCA Interpretation of Larceny Act 1916, s 1(1): 'fraudulently and without a claim of right'.

Williams, Wall v [1966] Crim LR 50t HC QBD Taxi-driver who briefly blocked road in badly executed 'U-turn' could validly be found to have caused unnecessary obstruction.

Williamson (Alan), R v (1978) 67 Cr App R 35; [1978] Crim LR 229; (1977) 127 NLJ 1205t; (1977) 121 SJ 812 CA Whether particular article an offensive weapon a question of fact for jury.

Williamson (Anthony Colin), R v; R v Ellerton (Stephen) (1978) 67 Cr App R 63; [1978] Crim LR 166; (1977) 127 NLJ 1177t CA On requisite intent for murder.

Willis (Christopher), R v; R v Wertheimer (Henry Joseph David); R v Linford (Michael Kevin); R v Willis (John Michael); R v Westbrook (Simon Jeffrey Edney) (1979) 68 Cr App R 265 CA Is no defence of entrapment; evidence obtained by 'entrapment' properly admitted.

Willmott v Atack [1976] 3 All ER 794; (1976) 63 Cr App R 207; [1976] Crim LR 575; (1977) 141 JP 35; (1976) 126 NLJ 719t; [1977] QB 498; (1976) 120 SJ 587; [1976] 3 WLR 753 HC QBD Must intend obstructing act to obstruct for it to be unlawful obstruction of police officer.

Wills v Bowley [1982] 2 All ER 654; [1983] 1 AC 57; (1982) 75 Cr App R 164; [1982] 3 WLR 10 HC QBD Police have power of arrest where reasonably suspect crime committed in their sight.

Wills v Bowley [1982] 2 All ER 654; [1983] 1 AC 57; (1982) 75 Cr App R 164; [1982] Crim LR 580; (1982) 146 JP 309; (1982) 126 SJ 411; [1982] TLR 286; [1982] 3 WLR 10 HL Police have power of arrest where reasonably suspect crime committed in their sight.

Wills, R v; R v Wills (Graham George) [1990] Crim LR 714; (1991) 92 Cr App R 297 CA Successful appeal against conviction for theft of debt (did not handle cheque in accordance with drawer's instructions).

Wilsher, Pym v (1901) 36 LJ 310; (1900-01) 45 SJ 578; (1900-01) XVII TLR 558; (1901) WN (I) 126; (1900-01) 49 WR 654 HC KBD Prosecution procedures under Vaccination Act 1898 did not apply to failure to vaccinate which occurred during lifetime of Vaccination Act 1867.

Wilson (Alan Thomas), R v [1996] 2 Cr App R 241; [1996] Crim LR 573; [1997] QB 47; (1996) 140 SJ LB 93; (1996) TLR 5/3/96; [1996] 3 WLR 125 CA Successful appeal against assault conviction as appellant's branding of wife's buttocks had been done with her consent.

Wilson (Alfred John), R v (1910-11) 6 Cr App R 207 CCA Sheer volume of accident claims was evidence were bogus.

Wilson (Clarence), R v; R v Jenkins (Edward John) and another [1983] 3 All ER 448; [1984] AC 242; (1984) 148 JP 435; (1983) 127 SJ 712; [1983] TLR 595 HL If indictment includes allegation of other offence can be convicted of that offence.

Wilson (Donald Theodore), R v (1984) 78 Cr App R 247; [1984] Crim LR 173; [1983] TLR 653 CA On what constitutes 'living on' earnings of prostitution contrary to Sexual Offences Act 1956, s 30(1) (2).

Wilson (Ernest), R v (1922-23) 17 Cr App R 130 CCA Leave to appeal against sentence for attempted suicide granted.

Wilson (George), R v (1916-17) 12 Cr App R 95 CCA Person who refuses to give information about self since prison release can be found habitual criminal.

Wilson (John Henry), R v; R v Marshall (Edward) (1912-13) 8 Cr App R 20 CCA On establishing that person a habitual criminal.

Wilson v Clark [1984] TLR 716 HC QBD On validity of arrest effected pursuant to the Immigration Act 1971.

Wilson v Coombe (1989) 88 Cr App R 322; (1988) 132 SJ 1300; [1989] 1 WLR 78 HC QBD Possession of firearms certificates apply to particular gun not type of gun: valid conviction of dealer who exchanged certificate-holders' guns for different gun of same class.

Wilson v Skeock (1949) 113 JP 295; (1949) LXV TLR 418 HC KBD Public Order Act 1936 not for prosecution of neighbours who had been abusive towards each other but binding over was nonetheless valid exercise of justices' inherent powers/powers under Justices of the Peace Act 1360.

Wilson, Bailey v [1968] Crim LR 617 Sessions Police officer making general enquiry was trespasser once remained on private property after told to leave; disorderly conduct to be offence must occur on public passageway: struggling from house/garden to police van not disorderly conduct.

Wilson, Cafferata v; Reeve v Wilson [1936] 3 All ER 149; (1934-39) XXX Cox CC 475; (1936) 100 JP 489; (1936) 155 LTR 510; (1936) 80 SJ 856; (1936-37) LIII TLR 34 HC KBD Fake revolver that could be converted into real revolver a firearm.

Wilson, Durose v (1907-09) XXI Cox CC 421; (1907) 71 JP 263; (1907) XCVI LTR 645 HC KBD Porter properly convicted as wilful party to use of flats/portion thereof as brothel.

Wilson, Farmer v (1899-1901) XIX Cox CC 502; (1900) 35 LJ 245; [1900] 69 LJCL 496; (1900) LXXXII LTR 566; (1899-1900) XVI TLR 309 HC QBD Was besetting of persons on board ship (irrespective of whether contract permitting persons to be there was legal or not).

Wilson, Hawkins v [1957] Crim LR 320 Magistrates Caravan not a building for purposes of Malicious Damage Act 1861, s 6.

Wilson, R v [1989] Crim LR 146 HC QBD Must be alteration of certificate upon exchange of particular firearm in respect of which certificate issued.

Wilson, R v (1911-12) XXVIII TLR 561 CCA Inadequate notice of evidence to be served led to habitual criminal conviction being quashed; evidence on lifestyle not confined to lifestyle during time between release from prison and committal of offence.

Wilson, R v [1997] 1 All ER 119 CA On elements of offence of carrying on illegal insurance business contrary to the Insurance Companies Act 1982.

Wiltshire v Barrett [1965] 2 All ER 271; [1965] Crim LR 295t; (1965) 129 JP 348; [1966] 1 QB 312; (1965) 109 SJ 274; [1965] 2 WLR 1195 CA Valid arrest if police officer has reasonable suspicion are committing road traffic offence/are released once discover innocent or no case.

Wiltshire, R v [1976] Crim LR 458 CA Four years' imprisonment for stockbroker guilty of theft from clients.

Wimperis v Griffin [1973] Crim LR 533 HC QBD Arrest under Road Traffic Act 1960 not rendered improper by virtue of immediately prior request for breath specimen under the Road Safety Act 1967.

Winder and others v Director of Public Prosecutions (1996) TLR 13/8/96 CA Running after hunt with intent of interfering with same an offence under the Criminal Justice and Public Order Act 1994, s 68.

Winder, Moses v [1980] Crim LR 232; [1981] RTR 37 HC QBD Failed attempt by diabetic to establish automatism defence to driving without due care and attention charge.

Windle, R v [1952] 2 All ER 1; (1952) 36 Cr App R 85; (1952) 116 JP 365; (1952) 102 LJ 303; [1952] 2 QB 826; (1952) 96 SJ 379; [1952] 1 TLR 1344; (1952) WN (I) 283 CCA If claiming insanity must show that did not know what were doing was unlawful.

Wines, R v [1953] 2 All ER 1497; (1953) 37 Cr App R 197; [1954] Crim LR 136; (1954) 118 JP 49; (1954) 98 SJ 14; [1954] 1 WLR 64 CCA Intending a deceit through falsifying accounts was sufficient intent to sustain accounts falsification charge.

Wing (Lee Cheung) v R; Yau (Lam Man) v R (1992) 94 Cr App R 355; [1992] Crim LR 440 PC Employees faking withdrawal slips guilty of falsification with view to gain where had not intended to account to company for profits made.

Wing-Siu (Chan) and others v R [1985] AC 168; (1985) 80 Cr App R 117; [1984] Crim LR 549; (1984) 128 SJ 685; [1984] TLR 411; [1984] 3 WLR 677 PC Person guilty of murder/grievous bodily harm if proved that entered premises as part of unlawful common enterprise and had contemplated that serious bodily harm might result.

Winn v Director of Public Prosecutions (1992) 156 JP 881; (1992) 142 NLJ 527 HC QBD On four different ways of committing offence created by Public Order Act 1986, s 4 (likely provocation of violence through use of threatening/abusive words or behaviour).

Winstanley, R v (1924-25) 69 SJ 777 CCA That person behaved in cruel and lustful way did not entitle them to succeed on insanity defence.

Winter v Woolfe [1930] All ER 623; (1931-34) XXIX Cox CC 214; (1931) 95 JP 20; [1931] 1 KB 549; (1930) 70 LJ 410; (1931) 144 LTR 311; (1930-31) XLVII TLR 145; (1930) WN (I) 266 HC KBD Need/need not show illicit sex/ that women involved are prostitutes to sustain charge of permitting premises to be used as brothel.

Winter v Woolfe (1931) 100 LJCL 92 CCA Need/need not show illicit sex/ that women involved are prostitutes to sustain charge of permitting premises to be used as brothel.

Wirral District Magistrates Court; ex parte Meikle, R v [1990] Crim LR 801; [1990] TLR 416 HC QBD Inapplicability of abuse of process doctrine to bail application (absent bad faith).

Wise (Philip), R v (1922-23) 17 Cr App R 17 CCA On granting of bail by CCA.

Wise v Dunning [1900-03] All ER 727; (1901-07) XX Cox CC 121; [1902] 71 LJCL 165; (1901-02) 46 SJ 152; (1901-02) XVIII TLR 85; (1901-02) 50 WR 317 HC KBD Justices can bind over provocative public speaker to keep the peace/be of good behaviour.

Wish, Anderton v (1981) 72 Cr App R 23; [1980] Crim LR 319/657 HC QBD Is appropriation to switch lower price tags to higher priced goods so as to pay lower price.

Withers and others, R v [1974] 1 All ER 101; (1974) 58 Cr App R 187; [1974] Crim LR 36t; (1974) 138 JP 123; (1973) 123 NLJ 1017t; [1974] QB 414; (1973) 117 SJ 834; [1974] 2 WLR 26 CA Public duty owed by bank can sustain conviction for conspiracy to effect public mischief; conspiracy to effect public mischief need not involve criminal or tortious acts/the state.

Withers v Director of Public Prosecutions [1974] 3 All ER 984; [1975] AC 842; (1975) 60 Cr App R 85; [1975] Crim LR 95; (1975) 139 JP 94; (1974) 124 NLJ 1157t; (1974) 118 SJ 862; [1974] 3 WLR 751 HL No offence of conspiracy to effect public mischief (though acts complained of may fall within definition of other criminal offence).

Witton (Edward), R v (1910-11) 6 Cr App R 149 CCA Conviction quashed where alibi established by means of fresh evidence upon appeal.

Wolverhampton Coroner, ex parte McCurbin, R v [1990] 2 All ER 759 CA Coroner's jury must be convinced beyond reasonable doubt of unlawful killing; otherwise death by misadventure on balance of probabilities.

Wood (Charles), R v (1919-20) 14 Cr App R 149; (1920) 84 JP 92; [1920] 89 LJCL 435; (1919-20) 64 SJ 409 CCA Seven months' hard labour (concurrent) for two convictions of indecent assault.

Wood (Ernest George), R v (1911-12) 7 Cr App R 56 CCA On housebreaking charge can infer felonious intent from circumstantial evidence.

Wood (William Douglas), R v (1987) 85 Cr App R 287; [1987] Crim LR 414; (1987) 131 SJ 840; [1987] 1 WLR 779 CA Evidence of earlier possession admissible in handling prosecution but not statements explaining same/description of how found.

Wood v Commissioner of the Metropolis [1986] 2 All ER 570; (1986) 83 Cr App R 145; [1986] Crim LR 481; (1986) 150 JP 236; (1986) 130 SJ 446; [1986] 1 WLR 796 HC QBD Piece of glass instrument for offensive use, not offensive weapon; use of instrument for offensive purpose must be premeditated.

Wood v Director of Public Prosecutions (1989) 153 JP 20 HC QBD On admissibility of expert medical evidence that was fact/opinion (here on defence of automatism).

Wood, Meaden v [1985] Crim LR 678 HC QBD On legislation pertaining to legitimate mode of effecting street collections.

Wood, R v [1957] Crim LR 54 Sessions Acts deemed to constitute attempt to procure act of gross indecency with another male.

Wood, R v [1975] Crim LR 236 CrCt Wife who surreptitiously placed sleeping tablets in husband's coffee to stop him from keeping her up at night not guilty of causing noxious thing to be taken.

Wood, R v (1981) 131 NLJ 929 CA Failed appeal against manslaughter conviction where claimed evidence did not prove had opportunity to commit crime.

Wood, Rogers v [1968] Crim LR 274t HC QBD Not keeping premises open where sold refreshments through window of coffee bar to persons on the street.

Woodage v Moss [1974] 1 All ER 584; [1974] Crim LR 104; (1974) 138 JP 253; (1974) 118 SJ 204; [1974] 1 WLR 411 HC QBD Person carrying uncertificated firearm from party to dealer is in possession/not dealer's servant (as no payment/obligation to so act).

Woodhall, Chief Constable of Blackpool v [1965] Crim LR 660 Magistrates On what is meant by publication for 'gain' under the Obscene Publications Acts 1959 and 1964.

Woodley v Woodley [1978] Crim LR 629 HC QBD Wife could be convicted of criminal damage of husband's property where husband was subject of exclusion order.

Woodman, R v [1974] 2 All ER 955; (1974) 59 Cr App R 200; [1974] Crim LR 441t; (1974) 138 JP 567; (1974) 124 NLJ 464t; [1974] QB 754; [1974] 2 WLR 821 CA Persons in control of property prima facie in control of materials there.

Woods (Sidney George), R v (1921) 85 JP 272 CCC Brother not acting in locus parenti guilty of manslaughter of brother whom struck in face and who died in consequence (as was in status lymphaticus - slight blow caused shock resulting in death).

Woods (Walter), R v (1982) 74 Cr App R 312; [1982] Crim LR 42 CA Self-induced drunkenness not defence to rape: 'relevant matters' in Sexual Offences (Amendment) Act 1976, s 1(2) means legally relevant.

Youden and others, Johnson v [1950] 1 KB 544 HC KBD Cannot be guilty of aiding and abetting where unaware of facts making up offence; once aware of some it is no defence to one's actions that did not know were acting unlawfully.

Young (Charles) and Young (Mark), R v [1979] Crim LR 651 CrCt Alibi notice not required where prosecution/defence alleging in context of road traffic offence that C/M was driving and M/C was aiding and abetting.

Young (Robert), R v (1943-45) 30 Cr App R 57 CCA On what constitutes public mischief.

Young (Tara Moira Lisa), R v (1993) 97 Cr App R 280; (1993) 137 SJ LB 32; [1992] TLR 641 CA Where jury convinced overall that was cruelty (even though disagree on specific incidents) can convict of cruelty to children.

Young and another, R v [1953] 1 All ER 21; (1952) 36 Cr App R 200; (1953) 117 JP 42 CCA On proof of theft in receiving stolen property trial.

Young and others v Peck (1913-14) XXIII Cox CC 270; (1912-13) 107 LTR 857 HC KBD Persons in crowd from which eggs thrown but who had not themselves thrown eggs properly convicted of intimidation.

Young, Hollis v (1908) 72 JP 199; (1908) XCVIII LTR 751; (1907-08) XXIV TLR 500 HC KBD State and colour of birds plus supporting evidence of witness could have grounded conviction for possession of recently taken wild birds contrary to Wild Birds Protection Act 1880, s 3.

Young, R v (1913-14) XXIII Cox CC 624; (1914) 78 JP 80; (1913-14) 109 LTR 753; (1913-14) 58 SJ 100; (1913-14) XXX TLR 69 CCA Must be leading criminal/dishonest life at time of arrest to sustain conviction; prosecution of person already convicted of offence to be closely monitored by court.

Young, R v [1984] 2 All ER 164; (1984) 78 Cr App R 288; [1984] Crim LR 363; (1984) 148 JP 492; (1984) 128 SJ 297; [1984] TLR 78; [1984] 1 WLR 654 CMAC Test whether knew or ought to have known was controlled drug is objective: self induced intoxication irrelevant to belief.

Young, R v; R v Kassim [1988] Crim LR 372; (1988) 152 JP 405 CA On what constitutes 'execution' of valuable security by deception (Theft Act 1968, s 20(2)).

Yu-Tsang (Wai) v R [1991] 4 All ER 664; [1992] 1 AC 269; (1992) 94 Cr App R 264; [1992] Crim LR 425; (1991) 135 SJ LB 164; [1991] TLR 451; [1991] 3 WLR 1006 PC Was conspiracy to defraud where intended to effect state of affairs that could deceive another into acting to his economic detriment even though that was not purpose of conspiracy.

Yule, R v [1963] 2 All ER 780; (1963) 47 Cr App R 229; [1963] Crim LR 564; (1963) 127 JP 469; (1963) 113 LJ 465; [1964] 1 QB 5; (1963) 107 SJ 497; [1963] 3 WLR 285 CCA Solicitor paying fees intended for other into own account commits fraudulent conversion; indictment defective but as no embarrassment to defendant was allowed.

Yuthiwattana (Helen), R v (1985) 80 Cr App R 55; [1984] Crim LR 562; (1984) 128 SJ 661; [1984] TLR 391 CA Lock-out of tenant for one day and night could be harassment/was not unlawful eviction of occupier.

Zabrovski v Palestine General Officer and Another [1947] 116 LJR 1053; (1947) 177 LTR 369 PC Habeas corpus relief if detained illegally and here though detained under emergency legislation was not illegal.

Zakos v R [1956] Crim LR 625t; (1956) 100 SJ 631 PC Interpretation of emergency regulations pertaining to carrying/discharging of firearms in Cyprus.

Zaman (Mohammed), R v (1975) 61 Cr App R 227; [1975] Crim LR 710; (1975) 125 NLJ 645; (1975) 119 SJ 657 CA Jurisdiction of CCA/trial judge to grant bail pending deportation.

Zeitlin (Leon), R v (1931-32) 23 Cr App R 163 CCA Bankrupt not guilty of obtaining credit where tells creditor of status as bankrupt within reasonable time before obtaining said credit.

Zezza v Government of Italy and another [1982] 2 All ER 513; [1983] 1 AC 46; (1982) 75 Cr App R 338; [1982] Crim LR 749; (1982) 132 NLJ 663; (1982) 126 SJ 398; [1982] TLR 284; [1982] 2 WLR 1077 HL Person whose extradition sought to be treated as convict if facts justify it.

Zossenheim, R v (1903-04) XX TLR 121 HC KBD On taking foreign depositions in extradition proceedings.